Essentials of Marketing

A Global-Managerial Approach

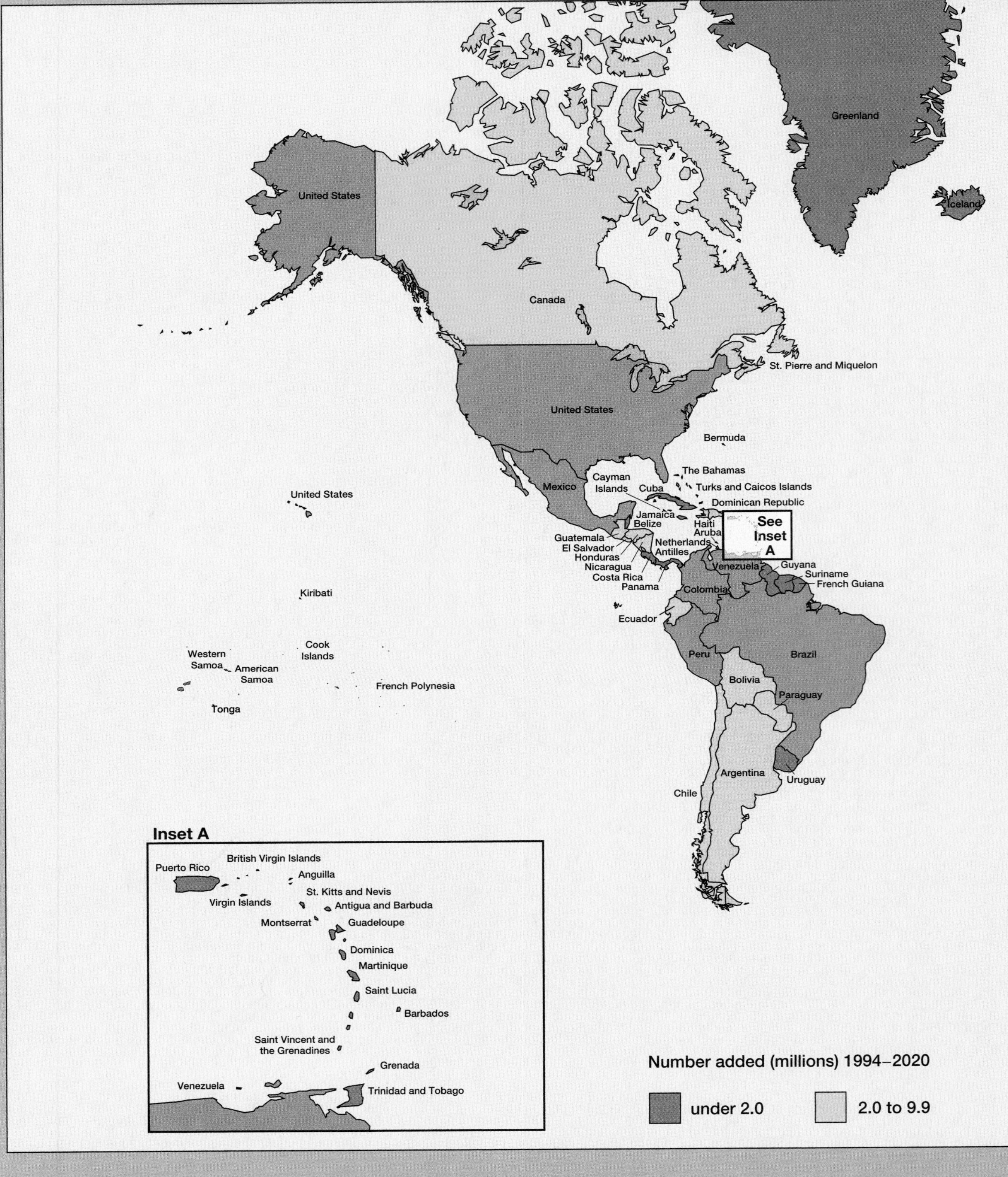
Greenland
Iceland
United States
Canada
St. Pierre and Miquelon
United States
Bermuda
The Bahamas
Turks and Caicos Islands
Cayman Islands
Cuba
Dominican Republic
Mexico
United States
Jamaica
Belize
Haiti
Aruba
See Inset A
Guatemala
El Salvador
Honduras
Nicaragua
Costa Rica
Panama
Netherlands Antilles
Venezuela
Guyana
Suriname
French Guiana
Colombia
Kiribati
Ecuador
Western Samoa
American Samoa
Cook Islands
French Polynesia
Tonga
Peru
Brazil
Bolivia
Paraguay
Argentina
Uruguay
Chile
Inset A
Puerto Rico
British Virgin Islands
Anguilla
Virgin Islands
St. Kitts and Nevis
Antigua and Barbuda
Montserrat
Guadeloupe
Dominica
Martinique
Saint Lucia
Barbados
Saint Vincent and the Grenadines
Grenada
Venezuela
Trinidad and Tobago
Number added (millions) 1994–2020
under 2.0
2.0 to 9.9

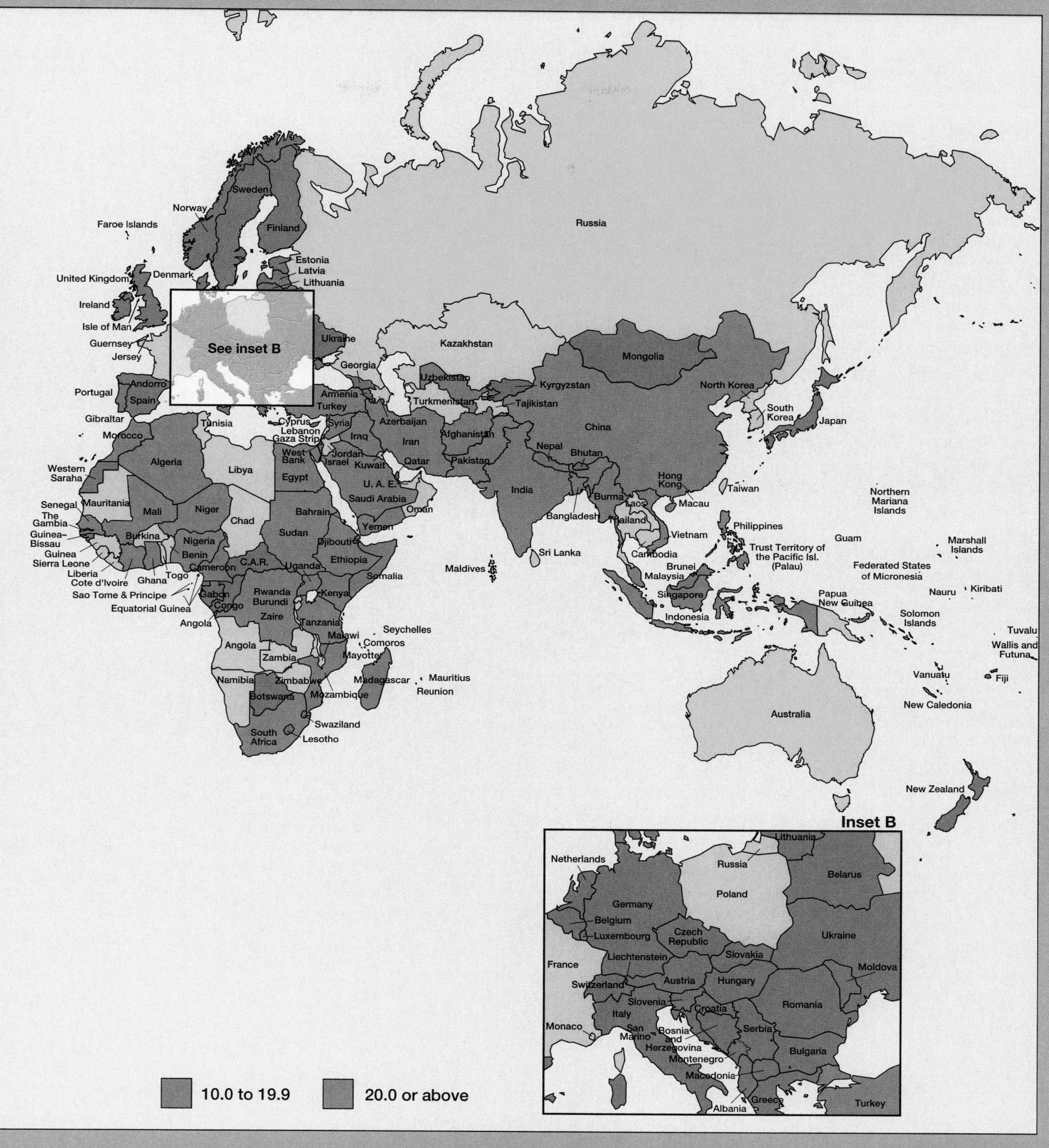

Russia
Faroe Islands
Norway
Sweden
Finland
Estonia
Latvia
Lithuania
United Kingdom
Denmark
Ireland
Isle of Man
Guernsey
Jersey
See inset B
Ukraine
Kazakhstan
Mongolia
Georgia
Portugal
Andorra
Spain
Armenia
Turkey
Uzbekistan
Kyrgyzstan
Turkmenistan
Tajikistan
North Korea
South Korea
Japan
Gibraltar
Tunisia
Cyprus
Lebanon
Gaza Strip
Syria
Azerbaijan
Morocco
Iraq
Iran
Afghanistan
China
Algeria
Libya
West Bank
Israel
Jordan
Kuwait
Qatar
Pakistan
Nepal
Bhutan
Western Sarah
Egypt
U. A. E.
Saudi Arabia
India
Hong Kong
Macau
Taiwan
Mauritania
Mali
Niger
Oman
Bahrain
Burma
Laos
Bangladesh
Thailand
Philippines
Northern Mariana Islands
Senegal
The Gambia
Guinea-Bissau
Guinea
Sierra Leone
Liberia
Cote d'Ivoire
Burkina
Ghana
Togo
Benin
Nigeria
Chad
Sudan
Yemen
Djibouti
Ethiopia
Vietnam
Guam
Marshall Islands
Cambodia
Sri Lanka
Trust Territory of the Pacific Isl. (Palau)
Cameroon
C.A.R.
Uganda
Somalia
Maldives
Brunei
Malaysia
Federated States of Micronesia
Sao Tome & Principe
Equatorial Guinea
Gabon
Congo
Rwanda
Burundi
Kenya
Singapore
Nauru
Kiribati
Papua New Guinea
Zaire
Tanzania
Indonesia
Solomon Islands
Angola
Malawi
Seychelles
Comoros
Mayotte
Tuvalu
Wallis and Futuna
Zambia
Namibia
Zimbabwe
Madagascar
Mauritius
Reunion
Vanuatu
Fiji
Botswana
Mozambique
New Caledonia
Australia
Swaziland
South Africa
Lesotho
New Zealand
Inset B
Lithuania
Netherlands
Russia
Belarus
Poland
Germany
Belgium
Luxembourg
Czech Republic
Ukraine
France
Liechtenstein
Slovakia
Moldova
Switzerland
Austria
Hungary
Slovenia
Croatia
Romania
Italy
Monaco
San Marino
Bosnia and Herzegovina
Serbia
Bulgaria
Montenegro
Macedonia
Albania
Greece
Turkey
10.0 to 19.9
20.0 or above

McGraw-Hill/Irwin Series in Marketing

Arens
Contemporary Advertising, 9/e

Arnould, Price, & Zinkhan
Consumers, 2/e

Bearden, Ingram, & LaForge
Marketing: Principles & Perspectives, 4/e

Belch & Belch
Advertising & Promotion: An Integrated Marketing Communications Approach, 6/e

Bingham & Gomes
Business Marketing Management, 2/e

Boyd, Walker, Mullins, & Larreche
Marketing Management: A Strategic Decision-Making Approach, 4/e

Cateora & Graham
International Marketing, 11/e

Cole & Mishler
Consumer and Business Credit Management, 11/e

Cravens & Piercy
Strategic Marketing, 7/e

Cravens, Lamb, & Crittenden
Strategic Marketing Management Cases, 7/e

Crawford & Di Benedetto
New Products Management, 7/e

Dolan
Marketing Management: Text and Cases, 1/e

Duncan
IMC: Using Advertising and Promotion to Build Brands, 1/e

Dwyer & Tanner
Business Marketing, 2/e

Eisenmann
Internet Business Models: Text and Cases, 1/e

Etzel, Walker, & Stanton
Marketing, 12/e

Forrest
Internet Marketing Intelligence, 1/e

Futrell
ABC's of Relationship Selling, 8/e

Futrell
Fundamentals of Selling, 7/e

Hair, Bush, & Ortinau
Marketing Research, 2/e

Hawkins, Best, & Coney
Consumer Behavior, 9/e

Johansson
Global Marketing, 3/e

Johnston & Marshall
Churchill/Ford/Walker's Sales Force Management, 7/e

Kerin, Berkowitz, Hartley, & Rudelius
Marketing, 7/e

Kerin, Hartley, & Rudelius
Marketing: The Core, 1/e

Lehmann & Winer
Analysis for Marketing Planning, 5/e

Lehmann & Winer
Product Management, 3/e

Levy & Weitz
Retailing Management, 5/e

Mason & Perreault
The Marketing Game!, 2/e

McDonald
Direct Marketing: An Integrated Approach, 1/e

Mohammed, Fisher, Jaworski, & Cahill
Internet Marketing: Building Advantage in a Networked Economy, 2/e

Monroe
Pricing, 3/e

Pelton, Strutton, & Lumpkin
Marketing Channels: A Relationship Management Approach, 2/e

Peppers & Rogers
Managing Customer Relationships to Build Competitive Advantage, 1/e

Perreault & McCarthy
Basic Marketing: A Global-Managerial Approach, 14/e

Perreault & McCarthy
Essentials of Marketing: A Global-Managerial Approach, 9/e

Peter & Donnelly
A Preface to Marketing Management, 9/e

Peter & Donnelly
Marketing Management: Knowledge and Skills, 7/e

Peter & Olson
Consumer Behavior, 6/e

Purvis & Burton
Which Ad Pulled Best?, 9/e

Rayport & Jaworski
Introduction to e-Commerce, 2/e

Rayport & Jaworski
e-Commerce, 1/e

Rayport & Jaworski
Cases in e-Commerce, 1/e

Richardson
Internet Marketing, 1/e

Roberts
Internet Marketing: Integrating Online and Offline Strategies, 1/e

Spiro, Stanton, & Rich
Management of a Sales Force, 11/e

Stock & Lambert
Strategic Logistics Management, 4/e

Ulrich & Eppinger
Product Design and Development, 2/e

Walker, Boyd, Mullins, & Larreche
Marketing Strategy: A Decision-Focused Approach, 4/e

Weitz, Castleberry, & Tanner
Selling: Building Partnerships, 5/e

Zeithaml & Bitner
Services Marketing, 3/e

Essentials of Marketing

9/e

A Global-Managerial Approach

William D. Perreault, Jr., Ph.D.
University of North Carolina

E. Jerome McCarthy, Ph.D.
Michigan State University

Boston Burr Ridge, IL Dubuque, IA Madison, WI New York San Francisco St. Louis
Bangkok Bogotá Caracas Kuala Lumpur Lisbon London Madrid Mexico City
Milan Montreal New Delhi Santiago Seoul Singapore Sydney Taipei Toronto

The McGraw·Hill Companies

ESSENTIALS OF MARKETING: A GLOBAL-MANAGERIAL APPROACH
Published by McGraw-Hill/Irwin, a business unit of The McGraw-Hill Companies, Inc., 1221 Avenue of the Americas, New York, NY, 10020.

This book is printed on acid-free paper.

domestic 2 3 4 5 6 7 8 9 0 VNH/VNH 0 9 8 7 6 5 4 3
International 2 3 4 5 6 7 8 9 0 VNH/VNH 0 9 8 7 6 5 4 3

ISBN 0-07-246420-8

Publisher: *John E. Biernat*
Executive editor: *Linda Schreiber*
Coordinating editor: *Lin Davis*
Managing developmental editor: *Nancy Barbour*
Marketing manager: *Kim Kanakes*
Media producer: *Craig Atkins*
Senior project manager: *Christine A. Vaughan*
Lead production supervisor: *Heather D. Burbridge*
Director of design BR: *Keith J. McPherson*
Photo research coordinator: *Jeremy Cheshareck*
Photo researcher: *Mike Hruby*
Lead supplement producer: *Cathy L. Tepper*
Senior digital content specialist: *Brian Nacik*
Cover illustrator: *Paul Turnbaugh*
Cover designer: *Keith J. McPherson*
Interior design: *Keith J. McPherson/Asylum Design*
Typeface: *10.5/12 Goudy*
Compositor: *GTS Graphics, Inc.*
Printer: *Von Hoffmann Press, Inc.*

Library of Congress Cataloging-in-Publication Data

Perreault, William D.
Essentials of marketing: a global-managerial approach / William D. Perreault, Jr., E. Jerome McCarthy. — 9th ed.
p. cm. — (McGraw-Hill/Irwin series in marketing)
Includes bibliographical references and indexes.
ISBN 0-07-246420-8 (alk. paper) — ISBN 0-07-119869-5 (international: alk. paper)
1. Marketing. I. McCarthy, E. Jerome (Edmund Jerome) II. Title. III. Series.
HF5415 .M378 2003
380.1—dc21 2002032682

INTERNATIONAL EDITION ISBN 0-07-119869-5

www.mhhe.com

About the Authors of *Essentials of Marketing, 9/e*

William D. Perreault, Jr., is currently Kenan Professor at the University of North Carolina Kenan-Flagler Business School. He has also taught at Stanford University, the University of Georgia, and North Carolina University and has been an invited speaker at over 80 universities. During 1997 he was the Arthur Andersen Distinguished Visitor at Cambridge University.

Dr. Perreault is the recipient of the two most prestigious awards in his field: the American Marketing Association Distinguished Educator Award and the Academy of Marketing Science Outstanding Educator Award. He also was selected for the Churchill Award, which honors career impact on marketing research. He was editor of the *Journal of Marketing Research* and has been on the review board of the *Journal of Marketing* and other journals. His research has also been published in many journals, and one *Journal of Marketing* article was recently voted one of the most influential articles on sales and sales management of the twentieth century.

The Decision Sciences Institute has recognized Dr. Perreault for innovations in marketing education, and at UNC he has received several awards for teaching excellence. His books include two other widely used texts: *Basic Marketing* and *The Marketing Game!*

Dr. Perreault is a past president of the American Marketing Association Academic Council and was on the AMA board. He was chair of an advisory committee to the U.S. Bureau of the Census, a trustee of the Marketing Science Institute, and on the Council of the Decision Sciences Institute. He is a Fellow of the Society for Marketing Advances. He has also worked as a consultant to organizations that range from GE and IBM to the Federal Trade Commission and Venezuelan Ministry of Education. He is on the advisory board for Copernicus: The Marketing Investment Strategy Group.

E. Jerome McCarthy received his Ph.D. from the University of Minnesota. He has taught at the Universities of Oregon, Notre Dame, and Michigan State. He was honored with the American Marketing Association's Trailblazer Award in 1987, and he was voted one of the "top five" leaders in Marketing Thought by marketing educators.

He has been deeply involved in teaching and developing new teaching materials. Besides writing various articles and monographs, he is the author of textbooks on data processing and social issues in marketing.

Dr. McCarthy is active in making presentations to business meetings and academic conferences. He has worked with groups of teachers throughout the country and has addressed international conferences in South America, Africa, and India.

He was also a Ford Foundation Fellow in 1963–64, studying the role of marketing in global economic development. In 1959–60 he was a Ford Foundation Fellow at the Harvard Business School working on mathematical methods in marketing.

Besides his academic interests, Dr. McCarthy has been involved in consulting for, and guiding the growth of, a number of businesses—both in the U.S. and overseas. He has worked with top managers from Steelcase, Dow Chemical, 3M, Bemis, Grupo Industrial Alfa, and many other companies. He is also active in executive education and is a director of several organizations. His primary interests, however, are in (1) "converting" students to marketing and marketing strategy planning and (2) preparing teaching materials to help others do the same. This is why he has spent a large part of his career developing, revising, and improving marketing texts to reflect the most current thinking in the field.

Preface

Essentials of Marketing Is Designed to Satisfy Your Needs

This book is about marketing and marketing strategy planning. And, at its essence, marketing strategy planning is about figuring out how to do a superior job of satisfying customers. We take that point of view seriously and believe in practicing what we preach. So you can trust that this new edition of *Essentials of Marketing*—and all of the other teaching and learning materials that accompany it—will satisfy *your* needs. We're excited about this edition of *Essentials of Marketing*, and we hope that you will be as well.

In developing this edition we've made hundreds of big and small additions, changes, and improvements in the text and all of the supporting materials that accompany it. We'll highlight some of those changes in this preface, but first it's useful to put this newest edition in a longer-term perspective.

A Shorter Text—for Flexibility and a Crisp Pace

Essentials of Marketing is a shortened version of our *Basic Marketing*, the most widely used text in the field. Our basic objectives in preparing a shorter text have always been:

- To make it easy, interesting, and fast for students to grasp the *essential* concepts of marketing.
- To provide a flexible text and choices from comprehensive support materials so that instructors can accomplish their objectives for their students even though the time available for the course is limited.

Accessibility is a key goal. In the whole text—and all of the supplements, ranging from the all new multimedia PowerPoints to the new edition of the *Learning Aid*—we spent much time and effort carefully defining terms and finding the right words, illustrations, and examples to speed understanding and motivate learning.

Building on Pioneering Strengths

Essentials of Marketing and *Basic Marketing* pioneered an innovative structure—using the "four Ps" with a managerial approach—for the introductory marketing course. They quickly became two of the most widely used business textbooks ever published because they organized the best ideas about marketing so that readers could both understand and apply them. The unifying focus of these ideas was on how to make the marketing decisions that a manager must make in deciding what customers to focus on and how best to meet their needs.

Over many editions of *Essentials of Marketing* there has been constant change in marketing management and the marketing environment. Some of the changes have been dramatic, and others have been subtle. As a result, we have made ongoing changes to the text to reflect marketing's best practices and ideas. Throughout all of these changes, *Essentials of Marketing* and *Basic Marketing* and the supporting materials that accompany them have been more widely used than any other teaching materials for introductory marketing. It is gratifying that the four Ps has proved to be an organizing structure that has worked well for millions of students and teachers.

Continuous Innovation and Improvement

The success of *Essentials of Marketing* is not the result of a single strength—or one long-lasting innovation. Rather, the text's four Ps framework, managerial orientation, and strategy planning focus have proved to be foundation pillars that are remarkably robust for supporting new developments in the field and innovations in the text and package. Thus, with each new edition of *Essentials of Marketing* we have continued to innovate to better meet the needs of students and faculty. In fact, we have made ongoing changes in how we develop the logic of the four Ps and the marketing strategy planning process. As always, though, our objective is to provide a flexible, high-quality text and choices from comprehensive and reliable support materials—so that instructors and students can accomplish their learning objectives. For example, included with the other innovations for this new edition are

- Integrated coverage, throughout the text, of the significant impacts that e-commerce, the Internet, and related information technologies are having on marketing.
- A complete revision of the *Student CD-ROM to Accompany Essentials of Marketing* that comes with the text, with a new interface that integrates the rich variety of multimedia learning resources it includes.
- A completely new and expanded archive of PowerPoint electronic lecture-support slides, with

links to full-motion videos, ads, and photos, to provide instructors with flexible support for lectures and presentations.

- The *Instructor CD-ROM to Accompany Essentials of Marketing* that provides Windows software and all of the text's teaching support materials in easy-to-use electronic form.
- A sharper focus, throughout the text, on how the strategy planning process should lead to decisions about a target market and marketing mix that represents the best opportunity and competitive advantage for the firm and superior value for consumers.
- Interesting new video cases and teaching videos focused on current marketing issues.
- High-involvement Internet exercises integrated throughout each chapter of the text.

We Believe in Continuous Quality Improvement

We have a commitment to ongoing improvements, and we're proud that we were implementing continuous quality improvements in preparing *Essentials of Marketing* long before the idea became popular in the world of business. We work to be creative in our coverage and approaches—because creativity is at the heart of the marketing spirit. The most creative teaching innovations are ones that meet students' needs and instructors' objectives. That's also why our first priority has always been, and always will be, producing quality materials that really work well for students and teachers. Students take the first marketing course only once. It is an investment and opportunity from which there should be a solid return. So we take it as a serious personal responsibility to support that investment with materials that are interesting and motivating—and that really build the skills and ideas that students need in their lives and careers.

Our belief that attention to continuous quality improvement in every aspect of the text and support materials *does make a difference* is consistently reaffirmed by the enthusiastic response of students and teachers alike to each new edition.

Leading Technology Innovations for Teaching and Learning

It has always been our belief that it is our responsibility to lead the marketing discipline in developing new, breakthrough approaches for teaching and learning in the first marketing course. Our constant thrust has been to use technology to provide better and easier options for teaching and richer and more interesting approaches for learning. Along with other innovations, we were the first to develop and offer spreadsheet-based computer-aided problems, custom-produced videos, a computerized test bank, a PC-based marketing simulation, a hypertext reference, bar-coded laser disks, CD-ROM–based interactive versions of the text, PowerPoint presentation slides with linking by objectives, CD-ROM multimedia archives and presentation software for instructors, multimedia case support, and the multimedia CD for students. Now we continue these traditions of innovation with a completely redesigned *Student CD-ROM to Accompany Essentials of Marketing*, *myPowerWeb* online readings, and a host of new and improved teaching and learning materials available at the *Essentials of Marketing* website at www.mhhe.com/fourps.

Critically Revised, Updated, and Rewritten

This new edition of *Essentials of Marketing* is the highest-quality teaching and learning resource ever published for the introductory marketing course. The whole text and all of the supporting materials have been critically revised, updated, and rewritten. As in past editions, clear and interesting communication has been a priority. *Essentials of Marketing* is designed to make it easy, interesting, and fast for students to grasp the key concepts of marketing. Careful explanations provide a crisp focus on the important "essentials" of marketing strategy planning. At the same time, we have thoroughly

- Researched and incorporated new concepts.
- Integrated hundreds of new examples that bring the concepts alive.
- Illustrated marketing ideas and "best practices" in a rich variety of contexts.

We have deliberately used marketing examples from a host of different contexts. Examples span organizations that have moved to e-commerce and those that have found other ways to innovate, profit and nonprofit organizations, large and small firms, domestic and international settings, purchases by organizations as well as by final consumers, services and ideas or "causes" as well as physical goods, and established products as well as new technologies—because this variety reinforces the point that effective marketing is critical to all organizations.

Clear Focus on Changes in Today's Dynamic Markets

This edition focuses special attention on changes taking place in today's dynamic markets. Throughout every chapter of the text we have integrated discussion and examples of

- Best practices in marketing, and how to avoid the mistakes of death-wish marketing (including errors and omissions all too common among many failed dot-com operators).
- Effective e-commerce innovations and changes in marketing over the Internet.
- The costs and benefits of different approaches for customer acquisition and retention.
- Relationship building and customer relationship management in marketing.
- The importance of providing superior customer value as the means to achieve customer satisfaction and competitive advantage.
- International perspectives.
- Ethical issues.

Similarly, we've also integrated new material on many important and fast-evolving topics. The following are but a sampling:

- Integrated marketing communications, direct-response promotion, and customer-initiated interactive marketing communications.
- Promotional campaigns that build "buzz" among consumers.
- The Euro, the World Trade Organization, exchange rates, and other topics central to international markets.
- The growth of business-to-business (B2B) exchanges on the Web and the expanding use of reverse auctions and interactive bidding.
- The circumstances when using a website for direct distribution or dual distribution makes sense and when it doesn't.
- The expanding role of sales technologies and self-service technology.
- The increasing channel power of large retail chains.
- Competitor analysis and how to develop competitive advantage.
- How to use flexible pricing and evaluate price sensitivity.

Driving Home Competitive Advantage

Throughout the 9th edition we've continued to put more emphasis on the *process* of marketing strategy planning. In today's dynamic markets it's not enough to simply figure out an attractive opportunity and an effective marketing mix. The real challenge is to quickly but logically zero in on the target market and marketing mix that is really best for the firm, while recognizing that strategies need to be refined and improved as market conditions change. This highlights the need for breakthrough opportunities, the problems with me-too imitation, and the crucial role of competitive advantage in providing customers with superior value. In other words, we sharpen the focus on how to figure out the best blend of the four Ps and crush the mistaken view fostered by some texts that the marketing job is just coming up with *some* marketing mix.

Coupled with this, you'll learn how breakthroughs in information technology are driving changes in all aspects of marketing—whether it's e-commerce ordering, getting marketing information, preparing salespeople to interact with customers, or analyzing the "fire-hydrant" flow of data on sales and costs. We'll also highlight the many ways that relationships among marketing partners are changing—ranging from coordination of logistics to alliances among firms focused on the same market opportunity. You'll see how intense competition, both in the United States and around the world, is affecting marketing strategy planning. You'll see what it takes to transform an effective new-product development process into profitable business.

Some other marketing texts are attempting to describe such changes. But that's not adequate. What sets *Essentials of Marketing* apart is that the explanations and examples equip students to see *why* these changes are taking place and what changes to expect in the future. That is an important distinction—because marketing is dynamic. Our objective is to prepare students to analyze marketing situations and develop exceptional marketing strategies—not just recite endless sets of lists.

A Fresh Design—to Make Important Concepts Even Clearer

Along with the new content, we've given the text a fresh design. The changes range from the new cover to hundreds of new photographs, ads, web pages, and illustrations. We've created many new exhibits—conceptual organizers, charts, and tables—and updated proven pieces from past editions, all with a fresh new design.

The aim of all this revising, refining, editing, and illustrating is to make important concepts and points even clearer to students. We want to make sure that each student really does get a good feel for a market-directed system and how he or she can help it—and some company—run better. We believe marketing is important and interesting—and we want every student who reads *Essentials of Marketing* to share our enthusiasm.

Eighteen Chapters—with an Emphasis on Marketing Strategy Planning

The emphasis of *Essentials of Marketing* is on marketing strategy planning. Eighteen chapters introduce the important concepts in marketing management and help the student see marketing through the eyes of the marketing manager. The organization of the chapters and topics is carefully planned. But we took special care in writing so that

- It is possible to rearrange and use the chapters in many different sequences—to fit different needs.
- All of the topics and chapters fit together into a clear, overall framework for the marketing strategy planning process.

Broadly speaking, the chapters fall into two groupings. The first seven chapters introduce marketing and a broad view of the marketing strategy planning process. They cover topics such as segmentation, differentiation, the marketing environment, and buyer behavior, as well as how marketing information systems and research provide information about these forces to improve marketing decisions. The second half of the text goes into the details of planning the four Ps, with specific attention to the key strategy decisions in each area. Then we conclude with an integrative review, including an assessment of marketing's challenges and opportunities.

The first two chapters deal with the nature of marketing—focusing both on its macro role in a global society and its micro role in businesses and other organizations. The first chapter stresses that the effectiveness of our macro-marketing system depends on the decisions of many producers and consumers. That sets the stage for the second chapter—and the rest of the book—which focuses on how businesspeople and, in particular, marketing managers develop marketing strategies to satisfy specific target markets. This chapter introduces the marketing concept and develops the customer value and four Ps frameworks.

Chapter 3 introduces an integrative model of the marketing strategy planning process that serves as an organizing framework for the whole text. Chapter 3 sets the stage by overviewing how analysis of the market and external market environment relate to segmentation and differentiation decisions as well as the criteria for narrowing down to a specific target market and marketing mix. Broadly speaking, it introduces a strategic planning view of how a manager leads his or her firm to new market opportunities and competitive advantage.

This strategic view alerts students to the importance of evaluating opportunities in the external environments affecting marketing—and these are discussed in Chapter 4. This chapter also highlights the critical role of screening criteria for narrowing down from possible opportunities to those that the firm will pursue.

The next two chapters take a closer look at *customers*—so students will better understand how to segment markets and satisfy target market needs. Chapter 5 introduces the behavioral aspects of the final consumer market. Chapter 6 looks at how business and organizational customers—like manufacturers, channel members, and government purchasers—are using e-commerce and the other ways that they are similar to and different from final consumers. You have to understand customers to understand marketing.

Chapter 7 is a contemporary view of getting information—from marketing information systems and marketing research—for marketing management planning. This chapter includes discussion of how information technology—ranging from intranets to speedy collection of market research data—is transforming the marketing manager's job. This sets the stage for discussions in later chapters about how research and marketing information improve each area of marketing strategy planning.

The next group of chapters—Chapters 8 to 17—is concerned with developing a marketing mix out of the four Ps: Product, Place (involving channels of distribution, logistics, and distribution customer service), Promotion, and Price. These chapters are concerned with developing the "right" Product and making it available at the "right" Place with the "right" Promotion and the "right" Price—to satisfy target customers and still meet the objectives of the business. These chapters are presented in an integrated, analytical way—as part of the overall framework for the marketing strategy planning process—so students' thinking about planning marketing strategies develops logically.

Chapters 8 and 9 focus on product planning for goods and services as well as new-product development and the different strategy decisions that are required at different stages of the product life cycle. We emphasize the value of an organized new-product development process for developing really new products that propel a firm to profitable growth.

Chapters 10 through 12 focus on Place. Chapter 10 introduces decisions a manager must make about using direct distribution (for example, selling from the firm's website) or working with other firms in a channel of distribution. We put special emphasis on the need for channel members to cooperate and coordinate to better meet the needs of customers. Chapter 11 focuses on the fast-changing arena of logistics and the strides that firms are making in using e-commerce to reduce the costs of storing, transporting, and handling products while improving the distribution service they provide customers.

Chapter 12 provides a clear picture of retailers, wholesalers, and their strategy planning—including exchanges taking place via the Internet. This composite chapter helps students see why the big changes taking place in retailing are reshaping the channel systems for many consumer products.

Chapters 13 to 15 deal with Promotion. These chapters build on the concepts of integrated marketing communications, direct-response promotion, and customer-initiated digital communication, which are introduced in Chapter 13. Chapter 14 deals with the role of personal selling and sales technology in the promotion blend. Chapter 15 covers advertising and sales promotion, including the ways that managers are taking advantage of the Internet to communicate more effectively and efficiently.

Chapters 16 and 17 deal with Price. Chapter 16 focuses on pricing objectives and policies, including use of information technology to implement flexible pricing, pricing in the channel, and the use of discounts, allowances, and other variations from a list price. Chapter 17 covers cost-oriented and demand-oriented pricing approaches and how they fit in today's competitive environments. The careful coverage of marketing costs helps equip students to deal with the renewed cost-consciousness of the firms they will join.

Chapter 18 reinforces the integrative nature of marketing management and reviews the marketing strategy planning process that leads to creative marketing plans. This final chapter also considers how efficient the marketing process is. Here we evaluate the effectiveness of both micro- and macro-marketing—and we consider the competitive, technological, ethical, and social challenges facing marketing managers now and in the future. After this chapter, many students want to look at Appendix C—which is about career opportunities in marketing.

Careful Integration of Special Topics

Some textbooks treat "special" topics—like e-commerce, relationship marketing, international marketing, services marketing, marketing over the Internet, marketing for nonprofit organizations, marketing ethics, and business-to-business marketing—in separate chapters. We deliberatively avoid doing that because we are convinced that treating such topics separately leads to an unfortunate compartmentalization of ideas. We think they are too important to be isolated in that way. For example, to simply tack on a new chapter on e-commerce or marketing applications on the Internet completely ignores the reality that these are not just isolated topics but rather must be considered broadly across the whole fabric of marketing decisions. In fact, the huge losses piled up by failed dot-com firms over the past few years are evidence of what happens when managers fail to understand the need to integrate marketing strategy planning decisions and don't come to grips with issues such as competitor analysis, customer value, and the marketing concept. Conversely, there is virtually no area of marketing decision making where it's safe to ignore the impact of e-commerce, the Internet, or information technology. The same is true with other topics. So they are interwoven and illustrated throughout the text to emphasize that marketing thinking is crucial in all aspects of our society and economy. This edition is again packaged with a grid that shows, in detail, how and where specific topics are integrated throughout the text. Talk is cheap, especially when it comes to the hype from some publishers about how important topics are treated in a new text. But the grid offers proof that in *Essentials of Marketing* we have delivered on the promise of integrated treatment.

Students Get "How-to-Do-It" Skill and Confidence

Really understanding marketing and how to plan marketing strategies can build self-confidence—and it can help prepare a student to take an active part in the business world. To move students in this direction, we deliberately include a variety of frameworks, models, classification systems, cases, and "how-to-do-it" techniques that relate to our overall framework for marketing strategy planning. Taken together, they should speed the development of "marketing sense" and enable the student to analyze marketing situations and develop marketing plans in a confident and meaningful way. They are practical and they work. In addition, because they are interesting and understandable, they motivate students to see marketing as the challenging and rewarding area it is.

Essentials of Marketing Motivates High-Involvement Learning

So students will see what is coming in each *Essentials of Marketing* chapter, behavioral objectives are included on the first page of each chapter. And to speed student understanding, important new terms are shown in red and defined immediately. Further, a glossary of these terms is presented at the end of the book. Within chapters, major section headings and second-level headings (placed in the margin for clarity) immediately show how the material is organized *and* summarize key points in the text. Further, we have placed annotated photos and ads near the concepts they illustrate to provide a visual reminder of the ideas and to show vividly how they apply in the current business world. In each chapter we have integrated Internet exercises related to the concepts being developed. The focus of these exercises is on important marketing issues, not just on "surfing the Net."

All of these aids help the student understand important concepts and speed review before exams. End-of-chapter questions and problems offer additional opportunities. They can be used to encourage students to investigate the marketing process and develop their own ways of thinking about it. These can be used for independent study or as a basis for written assignments or class discussion.

Varied Types of Cases

Understanding of the text material can be deepened by analysis and discussion of specific cases. *Essentials of Marketing* features several different types of cases. Each chapter starts with an in-depth case study developed specifically to highlight that chapter's teaching objectives and the specific marketing decision areas covered in that chapter. In addition, each chapter features a special case report in a highlighted box. These thought-provoking cases illustrate how companies handle topics covered in that chapter. All of these cases provide an excellent basis for critical evaluation and discussion. And we've included relevant Internet addresses so that it is easy for students to quickly get updated information about the companies and topics covered in the cases. Of course, website addresses referenced in the cases may change. Some companies change their websites to get a fresh look, to take advantage of new web capabilities, or just to update the information that's available. However, when that occurs, our *Essentials of Marketing* website at www.mhhe.com/fourps provides up-to-date links relevant to the chapters in the text. Our CD-ROMs also include links to the website so you can bookmark the site in your Internet browser.

In addition, there are several suggested cases at the end of each chapter. The focus of these cases is on problem solving. They encourage students to apply, and really get involved with, the concepts developed in the text. Each of the first 17 chapters also features a computer-aided problem. These case-based exercises stimulate a problem-solving approach to marketing strategy planning and give students hands-on experience that shows how logical analysis of alternative strategies can lead to improved decision making. For the convenience of students and faculty alike, printed versions of the cases for the computer-aided problems are incorporated in the book itself. Further, the award-winning spreadsheet software we developed specifically for use with these problems has been revised so that it is fully integrated with the other applications on the Student CD-ROM that comes with the text.

New Multimedia Video Cases Are Integrative

In the last edition we included a custom-produced set of exciting video cases. The response to them was great, and this time we've expanded the set and updated some of the best from the previous set. Each of these combines a written case with an accompanying video. These cases are a bit longer than the text-only cases and open up the opportunity for students to analyze an organization's whole marketing program in more depth and with even greater integration. Marketing professors wrote the scripts for both the videos and text portions of the cases—so the videos reinforce real content while bringing a high-involvement multimedia dimension to the learning experience. And to ensure consistency with all of the other *Essentials of Marketing* materials, we've carefully edited and coordinated the whole effort. These cases were developed so that they focus on different areas of the text, and thus they deal with a variety of issues:

- The expanding role of marketing in developing export opportunities for a raw material that was previously just viewed as a commodity.
- How a well-known company won profits and customer loyalty by developing a marketing mix that's carefully matched to the needs of its target market.
- New-product development for a major component part that is sold to producers who serve consumer markets.
- The growth strategy for a vineyard that is working to develop a major brand.
- The development of a new market awareness and strategy by a major nonprofit organization.
- A case on the promotional program for the introduction of an exciting new automobile.
- An integrated case on the marketing strategy for an innovative household appliance.

We designed these cases so that students can analyze them before or after seeing the video, or even without seeing the video at all. They can be used in a variety of ways, either for class discussion or individual assignments. To get the ball rolling, students get their own copy of segments of the case videos on the Student CD-ROM. We're proud of these video cases, and we're sure that they provide you with a valuable new way to learn about marketing.

Comprehensive, Current References for Independent Study

Some professors and students want to follow up on text readings. Each chapter is supplemented with detailed references—to both classic articles and current readings in business publications. These can guide more detailed study of the topics covered in a chapter.

Instructor Creates a System—with *Essentials of Marketing's P.L.U.S.*

Essentials of Marketing can be studied and used in many ways—the *Essentials of Marketing* text material is only the central component of our Professional Learning Units Systems (our *P.L.U.S.*) for students and teachers. Instructors (and students) can select from our units to develop their own personalized systems. Many combinations of units are possible—depending on course objectives. As a quick overview, in addition to the *Essentials of Marketing* text, the *P.L.U.S.* package includes a variety of new and updated supplements:

- A redesigned and updated *Student CD-ROM to Accompany Essentials of Marketing,* which includes clips for the video cases, a database of ads and annotations that illustrate keys concepts for each chapter, a new version of our computer-aided problems (CAP) spreadsheet software, self-test quizzes, and narrated self-study PowerPoint electronic slide shows, to introduce students to what's ahead. The CD also includes a revision of the *Essentials of Marketing Hypertext Reference* for use in developing marketing plans or reviewing for tests.
- An online learning center at our revised website (www.mhhe.com/fourps) for students and instructors, with features such as (constantly updated) links to just-published articles from myPowerWeb on topics in each chapter, chat rooms, software downloads, Internet website links, and other exciting features.
- A completely new and much expanded archive of PowerPoint lecture slides, incorporating full-motion video clips, photos, ads, interactive exercises, and other multimedia assets to support the professor.
- An improved *Instructor CD-ROM to Accompany Essentials of Marketing,* which includes all of the instructor resources available for *Essentials of Marketing* in electronic form.

In addition, we've completely revised and updated

- The *Multimedia Lecture Support Package.*
- The *Learning Aid* workbook.
- *Applications in Basic Marketing,* an annually updated book of marketing clippings from the popular press, free and shrinkwrapped with the text and, new to this edition, supplemented with myPowerWeb digital articles on the Web.
- Over 200 color acetates (also available in electronic form).
- Over 200 transparency masters (also available as PowerPoint slides).
- *Instructor's Manual.*
- Author-prepared *Manual of Tests*, accompanied by the *Diploma* test-generator software that supports both printed and online testing.
- A complete set of new and updated *teaching videos* and seven great video cases (and instructor's manual).
- A new Windows version of the *The Marketing Game!* (and instructor's manual) that offers password-protected digital plan and report files and supports working over the Internet.

We've been busy. You may not want to use all of this. Some people don't want any of it. But whatever you elect to use—and in whatever medium you like to work—the teaching and learning materials work well together. We've designed them that way.

Hypertext—a Marketing Knowledge Navigator

We introduced the innovative *Essentials of Marketing Hypertext Reference* with the 6th edition of *Essentials of Marketing* and have expanded its capabilities ever since. This easy-to-use Windows software puts almost all of the key concepts from *Essentials of Marketing* at your fingertips. It features hyperlinks, which means that when you are reading about a concept on screen you can instantly jump to more detail on any topic. You simply highlight the concept or topic and click with a mouse or press the enter key. Books assemble information in some specific order—but hypertext allows you to integrate thinking on any topic or combination of topics, regardless of where it is treated in the text.

The new version of the software provides an even clearer and easier way to search for ideas while developing a marketing plan. You can also use the software to review topics in "book order"—starting with learning objectives and then "paging" through each set of ideas.

Free Applications Book—Updated Each Year

It is a sign of the commitment of our publisher to the introductory marketing course that it will publish a new edition of *Applications in Basic Marketing* every year and provide it free of charge shrinkwrapped with each new copy of the 9th edition of *Essentials of Marketing.* This annually updated collection of marketing "clippings"—from publications such as *Business Week, The Wall Street Journal, Advertising Age,* and *Fortune*—provides convenient access to short, interesting, and current discussions of marketing issues. Each edition features about 100 articles. There are a variety of short clippings related to each chapter in *Essentials of Marketing*. In addition, because we revise this collection each year, it includes timely material that is available in no other text.

Learning Aid—Deepens Understanding

There are more components to *P.L.U.S.* A separate *Learning Aid* provides several more units and offers further opportunities to obtain a deeper understanding of the material. The *Learning Aid* can be used by the student alone or with teacher direction. Portions of the *Learning Aid* help students to review what they have studied. For example, there is a brief introduction to each chapter, a list of the important new terms (with page numbers for easy reference), true-false questions (with answers and page numbers) that cover all the important terms and concepts, and multiple-choice questions (with answers) that illustrate the kinds of questions that may appear in examinations. In addition, the *Learning Aid* has cases, exercises, and problems—with clear instructions and worksheets for the student to complete. The *Learning Aid* also features computer-aided problems that build on the computer-aided cases in the text. The *Learning Aid* exercises can be used as classwork or homework—to drill on certain topics and to deepen understanding of others by motivating application and then discussion. In fact, reading *Essentials of Marketing* and working with the *Learning Aid* can be the basic activity of the course.

Compete and Learn—with New Edition of *The Marketing Game!*

Another valuable resource is *The Marketing Game! The Marketing Game!* is a PC-based competitive simulation. It was developed specifically to reinforce the target marketing and marketing strategy-planning ideas discussed in *Essentials of Marketing*. Students make marketing management decisions—blending the four Ps to compete for the business of different possible target markets. The innovative design of *The Marketing Game!* allows the instructor to increase the number of decision areas involved as students learn more about marketing. In fact, many instructors use the advanced levels of the game as the basis for a second course. *The Marketing Game!* is widely heralded as the best marketing strategy simulation available—and the new Windows edition widens its lead over the others available. Competitors don't even need to be on the same continent. It works great with password-protected decisions submitted over the Internet and reports returned the same way.

Multimedia Support for Preparation, Lectures, and Discussion

Essentials of Marketing and all of our accompanying materials have been developed to promote student learning and get students involved in the excitement and challenges of marketing management. Additional elements of *P.L.U.S.* have been specifically developed to help an instructor offer a truly professional course that meets the objectives he or she sets for students. Complete instructor's manuals accompany all of the *P.L.U.S.* components.

Electronic Presentation Slides with Many Uses

With this edition we are providing instructors with a completely new, much-expanded set of PowerPoint electronic slide presentations. This flexible package features a large number of PowerPoint graphics developed for every chapter in the text. In addition, these new PowerPoints incorporate full-motion videos, ads, and interactive exercises for every chapter.

Because we provide the native-format PowerPoint files, instructors can modify or delete any slide or add other slides by using their own copy of PowerPoint. And, of course, if electronic projection equipment isn't available, the instructor can print out the images to customized color acetates or black and white transparencies. All of the overhead masters and color acetates are also available as PowerPoint slides.

While these electronic slides are intended mainly for instructor use in class discussions and lectures, they are easy to use and can be placed on the Internet, on the school's computer network, or in a computer lab as a supplement for independent review by students.

Complete Multimedia Lecture Support

With the PowerPoint electronic slide presentations we also provide detailed lecture notes, as well as lecture outlines. The PowerPoint slide show includes small versions of the slides for class handouts. All of these materials are packaged in our *Multimedia Lecture Support Package*. This supplement is available in an electronic form on the Instructor CD-ROM, and that makes it even more convenient to use. It gives instructors a great deal of flexibility and saves time that can be spent on other teaching activities. Instructors who prefer to use materials like those that were in the past included with our *Lecture Guide* won't be disappointed either. The new package will provide that material as well—in both printed form and in the form of word-processing files (which makes it easier for instructors to electronically cut and paste and incorporate their own materials or to save time and effort in creating a website for the course).

In addition, the *Multimedia Lecture Support Package* is accompanied by a high-quality selection of overhead masters and color transparencies—over 400 in all. The manual provides detailed suggestions about ways to use them. All of these items are also available on the CD-ROM.

Exciting New Video—Created by Marketing Experts

The newly revised and expanded *Essentials of Marketing Videos* are also available to all schools that adopt *Essentials of Marketing*. Half of the video modules are completely new—based on scripts written by expert marketing scholars and carefully linked to key topics in the text. In addition, several of the most popular video modules from the previous edition—the ones instructors and students said they most wanted to keep—have been thoroughly revised and updated. These new videos are really great, but it doesn't stop there! As we noted earlier, there are also seven great new videos to accompany the video cases.

Testing that Works for Faculty and Students

In addition, thousands of objective test questions—*written by the authors* to really work with the text—give instructors a high-quality resource. The *Diploma* program for Windows computers allows the instructor to select from any of these questions, change them as desired, or add new questions—and quickly print out a finished test customized to the instructor's course. As an added benefit, the instructor can publish questions to a website and students can take tests online.

The Responsibilities of Leadership

In closing, we return to a point raised at the beginning of this preface. *Essentials of Marketing* has been a leading textbook in marketing since its first edition. We take the responsibilities of that leadership seriously. We know that you want and deserve the very best teaching and learning materials possible. It is our commitment to bring you those materials—today with this edition and in the future with subsequent editions.

We recognize that fulfilling this commitment requires a process of continuous improvement. Improvements, changes, and development of new elements must be ongoing—because needs change. You are an important part of this evolution, of this leadership. We encourage your feedback. The most efficient way to get in touch with us is to send an e-mail message to Bill_Perreault @unc.edu. There's also a comment form built into the book's website, and if you prefer the traditional approach, send a letter to 2104 N. Lakeshore Dr., Chapel Hill, NC, 27514. Thoughtful criticisms and suggestions from students and teachers alike have helped to make *Essentials of Marketing* what it is. We hope that you will help make it what it will be in the future.

William D. Perreault, Jr.

E. Jerome McCarthy

Guided Tour

Marketing is now widely accepted by many nonprofit organizations, including the National Kidney Foundation, which wants to increase the number of organ donors.

THE ULTIMATE HAND-ME-DOWN.

SIGN AN ORGAN DONOR CARD. IT WON'T KILL YOU.

National Kidney Foundation of New York/New Jersey 1-800-63-DONATE

ways to prod
lower cost.
resolved, Harl
ing its objecti
its close relati
resource that
line of accesso
manufacturing
ing customers
should be co
strengths and weaknesses are discussed in the

Some opportunities require large amounts
may be required for R&D, production facilitie

Current and wide-ranging examples demonstrate that effective marketing is crucial to all organizations. Examples span profit and non-profit organizations, large and small firms, domestic and international settings, and every spot on the technology spectrum from traditional companies to dot-coms to bricks and clicks.

Adero wants marketers to keep in mind that a website that can attract prospects from all over the world won't be successful in turning them into customers if it ignores nationalism and cultural differences.

Perreault and McCarthy have achieved a truly global flavor by choosing to carefully integrate thorough international coverage throughout the text rather than confining it to one chapter.

Lipton is pursuing new customers and growth in over 100 countries. For example, its multilingual website in Belgium explains how to make exotic cocktails from Ice Tea, and in Asia it encourages consumer trial with free samples.

International Opportunities Should Be Considered

It's easy for a marketing manager to fall into the trap of ignoring international markets, especially when the firm's domestic market is prosperous. Yet, there are good reasons to go to the trouble of looking elsewhere for opportunities.

The world is getting smaller

International trade is increasing all around the world, and trade barriers are coming down. In addition, advances in e-commerce, transportation, and communications are making it easier and cheaper to reach international customers. With an Internet website, e-mail, and a fax machine, even the smallest firm can provide international customers with a great deal of information—and easy ways to order—at very little expense.

Develop a competitive advantage at home and abroad

If customers in other countries are interested in the products a firm offers—or could offer—serving them may improve economies of scale. Lower costs (and prices) may give a firm a competitive advantage both in its home markets *and* abroad. Black and Decker, for example, uses electric mot
By selling overseas as well as in the U.S.,
per motor is very low.

Many marketing managers who thought
national competition have been rudely surp
foreign producer is willing to pursue local
firm in Atlanta that makes air purification
[selling to an oil refinery] in Saudi Arabia
problem, then come attack me on my hom

Get an early start in a new market

Different countries are at different stag
have different needs at different times.

Exhibit 3-2
Four Basic Types of Opportunities

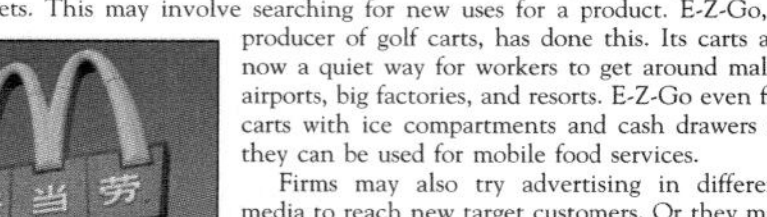

Market development means trying to increase sales by selling present products in new markets. This may involve searching for new uses for a product. E-Z-Go, a producer of golf carts, has done this. Its carts are now a quiet way for workers to get around malls, airports, big factories, and resorts. E-Z-Go even fits carts with ice compartments and cash drawers so they can be used for mobile food services.

Firms may also try advertising in different media to reach new target customers. Or they may add new stores in new areas. For example, to reach new customers, McDonald's has opened outlets in airports, zoos, casinos, and military bases. And it's rapidly expanded into international markets with outlets in places like Russia, Brazil, and China.[7]

Product development means offering new or improved products for present markets. By knowing the present market's needs, a firm may see new ways to satisfy customers. For example, Heinz figured out how ketchup could be more fun because kids are the biggest consumers. Producing ketchup in gross green and funky purple colors—in an EZ Squirt dispenser—increased sales so much that the factory had to run 24/7. Ski resorts have developed trails for hiking and biking to bring their winter ski customers back in the summer. Nike moved beyond shoes to offer its athletic target market a portable heart-rate monitor. And of course Intel boosts sales by developing newer and faster chips.[8]

Diversification means moving into totally different lines of business—perhaps entirely unfamiliar products, markets, or even levels in the production-marketing system. McDonald's, for example, is opening two four-star hotels in Switzerland. The plan is to serve families on the weekend, but the target market during the week is business travelers.

Products and customers that are very different from a firm's current base may look attractive to the optimists—but these opportunities are usually hard to evaluate. That's why diversification usually involves the biggest risk.[9]

Internet Exercise Go to the website for McDonald's hotel and review the information given (www.goldenarchhotel.com). Based on what you see, do you think that the hotels will appeal to the weekend target market of traveling families? Do you think they will appeal to business travelers during the week?

Most firms think first of greater market penetration. They want to increase profits where they already have experience and strengths. Many firms just try to do a better job of hanging onto the customers that they've already won. On the other hand, many firms are proving that market development—and the move into new international markets—is another profitable way to take advantage of current strengths.

Managers who compete in global markets need to be aware of how changes in the global economy will impact their strategies and opportunities.

Even a well-planned marketing strategy may fail if a country or region goes through a rapid business decline. As consumers' incomes drop, they must shift their spending patterns. They may simply have to do without some products. In the late 1990s this happened across countries in Asia, and many businesses collapsed. You can see how quickly this happens by considering Thailand. In a few months, the buying power of Thai money (the bhat) was cut by half. Imagine how *your* life would change if you suddenly had half as much money.

Economic changes are not always this dramatic. Consider the cooling off of the U.S. economy in 2000. The growth of the economy leading up to that time created a strong job market and increased incomes. Purchases of luxuries trended up because of this "wealth effect." This trend changed when the economy turned, but for most products demand declined more gradually.

Interest rates and inflation affect buying

Changes in the economy are often accompanied by changes in the interest rate—the charge for borrowing money. Interest rates directly affect the total price borrowers must pay for products. So the interest rate affects when, and if, they will buy. This is an especially important factor in some business markets. But it also affects consumer purchases of homes, cars, and other items usually bought on credit.

Interest rates usually increase during periods of inflation, and inflation is a fact of life in many economies. In some Latin American countries, inflation has exceeded 400 percent a year in recent years. In contrast, recent U.S. levels—3 to 20 percent—seem low. Still, inflation must be considered in strategy planning. When costs are rising rapidly and there are no more cost-cutting measures to take, a marketing manager may have to increase prices.

The global economy is connected

The economies of the world are connected—and changes in one economy quickly affect others. One reason for this is that the amount of international trade is increasing—and it is affected by changes in and between economies. For example, International Harvester (IH) was very successful selling its earth-moving equipment in Asia when construction was booming. However, when the "Asian flu" hit, many customers could no longer make payments and IH faced big losses.

Changes in the *exchange rate*—how much one country's money is worth in another country's money—have an important effect on international trade. When

Marketing's Role within the Firm or Nonprofit Organization 39

Exhibit 2-5
The Marketing Management Process

The **marketing management process** is the process of (1) *planning* marketing activities, (2) directing the *implementation* of the plans, and (3) *controlling* these plans. Planning, implementation, and control are basic jobs of all managers—but here we will emphasize what they mean to marketing managers.

As Exhibit 2-5 shows, the marketing management process is continuous. In the planning job, managers set guidelines for the implementing job—and specify expected results. They use these expected results in the control job—to determine if everything has worked out as planned. The link from the control job to the planning job is especially important. This feedback often leads to changes in the plans—or to new plans.

Marketing managers should seek new opportunities

Marketing managers cannot be satisfied just planning present activities. Markets are dynamic. Consumers' needs, competitors, and the environment keep changing. Consider Parker Brothers, a company that seemed to have a "Monopoly" in family games. While it continued selling board games, firms like Sega and Nintendo zoomed in with video game competition. Of course, not every opportunity is good for every company. Really attractive opportunities are those that fit with what the whole company wants to do and is able to do well.

Strategic management planning concerns the whole firm

The job of planning strategies to guide a whole company is called **strategic (management) planning**—the manage
match between an organization's resou
top-management job. It includes plann
duction, finance, human resources, an
On the other hand, company plan
keting plan often sets the tone and d
use *strategy planning* and *marketing stra*

What Is Marketing Strategy Planning?

Marketing strategy planning means
ing profitable marketing strategies. But
these words rather casually so far. Now
What is a marketing strategy?

Marketing Strategy Planning is introduced early and teaches students about the important concepts in marketing management. This coverage helps students see marketing through the eyes of a marketing manager.

Business and Organizational Customers and Their Buying Behavior 147

Exhibit 6-6 Examples of Different B2B E-Commerce Sites Used by Organizational Buyers and Sellers

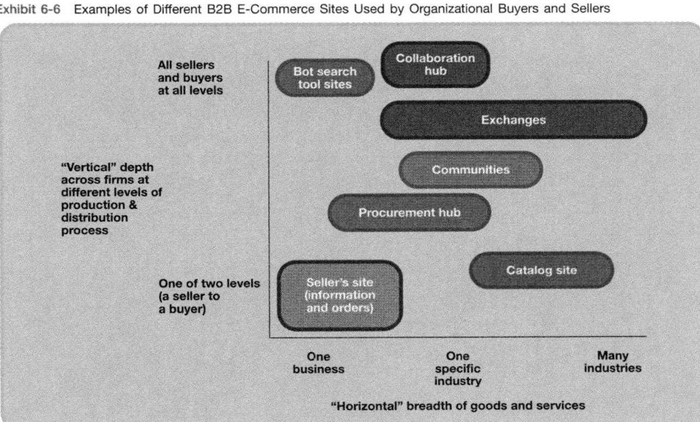

Some bots take things further and assemble price comparisons or a list of e-mail addresses.

Some purchasing managers are using search bots to locate hard-to-find, off-the-shelf products that eliminate the need for custom-produced items. For example, Allstates Rubber & Tools in the suburbs of Chicago is a small firm, but it's on the Internet. Allstates recently got a $1,000 order for rubber grommets (tiny rings used to protect electric wires) from a company in Saudi Arabia. If the customer had not been able to locate Allstates' website on the Internet it probably would have paid higher prices to have the grommets custom-produced—and Allstates would have missed the business.[17]

More progress is needed

As we've said from the start, business customers are usually interested in the total value of a supplier's marketing mix—not just in the product price in a single transaction. Earlier we reviewed why a buyer might prefer closer relationships with fewer sellers. So it is important to see that Internet tools that focus primarily on lowering the purchase price for a specific transaction do not necessarily lower total purchasing costs or apply to all types of purchases. So websites and Internet-based software tools that help both buyers and sellers work together in more efficient and effective relationships warrant attention. National Semiconductor's website is a good example. It is designed to create easy links between its customers, products, and distributors. Its large customers get special services, like access to a secure website that shows specific purchase histories and production or shipping status of their orders. Smaller customers can get all the product information they need and then link directly to the order page for the distributor that serves them. This system does not go as far as some, but it does illustrate how shared information and cooperation over the Internet is helping to create better relationships in business markets.[18]

The 9th edition features updated coverage of technology's impact on marketing thinking and processes, including ample discussion on the lessons learned from the successes and failures of dot-coms.

The interactive Student CD-ROM provides students additional help on more difficult topics, while reinforcing basic concepts from each chapter. The CD-ROM contains an electronic version of *Essentials of Marketing, 9/e;* computer-aided problems; chapter quizzes with instant feedback; eight narrated slide shows; seven complete videos; links to companies mentioned in the text; and sample advertisements from each chapter.

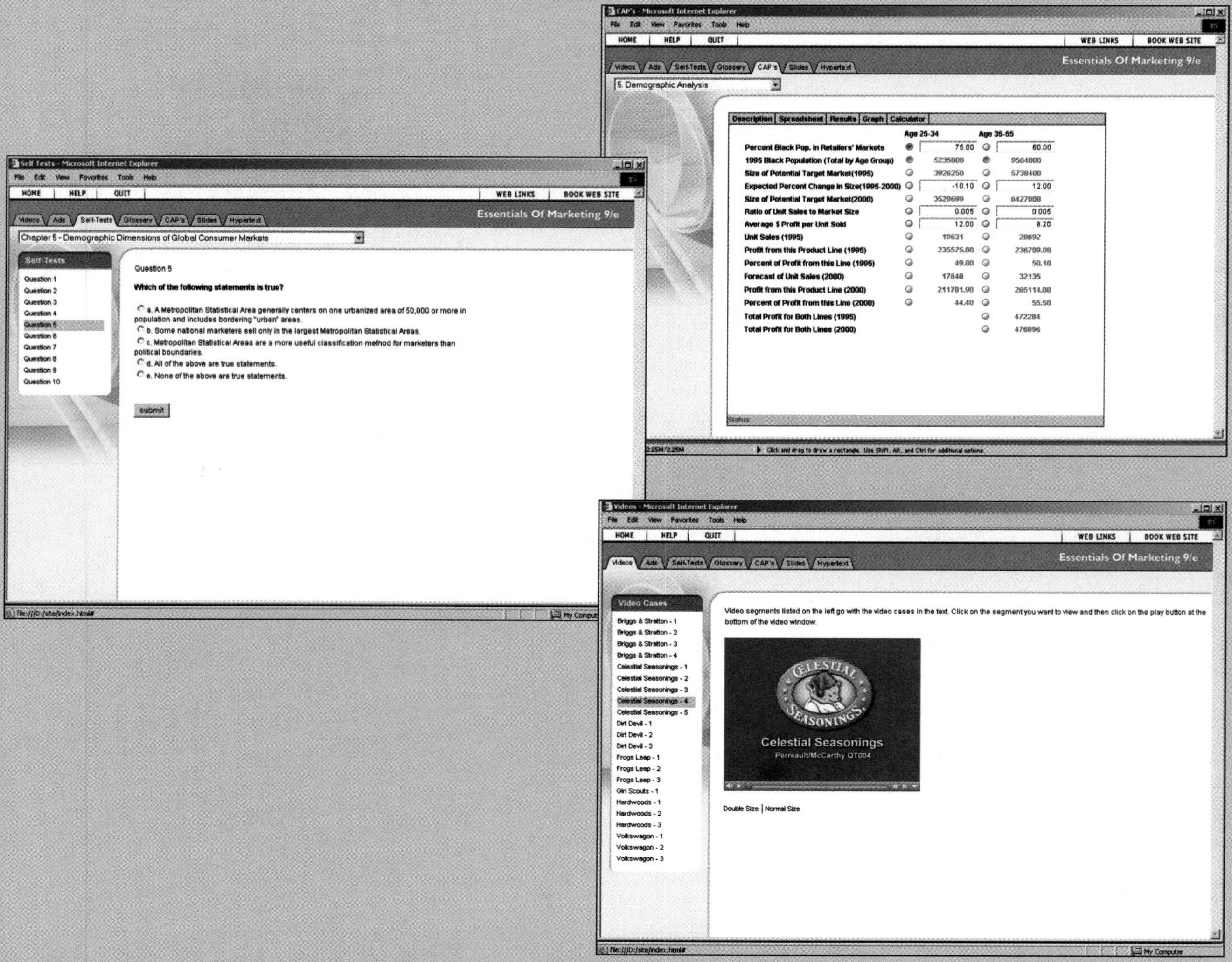

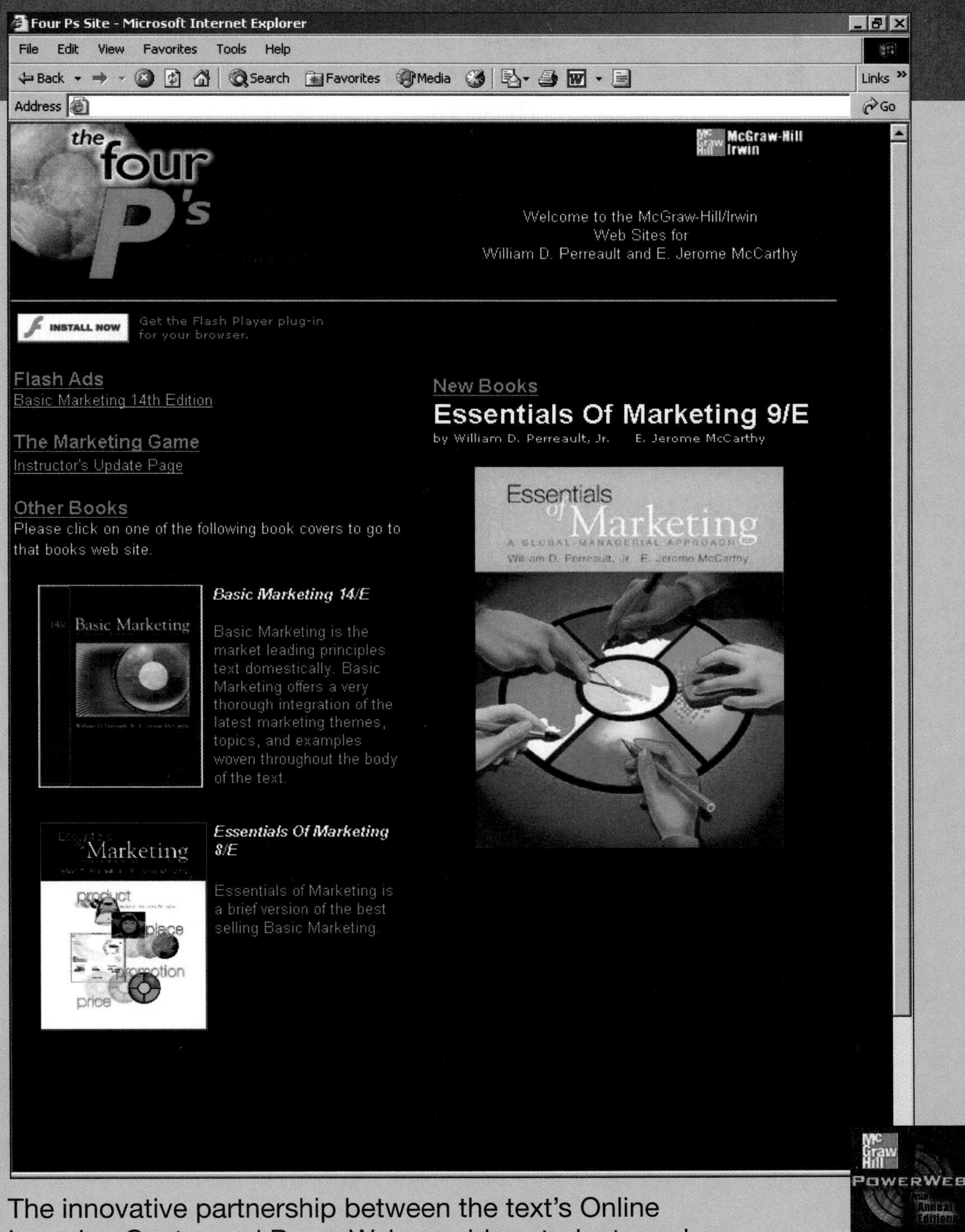

The innovative partnership between the text's Online Learning Center and PowerWeb provides students and instructors with unparalleled resources in the form of:

- Chapter quizzes
- Downloadable supplements
- Related links
- Current, application-oriented journal and periodical articles

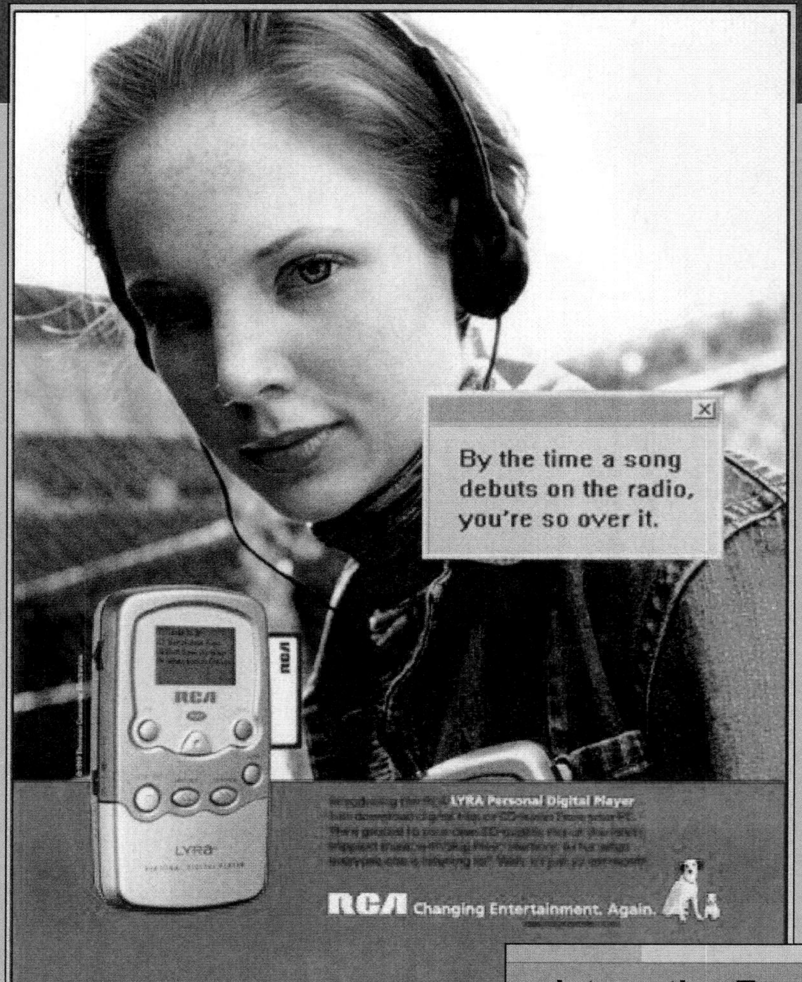

Completely new Interactive PowerPoint slides deliver graphically driven presentations of key chapter concepts and make use of text art, new artwork, graphs, advertisements, commercials, and interactive lecture demonstrations.

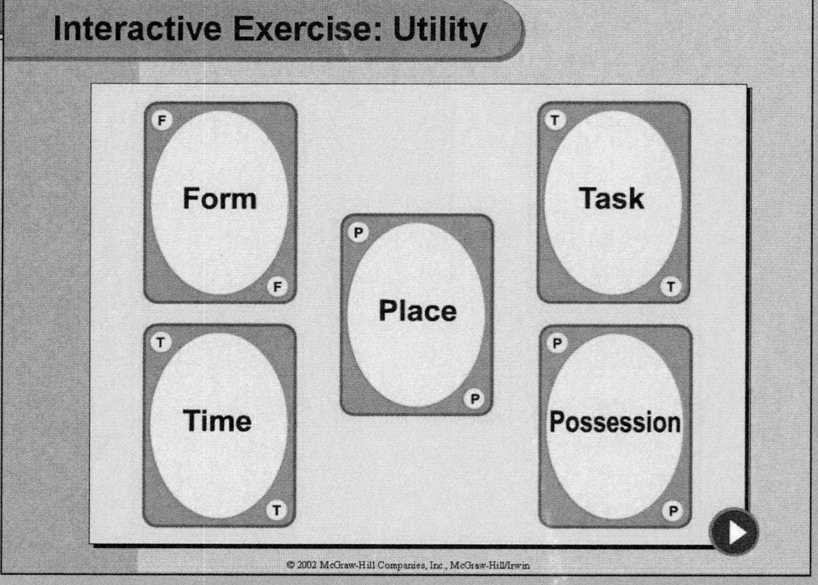

Each slide in the Interactive PowerPoint series comes complete with Notes to help instructors easily adapt the presentation to individual lecture styles.

An image Archive includes every text exhibit, the art from the acetate program, and 75 additional advertisements to allow the ultimate flexibility in PowerPoint customization.

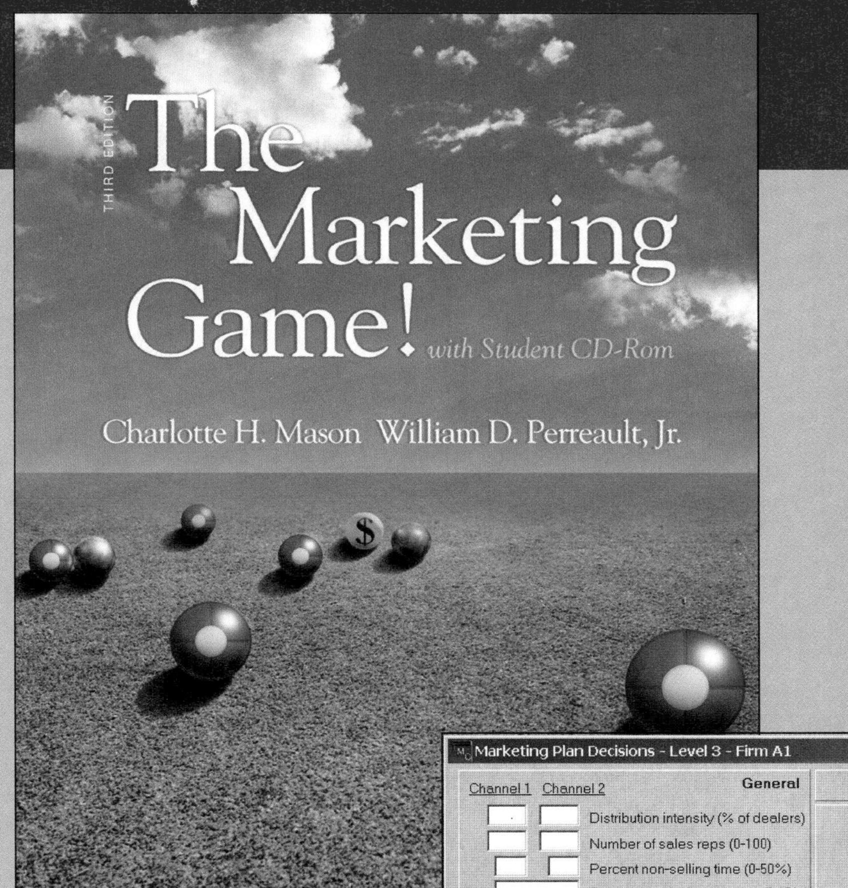

The Marketing Game! is a marketing strategy simulation that gives students the opportunity to compete against other students, individually or in teams, as they apply their marketing knowledge within a detailed, realistic company environment.

Features of *The Marketing Game!*

- Flexible instructor settings make adjusting the level of play and the marketing environment a matter of a couple of mouse clicks.
- The easy-to-use marketing plan form lets students submit their decisions.
- The instructor software evaluates the student plans and provides diagnostic reports in a matter of moments.
- Instructor support provided through video tutorials, PowerPoint slides, and a web resource.
- TMG! is offered at a significant discount when packaged with *Essentials of Marketing*.

There are 26 videos in the *Essentials of Marketing* 9/e teaching videos series. Over 10 in this edition are new or revised. In this set there are nineteen concept videos, designed to place chapter topics in a real-world context, and seven video cases. Two of the cases are completely new and designed specifically for this text. As always, an Instructor's Manual provides informative tips on how to incorporate these videos into your lectures and discussion.

Segment topics include:

- Gaining Market Share
- Responding to Market Opportunities
- Market Diversity
- Organizational Buying
- Product Management
- Logistic/Wholesaling
- Retailing
- Branding/Promotion
- Pricing
- New Product Development
- Marketing Planning
- Personal Selling
- Advertising
- Ethics
- Service Quality

Featured in the Video Cases: Frog's Leap Winery, Briggs and Stratton, Celestial Seasonings, Royal Appliance Mfg. Company, Volkswagen, and Girl Scouts of America.

Acknowledgments

Essentials of Marketing has been influenced and improved by the inputs of more people than it is possible to list. We do, however, want to express our appreciation to those who have played the most significant roles, especially in this edition.

We are especially grateful to our many students who have criticized and made comments about materials in *Essentials of Marketing*. Indeed, in many ways, our students have been our best teachers.

We owe our greatest debt of gratitude to Lin Davis. The book probably wouldn't exist if it weren't for her—because without her help it would have been just too overwhelming and we'd have quit! Lin has been part of this team for about 19 years. During that time she has made contributions in every aspect of the text and package. For this edition she spent countless hours researching photos and case histories, and she critiqued thousands of manuscript pages through countless revisions of the text and all the accompanying materials. She has reviewed, edited, and critiqued every word we've written. Her hard work, positive attitude, and dedication to quality throughout the whole process is without match. We could not have asked for a better friend and colleague.

Many improvements in the current edition were stimulated by feedback from a number of colleagues around the country. Their feedback took many forms. In particular, we would like to recognize the helpful contributions of

Mary Albrecht, Maryville University
Turina Bakken, University of Wisconsin
Jonathan Bohlman, Purdue University
John Brennan, Florida State University
Linda Jane Coleman, Salem State College
Brent Cunningham, Jacksonville State University
Phillip Downs, Florida State University
Michael Drake, College of DuPage
Lou Firenze, Northwood University
Thomas Giese, University of Richmond
Bobby Hall, Wayland Baptist University
Dorothy Harpool, Wichita State University
Pamela Homer, California State University—Long Beach
Timothy Johnston, University of Tennessee at Martin
Eileen Kearney, Montgomery County Community College
Jean Laliberte, Troy State University
Debra Laverie, Texas Tech University
W. J. Mahony, Southern Wesleyan University
Michael Mezja, University of Las Vegas
Robert Montgomery, University of Evansville
Todd Mooradian, College of William and Mary
Marlene Morris, Georgetown University
Brenda Moscool, California State University—Bakersfield
Reza Motameni, California State University—Fresno
Thomas Myers, University of Richmond
Esther S. Page-Wood, Western Michigan University
Lee Richardson, University of Baltimore
Robert Roe, University of Wyoming
Kenneth Shamley, Sinclair College
Doris Shaw, Kent State University
Donald Shifter, Fontbonne College
Janice Taylor, Miami University
Jeff Thieme, Syracuse University
Scott Thompson, University of Wisconsin—Oshkosh
M.G.M. Wetzeis, Universiteit Maastrict, The Netherlands

In addition, we appreciate people whose feedback on the previous edition had an ongoing influence on this revision. They are

David Andrus, Kansas State University at Manhattan
Scott Davis, University of California at Davis
Catherine Rich-Duval, Merrimack College
Sean Dwyer, Louisiana Technical University
J. Lee Goen, Oklahoma Baptist University
David Good, Central Missouri State University
Susan Gupta, University of Wisconsin at Milwaukee
John Hadjimarcou, University of Texas at El Paso
Deborah Baker Hulse, University of Texas at Tyler
James Kellaris, University of Cincinnati
James McAloon, Fitchburg State University
Philip S. Nitse, Idaho State University at Pocatello
J. R. Ogden, Kutztown University
Sam Okoroafo, University of Toledo
Daniel Rajaratnam, Baylor University
Carlos Rodriguez, Governors State University
Joel Saegert, University of Texas at San Antonio
Charles Schwepker, Central Missouri State University
Kimberly Taylor, Florida International University
A. J. Taylor, Austin Peay University
David Urban, Virginia Commonwealth University
Jane Wayland, Eastern Illinois University
Robert Witherspoon, Triton College
Joyce H. Wood, N. Virginia Community College
Newell Wright, James Madison University

Further, many of the ideas stimulated by thorough reviewers, diarists, and survey respondents for earlier editions were more fully implemented in this edition. For all of these suggestions and criticisms we are most appreciative.

We've always believed that the best way to build consistency and quality into the text and the other *P.L.U.S.* units is to do as much as possible ourselves. With the growth of multimedia technologies it's darn hard to be an expert on them all. But we've had spectacular help in that regard.

We're indebted to David Urban and Milt Pressley for their creative work on the new lecture-support PowerPoint presentation slides for this edition. Lewis Hershey participated in the effort on the previous edition. It's rare to find world-class marketing professors who also have their skill and experience with teaching technologies, so we are certainly fortunate that they've shared their brainwaves on this project.

John Gayle and David Hedstrom worked with us to redesign and program the new version of the CD-ROM. John also provided creative support on the PowerPoint slides. Nick Childers at Arthur Scott Productions has been the guru behind the scenes in production work on the video package for several editions. He also worked with us in developing the first versions of our CD-ROMs.

Judy Wilkinson played a big role as producer of the video series for this edition. In that capacity she worked closely with us to come up with ideas, and she provided guidance to the talented group of marketing professors who created or revised videos for this edition. Too much of the video footage used at all levels of education is full of glitz but devoid of content—because the people who produce it too often don't know the content. We've been able to conquer that challenge, but only because of the contributions made by Judy and other outstanding colleagues who have converted their marketing insights to the video medium. More specifically, we express respect for and deep appreciation to

Dave Burns, Youngstown State University
David Folsom, University of South Carolina—Aiken
Douglas Hausknecht, University of Akron
George Prough, University of Akron
Peter Rainsford, University of Denver
Judy Wilkinson, Youngstown State University

Of course, like other aspects of *Essentials of Marketing*, the video series has evolved and improved over time, and its current strength is partly due to the insights of Phil Niffenegger, who served as producer for our early video efforts. The video series also continues to benefit from the contributions of colleagues who developed videos in earlier editions. They are:

Gary R. Brockway, Murray State University
James Burley, Central Michigan University
Martha O. Cooper, Ohio State University
Carolyn Costley, University of Miami
Scott Johnson, University of Louisville
Gene R. Lazniak, Marquette University
Charles S. Madden, Baylor University
Don McBane, Central Michigan University
Robert Miller, Central Michigan University
W. Glynn Mangold, Murray State University
Michael R. Mullen, Florida Atlantic University
Phillip Niffenegger, Murray State University
Thomas G. Ponzurick, West Virginia University
Roger C. Shoenfeldt, Murray State University
Jeanne M. Simmons, Marquette University
Rollie O. Tillman, University of North Carolina at Chapel Hill
Robert Welsh, Central Michigan University
Holt Wilson, Central Michigan University
Poh-Lin Yeou, University of South Carolina

Faculty and students at our current and past academic institutions—Michigan State University, University of North Carolina, Notre Dame, University of Georgia, Northwestern University, University of Oregon, University of Minnesota, and Stanford University—have significantly shaped the book. Professor Andrew A. Brogowicz of Western Michigan University contributed many fine ideas to early editions of the text and supplements. Neil Morgan, Joe Cannon, Charlotte Mason, Val Zeithaml, Rollie Tillman, John Workman, Nicholas Didow, and Barry Bayus have provided a constant flow of helpful suggestions.

We are also grateful to the colleagues with whom we collaborate to produce international adaptations of the text. In particular, Stan Shapiro, Ken Wong, and Pascale G. Quester have all had a significant impact.

The designers, artists, editors, and production people at McGraw-Hill/Irwin who worked with us on this edition warrant special recognition. All of them have shared our commitment to excellence and brought their own individual creativity to the project. First we should salute Nancy Barbour, who has been the developmental editor on the project through a number of editions; her experience, hard work, friendship, and belief in our quality objectives have been an ongoing influence. Our projects create an enormous amount of work for her, and we appreciate what she does. Linda Schreiber is due special thanks. She took over as executive editor with this edition and has jumped in with creative ideas, energy, enthusiasm, and the instinct to quickly fix problems—all toward the objective of making the project all it should be. The positive attitude, attention, support, and hard work she contributed from her first day on the project have continued ever since.

Keith McPherson is a long-term contributor. He again took the creative lead in designing an attractive cover and inside for the book; he also put his personal touch on every piece of art in the text. What a talent, and what patience! We also appreciate Mike Hruby, who again was persistent in tracking down permissions for photos and ads we wanted to use to illustrate important ideas. Kim Kanakes Szum, marketing manager for the project, has been a constant source of valuable advice, feedback from the market, enthusiastic encouragement, and great marketing support. We also owe a debt of gratitude to Mark Christianson, Charles Pelto, and Craig Atkins, who have taken the internal lead at McGraw-Hill in producing all of the *Essentials of Marketing* technology initiatives. Craig Atkins has proved that he is a "technology hero" with his great initiatives on our new Student CD and Instructor CD.

Christine Vaughan has done a great job as production manager for the project. Without her adaptive problem solving we could not have succeeded with a (very) rapid-response production schedule—which is exactly what it takes to be certain that teachers and students get the most current information possible. Cathy Tepper is our hard-working supplements editor. We appreciate her dedication to all of the details involved in bringing such a complex project to market.

Rob Zwettler, Merrily Mazza, David Littlehale, Jerry Saykes, and Kurt Strand have all found time in their busy executive schedules to share their publishing insights—and they also gave us crucial top-management support. Steve Patterson is living proof that it is possible to survive and prosper after years as editor of this project, and his ongoing friendship and support is still much appreciated.

Our families have been patient and consistent supporters through all phases in developing *Essentials of Marketing*. The support has been direct and substantive. Pam Perreault has provided valuable assistance and more encouragement than you could imagine through many editions of the text. And Will and Suzanne Perreault continue to be patient and supportive while their dad spends time that was rightfully theirs meeting a never-ending set of deadlines.

We are indebted to all the firms that allowed us to reproduce their proprietary materials here. Similarly, we are grateful to associates from our business experiences who have shared their perspectives and feedback and enhanced our sensitivity to the key challenges of marketing management. In that regard, we especially acknowledge Kevin Clancy, Peter Krieg, and their colleagues at Copernicus: The Marketing Investment Strategy Group. The combination of pragmatic experience and creative insight they bring to the table is very encouraging. If you want to see great marketing, watch them create it.

A textbook must capsulize existing knowledge while bringing new perspectives and organization to enhance it. Our thinking has been shaped by the writings of literally thousands of marketing scholars and practitioners. In some cases it is impossible to give unique credit for a particular idea or concept because so many people have played important roles in anticipating, suggesting, shaping, and developing it. We gratefully acknowledge these contributors—from the early thought-leaders to contemporary authors—who have shared their creative ideas. We respect their impact on the development of marketing and more specifically this book.

To all of these persons—and to the many publishers who graciously granted permission to use their materials—we are deeply grateful. Responsibility for any errors or omissions is certainly ours, but the book would not have been possible without the assistance of many others. Our sincere appreciation goes to everyone who helped in their own special way.

William D. Perreault, Jr.
E. Jerome McCarthy

Contents

Chapter Nine
Product Management and New-Product Development

Chapter Ten
Place and Development of Channel Systems

Chapter Eleven
Logistics and Distribution Customer Service

Chapter Twelve
Retailers, Wholesalers, and Their Strategy Planning

Chapter One

Marketing's Role in the Global Economy

When You Finish This Chapter, You Should

1. Know what marketing is and why you should learn about it.

2. Understand the difference between micro-marketing and macro-marketing.

3. Know why and how macro-marketing systems develop.

4. Understand why marketing is crucial to economic development and our global economy.

5. Know why marketing specialists—including middlemen and facilitators—develop.

6. Know the marketing functions and who performs them.

7. Understand the important new terms (shown in red).

When it's time to roll out of bed in the morning, does your Sony alarm clock wake you with a buzzer or playing your favorite radio station? Is the station playing hip-hop, classical, or country music—or perhaps a Red Cross ad asking you to contribute blood? Will you slip into your Levi's jeans, your shirt from Abercrombie and Fitch, and your Nikes, or does the day call for your Brooks Brothers interviewing suit? Will breakfast be Lender's Bagels with cream cheese or Kellogg's Frosted Flakes—made with grain from America's heartland—or some extra-large eggs and Oscar Mayer bacon cooked in a Panasonic microwave oven imported from Japan? Will you drink Maxwell House decaf coffee grown in Colombia or some Tropicana Orange Juice? Will you eat at home or is this a day to meet a friend at the

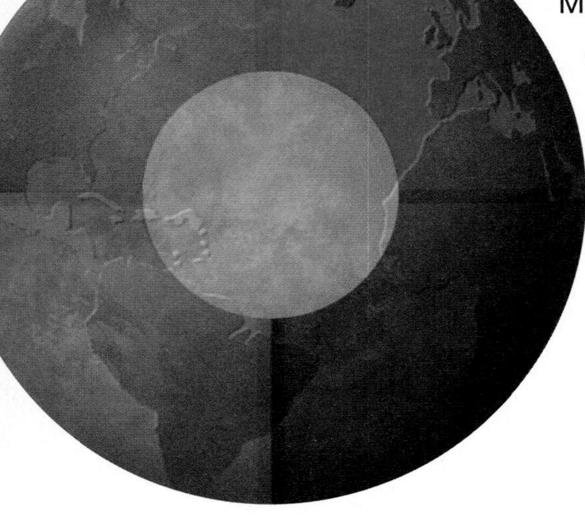

place

price

promotion

produ

school's cafeteria—where you'll pay someone else to serve your breakfast? To figure out what the day holds, will you need to log on to AOL to check your e-mail, or perhaps check the calendar on your Palm? Will you head off to school or work in a VW Beetle or on a bus that the city bought from General Motors, or is this the right kind of day to dust off your Razor scooter?

When you think about it, you can't get very far into a day without bumping into marketing—and what the whole marketing system does for you. It affects every aspect of our lives—often in ways we don't even consider.

In other parts of the world, people wake up each day to different kinds of experiences. A family in China may have little choice about what food they will eat or where their clothing will come from. A farmer in the mountains of Jamaica may awake in a barren hut with little more than the hope of raising enough to survive. A businessperson in a large city like Tokyo may have many choices but not be familiar with products that have names like Maxwell House, General Motors, and Oscar Mayer.

What explains these differences, and what do they have to do with marketing? In this chapter, we'll answer questions like these. You'll see what marketing is all about and why it's important to you. We'll also explore how marketing affects the quality of life in different societies and why it is so crucial to economic development and our global economy.

place price promotion product

The aim of marketing is to identify customers' needs—and to meet those needs so well that the product almost sells itself.

Marketing—What's It All About?

Marketing is more than selling or advertising

If forced to define marketing, most people, including some business managers, say that marketing means "selling" or "advertising." It's true that these are parts of marketing. But *marketing is much more than selling and advertising.*

How did all those bicycles get here?

To illustrate some of the other important things that are included in marketing, think about all the bicycles being peddled with varying degrees of energy by bike riders around the world. Most of us don't make our own bicycles. Instead, they are made by firms like Schwinn, Performance, Huffy, and Murray.

Most bikes do the same thing—get the rider from one place to another. But a bike rider can choose from a wide assortment of models. They are designed in different sizes and with or without gears. Off-road bikes have large knobby tires. Kids and older people may want more wheels—to make balancing easier. Some bikes need baskets or even trailers for cargo. You can buy a basic bike for less than $50. Or, you can spend more than $2,500 for a custom frame that you order over the Internet.

This variety complicates the production and sale of bicycles. The following list shows some of the things a firm should do before and after it decides to produce a bike.

1. Analyze the needs of people who might buy a bike and decide if they want more or different models.
2. Predict what types of bikes—handlebar styles, type of wheels, brakes, and materials—different customers will want and decide which of these people the firm will try to satisfy.
3. Estimate how many of these people will want to buy bicycles, and when.
4. Determine where in the world these bike riders will be and how to get the firm's bikes to them.
5. Estimate what price they are willing to pay for their bikes and if the firm can make a profit selling at that price.
6. Decide which kinds of promotion should be used to tell potential customers about the firm's bikes.

7. Figure out how to provide warranty service if a customer has a problem after buying a bike.

The above activities are not part of **production**—actually making goods or performing services. Rather, they are part of a larger process—called *marketing*—that provides needed direction for production and helps make sure that the right goods and services are produced and find their way to consumers.

Our bicycle example shows that marketing includes much more than selling or advertising. You'll learn much more about marketing activities in the next chapter. For now, it's enough to see that marketing plays an essential role in providing consumers with need-satisfying goods and services and, more generally, in creating customer satisfaction. Simply put, **customer satisfaction** is the extent to which a firm fulfills a customer's needs, desires, and expectations.

How Marketing Relates to Production

Production is a very important economic activity. Most people don't make most of the products they use. Picture yourself, for example, building a DVD player. We also turn to others to produce services—like health care and air transportation. Clearly, the high standard of living that most people in advanced economies enjoy is made possible by specialized production.

Bicycles, like mousetraps, don't sell themselves

Although production is a necessary economic activity, some people overrate its importance in relation to marketing. Their attitude is reflected in the old saying: "Make a better mousetrap and the world will beat a path to your door." In other words, they think that if you just have a good product, your business will be a success.

The "better mousetrap" idea probably wasn't true in Grandpa's time, and it certainly isn't true today. In modern economies, the grass grows high on the path to the Better Mousetrap Factory—if the new mousetrap is not properly marketed.

The point is that production and marketing are both important parts of a total business system aimed at providing consumers with need-satisfying goods and services. Together, production and marketing supply five kinds of economic utility—form, task, time, place, and possession utility—that are needed to provide consumer satisfaction. Here, **utility** means the power to satisfy human needs. See Exhibit 1-1.

Bicycles do not automatically provide utility

Form utility is provided when someone produces something tangible—for instance, a bicycle. **Task utility** is provided when someone performs a task for someone else—for instance, when a bank handles financial transactions. But just producing bicycles or handling bank accounts doesn't result in consumer satisfaction.

Exhibit 1-1
Types of Utility and How They Are Provided

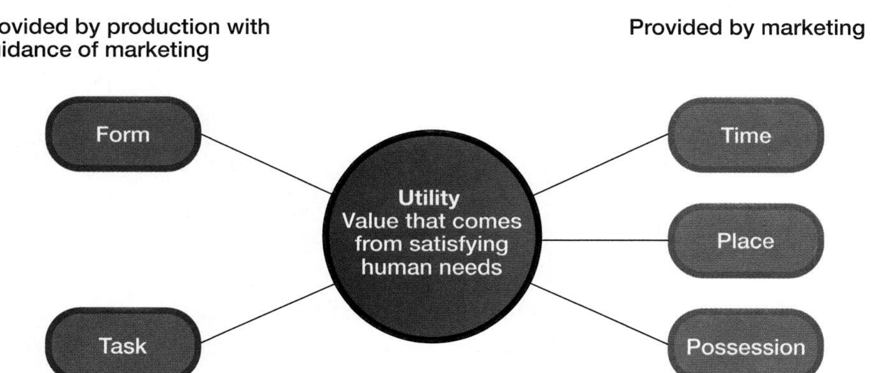

The product must be something that consumers want or there is no need to be satisfied—and no utility.

This is how marketing thinking guides the production side of business. Marketing focuses on what customers want and should guide what is produced and offered. It doesn't make sense to try to sell goods and services consumers don't want when there are so many things they do want. Let's take our "mousetrap" example a step further. Some customers don't want *any kind* of mousetrap. They may want someone else to exterminate the mice for them, or they may live where mice are not a problem.

Even when marketing and production combine to provide form or task utility, consumers won't be satisfied until time, place, and possession utility are also provided. **Time utility** means having the product available *when* the customer wants it. And **place utility** means having the product available *where* the customer wants it. Bicycles that stay at a factory don't do anyone any good. Time and place utility are very important for services too. For example, neighborhood health care clinics are popular because people can just walk in as soon as they feel sick, not a day later when their doctor can schedule an appointment.

Possession utility means obtaining a good or service and having the right to use or consume it. Customers usually exchange money or something else of value for possession utility.

We'll look at how marketing provides utility later in this chapter. First, we want to discuss why you should study marketing, and then we'll define marketing.

Marketing Is Important to You

Marketing is important to every consumer

You—as a consumer—pay for the cost of marketing activities. In advanced economies, marketing costs about 50 cents of each consumer dollar. For some goods and services, the percentage is much higher. Marketing affects almost every aspect of your daily life. All the goods and services you buy, the stores where you shop, and the radio and TV programs paid for by advertising are there because of

By working to understand the needs of its customers, wherever they are, Toyota has successfully adapted to markets all around the world.

Marketing Manager for Consumer Electronics

We've got a new opportunity that should help our business grow in the next decade. Put your college degree and experience in marketing consumer durables to work. Come help us analyze our markets and plan our marketing mix in a logical, creative, and enthusiastic way. This job offers income above industry standards, dynamic colleagues, relocation to desirable midwest suburb, and fast-track upward mobility. Check our website for more detail or reply in confidence, with a copy of your resume, to Box 4953.

marketing. Even your job résumé is part of a marketing campaign to sell yourself to some employer! Some courses are interesting when you take them but never relevant again once they're over. Not so with marketing—you'll be a consumer dealing with marketing for the rest of your life.

Marketing will be important to your job

Another reason for studying marketing is that it offers many exciting and rewarding career opportunities. Throughout this book you will find information about opportunities in different areas of marketing.

Even if you're aiming for a nonmarketing job, knowing about marketing will help you do your own job better. Marketing is important to the success of every firm and nonprofit organization. The same basic principles that firms use are also used to "sell" ideas, politicians, mass transportation, health care services, conservation, museums, and even colleges.[1]

Marketing affects economic growth

An even more basic reason for studying marketing is that marketing plays a big part in economic growth and development. Marketing stimulates research and new ideas—resulting in innovative new goods and services. Marketing gives customers a choice among products. If these products satisfy customers, fuller employment, higher incomes, and a higher standard of living can result. An effective marketing system is important to the future of all nations.[2]

How Should We Define Marketing?

Micro- or macro-marketing?

In our bicycle example, we saw that a producer of bicycles has to perform many customer-related activities besides just making bikes. The same is true for an insurance company, an art museum, or a family-service agency. This supports the idea of marketing as a set of activities done by an individual organization to satisfy the customers that it serves.

On the other hand, people can't survive on bicycles and art museums alone! In advanced economies, it takes goods and services from thousands of organizations to satisfy the many needs of society. A typical Wal-Mart store carries more than 100,000 different items. A society needs some sort of marketing system to organize the efforts of all the producers and middlemen needed to satisfy the varied needs of all its citizens. So marketing is also an important social process.

Internet

Internet Exercise You can check out the online shopping experience of Wal-Mart on the Web by going to the Wal-Mart home page (www.walmart.com) and clicking on "Go Shopping."

Marketing is both a set of activities performed by organizations and a social process. In other words, marketing exists at both the micro and macro levels. Therefore, we will use two definitions of marketing—one for micro-marketing and another for macro-marketing. Micro-marketing looks at customers and the organizations that serve them. Macro-marketing takes a broad view of our whole production–distribution system.

Micro-Marketing Defined

Micro-marketing is the performance of activities that seek to accomplish an organization's objectives by anticipating customer or client needs and directing a flow of need-satisfying goods and services from producer to customer or client.

Let's look at this definition.[3]

Applies to profit and nonprofit organizations

To begin with, this definition applies to both profit and nonprofit organizations. Profit is the objective for most business firms. But other types of organizations may seek more members—or acceptance of an idea. Customers or clients may be individual consumers, business firms, nonprofit organizations, government agencies, or even foreign nations. While most customers and clients pay for the goods and services they receive, others may receive them free of charge or at a reduced cost through private or government support.

Begins with customer needs

Marketing should begin with potential customer needs—not with the production process. Marketing should try to anticipate needs. And then marketing, rather than production, should determine what goods and services are to be developed—including decisions about product design and packaging; prices or fees; credit and collection policies; use of middlemen; transporting and storing policies; advertising and sales policies; and, after the sale, installation, customer service, warranty, and perhaps even disposal policies.

This does not mean that marketing should try to take over production, accounting, and financial activities. Rather, it means that marketing—by interpreting customers' needs—should provide direction for these activities and try to coordinate them.

Builds a relationship with the customer

When marketing helps everyone in a firm really meet the needs of a customer both before and after a purchase, the firm doesn't just get a single sale. Rather, it has a sale and an ongoing *relationship* with the customer. Then, in the future, when the customer has the same need again—or some other need that the firm can meet—other sales will follow. Often the marketing *flow* of need-satisfying goods and services is not just for a single transaction but rather is part of a lasting relationship that benefits both the firm and the customer.

The Focus of This Text—Management-Oriented Micro-Marketing

Since you are probably preparing for a career in management, the main focus of this text will be on micro-marketing. We will see marketing through the eyes of the marketing manager.

The micro-marketing ideas we will be discussing throughout this text apply to a wide variety of situations. They are important for new ventures started by one person as well as big corporations, in domestic and international markets, and regardless of whether the focus is on marketing physical goods, services, or an idea or cause. They are equally critical whether the relevant customers or clients are individual consumers, businesses, or some other type of organization. For editorial convenience, we will sometimes use the term *firm* as a shorthand way of referring to any type of organization, whether it is a political party, a religious organization, a government agency, or the like. However, to reinforce the point that the ideas apply to all types of organizations, throughout the book we will illustrate marketing concepts in a wide variety of situations.

Although micro-marketing is the primary focus of the text, marketing managers must remember that their organizations are just small parts of a larger macro-marketing system. Therefore, the rest of this chapter looks at the macro view of marketing.

Macro-Marketing Defined

Macro-marketing is a social process that directs an economy's flow of goods and services from producers to consumers in a way that effectively matches supply and demand and accomplishes the objectives of society.

Emphasis is on whole system

Like micro-marketing, macro-marketing is concerned with the flow of need-satisfying goods and services from producer to consumer. However, the emphasis with macro-marketing is not on the activities of individual organizations. Instead, the emphasis is on *how the whole marketing system works*. This includes looking at how marketing affects society, and vice versa.

Every society needs a macro-marketing system. Different producers in a society have different objectives, resources, and skills. Likewise, not all consumers share the same needs. So the basic role of a macro-marketing system is to effectively match heterogeneous supply and demand *and* at the same time accomplish society's objectives.[4]

Every society needs an economic system

All societies must provide for the needs of their members. Therefore, every society needs some sort of **economic system**—the way an economy organizes to use scarce resources to produce goods and services and distribute them for consumption by various people and groups in the society.

How an economic system operates depends on a society's objectives and the nature of its political institutions.[5] But regardless of what form these take, all economic systems must develop some method—along with appropriate economic institutions—to decide what and how much is to be produced and distributed by whom, when, to whom, and why. How these decisions are made may vary from nation to nation. But the macro-level objectives are basically similar: to create goods and services and make them available when and where they are needed—to maintain or improve each nation's standard of living or other socially defined objective.

How Economic Decisions Are Made

There are two basic kinds of economic systems: planned systems and market-directed systems. Actually, no economy is entirely planned or market-directed. Most are a mixture of the two extremes.

Government planners may make the decisions

In a **planned economic system,** government planners decide what and how much is to be produced and distributed by whom, when, to whom, and why. Producers generally have little choice about what goods and services to produce. Their main task is to meet their assigned production quotas. Prices are set by government planners and tend to be very rigid—not changing according to supply and demand. Consumers usually have some freedom of choice—it's impossible to control every single detail! But the assortment of goods and services may be quite limited.

Activities such as market research, branding, and advertising usually are neglected. Sometimes they aren't done at all.

Government planning may work fairly well as long as an economy is simple and the variety of goods and services is small. It may even be necessary under certain conditions—during wartime, drought, or political instability, for example. However, as economies become more complex, government planning breaks down. The collapse of communism in Eastern Europe dramatically illustrates this. Citizens of what was the Soviet Union were not satisfied with the government's plan—because products consumers wanted were not available. That brought about a revolution—one that is leading to the development of market-directed economies in the republics of Eastern Europe.[6]

Countries such as China, North Korea, and Cuba still rely primarily on planned economic systems. Even so, around the world there is a broad move toward market-directed economic systems—because they are more effective in meeting consumer needs.

A market-directed economy adjusts itself

In a **market-directed economic system,** the individual decisions of the many producers and consumers make the macro-level decisions for the whole economy. In a pure market-directed economy, consumers make a society's production decisions when they make their choices in the marketplace. They decide what is to be produced and by whom—through their dollar "votes."

Price is a measure of value

Prices in the marketplace are a rough measure of how society values goods and services. If consumers are willing to pay the market prices, then apparently they feel they are getting at least their money's worth. Similarly, the cost of labor and materials is a rough measure of the value of the resources used in the production of goods and services to meet these needs. New consumer needs that can be served profitably—not just the needs of the majority—will probably be met by some profit-minded businesses. Over time, the result is a balance of supply and demand and the coordination of the economic activity of many individuals and institutions.

Greatest freedom of choice

Consumers in a market-directed economy enjoy great freedom of choice. They are not forced to buy any goods or services, except those that must be provided for the good of society—things such as national defense, schools, police and fire protection, highway systems, and public-health services. These are provided by the community—and the citizens are taxed to pay for them.

Similarly, producers are free to do whatever they wish—provided that they stay within the rules of the game set by government *and* receive enough dollar "votes" from consumers. If they do their job well, they earn a profit and stay in business. But profit, survival, and growth are not guaranteed.

Conflicts can arise

Producers and consumers making free choices can cause conflicts and difficulties. This is called the **micro-macro dilemma.** What is "good" for some producers and consumers may not be good for society as a whole.

For example, many Americans want the convenience of disposable products and products in easy-to-use, small-serving packages. But these same "convenient" products and packages often lead to pollution of the environment and inefficient use of natural resources. Should future generations be left to pay the consequences of pollution that is the result of "free choice" by today's consumers?

Questions like these are not easy to answer. The basic reason is that many different people may have a stake in the outcomes—and social consequences—of the choices made by individual managers *and* consumers in a market-directed system. As you read this book and learn more about marketing, you will also learn more about social responsibility in marketing and why it must be taken seriously.

The role of government

The American economy and most other Western economies are mainly market-directed—but not completely. Society assigns supervision of the system to the government. For example, besides setting and enforcing the "rules of the game," government agencies control interest rates and the supply of money. They also set import and export rules that affect international competition. Government also tries to be sure that property is protected, contracts are enforced, individuals are not exploited, no one unfairly monopolizes markets, and producers deliver the kinds and quality of goods and services they claim to be offering.

You can see that we need some of these government activities to make sure the economy runs smoothly. However, too much government "guidance" can threaten the survival of a market-directed system and the economic and political freedom that goes with it.

Seeing this, many countries are reducing regulation and government control of markets. One indication of this is the trend toward privatization, which means that an activity previously owned and operated by the government is sold to private sector owners who manage it in a competitive market. For example, many countries that previously owned airlines have sold the airlines and encouraged more competition among various carriers.[7]

Socially responsible marketing managers are concerned about the environmental impact of their decisions, and some firms are finding innovative ways to both help the environment and improve customer satisfaction.

All Economies Need Macro-Marketing Systems

No economic system—whether centrally planned, market-directed, or a mix of the two—can achieve its objectives without an effective macro-marketing system. To see why this is true, we will look at the role of marketing in primitive societies. Then we will see how macro-marketing tends to become more and more complex in advanced economic systems.

Marketing involves exchange

In a **pure subsistence economy,** each family unit produces everything it consumes. There is no need to exchange goods and services. Each producer–consumer unit is totally self-sufficient, although usually its standard of living is relatively low. No marketing takes place because *marketing doesn't occur unless two or more parties are willing to exchange something for something else.*

What is a market?

The term *marketing* comes from the word **market**—which is a group of potential customers with similar needs who are willing to exchange something of value with sellers offering various goods and/or services—that is, ways of satisfying those needs. Of course, some negotiation may be needed. This can be done face-to-face at some physical location (for example, a farmers' market). Or it can be done indirectly—through a complex network that links middlemen, buyers, and sellers living far apart.

In primitive economies, exchanges tend to occur in central markets. **Central markets** are convenient places where buyers and sellers can meet one-on-one to exchange goods and services. In our information age, central markets take a variety of forms—ranging from suburban shopping centers to websites that operate in cyberspace. But you will understand macro-marketing better if you see how and why central markets develop. We'll start with a very simple case, but thinking about it will clarify what happens when a more complex system is involved.

Central markets help exchange

Imagine a small village of five families—each with a special skill for producing some need-satisfying product. After meeting basic needs, each family decides to specialize. It's easier for one family to make two pots and another to make two baskets than for each one to make one pot and one basket. Specialization makes

In advanced economies, a complex network of wholesalers, retailers, and other marketing specialists bring goods and services to consumers; in developing economies like Vietnam, central markets are often more basic.

Exhibit 1-2

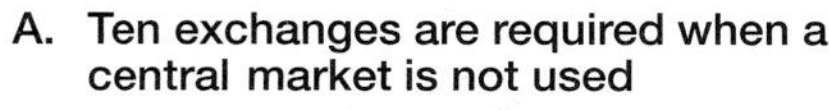

B. Only five exchanges are required when a middleman (intermediary) in a central market is used

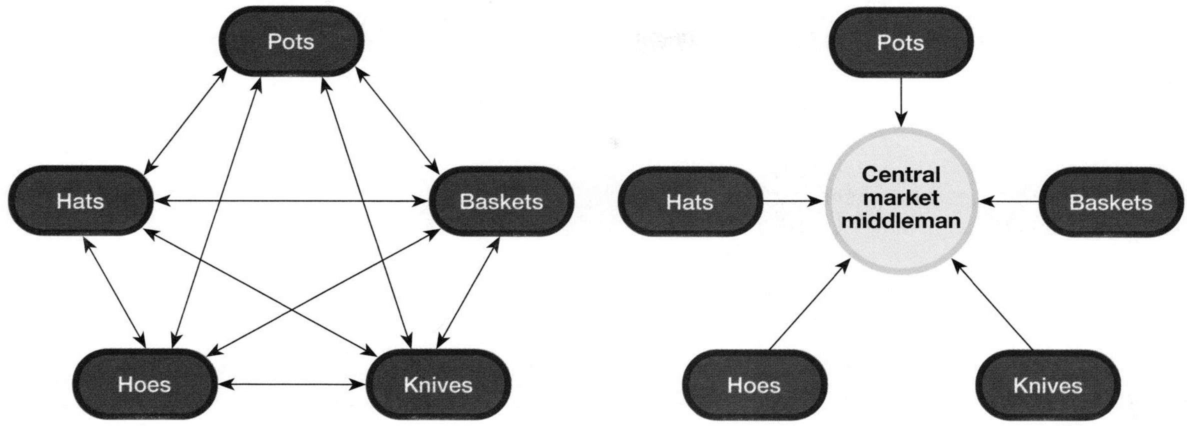

labor more efficient and increases the amount of form utility. Specialization also can increase task utility in producing services, but for now we'll focus on physical goods.

If these five families each specialize in one product, they will have to trade with each other. As Exhibit 1-2A shows, it will take the five families 10 separate exchanges to obtain some of each of the products. If the families live near each other, the exchange process is relatively simple. But if they are far apart, travel back and forth will take time. Who will do the traveling—and when?

Faced with this problem, the families may agree to come to a central market and trade on a certain day. Then each family makes only one trip to the market to trade with all the others. This reduces the total number of trips to five, which makes exchange easier, leaves more time for producing and consuming, and also provides for social gatherings.

A money system simplifies trading

While a central meeting place simplifies exchange, the individual bartering transactions still take a lot of time. Bartering only works when someone else wants what you have, and vice versa. Each trader must find others who have products of about equal value. After trading with one group, a family may find itself with extra baskets, knives, and pots. Then it has to find others willing to trade for these products.

A common money system changes all this. Sellers only have to find buyers who want their products and agree on the price. Then sellers are free to spend this income to buy whatever they want. If some buyers and sellers use *different* money systems—some use dollars and others use yen—they must also agree on the rate at which the money will be exchanged.

Middlemen intermediaries may help exchange even more

The development of a central market and a money system simplifies the exchange process among the five families in our imaginary village. But the families still need to make 10 separate transactions. So it still takes a lot of time and effort for the five families to exchange goods.

This clumsy exchange process is made much simpler by a **middleman** (or **intermediary**)—someone who specializes in trade rather than production. A middleman is willing to buy each family's goods and then sell each family whatever it needs. The middleman intermediary charges for this service, of course. But this charge may be more than offset by savings in time and effort.

High-Tech Access to Market Information in the Low-Tech World

When consumers in the U.S. think about technology and marketing, many think about shopping on the Internet. After all, 135 million people in the U.S. have online access to the Internet. Fancy shopping malls seem old hat. Contrast that with Bangladesh, one of the poorest countries in the world, where about 90 percent of the 68,000 villages don't even have access to a phone. But Grameen Bank, a private firm based in Dhaka, Bangladesh, is doing something about that problem. It is making loans so that someone in a village can buy a cell phone and then provide phone service to others. For example, Delora Begum bought a phone and now reigns as the "phone lady" in her village. And her business is helping the market system work better. For example, farmers pay to use the cell phone to learn the fair value of their rice and vegetables; often in the past they were exploited because they did not get a fair price. One local businessman routinely had to take a two-hour bus ride to order furnace oil for his brick factory. Now he can just call and place an order—and save a bone-jarring half day on a bus. Similarly, a local carpenter uses the cell phone to check the current price for wood so that he can make a profit when he prices the chairs and cabinets he makes. These are just a few examples, but in a country with an extremely ineffective macro-marketing system the Grameen Bank's cell phone venture is doing a lot to improve the quality of life of people in remote villages.[8]

In our simple example, using an intermediary at a central market reduces the necessary number of exchanges for all five families from 10 to 5. See Exhibit 1-2B. Each family has more time for production, consumption, and leisure. Also, each family can specialize in producing what it produces best—creating more form and task utility. Meanwhile, by specializing in trade, the intermediary provides additional time, place, and possession utility. In total, all the villagers may enjoy greater economic utility—and greater consumer satisfaction—by using an intermediary in the central market.

Central market and intermediaries may develop in cyberspace

The advantages of working with intermediaries multiply with increases in the number of producers and consumers, their distance from or difficulties in communicating with each other, and the number and variety of competing products. That is why there are so many wholesalers and retailers in modern economies.

On the other hand, technology is allowing some customers and sellers to meet for exchange in a central market that is located in "cyberspace"—that is, on the Internet—rather than in a mutually convenient geographic location. In fact, the Internet makes it possible for potential buyers from different parts of the world to bid against each other to determine the price that will ultimately be paid for a good or service. Obviously, this is a very different type of central market, but it is simply a variation of the same basic idea. From a macro-marketing perspective, the main purpose of markets and market intermediaries is to make exchange easier and allow greater time for production, consumption, and other activities—including leisure.[9]

Internet

Internet Exercise eBay features a number of online auctions in which different sellers auction off computers, consumer electronics, and other products to buyers. Visit the eBay website (www.ebay.com) and review an open auction for a consumer electronics product. What are the advantages and disadvantages of this market for sellers? For buyers?

The Role of Marketing in Economic Development

Effective marketing system is necessary

It is tempting to conclude that more effective macro-marketing systems are the result of greater economic development, but just the opposite is true. *An effective macro-marketing system is necessary for economic development.* Improved marketing is often the key to growth in less-developed nations.

Breaking the vicious circle of poverty

Without an effective macro-marketing system, many people in less-developed nations are not able to leave their subsistence way of life. They can't produce for the market because there are no buyers. And there are no buyers because everyone else is producing for their own needs. As a result, distribution systems and intermediaries do not develop.

Breaking this "vicious circle of poverty" may require major changes in the inefficient marketing systems that are typical in less-developed nations. At the least, more market-oriented middlemen are needed to move surplus output to markets—including foreign markets—where there is more demand.[10]

Less-developed nations have inefficient systems

Chapter 4 goes into more detail on how countries at different levels of economic development differ. However, to get a sense for these differences let's consider a case that involves India.

In India over 600 million people still live in rural farm areas. Many don't have life's basic comforts. For example, only about 40 percent have electricity, and less than 20 percent have piped water. Most can't afford a refrigerator. Workers in the sugarcane fields only earn about $1 a day. Many rural Indians have never even held a tube of toothpaste. Rather, they clean their mouths with charcoal powder and the stem of a local plant.

Colgate wants to introduce toothpaste in India, but it can't rely on U.S.-style ads—or the local drugstore—to do the selling job. Half of the rural people can't read, and very few have a TV. They also don't go to stores. Rather, once a week they go to a central market in a nearby village to get basic supplies they can't grow themselves. To reach these people, Colgate sends a van equipped with a generator and video gear into a village on market day. Music attracts the shoppers, and then an entertaining half-hour video (infomercial) explains the benefits of using Colgate toothpaste. Of course, most villagers can't spend a day's wages to buy a standard tube. So Colgate offers a small (30 gram) tube for six rupees (about 18¢).

Colgate's micro-marketing effort in India is expensive because the macro-marketing system is ineffective. It will take a long time before these villagers have basic comforts—or the type of efficient macro-marketing system—that those of us in developed economies take for granted.[11]

Nations' Macro-Marketing Systems Are Connected

As a nation grows, its international trade grows

All countries trade to some extent—we live in an interdependent world. Even so, the largest traders are highly developed nations. For example, the top industrial nations—the U.S., Canada, the countries of Western Europe, and Japan—account for about half of the world's total economic output, with the U.S. at about 23 percent, the countries of Western Europe at about 20 percent, and Japan at about 7 percent. These countries also account for about two-thirds of total world exports and about 63 percent of world imports.[12]

Because trade among nations is so important in economic development, most countries—whether highly developed or not—are eager to sell their goods and services in foreign markets. Yet they often don't want their local customers to spend cash on foreign-made products. They want the money—and the opportunities for jobs and economic growth—to stay in the local economy.

Tariffs and quotas may reduce trade

Taxes and restrictions at national or regional borders greatly reduce the free flow of goods and services between the macro-marketing systems of different countries. **Tariffs**—taxes on imported products—vary, depending on whether a country is trying to raise revenue or limit trade. Restrictive tariffs often block all movement. But even revenue-producing tariffs increase prices, discourage free movement of products, and cause red tape. This is what Caterpillar encounters trying to sell its construction equipment in Brazil. Brazil's 15 percent tariff adds nearly $40,000 to the cost of a $250,000 machine. Worse, Brazilian customs delays make it difficult for Caterpillar to honor its sales promise to deliver repair parts within 24 hours.[13]

Quotas act like restrictive tariffs. **Quotas** set the specific quantities of products that can move into or out of a country. Great market opportunities may exist in the markets of a unified Europe, for example, but import quotas (or export controls applied against a specific country) may discourage outsiders from entering.

The impact of such restrictions can be seen in the Russian market. At first it appeared that with the fall of communism, the Russian market would be more open to foreign automobile producers. And in a way it was. However, a Taurus that sold for about $22,000 in the U.S. cost over $48,000 in Russia. The price difference, due mainly to Russian import tariffs, severely limited the number of Russians able to pay that much. So, Ford set up assembly plants in Russia.[14]

The U.S. has held fast to some protectionist policies even though it is the world's cheerleader for free trade. For example, U.S. consumers pay more for Florida orange juice because orange juice concentrate from groves in Brazil gets hit with a 30 percent tariff. Similarly, the U.S. is a big exporter of services, but Japanese and European airlines are not allowed to land in a U.S. city, pick up paying passengers, and fly to another U.S. destination. You can see why trade restrictions are often a source of conflict between nations.[15]

Markets may rely on international countertrade

To overcome the problems of trade restrictions, many firms have turned to **countertrade**—a special type of bartering in which products from one country are traded for products from another country. For example, McDonnell Douglas Helicopter used countertrade when the Ugandan government wanted to buy 18 helicopters to help stamp out illegal elephant hunting. Uganda didn't have $25 million to pay for the helicopters, so a countertrade specialist for the helicopter company set up local projects to generate the money. One Ugandan factory now turns local pineapples and passion fruit into concentrated juice. The concentrate is sold to European buyers identified by the countertrade specialist.

This may seem unusual, but it isn't. Countertrade is an extremely important part of foreign trade for both large and small companies. In fact, about 20 to 25 percent of all U.S. exports rely on countertrade.[16]

Global trade is increasing

There are still many obstacles to free trade among nations. And trade "wars" among nations are likely to continue. Even so, there is a trend toward fewer restrictions on trade among different countries. Evidence of this is the creation in 1995 of the **World Trade Organization (WTO)**—the only international body dealing with the rules of trade between nations. At its heart are the WTO agreements, the legal ground rules for international commerce and for trade policy. The agreements have three main objectives: (1) to help trade flow as freely as possible, (2) to provide an impartial means of settling disputes, and (3) to facilitate further negotiation. The WTO agreements cover services and intellectual property as well as goods and in general try to encourage competition, discourage protectionism, and seek to provide more predictable policies.

With the formation of the WTO global trade is an even more important factor in economic development—and a more important source of opportunity for individual firms.[17]

Internet

Internet Exercise The World Trade Organization is a very important force behind the global move toward free trade, but sometimes there are still disputes. Go to the WTO website (www.wto.org) and find out how the WTO settles disputes. Do you think that this procedure favors the developed nations, the less-developed nations, or neither? Give your thinking.

Can Mass Production Satisfy a Society's Consumption Needs?

In advanced economies, most people depend on others to produce most of the goods and services they need to satisfy their basic needs. Many consumers can afford to satisfy higher-level needs as well as basic ones. Modern societies face a real challenge to satisfy all these needs.

Economies of scale mean lower cost

Fortunately, advanced economies can often take advantage of mass production with its **economies of scale**—which means that as a company produces larger numbers of a particular product, the cost for each of these products goes down. A one-of-a-kind car costs much more than a mass-produced model.

Of course, even in advanced societies, not all goods and services can be produced by mass production or with economies of scale. Consider medical care. It's difficult to get productivity gains in labor-intensive medical services—like brain surgery. Nevertheless, from a macro-marketing perspective, we are able to devote resources to these "quality-of-life" needs because we achieve efficiency in other areas.

Thus, modern production skills can help provide great quantities of goods and services to satisfy large numbers of consumers. But mass production alone does not solve the problem of satisfying consumers' needs. We also need effective marketing.

Effective marketing is needed to link producers and consumers

Effective marketing means delivering the goods and services that consumers want and need. It means getting products to them at the right time, in the right place, and at a price they're willing to pay. It means keeping consumers satisfied after the sale, and bringing them back to purchase again when they are ready. That's not an easy job—especially if you think about the variety of goods and services a highly developed economy can produce and the many kinds of goods and services consumers want.

Most consumers who drink tea live far from where it is grown. To overcome this spatial separation, someone must first perform a variety of marketing functions, like standardizing and grading the tea leaves, transporting and storing them, and buying and selling them.

Exhibit 1-3 Marketing Facilitates Production and Consumption

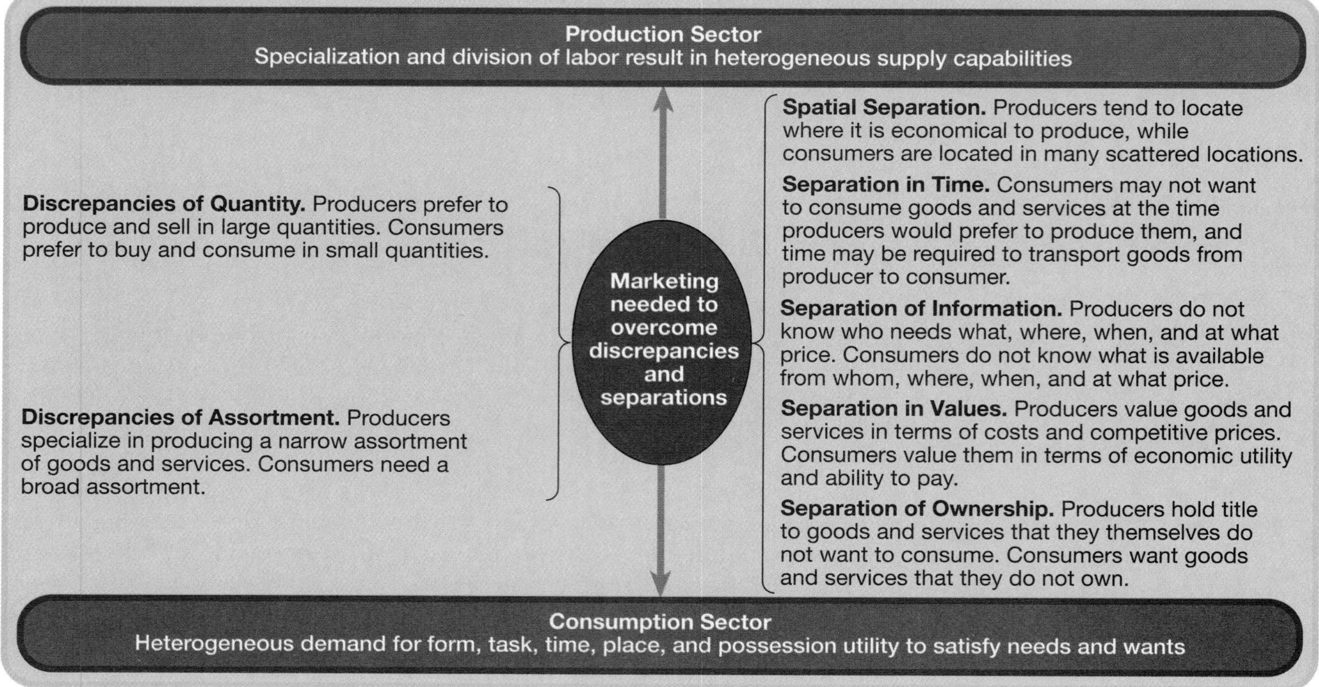

Effective marketing in an advanced economy is more difficult because producers and consumers are often separated in several ways. As Exhibit 1-3 shows, exchange between producers and consumers is hampered by spatial separation, separation in time, separation of information and values, and separation of ownership. "Discrepancies of quantity" and "discrepancies of assortment" further complicate exchange between producers and consumers. That is, each producer specializes in producing and selling large amounts of a narrow assortment of goods and services, but each consumer wants only small quantities of a wide assortment of goods and services.[18]

Marketing functions help narrow the gap

The purpose of a macro-marketing system is to overcome these separations and discrepancies. The "universal functions of marketing" help do this.

The **universal functions of marketing** are buying, selling, transporting, storing, standardization and grading, financing, risk taking, and market information. They must be performed in all macro-marketing systems. *How* these functions are performed—and *by whom*—may differ among nations and economic systems. But they are needed in any macro-marketing system. Let's take a closer look at them now.

Exchange usually involves buying and selling. The **buying function** means looking for and evaluating goods and services. The **selling function** involves promoting the product. It includes the use of personal selling, advertising, and other direct and mass-selling methods. This is probably the most visible function of marketing.

The **transporting function** means the movement of goods from one place to another. The **storing function** involves holding goods until customers need them.

Standardization and grading involve sorting products according to size and quality. This makes buying and selling easier because it reduces the need for inspection and sampling. **Financing** provides the necessary cash and credit to produce, transport, store, promote, sell, and buy products. **Risk taking** involves bearing the uncertainties that are part of the marketing process. A firm can never be sure that customers will want to buy its products. Products can also be damaged, stolen, or outdated. The **market information function** involves the collection, analysis, and distribution of all the information needed to plan, carry out, and control marketing activities, whether in the firm's own neighborhood or in a market overseas.

Who Performs Marketing Functions?

Producers, consumers, and marketing specialists

From a macro-level viewpoint, these marketing functions are all part of the marketing process and must be done by someone. None of them can be eliminated. In a planned economy, some of the functions may be performed by government agencies. Others may be left to individual producers and consumers. In a market-directed system, marketing functions are performed by producers, consumers, and a variety of marketing specialists (see Exhibit 1-4).

The macro-marketing systems for different nations may interact. For example, producers based in one nation may serve consumers in another country, perhaps with help from intermediaries and other specialists from both countries. What happened to food distribution in East Germany after the fall of the Berlin Wall illustrates this point. With the reunification of Germany, the political limits on trade were gone. Yet consumers still faced problems getting the food they wanted. Eastern Germany had no efficient wholesalers to supply the chain of 170 Konsum retail stores, which were previously state-owned. And it was expensive for producers in the West who wanted to reach the market in the East to do it without help. However, the Tegut grocery chain in the West saw the opportunity and established an automated warehouse in the East to supply the Konsum stores. The warehouse made it economical to assemble needed assortments of products from many different producers. Further, Tegut set up a computer network to provide timely reordering from the warehouse, online management of inventories and distribution, and even payment control. With the help of middlemen like Tegut, both local and foreign producers are better able to meet consumer needs.[19]

Intermediaries and facilitators develop and offer specialized services that facilitate exchange between producers and customers.

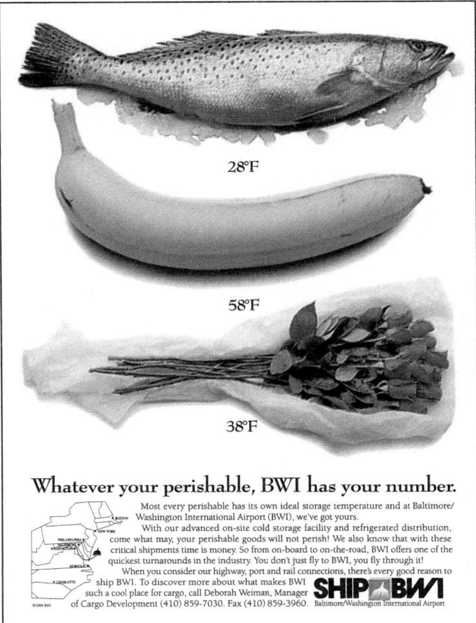

Exhibit 1-4
Model of a Market-Directed Macro-Marketing System

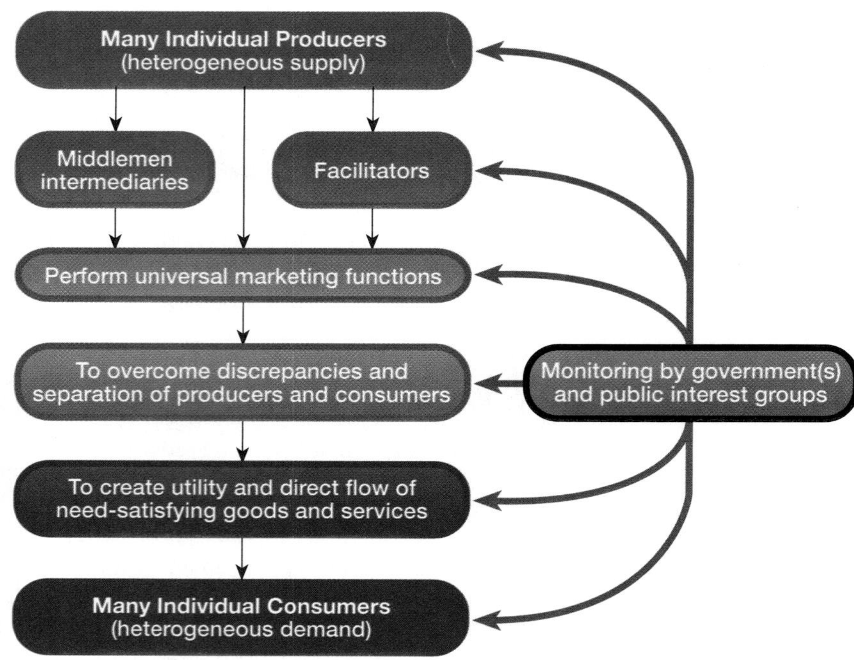

Specialists perform some functions

Marketing functions may be performed not only by middlemen but also by a variety of other **facilitators**—firms that provide one or more of the marketing functions other than buying or selling. These include advertising agencies, marketing research firms, independent product-testing laboratories, Internet service providers, public warehouses, transporting firms, communications companies, and financial institutions (including banks). Through specialization or economies of scale, marketing intermediaries and facilitators are often able to perform the marketing functions better—and at a lower cost—than producers or consumers can. This allows producers and consumers to spend more time on production and consumption.

Functions can be shifted and shared

From a macro viewpoint, all of the marketing functions must be performed by someone. But *from a micro viewpoint, not every firm must perform all of the functions. Further, not all goods and services require all the functions at every level of their production.* "Pure services"—like a plane ride—don't need storing, for example. But storing is required in the production of the plane and while the plane is not in service.

Some marketing specialists perform all the functions. Others specialize in only one or two. Marketing research firms, for example, specialize only in the market information function. Further, technology may make a certain function easier to perform. For example, the buying process may require that a customer first identify relevant sellers and where they are. Even though that might be accomplished quickly and easily on the Internet, the function hasn't been cut out. The important point to remember is this: *Responsibility for performing the marketing functions can be shifted and shared in a variety of ways, but no function can be completely eliminated.*

How Well Does Our Macro-Marketing System Work?

It connects remote producers and consumers

A macro-marketing system does more than just deliver goods and services to consumers—it allows mass production with its economies of scale. Also, mass communication, computer information systems, including the Internet, and mass

A market-directed, macro-marketing system encourages marketing managers to develop innovative ways to meet customers' needs.

transportation allow products to be shipped where they're needed. Oranges from California are found in Minnesota stores—even in December—and electronic parts made in Taiwan are used in making products all over the world.[20]

It encourages growth and new ideas

In addition to making mass production possible, a market-directed, macro-marketing system encourages **innovation**—the development and spread of new ideas and products. Competition for consumers' money forces firms to think of new and better ways of satisfying consumer needs. And the competition that marketing fosters drives down prices and gives consumers more choices and a higher standard of living.

Macro-marketing system is becoming more efficient

In combination, the forces of competition and the choices made by customers to support those firms that do the best job of meeting their needs drive our macro-marketing system to be more efficient.

Some changes come quickly. A good example is the speed with which firms have adopted e-commerce. **E-commerce** refers to exchanges between individuals or organizations—and activities that facilitate those exchanges—based on applications of information technology. E-commerce is helping to cut costs from almost every aspect of marketing while at the same time helping firms to better satisfy their customers. This has had a significant impact on our macro-marketing system. Most experts believe that the growth of the U.S. economy during the last decade, coupled with low levels of price increases (inflation), is due to the fact that e-commerce has helped sellers reduce costs.

Throughout this text we will detail how e-commerce is increasing the efficiency and effectiveness of marketing. On the other hand, the upward trend in the macro-marketing system does not ensure success for any *individual* firm or its customers. For example, many individual dot-com firms—companies established to do business over the Internet—failed. These companies were started by people who thought they had come up with "a better mousetrap," but customers didn't always see it that way. These failures are expensive, and ultimately that expense is shared by members of the society. So, throughout this text we will focus on how managers can make better decisions—to improve both micro-marketing performance and the performance of the whole macro-marketing system.

Exhibit 1-5 Sample Criticisms of Marketing

- Advertising is everywhere, and it's often annoying, misleading, or wasteful.
- The quality of products is poor and often they are not even safe.
- There are too many unnecessary products.
- Packaging and labeling are often confusing and deceptive.
- Middlemen add too much to the cost of distribution and just raise prices without providing anything in return.
- Marketing serves the rich and exploits the poor.
- Service stinks, and when a consumer has a problem nobody cares.
- Marketing creates interest in products that pollute the environment.
- Private information about consumers is collected and used to sell them things they don't want.
- Marketing makes people too materialistic and motivates them toward "things" instead of social needs.
- Easy consumer credit makes people buy things they don't need and can't afford.

Marketing has its critics

In explaining marketing's role in society, we described some of the benefits of a market-directed macro-marketing system. We can see this in the macro-marketing system of the United States. It provides—at least in material terms—one of the highest standards of living in the world. It seems to be "effective" and "fair" in many ways.

We must admit, however, that marketing—as it exists in the United States and other developed societies—has many critics. Marketing activity is especially open to criticism because it is the part of business most visible to the public.

A number of typical complaints about marketing are summarized in Exhibit 1-5. Think about these criticisms and whether you agree with them or not. What complaints do you have that are not covered by one of the categories in Exhibit 1-5?

Such complaints should not be taken lightly. They show that many people are unhappy with some parts of the marketing system. Certainly, the strong public support for consumer protection laws proves that not all consumers feel they are being treated like royalty.[21]

Is it an ethical issue?

Certainly some complaints about marketing arise because some firm intentionally cheated customers. But at other times, problems may arise because a manager did not fully consider the ethical implications of a decision. In either case, there is no excuse for sloppiness when it comes to **marketing ethics**—the moral standards that guide marketing decisions and actions. Each individual develops moral standards based on his or her own values. That helps explain why opinions about what is right or wrong often vary from one person to another and from one society to another. It is sometimes difficult to say whose opinions are "correct." Even so, such opinions may have a very real influence on whether an individual's (or a firm's) marketing decisions and actions are accepted or rejected. So marketing ethics are not only a philosophical issue, they are also a pragmatic concern. Throughout the text we will discuss the types of ethical issues individual marketing managers face. But we won't be moralizing and trying to tell you how you should think on any given issue. Rather, by the end of the course we hope that *you* will have some firm personal opinions about what is and is not ethical in micro-marketing activities.[22]

Keep in mind, however, that not all criticisms of marketing focus on ethical issues. Fortunately, most businesspeople work to be fair and honest. Moreover, not all criticisms are specific to the micro-marketing activities of individual firms. Some of the complaints about marketing really focus on the basic idea of a market-directed macro-marketing system. These criticisms often occur because people don't understand what marketing is—or how it works. As you go through this book, we'll discuss some of these criticisms. Then in our final chapter, we will return to a more complete appraisal of marketing in our consumer-oriented society.

Conclusion

In this chapter, we defined two levels of marketing: micro-marketing and macro-marketing. Macro-marketing is concerned with the way the whole global economy works. Micro-marketing focuses on the activities of individual firms. We discussed the role of marketing in economic development and the functions of marketing and who performs them. We ended by raising some of the criticisms of marketing—both of the whole macro system and of the way individual firms work.

We emphasized macro-marketing in this chapter, but the major thrust of this book is on micro-marketing. By learning more about market-oriented decision making, you will be able to make more efficient and socially responsible decisions. This will help improve the performance of individual firms and organizations (your employers). And eventually, it will help our macro-marketing system work better.

We'll see marketing through the eyes of the marketing manager—maybe *you* in the near future. And we will show how you can contribute to the marketing process. Along the way, we'll discuss the impact of micro-level decisions on society, and the ethical issues that marketing managers face. Then in Chapter 18—after you have had time to understand how and why producers and consumers think and behave the way they do—we will evaluate how well both micro-marketing and macro-marketing perform in a market-directed economic system.

Questions and Problems

1. List your activities for the first two hours after you woke up this morning. Briefly indicate how marketing affected your activities.
2. It is fairly easy to see why people do not beat a path to a mousetrap manufacturer's door, but would they be similarly indifferent if some food processor developed a revolutionary new food product that would provide all necessary nutrients in small pills for about $100 per year per person?
3. If a producer creates a really revolutionary new product and consumers can learn about it and purchase it at a website on the Internet, is any additional marketing effort really necessary? Explain your thinking.
4. Distinguish between macro- and micro-marketing. Then explain how they are interrelated, if they are.
5. Distinguish between how economic decisions are made in a planned economic system and how they are made in a market-directed economy.
6. A committee of the American Marketing Association defined marketing as "the process of planning and executing the conception, pricing, promotion, and distribution of ideas, goods, and services to create exchanges that satisfy individual and organizational objectives." Does this definition consider macro-marketing? Explain your answer.
7. Identify a "central market" in your city and explain how it facilitates exchange.
8. Identify a website on the Internet that serves as a "central market" for some type(s) of good(s) or service(s). Give the address (www.___.___) of the website and briefly explain the logic of your choice.
9. Explain why tariffs and quotas affect international marketing opportunities.
10. Discuss the nature of marketing in a socialist (planned) economy. Would the functions that must be provided and the development of wholesaling and retailing systems be any different from those in a market-directed economy?
11. Discuss how the micro-macro dilemma relates to each of the following products: high-powered engines in cars, nuclear power, bank credit cards, and pesticides that improve farm production.
12. Describe a recent purchase you made. Indicate why that particular product was available at a store and, in particular, at the store where you bought it.
13. Refer to Exhibit 1-3, and give an example of a purchase you made recently that involved separation of information and separation in time between you and the producer. Briefly explain how these separations were overcome.

14. Online computer shopping at websites on the Internet makes it possible for individual consumers to get direct information from hundreds of companies they would not otherwise know about. Consumers can place an order for a purchase that is then shipped to them directly. Will growth of these services ultimately eliminate the need for retailers and wholesalers? Explain your thinking, giving specific attention to what marketing functions are involved in these "electronic purchases" and who performs them.
15. Define the functions of marketing in your own words. Using an example, explain how they can be shifted and shared.
16. Explain, in your own words, why this text emphasizes micro-marketing.
17. Explain why a small producer might want a marketing research firm to take over some of its information-gathering activities.
18. Explain why a market-directed macro-marketing system encourages innovation. Give an example.

Suggested Cases

1. McDonald's "Seniors" Restaurant
4. Bidwell Carpet Cleaning, Inc.
17. myWedding.com

Computer-Aided Problem

1. **Revenue, Cost, and Profit Relationships**

This problem introduces you to the computer-aided problem (CAP) software—which is on the CD that accompanies this text—and gets you started with the use of spreadsheet analysis for marketing decision making. This problem is simple. In fact, you could work it without the software. But by starting with a simple problem, you will learn how to use the program more quickly and see how it will help you with more complicated problems. *Instructions for the CAP software are available at the end of this text.*

Sue Cline, the business manager at Magna University Student Bookstore, is developing plans for the next academic year. The bookstore is one of the university's nonprofit activities, but any "surplus" (profit) it earns is used to support the student activities center.

Two popular products at the bookstore are the student academic calendar and notebooks with the school name. Sue Cline thinks that she can sell calendars to 90 percent of Magna's 3,000 students, so she has had 2,700 printed. The total cost, including artwork and printing, is $11,500. Last year the calendar sold for $5.00, but Sue is considering changing the price this year.

Sue thinks that the bookstore will be able to sell 6,000 notebooks if they are priced right. But she knows that many students will buy similar notebooks (without the school name) from stores in town if the bookstore price is too high.

Sue has entered the information about selling price, quantity, and costs for calendars and notebooks in the spreadsheet program so that it is easy to evaluate the effect of different decisions. The spreadsheet is also set up to calculate revenue and profit, based on

$$\text{Revenue} = (\text{Selling price}) \times (\text{Quantity sold})$$

$$\text{Profit} = (\text{Revenue}) - (\text{Total cost})$$

Use the program to answer the questions below. Record your answers on a separate sheet of paper.

a. From the Spreadsheet Screen, how much revenue does Sue expect from calendars? How much revenue from notebooks? How much profit will the store earn from calendars? From notebooks?

b. If Sue increases the price of her calendars to $6.00 and still sells the same quantity, what is the expected revenue? The expected profit? (Note: Change the price from $5.00 to $6.00 on the spreadsheet and the program will recompute revenue and profit.) On your sheet of paper, show the calculations that confirm that the program has given you the correct values.

c. Sue is interested in getting an overview of how a change in the price of notebooks would affect revenue and profit, assuming that she sells all 6,000 notebooks she is thinking of ordering. Prepare a table—on your sheet of paper—with column headings for three variables: selling price, revenue, and profit. Show the *value for revenue and profit for different possible selling prices for a notebook—starting at a minimum price of $1.60 and adding 8 cents to the price until you reach a maximum of $2.40. At what price will selling 6,000 notebooks contribute $5,400.00 to profit? At what price would notebook sales contribute only $1,080.00? (Hint: Use the What If analysis feature to compute the new values. Start by selecting "selling price" for notebooks as the value to change, with a minimum value of $1.60 and a maximum value of $2.40. Select the revenue and profit for notebooks as the values to display. Then click the "Results" button at the top of the spreadsheet window.)*

For additional questions related to this problem, see Exercise 1-4 in the *Learning Aid for Use with Essentials of Marketing*, 9th edition.

When You Finish This Chapter, You Should

1. Know what the marketing concept is—and how it should affect strategy planning in a firm or nonprofit organization.

2. Understand what customer value is and why it is important to customer satisfaction.

3. Understand what a marketing manager does.

4. Know what marketing strategy planning is—and why it will be the focus of this book.

5. Understand target marketing.

6. Be familiar with the four Ps in a marketing mix.

7. Know the difference between a marketing strategy, a marketing plan, and a marketing program.

8. Understand the important new terms (shown in red).

Chapter Two

Marketing's Role within the Firm or Nonprofit Organization

As you saw in Chapter 1, marketing and marketing management are important in our society—and in business firms and nonprofit organizations. To get you thinking about the marketing strategy planning ideas we will be developing in this chapter and the rest of the book, let's consider Dell Computers.

As a freshman in college, Michael Dell started buying and reselling computers from his dorm room. At that time, the typical marketing mix for PCs emphasized distribution through specialized computer stores that sold to business users and some final consumers. Often the dealers' service quality didn't justify the high prices they charged, the features of the PCs they had in stock didn't match what customers wanted, and repairs were a hassle.

Dell decided there was a target market of price-conscious customers who would respond to a

place price promotion produc

different marketing mix. He used direct-response advertising in computer magazines—and customers called a toll-free number to order a computer with the exact features they wanted. Dell built computers to match the specific orders that came in and used UPS to quickly ship orders directly to the customer. Prices were low, too—because the direct channel meant there was no retailer markup and the build-to-order approach reduced inventory costs. This approach also kept Dell in constant contact with customers. Problems could be identified quickly and corrected. Dell also implemented the plan well—with constant improvements—to make good on its promise of reliable machines and superior service. For example, Dell pioneered a system of guaranteed on-site service—within 24 hours. Dell also set up ongoing programs to train all employees to work together to please customers.

Of course, it's hard to satisfy everyone all of the time. For example, profits fell when Dell's laptop design didn't measure up. Customers simply didn't see them as a good value. However, smart marketers learn from and fix mistakes. Dell quickly got its product line back on the bull's eye.

As sales grew, Dell put more money into advertising. Its ad agency crafted ads to position Dell in consumers' minds as an aggressive, value-oriented source of computers. At the same time, Dell added a direct sales force to call on big government and corporate buyers—because they expected in-person selling and a relationship, not just a telephone contact. And when these important customers said they wanted Dell to offer high-power machines to run their corporate networks, Dell put money into R&D to create what they needed.

price
place
promotion
product

Dell also saw the prospect for international growth. Many firms moved into Europe by exporting. But Dell set up its own operations there. Dell knew it would be tough to win over skeptical European buyers. They had never bought big-ticket items such as PCs on the phone. Yet, in less than five years, sales in Europe grew to 40 percent of Dell's total revenue and Dell pushed into Asian markets for more growth. That also posed challenges, so Dell's advertising manager invited major ad agencies to make presentations on how Dell could be more effective with its $80 million global advertising campaign.

By the mid-1990s, other firms were trying to imitate Dell's direct-order approach. For example, IBM set up Ambra, a direct-sales division. However, the retailers who were selling the bulk of IBM's computers were not happy about facing price competition from their own supplier! So IBM couldn't simply copy Dell's strategy. It was in conflict with the rest of IBM's marketing program.

As computer prices fell, many firms were worried about how to cope with slim profits. But Dell saw an opportunity for profitable growth by extending its direct model to a website (www.dell.com) that was soon generating about $1.5 billion in sales each month! Moreover, online selling lowered expenses and reduced supply and inventory costs. For example, when a customer ordered a PC produced in one factory and a monitor produced in another, the two pieces were brought together enroute to the customer. This cost cutting proved to be especially important when the economy softened and demand for PCs fell off. Building on its strengths, Dell cut prices in what many competitors saw as an "irrational" price war. But the design of Dell's website and sales system allowed it to charge different prices to different segments to match demand with supply. For example, high-margin laptops were priced lower to educational customers—to stimulate demand—than to government buyers who were less price sensitive. Similarly, if the supply of 17-inch monitors fell short, Dell could use an online promotion for 19-inch monitors and shift demand. To create more profit opportunities from its existing customers, Dell also put more emphasis on selling extended-care service agreements.

Clearly, the growth of the PC market is tapering off. That means that Dell's future profits will depend even more heavily on careful strategy planning. But perhaps Dell can continue to find new ways to satisfy customers' PC-related needs—or even identify other new, high-growth opportunities to pursue.[1]

We've mentioned only a few of many decisions marketing managers at Dell had to make in developing marketing strategies, but you can see that each of these decisions affects the others. Further, making marketing decisions is never easy and strategies may need to change. Yet, knowing what basic decision areas to consider helps you to plan a more successful strategy. This chapter will get you started by giving you a framework for thinking about all the marketing management decision areas—which is what the rest of this book is all about.

Marketing's Role Has Changed a Lot over the Years

From our Dell case, it's clear that marketing decisions are very important to a firm's success. But marketing hasn't always been so complicated. In fact, understanding how marketing thinking has evolved makes the modern view clearer. So, we will discuss four stages in marketing evolution: (1) the production era, (2) the sales era, (3) the marketing department era, and (4) the marketing company era. We'll talk about these eras as if they applied generally to all firms—but keep in mind that *some managers still have not made it to the final stages*. They are stuck in the past with old ways of thinking.

From the production to the sales era

From the Industrial Revolution until the 1920s, most companies were in the production era. The **production era** is a time when a company focuses on production of a few specific products—perhaps because few of these products are available in the market. "If we can make it, it will sell" is management thinking characteristic of the production era. Because of product shortages, many nations—including China and many of the post-communist republics of Eastern Europe—continue to operate with production era approaches.

By about 1930, most companies in the industrialized Western nations had more production capability than ever before. Now the problem wasn't just to produce—but to beat the competition and win customers. This led many firms to enter the sales era. The **sales era** is a time when a company emphasizes selling because of increased competition.

To the marketing department era

For most firms in advanced economies, the sales era continued until at least 1950. By then, sales were growing rapidly in most areas of the economy. The problem was deciding where to put the company's effort. Someone was needed to tie together the efforts of research, purchasing, production, shipping, and sales. As this situation became more common, the sales era was replaced by the marketing department era. The **marketing department era** is a time when all marketing activities are brought under the control of one department to improve short-run policy planning and to try to integrate the firm's activities.

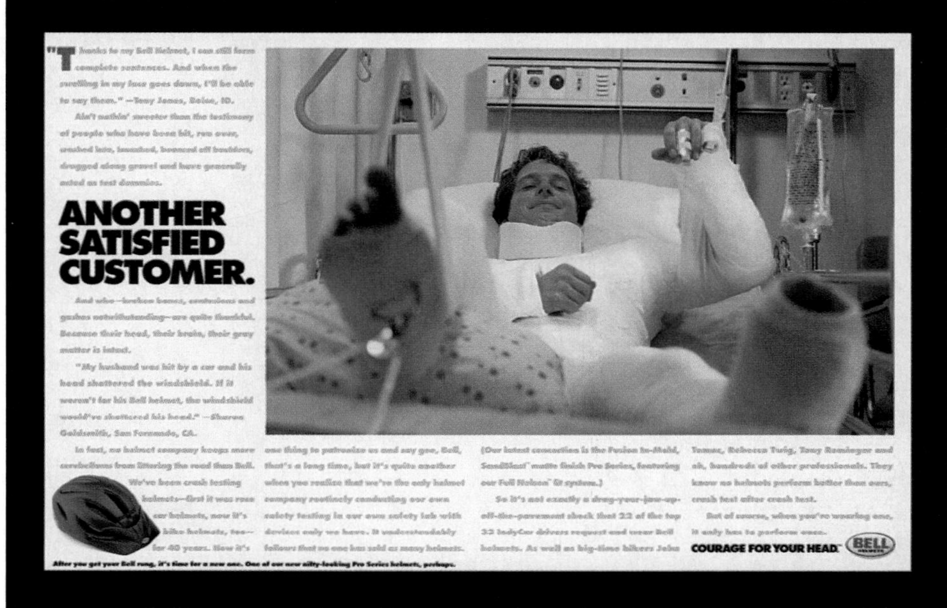

Customer satisfaction isn't always a life and death matter as it can be with Bell's bike helmets, but over time firms that can't satisfy their customers don't survive.

To the marketing company era

Since 1960, most firms have developed at least some managers with a marketing management outlook. Many of these firms have even graduated from the marketing department era into the marketing company era. The **marketing company era** is a time when, in addition to short-run marketing planning, marketing people develop long-range plans—sometimes five or more years ahead—and the whole company effort is guided by the marketing concept.

What Does the Marketing Concept Mean?

The **marketing concept** means that an organization aims *all* its efforts at satisfying its *customers*—at a profit. The marketing concept is a simple but very important idea. See Exhibit 2-1.

The marketing concept is not a new idea—it's been around for a long time. But some managers show little interest in customers' needs. These managers still have a **production orientation**—making whatever products are easy to produce and *then* trying to sell them. They think of customers existing to buy the firm's output rather than of firms existing to serve customers and—more broadly—the needs of society.

Well-managed firms have replaced this production orientation with a marketing orientation. A **marketing orientation** means trying to carry out the marketing concept. Instead of just trying to get customers to buy what the firm has produced, a marketing-oriented firm tries to offer customers what they need.

Three basic ideas are included in the definition of the marketing concept: (1) customer satisfaction, (2) a total company effort, and (3) profit—not just sales—as an objective. These ideas deserve more discussion.

Customer satisfaction guides the whole system

"Give the customers what they need" seems so obvious that it may be hard for you to see why the marketing concept requires special attention. However, people don't always do the logical—especially when it means changing what they've done in the past. In a typical company 35 years ago, production managers thought mainly about getting out the product. Accountants were interested only in balancing the books. Financial people looked after the company's cash position. And salespeople

Exhibit 2-1
Organizations with a Marketing Orientation Carry Out the Marketing Concept

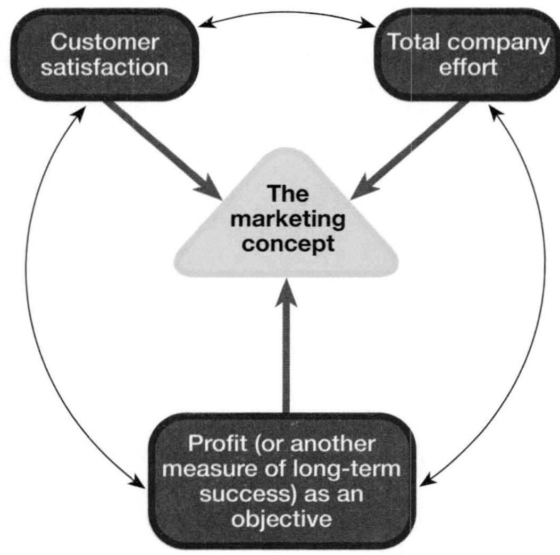

Firms that adopt the marketing concept want consumers and others in the channel of distribution to know that they provide superior customer value.

were mainly concerned with getting orders for whatever product was in the warehouse. Each department thought of its own activity as the center of the business. Unfortunately, this is still true in many companies today.

Work together to do a better job

Ideally, all managers should work together as a team. Every department may directly or indirectly impact customer satisfaction. But some managers tend to build "fences" around their own departments. There may be meetings to try to get them to work together—but they come and go from the meetings worried only about protecting their own turf.

We use the term *production orientation* as a shorthand way to refer to this kind of narrow thinking—and lack of a central focus—in a business firm. But keep in mind that this problem may be seen in sales-oriented sales representatives, advertising-oriented agency people, finance-oriented finance people, directors of nonprofit organizations, and so on. It is not a criticism of people who manage production. They aren't necessarily any more guilty of narrow thinking than anyone else.

The fences come down in an organization that has accepted the marketing concept. There may still be departments because specialization often makes sense. But the total system's effort is guided by what customers want—instead of what each department would like to do.

The marketing concept provides a guiding focus that *all* departments adopt. It should be a philosophy of the whole organization, not just an idea that applies to the marketing department.

Survival and success require a profit

Firms must satisfy customers. But keep in mind that it may cost more to satisfy some needs than any customers are willing to pay. Or, it may be much more costly to try to attract new customers than it is to build a strong relationship with—and repeat purchases from—existing customers. So profit—the difference between a firm's revenue and its total costs—is the bottom-line measure of the firm's success and ability to survive. It is the balancing point that helps the firm determine what needs it will try to satisfy with its total (sometimes costly!) effort.

Adoption of the Marketing Concept Has Not Been Easy or Universal

The marketing concept was first accepted by consumer products companies such as General Electric and Procter & Gamble. Competition was intense in their markets—and trying to satisfy customers' needs more fully was a way to win in this competition. Widespread publicity about the success of the marketing concept at these companies helped spread the message to other firms.[2]

Producers of industrial commodities—steel, coal, paper, glass, and chemicals—have accepted the marketing concept slowly if at all. Similarly, many traditional retailers have been slow to accept the marketing concept.

Service industries are catching up

Service industries—including airlines, power and telephone companies, banks, investment firms, lawyers, physicians, accountants, and insurance companies—were slow to adopt the marketing concept, too. But in recent years this has changed dramatically. This is partly due to changes in government regulations that forced many of these businesses to be more competitive.

Banks used to be open for limited hours that were convenient for bankers—not customers. Many closed during lunch hour! But now banks stay open longer, and also offer more services for their customers—automated teller machines, banking over the Internet, or a "personal banker" to give financial advice.[3]

It's easy to slip into a production orientation

The marketing concept may seem obvious, but it's very easy to slip into a production-oriented way of thinking. For example, a company might rush a new product to market—rather than first finding out if it will fill an unsatisfied need. Many firms in high-technology businesses fall into this trap. Consider the thousands of new dot-com firms that failed. They may have had a vision of what the technology could do, but they didn't stop to figure out all that it would take to satisfy customers or make a profit. Imagine how parents felt when eToys.com failed to deliver online purchases of Christmas toys on time. If you had that experience, would you ever shop there again? What would you tell others?

Take a look at Exhibit 2-2. It shows some differences in outlook between adopters of the marketing concept and typical production-oriented managers. As the exhibit suggests, the marketing concept forces the company to think through what it is doing—and why. And it motivates the company to develop plans for accomplishing its objectives.

The Marketing Concept and Customer Value

Take the customer's point of view

A manager who adopts the marketing concept sees customer satisfaction as the path to profits. And to better understand what it takes to satisfy a customer, it's useful to take the customer's point of view.

A customer may look at a market offering from two views. One deals with the potential benefits of that offering; the other concerns what the customer has to give up to get those benefits. Consider a student who has just finished an exam and is thinking about getting a cup of Mocha Latte from Starbucks. Our coffee lover might see this as a great-tasting snack, a personal reward, a quick pick-me-up, and even as a way to get to know an attractive classmate. Clearly, different needs are associated with these different benefits. The cost of getting these benefits would include the price of the coffee and any tip, but there might be other nondollar costs. For example, how difficult it will be to park is a convenience cost. Slow service would be an aggravation. And you might worry about another kind of cost if the professor whose exam you have the next day sees you "wasting time" at Starbucks.

Exhibit 2-2 Some Differences in Outlook between Adopters of the Marketing Concept and the Typical Production-Oriented Managers

Topic	Marketing Orientation	Production Orientation
Attitudes toward customers	Customer needs determine company plans.	They should be glad we exist, trying to cut costs and bringing out better products.
An Internet website	A new way to serve customers.	If we have a website customers will flock to us.
Product offering	Company makes what it can sell.	Company sells what it can make.
Role of marketing research	To determine customer needs and how well company is satisfying them.	To determine customer reaction, if used at all.
Interest in innovation	Focus on locating new opportunities.	Focus is on technology and cost cutting.
Importance of profit	A critical objective.	A residual, what's left after all costs are covered.
Role of packaging	Designed for customer convenience and as a selling tool.	Seen merely as protection for the product.
Inventory levels	Set with customer requirements and costs in mind.	Set to make production more convenient.
Focus of advertising	Need-satisfying benefits of goods and services.	Product features and how products are made.
Role of sales force	Help the customer to buy if the product fits customer's needs, while coordinating with rest of firm.	Sell the customer, don't worry about coordination with other promotion efforts or rest of firm.
Relationship with customer	Customer satisfaction before and after sale leads to a profitable long-run relationship.	Relationship ends when a sale is made.
Costs	Eliminate costs that do not give value to customer.	Keep costs as low as possible.

Customer value reflects benefits and costs

As this example suggests, both benefits and costs can take many different forms, perhaps ranging from economic to emotional. They also may vary depending on the situation. However, it is the customer's view of the various benefits and costs that is important. This leads us to the concept of **customer value**—the difference between the benefits a customer sees from a market offering and the costs of obtaining those benefits. A consumer is likely to be more satisfied when the customer value is higher—when benefits exceed costs by a larger margin. On the other hand, a consumer who sees the costs as greater than the benefits isn't likely to become a customer.

Some people think that low price and high customer value are the same thing. But that may not be the case at all. A good or service that doesn't meet a consumer's needs results in low customer value, even if the price is very low. Yet, a high price may be more than acceptable when it obtains the desired benefits. Think again about our Starbucks example. You can get a cup of coffee for a much lower price, but Starbucks offers more than *just* a cup of coffee.

Customer may not think about it very much

It's useful for a manager to evaluate ways to improve the benefits, or reduce the costs, of what the firm offers customers. However, this doesn't mean that customers stop and compute some sort of customer value score before making each purchase. If they did, there wouldn't be much time in life for anything else. So, a manager's objective and thorough analysis may not accurately reflect the customer's impressions. Yet, it is the customer's view that matters—even when the customer has not thought about it.

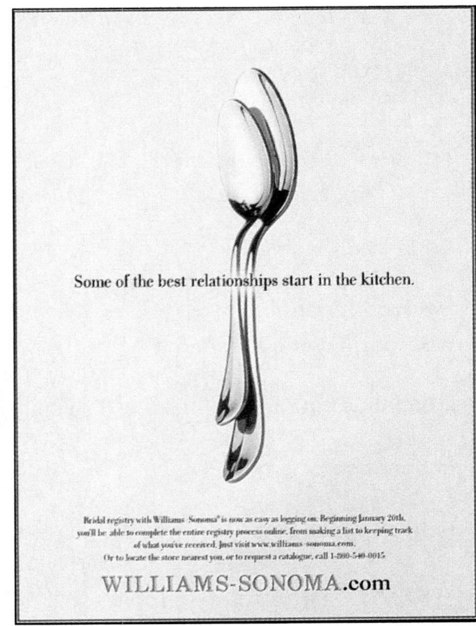

Many marketers are looking for ways to build long-term relationships with customers. For example, Payless Shoes gets the relationship off on the right foot by offering new parents a free pair of baby shoes. Williams-Sonoma offers a free online bridal registry, which builds relationships with newlyweds, a key target market.

Where does competition fit?

You can't afford to ignore competition. Consumers usually have choices about how they will meet their needs. So, a firm that offers superior customer value is likely to win and keep customers. Often the best way to improve customer value, and beat the competition, is to be first to satisfy a need that others have not even considered.

The competition between Pepsi and Coke illustrates this. Coke and Pepsi were spending millions of dollars on promotion—fighting head-to-head for the same cola customers. They put so much emphasis on the cola competition that they missed other opportunities. That gave firms like Snapple the chance to enter the market and steal away customers. For these customers, the desired benefits—and the greatest customer value—came from the variety of a fruit-flavored drink, not from one more cola.

Build relationships with customer value

Firms that embrace the marketing concept seek ways to build a profitable long-term relationship with each customer. Even the most innovative firm faces competition sooner or later. And trying to get new customers by taking them away from a competitor is usually more costly than retaining current customers by really satisfying their needs. Satisfied customers buy again and again. This makes their buying job easier, and it also increases the selling firm's profits.

Building relationships with customers requires that everyone in a firm works together to provide customer value before *and after* each purchase. If there is a problem with a customer's bill, the accounting people can't just leave it to the salesperson to straighten it out or, even worse, act like it's "the customer's problem." The long-term relationship with the customer—and the lifetime value of the customer's future purchases—is threatened unless everyone works together to make things right for the customer. The same ideas apply whether the issue is meeting promised delivery dates, resolving warranty problems, or giving a customer help on how to use a product.

In other words, any time the customer value is reduced—because the benefits to the customer decrease or the costs increase—the relationship is weakened.[4]

Exhibit 2-3 summarizes these ideas. In a firm that has adopted the marketing concept everyone focuses on customer satisfaction. They offer superior customer value. That helps attract customers in the first place—and keeps them satisfied after they buy. Because customers are satisfied, they want to purchase from the firm again. The relationship with customers is profitable, so the firm is encouraged to find better ways to offer superior customer value. In other words, when a firm adopts the marketing concept, it wins and so do its customers.

Exhibit 2-3
Satisfying Customers with Superior Customer Value to Build Profitable Relationships

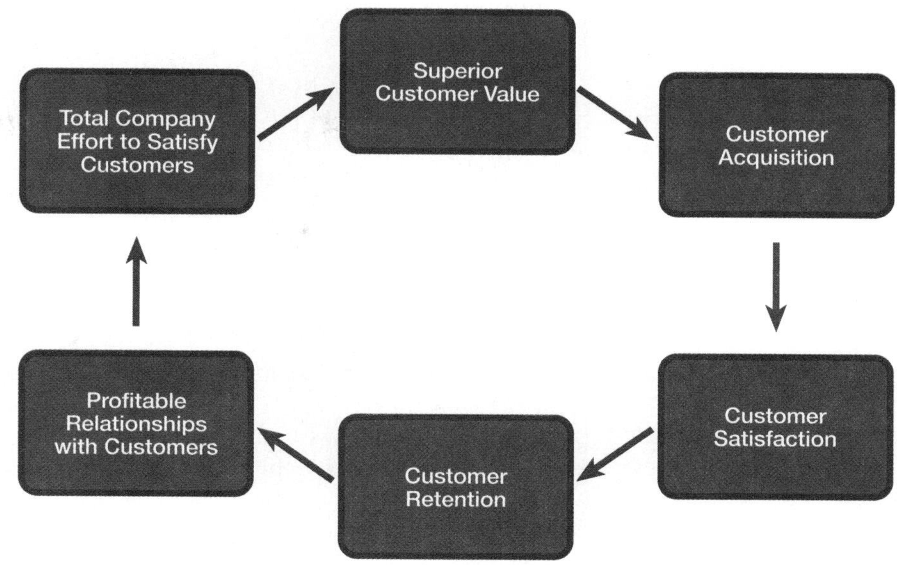

L. L. Bean delivers superior value

L. L. Bean illustrates these ideas. It is a firm that builds enduring relationships with its customers. It offers good customer value to consumers who are interested in enjoying the outdoors. Bean's quality products are well suited to a wide variety of outdoor needs—whether it's clothing for hikers or equipment for campers. The firm field-tests all its products—to be certain they live up to the firm's "100% satisfaction" guarantee. Although Bean operates a retail store in Freeport, Maine, its Internet website (www.llbean.com) and catalogs reach customers all over the world. Bean's computers track what each customer is buying, so new catalogs are mailed directly to the people who are most interested. Customers can call toll-free 24 hours a day—and get whatever advice they need because the salespeople are real experts on what they sell. Bean also makes it easy for consumers to return a product. Bean's prices are not low but Bean retains its loyal customers because they like the benefits of the relationship.[5]

Internet

Internet Exercise The L. L. Bean website (www.llbean.com) offers consumers a lot of information, including an "Outdoors Online" section with information about national parks. Do you think that this helps Bean to build relationships with its target customers?

The Marketing Concept Applies in Nonprofit Organizations

Newcomers to marketing thinking

The marketing concept is as important for nonprofit organizations as it is for business firms. In fact, marketing applies to all sorts of public and private nonprofit organizations—ranging from government agencies, health care organizations, educational institutions, and religious groups to charities, political parties, and fine arts organizations.

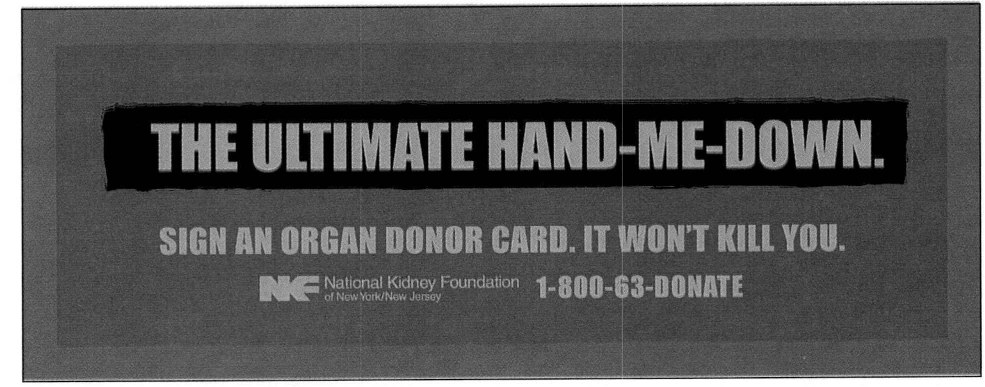

Marketing is now widely accepted by many nonprofit organizations, including the National Kidney Foundation, which wants to increase the number of organ donors.

Support may not come from satisfied "customers"

As with any business firm, a nonprofit organization needs resources and support to survive and achieve its objectives. Yet support often does not come directly from those who receive the benefits the organization produces. For example, the World Wildlife Fund protects animals. If supporters of the World Wildlife Fund are not satisfied with its efforts—don't think the benefits are worth what it costs to provide them—they will, and should, put their time and money elsewhere.

Just as most firms face competition for customers, most nonprofits face competition for the resources and support they need. The Air Force faces a big problem if it can't attract new recruits. A shelter for the homeless may fail if supporters decide to focus on some other cause, such as AIDS education.

What is the "bottom line"?

As with a business, a nonprofit must take in as much money as it spends or it won't survive. However, a nonprofit organization does not measure "profit" in the same way as a firm. And its key measures of long-term success are also different. The YMCA, colleges, symphony orchestras, and the post office, for example, all seek to achieve different objectives and need different measures of success.

Profit guides business decisions because it reflects both the costs and benefits of different activities. In a nonprofit organization, it is sometimes more difficult to be objective in evaluating the benefits of different activities relative to what they cost. However, if everyone in an organization agrees to *some* measure(s) of long-run success, it helps serve as a guide to where the organization should focus its efforts.

May not be organized for marketing

Some nonprofits face other challenges in organizing to adopt the marketing concept. Often no one has overall responsibility for marketing activities. Even when some leaders do the marketing thinking, they may have trouble getting unpaid volunteers with many different interests to all agree with the marketing strategy. Volunteers tend to do what they feel like doing![6]

Throughout this book, we'll be discussing the marketing concept and related ideas as they apply in many different settings. Often we'll simply say "in a firm" or "in a business"—but remember that most of the ideas can be applied in *any* type of organization.

The Marketing Concept, Social Responsibility, and Marketing Ethics

Society's needs must be considered

The marketing concept is so logical that it's hard to argue with it. Yet when a firm focuses its efforts on satisfying some consumers—to achieve its objectives—there may be negative effects on society. (Remember that we discussed this micro–macro dilemma in Chapter 1.) This means that marketing managers should be concerned with **social responsibility**—a firm's obligation to improve its positive effects on society and reduce its negative effects. Being socially responsible sometimes requires difficult trade-offs.

Consider, for example, the environmental problems created by CFCs, chemicals used in hundreds of critical products including fire extinguishers, cooling systems, and electronic circuit boards. We now know that CFCs deplete the earth's ozone layer. Yet when this was learned it was not possible to immediately stop producing and using all CFCs. For many products critical to society, there was no feasible short-term substitute for CFCs. Du Pont and other producers of CFCs worked hard to balance these conflicting demands. Yet you can see that there are no easy answers for how such conflicts should be resolved.[7]

The issue of social responsibility in marketing also raises other important questions—for which there are no easy answers.

Should all consumer needs be satisfied?

Some consumers want products that may not be safe or good for them in the long run. Some critics argue that businesses should not offer high-heeled shoes, alcoholic beverages, or sugar-coated cereals because they aren't "good" for consumers in the long run.

Similarly, bicycles and roller blades are among the most dangerous products identified by the Consumer Product Safety Commission. Who should decide if these products will be offered to consumers? Is this a micro-marketing issue or a macro-marketing issue?

What if it cuts into profits?

Being more socially conscious often seems to lead to positive customer response. For example, many consumers praise Wal-Mart as a "safe haven" for kids to shop because it does not carry CDs that are not suitable for children, lewd videos, plastic guns that look authentic, and video games judged to be too violent. Green Mountain Power has had a very good response to electric power produced with less pollution (even though the price is higher). And some consumers buy only from firms that certify that their overseas factories don't rely on child labor.[8]

Yet as the examples above show, there are times when being socially responsible conflicts with a firm's profit objective. Concerns about such conflicts have prompted critics to raise the basic question: Is the marketing concept really desirable?

Many socially conscious marketing managers are trying to resolve this problem. Their definition of customer satisfaction includes long-range effects—as well as immediate customer satisfaction. They try to balance consumer, company, *and* social interests.

The marketing concept guides marketing ethics

Firms that adopt the marketing concept are concerned about marketing ethics as well as broader issues of social responsibility. A firm cannot be truly consumer-oriented and at the same time intentionally unethical.

Problems may arise when some individual manager does not share the same marketing ethics as others in the organization. One person operating alone can damage a firm's reputation and even survival.

To be certain that standards for marketing ethics are as clear as possible, many organizations have developed their own written codes of ethics. These codes usually state—at least at a general level—the ethical standards that everyone in the firm should follow in dealing with customers and other people. Many professional societies also have such codes. For example, the American Marketing Association's code of ethics—see Exhibit 2-4—sets specific ethical standards for many aspects of marketing.[9]

The Management Job in Marketing

Now that you know about the marketing concept—a philosophy to guide the whole firm—let's look more closely at how a marketing manager helps a firm to achieve its objectives. The marketing manager is a manager, so let's look at the marketing management process.

Exhibit 2-4 Code of Ethics, American Marketing Association

CODE OF ETHICS

Members of the American Marketing Association (AMA) are committed to ethical professional conduct. They have joined together in subscribing to this Code of Ethics embracing the following topics:

Responsibilities of the Marketer

Marketers must accept responsibility for the consequences of their activities and make every effort to ensure that their decisions, recommendations, and actions function to identify, serve, and satisfy all relevant publics: customers, organizations and society.

Marketers' professional conduct must be guided by:

1. The basic rule of professional ethics: not knowingly to do harm;
2. The adherence to all applicable laws and regulations;
3. The accurate representation of their education, training and experience; and
4. The active support, practice and promotion of this Code of Ethics.

Honesty and Fairness

Marketers shall uphold and advance the integrity, honor, and dignity of the marketing profession by:

1. Being honest in serving consumers, clients, employees, suppliers, distributors and the public;
2. Not knowingly participating in conflict of interest without prior notice to all parties involved; and
3. Establishing equitable fee schedules including the payment or receipt of usual, customary and/or legal compensation for marketing exchanges.

Rights and Duties of Parties in the Marketing Exchange Process

Participants in the marketing exchange process should be able to expect that:

1. Products and services offered are safe and fit for their intended uses;
2. Communications about offered products and services are not deceptive;
3. All parties intend to discharge their obligations, financial and otherwise, in good faith; and
4. Appropriate internal methods exist for equitable adjustment and/or redress of grievances concerning purchases.

It is understood that the above would include, but is not limited to, the following responsibilities of the marketer:

In the area of product development and management,

- disclosure of all substantial risks associated with product or service usage;
- identification of any product component substitution that might materially change the product or impact on the buyer's purchase decision;
- identification of extra-cost added features.

In the area of promotions,

- avoidance of false and misleading advertising;
- rejection of high pressure manipulations, or misleading sales tactics;
- avoidance of sales promotions that use deception or manipulation.

In the area of distribution,

- not manipulating the availability of a product for purpose of exploitation;
- not using coercion in the marketing channel;
- not exerting undue influence over the reseller's choice to handle a product.

In the area of pricing,

- not engaging in price fixing;
- not practicing predatory pricing;
- disclosing the full price associated with any purchase.

In the area of marketing research,

- prohibiting selling or fund raising under the guise of conducting research;
- maintaining research integrity by avoiding misrepresentation and omission of pertinent research data;
- treating outside clients and suppliers fairly.

Organizational Relationships

Marketers should be aware of how their behavior may influence or impact on the behavior of others in organizational relationships. They should not demand, encourage or apply coercion to obtain unethical behavior in their relationships with others, such as employees, suppliers or customers.

1. Apply confidentiality and anonymity in professional relationships with regard to privileged information;
2. Meet their obligations and responsibilities in contracts and mutual agreements in a timely manner;
3. Avoid taking the work of others, in whole, or in part, and represent this work as their own or directly benefit from it without compensation or consent of the originator or owner;
4. Avoid manipulation to take advantage of situations to maximize personal welfare in a way that unfairly deprives or damages the organization or others.

Any AMA member found to be in violation of any provision of this Code of Ethics may have his or her Association membership suspended or revoked.

Exhibit 2-5
The Marketing Management Process

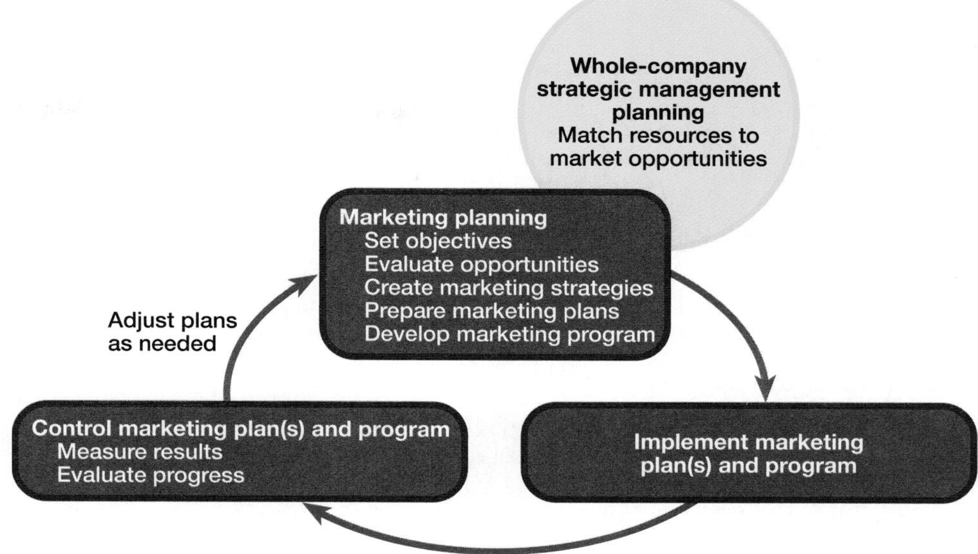

The **marketing management process** is the process of (1) *planning* marketing activities, (2) directing the *implementation* of the plans, and (3) *controlling* these plans. Planning, implementation, and control are basic jobs of all managers—but here we will emphasize what they mean to marketing managers.

As Exhibit 2-5 shows, the marketing management process is continuous. In the planning job, managers set guidelines for the implementing job—and specify expected results. They use these expected results in the control job—to determine if everything has worked out as planned. The link from the control job to the planning job is especially important. This feedback often leads to changes in the plans—or to new plans.

Marketing managers should seek new opportunities

Marketing managers cannot be satisfied just planning present activities. Markets are dynamic. Consumers' needs, competitors, and the environment keep changing. Consider Parker Brothers, a company that seemed to have a "Monopoly" in family games. While it continued selling board games, firms like Sega and Nintendo zoomed in with video game competition. Of course, not every opportunity is good for every company. Really attractive opportunities are those that fit with what the whole company wants to do and is able to do well.

Strategic management planning concerns the whole firm

The job of planning strategies to guide a whole company is called **strategic (management) planning**—the managerial process of developing and maintaining a match between an organization's resources and its market opportunities. This is a top-management job. It includes planning not only for marketing but also for production, finance, human resources, and other areas.

On the other hand, company plans should be market-oriented. And the marketing plan often sets the tone and direction for the whole company. So we will use *strategy planning* and *marketing strategy planning* to mean the same thing.[10]

What Is Marketing Strategy Planning?

Marketing strategy planning means finding attractive opportunities and developing profitable marketing strategies. But what is a "marketing strategy"? We have used these words rather casually so far. Now let's see what they really mean.

What is a marketing strategy?

Exhibit 2-6
A Marketing Strategy

A **marketing strategy** specifies a target market and a related marketing mix. It is a big picture of what a firm will do in some market. Two interrelated parts are needed:

1. A **target market**—a fairly homogeneous (similar) group of customers to whom a company wishes to appeal.
2. A **marketing mix**—the controllable variables the company puts together to satisfy this target group.

The importance of target customers in this process can be seen in Exhibit 2-6, where the customer—the "C"—is at the center of the diagram. The customer is surrounded by the controllable variables that we call the "marketing mix." A typical marketing mix includes some product, offered at a price, with some promotion to tell potential customers about the product, and a way to reach the customer's place.

The Learning Company's marketing strategy for its software aims at a specific group of target customers: young parents who have a computer at home and want their kids to learn while playing. The strategy calls for a variety of educational software products—like *Reader Rabbit* and *Where in the World Is Carmen Sandiego?* The firm's software is designed with entertaining graphics and sound, and it's tested on kids to be certain that it is easy to use. To make it convenient for target customers to buy the software, it can be ordered from the firm's own website (www.learningco.com) or from other retailers like Babbages. Promotion has helped build customer interest in the software. For example, when marketing managers released *Where in Time Is Carmen Sandiego?* they not only placed ads in family-oriented computer magazines but also sent direct-mail flyers to registered customers of the firm's other products. Some firms sell less-expensive games for kids, but parents are loyal to The Learning Co. because it caters to their needs and offers first-class customer service—including a 90-day, no-questions-asked guarantee that assures the buyer of good customer value.[11]

Selecting a Market-Oriented Strategy Is Target Marketing

Target marketing is not mass marketing

Note that a marketing strategy specifies some *particular* target customers. This approach is called "target marketing" to distinguish it from "mass marketing." **Target marketing** says that a marketing mix is tailored to fit some specific target customers. In contrast, **mass marketing**—the typical production-oriented approach—vaguely aims at "everyone" with the same marketing mix. Mass marketing assumes that everyone is the same—and it considers everyone to be a potential customer. See Exhibit 2-7.

Mass marketers may do target marketing

Commonly used terms can be confusing here. The terms *mass marketing* and *mass marketers* do not mean the same thing. Far from it! *Mass marketing* means trying to sell to "everyone," as we explained above. *Mass marketers* like Kraft Foods and Wal-Mart are aiming at clearly defined target markets. The confusion with mass marketing occurs because their target markets usually are large and spread out.

Target marketing can mean big markets and profits

Target marketing is not limited to small market segments—only to fairly homogeneous ones. A very large market—even what is sometimes called the "mass market"—may be fairly homogeneous, and a target marketer will deliberately aim at it. For example, a very large group of parents of young children are homogeneous on many dimensions—including their attitudes about changing baby diapers. In the United States alone, this group spends about $3.5 billion a year on disposable diapers—so it should be no surprise that it is a major target market for companies like Kimberly-Clark (Huggies) and Procter & Gamble (Pampers).

The basic reason to focus on some specific target customers is to gain a competitive advantage—by developing a more satisfying marketing mix that should also

Exhibit 2-7
Production-Oriented and Marketing-Oriented Managers Have Different Views of the Market

be more profitable for the firm. For example, Tianguis, a small grocery chain in Southern California, attracts Hispanic customers with special product lines and Spanish-speaking employees. E*trade uses an Internet site (www.etrade.com) to target knowledgeable investors who want a convenient, low-cost way to buy and sell stocks online without a lot of advice (or pressure) from a salesperson.

Developing Marketing Mixes for Target Markets

There are many marketing mix decisions

There are many possible ways to satisfy the needs of target customers. A product might have many different features. Customer service levels before or after the sale can be adjusted. The package, brand name, and warranty can be changed. Various advertising media—newspapers, magazines, cable, the Internet—may be used. A company's own sales force or other sales specialists can be used. The price can be changed, discounts can be given, and so on. With so many possible variables, is there any way to help organize all these decisions and simplify the selection of marketing mixes? The answer is yes.

The four "Ps" make up a marketing mix

It is useful to reduce all the variables in the marketing mix to four basic ones:

Product.
Place.
Promotion.
Price.

Exhibit 2-8
A Marketing Strategy—Showing the Four Ps of a Marketing Mix

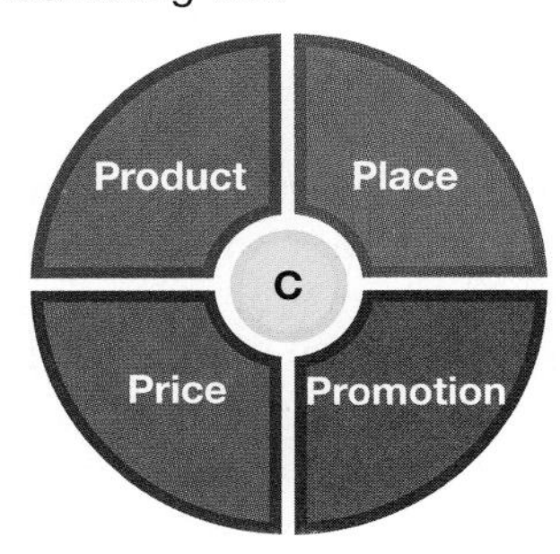

It helps to think of the four major parts of a marketing mix as the "four Ps." Exhibit 2-8 emphasizes their relationship and their common focus on the customer—"C."

Customer is not part of the marketing mix

The customer is shown surrounded by the four Ps in Exhibit 2-8. Some students assume that the customer is part of the marketing mix—but this is not so. The customer should be the *target* of all marketing efforts. The customer is placed in the center of the diagram to show this. The C stands for some specific customers—the target market.

Exhibit 2-9
Strategy Decision Areas Organized by the Four Ps

Product
Physical good
Service
Features
Benefits
Quality level
Accessories
Installation
Instructions
Warranty
Product lines
Packaging
Branding

Promotion
Objectives
Promotion blend
Salespeople
Kind
Number
Selection
Training
Motivation
Advertising
Targets
Kinds of ads
Media type
Copy thrust
Prepared by whom
Sales promotion
Publicity

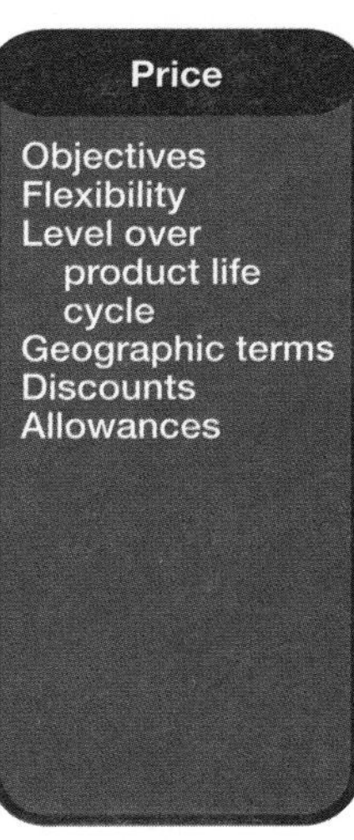

Exhibit 2-9 shows some of the strategy decision variables organized by the four Ps. These will be discussed in later chapters. For now, let's just describe each P briefly.

Product—the good or service for the target's needs

The Product area is concerned with developing the right "product" for the target market. This offering may involve a physical good, a service, or a blend of both. Keep in mind that Product is not limited to "physical goods." For example, the Product of H & R Block is a completed tax form. The Product of a political party is the set of causes it will work to achieve. The important thing to remember is that your good and/or service should satisfy some customers' needs.

Along with other Product-area decisions like branding, packaging, and warranties, we will talk about developing and managing new products and whole product lines.

Place—reaching the target

Place is concerned with all the decisions involved in getting the "right" product to the target market's Place. A product isn't much good to a customer if it isn't available when and where it's wanted.

A product reaches customers through a channel of distribution. A **channel of distribution** is any series of firms (or individuals) who participate in the flow of products from producer to final user or consumer.

Sometimes a channel system is quite short. It may run directly from a producer to a final user or consumer. This is especially common in business markets and in the marketing of services. The channel is direct when a producer uses an online website to handle orders by target customers, whether the customer is a final consumer or an organization. So, direct channels have become much more common since the development of the Internet.

On the other hand, often the channel system is much more complex—involving many different retailers and wholesalers. When a marketing manager has several different target markets, several different channels of distribution may be needed.

We will also see how physical distribution service levels and decisions concerning logistics (transporting, storing, and handling products) relate to the other Place decisions and the rest of the marketing mix.

Promotion—telling and selling the customer

The third P—Promotion—is concerned with telling the target market or others in the channel of distribution about the "right" product. Sometimes promotion is focused on acquiring new customers, and sometimes it's focused on retaining current customers. Promotion includes personal selling, mass selling, and sales promotion. It is the marketing manager's job to blend these methods of communication.

Personal selling involves direct spoken communication between sellers and potential customers. Personal selling usually happens face-to-face, but sometimes the

A firm's product may involve a physical good, a service, or a combination of both.

communication occurs over the telephone. Personal selling lets the salesperson adapt the firm's marketing mix to each potential customer. But this individual attention comes at a price; personal selling can be very expensive. Often this personal effort has to be blended with mass selling and sales promotion.

Mass selling is communicating with large numbers of customers at the same time. The main form of mass selling is **advertising**—any *paid* form of nonpersonal presentation of ideas, goods, or services by an identified sponsor. **Publicity**—any *unpaid* form of nonpersonal presentation of ideas, goods, or services—is another important form of mass selling. Mass selling may involve a wide variety of media, ranging from newspapers and billboards to the Internet.

Sales promotion refers to those promotion activities—other than advertising, publicity, and personal selling—that stimulate interest, trial, or purchase by final customers or others in the channel. This can involve use of coupons, point-of-purchase materials, samples, signs, catalogs, novelties, and circulars.

Price—making it right

In addition to developing the right Product, Place, and Promotion, marketing managers must also decide the right Price. Price setting must consider the kind of competition in the target market and the cost of the whole marketing mix. A manager must also try to estimate customer reaction to possible prices. Besides this, the manager must know current practices as to markups, discounts, and other terms of sale.

Each of the four Ps contributes to the whole

All four Ps are needed in a marketing mix. In fact, they should all be tied together. But is any one more important than the others? Generally speaking, the answer is no—all contribute to one whole. When a marketing mix is being developed, all (final) decisions about the Ps should be made at the same time.

Strategy jobs must be done together

It is important to stress—it cannot be overemphasized—that selecting a target market *and* developing a marketing mix are interrelated. The needs of a target market often virtually determine the nature of an appropriate marketing mix. Both parts of a marketing strategy must be decided together. It is *strategies* that must be evaluated against the company's objectives—not alternative target markets or alternative marketing mixes.

Lifetime Value of Customers Can Be Very High—or Very Low

Investors lost millions when stock market values of dot-com firms collapsed after an initial, frenzied run up. But why did values get so high in the first place, especially when most dot-coms were not yet profitable? The stock went up because many investors expected that the firms would earn profits in the future as more consumers went online and the early dot-coms accumulated customers. These hopes were fueled by dot-coms that made optimistic predictions about the lifetime value of the customers they were acquiring. The lifetime value of the customer concept is not new. For decades General Motors has known that a consumer who buys a GM car and is satisfied is likely to buy another one the next time. If that happens again and again, over a lifetime the happy customer would spend $250,000 on GM cars. Of course, this only works if the firm's marketing mix attracts the target customers and the relationship keeps them satisfied before, during, and after every purchase. If you don't satisfy and retain customers, they don't have high lifetime value and don't generate sales. Of course, sales revenue alone does not guarantee profits. For example, a firm can't give away so many products—or spend so much on promotion to acquire new customers (or keep the ones it has)—that the revenue will never be able to offset the costs. Unfortunately, that is what happened with many of the dot-coms. They saw how the financial arithmetic might work—*assuming* that new customers kept buying and costs came under control. But without a sensible marketing strategy, that assumption was not realistic.[12]

The Marketing Plan Is a Guide to Implementation and Control

Marketing plan fills out marketing strategy

A marketing strategy sets a target market and a marketing mix. It is a big picture of what a firm will do in some market. A marketing plan goes farther. A **marketing plan** is a written statement of a marketing strategy *and* the time-related details for carrying out the strategy. It should spell out the following in detail: (1) what marketing mix will be offered, to whom (that is, the target market), and for how long; (2) what company resources (shown as costs) will be needed at what rate (month by month perhaps); and (3) what results are expected (sales and profits perhaps monthly or quarterly, customer satisfaction levels, and the like). The plan should also include some control procedures—so that whoever is to carry out the plan will know if things are going wrong. This might be something as simple as comparing actual sales against expected sales—with a warning flag to be raised whenever total sales fall below a certain level.

Implementation puts plans into operation

After a marketing plan is developed, a marketing manager knows *what* needs to be done. Then the manager is concerned with **implementation**—putting marketing plans into operation. Strategies work out as planned only when they are effectively implemented. Many short-run decisions to help implement strategies may be needed.

Control is analyzing and correcting what you've done

The control job provides the feedback that leads managers to modify their marketing strategies. To maintain control, a marketing manager uses a number of tools—like computer sales analysis, marketing research surveys, and accounting analysis of expenses and profits.

Our focus in this text is on developing marketing strategies. But, eventually marketing managers must develop, implement, and control marketing plans. Thus, as we talk about each of the marketing decision areas, we will discuss some of the issues of implementation and control. This will help you understand how implementation and control keep the firm on course—or show the need to plan a new course.[13]

Several plans make a whole marketing program

Most companies implement more than one marketing strategy—and related marketing plan—at the same time. They may have several products—some of them quite different—that are aimed at different target markets. The other elements of the marketing mix may vary too. Gillette's Right Guard deodorant, its Mach3 razor

Exhibit 2-10
Elements of a Firm's Marketing Program

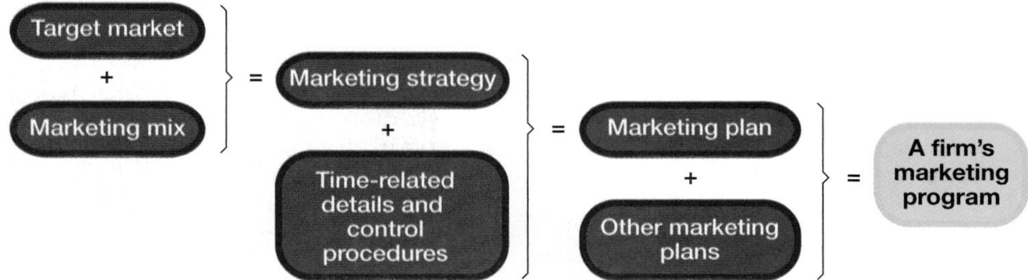

blades, and its Duracell Ultra batteries all have different marketing mixes. Yet the strategies for each must be implemented at the same time.[14]

A **marketing program** blends all of the firm's marketing plans into one "big" plan. See Exhibit 2-10. This program, then, is the responsibility of the whole company. Typically, the whole *marketing program* is an integrated part of the whole-company strategic plan we discussed earlier.

We will emphasize planning one marketing strategy at a time, rather than planning—or implementing—a whole marketing program. This is practical because it is important to plan each strategy carefully. Too many marketing managers fall into sloppy thinking. They try to develop too many strategies all at once—and don't develop any very carefully. However, when new strategies are evaluated, it makes sense to see how well they fit with the existing marketing program.

The Importance of Marketing Strategy Planning

We emphasize the planning part of the marketing manager's job for a good reason. The "one-time" strategy decisions—the decisions that decide what business the company is in and the strategies it will follow—usually determine success, or failure. An extremely good plan might be carried out badly and still be profitable, while a poor but well-implemented plan can lose money. The case history that follows shows why these decisions are so important.

Time for new strategies in the watch industry

The conventional watchmakers—both domestic and foreign—had always aimed at customers who thought of watches as high-priced, high-quality symbols to mark special events—like graduations or retirement. Advertising was concentrated around Christmas and graduation time and stressed a watch's symbolic appeal. Expensive jewelry stores were the main retail outlets.

This commonly accepted strategy of the major watch companies ignored people in the target market that just wanted to tell the time and were interested in a reliable, low-priced watch. So the U.S. Time Company developed a successful strategy around its Timex watches and became the world's largest watch company. Timex completely upset the watch industry not only by offering a good product (with a one-year repair or replace guarantee) at a lower price, but also by using new, lower-cost channels of distribution. Its watches were widely available in drugstores, discount houses, and nearly any other retail stores that would carry them.

Marketing managers at Timex soon faced a new challenge. Texas Instruments took competitors by surprise with its low-cost but very accurate electronic watches—using the same channels Timex had originally developed. But other firms quickly developed a watch that used a more stylish liquid crystal display for the digital readout. Texas Instruments could not change quickly enough to keep up, and the other companies took away its customers. The competition became so intense that Texas Instruments stopped marketing watches altogether.

To better meet the needs of a specific target market, Timex has developed a line of Rush sportwatches for women. It is also developing other watches to meet specific needs, such as its iControl watches that are very easy to program.

While Timex and others were focusing on lower-priced watches, Japan's Seiko captured a commanding share of the high-priced gift market for its stylish and accurate quartz watches by obtaining strong distribution. All of this forced many traditional watchmakers—like some of the once-famous Swiss brands—to close their factories.

Then Switzerland's Swatch launched its colorful, affordable plastic watches and changed what consumers see when they look at their watches. Swatch promoted its watches as fashion accessories and set them apart from those of other firms, whose ads squabbled about whose watches were most accurate. Swatch was also able to attract new retailers by focusing its distribution on upscale fashion and department stores. The total size of the watch market increased because many consumers bought several watches to match different fashions.

The economic downturn in the early 1990s brought more changes. Consumers were more cost conscious and less interested in expensive watches like those made by Rolex that were the "in" status symbol a few years earlier. The reemergence of value-seeking customers prompted Timex to return to its famous advertising tagline of the 1960s: "It takes a licking and keeps on ticking." Its position as the inexpensive-but-durable choice has helped it strengthen its distribution and has given it a leg up in getting shelf space for new products, such as its Indiglo line of watches.

By the turn of the century, the total market for watches was growing at only about 5 percent a year. To spark higher sales of its lines, Timex pushed to introduce more watches that combine time-telling and other needs. For example, its women's fitness watch includes a pulse timer and on-screen displays; and its Internet Messenger Watch, for about $100 and a monthly service charge, can receive short text messages, like an alert from the wearer's stock broker that it's time to sell. Of course, all the new features can make a watch more complicated to use, so Timex is refocusing on the need for simple convenience with its iControl technology, which it promotes with trendy ads and the tagline "Ridiculously easy to use." Competitors are on the move as well. For example, Casio has a watch with a global positioning system and Swatch is considering a watch with a smart chip that will also make it a debit card. With such changes always underway, marketing strategies must constantly be updated and revised.[15]

Internet

Internet Exercise Go to the Timex website (www.timex.com) and use the drop-down list or site map to go to the "Latest Products" section. Based on the needs that a product is designed to meet, can you identify the characteristics of the product's target market?

Creative Strategy Planning Needed for Survival

Dramatic shifts in strategy—like those described above—may surprise conventional, production-oriented managers. But such changes should be expected. Managers who embrace the marketing concept realize that they cannot just define their line of business in terms of the products they currently produce or sell. Rather, they have to think about the basic consumer needs they serve, how those needs may change in the future, and how they can improve the value they offer to customers. If they are too nearsighted, they may fail to see what's coming until too late.

Focus on "best practices" for improved results

The case studies and concepts in this chapter highlight effective marketing thinking. Throughout the text, we will continue with this thrust—focusing on marketing frameworks and concepts that produce good results. Some of these are new and innovative, and others are well established. What they have in common is that they all work well.

Sometimes we will warn you about marketing errors—so you can avoid them. But, we won't just give you laundry lists of different approaches and then leave it to you to guess what might work. Rather, our focus will be on "best-practices" marketing.

There is an important reason for this approach. In too many firms, managers do a poor job planning and implementing marketing strategies and programs. And, as shown in Exhibit 2-11, this type of "death-wish" marketing is both costly and

Exhibit 2-11 Distribution of Different Firms Based on Their Marketing Performance

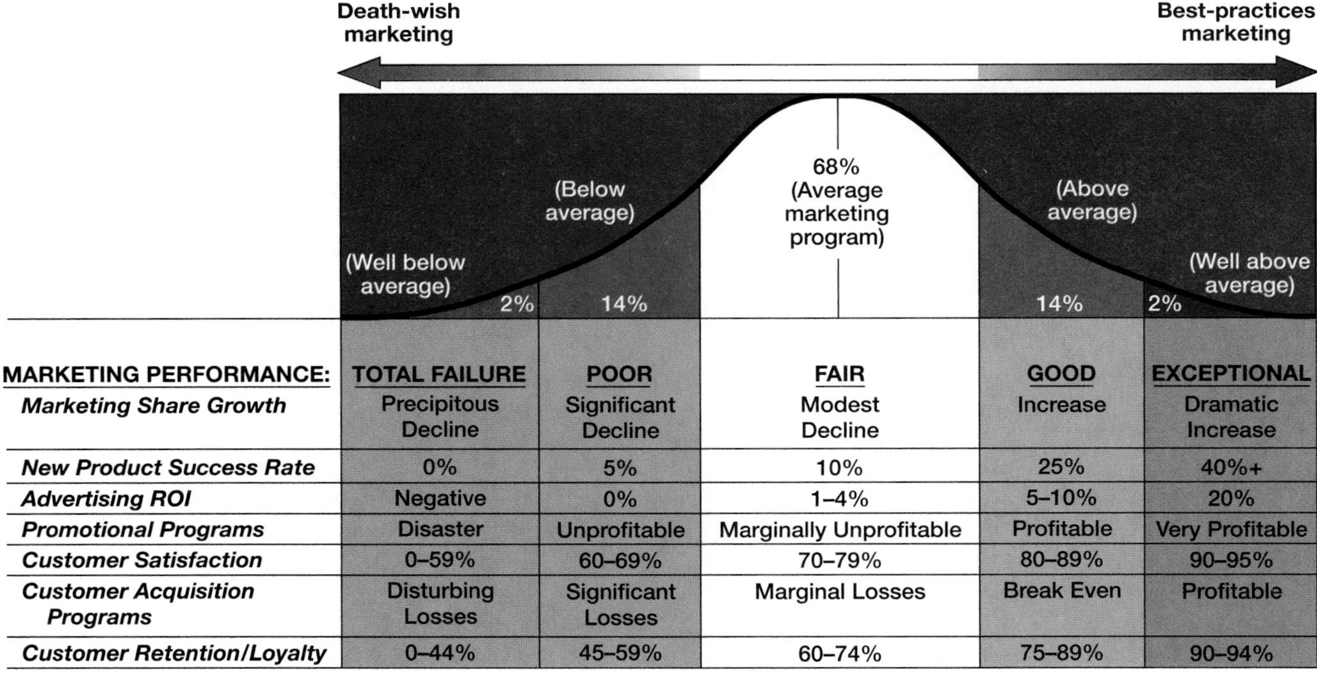

MARKETING PERFORMANCE:	TOTAL FAILURE	POOR	FAIR	GOOD	EXCEPTIONAL
Marketing Share Growth	Precipitous Decline	Significant Decline	Modest Decline	Increase	Dramatic Increase
New Product Success Rate	0%	5%	10%	25%	40%+
Advertising ROI	Negative	0%	1–4%	5–10%	20%
Promotional Programs	Disaster	Unprofitable	Marginally Unprofitable	Profitable	Very Profitable
Customer Satisfaction	0–59%	60–69%	70–79%	80–89%	90–95%
Customer Acquisition Programs	Disturbing Losses	Significant Losses	Marginal Losses	Break Even	Profitable
Customer Retention/Loyalty	0–44%	45–59%	60–74%	75–89%	90–94%

ineffective. In fact, you can see that even the average marketing program isn't producing great results—and that accounts for the majority of firms!

Exhibit 2-11 was developed by experts at Copernicus, one of the premier marketing consulting firms in the world. As these experts indicate in the chart, some managers are creating marketing programs that produce exceptional results for their companies. This book will help you do exactly that.

Conclusion

Marketing's role within a marketing-oriented firm is to provide direction for the firm. The marketing concept stresses that the company's efforts should focus on satisfying some target customers—at a profit. Production-oriented firms tend to forget this. The various departments within a production-oriented firm let their natural conflicts of interest get in the way of providing superior customer value.

The job of marketing management is one of continuous planning, implementing, and control. The marketing manager must constantly study the environment—seeking attractive opportunities and planning new strategies. Possible target markets must be matched with marketing mixes the firm can offer. Then, attractive strategies—really, whole marketing plans—are chosen for implementation. Controls are needed to be sure that the plans are carried out successfully. If anything goes wrong along the way, continual feedback should cause the process to be started over again—with the marketing manager planning more attractive marketing strategies.

A marketing mix has four major decision areas: the four Ps—Product, Place, Promotion, and Price. Most of this text is concerned with developing profitable marketing mixes for clearly defined target markets. So after several chapters on the marketing strategy planning process and several on analyzing target markets, we will discuss each of the four Ps in greater detail.

While market-oriented strategy planning is helpful to marketers, it is also needed by accountants, production and personnel people, and all other specialists. A market-oriented plan lets everybody in the firm know what ballpark they are playing in and what they are trying to accomplish.

We will use the term *marketing manager* for editorial convenience, but really, when we talk about marketing strategy planning, we are talking about the planning that a market-oriented manager should do when developing a firm's strategic plans. This kind of thinking should be done—or at least understood—by everyone in the organization.

Questions and Problems

1. Define the marketing concept in your own words and then explain why the notion of profit is usually included in this definition.
2. Define the marketing concept in your own words and then suggest how acceptance of this concept might affect the organization and operation of your college.
3. Give examples of some of the benefits and costs that might contribute to the customer value of each of the following products: (*a*) a wrist watch, (*b*) a weight-loss diet supplement, (*c*) a cruise on a luxury liner, and (*d*) a checking account from a bank.
4. Distinguish between production orientation and marketing orientation, illustrating with local examples.
5. Explain why a firm should view its internal activities as part of a total system. Illustrate your answer for (*a*) a large grocery products producer, (*b*) a plumbing wholesaler, and (*c*) a department store chain.
6. Give an example of a recent purchase you made where the purchase wasn't just a single transaction but rather part of an ongoing relationship with the seller. Discuss what the seller has done (or could do better) to strengthen the relationship and increase the odds of you being a loyal customer in the future.
7. Distinguish clearly between a marketing strategy and a marketing mix. Use an example.
8. Distinguish clearly between mass marketing and target marketing. Use an example.
9. Why is the customer placed in the center of the four Ps in the text diagram of a marketing strategy (Exhibit 2-8)? Explain, using a specific example from your own experience.

10. If a company sells its products only from a website, which is accessible over the Internet to customers from all over the world, does it still need to worry about having a specific target market? Explain your thinking.
11. Explain, in your own words, what each of the four Ps involves.
12. Distinguish between a strategy, a marketing plan, and a marketing program, illustrating for a local retailer.
13. Outline a marketing strategy for each of the following new products: (*a*) a radically new design for a toothbrush, (*b*) a new fishing reel, (*c*) a new wonder drug, and (*d*) a new industrial stapling machine.
14. Provide a specific illustration of why marketing strategy planning is important for all businesspeople, not just for those in the marketing department.

Suggested Cases

2. Healthy Foods, Inc.
5. Republic Polymer Company
16. Enviro Pure Water, Inc.
25. Metal Works, Inc.

Computer-Aided Problem

2. **Target Marketing**

Marko, Inc.'s managers are comparing the profitability of a target marketing strategy with a mass marketing "strategy." The spreadsheet gives information about both approaches.

The mass marketing strategy is aiming at a much bigger market. But a smaller percent of the consumers in the market will actually buy this product—because not everyone needs or can afford it. Moreover, because this marketing mix is not tailored to specific needs, Marko will get a smaller share of the business from those who do buy than it would with a more targeted marketing mix.

Just trying to reach the mass market will take more promotion and require more retail outlets in more locations—so promotion costs and distribution costs are higher than with the target marketing strategy. On the other hand, the cost of producing each unit is higher with the target marketing strategy—to build in a more satisfying set of features. But, because the more targeted marketing mix is trying to satisfy the needs of a specific target market, those customers will be willing to pay a higher price.

In the spreadsheet, "quantity sold" (by the firm) is equal to the number of people in the market who will actually buy one each of the product—multiplied by the share of those purchases won by the firm's marketing mix. Thus, a change in the size of the market, the percent of people who purchase, or the share captured by the firm will affect quantity sold. And a change in quantity sold will affect total revenue, total cost, and profit.

a. *On a piece of paper, show the calculations that prove that the spreadsheet "total profit" value for the target marketing strategy is correct. (Hint: Remember to multiply unit production cost and unit distribution cost by the quantity sold.) Which approach seems better—target marketing or mass marketing? Why?*
b. *If the target marketer could find a way to reduce distribution cost per unit by $.25, how much would profit increase?*
c. *If Marko, Inc., decided to use the target marketing strategy and better marketing mix decisions increased its share of purchases from 50 to 60 percent—without increasing costs—what would happen to total profit? What does this analysis suggest about the importance of marketing managers knowing enough about their target markets to be effective target marketers?*

For additional questions related to this problem, see Exercise 2-4 in the *Learning Aid for Use with Essentials of Marketing*, 9th edition.

When You Finish This Chapter, You Should

1. Understand why marketing strategy planning involves a process of narrowing down from broad opportunities to a specific target market and marketing mix.

2. Know about the different kinds of marketing opportunities.

3. Understand why opportunities in international markets should be considered.

4. Know about defining generic markets and product-markets.

5. Know what market segmentation is and how to segment product-markets into submarkets.

6. Know three approaches to market-oriented strategy planning.

7. Know dimensions that may be useful for segmenting markets.

8. Know what positioning is and why it is useful.

9. Understand the important new terms (shown in red).

Chapter Three

Focusing Marketing Strategy with Segmentation and Positioning

Polaroid desperately needed a profitable new opportunity. The firm had been losing money, so the objective of the new top executive was to quickly make Polaroid profitable again. That was a needed first step for Polaroid to be able to compete longer term.

Polaroid got its start with a breakthrough invention. Its instant picture cameras and films were unique and met the needs of different groups of customers. Realtors needed photos of just-listed homes for clients, colleges had to make IDs, and insurance adjusters had to document auto accidents. Over time, however, Polaroid faced competition from other types of goods and services. One-hour photo labs popped up everywhere. Then digital cameras made it even rougher. A hundred firms now offer all types of digital cameras. Digital pictures can be shared

place price promotion produc

by e-mail or a website—without costly film or printing. Increased competition wasn't the only problem. A bad economy eroded Polaroid's revenues in China and India.

Polaroid's new-product development manager helped overcome these weaknesses. He saw teens having fun at an instant photo booth in a Japanese airport and had an idea for an inexpensive new pocket-size camera that would appeal to teens with its instant, stamp-size photos. Some Polaroid engineers objected that the poor quality of the photos would hurt Polaroid's position as a technology leader. But marketers at Polaroid pressed on because the product would help attract a new generation of teen customers. Many teens viewed Polaroid cameras as clunky holdovers from the past. Besides, picture quality wasn't the benefit that determined their interest. They just wanted fun and quick pictures rather than a serious camera.

Polaroid's pocket camera proved to be right on target with the teen segment. It quickly became a best seller and new-product revenue was the highest it had been in a decade.

Targeted promotion helped to attract buyers, half of whom were girls age 13 to 17. Ads for Polaroid's I-Zone Pocket camera and film were placed in magazines like *Seventeen,* at clickclick.com and other websites popular with teens, and on TV shows like *Buffy the Vampire Slayer*. While ad media were slanted toward teen girls, the ad messages were broader so that they would appeal to a combined male and female teen market. To increase the opportunities for I-Zone Pocket camera fun, Polaroid came out with a special "sticky" film. The sticker-pictures could be attached to lockers, notebooks, and just about anything else. One funny ad featured a young man sticking instant pictures of his girlfriend to his bare chest. Reaching this younger target market also called for new distribution channels, including online toy and music stores and more emphasis on mass-merchandisers like Wal-Mart. Trade ads targeted at these retailers helped bring in the orders and make the film more widely available.

place price promotion product

Of course, Kodak didn't take this sitting down. Soon it was targeting teens with its one-use Max cameras. Marketers at Polaroid know that its teen target market can be fickle and that the I-Zone could become yesterday's fad. So it is introducing other new products for teens to strengthen its fun positioning. One is a camera that takes both digital and pocket pictures. Another is the Webster, a miniature scanner to turn I-Zone pictures into digital images. Teens can post pictures from either product at a special Polaroid website (www.i-zone.com).

Polaroid's new strategies and teen target market have boosted profits. But Polaroid's traditional customer segments—with a variety of other instant picture needs—still account for the bulk of its business. So if Polaroid is going to have a clear profit picture long term, it needs to find new ways to offer these segments superior customer value as they shift toward digital images.[1]

What Are Attractive Opportunities?

Breakthrough opportunities are best

As the Polaroid case suggests, attractive opportunities for a particular firm are those that match the firm's resources (what it can do) and objectives (what it wants to do).

Throughout this book, we will emphasize finding **breakthrough opportunities**—opportunities that help innovators develop hard-to-copy marketing strategies that will be very profitable for a long time. That's important because it's hard to continuously provide superior value to target customers if competitors can easily copy your marketing mix.

Competitive advantage is needed—at least

Even if a manager can't find a breakthrough opportunity, the firm should try to obtain a competitive advantage to increase its chances for profit or survival. **Competitive advantage** means that a firm has a marketing mix that the target market sees as better than a competitor's mix. Every firm needs some competitive advantage—

Attractive new opportunities are often fairly close to markets the firm already knows.

so the promotion people have something unique to sell and success doesn't just hinge on offering lower and lower prices. A competitive advantage may result from efforts in different areas of the firm—cost cutting in production, innovative R&D, financing for a new facility, or a well-known brand name. Whatever the source, an advantage only succeeds if it allows the firm to provide superior customer value.[2]

Marketing Strategy Planning Process Highlights Opportunities

From Chapter 2, you know that a marketing strategy requires decisions about the specific customers the firm will target and the marketing mix the firm will develop to appeal to that target market. However, the idea isn't just to come up with *some* strategy. After all, there are thousands of strategies that a firm might try. Rather, the challenge is to zero in on the best strategy.

Process narrows down from broad opportunities to specific strategy

As Exhibit 3-1 suggests, it is useful to think of the marketing strategy planning process as a narrowing-down process. Later in this chapter and Chapter 4 we will go into more detail about the terms in this figure. Then, throughout the rest of the book, we will present a variety of concepts and "how to" frameworks that will help you improve the way you make these strategy decisions. As a preview, let's briefly overview Exhibit 3-1.

The marketing strategy planning process starts with a broad look at a market—paying special attention to customer needs, the firm's objectives and resources, and competitors. This helps to identify new and unique opportunities that might be overlooked if the focus is narrowed too quickly.

Segmentation helps pinpoint the target

In the early stages of a search for opportunities we're looking for customers with needs that are not being satisfied as well as they might be. Of course, potential customers don't all have the same needs—nor do they always want to meet needs in the same way. Potential customers may also differ on attitudes, preferences for how to spend time, what shows to watch, and the like. In spite of the many possible differences, there often are subgroups (segments) of consumers who are similar

Exhibit 3-1
Overview of Marketing Strategy Planning Process

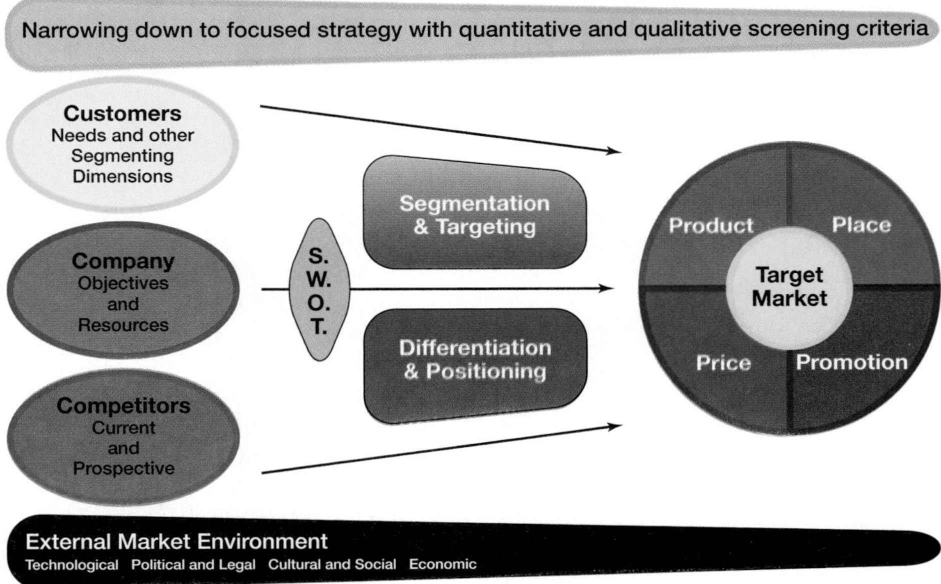

This Norwegian ad for the Audi Quattro simply says, "Sticks like quattro." Although it doesn't show the car at all, it helps to differentiate the Audi and its four-wheel drive system that holds the road especially well, even in the snow.

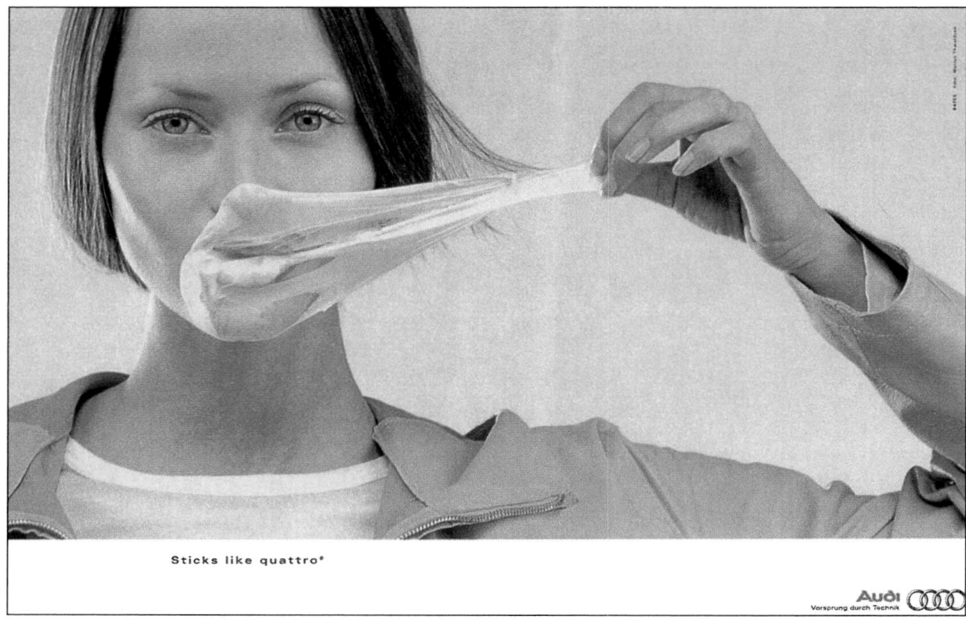

and could be satisfied with the same marketing mix. Thus, we try to identify and understand these different subgroups—with market segmentation. We will explain segmenting markets later in this chapter. Then, in Chapters 5 and 6, we delve deeper into customer behavior. For now, however, you should know that really understanding customers is at the heart of using market segmentation to narrow down to a specific target market to satisfy.

Narrow down to a superior marketing mix

A marketing mix won't get a competitive advantage if it *just* meets needs in the same way as some other firm. So, in evaluating possible strategies the marketing manager should look for ways to differentiate the marketing mix. **Differentiation** means that the marketing mix is distinct from and better than what is available from a competitor. Sometimes the difference is based mainly on one important element of the marketing mix—say, an improved product or faster delivery. Differentiation is more obvious to target customers, though, when all of the elements of its marketing mix are fine-tuned to the specific needs of a distinctive target market. Then target customers think of the firm as being in a unique position to meet their needs.

For example, in Norway, many auto buyers are particularly concerned about safety in the snow. So, Audi offers a four-wheel drive system, called quattro, that helps the car to hold the road. Audi ads emphasize this differentiation. Rather than show the car, however, the ads feature things that are very sticky (like bubblegum!) and the only text is the headline "sticks like quattro" and the Audi brand name. Of course, handling is not Audi's only strength, but it is an important one in helping to position Audi as better than competing brands with this target market.[3]

In this chapter, we'll introduce concepts relevant to this sort of positioning. Then, in Chapters 8 to 17, we'll cover the many ways in which the four Ps of the marketing mix can be differentiated. For now, you can see that the thrust is to narrow down from all possible marketing mixes to one that is differentiated to meet target customers' needs particularly well.

Screening criteria make it clear why you select a strategy

There are usually more different opportunities—and strategy possibilities—than a firm can pursue. Each one has its own strengths and weaknesses. Trends in the external market environment may make a potential opportunity more or less attractive. These complications can make it difficult to zero in on the best target market and marketing mix. However, developing a set of specific screening criteria can help a manager eliminate potential strategies that are not well suited for the firm.

S.W.O.T. analysis highlights advantages and disadvantages

A useful aid for identifying relevant screening criteria and for zeroing in on a feasible strategy is **S.W.O.T. analysis**—which identifies and lists the firm's strengths and weaknesses and its opportunities and threats. The name S.W.O.T. is simply an abbreviation for the first letters of the words *s*trengths, *w*eaknesses, *o*pportunities, and *t*hreats. A good S.W.O.T. analysis helps the manager focus on a strategy that takes advantage of the firm's opportunities and strengths while avoiding its weaknesses and threats.

The marketing strategy developed by Amilya Antonetti illustrates the basic ideas behind a S.W.O.T. analysis. Her son was allergic to the chemicals in standard laundry detergents. Her research showed that many other children had the same problem. So she started SoapWorks and developed a line of hypoallergenic cleaning products. Unlike the big firms, she didn't have relations with grocery chains or money for national TV ads. To get around these weaknesses, she used inexpensive radio ads in local markets and touted SoapWorks as a company created for moms by a mom who cared about kids. She had a credible claim that the big corporations couldn't make. Her ads also helped her get shelf space because they urged other mothers to ask for SoapWorks products and to tell friends about stores that carried them. This wasn't the fastest possible way to introduce a new product line, but her cash-strapped strategy played to her unique strengths with her specific target market.[4]

Exhibit 3-1 focuses on planning each strategy carefully. Of course, this same approach works well when several strategies are to be planned. Then, having an organized evaluation process is even more important. It forces everyone involved to think through how the various strategies fit together as part of an overall marketing program.[5]

Types of Opportunities to Pursue

Some alert marketers spot attractive opportunities everywhere they look. This seems reasonable when you recognize that most people have unsatisfied needs. Unfortunately, many opportunities seem "obvious" only after someone else identifies them. So, early in the marketing strategy planning process it's useful for marketers to have a framework for thinking about the broad kinds of opportunities they may find. Exhibit 3-2 shows four broad possibilities: market penetration, market development, product development, and diversification.

Market penetration

Market penetration means trying to increase sales of a firm's present products in its present markets—probably through a more aggressive marketing mix. The firm may try to strengthen its relationship with customers to increase their rate of use or repeat purchases, or try to attract competitors' customers or current nonusers. For example, Coleman got a 50 percent increase in sales of its outdoor equipment, like camping lanterns and stoves, by reaching its target market with special promotional displays at outdoor events like concerts, fishing tournaments, and campsites for Nascar races.[6]

New promotion appeals alone may not be effective. A firm may need to add an Internet website to make it easier for customers to place an order. Or, it may need to add more stores in present areas for greater convenience.

Exhibit 3-2
Four Basic Types of Opportunities

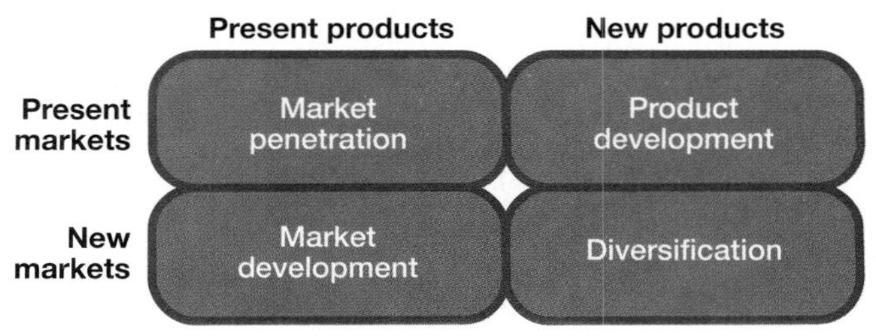

Market development

Market development means trying to increase sales by selling present products in new markets. This may involve searching for new uses for a product. E-Z-Go, a producer of golf carts, has done this. Its carts are now a quiet way for workers to get around malls, airports, big factories, and resorts. E-Z-Go even fits carts with ice compartments and cash drawers so they can be used for mobile food services.

Firms may also try advertising in different media to reach new target customers. Or they may add new stores in new areas. For example, to reach new customers, McDonald's has opened outlets in airports, zoos, casinos, and military bases. And it's rapidly expanded into international markets with outlets in places like Russia, Brazil, and China.[7]

Product development

Product development means offering new or improved products for present markets. By knowing the present market's needs, a firm may see new ways to satisfy customers. For example, Heinz figured out how ketchup could be more fun because kids are the biggest consumers. Producing ketchup in gross green and funky purple colors—in an EZ Squirt dispenser—increased sales so much that the factory had to run 24/7. Ski resorts have developed trails for hiking and biking to bring their winter ski customers back in the summer. Nike moved beyond shoes to offer its athletic target market a portable heart-rate monitor. And of course Intel boosts sales by developing newer and faster chips.[8]

Diversification

Diversification means moving into totally different lines of business—perhaps entirely unfamiliar products, markets, or even levels in the production-marketing system. McDonald's, for example, is opening two four-star hotels in Switzerland. The plan is to serve families on the weekend, but the target market during the week is business travelers.

Products and customers that are very different from a firm's current base may look attractive to the optimists—but these opportunities are usually hard to evaluate. That's why diversification usually involves the biggest risk.[9]

Internet

Internet Exercise Go to the website for McDonald's hotel and review the information given (www.goldenarchhotel.com). Based on what you see, do you think that the hotels will appeal to the weekend target market of traveling families? Do you think they will appeal to business travelers during the week?

Which opportunities come first?

Most firms think first of greater market penetration. They want to increase profits where they already have experience and strengths. Many firms just try to do a better job of hanging onto the customers that they've already won. On the other hand, many firms are proving that market development—and the move into new international markets—is another profitable way to take advantage of current strengths.

Lipton is pursuing new customers and growth in over 100 countries. For example, its multilingual website in Belgium explains how to make exotic cocktails from Ice Tea, and in Asia it encourages consumer trial with free samples.

International Opportunities Should Be Considered

It's easy for a marketing manager to fall into the trap of ignoring international markets, especially when the firm's domestic market is prosperous. Yet, there are good reasons to go to the trouble of looking elsewhere for opportunities.

The world is getting smaller

International trade is increasing all around the world, and trade barriers are coming down. In addition, advances in e-commerce, transportation, and communications are making it easier and cheaper to reach international customers. With an Internet website, e-mail, and a fax machine, even the smallest firm can provide international customers with a great deal of information—and easy ways to order—at very little expense.

Develop a competitive advantage at home and abroad

If customers in other countries are interested in the products a firm offers—or could offer—serving them may improve economies of scale. Lower costs (and prices) may give a firm a competitive advantage both in its home markets *and* abroad. Black and Decker, for example, uses electric motors in many of its tools and appliances. By selling overseas as well as in the U.S., it gets economies of scale and the cost per motor is very low.

Many marketing managers who thought they could avoid the struggles of international competition have been rudely surprised to find that an aggressive, low-cost foreign producer is willing to pursue local customers. The owner of Purafil, a small firm in Atlanta that makes air purification equipment, puts it this way: "If I'm not [selling to an oil refinery] in Saudi Arabia, somebody else is going to solve their problem, then come attack me on my home turf."[10]

Get an early start in a new market

Different countries are at different stages of development, and their consumers have different needs at different times.

A company facing tough competition, thin profit margins, and slow sales growth at home may get a fresh start in another country where demand for its product is just beginning to grow. A marketing manager may be able to transfer marketing know-how—or some other competitive advantage—the firm has already developed. Consider JLG, a U.S.-based producer of equipment used to lift workers and tools at construction sites. In the early 1990s competition was tough and JLG's profits all but evaporated. By cutting costs, the company improved its domestic sales. But it got an even bigger boost from expanding overseas. By 2000 its international sales were greater than its total sales five years before. Now that JLG has stronger distribution, international sales should soon account for half of its business.[11]

Find better trends in variables

Unfavorable trends in the marketing environment at home—or favorable trends in other countries—may make international marketing particularly attractive. For example, population growth in the United States has slowed and income is leveling off. In other places in the world, population and income are increasing rapidly.[12]

Search for Opportunities Can Begin by Understanding Markets

What is a company's market?

Identifying a company's market is an important but sticky issue. In general, a **market** is a group of potential customers with similar needs who are willing to exchange something of value with sellers offering various goods and/or services—that is, ways of satisfying those needs.

Marketing-oriented managers develop marketing mixes for *specific* target markets. Getting the firm to focus on specific target markets is vital. As shown in Exhibit 3-3, deciding on a specific target market involves a narrowing-down process—to get beyond production-oriented mass market thinking. But some managers don't understand this narrowing-down process.

Don't just focus on the product

Some production-oriented managers get into trouble because they ignore the tough part of defining markets. To make the narrowing-down process easier, they just describe their markets in terms of *products* they sell. For example, producers and retailers of greeting cards might define their market as the "greeting-card" market. But this production-oriented approach ignores customers—and customers make a market! This also leads to missed opportunities. Hallmark isn't missing these opportunities. Instead, Hallmark aims at the "personal-expression" market. Hallmark stores offer all kinds of products that can be sent as "memory makers"—to express one person's feelings toward another. And as opportunities related to these needs change, Hallmark changes too. For example, at the Hallmark website (www.hallmark.com) it is easy to get shopping suggestions

The Olympus pocket camera competes directly with other 35-mm cameras, but it may also compete in a broader product-market against Vivitar's digital camera for kids or even Sony's innovative Mavica, which stores digital pictures on a 3-inch CD-R.

Exhibit 3-3
Narrowing Down to Target Markets

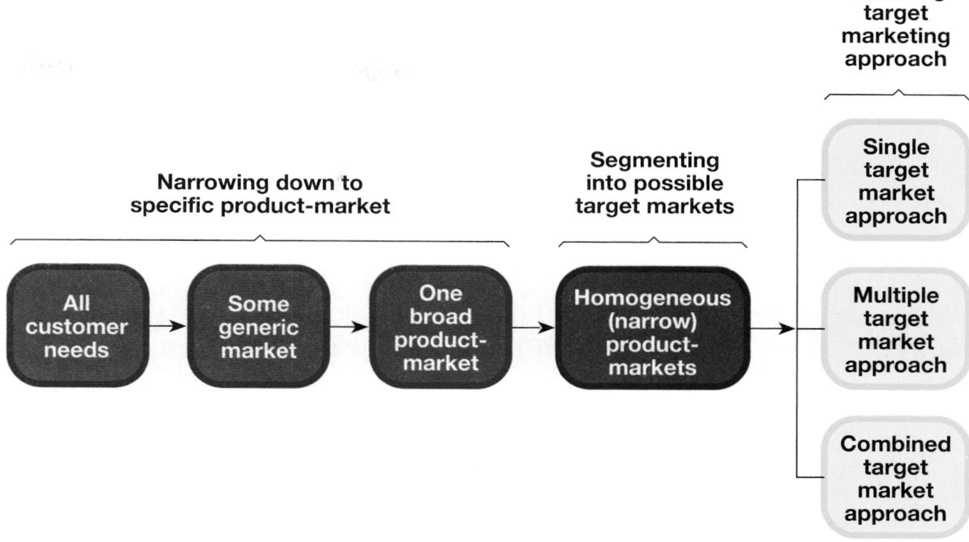

from an online "gift assistant," to order flowers, or to personalize an electronic greeting card to send over the Internet.[13]

From generic markets to product-markets

To understand the narrowing-down process, it's useful to think of two basic types of markets. A **generic market** is a market with *broadly* similar needs—and sellers offering various—*often diverse*—ways of satisfying those needs. In contrast, a **product-market** is a market with *very* similar needs and sellers offering various *close substitute* ways of satisfying those needs.[14]

A generic market description looks at markets broadly and from a customer's viewpoint. Entertainment-seekers, for example, have several very different ways to satisfy their needs. An entertainment-seeker might buy a Sony satellite receiving system for a TV, sign up for a cruise on the Carnival Line, or reserve season tickets for the symphony. Any one of these *very different* products may satisfy this entertainment need.

It is sometimes hard to understand and define generic markets because *quite different product types may compete with each other*. For example, a person on a business trip to Italy might want a convenient way to record memories of the trip. Minolta's APS camera, Sony's digital camcorder, Kodak's PalmPix digital accessory for a Palm, and even postcards from local shops may all compete to serve our traveler's needs. If customers see all these products as substitutes—as competitors in the same generic market—then marketers must deal with this complication.

Suppose, however, that our traveler decides to satisfy this need with an APS camera. Then—in this product-market—Minolta, Kodak, Nikon, and many other brands may compete with each other for the customer's dollars. In this *product*-market concerned with APS format cameras *and* needs to conveniently record memories, consumers compare similar products to satisfy their image needs.

Broaden market definitions to find opportunities

Broader market definitions—including both generic market definitions and product-market definitions—can help firms find opportunities. But deciding *how* broad to go isn't easy. Too narrow a definition limits a firm's opportunities—but too broad a definition makes the company's efforts and resources seem insignificant. Consider, for example, the mighty Coca-Cola Company. It has great success and a huge market share in the U.S. cola-drinkers' market. On the other hand, its share of all beverage drinking worldwide is very small.

Here we try to match opportunities to a firm's resources and objectives. So the *relevant market for finding opportunities* should be bigger than the firm's present product-market—but not so big that the firm couldn't expand and be an important competitor. A small manufacturer of screwdrivers in Mexico, for example, shouldn't define its market as broadly as "the worldwide tool users market" or as narrowly as "our present screwdriver customers." But it may have the production and/or marketing potential to consider "the handyman's hand-tool market in North America." Carefully naming your product-market can help you see possible opportunities.

Naming Product-Markets and Generic Markets

Some managers think about markets just in terms of the product they already produce and sell. But this approach can lead to missed opportunities. Think about all of the minivans and SUVs that you see and how many cars they've replaced on the road. If Chrysler had been thinking only about the "car" market, the minivan opportunity might have been missed altogether.

Product-related terms do not—by themselves—adequately describe a market. A complete product-market definition includes a four-part description.

What:	**1. Product type (type of good and type of service)**
To meet what:	**2. Customer (user) needs**
For whom:	**3. Customer types**
Where:	**4. Geographic area**

We refer to these four-part descriptions as product-market "names" because most managers label their markets when they think, write, or talk about them. Such a four-part definition can be clumsy, however, so we often use a nickname. And the nickname should refer to people—not products—because, as we emphasize, people make markets!

Product type should meet customer needs

Product type describes the goods and/or services that customers want. Sometimes the product type is strictly a physical good or strictly a service. But marketing managers who ignore the possibility that *both* are important can miss opportunities.

Customer (user) needs refer to the needs the product type satisfies for the customer. At a very basic level, product types usually provide functional benefits such as nourishing, transporting, holding, saving time, and so forth. Although we need to identify such "basic" needs first, in advanced economies, we usually go on to emotional needs—such as needs for fun, excitement, or status. Correctly defining the need(s) relevant to a market is crucial and requires a good understanding of customers. We discuss these topics more fully in Chapters 5 and 6.

Customer type refers to the final consumer or user of a product type. Here we want to choose a name that describes all present (possible) types of customers. To define customer type, marketers should identify the final consumer or user of the product type, rather than the buyer—if they are different. For instance, producers should avoid treating middlemen as a customer type—unless middlemen actually use the product in their own business.

The *geographic area* is where a firm competes—or plans to compete—for customers. Naming the geographic area may seem trivial, but understanding geographic boundaries of a market can suggest new opportunities. A firm aiming only at the domestic market, for example, may want to expand into world markets.

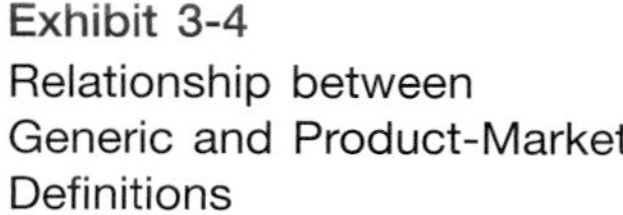

Exhibit 3-4
Relationship between Generic and Product-Market Definitions

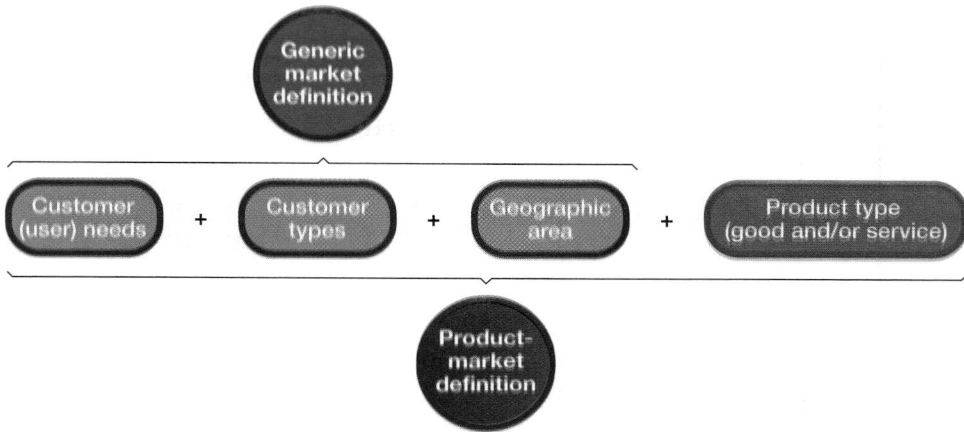

No product type in generic market names

A generic market description *doesn't include any product-type terms*. It consists of only three parts of the product-market definition—without the product type. This emphasizes that any product type that satisfies the customer's needs can compete in a generic market. Exhibit 3-4 shows the relationship between generic market and product-market definitions.

Later we'll study the many possible dimensions for segmenting markets. But for now you should see that defining markets only in terms of current products is not the best way to find new opportunities.

Market Segmentation Defines Possible Target Markets

Market segmentation is a two-step process

Market segmentation is a two-step process of: (1) *naming* broad product-markets and (2) *segmenting* these broad product-markets in order to select target markets and develop suitable marketing mixes.

This two-step process isn't well understood. First-time market segmentation efforts often fail because beginners start with the whole mass market and try to find one or two demographic characteristics to segment this market. Customer behavior is usually too complex to be explained in terms of just one or two demographic characteristics. For example, not all elderly men buy the same products or brands. Other dimensions usually must be considered—starting with customer needs.

Naming broad product-markets is disaggregating

The first step in effective market segmentation involves naming a broad product-market of interest to the firm. Marketers must break apart—disaggregate—all possible needs into some generic markets and broad product-markets in which the firm may be able to operate profitably. See Exhibit 3-3. No one firm can satisfy everyone's needs. So the naming—disaggregating—step involves brainstorming about very different solutions to various generic needs and selecting some broad areas—broad product-markets—where the firm has some resources and experience. This means that a car manufacturer would probably ignore all the possible opportunities in food and clothing markets and focus on the generic market, "transporting people in the world," and probably on the broad product-market, "cars, trucks, and utility vehicles for transporting people in the world."

This approach tries to narrow down the marketing focus to product-market areas where the firm is more likely to have a competitive advantage or even to find breakthrough opportunities.

Exhibit 3-5
A Market Grid Diagram with Submarkets

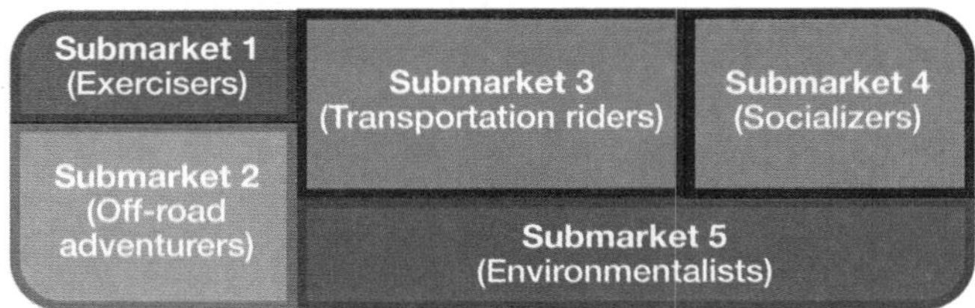

Market grid is a visual aid to market segmentation

Assuming that any broad product-market (or generic market) may consist of submarkets, picture a market as a rectangle with boxes that represent the smaller, more homogeneous product-markets.

Exhibit 3-5, for example, represents the broad product-market of bicycle riders. The boxes show different submarkets. One submarket might focus on people who want basic transportation, another on people who want exercise, and so on. Alternatively, in the generic "transporting market" discussed earlier, we might see different product-markets of customers for bicycles, motorcycles, cars, airplanes, ships, buses, and "others."

Segmenting is an aggregating process

Marketing-oriented managers think of **segmenting** as an aggregating process—clustering people with similar needs into a "market segment." A **market segment** is a (relatively) homogeneous group of customers who will respond to a marketing mix in a similar way.

This part of the market segmentation process (see Exhibit 3-3) takes a different approach from the naming part. Here we look for similarities rather than basic differences in needs. Segmenters start with the idea that each person is one of a kind but that it may be possible to aggregate some similar people into a product-market.

Segmenters see each of these one-of-a-kind people as having a unique set of dimensions. Consider a product-market in which customers' needs differ on two important segmenting dimensions: need for status and need for dependability. In Exhibit 3-6A, each dot shows a person's position on the two dimensions. While each person's position is unique, many of these people are similar in terms of how much status and dependability they want. So a segmenter may aggregate them into three (an arbitrary number) relatively homogeneous submarkets—A, B, and C. Group A might be called "status-oriented" and Group C "dependability-oriented." Members of Group B want both and might be called the "demanders."

How far should the aggregating go?

The segmenter wants to aggregate individual customers into some workable number of relatively homogeneous target markets and then treat each target market differently.

Look again at Exhibit 3-6A. Remember we talked about three segments. But this was an arbitrary number. As Exhibit 3-6B shows, there may really be six segments. What do you think—does this broad product-market consist of three segments or six?

Exhibit 3-6
Every Individual Has His or Her Own Unique Position in a Market—Those with Similar Positions Can Be Aggregated into Potential Target Markets

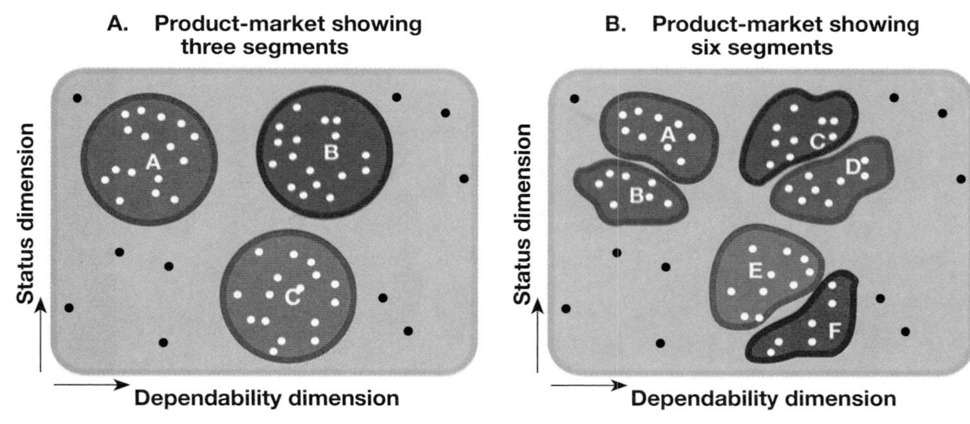

Heinz Introduced "talking labels" on the bottles of its popular ketchup—and featured the change in print ads—as part of a global campaign to give the brand an edgy attitude and increase consumption among Heinz's teen target market.

Another difficulty with segmenting is that some potential customers just don't fit neatly into market segments. For example, not everyone in Exhibit 3-6B was put into one of the groups. Forcing them into one of the groups would have made these segments more heterogeneous and harder to please. Further, forming additional segments for them probably wouldn't be profitable. They are too few and not very similar in terms of the two dimensions. These people are simply too unique to be catered to and may have to be ignored—unless they are willing to pay a high price for special treatment.

The number of segments that should be formed depends more on judgment than on some scientific rule. But the following guidelines can help.

Criteria for segmenting a broad product-market

Ideally, "good" market segments meet the following criteria:

1. *Homogeneous (similar) within*—the customers in a market segment should be as similar as possible with respect to their likely responses to marketing mix variables *and* their segmenting dimensions.
2. *Heterogeneous (different) between*—the customers in different segments should be as different as possible with respect to their likely responses to marketing mix variables *and* their segmenting dimensions.
3. *Substantial*—the segment should be big enough to be profitable.
4. *Operational*—the segmenting dimensions should be useful for identifying customers and deciding on marketing mix variables.

It is especially important that segments be *operational.* This leads marketers to include demographic dimensions such as age, sex, income, location, and family size. In fact, it is difficult to make some Place and Promotion decisions without such information.

Target marketers aim at specific targets

Once you accept the idea that broad product-markets may have submarkets, you can see that target marketers usually have a choice among many possible target markets.

There are three basic ways to develop market-oriented strategies in a broad product-market.

1. The **single target market approach**—segmenting the market and picking one of the homogeneous segments as the firm's target market.
2. The **multiple target market approach**—segmenting the market and choosing two or more segments, then treating each as a separate target market needing a different marketing mix.
3. The **combined target market approach**—combining two or more submarkets into one larger target market as a basis for one strategy.

Exhibit 3-7
Target Marketers Have Specific Aims

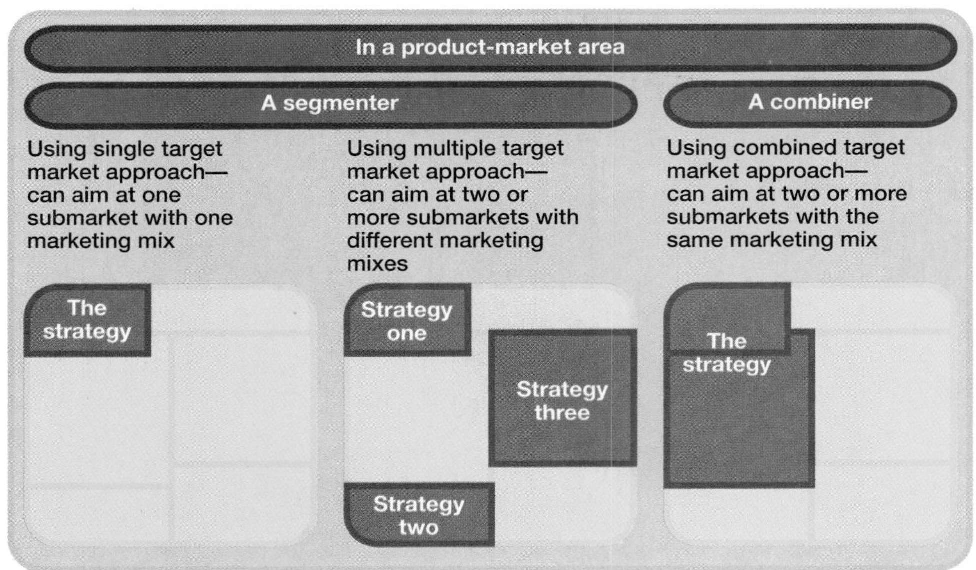

Note that all three approaches involve target marketing. They all aim at specific, clearly defined target markets. See Exhibit 3-7. For convenience, we call people who follow the first two approaches the "segmenters" and people who use the third approach the "combiners."

Combiners try to satisfy "pretty well"

Combiners try to increase the size of their target markets by combining two or more segments. Combiners look at various submarkets for similarities rather than differences. Then they try to extend or modify their basic offering to appeal to these "combined" customers with just one marketing mix. See Exhibit 3-7.

A combined target market approach may help achieve some economies of scale. It may also require less investment than developing different marketing mixes for different segments—making it especially attractive for firms with limited resources.

Too much combining is risky

It is tempting to aim at larger combined markets instead of using different marketing mixes for smaller segmented markets. But this makes it harder to develop marketing mixes that can satisfy each potential customer. So, a combiner faces the continual risk of innovative segmenters chipping away at the various segments of the combined target market—by offering more attractive marketing mixes to more homogeneous submarkets. ATI Technologies, a firm that is a leader in making graphics chips for PCs, saw this happen. It produces high-quality products with features desired by a very wide variety of computer users. But ATI has lost business to more specialized competitors like Nvidia Corp. By focusing on the needs of video-game lovers who don't want to compromise when it comes to realistic special effects, Nvidia has developed chips that do fewer things. Still, Nividia's chips do those fewer specialized things really well.

Segmenters try to satisfy "very well"

Segmenters aim at one or more homogeneous segments and try to develop a different marketing mix for each segment. Segmenters usually adjust their marketing mixes for each target market—perhaps making basic changes in the product itself. They believe that aiming at one—or some—of these smaller markets makes it possible to provide superior value and satisfy them better.

Segmenting may produce bigger sales

Note that segmenters are not settling for a smaller sales potential or lower profits. Instead, they hope to increase sales by getting a much larger share of the business in the market(s) they target. A segmenter who really satisfies the target market can often build such a close relationship with customers that it faces no real competition.

A segmenter that offers a marketing mix precisely matched to the needs of the target market can often charge a higher price that produces higher profits.

Check Point Software Technologies, a company that makes firewall software to protect websites from hackers, is a good example. Microsoft, Cisco Systems, and most other firms that compete in Check Point's "computer security needs" market create sweeping sets of products to cover a host of corporate computing needs. But by focusing on a particular set of needs Check Point has become the leader in its market. The payoff is that its profit margins are even higher than those earned by Microsoft.[15]

Should you segment or combine?

Which approach should a firm use? This depends on the firm's resources, the nature of competition, and—most important—the similarity of customer needs, attitudes, and buying behavior.

In general, it's usually safer to be a segmenter—that is, to try to satisfy some customers *very* well instead of many just *fairly* well. That's why many firms use the single or multiple target market approach instead of the combined target market approach. Procter & Gamble, for example, offers many products that seem to compete directly with each other (e.g., Tide versus Cheer or Crest versus Gleem). However, P&G offers tailor-made marketing mixes to each submarket large—and profitable—enough to deserve a separate marketing mix. A smaller firm with more limited resources may have to use the single target market approach—focusing all its efforts at the one submarket niche where it sees the best opportunity.[16]

Profit is the balancing point

In practice, cost considerations probably encourage more aggregating—to obtain economies of scale—while demand considerations suggest less aggregating—to satisfy needs more exactly.

Profit is the balancing point. It determines how unique a marketing mix the firm can afford to offer to a particular group.

What Dimensions Are Used to Segment Markets?

Segmenting dimensions guide marketing mix planning

Market segmentation forces a marketing manager to decide which product-market dimensions might be useful for planning marketing strategies. The dimensions should help guide marketing mix planning. Exhibit 3-8 shows the basic kinds of dimensions we'll be talking about in Chapter 5—and their probable effect on the four Ps. Ideally, we want to describe any potential product-market in terms of all three types of customer-related dimensions—plus a product type description—because these dimensions help us develop better marketing mixes.

Exhibit 3-8 Relation of Potential Target Market Dimensions to Marketing Strategy Decision Areas

Potential Target Market Dimensions	Effects on Strategy Decision Areas
1. Behavioral needs, attitudes, and how present and potential goods and services fit into customers' consumption patterns.	Affects *Product* (features, packaging, product line assortment, branding) and *Promotion* (what potential customers need and want to know about the firm's offering, and what appeals should be used).
2. Urgency to get need satisfied and desire and willingness to seek information, compare, and shop.	Affects *Place* (how directly products are distributed from producer to customer, how extensively they are made available, and the level of service needed) and *Price* (how much potential customers are willing to pay).
3. Geographic location and other demographic characteristics of potential customers.	Affects size of *Target Markets* (economic potential), *Place* (where products should be made available), and *Promotion* (where and to whom to target advertising and personal selling).

Exhibit 3-9 Possible Segmenting Dimensions and Typical Breakdowns for Consumer Markets

Behavioral	
Needs	Economic, functional, physiological, psychological, social, and more detailed needs.
Benefits sought	Situation specific, but to satisfy specific or general needs.
Thoughts	Favorable or unfavorable attitudes, interests, opinions, beliefs.
Rate of use	Heavy, medium, light, nonusers.
Purchase relationship	Positive and ongoing, intermittent, no relationship, bad relationship.
Brand familiarity	Insistence, preference, recognition, nonrecognition, rejection.
Kind of shopping	Convenience, comparison shopping, specialty, none (unsought product).
Type of problem-solving	Routinized response, limited, extensive.
Information required	Low, medium, high.
Geographic	
Region of world, country	North America (United States, Canada), Europe (France, Italy, Germany), and so on.
Region in country	(Examples in United States): Pacific, Mountain, West North Central, West South Central, East North Central, East South Central, South Atlantic, Middle Atlantic, New England.
Size of city	No city; population under 5,000; 5,000–19,999; 20,000–49,999; 50,000–99,999; 100,000–249,999; 250,000–499,999; 500,000–999,999; 1,000,000–3,999,999; 4,000,000 or over.
Demographic	
Income	Under \$5,000; \$5,000–9,999; \$10,000–14,999; \$15,000–19,999; \$20,000–29,999; \$30,000–39,999; \$40,000–59,999; \$60,000 and over.
Sex	Male, female.
Age	Infant; under 6; 6–11; 12–17; 18–24; 25–34; 35–49; 50–64; 65 or over.
Family size	1, 2, 3–4, 5 or more.
Family life cycle	Young, single; young, married, no children; young, married, youngest child under 6; young, married, youngest child over 6; older, married, with children; older, married, no children under 18; older, single; other variations for single parents, divorced, etc.
Occupation	Professional and technical; managers, officials, and proprietors; clerical sales; craftspeople, foremen; operatives; farmers; retired; students; housewives; unemployed.
Education	Grade school or less; some high school; high school graduate; some college; college graduate.
Ethnicity	Asian, Black, Hispanic, Native American, White, Multiracial.
Social class	Lower-lower, upper-lower, lower-middle, upper-middle, lower-upper, upper-upper.

Note: Terms used in this table are explained in detail later in the text.

Many segmenting dimensions may be considered

Customers can be described by many specific dimensions. Exhibit 3-9 shows some dimensions useful for segmenting consumer markets. A few are behavioral dimensions, others are geographic and demographic. Exhibit 3-10 shows some additional dimensions for segmenting markets when the customers are businesses, government agencies, or other types of organizations. Regardless of whether customers are final consumers or organizations, segmenting a broad product-market may require using several different dimensions at the same time.[17]

What are the qualifying and determining dimensions?

To select the important segmenting dimensions, think about two different types of dimensions. **Qualifying dimensions** are those relevant to including a customer type in a product-market. **Determining dimensions** are those that actually affect the customer's purchase of a specific product or brand in a product-market.

A prospective car buyer, for example, has to have enough money—or credit—to buy a car and insure it. Our buyer also needs a driver's license. This still doesn't guarantee a purchase. He or she must have a real need—like a job that requires

Any hiking boot should repel water, and a product that doesn't meet that "qualifying need" probably wouldn't appeal to many hikers. Sorel wants its target customers to know that its boots go further in keeping feet dry because that difference may determine which brand of boot they buy.

"wheels" or kids who have to be carpooled. This need may motivate the purchase of *some* car. But these qualifying dimensions don't determine what specific brand or model car the person might buy. That depends on more specific interests—such as the kind of safety, performance, or appearance the customer wants. Determining dimensions related to these needs affect the specific car the customer purchases. If safety is a determining dimension for a customer, a Volvo wagon that offers side impact protection, airbags, and all-wheel drive might be the customer's first choice.

Determining dimensions may be very specific

How specific the determining dimensions are depends on whether you are concerned with a general product type or a specific brand. See Exhibit 3-11. The more

Exhibit 3-10 Possible Segmenting Dimensions for Business/Organizational Markets

Kind of relationship	Weak loyalty → strong loyalty to vendor Single source → multiple vendors "Arm's length" dealings → close partnership No reciprocity → complete reciprocity
Type of customer	Manufacturer, service producer, government agency, military, nonprofit, wholesaler or retailer (when end user), and so on.
Demographics	Geographic location (region of world, country, region within country, urban → rural) Size (number of employees, sales volume) Primary business or industry (North American Industry Classification System) Number of facilities
How customer will use product	Installations, components, accessories, raw materials, supplies, professional services
Type of buying situation	Decentralized → centralized Buyer → multiple buying influence Straight rebuy → modified rebuy → new-task buying
Purchasing methods	Vendor analysis, purchasing specifications, Internet bids, negotiated contracts, long-term contracts, e-commerce websites

Note: Terms used in this table are explained in detail later in the text.

Exhibit 3-11 Finding the Relevant Segmenting Dimensions

All potential dimensions	Qualifying dimensions	Determining dimensions (product type)	Determining dimensions (brand specific)
Dimensions generally relevant to purchasing behavior	Dimensions relevant to including a customer type in the product-market	Dimensions that affect the customer's purchase of a specific type of product	Dimensions that affect the customer's choice of a specific brand

Segmenting dimensions become more specific to reasons why the target segment chooses to buy a particular brand of the product

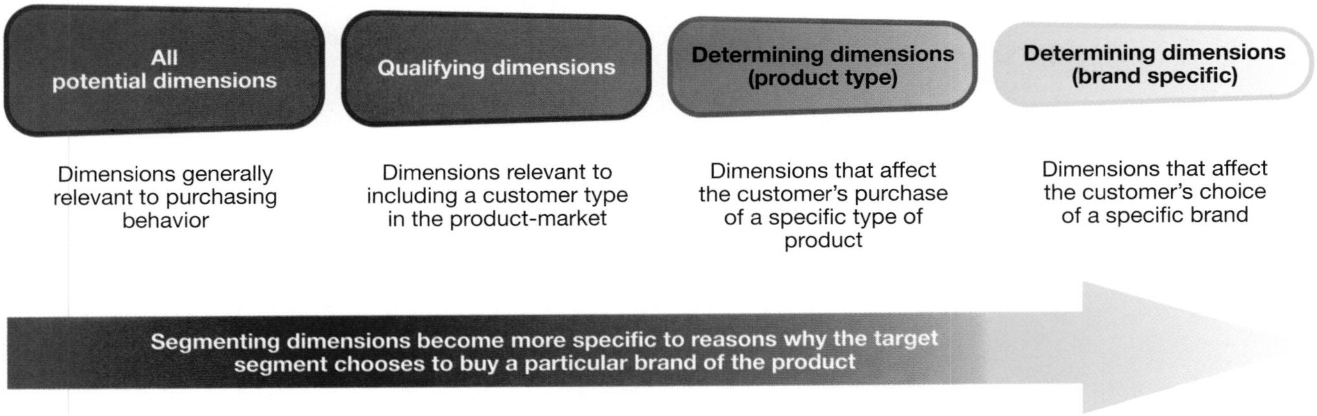

specific you want to be, the more particular the determining dimensions may be. In a particular case, the determining dimensions may seem minor. But they are important because they *are* the determining dimensions.

Marketers at General Mills know this. Lots of people try to check e-mail or drive a car while eating breakfast or lunch. General Mills has figured out that for many of these target customers the real determining dimension in picking a snack is whether it can be eaten "one-handed."[18]

Different dimensions needed for different submarkets

Note that each different submarket within a broad product-market may be motivated by a different set of dimensions. In the snack food market, for example, health food enthusiasts are interested in nutrition, dieters worry about calories, and economical shoppers with lots of kids may want volume to "fill them up."

Ethical issues in selecting segmenting dimensions

Marketing managers sometimes face ethical decisions when selecting segmenting dimensions. Problems may arise if a firm targets customers who are somehow at a disadvantage in dealing with the firm or who are unlikely to see the negative effects of their own choices. For example, some people criticize shoe companies for targeting poor, inner-city kids who see expensive athletic shoes as an important status symbol. Encyclopedia publishers have been criticized for aggressive selling to less-educated parents who don't realize that the "pennies a day" credit terms are more than they can afford. Some nutritionists criticize firms that market snack foods to children.

Sometimes a marketing manager must decide whether a firm should serve customers it really doesn't want to serve. For example, banks sometimes offer marketing mixes that basically drive off low-income consumers.

People often disagree about what segmenting dimensions are ethical in a given situation. A marketing manager needs to consider not only his or her own views but also the views of other groups in society. Even when there is no clear "right" answer, negative publicity may be very damaging. This is what Amazon.com encountered when it was revealed that it was charging some regular customers higher prices than new customers at its site.[19]

International marketing requires even more segmenting

Success in international marketing requires even more attention to segmenting. There are over 228 nations with their own unique cultures! And they differ greatly in language, customs (including business ethics), beliefs, religions, race, and income distribution patterns. (We'll discuss some of these differences in Chapters 4 and 5.) These additional differences can complicate the segmenting process. Even worse, critical data are often less available as firms move into international markets. This is one reason why some firms insist that local operations and decisions be handled by natives. They, at least, have a feel for their markets.

There are more dimensions—but there is a way

Segmenting international markets may require more dimensions. But one practical method adds just one step to the approach discussed above. First, marketers segment by country or region—looking at demographic, cultural, and other characteristics, including stage of economic development. This may help them find regional or national submarkets that are fairly similar. Then they apply the same basic approaches discussed earlier.

More Sophisticated Techniques May Help in Segmenting

Marketing researchers and managers often turn to computer-aided methods for help with the segmenting job. A detailed review of the possibilities is beyond the scope of this book. But a brief discussion will give you a flavor of how computer-aided methods work.

Clustering usually requires a computer

Clustering techniques try to find similar patterns within sets of data. Clustering groups customers who are similar on their segmenting dimensions into homogeneous segments. Clustering approaches use computers to do what previously was done with much intuition and judgment.

The data to be clustered might include such dimensions as demographic characteristics, the importance of different needs, attitudes toward the product, and past buying behavior. The computer searches all the data for homogeneous groups of people. The results sometimes suggest new, or better, marketing strategies.[20]

A cluster analysis of the toothpaste market, for example, might show that some people buy toothpaste because it tastes good (the sensory segment), while others are concerned with the effect of clean teeth and fresh breath on their social image (the sociables). Still others worry about decay or tartar (the worriers), and some are just interested in the best value for their money (the value seekers). Each of these market segments calls for a different marketing mix—although some of the four Ps may be similar.

It is usually better to focus on the needs satisfied by products rather than on the product characteristics themselves.

Herman Miller Takes a Back Seat to No One

Herman Miller (HM) is a 75-year-old company that makes office furniture. Boring stuff? Marketing managers at HM know that some office furniture customers feel that way. So, they decided to do something about it. Consider the success of the company's Aeron desk chair. In an e-commerce world even top executives sit at computers and need a desk chair created for both work and looks. To satisfy this upscale segment, HM designed a new type of chair from scratch. There's no fabric or padding, but everything about it adjusts to your body. It's so comfortable that HM positions it as "the chair you can wear." With a price tag close to $1,000, it became a status symbol for high-tech managers and was as profitable as it was popular. But with the cooling off of the economy and collapse of the dot-coms, HM is looking for other new opportunities for growth. It's finding them with a new line, called Red, that targets new firms and small businesses. HM created a new division, SQA (which stands for Simple, Quick, Affordable), to serve this segment. The SQA factory does not offer the thousands of choices in fabrics and styles that were popular with HM's traditional, big corporate buyers. Nor do customers get extensive help from sales reps and dealers. However, HM's Red product line does offer bold colors and chic styles that give HM an advantage over suppliers like OfficeMax. Buyers place orders at a slick website (www.hermanmillerred.com) that displays a 3-D drawing of the buyer's office space and furniture choices. The orders are immediately linked into the factory production schedule, so delivery times are very fast. This system also reduces selling costs, so the line is profitable even at Red's affordable price point. Competing firms are now chasing this same market segment, but with HM's head start a lot of them are just taking a back seat.[21]

Customer database can focus the effort

A variation of the clustering approach is based on customer relationship management methods. With **customer relationship management (CRM),** the seller fine-tunes the marketing effort with information from a detailed customer database. This usually includes data on a customer's past purchases as well as other segmenting information. For example, a florist that keeps a database of customers who have ordered flowers for Mother's Day or Valentine's Day can call them in advance with a special offer. Firms that operate over the Internet may have a special advantage with these database-focused approaches. They are able to communicate with customers via a website or e-mail, which means that the whole effort is not only targeted but also very inexpensive. Further, it's fast and easy for a customer to reply.[22]

Amazon.com takes this even further. When a customer orders a book, the Amazon CRM system at the website recommends other related books that have been purchased by other customers who bought that book.

Differentiation and Positioning Take the Customer Point of View

Differentiate the marketing mix—to serve customers better

The reason for focusing on a specific target market is so that you can fine-tune the whole marketing mix to provide some group of potential customers with superior value. By *differentiating* the marketing mix to do a better job meeting customers' needs, the firm builds a competitive advantage. When this happens, target customers view the firm's position in the market as uniquely suited to their preferences and needs. Further, because everyone in the firm is clear about what position it wants to achieve with customers, the Product, Promotion, and other marketing mix decisions can be blended better to achieve the desired objectives.

Positioning is based on customers' views

Positioning refers to how customers think about proposed and/or present brands in a market. A marketing manager needs a realistic view of how customers think about offerings in the market. Without that, it's hard to differentiate. At the same time, the manager should know how he or she *wants* target customers to think about the firm's marketing mix. Positioning issues are especially important when competitors in a market appear to be very similar. For example, many people think that there isn't much difference between one brand of TV and another. But Sony wants TV buyers to see its Wega flat-screen as offering the very best picture.

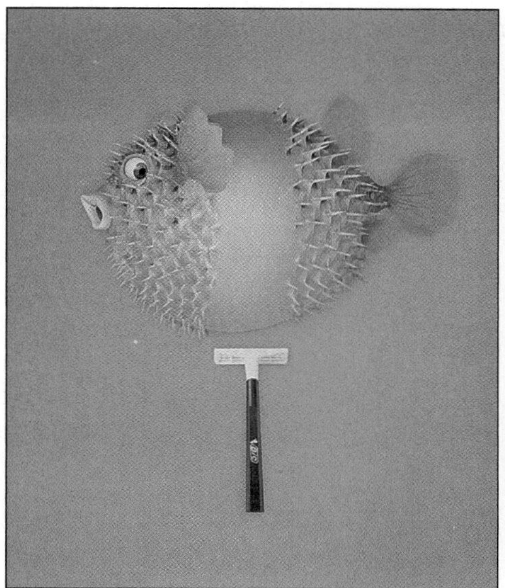

Firms often use promotion to help "position" how a marketing mix meets target customers' specific needs. For example, Bic ads along the roadside in Thailand highlight an ultra-close shave. In the U.S., Target wants consumers to remember not only its soft goods but also its houseware lines.

Once you know what customers think, then you can decide whether to leave the product (and marketing mix) alone or reposition it. This may mean *physical changes* in the product or simply *image changes based on promotion*. For example, most cola drinkers can't pick out their favorite brand in a blind test—so physical changes might not be necessary (and might not even work) to reposition a cola. Yet, ads that portray Pepsi drinkers in funny situations help position "the Joy of Pepsi."

Internet

Internet Exercise For years, Volvo has had a reputation as a particularly safe car and much of its advertising has reinforced that positioning. Go to the website for Volvo cars (www.volvocars.com) and select the link for the U.S. website. Consider whether the U.S. website successfully reinforces a positioning of Volvo as a "safe" alternative. Why or why not?

Figuring out what customers really think about competing products isn't easy, but there are approaches that help. Most of them require some formal marketing research. The results are usually plotted on graphs to help show how consumers view the competing products. Usually, the products' positions are related to two or three product features that are important to the target customers.

Managers make the graphs for positioning decisions by asking consumers to make judgments about different brands—including their "ideal" brand—and then use computer programs to summarize the ratings and plot the results. The details of positioning techniques—sometimes called "perceptual mapping"—are beyond the scope of this text. But Exhibit 3-12 shows the possibilities.[23]

Exhibit 3-12 shows the "product space" for different brands of bar soap using two dimensions—the extent to which consumers think the soaps moisturize and deodorize their skin. For example, consumers see Dial as quite low on moisturizing but high on deodorizing. Lifebuoy and Dial are close together—implying that consumers think of them as similar on these characteristics. Dove is viewed as different and is further away on the graph. Remember that positioning maps are based on *customers' perceptions*. The actual characteristics of the products (as determined by a chemical test) might be different!

Each segment may have its own preferences

The circles in Exhibit 3-12 show different segments (submarkets) of consumers clustered near their ideal soap preferences. Groups of respondents with a similar ideal product are circled to show apparent customer concentrations. In

Exhibit 3-12
"Product Space" Representing Consumers' Perceptions for Different Brands of Bar Soap

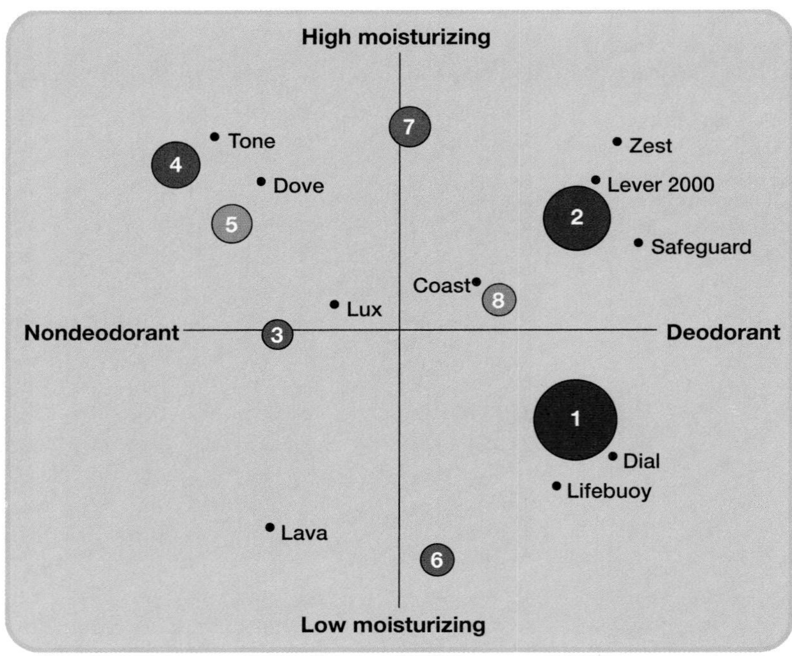

this graph, the size of the circles suggests the size of the segments for the different ideals.

Ideal clusters 1 and 2 are the largest and are close to two popular brands—Dial and Lever 2000. It appears that customers in cluster 1 want more moisturizing than they see in Dial and Lifebuoy. However, exactly what these brands should do about this isn't clear. Perhaps both of these brands should leave their physical products alone—but emphasize moisturizing more in their promotion to make a stronger appeal to those who want moisturizers. A marketing manager talking about this approach might simply refer to it as "positioning the brand as a good moisturizer." Of course, whether the effort is successful depends on whether the whole marketing mix delivers on the promise of the positioning communication.

Note that ideal cluster 7 is not near any of the present brands. This may suggest an opportunity for introducing a new product—a strong moisturizer with some deodorizers. A firm that chooses to follow this approach would be making a segmenting effort.

Combining versus segmenting

Positioning analysis may lead a firm to combining—rather than segmenting—if managers think they can make several general appeals to different parts of a "combined" market. For example, by varying its promotion, Coast might try to appeal to segments 8, 1, and 2 with one product. These segments are all quite similar (close together) in what they want in an ideal brand. On the other hand, there may be clearly defined submarkets—and some parts of the market may be "owned" by one product or brand. In this case, segmenting efforts may be practical—moving the firm's own product into another segment of the general market area where competition is weaker.

Positioning as part of broader analysis

A positioning analysis helps managers understand how customers see their market. It is a visual aid to understanding a product-market. The first time such an analysis is done, managers may be shocked to see how much customers' perceptions of a market differ from their own. For this reason alone, positioning analysis may be crucial. But, a positioning analysis usually focuses on specific product features and brands that are close competitors in the product-market. Thus, it is a product-oriented approach. Important *customer*-related dimensions—including needs and attitudes—may be overlooked.

Premature emphasis on product features is dangerous in other ways as well. As our bar soap example shows, starting with a product-oriented definition of a market and how bar soaps compete against other bar soaps can make a firm miss more basic shifts in markets. For example, bars might be losing popularity to liquid soaps. Or other products, like bath oils or body shampoos for use in the shower, may be part of the relevant competition. Managers wouldn't see these shifts if they looked only at alternative bar soap brands—the focus is just too narrow.

It's also important to realize that the way consumers look at a product isn't just a matter of chance. Let's return to our bar soap example. While many consumers do think about soap in terms of moisturizing and deodorizing, other needs shouldn't be overlooked. For example, some consumers are especially concerned about wiping out germs. Marketers for Dial soap recognized this need and developed ads that positioned Dial as "the choice" for these target customers.

Customers won't always be conscious of all of the detailed ways that a firm's marketing mix might be different, but careful positioning can help highlight a unifying theme or benefits that relate to the determining dimensions of the target market. Thus, positioning should be part of the broader strategy planning process and ensure that the whole marketing mix is viewed as offering target customers superior value.

Conclusion

Firms need creative strategy planning to survive in our increasingly competitive markets. In this chapter, we discussed how to find attractive target market opportunities. We started by considering four basic types of opportunities—market penetration, market development, product development, and diversification—with special emphasis on opportunities in international markets. We also saw that carefully defining generic markets and product-markets can help find new opportunities. We stressed the shortcomings of a too narrow, product-oriented view of markets.

We also discussed market segmentation—the process of naming and then segmenting broad product-markets to find potentially attractive target markets. Some people try to segment markets by starting with the mass market and then dividing it into smaller submarkets based on a few dimensions. But this can lead to poor results. Instead, market segmentation should first focus on a broad product-market and then group similar customers into homogeneous submarkets. The more similar the potential customers are, the larger the submarkets can be. Four criteria for evaluating possible product-market segments were presented.

Once a broad product-market is segmented, marketing managers can use one of three approaches to market-oriented strategy planning: (1) the single target market approach, (2) the multiple target market approach, and (3) the combined target market approach. In general, we encouraged marketers to be segmenters rather than combiners.

We also discussed some computer-aided approaches—clustering techniques, CRM, and positioning.

In summary, good marketers should be experts on markets and likely segmenting dimensions. By creatively segmenting markets, they may spot opportunities—even breakthrough opportunities—and help their firms succeed against aggressive competitors offering similar products. Segmenting is basic to target marketing.

Questions and Problems

1. Distinguish between an attractive opportunity and a breakthrough opportunity. Give an example.
2. Explain how new opportunities may be seen by defining a firm's markets more precisely. Illustrate for a situation where you feel there is an opportunity—namely, an unsatisfied market segment—even if it is not very large.
3. In your own words, explain why the book suggests that you should think of marketing strategy planning as a narrowing down process.

4. Distinguish between a generic market and a product-market. Illustrate your answer.
5. Explain the major differences among the four basic types of opportunities discussed in the text and cite examples for two of these types of opportunities.
6. Explain why a firm may want to pursue a market penetration opportunity before pursuing one involving product development or diversification.
7. In your own words, explain several reasons why marketing managers should consider international markets when evaluating possible opportunities.
8. Give an example of a foreign-made product (other than an automobile) that you personally have purchased. Give some reasons why you purchased that product. Do you think that there was a good opportunity for a domestic firm to get your business? Explain why or why not.
9. Explain what market segmentation is.
10. List the types of potential segmenting dimensions and explain which you would try to apply first, second, and third in a particular situation. If the nature of the situation would affect your answer, explain how.
11. Explain why segmentation efforts based on attempts to divide the mass market using a few demographic dimensions may be very disappointing.
12. Illustrate the concept that segmenting is an aggregating process by referring to the admissions policies of your own college and a nearby college or university.
13. Review the types of segmenting dimensions listed in Exhibits 3-9 and 3-10, and select the ones you think should be combined to fully explain the market segment you personally would be in if you were planning to buy a new watch today. List several dimensions and try to develop a shorthand name, like "fashion-oriented," to describe your own personal market segment. Then try to estimate what proportion of the total watch market would be accounted for by your market segment. Next, explain if there are any offerings that come close to meeting the needs of your market. If not, what sort of a marketing mix is needed? Would it be economically attractive for anyone to try to satisfy your market segment? Why or why not?
14. Identify the determining dimension or dimensions that explain why you bought the specific brand you did in your most recent purchase of a *(a)* soft drink, *(b)* shampoo, *(c)* shirt or blouse, and *(d)* larger, more expensive item, such as a bicycle, camera, or boat. Try to express the determining dimension(s) in terms of your own personal characteristics rather than the product's characteristics. Estimate what share of the market would probably be motivated by the same determining dimension(s).
15. Consider the market for off-campus apartments in your city. Identify some submarkets that have different needs and determining dimensions. Then evaluate how well the needs in these market segments are being met in your geographic area. Is there an obvious breakthrough opportunity waiting for someone?
16. Explain how positioning analysis can help a marketing manager identify target market opportunities.

Suggested Cases

7. Lilybank Lodge
10. Runners World
25. Metal Works, Inc.
26. Deluxe Foods, Ltd.

Computer-Aided Problem

3. Segmenting Customers

The marketing manager for Audiotronics Software Company is seeking new market opportunities. He is focusing on the voice recognition market and has narrowed down to three segments: the Fearful Typists, the Power Users, and the Professional Specialists. The Fearful Typists don't know much about computers—they just want a fast way to create e-mail messages, letters, and simple reports without errors. They don't need a lot of special features. They want simple instructions and a program that's easy to learn. The Power Users know a lot about computers, use them often, and want a voice recognition program with many special features. All computer programs seem easy to them—so they aren't worried about learning to use the various features. The Professional Specialists have jobs that require a lot of writing. They don't know much about computers but are willing to learn. They want special features needed for their work—but only if they aren't too hard to learn and use.

The marketing manager prepared a table summarizing the importance of each of three key needs in the three segments (see table below).

	Importance of Need (1 = Not Important; 10 = Very Important)		
Market Segment	Features	Easy to Use	Easy to Learn
Fearful Typists	3	8	9
Power Users	9	2	2
Professional Specialists	7	5	6

Audiotronics' sales staff conducted interviews with seven potential customers who were asked to rate how important each of these three needs were in their work. The manager prepared a spreadsheet to help him cluster (aggregate) each person into one of the segments—along with other similar people. Each person's ratings are entered in the spreadsheet, and the clustering procedure computes a similarity score that indicates how similar (a low score) or dissimilar (a high score) the person is to the typical person in each of the segments. The manager can then "aggregate" potential customers into the segment that is most similar (that is, the one with the *lowest* similarity score).

a. *The ratings for a potential customer appear on the first spreadsheet. Into which segment would you aggregate this person?*

b. *The responses for seven potential customers who were interviewed are listed in the table below. Enter the ratings for a customer in the spreadsheet and then write down the similarity score for each segment. Repeat the process for each customer. Based on your analysis, indicate the segment into which you would aggregate each customer. Indicate the size (number of customers) of each segment.*

c. *In the interview, each potential customer was also asked what type of computer he or she would be using. The responses are shown in the table along with the ratings. Group the responses based on the customer's segment. If you were targeting the Fearful Typists segment, what type of computer would you focus on when developing your software?*

d. *Based on your analysis, which customer would you say is least like any of the segments? Briefly explain the reason for your choice.*

For additional questions related to this problem, see Exercise 3-4 in the *Learning Aid for Use with Essentials of Marketing*, 9th edition.

	Importance of Need (1 = Not Important; 10 = Very Important)			
Potential Customer	Features	Easy to Use	Easy to Learn	Type of Computer
A.	8	1	2	Dell laptop
B.	6	6	5	IBM desktop
C.	4	9	8	Apple
D.	2	6	7	Apple
E.	5	6	5	IBM desktop
F.	8	3	1	Dell laptop
G.	4	6	8	Apple

When You Finish This Chapter, You Should

1. Know the variables that shape the environment of marketing strategy planning.

2. Understand why company objectives are important in guiding marketing strategy planning.

3. See how the resources of a firm affect the search for opportunities.

4. Know how the different kinds of competitive situations affect strategy planning.

5. Understand how the economic and technological environment can affect strategy planning.

6. Know why you might be sent to prison if you ignore the political and legal environment.

7. Know about the cultural and social environment and key population and income trends that affect it.

8. Understand how to screen and evaluate marketing strategy opportunities.

9. Understand the important new terms (shown in red).

Chapter Four

Evaluating Opportunities in the Changing Marketing Environment

UPS is on a roll. But if you think it's just those clean brown trucks that are moving, think again. Top management's objective isn't just to be the leader in delivering packages, but also to be the world leader in delivering services and information to corporate clients to help them pare shipping, inventory, and handling costs, manage relationships with suppliers, and even bill their customers. To achieve these objectives, marketing managers at UPS are developing completely new marketing strategies for new services and markets, like logistics consulting and handling of digital invoices and payments.

This means that UPS is no longer just competing with package-delivery rivals like FedEx and DHL. It also competes with a host of other firms that market information technology solutions for business problems. But UPS has resources

place price promotion produc

and strengths that help in this competition. It has already earned the trust of many business customers with whom it has close working relationships. Its experience and expertise are a competitive advantage also. A decade ago, UPS began to make huge investments in information systems, mainly to make its own operations more efficient. However, UPS quickly took advantage of this technology to make its package tracking databases available to customers over the Internet (www.ups.com). For final consumers, this was just a nice benefit of using UPS. But for many business customers, knowing precisely where stuff was meant saving millions of dollars in inventory costs. That opened customers' eyes to the possibilities. Then UPS set up a special sales force to help firms link their e-commerce websites directly to UPS shipping data. That gave it more opportunities to see ways that UPS could improve a customer's distribution system. Now, for example, if you order a pair of Air Jordans at Nike.com, the order is instantly filled by UPS from Nike inventory maintained at a UPS warehouse in Kentucky—and UPS delivers the sneakers directly to you the next day. In fact, if there is any problem and you call the toll-free number on Nike's website, it's a UPS employee at a call center in San Antonio who answers your call.

Sometimes UPS logistics solutions don't even rely on UPS trucks. For example, Ford Motor Company gave UPS a contract to manage the transportation and distribution of over 4 million cars and trucks a year—from 21 different factories to 6,000 dealers across North America. Now a Ford dealer who wants to find a metallic blue Mustang convertible can instantly do it online. The UPS system also reduces transit time for a new Mustang from 16 days to 12. That frees up $1 billion worth of inventory and saves Ford $125 million a year in inventory carrying costs.

These successes are earning profits for UPS, but it still must cope with the challenges of a weakened economy. However, even when demand for package deliveries is low UPS has a profit advantage over competitors who are less efficient. A weak economy may even help the UPS strategic business unit that offers logistics consulting services because customer firms have an even greater need to pare costs. Moreover, the trend toward free trade is helping UPS expand revenue from both international airfreight and the broker services it now offers to help firms cope with local customs laws.[1]

The Marketing Environment

The UPS case shows that a marketing manager must analyze customer needs and choose marketing strategy variables within the framework of the marketing environment and how it is changing.

A large number of forces shape the marketing environment. The direct environment of a market includes customers, the company, and competitors. The external market environment is broader and includes four major areas:

1. Economic environment.
2. Technological environment.
3. Political and legal environment.
4. Cultural and social environment.

The marketing manager can't control the variables of the marketing environment. That's why it's useful to think of them as uncontrollable variables. On the other hand, the marketing manager should analyze the environment when making decisions that can be controlled. For example, a manager can select strategies that lead the firm into product-markets where competition is not yet strong.

In creating its new website, Gap's objective was to complement and support its bricks and mortar stores rather than just cannibalize in-store sales. So, Gap Online features sizes and styles, like maternity clothes, that are not in stock in regular stores.

Objectives Should Set Firm's Course

A company must decide where it's going, or it may fall into the trap expressed so well by the quotation: "Having lost sight of our objective, we redoubled our efforts." Company objectives should shape the direction and operation of the whole business.

It is difficult to set objectives that really guide the present and future development of a company. The marketing manager should be heard when the company is setting objectives. But setting whole-company objectives—within resource limits—is ultimately the responsibility of top management. Top management must look at the whole business, relate its present objectives and resources to the external environment, and then decide what the firm wants to accomplish in the future.

Three basic objectives provide guidelines

The following three objectives provide a useful starting point for setting a firm's objectives. They should be sought *together* because in the long run a failure in even one of the three areas can lead to total failure of the business. A business should:

1. Engage in specific activities that will perform a socially and economically useful function.
2. Develop an organization to carry on the business and implement its strategies.
3. Earn enough profit to survive.[2]

A mission statement helps set the course

Our three general objectives provide guidelines, but a firm should develop its own objectives. This is important, but top executives often don't state their objectives clearly. If objectives aren't clear from the start, different managers may hold unspoken and conflicting objectives.

Many firms try to avoid this problem by developing a **mission statement,** which sets out the organization's basic purpose for being. For example, the mission of the Fort Smith Public Library (www.fspl.lib.ar.us) is "to serve the minds of the citizens in our community by providing easy access to resources that meet their informational and recreational needs." A good mission statement should focus on a few key goals rather than embracing everything. It should also supply guidelines when managers face difficult decisions. For example, if an employee of the library is trying to decide whether or not to write a proposal for the funding of a Spanish language story time or new computers that provide Internet access, it should be clear that these services are within the scope of the library's stated mission. A mission statement may need to be revised as new market needs arise or as the marketing environment changes. But this would be a fundamental change and not one that is made casually.[3]

The whole firm must work toward the same objectives

A mission statement is important, but it is not a substitute for more specific objectives that provide guidance in screening possible opportunities. For example, top management might set objectives such as "earn 25 percent annual return on investment" and "introduce at least three innovative and successful products in the next two years."

Of course, when there are a number of specific objectives stated by top management, it is critical that they be compatible. For example, the objective of introducing new products is reasonable. However, if the costs of developing and introducing the new products cannot be recouped within one year, the return on investment objective is impossible.[4]

Exhibit 4-1 A Hierarchy of Objectives

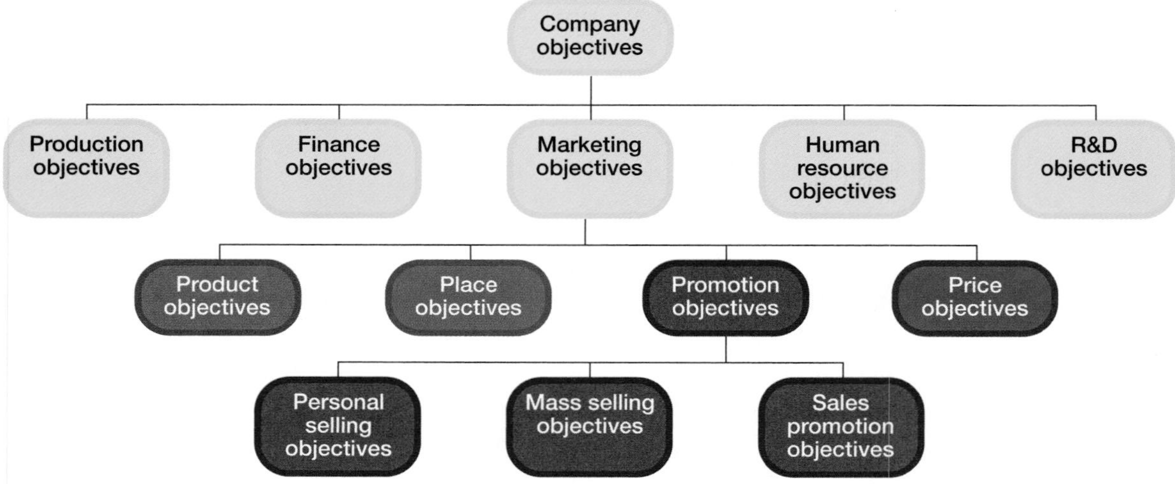

Company objectives should lead to marketing objectives

To avoid such problems, the marketing manager should at least be involved in setting company objectives. Company objectives guide managers as they search for and evaluate opportunities—and later plan marketing strategies. Particular *marketing* objectives should be set within the framework of larger company objectives. As shown in Exhibit 4-1, firms need a hierarchy of objectives—moving from company objectives to marketing department objectives. For each marketing strategy, firms also need objectives for each of the four Ps—as well as more detailed objectives. For example, in the Promotion area, we need objectives for advertising, sales promotion, *and* personal selling.

Toyota provides a good example. One of its company objectives is to achieve high customer satisfaction. So, the R&D people design vehicles to meet specific reliability objectives. Similarly, the production people work to cut manufacturing defects. The marketing department, in turn, sets specific customer satisfaction objectives for every product. That leads to specific promotion objectives to ensure that the sales and advertising people don't promise more than the company can deliver. Dealers' service people, in turn, work to fix any problem the first time it's reported.

Both company objectives and marketing objectives should be realistic and achievable. Overly ambitious objectives are useless if the firm lacks the resources to achieve them.

Company Resources May Limit Search for Opportunities

Every firm has some resources—hopefully some unique ones—that set it apart. Breakthrough opportunities—or at least some competitive advantage—come from making use of these strengths while avoiding direct competition with firms having similar strengths.

To find its strengths, a firm must evaluate its functional areas (production, research and engineering, marketing, general management, and finance) as well as its present products and markets. The knowledge of people at the firm can also be a unique resource. By analyzing successes or failures in relation to the firm's resources, management can discover why the firm was successful—or why it failed—in the past.

Harley-Davidson's motorcycle business was on the ropes, and it was losing customers to Japanese competitors. Studying the Japanese firms helped Harley identify

ways to produce higher-quality motorcycles at lower cost. With these resource-use problems resolved, Harley was again on the road to achieving its objectives. As its sales and reputation grew, its close relationship with Harley owners became a resource that helped Harley introduce a profitable line of accessories. The Harley case highlights both manufacturing quality and relationships with existing customers as resources. Other resources that should be considered as part of an evaluation of strengths and weaknesses are discussed in the following sections.[5]

Financial strength

Some opportunities require large amounts of capital just to get started. Money may be required for R&D, production facilities, marketing research, or advertising before a firm makes its first sale. And even a really good opportunity may not be profitable for years. So lack of financial strength is often a barrier to entry into an otherwise attractive market.

Producing capability and flexibility

In many businesses, the cost of producing and selling each unit decreases as the quantity increases. Therefore, smaller firms can be at a great cost disadvantage if they try to win business from larger competitors.

On the other hand, new—or smaller—firms sometimes have the advantage of flexibility. They are not handicapped with large, special-purpose facilities that are obsolete or poorly located.

Some firms are finding that they have the greatest flexibility by not having any "in house" manufacturing at all. Sara Lee, the company that markets brands like Hanes and L'Eggs, is a good example. Sara Lee sold its manufacturing facilities for many of these textile-related markets. Sara Lee says it doesn't have a competitive advantage in manufacturing. Further, as its needs change in various markets around the world it will buy products from whatever suppliers are best able to meet its specifications.

Marketing strengths

Our marketing strategy planning framework (Exhibit 3-1) helps in analyzing current marketing resources. In the product area, for example, a familiar brand can be

A familiar brand name—and other marketing strengths—can be an advantage in seeking new opportunities.

a big strength. Starbucks is famous for its coffee beverages. When Starbucks introduced Coffee Ice Cream, many people quickly tried it because they knew what Starbucks flavor meant.[6] A new idea or process may be protected by a *patent*. A patent owner has a 20-year monopoly to develop and use its new product, process, or material. If one firm has a strong patent, competitors may be limited to second-rate offerings—and their efforts may be doomed to failure.[7]

Good relations with established middlemen—or control of good locations—can be important resources. When marketing managers at Microsoft decided to introduce the Xbox game console, Microsoft software and computer accessories had already proved profitable for retailers like Best Buy that could reach the target market. So these retailers were willing to give the new product shelf space even if they were already carrying competing products from Nintendo or Sony.[8]

Promotion and price resources must be considered too. Fidelity Investments already has a skilled sales force. Marketing managers know these sales reps can handle new products and customers. And expertise to create an Internet website for online orders may enable a firm to expand its market and undercut competitors' prices.

Finally, thorough understanding of a target market can give a company an edge. Many companies fail in new product-markets because they don't really understand the needs of the new customers or the new competitive environment.

Analyzing Competitors and the Competitive Environment

Choose opportunities that avoid head-on competiton

The **competitive environment** affects the number and types of competitors the marketing manager must face and how they may behave. Although marketing managers usually can't control these factors, they can choose strategies that avoid head-on competition. And where competition is inevitable, they can plan for it.

Economists describe four basic kinds of market (competitive) situations: pure competition, oligopoly, monopolistic competition, and monopoly. Understanding the differences among these market situations is helpful in analyzing the competitive environment, and our discussion assumes some familiarity with these concepts. (For a review, see Exhibit A-11 and the related discussion in Appendix A, which follows Chapter 18.)

Most product-markets head toward pure competition—or oligopoly—over the long run. In these situations, competitors offer very similar products. Because customers see the different available products (marketing mixes) as close substitutes, managers just compete with lower and lower prices, and profit margins shrink. Sometimes managers do this much too quickly, without really thinking through the question of how to add more customer value.

Competitor-free environments are rare

Monopoly situations, in which one firm completely controls a broad product-market, are rare in market-directed economies. Further, governments commonly regulate monopolies. For example, in many parts of the world prices set by utility companies must be approved by a government agency. Although most marketing managers can't expect to operate with complete control in an unregulated monopoly, they can move away from head-on competition.

Monopolistic competition is typical—and a challenge

In monopolistic competition, a number of different firms offer marketing mixes that at least some customers see as different. Each competitor tries to get control (a monopoly) in its "own" target market. But competition still exists because some customers see the various alternatives as substitutes. Most marketing managers in developed economies face monopolistic competition.

When AOL got started in the U.S., it faced relatively little competition in the new market for online services. However, in entering the European market, it has faced more competition from subscription-free Internet service providers; so promotion focused on AOL's superior support.

In monopolistic competition, marketing managers sometimes try to differentiate very similar products by relying on other elements of the marketing mix. For example, Clorox Bleach uses the same basic chemicals as other bleaches. But marketing managers for Clorox may help to set it apart from other bleaches by offering an improved pouring spout, by producing ads that demonstrate its stain-killing power, or by getting it better shelf positions in supermarkets. Yet such approaches may not work, especially if competitors can easily imitate each new idea.

Analyze competitors to find a competitive advantage

The best way for a marketing manager to avoid head-on competition is to find new or better ways to satisfy customers' needs and provide value. The search for a breakthrough opportunity—or some sort of competitive advantage—requires an understanding not only of customers but also of competitors. That's why marketing managers turn to **competitor analysis**—an organized approach for evaluating the strengths and weaknesses of current or potential competitors' marketing strategies.

The basic approach to competitor analysis is simple. You compare the strengths and weaknesses of your current (or planned) target market and marketing mix with what competitors are currently doing or are likely to do in response to your strategy.

The initial step in competitor analysis is to identify potential competitors. It's useful to start broadly and from the viewpoint of target customers. Companies may offer quite different products to meet the same needs, but they are competitors if customers see them as offering close substitutes. For example, disposable diapers, cloth diapers, and diaper rental services all compete in the same generic market concerned with baby care. Identifying a broad set of potential competitors helps marketing managers understand the different ways customers are currently meeting needs and sometimes points to new opportunities. For example, even parents who usually prefer the economy of cloth diapers may be interested in the convenience of disposables when they travel.

Usually, however, marketing managers quickly narrow the focus of their analysis to the set of **competitive rivals**—firms that will be the closest competitors. Rivals offering similar products are usually easy to identify. However, with a really new and different product concept, the closest competitor may be a firm that is currently serving similar needs with a different type of product. Although such firms may not appear to be close competitors, they are likely to fight back—perhaps with a directly competitive product—if another firm starts to take away customers.

Anticipate competition that will come

A successful new strategy attracts copycats who jump in for a share of the profit. Sometimes a creative imitator figures out a way to provide customers with superior value. Then, sales may disappear before the pioneer even knows what's happened.

Exhibit 4-2 Competitor Analysis (summary): Disposable Diaper Competition in Japan

	P&G's Current and Planned Strategy	Kao's Strengths (+) and Weaknesses (−)	Uni-Charm's Strengths (+) and Weaknesses (−)
Target Market(s)	Upscale, modern parents who can afford disposable diapers	Same as for P&G	Same as for P&G, but also budget-conscious segment that includes cloth diaper users (+)
Product	Improved fit and absorbency (+); brand name imagery weak in Japan (−)	Brand familiarity (+), but no longer the best performance (−)	Two brands—for different market segments—and more convenient package with handles (+)
Place	Distribution through independent wholesalers to both food stores and drugstores (+), but handled by fewer retailers (−)	Close relations with and control over wholesalers who carry only Kao products (+); computerized inventory reorder system (+)	Distribution through 80% of food stores in best locations (+); shelf space for two brands (+)
Promotion	Heaviest spending on daytime TV, heavy sales promotion, including free samples (+); small sales force (−)	Large efficient sales force (+); lowest advertising spending (−) and out-of-date ad claims (−)	Advertising spending high (+); effective ads that appeal to Japanese mothers (+)
Price	High retail price (−), but lower unit price for larger quantities (+)	Highest retail price (−), but also best margins for wholesalers and retailers (+)	Lowest available retail price (+); price of premium brand comparable to P&G (−)
(Potential) Competitive Barriers	Patent protection (+), limits in access to retail shelf space (−)	Inferior product (−), excellent logistics support system (+)	Economies of scale and lower costs (+); loyal customers (+)
Likely Response(s)	Improve wholesaler and retailer margins; faster deliveries in channel; change package to require less shelf space	Press retailers to increase in-store promotion; change advertising and/or improve product	Increase short-term sales promotions; but if P&G takes customers, cut price on premium brand

Finding a sustainable competitive advantage requires special attention to competitor strengths and weaknesses. For example, it is very difficult to dislodge a firm that is already a market leader simply by attacking with a similar strategy. The leader can usually defend its position by quickly copying the best parts of what a new competitor is trying to do. On the other hand, an established competitor may not be able to defend quickly if it is attacked where it is weak. For example, Sony Walkman CD players had a large market share. When RCA added a feature so its CD players could also handle MP3 music files, Sony was slow to respond. Sony executives were worried that more widespread use of MP3 files could hurt profits from the firm's music recording business.[9]

Watch for competitive barriers

In a competitor analysis, you also consider **competitive barriers**—the conditions that may make it difficult, or even impossible, for a firm to compete in a market. Such barriers may limit your own plans or, alternatively, block competitors' responses to an innovative strategy.

For example, Exhibit 4-2 summarizes a competitor analysis in the Japanese market for disposable diapers. P&G was about to replace its original Pampers, which were selling poorly, with a new version that offered improved fit and better absorbency. Kao and Uni-Charm, the two leading Japanese producers, both had better distribution networks. Kao also had a better computer system to handle reorders. Because most Japanese grocery stores and drugstores are very small, frequent restocking by wholesalers is critical. So getting cooperation in the channel was a potential competitive barrier for P&G. To overcome this problem, P&G changed its packaging to take up less space and offered wholesalers and retailers better markups.[10]

Seek information about competitors

A marketing manager should actively seek information about current or potential competitors. Although most firms try to keep the specifics of their plans secret, much public information may be available. Sources of competitor information include trade publications, alert sales reps, middlemen, and other industry experts. In business markets, customers may be quick to explain what competing suppliers are offering.

The Internet is a powerful way to get information about competitors. A firm that puts all of its marketing information on a website for customers also makes it readily available to competitors. Similarly, it's easy to search through thousands of online publications and databases for any mention of a competitor. It's also increasingly common to specify what you want and instruct a software "robot" to send you a copy as soon as it's available. For more information about this type of Internet news service, check out www.infogate.com or www.companysleuth.com.

Internet

Internet Exercise If you were a new marketing manager at Rubbermaid, you might be interested in finding out more about Tupperware, an important competitor in some markets. What type of relevant information could you get by going to the Tupperware website (www.tupperware.com)?

Ethical issues may arise

The search for information about competitors sometimes raises ethical issues. For example, people who change jobs and move to competing firms may have a great deal of information, but is it ethical for them to use it? Similarly, some firms have been criticized for going too far—like waiting at a landfill for competitors' trash to find copies of confidential company reports. And the high-tech version of that occurs when computer "hackers" use the Internet to break into a competitor's computer network.

Beyond the moral issues, spying on competitors to obtain trade secrets is illegal. Damage awards can be huge. The courts ordered competing firms to pay Procter & Gamble about $125 million in damages for stealing secrets about its Duncan Hines soft cookies.[11]

Competition may vary from country to country

A firm that faces very stiff competition may find that the competitive environment—and the opportunities—are much better in another region or country. For instance, eight years of slow growth and deregulation made the Japanese market extremely competitive. So, the Iris Ohyama Company, a maker of plastic storage containers, started exporting to North America. Within three years, its sales to U.S. retailers like Staples were $60 million.[12]

The Economic Environment

The **economic and technological environment** affects the way firms—and the whole economy—use resources. We will treat the economic and technological environments separately to emphasize that the technological environment provides a *base* for the economic environment. Technical skills and equipment affect the way companies convert an economy's resources into output. The economic environment, on the other hand, is affected by the way all of the parts of a macro-economic system interact. This then affects such things as national income, economic growth, and inflation. The economic environment may vary from one country to another, but economies around the world are linked.

Economic conditions change rapidly

The economic environment can, and does, change quite rapidly. The effects can be far-reaching and require changes in marketing strategy.

Managers who compete in global markets need to be aware of how changes in the global economy will impact their strategies and opportunities.

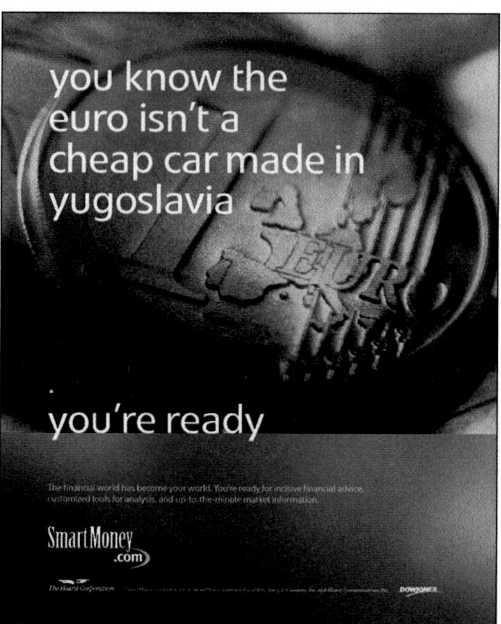

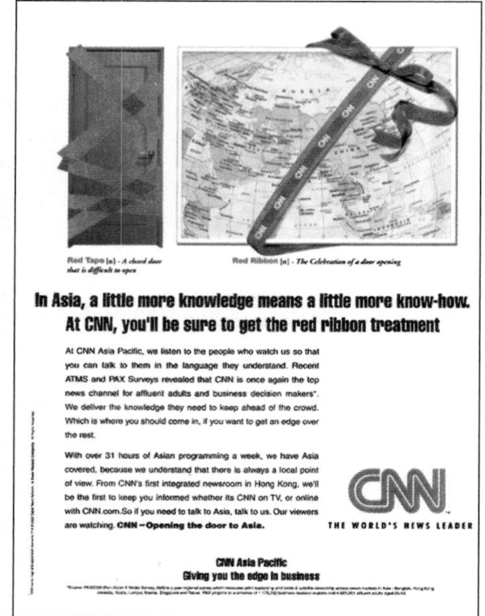

Even a well-planned marketing strategy may fail if a country or region goes through a rapid business decline. As consumers' incomes drop, they must shift their spending patterns. They may simply have to do without some products. In the late 1990s this happened across countries in Asia, and many businesses collapsed. You can see how quickly this happens by considering Thailand. In a few months, the buying power of Thai money (the bhat) was cut by half. Imagine how *your* life would change if you suddenly had half as much money.

Economic changes are not always this dramatic. Consider the cooling off of the U.S. economy in 2000. The growth of the economy leading up to that time created a strong job market and increased incomes. Purchases of luxuries trended up because of this "wealth effect." This trend changed when the economy turned, but for most products demand declined more gradually.

Interest rates and inflation affect buying

Changes in the economy are often accompanied by changes in the interest rate—the charge for borrowing money. Interest rates directly affect the total price borrowers must pay for products. So the interest rate affects when, and if, they will buy. This is an especially important factor in some business markets. But it also affects consumer purchases of homes, cars, and other items usually bought on credit.

Interest rates usually increase during periods of inflation, and inflation is a fact of life in many economies. In some Latin American countries, inflation has exceeded 400 percent a year in recent years. In contrast, recent U.S. levels—3 to 20 percent—seem low. Still, inflation must be considered in strategy planning. When costs are rising rapidly and there are no more cost-cutting measures to take, a marketing manager may have to increase prices.

The global economy is connected

The economies of the world are connected—and changes in one economy quickly affect others. One reason for this is that the amount of international trade is increasing—and it is affected by changes in and between economies. For example, International Harvester (IH) was very successful selling its earth-moving equipment in Asia when construction was booming. However, when the "Asian flu" hit, many customers could no longer make payments and IH faced big losses.

Changes in the *exchange rate*—how much one country's money is worth in another country's money—have an important effect on international trade. When the dollar is strong, it's worth more in foreign countries. This sounds good—but it makes U.S. products more expensive overseas and foreign products cheaper in the United States. New domestic competition arises as foreign products gain a competitive edge with lower prices.

Marketing managers must watch the economic environment carefully. In contrast to the cultural and social environment, economic conditions can move rapidly and require immediate strategy changes.[13]

The Technological Environment

Technology affects opportunities

Technology is the application of science to convert an economy's resources to output. Technology affects marketing in two basic ways: with new products and with new processes (ways of doing things). For example, advances in information technology make it possible for people in different parts of the world to communicate with satellite video-conferencing and to transmit complex design drawings over the Internet. Websites enable sophisticated e-commerce exchanges between remote firms. These process changes are accompanied by an exciting explosion of high-tech products—from genome-based medicines to cars that contact the police if they are stolen.

Technology transfer is rapid

New technologies have created important industries that didn't even exist a few years ago. Fifteen years ago AOL didn't exist. Now it's one of the best known brands in the world. With such big opportunities at stake, you can also see why there is such rapid transfer of technology from one part of the world to another. But technology transfer is not automatic. Someone—perhaps you—has to see the opportunity.

Internet technologies are reshaping marketing

Many of the big advances in business have come from early recognition of new ways to do things. There is perhaps no better example of this than the World Wide Web and the Internet. The **Internet** is a system for linking computers around the world. The idea of linking computers in a network is not new. Even so, the Internet expands the network concept to include any computer anywhere and it makes the exchange of information easy. As a result, this new technology is radically changing just about every aspect of marketing.

Consider the arena of promotion. The invention of TV changed marketing because it suddenly made it possible for a sponsor to broadcast a vivid message to millions of people at the same time. Now, the Internet makes it possible for that sponsor to select any of millions of messages and to simultaneously narrowcast any of them to millions of different individuals. It is just as easy for customers to request the information in the first place, or to respond electronically once they have it. Thus, the Internet's capability radically changes our ideas about how firms communicate with customers, and vice versa. Similarly, the Internet is creating totally different approaches to pricing. Airlines are now running online auctions of seats that might otherwise go unsold. To check out an online auction, go to www.ebay.com.

In hindsight, new approaches such as these seem obvious—given that the technology is available. But they are not obvious up front—unless you're really looking for them.[14]

Technology and ethical issues

Marketers often must help their firms decide what technological developments are ethically acceptable. For example, firms that operate on the Internet can track information about who "hits" the company web page and what website they came from. The firm can then sell this information to whoever wants to use it to send promotional e-mail. Yet uninvited e-mail is just another form of invasion of privacy.

Some attractive technological developments may be rejected because of their long-run effects on the environment. Aseptic drink boxes, for example, are convenient but difficult to recycle. In a case like this, what's good for the firm and some customers may not be good for the cultural and social environment or acceptable in the political and legal environment. Being close to the market should give marketers a better feel for current trends and help firms avoid serious mistakes.[15]

The Political Environment

The attitudes and reactions of people, social critics, and governments all affect the political environment. Consumers in the same country usually share a common political environment, but the political environment can also affect opportunities at a local or international level.

Nationalism can be limiting in international markets

Strong sentiments of **nationalism**—an emphasis on a country's interests before everything else—affect how macro-marketing systems work. They can affect how marketing managers work as well. Nationalistic feelings can reduce sales—or even block all marketing activity—in some international markets. For many years, Japan has made it difficult for outside firms to do business there—in spite of the fact that Japanese producers of cars, TVs, digital cameras, and other products have established profitable markets in the United States, Europe, and other parts of the world.

The "Buy American" policy in many government contracts and business purchases reflects this same attitude in the U.S. There is broad support for protecting U.S. producers—and jobs—from foreign competition.[16]

Regional groupings are becoming more important

Important dimensions of the political environment are likely to be similar among nations that have banded together to have common regional economic boundaries. The unification of Europe and free trade among the nations of North America are examples of this sort of regional grouping.

The unification of European markets

In the past, each country in Europe had its own unique trade rules and regulations. These differences made it difficult and expensive to move products from one country to the others. Now, the countries of the European Union (EU) are reducing conflicting laws, taxes, and other obstacles to trade within Europe. This is reducing costs and the prices European consumers pay. Even bigger changes may come if Britain decides to join other countries that have moved to the euro, a new unified money system for the EU.

Although Europe is becoming the largest unified market in the world, marketers will still encounter differences among European countries. What happened to Lands' End, the Wisconsin-based Internet and mail-order retailer, illustrates the issues. To better reach European consumers, Lands' End set up shop in England and Germany. As in the U.S., its website touted the unconditional lifetime guarantee that is a key part of its strategy. However, German consumer protection rules prohibited promotion of the guarantee; the Germans argued that the promotion was misleading (on the logic that the cost of the guarantee was "hidden" in higher prices that consumers would pay). German officials wanted this ban to apply even if the German consumer purchased the product from a Lands' End website in England. If quirky local rules like this are allowed to prevail, companies that want to use e-commerce to efficiently reach the whole European market will have to comply with different laws in every country. This could erode benefits that should come from more European unification.[17]

NAFTA is building trade cooperation

The international competition fostered by the moves to unify Europe provided impetus for the U.S., Mexico, and Canada to develop more cooperative trade

Adero wants marketers to keep in mind that a website that can attract prospects from all over the world won't be successful in turning them into customers if it ignores nationalism and cultural differences.

agreements. The **North American Free Trade Agreement (NAFTA)** lays out a plan to reshape the rules of trade among the U.S., Canada, and Mexico. NAFTA basically enlarges the free-trade pact that had already knocked down most barriers to U.S.–Canada trade, and over a 15-year period it will eliminate most such barriers with Mexico. It also establishes a forum for resolving future trade disputes.

The changes that result from NAFTA may ultimately be as significant as those in Europe. Talks are underway to explore the concept of expanding NAFTA to create a free-trade zone for 34 countries across North, South, and Central America.

Of course, removal of some economic and political barriers—whether across all of the Americas or Europe—will not eliminate the need to adjust strategies to reach submarkets of consumers. Centuries of cultural differences will not disappear overnight. Some may never disappear.[18]

Some dramatic changes in the political environment—like the fall of communism in Eastern Europe—happen fast and are hard to predict. Yet many important political changes—both within and across nations—evolve more gradually. The development of consumerism is a good example.

Consumerism is here—and basic

Consumerism is a social movement that seeks to increase the rights and powers of consumers. In the last 40 years, consumerism has emerged as a major political force. Although the consumer movement has spread to many different countries, it was born in America.

The basic goals of modern consumerism haven't changed much since 1962, when President Kennedy's "Consumer Bill of Rights" affirmed consumers' rights to safety, to be informed, to choose, and to be heard.

Thirty-five years ago, U.S. consumerism was much more visible. Consumers staged frequent boycotts and protest marches and attracted much media attention. Today, consumer groups provide information and work on special projects like product safety standards. Publications like *Consumer Reports* provide product comparisons and information on other consumer concerns.

Clearly, top management—and marketing managers—must continue to pay attention to consumer concerns. The old, production-oriented ways of doing things are no longer acceptable.[19]

The Legal Environment

Changes in the political environment often lead to changes in the legal environment and in the way existing laws are enforced. The legal environment sets the basic rules for how a business can operate in society. To illustrate the effects of the legal environment, we will discuss how it has evolved in the United States. However, laws often vary from one country to another.

Trying to encourage competition

American economic and legislative thinking is based on the idea that competition among many small firms helps the economy. Therefore, attempts by business to limit competition are considered contrary to the public interest.

Starting in 1890, Congress passed a series of antimonopoly laws. Exhibit 4-3 shows the names and dates of these laws. Although the specific focus of each law is different, in general they are all intended to encourage competition.

Antimonopoly law and marketing mix planning

In later chapters, we will specifically apply antimonopoly law to the four Ps. For now you should see in Exhibit 4-3 what kind of proof the government must have to get a conviction under each of the major laws. You should also know which of the four Ps are most affected by each law.

Prosecution is serious—you can go to jail

Businesses and *individual managers* are subject to both criminal and civil laws. Penalties for breaking civil laws are limited to blocking or forcing certain actions—along with fines. Where criminal law applies, jail sentences can be imposed. For example, several managers at Beech-Nut Nutrition Company were fined $100,000 each and sent to jail. In spite of ads claiming that Beech-Nut's apple juice was 100 percent natural, they tried to bolster profits by secretly using low-cost artificial ingredients.[20]

Consumer protection laws are not new

Although antimonopoly laws focus on protecting competition, the wording of the laws in Exhibit 4-3 has, over time, moved toward protecting consumers. Some consumer protections are also built into the English and U.S. common law systems. A seller has to tell the truth (if asked a direct question), meet contracts, and stand behind the firm's product (to some reasonable extent). Beyond this, it is expected that vigorous competition in the marketplace will protect consumers—*so long as they are careful.*

Yet focusing only on competition didn't protect consumers very well in some areas. So the government found it necessary to pass other laws. For example, various laws regulate packaging and labels, credit practices, and environmental issues. Usually, however, the laws focus on specific types of products.

Foods and drugs are controlled

Consumer protection laws in the United States go back to 1906 when Congress passed the Pure Food and Drug Act. Unsanitary meat-packing practices in the Chicago stockyards stirred consumer support for this act. Before the law, it was assumed that common law and the old warning "let the buyer beware" would take care of consumers.

Product safety is controlled

The Consumer Product Safety Act (of 1972), another important consumer protection law, set up the Consumer Product Safety Commission. This group has broad power to set safety standards and can impose penalties for failure to meet these standards. There is some question as to how much safety consumers really want—the commission found the bicycle the most hazardous product under its control!

But given that the commission has the power to *force* a product off the market—or require expensive recalls to correct problems—it is obvious that

Exhibit 4-3 Focus (mostly prohibitions) of Federal Antimonopoly Laws on the Four Ps

Law	Product	Place	Promotion	Price
Sherman Act (1890) Monopoly or conspiracy in restraint of trade	Monopoly or conspiracy to control a product	Monopoly or conspiracy to control distribution channels		Monopoly or conspiracy to fix or control prices
Clayton Act (1914) Substantially lessens competition	Forcing sale of some products with others—tying contracts	Exclusive dealing contracts (limiting buyers' sources of supply)		Price discrimination by manufacturers
Federal Trade Commission Act (1914) Unfair methods of competition		Unfair policies	Deceptive ads or selling practices	Deceptive pricing
Robinson-Patman Act (1936) Tends to injure competition		Prohibits paying allowances to "direct" buyers in lieu of middlemen costs (brokerage charges)	Prohibits "fake" advertising allowances or discrimination in help offered	Prohibits price discrimination on goods of "like grade and quality" without cost justification, and limits quantity discounts
Wheeler-Lea Amendment (1938) Unfair or deceptive practices	Deceptive packaging or branding		Deceptive ads or selling claims	Deceptive pricing
Antimerger Act (1950) Lessens competition	Buying competitors	Buying producers or distributors		
Magnuson-Moss Act (1975) Unreasonable practices	Product warranties			

safety must be considered by marketing managers. There is no more tragic example of this than the recent recalls of Firestone tires used as original equipment on Ford's Explorer SUV. Hundreds of consumers were killed or seriously injured in accidents. Consumer faith in the Firestone brand is so low that it may not survive—even if the company isn't bankrupted by the costs of the recalls and lawsuit damages.[21]

Internet

Internet Exercise The Consumer Product Safety Commission sometimes requires auto makers to issue recalls. However, not all consumers learn about the recalls. Go to the *Consumer Reports* website (www.consumerreports.org) and select the link for recalls. Then check to see if there has been a recall on a year and model of car or truck that is of interest to you (say, one owned by your family).

State and local laws vary

Besides federal legislation—which affects interstate commerce—marketers must be aware of state and local laws. There are state and city laws regulating minimum prices and the setting of prices, regulations for starting up a business (licenses, examinations, and even tax payments), and in some communities, regulations prohibiting certain activities—such as telephone selling or selling on Sundays or during evenings.

Consumerists and the law say "Let the seller beware"

The old rule about buyer–seller relations—*let the buyer beware*—has changed to *let the seller beware*. The current shift to proconsumer laws and court decisions suggests that lawmakers are more interested in protecting consumers. This may upset production-oriented managers. But times have changed—and managers must adapt to this new political and legal environment.[22]

The Cultural and Social Environment

The **cultural and social environment** affects how and why people live and behave as they do—which affects customer buying behavior and eventually the economic, political, and legal environment. Many variables make up the cultural and social environment. Some examples are the languages people speak, the type of education they have, their religious beliefs, what type of food they eat, the style of clothing and housing they have, and how they view work, marriage, and family.

Demographic data and trends tell us a lot about a society and its culture. Understanding the demographic dimensions is also important to marketing strategy planning, so it's useful to look at some key demographic patterns.

Where people are around the world

Exhibit 4-4 summarizes data for representative countries from different regions around the world. Even with a population of over 281 million, the United States makes up less than 5 percent of the total world population—which is now over 6 billion.

Although the size of a market is important, the population trend is also important. The world's population is growing fast, but that population growth varies dramatically from country to country. In general, less-developed countries experience the fastest rate of growth. The populations of Pakistan, Nicaragua, Nigeria, and Saudi Arabia are expected to double in 25 years or less. It will take about five times as long for the population of the U.S. to double. Population growth is even slower in Canada, Japan, and the European countries.[23] You can see why so many marketers who face slow growth in their domestic markets have turned to international markets where population and sales revenues continue to grow.

Information about demographic characteristics of consumer markets is readily available and can help marketing managers plan more successful strategies.

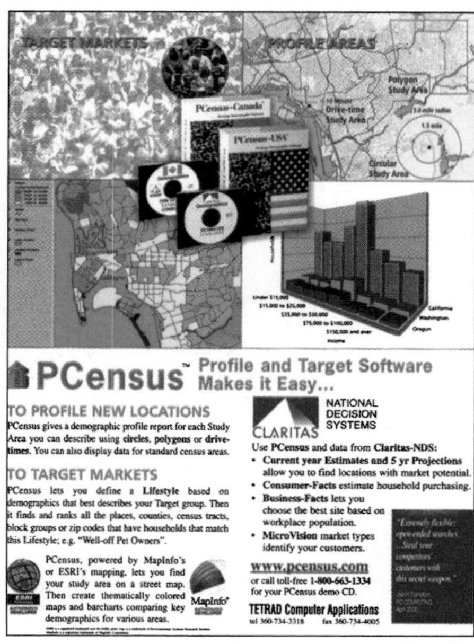

Exhibit 4-4 Demographic Dimensions for Representative Countries

Country	2000 Population (000s)	1990–2000 Annual Percent Population Growth	2000 Years for Population to Double	2000 Population Density (people/ square mile)	1999 Percent of Population In Urban Areas	1999 GNP (millions of $U.S.)	1999 GNP per Capita	1999 GDP (millions of $U.S.)	1999 Illiteracy Percent
Algeria	31,194	2.1	29	34	60	46,455	1,550	47,015	33
Argentina	36,955	1.2	62	35	90	277,882	7,600	281,942	3
Australia	19,165	1.2	110	6	85	380,791	20,050	389,691	0
Bangladesh	129,194	1.6	38	2,305	24	46,960	370	45,779	59
Brazil	172,860	1.3	45	52	81	742,819	4,420	760,345	15
Canada	31,278	1.2	178	8	77	591,354	19,320	612,049	0
China	1,261,832	1.0	79	342	32	980,246	780	991,203	17
Egypt	68,360	2.0	35	177	45	87,530	1,400	92,413	45
Ethiopia	64,117	2.8	29	150	17	6,578	100	6,534	63
Finland	5,167	0.4	433	40	67	122,874	23,780	126,130	0
France	59,330	0.4	204	279	75	1,427,160	23,480	1,410,260	0
Germany	82,797	0.4	no	596	87	2,079,230	25,350	2,081,200	0
Greece	10,602	0.4	no	208	60	124,010	11,770	123,934	3
India	1,014,004	1.8	39	789	28	442,233	450	459,765	44
Israel	5,842	2.6	45	766	91	104,081	17,450	125,031	4
Italy	57,634	0.2	no	497	67	1,135,990	19,710	1,149,960	2
Japan	126,550	0.2	462	870	79	4,078,920	32,230	4,395,080	0
Kuwait	1,974	−0.8	32	318	97	32,270	19,020	29,572	18
Mexico	100,350	1.7	36	132	74	428,794	4,400	474,951	9
Morocco	30,122	2.0	41	167	55	33,816	1,200	35,238	52
Mozambique	19,105	2.9	32	62	39	3,889	230	4,169	57
Nepal	24,702	2.5	28	421	12	5,091	220	4,904	60
Nicaragua	4,813	2.8	23	101	56	2,110	430	2,302	32
Nigeria	123,338	2.9	24	346	43	37,882	310	43,286	37
Norway	4,481	0.5	217	36	75	146,430	32,880	145,449	0
Pakistan	141,554	2.2	25	490	36	63,971	470	59,880	55
Romania	22,411	−0.2	no	244	56	34,188	1,520	33,750	2
Saudi Arabia	22,024	3.3	23	26	85	143,361	6,910	128,892	24
Singapore	4,152	3.2	84	16,714	100	95,429	29,610	84,945	8
Spain	39,997	0.2	6,931	202	77	551,560	14,000	562,245	2
Switzerland	7,262	0.6	315	448	68	273,061	38,350	260,299	0
Tanzania	35,306	3.0	24	97	32	8,027	240	8,777	25
Thailand	61,231	1.1	70	313	21	121,019	1,960	123,887	5
Uganda	23,318	3.1	24	251	14	6,786	320	6,349	34
United Kingdom	59,508	0.3	546	632	89	1,338,080	22,640	1,373,610	0
United States	281,422	1.0	120	77	77	8,350,960	30,600	8,708,870	0
Venezuela	23,543	2.0	34	69	87	86,963	3,670	103,918	8

The shift to urban and suburban areas

The extent to which a country's population is clustered around urban areas varies a lot. In the United Kingdom, Argentina, Australia, Israel, and Singapore, for example, more than 85 percent of people live in urban areas. See Exhibit 4-4. By contrast, in Ethiopia, Nepal, and Uganda less than 17 percent of the people live in major urban areas.

In the U.S., migration from rural to urban areas has been continuous. In 1920, about half the population lived in rural areas. By 1950, the number living on farms dropped to 15 percent. Now it is less than 2 percent. We have become an urban and suburban society.[24]

For many firms, the concentration of people in major cities simplifies Place and Promotion strategy decisions—especially for major cities in the wealthiest nations. Affluent, big-city consumers often have similar lifestyles and needs. Thus, many of the products successful in Toronto, New York, or Paris are likely to be successful in Caracas and Tokyo. The spread of the Internet, satellite TV, and other communication technologies will accelerate this trend.

However, keep in mind that many of the world's consumers—whether crowded in cities or widely spread in rural areas—live in deplorable conditions. These people have little hope of escaping the crush of poverty. They certainly have needs—but they don't have the income to do anything about the needs.

There's no market when there's no income

Profitable markets require income—as well as people. The amount of money people can spend affects the products they are likely to buy. When considering international markets, income is often one of the most important demographic dimensions.

There are a variety of different measures of national income. One widely used measure is **gross national product (GNP)**—the total market value of goods and services produced by a country's economy in a year. Gross domestic product (GDP) is a similar measure that often is used to describe the U.S. economy. The difference between the two measures is that GNP for a nation does not include income earned by foreigners who own resources in that nation. By contrast, the GDP does include foreign income. The measure you use can make a difference, especially when

This chart from Monsanto's annual report shows how the firm wants to build its presence in countries with large populations and projected strong economic growth. India is an example of a key target.

Countries/ World Areas	Real GDP* Levels (Percent of world total)	Projected GDP* Growth	Population (Percent of world total)	Monsanto Growth Opportunity
Canada, United States, European Union (EU), Australia and Japan	Roughly $17.5 trillion (80%)	Between 2% and 2.7%	817.4 million (18%)	Presence established; targeted growth expected near term
Mexico, Brazil, Argentina, India, China and Indonesia	More than $2.1 trillion (10%)	Ranges from more than 9% in China, to roughly 7% in Indonesia, 6% in India and 2% to 3% in Latin America	2,718.3 million (61%)	Presence not as established; near-term growth potential high
Developing Asian, non-EU European and Latin American countries (if not listed elsewhere)	More than $1.6 trillion (7%)	Ranges from 2% to 8%	345.7 million (8%)	Presence not as established; medium growth potential near term
Middle East, Pakistan, Africa and Philippines	Roughly $700 billion (3%)	Ranges from roughly 3.5% to 5.5%	559.6 million (13%)	Presence not established; growth potential longer term

* Gross Domestic Product

Computer Company Creates Legendary Success in China

China is the home of almost 1.3 billion people and accounts for about 25 percent of the world's population. Its population would be even larger, but about 20 years ago the communist government set a rule that most families could have only one child. Although the Chinese economy is changing rapidly, the gross national product per capita in China is only about 2.5 percent what it is in the U.S. and Japan. To put that in perspective, the average per capita income in China is less than $70 per month. Yet, not everyone in China is on the low end of the income distribution, and with so many people the demand for some goods and services is huge. In fact, China is becoming the world's fastest growing market for personal computers and mobile phones. By 2005 it is expected that one out of four mobile phones in the world will be in China. Similarly, although only about 1 out of every 175 Chinese currently has a personal computer, sales in China are already over 1.5 million units a year. It's easy to see why firms like Dell want to capture more of this market. But they are finding it difficult to compete with Legend, a Chinese computer maker. One reason is that managers at Legend understand their customers better. For example, unlike customers in more developed markets, most Chinese are first-time buyers who want a lot of hand-holding and service. So Legend developed easy-to-use software and Chinese language tutorials for its high-quality computers. Legend also installs speech recognition software; that helps because there are many more characters in the Chinese language than letters in the English alphabet (and keys on the typical keyboard). Legend also has a big advantage in reaching customers. It has over 1,800 local distributors and more than 50 of its own stores. They help overcome distribution problems caused by China's inefficient highway and rail system, and they support customers with good service and free training.[25]

www.mhhe.com/fourps

comparing countries with different patterns of international investment. For example, Ford has a factory in Thailand. The GDP measure for Thailand would include the profits from that factory because they were earned in that country. However, Ford is not a Thai firm and most of its profit will ultimately flow out of Thailand. Thus, the Thai GNP would not include those profits. You should see that using GDP income measures can give the impression that people in less-developed countries have more income than they really do. For that reason, we'll focus on comparisons based on GNP.

Exhibit 4-4 gives an estimate of GNP and GDP for each country listed. You can see that the more developed industrial nations—including the U.S., Japan, and Germany—have the biggest share of the world's GNP. This is why so much trade takes place between these countries—and why many firms see them as the more important markets.[26]

People can't spend what they don't have

GNP tells us about the income of a whole nation, but in a country with a large population that income must be spread over more people. GNP per person is a useful figure because it gives some idea of the income level of people in a country. Exhibit 4-4 shows, for example, that GNP per capita in the U.S. is quite high—about $30,600. Japan, Norway, Switzerland, and Singapore are among those with the highest GNP per capita. In general, markets like these offer the best potential for products that are targeted at consumers with higher income levels.

Many managers, however, see great potential—and less competition—where GNP per capita is low. For example, Mars is promoting its candy in Eastern Europe. As with many other firms, it hopes to establish a relationship with consumers now, and then turn brand loyalty into profitable growth as consumer incomes increase.

Reading, writing, and marketing problems

The ability of a country's people to read and write has a direct influence on the development of its economy—and on marketing strategy planning. The degree of literacy affects the way information is delivered—which in marketing means promotion. Unfortunately, only about three-fourths of the world's population can read and write. You may be surprised by the high illiteracy rates for some of the countries in Exhibit 4-4.[27]

Much segmenting may be required

This exhibit shows that marketers can learn a great deal about possible opportunities in different countries by studying available demographic data and trends. Many useful data are available. For example, *The World Factbook* is prepared by the Central Intelligence Agency (CIA) for the use of U.S. government officials, but it is available to everyone. It gives facts and statistics on each country in the world. It can be accessed at the CIA's website (www.odci.gov/cia/publications/factbook). The World Bank publishes *The World Development Indicators*, another excellent source for statistics on individual countries. It is available at the World Bank's website (www.worldbank.org/data/wdi). The International Programs Center of the U.S. Census Bureau also publishes an analysis on world population and related topics called *World Population Profile*. You can also access useful statistics for individual countries at the Census Bureau's website (www.census.gov/ipc).

Internet

Internet Exercise Visit the website for the CIA's *World Factbook* (www.odci.gov/cia/publications/factbook) and compare the profile data for Canada and Australia. How are they similar and how are they different?

After finding some countries or regions of possible interest (and eliminating unattractive ones), much more segmenting may be required. To illustrate how useful demographic dimensions can be in this effort, we will consider specific characteristics of the U.S. market in some detail. For additional data on the U.S. market, you can go to the Census Bureau's website (www.census.gov). Similar ideas apply to other markets around the world.

The U.S. population is shifting

We've said that the U.S. population is not growing as fast as in some other countries, but Exhibit 4-5 shows that population growth varies a lot in different regions of the country. The states with the darkest shading are growing at the fastest rate. Note that the greatest growth is in the West—in states such as Nevada, Arizona, Idaho, Utah, and Colorado. Growth continued in the Sun Belt states of the South as well, with Georgia leading the way with 26 percent, and other Sun Belt states like Florida, Texas, North Carolina, and Tennessee growing rapidly.[28]

These different rates of growth are especially important to marketers. Sudden growth in one area may create a demand for many new shopping centers—while retailers in declining areas face tougher competition for a smaller number of customers.

The mobile ones are an attractive market

As these shifts in population suggest, people move, stay awhile, and then move again. In fact, about 16 percent of Americans move each year. Although about 6 out of 10 moves are within the same county, both the local and long-distance mobiles are important market segments. Many market-oriented decisions have to be made fairly quickly after a move. Alert marketers try to locate these potential customers early—to inform them of offerings before they make their purchase decisions. Retail chains, "national" brands, and franchised services available in different areas have a competitive advantage with mobiles. The customer who moves to a new town may find the familiar CVS sign down the street and never even try its local competitors.[29]

Local political boundaries don't define market areas

Marketers are more interested in the size of homogeneous *marketing* areas than in the number of people within political boundaries of a city or county. To meet this need, the U.S. Census Bureau has developed a separate population classification based on metropolitan statistical areas. Many data are reported on the characteristics of people in these areas. The technical definition of these areas has changed over time. But basically a **Metropolitan Statistical Area (MSA)** is an integrated economic and social unit with a large population nucleus. Generally, an MSA

Exhibit 4-5 2000 Population (in thousands) and Percent Change in Population by State, 1990–2000

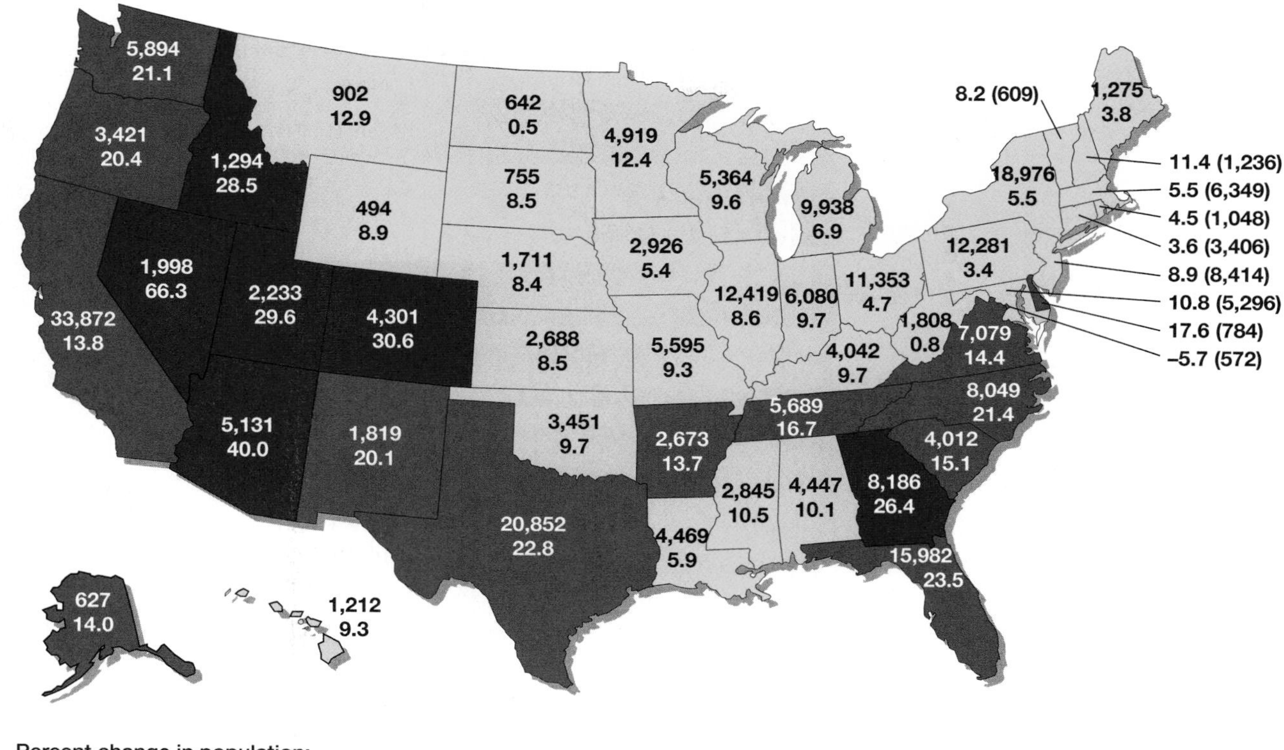

centers on one city or urbanized area of 50,000 or more inhabitants and includes bordering urban areas.

The largest MSAs—basically those with a population of more than a million—are called Consolidated Metropolitan Statistical Areas. Over three-fourths of all Americans live in MSAs and almost 40 percent live in the 18 largest CMSAs. More detailed data are available for areas within these sprawling, giant urban areas.

Big targets are attractive—but very competitive

Some national marketers sell only in these metro areas because having so many customers packed into a small area can simplify the marketing effort. They can use fewer middlemen and still offer products conveniently. One or two local advertising media—a city newspaper or TV station—can reach most residents. If a sales force is needed, it will incur less travel time and expense because people are closer together.

Metro areas are also attractive markets because they offer greater sales potential than their large population alone suggests. On the other hand, competition for consumer dollars is usually stiff in an MSA.[30]

The graying of America

Another important dimension of U.S. society is the age distribution. Because the U.S. population is growing slowly, the average age is rising. In 1970, the average age of the population was 28—but by the year 2000 the average age jumped to about 36.

Stated another way, the percentage of the population in different age groups is changing. Exhibit 4-6 shows the number of people in different age groups in 1990 and 2000—and how the size of these groups will look in 2010. Note the big increases in the 45–64 age group from 1990 to 2000 and also 2000 to 2010.

The major reason for this change is that the post–World War II baby boom produced about one-fourth of the present U.S. population. Some of the effects of this

Exhibit 4-6
Population Distribution (and percent growth rate) by Age Groups for Different 10-Year Periods

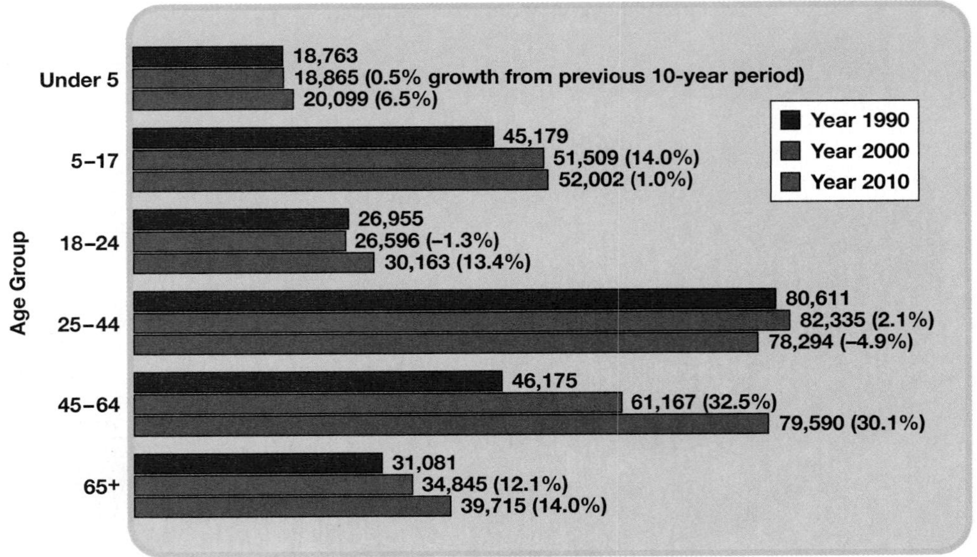

big market are very apparent. For example, recording industry sales exploded—to the beat of rock and roll music and the Beatles—as the baby boom group moved into their record-buying teens. Soon after, colleges added facilities and faculty to handle the surge—then had to cope with excess capacity and loss of revenue when the student-age population dwindled. To relieve financial strain many colleges now add special courses and programs for adults to attract the now-aging baby boom students. On the other hand, the fitness industry and food producers who offer low-calorie foods are reaping the benefit of a middle-aged "bulge" in the population.

Medical advances help people live longer and are also adding to the proportion of the population in the **senior citizen** group—people aged 65 and over. Note from Exhibit 4-6 that the over-65 age group will grow another 14 percent by 2010. Even more dramatic, by 2030 the over-65 group will double in size and they will be almost 20 percent of the total U.S. population. This ongoing growth creates new opportunities for such industries as tourism, health care, and financial services.[31]

The teen cycle is starting again

While society—and many marketers—has been fixated on the aging baby boomers, the ranks of teenagers have started to grow again. This is in part reflected in the 14.0 percent growth of the 5–17 age group between 1990 and 2000 and the 13.4 percent growth rate of the 18–24 age group in this decade (see Exhibit 4-6). But the coming changes are even bigger than this suggests. For 15 years, there was a steady decline in the number of teenagers. Now that has reversed. Between 1995 and 2005, the teenage group will grow at close to twice the rate of the overall population. By the time the number of teens peaks in 2010, the size of this group will top the baby boom–fueled teen explosion of the 1970s. In 2010, there will be over 35 million U.S. teens—and along the way a new teen-oriented culture will reshape society and markets. However, marketers who simultaneously try to appeal to aging baby boomers and to teens may find themselves right in the middle of a real clash of cultures.[32]

Changes come slowly

The demographic data we've been reviewing show that changes in basic cultural values and social attitudes come slowly. As a result, an individual firm can't hope to encourage big changes in the short run. Instead, it should identify current attitudes and work within these constraints—as it seeks new and better opportunities.[33]

Exhibit 4-7 An Example of Product-Market Screening Criteria for a Small Retail and Wholesale Distributor ($10 million annual sales)

1. Quantitative criteria
   a. Increase sales by $1,500,000 per year for the next five years.
   b. Earn ROI of at least 25 percent before taxes on new ventures.
   c. Break even within one year on new ventures.
   d. Opportunity must be large enough to justify interest (to help meet objectives) but small enough so company can handle with the resources available.
   e. Several opportunities should be pursued to reach the objectives—to spread the risks.

2. Qualitative criteria
   a. Nature of business preferred.
      (1) Should take advantage of our online Internet order system and website promotion.
      (2) New goods and services for present customers to strengthen relationships and revenue.
      (3) "Quality" products that do not cannibalize sales of current products.
      (4) Competition should be weak and opportunity should be hard to copy for several years.
      (5) There should be strongly felt (even unsatisfied) needs—to reduce promotion costs and permit "high" prices.
   b. Constraints.
      (1) Nature of businesses to exclude.
         (a) Manufacturing.
         (b) Any requiring large fixed capital investments.
         (c) Any requiring many support people who must be "good" all the time and would require much supervision.
      (2) Geographic.
         (a) United States, Mexico, and Canada only.
      (3) General.
         (a) Make use of current strengths.
         (b) Attractiveness of market should be reinforced by more than one of the following basic trends: technological, demographic, social, economic, political.
         (c) Market should not be bucking any basic trends.

Using Screening Criteria to Narrow Down to Strategies

Developing and applying screening criteria

After you analyze the firm's resources (for strengths and weaknesses), the environmental trends the firm faces, and the objectives of top management, you merge them all into a set of product-market screening criteria. These criteria should include both quantitative and qualitative components. The quantitative components summarize the firm's objectives: sales, profit, and return on investment (ROI) targets. (Note: ROI analysis is discussed briefly in Appendix B, which comes after Chapter 18.) The qualitative components summarize what kinds of businesses the firm wants to be in, what businesses it wants to exclude, what weaknesses it should avoid, and what resources (strengths) and trends it should build on.[34]

Developing screening criteria is difficult but worth the effort. They summarize in one place what the firm wants to accomplish. When a manager can explain the specific criteria that are relevant to selecting (or screening out) an opportunity, others can understand the manager's logic. Thus, marketing decisions are not just made or accepted based on intuition and gut feel.

The criteria should be realistic—that is, they should be achievable. Opportunities that pass the screen should be able to be turned into strategies that the firm can implement with the resources it has. For example, Exhibit 4-7 illustrates some product-market screening criteria for a small retail and wholesale distributor.

Whole plans should be evaluated

You need to forecast the probable results of implementing a marketing strategy to apply the quantitative part of the screening criteria because only implemented plans generate sales, profits, and return on investment (ROI). For a rough screening, you only need to estimate the likely results of implementing each opportunity

Exhibit 4-8
Expected Sales and Cost Curves of Two Strategies over Five-Year Planning Periods

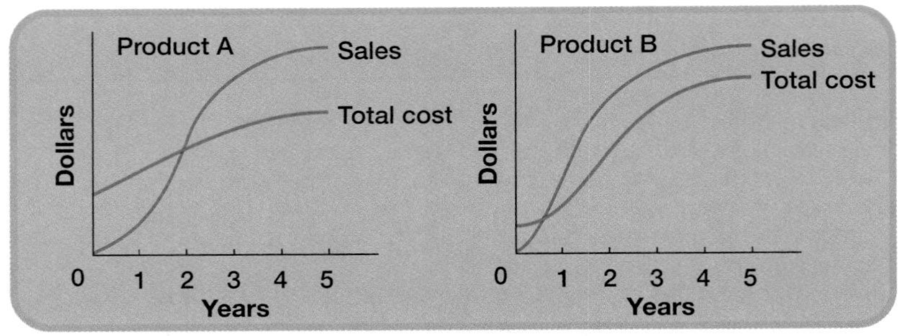

over a logical planning period. If a product's life is likely to be three years, for example, a good strategy may not produce profitable results for 6 to 12 months. But evaluated over the projected three-year life, the product may look like a winner. When evaluating the potential of possible opportunities (product-market strategies), it is important to evaluate similar things—that is, *whole* plans.

Total profit approach can help evaluate possible plans

Note that managers can evaluate different marketing plans at the same time. Exhibit 4-8 compares a much improved product and product concept (Product A) with a "me-too" product (Product B) for the same target market. In the short run, the me-too product will make a profit sooner and might look like the better choice—if managers consider only one year's results. The improved product, on the other hand, will take a good deal of pioneering—but over its five-year life will be much more profitable.

Planning Grids Help Evaluate a Portfolio of Opportunities

When a firm has many possibilities to evaluate, it usually has to compare quite different ones. This problem is easier to handle with graphical approaches—such as the nine-box strategic planning grid developed by General Electric and used by many other companies. Such grids can help evaluate a firm's whole portfolio of strategic plans or businesses.

General Electric looks for green positions

General Electric's strategic planning grid—see Exhibit 4-9—forces company managers to make three-part judgments (high, medium, and low) about the business strengths and industry attractiveness of all proposed or existing product-market plans. As you can see from Exhibit 4-9, this approach helps a manager organize information about the company's marketing environments (discussed earlier in this chapter) along with information about its strategy and translate it into relevant screening criteria.

GE feels opportunities that fall into the green boxes in the upper left-hand corner of the grid are its best growth opportunities. Managers give these opportunities high marks on both industry attractiveness and business strengths. The red boxes in the lower right-hand corner of the grid, on the other hand, suggest a no-growth policy. Existing red businesses may continue to generate earnings, but they no longer deserve much investment. Yellow businesses are borderline cases—they can go either way. GE may continue to support an existing yellow business but will probably reject a proposal for a new one. It simply wouldn't look good enough on the relevant screening criteria.

GE's "stoplight" evaluation method is a subjective, multiple-factor approach. It avoids the traps and possible errors of trying to use oversimplified, single-number screening criteria—like ROI or market share. Instead, top managers review detailed written summaries of many different screening criteria that help them

Exhibit 4-9
General Electric's Strategic Planning Grid

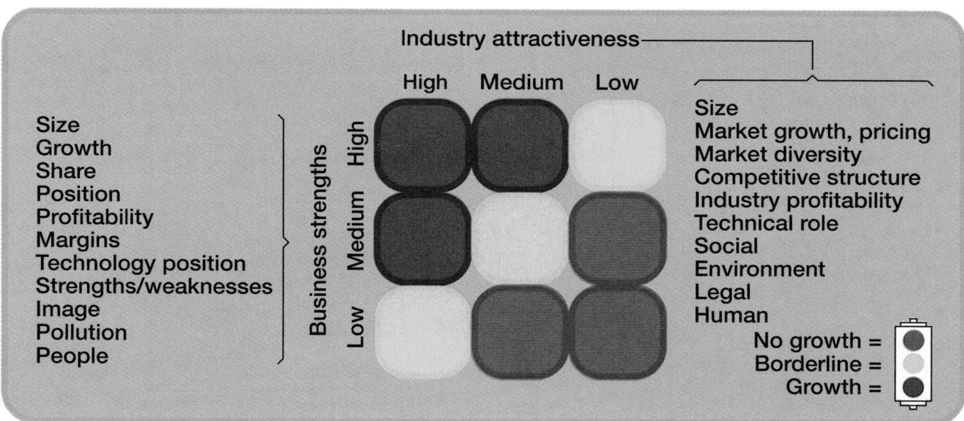

make summary judgments. This approach helps everyone understand why the company supports some new opportunities and not others.[35]

General Electric considers factors that reflect its objectives. Another firm might modify the evaluation to emphasize other screening criteria—depending on its objectives and the type of product-market plans it is considering.

Multiproduct Firms Have a Difficult Strategy Planning Job

Multiproduct firms, like General Electric, obviously have a more difficult strategic planning job than firms with only a few products or product lines aimed at the same target market. Multiproduct firms have to develop strategic plans for very different businesses. And they have to balance plans and resources so the whole company reaches its objectives. This means they must approve plans that make sense for the whole company—even if it means getting needed resources by milking some businesses and eliminating others.

Details on how to manage a complicated multiproduct firm are beyond our scope. But you should be aware that the principles in this text are applicable—they just have to be extended. For example, some multiproduct firms form strategic business units (SBUs) to improve their operations.

Strategic business units many help

A **strategic business unit (SBU)** is an organizational unit (within a larger company) that focuses on some product-markets and is treated as a separate profit center. By forming SBUs, a company formally acknowledges its very different activities. One SBU of Sara Lee, for example, produces baked goods for consumers and restaurants—another produces and markets Hanes brand T-shirts and underwear.

Some SBUs grow rapidly and require a great deal of attention and resources. Others produce only average profits and should be *milked*—that is, allowed to generate cash for the businesses with more potential. Product lines with poor market position, low profits, and poor growth prospects should be dropped or sold.

Evaluating Opportunities in International Markets

Evaluate the risks

The approaches we've discussed so far apply to international markets just as they do to domestic ones. But in international markets it is often harder to fully understand the marketing environment variables. This may make it harder to see the risks

Some products, like industrial motors made by Baldor, are used the same way all over the world. Other products are much more sensitive to cultural differences.

involved in particular opportunities. Some countries are politically unstable; their governments and constitutions come and go. An investment safe under one government might become a takeover target under another.

To reduce the risk of missing some basic variable that may help screen out a risky opportunity, marketing managers sometimes need a detailed analysis of the market environment they are considering entering. Such an analysis can reveal facts about an unfamiliar market that a manager in a distant country might otherwise overlook. Further, a local citizen who knows the marketing environment may be able to identify an "obvious" problem ignored even in a careful analysis. Thus, it is very useful for the analysis to include inputs from locals—perhaps cooperative middlemen.[36]

Risks vary with environmental sensitivity

The farther you go from familiar territory, the greater the risk of making big mistakes. But not all products, or marketing mixes, involve the same risk. Think of the risks as running along a "continuum of environmental sensitivity." See Exhibit 4-10.

Some products are relatively insensitive to the economic and cultural environment they're placed in. These products may be accepted as is—or they may require just a little adaptation to make them suitable for local use. Most industrial products are near the insensitive end of this continuum.

At the other end of the continuum, we find highly sensitive products that may be difficult or impossible to adapt to all international situations. Consumer products closely linked to other social or cultural variables are at this end. For example, some cultures view dieting as unhealthy; that explains why products like Diet Pepsi that are popular in the United States have done poorly there.

This continuum helps explain why many of the early successes in international marketing were basic commodities such as gasoline, soap, transportation vehicles, mining equipment, and agricultural machinery. It also helps explain why some consumer products firms have been successful with basically the same promotion and products in different parts of the globe.

Yet some managers don't understand the reason for these successes. They think they can develop a global marketing mix for just about *any* product. They fail to see that firms producing and/or selling products near the sensitive end of the continuum should carefully analyze how their products will be seen and used in new environments—and plan their strategies accordingly.[37]

Exhibit 4-10
Continuum of Environmental Sensitivity

Insensitive		Sensitive
Industrial products	Basic commodity-type consumer products	Consumer products that are linked to cultural variables

What if risks are still hard to judge?

If the risks of an international opportunity are hard to judge, it may be wise to look first for opportunities that involve exporting. This gives managers a chance to build experience, know-how, and confidence over time. Then the firm will be in a better position to judge the prospects and risks of taking further steps.

Conclusion

Businesses need innovative strategy planning to survive in our increasingly competitive markets. In this chapter, we discussed the variables that shape the environment of marketing strategy planning and how they may affect opportunities. First we looked at how the firm's own resources and objectives may help guide or limit the search for opportunities. Then, we went on to look at the need to understand competition and how to do a competitive analysis. Then, we shifted our focus to the external market environments. They are important because changes in these environments present new opportunities, as well as problems, that a marketing manager must deal with in marketing strategy planning.

The economic environment—including chances of recessions or inflation—also affects the choice of strategies. And the marketer must try to anticipate, understand, and deal with these changes—as well as changes in the technology underlying the economic environment.

The marketing manager must also be aware of legal restrictions and be sensitive to changing political climates. The acceptance of consumerism has already forced many changes.

The cultural and social environment affects how people behave and what marketing strategies will be successful.

Developing good marketing strategies within all these environments isn't easy. You can see that marketing management is a challenging job that requires integration of information from many disciplines.

Eventually, managers need procedures for screening and evaluating opportunities. We explained an approach for developing qualitative and quantitative screening criteria—from an analysis of the strengths and weaknesses of the company's resources, the environmental trends it faces, and top management's objectives. We also discussed ways for evaluating and managing quite different opportunities—using the GE strategic planning grid and SBUs.

Now we can go on in the rest of the book to discuss how to turn opportunities into profitable marketing plans and programs.

Questions and Problems

1. Do you think it makes sense for a firm to base its mission statement on the type of product it produces? For example, would it be good for a division that produces electric motors to have as its mission. "We want to make the best (from our customers' point of view) electric motors available anywhere in the world"?
2. Explain how a firm's objectives may affect its search for opportunities.
3. Specifically, how would various company objectives affect the development of a marketing mix for a new type of Internet browser software? If this company were just being formed by a former programmer with limited financial resources, list the objectives the programmer might have. Then discuss how they would affect the development of the programmer's marketing strategy.

4. Explain how a firm's resources may limit its search for opportunities. Cite a specific example for a specific resource.
5. In your own words, explain how a marketing manager might use a competitor analysis to avoid situations that involve head-on competition.
6. The owner of a small hardware store—the only one in a medium-sized town in the mountains—has just learned that a large home improvement chain plans to open a new store nearby. How difficult will it be for the owner to plan for this new competitive threat? Explain your answer.
7. Discuss the probable impact on your hometown if a major breakthrough in air transportation allowed foreign producers to ship into any U.S. market for about the same transportation cost that domestic producers incur.
8. Will the elimination of trade barriers between countries in Europe eliminate the need to consider submarkets of European consumers? Why or why not?
9. What and who is the U.S. government attempting to protect in its effort to preserve and regulate competition?
10. For each of the *major* laws discussed in the text, indicate whether in the long run the law will promote or restrict competition (see Exhibit 4-3). As a consumer without any financial interest in business, what is your reaction to each of these laws?
11. Drawing on data in Exhibit 4-4, do you think that Romania would be an attractive market for a firm that produces home appliances? What about Finland? Discuss your reasons.
12. Discuss how the worldwide trend toward urbanization is affecting opportunities for international marketing.
13. Discuss how slower population growth will affect businesses in your local community.
14. Discuss the impact of the new teen cycle on marketing strategy planning in the U.S.
15. Name three specific examples of firms that developed a marketing mix to appeal to senior citizens. Name three examples of firms that developed a marketing mix to appeal to teenagers.
16. Explain the components of product-market screening criteria that can be used to evaluate opportunities.

Suggested Cases

2. Healthy Foods, Inc.
6. Three Rivers Steel Company
18. Outdoor World, Inc.
27. Expert Nursing Services, Inc. (ENS)

Computer-Aided Problem

4. Competitor Analysis

Mediquip, Inc., produces medical equipment and uses its own sales force to sell the equipment to hospitals. Recently, several hospitals have asked Mediquip to develop a laser-beam "scalpel" for eye surgery. Mediquip has the needed resources, and 200 hospitals will probably buy the equipment. But Mediquip managers have heard that Laser Technologies—another quality producer—is thinking of competing for the same business. Mediquip has other good opportunities it could pursue—so it wants to see if it would have a competitive advantage over Laser Tech.

Mediquip and Laser Tech are similar in many ways, but there are important differences. Laser Technologies already produces key parts that are needed for the new laser product—so its production costs would be lower. It would cost Mediquip more to design the product—and getting parts from outside suppliers would result in higher production costs.

On the other hand, Mediquip has marketing strengths. It already has a good reputation with hospitals—and its sales force calls on only hospitals. Mediquip thinks that each of its current sales reps could spend some time selling the new product and that it could adjust sales territories so only four more sales reps would be needed for good coverage in the market. In contrast, Laser Tech's sales reps call on only industrial customers, so it would have to add 14 reps to cover the hospitals.

Hospitals have budget pressures—so the supplier with the lowest price is likely to get a larger share of the business. But Mediquip knows that either supplier's price will be set high enough to cover the added costs of designing, producing, and selling the new product—and leave something for profit.

Mediquip gathers information about its own likely costs and can estimate Laser Tech's costs from industry studies and Laser Tech's annual report. Mediquip has set up a spreadsheet to evaluate the proposed new product.

a. *The initial spreadsheet results are based on the assumption that Mediquip and Laser Tech will split the business 50/50. If Mediquip can win at least 50 percent of the market, does Mediquip have a competitive advantage over Laser Tech? Explain.*
b. *Because of economies of scale, both suppliers' average cost per machine will vary depending on the quantity sold. If Mediquip had only 45 percent of the market and Laser Tech 55 percent, how would their costs (average total cost per machine) compare? What if Mediquip had 55 percent of the market and Laser Tech only 45 percent? What conclusion do you draw from these analyses?*
c. *It is possible that Laser Tech may not enter the market. If Mediquip has 100 percent of the market, and quantity purchases from its suppliers will reduce the cost of producing one unit to $6,500, what price would cover all its costs and contribute $1,125 to profit for every machine sold? What does this suggest about the desirability of finding your own unsatisfied target markets? Explain.*

For additional questions related to this problem, see Exercise 4-4 in the *Learning Aid for Use with Essentials of Marketing*, 9th edition.

Chapter Five

Final Consumers and Their Buying Behavior

When You Finish This Chapter, You Should

1. Know how income affects consumer behavior and spending patterns.

2. Understand the economic-buyer model of buyer behavior.

3. Understand how psychological variables affect an individual's buying behavior.

4. Understand how social influences affect an individual's and household's buying behavior.

5. See why the purchase situation has an effect on consumer behavior.

6. Know how consumers use problem-solving processes.

7. Have some feel for how a consumer handles all the behavioral variables and incoming stimuli.

8. Understand the important new terms (shown in red).

In the 1970s, yogurt was popular in Europe but for the most part unknown in the U.S. culture. Most consumers were not aware of it, had never tried it, and didn't know if they would like it. All of that changed when Dannon began to promote yogurt in the U.S. Sales grew slowly at first, but that changed in the 1980s as more adults became interested in healthy eating. For lots of people, yogurt was an economical lunch that tasted good and saved time. It didn't require preparation or cleanup, and it could be eaten almost anywhere. All you needed was a plastic spoon.

By the 1990s, many brands of yogurt were on the market. Most consumers couldn't tell the difference between brands. When it was time to buy, they just picked up their routine brand or perhaps whatever was on sale. Growth in the yogurt category seemed to be pretty much tapped out. But by carefully studying consumer behavior, Ian Friendly and others on his marketing team at Yoplait changed all of

place price promotion produ

Splash and Watermelon Meltdown.

Go-Gurt's introductory ads were placed on media like Nickelodeon so they'd reach kids directly. Then it was up to them to ask their parents to buy Go-Gurt at the store. The ads positioned Go-Gurt not just as a food but as a lifestyle accessory for kids. To build awareness of the benefits of the package and interest in the product, the ads conveyed the idea that it was OK to play with your food.

To follow up on the awareness and interest generated by the ads, a heavy sampling program played a crucial role in building product trial. Kids on skateboards and scooters passed out the samples from backpacks at festivals, theme parks, soccer games, and local parks.

Go-Gurt has been such a success that Yoplait has given adult yogurt eaters something else to think about when they visit the yogurt aisle—four flavors of a comparable yogurt in a tube, Yoplait Expresse.[1]

that. Their marketing plan for a new product, Go-Gurt, racked up $100 million in sales in the first year. Much of that represented new demand in the yogurt category because the percentage of kids eating yogurt doubled. That was no accident. They created Go-Gurt to have kid appeal.

Kids need nutritious food, but research showed that what they want in snacks is great taste, convenience, and fun. Go-Gurt made on-the-go snacking more convenient by putting the yogurt in a 9-inch-long, one-handed squeeze tube. Kids didn't have a positive attitude about standard yogurt flavors, so the foil-embossed Go-Gurt tube was filled with flavors kids could learn to love—like Strawberry

Consumer Behavior—Why Do They Buy What They Buy?

Our Go-Gurt example shows that many variables can influence consumers and their buying behavior. Specific consumer behaviors vary a great deal for different products and from one target market to the next. In today's global markets, the variations are countless. That makes it impractical to try to catalog all the detailed possibilities for every different market situation. But there are *general* behavioral principles—frameworks—that marketing managers can apply to learn more about their specific target markets. In this chapter, our approach focuses on developing your skill in working with these frameworks by exploring thinking from economics, psychology, sociology, and the other behavioral disciplines.

Consumer Spending Patterns Are Related to Income

Markets are made up of people with money to spend. So consumer spending patterns are related to income. Consumer budget studies show that most consumers spend their incomes as part of family or household units. So, our brief discussion will concern how families or households spend their income.

Discretionary income is elusive

Most families spend a good portion of their income on such "necessities" as food, rent or house payments, car and home furnishings payments, and insurance. A family's purchase of "luxuries" comes from **discretionary income**—what is left of income after paying taxes and paying for necessities.

Discretionary income is an elusive concept because the definition of necessities varies from family to family and over time. It depends on what they think is necessary for their lifestyle. A cable TV service might be purchased out of discretionary income by a lower-income family but be considered a necessity by a higher-income family.[2]

Marketers are very aware that spending varies with income and other demographic dimensions.

Exhibit 5-1
Percent of Total Income Going to Different Income Groups in 1999

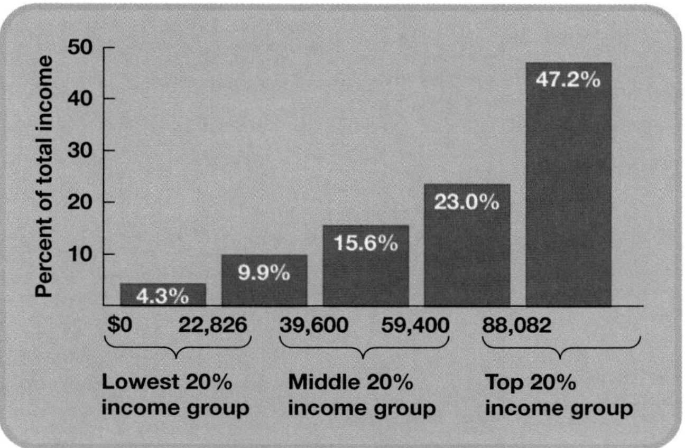

The higher-income groups receive a big share

Higher-income groups in the U.S. receive a very large share of total income, as you can see in Exhibit 5-1, which divides all families into five equal-sized groups—from lowest income to highest. Note that although the median income of U.S. families in 1999 was about $48,950, the top 20 percent of the families—those with incomes over $88,082—received over 47 percent of the total income. This gave them extra buying power, especially for luxury items like cellular phones, memberships in country clubs, and yachts. Well-to-do families with incomes over $155,040—the top 5 percent nationally—got more than 20 percent of the total income.

At the lower end of the scale, over 14 million families had less than $22,826 income. They account for 20 percent of all families but receive only 4.3 percent of total income. Even this low-income group is an attractive market for some basic commodities, especially food and clothing—even though almost half of them live below the poverty level of $17,029 for a family of four. These consumers may receive food stamps, medicare, and public housing, which increases their buying power.[3]

Basic data on consumer income and spending patterns can help forecast general *trends* in consumer buying. But when many firms sell similar products, basics aren't much help in predicting which *specific* products and brands consumers will purchase. That requires a better understanding of the buying process.

The Behavioral Sciences Help You Understand the Buying Process

Economic needs affect most buying decisions

Most economists assume that consumers are **economic buyers**—people who know all the facts and logically compare choices in terms of cost and value received to get the greatest satisfaction from spending their time and money.

This view assumes that economic needs guide most consumer behavior. **Economic needs** are concerned with making the best use of a consumer's time and money—as the consumer judges it. Some consumers look for the lowest price. Others will pay extra for convenience. And others may weigh price and quality for the best value. Some economic needs are economy of purchase or use, convenience, efficiency in operation or use, dependability in use, and improvement of earnings.

Clearly, marketing managers must be alert to new ways to appeal to economic needs. Most consumers appreciate firms that offer them improved value for the money they spend. But improved value does not just mean offering lower and lower prices. For example, many consumers face a "poverty of time." Carefully planned

Economic needs affect many buying decisions, but for some purchases the behavioral influences on a consumer are more important.

Place decisions can make it easier and faster for customers to make a purchase. And products designed to work better, require less service, or last longer are worth more to the consumer.

The economic value that a purchase offers a customer is an important factor in many purchase decisions. But most buyer behavior is not as simple as the economic-buyer model suggests. A product that one person sees as a good value—and is eager to buy—is of no interest to someone else. So we can't expect to understand buying behavior without taking a broader view.

How we will view consumer behavior

Many behavioral dimensions influence consumers. Let's try to combine these dimensions into a model of how consumers make decisions. Exhibit 5-2 shows that psychological variables, social influences, and the purchase situation all affect a person's buying behavior. We'll discuss these topics in the next few pages. Then we'll expand the model to include the consumer problem-solving process.

Exhibit 5-2
A Model of Buyer Behavior

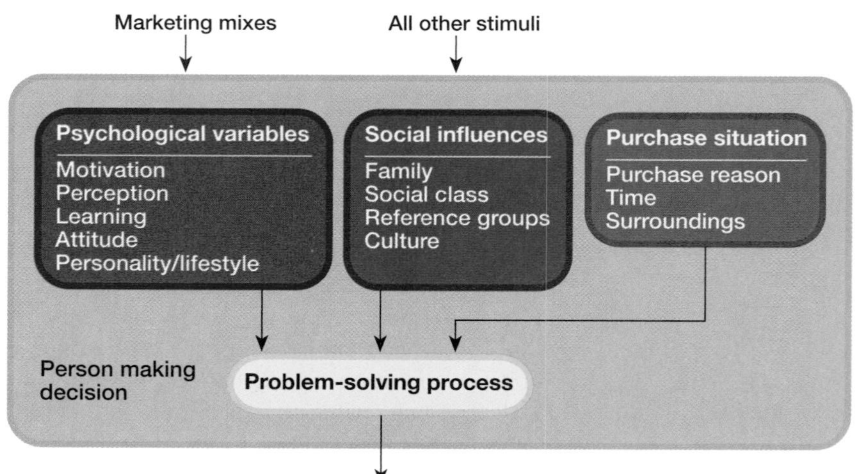

Psychological Influences within an Individual

Needs motivate consumers

Everybody is motivated by needs and wants. **Needs** are the basic forces that motivate a person to do something. Some needs involve a person's physical well-being, others the individual's self-view and relationship with others. Needs are more basic than wants. **Wants** are "needs" that are learned during a person's life. For example, everyone needs water or some kind of liquid, but some people also have learned to want Clearly Canadian's raspberry-flavored sparkling water on the rocks.

When a need is not satisfied, it may lead to a drive. The need for liquid, for example, leads to a thirst drive. A **drive** is a strong stimulus that encourages action to reduce a need. Drives are internal—they are the reasons behind certain behavior patterns. In marketing, a product purchase results from a drive to satisfy some need.

Some critics imply that marketers can somehow manipulate consumers to buy products against their will. But trying to get consumers to act against their will is a waste of time. Instead, a good marketing manager studies what consumer drives, needs, and wants already exist and how they can be satisfied better.

Consumers seek benefits to meet needs

We're all a bundle of needs and wants. Exhibit 5-3 lists some important needs that might motivate a person to some action. This list, of course, is not complete. But thinking about such needs can help you see what *benefits* consumers might seek from a marketing mix.

When a marketing manager defines a product-market, the needs may be quite specific. For example, the food need might be as specific as wanting a Domino's thick-crust pepperoni pizza—delivered to your door hot and ready to eat.

Several needs at the same time

Some psychologists argue that a person may have several reasons for buying—at the same time. Maslow is well known for his five-level hierarchy of needs. We will discuss a similar four-level hierarchy that is easier to apply to consumer behavior. Exhibit 5-4 illustrates the four levels along with an advertising slogan showing how

Exhibit 5-3 Possible Needs Motivating a Person to Some Action

Types of Needs	Specific Examples			
Physiological needs	Hunger	Thirst	Activity	Sleep
	Sex	Body elimination	Self-preservation	Warmth/coolness
	Rest			
Psychological needs	Aggression	Curiosity	Being responsible	Dominance
	Family preservation	Imitation	Independence	Love
	Nurturing	Order	Personal fulfillment	Playing-competition
	Playing-relaxing	Power	Pride	Self-expression
	Self-identification	Tenderness		
Desire for . . .	Acceptance	Achievement	Acquisition	Affection
	Affiliation	Appreciation	Beauty	Companionship
	Comfort	Leisure	Distance—"space"	Distinctiveness
	Esteem	Fame	Happiness	Identification
	Knowledge	Prestige	Pleasure	Recognition
	Respect	Retaliation	Self-satisfaction	Sociability
	Status	Sympathy	Variety	Fun
Freedom from . . .	Fear	Depression	Discomfort	Anxiety
	Pain	Stress	Loss	Illness
	Harm	Ridicule	Sadness	Pressure

Exhibit 5-4 The PSSP Hierarchy of Needs

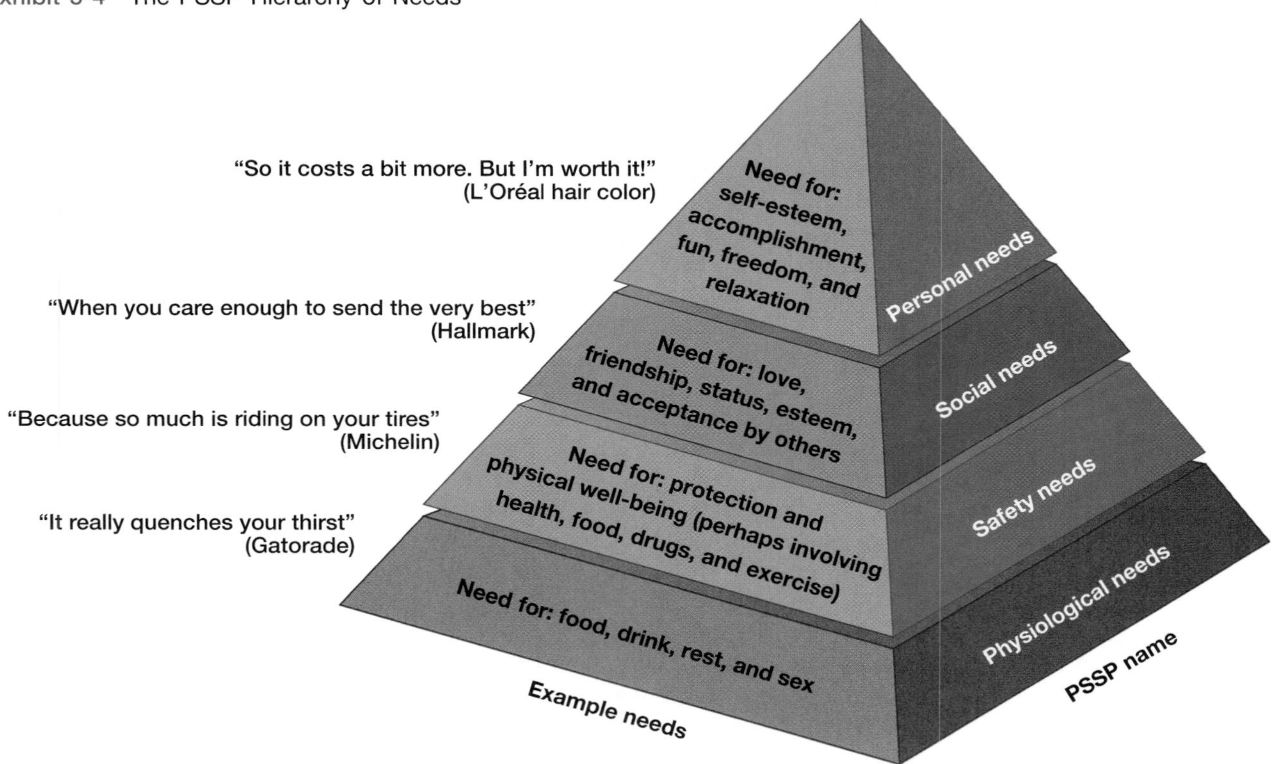

a company has tried to appeal to each need. The lowest-level needs are physiological. Then come safety, social, and personal needs. As a study aid, think of the PSSP needs.[4]

Physiological needs are concerned with biological needs—food, drink, rest, and sex. **Safety needs** are concerned with protection and physical well-being (perhaps involving health, food, medicine, and exercise). **Social needs** are concerned with love, friendship, status, and esteem—things that involve a person's interaction with others. **Personal needs,** on the other hand, are concerned with an individual's need for personal satisfaction—unrelated to what others think or do. Examples include self-esteem, accomplishment, fun, freedom, and relaxation.

Motivation theory suggests that we never reach a state of complete satisfaction. As soon as we get our lower-level needs reasonably satisfied, those at higher levels become more dominant. This explains why marketing efforts targeted at affluent consumers in advanced economies often focus on higher-level needs. It also explains why these approaches may be useless in parts of the world where consumers' basic needs are not being met.

A particular product may satisfy more than one need at the same time. In fact, most consumers try to fill a *set* of needs rather than just one need or another in sequence. Discovering which needs to satisfy may require careful analysis. Consider, for example, the lowly vegetable peeler. Marketing managers for OXO International realized that many people, especially young children and senior citizens, have trouble gripping the handle of a typical peeler. OXO redesigned the peeler with a bigger handle that addressed this physical need. OXO also coated the handle with dishwasher-safe rubber. This makes cleanup more convenient—and the sharp peeler is safer to use. The attractively designed grip also appeals to consumers who get personal satisfaction from cooking. The premium-priced peeler has sold well because it appeals to people with a variety of needs.[5]

How consumers perceive a product or marketing communication may depend on consumer interest and the urgency of the need.

Perception determines what consumers see and feel

Consumers select varying ways to meet their needs sometimes because of differences in **perception**—how we gather and interpret information from the world around us.

We are constantly bombarded by stimuli—ads, products, stores—yet we may not hear or see anything. This is because we apply the following selective processes:

1. **Selective exposure**—our eyes and minds seek out and notice only information that interests us.
2. **Selective perception**—we screen out or modify ideas, messages, and information that conflict with previously learned attitudes and beliefs.
3. **Selective retention**—we remember only what we want to remember.

These selective processes help explain why some people are not affected by some advertising—even offensive advertising. They just don't see or remember it! Even if they do, they may dismiss it immediately.

Our needs affect these selective processes. And current needs receive more attention. For example, Goodyear tire retailers advertise some sale in the newspaper almost weekly. Most of the time we don't even notice these ads—until we need new tires. Only then do we tune in to Goodyear's ads.

Learning determines what response is likely

Learning is a change in a person's thought processes caused by prior experience. Learning is often based on direct experience: A little girl tastes her first cone of Ben & Jerry's Concession Obsession flavor ice cream, and learning occurs! Learning may also be based on indirect experience or associations. If you watch an ad that shows other people enjoying Ben & Jerry's Chocolate Fudge Brownie low-fat frozen yogurt, you might conclude that you'd like it too.

Consumer learning may result from things that marketers do, or it may result from stimuli that have nothing to do with marketing. Either way, almost all consumer behavior is learned.[6]

Experts describe a number of steps in the learning process. We've already discussed the idea of a drive as a strong stimulus that encourages action. Depending on the **cues**—products, signs, ads, and other stimuli in the environment—an individual chooses some specific response. A **response** is an effort to satisfy a drive. The specific response chosen depends on the cues and the person's past experience.

Exhibit 5-5
The Learning Process

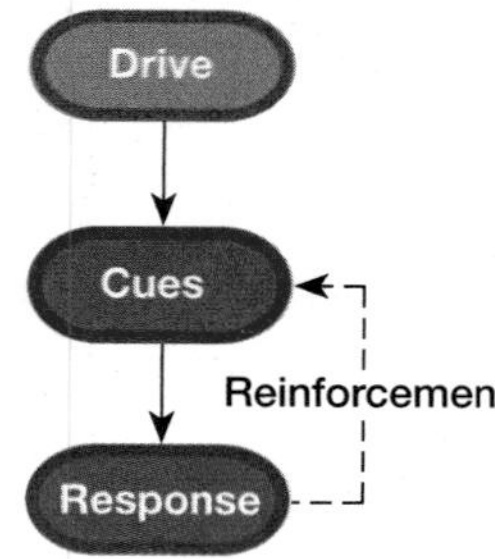

Reinforcement of the learning process occurs when the response is followed by satisfaction—that is, reduction in the drive. Reinforcement strengthens the relationship between the cue and the response. And it may lead to a similar response the next time the drive occurs. Repeated reinforcement leads to development of a habit—making the individual's decision process routine. Exhibit 5-5 shows the relationships of the important variables in the learning process.

The learning process can be illustrated by a thirsty person. The thirst *drive* could be satisfied in a variety of ways. But if the person happened to walk past a vending machine and saw a Mountain Dew sign—a *cue*—then he might satisfy the drive with a *response*—buying a Mountain Dew. If the experience is satisfactory, positive *reinforcement* will occur, and our friend may be quicker to satisfy this drive in the same way in the future. This emphasizes the importance of developing good products that live up to the promises of the firm's advertising. People can learn to like or dislike Mountain Dew—reinforcement and learning work both ways. Unless marketers satisfy their customers, they must constantly try to attract new ones to replace the dissatisfied ones who don't come back.

Positive cues help a marketing mix

Sometimes marketers try to identify cues or images that have positive associations from some other situation and relate them to their marketing mix. Many people associate the smell of lemons with a fresh, natural cleanliness. So companies often add lemon scent to household cleaning products—Clorox bleach and Pledge furniture polish, for example—because it has these associations. Similarly, firms like Calvin Klein use ads suggesting that people who use their products have more appeal to the opposite sex.

Many needs are culturally learned

Many needs are culturally learned. The need for food, for instance, may lead to many specific food wants. Many Japanese enjoy sushi (raw fish), and their children learn to like it. Fewer Americans, however, have learned to enjoy it.

Some critics argue that marketing efforts encourage people to spend money on learned wants totally unrelated to any basic need. For example, Europeans are less concerned about perspiration, and fewer buy antiperspirants. Yet Americans spend millions of dollars on such products. Advertising says that using Ban deodorant "takes the worry out of being close." But is marketing activity the cause of the difference in the two cultures? Most research says that advertising can't convince buyers of something contrary to their basic attitudes.

Attitudes relate to buying

An **attitude** is a person's point of view toward something. The "something" may be a product, an advertisement, a salesperson, a firm, or an idea. Attitudes are important because they affect the selective processes, learning, and buying decisions.

Because attitudes involve liking or disliking, they have some action implications. Beliefs are not so action-oriented. A **belief** is a person's opinion about something. Beliefs may help shape a consumer's attitudes but don't necessarily involve any liking or disliking. It is possible to have a belief—say, that Listerine has a medicinal taste—without really caring what it tastes like. On the other hand, beliefs about a product may have a positive or negative effect in shaping consumers' attitudes. For example, a person with allergies is unlikely to switch to a new medicine like Claritin unless she believes it will be more effective than what she used in the past.

In an attempt to relate attitude more closely to purchase behavior, some marketers stretched the attitude concept to include consumer "preferences" or "intention to buy." Managers who must forecast how much of their brand customers will buy are particularly interested in the intention to buy. Forecasts would be easier if attitudes were good predictors of intentions to buy. Unfortunately, the relationships usually are not that simple. A person may have positive attitudes toward Jacuzzi whirlpool bathtubs but no intention of buying one.

Companies that sell soy-based products are developing new marketing mixes to help overcome negative attitudes that some consumers have about the taste of soy. For example, White Wave Silk is now packaged like milk and promotion focuses on the health benefits. In the same vein, CardioLink's name and trade ads help position its soy powder as healthy for the heart.

Try to understand attitudes and beliefs

Research on consumer attitudes and beliefs can sometimes help a marketing manager get a better picture of markets. For example, research showed that some consumers thought that Purina Dog Chow was a great dog food, but they didn't buy it all of the time. They believed that their dogs would get bored with it. But vets have found dogs benefit from a consistent diet. So, Purina developed an ad campaign to convince these dog owners that what they believed was not true. Each ad gives a dog's-eye-view reaction to being fed a different dog food. In one ad, after taking a few bites, the dog looks into the camera with a pained expression and walks away. He returns with a packet of antacid, which he drops in his water bowl. Such ads helped convince customers that switching foods was not good and Dog Chow sales increased. Consumer beliefs—right or wrong—can have a significant impact on whether a strategy succeeds.[7]

Most marketers work with existing attitudes

Changing present attitudes—especially negative ones—is sometimes necessary. But that's probably the most difficult job marketers face. It's usually more economical to work with consumer attitudes than to try to change them. Attitudes tend to be enduring.[8]

Ethical issues may arise

Part of the marketing job is to inform and persuade consumers about a firm's offering. An ethical issue sometimes arises, however, if consumers have *inaccurate* beliefs. For example, many consumers are confused about what foods are really healthy. Marketers for a number of food companies have been criticized for packaging and promotion that take advantage of inaccurate consumer perceptions about the meaning of the words *lite* or *low-fat*. A firm's lite donuts may have less fat or fewer calories than its other donuts—but that doesn't mean that the donut is *low* in fat. Similarly, promotion of a "children's cold formula" may play off parents' fears that adult medicines are too strong—even though the basic ingredients in the children's formula are the same.

Marketers must also be careful about promotion that might encourage false beliefs, even if the advertising is not explicitly misleading. For example, ads for Ultra Slim-Fast beverage don't claim that anyone who buys the product will lose weight and look like the slim models who appear in the ads—but some critics argue that the advertising gives that impression.[9]

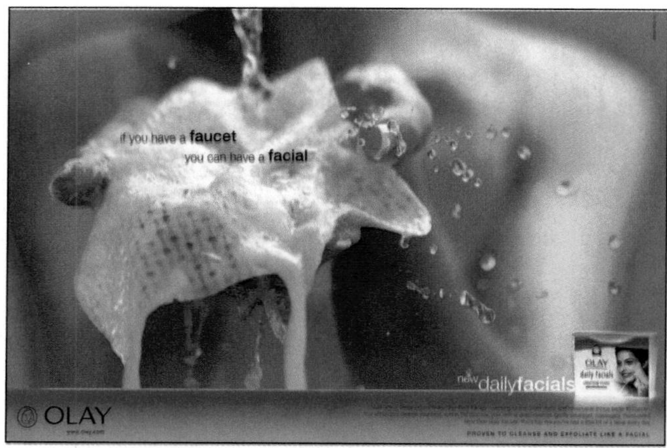

Marketing managers for new Olay Cleansing Cloths (and other Olay skin care products) wanted to take advantage of the familiar Oil of Olay brand name, but realized that many consumers didn't have a positive association between "oil" and beauty. So, the brand name was updated to just Olay and the logo of a woman's figure was changed slightly to appeal to younger women.

Meeting expectations is important

Attitudes and beliefs sometimes combine to form an **expectation**—an outcome or event that a person anticipates or looks forward to. Consumer expectations often focus on the benefits or value that the consumer expects from a firm's marketing mix. A consumer is likely to be dissatisfied if his or her expectations are not met. For example, when Dryel home dry cleaning kits were introduced, ads portrayed Dryel as an alternative to expensive dry-cleaner services. Many consumers who tried it were disappointed because clothing still needed to be pressed.[10]

A key point here is that consumers may evaluate a product on how it performs *relative to their expectations*. A product that otherwise might get high marks from a consumer may be a disappointment if there's a gap between what the consumer gets and what the consumer expects. Promotion that overpromises can create this problem. Finding the right balance, however, can be difficult. A few years ago Van Heusen came up with a new way to treat its shirts so that they look better than previous wash-and-wear shirts. Van Heusen promotes these shirts as "wrinkle-free" and the label shows an iron stuffed in a garbage can. Most people agree that the new shirt is an improvement. Even so, consumers who buy a shirt expecting it to look as crisp as if it had just been ironed are disappointed.[11]

Personality affects how people see things

Many researchers study how personality affects people's behavior, but the results have generally been disappointing to marketers. A trait like neatness can be associated with users of certain types of products—like cleaning materials. But marketing managers have not found a way to use personality in marketing strategy planning.[12] As a result, they've stopped focusing on personality measures borrowed from psychologists and instead developed lifestyle analysis.

Psychographics focus on activities, interests, and opinions

Psychographics or **lifestyle analysis** is the analysis of a person's day-to-day pattern of living as expressed in that person's Activities, Interests, and Opinions—sometimes referred to as AIOs. Exhibit 5-6 shows a number of variables for each of the AIO dimensions—along with some demographics used to add detail to the lifestyle profile of a target market.

Understanding the lifestyle of target customers has been especially helpful in providing ideas for advertising themes. Let's see how it adds to a typical demographic description. It may not help Mercury marketing managers much to know that an average member of the target market for a Mountaineer SUV is 34.8 years old,

Would You Like Those Peanuts with Sugar and Cream?

Marketing managers for Planters' peanuts wanted a new package that would keep peanuts fresh. They also wanted the package to be a cue to promote freshness to consumers. They thought that they had the right idea when they put Planters Fresh Roast Salted Peanuts in a vacuum-packed bric-pac, like the ones that coffee comes in. They were confident that when consumers saw the vacuum-packed peanuts it would remind them that they were fresh roasted, just like with fresh-roasted coffee. To reinforce that message, Planters put the words "Fresh Roast" in large print on the front of the package—right under the Planters name and over the words "salted peanuts." The familiar Mr. Peanut trademark character was there too. This all seemed like a good idea, but it didn't work as planned.

One problem was that the peanuts weren't the same size and shape as coffee, so the bags were pretty lumpy. That made the words harder to read on supermarket shelves. Also, the bags were supposed to be resealable. But that didn't work well because of the lumps. So, once the bag was opened, the peanuts got stale. Consumers who expected extra freshness were disappointed. But, other shoppers had a bigger surprise before they even left the store.

Some consumers opened the bag and put the contents into the grocery store's coffee grinder. You can imagine the gooey peanut butter mess that made. You can also imagine that the store manager was not happy with Planters. Were the consumers trying to make peanut butter? No. Everything on the bag made it clear that it was peanuts. However, the link of the bag with coffee was so strong that consumers didn't stop to think about it. Moreover, the new package came out at about the same time that flavored coffees were just becoming popular. Hey, if some ad is telling you to try hazelnut-flavored coffee, why not peanut-flavored coffee too? No, Planters doesn't want to compete with Starbucks, so this package is off the market.[13]

www.mhhe.com/fourps

married, lives in a three-bedroom home, and has 2.3 children. Lifestyles help marketers paint a more human portrait of the target market. For example, lifestyle analysis might show that the 34.8-year-old is also a community-oriented consumer with traditional values who especially enjoys spectator sports and spends much time in other family activities. An ad might show the Mountaineer being used by a happy family at a ball game so the target market could really identify with the ad. And the ad might be placed on an ESPN show whose viewers match the target lifestyle profile.[14]

Marketing managers who want to learn more about the lifestyle of a target market sometimes turn to a research firm like SRI Consulting. SRI offers a service called geoVALS (VALS is an abbreviation for values, attitudes, and lifestyles). GeoVALS uses psychographics to show where customers live and why they behave as they do; it is especially useful for targeting direct-mail ad campaigns. With another service, VALS 2, SRI describes a firm's target market in terms of a set of typical VALS lifestyle groups (segments). An advantage of this

Exhibit 5-6
Lifestyle Dimensions (and some related demographic dimensions)

Dimension	Examples		
Activities	Work Hobbies Social events	Vacation Entertainment Club membership	Surfing Web Shopping Sports
Interests	Family Home Job	Community Recreation Fashion	Food Media Achievements
Opinions	Themselves Social issues Politics	Business Economics Education	Products Future Culture
Demographics	Income Age Family life cycle	Geographic area Ethnicity Dwelling	Occupation Family size Education

1965

1972

The original Betty, 1936 — 1980 — 1986 — Betty Crocker 2000

General Mills has changed "Betty Crocker's" appearance as consumer attitudes and lifestyles have changed. The face of the newest Betty Crocker reflects her multicultural background.

approach is that SRI has developed very detailed information about the various VALS groups. For example, the VALS approach has been used to profile consumers in the United Kingdom, Germany, Japan, and Canada as well as the United States.[15]

Internet

Internet Exercise Go to the SRI Internet site (http://future.sri.com), click on VALS, and then click on "To the Survey" to review the VALS questionnaire. If you wish, complete the short questionnaire online. SRI will provide you with your VALS profile.

Social Influences Affect Consumer Behavior

We've been discussing some of the ways needs, attitudes, and other psychological variables influence the buying process. Now we'll look at how the individual interacts with family, social class, and other groups who may have influence.

Family life cycle influences needs

Relationships with other family members influence many aspects of consumer behavior. Family members may also share many attitudes and values, consider each other's opinions, and divide various buying tasks.

Income has a direct bearing on family spending patterns, but many other demographic dimensions are also useful in understanding consumer buying. Marital status, age, and the age of any children in the family have an especially important effect on how people spend their income. Put together, these dimensions tell us about the life-cycle stage of a family. Exhibit 5-7 shows a summary of stages in the family life cycle.[16]

Young people and families accept new ideas

Singles and young couples seem to be more willing to try new products and brands—and they are careful, price-conscious shoppers. Although many young people are waiting longer to marry, most do tie the knot eventually. These younger families—especially those with no children—are still accumulating durable goods, such as automobiles and home furnishings. Only as children arrive and grow does family spending shift to soft goods and services, such as education, medical, and

Exhibit 5-7 Stages in Modern Family Life Cycles

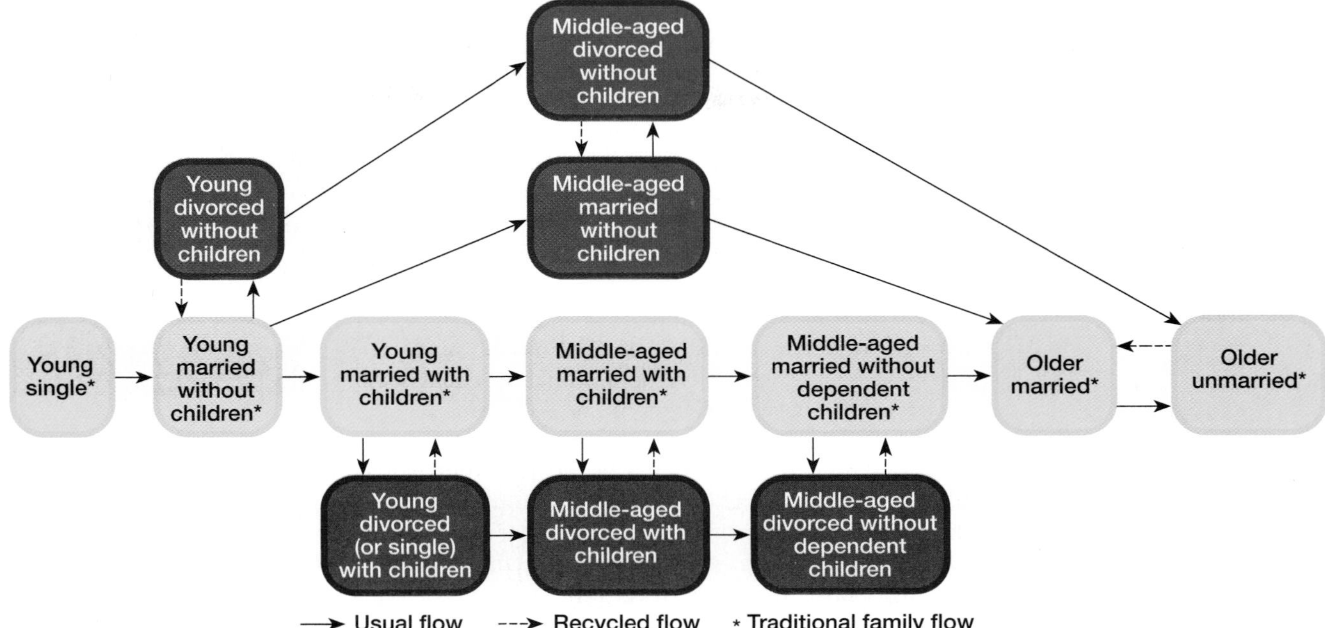

personal care. This usually happens when the family head reaches the 35–44 age group. To meet expenses, people in this age group often make more purchases on credit, and they save less.

Divorce—increasingly a fact of American life—disrupts the family life-cycle pattern. The mother usually has custody of the children, and the father may pay child support. The mother and children typically have much less income than two-parent families. Such families spend a larger percent of their income on housing, child care, and other necessities—with little left for discretionary purchases. If a single parent remarries, the family life cycle may start over again.[17]

Reallocation for teenagers

Once children become teenagers, further shifts in spending occur. Teenagers eat more, want to wear expensive clothes, and develop recreation and education needs that are hard on the family budget. Further, teens play an increasingly important role in shopping and shaping family purchases.

America's teens currently spend over $150 billion a year. They are a target for many firms. For example, Siemens added an MP3 player to its wireless phone to help it win teen preference away from Nokia.[18]

Selling to the empty nesters

Another important category is the **empty nesters**—people whose children are grown and who are now able to spend their money in other ways. Usually these people are in the 50–64 age group and this is often a high-income period—especially for white-collar workers. Empty nesters are an attractive market for many items. They often spend more on travel and other things they couldn't afford before.[19]

Who is the real decision maker in family purchases?

In years past, most marketers in the United States targeted the wife as the family purchasing agent. Now, with sex-role stereotypes changed and with night and weekend shopping more popular, men and older children may take more responsibility for shopping and decision making. In other countries, family roles vary. For example, in Norway women still do most of the family shopping.

Buying responsibility and influence vary greatly depending on the product and the family. Although only one family member may go to the store and make a specific purchase, other family members may have influenced the decision or really decided what to buy. Still others may use the product. That's why the box for Post's Oreo O's cereal looks like the wrapper on the cookies, to get kid's attention in the store.[20]

Social class affects attitudes, values, and buying

Up to now, we've been concerned with individuals and their family relationships. Now let's consider how society looks at an individual and perhaps the family—in terms of social class. A **social class** is a group of people who have approximately equal social position as viewed by others in the society.

Almost every society has some social class structure. In most countries social class is closely related to a person's occupation, but it may also be influenced by education, community participation, where a person lives, income, possessions, social skills, and other factors—including what family a person is born into.

In most countries—including the United States—there is *some* general relationship between income level and social class. But people with the same income level may be in different social classes. And people in different social classes may spend, save, and borrow money in very different ways.

Exhibit 5-8 Characteristics and Relative Sizes of Different Social Class Groups in the United States

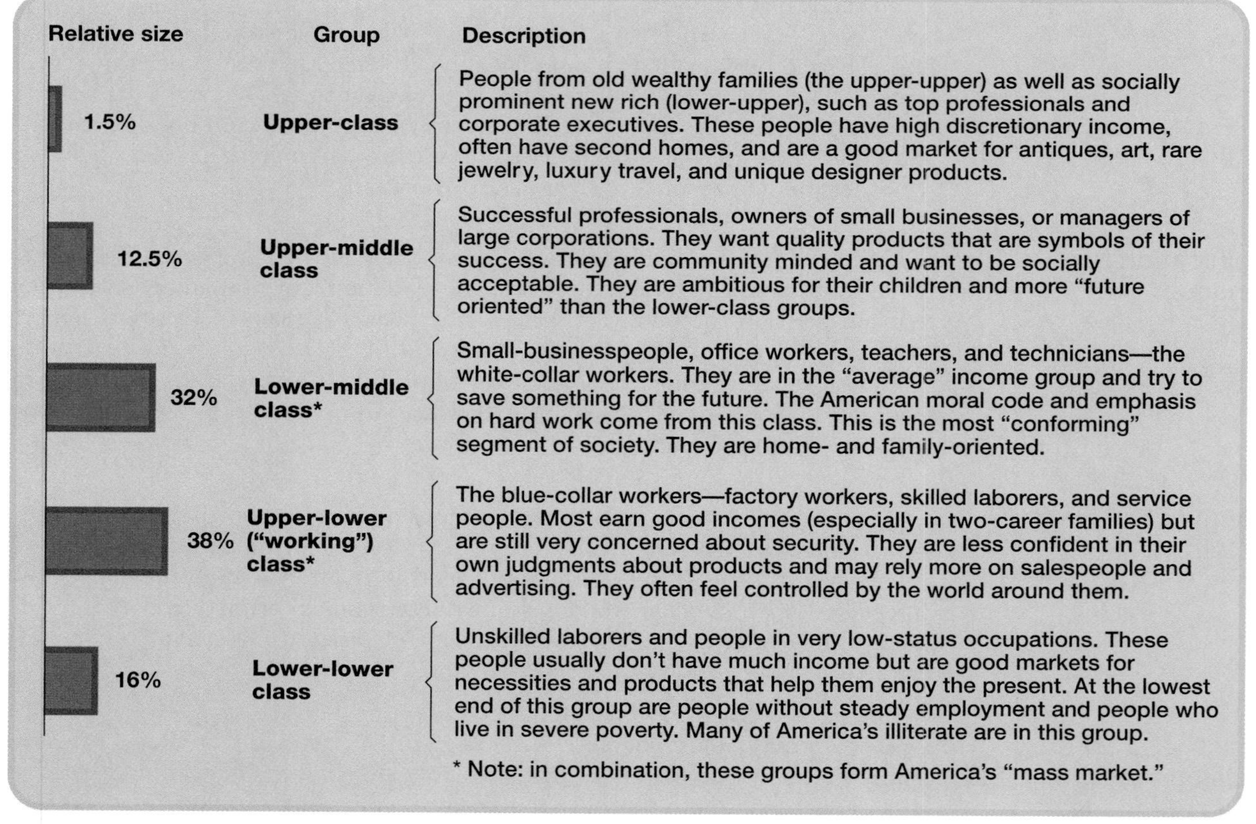

Relative size	Group	Description
1.5%	Upper-class	People from old wealthy families (the upper-upper) as well as socially prominent new rich (lower-upper), such as top professionals and corporate executives. These people have high discretionary income, often have second homes, and are a good market for antiques, art, rare jewelry, luxury travel, and unique designer products.
12.5%	Upper-middle class	Successful professionals, owners of small businesses, or managers of large corporations. They want quality products that are symbols of their success. They are community minded and want to be socially acceptable. They are ambitious for their children and more "future oriented" than the lower-class groups.
32%	Lower-middle class*	Small-businesspeople, office workers, teachers, and technicians—the white-collar workers. They are in the "average" income group and try to save something for the future. The American moral code and emphasis on hard work come from this class. This is the most "conforming" segment of society. They are home- and family-oriented.
38%	Upper-lower ("working") class*	The blue-collar workers—factory workers, skilled laborers, and service people. Most earn good incomes (especially in two-career families) but are still very concerned about security. They are less confident in their own judgments about products and may rely more on salespeople and advertising. They often feel controlled by the world around them.
16%	Lower-lower class	Unskilled laborers and people in very low-status occupations. These people usually don't have much income but are good markets for necessities and products that help them enjoy the present. At the lowest end of this group are people without steady employment and people who live in severe poverty. Many of America's illiterate are in this group.

* Note: in combination, these groups form America's "mass market."

Reference group influence is usually more important when others will be able to see which product a consumer is using, but Jockey wants young people to view its underwear as in fashion and encourages them to "Let 'em know you're Jockey."

The U.S. class system is far less rigid than those in most countries. Children start out in the same social class as their parents—but they can move to a different class depending on their education or jobs. By contrast, India's social structure is more rigid, and individuals can't easily move up in the class system.

Marketers want to know what buyers in various social classes are like. In the United States, simple approaches for measuring social class groupings are based on a person's *occupation*, *education*, and *type and location of housing*. By using marketing research surveys or available census data, marketers can get a feel for the social class of a target market. Exhibit 5-8 illustrates a multilevel social class structure for the United States. Note the relative sizes of the groupings and how they differ.

Many people think of America as a middle-class society. But in many marketing situations the social class groups are distinct, and they have different attitudes.

Reference groups are relevant too

A **reference group** is the people to whom an individual looks when forming attitudes about a particular topic. People normally have several reference groups for different topics. Some they meet face-to-face. Others they just wish to imitate. In either case, they may take values from these reference groups and make buying decisions based on what the group might accept.

Reference influence is stronger for products that others see and which relate to status in the group. For one group, owning an expensive fur coat may be a sign of "having arrived." A group of animal lovers might view it as a sign of bad judgment.[21]

Reaching the opinion leaders who are buyers

An **opinion leader** is a person who influences others. Opinion leaders aren't necessarily wealthier or better educated. And opinion leaders on one subject aren't necessarily opinion leaders on another. For example, you may have a friend who is ahead of the curve in knowing about computer products, but you might not want that friend's opinion about new clothing styles and cosmetics. On the other hand, sometimes a leader in one area earns respect in another. For example, George Foreman, former heavyweight champion of the world, has become a household name representing his line of Foreman grills. Some marketing mixes aim especially at opinion leaders since their opinions affect others and they have many product-related discussions with "followers." Favorable word-of-mouth publicity from opinion leaders can really help a marketing mix. But the opposite is also true. If opinion leaders aren't satisfied, they're likely to talk about it.[22]

Culture surrounds the other influences

Culture is the whole set of beliefs, attitudes, and ways of doing things of a reasonably homogeneous set of people. In Chapter 4 we looked at the broad impact of culture.

We can think of the American culture, the French culture, or the Latin American culture. People within these cultural groupings tend to be more similar in outlook and behavior. But sometimes it is useful to think of subcultures within such groupings. For example, within the American culture, there are various religious and ethnic subcultures.

Failure to consider cultural differences, even subtle ones, can result in problems. To promote their product and get people to try it, marketers for Pepto-Bismol often provide free samples at festivals and street fairs. Their idea is that people tend to overindulge at such events. However, when they distributed sample packets at a festival in San Francisco's Chinatown, they insulted many of the people they wanted to influence. Booths with Chinese delicacies lined the streets, and many of the participants interpreted the sample packets (which featured the word "Nauseous" in large letters) as suggesting that Chinese delicacies were nauseating. The possibility of this misinterpretation may seem obvious in hindsight, but if it had been that obvious in advance the whole promotion would have been handled differently.[23]

Multicultural diversity is replacing the melting pot

People from different ethnic groups may be influenced by very different cultural variables. They may have quite different needs and their own ways of thinking. Moreover, Americans are beginning to recognize the value of multicultural diversity. The U.S. is becoming a multicultural market. As a result, rather than disappearing in a melting pot, some important cultural and ethnic dimensions are being preserved and highlighted. This creates both opportunities and challenges for marketers.

Some important ethnic differences are obvious. For example, more than 1 out of 10 families in the U.S. speaks a language other than English at home. Some areas have a much higher rate. In Miami and San Antonio, for example, about one out of three families speaks Spanish. This obviously affects promotion planning.

Internet

Internet Exercise Visit the website for Ethnic Grocer (www.ethnicgrocer.com), select "Shop by Country," and then "Mexico." Are any of the carbonated beverages listed for Mexico likely to become popular in the U.S.? Why or why not?

Stereotypes are common—and misleading

A marketer needs to study ethnic dimensions very carefully because they can be subtle and fast-changing. This is also an area where stereotyped thinking is the most common—and misleading. Many firms make the mistake of treating all consumers in a particular ethnic group as homogeneous. For example, some marketing managers treat all 35 million African American consumers as "the Black market," ignoring the great variability among African-American households on other segmenting dimensions.

Many firms are developing new strategies to appeal to fast-growing ethnic markets in the U.S. For example, this Spanish-language ad promotes Suavitel fabric softener, which has a special fragrance that appeals to many Hispanic-American consumers.

Ethnic markets are becoming more important

More marketers pay attention to ethnic groups now because the number of ethnic consumers is growing at a much faster rate than the overall society. For example, the Asian American population (about 11.6 million, or 3.6 percent of the total population) has tripled since 1980—one of the fastest growth rates for any segment of the population. Similarly, the Hispanic population, now over 35 million and about 12.5 percent of the total population, surged by more than 60 percent since 1990. To put this in perspective, there are now more Hispanics in the U.S. than there are Canadians in Canada and more Hispanics in the U.S. than African Americans, previously the largest minority group. Already, more than 36 percent of American children are African American, Hispanic, or Asian. Longer term, whites are expected to become a minority by 2050.[24]

Culture varies in international markets

Planning strategies that consider cultural differences in international markets can be even harder—and such cultures usually vary more. Each foreign market may need to be treated as a separate market with its own submarkets. Ignoring cultural differences—or assuming that they are not important—almost guarantees failure in international markets.

For example, Japanese consumers tend to snap up the latest gadgets, but only about 7 percent of Japanese households have a dishwasher (compared to about 50 percent in the U.S.). Appliance manufacturers who have tried to export their standard models to Japan have met with failure. One reason is that Japanese kitchens are much too small for units that are standard in the U.S. Another problem is that fermented soybeans and other common Japanese foods tend to be very sticky. A standard dishwasher won't clean the dishes well. To address these cultural differences, manufacturers have developed small countertop machines with powerful jets to do the cleaning. But another obstacle remains. Many traditional Japanese feel that it is the woman's duty to wash the dishes. For many housewives, the guilt of having dishes done by a machine is worse than the aggravation of doing the job. Foreign firms seem to have missed that. But it became more obvious when Matsushita, the Japanese firm whose washers lead the market, got increases in sales by focusing its promotion on conservation of hot water and hygiene—rather than convenience—as the important reasons to buy a dishwasher.[25]

From a target marketing point of view, a marketing manager probably wants to aim at people within one culture or subculture. A firm developing strategies for two cultures often needs two different marketing plans.[26]

Individuals Are Affected by the Purchase Situation

Purchase reason can vary

Why a consumer makes a purchase can affect buying behavior. For example, a student buying a pen to take notes might pick up an inexpensive Bic. But the same student might choose a Cross pen as a gift for a friend.

Time affects what happens

Time influences a purchase situation. *When* consumers make a purchase—and the time they have available for shopping—will influence their behavior. Socializing with friends at a Starbucks induces different behavior than grabbing a quick cup of 7-Eleven coffee on the way to work.

The urgency of the need is another time-related factor. A sports buff who needs a VCR in time for the Super Bowl—that evening—might spend an hour driving across town in heavy traffic to get the right unit. In a different circumstance, the same person might order the VCR online from a website and figure that the extra time for it to be shipped is well worth the money saved.

On the other hand, how long something takes may be relative. Our online shopper might be frustrated by a web page that takes two minutes to load and abandon his virtual shopping cart after the VCR is already selected. This happens all of the time online. On the other hand, you don't often see a consumer walk away from a shopping cart because of a two-minute wait in a checkout line at a store.

Surroundings affect buying too

Surroundings can affect buying behavior. The excitement at an auction may stimulate impulse buying. Checking out an auction online might lead to a different response.

Surroundings may discourage buying too. For example, some people don't like to stand in a checkout line where others can see what they're buying—even if the other shoppers are complete strangers.[27]

Needs, benefits sought, attitudes, motivation, and even how a consumer selects certain products all vary depending on the purchase situation. So different purchase situations may require different marketing mixes—even when the same target market is involved.

The nature of the purchase situation and the problem-solving processes that consumers use are typically different when they are shopping on the Internet rather than at a store.

Consumers Use Problem-Solving Processes

The variables discussed affect *what* products a consumer finally decides to purchase. Marketing managers also need to understand *how* buyers use a problem-solving process to select particular products.

Most consumers seem to use the following five-step problem-solving process:

1. Becoming aware of—or interested in—the problem.
2. Recalling and gathering information about possible solutions.
3. Evaluating alternative solutions—perhaps trying some out.
4. Deciding on the appropriate solution.
5. Evaluating the decision.[28]

Exhibit 5-9 presents an expanded version of the buyer behavior model shown in Exhibit 5-2. Note that this exhibit integrates the problem-solving process with the whole set of variables we've been reviewing.

Exhibit 5-9
An Expanded Model of the Consumer Problem-Solving Process

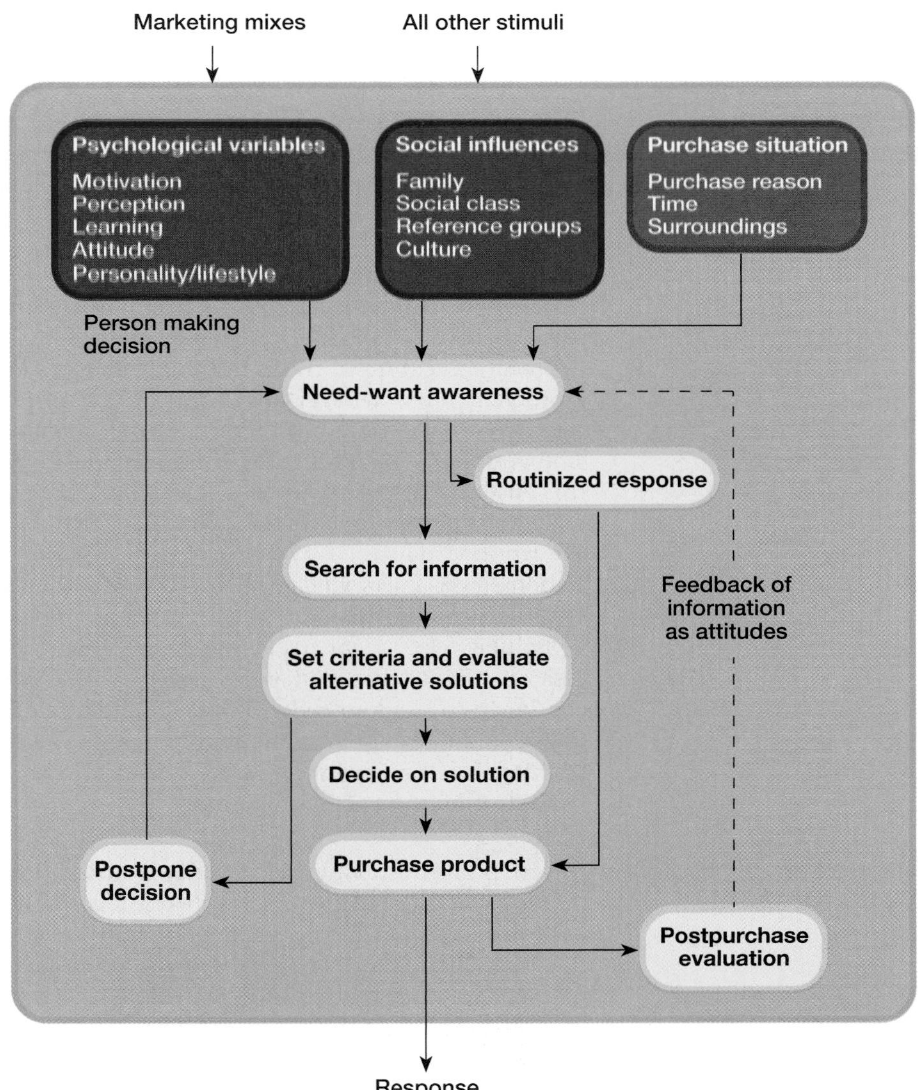

Exhibit 5-10
Grid of Evaluative Criteria for Three Car Brands

Brands	Common features			
	Gas mileage	Ease of service	Comfortable interior	Styling
Nissan	[−]	+	+	−
Saab	+	[−]	+	+
Toyota	+	+	[+]	[−]

Note: Pluses and minuses indicate a consumer's evaluation of a feature for a brand.

When consumers evaluate information about purchase alternatives, they may weigh differences in brands within a product type *and* where the products are available. This can be a very complicated evaluation procedure, and, depending on their choice of criteria, consumers may make seemingly irrational decisions. If convenient service is crucial, for example, a buyer might pay list price for an unexciting car from a very convenient dealer. Marketers need a way to analyze these decisions.

Grid of evaluative criteria helps

Based on studies of how consumers seek out and evaluate product information, researchers suggest that marketing managers use an evaluative grid showing features common to different products (or marketing mixes). For example, Exhibit 5-10 shows some of the features common to three different cars a consumer might consider.

The grid encourages marketing managers to view each product as a bundle of features or attributes. The pluses and minuses in Exhibit 5-10 indicate one consumer's attitude toward each feature of each car. If members of the target market don't rate a feature of the marketing manager's brand with pluses, it may indicate a problem. The manager might want to change the product to improve that feature or perhaps use more promotion to emphasize an already acceptable feature. The consumer in Exhibit 5-10 has a minus under gas mileage for the Nissan. If the Nissan really gets better gas mileage than the other cars, promotion might focus on mileage to improve consumer attitudes toward this feature and toward the whole product.

Some consumers will reject a product if they see *one* feature as substandard—regardless of how favorably they regard the product's other features. The consumer in Exhibit 5-10 might avoid the Saab, which he saw as less than satisfactory on ease of service, even if it were superior in all other aspects. In other instances, a consumer's overall attitude toward the product might be such that a few good features could make up for some shortcomings. The comfortable interior of the Toyota (Exhibit 5-10) might make up for less exciting styling—especially if the consumer viewed comfort as really important.[29]

Three levels of problem solving are useful

The problem-solving process shown in Exhibit 5-9 doesn't show how long this process will take or how much thought a consumer will give to each step. Individuals who have had a lot of experience may move quickly through some of the steps.

It is helpful, therefore, to recognize three levels of problem solving: extensive problem solving, limited problem solving, and routinized response behavior. See Exhibit 5-11. Consumers use **extensive problem solving** for a completely new or important need—when they put much effort into deciding how to satisfy it. For example, a music lover who wants an MP3 player might talk with friends about

Exhibit 5-11 Problem-Solving Continuum

Low involvement Frequently purchased Inexpensive Little risk Little information needed	Routinized response behavior	Limited problem solving	Extensive problem solving	High involvement Infrequently purchased Expensive High risk Much information desired

different models and search the Internet to get a more detailed review and compare prices. She might visit a local dealer to listen to a Panasonic unit with an optional memory card to hold more tracks. If the store has an extended service guarantee at the right price—she might buy it. This is not exactly an impulse purchase!

Consumers use **limited problem solving** when they're willing to put *some* effort into deciding the best way to satisfy a need. Limited problem solving is typical when a consumer has some previous experience in solving a problem but isn't certain which choice is best at the current time. If our music lover also wanted some new compact discs for her car CD player, she might go to a familiar store and evaluate what they had in stock for her favorite types of music.

Consumers use **routinized response behavior** when they regularly select a particular way of satisfying a need when it occurs. Routinized response behavior is typical when a consumer has considerable experience in how to meet a need and has no need for additional information. For example, our music lover might routinely buy the latest recording by her favorite band as soon as it's available.

Most marketing managers would like their target consumers to buy their products in this routinized way. Some firms provide special services for frequent buyers, encourage repeat business with discounts, or do other things to build a good relationship so that the customer purchases from them in a routinized way.

Routinized response behavior is also typical for **low-involvement purchases**—purchases that have little importance or relevance for the customer. Let's face it, buying a box of salt is probably not one of the burning issues in your life.[30]

New concepts require an adoption process

When consumers face a really new concept, their previous experience may not be relevant. These situations involve the **adoption process**—the steps individuals go through on the way to accepting or rejecting a new idea. Although the adoption process is similar to the problem-solving process, learning plays a clearer role and promotion's contribution to a marketing mix is more visible.

In the adoption process, an individual moves through some fairly definite steps:

1. *Awareness*—the potential customer comes to know about the product but lacks details. The consumer may not even know how it works or what it will do.
2. *Interest*—*if* the consumer becomes interested, he or she will gather general information and facts about the product.
3. *Evaluation*—a consumer begins to give the product a mental trial, applying it to his or her personal situation.
4. *Trial*—the consumer may buy the product to experiment with it in use. A product that is either too expensive to try or isn't available for trial may never be adopted.
5. *Decision*—the consumer decides on either adoption or rejection. A satisfactory evaluation and trial may lead to adoption of the product and regular use. According to psychological learning theory, reinforcement leads to adoption.
6. *Confirmation*—the adopter continues to rethink the decision and searches for support for the decision—that is, further reinforcement.[31]

Marketers often want to make it easier for consumers to adopt a product. Colgate offers free samples to encourage consumers in Colombia to try its Protex Fresh soap bars; AOL gives away free diskettes in dozens of ways, including with newspapers.

Internet

Internet Exercise To make it easier for consumers to visualize how certain fashions will look, the Lands' End website (www.landsend.com) has an interactive "virtual model" feature. Go to the Lands' End website, click on "My Model," and check out this feature. Do you think that it makes it easier to evaluate a potential purchase?

Dissonance may set in after the decision

A buyer may have second thoughts after making a purchase decision. The buyer may have chosen from among several attractive alternatives—weighing the pros and cons and finally making a decision. Later doubts, however, may lead to **dissonance**—tension caused by uncertainty about the rightness of a decision. Dissonance may lead a buyer to search for additional information to confirm the wisdom of the decision. Without this confirmation, the adopter might buy something else next time.[32]

Consumer Behavior in International Markets

All the influences interact—often in subtle ways

You're a consumer, so you probably have very good intuition about the many influences on consumer behavior that we've been discussing. That's good, but it's also a potential trap—especially when developing marketing mixes for consumers in international markets. The less a marketing manager knows about the *specific* social and intrapersonal variables that shape the behavior of target customers, the more likely it is that relying on intuition will be misleading. Many specific influences do not generalize from one culture to another.

Cadbury's effort to develop a Japanese market for its Dairy Milk Chocolate candy bar illustrates the point. In marketing research Japanese consumers said that they didn't like the high milk-fat content of Cadbury's bar. Cadbury's managers, however, reasoned that this was because they were not accustomed to the candy. After all, in most other countries it's the rich taste of the candy that turns consumers into "chocoholics." When Cadbury introduced the bar in Japan, it was a real flop. Taste preferences in other countries simply didn't generalize to Japan.

Sometimes important influences are more subtle. When P&G first introduced disposable diapers in Japan, interest was limited. Research suggested that price and product fit were sticking points. However, another powerful cultural force was also at work. At that time, most Japanese mothers were expected to dedicate themselves to caring for their babies. Many women who could afford the convenience of disposable diapers felt guilty using them. Japanese firms that entered the market later used ads to emphasize that disposables were best *for the baby*. That appeal relieved the mother's guilt.

Watch out for stereotypes, and change

Our diaper example can also serve as a reminder to watch out for oversimplifying stereotypes. Consumers in a foreign culture may be bound by some similar cultural forces, but that doesn't mean that they are all the same. Further, changes in the underlying social forces may make outdated views irrelevant.

The stereotype that the typical Japanese executive works very long hours and devotes very little time to family life has been highlighted in the Western media. Yet in today's Japan, many young executives want a more balanced family life. A marketer who didn't recognize this change probably wouldn't fully understand these people, their needs, or buying behavior in their families.

Developing a marketing mix that really satisfies the needs of a target market takes a real understanding of consumer behavior and the varied forces that shape it. So when planning strategies for international markets, it's best to involve locals who have a better chance of understanding the experience, attitudes, and interests of your customers.[33]

Conclusion

In this chapter, we analyzed the individual consumer as a problem solver who is influenced by psychological variables, social influences, and the purchase situation. All of these variables are related, and our model of buyer behavior helps integrate them into one process. Marketing strategy planning requires a good grasp of this material.

Assuming that everyone behaves the way you do—or even like your family or friends do—can lead to expensive marketing errors. Consumer buying behavior results from the consumer's efforts to satisfy needs and wants. We discussed some reasons why consumers buy and saw that consumer behavior can't be fully explained by only a list of needs.

We also saw that most societies are divided into social classes, a fact that helps explain some consumer behavior. And we discussed the impact of reference groups and opinion leaders.

We presented a buyer behavior model to help you interpret and integrate the present findings—as well as any new data you might get from marketing research. As of now, the behavioral sciences can only offer insights and theories, which the marketing manager must blend with intuition and judgment to develop marketing strategies.

Companies may have to use marketing research to answer specific questions. But if a firm has neither the money nor the time for research, then marketing managers have to rely on available descriptions of present behavior and guesstimates about future behavior. Popular magazines and leading newspapers often reflect the public's shifting attitudes. And many studies of the changing consumer are published regularly in the business and trade press. This material—coupled with the information in these last two chapters—will help your marketing strategy planning.

Remember that consumers—with all their needs and attitudes—may be elusive, but they aren't invisible. Research has provided more data and understanding of consumer behavior than business managers generally use. Applying this information may help you find your breakthrough opportunity.

Questions and Problems

1. In your own words, explain economic needs and how they relate to the economic-buyer model of consumer behavior. Give an example of a purchase you recently made that is consistent with the economic-buyer model. Give another that is not explained by the economic-buyer model. Explain your thinking.
2. Explain what is meant by a hierarchy of needs and provide examples of one or more products that enable you to satisfy each of the four levels of need.
3. Cut out (or copy) two recent advertisements: one full-page color ad from a magazine and one large

display from a newspaper. In each case, indicate which needs the ads are appealing to.

4. Explain how an understanding of consumers' learning processes might affect marketing strategy planning. Give an example.
5. Briefly describe your own *beliefs* about the potential value of wearing automobile seat belts, your *attitude* toward seat belts, and your *intention* about using a seat belt the next time you're in a car.
6. Give an example of a recent purchase experience in which you were dissatisfied because a firm's marketing mix did not meet your expectations. Indicate how the purchase fell short of your expectations—and also explain whether your expectations were formed based on the firm's promotion or on something else.
7. Explain psychographics and lifestyle analysis. Explain how they might be useful for planning marketing strategies to reach college students, as opposed to average consumers.
8. A supermarket chain is planning to open a number of new stores to appeal to Hispanics in southern California. Give some examples that indicate how the four Ps might be adjusted to appeal to the Hispanic subculture.
9. How should the social class structure affect the planning of a new restaurant in a large city? How might the four Ps be adjusted?
10. What social class would you associate with each of the following phrases or items? In each case, choose one class if you can. If you can't choose one class but rather feel that several classes are equally likely, then so indicate. In those cases where you feel that all classes are equally interested or characterized by a particular item, choose all five classes.
    a. A gun rack in a pickup truck.
    b. The *National Enquirer*.
    c. *New Yorker* magazine.
    d. *Working Woman* magazine.
    e. People watching soap operas.
    f. Jaguar automobile.
    g. Men who drink beer after dinner.
    h. Families who vacation at a Disney theme park.
    i. Families who distrust banks (keep money in socks or mattresses).
    j. Owners of pit bulls.
11. Illustrate how the reference group concept may apply in practice by explaining how you personally are influenced by some reference group for some product. What are the implications of such behavior for marketing managers?
12. Give two examples of recent purchases where the specific purchase situation influenced your purchase decision. Briefly explain how your decision was affected.
13. Give an example of a recent purchase in which you used extensive problem solving. What sources of information did you use in making the decision?
14. On the basis of the data and analysis presented in Chapters 4 and 5, what kind of buying behavior would you expect to find for the following products: *(a)* a haircut, *(b)* a dishwasher detergent, *(c)* a printer for a personal computer, *(d)* a tennis racket, *(e)* a dress belt, *(f)* a telephone answering machine, *(g)* life insurance, *(h)* an ice cream cone, and *(i)* a new checking account? Set up a chart for your answer with products along the left-hand margin as the row headings and the following factors as headings for the columns: *(a)* how consumers would shop for these products, *(b)* how far they would travel to buy the product, *(c)* whether they would buy by brand, *(d)* whether they would compare with other products, and *(e)* any other factors they should consider. Insert short answers—words or phrases are satisfactory—in the various boxes. Be prepared to discuss how the answers you put in the chart would affect each product's marketing mix.
15. Review the Go-Gurt case that introduces this chapter, and identify which of the key terms (that appear in red) from the text of the chapter that you think are illustrated in the case. Write down each key term you identify and briefly explain how it is illustrated.

Suggested Cases

3. Pillsbury's Häagen-Dazs
8. Sophia's Ristorante
9. Sleepy Time Motel
10. Runners World
26. Deluxe Foods, Ltd.

Computer-Aided Problem

5. **Selective Processes**

Submag, Inc., uses direct-mail promotion to sell magazine subscriptions. Magazine publishers pay Submag $3.12 for each new subscription. Submag's costs include the expenses of printing, addressing, and mailing each direct-mail advertisement plus the cost of using a mailing list. There are many suppliers of mailing lists, and the cost and quality of different lists vary.

Submag's marketing manager, Shandra Debose, is trying to choose between two possible mailing lists. One list has been generated from phone directories. It is less expensive than the other list, but the supplier acknowledges that about 10 percent of the names are out-of-date (addresses where people have moved away.) A competing supplier offers a list of active members of professional associations. This list costs 4 cents per name more than the phone list, but only 8 percent of the addresses are out-of-date.

In addition to concerns about out-of-date names, not every consumer who receives a mailing buys a subscription. For example, *selective exposure* is a problem. Some target customers never see the offer—they just toss out junk mail without even opening the envelope. Industry studies show that this wastes about 10 percent of each mailing—although the precise percentage varies from one mailing list to another.

Selective perception influences some consumers who do open the mailing. Some are simply not interested. Others don't want to deal with a subscription service. Although the price is good, these consumers worry that they'll never get the magazines. Submag's previous experience is that selective perception causes more than half of those who read the offer to reject it.

Of those who perceive the message as intended, many are interested. But *selective retention* can be a problem. Some people set the information aside and then forget to send in the subscription order.

Submag can mail about 25,000 pieces per week. Shandra Debose has set up a spreadsheet to help her study effects of the various relationships discussed above and to choose between the two mailing lists.

a. *If you were Debose, which of the two lists would you buy based on the initial spreadsheet? Why?*
b. *For the most profitable list, what is the minimum number of items that Submag will have to mail to earn a profit of at least $3,500?*
c. *For an additional cost of $.01 per mailing, Submag can include a reply card that will reduce the percent of consumers who forget to send in an order (Percent Lost—Selective Retention) to 45 percent. If Submag mails 25,000 items, is it worth the additional cost to include the reply card? Explain your logic.*

For additional questions related to this problem, see Exercise 5-5 in the *Learning Aid for Use with Essentials of Marketing*, 9th edition.

Chapter Six

Business and Organizational Customers and Their Buying Behavior

When You Finish This Chapter, You Should

1. Know who the business and organizational customers are.

2. See why multiple influence is common in business and organizational purchase decisions.

3. Understand the problem-solving behavior of organizational buyers.

4. Understand the different types of buyer–seller relationships and their benefits and limitations.

5. Know the basic e-commerce methods used in organizational buying.

6. Know about the number and distribution of manufacturers and why they are an important customer group.

7. Know how buying by service firms, retailers, wholesalers, and governments is similar to—and different from—buying by manufacturers.

8. Understand the important new terms (shown in red).

MetoKote Corp. specializes in protective coatings, like powder-coat and liquid paint, that other manufacturers need for the parts and equipment they make. When you see John Deere (JD) agricultural or construction equipment, its familiar green finish probably came from MetoKote. In fact, John Deere and MetoKote have a close buyer–seller relationship. While purchasing managers at Deere use Internet portals to identify suppliers and get competitive bids for many items they need, it's different with MetoKote. Deere isn't going to switch to some other supplier just because an Internet search identifies some cheaper coating. MetoKote doesn't just supply Deere with coatings; it handles the

place price promotion produ

whole coating job for Deere. In fact, it has built facilities right next to some Deere plants. When it's time for a part to be coated, a conveyor belt moves it out of the JD plant and into the MetoKote facility. Four hours later it's back—and it's green. Many people were involved in the decision to purchase coating services this way. JD's production people like it that MetoKote's experts keep up with all of the environmental regulations and new technologies for coatings. Deere's finance people like the idea that a Deere plant can be less costly to build and maintain if it doesn't need space for big spray booths. Because MetoKote does not have to ship the parts to Deere after they are coated, there are fewer scratches and dents—which the quality people like. And the purchasing people don't have to worry about parts being there when they're needed. Of course, this was not a simple sale for MetoKote—and on an ongoing basis many people cooperate and share information to make it work for both firms.

John Deere needs high-quality protective finishes because the buyers for its customers want durable, long-lasting equipment. Like Deere, they want good value from their suppliers. That means that marketers at Deere need to think about the quality of Deere service as well as the quality of Deere equipment. For example, when a huge commercial farm in California or Brazil needs a repair part, they can't afford delays. Deere helps them, and the dealers who sell its parts and equipment, with information technology. At any hour an equipment customer can check Deere's website (www.deere.com) to see which dealers have a needed part in

www.mhhe.com/fourps

inventory, to check the price, and to place an order for fast delivery. But helping its customers earn better profits in their own operations doesn't stop there. Some Deere farm equipment includes global positioning devices that track exactly where the equipment goes. That makes it possible for the owner to use JD's VantagePoint Network to collect, store, and interpret detailed data generated by their farming operations online, right down to creation of maps of fields that need to be plowed, seeded, or cut. It is benefits like this that make Deere the supplier of choice for many business customers.[1]

Business and Organizational Customers—A Big Opportunity

As the John Deere case illustrates, the buying behavior of organizational customers can be very different from the buying behavior of final consumers. Developing marketing strategies for these markets requires a solid understanding of who these customers are and how they buy. That is the focus of this chapter.

What types of customers are involved?

Business and organizational customers are any buyers who buy for resale or to produce other goods and services. Exhibit 6-1 shows the different types of customers in these markets. As you can see, not all of the organizational customers in these markets are business firms. Even so, to distinguish them from the final consumer market, managers sometimes refer to them collectively as the "business-to-business" market, or simply the *B2B market*. Similarly, the different kinds of organizational customers are sometimes loosely called "business buyers," "intermediate buyers," or "industrial buyers."

Organizational Customers Are Different

Organizations buy for a basic purpose

Like final consumers, organizations make purchases to satisfy needs. But the needs are often easier to understand because most organizations buy goods and services that will help them meet the demand for the goods and services that they in turn supply to their markets.

Basic purchasing needs are economic

Organizational buyers typically focus on economic factors when they make purchase decisions. They are usually less emotional in their buying than final consumers.

Buyers try to consider the total cost of selecting a supplier and its particular marketing mix, not just the initial price of the product. For example, a hospital that needs a new type of X-ray equipment might look at both the original cost and ongoing costs, how it would affect doctor productivity, and of course the quality of the images it produces. The hospital might also consider the seller's reliability and ability to provide speedy maintenance and repair.

The matter of dependability deserves emphasis. An organization may not be able to function if purchases don't arrive when they're expected. A manufacturer may have to shut down a production line if sellers haven't delivered the goods. Dependable product quality is important too. A bug in e-commerce software purchased by a firm might cause the firm's online order system to shut down. The costs of finding and correcting the problem—to say nothing about the cost of the lost business—could be completely out of proportion to the original cost of the software.

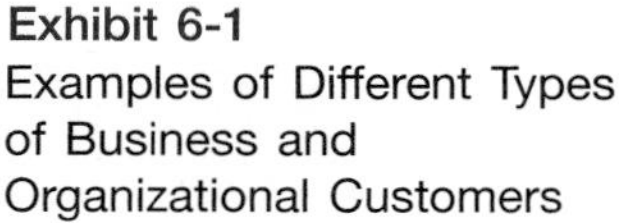

Exhibit 6-1
Examples of Different Types of Business and Organizational Customers

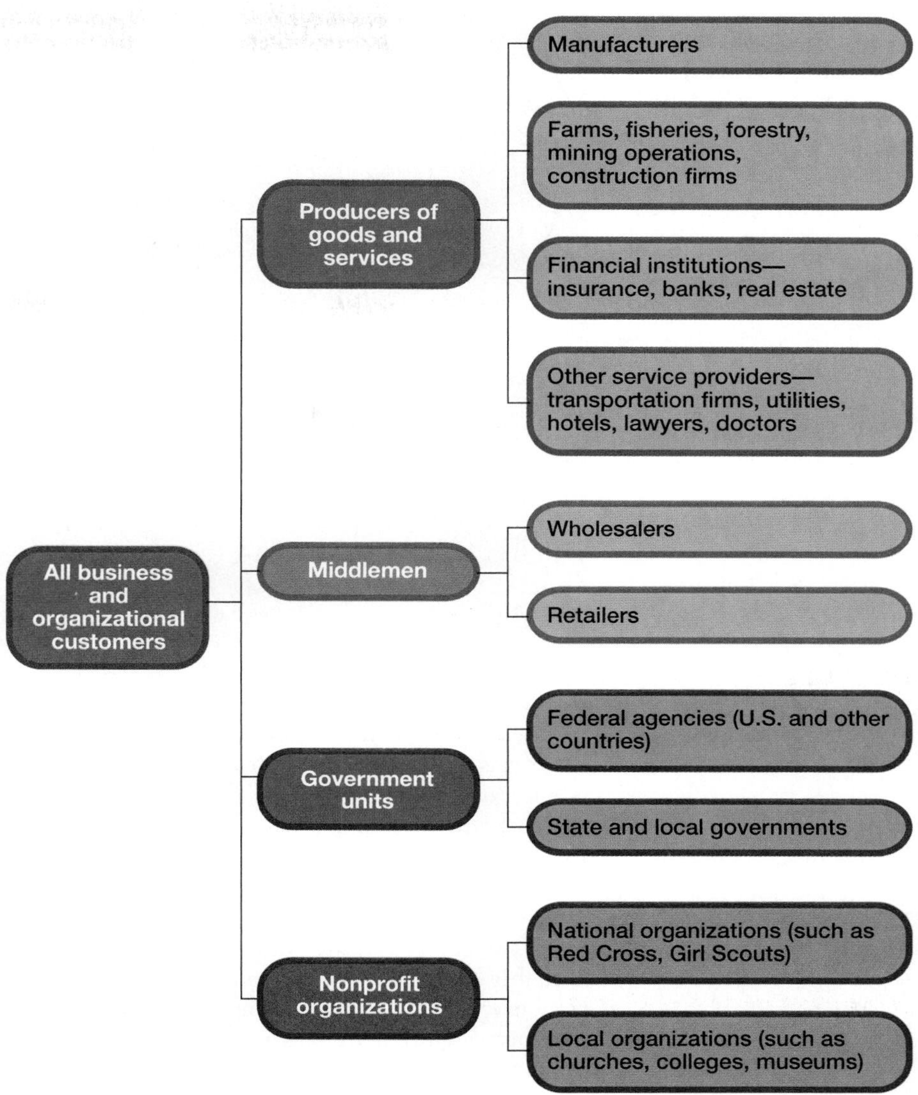

Even small differences are important

Understanding how the buying behavior of a particular organization differs from others can be very important. Even seemingly trivial differences in buying behavior may be important because success often hinges on fine-tuning the marketing mix.

Sellers often approach each organizational customer directly, usually through a sales representative. This gives the seller more chance to adjust the marketing mix for each individual customer. This carries target marketing to its extreme. But sellers often need unique strategies to compete for large-volume purchases.

In such situations, the individual sales rep takes much responsibility for strategy planning and coordinates the relationship with the customer. That may involve working with many people—including top management—in both firms. This is relevant to your career planning since these interesting jobs are very challenging and pay well.

Serving customers in international markets

There are often good opportunities to serve business customers in different countries around the world. Specific business customs do vary from one country to another—and the differences can be important. For example, a salesperson working in Japan must know how to handle a customer's business card with respect. Japanese consider it rude to write notes on the back of a card or put it in a wallet while the person who presented it is still in the room. But the basic approaches

Steel bearings are a small portion of the cost of producing an airplane, but Timken wants decision makers to keep in mind that it's critical to get the proven quality of its products.

marketers use to deal with business customers in different parts of the world are much less varied than those required to reach individual consumers.

This is one reason the shift to a global economy has been so rapid for many firms. Their business customers in different countries buy in similar ways and can be reached with similar marketing mixes. Moreover, business customers are often willing to work with a distant supplier who has developed a superior marketing mix.

Specifications describe the need

Organizational buyers often buy on the basis of a set of **purchasing specifications**—a written (or electronic) description of what the firm wants to buy. When quality is highly standardized, as is often the case with manufactured items, the specification may simply consist of a brand name or part number. Often, however, the purchase requirements are more complicated; then the specifications may set out detailed information about the performance standards the product must meet. This often applies to services because they tend to be less standardized and usually are not performed until after they're purchased.

Customers may expect quality certification

Organizational customers considering a new supplier or one from overseas may be concerned about product quality. However, this is becoming less of an obstacle because of ISO 9000. **ISO 9000** is a way for a supplier to document its quality procedures according to internationally recognized standards.

ISO 9000 assures a customer that the supplier has effective quality checks in place, without the customer having to conduct its own costly and time-consuming audit. Some customers won't buy from any supplier who doesn't have it. To get ISO 9000 certified, a supplier basically must prove to outside auditors that it documents in detail how the company operates and who is responsible for quality every step of the way.[2]

Many Different People May Influence a Decision

Purchasing managers are specialists

Many organizations rely on specialists to ensure that purchases are handled sensibly. These specialists have different titles in different firms (such as purchasing agent, procurement officer, or buyer), but basically they are all **purchasing managers**—

A person who works on a utility firm's high-power wires needs safe, durable climbing gear. A number of different people may influence the decision about which gear the firm should buy.

buying specialists for their employers. In large organizations, they usually specialize by product area and are real experts.

Some people think purchasing is handled by clerks who sit in cubicles and just do the paperwork to place orders. That view is out-of-date. Today, most firms look to their purchasing departments to help cut costs and provide competitive advantage. These purchasing people have a lot of clout. And there are good job opportunities in purchasing for capable business graduates.

Salespeople often have to see a purchasing manager first—before they contact any other employee. These buyers hold important positions and take a dim view of sales reps who try to go around them. Rather than being "sold," these buyers want salespeople to provide accurate information that will help them buy wisely. They like information on new goods and services, and tips on potential price changes, supply shortages, and other changes in market conditions. Sometimes all it takes for a sales rep to keep a buyer up-to-date is to send an occasional e-mail. But a buyer can tell when a sales rep has the customer firm's interest at heart.[3]

Multiple buying influence in a buying center

Multiple buying influence means that several people—perhaps even top management—share in making a purchase decision. An example shows how the different buying influences work.

Suppose Electrolux, the Swedish firm that produces vacuum cleaners, wants to buy a machine to stamp out the various metal parts it needs. An assistant to the purchasing manager does an Internet search to identify possible vendors. However, the list that the assistant (a gatekeeper) prepares for the manager excludes a few vendors based on an initial review of their websites. The manager e-mails vendors on the list. Each of them is eager to get the business and submits a proposal. Several people (influencers) at Electrolux help to evaluate the vendors' proposals. A finance manager worries about the high cost and suggests leasing the machine. The quality control people want a machine that will do a more accurate job—although it's more expensive. The production line workers want the machine that is easiest to use so they can continue to rotate jobs.

The company president (the decider) asks the purchasing department to assemble all the information but retains the power to select and approve the supplier.

Exhibit 6-2
Multiple Influence and Roles in the Buying Center

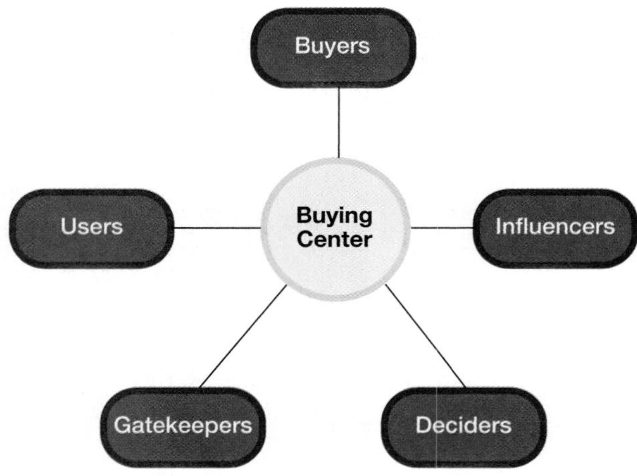

The purchasing manager's assistant schedules visits for salespeople. After all these buying influences are considered, one of the purchasing agents for the firm (the buyer) will be responsible for making recommendations and arranging the terms of the sale.

It is helpful to think of a **buying center** as all the people who participate in or influence a purchase. Different people may make up a buying center from one decision to the next. The salesperson must study each case carefully. Just learning who to talk with may be hard, but thinking about the various roles in the buying center can help. See Exhibit 6-2.

The salesperson may have to talk to every member of the buying center—stressing different topics for each. This complicates the promotion job and lengthens it. On important purchases—a new building or major equipment—the selling period may take a year or more.[4]

Vendor analysis considers all of the influences

Considering all of the factors relevant to a purchase decision is sometimes complex. A supplier or product that is best in one way may not be best in others. To try to deal with these situations, many firms use **vendor analysis**—a formal rating of suppliers on all relevant areas of performance. The purpose isn't just to get a low price from the supplier on a given part or service. Rather, the goal is to lower the *total costs* associated with purchases. Analysis might show that the best vendor is the one that helps the customer reduce costs of excess inventory, retooling of equipment, or defective parts.[5]

Internet

Internet Exercise At the Computer Discount Warehouse website (www.cdw.com) a buyer can compare the features and prices of alternative products. Click on "Notebooks" (under the PRODUCTFINDER heading) and then search for notebooks with a Processor Speed of at least 1GHz. Select two notebooks from two different manufacturers and click compare. How helpful would this analysis be if you were a computer buyer?

Behavioral needs are relevant too

Vendor analysis focuses on economic factors, but purchasing in organizations may also involve many of the same behavioral dimensions we discussed in Chapter 5. Purchasing managers and others involved in buying decisions are human, and they want friendly relationships with suppliers.

The different people involved in purchase decisions are also human with respect to protecting their own interests. That's one reason people from different departments may have different priorities in trying to influence what is purchased. Similarly, purchasing managers may want to avoid taking risks that might reflect

Organizational customers want reliable suppliers who will deliver on their promises and not reflect badly on the buyer's decisions.

badly on their decisions. If a new source delivers late or quality is poor, you can guess who will be blamed. Marketers who can help the buyer avoid risk have a definite appeal.

Ethical conflicts may arise

Most organizational buyers are serious professionals who are careful to avoid a conflict between their own self-interest and company outcomes. Marketers must be careful here. A salesperson who offers a company pen to a prospect may view the giveaway as part of the promotion effort—but the customer firm may have a policy against any employee accepting *any* gift from a supplier. For example, General Motors developed an ethics policy that forbids employees from accepting anything of value from a vendor, including things like a golf outing, a steak dinner, or tickets to a sporting event.

Marketers need to take concerns about conflict of interest very seriously. The whole marketing effort may be tainted if it even *appears* that a marketer has encouraged a person who influences a decision to put personal gain ahead of company interest.[6]

Purchasing may be centralized

If an organization has facilities at many locations, much of the purchasing work may be done at a central location. Wal-Mart handles most of the purchase decisions for stores in its retail chain from its headquarters in Arkansas. Many purchasing decisions for agencies of the U.S. government are handled in Washington, D.C.

Many firms also have centralized controls on who can make purchases. A person who needs to purchase something usually completes a **requisition**—a request to buy something. This is frequently handled online to cut time and paper shuffling. Even so, there may be delays before a supervisor authorizes the requisition and a purchasing manager can select the "best" seller and turn the authorization into a purchase order. The process may take a few hours for a simple purchase—but it may turn into months for a complex purchase.

Organizational Buyers Are Problem Solvers

Three kinds of buying processes are useful

In Chapter 5, we discussed problem solving by consumers and how it might vary from extensive problem solving to routine buying. In organizational markets, we can adapt these concepts slightly and work with three similar buying processes: a new-task buying process, a modified rebuy process, or a straight rebuy.[7] See Exhibit 6-3.

New-task buying occurs when an organization has a new need and the customer wants a great deal of information. New-task buying can involve setting product specifications, evaluating sources of supply, and establishing an order routine that

Exhibit 6-3
Organizational Buying Processes

Characteristics	Type of Process		
	New-Task Buying	Modified Rebuy	Straight Rebuy
Time Required	Much	Medium	Little
Multiple Influence	Much	Some	Little
Review of Suppliers	Much	Some	None
Information Needed	Much	Some	Little

can be followed in the future if results are satisfactory. Multiple buying influence is typical in new-task buying.

A **straight rebuy** is a routine repurchase that may have been made many times before. Buyers probably don't bother looking for new information or new sources of supply. Most of a company's small or recurring purchases are of this type—but they take only a small part of an organized buyer's time. Important purchases may be made this way too—but only after the firm has decided what procedure will be "routine."

The **modified rebuy** is the in-between process where some review of the buying situation is done—though not as much as in new-task buying. Sometimes a competitor will get lazy enjoying a straight rebuy situation. An alert marketer can turn these situations into opportunities by providing more information or a better marketing mix.

New-task buying requires information

Customers in a new-task buying situation are likely to seek information from a variety of sources. See Exhibit 6-4. Many of the impersonal sources are readily available in digital form online as well as in other formats. How much information a customer collects depends on the importance of the purchase and the level of uncertainty about what choice might be best. The time and expense of searching for information may not be justified for a minor purchase. But a major purchase often involves real detective work by the buyer.

Of course, the flip side of the new-task buying situation is that a seller's promotion has much more chance to have an impact. At the very least, the marketer needs to be certain that his or her firm will turn up in the buyer's search. In this regard, a good website is a crucial piece of insurance. Even a simple website is likely to turn up in a buyer's Internet search.[8]

What buying procedure becomes routine is critical

Once a buying firm gets beyond the early stages of a new-task buying decision, it needs to make important decisions about how it is going to deal with one or more suppliers to meet its needs. At one extreme, a buyer might want to rely on competition

Exhibit 6-4
Major Sources of Information Used by Organizational Buyers

	Marketing sources	Nonmarketing sources
Personal sources	• Salespeople • Others from supplier firms • Trade shows	• Buying center members • Outside business associates • Consultants and outside experts
Impersonal sources	• Advertising in trade publications • Sales literature • Sales catalogs • Web page	• Rating services • Trade associations • News publications • Product directories • Internet news pointcasts

among all available vendors to get the best price on each and every order it places. At the other extreme, it might just routinely buy from one vendor with whom it already has a good relationship. In practice, there are many variations between these extremes. To better understand the variations, let's take a closer look at the benefits and limitations of different types of buyer–seller relationships. That will also help you to see why new e-commerce developments have become so important.

Buyer–Seller Relationships in Business Markets

Close relationships may produce mutual benefits

There are often significant benefits of a close working relationship between a supplier and a customer firm. And such relationships are becoming common. Many firms are reducing the number of suppliers with whom they work—expecting more in return from the suppliers that remain. The best relationships involve real partnerships where there's mutual trust and a long-term outlook.

The partnership between AlliedSignal and Betz Laboratories shows the benefits of a good relationship. A while back, Betz was just one of several suppliers that sold Allied chemicals to keep the water in its plants from gunking up pipes and rusting machinery. But Betz didn't stop at selling commodity powders. Teams of Betz experts and engineers from Allied studied each plant to find places where water was being wasted. For example, by adding a few valves to recycle the water in a cooling tower, Betz was able to save 300 gallons of water a minute, which resulted in savings of over $100,000 a year and reduced environmental impact. Because of ideas like this, Allied's overall use of water treatment chemicals decreased. However, Betz sales to Allied doubled because it became Allied's sole supplier.[9]

Relationships may not make sense

Although close relationships can produce benefits, they are not always best. A long-term commitment to a partner may reduce flexibility. When competition drives down prices and spurs innovation, the customer may be better off letting suppliers compete for the business. It may not be worth the customer's time to build a relationship for purchases that are unimportant or infrequent.

In today's business markets, suppliers of both goods and services are working to build closer relationships with their business customers—to meet needs better and create a competitive advantage.

Exhibit 6-5
Key Dimensions of Relationships in Business Markets

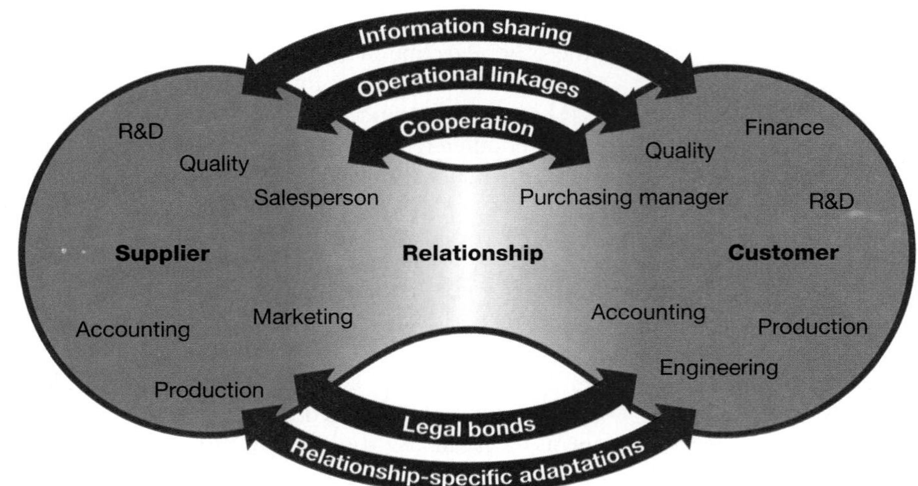

It may at first appear that a seller would *always* prefer to have a closer relationship with a customer, but that is not so. Some customers may place orders that are too small or require so much special attention that the relationship would never be profitable for the seller. If a customer doesn't want a relationship, trying to build one may cost more than it's worth. Further, many small suppliers have made the mistake of relying too heavily on relationships with too few customers. One failed relationship may bankrupt the business.[10]

Relationships have many dimensions

Relationships are not "all or nothing" arrangements. Firms may have a close relationship in some ways and not in others. Thus, it's useful to know about five key dimensions that help characterize most buyer–seller relationships: cooperation, information sharing, operational linkages, legal bonds, and relationship-specific adaptations. Purchasing managers for the buying firm and salespeople for the supplier usually coordinate the different dimensions of a relationship. However, as shown in Exhibit 6-5, close relationships often involve direct contacts between a number of people from other areas in both firms.[11]

Cooperation treats problems as joint responsibilities

In cooperative relationships, the buyer and seller work together to achieve both mutual and individual objectives. The two firms treat problems that arise as a joint responsibility. National Semiconductor (NS) and Siltec, a supplier of silicon wafers, have found clever ways to cooperate and cut costs. For example, workers at the NS plant used to throw away the expensive plastic cassettes that Siltec uses to ship the silicon wafers. Now Siltec and NS cooperate to recycle the cassettes. This helps the environment and also saves more than $300,000 a year. Siltec passes along most of that to NS as lower prices.[12]

Shared information is useful but may be risky

Some relationships involve sharing of information. This might include the exchange of proprietary cost data, discussion of demand forecasts, and joint work on new product designs. Information might be shared through information systems or over the Internet. This is often a key facet of relationships that involve e-commerce.

Many firms provide relationship partners with access to password-protected websites. One big advantage of this approach is that it is fast and easy to update the information. A customer can check detailed product specs or the status of a job on the production line without having to wait for someone to answer the question. Information sharing can lead to better decisions, reduced uncertainty about the future, and better planning. However, firms don't want to share information if there's a risk that a partner might misuse it. For example, some suppliers claim that General

Motors' former purchasing chief showed blueprints of their secret technology to competing suppliers. Violations of trust in a relationship are an ethical matter and should be taken seriously.

Operational linkages share functions between firms

Operational linkages are direct ties between the internal operations of the buyer and seller firms. These usually involve ongoing coordination of activities between the firms. Shared activities are especially important when neither firm, working on its own, can perform a task as well as the two firms can working together. John Deere's relationship with MetoKote, described at the start of this chapter, involves operational linkages.

Operational linkages are often required to reduce total inventory costs. Business customers want enough inventory to prevent stock-outs and keep production lines moving. On the other hand, keeping too much inventory is expensive. Providing a customer with inventory when it's needed may require that a supplier be able to provide **just-in-time delivery**—reliably getting products there *just* before the customer needs them. We'll discuss just-in-time systems in more detail in Chapter 11. For now, it's enough to see that just-in-time relationships between buyers and sellers usually require operational linkages (as well as information sharing). For example, Wal-Mart might want a producer of socks to pack cartons so that when they are unloaded at a Wal-Mart distribution facility all of the cartons for a certain store or district are grouped together. This makes it faster for forklifts to "cross dock" the cartons onto an outbound truck. However, it means that the supplier's production and packing of socks in different colors and sizes must be closely linked to the precise store in the Wal-Mart chain that places each order.

Operational linkages may also involve the routine activities of individuals who almost become part of the customer's operations. Design engineers, salespeople, and service representatives may develop solutions to problems, conduct maintenance checks, or coordinate orders. At the DaimlerChrysler design center, for example, 30 offices are set aside for full-time use by people employed by suppliers.

Contracts spell out obligations

Many purchases are simple transactions. The seller's responsibility is to provide goods or services, and the buyer's responsibility is to pay the agreed price. However, more complex relationships may be spelled out in a detailed legal contract. An agreement may apply only for a short period, but long-term contracts are also common.

For example, a customer might ask a supplier to guarantee a 6 percent price reduction for a particular part for each of the next three years and pledge to virtually eliminate defects. In return, the customer might offer to double its orders and help the supplier boost productivity.

Sometimes the buyer and seller know roughly what is needed but can't fix all the details in advance. For example, specifications or total requirements may change over time. Then the relationship may involve **negotiated contract buying,** which means agreeing to a contract that allows for changes in the purchase arrangements. In such cases, the general project and basic price is described but with provision for changes and price adjustments up or down.

Some managers think that even a detailed contract isn't a good substitute for regular, good-faith reviews to make sure that neither party gets hurt by changing business conditions. Harley-Davidson used this "operate on a handshake" approach when it moved toward closer relationships with a smaller number of suppliers. Purchasing executives tossed out detailed contracts and replaced them with a short statement of principles to guide relationships between Harley and its suppliers. This approach is typical of relationships with Japanese firms.

Specific adaptations invest in the relationship

Relationship-specific adaptations involve changes in a firm's product or procedures that are unique to a relationship partner. Industrial suppliers often custom design a new product for just one customer; this may require investments in R&D

or new manufacturing technologies. Donnelly Corp. is an extreme example. It had been supplying Honda with mirrors for the interiors of its cars. Honda's purchasing people liked Donnelly's collaborative style, so they urged Donnelly to supply exterior mirrors as well. Donnelly had never been in that business—so it had to build a factory to get started.

Buying firms may also adapt to a particular supplier; a computer maker may design around Intel's Pentium chip. However, buyers are often hesitant about increased dependence on a specific supplier. Typically, they do it only when there isn't a good alternative—perhaps because only one supplier is available to meet a need.[13]

Powerful customer may control the relationship

Although a marketing manager may want to work in a cooperative partnership, that may be impossible with large customers who have the power to dictate how the relationship will work. For example, Duall/Wind was a supplier of small plastic parts for Polaroid instant cameras. When Duall/Wind wanted to raise its prices to cover increasing costs, Polaroid's purchasing manager demanded that Duall/Wind show a breakdown of all its costs, from materials to labor to profit. As Duall/Wind's president said, "I had a tough time getting through my head that Polaroid wanted to come right in here and have us divulge all that." But Polaroid is a big account—and it got the information it wanted.[14]

Buyers may still use several sources to spread their risk

Even if a marketing manager develops the best marketing mix possible and cultivates a close relationship with the customer, the customer may not give *all* of its business to one supplier. Buyers often look for several dependable sources of supply to protect themselves from unpredictable events such as strikes, fires, or floods in one of their suppliers' plants. A good marketing mix is still likely to win a larger share of the total business—which can prove to be very important. From a buyer's point of view, it may not seem like a big deal to give a particular supplier a 30 percent share of the orders rather than a 20 percent share. But for the supplier that's a 50 percent increase in sales![15]

Reciprocity may influence relationship

We've emphasized that most buyer–seller relationships are based on reducing the customer's total procurement costs. However, some relationships are based on reciprocity. **Reciprocity** means trading sales for sales—that is, "if you buy from me, I'll buy from you." If a company's customers also can supply products that the firm buys, then the sales departments of both buyer and seller may try to trade sales for sales. Purchasing managers generally resist reciprocity but often face pressure from their sales departments.

Reciprocity is often a bigger factor in other countries than it is in the United States. In Japan, for example, reciprocity is very common.[16]

Internet E-Commerce Is Reshaping Many Business Markets

New types of B2B e-commerce websites have quickly changed the way that buyers make decisions and relate to suppliers. The Web makes it possible for all types of information to flow between buyers and sellers much more quickly and efficiently. This often lowers the cost of the search for market information and the cost of transactions. For example, online order systems can cut out paper-shuffling bottlenecks, speed delivery of purchases, and reduce inventory costs. We'll discuss these distribution service issues in more detail in Chapter 11.

Here, we'll cover the e-commerce website resources that many buyers use and the role that they play. We'll consider them separately, but often one website (or linked set of websites) combines them.

Community sites mainly offer digital information

Like online trade magazines (or online trade associations), community websites offer information and communications of interest for specific industries. A site may focus on a single "community" or feature different sections for many industries. For example, www.verticalnet.com has separate communities for different industries, ranging from food processing and solid-waste management to health care and utilities. Community sites were among the first on the Web; many just put in digital form information that was already distributed in other ways. Initially they relied on advertising revenue to operate, but now some are trying to earn commissions based on sales referrals.

Catalog sites make it convenient to search for products

Catalog sites, as the name implies, offer digital product catalogs, usually for a number of different sellers. Catalog sites make it easy for industrial buyers to search for a product and do one-stop shopping. For example, PlasticsNet.com focuses on chemicals used in the plastic industry. Grainger's OrderZone.com features a vast array of supply items that are used across many different industries. Some catalog sites are upgrading their service to make it easier for a buyer to place an order, track delivery status, and update inventory information. Others are improving the quality of the information available. For example, rather than just describe an electric motor a site might allow the buyer to download detailed engineering drawings.

Exchanges bring buyers and sellers together

Exchanges operate much like a stock exchange (for example, the New York Stock Exchange) by bringing buyers and sellers together, usually anonymously, to agree on prices for commodities such as energy (see, for example, www.altranet.com) or telecommunications capacity. Some exchanges act as independent intermediaries. Others are backed by major firms in the industry. Either way, an exchange must maintain a neutral role and not favor either buyers or sellers if it expects return visits.

Procurement hubs operate for the benefit of buyers

A procurement hub site gives potential suppliers a central source of information for the purchasing needs of a firm or industry. Some large firms have created procurement hubs to handle purchasing for all of their own divisions. In some industries, firms band together to create a procurement hub. The big three automakers in the U.S. do this.

These hubs are becoming an important, buyer-driven force in e-commerce. They make it easier and less costly for suppliers to find out about and pursue sales

In business-to-business markets, the Internet has prompted explosive growth in e-commerce and new central market "portals" that bring buyers and sellers together more quickly and at lower cost.

opportunities in target firms and industries. As a result, the number of suppliers competing for a buyer's business often increases. This tends to drive down selling prices or provide benefits to the buyer with respect to other terms of the sale.

Interactive competitive bidding systems drive down prices

Most procurement hubs use an interactive system to get competitive bids. **Competitive bids** are the terms of sale offered by different suppliers in response to the purchase specifications posted by the buyer. Usually, the focus is on the supplier's price. Firms have relied on competitive bidding for a long time. However, before the Internet it usually took too long to go through several rounds of bids. The Internet makes it fast and easy for the customer firm to run a *reverse auction*. Vendors are invited (via e-mail or at the procurement hub) to place a bid for a purchase with a given specification. The bidding still focuses on price, but sometimes other terms of sales (like warranty period or delivery time) are also important. Each bid, and who made it, is typically visible to all potential bidders via the website. That way, other bidders can decide whether or not to offer the customer a lower price.

Auction sites focus on unique items

Auction sites tend to be more seller-driven and are especially popular for items such as used equipment and vehicles, perishable products, and surplus inventory (such as unsold advertising space) that are unique and only available for sale once. For example, www.avbid.net runs auctions related to aircraft parts and services. At these auctions the seller lists and describes what's for sale, and potential buyers place their bids (what they would pay) at a website. Auctions use a variety of formats, but in general the highest bidder (prior to the deadline) purchases the product. Some auction sites also handle reverse auctions for the benefit of buyers.

Collaboration hubs support cooperation

Collaboration hubs go beyond matching buyers and sellers for a one-time transaction and instead are designed to help firms work together. The collaboration might involve design, manufacturing, and distribution. Many of these sites focus on the needs of smaller firms in a specific industry. For instance, Citadon (www.citadon.com) provides a single online workplace for construction contractors to collaborate with architects, store blueprints, work through building permit requirements, and purchase building materials.

Websites within and across industries

As the examples above suggest, some B2B e-commerce websites are specialized for firms at different levels of production and distribution within a particular industry. For example, a "vertical" site that specializes on the plastics industry might be of interest to firms that make the basic chemicals from which plastics are formed, firms that create plastic injection molding equipment, and firms that use that equipment to make finished goods. On the other hand, some websites are designed to serve a broad ("horizontal") cross section of firms from different industries. For example, a horizontal site might serve manufacturers regardless of whether they produce bearings, truck frames, or construction equipment. See Exhibit 6-6.

One consequence of these differences in focus is that there are many sites with potentially overlapping coverage. While some industries are not covered well, in other industries many sites compete to be *the* central market. As a result, this is an arena in which there are still many ongoing changes. Hundreds, or perhaps thousands, of B2B websites that were established just a few years ago have already disappeared, and consolidation is still underway.

Internet (ro)bots search for products—by description

Because of such problems, purchasing managers often turn to special software packages to help with their search effort. For example, if a purchasing manager can specify a certain model of a product the search "bot" (short for *robot*) looks at all of the websites on the Internet to find everywhere that the product is mentioned.

Exhibit 6-6 Examples of Different B2B E-Commerce Sites Used by Organizational Buyers and Sellers

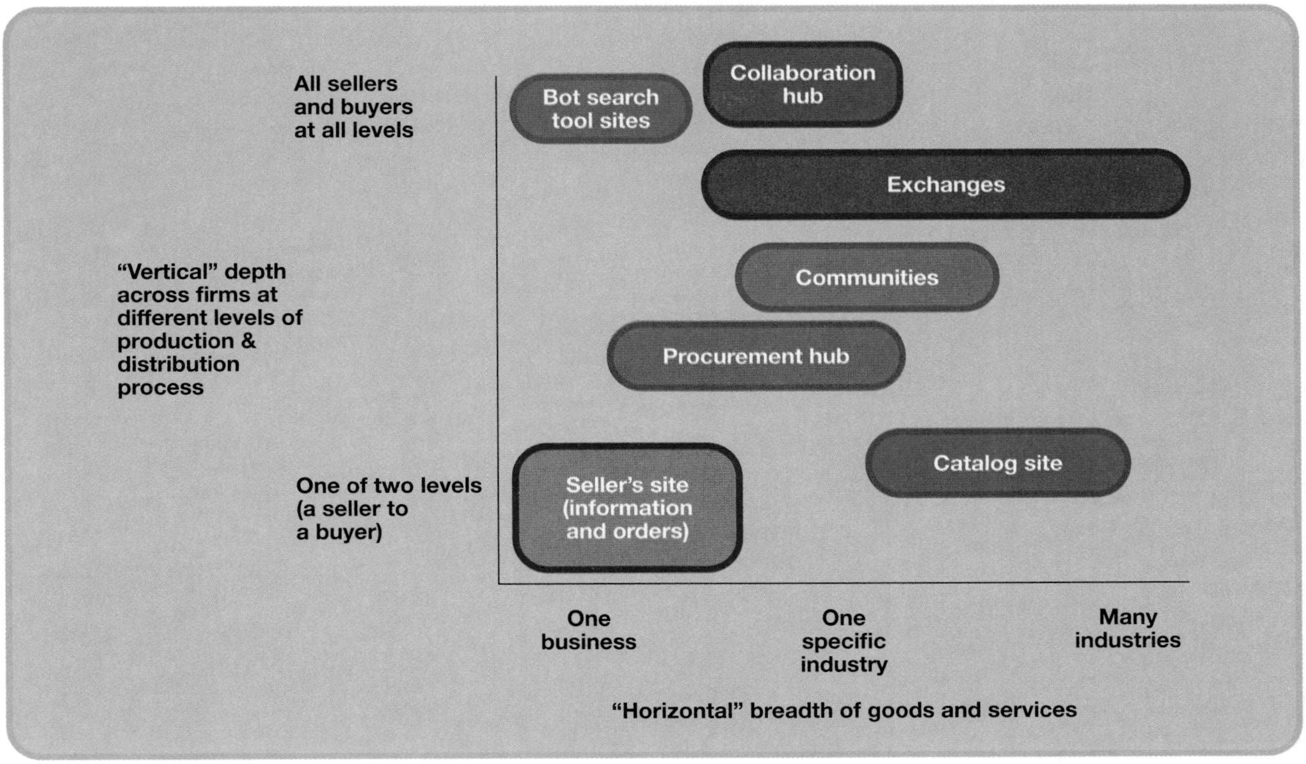

Some bots take things further and assemble price comparisons or a list of e-mail addresses.

Some purchasing managers are using search bots to locate hard-to-find, off-the-shelf products that eliminate the need for custom-produced items. For example, Allstates Rubber & Tools in the suburbs of Chicago is a small firm, but it's on the Internet. Allstates recently got a $1,000 order for rubber grommets (tiny rings used to protect electric wires) from a company in Saudi Arabia. If the customer had not been able to locate Allstates' website on the Internet it probably would have paid higher prices to have the grommets custom-produced—and Allstates would have missed the business.[17]

More progress is needed

As we've said from the start, business customers are usually interested in the total value of a supplier's marketing mix—not just in the product price in a single transaction. Earlier we reviewed why a buyer might prefer closer relationships with fewer sellers. So it is important to see that Internet tools that focus primarily on lowering the purchase price for a specific transaction do not necessarily lower total purchasing costs or apply to all types of purchases. So websites and Internet-based software tools that help both buyers and sellers work together in more efficient and effective relationships warrant attention. National Semiconductor's website is a good example. It is designed to create easy links between its customers, products, and distributors. Its large customers get special services, like access to a secure website that shows specific purchase histories and production or shipping status of their orders. Smaller customers can get all the product information they need and then link directly to the order page for the distributor that serves them. This system does not go as far as some, but it does illustrate how shared information and cooperation over the Internet is helping to create better relationships in business markets.[18]

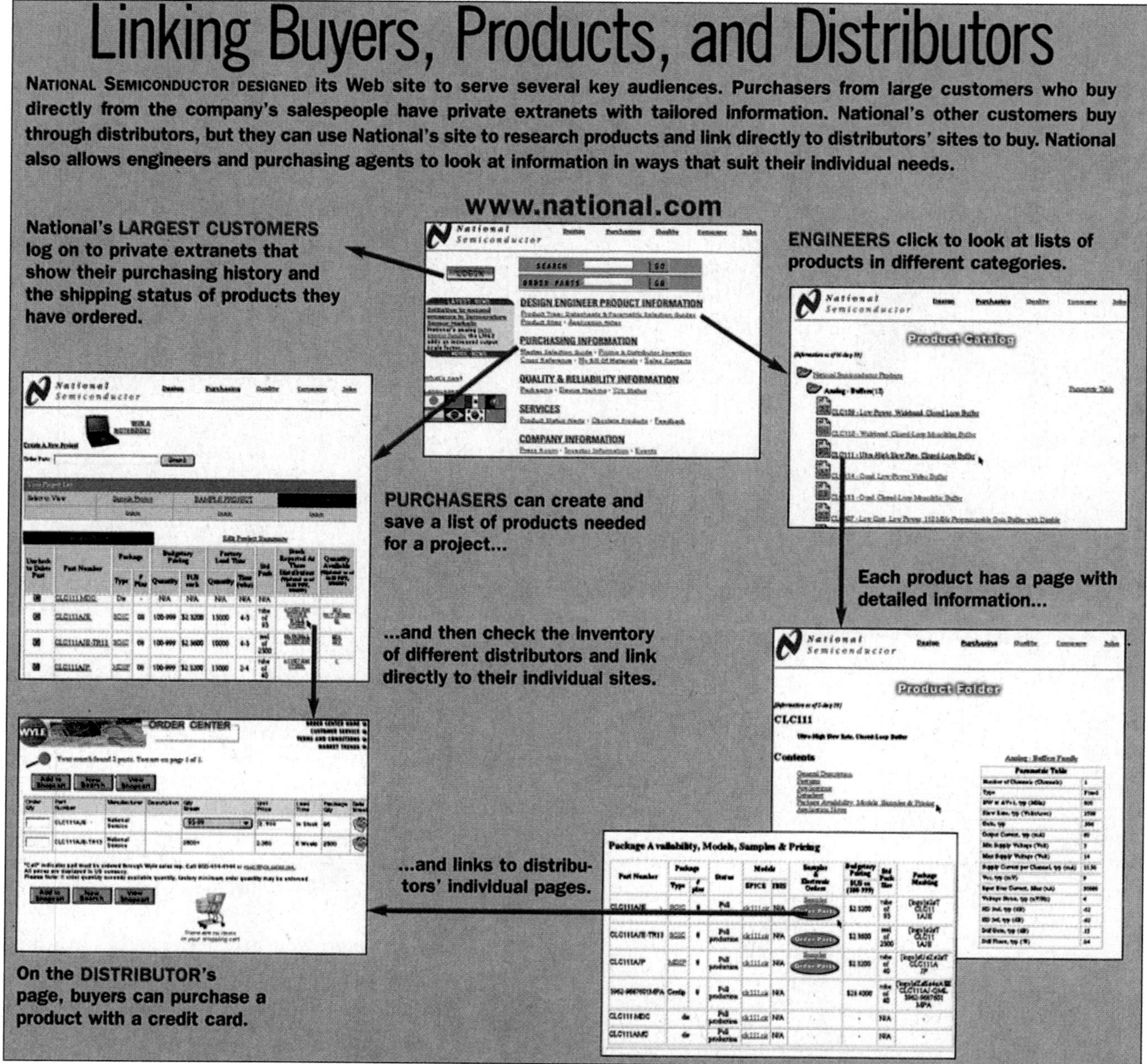

E-commerce order systems are common

E-commerce computer systems now *automatically* handle a large portion of routine order-placing. Buyers program decision rules that tell the computer how to order and leave the details of routine following through to the machine. For example, when an order comes in that requires certain materials or parts, the computer system automatically orders them from the appropriate suppliers, the delivery date is set, and production is scheduled.

In a routine order situation, it's very important to be one of the regular sources of supply. For straight rebuys, the buyer (or computer) may place an order without even considering other potential sources. Obviously, it's a big sale to be selected as the major supplier that routinely receives all of a customer's electronic orders for the products you sell. Often this type of customer will be more impressed by an attractive marketing mix for a whole *line* of products than just a lower price for a particular item. Further, it may be too expensive and too much trouble to

GE Lights the Way for E-Commerce

General Electric is a true pioneer in e-commerce—and its successes provide evidence of what is possible. Even so, some of its early efforts didn't work. When it first tried to solicit bids from vendors over the Internet, it only focused on price. So it got a lot of lowball quotes from firms that didn't have the ability to fill orders. By 1995 GE was on a smarter track. It developed an Internet-based system called the Trading Process Network (TPN) that eliminated the delays of traditional purchasing approaches using paper documents and snail mail. With TPN, a buyer for GE's lighting division could search the Net to find possible suppliers for the custom-made machine tools it needed. To eliminate the paper shuffle, electronic blueprints could be sent with a bid request via e-mail. As a GE purchasing manager put it, they could "simply point and click and send out a bid package to suppliers around the world." Suppliers could respond quickly, too. So a bid process that previously took about a month could be reduced to only days, or even hours.

When GE executives saw how e-commerce was improving their purchasing, they decided to offer the TPN service to outside companies. A small firm could try the TPN Web (www.getradeweb.com) for a fee of only $65 a month. However, the monthly fee for a large company was $70,000. That pricing gives a hint of the kind of savings big purchasers could reap—and why GE's Global eXchange Services (GXS) division pushed to develop a full-service Internet portal (www.gegxs.com). GSX now operates one of the largest B2B e-commerce networks in the world. It has more than 100,000 trading partners. The network handles 1 billion transactions a year for goods and services worth $1 trillion.

GE has continued to drive down its own purchasing costs with e-commerce. In the first six months that it used real-time, online competitive bidding, GE saved $480 million. However, even GE does not purchase everything this way. Its current target is to do about 30 percent of purchases online. And even with online competitive bidding it does not always select the lowest bid. A supplier with a higher bid may get the business when it offers service or other value that GE needs.[19]

www.mhhe.com/fourps

change the whole buying system just because somebody is offering a low price on a particular day.

However, if a buyer believes that there are several suppliers who could meet the specs, the buyer may request competitive bids. If different suppliers' quality, dependability, and delivery schedules all meet the specs, the buyer will select the low-price bid. But a creative marketer needs to look carefully at the purchaser's specs—and the need—to see if other elements of the marketing mix could provide a competitive advantage.

Sellers' sales reps (and perhaps whole teams of people) regularly call on these customers, but *not* to sell a particular item. Rather, they want to maintain relations, become a preferred source, or point out new developments that might cause the buyer to reevaluate the present straight rebuy procedure and give more business to the sales rep's company.

Variations in buying by customer type

We've been discussing aspects of relationships and e-commerce that generally apply with different types of customer organizations—in both the U.S. and internationally. However, it's also useful to have more detail about specific types of customers.

Manufacturers Are Important Customers

There are not many big ones

One of the most striking facts about manufacturers is how few there are compared to final consumers. This is true in every country. In the United States, for example, there are about 366,000 factories. Exhibit 6-7 shows that the majority of these are quite small—over half have less than 10 workers. But these small firms account for less than 3 percent of manufacturing value. In small plants, the owners often do the buying. And they buy less formally than buyers in the relatively few large manufacturing plants—which employ most of the workers and produce a large share of the value added by manufacturing. For example, plants with 250 or more employees make up less than 4 percent of the total—yet they employ nearly half of the production employees and produce about 61 percent of the value added by manufacturers.

Exhibit 6-7 Size Distribution of Manufacturing Establishments

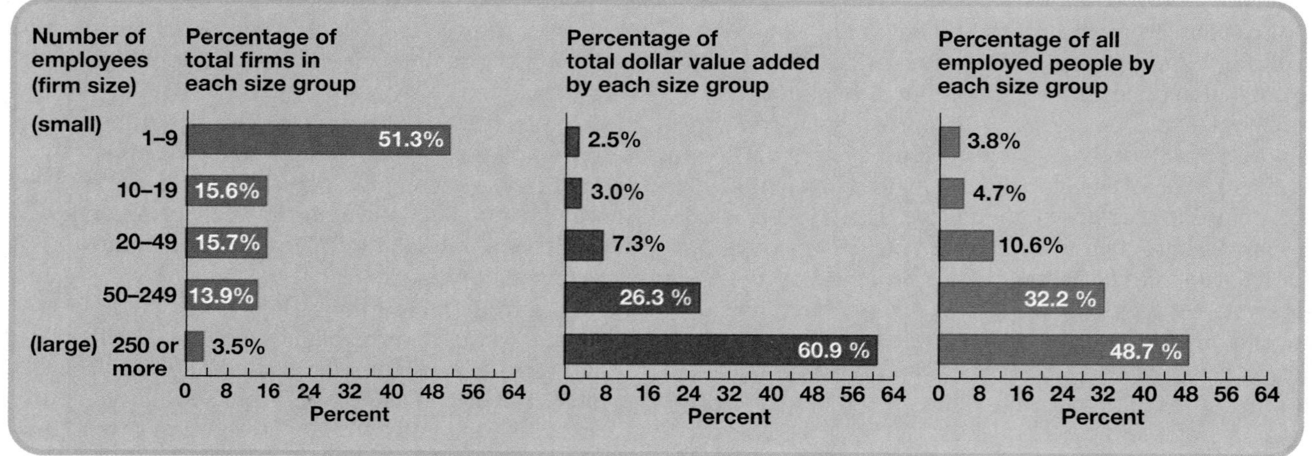

In other countries, the size distribution of manufacturers varies. But across different countries, the same general conclusion holds: It is often desirable to segment industrial markets on the basis of customer size because large firms do so much of the buying.

Customers cluster in geographic areas

In addition to concentration by company size, industrial markets are concentrated in certain geographic areas. Internationally, industrial customers are concentrated in countries that are at the more advanced stages of economic development. From all the talk in the news about the U.S. shifting from an industrial economy to a service economy or an information economy you might conclude that the U.S. is an exception—that the U.S. industrial market is shrinking. But that's a myth. U.S. manufacturing output is higher than at any other time in history.

Within a country, there is often further concentration in specific areas. In the U.S., many factories are concentrated in big metropolitan areas—especially in New York, Pennsylvania, Ohio, Illinois, Texas, and California. There is also concentration by industry. In Germany, for example, the steel industry is concentrated in the Ruhr Valley. Similarly, U.S. manufacturers of high-tech electronics are concentrated in California's famous Silicon Valley near San Francisco and also along Boston's Route 128.[20]

Business data often classify industries

The products an industrial customer needs to buy depend on the business it is in. Because of this, sales of a product are often concentrated among customers in similar businesses. For example, apparel manufacturers are the main customers for buttons. Marketing managers who can relate their own sales to their customers' type of business can focus their efforts.

Detailed information is often available to help a marketing manager learn more about customers in different lines of business. The U.S. government collects and publishes data by the **North American Industry Classification System (NAICS) codes**—groups of firms in similar lines of business. (NAICS is pronounced like "nakes.") The number of establishments, sales volumes, and number of employees—broken down by geographic areas—are given for each NAICS code. A number of other countries collect similar data, and some of them try to coordinate their efforts with an international variation of the NAICS system.

The U.S. adopted NAICS as a standard in 1997 and it is being phased in over time. The phase-in makes it easier to use the system because in the past data were reported using Standard Industrial Classification (SIC) codes. Many of the codes are similar; check the website at www.naics.com for details. However, the move to the new system should help business marketers. The NAICS system is suited for identifying new or fast-changing industries—and for marketers that spells opportunity. NAICS is also more detailed than SIC and works better for services such as financial institutions,

A firm like Alcoa Aluminum is likely to find that the majority of its customers are concentrated within a few industries that it can identify by Industry Classification System code number.

health care providers, and firms in the entertainment business. The general logic of NAICS and SIC is similar. So let's take a closer look at how the NAICS codes work.

The NAICS code breakdowns start with broad industry categories such as construction (23), manufacturing (31), wholesale trade (42), finance and insurance (52), and so on. Within each two-digit industry breakdown, much more detailed data may be available for three-digit industries (that is, subindustries of the two-digit industries). For example, within the two-digit manufacturing industry (code 31) there are manufacturers of food (311), beverages and tobacco (312), and others, including apparel manufacturers (315). Then each three-digit group of firms is further subdivided into more detailed four-, five-, and six-digit classifications. For instance, within the three-digit (315) apparel manufacturers there are four-digit subgroups for knitting mills (3151), cut and sew firms (3152), and producers of apparel accessories (3159). Exhibit 6-8 illustrates that breakdowns are more detailed as you move to codes with more digits. However, detailed data (say, broken down at the four-digit level) aren't available for all industries in every geographic area. The government does not provide detail when only one or two plants are located in an area.[21]

Internet

Internet Exercise Comprehensive information about NAICS codes is available online (www.naics.com). At the website select "Find Your NAICS Code" and when the search page appears submit a query for the keyword "welding." If your firm was interested in selling its lasers to manufacturers of laser welding equipment, what is the NAICS code of the industry for which you would want to get a list of manufacturers?

Producers of Services—Smaller and More Spread Out

The service side of the U.S. economy is large and has been growing fast. Service operations are also growing in some other countries. There are many good opportunities to provide these companies with the products they need to support their operations. But there are also challenges.

The United States has about 2.5 million service firms—over six times as many as it has manufacturers. Some of these are big companies with international operations. Examples include AT&T, Hilton Hotels, Prudential Insurance, CitiGroup, and

Exhibit 6-8 Illustrative NAICS Code Breakdown for Apparel Manufacturers

Sector	Construction (23)	Manufacturing (31)	others...	
Subsector	Food (311)	Apparel (315)	others...	
Industry group	Knitting mills (3151)	Cut and sew apparel (3152)	Apparel accessories (3159)	others...
Industry	Women's & girls' (31523)	Men's & boys' (31522)	Other cut & sew (31529)	others...
U.S. industry	Underwear & nightwear (315221)	Suits and coats (315222)	Shirts (315223)	others...

EDS (Electronic Data Systems). These firms have purchasing departments that are like those in large manufacturing organizations. But most service firms are small. They're also more spread out than manufacturing concerns. Factories often locate where it is less costly to produce goods in quantity. Service operations, in contrast, often have to be close to their customers.

Buying may not be as formal

Purchases by small service firms are often handled by whoever is in charge. This may be a doctor, lawyer, owner of a local insurance agency, or manager of a hotel. Suppliers who usually deal with purchasing specialists in large organizations may have trouble adjusting to this market. Personal selling is still an important part of promotion, but reaching these customers in the first place often requires more advertising. And small service firms may need much more help in buying than a large corporation.

Canon, the familiar name in office copiers, was very successful serving the needs of smaller service firms like law offices. Canon developed promotion materials to help first-time buyers understand differences in copiers. It emphasized that its machines were easy to use and maintain. And Canon also used retail channels to make the copiers available in smaller areas where there wasn't enough business to justify using a sales rep.[22]

Retailers and Wholesalers Buy for Their Customers

Most retail and wholesale buyers see themselves as purchasing agents for their target customers—remembering the old saying that "Goods well bought are half sold." Typically, retailers do *not* see themselves as sales agents for particular manufacturers. They buy what they think they can profitably sell. For example, the buying specialist at Walgreens Drugstores who handles products targeted at ethnic consumers is a real expert. He knows what ethnic customers want and won't be persuaded by a sales rep for a manufacturer who can't provide it. Of course, there is a place for collaboration, as when the Walgreens buyer works with people at Soft Sheen Products to develop a new product for the African American target market. That's profitable for both firms.

Committee buying is impersonal

Space in retail stores is limited and buyers for retail chains simply are not interested in carrying every product that some salesperson wants them to sell. In an average week, 150 to 250 new items are offered to the buying offices of a large chain like Safeway. If the chain accepted all of them, it would add 10,000 new items during a single year! Obviously, these firms need a way to deal with this overload.[23]

Decisions to add or drop lines or change buying policies may be handled by a *buying committee*. The seller still calls on and gives a pitch to a buyer—but the buyer does not have final responsibility. Instead, the buyer prepares forms summarizing proposals for new products and passes them on to the committee for evaluation. This rational, almost cold-blooded approach certainly reduces the impact of a persuasive salesperson. On the other hand, it may favor a firm that has hard data on how its whole marketing mix will help the retailer to attract and keep customers.

Reorders are straight rebuys

Retailers and wholesalers usually carry a large number of products. A drug wholesaler, for example, may carry up to 125,000 products. Because they deal with so many products, most middlemen buy their products on a routine, automatic reorder basis—straight rebuys—once they make the initial decision to stock specific items. Sellers to these markets must understand the size of the buyer's job and have something useful to say and do when they call.

Buyers watch computer output closely

Most wholesalers and retailers now use computerized inventory replenishment systems. Scanners at retail checkout counters keep track of what goes out the door—and computers use this data to update the records. Even small retailers and wholesalers use automated control systems that create daily reports showing sales of every product. Buyers with this kind of information know, in detail, the profitability of the different competing products. If a product isn't moving, the retailer isn't likely to be impressed by a salesperson's request for more in-store attention or added shelf space.

Colgate and Carrefour executives in France work together to create mutually beneficial programs not only for the retailer's home country but for the many other countries where Carrefour is expanding.

Some are not "open to buy"

Retail buyers are sometimes controlled by a miniature profit and loss statement for each department or merchandise line. In an effort to make a profit, the buyer tries to forecast sales, merchandise costs, and expenses. The figure for "cost of merchandise" is the amount buyers have budgeted to spend over the budget period. If the money has not yet been spent, buyers are **open to buy**—that is, the buyers have budgeted funds that can be spent during the current period. However, if the budget has been spent, they are no longer in the market and no amount of special promotion or price-cutting is likely to induce them to buy.[24]

Buying and selling are closely related

In wholesale and retail firms, there is usually a very close relationship between buying and selling. Buyers are often in close contact with their firm's salespeople and with customers. The housewares buyer for a local department store, for example, may even supervise the salespeople who sell housewares. Salespeople are quick to tell the buyer if a customer wants a product that is not available—especially if the salespeople work on commission.

Resident buyers may help a firm's buyers

Resident buyers are independent buying agents who work in central markets (New York City, Paris, Rome, Hong Kong, Chicago, Los Angeles) for several retailer or wholesaler customers based in outlying areas or other countries. They buy new styles and fashions and fill-in items as their customers run out of stock during the year.

Resident buying organizations fill a need. They help small channel members (producers and middlemen) reach each other inexpensively. Resident buyers usually are paid an annual fee based on their purchases.

The Government Market

Size and diversity

Some marketers ignore the government market because they think that government red tape is more trouble than it's worth. They probably don't realize how big the government market really is. Government is the largest customer group in many countries—including the United States. About 35 percent of the U.S. gross national product is spent by various government units; the figure is much higher in some economies. Different government units in the United States spend about $2,866,000,000,000 (think about it!) a year to buy almost every kind of product. They run not only schools, police departments, and military organizations, but also supermarkets, public utilities, research laboratories, offices, hospitals, and even liquor stores. These huge government expenditures cannot be ignored by an aggressive marketing manager.

Competitive bids may be required

Government buyers in the United States are expected to spend money wisely—in the public interest. To avoid charges of favoritism, most government customers buy by specification using a mandatory bidding procedure. Often the government buyer must accept the lowest bid that meets the specifications. You can see how important it is for the buyer to write precise and complete specifications. Otherwise, sellers may submit a bid that fits the specs but doesn't really match what is needed. By law, a government unit might have to accept the lowest bid—even for an unwanted product. Writing specifications is not easy—and buyers usually appreciate the help of well-informed salespeople.

Rigged specs are an ethical concern

At the extreme, a government customer who wants a specific brand or supplier may try to write the description so that no other supplier can meet all the specs. The buyer may have good reasons for such preferences—a more reliable product, prompt delivery, or better service after the sale. This kind of loyalty sounds great, but marketers must be sensitive to the ethical issues involved. Laws that require government customers to get bids are intended to increase competition among suppliers, not reduce it. Specs that are written primarily to defeat the purpose of these laws may be viewed as illegal bid rigging.

The approved supplier list

Specification and bidding difficulties aren't problems in all government orders. Some items that are bought frequently—or for which there are widely accepted standards—are purchased routinely. The government unit simply places an order at a previously approved price. To share in this business, a supplier must be on the list of approved suppliers. The list is updated occasionally, sometimes by a bid procedure.

Negotiated contracts are common too

Negotiation is often necessary when there are many intangible factors. Unfortunately, this is exactly where favoritism and influence can slip in. And such influence is not unknown—especially in city and state government contracts. Nevertheless, negotiated contracts are an important buying method in government sales—so a marketing mix should emphasize more than just low price.[25]

Learning what government wants

In the United States, there are more than 85,000 local government units (school districts, cities, counties, and states) as well as many federal agencies that make purchases. Keeping on top of all of them is nearly impossible. Potential suppliers should focus on the government units they want to cater to and learn the bidding methods of those units. Then it's easier to stay informed since most government contracts are advertised.

A marketer can learn a lot about potential government target markets from various government publications and by using the Internet. For example, there is an online government contractors' resource center at www.govcon.com. It includes a link to the online version of the U.S. federal government's *Commerce Business Daily*, which lists most current purchase bid requests. The Small Business Administration (www.sba.gov) offers many resources, including the *U.S. Purchasing, Specifications, and Sales Directory*. It explains government procedures to encourage competition for such business. Various state and local governments also offer guidance, as do government units in many other countries.

Dealing with foreign governments

Selling to government units in foreign countries can be a real challenge. In many cases, a firm must get permission from the government in its own country to sell to a foreign government. Moreover, most government contracts favor domestic suppliers if they are available. Public sentiment may make it very difficult for a foreign competitor to get a contract. Or the government bureaucracy may simply bury a foreign supplier in so much red tape that there's no way to win.

Is it unethical to "buy help"?

In some countries, government officials expect small payments (grease money) just to speed up processing of routine paperwork, inspections, or decisions from the local bureaucracy. Outright influence peddling—where government officials or their friends request bribe money to sway a purchase decision—is common in some markets. In the past, marketers from some countries have looked at such bribes as a cost of doing business. However, the **Foreign Corrupt Practices Act**, passed by the U.S. Congress in 1977, prohibits U.S. firms from paying bribes to foreign officials. A person who pays bribes, or authorizes an agent to pay them, can face stiff penalties. However, the law was amended in 1988 to allow small grease money payments if they are customary in a local culture. Further, a manager isn't held responsible if an agent in the foreign country secretly pays bribes.[26]

Conclusion

In this chapter, we considered the number, size, location, and buying behavior of various types of organizational customers—to try to identify logical dimensions for segmenting markets and developing marketing mixes. We looked at who makes and influences organizational buying decisions, and how multiple influence may make the marketing job more difficult. We also saw that the problem-solving models of buyer behavior introduced in Chapter 5 apply here, with modifications.

Buying behavior—and marketing opportunities—may change when there's a close relationship between a supplier and a customer. However, close relationships are not an all-or-nothing thing. There are different ways that a supplier can build a closer relationship with its customers. We identified key dimensions of relationships and their benefits and limitations.

We also looked at how buyers use e-commerce in the buying process. Some capabilities, like interactive competitive bidding, have already had a major impact. And much progress is underway toward fostering more efficient relationships.

The chapter focuses on aspects of buying behavior that often apply to different types of organizational customers. However, we discussed some key differences in the manufacturer, services, middleman, and government markets.

A clear understanding of organizational buying habits, needs, and attitudes can aid marketing strategy planning. And since there are fewer organizational customers than final consumers, it may even be possible for some marketing managers (and their salespeople) to develop a unique strategy for each potential customer.

This chapter offers some general principles that are useful in strategy planning—but the nature of the products being offered may require adjustments in the plans. Different product classes are discussed in Chapter 8. Variations by product may provide additional segmenting dimensions to help a marketing manager fine-tune a marketing strategy.

Questions and Problems

1. In your own words, explain how buying behavior of business customers in different countries may have been a factor in speeding the spread of international marketing.
2. Compare and contrast the buying behavior of final consumers and organizational buyers. In what ways are they most similar and in what ways are they most different?
3. Briefly discuss why a marketing manager should think about who is likely to be involved in the buying center for a particular purchase. Is the buying center idea useful in consumer buying? Explain your answer.
4. If a nonprofit hospital were planning to buy expensive MRI scanning equipment (to detect tumors), who might be involved in the buying center? Explain your answer and describe the types of influence that different people might have.
5. Describe the situations that would lead to the use of the three different buying processes for a particular product—lightweight bumpers for a pickup truck.
6. Why would an organizational buyer want to get competitive bids? What are some of the situations when competitive bidding can't be used?
7. How likely would each of the following be to use competitive bids: *(a)* a small town that needed a road resurfaced, *(b)* a scouting organization that needed a printer to print its scouting handbook, *(c)* a hardware retailer that wants to add a new lawn mower line, *(d)* a grocery store chain that wants to install new checkout scanners, and *(e)* a sorority that wants to buy a computer to keep track of member dues? Explain your answers.
8. Discuss the advantages and disadvantages of just-in-time supply relationships from an organizational buyer's point of view. Are the advantages and disadvantages merely reversed from the seller's point of view?
9. Explain why a customer might be willing to work more cooperatively with a small number of suppliers rather than pitting suppliers in a competition against each other. Give an example that illustrates your points.
10. Would a tool manufacturer need a different marketing strategy for a big retail chain like Home Depot than for a single hardware store run by its owner? Discuss your answer.
11. How do you think a furniture manufacturer's buying habits and practices would be affected by the specific type of product to be purchased? Consider fabric for upholstered furniture, a lathe for the

production line, cardboard for shipping cartons, and lubricants for production machinery.

12. Discuss the importance of target marketing when analyzing organizational markets. How easy is it to isolate homogeneous market segments in these markets?
13. Explain how NAICS codes might be helpful in evaluating and understanding business markets. Give an example.
14. Considering the nature of retail buying, outline the basic ingredients of promotion to retail buyers. Does it make any difference what kinds of products are involved? Are any other factors relevant?
15. The government market is obviously an extremely large one, yet it is often slighted or even ignored by many firms. Red tape is certainly one reason, but there are others. Discuss the situation and be sure to include the possibility of segmenting in your analysis.
16. Some critics argue that the Foreign Corrupt Practices Act puts U.S. businesses at a disadvantage when competing in foreign markets with suppliers from other countries that do not have similar laws. Do you think that this is a reasonable criticism? Explain your answer.

Suggested Cases

5. Republic Polymer Company
6. Three Rivers Steel Company
19. Chemical International, Inc.
29. Huntoon & Balbiera, P.C.

Computer-Aided Problem

6. **Vendor Analysis**

CompuTech, Inc., makes circuit boards for microcomputers. It is evaluating two possible suppliers of electronic memory chips.

The chips do the same job. Although manufacturing quality has been improving, some chips are always defective. Both suppliers will replace defective chips. But the only practical way to test for a defective chip is to assemble a circuit board and "burn it in"—run it and see if it works. When one chip on a board is defective at that point, it costs $2.00 for the extra labor time to replace it. Supplier 1 guarantees a chip failure rate of not more than 1 per 100 (that is, a defect rate of 1 percent). The second supplier's 2 percent defective rate is higher, but its price is lower.

Supplier 1 has been able to improve its quality because it uses a heavier plastic case to hold the chip. The only disadvantage of the heavier case is that it requires CompuTech to use a connector that is somewhat more expensive.

Transportation costs are added to the price quoted by either supplier, but Supplier 2 is further away so transportation costs are higher. And because of the distance, delays in supplies reaching CompuTech are sometimes a problem. To ensure that a sufficient supply is on hand to keep production going, CompuTech must maintain a backup inventory—and this increases inventory costs. CompuTech figures inventory costs—the expenses of finance and storage—as a percentage of the total order cost.

To make its vendor analysis easier, CompuTech's purchasing agent has entered data about the two suppliers on a spreadsheet. He based his estimates on the quantity he thinks he will need over a full year.

a. *Based on the results shown in the initial spreadsheet, which supplier do you think CompuTech should select? Why?*
b. *CompuTech estimates it will need 100,000 chips a year if sales go as expected. But if sales are slow, fewer chips will be needed. This isn't an issue with Supplier 2; its price is the same at any quantity. However, Supplier 1's price per chip will be $1.95 if CompuTech buys less than 90,000 during the year. If CompuTech only needs 84,500 chips, which supplier would be more economical? Why?*
c. *If the actual purchase quantity will be 84,500 and Supplier 1's price is $1.95, what is the highest price at which Supplier 2 will still be the lower-cost vendor for CompuTech? (Hint: You can enter various prices for Supplier 2 in the spreadsheet—or use the results feature to vary Supplier 2's price and display the total costs for both vendors.)*

For additional questions related to this problem, see Exercise 6-3 in the *Learning Aid for Use with Essentials of Marketing*, 9th edition.

When You Finish This Chapter, You Should

1. Know about marketing information systems.

2. Understand a scientific approach to marketing research.

3. Know how to define and solve marketing problems.

4. Know about getting secondary and primary data.

5. Understand the role of observing, questioning, and using experimental methods in marketing research.

6. Understand the important new terms (shown in red.)

Chapter Seven

Improving Decisions with Marketing Information

With over 860 stores, LensCrafters has quickly become one of the largest chains of eyewear stores in the United States, Canada, and Puerto Rico.

A key to LensCrafters' success is that its managers use marketing research to better understand target market needs and to plan strategies. It's also easy for managers to get—and share—marketing information. That's because the company has its own intranet, and the information on it is constantly updated.

When LensCrafters was first evaluating the eye care market, a situation analysis revealed that there was a big opportunity. For example, library research revealed that 57 percent of people aged 18 or older wear eyeglasses, contact lenses, or both. Many also get sunglasses. Similarly, government statistics showed that demographic trends were favorable to long-run growth in the $10 billion a year eye care market.

Subsequent LensCrafters research provided guidance for

place price promotion produ

turning this opportunity into a marketing strategy. Focus group interviews and consumer surveys confirmed that most consumers viewed shopping for glasses as very inconvenient. Frame selections were too small, opticians' shops were typically closed when customers were off work and had time to shop, and the whole process usually required long waits and repeat trips. So LensCrafters put the labs that make the glasses right in its stores and kept the stores open nights and weekends. Ads tout LensCrafters' high-quality, one-hour service. With LensCrafters' new, patented Accu-Fit Measuring System, customers are assured of a perfect-fitting pair of glasses.

To be sure that service quality lives up to the advertising promises, LensCrafters sends a customer satisfaction survey to every customer. Surveys are analyzed by store and used to find out what's going on where. LensCrafters even ties satisfaction results to employee bonuses.

To make it convenient for more consumers to shop at LensCrafters, the chain has been aggressively opening new stores. The firm's Internet website (www.lenscrafters.com) offers a store locator. Because the size and growth rate of various age groups in a geographic market drive demand for vision products, LensCrafters analyzes demographic data to locate new stores where profit potential is greatest. And each store carries a very large selection of frame styles, lenses, and sunglasses tailored to the age, gender, and ethnic makeup of the local market.

Managers at LensCrafters also routinely analyze sales data that are available in the firm's marketing information system. By breaking down sales by product, store, and time period, they can spot buying trends early and plan

www.mhhe.com/fourps

for them. This is especially important now that LensCrafters is putting more emphasis on eyewear fashion.

Research also guides promotion decisions. For example, LensCrafters uses direct-mail advertising targeted to customers in segments where interest in its fashionable eyeglasses is highest.[1]

Radical Changes Are Underway in Marketing Information

The LensCrafters case shows that successful marketing strategies require information about potential target markets and their likely responses to marketing mixes as well as about competition and other marketing environment variables. Managers also need information for implementation and control. Without good information, managers are left to guess—and in today's fast-changing markets, that invites failure.

MIS makes information available and accessible

Firms like LensCrafters realize that it doesn't pay to wait until you have important questions you can't answer. They anticipate the information they will need. They work to develop a *continual flow of information* that is available and quickly accessible when it's needed.

A **marketing information system (MIS)** is an organized way of continually gathering, accessing, and analyzing information that marketing managers need to make decisions.

We won't cover all of the technical details of planning for an MIS. But you should understand what an MIS is so you know some of the possibilities. So, we'll be discussing the elements of a complete MIS as shown in Exhibit 7-1. As part of that review, we'll highlight how technology is changing MIS use.

Get more information—faster and easier

Recent developments in information technology are having a *radical* impact on what information is available to marketing managers and how quickly. A short

New developments in computer networks and software are making it easier for companies to gather and analyze marketing information.

Exhibit 7-1
Elements of a Complete Marketing Information System

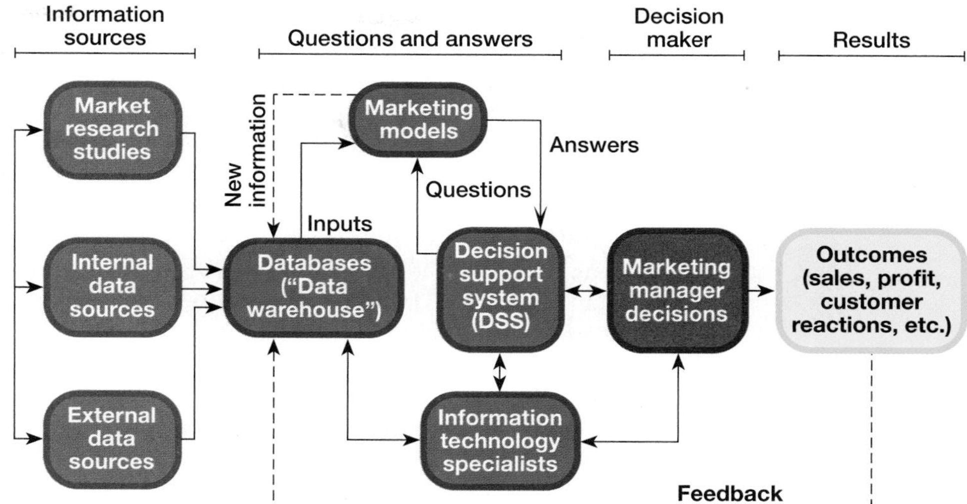

time ago, connecting remote computers or exchanging data over networks was very difficult. Now, it's standard. And even a manager with little computer experience can quickly learn to use an MIS. As a result, managers everywhere have access to much more information. It's instantly available, and often just a mouse click away.

An intranet is easy to update

Many firms, even very small ones, have their own **intranet**—a system for linking computers within a company. An intranet works like the Internet. However, to maintain security, access to websites on an intranet is usually limited to employees. Even so, information is available on demand. Further, it's a simple matter to "publish" new information to a website as it becomes available.

The *type* of information available is changing dramatically. As recently as 1995, most marketing managers with information needs relied on computers mainly for number crunching. The multimedia revolution in computing has quickly lifted that limitation. Now it doesn't matter whether marketing information takes the form of a marketing plan, report, memo, spreadsheet, database, presentation, photo, graphic, or table of statistics. It is all being created on computer. So it can be easily stored and accessed by computer.

Marketing managers must help develop an MIS

In most companies, an MIS is set up by a person or group that provides *all* departments in the firm with information technology support. These specialists are important, but the marketing manager should play an important role, too. Marketing managers know what data they've routinely used or needed in the past. They can also foresee what types of data might be useful. They should communicate these needs to the specialists so the information will be there when they want it and in the form they want it.

Decision support systems put managers online

An MIS organizes incoming information into a **data warehouse**—a place where databases are stored so that they are available when needed. You can think of a data warehouse as a sort of electronic library, where all of the information is indexed extremely well. Firms with an MIS often have information technology specialists who help managers get specialized reports and output from the warehouse. However, to get better decisions, most MIS systems now provide marketing managers with a decision support system. A **decision support system (DSS)** is a computer program that makes it easy for a marketing manager to get and use information *as he or she is making decisions*.

A decision support system usually involves some sort of **search engine**—a computer program that helps a marketing manager find information that is needed. For example, a manager who wants sales data for the previous week or day might search for any database or computer file that references the term *unit sales* as well as the relevant data. The search engine would identify any files where that term appeared. If there were many, the manager could narrow the search further (say by specifying the product of interest).

When the search is focused on numerical data, simply finding the information may not go far enough. Thus, a DSS typically helps change raw data—like product sales for the previous day—into more *useful information*. For example, it may draw graphs to show relationships in data—perhaps comparing yesterday's sales to the sales on the same day in the last four weeks. The MIS that managers at Frito-Lay use illustrates the possibilities.

All of Frito-Lay's salespeople are equipped with hand-held computers. Throughout the day they input sales information at the stores they visit. In the evening they send all the data over telephone lines to a central computer, where it is analyzed. Within 24 hours marketing managers at headquarters and in regional offices get reports and graphs that summarize how sales went the day before—broken down by brands and locations. The information system even allows a manager to zoom in and take a closer look at a problem in Peoria or a sales success in Sacramento.[2]

Some decision support systems go even further. They allow the manager to see how answers to questions might change in various situations. For example, a manager at Kraft Foods may want to estimate how much sales will increase if the firm uses a certain type of promotion in a specific market area. The DSS will ask the manager for a *personal* judgment about how much business could be won from each competitor in that market. Then, using this input and drawing on data in the database about how the promotion had worked in other markets, the system will make a sales estimate using a marketing model. A **marketing model** is a statement of relationships among marketing variables.[3]

Many firms are not there yet

Of course, not every firm has a complete MIS system. And in some firms that do, managers don't know how to use what's there. A major problem is that many managers are used to doing it the old way—and they don't think through what information they need.

One sales manager thought he was progressive when he asked his assistant for a report listing each sales rep's sales for the previous month and the current month. The assistant quickly found the relevant information on the firm's intranet, put it into an Excel spreadsheet, and printed out the report. Later, however, she was surprised to see the sales manager working on the list with a calculator. He was figuring the percentage change in sales for the month and ranking the reps from largest increase in sales to smallest. The spreadsheet software could have done all of that—instantly—but the sales manager got what he *asked for*, not what he really needed. An MIS can provide information—but only the marketing manager knows what problem needs solving. It's the job of the manager—not the computer or the MIS specialist—to ask for the right information in the right form.[4]

New questions require new answers

MIS systems tend to focus on recurring information needs. Routinely analyzing such information can be valuable to marketing managers. But it shouldn't be their only source of information for decision making. They must try to satisfy ever-changing needs in dynamic markets. So marketing research must be used—to supplement data already available and accessible through the MIS.

What Is Marketing Research?

Research provides a bridge to customers

The marketing concept says that marketing managers should meet the needs of customers. Yet today, many marketing managers are isolated in company offices—far from potential customers. This means marketing managers have to rely on help from **marketing research**—procedures to develop and analyze new information to help marketing managers make decisions. One of the important jobs of a marketing researcher is to get the "facts" that are not currently available.

Who does the work?

Most large companies have a separate marketing research department to plan and carry out research projects. These departments often use outside specialists—including interviewing and tabulating services—to handle technical assignments. Further, they may call in specialized marketing consultants and marketing research organizations to take charge of a research project.

Small companies (those with less than $4 or $5 million in sales) usually don't have separate marketing research departments. They often depend on their salespeople or managers to conduct what research they do.

Some nonprofit organizations have begun to use marketing research—usually with the help of outside specialists. For example, many politicians rely on research firms to conduct surveys of voter attitudes.[5]

Ethical issues in marketing research

The basic reason for doing marketing research is to get information that people can trust in making decisions. But research often involves many hidden details. A person who wants to misuse marketing research to pursue a personal agenda can often do so.

Perhaps the most common ethical issues concern decisions to withhold certain information about the research. For example, a manager might selectively share only those results that support his or her viewpoint. Others involved in a decision might never know that they are getting only partial truths. Or during a set of interviews, a researcher may discover that consumers are interpreting a poorly worded question many different ways. If the researcher doesn't admit the problem, an unknowing manager may rely on meaningless results.

Another problem involves more blatant abuses. It is unethical for a firm to contact consumers under the pretense of doing research when the real purpose is to sell something. For example, some political organizations have been criticized for surveying voters to find out their attitudes about various political candidates and issues. Then, armed with that information, someone else calls back to solicit donations. Legitimate marketing researchers don't do this!

The relationship between the researcher and the manager sometimes creates an ethical conflict. Managers must be careful not to send a signal that the only acceptable results from a research project are ones that confirm their existing viewpoints. Researchers are supposed to be objective, but that objectivity may be swayed if future jobs depend on getting the "right" results.[6]

Effective research usually requires cooperation

Good marketing research requires cooperation between researchers and marketing managers. Researchers must be sure their research focuses on real problems.

Marketing managers must be able to explain what their problems are and what kinds of information they need. They should be able to communicate with specialists in the specialists' language. They should also know about some of the basic decisions made during the research process so they know the limitations of the findings.

Developments in information technology are making it easier to gather information about customers, but marketers need to be sensitive to concerns that some consumers and critics have about privacy. Zero-Knowledge, the Canadian company featured here, positions itself as the "consumer's advocate on privacy."

For this reason, our discussion of marketing research won't emphasize mechanics but rather how to plan and evaluate the work of marketing researchers.[7]

The Scientific Method and Marketing Research

The scientific method can help marketing managers make better decisions. The **scientific method** is a decision-making approach that focuses on being objective and orderly in *testing* ideas before accepting them. With the scientific method, managers don't just *assume* that their intuition is correct. Instead, they use their intuition and observations to develop **hypotheses**—educated guesses about the relationships between things or about what will happen in the future. Then they test their hypotheses before making final decisions.

A manager who relies only on intuition might introduce a new product without testing consumer response. But a manager who uses the scientific method might say, "I think (hypothesize) that consumers currently using the most popular brand will prefer our new product. Let's run some consumer tests. If at least 60 percent of the consumers prefer our product, we can introduce it in a regional test market. If it doesn't pass the consumer test there, we can make some changes and try again."

The scientific method forces an orderly research process. Some managers don't carefully specify what information they need. They blindly move ahead—hoping that research will provide "the answer." Other managers may have a clearly defined problem or question but lose their way after that. These hit-or-miss approaches waste both time and money.

Five-Step Approach to Marketing Research

The **marketing research process** is a five-step application of the scientific method that includes:

1. Defining the problem.
2. Analyzing the situation.
3. Getting problem-specific data.

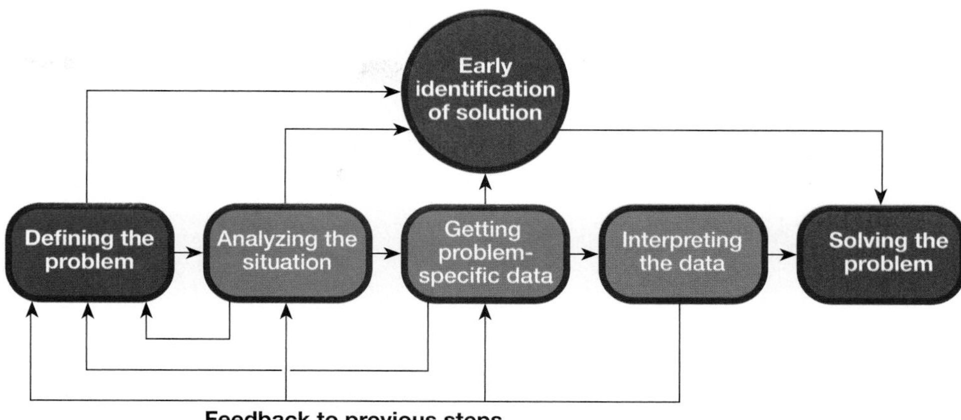

Exhibit 7-2
Five-Step Scientific Approach to Marketing Research Process

4. Interpreting the data.
5. Solving the problem.

Exhibit 7-2 shows the five steps in the process. Note that the process may lead to a solution before all of the steps are completed. Or as the feedback arrows show, researchers may return to an earlier step if needed. For example, the interpreting step may point to a new question—or reveal the need for additional information—before a final decision can be made.

Defining the Problem—Step 1

Defining the problem is often the most difficult step in the marketing research process. But it's important for the objectives of the research to be clearly defined. The best research job on the wrong problem is wasted effort.

Finding the right problem level almost solves the problem

Our strategy planning framework is useful for guiding the problem definition step—as well as the whole marketing research process. First, a marketing manager should understand the target market and what needs the firm can satisfy. Then the manager can focus on lower-level problems—namely, how sensitive the target market is to a change in one or more of the marketing mix ingredients. Without such a framework, marketing researchers can waste time, and money, working on the wrong problem.[8]

Don't confuse problems with symptoms

The problem definition step sounds simple—and that's the danger. It's easy to confuse symptoms with the problem. Suppose a firm's MIS shows that the company's sales are decreasing in certain territories while expenses are remaining the same—resulting in a decline in profits. Will it help to define the problem by asking: How can we stop the sales decline? Probably not. This would be like fitting a hearing-impaired patient with a hearing aid without first trying to find out *why* the patient was having trouble hearing.

It's easy to fall into the trap of mistaking symptoms for the problem. When this happens, the research objectives are not clear, and researchers may ignore relevant questions—while analyzing unimportant questions in expensive detail.

Setting research objectives may require more understanding

Sometimes the research objectives are very clear. A manager wants to know if the targeted households have tried a new product and what percent of them bought it a second time. But research objectives aren't always so simple. The manager might also want to know *why* some didn't buy or whether they had even heard of the product. Companies rarely have enough time and money to study everything. A manager must narrow the research objectives. One good way is to develop a list of research questions that includes all the possible problem areas. Then the manager can consider the items on the list more completely—in the situation analysis step—before narrowing down to final research objectives.

Analyzing the Situation—Step 2

What information do we already have?

When the marketing manager thinks the real problem has begun to surface, a situation analysis is useful. A **situation analysis** is an informal study of what information is already available in the problem area. It can help define the problem and specify what additional information, if any, is needed.

Pick the brains around you

The situation analysis usually involves informal talks with informed people. Informed people can be others in the firm, a few good middlemen who have close contact with customers, or others knowledgeable about the industry. In industrial markets—where relationships with customers are close—researchers may even call the customers themselves.

Situation analysis helps educate a researcher

The situation analysis is especially important if the researcher is a research specialist who doesn't know much about the management decisions to be made or if the marketing manager is dealing with unfamiliar areas. They both must be sure they understand the problem area—including the nature of the target market, the marketing mix, competition, and other external factors. Otherwise, the researcher may rush ahead and make costly mistakes or simply discover facts that management already knows. The following case illustrates this danger.

A marketing manager at the home office of a large retail chain hired a research firm to do in-store interviews to learn what customers liked most, and least, about some of its stores in other cities. Interviewers diligently filled out their questionnaires. When the results came in, it was apparent that neither the marketing manager nor the researcher had done their homework. No one had even talked with the local store managers! Several of the stores were in the middle of some messy remodeling—so all the customers' responses concerned the noise and dust from the construction. The research was a waste of money.

Secondary data may provide the answers—or some background

The situation analysis should also find relevant **secondary data**—information that has been collected or published already. Later, in Step 3, we will cover **primary data**—information specifically collected to solve a current problem. Too often researchers rush to gather primary data when much relevant secondary information is already available—at little or no cost! See Exhibit 7-3.

A lot of secondary data is available

Ideally, a lot of secondary data is already available from the firm's MIS. Data that have not been organized in an MIS may be available from the company's files and reports. Secondary data also are available from libraries, trade associations, government agencies, and private research organizations; increasingly, these organizations are putting their information online. So one of the first places a researcher should look for secondary data is on the Internet.

Search engines find information on the Internet

Although much information relevant to your situation analysis may be on the Internet, it won't do you much good if you can't find it. Fortunately, there are a number of good tools for searching on the Internet and reference books that explain the details of the different tools. However, the basic idea is simple. And, usually, the best way to start is to use a search engine.

Exhibit 7-3 Sources of Secondary and Primary Data

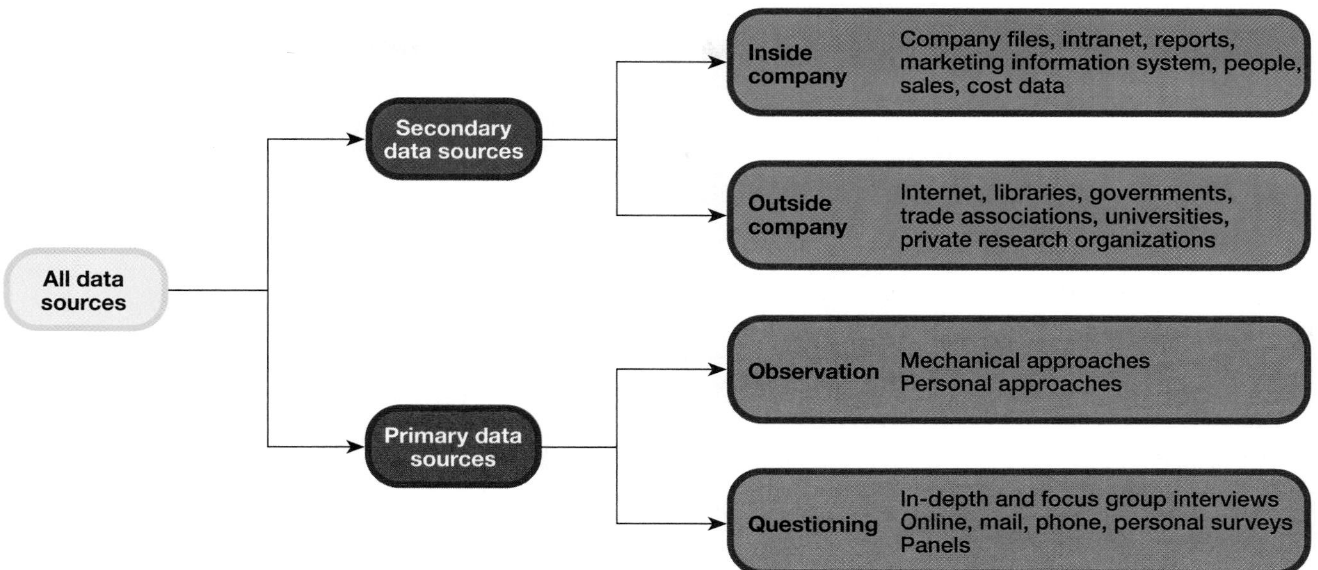

Most popular Internet browsers, like Netscape Navigator and Microsoft Internet Explorer, have a menu selection or button to activate an Internet search. In addition, there are hundreds of more specialized search engines. In general a user specifies words or a phrase to find and the search engine produces a list of hyperlinks to websites where that search string is found. Usually all you do is click on the hyperlink of interest, and the browser shows the relevant page for that hyperlink on screen. If you want, you can go back to the list and check out another hyperlink.

One popular and useful search engine is at the website for Yahoo (www.yahoo.com). It is especially good at searching for web pages. Another very useful search engine is at the AltaVista website (www.altavista.digital.com); it does a good job of classifying online documents that include the search string. A search engine that is particularly useful for locating specific people or businesses is at www.hotbot.lycos.com. The Northern Light search engine (www.northernlight.com) is very good at identifying published articles on the search topic. Keep in mind, however, that these are just a few of the popular search engines. In fact, if you want to get an idea of how many are available—and how they are different—go to www.yahoo.com and do a search on the term *search engine*.[9]

Most computerized database and index services are now available over the Internet. Some of these are provided by libraries and private firms. For instance, for a fee a user can use Dow Jones' interactive news retrieval system (www.djnr.com) to search the full text of hundreds of publications, including newspapers from around the world. ProQuest Direct, at www.proquest.com, is another valuable research tool. It provides access to one of the world's largest collections of information, including summaries of articles from over 5,000 publications. Many articles are available in full text, full image format.

Internet

Internet Exercise Assume that your boss has asked you to do a customer satisfaction survey. As part of a situation analysis, you want to get ideas about what others have done in this area. Go to the website for the Yahoo search engine (www.yahoo.com). In the dialogue box type 'customer satisfaction survey' (include the single quote marks) and click on search. Look at some of the websites identified. How helpful is this? How could it be improved?

The Internet is dramatically changing how marketing managers get both primary and secondary data.

Government data are inexpensive

Federal and state governments publish data on many subjects. Government data are often useful in estimating the size of markets. In Chapter 4 we gave a number of examples of the different types of data that are available and suggested websites. Distribution of government data is not limited to the Internet, however. Almost all government data are available in inexpensive publications. Much of it is also available in computer form ready for further analysis.

Sometimes it's more practical to use summary publications for leads to more detailed reports. For the U.S. market, one of the most useful summary references is the *Statistical Abstract of the United States*. Like an almanac, it is issued in print form each year and gives 1,500 summary tables from more than 200 published sources. Detailed footnotes guide readers to more specific information on a topic. The abstract and much of the source material on which it is based are available online at www.census.gov. Similarly, the *United Nations Statistical Yearbook* is one of the finest summaries of worldwide data; like many other international statistical references, it is available on CD-ROM and online (www.un.org/depts/unsd).

Secondary data are very limited on some international markets. However, most countries with advanced economies have government agencies that help researchers get the data they need. For example, Statistics Canada (www.statcan.ca) compiles a great deal of information on the Canadian market. Eurostat (europa.eu.int/comm/eurostat), the statistical office for the European Union countries, and the Organization for Economic Cooperation (in Paris) offer many publications packed with data on Europe. In the United States, the Department of Commerce (www.doc.gov) distributes statistics compiled by all other federal departments. Some city and state governments have similar agencies for local data. The Yahoo website (www.yahoo.com) provides an index to a large amount of information about different governments.

Private sources are useful too

Many private research organizations—as well as advertising agencies, newspapers, and magazines—regularly compile and publish data. A good business library is valuable for sources such as *Sales & Marketing Management*, *Advertising Age*, *Journal of Global Marketing*, and the publications of the National Industrial Conference Board.

The *Encyclopedia of Associations* lists 75,000 U.S. and international trade and professional associations that can be a good source of information. For example, the American Marketing Association (www.ama.org) has an information center with many marketing publications.[10]

Situation analysis yields a lot—for very little

The virtue of a good situation analysis is that it can be very informative but takes little time. And it's inexpensive compared with more formal research efforts—like a large-scale survey. Situation analysis can help focus further research or even eliminate the need for it entirely. The situation analyst is really trying to determine the exact nature of the situation and the problem.

Determine what else is needed

At the end of the situation analysis, you can see which research questions—from the list developed during the problem definition step—remain unanswered. Then you have to decide exactly what information you need to answer those questions and how to get it.

This may require discussion between technical experts and the marketing manager. Often companies use a written **research proposal**—a plan that specifies what information will be obtained and how—to be sure no misunderstandings occur later. The research plan may include information about costs, what data will be collected, how it will be collected, who will analyze it and how, and how long the process will take. Then the marketing manager must decide if the time and costs involved are worthwhile. It's foolish to pay $100,000 for information to solve a $50,000 problem!

Getting Problem-Specific Data—Step 3

Gathering primary data

The next step is to plan a formal research project to gather primary data. There are different methods for collecting primary data. Which approach to use depends on the nature of the problem and how much time and money are available.

In most primary data collection, the researcher tries to learn what customers think about some topic or how they behave under some conditions. There are two basic methods for obtaining information about customers: *questioning* and *observing*. Questioning can range from qualitative to quantitative research. And many kinds of observing are possible.

Qualitative questioning—open-ended with a hidden purpose

Qualitative research seeks in-depth, open-ended responses, not yes or no answers. The researcher tries to get people to share their thoughts on a topic—without giving them many directions or guidelines about what to say.

A researcher might ask different consumers, "What do you think about when you decide where to shop for food?" One person may talk about convenient location, another about service, and others about the quality of the fresh produce. The real advantage of this approach is *depth*. Each person can be asked follow-up questions so the researcher really understands what *that* respondent is thinking. The depth of the qualitative approach gets at the details—even if the researcher needs a lot of judgment to summarize it all.

Focus groups stimulate discussion

The most widely used form of qualitative questioning in marketing research is the **focus group interview,** which involves interviewing 6 to 10 people in an informal group setting. The focus group also uses open-ended questions, but here the interviewer wants to get group interaction—to stimulate thinking and get immediate reactions.

A skilled focus group leader can learn a lot from this approach. A typical session may last an hour, so participants can cover a lot of ground. Sessions are often videotaped (or broadcast over the Internet or by satellite) so different managers can form their own impressions of what happened. Some research firms create electronic focus groups in which participants log onto a specified website and with others participate in a chat session; each person types in comments that are shared on the computer screen of each of the other participants. What they type is the record of the session.[11]

Regardless of how a focus group is conducted, conclusions reached from a session usually vary depending on who watches it. A typical problem—and serious limitation—with qualitative research is that it's hard to measure the results objectively.

Focus groups can be conducted quickly and at relatively low cost—an average of about $3,500 each. This is part of their appeal. But focus groups are probably being overused. It's easy to fall into the trap of treating an idea arising from a focus group as a "fact" that applies to a broad target market. For example, it's trendy for food product firms in Japan to do focus groups with teenage girls. The logic is that girls will be brutally honest about what they think and that they are good at predicting what will be a hit. So based on a girl's comments in a focus group, Meiji Milk Products substituted oolong tea for fruit juice in a new drink it was developing. The suggested change might or might not be a good one. But there's no way to know if one girl's point of view is representative.[12]

To avoid this trap, some researchers use qualitative research to prepare for quantitative research. For example, the Jacksonville Symphony Orchestra wanted to broaden its base of support and increase ticket sales. It hired a marketing research firm to conduct focus group interviews. These interviews helped the marketing managers refine their ideas about what these target "customers" liked and did not like about the orchestra. The ideas were then tested with a larger, more representative sample.[13]

Qualitative research can provide good ideas—hypotheses. But we need other approaches—perhaps based on more representative samples and objective measures—to *test* the hypotheses.

Structured questioning gives more objective results

When researchers use identical questions and response alternatives, they can summarize the information quantitatively. Samples can be larger and more representative, and various statistics can be used to draw conclusions. For these reasons, most survey research is **quantitative research**—which seeks structured responses that can be summarized in numbers, like percentages, averages, or other statistics. For example, a

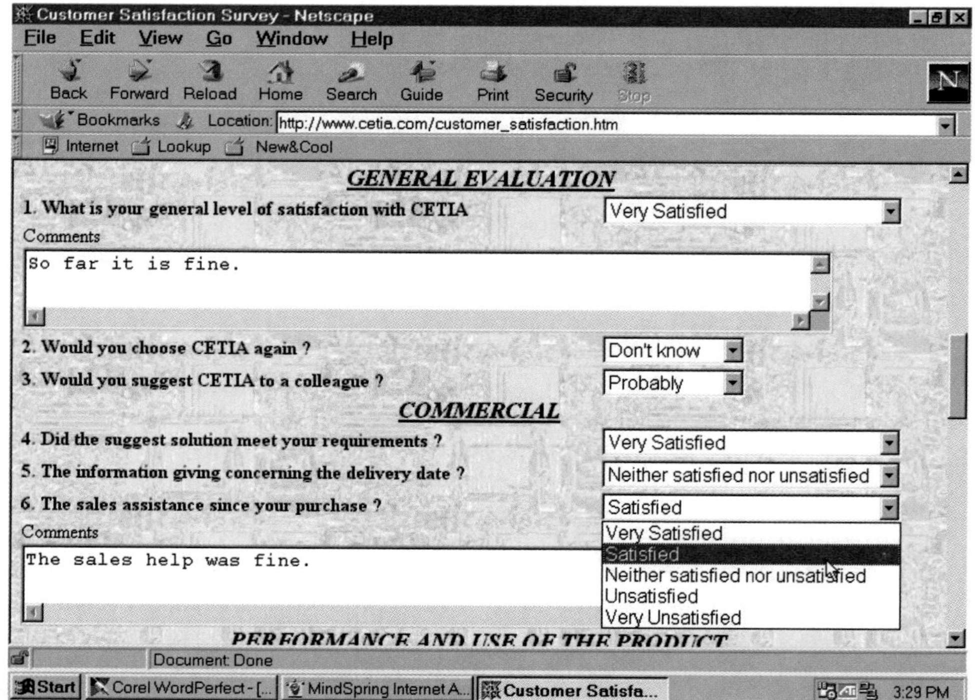

CETIA is a European manufacturer of minicomputers. When it delivers a product, it asks the customer to complete this interactive customer satisfaction survey, which is located at CETIA's Internet website. The survey uses a combination of fixed response questions and open-ended comments.

marketing researcher might calculate what percentage of respondents have tried a new product and then figure an average score for how satisfied they were.

Fixed responses speed answering and analysis

Survey questionnaires usually provide fixed responses to questions to simplify analysis of the replies. This multiple-choice approach also makes it easier and faster for respondents to reply. Simple fill-in-a-number questions are also widely used in quantitative research. Fixed responses are also more convenient for computer analysis, which is how most surveys are analyzed.

Surveys come in many forms

Decisions about what specific questions to ask and how to ask them usually depend on how respondents will be contacted—by mail (or electronic mail), via a website, on the phone, or in person. What question and response approach is used may also affect the survey. There are many possibilities. For example, whether the survey is self-administered or handled by an interviewer, the questionnaire may be on paper or in an interactive computer format (perhaps distributed on a CD or disk or displayed on a website). The computer can be programmed to skip certain questions, depending on answers given. Computerized questionnaires also allow the research to show pictures or play audio/video clips (for example, to get reactions to an advertising jingle). In an automated telephone interview, questions may be prerecorded on an audio tape or computer and the subject responds by pushing touch-tone buttons on the phone.

Mail and online surveys are common and convenient

A questionnaire distributed by mail, e-mail, or online is useful when extensive questioning is necessary. Respondents can complete the questions at their convenience. They may be more willing to provide personal information—since a questionnaire can be completed anonymously. But the questions must be simple and easy to follow since no interviewer is there to help. If the respondent is likely to be a computer user, it may be possible to send the questionnaire on a disk (or put it on a website) and include a help feature with additional directions for people who need them.

A big problem with questionnaires is that many people don't complete them. The **response rate**—the percentage of people contacted who complete the questionnaire—is often low and respondents may not be representative. Mail, e-mail, and online

Online surveys provide fast feedback and often at a lower cost than the old-fashioned way. Of course, as always, the manager needs to be certain that the sample used is representative.

surveys are economical if a large number of people respond. But they may be quite expensive if the response rate is low. Worse, the results may be misleading if the respondents are not representative.

Distributing questionnaires by e-mail, or at a website, is popular. It is quick—and the responses come back in computer form. Surveys sent by regular mail usually take a lot longer. In business markets, questionnaires can sometimes be sent by fax.

Regardless of how quickly a questionnaire is distributed, it often takes a month or more to get the data back, which is too slow for some decisions. Moreover, it is difficult to get respondents to expand on particular points. In markets where illiteracy is a problem, it may not be possible to get any response. In spite of these limitations, the convenience and economy of self-administered surveys makes them popular for collecting primary data.

Internet

Internet Exercise Perseus Development Corporation sells software that allows a user to create online questionnaires that can be distributed by e-mail or used on the Internet. To see samples of online questions, go to the Perseus website (www.perseus.com) and then click on *Sample Surveys*. Do you think that it's more convenient for a consumer to complete a survey online or with pencil and paper?

Telephone surveys—fast and effective

Telephone interviews are also popular. They are effective for getting quick answers to simple questions. In addition, with computer-aided telephone interviewing, answers are immediately recorded on a computer, resulting in fast data analysis. On the other hand, many consumers find calls intrusive—and about a third refuse to answer any questions. Moreover, respondents can't be certain who is calling or how personal information might be used.

Personal interview surveys—can be in-depth

A personal interview survey is usually much more expensive per interview than e-mail, mail, or telephone surveys. But it's easier to get and keep the respondent's attention when the interviewer is right there. The interviewer can also help explain complicated directions and perhaps get better responses. For these reasons, personal interviews are commonly used for research on business customers. To reduce the cost of locating consumer respondents, interviews are sometimes done at a store or shopping mall. This is called a mall intercept interview because the interviewer stops a shopper and asks for responses to the survey.

Researchers have to be careful that having an interviewer involved doesn't affect the respondent's answers. Sometimes people won't give an answer they consider embarrassing. Or they may try to impress or please the interviewer. Further, in some cultures people don't want to give any information. For example, many people in Africa, Latin America, and Eastern Europe are reluctant to be interviewed.[14]

Observing—what you see is what you get

Observing—as a method of collecting data—focuses on a well-defined problem. Here we are not talking about the casual observations that may stimulate ideas in

Whirlpool Heats Up Sales with Marketing Research

Marketing managers at Whirlpool want to satisfy customers. So they do a lot of research to find out how satisfied customers really are. For example, Whirlpool participates in a survey that results in the American Satisfaction Index. This survey of 50,000 consumers allows Whirlpool to benchmark what customers think about its quality with ratings for other firms, including competitors. The ratings published in 2000, for example, put Whirlpool among the top companies studied, and its rating was up 2 points from the year before. But the research doesn't stop there. Each year Whirlpool sends an appliance satisfaction survey to 180,000 households. Respondents rate all of their appliances on dozens of dimensions. When a competing product scores higher, Whirlpool engineers take it apart to see why and build the best ideas into their new models. However, they don't just wait for competitors to figure things out first.

A recently introduced oven, now one of Whirlpool's hottest sellers, illustrates their approach. A survey showed that consumers wanted an oven with easy-to-clean controls. That didn't seem consistent with previous sales patterns; the firm's MIS showed that models with knobs consistently outsold models with easier-to-clean push buttons. Rather than disregard the survey, Whirlpool designed a range with touch pad controls by listening to consumers at every step along the way. Consumers who played with computer simulations of the touch pad explained what they liked and didn't like. Videotapes of consumers who tried prototype models in mall intercept interviews provided ideas to further refine the design. The result is a touch pad control that is easy to clean and so easy to use that consumers don't even need to read the manual.

Consumer research has been an even more important factor in Whirlpool's growth overseas. For example, until recently only about one-third of European households had a microwave oven. Whirlpool researchers learned that more people would buy a microwave oven if it could crisp food as it heated the food. Whirlpool designed a microwave with a broiler coil and other innovations. The result is an oven that is popular in Britain for frying bacon and eggs and in Italy for crisping pizza crusts.[15]

www.mhhe.com/fourps

the early steps of a research project. With the observation method, researchers try to see or record what the subject does naturally. They don't want the observing to *influence* the subject's behavior. For example, many franchise companies use the observation method—to check how well a franchisee is performing. KFC hires people to go to different KFC stores and act like normal customers. Then these "secret shoppers" report back to KFC on how they were treated, the quality of the service and food, and the cleanliness of the store.

In some situations, consumers are recorded on videotape. Later, researchers can study the tape by running the film at very slow speed or actually analyzing each frame. Researchers use this technique to study the routes consumers follow through a grocery store or how they select products in a department store. Similarly, firms that have online shopping services on the Internet can use software to "watch" how consumers use the website.

Observing is common in advertising research

Observation methods are common in advertising research. For example, Nielsen Media Research (www.nielsenmedia.com) uses a device called the "people meter" that adapts the observation method to television audience research. This device is attached to the TV set in the homes of selected families. It records when the set is on and what station is tuned in.

Checkout scanners see a lot

Computerized scanners at retail checkout counters, a major breakthrough in observing, help researchers collect very specific, and useful, information. Often this type of data feeds directly into a firm's MIS. Managers of a large chain of stores can see exactly what products have sold each day and how much money each department in each store has earned. But the scanner also has wider applications for marketing research.

Information Resources, Inc. (www.infores.com), and ACNielsen (acnielsen.com) use **consumer panels**—a group of consumers who provide information on a continuing basis. Whenever a panel member shops for groceries, he or she gives an ID card to the clerk who scans the number. Then the scanner records every purchase—

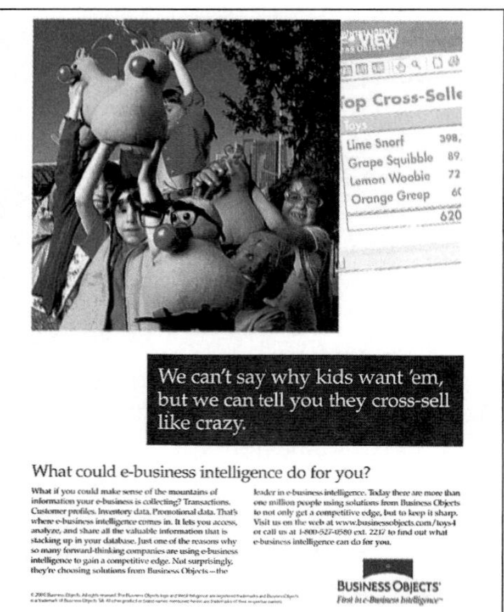

A firm's own data on customers' past purchases, if properly analyzed, can be an important source of information for evaluating new opportunities.

including brands, sizes, prices, and any coupons used. In a variation of this approach, consumers use a hand-held scanner to record purchases once they get home. For a fee, clients can evaluate actual customer purchase patterns and answer questions. If consumers switched from another brand, did they go back to their old brand the next time?

Some members of the consumer panel are also tied into a special TV cable system. With this system, a company can direct advertisements to some houses and not others. Then researchers can evaluate the effect of the ads by comparing the purchases of consumers who saw the ads with those who didn't.

Data captured by electronic scanners are equally important to e-commerce in business-to-business markets. Increasingly, firms mark their shipping cartons and packages with computer-readable bar codes that make it fast and easy to track inventory, shipments, orders, and the like. As information about product sales or shipments becomes available, it is instantly included in the MIS and accessible over the Internet.[16]

Experimental method controls conditions

A marketing manager can get a different kind of information—with either questioning or observing—using the experimental method. With the **experimental method,** researchers compare the responses of two (or more) groups that are similar except on the characteristic being tested. Researchers want to learn if the specific characteristic—which varies among groups—*causes* differences in some response among the groups. For example, a researcher might be interested in comparing responses of consumers who had seen an ad for a new product with consumers who had not seen the ad. The "response" might be an observed behavior—like the purchase of a product—or the answer to a specific question—like "How interested are you in this new product?" See Exhibit 7-4.

Marketing managers for Mars—the company that makes Snickers candy bars—used the experimental method to help solve a problem. They wanted to know if making their candy bar bigger would increase sales enough to offset the higher cost. To decide, they conducted a marketing experiment in which the company carefully varied the size of candy bars sold in *different* markets. Otherwise, the marketing mix stayed the same. Then researchers tracked sales in each market area to see the effect of the different sizes. They saw a big difference immediately: The added sales more than offset the cost of a bigger candy bar.

Simmons' ad agency used an experiment to improve a new print ad for the Beautyrest mattress. Groups of consumers saw two different ads. The ads were the same, except that one featured a father holding a baby and the other featured a mother. The ad with the father earned higher recall scores.

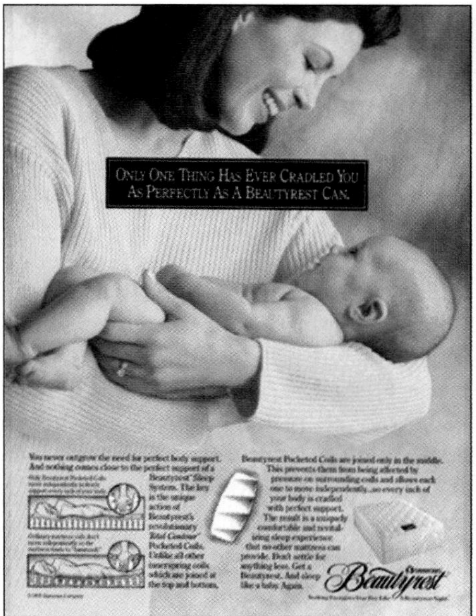

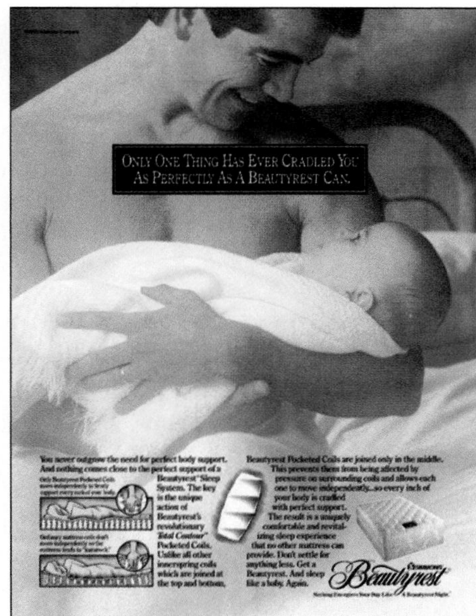

Test-marketing of new products is another type of marketing experiment. In a typical approach, a company tries variations on its planned marketing mix in a few geographic market areas. The results of the tests help to identify problems or refine the marketing mix—before the decision is made to go to broader distribution. However, alert competitors may disrupt such tests—perhaps by increasing promotion or offering retailers extra discounts.[17]

Syndicated research shares data collection costs

Some private research firms collect data and then sell it to many different client firms. Often the marketing manager subscribes to the research service and gets regular updates. This can be an economical approach when marketing managers from different firms need the same type of data. For example, many different auto producers use J. D. Power's (www.jdpa.com) surveys of customer satisfaction—often as the basis for advertising claims.[18]

Exhibit 7-4 Illustration of Experimental Method in Comparing Effectiveness of Two Ads

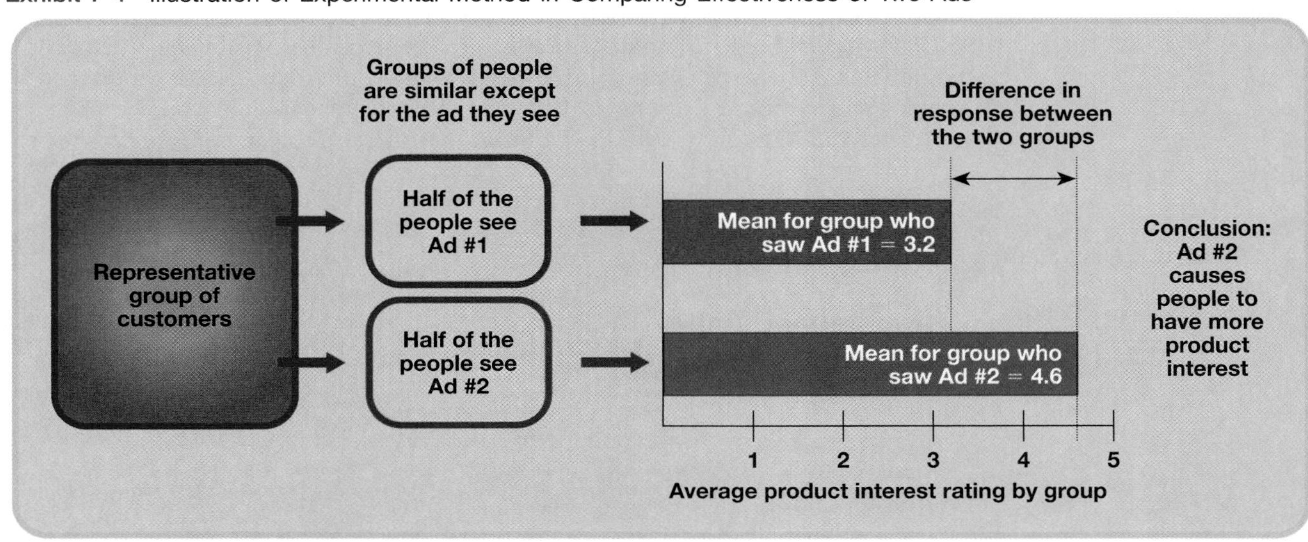

Interpreting the Data—Step 4

What does it really mean?

After someone collects the data, it has to be analyzed to decide what it all means. In quantitative research, this step usually involves statistics. **Statistical packages**—easy-to-use computer programs that analyze data—have made this step easier. As we noted earlier, some firms provide *decision support systems* so managers can use a statistical package to interpret data themselves. More often, however, technical specialists are involved at the interpretation step.

Cross-tabulation is one of the most frequently used approaches for analyzing and interpreting marketing research data. It shows the relationship of answers to two different questions. Exhibit 7-5 is an example. The cross-tab analysis showed that customers who had moved in the last year were much more likely than nonmovers to have adopted "Caller ID" on their phones at home.

There are many other approaches for statistical analysis—the best one depends on the situation. The details of statistical analysis are beyond the scope of this book. But a good manager should know enough to understand what a research project can and can't do.[19]

Is your sample really representative?

It's usually impossible for marketing managers to collect all the information they want about everyone in a **population**—the total group they are interested in. Marketing researchers typically study only a **sample,** a part of the relevant population. How well a sample *represents* the total population affects the results. Results from a sample that is not representative may not give a true picture.

The manager of a retail store might want a phone survey to learn what consumers think about the store's hours. If interviewers make all of the calls during the day, those interviewed might say the limited store hours are "satisfactory." Yet it would be a mistake to assume that *all* consumers are satisfied. Consumers who work outside the home during the day won't be represented.

Research results are not exact

An estimate from a sample, even a representative one, usually varies somewhat from the true value for a total population. Managers sometimes forget this. They assume that survey results are exact. Instead, when interpreting sample estimates, managers should think of them as *suggesting* the approximate value.[20]

Validity problems can destroy research

Even if the sampling is carefully planned, it is also important to evaluate the quality of the research data itself.

Managers and researchers should be sure that research data really measures what it is supposed to measure. Many of the variables marketing managers are interested in are difficult to measure accurately. Questionnaires may let us assign numbers to consumer responses, but that still doesn't mean that the result is precise. An interviewer

Exhibit 7-5
Cross-Tabulation Breakdown of Responses to a Phone Company Consumer Survey

		Have You Moved in the Last Year?		
	Answers:	No	Yes	Total
Do you have "Caller ID" on your phone at home?	*Yes*	10.2%	23.4%	15.5%
	No	89.8	76.6	84.5
	Total	100.0%	100.0%	100.0%

Interpretation: 15.5 percent of people in the survey said that they had "Caller ID" on their phone at home. However, the percentage was much higher (23.4%) among people who had moved in the last year, and lower (10.2%) among people who had not moved.

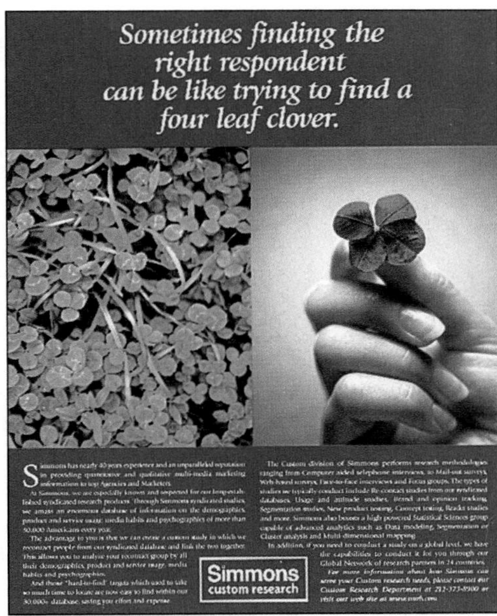

Survey Sampling, Inc., and Simmons Custom Research help marketing researchers develop samples that are really representative of the target market.

might ask "How much did you spend on soft drinks last week?" A respondent may be perfectly willing to cooperate—and be part of the representative sample—but just not be able to remember.

Validity concerns the extent to which data measures what it is intended to measure. Validity problems are important in marketing research because many people will try to answer even when they don't know what they're talking about. Further, a poorly worded question can mean different things to different people and invalidate the results. Often, pretests of a research project are required to evaluate the quality of the questions and measures and to ensure that potential problems have been identified.

Poor interpretation can destroy research

Besides sampling and validity problems, a marketing manager must consider whether the analysis of the data supports the *conclusions* drawn in the interpretation step. Sometimes technical specialists pick the right statistical procedure—their calculations are exact—but they misinterpret the data because they don't understand the management problem. In one survey, car buyers were asked to rank five cars in order from "most preferred" to "least preferred." One car was ranked first by slightly more respondents than any other car so the researcher reported it as the "most liked car." That interpretation, however, ignored the fact that 70 percent of the respondents ranked the car *last*!

Interpretation problems like this can be subtle but crucial. Some people draw misleading conclusions on purpose to get the results they want. Marketing managers must decide whether *all* of the results support the interpretation and are relevant to their problem.

Solving the Problem—Step 5

The last step is solving the problem

In the problem solution step, managers use the research results to make marketing decisions.

Some researchers, and some managers, are fascinated by the interesting tidbits of information that come from the research process. They are excited if the research reveals something they didn't know before. But if research doesn't have action implications, it has little value and suggests poor planning by the researcher and the manager.

When the research process is finished, the marketing manager should be able to apply the findings in marketing strategy planning—the choice of a target market or the mix of the four Ps. If the research doesn't provide information to help guide these decisions, the company has wasted research time and money.

We emphasize this step because it is the reason for and logical conclusion to the whole research process. This final step must be anticipated at each of the earlier steps.

International Marketing Research

Research contributes to international success

Marketing research on overseas markets is often a major contributor toward international marketing success. Conversely, export failures are often due to a lack of home office expertise concerning customer interests, needs, and other segmenting dimensions as well as environmental factors such as competitors' prices and products. Effective marketing research can help to overcome these problems.

Avoid mistakes with local researchers

Whether a firm is small and entering overseas markets for the first time or already large and well established internationally, there are often advantages to working with local market research firms. These research suppliers know the local situation and are less likely to make mistakes based on misunderstanding the customs, language, or circumstances of the customers they study.

Many large research firms have a network of local offices around the world to help with such efforts. Similarly, multinational or local advertising agencies and middlemen can often provide leads on identifying the best research suppliers.

There are a large number of international marketing research firms that offer specialized services to marketing managers.

Some coordination and standardization makes sense

When a firm is doing similar research projects in different markets around the world, it makes sense for the marketing manager to coordinate the efforts. If the manager doesn't establish some basic guidelines at the outset, the different research projects may all vary so much that the results can't be compared from one market area to another. Such comparisons give a home office manager a better chance of understanding how the markets are similar and how they differ.

Companies with operations in various countries often attempt to centralize some market research functions. One reason is to reduce costs or achieve research economies of scale. The centralized approach also improves the firm's ability to transfer experience and know-how from one market area or project to another. For example, one of Eastman Kodak's International Divisions appointed a market research specialist in each subsidiary company throughout the Asian region. The specialists report to local marketing managers but also receive research direction from expert research managers in the head office in the U.S.

There is even greater opportunity and need to standardize and coordinate elements of a marketing information system in an international marketing operation. Computer databases and information systems are most useful when they are designed to include the same variables organized consistently over time. Without this, it is impossible for the manager to go into much depth in comparing and contrasting data from different markets.[21]

How Much Information Do You Need?

What is the value of information?

The high cost of good information must be balanced against its probable value to management. Marketing managers must take risks because of incomplete information. That's part of their job and always will be. But they must weigh the cost of getting more data against its likely value. If the risk is not too great, the cost of getting more information may be greater than the potential loss from a poor decision. A decision to expand into a new territory with the present marketing mix, for example, might be made with more confidence after a $75,000 survey. But just sending a sales rep into the territory for a few weeks to try to sell potential customers would be a lot cheaper. And, if successful, the answer is in and so are some sales.[22]

Conclusion

Marketing managers face difficult decisions in selecting target markets and managing marketing mixes. And managers rarely have all the information they would like to have. This problem is usually worse for managers who work with international markets. But they don't have to rely only on intuition. They can usually obtain good information to improve the quality of their decisions.

Computers and computer networks, like the Internet, are helping marketing managers become full-fledged members of the information age. Both large and small firms are setting up intranets and marketing information systems (MIS)—to be certain that routinely needed data are available and accessible quickly.

Marketing managers deal with rapidly changing environments. Available data are not always adequate to answer the detailed questions that arise. Then a marketing research project may be required to gather new information.

Marketing research should be guided by the scientific method. The scientific approach to solving marketing problems involves five steps: defining the problem, analyzing the situation, obtaining data, interpreting data, and solving the problem. This objective and organized approach helps to keep research on target—reducing the risk of doing costly research that isn't necessary or doesn't solve the problem.

Our strategy planning framework can be helpful in finding the real problem. By finding and focusing on the real problem, the researcher and marketing manager may be able to move quickly to a useful solution—without the cost and risks of gathering primary data in a formal research project. With imagination, they may even be able to find the answers in their MIS or in other readily available secondary data.

Questions and Problems

1. Discuss the concept of a marketing information system and why it is important for marketing managers to be involved in planning the system.
2. In your own words, explain why a decision support system (DSS) can add to the value of a marketing information system. Give an example of how a decision support system might help.
3. If a firm's intranet and marketing decision support system do not include a search engine, would they still be useful to a marketing manager? Why?
4. Discuss how output from a marketing information system (MIS) might differ from the output of a typical marketing research department.
5. Discuss some of the likely problems facing the marketing manager in a small firm that has just purchased a personal computer with a cable modem to search the Internet for information on competitors' marketing plans.
6. Explain the key characteristics of the scientific method and show why these are important to managers concerned with research.
7. How is the situation analysis different from the data collection step? Can both these steps be done at the same time to obtain answers sooner? Is this wise?
8. Distinguish between primary data and secondary data and illustrate your answer.
9. With so much secondary information now available free or at low cost over the Internet, why would a firm ever want to spend the money to do primary research?
10. If a firm were interested in estimating the distribution of income in the state of California, how could it proceed? Be specific.
11. If a firm were interested in estimating sand and clay production in Georgia, how could it proceed? Be specific.
12. Go to the library (or get on the Internet) and find (in some government publication or website) three marketing-oriented "facts" on international markets that you did not know existed or were available. Record on one page and show sources.
13. Explain why a company might want to do focus group interviews rather than individual interviews with the same people.
14. Distinguish between qualitative and quantitative approaches to research—and give some of the key advantages and limitations of each approach.
15. Define response rate and discuss why a marketing manager might be concerned about the response rate achieved in a particular survey. Give an example.
16. Prepare a table that summarizes some of the key advantages and limitations of mail, e-mail, telephone, and personal interview approaches for administering questionnaires.
17. Would a firm want to subscribe to a shared cost data service if the same data were going to be available to competitors? Discuss your reasoning.
18. Explain how you might use different types of research (focus groups, observation, survey, and experiment) to forecast market reaction to a new kind of disposable baby diaper, which is to receive no promotion other than what the retailer will give it. Further, assume that the new diaper's name will not be associated with other known products. The product will be offered at competitive prices.
19. Marketing research involves expense—sometimes considerable expense. Why does the text recommend the use of marketing research even though a highly experienced marketing executive is available?
20. A marketing manager is considering opportunities to export her firm's current consumer products to several different countries. She is interested in getting secondary data that will help her narrow down choices to countries that offer the best potential. The manager then plans to do more detailed primary research with consumers in those markets. What suggestions would you give her about how to proceed?
21. Discuss the concept that some information may be too expensive to obtain in relation to its value. Illustrate.

Suggested Cases

8. Sophia's Ristorante
9. Sleepy Time Motel
24. PCT, Inc.

Computer-Aided Problem

7. Marketing Research

Texmac, Inc., has an idea for a new type of weaving machine that could replace the machines now used by many textile manufacturers. Texmac has done a telephone survey to estimate how many of the old-style machines are now in use. Respondents using the present machines were also asked if they would buy the improved machine at a price of $10,000.

Texmac researchers identified a population of about 5,000 textile factories as potential customers. A sample of these were surveyed, and Texmac received 500 responses. Researchers think the total potential market is about 10 times larger than the sample of respondents. Two hundred twenty of the respondents indicated that their firms used old machines like the one the new machine was intended to replace. Forty percent of those firms said that they would be interested in buying the new Texmac machine.

Texmac thinks the sample respondents are representative of the total population, but the marketing manager realizes that estimates based on a sample may not be exact when applied to the whole population. He wants to see how sampling error would affect profit estimates. Data for this problem appear in the spreadsheet. Quantity estimates for the whole market are computed from the sample estimates. These quantity estimates are used in computing likely sales, costs, and profit contribution.

a. *An article in a trade magazine reports that there are about 5,200 textile factories that use the old-style machine. If the total market is really 5,200 customers—not 5,000 as Texmac originally thought—how does that affect the total quantity estimate and profit contribution?*

b. *Some of the people who responded to the survey didn't know much about different types of machines. If the actual number of old machines in the market is really 200 per 500 firms—not 220 as estimated from survey responses—how much would this affect the expected profit contribution (for 5,200 factories)?*

c. *The marketing manager knows that the percentage of textile factories that would actually buy the new machine might be different from the 40 percent who said they would in the survey. He estimates that the proportion that will replace the old machine might be as low as 36 and as high as 44 percent—depending on business conditions. Use the results feature to prepare a table that shows how expected quantity and profit contribution change when the sample percent varies between a minimum of 36 and a maximum of 44 percent. What does this analysis suggest about the use of estimates from marketing research samples? (Note: Use 5,200 for the number of potential customers and use 220 as the estimate of the number of old machines in the sample.)*

For additional questions related to this problem, see Exercise 7-4 in the *Learning Aid for Use with Essentials of Marketing*, 9th edition.

When You Finish This Chapter, You Should

1. Understand what "Product" really means.

2. Know the key differences between goods and services.

3. Know the differences among the various consumer and business product classes.

4. Understand how the product classes can help a marketing manager plan marketing strategies.

5. Understand what branding is and how to use it in strategy planning.

6. Understand the importance of packaging in strategy planning.

7. Understand the role of warranties in strategy planning.

8. Understand the important new terms (shown in red).

Chapter Eight

Elements of Product Planning for Goods and Services

For decades, 35mm cameras have been the photographic standard. The technical quality of the films is excellent. They capture subtle colors and fine details. And there's a lot of choice among cameras for serious photographers who study all of the details. Unfortunately, this doesn't satisfy many amateur photographers. For them, one camera seems pretty much like another. They often botch their snapshots because of errors loading the film or the wrong light. Sometimes the shape of the picture just doesn't fit the subject. Or if there's one great picture and someone wants a reprint, the negative can't be found. These problems have been around for a long time. So to address them—and get new sales of films and cameras—Kodak and its four global rivals agreed on a new photo standard, the Advanced Photo System (APS).

When Kodak was ready to introduce its new Advantix brand APS film and cameras in 1996, it looked like a winning idea. A new film cartridge made it

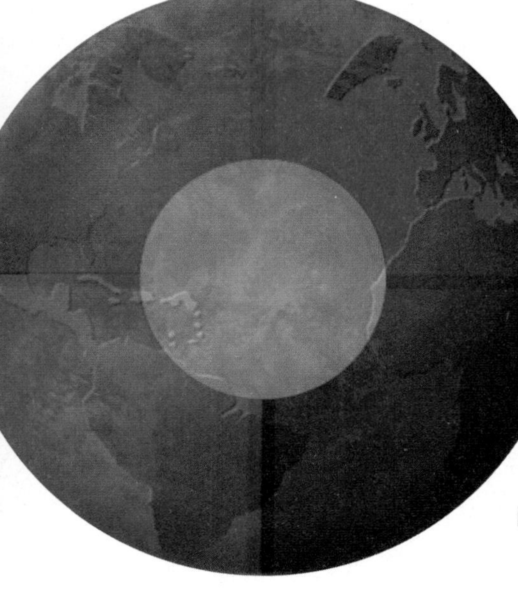

place price promotion produ

easy to load the film. Photos could be shot in any of three sizes, including an extrawide format. The film adjusted for differences in light. And developed film came back protected in the cartridge. Reprints were easy to order too because a numbered proof sheet came with each set of prints. Customers liked these benefits. What they really wanted was good snapshots—so Advantix seemed worth the 15 percent higher price.

However, in its rush to beat rivals to market, Kodak ran into production problems. It could not get enough cameras to retailers. So the big ad campaign to build familiarity with the Advantix brand of film and cameras was wasted. Worse, because of a confusing package, many people bought Advantix film expecting it to work in a 35mm camera; it wouldn't. Initially, getting Advantix pictures developed was also a hassle. Retailers were slow to put money into new equipment to develop Advantix film; they waited to see if customers wanted it. And it added to consumer confusion that Fuji, Minolta, and other firms each had their own brand names for APS products.

By 1998, these problems were smoothing out. But sales were slow because too few consumers knew about Advantix. So Kodak relaunched the product. Kodak stuck with the Advantix name but used a new package design. Ads directly pitted Advantix against the problems with 35mm pictures, even though that risked eating into Kodak's 35mm sales. Camera giveaway promotions on the Kodak website (www.kodak.com) stirred interest too. And price-off discounts on three-roll packages got consumers to take more pictures.

www.mhhe.com/fourps

As demand grew, retailers also gave Advantix more attention. For example, Wal-Mart put Kodak's $50 camera on special display. And many photo labs offered consumers a money-back guarantee on any Advantix prints that were not completely satisfactory.

For many customers in the target market, Kodak's Advantix line offers new benefits that they couldn't get before. But it involves new products that are basically incremental to what Kodak was already selling and what customers were already buying. Digital cameras and pictures are a more revolutionary type of new product. Consumers who adopt them will change their picture-taking behavior, and, as Kodak knows, they'll certainly change their film-buying and film-processing behavior too. It won't happen overnight, but digital cameras will make traditional cameras obsolete. And in the process the competition that Kodak faces has already changed, in some cases dramatically. Take, for example, HP's DeskJet brand color printers. If you buy a digital camera, the odds are that you'll print out the pictures on a DeskJet, not on a Kodak printer. So just as Kodak is fighting for shelf space against low-price Fuji and dealer brands in the mature market for 35mm film, it is fighting new and very different competitors in the fast-growing market related to digital photography.[1]

The Product Area Involves Many Strategy Decisions

The Kodak case highlights some important topics we'll discuss in this chapter and the next. Here we'll start by looking at how customers see a firm's product. Then we'll talk about product classes to help you better understand marketing strategy planning. We'll also talk about branding, packaging, and warranties. As shown in Exhibit 8-1, there are many strategy decisions related to the Product area.

What Is a Product?

Customers buy satisfaction, not parts

When Volkswagen sells a new Beetle, is it just selling a certain number of nuts and bolts, some sheet metal, an engine, and four wheels?

When Air Jamaica sells a ticket for a flight to the Caribbean, is it just selling so much wear and tear on an airplane and so much pilot fatigue?

The answer to these questions is *no*. Instead, what these companies are really selling is the satisfaction, use, or benefit the customer wants.

All consumers care about is that their new Beetles look cute and keep running. And when they take a trip on Air Jamaica, they really don't care how hard it is on the plane or the crew. They just want a safe, comfortable trip. In the same way, when producers and middlemen buy a product, they're interested in the profit they can make from its purchase—through use or resale.

Product means the need-satisfying offering of a firm. The idea of "Product" as potential customer satisfaction or benefits is very important. Many business managers get wrapped up in the technical details involved in producing a product. But

Exhibit 8-1
Strategy Planning for Product

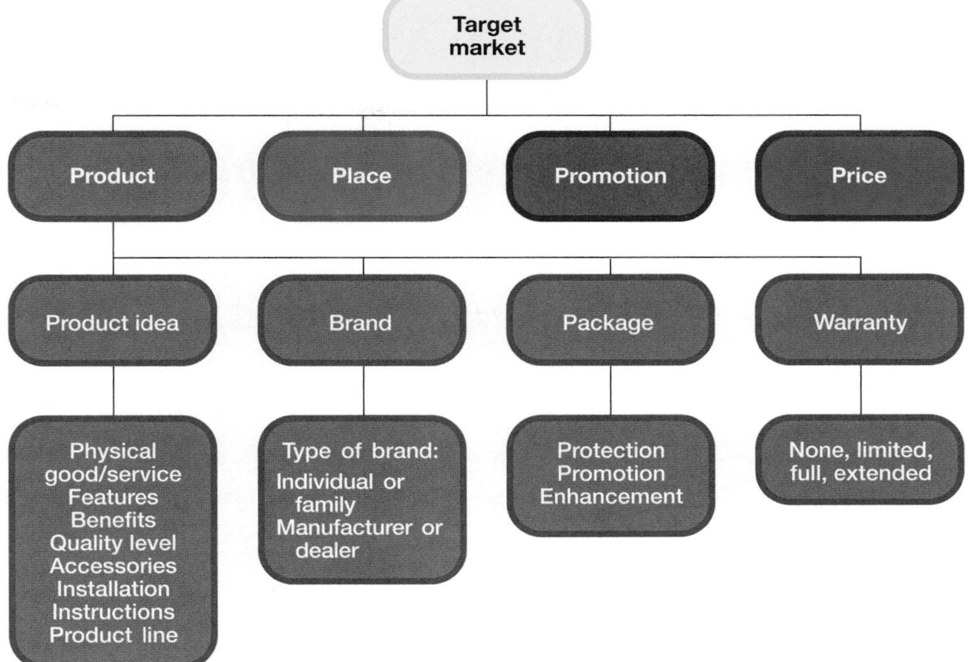

most customers think about a product in terms of the total satisfaction it provides. That satisfaction may require a "total" product offering that is really a combination of excellent service, a physical good with the right features, useful instructions, a convenient package, a trustworthy warranty, and perhaps even a familiar name that has satisfied the consumer in the past. For example, Hertz targets business travelers with a product that includes a choice of quality cars, convenient reservations, fast pickup and drop-off, availability at most major airports, and a premium price.[2]

Product quality and customer needs

Product quality should also be determined by how customers view the product. From a marketing perspective, **quality** means a product's ability to satisfy a customer's needs or requirements. This definition focuses on the customer—and how the customer thinks a product will fit some purpose. For example, the "best" satellite TV service may not be the one with the highest number of channels but the one that includes a local channel that a consumer wants to watch. Similarly, the best-quality clothing for casual wear on campus may be a pair of jeans, not a pair of dress slacks made of a higher-grade fabric.

Among different types of jeans, the one with the most durable fabric might be thought of as having the highest grade or *relative quality* for its product type. Marketing managers often focus on relative quality when comparing their products to competitors' offerings. However, a product with better features is not a high-quality product if the features aren't what the target market wants.[3]

Goods and/or services are the product

A product may be a physical *good* or a *service* or a *blend* of both. Exhibit 8-2 shows that a product can range from a 100 percent emphasis on physical goods—for commodities like steel pipe—to a 100 percent emphasis on service, like dial-up

To better satisfy its customers' needs and make traveling more enjoyable, this French railroad's service includes door-to-door delivery of the passenger's luggage. The ad says "your luggage is old enough to travel by itself. It's up to us to ensure you'd rather go by train."

Internet access from EarthLink. Regardless of the emphasis involved, the marketing manager must consider most of the same elements in planning products and marketing mixes. Given this, we usually won't make a distinction between goods and services but will call all of them *Products*. Sometimes, however, understanding the differences in goods and services can help fine-tune marketing strategy planning. So let's look at some of these differences next.

Differences in Goods and Services

How tangible is the product?

Because a good is a physical thing, it can be seen and touched. You can try on a pair of Timberland shoes or smell Colombian coffee as it brews. A good is *tangible*. When you buy it, you own it. And it's usually pretty easy to see exactly what you'll get.

On the other hand, a **service** is a deed performed by one party for another. When you provide a customer with a service, the customer can't keep it. Rather, a service is experienced, used, or consumed. You go see a DreamWorks Pictures movie, but afterward all you have is a memory. Services are *intangible*. You

Exhibit 8-2
Examples of Possible Blends of Physical Goods and Services in a Product

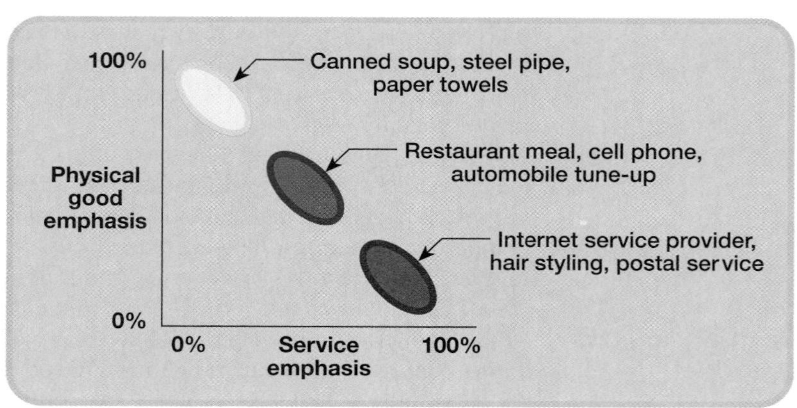

Providing consistent, high-quality service is a challenge, so many firms are using technology to make it easier and quicker for customers to get the services they want by themselves.

can't "hold" a service. And it may be hard to know exactly what you'll get when you buy it.

Is the product produced before it's sold?

Goods are usually produced in a factory and then sold. By contrast, services are often sold first, then produced. And they're produced and consumed in the same time frame. Thus, goods producers may be far away from the customer, but service providers often work in the customer's presence.

A worker in a Magnavox TV factory can be in a bad mood—and customers will never know. But a rude bank teller can drive customers away.

Services can't be stored or transported

Services are perishable—they can't be stored. This makes it harder to balance supply and demand. As an example, consider MCI's long-distance telephone services. Even on Mother's Day when demand is high customers expect good service. They don't want to hear "Sorry, all lines are busy." So MCI must have enough equipment and employees to deal with peak demand times. But when customers aren't making many calls, MCI's facilities are idle and the unused capacity can't be saved and sold later.

It's often difficult to have economies of scale when the product emphasis is on service. *Services often have to be produced in the presence of the customer.* Merrill Lynch's investment advice could, perhaps, be produced more economically in a single building in New York City and made available only on its website. But Merrill Lynch has offices all over the world because many customers want a personal touch from their stockbroker.[4]

Whole Product Lines Must Be Developed Too

A **product assortment** is the set of all product lines and individual products that a firm sells. A **product line** is a set of individual products that are closely related. The seller may see the products in a line as related because they're produced and/or operate in a similar way, sold to the same target market, sold through the same types of outlets, or priced at about the same level. Sara Lee, for example, has many product lines in its product assortment—including desserts, snacks, hosiery, sportswear, lingerie, and shoe polish. But Enterprise has one product line—different types of vehicles to rent. An **individual product** is a particular product within a product line.

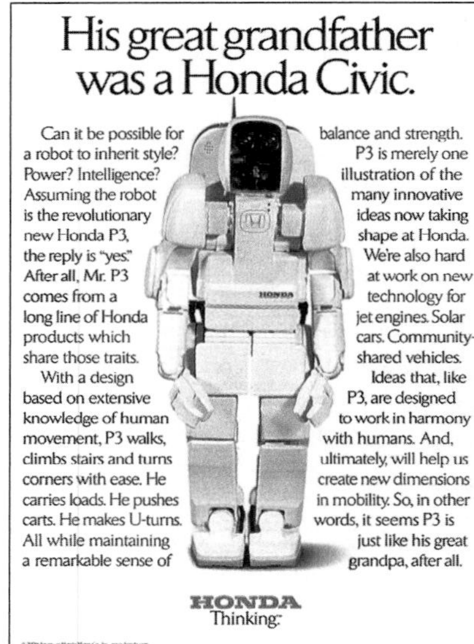

At companies like Honda, managers must develop marketing plans for individual products that are consistent with the marketing program for the whole product assortment.

It usually is differentiated by brand, level of service offered, price, or some other characteristic. For example, each size and flavor of a brand of soap is an individual product. Middlemen usually think of each separate product as a stock-keeping unit (sku) and assign it a unique sku number.

Each individual product and target market may require a separate strategy. So a marketing manager may have to plan *several* strategies to develop an effective marketing program for a whole company.[5]

Product Classes Help Plan Marketing Strategies

You don't have to treat *every* product as unique when planning strategies. Some product classes require similar marketing mixes. These product classes are a useful starting point for developing marketing mixes for new products and evaluating present mixes.

Product classes start with type of customer

All products fit into one of two broad groups—based on the type of customer that will use them. **Consumer products** are products meant for the final consumer. **Business products** are products meant for use in producing other products. Thus, the big difference in the business products market is **derived demand**—the demand for business products derives from the demand for consumer products. For example, if consumer demand for cars drops, car makers buy less steel.[6]

The same product—like Bertolli Olive Oil—*might* be in both groups. Consumers buy it to use in their own kitchens, but food processing companies buy it in large quantities as an ingredient in the products they sell. Selling the same product to both final consumers and business customers requires (at least) two different strategies.

There are product classes within each group. Consumer product classes are based on *how consumers think about and shop for products*. Business product classes are based on *how buyers think about products and how they'll be used*.[7]

Exhibit 8-3 Consumer Product Classes and Marketing Mix Planning

Consumer Product Class	Marketing Mix Considerations	Consumer Behavior
Convenience products		
Staples	Maximum exposure with widespread, low-cost distribution; mass selling by producer; usually low price; branding is important.	Routinized (habitual), low effort, frequent purchases; low involvement.
Impulse	Widespread distribution with display at point of purchase.	Unplanned purchases bought quickly.
Emergency	Need widespread distribution near probable point of need; price sensitivity low.	Purchase made with time pressure when a need is great.
Shopping products		
Homogeneous	Need enough exposure to facilitate price comparison; price sensitivity high.	Customers see little difference among alternatives, seek lowest price.
Heterogeneous	Need distribution near similar products; promotion (including personal selling) to highlight product advantages; less price sensitivity.	Extensive problem solving; consumer may need help in making a decision (salesperson, website, etc.).
Specialty products	Price sensitivity is likely to be low; limited distribution may be acceptable, but should be treated as a convenience or shopping product (in whichever category product would typically be included) to reach persons not yet sold on its specialty product status.	Willing to expend effort to get specific product, even if not necessary; strong preferences make it an important purchase; Internet becoming important information source.
Unsought products		
New unsought	Must be available in places where similar (or related) products are sought; needs attention-getting promotion.	Need for product not strongly felt; unaware of benefits or not yet gone through adoption process.
Regularly unsought	Requires very aggressive promotion, usually personal selling.	Aware of product but not interested; attitude toward product may even be negative.

Consumer Product Classes—How They Are Defined

Consumer product classes divide into four groups: (1) convenience, (2) shopping, (3) specialty, and (4) unsought. *Each class is based on the way people buy products.* See Exhibit 8-3 for a summary of how these product classes relate to marketing mixes.

Convenience products—purchased quickly with little effort

Convenience products are products a consumer needs but isn't willing to spend much time or effort shopping for. These products are bought often, require little service or selling, don't cost much, and may even be bought by habit. A convenience product may be a staple, impulse product, or emergency product.

Staples are products that are bought often, routinely, and without much thought—like breakfast cereal, canned soup, and most other packaged foods used almost every day in almost every household.

Impulse products are products that are bought quickly—as *unplanned* purchases—because of a strongly felt need. True impulse products are items that the customer hadn't planned to buy, decides to buy on sight, may have bought the same way many

Many consumers shop for plates and other tableware as if they were homogeneous products, but Crate & Barrel wants customers to see its distinctive offerings as heterogeneous shopping products, or perhaps even specialty items.

times before, and wants right now. If the buyer doesn't see an impulse product at the right time, the sale may be lost.[8]

Emergency products are products that are purchased immediately when the need is great. The customer doesn't have time to shop around when a traffic accident occurs, a thunderstorm begins, or an impromptu party starts. The price of the ambulance service, raincoat, or ice cubes won't be important.

Shopping products—are compared

Shopping products are products that a customer feels are worth the time and effort to compare with competing products. Shopping products can be divided into two types, depending on what customers are comparing: (1) homogeneous or (2) heterogeneous shopping products.

Homogeneous shopping products are shopping products the customer sees as basically the same and wants at the lowest price. Some consumers feel that certain sizes and types of computers, television sets, washing machines, and even cars are very similar. So they shop for the best price. For some products, the Internet has become a way to do that quickly.

Firms may try to promote their product differences to avoid head-to-head price competition. For example, EarthLink says that with its dial-up Internet service you get fewer busy signals and lost connections. But if consumers don't think the differences are important, they'll just look at price.

Heterogeneous shopping products are shopping products the customer sees as different and wants to inspect for quality and suitability. Furniture, clothing, and membership in a spa are good examples. Often the consumer expects help from a knowledgeable salesperson. Once the customer finds the right product, price may not matter as long as it's reasonable. Some retailers carry competing brands so consumers won't go to a competitor to compare items.

Specialty products—no substitutes please!

Specialty products are consumer products that the customer really wants and makes a special effort to find. Shopping for a specialty product doesn't mean comparing—the buyer wants that special product and is willing to search for it. It's the customer's *willingness to search*—not the extent of searching—that makes it a specialty product.

Any branded product that consumers insist on by name is a specialty product. Marketing managers want customers to see their products as specialty products and ask for them over and over again. Building that kind of relationship isn't easy. It means satisfying the customer every time. However, that's easier and a lot less costly than trying to win back dissatisfied customers or attract new customers who are not seeking the product at all.

Unsought products—need promotion

Unsought products are products that potential customers don't yet want or know they can buy. So they don't search for them at all. In fact, consumers probably won't buy these products if they see them—unless Promotion can show their value.

New unsought products are products offering really new ideas that potential customers don't know about yet. Informative promotion can help convince customers to accept the product, ending its unsought status. Dannon's yogurt, Litton's microwave ovens, and Netscape's browser are all popular items now, but initially they were new unsought products.

Regularly unsought products are products—like gravestones, life insurance, and encyclopedias—that stay unsought but not unbought forever. There may be a need, but potential customers aren't motivated to satisfy it. For this kind of product, personal selling is *very* important.

Many nonprofit organizations try to "sell" their unsought products. For example, the Red Cross regularly holds blood drives to remind prospective donors of how important it is to give blood.

One product may be seen several ways

The same product might be seen in different ways by different target markets. For example, a product viewed as a staple by affluent consumers in the U.S. might be seen as a heterogeneous shopping product by consumers in another country. Similarly, a convenient place to shop often means very different things in different countries. In Japan, for example, retail stores tend to be smaller and carry smaller selections of products.

Business Product Classes—How They Are Defined

Business product classes are based on how buyers see products and how the products will be used. The classes of business products are (1) installations, (2) accessories, (3) raw materials, (4) components, (5) supplies, and (6) professional services. Exhibit 8-4 relates these product classes to marketing mix planning.

Installations—a boom-or-bust business

Installations—such as buildings, land rights, and major equipment—are important capital items. A **capital item** is a long-lasting product that can be used and depreciated for many years. Often it's very expensive. One-of-a-kind installations—like custom-made machines—generally require special negotiations for each sale.

Businesses buy the goods and services they need to produce products for their own customers, so the demand for GE's special plastic resins, used to make lightweight and impact-resistant body panels, is derived from consumer demand for VW's unique car.

Exhibit 8-4 Business Product Classes and Marketing Mix Planning

Business Product Classes	Marketing Mix Considerations	Buying Behavior
Installations	Usually requires skillful personal selling by producer, including technical contacts, and/or understanding of applications; leasing and specialized support services may be required.	Multiple buying influence (including top management) and new-task buying are common; infrequent purchase, long decision period, and boom-or-bust demand are typical.
Accessory equipment	Need fairly widespread distribution and numerous contacts by experienced and sometimes technically trained personnel; price competition is often intense, but quality is important.	Purchasing and operating personnel typically make decisions; shorter decision period than for installations; Internet sourcing.
Raw materials	Grading is important, and transportation and storing can be crucial because of seasonal production and/or perishable products; markets tend to be very competitive.	Long-term contract may be required to ensure supply; online auctions.
Component parts and materials	Product quality and delivery reliability are usually extremely important; negotiation and technical selling typical on less-standardized items; replacement after market may require different strategies.	Multiple buying influence is common; online competitive bids used to encourage competitive pricing.
Maintenance, repair, and operating (MRO) supplies	Typically require widespread distribution or fast delivery (repair items); arrangements with appropriate middlemen may be crucial.	Often handled as straight rebuys, except important operating supplies may be treated much more seriously and involve multiple buying influence.
Professional services	Services customized to buyer's need; personal selling very important; inelastic demand often supports high prices.	Customer may compare outside service with what internal people could provide; needs may be very specialized.

Negotiations often involve top management and can stretch over months or even years. Standardized major equipment is treated more routinely.

Installations are a boom-or-bust business. During growth periods, firms buy installations to increase capacity. But during a downswing, sales fall off sharply.[9]

Specialized services are needed as part of the product

Suppliers sometimes include special services with an installation at no extra cost. A firm that sells (or leases) equipment to dentists, for example, may install it and help the dentist learn to use it.

Accessories—important but short-lived capital items

Accessories are short-lived capital items—tools and equipment used in production or office activities—like Canon's small copy machines, Rockwell's portable drills, and Steelcase's filing cabinets. Accessories are more standardized than installations. And they're usually needed by more customers.

Since these products cost less and last a shorter time than installations, multiple buying influence is less important. Operating people and purchasing agents, rather than top managers, may make the purchase decision. As with installations, some customers may wish to lease or rent—to spread the cost over time.

Raw materials become part of a physical good

Raw materials are unprocessed expense items—such as logs, iron ore, and wheat—that are moved to the next production process with little handling. An **expense item** is a product whose total cost is treated as a business expense in the year it's purchased. Unlike installations and accessories, *raw materials become part of a physical good.*

There are two types of raw materials. **Farm products** are grown by farmers—examples are oranges, oats, sugar cane, and cattle. **Natural products** are products that occur in nature—such as timber, iron ore, oil, and coal.

The need for grading is one of the important differences between raw materials and other business products. Nature produces what it will—and someone must sort and grade raw materials to satisfy various market segments. Most buyers of raw materials want ample supplies in the right grades for specific uses—fresh vegetables for Green Giant's production lines or logs for Weyerhaeuser's paper mills.

Component parts and materials must meet specifications

Components are processed expense items that become part of a finished product. Component *parts* are finished (or nearly finished) items that are ready for assembly into the final product. ATI's graphics cards included in personal computers and TRW's air bags in cars are examples. Component *materials* are items such as wire, plastic, textiles, or cement. They have already been processed but must be processed further before becoming part of the final product. Quality is important with components because they affect the firm's own product quality.

Some components are custom-made. Then teamwork between the buyer and seller may be needed to arrive at the right specifications. So a buyer may develop a close partnership with a dependable supplier. In contrast, standardized component materials are more likely to be purchased online using a competitive bidding system.

Since component parts go into finished products, a replacement market often develops. Car tires are components originally sold to an *original equipment manufacturer (OEM)* that become consumer products in the after market.[10]

Supplies for maintenance, repair, and operations

Supplies are expense items that do not become part of a finished product. Supplies can be divided into three types: (1) maintenance, (2) repair, and (3) operating supplies—giving them their common name: MRO supplies.

Maintenance and small operating supplies are like convenience products. The item will be ordered because it is needed—but buyers won't spend much time on it. For such "nuisance" purchases, branding is important and so are breadth of assortment and the seller's dependability. Middlemen usually handle the many supply items, and now they are often purchased via online catalog sites.[11]

Important operating supplies, like coal or fuel oil, receive special treatment. Usually there are several sources for such commodity products—and large volumes may be purchased at global exchanges on the Internet.

Professional services—pay to get it done

Professional services are specialized services that support a firm's operations. They are usually expense items. Management consulting services can improve the company's efficiency. Information technology services can maintain a company's networks and websites. And food services can improve morale.

Managers compare the cost of buying professional services outside the firm ("outsourcing") to the cost of having company people do them. For special skills needed only occasionally, an outsider can be best. So, the number of service specialists is growing in our complex economy.

Branding Needs a Strategy Decision Too

There are so many brands—and we're so used to seeing them—that we take them for granted. But branding is an important decision area, so we will treat it in some detail.

What is branding?

Branding means the use of a name, term, symbol, or design—or a combination of these—to identify a product. It includes the use of brand names, trademarks, and practically all other means of product identification.

Exhibit 8-5 Recognized Trademarks and Symbols Help in Promotion

Brand name has a narrower meaning. A **brand name** is a word, letter, or a group of words or letters. Examples include America Online (AOL), WD-40, 3M Post-its, and PT Cruiser.

The name Google is the brand name (for an Internet search engine). However, when the name appears in the style shown in Exhibit 8-5 it is a trademark. Trademark is a legal term. A **trademark** includes only those words, symbols, or marks that are legally registered for use by a single company. A **service mark** is the same as a trademark except that it refers to a service offering.

These differences may seem technical. But they are very important to business firms that spend a lot of money to protect and promote their brands. Sometimes a firm's brand name is the only element in its marketing mix that a competitor can't copy.

Brands meet needs

Well-recognized brands make shopping easier. Think of trying to buy groceries, for example, if you had to evaluate each of 25,000 items every time you went to a supermarket.

Brand promotion has advantages for branders as well as customers. A good brand reduces the marketer's selling time and effort. Good brands can also improve the company's image—speeding acceptance of new products marketed under the same name.[12]

Conditions Favorable to Branding

Can you recall a brand name for file folders, bed frames, electric extension cords, or nails? As these examples suggest, it's not always easy to establish a respected brand.

The following conditions are favorable to successful branding:

1. The product is easy to identify by brand or trademark.
2. Product quality is easy to maintain and the best value for the price.
3. Dependable and widespread availability is possible. When customers start using a brand, they want to be able to continue using it.
4. Demand is strong enough that the market price can be high enough to make the branding effort profitable.
5. There are economies of scale. If the branding is really successful, costs should drop and profits should increase.
6. Favorable shelf locations or display space in stores will help. This is something retailers can control when they brand their own products.

In general, these conditions are less common in less-developed economies, and that may explain why efforts to build brands in less-developed nations often fail.

Achieving Brand Familiarity Is Not Easy

Today, well-known brands exist for most product categories, ranging from crayons (Crayola) to real estate services (Century 21). However, what brand is familiar often varies from one country to another.

Brand acceptance must be earned with a good product and regular promotion. **Brand familiarity** means how well customers recognize and accept a company's brand. The degree of brand familiarity affects the planning for the rest of the marketing mix—especially where the product should be offered and what promotion is needed.

Five levels of brand familiarity

Five levels of brand familiarity are useful for strategy planning: (1) rejection, (2) nonrecognition, (3) recognition, (4) preference, and (5) insistence.

Some brands have been tried and found wanting. **Brand rejection** means that potential customers won't buy a brand unless its image is changed. Rejection may suggest a change in the product or perhaps only a shift to target customers who have a better image of the brand. Overcoming a negative image is difficult and can be very expensive.

Brand rejection is a big concern for service-oriented businesses because it's hard to control the quality of service. A business traveler who gets a dirty room in a Hilton Hotel in Caracas, Venezuela, might not return to a Hilton anywhere. Yet it's difficult for Hilton to ensure that every maid does a good job every time.

Some products are seen as basically the same. **Brand nonrecognition** means final consumers don't recognize a brand at all—even though middlemen may use the brand name for identification and inventory control. Examples include school supplies, inexpensive dinnerware, many of the items that you'd find in a hardware store, and thousands of dot-coms on the Internet.

Brand recognition means that customers remember the brand. This may not seem like much, but it can be a big advantage if there are many "nothing" brands on the market. Even if consumers can't recall the brand without help, they may be reminded when they see it in a store among other less familiar brands.

It takes time and money to build brand awareness, so sometimes brands can be extended. Both Bounce and Mr. Clean have recently introduced new products that benefit from their well-recognized brand names.

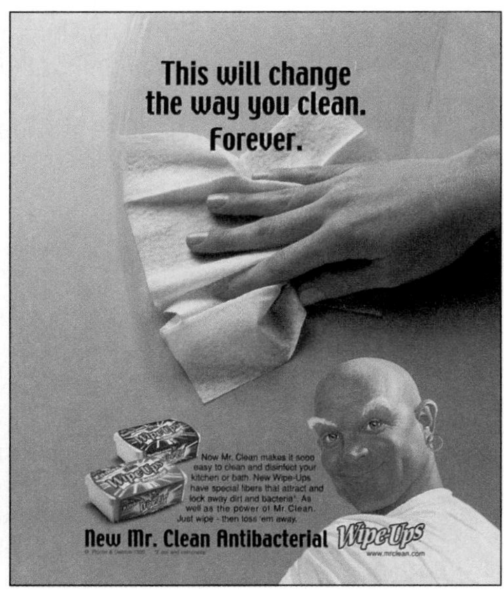

Exhibit 8-6
Characteristics of a Good Brand Name

- Short and simple
- Easy to spell and read
- Easy to recognize and remember
- Easy to pronounce
- Can be pronounced in only one way
- Can be pronounced in all languages (for international markets)
- Suggestive of product benefits
- Adaptable to packaging/labeling needs
- No undesirable imagery
- Always timely (does not go out-of-date)
- Adaptable to any advertising medium
- Legally available for use (not in use by another firm)

Most branders would like to win **brand preference**—which means that target customers usually choose the brand over other brands, perhaps because of habit or favorable past experience.

Brand insistence means customers insist on a firm's branded product and are willing to search for it. This is an objective of many target marketers.

The right brand name can help

A good brand name can help build brand familiarity. It can help tell something important about the company or its product. Exhibit 8-6 lists some characteristics of a good brand name.

Companies that compete in international markets face a special problem in selecting brand names. A name that conveys a positive image in one language may be meaningless in another. Or, worse, it may have unintended meanings. GM's Nova car is a classic example. GM stuck with the Nova name when it introduced the car in South America. It seemed like a sensible decision because *nova* is the Spanish word for star. However, Nova also sounds the same as the Spanish words for "no go." Consumers weren't interested in a no-go car, and sales didn't pick up until GM changed the name.[13]

A respected name builds brand equity

Because it's costly to build brand recognition, some firms prefer to acquire established brands rather than try to build their own. The value of a brand to its current owner or to a firm that wants to buy it is sometimes called **brand equity**—the value of a brand's overall strength in the market. For example, brand equity is likely to be higher if many satisfied customers insist on buying the brand and if retailers are eager to stock it. That almost guarantees ongoing profits.

The financial value of the Yahoo brand name illustrates the brand equity idea. In 1994, Yahoo was just a tiny start-up trying to make it with a directory site on the Internet. Most people had never heard the name, and few even knew what the Internet was or why you'd need a directory site. As interest in the Internet grew, Yahoo promoted its brand name on TV and in magazines. It was often the only website name that newcomers to the Web knew, so for many it was a good place from which to start their surfing. Within a few years, Yahoo was attracting 30 million different people a month. Since Yahoo charged fees to advertisers eager to reach these users, the familiarity of its brand translated directly into ad revenues.[14]

Protecting Brand Names and Trademarks

U.S. common law and civil law protect the rights of trademark and brand name owners. The **Lanham Act** (of 1946) spells out what kinds of marks (including brand names) can be protected and the exact method of protecting them. The law applies to goods shipped in interstate or foreign commerce.

The Lanham Act does not force registration. But registering under the Lanham Act is often a first step toward protecting a trademark to be used in international markets. That's because some nations require that a trademark be registered in its home country before they will register or protect it.

How to Blow Out a Relationship with Customers

There are few brand names that are more familiar to U.S. consumers than Firestone and Ford Explorer. Yet in the aftermath of tread separations on tires that resulted in many rollovers and tragic deaths, the reputations of these once lofty brand names are tarnished. Millions of consumers say that they will never again buy any tire with the Firestone name on it. The Firestone brand may not survive. The plant where many of the unsafe tires were produced has already been shut down. What automaker would buy from that plant and risk its own image and sales. Tire retailers who sell replacement tires in the consumer market face similar reactions. It's easier for them to just sell Michelins, a brand that positions itself on safety benefits.

In part to protect its customers, Ford recalled millions of Firestone tires, including many designs that Firestone says are not a problem. Who should pay the cost? Unlike most of the components used in building a car, the tires are covered by a Firestone warranty, not by Ford's warranty. Responsibility is clearer in government recalls. But staff shortages at the National Highway Traffic Safety Administration contributed to delays in figuring out who was really at fault.

The long-standing relationship between Ford and Firestone is severed. Imagine how you would feel if you were Bill Ford, chairman of Ford. Firestone was his grandfather. That aside, questions about rollovers have eroded the brand equity of one of the best-sellers in Ford's whole product line. Rebuilding profits won't be easy. With all the bad publicity many customers are concerned about rollover hazards of the Explorer. Even if a complete redesign would help reassure them, that's not an option. The new-product development process for a big change in the Explorer will take years.[15]

www.mhhe.com/fourps

You must protect your own

A brand can be a real asset to a company. Each firm should try to see that its brand doesn't become a common descriptive term for its kind of product. When this happens, the brand name or trademark becomes public property—and the owner loses all rights to it. This happened with the names cellophane, aspirin, shredded wheat, and kerosene.[16]

Counterfeiting is accepted in some cultures

Even when products are properly registered, counterfeiters may make unauthorized copies. Many well-known brands—ranging from Levi's jeans to Rolex watches to Zantax ulcer medicine—face this problem. Counterfeiting is especially common in developing nations. In China, most videotapes and CDs are bootleg copies. Counterfeiting is big business in some countries, so efforts to stop it may meet with limited success. There are also differences in cultural values. In South Korea, for example, many people don't see counterfeiting as unethical.[17]

What Kind of Brand to Use?

Keep it in the family

Branders of more than one product must decide whether they are going to use a **family brand**—the same brand name for several products—or individual brands for each product. Examples of family brands are Keebler snack food products and Sears' Kenmore appliances.

The use of the same brand for many products makes sense if all are similar in type and quality. The main benefit is that the goodwill attached to one or two products may help the others. Money spent to promote the brand name benefits more than one product, which cuts promotion costs for each product.

A special kind of family brand is a **licensed brand**—a well-known brand that sellers pay a fee to use. For example, the familiar Sunkist brand name has been licensed to many companies for use on more than 400 products in 30 countries.[18]

Individual brands for outside and inside competition

A company uses **individual brands**—separate brand names for each product—when it's important for the products to each have a separate identity, as when products vary in quality or type.

If the products are really different, such as Elmer's glue and Borden's ice cream, individual brands can avoid confusion. Some firms use individual brands with similar

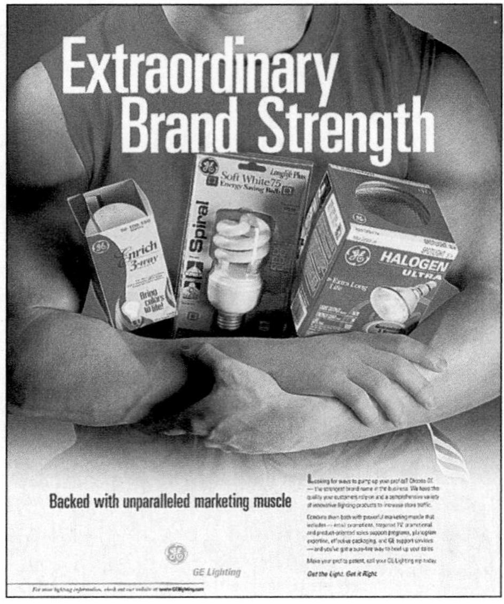

As these trade ads suggest, both Del Monte and GE want retailers to remember that many consumers already know and trust their brand names.

products to make segmentation and positioning efforts easier. Unilever, for example, markets Aim, Close-Up, and Pepsodent toothpastes, but each involves different positioning efforts.[19]

Internet

Internet Exercise Go to the Procter & Gamble website (www.pg.com) and click on *Product List and Info* and then on *Beauty Care.* Find out the brand names of the different shampoos that P&G makes. How are the different brands positioned, and what target markets do they appeal to?

Generic "brands"

Products that some consumers see as commodities may be difficult or expensive to brand. Some manufacturers and middlemen have responded to this problem with **generic products**—products that have no brand at all other than identification of their contents and the manufacturer or middleman. Generic products are usually offered in plain packages at lower prices. They are quite common in less-developed nations.[20]

Who Should Do the Branding?

Manufacturer brands versus dealer brands

Manufacturer brands are brands created by producers. These are sometimes called *national brands* because the brand is promoted all across the country or in large regions. Note, however, that many manufacturer brands are now distributed globally. Such brands include Nabisco, Campbell's, Whirlpool, Ford, and IBM. Many creators of service-oriented firms—like McDonald's, Orkin Pest Control, and Bank of America—promote their brands this way too.

Dealer brands, also called **private brands,** are brands created by middlemen. Examples of dealer brands include the brands of Kroger, Ace Hardware, Radio Shack, Wal-Mart, and Sears. Some of these are advertised and distributed more widely than many national brands. For example, national TV ads have helped Original Arizona Jeans (by JCPenney) and Canyon River Blues (by Sears) compete with Levi's and Wrangler.

From the middleman's perspective, the major advantage of selling a popular manufacturer brand is that the product is already presold to some target customers. The major disadvantage is that manufacturers normally offer lower gross margins than the middleman might be able to earn with a dealer brand.

Who's winning the battle of the brands?

The **battle of the brands,** the competition between dealer brands and manufacturer brands, is just a question of whose brands will be more popular and who will be in control.

At one time, manufacturer brands were much more popular than dealer brands. Now sales of both kinds of brands are about equal—but sales of dealer brands are expected to continue growing. Middlemen have some advantages in this battle. With the number of large retail chains growing, they are better able to arrange reliable sources of supply at low cost. They can also give the dealer brand special shelf position or promotion.

Consumers benefit from the battle. Competition has already narrowed price differences between manufacturer brands and well-known dealer brands.[21]

The Strategic Importance of Packaging

Packaging involves promoting, protecting, and enhancing the product. Packaging can be important to both sellers and customers. See Exhibit 8-7. It can make a product more convenient to use or store. It can prevent spoiling or damage. Good packaging makes products easier to identify and promotes the brand at the point of purchase and even in use.

Packaging can enhance the product

A new package can make *the* important difference in a new marketing strategy—by meeting customers' needs better. Sometimes a new package makes the product easier or safer to use. For example, most drug and food products now have special seals to prevent product tampering.

Clever packaging is an important part of an effort by Dean's Foods to pump new life into an old product—milk. Dean is selling six-packs of chocolate-flavored milk in bottles called chugs—lightweight plastic bottles designed like old-fashioned milk bottles with a wide mouth, but with resealable twist-off caps. The shape of the new package also helps Dean get distribution in convenience stores and vending machines. Of course, storing milk for long or shipping it large distances is still a problem because milk is perishable. But Dean is working on packaging technology that will keep milk fresh for 60 days.[22]

Packaging sends a message

Packaging can tie the product to the rest of the marketing strategy. Packaging for Energizer batteries features the pink bunny seen in attention-getting TV ads. Customers see the package in stores, when they're actually buying.

Packaging may lower distribution costs

Better protective packaging is very important to manufacturers and wholesalers. They sometimes have to pay the cost of goods damaged in shipment. Retailers need protective packaging too. It can reduce storing costs by cutting breakage, spoilage, and theft. Good packages save space and are easier to handle and display.[23]

Exhibit 8-7 Some Ways Packaging Benefits Consumers and Marketers

Opportunity to Add Value	Some Decision Factors	Examples
Promotion	Link product to promotion	The bunny on the Energizer battery package is a reminder that it "keeps going and going."
	Branding at point of purchase or consumption	Coke's logo greets almost everyone each time the refrigerator is opened.
	Product information	Kraft's nutrition label helps consumers decide which cheese to buy, and a UPC code reduces checkout time and errors.
Protection	For shipping and storing	Sony's MP3 player is kept safe by Styrofoam inserts.
	From spoiling	Tylenol's safety seal prevents tampering.
	From shoplifting	Cardboard hang-tag on Gillette razor blades is too large to hide in hand.
Enhance product	The environment	Tide detergent bottle can be recycled.
	Convenience in use	Squeezable tube of Yoplait Go-Gurt is easy to eat on the go and in new situations.
	Added product functions	Plastic tub is useful for refrigerator leftovers after the Cool Whip is gone.

Universal product codes speed handling

To speed handling of fast-selling products, government and industry representatives have developed a **universal product code (UPC)** that identifies each product with marks readable by electronic scanners. A computer then matches each code to the product and its price. These codes speed the checkout process and reduce the need to mark the price on every item. They also reduce errors by cashiers and make it easy to control inventory and track sales of specific products.[24]

What Is Socially Responsible Packaging?

Laws reduce confusion and clutter

In the United States, consumer criticism finally led to the passage of the **Federal Fair Packaging and Labeling Act** (of 1966)—which requires that consumer goods be clearly labeled in easy-to-understand terms—to give consumers more information. The law also calls on industry to try to reduce the number of package sizes and make labels more useful. Since then there have been further guidelines. The most far-reaching are based on the Nutrition Labeling and Education Act of 1990. It requires food manufacturers to use a uniform format that allows consumers to compare the nutritional value of different products.[25]

Internet

Internet Exercise The FDA's website has a page on the food label requirements that proclaims "grocery store aisles have become avenues to greater nutritional knowledge." Go to that page at Internet address (www.fda.gov/opacom/backgrounders/foodlabel/newlabel.html) and review the actual label requirements. Do you use this information in deciding what products to buy?

Current laws also offer more guidance on environmental issues. Some states require a consumer to pay a deposit on bottles and cans until they're returned. These laws mean well, but they can cause problems. Channels of distribution are usually set up to distribute products, not return empty packages.[26]

Food label requirements help some consumers make healthier purchases, but many consumers don't understand or use the information.

GRADE A • PASTEURIZED • HOMOGENIZED

Nutrition Facts
Serving Size 1 cup (240mL)
Servings Per Container 4

Amount Per Serving	
Calories 80	Calories from Fat 0
	% Daily Value*
Total Fat 0g	0%
Saturated Fat 0g	0%
Cholesterol 5mg	2%
Sodium 110mg	5%
Total Carbohydrate 11g	4%
Dietary Fiber 0g	0%
Sugars 11g	
Protein 8g	16%

Vitamin A 10% • Vitamin C 2%
Calcium 25% • Iron 0% • Vitamin D 25%

*Percent Daily Values are based on a 2,000 calorie diet. Your daily values may be higher or lower depending on your calorie needs:

	Calories:	2,000	2,500
Total Fat	Less than	65g	80g
Sat.Fat	Less than	20g	25g
Cholesterol	Less than	300mg	300mg
Sodium	Less than	2,400mg	2,400mg
Total Carbohydrate		300g	375g
Dietary Fiber		25g	30g
Protein		50g	65g

Calories per gram:
Fat 9 • Carbohydrate 4 • Protein 4

INGREDIENTS: SKIM MILK, VITAMIN A PALMITATE, AND VITAMIN D_3.

Ethical decisions remain

Although various laws provide guidance on many packaging issues, many areas still require marketing managers to make ethical choices. For example, some firms have been criticized for designing packages that conceal a downsized product, giving consumers less for the money. Similarly, some retailers design packages and labels for their private-label products that look just like, and are easily confused with, manufacturer brands. Are efforts such as these unethical, or are they simply an attempt to make packaging a more effective part of a marketing mix? Different people will answer differently.

Empty packages now litter our streets, and some plastic packages will lie in a city dump for decades. But some consumers like the convenience that accompanies these problems. Is it unethical for a marketing manager to give consumers with different preferences a choice? Some critics argue that it is; others praise firms that give consumers a choice.

Many critics feel that labeling information is too often incomplete or misleading. But how far should a marketing manager go in putting potentially negative information on a package? For example, should Häagen-Dazs affix a label that says "this product will clog your arteries"? That sounds extreme, but what type of information *is* appropriate?[27]

Unit-pricing is a possible help

Some retailers, especially supermarkets, make it easier for consumers to compare packages with different weights or volumes. They use **unit-pricing**—which involves placing the price per ounce (or some other standard measure) on or near the product. This makes price comparison easier.[28]

Warranty Policies Are a Part of Strategy Planning

Warranty puts promises in writing

A **warranty** explains what the seller promises about its product. A marketing manager should decide whether to offer a specific warranty, and if so what the warranty will cover and how it will be communicated to target customers. This is an area where the legal environment—as well as customer needs and competitive offerings—must be considered.

In a competitive market, a product warranty or a service guarantee can be a very important part of the marketing mix.

U.S. common law says that producers must stand behind their products—even if they don't offer a specific warranty. A written warranty provided by the seller may promise more than the common law provides. However, it may actually *reduce* the responsibility a producer would have under common law.

The federal **Magnuson-Moss Act** (of 1975) says that producers must provide a clearly written warranty if they choose to offer any warranty. The warranty does not have to be strong. However, Federal Trade Commission (FTC) guidelines try to ensure that warranties are clear and definite and not deceptive or unfair.

Warranty may improve the marketing mix

Some firms use warranties to improve the appeal of their marketing mix. They design more quality into their goods or services and offer refunds or replacement, not just repair, if there is a problem. Xerox Corp. uses this approach with its copy machines. Its three-year warranty says that a customer who is not satisfied with a copier—for *any* reason—can trade it for another model.

Service guarantees

Customer service guarantees are becoming more common as a way to attract, and keep, customers. Pizza Hut guarantees a luncheon pizza in five minutes or it's free. General Motors set up a fast-oil-change guarantee to compete with fast-lube specialists who were taking customers away from dealers. If the dealer doesn't get the job done in 29 minutes or less, the next oil change is free.

There's more risk in offering a service guarantee than a warranty on a physical product. A lazy employee or a service breakdown can create a big expense. However, without the guarantee, dissatisfied customers may just go away mad without ever complaining.

Warranty support can be costly

The cost of warranty support ultimately must be covered by the price that consumers pay. This has led some firms to offer warranty choices. The basic price for a product may include a warranty that covers a short time period or that covers parts but not labor. Consumers who want more or better protection pay extra for an extended warranty or a service contract.[29]

Conclusion

In this chapter, we looked at Product very broadly. We saw that a firm's Product is *what satisfies the needs of its target market*. A product may be a physical good, a service, or some combination.

We introduced consumer product and business product classes and showed their affect on planning marketing mixes. Consumer product classes are based on consumers' buying behavior. Business product classes are based on how buyers see the products and how they are used.

Branding and packaging can create new and more satisfying products. Packaging offers special opportunities to promote the product and inform customers. Variations in packaging can make a product attractive to different target markets.

Customers see brands as a guarantee of quality, and this leads to repeat purchasing. For marketers, such routine buying means lower promotion costs and higher sales.

Marketing managers use individual or family brands. In the end, however, customers express their approval or disapproval of the whole Product (including the brand). The degree of brand familiarity is a measure of the marketing manager's ability to carve out a separate market. And brand familiarity affects Place, Price, and Promotion decisions.

Warranties are also important in strategy planning. A warranty need not be strong—it just has to be clearly stated. But some customers find strong warranties attractive.

Product is concerned with much more than physical goods and services. To succeed in our increasingly competitive markets, the marketing manager must also be concerned about packaging, branding, and warranties.

Questions and Problems

1. Define, in your own words, what a Product is.
2. Discuss several ways in which physical goods are different from pure services. Give an example of a good and then an example of a service that illustrates each of the differences.
3. What products are being offered by a shop that specializes in bicycles? By a travel agent? By a supermarket? By a new car dealer?
4. What kinds of consumer products are the following: *(a)* watches, *(b)* automobiles, and *(c)* toothpastes? Explain your reasoning.
5. Consumer services tend to be intangible, and goods tend to be tangible. Use an example to explain how the lack of a physical good in a pure service might affect efforts to promote the service.
6. How would the marketing mix for a staple convenience product differ from the one for a homogeneous shopping product? How would the mix for a specialty product differ from the mix for a heterogeneous shopping product? Use examples.
7. Give an example of a product that is a *new* unsought product for most people. Briefly explain why it is an unsought product.
8. In what types of stores would you expect to find *(a)* convenience products, *(b)* shopping products, *(c)* specialty products, and *(d)* unsought products?
9. Cite two examples of business products that require a substantial amount of service in order to be useful.
10. Explain why a new law office might want to lease furniture rather than buy it.
11. Would you expect to find any wholesalers selling the various types of business products? Are retail stores required (or something like retail stores)?
12. What kinds of business products are the following: *(a)* lubricating oil, *(b)* electric motors, and *(c)* a firm that provides landscaping and grass mowing for an apartment complex? Explain your reasoning.
13. How do raw materials differ from other business products? Do the differences have any impact on their marketing mixes? If so, what specifically?
14. For the kinds of business products described in this chapter, complete the following table (use one or a few well-chosen words).
    a. *Kind of distribution facility(ies) needed and functions they will provide.*
    b. *Caliber of salespeople required.*
    c. *Kind of advertising required.*

Products	1	2	3
Installations			
Buildings and land rights			
Major equipment			
Standard			
Custom-made			
Accessories			
Raw materials			
Farm products			
Natural products			
Components			
Supplies			
Maintenance and small operating supplies			
Operating supplies			
Professional services			

15. Is there any difference between a brand name and a trademark? If so, why is this difference important?
16. Is a well-known brand valuable only to the owner of the brand?
17. Suggest an example of a product and a competitive situation where it would *not* be profitable for a firm to spend large sums of money to establish a brand.
18. List five brand names and indicate what product is associated with the brand name. Evaluate the strengths and weaknesses of the brand name.
19. Explain family brands. Should Toys "R" Us carry its own dealer brands to compete with some of the popular manufacturer brands it carries? Explain your reasons.
20. In the past, Sears emphasized its own dealer brands. Now it is carrying more well-known manufacturer brands. What are the benefits to Sears of carrying more manufacturer brands?
21. What does the degree of brand familiarity imply about previous and future promotion efforts? How does the degree of brand familiarity affect the Place and Price variables?
22. You operate a small hardware store with emphasis on manufacturer brands and have barely been breaking even. Evaluate the proposal of a large wholesaler who offers a full line of dealer-branded hardware items at substantially lower prices. Specify any assumptions necessary to obtain a definite answer.
23. Give an example where packaging costs probably *(a)* lower total distribution costs and *(b)* raise total distribution costs.
24. Is it more difficult to support a warranty for a service than for a physical good? Explain your reasons.

Suggested Cases

3. Pillsbury's Häagen-Dazs
7. Lilybank Lodge
12. Paper Supplies Corporation
16. Enviro Pure Water, Inc.
27. Expert Nursing Services, Inc. (ENS)

Computer-Aided Problem

8. **Branding Decision**

Wholesteen Dairy, Inc., produces and sells Wholesteen brand condensed milk to grocery retailers. The overall market for condensed milk is fairly flat, and there's sharp competition among dairies for retailers' business. Wholesteen's regular price to retailers is $8.88 a case (24 cans). FoodWorld—a fast-growing supermarket chain and Wholesteen's largest customer—buys 20,000 cases of Wholesteen's condensed milk a year. That's 20 percent of Wholesteen's total sales volume of 100,000 cases per year.

FoodWorld is proposing that Wholesteen produce private label condensed milk to be sold with the FoodWorld brand name. FoodWorld proposes to buy the same total quantity as it does now, but it wants half (10,000 cases) with the Wholesteen brand and half with the FoodWorld brand. FoodWorld wants Wholesteen to reduce costs by using a lower-quality can for the

FoodWorld brand. That change will cost Wholesteen $.01 less per can than it costs for the cans that Wholesteen uses for its own brand. FoodWorld will also provide preprinted labels with its brand name—which will save Wholesteen an additional $.02 a can.

Wholesteen spends $70,000 a year on promotion to increase familiarity with the Wholesteen brand. In addition, Wholesteen gives retailers an allowance of $.25 per case for their local advertising, which features the Wholesteen brand. FoodWorld has agreed to give up the advertising allowance for its own brand, but it is only willing to pay $7.40 a case for the milk that will be sold with the FoodWorld brand name. It will continue under the old terms for the rest of its purchases.

Sue Glick, Wholesteen's marketing manager, is considering the FoodWorld proposal. She has entered cost and revenue data on a spreadsheet—so she can see more clearly how the proposal might affect revenue and profits.

a. *Based on the data in the initial spreadsheet, how will Wholesteen profits be affected if Glick accepts the FoodWorld proposal?*

b. *Glick is worried that FoodWorld will find another producer for the FoodWorld private label milk if Wholesteen rejects the proposal. This would immediately reduce Wholesteen's annual sales by 10,000 cases. FoodWorld might even stop buying from Wholesteen altogether. What would happen to profits in these two situations?*

c. *FoodWorld is rapidly opening new stores and sells milk in every store. The FoodWorld buyer says that next year's purchases could be up to 25,000 cases of Wholesteen's condensed milk. But Sue Glick knows that FoodWorld may stop buying the Wholesteen brand and want all 25,000 cases to carry the FoodWorld private label brand. How will this affect profit? (Hint: enter the new quantities in the "proposal" column of the spreadsheet.)*

d. *What should Wholesteen do? Why?*

For additional questions related to this problem, see Exercise 8-5 in the *Learning Aid for Use with Essentials of Marketing*, 9th edition.

When You Finish This Chapter, You Should

1. Understand how product life cycles affect strategy planning.

2. Know what is involved in designing new products and what "new products" really are.

3. Understand the new-product development process.

4. See why product liability must be considered in screening new products.

5. Understand the need for product or brand managers.

6. Understand how total quality management can improve goods and services.

7. Understand the important new terms (shown in red).

Chapter Nine

Product Management and New-Product Development

In today's markets, a few years can bring a lot of changes. When Palm introduced its first personal digital assistant (PDA), it was a really new product concept—even in the eyes of its target market of gadget-loving, on-the-go executives. It didn't do anything radical, but it did a few important things really well. It could store names and addresses, track expenses, schedule meetings and priorities, and program calculations. And it was easy to use, which helped Palm sell a million units in just the first two years. As sales growth accelerated, Palm introduced new models with more features—like its connected organizer that could "beam" data to another Palm or a computer and even connect to e-mail anywhere anytime.

During those early years, Palm had little direct competition. Customers around the world

place price promotion produc

bought 13 million PDAs in five years, and 75 percent of them were Palms. Business customers were not very price-sensitive, so without much competition Palm also enjoyed great profit margins.

Palm's marketing plan for its new m500 series (www.palm.com) was to improve graphics and power and add modular features like a digital camera and digital notepad for handwritten e-mail. While these were not big changes for the PDA market, they probably looked revolutionary to the marketing managers for DayTimer's pen-and-paper organizers, Timex's DataLink watches, HP's programmable calculators, IBM's Thinkpad laptops, and Motorola's digital pagers. The marketing managers for these products may not have seen the changes to the new m500 or the original PDA as a competitor. Yet when a firm finds a better way to meet customer needs, it disrupts old ways of doing things. And PDAs were taking business from other categories, even digital cameras.

But Palm wasn't immune to the forces of competition either. Its profits, and the growth of the PDA market, attracted rivals. Casio, IBM, Sharp, Psion, HP, and others jumped into the fray. For example, just as Palm was hoping to get growth from sales to students and other price-sensitive consumers, Handspring made big inroads with colorful, low-priced models. Similarly, Compaq's iPaq and other brands chipped away at the high end of the market with units using Microsoft's new Pocket PC operating system. Many users who wanted feature-packed PDAs with more power and better screens thought the Pocket PC had benefits that Palm's system missed. As a weak economy eroded demand, price competition on high-end PDAs wiped out Palm's profit margins. It also didn't help that Palm's new-product development process hit delays. When its new model didn't come out on schedule, even loyal customers looked elsewhere.

Given the fast changes in this market environment, it's hard to know what will happen in the future or how marketing strategies may change. Soon a PDA may just be a promotional giveaway with a subscription to some service—like wireless video teleconferencing over the Internet. Or the really big market may be kids—if PDA makers build in more interactive gaming features.[1]

Managing Products over Their Life Cycles

The life and death cycle seen in our Palm case is being repeated over and over again in product-markets worldwide. Cellular phones are replacing shortwave radios and CBs and also making it possible for people to communicate from places where it was previously impossible. Cellular linkups over the Internet are coming on strong. Cassette tapes replaced vinyl records, and now CDs, digital minidiscs, and VHS tapes are challenged by DVD and downloaded MP3 digital files stored on memory cards.

Revolutionary products create new product-markets. Competitors are always developing and copying new ideas and products—making existing products out-of-date more quickly than ever. Products, like consumers, go through life cycles. So developing new products and managing existing products to meet changing conditions is important to the success of every firm.

Product life cycle has four major stages

The **product life cycle** describes the stages a really new product idea goes through from beginning to end. The product life cycle is divided into four major stages: (1) market introduction, (2) market growth, (3) market maturity, and (4) sales decline. The product life cycle is concerned with new types (or categories) of product in the market, not just what happens to an individual brand.

A particular firm's marketing mix usually must change during the product life cycle. The product may be aimed at entirely different target markets at different stages. Customers' attitudes and needs may change over the product life cycle. And the nature of competition may move toward pure competition or oligopoly.

Further, total sales of the product—by all competitors in the industry—vary in each of its four stages. They move from very low in the market introduction stage to high at market maturity and then back to low in the sales decline stage. More important, the profit picture changes too. These general relationships can be seen in Exhibit 9-1. Note that sales and profits do not move together over time. *Industry profits decline while industry sales are still rising.*[2]

Market introduction—investing in the future

In the **market introduction** stage, sales are low as a new idea is first introduced to a market. Customers aren't looking for the product. Even if the product offers superior value, customers don't even know about it. Informative promotion is needed to tell potential customers about the advantages and uses of the new product concept.

Even though a firm promotes its new product, it takes time for customers to learn that the product is available. Most companies experience losses during the introduction stage because they spend so much money for Promotion, Product, and Place development. Of course, they invest the money in the hope of future profits.

Exhibit 9-1
Typical Life Cycle of a New Product Concept

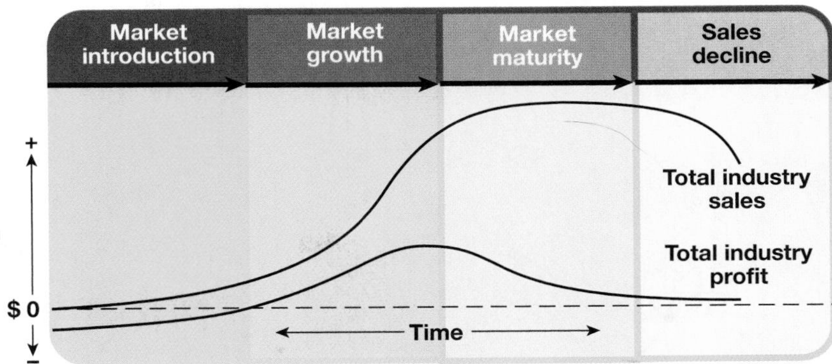

Market growth—profits go up and down

In the **market growth** stage, industry sales grow fast—but industry profits rise and then start falling. The innovator begins to make big profits as more and more customers buy. But competitors see the opportunity and enter the market. Some just copy the most successful product or try to improve it to compete better. Others try to refine their offerings to do a better job of appealing to some target markets. The new entries result in much product variety.

This is the time of biggest profits *for the industry*. It is also a time of rapid sales and earnings growth for companies with effective strategies. *But it is toward the end of this stage when industry profits begin to decline* as competition and consumer price sensitivity increase. See Exhibit 9-1.

Some firms make big strategy planning mistakes at this stage by not understanding the product life cycle. They see the big sales and profit opportunities of the early market growth stage but ignore the competition that will soon follow. When they realize their mistake, it may be too late. This happened with many dot-coms during the late 1990s.

Market maturity—sales level off, profits continue down

The **market maturity** stage occurs when industry sales level off and competition gets tougher. Many aggressive competitors have entered the race for profits—except in oligopoly situations. Industry profits go down throughout the market maturity stage because promotion costs rise and some competitors cut prices to attract business. Less efficient firms can't compete with this pressure—and they drop out of the market.

New firms may still enter the market at this stage—increasing competition even more. Note that late entries completely miss the profitable market growth stage. And they must try to take a share of the saturated market from established firms, which is difficult and expensive. The market leaders have a lot at stake, so they fight hard to defend their markets. Customers who are happy with their current relationship won't switch to a new brand. So late entrants usually have a tough battle.

Persuasive promotion becomes more important during the market maturity stage. Products may differ only slightly. Most competitors have discovered effective appeals or just copied the leaders. By then, price sensitivity is a real factor.

In the United States, the markets for most cars, boats, television sets, and many household appliances are in market maturity. This stage may continue for many years—until a basically new product idea comes along—even though individual brands or models come and go. For example, high-definition digital TV (HDTV) is coming on now, and over time it will make old-style TVs obsolete.[3]

Sales decline—a time of replacement

During the **sales decline** stage, new products replace the old. Price competition from dying products becomes more vigorous—but firms with strong brands may make profits until the end because they successfully differentiated their

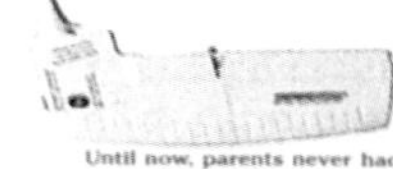

New products that do a better job of meeting the needs of specific target customers are more likely to move quickly and successfully through the introductory stage of the product life cycle.

products. They may keep some sales by appealing to the most loyal customers or those who are slow to try new ideas. These conservative buyers might switch later—smoothing the sales decline.

Product Life Cycles Should Be Related to Specific Markets

Remember that product life cycles describe industry sales and profits for a *product idea* within a particular product-market. The sales and profits of an individual brand may not, and often do not, follow the life-cycle pattern. They may vary up and down throughout the life cycle—sometimes moving in the opposite direction of industry sales and profits. Further, a product idea may be in a different life-cycle stage in different markets.

Individual brands may not follow the pattern

A given firm may introduce or drop a specific product during any stage of the product life cycle. A "me-too" brand introduced during the market growth stage, for example, may never get any sales and suffer a quick death. But market leaders may enjoy high profits during the market maturity stage—even though industry profits are declining.

Strategy planners who naively expect sales of an individual product to follow the general product life-cycle pattern are likely to be rudely surprised. In fact, it might be more sensible to think in terms of "product-market life cycles" rather than product life cycles—but we will use the term *product life cycle* because it is commonly accepted and widely used.

Each market should be carefully defined

How we see product life cycles depends on how broadly we define a product-market. For example, about 80 percent of all U.S. households own microwave ovens which are at the market maturity stage here. In many other countries they're still early in the growth stage. Even in European countries like Italy and Spain, fewer than 20 percent of all households own microwave ovens.[4] As this example suggests, a firm with a mature product can sometimes find new growth in international markets.

How broadly we define the needs of customers in a product-market also affects how we view product life cycles—and who the competitors are. Consider the needs related to storing and preparing foods. Sales of Saran Wrap (and other similar products) fell sharply when small plastic storage bags became popular. However, sales

Marketing managers for Kellogg and Nabisco have found many opportunities for new growth in international markets.

picked up again later when microwave cooking become popular. In the last few years, resealable bags like those from Ziploc have taken over because they can be used in both the freezer and the microwave.

If a market is defined broadly, there may be many competitors—and the market may appear to be in market maturity. On the other hand, if we focus on a narrow submarket—and a particular way of satisfying specific needs—then we may see much shorter product life cycles as improved product ideas come along to replace the old.

Product Life Cycles Vary in Length

How long a whole product life cycle takes—and the length of each stage—varies a lot across products. The cycle may vary from 90 days—in the case of toys like the Ghostbusters line—to possibly 100 years for gas-powered cars.

Some products move fast

A new product idea will move through the early stages of the life cycle more quickly when it has certain characteristics. For example, the greater the *comparative advantage* of a new product over those already on the market, the more rapidly its sales will grow. Sales growth is also faster when the product is *easy to use* and if its advantages are *easy to communicate*. If the product *can be tried* on a limited basis—without a lot of risk to the customer—it can usually be introduced more quickly. Finally, if the product is *compatible* with the values and experiences of target customers, they are likely to buy it more quickly.

The fast adoption of the Netscape Navigator browser is a good example. Compared to earlier ways for computers to communicate on the Internet, Navigator was easy to use with both pictures and text. It also offered a simple way to customize to the user's preferences. Free downloads made it easy for consumers to try the software. And Navigator worked like other Windows software that users already knew, so it was easy to install—and it was already compatible with their computers.[5]

Internet

Internet Exercise A number of software, hardware, and programming firms are working on products that deliver Internet information via TV. Explore the WebTV website (www.webtv.com) to find out about one aspect of this idea. How does WebTV stack up when you consider the characteristics of an innovation reviewed earlier?

Product life cycles are getting shorter

Although the life of different products varies, in general product life cycles are getting shorter. This is partly due to rapidly changing technology. One new invention may make possible many new products that replace old ones. Tiny electronic microchips led to hundreds of new products—from Texas Instruments calculators in the early days to microchip-controlled heart valves now.

Patents for a new product may not be much protection in slowing down competitors. Competitors can often find ways to copy the product idea without violating a specific patent. Worse, some unethical firms simply disregard the patent. Patent violations by foreign competitors are very common. A product's life may be over before a case can get through patent-court bottlenecks.[6]

Although life cycles keep moving in the advanced economies, many advances bypass most consumers in less-developed economies. These consumers struggle at the subsistence level, without an effective macro-marketing system to stimulate innovation.

The early bird usually makes the profits

The product life cycle means that firms must be developing new products all the time. Further, they must try to have marketing mixes that will make the most of the market growth stage—when profits are highest.

During the growth stage, competitors are likely to rapidly introduce product improvements. Fast changes in marketing strategy may be required here because profits don't necessarily go to the innovator. Sometimes fast copiers of the basic idea will share in the market growth stage. Copiers can be even faster than the innovator in adapting to the market's needs. Marketers must be flexible, *but also* they must fully understand the needs and attitudes of their target markets.[7]

A certain color or style may be in fashion one season and outdated the next.

The short happy life of fashions

The sales of some products are influenced by **fashion**—the currently accepted or popular style. Fashion-related products tend to have short life cycles. What is currently popular can shift rapidly. Marketing managers who work with fashions often have to make really fast product changes.[8]

How fast is fast enough? Zara, a women's fashion retailer based in Spain, takes only about two weeks to go from a new fashion concept to having items on the racks of its stores. Zara's market-watching designers get a constant flow of new fashion ideas from music videos, fashion shows, and magazines. Zara quickly produces just enough of a design to test the waters and then sends it out for overnight delivery to some of its 449 stores around the world. Stores track consumer preferences every day through point-of-sale computers and designers get online summaries of what's selling and where. If an item is hot, more is produced and shipped. Otherwise it's dropped. With this system items are rarely on the shelves of Zara stores for more than a week or two.[9]

Planning for Different Stages of the Product Life Cycle

Length of cycle affects strategy planning

Where a product is in its life cycle—and how fast it's moving to the next stage—should affect marketing strategy planning. Marketing managers must make realistic plans for the later stages. Exhibit 9-2 shows the relationship of the product life cycle to the marketing mix variables. The technical terms in this figure are discussed later in the book.

Introducing new products

Exhibit 9-2 shows that a marketing manager has to do a lot of work to introduce a really new product. Money must be spent developing the new product. The firm will have to build channels of distribution—perhaps offering special incentives to win cooperation. Promotion is needed to build demand *for the whole idea* not just to sell a specific brand. Because all this is expensive, it may lead the marketing manager to try to "skim" the market—charging a relatively high price to help pay for the introductory costs.

The correct strategy, however, depends on how quickly the new idea will be accepted by customers—and how quickly competitors will follow with their own versions of the product. When the early stages of the cycle will be fast, a low initial (penetration) price may make sense to help develop loyal customers early and keep competitors out.

Pioneer may need help from competitors

Sometimes it's not in the best interest of the market pioneer for competitors to stay out of the market. Building customer interest in a really new product idea—and obtaining distribution to make the product available—can be too big a job for a single company. Two or more companies investing in promotion to build demand may help to stimulate the growth of the whole product-market. Similarly, a new product may languish if it is not compatible with other products that customers rely on. This is what recently happened with Digital Video Express (Divx) video disks. When Divx came out, many consumer-electronics firms were launching DVD format products. Divx had advantages, but it was not compatible with many DVD players already on the market. Video stores didn't want to stock movies in both formats so Divx fizzled.[10]

New product sales may not take off

Not all new product ideas catch on. Customers may conclude that the marketing mix doesn't satisfy their needs, or other new products may meet the same need better. But the success that eludes a firm with its initial strategy can sometimes be achieved by modifying the strategy.[11]

Exhibit 9-2
Typical Changes in Marketing Variables over the Product Life Cycle

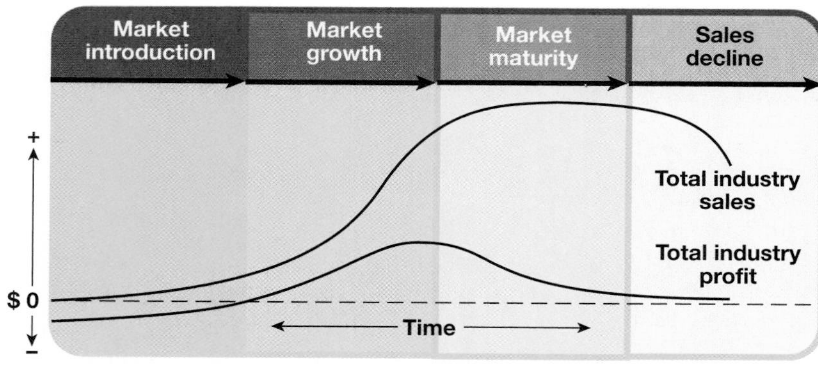

Competitive situation	Monopoly or monopolistic competition	Monopolistic competition or oligopoly	Monopolistic competition or oligopoly heading toward pure competition →	
Product	One or few	Variety—try to find best product Build brand familiarity	All "same" Battle of brands	Some drop out
Place	Build channels Maybe selective distribution →		Move toward more intensive distribution →	
Promotion	Build primary demand Pioneering-informing	Build selective demand → Informing/Persuading → Persuading/Reminding (frantically competitive)		
Price	Skimming or penetration	Meet competition (especially in oligopoly) → or Price dealing and price cutting →		

Managing maturing products

It's important for a firm to have some competitive advantage as it moves into market maturity. Even a small advantage can make a big difference. For example, graham crackers were competing in a mature market and sales were flat. Nabisco used the same ingredients to create bite-sized Teddy Grahams and then promoted them heavily. These changes captured new sales and profits for Nabisco.[12]

Industry profits are declining in market maturity. Top managers must see this, or they will expect profits that are no longer possible. They may place impossible burdens on the marketing department—causing marketing managers to think about deceptive advertising or some other desperate attempt to reach impossible objectives.

Product life cycles keep moving. But that doesn't mean a firm should just sit by as its sales decline. There are other choices. A firm can improve its product or develop an innovative new product for the same market. Or it can develop a strategy for its product (perhaps with modifications) targeted at a new market. For example, it might find a market in a country where the life cycle is not so far along, or it might try to serve a new need. Or the firm can withdraw the product before it completes the cycle and refocus on better opportunities. See Exhibit 9-3.

Improve the product or develop a new one

Even in a mature market, continued improvements may be needed to keep customers satisfied. An example is Procter & Gamble's Tide. Introduced in 1947, Tide led to a whole new generation of detergents that cleaned better with fewer suds.

Some companies continue to do well in market maturity by improving their products. Lipton has developed a cold brew tea and Nintendo's Game Boy remains popular with new color features.

But Tide continues to change because of new washing machines and fabrics—so the Tide sold today has had at least 55 modifications.[13]

Develop new strategies for different markets

In a mature market, a firm may be fighting to keep or increase its market share. But if the firm finds a new use for the product, it may need to try to stimulate overall demand. Du Pont's Teflon is a good example. It was developed more than 50 years ago and has enjoyed sales growth as a nonstick coating for cookware and as a lining for chemically resistant equipment. But marketing managers for Teflon are not waiting to be stuck with declining profits in those mature markets. They are constantly developing strategies for new markets. For example, Teflon is now selling well as a special coating for the wires used in high-speed communications between computers.[14]

Phasing out dying products

Not all strategies have to be exciting growth strategies. If prospects are poor in some product-market, a phase-out strategy may be needed. The need for phasing out becomes more obvious as the sales decline stage arrives.

Marketing plans are implemented as ongoing strategies. Salespeople make calls, inventory moves in the channel, advertising is scheduled for several months into the future, and so on. So the firm usually experiences losses if managers end a plan too abruptly. Because of this, it's sometimes better to phase out the product gradually.

Phasing out a product may involve some difficult implementation problems. But phase-out is also a *strategy*—and it must be market-oriented to cut losses. In fact, it is possible to milk a dying product for some time if competitors move out more

Exhibit 9-3
Examples of Three Marketing Strategy Choices for a Firm in a Mature Product-Market

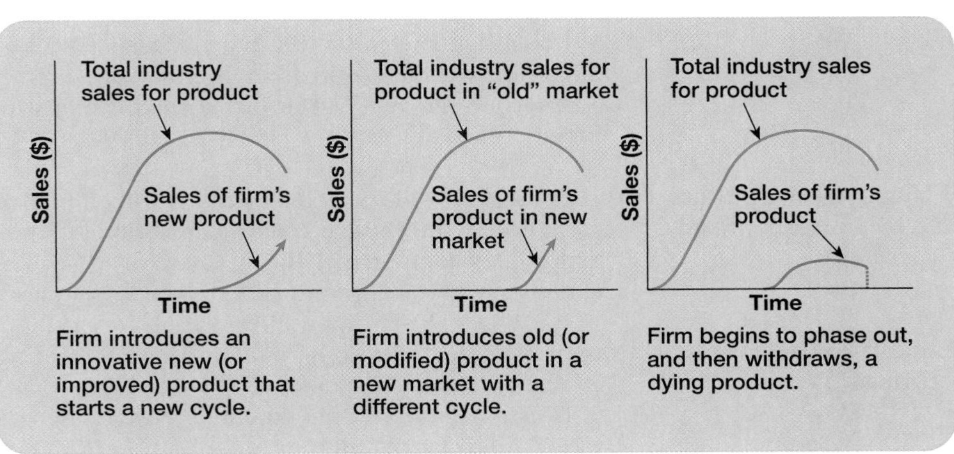

Tide detergent has been improved many times over the years, and now has a new WearCare formula that helps protect cotton threads from damage. By contrast, Dryel is a completely new type of product and being able to dry clean delicate clothes at home is a new idea.

quickly and there is ongoing (though declining) demand. Some customers may be willing to pay attractive prices to get their old favorite.

New-Product Planning

In most markets, progress marches on. So not having an active new-product development process means that consciously, or subconsciously, the firm has decided to milk its current products and go out of business. New-product planning is not an optional matter. It has to be done just to survive in today's dynamic markets.

What is a new product?

In discussing the introductory stage of product life cycles, we focused on the type of really new product innovations that tend to disrupt old ways of doing things. However, each year firms introduce many products that are basically refinements of existing products. So a **new product** is one that is new *in any way* for the company concerned.

A product can become "new" in many ways. A fresh idea can be turned into a new product and start a new product life cycle. For example, Alza Corporation's time-release skin patches are replacing pills and injections for some medications.

Variations on an existing product idea can also make a product new. Colgate redesigned the conventional toothbrush with a soft handle and angled bristles to do a better job removing tartar. Even small changes in an existing product can make it new.

FTC says product is "new" only six months

A firm can call its product new for only a limited time. Six months is the limit according to the **Federal Trade Commission (FTC)**—the federal government agency that polices antimonopoly laws. To be called new, says the FTC, a product must be entirely new or changed in a "functionally significant or substantial respect."

Ethical issues in new-product planning

New product decisions—and decisions to abandon old products—often involve ethical considerations. For example, some firms (including firms that develop drugs to treat AIDS) have been criticized for holding back important new product innovations until patents run out, or sales slow down, on their existing products.

At the same time, others have been criticized for "planned obsolescence"—releasing new products that the company plans to soon replace with improved new versions. Similarly, wholesalers and middlemen complain that producers too often keep their new-product introduction plans a secret and leave middlemen with dated inventory that they can sell only at a loss.

Criticisms are also leveled at firms that constantly release minor variations of products that already saturate markets. Consider what happened with disposable diapers. Marketing managers thought that they were serving some customers' needs better when they offered diapers in boys' and girls' versions and in a variety of sizes and colors. But many retailers felt that the new products were simply a ploy to get more shelf space. Further, some consumers complained that the bewildering array of choices made it impossible to make an informed decision.

Different marketing managers might have very different reactions to such criticisms. However, product management decisions often have a significant effect on customers and middlemen. A too casual decision may lead to a negative backlash that affects the firm's strategy or reputation.[15]

An Organized New-Product Development Process Is Critical

Identifying and developing new-product ideas—and effective strategies to go with them—is often the key to a firm's success and survival. But the risks and costs of new-product development failure are high. Experts estimate that consumer packaged-goods companies spend at least $20 million to introduce a new brand—and 70 to 80 percent of these new brands flop. That's a big expense—and a waste. In the service sector, the front-end cost of a failed effort may not be as high, but it can have a devastating long-term effect if dissatisfied consumers turn elsewhere for help.[16]

Internet

Internet Exercise Marketing Intelligence Service, Ltd., is a U.S.-based firm that tracks new consumer packaged goods—both successes and failures. Enter its website (www.productscan.com) and click on the *What's New* button, then review its selections for new product innovations of the year. Do you think that these products offer customers superior value, or are they just me-too imitations?

A new product may fail for many reasons. Most often, companies fail to offer a unique benefit or underestimate the competition. Sometimes the idea is good but the company has design problems—or the product costs much more to produce than was expected. Some companies rush to get a product on the market without developing a complete marketing plan.[17]

But moving too slowly can be a problem too. With the fast pace of change for many products, speedy entry into the market can be a key to competitive advantage. Marketing managers at Xerox learned this the hard way. Japanese competitors were taking market share with innovative new models of copiers. It turned out that the competitors were developing new models twice as fast as Xerox and at half the cost. For Xerox to compete, it had to slash its five-year product development cycle. Many other companies—ranging from manufacturers like Chrysler Corporation to Internet service firms like E*Trade—are working to speed up the new-product development process.[18]

To move quickly and also avoid expensive new-product failures, companies should follow an organized new-product development process. The following pages describe such a process, which moves logically through five steps: (1) idea generation,

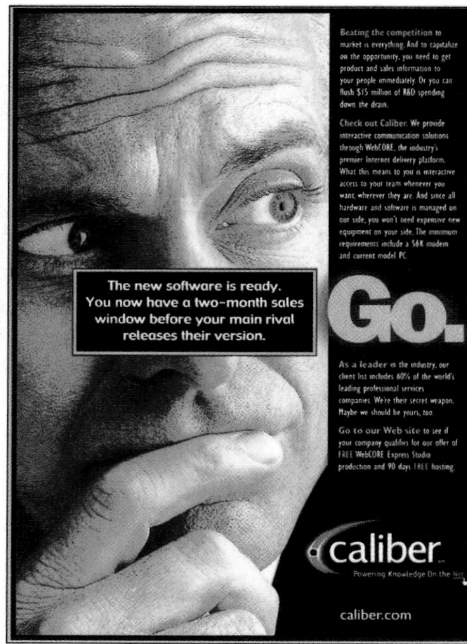

Generating innovative and profitable new products requires an understanding of customer needs—and an organized new-product development process.

(2) screening, (3) idea evaluation, (4) development (of product and marketing mix), and (5) commercialization.[19] See Exhibit 9-4.

The general process is similar for both consumer and business markets—and for both goods and services. There are some significant differences, but we will emphasize the similarities in the following discussion.

Process tries to kill new ideas—economically

An important element in this new-product development process is continued evaluation of a new idea's likely profitability and return on investment. The hypothesis tested is that the new idea will *not* be profitable. This puts the burden on the new idea—to prove itself or be rejected. Such a process may seem harsh, but experience shows that most new ideas have some flaw. Marketers try to discover those flaws early, and either find a remedy or reject the idea completely. Applying this process requires much analysis of the idea *before* the company spends money to develop and market a product. This is a major departure from the usual production-oriented approach—in which a company develops a product first and then asks sales to "get rid of it."

Step 1: Idea generation

Finding new product ideas can't be left to chance. Companies need a formal procedure for seeking new ideas. Although later steps eliminate many ideas, a company must identify some that succeed.

Exhibit 9-4 New-Product Development Process

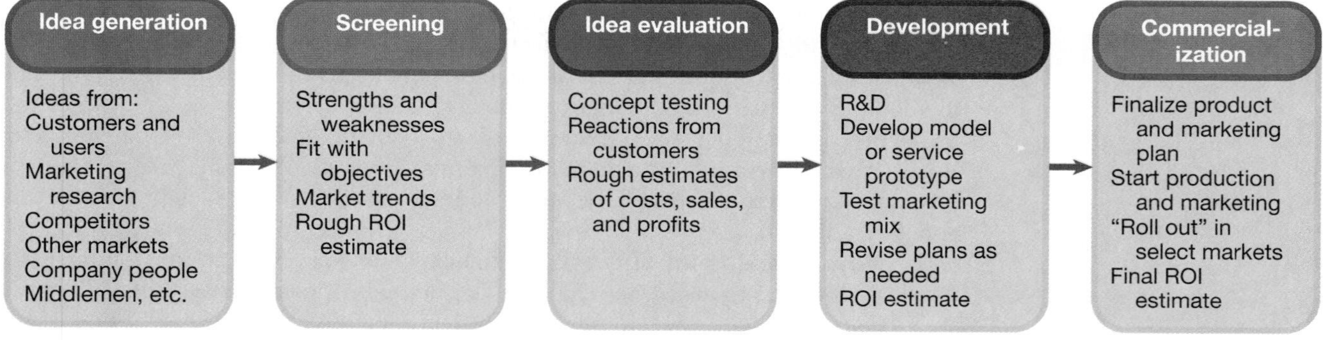

Exhibit 9-5
Types of New-Product Opportunities

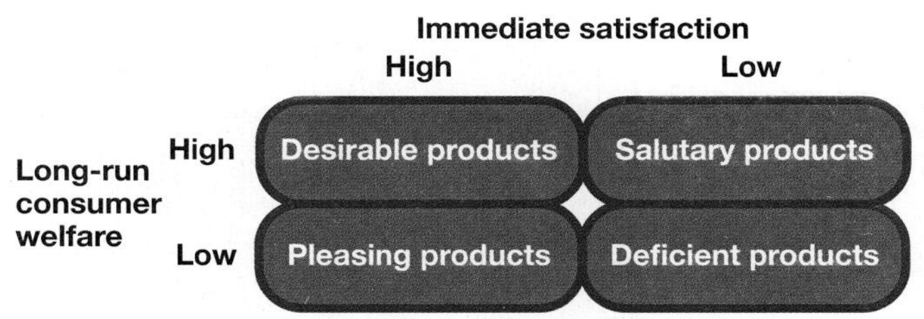

New ideas can come from a company's own sales or production staff, middlemen, competitors, consumer surveys, or other sources such as trade associations, advertising agencies, or government agencies. By analyzing new and different views of the company's markets and studying present consumer behavior, a marketing manager can spot opportunities that have not yet occurred to competitors or even to potential customers. For example, ideas for new service concepts may come directly from analysis of consumer complaints.

No one firm can always be first with the best new ideas. So in their search for ideas, companies should pay attention to what competitors are doing. Some firms use what's called reverse engineering. For example, new-product specialists at Ford Motor Company buy other firms' cars as soon as they're available. Then they take the cars apart to look for new ideas or improvements.[20]

Many firms now "shop" in international markets for new ideas. For instance, food companies in Europe are experimenting with a clear, odorless, natural film for wrapping food that was introduced in Japan. Consumers don't have to unwrap it; when they put the product in boiling water or a microwave, the wrapper vanishes.[21]

Research shows that many new ideas in business markets come from customers who identify a need they have. Then they approach a supplier with the idea and perhaps even with a particular design or specification. These customers become the lead users of the product, but the supplier can pursue the opportunity in other markets.[22]

Step 2: Screening

Screening involves evaluating the new ideas with the type of S.W.O.T analysis described in Chapter 3 and the product-market screening criteria described in Chapter 4. Recall that these criteria include the combined output of a resources (strengths and weaknesses) analysis, a long-run trends analysis, and a thorough understanding of the company's objectives. See Exhibit 3-1 and Exhibit 4-7. Further, a "good" new idea should eventually lead to a product (and marketing mix) that will give the firm a competitive advantage—hopefully, a lasting one.

Some companies screen based on consumer welfare

Screening should also consider how a new product will affect consumers over time. Ideally, the product should increase consumer welfare, not just satisfy a whim. Exhibit 9-5 shows different kinds of new-product opportunities. Obviously, a socially responsible firm tries to find desirable opportunities rather than deficient ones. This may not be as easy as it sounds, however. Some consumers want pleasing products and give little thought to their own long-term welfare. And some competitors will offer consumers whatever they will buy.

Safety must be considered

Real acceptance of the marketing concept certainly leads to safe products. The U.S. **Consumer Product Safety Act** (of 1972) set up the Consumer Product Safety Commission to encourage safety in product design and better quality control. The commission has a great deal of power. It can set safety standards for products. It can order costly repairs or return of unsafe products. And it can back up its orders with

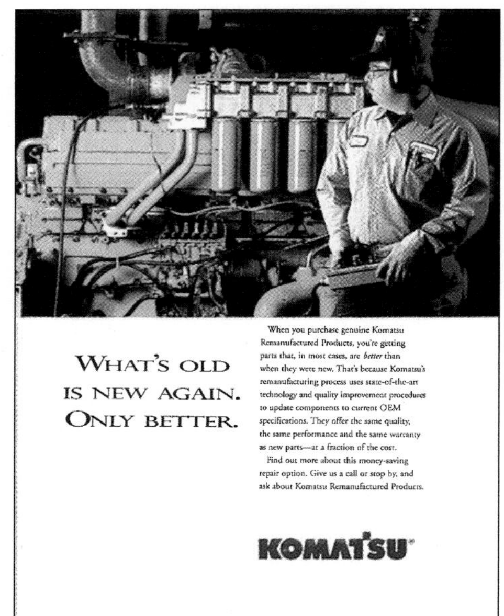

Products that can be regenerated or remanufactured provide both immediate satisfaction and long-run consumer welfare.

fines and jail sentences. The Food and Drug Administration has similar powers for food and drugs.

Product safety complicates strategy planning because not all customers—even those who want better safety features—are willing to pay more for safer products. Some features cost a lot to add and increase prices considerably. These safety concerns must be considered at the screening step because a firm can later be held liable for unsafe products.

Products can turn to liabilities

Product liability means the legal obligation of sellers to pay damages to individuals who are injured by defective or unsafe products. Product liability is a serious matter. Liability settlements may exceed not only a company's insurance coverage but its total assets!

Relative to most other countries, U.S. courts enforce a very strict product liability standard. Producers may be held responsible for injuries related to their products no matter how the items are used or how well they're designed. Riddell—whose football helmets protect the pros—was hit with a $12 million judgment for a high school football player who broke his neck. The jury concluded that Riddell should have put a sticker on the helmet to warn players of the danger of butting into opponents!

Cases and settlements like this are common. Some critics argue that the U.S. rules are so tough that they discourage innovation and economic growth. In contrast, Japan may be too slack. Japan's system discourages consumers from filing complaints because they are required to pay a percentage of any damages they seek as court costs—regardless of whether they win or lose.

Product liability is a serious ethical and legal matter. Many countries are attempting to change their laws so that they will be fair to both firms and consumers. But until product liability questions are resolved, marketing managers must be even more sensitive when screening new-product ideas.[23]

Step 3: Idea evaluation

When an idea moves past the screening step, it is evaluated more carefully. Companies can often estimate likely costs, revenue, and profitability at this stage. And market research can help identify the size of potential markets. Note that an actual product has not yet been developed—and this can handicap the firm in getting feedback from customers. For help in idea evaluation, firms use **concept testing**—getting reactions from customers about how well a new product idea fits their needs. Concept testing uses market research—ranging from informal focus groups to formal surveys of potential customers.

Product planners must think about wholesaler and retailer customers as well as final consumers. Middlemen may have special concerns about handling a proposed product. A Utah ice-cream maker was considering a new line of ice-cream novelty products—and he had visions of a hot market in California. But he had to drop his idea when he learned that grocery store chains wanted payments of $20,000 each just to stock his frozen novelties in their freezers.[24]

Whatever research methods are used, the idea evaluation step should gather enough information to help decide whether there is an opportunity, whether it fits with the firm's resources, *and* whether there is a basis for developing a competitive advantage. With such information, the firm can estimate likely ROI (return on investment) in the various market segments and decide whether to continue the new-product development process.[25]

Step 4: Development

Product ideas that survive the screening and idea evaluation steps must now be analyzed further. Usually, this involves some research and development (R&D) and engineering to design and develop the physical part of the product. In the case of a new service offering, the firm will work out the details of what training, equipment, staff, and so on will be needed to deliver on the idea. Input from the earlier efforts helps guide this technical work.

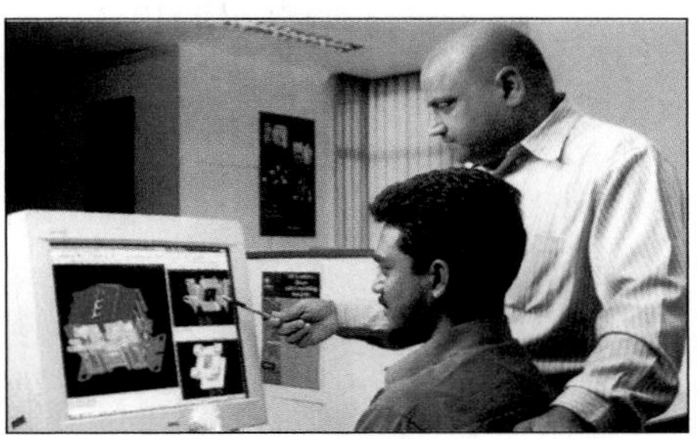

New computer-aided design (CAD) systems are sparking a revolution in design work. Designers can develop lifelike 3-D color drawings of packages and products. Changes can be made almost instantly. They can be sent by e-mail to managers all over the world for immediate review. They can even be put on a website for marketing research with remote customers. Then once the designs are finalized, they feed directly into computer-controlled manufacturing systems. Companies like Motorola and Timex have found that these systems cut their new-product development time in half—giving them a leg up on many competitors.

Even so, it is still useful to test models and early versions of the product in the market. This process may have several cycles. A manufacturer may build a model of a physical product or produce limited quantities; a service firm may try to train a small group of service providers. Product tests with customers may lead to revisions—*before* the firm commits to full-scale efforts.

With actual goods or services, potential customers can react to how well the product meets their needs. Focus groups, panels, and larger surveys can react to specific features and to the whole product idea. Sometimes that reaction kills the idea. For example, Coca-Cola Foods believed it had a great idea with Minute Maid Squeeze-Fresh, frozen orange juice concentrate in a squeeze bottle. In tests, however, Squeeze-Fresh bombed. Consumers loved the idea but hated the product. It was messy to use, and no one knew how much concentrate to squeeze in the glass.[26]

In other cases, testing can lead to revision of product specifications for different markets. Sometimes a complex series of revisions may be required. Months or even years of research may be necessary to focus on precisely what different market segments will find acceptable. For example, Gillette's Mach3 razor blade took over a decade and $750 million in development and tooling costs.[27]

Firms often take apart competitors' products to look for ideas that they can apply or adapt in their own products.

Firms often use full-scale market testing to get reactions in real market conditions or to test variations in the marketing mix. For example, a firm may test alternative brands, prices, or advertising copy in different test cities. Note that the firm is testing the whole marketing mix, not just the product. For example, a hotel chain might test a new service offering at one location to see how it goes over.

Running market tests is costly, but *not* testing is sometimes even more expensive. Frito-Lay was so sure it understood consumers' snack preferences that it introduced a three-item cracker line without market testing. Even with network TV ad support, MaxSnax met with overwhelming consumer indifference. By the time Frito-Lay pulled the product from store shelves, it had lost $52 million.[28]

After the market test, the firm can estimate likely ROI for various strategies to determine whether the idea moves on to commercialization.[29]

Step 5: Commercialization

A product idea that survives this far can finally be placed on the market. Putting a product on the market is expensive. Manufacturing or service facilities have to be set up. Goods have to be produced to fill the channels of distribution, or people must be hired and trained to provide services. Further, introductory promotion is costly—especially if the company is entering a very competitive market.

Because of the size of the job, some firms introduce their products city by city or region by region—in a gradual "rollout"—until they have complete market coverage. Sprint used this approach in introducing its broadband wireless service that included a rooftop transmission device. Detroit, Phoenix, and San Francisco were targeted first. Rollouts also permit more market testing—although that is not their purpose. Rather, the purpose is to do a good job implementing the marketing plan. But marketing managers also need to pay close attention to control—to ensure that the implementation effort is working and that the strategy is on target.

New-Product Development: A Total Company Effort

We've been discussing the steps in a logical, new-product development process. However, as shown in Exhibit 9-6, many factors can impact the success of the effort.

Top-level support is vital

Companies that are particularly successful at developing new goods and services seem to have one key trait in common: enthusiastic top-management support for new-product development.[30]

Put someone in charge

In addition, rather than leaving new-product development to someone in engineering, R&D, or sales who happens to be interested in taking the initiative, successful companies put someone in charge. It may be a person, department, or team.

A new-product development team with people from different departments helps ensure that new ideas are carefully evaluated and profitable ones quickly brought to market. It's important to choose the right people for the job. Overly conservative managers may kill too many, or even all, new ideas. Or committees may create bureaucratic delays that make the difference between a product's success or failure.

Market needs guide R&D effort

From the idea generation stage to the commercialization stage, the R&D specialists, the operations people, and the marketing people must work together to evaluate the feasibility of new ideas. They may meet in person, or communicate with e-mail or intranet sites, or perhaps via teleconferencing or some other technology. There are many ways to share ideas. So it isn't sensible for a marketing manager to develop elaborate marketing plans for goods or services that the firm simply can't produce—or produce profitably. It also doesn't make sense for R&D people to develop a technology or product that does not have potential for the firm

Exhibit 9-6 New-Product Development Success Factors

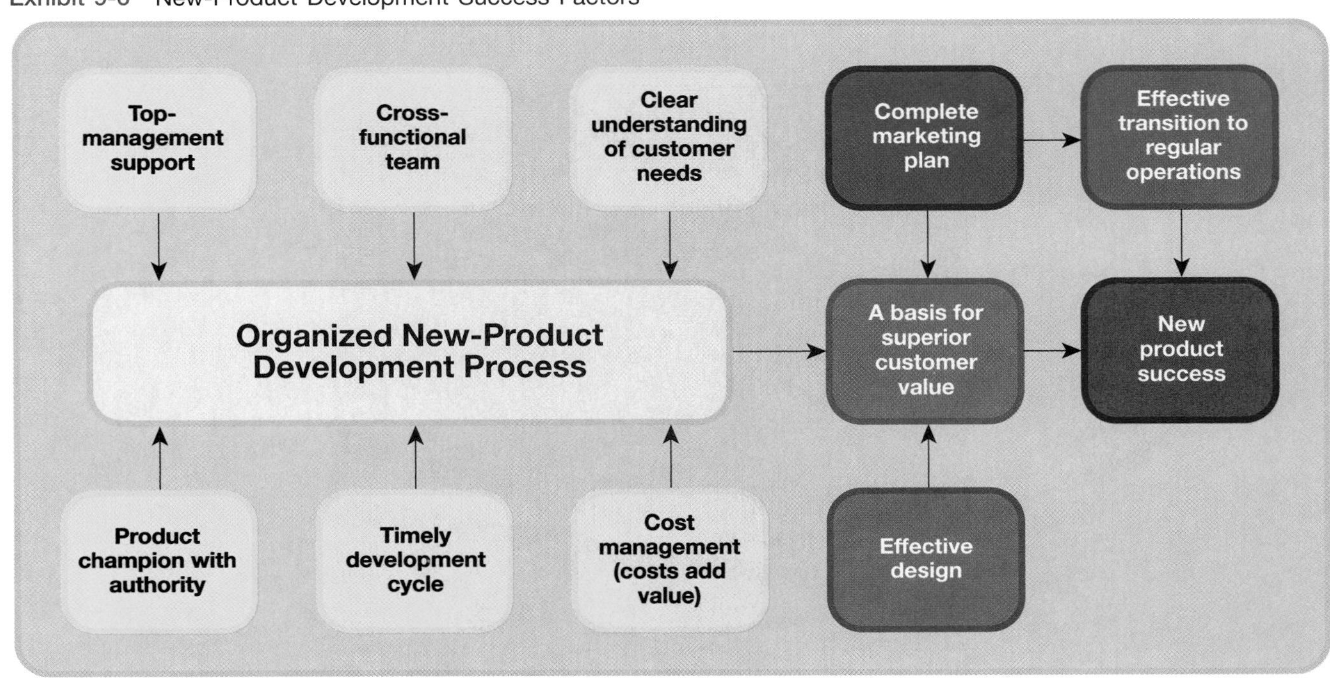

and its markets. Clearly, a balancing act is involved here. But the critical point is the basic one we've been emphasizing throughout the whole book: marketing-oriented firms seek to satisfy customer needs at a profit with an integrated, whole company effort.

Need for Product Managers

Product variety leads to product managers

When a firm has only one or a few related products, everyone is interested in them. But when a firm has products in several different product categories, management may decide to put someone in charge of each category, or each brand, to be sure that attention to these products is not lost in the rush of everyday business. **Product managers** or **brand managers** manage specific products—often taking over the jobs formerly handled by an advertising manager. That gives a clue to what is often their major responsibility—Promotion—since the products have already been developed by the new-product people. However, some brand managers start at the new-product development stage and carry on from there.

Product managers are especially common in large companies that produce many kinds of products. Several product managers may serve under a marketing manager. Sometimes these product managers are responsible for the profitable operation of a particular product's whole marketing effort. Then they have to coordinate their efforts with others—including the sales manager, advertising agencies, production and research people, and even channel members. This is likely to lead to difficulties if product managers have no control over the marketing strategy for other related brands or authority over other functional areas whose efforts they are expected to direct and coordinate.

To avoid these problems, in some companies the product manager serves mainly as a "product champion"—concerned with planning and getting the promotion effort implemented. A higher-level marketing manager with more authority coordinates the efforts and integrates the marketing strategies for different products into an overall plan.

Consumer packaged goods companies, like Nabisco, usually assign brand managers who are responsible for individual products. However, when there are a number of products in the same product category there is often a higher-level manager who ensures that the marketing program for the whole category is effective.

3M Sticks to Its Focus on Innovation

Minnesota Mining & Manufacturing (3M) is fast and successful in spinning out new products. This isn't just by chance. 3M's top executive set an objective that 30 percent of sales should come from products that didn't exist four years ago. You see the emphasis on innovation in even the quickest visit to 3M's website (www.3m.com). For example, current 3M innovations include radiant light film (for uses ranging from graphical signage to glittery toys) and electrostatic fibers (that filter dust out of heating vents). You can see why 3M says, "we are always new."

3M motivates innovation by staying close to customers, rewarding new-product champions, and sharing ideas among divisions. Teams from marketing, operations, and R&D screen new-product concepts for the ones with the highest profit potential. Then everyone works to bring the best ones to market fast. 3M's Scotch-Brite Never Rust Wool Soap Pads show how this approach can succeed. Consumers told 3M marketing researchers that they wanted an improved soap pad. Ordinary steel wool pads leave rust stains on sinks and tiny metal splinters in dishpan hands. 3M screens new products for their environmental impact, so the R&D people developed a pad using fibers from recycled plastic bottles. Experts from 3M's abrasives division figured out how to coat the fibers with fine abrasives and biodegradable soap. Further marketing research refined the shape of the pads, and test markets confirmed that consumers would pay more for Never Rust pads than they did for Brillo.

The managers varied the marketing plan for different countries. In mature markets such as the U.S. and Brazil where steel wool pads already had a large consumer base, the objective was to capture share. In Japan, where steel wool is not commonly used, the objective was to pioneer the market and attract new customers. In a firm renowned for innovation, the launch of Never Rust pads was one of 3M's most profitable ever.

3M is also serious about how its innovations affect consumer welfare. When managers learned that traces of a chemical in 3M's Scotchgard fabric protector might persist in the environment, they didn't wait for scientists to do more tests. They voluntarily pulled the popular product off the market—before they even knew if R&D could find a substitute chemical.[31]

The activities of product managers vary a lot depending on their experience and aggressiveness and the company's organizational philosophy. Today companies are emphasizing marketing *experience*—because this important job takes more than academic training and enthusiasm. But it is clear that someone must be responsible for developing and implementing product-related plans—especially when a company has many products.[32]

Managing Product Quality

Total quality management meets customer requirements

In Chapter 8, we explained that product quality means the ability of a product to satisfy a customer's needs or requirements. Now we'll expand that idea and discuss some ways a manager can improve the quality of a firm's goods and services. We'll develop these ideas from the perspective of **total quality management (TQM),** the philosophy that everyone in the organization is concerned about quality, throughout all of the firm's activities, to better serve customer needs.

The cost of poor quality is lost customers

Most of the early attention in quality management focused on reducing defects in goods produced in factories. At one time most firms assumed defects were an inevitable part of mass production. They saw the cost of replacing defective parts or goods as just a cost of doing business—an insignificant one compared to the advantages of mass production. However, many firms were forced to rethink this assumption when Japanese producers of cars, electronics, and cameras showed that defects weren't inevitable. Much to the surprise of some production-oriented managers, the Japanese experience showed that it is less expensive to do something right the first time than to pay to do it poorly and *then* pay again to fix problems. And the success of Japanese producers in taking customers away from established competitors made it clear that the cost of defects wasn't just the cost of replacement!

From the customer's point of view, getting a defective product and having to complain about it is a big headache. The customer can't use the defective product and suffers the inconvenience of waiting for someone to fix the problem—if *someone* gets around to it. It certainly doesn't deliver superior value. Rather, it erodes goodwill and leaves customers dissatisfied. The big cost of poor quality is the cost of lost customers.

Firms that adopted TQM methods to reduce manufacturing defects soon used the same approaches to overcome many other problems. Their success brought attention to what is possible with TQM—whether the problem concerns poor customer service, flimsy packaging, or even salespeople who can't answer customers' questions.

Getting a handle on doing things right the first time

The idea of identifying customer needs and doing things right the first time seems obvious, but it's easier said than done. Problems always come up, and it's not always clear what isn't being done as well as it could be. Most people tend to ignore problems that don't pose an immediate crisis. But firms that adopt TQM always look for ways to improve implementation with **continuous improvement**—a commitment to constantly make things better one step at a time. Once you accept the idea that there *may* be a better way to do something and you look for it, you may just find it! The place to start is to clearly define "defects"—from the customer's point of view.

Things gone right and things gone wrong

Managers who use the TQM approach think of quality improvement as a sorting process—a sorting out of things gone right and things gone wrong. The sorting process calls for detailed measurements related to a problem. Then managers use a set of statistical tools to analyze the measurements and identify the problem areas that are the best candidates for fixing. The statistical details are beyond our focus here, but it's useful to get a feel for how managers use the tools.

Starting with customer needs

Let's consider the case of a restaurant that does well during the evening hours but wants to improve its lunch business. The restaurant develops a strategy that targets local businesspeople with an attractive luncheon buffet. The restaurant decides on a buffet because research shows that target customers want a choice of good healthy food and are willing to pay reasonable prices for it—as long as they can eat quickly and get back to work on time.

As the restaurant implements its new strategy, the manager wants a measure of how things are going. So she encourages customers to fill out comment cards that ask "How did we do today?" After several months of operation, things seem to be going reasonably well—although business is not as brisk as it was at first. The manager reads the comment cards and divides the ones with complaints into categories—to count up different reasons why customers weren't satisfied.

Slay the dragons first

Then the manager creates a graph (see Exhibit 9-7) showing a frequency distribution for the different types of complaints. Quality people call this a **Pareto chart**—a graph that shows the number of times a problem cause occurs, with problem causes ordered from most frequent to least frequent. The manager's Pareto chart reveals that customers complain most frequently that they have to wait for a seat. There were other common complaints—the buffet was not well organized, the table was not clean, and so on. However, the first complaint is much more common than the next most frequent.

This is typical. The worst problems often occur over and over again. This focuses the manager's attention on which quality problem to fix first. A rule of quality management is to slay the dragons first—which simply means start with the biggest

Exhibit 9-7
Pareto Chart Showing Frequency of Different Complaints

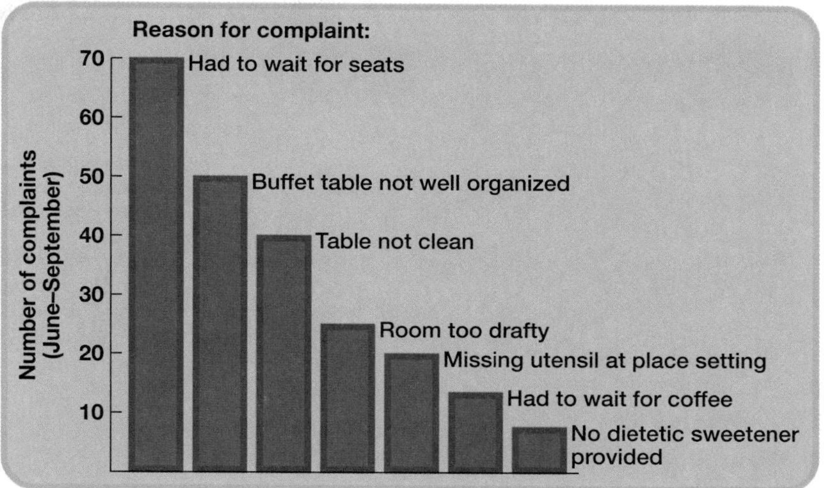

problem. After removing that problem, the battle moves on to the next most frequent problem. If you do this *continuously,* you solve a lot of problems—and you don't just satisfy customers, you delight them.

Internet

Internet Exercise BaRaN Systems Ltd. has developed a software product called SQC for Excel that works with the Microsoft Excel spreadsheet program and makes it easy to do the types of analyses that are useful for quality management. Go to its website (www.baran-systems.com) and click on the link for *SQC for Excel.* Then at that page scroll down and look at the "Quick Tour" section. What is it about the graphs that makes it easy to see which areas need special attention?

Figure out why things go wrong

So far, our manager has only identified the problem. To solve it, she creates a **fishbone diagram**—a visual aid that helps organize cause-and-effect relationships for "things gone wrong." See Exhibit 9-8. With this diagram our restaurant manager discovers that customers wait to be seated because tables aren't cleared soon enough. In fact, the Pareto chart (Exhibit 9-7) shows that customers also complain frequently about tables not being clean. So the two implementation problems may be related.

The manager's fishbone diagram also summarizes other causes for tables not being cleaned quickly. There are different basic categories of causes—restaurant policy, procedures, people problems, and the physical environment. With this overview of different ways the service operation is going wrong, the manager can decide what to fix. She establishes different formal measures. For example, she counts how frequently different causes delay customers from being seated. She finds that the cashier's faulty credit card scanning machine holds up check processing. About half the time the cashier has to stop and enter the credit card information by hand. The fishbone diagram shows that restaurant policy is to clear the table after the entire party leaves. But customers have to wait at their tables while the staff deals with the faulty credit card machine, and cleaning is delayed. With the credit card machine replaced, the staff can clear the tables sooner—and because they're not so hurried they do a better cleaning job. Two dragons are on the way to being slayed!

Our case shows that people in different areas of the restaurant affect customer satisfaction. The waitperson couldn't do what was needed to satisfy customers because the cashier had trouble with the credit card machine. The TQM approach

Exhibit 9-8 Fishbone Diagram Showing Cause and Effect for "Why Tables Are Not Cleared Quickly"

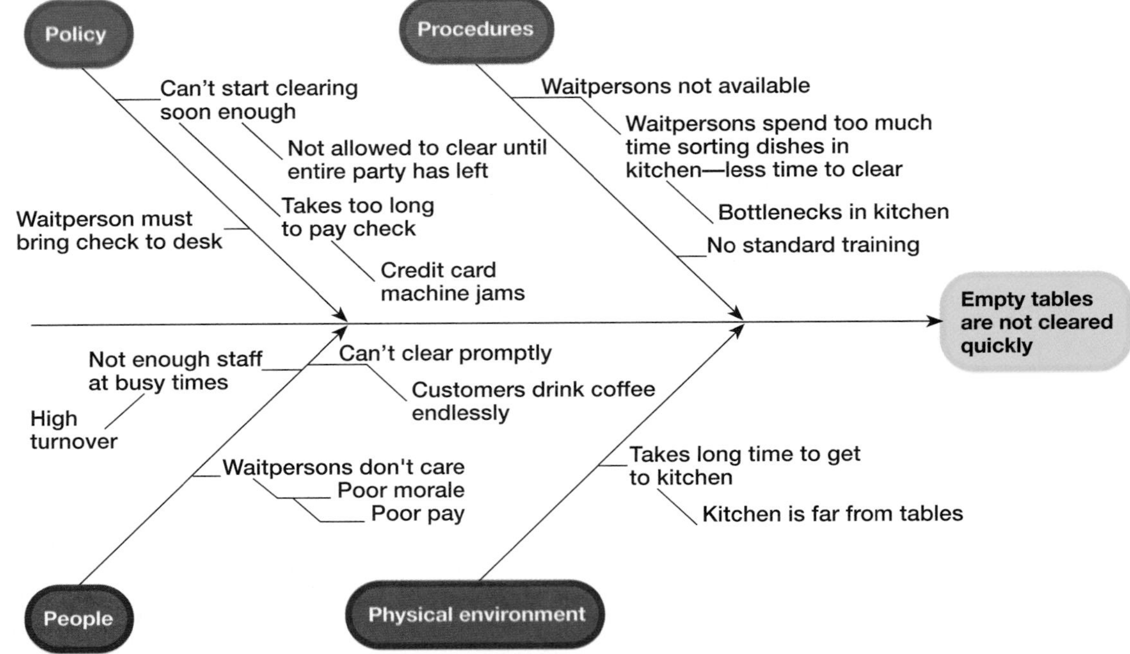

helps everyone see and understand how their job affects what others do and the customer's satisfaction.[33]

Building quality into services

The restaurant case illustrates how a firm can improve product quality with TQM approaches. We used a service example to highlight the point that almost every firm must consider service quality in developing its strategy—whether its product is primarily a service, primarily a physical good, or a blend of both. For example, a manufacturer of ball bearings isn't just providing wholesalers or producers with round pieces of steel. Customers need information about deliveries, they need orders filled properly, and they may have questions to ask the firm's accountant, receptionist, or engineers. Because almost every firm must manage the service it provides customers, let's consider some of the special concerns of managing service quality.

Train people and empower them to serve

It's difficult to maintain consistent quality in services because the server is inseparable from the service. A person doing a specific service job may perform one specific task correctly but still annoy the customer in a host of other ways. So two keys to improving service quality are: (1) training and (2) empowerment.

All employees who have any contact with customers need training—many firms see 40 hours a year of training as a minimum. Good training usually includes role-playing on handling different types of customer requests and problems. A rental car attendant who is rude when a customer is trying to turn in a car may leave the customer dissatisfied—even if the rental car was perfect.

Companies can't afford an army of managers to inspect how each employee implements a strategy—and such a system usually doesn't work anyway. Quality cannot be "inspected in." It must come from the people who do the service jobs. So firms that commit to service quality empower employees to satisfy customers' needs. **Empowerment** means giving employees the authority to correct a problem without first checking with management. At a Guest Quarters hotel, an empowered room-service employee knows it's OK to run across the street to buy the specific bottled water a guest requests. In the Saturn car manufacturing plant, employees can stop the assembly line to correct a problem rather than passing it down the line.

Managers lead the quality effort

Managers must show that they are committed to doing things right to satisfy customers and that quality is everyone's job. Without top-level support, some people won't get beyond their business-as-usual attitude—and TQM won't work.

Specify jobs and benchmark performance

Managers who develop successful quality programs clearly specify and write out exactly what tasks need to be done, how, and by whom. This may seem unnecessary. After all, most people know, in general, what they're supposed to do. However, if the tasks are clearly specified, it's easier to see what criteria should be used to measure performance.

Once criteria are established, there needs to be some basis on which to evaluate the job being done. In our restaurant example, one part of the job specification for the cashier is to process credit card payments. In that case, relevant criteria might include the amount of time that it takes and the number of people waiting in line to pay. If the restaurant manager had seen a record of how long it was taking to process credit cards, she would have known that for many customers it was taking too long. Without the measure, the precise nature of the problem was hidden.

That takes us to the issue of **benchmarking**—picking a basis of comparison for evaluating how well a job is being done. For example, consider a case in which an airline asks customers to rate their satisfaction with a flight. Then the company might benchmark each route against the others on average customer satisfaction. But, if the service of all the airline's flights is poor, that isn't a sensible approach. The ones that stink the least would look good on a relative basis. So many firms try to benchmark against some external standard. For example, an airline might want to benchmark against a competitor. Or better, the manager might identify other travel firms that earn superlative customer satisfaction ratings—and benchmark against them.

Getting a return on quality is important

While the cost of poor quality is lost customers, the type of quality efforts we've been discussing also result in costs. It's easy to fall into the trap of running up *unnecessary costs* trying to improve some facet of quality that really isn't that important to customer satisfaction or customer retention. When that happens, customers may still be satisfied, but the firm can't make a profit because of the extra costs. In other words, there isn't a financial return on the money spent to improve quality. A manager should focus on quality efforts that really provide the customer with superior value—quality that costs no more to provide than customers will ultimately be willing to pay.[34]

Conclusion

New-product planning is an increasingly important activity in a modern economy because it is no longer very profitable to just sell me-too products in highly competitive markets. Markets, competition, and product life cycles are changing at a fast pace.

The product life cycle concept is especially important to marketing strategy planning. It shows that a firm needs different marketing mixes—and even strategies—as a product moves through its cycle. This is an important point because profits change during the life cycle—with most of the profits going to the innovators or fast copiers.

We pointed out that a product is new to a firm if it is new in any way or to any target market. But the Federal Trade Commission takes a narrower view of what you can call "new."

New products are so important to business survival that firms need some organized process for developing them. We discuss such a process and emphasize that it requires a total company effort to be successful.

The failure rate of new products is high—but it is lower for better-managed firms that recognize product development and management as vital processes. Some firms appoint product managers to manage individual products and new-product teams to ensure that the process is carried out successfully.

Poor product quality results in dissatisfied customers. So, alert marketers look for ways to design better quality into new products and to improve the quality of ones they already have. Approaches developed in the total quality management movement can be a big help in this regard. Ultimately, the challenge is for the manager to focus on aspects of quality that really matter to the target customer. Otherwise, the cost of the quality offered may be higher than what target customers are willing to pay.

Questions and Problems

1. Explain how industry sales and industry profits behave over the product life cycle.
2. Cite two examples of products that you feel are currently in each of the product life-cycle stages. Consider services as well as physical goods.
3. Explain how you might reach different conclusions about the correct product life-cycle stage(s) in the worldwide automobile market.
4. Explain why individual brands may not follow the product life-cycle pattern. Give an example of a new brand that is not entering the life cycle at the market introduction stage.
5. Discuss the life cycle of a product in terms of its probable impact on a manufacturer's marketing mix. Illustrate using personal computers.
6. What characteristics of a new product will help it to move through the early stages of the product life cycle more quickly? Briefly discuss each characteristic—illustrating with a product of your choice. Indicate how each characteristic might be viewed in some other country.
7. What is a new product? Illustrate your answer.
8. Explain the importance of an organized new-product development process and illustrate how it might be used for *(a)* a new hair care product, *(b)* a new children's toy, and *(c)* a new subscribers-only cable television channel.
9. Discuss how you might use the new-product development process if you were thinking about offering some kind of summer service to residents in a beach resort town.
10. Explain the role of product or brand managers. When would it make sense for one of a company's current brand managers to be in charge of the new-product development process? Explain your thinking.
11. If a firm offers one of its brands in a number of different countries, would it make sense for one brand manager to be in charge, or would each country require its own brand manager? Explain your thinking.
12. Discuss the social value of new-product development activities that seem to encourage people to discard products that are not all worn out. Is this an economic waste? How worn out is all worn out? Must a shirt have holes in it? How big?
13. What are the major advantages of total quality management approaches for improving the quality of goods and services? What limitations can you think of?

Suggested Cases

3. Pillsbury's Häagen-Dazs
11. ChemTech
18. Outdoor World, Inc.

Computer-Aided Problem

9. Growth Stage Competition

AgriChem, Inc., has introduced an innovative new product—a combination fertilizer, weed killer, and insecticide that makes it much easier for soybean farmers to produce a profitable crop. The product introduction was quite successful, with 1 million units sold in the year of introduction. And AgriChem's profits are increasing. Total market demand is expected to grow at a rate of 200,000 units a year for the next five years. Even so, AgriChem's marketing managers are concerned about what will happen to sales and profits during this period.

Based on past experience with similar situations, they expect one new competitor to enter the market during each of the next five years. They think this competitive pressure will drive prices down about 6 percent a year. Further, although the total market is growing, they know that new competitors will chip away at AgriChem's market share—even with the 10 percent a year increase planned for the promotion budget. In spite of the competitive pressure, the marketing managers are sure that familiarity with AgriChem's brand will help it hold a large share of the total market and give AgriChem greater economies of scale than competitors. In fact, they expect that the ratio of profit to dollar sales for AgriChem should be about 10 percent higher than for competitors.

AgriChem's marketing managers have decided the best way to get a handle on the situation is to organize the data in a spreadsheet. They have set up the spreadsheet so they can change the "years in the future" value and see what is likely to happen to AgriChem and the rest of the industry. The starting spreadsheet shows the current situation with data from the first full year of production.

a. *Compare AgriChem's market share and profit for this year with what is expected next year—given the marketing managers' current assumptions. What are they expecting? (Hint: Set number of years in the future to 1.)*

b. *Prepare a table showing AgriChem's expected profit, and the expected industry revenue and profit, for the current year and the next five years. Briefly explain what happens to industry sales and profits and why. (Hint: Do an analysis to vary the number of years in the future value in the spreadsheet from a minimum of 0—the current year—to a maximum of 5. Display the three values requested.)*

c. *If market demand grows faster than expected—say, at 280,000 units a year—what will happen to AgriChem's profits and the expected industry revenues and profits over the next five years? What are the implications of this analysis?*

For additional questions related to this problem, see Exercise 9-4 in the *Learning Aid for Use with Essentials of Marketing*, 9th edition.

Chapter Ten

Place and Development of Channel Systems

When You Finish This Chapter, You Should

1. Understand what product classes suggest about Place objectives.

2. Understand why some firms use direct channel systems while others rely on intermediaries and indirect systems.

3. Understand how and why marketing specialists develop to make channel systems more effective.

4. Understand how to develop cooperative relationships and avoid conflict in channel systems.

5. Know how channel members in vertical marketing systems shift and share functions—to meet customer needs.

6. Understand the differences between intensive, selective, and exclusive distribution.

7. Understand the important new terms (shown in red).

Steve Bollic's small firm creates video game software. In the summer of 2001, he learned that Ingram Book Group, a book wholesaler, had formed an alliance with Valley Media, Inc., a distributor of music and entertainment products. Most people in his product-market would have glossed over that news, but in his previous job Bollic had gotten a taste of what it might mean: tough new competition from game producers whose distribution channels focused on the big retail chains.

Bollic had been a manager for the Intimate Bookshops, a small chain of shops that for decades had been *the* place to buy books in his college-town market. He moved on to start his video game business even before the Intimate had its final clearance sale and closed its doors for good. After all, sales of books through independent bookshops dropped by over 25 percent in the 1990s. Like the Intimate, many went out of business because of changes in the channels of distribution for books. Many

place price promotion produ

small publishers with whom they worked also had troubles.

At the Intimate, competitors had chipped away at sales over the years. But the coffin nail was not driven by mail-order book clubs, or by the religious book store that opened in town, or even by used textbook brokers who ate into that business. Rather, the bigger issue was the big national chains. They had buying clout with publishers and could demand lower prices for larger quantities. They also had aggressive marketing programs to woo consumers. The Intimate had lost some customers to the frequent-buyer discount and special-order service at Walden Books. Others went to Barnes and Noble for the selection—and the coffee bar. Wal-Mart carried only a few best-sellers, but its low prices turned shoppers into impulse buyers. Some of the Intimate's ex-customers were no longer shopping in any store. Rather, they were ordering books online from Amazon.com.

Operating from its website, Amazon offers consumers an amazing selection of over two million books. As Amazon ads pop up on-screen, web surfers may think the selection is even greater. But Bollic knew that in reality Amazon's warehouse keeps inventory on only a couple thousand of the fastest-selling books. That's because Amazon fills most orders through wholesalers. And that takes us back to Ingram Book Group. It has been the hidden giant behind many big book retailers, including Internet sellers. For example, in 1998 it handled more than 60 percent of Amazon's orders. At the same time it was a major supplier for Barnes and Noble. There are good reasons. Its distribution customer service is hard to match. Orders flow into Ingram's computers electronically, and most are assembled and shipped the same day from its inventory of 500,000 titles. With a half-dozen warehouses spread across the country, Ingram gets 95 percent of its shipments to the retailer within 48 hours. You can see why Barnes and Noble wanted to merge with Ingram; this vertical integration would have made the combined firm even more efficient and powerful.

When that merger fell through, Barnes and Noble expanded its own distribution centers, inventory, and logistics systems to become more efficient on its own. Ingram, in turn, is getting new business by offering its retailer-customers new services—like sending books directly to the consumer. But Ingram is also adding music and entertainment products, like video games, to its line. That's because many of the retailer-customers it serves are scrambling their product lines to include the best sellers among these categories. With video games becoming a mature product, it is not a complete surprise that distribution intensity is expanding. But it may mean that Bollic will need to decide whether to join one of these new channel systems or stick with the specialists who helped him get started.[1]

Place Decisions Are an Important Part of Marketing Strategy

This case shows that offering customers a good product at a reasonable price is not the whole story. Managers must also think about **Place**—making goods and services available in the right quantities and locations—when customers want them. And when different target markets have different needs, a number of Place variations may be required. Our opening case also makes it clear that new Place arrangements

Exhibit 10-1
Strategy Decision Areas in Place

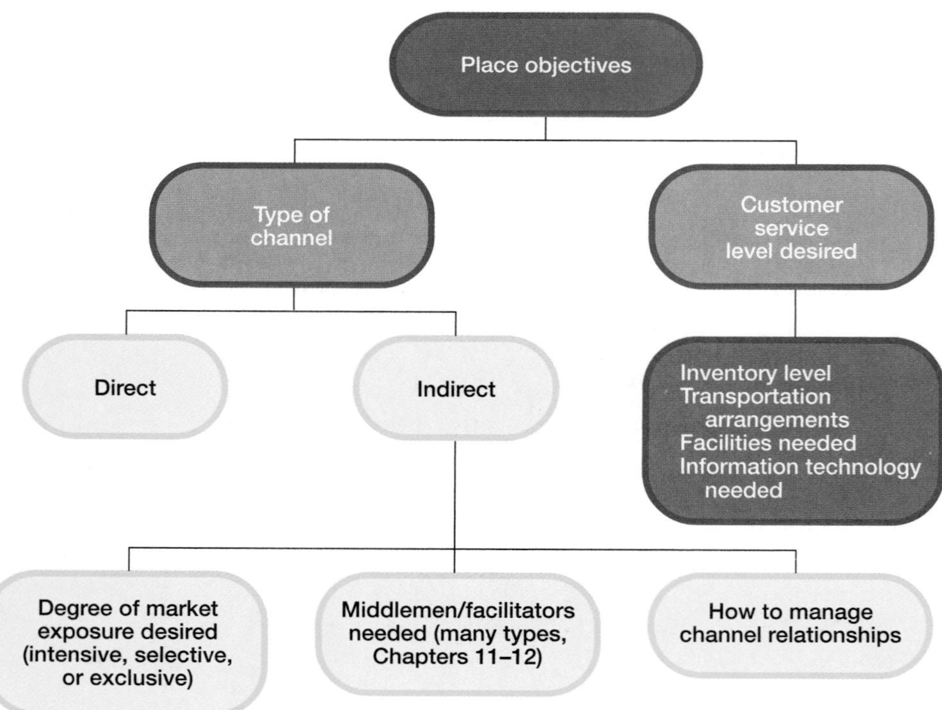

can dramatically change the competition in a product-market. This is especially important in business today because many firms are trying to use new information technologies, including websites and e-commerce, to reach customers more efficiently.

In the next three chapters, we'll deal with the many important strategy decisions that a marketing manager must make concerning Place. Exhibit 10-1 gives an overview. We'll start in this chapter with a discussion of the type of channel that's needed to meet customers' needs. We'll show why specialists are often involved and how they come together to form a **channel of distribution**—any series of firms or individuals who participate in the flow of products from producer to final user or consumer. We'll also consider how to manage relations among channel members to reduce conflict and improve cooperation.

Place Decisions Are Guided by "Ideal" Place Objectives

All marketing managers want to be sure that their goods and services are available in the right quantities and locations—when customers want them. But customers may have different needs with respect to time, place, and possession utility as they make different purchases.

Product classes suggest Place objectives

In Chapter 8 we introduced the product classes—which summarize consumers' urgency to have needs satisfied and willingness to seek information, shop, and compare. Now you should be able to use the product classes to handle Place decisions.

Exhibit 8-3 shows the relationship between consumer product classes and ideal Place objectives. Similarly, Exhibit 8-4 shows the business product classes and how they relate to customer needs. Study these exhibits carefully. They set the framework for making Place decisions. In particular, the product classes help us decide how much market exposure we'll need in each geographic area.

Place system is not automatic

Several different product classes may be involved if different market segments view a product in different ways. Thus, a marketing manager may need to develop several strategies, each with its own Place arrangements. There may not be one Place arrangement that is best.

Most pet food companies focus on distribution through grocery stores, but Science Diet brand premium pet foods reach consumers in the U.S., Japan, and Italy through a different channel—veterinary offices and pet stores. Because Science Diet has developed cooperative relationships with other members of this channel, Science Diet products often get special promotion support at the point of purchase.

Place decisions have long-run effects

The marketing manager must also consider Place objectives in relation to the product life cycle; see Exhibit 9-2. Place decisions often have long-run effects. They're usually harder to change than Product, Price, and Promotion decisions. Many firms that thought they could quickly establish effective websites for direct online sales, for example, found that it took several years and millions of dollars to work out the kinks. It can take even longer and a great deal of money to develop effective working relationships with others in the channel. Legal contracts with channel partners may limit changes. And it's hard to move retail stores and wholesale facilities once they are set up. Yet as products mature, they typically need broader distribution to reach different target customers.

The distribution of premium pet foods followed this pattern. A decade ago, supermarkets wouldn't carry specialized pet foods because there wasn't much demand. So marketing managers for Science Diet products concentrated on getting distribution through pet shops and veterinary offices. Science Diet's sales in this channel grew rapidly. What's more, profit margins on the specialty foods were much higher than on traditional fare. Seeing this growth, Purina, Kal Kan, and other producers developed new products and worked with their supermarket channels to set up special "nutrition centers" on the pet food aisle. As market growth continued, P&G bought Iams and pushed for distribution in pet superstores, at mass-merchandisers, and online.[2]

Channel System May Be Direct or Indirect

One of the most basic Place decisions producers must make is whether to handle the whole distribution themselves—perhaps by relying on direct-to-customer e-commerce selling—or use wholesalers, retailers, and other specialists. Middlemen, in turn, must select the producers they'll work with.

Why a firm might want to use direct distribution

Many firms prefer to distribute directly to the final customer because they want to control the whole marketing job. They may think that they can serve target customers at a lower cost or do the work more effectively than middlemen. Since middlemen often carry products of several competing producers, they might not give any one item the special emphasis its producer wants.

The Internet makes direct distribution easier

Website-based e-commerce systems give many firms direct access to customers whom it would have been impossible to reach in the past. Even small, specialized firms may be able to establish a web page and draw customers from all over the world. Of course, there are limitations. If a customer wants a salesperson to demonstrate a product, then a "virtual store" may not be adequate. However, distribution via the

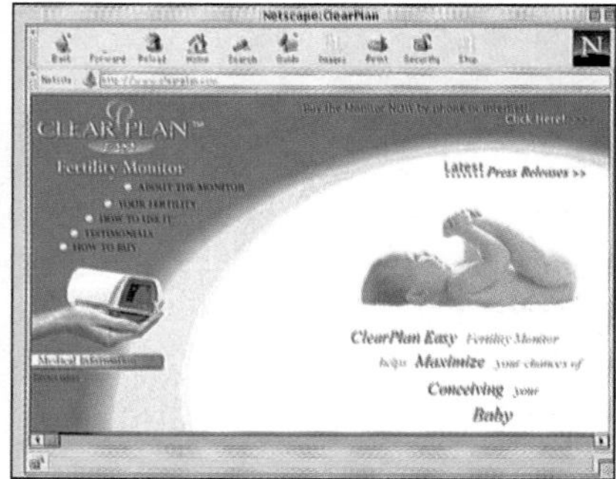

In the U.S. and many other developed nations, Unilever relies primarily on indirect distribution through a variety of wholesalers and retailers. However, in Spain it delivers frozen foods directly to consumer homes, and in Vietnam a mobile store brings products to local consumers. And now some products are sold direct to consumers from an Internet website.

When Snapple bought SoBe's main wholesaler in New Jersey, other goods wholesalers were not available and SoBe was left with limited distribution. So marketers for SoBe sold directly to retailers. Getting retailer cooperation and good shelf space was easier when SoBe provided its own coolers.

Internet is still evolving. Some firms now use live camera "feeds" while talking with the customer over an Internet video phone. Other innovations are being tested. Regardless, if it's with the help of technology or by other more traditional means, there often *are* great advantages in selling directly to the final user or consumer.

Direct contact with customers

If a firm is in direct contact with its customers, it is more aware of changes in customer attitudes. It is in a better position to adjust its marketing mix quickly because there is no need to convince other channel members to help. If a product needs an aggressive selling effort or special technical service, the marketing manager can ensure that salespeople receive the necessary training and motivation.

Suitable middlemen are not available

A firm may have to go direct if suitable middlemen are not available or will not cooperate. For example, Apple is again opening its own stores in hopes of getting more in-store promotional emphasis on what's different about its iMac computers.[3]

Middlemen who have the best contacts with the target market may be hesitant to add unproven vendors or new products, especially really new products that don't fit well with their current business.

Common with business customers and services

Many business products are sold direct-to-customer. Rolm, for example, sells its computerized voice mail systems direct. Alcan sells aluminum to General Motors direct. This is understandable since in business markets there are fewer transactions, orders are larger, and customers may be concentrated in one geographic area. Further, once relationships are established e-commerce systems can efficiently handle orders, inventory replenishment, and routine information (such as delivery schedules).

Service firms often use direct channels. If the service must be produced in the presence of customers, there may be little need for middlemen. An accounting firm like Price-Waterhouse, for example, must deal directly with its customers. However, many firms that produce physical goods turn to middlemen specialists to help provide the services customers expect. Maytag may hope that its authorized dealers don't get many repair calls, but the service is available when customers need it. Here the middleman produces the service.[4]

Some consumer products are sold direct

Many companies that produce consumer products have websites where a consumer can place a direct order. But for most consumer products this is still a small part of total sales. Most consumer products are sold through middlemen.[5]

Internet

Internet Exercise Gateway is a computer company that uses direct distribution to its customers in the U.S. Go to the Gateway website (www.gateway.com) and think about how it is organized. Is the website organized well to help Gateway reach different segments of customers in the U.S.?

Don't be confused by the term *direct marketing*

Even though most consumer products are sold through middlemen, an increasing number of firms now rely on **direct marketing**—direct communication between a seller and an individual customer using a promotion method other than face-to-face personal selling. Sometimes direct marketing promotion is coupled with direct distribution from a producer to consumers. Park Seed Company, for example, sells the seeds it grows directly to consumers with a mail catalog and website. However, many firms that use direct marketing promotion distribute their products through middlemen. So the term *direct marketing* is primarily concerned with the Promotion area, not Place decisions. We'll talk about direct marketing promotion in more detail in Chapter 13.[6]

When indirect channels are best

Even if a producer wants to handle the whole distribution job, sometimes it's simply not possible. Customers often have established buying patterns. For example, Square D, a producer of electrical supplies, might want to sell directly to electrical contractors. It can certainly set up a website for online orders or even open sales offices in key markets. But if contractors like to make all of their purchases in one convenient stop—at a local electrical wholesaler—the only practical way to reach them is through a wholesaler.

Similarly, consumers are spread throughout many geographic areas and often prefer to shop for certain products at specific places. Some consumers, for instance, see Sears as *the* place to shop for tires, so they'll only buy the brands that Sears carries. This is one reason why most firms that produce consumer products rely so heavily on indirect channels (see Exhibit 10-2).[7]

Direct distribution usually requires a significant investment in facilities, people, and information technology. A company may want to avoid that investment by working with established middlemen. Middlemen may further reduce a producer's need for working capital by buying the producer's output and carrying it in inventory until it's sold. If customers want a good "right now," there must be an inventory available to make the sale. And if customers are spread over a large area, it will probably be necessary to have widespread distribution.

Exhibit 10-2
Four Examples of Basic Channels of Distribution for Consumer Products

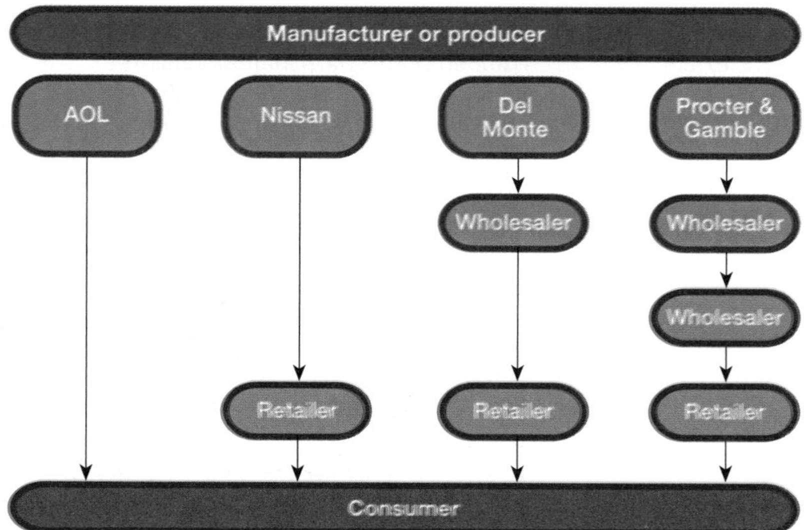

Some middlemen play a critical role by providing credit (working capital) to customers at the end of the channel. A middleman who knows local customers can help reduce credit risks. As sales via the Internet grow, sellers are looking for faster and better ways to check the credit ratings of distant customers. It's an unhappy day when the marketing manager learns that a customer who was shipped goods based on an online order can't pay the invoice.

The most important reason for using an indirect channel of distribution is that an intermediary can often help producers serve customer needs better and at lower cost. Remember that we discussed this briefly in Chapter 1. Now we'll go into more detail.

Channel Specialists May Reduce Discrepancies and Separations

The assortment and quantity of products customers want may be different from the assortment and quantity of products companies produce. Producers are often located far from their customers and may not know how best to reach them. Customers in turn may not know about their choices. Specialists develop to adjust these discrepancies and separations (see Exhibit 1-3).[8]

Middlemen may supply needed information

Specialists often help provide information to bring buyers and sellers together. For example, most consumers don't know much about the wide variety of home and auto insurance policies available from many different insurance companies. A local independent insurance agent may help them decide which policy, and which insurance company, best fits their needs.

Middlemen who are close to their customers are often able to forecast demand more accurately. This information can help reduce inventory costs in the whole channel—and it may help the producer smooth out production.

Most producers seek help from specialists when they first enter international markets. Specialists can provide crucial information about customer needs and insights into differences in the marketing environment.

Discrepancies of quantity and assortment

Discrepancy of quantity means the difference between the quantity of products it is economical for a producer to make and the quantity final users or consumers normally want. For example, most manufacturers of golf balls produce large quantities—perhaps

Office Depot, a large office supplies chain, accumulates products from many producers at its distribution center and then breaks bulk to provide the convenient assortments that consumers expect to find at individual Office Depot stores.

To reach its place objectives, Sprint sells PCS phones and its wireless services through 12,000 outlets, including retail chains like Staples and its own Sprint PCS Centers.

200,000 to 500,000 in a given time period. The average golfer, however, wants only a few balls at a time. Adjusting for this discrepancy usually requires middlemen—wholesalers and retailers.

Producers typically specialize by product—and therefore another discrepancy develops. **Discrepancy of assortment** means the difference between the lines a typical producer makes and the assortment final consumers or users want. Most golfers, for example, need more than golf balls. They want golf shoes, gloves, clubs, a bag, and, of course, a golf course to play on. And they usually don't want to shop for each item separately. So, again, there is a need for wholesalers and retailers to adjust these discrepancies.

Channel specialists adjust discrepancies with regrouping activities

Regrouping activities adjust the quantities and/or assortments of products handled at each level in a channel of distribution.

There are four regrouping activities: accumulating, bulk-breaking, sorting, and assorting. When one or more of these activities is needed, a marketing specialist may develop to fill this need.

Adjusting quantity discrepancies by accumulating and bulk-breaking

Accumulating involves collecting products from many small producers. Much of the coffee that comes from Colombia is grown on small farms in the mountains. Accumulating the small crops into larger quantities is a way of getting the lowest transporting rate and making it more convenient for distant food processing companies to buy and handle it. Accumulating is especially important in less-developed countries and in other situations, like agricultural markets, where there are many small producers.

Accumulating is also important with professional services because they often involve the combined work of a number of individuals, each of whom is a specialized producer. A hospital makes it easier for patients by accumulating the services of a number of health care specialists, many of whom may not actually work for the hospital.

Many middlemen who operate from Internet websites focus on accumulating. Specialized sites for everything from Chinese art to Dutch flower bulbs bring together the output of many producers.

Bulk-breaking involves dividing larger quantities into smaller quantities as products get closer to the final market. The bulk-breaking may involve several levels of middlemen. Wholesalers may sell smaller quantities to other wholesalers or directly to retailers. Retailers continue breaking bulk as they sell individual items to their customers.

Adjusting assortment discrepancies by sorting and assorting

Different types of specialists adjust assortment discrepancies. They perform two types of regrouping activities: sorting and assorting.

Sorting means separating products into grades and qualities desired by different target markets. For example, a wholesaler that specializes in serving convenience stores may focus on smaller packages of frequently used products, whereas a wholesaler working with restaurants and hotels might handle only very large institutional sizes.

Assorting means putting together a variety of products to give a target market what it wants. This usually is done by those closest to the final consumer or user—retailers or wholesalers who try to supply a wide assortment of products for the convenience of their customers. Thus, a wholesaler selling Yazoo tractors and mowers to golf courses might also carry Pennington grass seed and Scott fertilizer.

Watch for changes

Sometimes these discrepancies are adjusted badly—especially when consumer wants and attitudes shift rapidly. When cellular phones suddenly became popular, an opportunity developed for a new specialist. Cellular phone dealers came on the scene to help customers figure out what type of cellular phone and service would meet their needs. It cost the sellers of cellular services about $300 per customer to sell through dealers. However, as the market grew, competition for customers heated up and electronics stores wanted a piece of the action. They were willing to take a smaller markup. Now that the cellular market is established, many cellular service providers are finding it cheaper to sell from a website or use their own salespeople.[9]

Specialists should develop to adjust discrepancies *if they must be adjusted.* But there is no point in having middlemen just because that's the way it's been done in the past. Sometimes a breakthrough opportunity can come from finding a better way to reduce discrepancies. Some manufacturers of business products can now reach more customers in distant markets with an Internet website than it was previously possible for them to reach with independent manufacturers reps who sold on commission (but otherwise left distribution to the firm). The website cost advantage can translate to lower prices and a marketing mix that is a better value for some target segments.[10]

Channel Relationship Must Be Managed

Marketing manager must choose type of channel relationship

Middlemen specialists can help make a channel more efficient. But there may be problems getting the different firms in a channel to work together well. How well they work together depends on the type of relationship they have. This should be carefully considered since marketing managers usually have choices about what type of channel system to join or develop.

The whole channel should have a product-market commitment

Ideally, all of the members of a channel system should have a shared *product-market commitment*—with all members focusing on the same target market at the end of the channel and sharing the various marketing functions in appropriate ways. Unfortunately, many marketing managers overlook this idea because it's not the way their firms have traditionally handled channel relationships.

Traditional channel systems involve weak relationships

In **traditional channel systems,** the various channel members make little or no effort to cooperate with each other. They buy and sell from each other—and that's the extent of their relationship. Each channel member does only what it considers to be in its own best interest. It doesn't worry about other members of the channel. This is shortsighted, but it's easy to see how it can happen. The objectives of the various channel members may be different. For example, General Electric wants a wholesaler of electrical building supplies to sell GE products. But a wholesaler who works with different producers may not care whose products get sold. The wholesaler just wants happy customers and a good profit margin.

Conflict gets in the way

Specialization can make a channel more efficient—but not if the specialists are so independent that the channel doesn't work smoothly. Because members of traditional channel systems often have different objectives—and different ideas about how things should be done—conflict is common.

There are two basic types of conflict in channels of distribution. Vertical conflicts occur between firms at different levels in the channel of distribution. For example, a producer and a retailer may disagree about how much shelf space or promotion effort the retailer should give the producer's product. For instance, when Wherehouse Entertainment (a large retail music chain) started to sell used CDs—at about half the price of new ones—several recording companies said that they would halt cooperative advertising payments to any retailer that sold used CDs. The recording companies felt that the used CDs hurt their sales.[11]

Horizontal conflicts occur between firms at the same level in the channel of distribution. For example, a furniture store that keeps a complete line of furniture on display isn't happy to find out that a store down the street is offering customers lower prices on special orders of the same items. The discounter is getting a free ride from the competing store's investment in inventory.

Traditional channel systems are still typical in some industries. The members of these channels have their independence, but they may pay for it too. As we will see, such channels are declining in importance—with good reason.[12]

Cooperative relationships share common objectives

Usually the best way to avoid conflict is to get everyone in the channel focused on the same basic objective—satisfying the customer at the end of the channel. This leads us away from traditional channels to cooperative channel relationships and the channel captain concept.

Channel captain can guide channel relationships

Each channel system should act as a unit, where each member of the channel collaborates to serve customers at the end of the channel. In this view, cooperation is everyone's responsibility. However, some firms are in a better position to take the lead in the relationship and in coordinating the whole channel effort. This situation calls for a **channel captain**—a manager who helps direct the activities of a whole channel and tries to avoid or solve channel conflicts.

For example, when Harley-Davidson wanted to expand sales of fashion accessories, it was difficult for motorcycle dealers to devote enough space to all of the different styles. Harley considered selling the items directly from its own website, but that would take sales away from dealers who were working hard to help Harley sell both cycles and fashions. So Harley's president asked a group of dealers and Harley managers to work together to come up with a plan they all liked. The result was a website that sells Harley products through the dealer that is closest to the customer.[13]

The concept of a single channel captain is logical. But most traditional channels don't have a recognized captain. The various firms don't act as a coordinated system. Yet firms are interrelated, even if poorly, by their policies. So it makes sense to try to avoid channel conflicts by planning for channel relations. The channel captain arranges for the necessary functions to be performed in the most effective way.

The situation faced by Goodyear is a good example. The Goodyear brand was sold almost exclusively through its own stores and its 2,500 independent tire dealers. But sales were falling. There were many reasons. France's Michelin and Japan's Bridgestone had aggressively expanded distribution in North America. Moreover, many consumers were shopping at discount outlets. Goodyear decided it had no choice but to expand distribution and sell Goodyear tires to Kmart's Penske autocenters and other big retail chains. To reach discount shoppers, Goodyear also converted many of its own autocenters to no-frills stores operated under the Just Tires name. However, to reduce the conflict that these changes caused with its independent dealers, Goodyear introduced the new Aquatred and other specialized tires that appealed to the dealers' target market. Goodyear also created the Gemini brand name and increased advertising to help promote service by Goodyear dealers. As a result, Goodyear's sales increased and so did the sales of its dealers.[14]

Some producers lead their channels

As the Goodyear case suggests, in the U.S. producers frequently take the lead in channel relations. Middlemen often wait to see what the producer intends to do and wants them to do.

Some middlemen are channel captains

However, some wholesalers or retailers do take the lead. They are closer to the final user or consumer and are in an ideal position to assume the channel captain role. These middlemen analyze their customers' needs and then seek out producers who can provide these products at reasonable prices. With the growth of powerful chains, like Wal-Mart and Toys "R" Us, retailers now dominate the channel systems for many products in the United States. In Japan, very large wholesalers (trading companies) are often the channel captains.

Retailers like Sears and wholesalers like Ace Hardware that develop their own dealer brands in effect act like producers. They specify the whole marketing mix for a product and merely delegate production to a factory.[15]

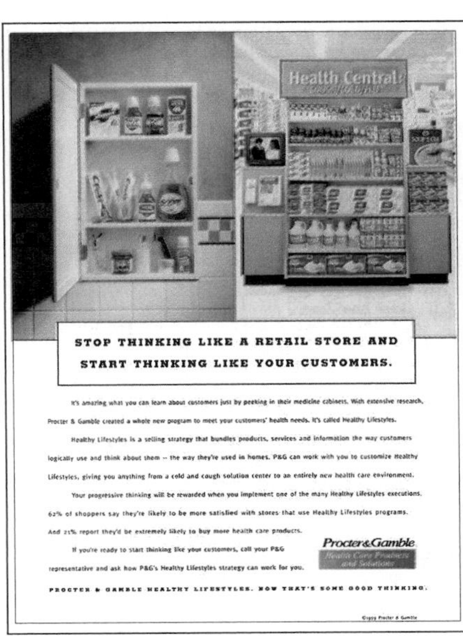

A channel captain can improve the performance of the whole channel—by developing strategies that help everyone in the channel do a better job of meeting the needs of target customers at the end of the channel.

Kimberly-Clark Boosts Bottom Line for Disposable Diapers

It's a messy problem when a busy parent makes a special trip to a Costco store to buy Huggies disposable diapers and they're out of stock. It can be costly too. The average retailer's loss from out-of-stocks on high-volume items, like diapers, is about 11 percent of annual sales. So what should a Costco manager do to avoid the problem? Nothing. That job is handled by Kimberly-Clark (KC), the firm that makes Huggies. Costco has a system that it calls "vendor managed inventory" in which key suppliers take over responsibility for managing a set of products, often a whole product category. Every day an analyst at KC's headquarters studies Costco's online data that detail Huggies' sales and inventory at every Costco store. The analyst studies how much is sold of each item in each store in the average week. If inventory is getting low, a new order is placed and shipping is scheduled. It's also important not to order too much or too early. KC absorbs all of the inventory and delivery costs required to keep Huggies on the shelves at Costco. When KC does this job well, it makes more money and so does Costco. Costco is a powerful customer, but KC is the channel captain for this category. Costco could do the job itself, but it handles such a wide assortment of products that it would be costly to do all the work required in every high-volume category. Many large retailers use similar approaches. Smaller retailers, however, may find that vendors are not as eager to provide this kind of extra support. The benefits justify the costs when the vendor is more selective about where the service is provided.[16]

Vertical Marketing Systems Focus on Final Customers

Many marketing managers accept the view that a coordinated channel system can help everyone in the channel. These managers are moving their firms away from traditional channel systems and instead developing or joining vertical market systems.

Vertical marketing systems are channel systems in which the whole channel focuses on the same target market at the end of the channel. Such systems make sense, and are growing, because if the final customer doesn't buy the product, the whole channel suffers. There are three types of vertical marketing systems—corporate, administered, and contractual. Exhibit 10-3 summarizes some characteristics of these systems and compares them with traditional systems.

Corporate channel systems shorten channels

Some corporations develop their own vertical marketing systems by internal expansion and/or by buying other firms. With **corporate channel systems**—corporate ownership all along the channel—we might say the firm is going "direct." But

Exhibit 10-3
Characteristics of Traditional and Vertical Marketing Systems

	Type of Channel			
		Vertical Marketing Systems		
Characteristics	Traditional	Administered	Contractual	Corporate
Amount of cooperation	Little or none	Some to good	Fairly good to good	Complete
Control maintained by	None	Economic power and leadership	Contracts	Ownership by one company
Examples	Typical channel of "independents"	General Electric, Miller Beer, O.M. Scott & Sons (lawn products)	McDonald's, Holiday Inn, IGA, Ace Hardware, Super Valu, Coca-Cola, Chevrolet	Florsheim Shoes, Sherwin-Williams, Mothers Work

actually the firm may be handling manufacturing, wholesaling, *and* retailing—so it's more accurate to think of the firm as a vertical marketing system.

Corporate channel systems often develop by **vertical integration**—acquiring firms at different levels of channel activity. In England, most of the quaint local pubs are now actually owned and operated by the large beer breweries.

Corporate channel systems are sometimes started by retailers. Mothers Work is a good example. It started as a mail-order catalog specializing in maternity clothes. Now it sells more than a third of all maternity clothes in the U.S. Vertical integration has been a key factor in its ability to give its customers what they want. It has over 700 company-run stores, its own designers, fabric-cutting operations, warehouses, and information systems to tie them all together.[17]

Vertical integration has potential advantages—stable sources of supply, better control of distribution and quality, greater buying power, and lower executive overhead. Provided that the discrepancies of quantity and assortment are not too great at each level in a channel, vertical integration can be profitable. However, many managers have found that it's hard to be really good at running manufacturing, wholesaling, and retailing businesses that are very different from each other. Instead, they try to be more efficient at what they do best and focus on ways to get cooperation in the channel for the other activities.

Administered and contractual systems may work well

Firms can often gain the advantages of vertical integration without building a costly corporate channel. A manager can develop administered or contractual channel systems instead. In **administered channel systems,** the channel members informally agree to cooperate with each other. They can agree to routinize ordering, share inventory and sales information over computer networks, standardize accounting, and coordinate promotion efforts. In **contractual channel systems,** the channel members agree by contract to cooperate with each other. With both of these systems, the members retain some of the flexibility of a traditional channel system. Moreover, the opportunities to provide customers with superior value are growing because of help from new information technologies. For example, in the hardware business, computerized checkout systems track sales. The information is sent to the wholesaler's computer, which enters orders automatically when needed. Shipping cartons with computer-readable bar codes track the status of shipments and reduce errors. This reduces buying and selling costs, inventory investment, and customer frustration with out-of-stock items throughout the channel.

Vertical marketing systems—new wave in the marketplace

Vertical systems in the consumer products area have a healthy majority of retail sales and should continue to increase their share in the future. Vertical marketing systems are becoming the major competitive units in the U.S. distribution system—and they are growing rapidly in other parts of the world as well.[18]

Short-term alliances are also popular

Firms that cooperate to build vertical marketing systems typically share a longer-term commitment. Sometimes, however, what a firm wants is a short-term collaboration to accomplish a specific objective. This may lead to an alliance, a partnership (usually informal) in which firms agree to work together to achieve an objective. An alliance may involve two firms, or a whole network. The firms may be at the same level in the channel or at different levels. For example, a number of hardware, software, and service firms in the computer business have formed alliances to build a market for the Linux operating system. Some of these firms produce hardware, some produce software, and some focus on distribution. Without the alliance, it would be difficult for any one of these firms to compete with Microsoft.[19]

The Best Channel System Should Achieve Ideal Market Exposure

You may think that all marketing managers want their products to have maximum exposure to potential customers. This isn't true. Some product classes require much less market exposure than others. **Ideal market exposure** makes a product available widely enough to satisfy target customers' needs but not exceed them. Too much exposure only increases the total cost of marketing.

Ideal exposure may be intensive, selective, or exclusive

Intensive distribution is selling a product through all responsible and suitable wholesalers or retailers who will stock and/or sell the product. **Selective distribution** is selling through only those middlemen who will give the product special attention. **Exclusive distribution** is selling through only one middleman in a particular geographic area. As we move from intensive to exclusive distribution, we give up exposure in return for some other advantage—including, but not limited to, lower cost.

Intensive distribution—sell it where they buy it

Intensive distribution is commonly needed for convenience products and business supplies—such as laser printer cartridges, ring binders, and copier paper—used by all offices. Customers want such products nearby.

The seller's intent is important here. Intensive distribution refers to the desire to sell through *all* responsible and suitable outlets. What this means depends on customer habits and preferences. If customers preferred to buy Sharp portable TVs only at electronics stores, you would try to sell through all electronics stores to achieve intensive distribution. Today, however, many customers buy small portable TVs at a variety of convenient outlets—including Eckerd drugstores, a local Target, over the phone from the Sharper Image catalog, or perhaps from a website on the Internet. This means that an intensive distribution policy requires use of all these outlets, and more than one channel, to reach one target market.

Rayovac batteries were not selling well even though their performance was very similar to other batteries. Part of that was due to heavier advertising by Duracell and Energizer. But consumers usually don't go shopping for batteries. They're purchased on impulse 83 percent of the time. To get a larger share of purchases, Rayovac had to be in more stores. It offered retailers a marketing mix with less advertising and a lower price. In three years, the brand moved from being available in 36,000 stores to 82,000 stores—and that increase gave sales a big charge.[20]

Selective distribution—sell it where it sells best

Selective distribution covers the broad area of market exposure between intensive and exclusive distribution. It may be suitable for all categories of products. Only the better middlemen are used here. Companies usually use selective distribution to gain some of the advantages of exclusive distribution—while still achieving fairly widespread market coverage.

Reduce costs and get better partners

A selective policy might be used to avoid selling to wholesalers or retailers who (1) place orders that are too small to justify making calls, (2) make too many returns or request too much service, (3) have a poor credit rating, or (4) are not in a position to do a satisfactory job.

Selective distribution is becoming more popular than intensive distribution as firms see that they don't need 100 percent coverage of a market to support national advertising. Often the majority of sales come from relatively few customers—and the others buy too little compared to the cost of working with them. This is called the 80/20 rule—80 percent of a company's sales often come from only 20 percent of its customers *until it becomes more selective in choosing customers*.

As the percentage of people and firms adopting personal computers has increased, Microsoft has moved to more intensive distribution of its products worldwide.

Esprit—a producer of colorful, trendy clothing—was selling through about 4,000 department stores and specialty shops nationwide. But Esprit found that about half of the stores generated most of the sales. Sales analysis also showed that sales in Esprit's own stores were about 400 percent better than sales in other sales outlets. Profits increased when Esprit cut back to about 2,000 outlets and opened more of its own stores and a website.[21]

Get special effort from channel members

Selective distribution can produce greater profits not only for the producer but for all channel members. Wholesalers and retailers are more willing to promote products aggressively if they know they're going to obtain the majority of sales through their own efforts. They may carry wider lines and provide more service—both of which lead to more sales.

Selective often moves to intensive as market grows

In the early part of the life cycle of a new unsought good, a producer may have to use selective distribution. Well-known middlemen may have the power to get such a product introduced but sometimes on their own terms—which often include limiting the number of competing wholesalers and retailers. The producer may be happy with such an arrangement at first but dislike it later when more retailers want to carry the product.

Exclusive distribution sometimes makes sense

Exclusive distribution is just an extreme case of selective distribution—the firm selects only one middleman in each geographic area. Besides the various advantages of selective distribution, producers may want to use exclusive distribution to help control prices and the service offered in a channel. It's also attractive to middlemen because they don't face local competition selling the same products.

Is limiting market exposure legal?

Exclusive distribution is a vague area under U.S. antimonopoly laws. Courts currently focus on whether an exclusive distribution arrangement hurts competition.

Horizontal arrangements—among *competing* retailers, wholesalers, or producers—to limit sales by customer or territory have consistently been ruled illegal by the U.S. Supreme Court. Courts consider such arrangements obvious collusion that reduces competition and harms customers.

The legality of vertical arrangements—between producers and middlemen—is not as clear-cut. A 1977 Supreme Court decision (involving Sylvania and the distribution of TV sets) reversed an earlier ruling that it was always illegal to set up vertical relationships limiting territories or customers. Now courts can weigh the possible good effects against the possible restrictions on competition. They look at competition between whole channels rather than just focusing on competition at one level of distribution.

The Sylvania decision does not mean that all vertical arrangements are legal. Rather, it says that a firm has to be able to legally justify any exclusive arrangements. Thus, firms should be cautious about entering into *any* exclusive distribution arrangement. The courts can force a change in relationships that were expensive to develop. And even worse, the courts can award triple damages if they rule that competition has been hurt.

The same cautions apply to selective distribution. Here, however, less formal arrangements are typical—and the possible impact on competition is more remote. It is now more acceptable to carefully select channel members when building a channel system. Refusing to sell to some middlemen, however, should be part of a logical plan with long-term benefits to consumers.[22]

Channel Systems Can Be Complex

Trying to achieve the desired degree of market exposure can lead to complex channels of distribution. Firms may need different channels to reach different segments of a broad product-market or to be sure they reach each segment. Sometimes this results in competition between different channels.

Consider the different channels used by a company that publishes computer books. See Exhibit 10-4. This publisher sells through a general book wholesaler who in turn sells to Internet book retailers and independent book retailers. The publisher may have some direct sales of its best-selling books to a large chain or even to consumers who order directly from its website. However, it might also sell through a computer supplies wholesaler that serves electronics superstores like Best Buy. This

Exhibit 10-4 An Example of Dual Distribution by a Publisher of Computer Books

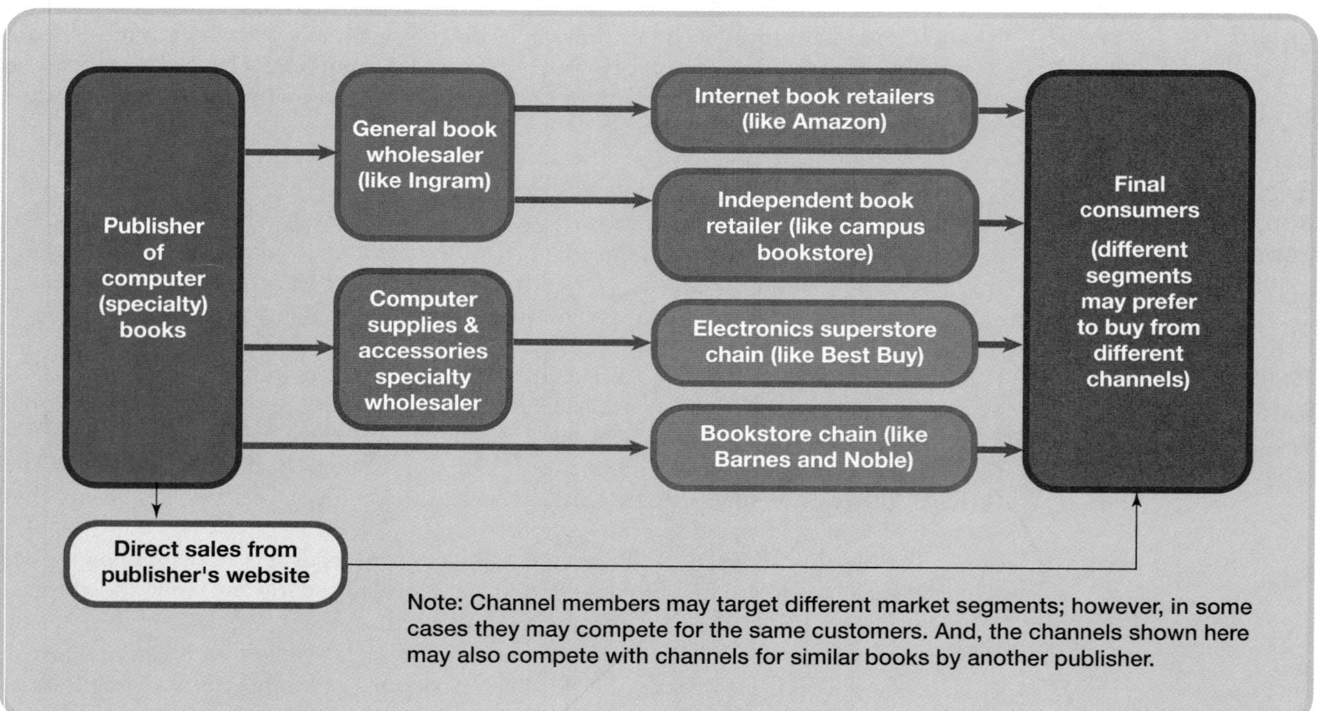

can cause problems because different wholesalers and retailers want different markups. It also increases competition, including price competition. And the competition among different middlemen may result in conflicts between the middlemen and the publisher.

Dual distribution systems may be needed

Dual distribution occurs when a producer uses several competing channels to reach the same target market—perhaps using several middlemen in addition to selling directly. Dual distribution is becoming more common. Big retail chains want to deal directly with producers. They want large quantities and low prices. The producer sells directly to retail chains and relies on wholesalers to sell to smaller accounts. Some established middlemen resent this because they don't appreciate *any* competition—especially price competition set up by their own suppliers.

Other times, producers are forced to use dual distribution because their present channels are doing a poor job or aren't reaching some potential customers. For example, Reebok International had been relying on local sporting goods stores to sell its shoes to high school and college athletic teams. But Reebok wasn't getting much of the business. When it set up its own team-sales department to sell directly to the schools, it got a 30,000-unit increase in sales.[23]

Ethical decisions may be required

If customers' Place requirements change, a firm's current channel system may not be effective. The changes required to serve customer needs may hurt one or more members of the channel. Ethical dilemmas arise in situations like this—because not everyone in the channel can win.

For example, wholesalers and the independent retailers that they serve in a channel of distribution may trust a producer channel-captain to develop marketing strategies that will work for the whole channel. However, the producer may decide that consumers, and its own business, are best served by a change (say, dropping current middlemen and selling directly to big retail chains). A move of this sort, if implemented immediately, may not give current middlemen-partners a chance to make adjustments of their own. The more dependent they are on the producer, the more severe the impact is likely to be. It's not easy to determine the best or most ethical solution in these situations. However, marketing managers must think carefully about the consequences of Place strategy changes for other channel members. In channels, as in any business dealing, relationships of trust must be treated with care.[24]

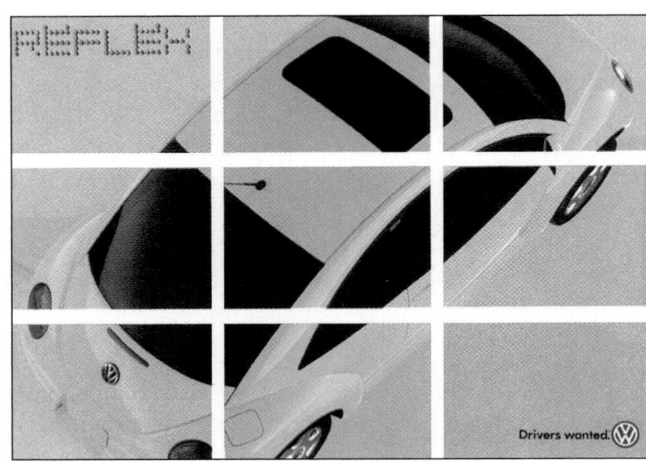

Some special models of the Beetle could only be ordered online direct from VW's website. However, the customer was then directed to a VW dealer who completed the transaction—an arrangement that avoids conflict between VW and its dealers.

Internet

Internet Exercise Avon sells cosmetics and other products through independent sales representatives (agents), in kiosks and stores, and also through a catalog (both online and printed). Review the Avon website (www.avon.com). Do you think that Avon's independent sales representatives would view the website as competing for their customers' purchases and a source of conflict, or would they think that it helps them promote the product and identify new prospects? Explain your thinking.

Reverse channels should be planned

Most firms focus on getting products to their customers. But some marketing managers must also plan for **reverse channels**—channels used to retrieve products that customers no longer want. The need for reverse channels may arise in a variety of different situations. Some companies have to recall products because of safety problems. A producer that makes an error in completing an order may have to take returns. If a product breaks while it's still under warranty, someone needs to get it to the repair center. And sometimes consumers buy something in error and want to return it. For example, this is quite common with online purchases where consumers can't see, touch, or try the actual product before purchasing it.[25]

Another problem arises from products that are damaged in shipping or discontinued. Most manufacturers take them back. A grocery products trade group says that the cost of such unsalable products, in total, may be as much as $4 billion a year.

When marketing managers don't plan for reverse channels, the firm's customers may be left to solve "their" problem. That usually doesn't make sense. So a complete plan for Place may need to consider an efficient way to return products—with policies that different channel members agree on. It may also require specialists who were not involved in getting the product to the consumer. But if that's what it takes to satisfy customers, it should be part of marketing strategy planning.[26]

Conclusion

In this chapter, we discussed the role of Place and noted that Place decisions are especially important because they may be difficult and expensive to change.

Marketing specialists, and channel systems, develop to adjust discrepancies of quantity and assortment. Their regrouping activities are basic in any economic system. And adjusting discrepancies provides opportunities for creative marketers.

Channel planning requires firms to decide on the degree of market exposure they want. The ideal level of exposure may be intensive, selective, or exclusive. They also need to consider the legality of limiting market exposure to avoid having to undo an expensively developed channel system or face steep fines.

The importance of planning channel systems was discussed—along with the role of a channel captain. We stressed that channel systems compete with each other and that vertical marketing systems seem to be winning.

In this broader context, the "battle of the brands" is only a skirmish in the battle between various channel systems. And we emphasized that producers aren't necessarily the channel captains. Often middlemen control or even dominate channels of distribution.

Questions and Problems

1. Review the case at the beginning of the chapter and explain why Amazon.com would use a wholesaler like Ingram.
2. Give two examples of service firms that work with other channel specialists to sell their products to final consumers. What marketing functions is the specialist providing in each case?

3. Discuss some reasons why a firm that produces installations might use direct distribution in its domestic market but use middlemen to reach overseas customers.
4. Explain discrepancies of quantity and assortment using the clothing business as an example. How does the application of these concepts change when selling steel to the automobile industry? What impact does this have on the number and kinds of marketing specialists required?
5. Explain the four regrouping activities with an example from the building supply industry (nails, paint, flooring, plumbing fixtures, etc.). Do you think that many specialists develop in this industry, or do producers handle the job themselves? What kinds of marketing channels would you expect to find in this industry, and what functions would various channel members provide?
6. Insurance agents are middlemen who help other members of the channel by providing information and handling the selling function. Does it make sense for an insurance agent to specialize and work exclusively with one insurance provider? Why or why not?
7. Discuss the Place objectives and distribution arrangements that are appropriate for the following products (indicate any special assumptions you have to make to obtain an answer):
   a. *A postal scale for products weighing up to 2 pounds.*
   b. *Children's toys: (1) radio-controlled model airplanes costing $80 or more, (2) small rubber balls.*
   c. *Heavy-duty, rechargeable, battery-powered nut tighteners for factory production lines.*
   d. *Fiberglass fabric used in making roofing shingles.*
8. Give an example of a producer that uses two or more different channels of distribution. Briefly discuss what problems this might cause.
9. Explain how a channel captain can help traditional independent firms compete with a corporate (integrated) channel system.
10. What would happen if retailer-organized channels (either formally integrated or administered) dominated consumer product marketing?
11. How does the nature of the product relate to the degree of market exposure desired?
12. Why would middlemen want to be exclusive distributors for a product? Why would producers want exclusive distribution? Would middlemen be equally anxious to get exclusive distribution for any type of product? Why or why not? Explain with reference to the following products: candy bars, batteries, golf clubs, golf balls, steak knives, televisions, and industrial woodworking machinery.
13. Discuss the promotion a new grocery products producer would need in order to develop appropriate channels and move products through those channels. Would the nature of this job change for a new producer of dresses? How about for a new, small producer of installations?

Suggested Cases

12. Paper Supplies Corporation
14. Modern Horizons, Inc.
15. Morgan Company
30. Aluminum Basics Co.

Computer-Aided Problem

10. **Intensive versus Selective Distribution**

Hydropump, Inc., produces and sells high-quality pumps to business customers. Its marketing research shows a growing market for a similar type of pump aimed at final consumers—for use with Jacuzzi-style tubs in home remodeling jobs. Hydropump will have to develop new channels of distribution to reach this target market because most consumers rely on a retailer for advice about the combination of tub, pump, heater, and related plumbing fixtures they need. Hydropump's marketing manager, Robert Black, is trying to decide between intensive and selective distribution. With intensive distribution, he would try to sell through all the plumbing supply, bathroom fixture, and hot-tub retailers who will carry the pump. He estimates that about 5,600 suitable retailers would be willing to carry a new pump.

With selective distribution, he would focus on about 280 of the best hot-tub dealers (2 or 3 in the 100 largest metropolitan areas).

Intensive distribution would require Hydropump to do more mass selling—primarily advertising in home renovation magazines—to help stimulate consumer familiarity with the brand and convince retailers that Hydropump equipment will sell. The price to the retailer might have to be lower too (to permit a bigger markup) so they will be motivated to sell Hydropump rather than some other brand offering a smaller markup.

With intensive distribution, each Hydropump sales rep could probably handle about 300 retailers effectively. With selective distribution, each sales rep could handle only about 70 retailers because more merchandising help would be necessary. Managing the smaller sales force and fewer retailers, with the selective approach, would require less manager overhead cost.

Going to all suitable and available retailers would make the pump available through about 20 times as many retailers and have the potential of reaching more customers. However, many customers shop at more than one retailer before making a final choice—so selective distribution would reach almost as many potential customers. Further, if Hydropump is using selective distribution, it would get more in-store sales attention for its pump and a larger share of pump purchases at each retailer.

Black has decided to use a spreadsheet to analyze the benefits and costs of intensive versus selective distribution.

a. *Based on the initial spreadsheet, which approach seems to be the most sensible for Hydropump? Why?*
b. *A consultant points out that even selective distribution needs national promotion. If Black has to increase advertising and spend a total of $100,000 on mass selling to be able to recruit the retailers he wants for selective distribution, would selective or intensive distribution be more profitable?*
c. *With intensive distribution, how large a share (percent) of the retailers' total unit sales would Hydropump have to capture to sell enough pumps to earn $200,000 profit?*

For additional questions related to this problem, see Exercise 10-3 in the *Learning Aid for Use with Essentials of Marketing*, 9th edition.

When You Finish This Chapter, You Should

1. Understand why logistics (physical distribution) is such an important part of Place *and* marketing strategy planning.

2. Understand why the physical distribution customer service level is a key marketing strategy variable.

3. Understand the physical distribution concept and why it requires coordination of storing, transporting, and related activities.

4. See how firms can cooperate and share logistics activities to improve value to the customer at the end of the channel.

5. Know about the advantages and disadvantages of the various transporting methods.

6. Know how inventory decisions and storing affect marketing strategy.

7. Understand the distribution center concept.

8. Understand the important new terms (shown in red).

Chapter Eleven

Logistics and Distribution Customer Service

If you want a Coca-Cola, there's usually one close by—no matter where you might be in the world. And that's no accident. An executive for the best-known brand name in the world stated the objective simply: "Make Coca-Cola available within an arm's reach of desire." To achieve that objective, Coke works with many different channels of distribution. But that's just the start. Think about what it takes for a bottle, can, or cup of Coke to be there whenever you're ready. In warehouses and distribution centers, on trucks, in gyms and sports arenas, and thousands of other retail outlets, Coke handles, stores, and transports over 250 billion servings of soft drink a year. Getting all of that product to consumers could be a logistical nightmare, but Coke does it effectively and at a low cost. Think about it: A can of Coke at the store costs about what you pay to have the post office deliver a 2-ounce letter.

Fast information about what the market needs helps keep Coke's distribution on target. In the

place price promotion produ

United States, computer systems show Coke managers exactly what's selling in each market; that allows Coke to plan inventories and deliveries. Coke also operates a 24-hour-a-day communications center to respond to the two million requests it gets from channel members each year. Orders are processed instantly—so sales to consumers at the end of the channel aren't lost because of stock-outs. And Coke products move efficiently through the channel. In Cincinnati, for example, Coke built the beverage industry's first fully automated distribution center. Forklifts were replaced with automatically guided vehicles that speed up the product flow and reduce labor costs.

Coke's strategies in international markets rely on many of the same ideas. But the stage of market development varies in different countries, so Coke's emphasis varies as well. To increase sales in France, for example, Coke is installing thousands of soft-drink coolers in French supermarkets. In Great Britain, Coke is using multipacks because it wants to have more inventory at the point of consumption—in consumers' homes. In Japan, by contrast, single-unit vending machine sales are very important—so Coke uses an army of truck drivers to constantly restock its 870,000 vending machines, more per capita than anywhere else in the world. Coke is even testing vending machines that raise the price when it's hot or when few cans are left. In less-developed areas, the Place system is not always so sophisticated. In China, for example, the Communist Party won't let Coke control all of the details, but a local manager struck a deal. For some cash, the Communist Party keeps inventories in some of its local offices. Then retired party members use bicycle-powered pushcarts to sell the Coke inventory at densely populated housing projects.

To increase fountain-drink sales in domestic and

www.mhhe.com/fourps

international markets, Coke equips restaurants and food outlets with Coke dispensers. Once a Coke dispenser is installed, the retailer usually doesn't have room for a competitor's dispenser. And when a consumer wants a fountain drink, Coke isn't just "the real thing," it's the only thing. The number of fountain outlets has grown so rapidly that one Coke account rep serves as many as 1,000 customers in a geographic area. That means that the little guys could get lost in the shuffle. However, to give them the service they need at a reasonable cost, Coke recently initiated Coke.net, a password-protected web portal where fountain customers can access account managers online, track syrup orders, request equipment repairs, or download marketing support materials.

Of course, Pepsi is a tough competitor and isn't taking all of this sitting down. In recent years it has added more noncola products, and its edgy ads for Mountain Dew and other products are helping it gain market share—which means it gets more shelf space and more Pepsi stocked at the point of purchase. Coke is pushing on new fronts as well. So the competition is becoming even more intense. It's not just the "Cola Wars" any more but rather the wars for cola, juice, water, sports drinks, tea, and many other beverages. And who wins customers and profits in this broader competition will depend on overall marketing programs—but clearly Place has an important role to play.[1]

Physical Distribution Gets It to Customers

Choosing the right channel of distribution is crucial in getting products to the target market's Place. But as the Coke case shows, that alone is usually not enough to ensure that products are available at the right time and in the right quantities. Whenever the product includes a physical good, Place requires logistics decisions. **Logistics** is the transporting, storing, and handling of goods to match target customers' needs with a firm's marketing mix—both within individual firms and along a channel of distribution. **Physical distribution (PD)** is another common name for logistics. PD provides time and place utility and makes possession utility possible.

Logistics costs are very important to both firms and consumers. These costs vary from firm to firm and, from a macro-marketing perspective, from country to country. However, for many physical goods, firms spend half or more of their total marketing dollars on physical distribution activities. The total amount of money involved is so large that even small improvements in this area can have a big effect on a whole macro-marketing system and consumers' quality of life. For example, during the past decade many supermarket chains and producers that supply them collaborated to create a system called Efficient Consumer Response (ECR) that cut grocers' costs, and prices, by about 11 percent. That translates to savings of about $30 *billion* a year for U.S. consumers! The basic idea of ECR involves paperless, computerized links between grocers and their suppliers, which leads to continuous replenishment of shelves based on what actually sells each day. Although the ECR movement started in the U.S. and Canada, it quickly spread across Europe and in other regions. Now, 50 consumer packaged goods companies have banned together to create Transora, a web portal (www.transora.com), to bring more e-commerce benefits to the ECR concept. Innovations like these have the potential to save firms, and their customers, massive amounts of money.[2]

The physical distribution customer service level—including fast and reliable delivery of whatever assortment is needed—is critical to many business customers.

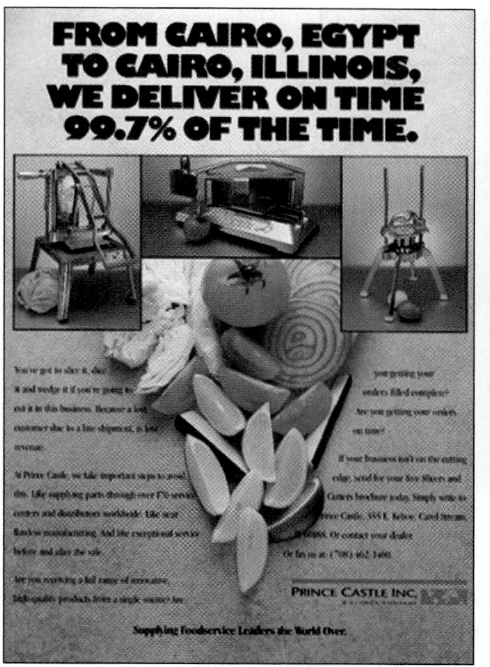

Physical Distribution Customer Service

From the beginning, we've emphasized that marketing strategy planning is based on meeting customers' needs. Planning for logistics and Place is no exception. So let's start by looking at logistics through a customer's eyes.

Customers want products, not excuses

Customers don't care how a product was moved or stored or what some channel member had to do to provide it. Rather, customers think in terms of the physical distribution **customer service level**—how rapidly and dependably a firm can deliver what they, the customers, want. Marketing managers need to understand the customer's point of view.

What does this really mean? It means that Toyota wants to have enough windshields delivered to make cars *that* day—not late so production stops *or* early so there are a lot of extras to move around or store. It means that executives who rent cars from Hertz want them to be ready when they get off their planes. It means that when you order a blue shirt at the Lands' End website you receive blue, not pink. It means you want your Lay's Baked Potato Chips to be whole when you buy a bag at the snack bar—not crushed into crumbs from rough handling in a warehouse.

Physical distribution is invisible to most consumers

PD is, and should be, a part of marketing that is "invisible" to most consumers. It only gets their attention when something goes wrong. At that point, it may be too late to do anything that will keep them happy.

In countries where physical distribution systems are inefficient, consumers face shortages of the products they need. By contrast, most consumers in the United States and Canada don't think much about physical distribution. This probably means that these market-directed macro-marketing systems work pretty well—that a lot of individual marketing managers have made good decisions in this area. But it doesn't mean that the decisions are always clear-cut or simple. In fact, many trade-offs may be required.

Exhibit 11-1
Trade-Offs among Physical Distribution Costs, Customer Service Level, and Sales

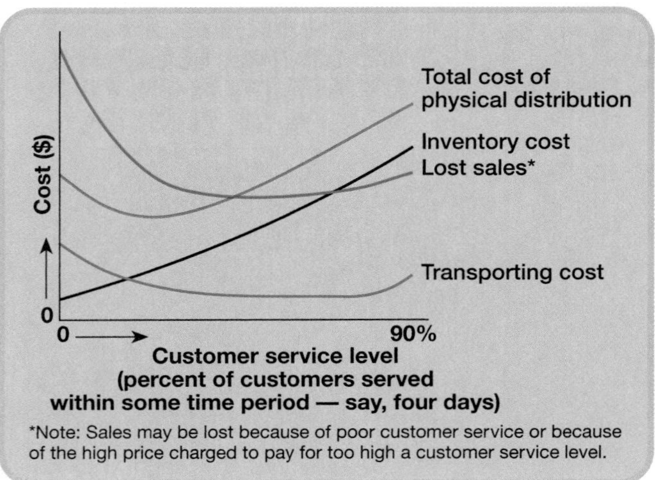

Trade-offs of costs, service, and sales

Most customers would prefer very good service at a very low price. But that combination is hard to provide because it usually costs more to provide higher levels of service. So most physical distribution decisions involve trade-offs between costs, the customer service level, and sales.

If you want a new Compaq computer and the Best Buy store where you would like to buy it doesn't have it on hand, you're likely to buy it elsewhere; or if that model Compaq is hard to get you might just switch to some other brand. Perhaps the Best Buy store could keep your business by guaranteeing two-day delivery of your computer—by using airfreight from Compaq's factory. In this case, the manager is trading the cost of storing inventory for the extra cost of speedy delivery—assuming that the computer is available in inventory *somewhere* in the channel. In this example, missing one sale may not seem that important, but it all adds up. In fact, using Compaq Computer to illustrate this point is quite purposeful. A few years ago Compaq lost over $500 million in sales because its computers weren't available when and where customers were ready to buy them.

Exhibit 11-1 illustrates trade-off relationships like those highlighted in the Compaq example. For example, faster but more expensive transportation may reduce the need for a costly inventory of computers. If the service level is too low, customers will buy elsewhere and sales will be lost. Alternatively, the supplier may hope that a higher service level will attract more customers. But if the service level is higher than customers want or are willing to pay for, sales will be lost to a competitor.

The trade-offs that must be made in the PD area can be complicated. The lowest-cost approach may not be best—if customers aren't satisfied. If different target markets want different customer service levels, several different strategies may be needed.[3]

Many firms are trying to address these complications with e-commerce. Information technology can improve service levels and cut costs at the same time. Better information flows help to improve efficiency and add value for the customer.

Physical Distribution Concept Focuses on the Whole Distribution System

The physical distribution concept

The **physical distribution (PD) concept** says that all transporting, storing, and product-handling activities of a business and a whole channel system should be coordinated as one system that seeks to minimize the cost of distribution for a given

Exhibit 11-2
Examples of Factors that Affect PD Service Levels

- Advance information on product availability
- Time to enter and process orders
- Backorder procedures
- Where inventory is stored
- Accuracy in filling orders
- Damage in shipping, storing, and handling
- Online status information
- Advance information on delays
- Time needed to deliver an order
- Reliability in meeting delivery date
- Complying with customer's instructions
- Defect-free deliveries
- How needed adjustments are handled
- Procedures for handling returns

customer service level. Both lower costs and better service help to increase customer value. It may be hard to see this as a startling development. But until just a few years ago, even the most progressive companies treated physical distribution functions as separate and unrelated activities.

Within a firm, responsibility for different distribution activities was spread among various departments—production, shipping, sales, warehousing, and others. No one person was responsible for coordinating storing and shipping decisions or customer service levels.[4]

Decide what service level to offer

With broader adoption of the physical distribution concept, this is changing. Firms work together to decide what aspects of service are most important to customers at the end of the channel. Then they focus on finding the least expensive way to achieve the target level of service.

Exhibit 11-2 shows a variety of factors that may influence the customer service level (at each level in the channel). The most important aspects of customer service depend on target market needs. Xerox might focus on how long it takes to deliver copy machine repair parts once it receives an order. When a copier breaks down, customers want the repair "yesterday." The service level might be stated as "we will deliver 90 percent of all emergency repair parts within 24 hours." This might require that commonly needed parts be available on service trucks, that order processing be very fast, and that parts not available locally be sent by airfreight. This service level will affect the total cost of the PD system. But it may also beat competitors.

Marketing managers at Clorox, for example, must do everything they can to develop and keep strong partnerships with middlemen. Many other firms sell products with precisely the same ingredients and are constantly trying to steal customers. Yet Clorox's high standards for customer service help it obtain a competitive advantage. For example, when the bleach buyer for a major retail chain went on vacation, the chain's central distribution center almost ran out of Clorox liquid bleach. But Clorox people identified the problem themselves—because of a computer system that allowed Clorox to access the chain's inventory records. Clorox rearranged production and got a shipment out fast enough to prevent the chain, and Clorox, from losing sales. In the future when another bleach supplier tells buyers for the chain that "bleach is bleach," they'll remember the distribution service Clorox provides.[5]

Find the lowest total cost for the right service level

In selecting a PD system, the **total cost approach** involves evaluating each possible PD system and identifying *all* of the costs of each alternative. This approach uses the tools of cost accounting and economics. Costs that otherwise might be ignored—like inventory carrying costs—are considered. The possible costs of lost sales due to a lower customer service level may also be considered. The following simple example clarifies why the total cost approach is important.

Both Business Objects and Sauder try to help customer firms do a better job of tracking the status of orders and making certain that products are where they are needed at the right time.

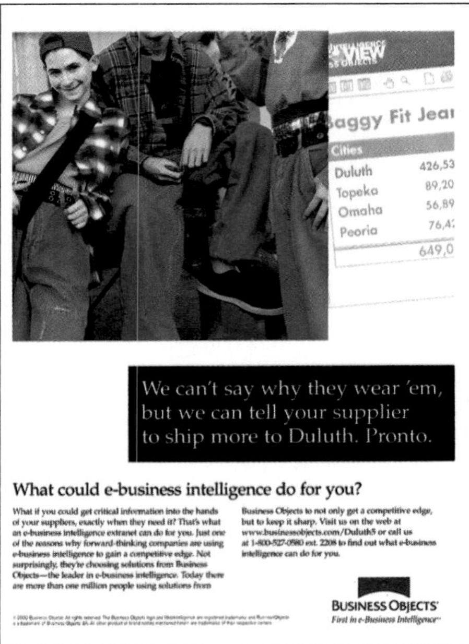

A cost comparison of alternative systems

The Good Earth Vegetable Company was shipping produce to distant markets by train. The cost of shipping a ton of vegetables by train averaged less than half the cost of airfreight so the company assumed that rail was the best method. But then Good Earth managers did a more complete analysis. To their surprise, they found the airfreight system was faster and cheaper.

Exhibit 11-3 compares the costs for the two distribution systems—airplane and railroad. Because shipping by train was slow, Good Earth had to keep a large inventory in a warehouse to fill orders on time. And the company was also surprised at the extra cost of carrying the inventory in transit. Good Earth's managers also found that the cost of spoiled vegetables during shipment and storage in the warehouse was much higher when they used rail shipping.

In this case, total cost analyses showed that airfreight, while more costly by itself, provided better service than the conventional means—and at a lower total

Exhibit 11-3
Comparative Costs of Airplane versus Rail and Warehouse

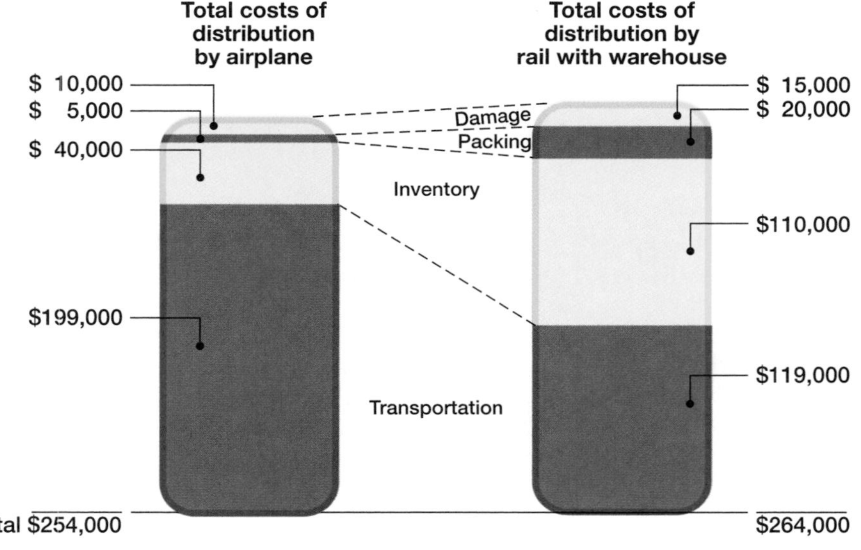

distribution cost. The case also illustrates why it is important to get beyond a focus on individual functional elements of PD and instead consider the costs and service level of a whole system. This broader focus should consider how the whole channel operates, not just individual firms.

Many firms are now applying this type of thinking to improve value to customers and profits. For example, applying the total cost approach, National Semiconductor cut its standard delivery time in half, reduced distribution costs 2.5 percent, and increased sales by 34 percent. In the process it shut down six warehouses around the globe and started to airfreight microchips to its worldwide customers from a new 125,000-square-foot distribution center in Singapore. In advance of these changes, no one would have said that this was an obvious thing to do. But it proved to be the smart thing.[6]

Coordinating Logistics Activities among Firms

Functions can be shifted and shared in the channel

As a marketing manager develops the Place part of a strategy, it is important to decide how physical distribution functions can and should be divided within the channel. Who will store, handle, and transport the goods—and who will pay for these services? Who will coordinate all of the PD activities?

There is no right sharing arrangement. Physical distribution can be varied endlessly in a marketing mix and in a channel system. And competitors may share these functions in different ways—with different costs and results.

How PD is shared affects the rest of a strategy

How the PD functions are shared affects the other three Ps—especially Price. The sharing arrangement can also make (or break) a strategy. Consider Channel Master, a firm that wanted to take advantage of the growing market for the dishlike antennas used to receive TV signals from satellites. The product looked like it could be a big success, but the small company didn't have the money to invest in a large inventory. So Channel Master decided to work only with wholesalers who were willing to buy (and pay for) several units—to be used for demonstrations and to ensure that buyers got immediate delivery.

In the first few months Channel Master earned $2 million in revenues—just by providing inventory for the channel. And the wholesalers paid the interest cost of carrying inventory—over $300,000 the first year. Here the wholesalers helped share the risk of the new venture—but it was a good decision for them too. They won many sales from a competing channel whose customers had to wait several months for delivery. And by getting off to a strong start, Channel Master became a market leader.

A coordinated effort reduces conflict

If firms in the channel do not plan and coordinate how they will share PD activities, PD is likely to be a source of conflict rather than a basis for competitive advantage. Let's consider this point by taking a closer look at just-in-time (JIT) delivery systems (which we introduced in Chapter 6).

JIT requires a close, cooperative relationship

A key advantage of JIT for business customers is that it reduces their PD costs—especially storing and handling costs. However, if the customer doesn't have any backup inventory, there's no security blanket if a supplier's delivery truck gets stuck in traffic, there's an error in what's shipped, or there are any quality problems. Thus, a JIT system requires that a supplier have extremely high quality control in every PD activity.

A JIT system usually requires that a supplier respond to very short order lead times and the customer's production schedule. Thus, e-commerce order systems and information sharing over computer networks are often required. JIT suppliers often

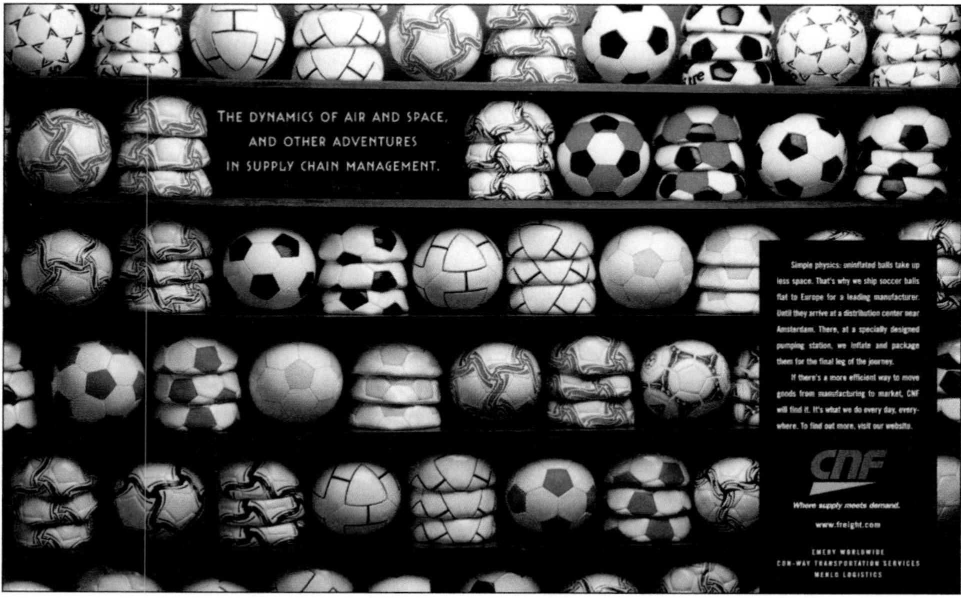

To help a manufacturer of soccer balls reduce its logistics costs, CNF ships the balls to Europe uninflated and then pumps them up before the last leg of their journey to individual outlets.

locate their facilities close to important customers. Trucks may make smaller and more frequent deliveries—perhaps even several times a day.

A JIT system shifts greater responsibility for PD activities backward in the channel. If the supplier can be more efficient than the customer could be in controlling PD costs—and still provide the customer with the service level required—this approach can work well for everyone in the channel. However, JIT is not always the best approach. It may be better for a supplier to produce and ship in larger, more economical quantities—if the savings offset the distribution system's total inventory and handling costs.[7]

Chain of supply may involve even more firms

In our discussion, we have taken the point of view of a marketing manager. This focuses on how logistics should be coordinated to meet the needs of customers at the end of the channel of distribution. Now, however, we should broaden the picture somewhat because the relationships within the distribution channel are sometimes part of a broader network of relationships in the **chain of supply**—the complete set of firms and facilities and logistics activities that are involved in procuring materials, transforming them into intermediate or finished products, and distributing them to customers. For example, Toyota not only works with dealers and customers but also with the supplier firms from which it buys parts. Those firms, in turn, coordinate with their own suppliers. What happens at each link can impact the whole chain. If the firm that produces seats for Toyota doesn't get the fabric from its supplier on time, the seats will be delayed in route to Toyota and the car will be slow getting to the dealer and consumer.

Ideally, all of the firms in the chain of supply should work together to meet the needs of the customer at the very end of the chain. That way, at each link along the chain the shifting and sharing of logistics functions and costs are handled to result in maximum value for the final customer. Further, all of the firms in the whole chain of supply are able to do a better job of competing against competitors who are involved in other chains of supply.

It's difficult for a manager in any one company to know what kind of logistics sharing arrangement will work best, or even be possible, in a whole series of other companies. Because of that, many firms turn to outside experts for help. For example, specialists have developed to design e-commerce computer systems that link all of the firms in a chain of supply. In other cases, firms sometimes outsource the whole job of planning *and* implementing their logistics systems.[8]

Internet

Internet Exercise Large corporations often turn to other firms that specialize in logistics—transportation and warehousing services, consultants, developers of software for e-commerce, and the like—to help implement the physical distribution aspects of their marketing strategies. The website of the Virtual Logistics Directory (www.logisticdirectory.com) lists many logistics specialists and what they do. Go to the website and select the *Integrated Logistics* category. Review the descriptions of some of the firms listed, and then pick one. Explain why a large corporation with a logistics problem might seek its help rather than just trying to tackle the problem internally.

Better information helps coordinate PD

Coordinating all of the elements of PD has always been a challenge—even in a single firm. Trying to coordinate PD throughout the whole supply chain is even tougher. Keeping track of inventory levels, when to order, and where goods are when they move continues to improve as more firms are able to have their computers "talk to each other" directly and as managers can get information from a website whenever they need it.

Electronic data interchange sets a standard

Until recently, differences in computer systems from one firm to another hampered the flow of information. Many firms attacked this problem by adopting **electronic data interchange (EDI)**—an approach that puts information in a standardized format easily shared between different computer systems. Purchase orders, shipping reports, and other paper documents were replaced with computerized EDI. With EDI, a customer transmits its order information directly to the supplier's computer. The supplier's computer immediately processes the order and schedules production, order assembly, and transportation. Inventory information is automatically updated, and status reports are available instantly. The supplier might then use EDI to send the updated information to the transportation provider's computer. This type of system is now very common. In fact, almost all international transportation firms rely on EDI links with their customers.

EDI systems were originally developed and popularized before the World Wide Web and Internet gained widespread use. Most traditional EDI systems are expensive to develop, rely on proprietary computer networks, and use specialized software to exchange data securely. Alternatives to this approach that rely on the Internet are gaining in popularity.[9]

Better information is a key reason for the success of Pepperidge Farm's line of premium cookies. Many of the company's 2,200 drivers use hand-held computers to record the inventory at each stop along their routes. They use the Internet to transmit the information into a computer at the bakeries—so that cookies in short supply will be produced. The right assortment of fresh cookies is quickly shipped to local markets, and delivery trucks are loaded with what retailers need that day. That means fresher cookies for consumers and helps to support Pepperidge Farm's high-quality positioning and premium price.[10]

Ethical issues may arise

Most of the ethical issues that arise in the PD area concern communications about product availability. For example, some critics say that Internet sellers too often take orders for products that are not available or which they cannot deliver as quickly as customers expect. Yet a marketing manager can't always know precisely how long it will take before a product will be available. It doesn't make sense for the marketer to lose a customer if it appears that he or she can satisfy the customer's needs. But the customer may be inconvenienced or face added cost if the marketer's best guess isn't accurate.

Some suppliers criticize customers for abusing efforts to coordinate PD activities in the channel. For example, some retailers hedge against uncertain demand by telling suppliers that they plan to place an order, but then they don't confirm the order until the last minute. This shifts the uncertainty to the supplier. Is this unethical? Some think it is. However, a marketing manager should realize that the firm's order policies can reduce such problems—if the cost of providing the service customers want is higher than what they will pay.[11]

Now that you see why the coordination of physical distribution activities is so important, let's take a closer look at some of the PD decision areas.

The Transporting Function Adds Value to a Marketing Strategy

Transporting aids economic development and exchange

Transporting is the marketing function of moving goods. Transportation provides time and place utilities—at a cost. But the cost is less than the value added to products by moving them or there is little reason to ship in the first place.

Transporting can help achieve economies of scale in production. If production costs can be reduced by producing larger quantities in one location, these savings may more than offset the added cost of transporting the finished products to customers. Without low-cost transportation, both within countries and internationally, there would be no mass distribution as we know it today.

Transporting can be costly

Transporting costs limit the target markets a marketing manager can serve. Shipping costs increase delivered cost—and that's what really interests customers. Transport costs add little to the cost of products that are already valuable relative to their size and weight. A case of medicine, for example, might be shipped to a drugstore at low cost. But transporting costs can be a large part of the total cost for heavy products of low value—like many minerals and raw materials. You can imagine that shipping a massive roll of aluminum to a producer of soft-drink cans is an expensive proposition.[12]

Governments may influence transportation

Government often plays an important role in the development of a country's transportation system—including its roads, harbors, railroads, and airports. And different countries regulate transportation differently—although regulation has in general been decreasing.

For example, as part of their move toward unification, most European countries are reducing their transporting regulations. The construction of the tunnel under the English Channel is a dramatic example of the changes taking place. The "chunnel" allows trains to speed between England and the rest of Europe.

As regulations decreased in the U.S., competition in the transportation industry increased. As a result, a marketing manager generally has many carriers in one or more modes competing for the firm's transporting business. Or a firm can do its own transporting. So knowing about the different modes is important.[13]

Which Transporting Alternative Is Best?

Transporting function must fit the whole strategy

The transporting function should fit into the whole marketing strategy. But picking the best transporting alternative depends on the product, other physical distribution decisions, and what service level the company wants to offer. Exhibit 11-4 shows that different modes of transportation have different strengths and weaknesses.

Exhibit 11-4 Benefits and Limitations of Different Transport Modes

	Transporting Features					
Mode	Cost	Delivery Speed	Number of Locations Served	Ability to Handle a Variety of Goods	Frequency of Scheduled Shipments	Dependability in Meeting Schedules
Truck	High	Fast	Very extensive	High	High	High
Rail	Medium	Average	Extensive	High	Low	Medium
Water	Very low	Very slow	Limited	Very high	Very low	Medium
Air	Very high	Very fast	Extensive	Limited	High	High
Pipeline	Low	Slow	Very limited	Very limited	Medium	High

Low transporting cost is *not* the only criterion for selecting the best mode. You can find more detail at the website of the Bureau of Transportation Statistics (www.bts.gov).[14]

Railroads—large loads moved at low cost

Railroads are still the workhorse of the U.S. transportation system. They carry more freight over more miles than any other mode. However, they account for less than 10 percent of transport revenues. They carry heavy and bulky goods—such as coal, steel, and chemicals—over long distances at relatively low cost. Because railroad freight moves more slowly than truck shipments, it is not as well suited for perishable items or those in urgent demand. Railroads are most efficient at handling full carloads of goods. Less-than-carload (LCL) shipments take a lot of handling, which means they usually move more slowly and at a higher price per pound than carload shipments.[15]

Trucks are more expensive, but flexible and essential

The flexibility and speed of trucks make them better at moving small quantities of goods for shorter distances. They can travel on almost any road. They go where the rails can't. They are also reliable in meeting delivery schedules, which is an

Mercedes recently introduced a new, smaller truck that is designed to be more flexible in making deliveries in congested cities like Istanbul, where this ad appeared.

Babbages Changes the Rules to Win Game Lovers' Business

Winning the hearts, wallets, and loyalty of electronic game fanatics isn't easy, but Babbages' marketing strategy has done just that. Imagine, for instance, the week in which the folks at Babbages shipped 500,000 units of 73 different games by overnight delivery to 900 different stores. Or there was the time they filled tractor-trailer trucks at Nintendo's loading dock, at midnight, and then rushed to a chartered jet so that a highly anticipated game would be available in stores the same day it was released. Have they lost their minds? No, but some people think that their customers have. Big-spending game enthusiasts want to be the very first to get a new game when it comes out. So Babbages ships every new game for overnight delivery. While Wal-Mart and Best Buy stores can stock more at a lower price, it takes longer for games to work through their distribution centers and get to store shelves. By then, Babbages would like to be sold out. The shelf life of a new game is only about 15 weeks, and most sales are at the beginning. So gamers will drive across town to get a game sooner at Babbages, even if it's more pricey. That way, when someone asks their opinions about a new game, they will be in the know. In fact, game manufacturers like Nintendo know that avid gamers post reviews of a game on the Internet within 24 hours of when it gets to Babbages. If reviews say that a game is really hot, the manufacturer can ramp up production. That saves time because the factories are in Asia, and it takes about three weeks to reorder and get more product on shelves.[16]

essential requirement for logistics systems that require rapid replenishment of inventory after a sale. In combination these factors explain why at least 75 percent of U.S. consumer products travel at least part of the way from producer to consumer by truck. And in countries with good highway systems, trucks can give extremely fast service. Trucks compete for high-value items.[17]

Ship it overseas—but slowly

Water transportation is the slowest shipping mode—but usually the lowest-cost way of shipping heavy freight. Water transportation is very important for international shipments and often the only practical approach. This explains why port cities like Boston, New York City, Rotterdam, Osaka, and Singapore are important centers for international trade.

Inland waterways are important too

Inland waterways (such as the Mississippi River and Great Lakes in the United States and the Rhine and Danube in Europe) are also important, especially for bulky,

The growth of airfreight has made it easier and faster for firms to serve customers in foreign markets.

nonperishable products such as iron ore, grain, and gravel. However, when winter ice closes freshwater harbors, alternate transportation must be used.

Pipelines move oil and gas

Pipelines are used primarily to move oil and natural gas. So pipelines are important both in the oil-producing and oil-consuming countries. Only a few major cities in the United States, Canada, Mexico, and Latin America are more than 200 miles from a major pipeline system.

Airfreight is expensive but fast and growing

The most expensive cargo transporting mode is airplane—but it is fast! Airfreight rates are on average three times higher than trucking rates—but the greater speed may offset the added cost.

High-value, low-weight goods—like high-fashion clothing and parts for the electronics industry—are often shipped by air. Perishable products that previously could not be shipped are now being flown across continents and oceans. Flowers and bulbs from Holland, for example, now are jet-flown to points all over the world.

Internet

Internet Exercise A firm that is just starting to export to international markets may want help figuring out what shipping services are available. The North Carolina Ports Authority's website (www.ncports.com) helps provide such information. Go to the website, select *Ports Directory,* and review the different firms and agencies that might be able to provide you with help if you had to ship a large quantity of furniture to the Middle East. Identify an organization from those listed that you might want to contact first, and indicate why.

But airplanes may cut the total cost of distribution

Using planes may reduce the cost of packing, unpacking, and preparing goods for sale and may help a firm reduce inventory costs by eliminating outlying warehouses. Valuable benefits of airfreight's speed are less spoilage, theft, and damage. Although the *transporting* cost of air shipments may be higher, the *total* cost of distribution may be lower. As more firms realize this, airfreight firms—like DHL Worldwide Express, FedEx, and Emery Air Freight—have enjoyed rapid growth. These firms play an especially important role in the growth of international business.[18]

Put it in a container—and move between modes easily

Products often move by several different modes and carriers during their journey. This is especially common for international shipments. Japanese firms—like Sony—ship stereos to the United States, Canada, and Europe by boat. When they arrive at the dock, they are loaded on trains and sent across the country. Then the units are delivered to a wholesaler by truck or rail.

Loading and unloading goods several times used to be a real problem. Parts of a shipment would become separated, damaged, or even stolen. And handling the goods—perhaps many times—raised costs and slowed delivery. Many of these problems are reduced with **containerization**—grouping individual items into an economical shipping quantity and sealing them in protective containers for transit to the final destination.

Piggyback—a ride on two or more modes

Piggyback service means loading truck trailers—or flatbed trailers carrying containers—on railcars to provide both speed and flexibility. Railroads now pick up truck trailers at the producer's location, load them onto specially designed rail flatcars, and haul them as close to the customer as rail lines run. The trailers are then hooked up to a truck tractor and delivered to the buyer's door. Similar services are offered on ocean-going ships—allowing door-to-door service between cities around the world.[19]

Transportation choices affect environmental costs too

Marketing managers must be sensitive to the environmental effects of transportation decisions. Some say trucks cause air pollution in already crowded cities. People who live near airports suffer from noise pollution. A damaged pipeline can spew thousands of gallons of oil before it can be repaired. The Exxon *Valdez* oil spill in Alaska is a dramatic example of the kind of environmental disaster that can happen when a transportation accident occurs.

Today, the public *expects* companies to manufacture, transport, sell, and dispose of products in an environmentally sound manner. If companies are environmentally unsafe, consumers will show their dissatisfaction through their market choices. However, these environmental efforts increase the cost of distribution.

The Storing Function and Marketing Strategy

Store it and smooth out sales, increase profits and consumer satisfaction

Storing is the marketing function of holding goods. It provides time utility. **Inventory** is the amount of goods being stored.

Maintaining the right inventory level is difficult when it's hard to forecast likely demand. Even so, a firm that is stocked out when customers are ready to buy may not only lose the sale but may also damage the relationship and the possibility of future sales. Kmart ran into this problem. Many consumers decided it was no longer a convenient place to shop when stores repeatedly ran out of basic staples that consumers expected to find.

Storing is necessary when production of goods doesn't match consumption. This is common with mass production. Nippon Steel, for example, might produce thousands of steel bars of one size before changing the machines to produce another size. It's often cheaper to produce large quantities of one size, and store the unsold quantity, than to have shorter production runs. Thus, storing goods allows the producer to achieve economies of scale in production.

Storing varies the channel system

Storing allows producers and middlemen to keep stocks at convenient locations—ready to meet customers' needs. In fact, storing is one of the major activities of some middlemen.

Most channel members provide the storing function for some length of time. Even final consumers store some things for their future needs.

Which channel members store the product, and for how long, affects the behavior of all channel members. For example, the producer of Snapper lawn mowers tries

Logistics activities are often invisible to consumers, but a breakdown in distribution customer service can result in dissatisfied consumers and lost business.

Exhibit 11-5 Many Expenses Contribute to Total Inventory Cost

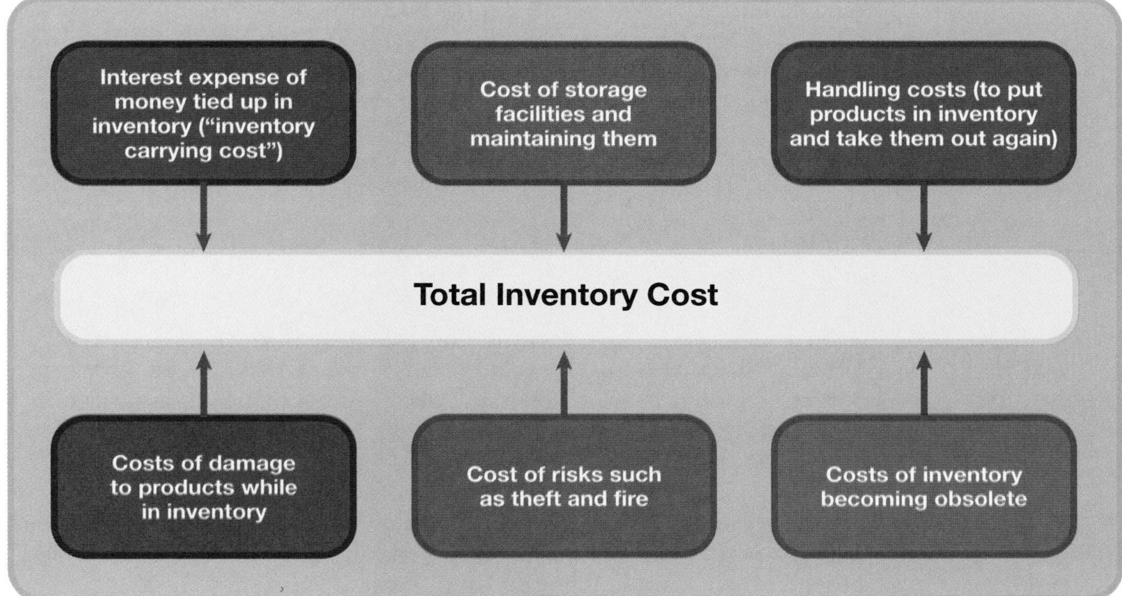

to get wholesalers to inventory a wide selection of its machines. That way, retailers can carry smaller inventories since they can be sure of dependable local supplies. And they might decide to sell Snapper—rather than Toro or some other brand that they would have to store at their own expense.

If final customers "store" the product, more of it may be used or consumed. Coke wants customers to buy six packs and 2-liter bottles. Then consumers have an "inventory" in the refrigerator when thirst hits. Of course, consumers aren't always willing to hold the inventory. In China, for example, Coke had little success until it gave up pushing 2-liter bottles and switched to single-serving 75-ml bottles. Only 1 out of 10 Chinese families has a refrigerator—so they didn't have a good way to store a bottle once it was open.

Goods are stored at a cost

Storing can increase the value of goods, but *storing always involves costs* too. These costs are typically 20 to 40 percent of the value of the inventory. So, different kinds of cost are involved. See Exhibit 11-5. Car dealers, for example, must store cars on their lots—waiting for the right customer. The interest expense of money tied up in the inventory is a major cost. In addition, if a new car on the lot is dented or scratched, there is a repair cost. If a car isn't sold before the new models come out, its value drops. There is also a risk of fire or theft—so the retailer must carry insurance. And, of course, dealers incur the cost of leasing or owning the display lot where they store the cars.

In today's competitive markets, most firms watch their inventories closely. Taken in total, the direct and indirect costs of unnecessary inventory can make the difference between a profitable strategy and a loser.[20]

Rapid response cuts inventory costs

Many firms are finding that they can cut inventory costs and still provide the desired customer service—if they can reduce the time it takes to replace items that are sold. This is one important reason that the JIT and ECR approaches have been widely adopted. The firms involved use EDI, the Internet, and similar computerized approaches to share information and speed up the order cycle and delivery process.

JIT and ECR systems can also help firms see the benefit of dropping some of the items that they stock and sell. P&G is a vivid example. Between 1991 and 1996 it introduced many new products but cut its total number of skus (individual stock-keeping units) by 34 percent, mainly by cutting the number of sizes and colors for some of its brands. After the cuts, sales of the remaining products went up and costs came down. With fewer products, P&G put more marketing effort behind those it kept, and its retailers were more willing to push products that turn over quickly.[21]

Specialized Storing Facilities May Be Required

New cars can be stored outside on the dealer's lot. Fuel oil can be stored in a specially designed tank. Coal and other raw materials can be stored in open pits. But most products must be stored inside protective buildings. Often, firms can choose among different types of specialized storing facilities. The right choice may reduce costs and serve customers better.

Private warehouses are common

Private warehouses are storing facilities owned or leased by companies for their own use. Most manufacturers, wholesalers, and retailers have some storing facilities either in their main buildings or in a separate location.

Firms use private warehouses when a large volume of goods must be stored regularly. Yet private warehouses can be expensive. If the need changes, the extra space may be hard, or impossible, to rent to others.

Public warehouses fill special needs

Public warehouses are independent storing facilities. They can provide all the services that a company's own warehouse can provide. A company might choose a public warehouse if it doesn't have a regular need for space. For example, Tonka Toys uses public warehouses because its business is seasonal. Tonka pays for the space only when it is used. Public warehouses are also useful for manufacturers who must maintain stocks in many locations—including foreign countries. See Exhibit 11-6 for a comparison of private and public warehouses.[22]

Warehousing facilities cut handling costs too

The cost of physical handling is a major storing cost. Goods must be handled once when put into storage and again when removed to be sold. To reduce these costs, modern one-story buildings away from downtown traffic are replacing the old multistory warehouses. They eliminate the need for elevators and permit the use

Exhibit 11-6
A Comparison of Private Warehouses and Public Warehouses

	Type of Warehouse	
Characteristics	Private	Public
Fixed investment	Very high	No fixed investment
Unit cost	High if volume is low Very low if volume is very high	Low: charges are made only for space needed
Control	High	Low managerial control
Adequacy for product line	Highly adequate	May not be convenient
Flexibility	Low: fixed costs have already been committed	High: easy to end arrangement

of power-operated lift trucks, battery-operated motor scooters, roller-skating order pickers, electric hoists for heavy items, and hydraulic ramps to speed loading and unloading. Bar codes and UPC (uniform product code) numbers make it easy for computers to monitor inventory, order needed stock, and track storing and shipping costs. Some warehouses have computer-controlled order-picking systems or conveyor belts that speed the process of locating and assembling the assortment required to fill an order.[23]

The Distribution Center—A Different Kind of Warehouse

Is storing really needed?

Discrepancies of assortment or quantity between one channel level and another are often adjusted at the place where goods are stored. It reduces handling costs to regroup and store at the same place—*if both functions are required.* But sometimes regrouping is required when storing isn't.

Don't store it, distribute it

A **distribution center** is a special kind of warehouse designed to speed the flow of goods and avoid unnecessary storing costs. Anchor Hocking moves over a million pounds of its housewares products through its distribution center each day. Faster inventory turnover and easier bulk-breaking reduce the cost of carrying inventory.

Today, the distribution center concept is widely used by firms at all channel levels. Many products buzz through a distribution center without ever tarrying on a shelf; workers and equipment immediately sort the products as they come in and then move them to an outgoing loading dock and the vehicle that will take them to their next stop.

Managers must be innovative to provide customers with superior value

More competitive markets, improved technology, coordination among firms, and efficient new distribution centers are bringing big improvements to the PD area. Yet the biggest challenges may be more basic. As we've emphasized here, physical distribution activities transcend departmental, corporate, and even national boundaries. So, taking advantage of ways to improve often requires cooperation all

McKesson is a leading distributor of drugs, and effective use of technology has been a key reason for its success. The space-age gizmo on this man's arm combines a scanner, computer, and two-way radio—to speed up order assembly and delivery from McKesson's distribution center.

along the channel system. Too often, such cooperation doesn't exist—and changing ingrained ways of doing things is hard. But marketing managers who push for innovations in these areas are likely to win customers away from firms and whole channel systems that are stuck doing things in the old way.[24]

Conclusion

This chapter deals with logistics activities and how they provide *time* and *place* utility to improve value to the customer. We looked at the customer service level and why it is important.

We emphasized the relation between customer service level, transporting, and storing. The physical distribution concept focuses on coordinating all the storing, transporting, and product handling activities into a smoothly working system—to deliver the desired service level and customer value at the lowest cost.

Marketing managers often want to improve service and may select a higher-cost alternative to improve their marketing mix. The total cost approach might reveal that it is possible *both* to reduce costs and to improve service—perhaps by identifying creative new distribution alternatives.

We discussed various modes of transporting and their advantages and disadvantages. We also discussed ways to reduce inventory costs. We explained why distribution centers are an important way to cut storing and handling costs, and we explained how computerized information links—within firms and among firms in the channel—are increasingly important in blending all of the activities into a smooth-running system.

Effective marketing managers make important strategy decisions about physical distribution. Creative strategy decisions may result in lower PD costs while maintaining or improving the customer service level. And production-oriented competitors may not even understand what is happening.

Questions and Problems

1. Explain how adjusting the customer service level could improve a marketing mix. Illustrate.
2. Briefly explain which aspects of customer service you think would be most important for a producer that sells fabric to a firm that manufactures furniture.
3. Briefly describe a purchase you made where the customer service level had an effect on the product you selected or where you purchased it.
4. Discuss the types of trade-offs involved in PD costs, service levels, and sales.
5. Give an example of why it is important for different firms in the chain of supply to coordinate logistics activities.
6. Discuss some of the ways computers are being used to improve PD decisions.
7. Explain why a just-in-time delivery system would require a supplier to pay attention to quality control. Give an example to illustrate your points.
8. Discuss the problems a supplier might encounter in using a just-in-time delivery system with a customer in a foreign country.
9. Review the list of factors that affect PD service level in Exhibit 11-2. Indicate which ones are most likely to be improved by EDI links between a supplier and its customers.
10. Explain the total cost approach and why it may cause conflicts in some firms. Give examples of how conflicts might occur between different departments.
11. Discuss the relative advantages and disadvantages of railroads, trucks, and airlines as transporting methods.
12. Discuss some of the ways that air transportation can change other aspects of a Place system.
13. Indicate the nearest location where you would expect to find large storage facilities. What kinds of products would be stored there? Why are they stored there instead of some other place?

14. When would a producer or middleman find it desirable to use a public warehouse rather than a private warehouse? Illustrate, using a specific product or situation.

15. Clearly differentiate between a warehouse and a distribution center. Explain how a specific product would be handled differently by each.

16. If a retailer operates only from a website and ships all orders by UPS, is it freed from the logistics issues that face traditional retailers? Explain your thinking.

Suggested Cases

15. Morgan Company

23. Rainbow Packers, Inc.

Computer-Aided Problem

11. Total Distribution Cost

Proto Company has been producing various items made of plastic. It recently added a line of plain plastic cards that other firms (such as banks and retail stores) will imprint to produce credit cards. Proto offers its customers the plastic cards in different colors, but they all sell for $40 per box of 1,000. Tom Phillips, Proto's product manager for this line, is considering two possible physical distribution systems. He estimates that if Proto uses airfreight, transportation costs will be $7.50 a box, and its cost of carrying inventory will be 5 percent of total annual sales dollars. Alternatively, Proto could ship by rail for $2 a box. But rail transport will require renting space at four regional warehouses—at $26,000 a year each. Inventory carrying cost with this system will be 10 percent of total annual sales dollars. Phillips prepared a spreadsheet to compare the cost of the two alternative physical distribution systems.

a. *If Proto Company expects to sell 20,000 boxes a year, what are the total physical distribution costs for each of the systems?*
b. *If Phillips can negotiate cheaper warehouse space for the rail option so that each warehouse costs only $20,000 per year, which physical distribution system has the lowest overall cost?*
c. *Proto's finance manager predicts that interest rates are likely to be lower during the next marketing plan year and suggests that Tom Phillips use inventory carrying costs of 4 percent for airfreight and 7.5 percent for railroads (with warehouse cost at $20,000 each). If interest rates are in fact lower, which alternative would you suggest? Why?*

For additional questions related to this problem, see Exercise 11-3 in the *Learning Aid for Use with Essentials of Marketing*, 9th edition.

Chapter Twelve

Retailers, Wholesalers, and Their Strategy Planning

When You Finish This Chapter, You Should

1. Understand how retailers plan their marketing strategies.

2. Know about the many kinds of retailers that work with producers and wholesalers as members of channel systems.

3. Understand the differences among the conventional and nonconventional retailers—including Internet merchants and others who accept the mass-merchandising concept.

4. Understand scrambled merchandising and the "wheel of retailing."

5. See why size or belonging to a chain can be important to a retailer.

6. Know what progressive wholesalers are doing to modernize their operations and marketing strategies.

7. Know the various kinds of merchant wholesalers and agent middlemen and the strategies that they use.

8. Understand why retailing and wholesaling have developed in different ways in different countries.

9. See why the Internet is impacting both retailing and wholesaling.

10. Understand the important new terms (shown in red).

Frieda's, Inc., is a family-owned wholesale firm that each year supplies supermarkets with $30 million worth of exotic fruits and vegetables. It was started by Frieda Caplan in 1962; now, her daughters Karen and Jackie run the company. It is a sign of the marketing savvy of these women that kiwi fruit, artichokes, Chinese donut peaches, alfalfa sprouts, spaghetti squash, pearl onions, and mushrooms no longer seem very exotic. All of these crops were once viewed as unusual. Few farmers grew them, and consumers didn't know about them. Supermarkets and traditional produce wholesalers didn't want to handle them because they had a limited market. Frieda's helped to change all that.

Caplan realized that some supermarkets wanted to put more emphasis on their produce departments. These retailers were targeting consumers who were less price-sensitive and

place

price

promotion

produc

wanted more choices in the hard-to-manage produce department. So she looked for products that would help her retailer-customers meet this need. For example, the funny looking kiwi fruit with its fuzzy brown skin was popular in New Zealand but virtually unknown to other consumers. Caplan worked with small farmer-producers to ensure that she could provide her retailer-customers with a steady supply. She packaged kiwi with interesting recipes and promoted kiwi *and* her brand name to consumers. Because of her efforts, most supermarkets now carry kiwi—which has become a $40 million crop for California farmers.

Because demand has grown, many larger wholesalers now handle kiwi. But that doesn't bother the Caplans. When one of Frieda's specialty items becomes a commodity with low profit margins, another novel item replaces it. The Frieda's label is now on 400 products—like Asian pears, kiwano melons, sun-dried yellow tomatoes, and hot Asian chiles.

A few years ago, some skeptics said that specialty wholesalers like Frieda's would bite the dust because online market exchanges, like Produce.com, would make them obsolete. However, Produce.com is out of business and Frieda's is growing faster than ever—by taking advantage of its own website (www.friedas.com) and by providing value-adding services that get supermarket buyers to think beyond just getting the lowest bid on some commodity.

The Caplans recently established an online retail operation, Shop@Friedas, but it doesn't compete directly with supermarkets. Rather, from its website the firm sells a limited-line of *gift* selections like the "Chile Lover's Basket."

price
place
promotion
product

The website also has a Club Frieda section where consumer-members get recipes and information about new products and local promotions. The website also invites consumers to be the "eyes and ears of the company" and send in ideas about interesting new products.

Building relationships with consumers isn't new at Frieda's. Earlier the Caplans developed a database with detailed information about buying habits of 100,000 consumers who responded to an invitation on Frieda's label.

Frieda's continues to have an advantage with many supermarkets because consumers love its products and it constantly offers new services that add value in the channel. For example, Frieda's "El Mercado de Frieda" line helps retailers do a better job attracting Hispanic customers.[1]

Wholesalers and Retailers Plan Their Own Strategies

In Chapter 10, we discussed the vital role that wholesalers and retailers perform in channel systems. Now we'll look at the decisions that retailers and wholesalers make in developing their own strategies. We'll also highlight how their strategies have evolved.

Understand how retailing and wholesaling are evolving

Understanding the how and why of these changes will help you know what to expect in the future. It will also make it clear that it is the whole strategy, not just one aspect of it, that ultimately is a success or failure. This may seem obvious, but it's a point that many people have ignored—at great cost.

Consider the dramatic changes prompted by the Internet. A few years ago many people were proclaiming that it would quickly change everything we thought about successful retailing. Yet, many creative ideas for online retailing bombed precisely because managers of dot-coms failed to understand why retailing has evolved as it has. For many consumers and many types of purchases, it doesn't matter if an online retailer posts low prices for an incredible assortment when there's no way to get customer service, products are not actually available, or it's a hassle to return a green shirt that looked blue on the website. *You* want to avoid the trap of this sort of incomplete thinking!

So in this chapter we focus on decisions that apply to *all* retailers and wholesalers, while highlighting how their strategies are changing.

The Nature of Retailing

Retailing covers all of the activities involved in the sale of products to final consumers. Retailers range from large chains of specialized stores—like Toys "R" Us—to individual merchants like the woman who sells baskets from an open stall in the central market in Ibadan, Nigeria. Some retailers operate from stores and others operate without a store—by selling online, on TV, with a printed catalog, from vending machines, or even in consumers' homes. Most retailers sell goods produced by someone else. But in the case of service retailing—like dry cleaning, fast food, online bank accounts, or one-hour photo processing, for example—the retailer is also the producer.

Retailing is crucial to consumers in every macro-marketing system. For example, consumers spend $3.2 *trillion* (that's $3,200,000,000,000!) a year buying goods and services from U.S. retailers.

The nature of retailing and its rate of change are generally related to the stage and speed of a country's economic development. In the U.S., retailing is more varied and dynamic than in most other countries. By studying the U.S. system, you will better understand where retailing is headed in other parts of the world.

Planning a Retailer's Strategy

Retailers interact directly with final consumers—so strategy planning is critical to their survival. If a retailer loses a customer to a competitor, the retailer is the one who suffers. Producers and wholesalers still make *their* sale regardless of which retailer sells the product.

Consumers have reasons for buying from particular retailers

Different consumers prefer different kinds of retailers. But many retailers either don't know or don't care why. All too often, beginning retailers just rent a store and assume customers will show up. As a result, in the U.S. about three-fourths of new retailing ventures fail during the first year. Even an established retailer will quickly lose if its customers find a better way to meet their needs. To avoid this fate, a retailer needs to carefully identify possible target markets and try to understand why these people buy where they do. That helps the retailer tune its marketing mix to the needs of specific target markets.[2]

Retailer's whole offering is its Product

Most retailers in developed nations sell more than one kind of product. So the brands and product assortment carried can be critical to their success. Yet it's best to take a broader view in thinking about the Product strategy decisions for a retailer's marketing mix. The retailer's *whole* offering—assortment of goods and services, advice from salesclerks, convenience, and the like—is its "Product."

Different consumers have different needs—and needs vary from one purchase situation to another. Which retailer's Product offers the best customer value depends on the needs that a customer wants to satisfy. Whatever the effect of other consumer needs, economic needs are usually very important in shaping the choice of a retailer. Social and individual needs may also come into play. Our discussion of consumer behavior in Chapter 5 applies here.

Features of offering relate to needs

Features of a retailer's offering that relate to economic needs include

- *Convenience* (available hours, finding needed products, fast checkout, location, parking).
- *Product selection* (width and depth of assortment, quality).
- *Special services* (special orders, home delivery, gift wrap, entertainment).
- *Fairness in dealings* (honesty, correcting problems, return privileges, purchase risks).
- *Helpful information* (courteous sales help, displays, demonstrations, product information).
- *Prices* (value, credit, special discounts, taxes or extra charges).

Some features that relate to social and emotional factors include

- *Social image* (status, prestige, "fitting in" with other shoppers).
- *Shopping atmosphere* (comfort, safety, excitement, relaxation, sounds, smells).

In later chapters we'll go into much more detail on the price and promotion decisions that all firms—including retailers and wholesalers—make.

Strategy requires carefully set policies

In developing a strategy a retailer should consciously make decisions that set policies on *all* of these factors. Each of them can impact a customer's view of the costs

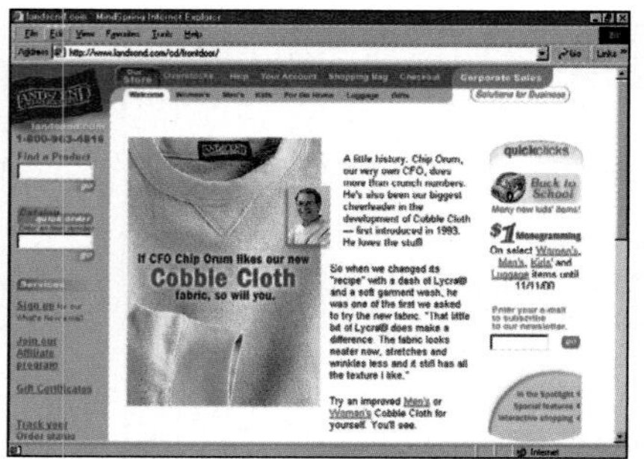

It's best of think of a retailer's Product as its whole offering—including its assortment of goods and services, advice from salespeople, the convenience of shopping, and hours it is available.

and benefits of choosing that retailer. And in combination they differentiate one retailer's offering and strategy from another. If the combination doesn't provide superior value to some target market, the retailer will fail.

Consumer needs relate to segmentation and positioning

Segmentation and positioning decisions are important to retailers. And ignoring either economic or social and emotional values in those decisions can lead to serious errors in a retailer's strategy planning.

Consider, for example, how the shopping atmosphere may have an emotional effect on a consumer's view of a retailer. How merchandise is displayed, what decorations, colors, and finishes are used, and even the temperature, sounds, and smell of a store all contribute to its "atmospherics" and store image. The right combination may attract more target customers and encourage them to spend more. Tiffany's, for example, offers luxury surroundings and inventive displays to attract upscale consumers. But Tiffany's may also appeal to consumers who get an ego boost from Tiffany's prestige image and very attentive staff. Of course, interesting surroundings are usually costly, and the prices that consumers pay must cover that expense. An online jewelry retailer avoids those costs but offers a completely different shopping experience and deals with a different set of needs. So a retailer's atmosphere and image may be a plus or a minus, depending on the target market. And there's no single right answer about which target market is best. Like Tiffany's, Dollar General has been very profitable. But it has a "budget" image and atmosphere that appeals to working-class customers, many of whom just prefer to shop where they don't feel out of place.[3]

Different types of retailers emphasize different strategies

Retailers have an almost unlimited number of ways in which to alter their offerings—their marketing mixes—to appeal to a target market. Because of all the variations, it's oversimplified to classify retailers and their strategies on the basis of a single characteristic—such as merchandise, services, sales volume, or even whether they operate in cyberspace. But a good place to start is by considering basic types of retailers and some differences in their strategies.

Let's look first at conventional retailers. Then we'll see how other retailers successfully modify conventional offerings to better meet the needs of *some* consumers. Think about *why* the changes take place. That will help you identify opportunities and plan better marketing strategies.

Conventional Retailers—Try to Avoid Price Competition

Single-line, limited-line retailers specialize by product

A hundred and fifty years ago, **general stores**—which carried anything they could sell in reasonable volume—were the main retailers in the United States. But with the growing number of consumer products after the Civil War, general stores

In spite of consumer interest in Western products and new retailing formats, most retailing in Asia is still handled by small limited-line stores, like the independently owned Filipino store on the left and the Japanese electronics one on the right.

couldn't offer enough variety in all their traditional lines. So some stores began specializing in dry goods, apparel, furniture, or groceries.

Now most conventional retailers are **single-line** or **limited-line stores**—stores that specialize in certain lines of related products rather than a wide assortment. Many stores specialize not only in a single line, such as clothing, but also in a *limited-line* within the broader line. Within the clothing line, a retailer might carry *only* shoes or even neckties but offer depth in that limited line.

Single-line, limited-line stores are being squeezed

The main advantage of such retailers is that they can satisfy some target markets better because they adjust to suit specific customers. They try to build a long-term relationship with their customers and earn a position as *the* place to shop for a certain type of product. But single-line and limited-line stores face the costly problem of having to stock some slow-moving items in order to satisfy the store's target market. Many of these stores are small—with high expenses relative to sales. So they try to keep their prices up by avoiding competition on identical products.

Conventional retailers like this have been around for a long time and are still found in every community. In most countries conventional retailers still handle the vast majority of all retailing sales. However, this situation is changing fast. Nowhere is the change clearer than in the United States. Conventional retailers are being squeezed by retailers who modify their mixes in the various ways suggested in Exhibit 12-1. Let's look closer at some of these other types of retailers.

Expand Assortment and Service—To Compete at a High Price

Specialty shops usually sell shopping products

A **specialty shop**—a type of conventional limited-line store—is usually small and has a distinct "personality." Specialty shops sell special types of shopping products—such as high-quality sporting goods, exclusive clothing, cameras, or even antiques. They aim at a carefully defined target market by offering a unique product assortment, knowledgeable salesclerks, and better service.

Catering to certain types of customers simplifies buying, speeds turnover, and cuts costs due to obsolescence and style changes. Specialty shops probably will continue to be a part of the retailing scene as long as customers have varied tastes and the money to satisfy them.[4]

Exhibit 12-1 Types of Retailers and the Nature of Their Offerings

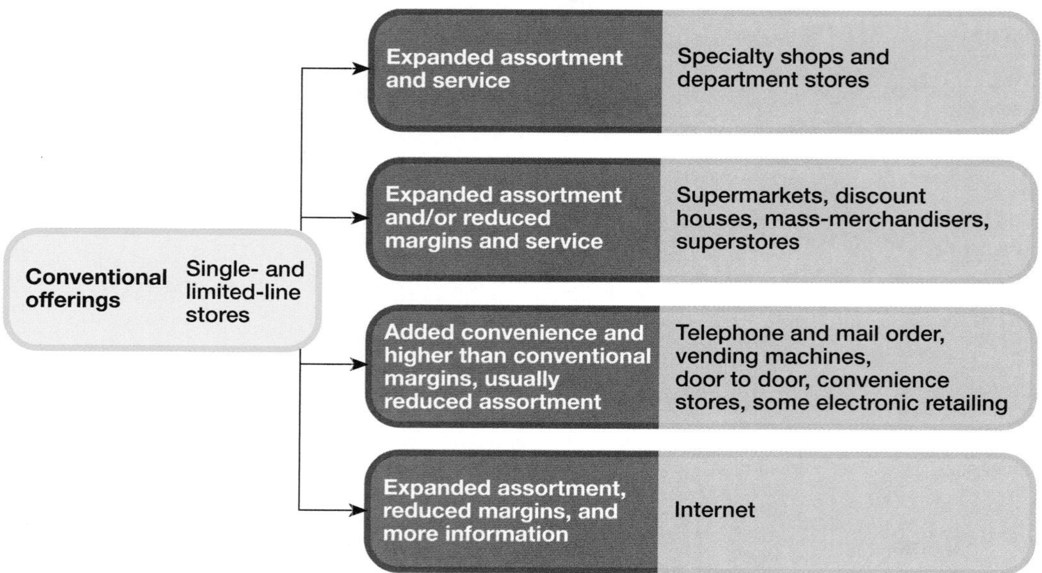

Department stores combine many limited-line stores and specialty shops

Department stores are larger stores that are organized into many separate departments and offer many product lines. Each department is like a separate limited-line store and handles a wide variety of shopping products—such as men's wear or housewares. They are usually strong in customer services—including credit, merchandise return, delivery, and sales help.

Department stores are still a major force in big cities. But in the U.S., the number of department stores, the average sales per store, and their share of retail business has declined continuously since the 1970s. Well-run limited-line stores compete with good service and often carry the same brands. In the U.S. and many other countries, mass-merchandising retailers have posed an even bigger threat.[5]

Evolution of Mass-Merchandising Retailers

Mass-merchandising is different from conventional retailing

Conventional retailers think that demand in their area is fixed—and they have a "buy low and sell high" philosophy. Many modern retailers reject these ideas. They accept the **mass-merchandising concept**—which says that retailers should offer low prices to get faster turnover and greater sales volumes—by appealing to larger markets. The mass-merchandising concept applies to many types of retailers—including both those that operate stores and those that sell online. But to understand mass-merchandising better, let's look at its evolution from the development of supermarkets and discounters to modern mass-merchandisers like Wal-Mart in the U.S., Tesco in the U.K., and Amazon.com on the Internet.

Supermarkets started the move to mass-merchandising

From a world view, most food stores are small limited-line operations. Shopping for food is inconvenient and expensive. Many Italians, for example, still go to one shop for pasta, another for meat, and yet another for milk. This may seem outdated, but most of the world's consumers don't have access to **supermarkets**—large stores specializing in groceries with self-service and wide assortments.

The basic idea for supermarkets developed in the U.S. during the 1930s Depression. Some innovators introduced self-service to cut costs but provided a broad assortment in large bare-bones stores. Profits came from large-volume sales—not from high traditional markups.[6]

Newer supermarkets carry 40,000 product items and stores average around 45,000 square feet. To be called a supermarket, a store must have annual sales of at least $2 million, but the average supermarket has annual sales of about $17 million a year. In the U.S., there are about 32,000 supermarkets and in most areas they are at the saturation level. In many other countries, however, they are just becoming a force.[7]

Modern supermarkets are planned for maximum efficiency. Scanners at checkout make it possible to carefully analyze the sales of each item and allocate more shelf space to faster-moving and higher-profit items. *Survival* depends on such efficiency. Net profits in supermarkets usually run a thin 1 percent of sales *or less!*

Some supermarket operators have opened "super warehouse" stores. These 50,000- to 100,000-square-foot stores carry more items than supermarkets, but they usually put less emphasis on perishable items like produce or meat.[8]

Discount houses upset some conventional retailers

Right after World War II, some retailers started to focus on discount prices. These **discount houses** offered "hard goods" (cameras, TVs, appliances) at substantial price cuts to customers who would go to the discounter's low-rent store, pay cash, and take care of any service or repair problems themselves. These retailers sold at 20 to 30 percent off the list price being charged by conventional retailers.

In the early 1950s, with war shortages finally over, manufacturer brands became more available. The discount houses were able to get any brands they wanted and to offer wider assortments. At this stage, many discounters turned respectable—moving to better locations and offering more services and guarantees. It was from these origins that today's mass-merchandisers developed.

Mass-merchandisers are more than discounters

Mass-merchandisers are large, self-service stores with many departments that emphasize "soft goods" (housewares, clothing, and fabrics) and staples (like health and beauty aids) but still follow the discount house's emphasis on lower margins to get faster turnover. Mass-merchandisers—like Wal-Mart and Target—have checkout counters in the front of the store and little sales help on the floor. Today the average mass-merchandiser has nearly 60,000 square feet of floor space, but many new stores are 100,000 square feet or more.

Mass-merchandisers grew rapidly—and they've become the primary nonfood place to shop for many frequently purchased consumer products. By itself, Wal-Mart handles a whopping 20 percent or more of the total national sales for whole categories of products.

Although mass-merchandisers are the driving force in much of retailing in the U.S. today, their growth rate has slowed substantially and, for future growth, they're expanding internationally.[9]

Supercenters meet all routine needs

Some supermarkets and mass-merchandisers have moved toward becoming **supercenters (hypermarkets)**—very large stores that try to carry not only food and drug items but all goods and services that the consumer purchases *routinely*. These superstores look a lot like a combination of the supermarkets, drugstores, and mass-merchandisers from which they have evolved, but the concept is different. A supercenter is trying to meet *all* the customer's routine needs at a low price. Supercenter operators include Wal-Mart, Meijer, Fred Meyer, and Super Target.

Supercenters average more than 150,000 square feet and carry about 50,000 items. Their assortment in one place is convenient, but many time-pressured consumers think that the crowds, lines, and "wandering around" time in the store are not.[10]

Although U.S. supermarkets were the first mass-merchandisers, the mass-merchandising concept has now been introduced by many retailers. Single-line mass-merchandisers like Office Depot offer selections and prices that make it difficult for traditional retailers to compete.

New mass-merchandising formats keep coming

The warehouse club is another retailing format that quickly gained popularity. Sam's Club and Costco are two of the largest. Consumers usually pay an annual membership fee to shop in these large, no-frills facilities. Among the 3,500 items per store, they carry food, appliances, yard tools, tires, and other items that many consumers see as homogeneous shopping items and want at the lowest possible price. The growth of these clubs has also been fueled by sales to small-business customers. That's why some people refer to these outlets as wholesale clubs. However, when half or more of a firm's sales are to final consumers, it is classified as a retailer, not a wholesaler.[11]

Single-line mass-merchandisers are coming on strong

Since 1980 some retailers—focusing on single product lines—have adopted the mass-merchandisers' approach with great success. Toys "R" Us pioneered this trend. Similarly, Ikea (furniture), Home Depot (home improvements), Best Buy (electronics), and Office Depot attract large numbers of customers with their large assortment and low prices in a specific product category. These stores are called category killers because it's so hard for less specialized retailers to compete.[12]

It's reasonable to think about the move to 24-hour-a-day online selling—by the established retailers, new firms that never relied on stores, or both—as a next step in the evolution of mass-merchandising. But we'll have a more complete basis for evaluating the strengths and limitations of selling and shopping on the Web if we first look at some retailers who have targeted consumers who want more convenience, even if the price is higher.

Some Retailers Focus on Added Convenience

Convenience (food) stores must have the right assortment

Convenience (food) stores are a convenience-oriented variation of the conventional limited-line food stores. Instead of expanding their assortment, however, convenience stores limit their stock to pickup or fill-in items like bread, milk, beer,

and eat-on-the-go snacks. Many also sell gas. Stores such as 7-Eleven and Stop-N-Go aim to fill consumers' needs between major shopping trips to a supermarket. They often charge prices 10 to 20 percent higher than nearby supermarkets.[13]

Vending machines are convenient

Automatic vending is selling and delivering products through vending machines. Vending machine sales account for only about 1.5 percent of total U.S. retail sales. Yet for some target markets this retailing method can't be ignored.

The major disadvantage to automatic vending is high cost. The machines are expensive to buy, stock, and repair relative to the volume they sell. So vendors must charge higher prices.[14]

Shop at home—in a variety of ways

In-home shopping in the U.S. started in the pioneer days with **door-to-door selling**—a salesperson going directly to the consumer's home. Variations on this approach are still important for firms like Amway and Mary Kay. It meets some consumers' need for convenient personal attention. It is also growing in popularity in some international markets, like China, where it provides salespeople with a good income. In the U.S., it now accounts for less than 1 percent of retail sales. It's getting harder to find someone at home during the day.

On the other hand, time-pressured dual-career families are a prime target market for **telephone and direct-mail retailing** that allows consumers to shop at home—usually placing orders by mail or a toll-free long-distance telephone call and charging the purchase to a credit card. Typically, catalogs and ads on TV let customers see the offerings, and purchases are delivered by UPS. Some consumers really like this convenience—especially for products not available in local stores.

This approach reduces costs by using computer mailing lists to target specific customers and by using warehouse-type buildings and limited sales help. And shoplifting—a big expense for most retailers—isn't a problem. In recent years, many of these firms have faced increased competition, slower sales growth, and lower profits. However, the Internet is opening up new growth opportunities for many of these firms.[15]

Many retailers are looking for ways to make shopping faster and more convenient. With Mobil's SpeedPass system, a miniature electronic device identifies the driver and turns on the pump; the customer doesn't even need a credit card.

Put the catalog on cable TV or computer

QVC, Home Shopping Network, and others are succeeding by devoting cable TV channels to home shopping. Some experts think that the coming explosion in the number of available cable channels and interactive cable services will make sales from this approach grow even faster. In addition, QVC has opened a major website on the Internet. However, selling on the Internet is turning into something much more than just a variation of selling on TV or from a catalog.[16]

Retailing on the Internet

Most mass-merchandisers now sell on the Web, so one could view that development as just another aspect of how low-margin sellers try to appeal to a large target market with wide assortments at discount prices. Or one might view the Internet as just another way to add convenient in-home shopping, with an electronic catalog and ordering on a remote computer. After all, that's the way most people saw pre-Internet dial-up systems such as Prodigy—a joint venture between Sears and IBM that fizzled because it was too complicated.

Yet both of these views are incomplete and probably misleading. Rather than just treat it as a new way that some types of retailers are incrementally varying their old strategies, let's look at what is *really* different about it.

It's still in its infancy

Internet retailing is still in the growth stages. On the one hand, Internet usage and consumer e-commerce sales have grown at a fast rate. In 1997, consumers spent about $2.7 billion on the Internet. To put that in perspective, it took about 3 percent of Wal-Mart's stores to rack up the same sales. By 2001 that number leaped to about $144 billion. But don't confuse the effect that the Internet may have on retailing with the reality of its immediate economic impact. So far, it accounts for less than 5 percent of retailing sales dollars. So in absolute dollars, retailing on the Internet is in its infancy. Thus, it's useful to consider what's different about it today and how it will evolve. See Exhibit 12-2.

Moving information versus moving goods

Stripped to its essence, the Internet dramatically lowers the cost of communication while making it faster. The Internet produces the biggest gains in businesses where better information flows result in more efficiency. That's what happens in much online B2B e-commerce. On the other hand, Place decisions for consumer markets need to deal with the challenge of getting many small purchases to the *consumer's* place. Much of the investment in Internet retailing systems has been directed toward moving information (like orders), not physical goods. It takes, for

Exhibit 12-2 Some Illustrative Differences between Online and In-Store Shopping

Characteristics	Online Shopping	In-Store Shopping
Customer characteristics	Younger, better educated, more upscale	Cross section; depends on store
Day-of-week emphasis	Higher percent of purchases during weekdays	Higher percent of purchases on the weekend
Customer service	Weak but improving	Varies, but usually better than online
Products purchased	More emphasis on one-time purchases	More emphasis on routine purchases
Availability of product	Not available for inspection or immediate use	Usually available for inspection and immediate use
Comparative information about products	Much more extensive, but sometimes poorly organized	Often weak (for example, limited to what is on packages)
Entertainment value	A media experience	Often a social experience
Charges	Product prices often lower, but shipping and handling costly	Product prices and taxes higher, but usually no delivery expense
Shopping hours and preparation	Completely flexible if online access is available	Depends on store and available transportation

example, about $20 million to build a world-class website for consumer e-commerce. But it costs about $150 million to build a distribution center and systems to support a large-scale consumer web operation. Therefore, much of the attention so far has been on the "front door" of the Internet "store" and not on the back end of retailing operations where more of the big costs accumulate.

The investment and innovations will come into balance over time, just as they have with other retailing innovations. But demand is what will shape investments in new supply capabilities. So far, the basic patterns of consumer demand have not changed that much.

Convenience takes on new meanings

Traditional thinking about retail stores looked at shopping conveniences from the perspective of product assortments and location. On the Internet, by contrast, a consumer can get to a very wide assortment, perhaps from different sellers, by clicking from one website to another. The assortment moves toward being unlimited.

But the Internet makes shopping inconvenient in other ways. You have to plan ahead. You can't touch a product. When you buy something, you've actually just ordered it and you don't have it to use. Someone else has to deliver it, and that involves delays and costs.

Surfing around the Internet is convenient for people who are facile with computers, but many consumers are not. At present, people who actually shop on the Web are better educated, younger, and more well to do. It should be no surprise that the majority of retail dollars spent on the Internet are for computer-related stuff. That target market visits the Internet store. But many people don't.

Of course, use of the Internet is growing. Cable and telephone companies are in a race to provide more consumers with faster access. WebTV already makes it easy, but it is just the start. Costs will continue to come down.

More and less information at the same time

On the Internet a consumer can't really inspect a product. Many consumers see that as a disadvantage. On the other hand, in a retail store it's often hard to get good information. At a website detailed product information is usually just a mouse-click away.

Why eToys.com Is eToys.Gone

eToys was founded in 1997 with the dream of becoming the premier site on the Internet for the kids' product market. Many investors bought into its vision of unlimited growth; at one time its stock market value was 35 percent greater than its long-established profitable competitor, Toys "R" Us. eToys did deliver in producing one of the slickest e-commerce websites. Parents could search for toys by age group or theme or product. Kids could create and send "gift wish lists." But eToys failed to consider some basic marketing ideas. For example, toys are a mature category, so a user-friendly website doesn't increase total consumer demand. eToys also underestimated how competitors would react to its plan to take most of their customers—which is what it would have taken to even cover eToys' costs. Wal-Mart copied some of eToys' best ideas but also had the buying clout to create its own brands and sell toys cheaper. Toys "R" Us teamed up with Amazon. Worse, eToys assumed that once it got customers to its site—by spending huge amounts on advertising—those customers would be loyal. When 5 percent of its orders didn't go out on time during the 1999 holiday season, customers bolted. Every parent who let a kid down told everyone they knew. When eToys tried to improve its distribution systems, costs spiraled out of control because of the hassles of handling breakable toys that come in all sorts of sizes and shapes. In the end, the total costs of efforts were so high that it would have taken four or five years of constantly improving sales just to break even on operations—say nothing about making up millions in losses. You can build a better mousetrap, but if it doesn't meet customer needs at a profit you're in trouble.[17]

It's also possible to access a much broader array of information. Ziff-Davis Publishing, for example, has a comprehensive website (www.zdnet.com) with product reviews, feature comparisons, and performance tests on almost every computer-related product. Similar sites exist for everything from automobiles to vitamins. Better information can make many consumers better shoppers, even if they buy in a store rather than online. That's what many web surfers do now. That reduces the risk of not getting what they thought they were buying and the hassles of returning it if there's a problem.

More powerful computers are also opening up many more possibilities for multimedia information—pictures, product-demo videos, and audio explanations.

The Internet is also a good medium for video-conferencing. Many computers now come with a videocam. So, in the future, it will be easier for a consumer to get help from a real person while at a website. Many failed dot-com retailers figured out too late that cutting costs by dropping human customer service support was a big mistake. They ignored the lessons learned by mass-merchandisers when they tried to do the same thing in their early days.

Lost in the "aisles" of the Internet

If you know what you want, you can usually find it fast on the Internet. You can look for "Revo sunglasses" and get a list of sellers and see pictures of every style made. However, you may get too much information or the wrong information when you do a search. So, there will need to be better "virtual malls"—databases with lots of information that can be viewed lots of ways—to make it easier to get information you want and avoid the irrelevant clutter.

Internet

Internet Exercise INTERSHOP Communications develops and sells software that companies use to create "virtual stores" for Internet retailing. For example, it allows a seller to create an online catalog that is easy for consumers to use, and it has tools for analyzing sales and keeping track of customers. Go to the firm's website (www.intershop.com) and select *Products* and then *Enfinity*. Review the information provided. Do you think it would be easier for consumers if all Internet sellers used a common system, such as this one, rather than coming up with many different arrangements? Briefly explain your thinking.

The costs are still deceptive

The Internet makes it easy to compare prices from different sellers. That is putting price pressure on Internet sellers who have not figured out how else to differentiate what they offer. For more expensive items, a discount price may offset

Many established retailers, like Barnes & Noble, are trying to figure out how to combine "clicks and mortar" to meet consumers' needs better than would be possible with only an online website or only a store.

delivery costs. That often isn't the case with less expensive items. Low-cost ways of handling post-purchase deliveries need to be developed for the Internet to be really practical for everyday purchases. We'll return to this issue at the end of the chapter. For now, though, we should note that a large number of people are working on that problem. Some firms have partial solutions. For example, in England Tesco sells groceries from a website and delivers them within 24 hours. But other firms, like Webvan, collapsed under the problems of trying to do that in a way that satisfies consumers' needs.

Another cost occurs if a product must be returned. That, of course, assumes you get what you order. The Internet is the ultimate weapon for fly-by-night operators. Fraud is already a big problem.

Competitive effects will influence other retailers

Retailers of every type are experimenting with selling on the Internet. They range from department stores like Bloomingdale's to discounters like Target to limited-line retailers like Virtual Vineyards (wine) to service providers like American Express.

None of these retailers knows what longer-term impact Internet selling will have on their markets. However, as new retailing formats and concepts are refined, they increase the competitive pressure on existing companies.[18]

Why Retailers Evolve and Change

The wheel of retailing keeps rolling

The **wheel of retailing theory** says that new types of retailers enter the market as low-status, low-margin, low-price operators and then—if successful—evolve into more conventional retailers offering more services with higher operating costs and higher prices. Then they're threatened by new low-status, low-margin, low-price retailers—and the wheel turns again. Department stores, supermarkets, and mass-merchandisers went through this cycle. Some Internet sellers are on this path.

The wheel of retailing theory, however, doesn't explain all major retailing developments. Vending machines entered as high-cost, high-margin operations. Convenience food stores are high-priced. Suburban shopping centers don't emphasize low

Some manufacturers have always had outlet stores near their factories, but outlet malls are emerging as a new retailing format that is popular with some consumers.

price. Current retailers who are adding websites are likely to face competitors who cut operating expenses even deeper.

Scrambled merchandising—mixing product lines for higher profits

Conventional retailers tend to specialize by product line. But most modern retailers are moving toward **scrambled merchandising**—carrying any product lines they think they can sell profitably. Supermarkets and drugstores sell anything they can move in volume—panty hose, phone cards, one-hour photo processing, motor oil, potted plants, and computer software. Mass-merchandisers don't just sell everyday items but also cellular phones, computer printers, and jewelry.[19]

Product life cycle concept applies to retailer types too

A retailer with a new idea may have big profits—for a while. But if it's a really good idea, the retailer can count on speedy imitation and a squeeze on profits. Other retailers will copy the new format or scramble their product mix to sell products that offer them higher margins or faster turnover. That puts pressure on the original firm to change or lose its market.

Some conventional retailers are in decline as these life and death cycles continue. Recent innovators, like the Internet merchants, are still in the market growth stage. See Exhibit 12-3. Some retailing formats that are mature in the United States are only now beginning to grow in other countries.

Ethical issues may arise

Most retailers face intense competitive pressure. The desperation that comes with such pressure has pushed some retailers toward questionable marketing practices.

Critics argue, for example, that retailers too often advertise special sale items to bring price-sensitive shoppers into the store or to a website but then don't stock enough to meet demand. Other retailers are criticized for pushing consumers to trade up to more expensive items. What is ethical and unethical in situations like these, however, is subject to debate. Retailers can't always anticipate demand perfectly, and deliveries may not arrive on time. Similarly, trading up may be a sensible part of a strategy—if it's done honestly.

The marketing concept should guide firms away from unethical treatment of customers. However, a retailer on the edge of going out of business may lose perspective on the need to satisfy customers.[20]

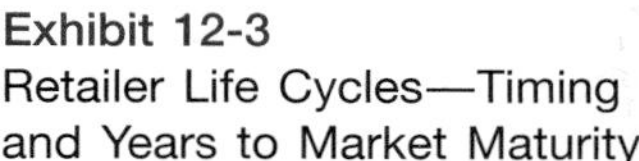

Exhibit 12-3
Retailer Life Cycles—Timing and Years to Market Maturity

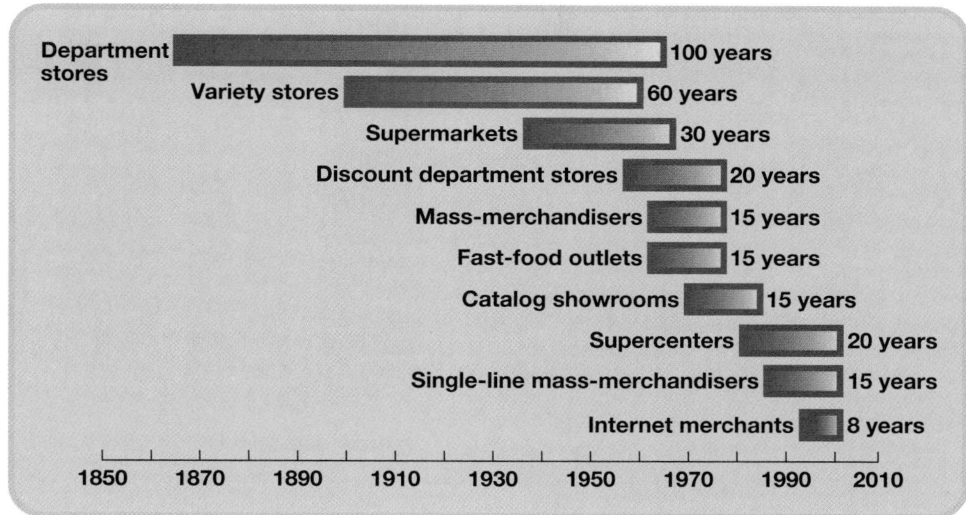

Retailer Size and Profits

A few big retailers do most of the business

The large number of retailers (1,113,137) might suggest that retailing is a field of small businesses. To some extent this is true. As shown in Exhibit 12-4, when the last census of retailers was published over 62 percent of all the retail stores in the United States had annual sales of less than $1 million. But that's only part of the story. Those same retailers accounted for only about 10 cents of every $1 in retail sales!

The larger retail stores—those selling more than $5 million annually—do most of the business. Less than 10 percent of the retail stores are this big, yet they account for over 65 percent of all retail sales. Many small retailers are being squeezed out of business.[21]

Big chains are building market clout

The main way for a retailer to achieve economies of scale is with a corporate chain. A **corporate chain** is a firm that owns and manages more than one store—and often it's many. Chains have grown rapidly and now account for about half of all retail sales. You can expect chains to continue to grow and take business from independent stores.

Large chains use central buying for different stores. They take advantage of quantity discounts or opportunities to develop their own efficient distribution centers. They use computer networks to control inventory costs and stock-outs. They may also spread promotion, information technology, and management costs to many stores. Retail chains also have their own dealer brands.[22]

Independents form chains too

Competitive pressure from corporate chains encouraged the development of both cooperative chains and voluntary chains. **Cooperative chains** are retailer-sponsored groups—formed by independent retailers—that run their own buying organizations and conduct joint promotion efforts. Cooperative chains face a tough battle. Some, like True Value Hardware, are still adapting as they identify the weakness of corporate chains. For example, ads remind consumers that they don't need to waste a half-hour lost in a big store to pick up some simple item.

Voluntary chains are wholesaler-sponsored groups that work with "independent" retailers. Some are linked by contracts stating common operating procedures and requiring the use of common storefront designs, store names, and joint promotion efforts. Examples include SuperValu in groceries and Ace in hardware.

Exhibit 12-4 Distribution of Stores by Size and Share of Total U.S. Retail Sales

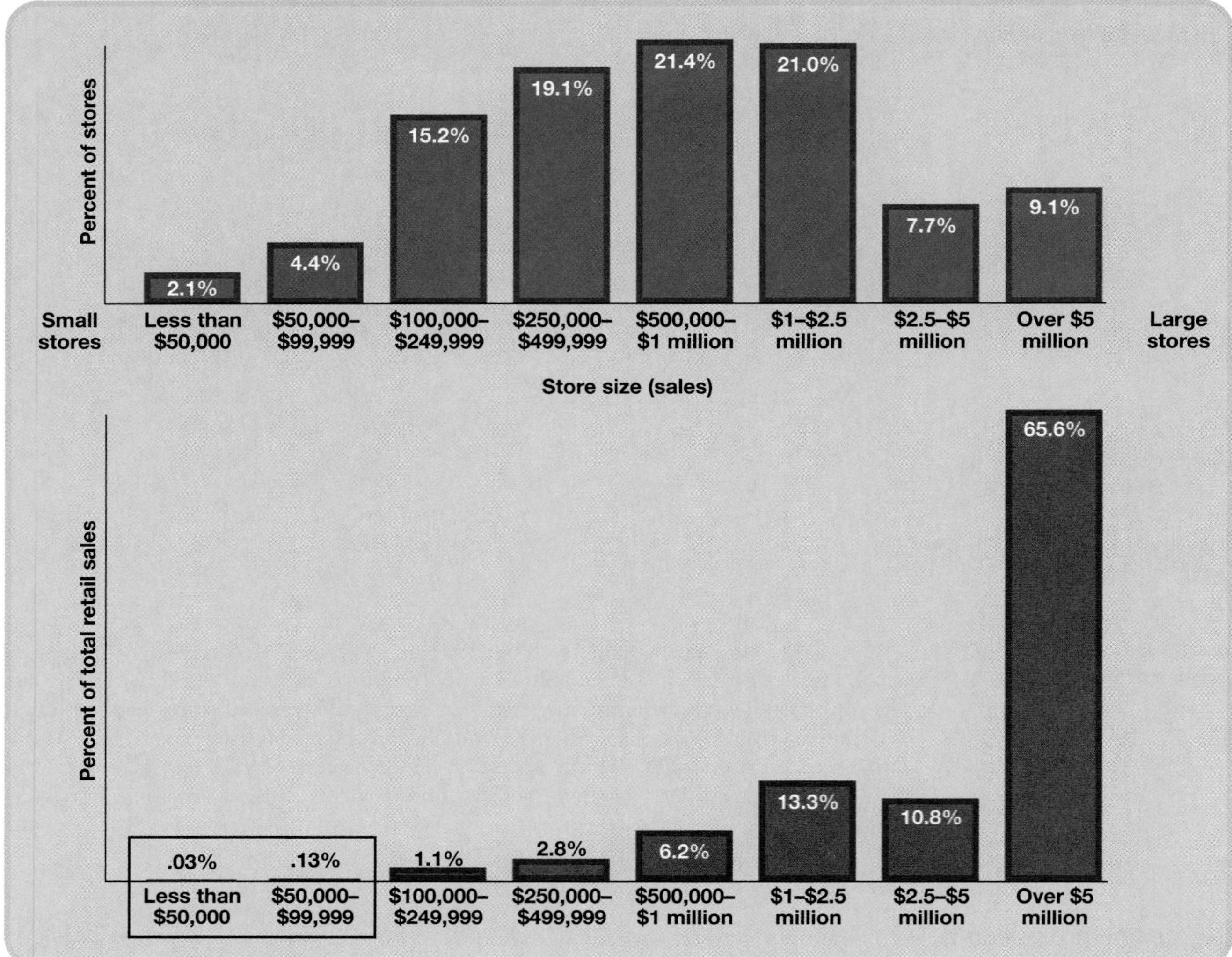

Franchisors form chains too

In a **franchise operation,** the franchisor develops a good marketing strategy, and the retail franchise holders carry out the strategy in their own units. Each franchise holder benefits from its relationship with the larger company and its experience, buying power, promotion, and image. In return, the franchise holder usually signs a contract to pay fees and commission and to strictly follow franchise rules designed to continue the successful strategy.

Franchise holders' sales account for about half of all retail sales. One reason is that franchising is especially popular with service retailers, a fast-growing sector of the economy.[23]

Differences in Retailing in Different Nations

New ideas spread across countries

New retailing approaches that succeed in one part of the world are often quickly adapted to other countries. Self-service approaches that started with supermarkets in the United States are now found in retail operations worldwide. The supercenter concept, on the other hand, initially developed in Europe.

Some mass-merchandiser chains, like Tesco in the U.K., are looking for growth by opening small stores—which will put even more pressure on conventional retailers.

Mass-merchandising requires mass markets

The low prices, selections, and efficient operations offered by mass-merchandisers might be attractive to consumers everywhere. But consumers in less-developed nations often don't have the income to support mass distribution. The small shops that survive in these economies sell in very small quantities, often to a small number of consumers.

Some countries block change

The political and legal environment severely limits the evolution of retailing in some nations. Japan is a prime example. For years its Large Store Law—aimed at protecting the country's politically powerful small shopkeepers—has been a real barrier to retail change. The law restricts development of large stores by requiring special permits, which are routinely denied.

Japan is taking steps to change the Large Store Law. Even so, most experts believe that it will be years before Japan moves away from its system of small, limited-line shops.[24]

What Is a Wholesaler?

It's hard to define what a wholesaler is because there are so many different wholesalers doing different jobs. Some of their activities may even seem like manufacturing. As a result, some wholesalers describe themselves as "manufacturer and dealer." Some like to identify themselves with such general terms as *merchant, jobber, dealer,* or *distributor.* And others just take the name commonly used in their trade—without really thinking about what it means.

To avoid a long technical discussion on the nature of wholesaling, we'll use the U.S. Bureau of the Census definition:

Wholesaling is concerned with the *activities* of those persons or establishments that sell to retailers and other merchants, and/or to industrial, institutional, and commercial users, but that do not sell in large amounts to final consumers.

So **wholesalers** are firms whose main function is providing wholesaling activities. Wholesalers sell to all of the different types of organizational customers shown in Exhibit 6-1.

Wholesaling activities are just variations of the basic marketing functions—gathering and providing information, buying and selling, grading, storing, transporting, financing, and risk taking—we discussed in Chapter 1. You can understand wholesalers' strategies better if you look at them as members of channels. They add value by doing jobs for their customers and for their suppliers.

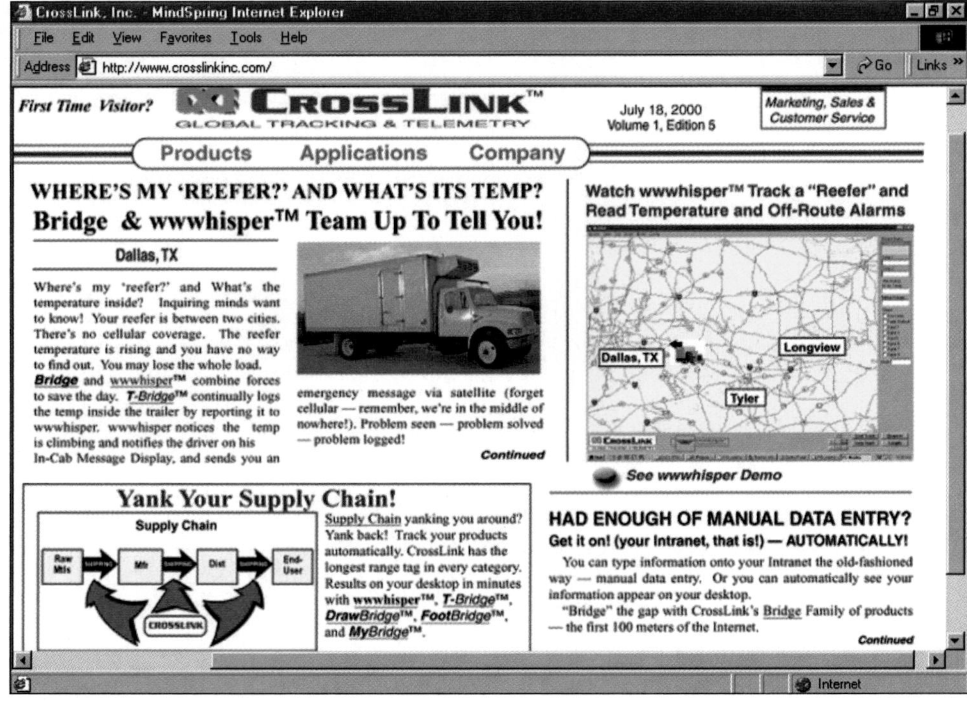

Many modern wholesalers are adopting new technologies to become more effective. For example, CrossLink's satellite communication system tracks the temperature of refrigerated deliveries and notifies the central office if there is any risk that products will be spoiled.

Wholesaling Is Changing with the Times

A hundred years ago wholesalers dominated distribution channels in the United States and most other countries. The many small producers and small retailers needed their services. This situation still exists in less-developed economies. However, in the developed nations, as producers became larger many bypassed the wholesalers. Similarly, large retail chains often take control of functions that had been handled by wholesalers. Now e-commerce is making it easier for producers and customers to "connect" without having a wholesaler in the middle of the exchange.

In light of these changes, many people have predicted a gloomy future for wholesalers. In the 1970s and 1980s that seemed to be the pattern. Now, however, many wholesalers are adapting rapidly and finding new ways to add value in the channel. For example, some of the biggest B2B e-commerce sites on the Internet are wholesaler operations. And many wholesalers are enjoying significant growth.

Producing profits, not chasing orders

Progressive wholesalers are becoming more concerned with channel relationships. Many are using technology to offer better service. Others develop voluntary chains that bind them more closely to their customers.

Modern wholesalers no longer require all customers to pay for all the services they offer simply because certain customers use them. Many offer a basic service at minimum cost—then charge additional fees for any special services required. They've also streamlined their operations to cut unnecessary costs and improve profits. In fact, wholesalers pioneered many of the logistics innovations we discussed in Chapter 11. They use computers to track inventory and reorder only when it's really needed. Computerized sales analysis helps them identify and drop unprofitable products and customers. This sometimes leads to a selective distribution policy. Then they can fine-tune how they add value for their profitable customers.

Perhaps good-bye to some

Not all wholesalers are progressive, and some less efficient ones will fail. Efficiency and low cost, however, are not all that's needed for success. Some wholesalers will disappear as the functions they provided in the past are shifted and shared in different ways in the channel. Cost-conscious buyers for Wal-Mart, Lowe's, and other chains are refusing to deal with some of the middlemen who represent small producers. They want to negotiate directly with the producer. Similarly, producers see advantages in having closer direct relationships with fewer suppliers—and they're paring out weaker vendors. Efficient delivery services like UPS are also making it easy for many producers to ship directly to their customers—even ones in foreign markets. The Internet is putting pressure on wholesalers whose primary role is providing information to bring buyers and sellers together.[25]

Is it an ethical issue?

All of this is squeezing some wholesalers out of business. Some critics—including many of the wounded wholesalers—argue that it's unethical for powerful suppliers or customers to simply cut out wholesalers who spend money and time, perhaps decades, developing markets.

For example, Amana notified Cooper Distributing Co. that it intended to cancel their distribution agreement in 10 days. Cooper had handled Amana appliances for 30 years, and Amana products represented 85 percent of Cooper's sales. Amana's explanation to Cooper? "We just think we can do it better."

Situations like this arise often. They may be cold-hearted, but are they unethical? We argue that it isn't fair to cut off the relationship with such short notice. But most wholesalers realize that their business is *always* at risk—if they don't perform channel functions better or cheaper than their suppliers or customers can do themselves.[26]

Survivors will need effective strategies

The wholesalers who do survive will need to be efficient, but that doesn't mean they'll all have low costs. Some wholesalers' higher operating expenses result from the strategies they select—including the special services they offer to *some* customers.

Wholesalers Add Value in Different Ways

Exhibit 12-5 compares the number, sales volume, and operating expenses of some major types of wholesalers. The differences in operating expenses suggest that each of these types performs, or does not perform, certain wholesaling functions. But which ones and why? And why do manufacturers use merchant wholesalers—costing 14.1 percent of sales—when agent middlemen cost only 4.2 percent?

Exhibit 12-5 U.S. Wholesale Trade by Type of Wholesale Operation

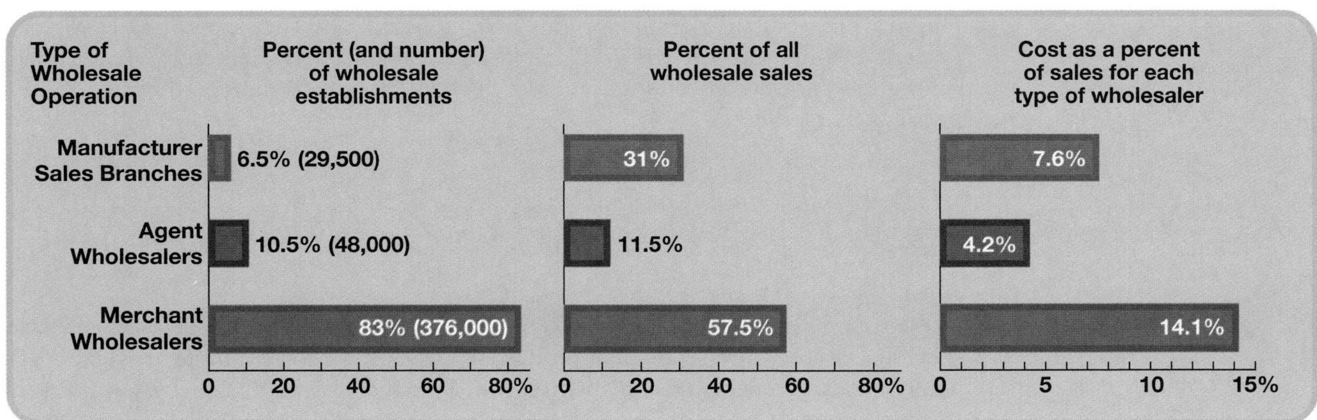

Exhibit 12-6 Types of Wholesalers

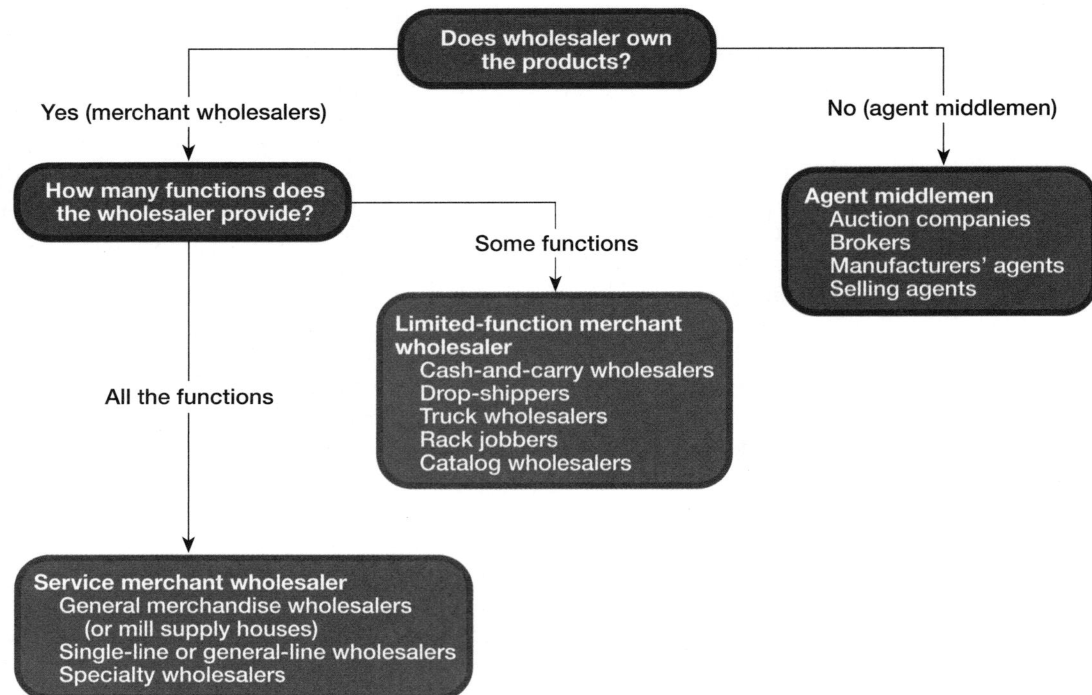

To answer these questions, we must understand what these wholesalers do and don't do. Exhibit 12-6 gives a big-picture view of the major types of wholesalers we'll be discussing. Note that a major difference between merchant and agent wholesalers is whether they *own* the products they sell. Before discussing these wholesalers, we'll briefly consider producers who handle their own wholesaling activities.

Manufacturers' sales branches are considered wholesalers

Manufacturers who just take over some wholesaling activities are not considered wholesalers. However, when they have **manufacturers' sales branches**—warehouses that producers set up at separate locations away from their factories—they're classified as wholesalers by the U.S. Census Bureau and by government agencies in many other countries.

In the United States, these manufacturer-owned branch operations account for about 6.5 percent of wholesale facilities—but they handle 31 percent of total wholesale sales. One reason sales per branch are so high is that the branches are usually placed in the best market areas. This helps explain why their operating costs, as a percent of sales, are often lower. It's also easier for a manufacturer to coordinate information and logistics functions with its own branch operations than with independent wholesalers.[27]

Merchant Wholesalers Are the Most Numerous

Merchant wholesalers own (take title to) the products they sell. They often specialize by certain types of products or customers. For example, Fastenal is a wholesaler that specializes in distributing threaded fasteners used by a variety of manufacturers. It owns (takes title to) the fasteners for some period before selling

Merchant wholesalers in Africa are often smaller, carry narrower product lines, and deal with fewer customers than their counterparts in North America.

to its customers. If you think all merchant wholesalers are fading away, Fastenal is proof that they can serve a needed role. In the last decade Fastenal's profits have grown at about the same pace as Microsoft's.

Internet

Internet Exercise Check out the different aspects of the Fastenal website (www.fastenal.com). Give examples of ways that the website is intended to help Fastenal's customers and suppliers.

Exhibit 12-5 shows that over 80 percent of the wholesaling establishments in the United States are merchant wholesalers—and they handle over 57 percent of wholesale sales. Merchant wholesalers are even more common in other countries. Japan is an extreme example. Products are often bought and sold by a series of merchant wholesalers on their way to the business user or retailer.[28]

Service wholesalers provide all the functions

Service wholesalers are merchant wholesalers who provide all the wholesaling functions. Within this basic group are three types: (1) general merchandise, (2) single-line, and (3) specialty.

General merchandise wholesalers are service wholesalers who carry a wide variety of nonperishable items such as hardware, electrical supplies, drugs, cosmetics, and automobile equipment. With their broad line of convenience and shopping products, they serve hardware stores, drugstores, and small department stores. *Mill supply houses* operate in a similar way, but they carry a broad variety of accessories and supplies to serve the needs of manufacturers.

Single-line (or general-line) wholesalers are service wholesalers who carry a narrower line of merchandise than general merchandise wholesalers. For example, they might carry only food, apparel, or certain types of industrial tools or supplies. In consumer products, they serve the single- and limited-line stores. In business products, they cover a wider geographic area and offer more specialized service.

Specialty wholesalers are service wholesalers who carry a very narrow range of products and offer more information and service than other service wholesalers. A consumer products specialty wholesaler might carry only health foods or oriental foods instead of a full line of groceries. Some limited-line and specialty wholesalers are growing by helping independent retailer-customers find better ways to compete

3M produces 1,600 products that are used by auto body repair shops in the U.S., Europe, Japan, and other countries. To reach this target market, 3M works with hundreds of specialty wholesalers.

with mass-merchandisers. But in general, many consumer products wholesalers have been hit hard by the growth of retail chains that set up their own distribution centers and deal directly with producers.

A specialty wholesaler of business products might limit itself to fields requiring special technical knowledge or service. Richardson Electronics is an interesting example. It specializes in distributing replacement parts, such as electron tubes, for old equipment that many manufacturers still use on the factory floor. Many of its customers operate in countries where new technologies are not yet common, but Richardson gives them easy access to information from its website (www.rell.com) and makes its products available quickly by stocking them in locations around the world.[29]

Limited-function wholesalers provide some functions

Limited-function wholesalers provide only *some* wholesaling functions. In the following paragraphs, we briefly discuss the main features of these wholesalers. Although less numerous in some countries, these wholesalers are very important for some products.

Cash-and-carry wholesalers want cash

Cash-and-carry wholesalers operate like service wholesalers—except that the customer must pay cash. In the U.S., big warehouse clubs have taken much of this business. But cash-and-carry operators are common in less-developed nations where very small retailers handle the bulk of retail transactions.

Drop-shippers do not handle the products

Drop-shippers own (take title to) the products they sell—but they do *not* actually handle, stock, or deliver them. These wholesalers are mainly involved in selling. They get orders and pass them on to producers. Then the producer ships the order directly to the customer. Drop-shippers commonly sell bulky products (like lumber) for which additional handling would be expensive and possibly damaging. Drop-shippers in the U.S. are already feeling the squeeze from buyers and sellers connecting directly via the Internet. But the progressive ones are fighting back by setting up their own websites and getting fees for referrals.

Truck wholesalers deliver—at a cost

Truck wholesalers specialize in delivering products that they stock in their own trucks. Their big advantage is that they promptly deliver perishable products that regular wholesalers prefer not to carry. A 7-Eleven store that runs out of potato chips on a busy Friday night doesn't want to be out of stock all weekend!

Rack jobbers sell hard-to-handle assortments

Rack jobbers specialize in hard-to-handle assortments of products that a retailer doesn't want to manage—and rack jobbers usually display the products on their own wire racks. For example, a grocery store or mass-merchandiser might rely on a rack jobber to decide which paperback books or magazines it sells. The wholesaler knows which titles sell in the local area and applies that knowledge in many stores.

Catalog wholesalers reach outlying areas

Catalog wholesalers sell out of catalogs that may be distributed widely to smaller industrial customers or retailers who might not be called on by other middlemen. Customers place orders at a website or by mail, e-mail, fax, or telephone. These wholesalers sell lines such as hardware, jewelry, sporting goods, and computers. For example, Inmac uses a catalog that is printed in six languages and a website (www.inmac.com) to sell a complete line of computer accessories. Many of these customers don't have a local wholesaler, but they can place orders from anywhere in the world. Most catalog wholesalers quickly adapted to the Internet. But they're facing more competition too; the Internet allows customers to compare prices from more sources of supply.[30]

Agent Middlemen Are Strong on Selling

They don't own the products

Agent middlemen are wholesalers who do *not* own the products they sell. Their main purpose is to help in buying and selling. Agent middlemen normally specialize by customer type and by product or product line. But they usually provide even fewer functions than the limited-function wholesalers. They operate at relatively low cost—sometimes 2 to 6 percent of their selling price—or less in the case of website-based agents who simply bring buyers and sellers together. Worldwide, the role of agent middlemen is rapidly being transformed by the Internet. Those who didn't get on board this fast-moving train were left behind.

They are important in international trade

Agent middlemen are common in international trade. Many markets have only a few well-financed merchant wholesalers. The best many producers can do is get local representation through agents and then arrange financing through banks that specialize in international trade.

Agent middlemen are usually experts on local business customs and regulations in their own countries. Sometimes a marketing manager can't work through a foreign government's red tape without the help of a local agent.

Manufacturers' agents—free-wheeling sales reps

A **manufacturers' agent** sells similar products for several noncompeting producers—for a commission on what is actually sold. Such agents work almost as members of each company's sales force—but they're really independent middlemen. More than half of all agent middlemen are manufacturers' agents.

Their big plus is that they already call on some customers and can add another product line at relatively low cost—and at no cost to the producer until something sells!

Agents can be especially useful for introducing new products. For this service, they may earn 10 to 15 percent commission. (In contrast, their commission on large-volume established products may be quite low—perhaps only 2 percent.) A 10 to 15 percent commission rate may seem small for a new product with low sales. Once a product sells well, however, a producer may think the rate is high and begin using its own sales reps.

Export or import agents are basically manufacturers' agents who specialize in international trade. These agent middlemen operate in every country and help international firms adjust to unfamiliar market conditions in foreign markets.

Manufacturers' reps will continue to play an important role in businesses that need an agent to perform order-getting tasks. But manufacturers' reps everywhere

Innovative wholesalers are using multilingual bar codes to reduce costs and errors in overseas markets.

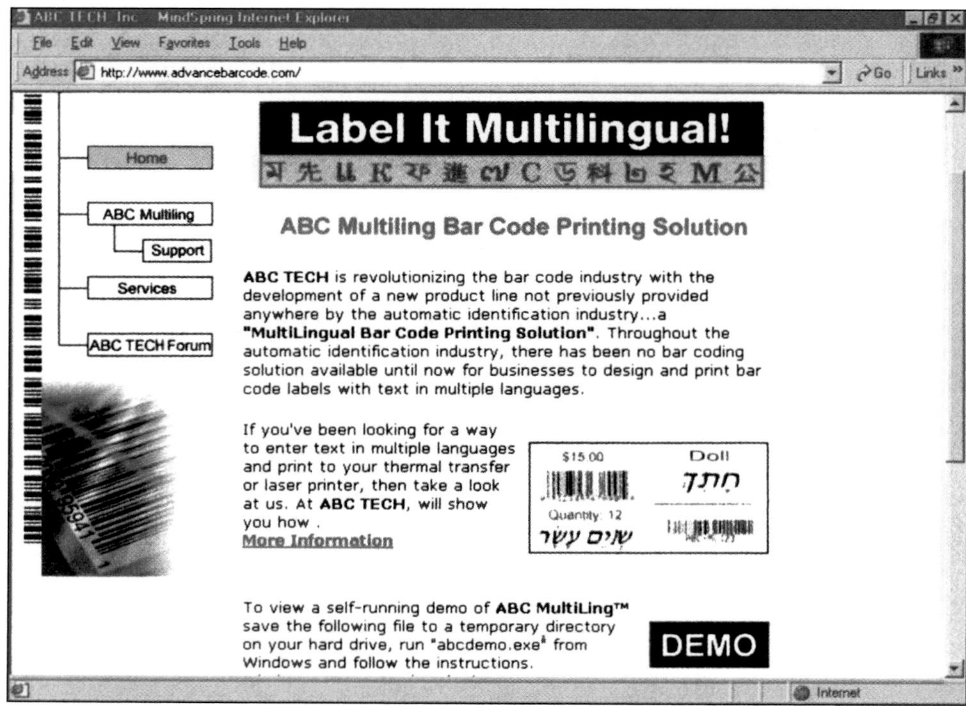

are feeling pressure when it comes to routine business contacts. More producers are turning to telephone selling, websites, e-mail, teleconferencing, and faxes to contact customers directly.[31]

Brokers provide information

Brokers bring buyers and sellers together. Brokers usually have a *temporary* relationship with the buyer and seller while a particular deal is negotiated. They are especially useful when buyers and sellers don't come into the market very often. The broker's product is information about what buyers need and what supplies are available. If the transaction is completed, they earn a commission from whichever party hired them. **Export and import brokers** operate like other brokers, but they specialize in bringing together buyers and sellers from different countries. Smart brokers quickly saw new opportunities to expand their reach by using the Internet. As the Internet causes consolidation, it will also provide more value. A smaller number of cyber-brokers will cut costs and dominate the business with larger databases of buyers and sellers.

Selling agents—almost marketing managers

Selling agents take over the whole marketing job of producers—not just the selling function. A selling agent may handle the entire output of one or more producers—even competing producers—with almost complete control of pricing, selling, and advertising. In effect, the agent becomes each producer's marketing manager.

Financial trouble is one of the main reasons a producer calls in a selling agent. The selling agent may provide working capital but may also take over the affairs of the business. But selling agents also work internationally. A **combination export manager** is a blend of manufacturers' agent and selling agent—handling the entire export function for several producers of similar but noncompeting lines.

Auction companies—speed up the sale

Auction companies provide a place where buyers and sellers can come together and bid to complete a transaction. Traditionally they were important in certain lines—such as livestock, tobacco, and used cars where demand and supply conditions change rapidly. Customer bids determine the price.

Aucnet is a good example of a progressive auction company that put the bid process on the Internet. Its very successful used car auction runs from a website (www.aucnet.com). The key to its success is that it provides bidders with a very thorough online rating of the quality of each car. Because the ratings add value, Aucnet attracts dealers from all over the country. The Internet has spurred growth of all sorts of auction companies in lines of business where auctions have previously not been common.[32]

What Will Happen to Retailers and Wholesalers in the Future?

A common theme in this chapter—and the two before it—is that channels of distribution are in the midst of dynamic changes. There have been dramatic improvements in logistics, the Internet, and e-commerce. But before all of this, the evolution of retailing and wholesaling was ongoing. Middlemen who find new and better ways to add value prosper.

A variety of firms are trying to figure out how to have a presence on the Web. Many of them are reshaping competition in the product-markets in which they compete. On the other hand, much of the initial change has simply been an adjustment to what was done in the past. The catalog becomes electronic. E-mail supplements toll-free phone orders. A retailer opens a new website instead of a new store. The technology is revolutionary and exciting, but much of what firms are doing with it so far is evolutionary.

In time, more revolutionary change may come. Imagine, for example, what it would take for you—and everyone you know—to do most of your routine shopping on the Internet. What new marketing functions would be needed, and who would provide them? Let's consider one scenario.

You put products in your virtual shopping basket at several websites. The seller assembles your items in a carton with a bar code for your personal name, address, and account. Then that carton and cartons for all of the other orders that come into that website would be quickly taken in large economical batches to an intermediary. The computer-controlled sorting system going into the intermediary's 5-acre facility would scan each carton's bar code and route it to the sorting area for a truck that serves you and each of your neighbors. After a night of accumulating all the cartons that are directed to you from different sellers, the intermediary would place the cartons on a delivery vehicle in the right sequence so they can be efficiently unloaded as the truck passes each customer on its route.[33]

Something like this probably isn't far off. Specialists will develop to make distribution *after* an Internet purchase more efficient, just as middlemen developed to make distribution more efficient *prior* to purchases in retail stores. What is described above isn't very different from what UPS does, but the cost per package is much higher than it would be if everybody got deliveries every day.

If the after-purchase distribution problem is handled, who will the seller be? Will the Internet merchants of tomorrow be an evolved form of the retailers of today? Or will current-day wholesalers be in a better position to catch that prize? Some wholesalers are already working with very large assortments. Or, in a world where you can conveniently surf from one specialized seller to another, will the breadth of assortment from any one seller be irrelevant? That could put producers in a stronger position. Perhaps none of these traditional forms of business will lead the way, but rather it will be a unique new type of specialist that is born on the Internet. The answers to these questions will take time, but already new intermediaries are coming on the scene.

Let's admit it. You can only speculate about where e-commerce will lead. But perhaps it's good to speculate a little. The way markets work in the future will depend on the creative innovations that people like you imagine, analyze, and ultimately turn into profitable marketing strategies.

Conclusion

Modern retailing is scrambled—and we'll probably see more changes in the future. In such a dynamic environment, a producer's marketing manager must choose very carefully among the available kinds of retailers. And retailers must plan their marketing mixes with their target customers' needs in mind—while at the same time becoming part of an effective channel system.

We described many types of retailers—and we saw that each has its advantages and disadvantages. We also saw that modern retailers have discarded conventional practices. The old "buy low and sell high" philosophy is no longer a safe guide. Lower margins with faster turnover is the modern philosophy as more retailers move into mass-merchandising. But even this is no guarantee of success as retailers' life cycles move on.

Growth of chains and scrambled merchandising will continue as retailing evolves to meet changing consumer demands. But important breakthroughs are possible—perhaps with the Internet—and consumers probably will continue to move away from conventional retailers.

Wholesalers can provide functions for those both above and below them in a channel of distribution. These services are closely related to the basic marketing functions. There are many types of wholesalers. Some provide all the wholesaling functions—while others specialize in only a few. Eliminating wholesalers does not eliminate the need for the functions they now provide, but technology is helping firms to perform these functions in more efficient ways.

Merchant wholesalers are the most numerous and account for the majority of wholesale sales. Their distinguishing characteristic is that they take title to (own) products. Agent middlemen, on the other hand, act more like sales representatives for sellers or buyers—and they do not take title.

Despite dire predictions, wholesalers continue to exist. The more progressive ones are adapting to a changing environment. But some less progressive wholesalers will fail. The Internet is already taking its toll. On the other hand, new types of intermediaries are evolving. Some are creating new ways of helping producers and their customers achieve their objectives by finding new ways to add value.

Questions and Problems

1. What sort of a "product" are specialty shops offering? What are the prospects for organizing a chain of specialty shops?
2. Distinguish among discount houses, price-cutting by conventional retailers, and mass-merchandising. Forecast the future of low-price selling in food, clothing, and appliances. How will the Internet affect that future?
3. Discuss a few changes in the marketing environment that you think help to explain why telephone, mail-order, and Internet retailing have been growing so rapidly.
4. What are some advantages and disadvantages to using the Internet for shopping?
5. Apply the wheel of retailing theory to your local community. What changes seem likely? Will established retailers see the need for change, or will entirely new firms have to develop?
6. What advantages does a retail chain have over a retailer who operates with a single store? Does a small retailer have any advantages in competing against a chain? Explain your answer.
7. Many producers are now seeking new opportunities in international markets. Are the opportunities for international expansion equally good for retailers? Explain your answer.
8. Discuss how computer systems affect wholesalers' and retailers' operations.

9. Consider the evolution of wholesaling in relation to the evolution of retailing. List several changes that are similar, and several that are fundamentally different.
10. Do wholesalers and retailers need to worry about new-product planning just as a producer needs to have an organized new-product development process? Explain your answer.
11. How do you think a retailer of Maytag washing machines would react if Maytag set up a website, sold direct to consumers, and shipped direct from its distribution center? Explain your thinking.
12. What risks do merchant wholesalers assume by taking title to goods? Is the size of this risk about constant for all merchant wholesalers?
13. Why would a manufacturer set up its own sales branches if established wholesalers were already available?
14. What is an agent middleman's marketing mix?
15. Why do you think that many merchant middlemen handle competing products from different producers, while manufacturers' agents usually handle only noncompeting products from different producers?
16. What alternatives does a producer have if it is trying to expand distribution in a foreign market and finds that the best existing merchant middlemen won't handle imported products?
17. Discuss the future growth and nature of wholesaling if chains, scrambled merchandising, and the Internet continue to become more important. How will wholesalers have to adjust their mixes? Will wholesalers be eliminated? If not, what wholesaling functions will be most important? Are there any particular lines of trade where wholesalers may have increasing difficulty?

Suggested Cases

10. Runners World
13. Mixed Media Technologies, Inc.
14. Modern Horizons, Inc.
15. Morgan Company
30. Aluminum Basics Co.

Computer-Aided Problem

12. Selecting Channel Intermediaries

Art Glass Productions, a producer of decorative glass gift items, wants to expand into a new territory. Managers at Art Glass know that unit sales in the new territory will be affected by consumer response to the products. But sales will also be affected by which combination of wholesalers and retailers Art Glass selects. There is a choice between two wholesalers. One wholesaler, Giftware Distributing, is a merchant wholesaler that specializes in gift items; it sells to gift shops, department stores, and some mass-merchandisers. The other wholesaler, Margaret Degan & Associates, is a manufacturers' agent that calls on many of the gift shops in the territory.

Art Glass makes a variety of glass items, but the cost of making an item is usually about the same—$5.20 a unit. The items would sell to Giftware Distributing at $12.00 each—and in turn the merchant wholesaler's price to retailers would be $14.00—leaving Giftware with a $2.00 markup to cover costs and profit. Giftware Distributing is the only reputable merchant wholesaler in the territory, and it has agreed to carry the line only if Art Glass is willing to advertise in a trade magazine aimed at retail buyers for gift items. These ads will cost $8,000 a year.

As a manufacturers' agent, Margaret Degan would cover all of her own expenses and would earn 8 percent of the $14.00 price per unit charged the gift shops. Individual orders would be shipped directly to the retail gift shops by Art Glass, using United Parcel Service (UPS). Art Glass would pay the UPS charges at an average cost of $2.00 per item. In contrast, Giftware Distributing would anticipate demand and place larger orders in advance. This would reduce the shipping costs, which Art Glass would pay, to about $.60 a unit.

Art Glass' marketing manager thinks that Degan would only be able to sell about 75 percent as many items as Giftware Distributing—since she doesn't have time to call on all of the smaller shops and doesn't call on any department stores. On the other hand, the merchant wholesaler's demand for $8,000 worth of supporting advertising requires a significant outlay.

The marketing manager at Art Glass decided to use a spreadsheet to determine how large sales would have to be to make it more profitable to work with Giftware and to see how the different channel arrangements would contribute to profits at different sales levels.

a. *Given the estimated unit sales and other values shown on the initial spreadsheet, which type of wholesaler would contribute the most profit to Art Glass Productions?*
b. *If sales in the new territory are slower than expected, so that the merchant wholesaler was able to sell only 3,000 units—or the agent 2,250 units—which wholesaler would contribute the most to Art Glass' profits? (Note: Assume that the merchant wholesaler only buys what it can sell; that is, it doesn't carry extra inventory beyond what is needed to meet demand.)*
c. *Prepare a table showing how the two wholesalers' contributions to profit compare as the quantity sold varies from 3,500 units to 4,500 units for the merchant wholesaler and 75 percent of these numbers for the manufacturers' agent. Discuss these results. (Note: Use the results feature to vary the quantity sold by the merchant wholesaler, and the program will compute 75 percent of that quantity as the estimate of what the agent will sell.)*

For additional questions related to this problem, see Exercise 12-4 in the *Learning Aid for Use with Essentials of Marketing*, 9th edition.

When You Finish This Chapter, You Should

1. Know the advantages and disadvantages of the promotion methods a marketing manager can use in strategy planning.

2. Understand the integrated marketing communications concept and why most firms use a blend of different promotion methods.

3. Understand the importance of promotion objectives.

4. Know how the communication process affects promotion planning.

5. Understand how direct-response promotion is helping marketers develop more targeted promotion blends.

6. Understand how new customer-initiated interactive communication is different.

7. Know how typical promotion plans are blended to get an extra push from middlemen and help from customers in pulling products through the channel.

8. Understand how promotion blends typically vary over the adoption curve and product life cycle.

9. Understand how to determine how much to spend on promotion efforts.

10. Understand the important new terms (shown in red).

Chapter Thirteen

Promotion—Introduction to Integrated Marketing Communications

Chrysler's management challenged the new-product development team to come up with an exciting vehicle that would generate a lot of interest and draw consumers into showrooms. The objective wasn't just to sell the new car but to improve the image and sales of other cars in the line. Management also wanted the new design to cut costs by sharing parts with the Dodge Neon, a not-so-popular economy sedan, and to qualify as a truck to help meet government gas mileage requirements for its truck line. That's a tall order, but out of it came the PT Cruiser and a big marketing success.

The PT Cruiser's unique retro-look styling played a big role in generating baby-boomer interest. And if the design was the bait, the interior is the hook. It's very flexible—with 26 seat configurations, a flat cargo area, and easy hatchback access. The Cruiser

place price promotion produc

really came across as something unique—a “personal transportation” (PT) vehicle. Carefully planned promotion leveraged the whole PT strategy to earn more profit than was expected.

Chrysler marketers introduced a PT Cruiser concept car at the 1999 Detroit Auto Show. To take advantage of the heavy news coverage at the show, they staged a surprise event to announce that a production version would be available for the 2000 model year. Immediately, the funky new PT got free publicity in national news media that would have cost many millions of dollars. As the PT concept car made the car show circuit, it drew in large crowds and interested consumers registered to receive more information. Chrysler also ran teaser-type print ads that showed a picture of the Cruiser and a big Chrysler logo with simple copy that positioned the Cruiser as “an antidote for the daily grind” and listed both a toll-free number and website for consumers to contact.

Before the PT was even available, 225,000 people who had asked for more information were in a direct-response promotion database. Chrysler sent these “hand raisers” a series of three mail brochures highlighting different benefits of the Cruiser and inviting them to visit a dealer. They were also invited to special previews to see the car in person. For example, 10 of these were scheduled at major sporting events and each attracted over 10,000 consumers. People hired to staff the previews were trained to answer questions on the whole Chrysler line, refer consumers to local dealers, and get visitors started with interactive digital kiosks that provided in-depth multimedia promotion on every Chrysler model.

Chrysler marketers also worked on many other special sales promotions to build interest, prompt word of mouth, and encourage dealer visits. For instance, they offered a $50 gift certificate to Macy's department store and promised to make charity contributions for each test drive.

By the time Cruisers were shipped from the factory, dealer sales reps had closed sales on almost all of the year's production capacity. Dealers couldn't even keep copies of promotional brochures in stock. In light of the overwhelming demand, Chrysler cut back on its planned spending for TV ads. It also had its agency's creative people change ads to put even more emphasis on the whole Chrysler line.

When Cruiser demand continued to grow for the 2001 model, Chrysler expanded production capacity and added a plant in Austria to serve the European market. It also raised prices—especially on fancy options like heated seats—to improve profit margins on units it was selling. And to take advantage of the investments in Cruiser development and promotion, and to keep the buzz going, Chrysler marketers added a convertible for 2003 (www.chrysler.com/pt-cruiser).

While the promotion blend is selling Cruisers and pulling customers into dealerships, sales on the rest of the Chrysler line have not picked up. Alas, promotion can't carry the whole load of the marketing mix. So marketing managers at Chrysler will have to adjust other aspects of their marketing program if they are going to achieve similar success with other products in its line.[1]

Several Promotion Methods Are Available

Promotion is communicating information between seller and potential buyer or others in the channel to influence attitudes and behavior. The marketing manager's main promotion job is to tell target customers that the right Product is available at the right Place at the right Price.

As the PT Cruiser example shows, a marketing manager can choose from several promotion methods—personal selling, mass selling, and sales promotion (see Exhibit 13-1). Further, because the different promotion methods have different strengths and limitations, a marketing manager usually uses them in combination. And, as with other marketing mix decisions, it is critical that the marketer manage and coordinate the different promotion methods as an integrated whole, not as separate and unrelated parts.

Personal selling—flexibility is its strength

Personal selling involves direct spoken communication between sellers and potential customers. Salespeople get immediate feedback—which helps them to adapt. Although some personal selling is included in most marketing mixes, it can be very expensive. So it's often desirable to combine personal selling with mass selling and sales promotion.

Mass selling involves advertising and publicity

Mass selling is communicating with large numbers of potential customers at the same time. It's less flexible than personal selling, but when the target market is large and scattered, mass selling can be less expensive.

Advertising is the main form of mass selling. **Advertising** is any *paid* form of nonpersonal presentation of ideas, goods, or services by an identified sponsor. It includes the use of traditional media like magazines, newspapers, radio and TV, signs, and

Colgate-Palmolive's director of promotions holds meetings to help managers see how to match promotion techniques to marketing objectives.

direct mail as well as new media such as the Internet. While advertising must be paid for, another form of mass selling—publicity—is "free."

Publicity avoids media costs

Publicity is any *unpaid* form of nonpersonal presentation of ideas, goods, or services. Of course, publicity people are paid. But they try to attract attention to the firm and its offerings *without having to pay media costs*. For example, movie studios try to get celebrities on TV talk shows because this generates a lot of interest and sells tickets to new movies without the studio paying for TV time.

Publicity generated for *Harry Potter and the Goblet of Fire* is a classic example. There was already interest in the Potter series. But Scholastic, Inc., the distributor of the books, got a bigger bang, and worldwide media coverage, by notifying bookstores and the media that no store could sell the book before July 8. Deliveries were scheduled to make that stick. And Scholastic kept the title and plot shrouded in secrecy. As interest in the secrecy spread, national media picked up on the story and devoted a huge amount of attention to it. For example, Harry was on the cover of *Newsweek* and a feature article explained why it was going to be one of the fastest-selling books in history. With publicity like that, even people who had never heard of the series wanted to find out what they were missing.[2]

If a firm has a really new message, publicity may be more effective than advertising. Trade magazines, for example, may carry articles featuring the newsworthy

Exhibit 13-1
Basic Promotion Methods and Strategy Planning

Exhibit 13-2
Example of Sales Promotion Activities

Aimed at final consumers or users	Aimed at middlemen	Aimed at company's own sales force
Contests	Price deals	Contests
Coupons	Promotion allowances	Bonuses
Aisle displays	Sales contests	Meetings
Samples	Calendars	Portfolios
Trade shows	Gifts	Displays
Point-of-purchase materials	Trade shows	Sales aids
Banners and streamers	Meetings	Training materials
Frequent buyer programs	Catalogs	
Sponsored events	Merchandising aids	

products of regular advertisers—in part because they *are* regular advertisers. The firm's publicity people write the basic copy and then try to convince magazine editors to print it. A consumer might carefully read a long magazine story but ignore an ad with the same information.

Some companies prepare videotapes designed to get free publicity for their products on TV news shows. For example, after learning that Seattle Mariner Jay Buhner loves Cheerios, a General Mills marketing manager had 162 boxes of the cereal stuffed into his spring-training locker and videotaped Buhner's surprise on opening his locker. TV news programs in 12 major markets showed the video. It would have cost hundreds of thousands of dollars to get as much attention with advertising.[3]

Sales promotion tries to spark immediate interest

Sales promotion refers to promotion activities—other than advertising, publicity, and personal selling—that stimulate interest, trial, or purchase by final customers or others in the channel. Sales promotion may be aimed at consumers, at middlemen, or at a firm's own employees. Examples are listed in Exhibit 13-2. Relative to other promotion methods, sales promotion can usually be implemented quickly and get results sooner. In fact, most sales promotion efforts are designed to produce immediate results.

Less is spent on advertising than personal selling or sales promotion

Many people incorrectly think that promotion money gets spent primarily on advertising—because advertising is all around them. But all the special sales promotions—coupons, sweepstakes, trade shows, and the like—add up to even more money. Similarly, much personal selling goes on in the channels and in other business markets. In total, firms spend less money on advertising than on personal selling or sales promotion.

Someone Must Plan, Integrate, and Manage the Promotion Blend

Each promotion method has its own strengths and weaknesses. In combination, they complement each other. Yet, each method also involves its own distinct activities and requires different types of expertise. As a result, it's usually the responsibility of specialists—such as sales managers, advertising managers, and promotion managers—to develop and implement the detailed plans for the various parts of the overall promotion blend.

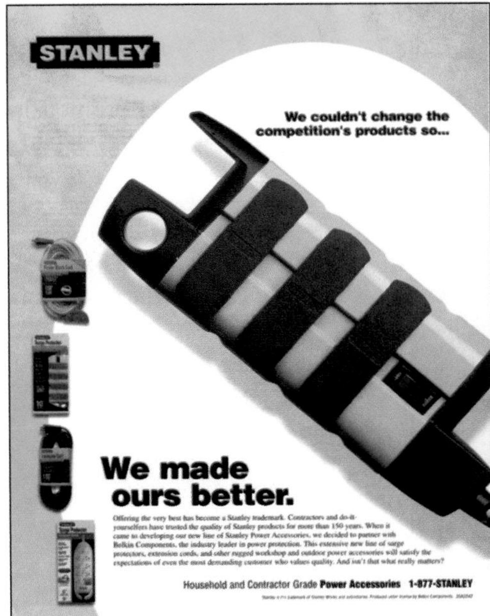

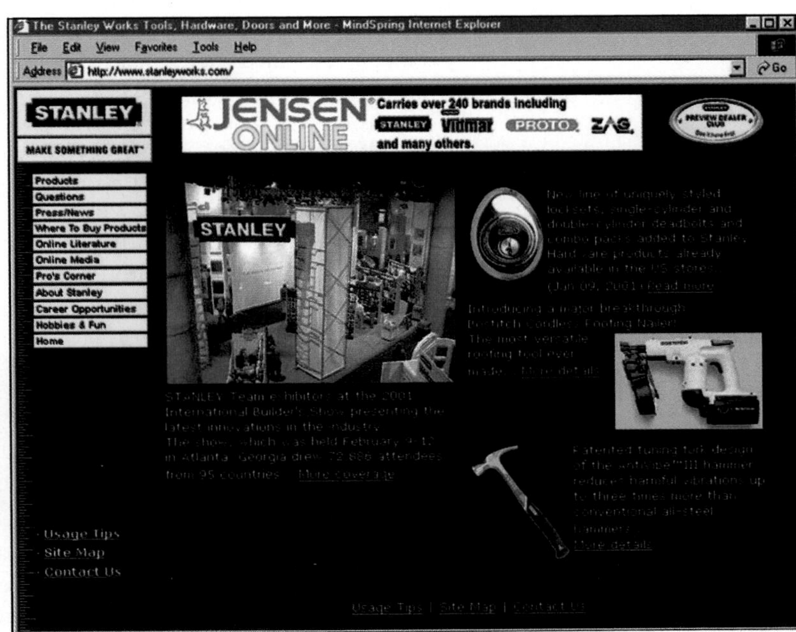

Stanley Works depends on a blend of integrated marketing communications, including sales presentations and product demonstration tours, trade ads focused on retailers, ads targeted at end-users, and a website that provides information on the whole line.

Sales managers manage salespeople

Sales managers are concerned with managing personal selling. Often the sales manager is responsible for building good distribution channels and implementing Place policies. In smaller companies, the sales manager may also act as the marketing manager and be responsible for advertising and sales promotion.

Advertising managers work with ads and agencies

Advertising managers manage their company's mass-selling effort—in television, newspapers, magazines, and other media. Their job is choosing the right media and developing the ads. Advertising departments within their own firms may help in these efforts—or they may use outside advertising agencies. The advertising manager may handle publicity too. Or it may be handled by an outside agency or by whoever handles **public relations**—communication with noncustomers, including labor, public interest groups, stockholders, and the government.

Sales promotion managers need many talents

Sales promotion managers manage their company's sales promotion effort. In some companies, a sales promotion manager has independent status and reports directly to the marketing manager. If a firm's sales promotion spending is substantial, it probably *should* have a specific sales promotion manager. Sometimes, however, the sales or advertising departments handle sales promotion efforts—or sales promotion is left as a responsibility of individual brand managers. Regardless of who the manager is, sales promotion activities vary so much that many firms use both inside and outside specialists.

Marketing manager talks to all, blends all

Although many specialists may be involved in planning for and implementing specific promotion methods, determining the blend of promotion methods is a strategy decision—and it is the responsibility of the marketing manager.

The various promotion specialists tend to focus on what they know best and their own areas of responsibility. A creative web page designer or advertising copywriter in New York may have no idea what a salesperson does during a call on a wholesaler. In addition, because of differences in outlook and experience, the advertising, sales, and sales promotion managers often have trouble working with each other as partners. Too often they just view other promotion methods as using up budget money they want.

The marketing manager must weigh the pros and cons of the various promotion methods, then devise an effective promotion blend—fitting in the various departments and personalities and coordinating their efforts.

Send a consistent and complete message with integrated marketing communications

Effective blending of all of the firm's promotion efforts should produce **integrated marketing communications**—the intentional coordination of every communication from a firm to a target customer to convey a consistent and complete message.

Internet

Internet Exercise Sony produces a very wide variety of products. Does the information available on its website (www.sony.com) appear to be part of an integrated marketing communications effort? Explain your thinking.

It seems obvious that a firm's different communications to a target market should be consistent. However, when a number of different people are working on different promotion elements, they are likely to see the same big picture only if a marketing manager ensures that it happens. Getting consistency is harder when different firms handle different aspects of the promotion effort. For example, different firms in the channel may have conflicting objectives.

To get effective coordination, everyone involved with the promotion effort must clearly understand the plan for the overall marketing strategy. They all need to understand how each promotion method will contribute to achieve specific promotion objectives.[4]

Which Methods to Use Depends on Promotion Objectives

Overall objective is to affect behavior

The different promotion methods are all different forms of communication. They should encourage customers to choose a *specific* product. Therefore, promotion must (1) reinforce present attitudes or relationships that might lead to favorable behavior

This trade ad for Kellogg's new Snack 'Ums informs potential channel members that the new product is available and that market testing gives evidence that it will be profitable for the retailer. With its ad Beech-Nut wants to persuade parents that its natural baby food is superior to other products.

or (2) actually change the attitudes and behavior of the firm's target market. Affecting buyer behavior is a tough job—but that is exactly the objective of Promotion.

Informing, persuading, and reminding are basic promotion objectives

Promotion objectives must be clearly defined—because the right promotion blend depends on what the firm wants to accomplish. It's helpful to think of three basic promotion objectives: *informing*, *persuading*, and *reminding* target customers about the company and its marketing mix. All try to affect buyer behavior by providing more information.

It's also useful to set more specific promotion objectives that state *exactly who* you want to inform, persuade, or remind, and *why*. This is unique to each company's strategy—and specific objectives vary by promotion method. We'll talk about more specific promotion objectives in the next two chapters. Here we'll focus on the three basic promotion objectives and how you can reach them.

Informing is educating

Potential customers must know something about a product if they are to buy at all. A firm with a really new product may not have to do anything but *inform* consumers about it and show that it meets consumer needs better than other products.

Persuading usually becomes necessary

When competitors offer similar products, the firm must not only inform customers that its product is available but also persuade them to buy it. A *persuading* objective means the firm will try to develop a favorable set of attitudes so customers will buy, and keep buying, its product. A persuading objective often focuses on reasons why one brand is better than others. To convince consumers to buy Tylenol, Johnson & Johnson's ads position Tylenol as the safe and effective pain relief medicine most often used by hospitals.

Reminding may be enough, sometimes

If target customers already have positive attitudes about a firm's marketing mix—or a good relationship with a firm—a *reminding* objective might be suitable. This objective can be extremely important. Customers who have been attracted and sold once are still targets for competitors' appeals. Reminding them of their past satisfaction may keep them from shifting to a competitor. Campbell realizes that most people know about its soup—so much of its advertising is intended to remind.

Promotion objectives relate to adoption process

In Chapter 5, we looked at consumer buying as a problem-solving process in which buyers go through six steps on the way to adopting (or rejecting) an idea or product. The three basic promotion objectives relate to these six steps. See Exhibit 13-3.

Exhibit 13-3
Relation of Promotion Objectives, Adoption Process, and AIDA Model

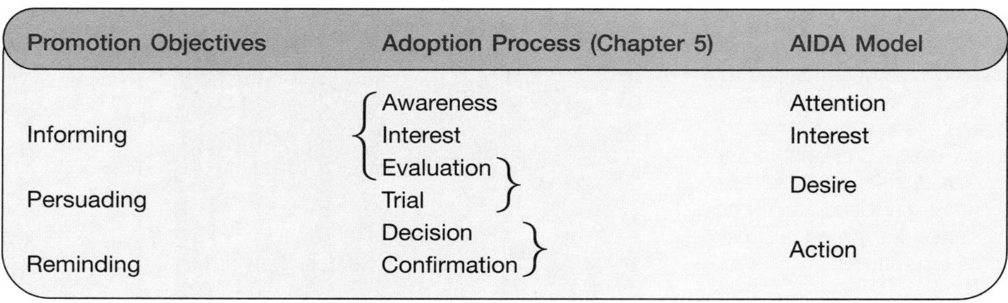

Promotion Objectives	Adoption Process (Chapter 5)	AIDA Model
Informing	Awareness Interest Evaluation	Attention Interest
Persuading	Evaluation Trial	Desire
Reminding	Decision Confirmation	Action

Informing and *persuading* may be needed to affect the potential customer's knowledge and attitudes about a product and then bring about its adoption. Later promotion can simply *remind* the customer about that favorable experience and confirm the adoption decision.

The AIDA model is a practical approach

The basic promotion objectives and adoption process fit very neatly with another action-oriented model—called AIDA—that we will use in this and the next two chapters to guide some of our discussion.

The **AIDA model** consists of four promotion jobs: (1) to get *Attention*, (2) to hold *Interest*, (3) to arouse *Desire*, and (4) to obtain *Action*. (As a memory aid, note that the first letters of the four key words spell AIDA, the well-known opera.)

Exhibit 13-3 shows the relationship of the adoption process to the AIDA jobs. Getting attention is necessary to make consumers aware of the company's offering. Holding interest gives the communication a chance to build the consumer's interest in the product. Arousing desire affects the evaluation process—perhaps building preference. And obtaining action includes gaining trial, which may lead to a purchase decision. Continuing promotion is needed to confirm the decision and encourage an ongoing relationship and additional purchases.

Promotion Requires Effective Communication

Communication can break down

There are many reasons why a promotion message can be misunderstood or not heard at all. To understand this, it's useful to think about a whole **communication process**—which means a source trying to reach a receiver with a message. Exhibit 13-4 shows the elements of the communication process. Here we see that a **source**—the sender of a message—is trying to deliver a message to a **receiver**—a potential customer. Customers evaluate both the message and the source of the message in terms of trustworthiness and credibility. For example, American Dental Association (ADA) studies show that Listerine mouthwash helps reduce plaque buildup on

Exhibit 13-4
The Traditional Communication Process

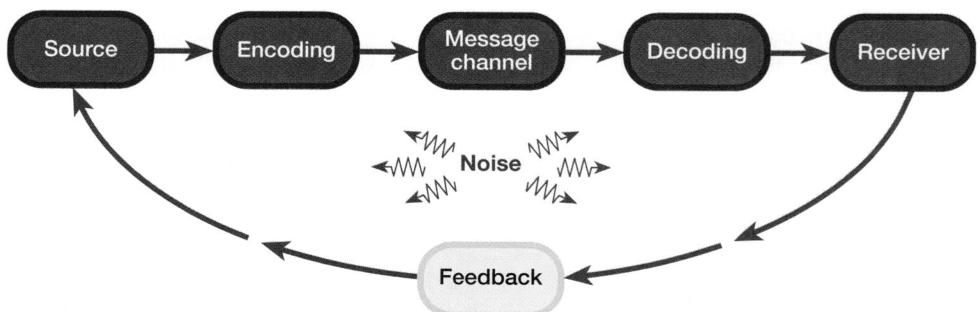

teeth. Listerine mentions the ADA endorsement in its ads to help make the message credible.

A major advantage of personal selling is that the source—the seller—can get immediate feedback from the receiver. It's easier to judge how the message is being received and to change it if necessary. Mass sellers usually must depend on marketing research or total sales figures for feedback—and that can take too long. Many marketers include toll-free telephone numbers and website addresses as ways of building direct-response feedback from consumers into their mass-selling efforts.

The **noise**—shown in Exhibit 13-4—is any distraction that reduces the effectiveness of the communication process. Conversations and snack-getting during TV ads are noise. The clutter of competing ads on the Internet is noise. Advertisers who plan messages must recognize that many possible distractions—noise—can interfere with communications.

Encoding and decoding depend on a common frame of reference

The basic difficulty in the communication process occurs during encoding and decoding. **Encoding** is the source deciding what it wants to say and translating it into words or symbols that will have the same meaning to the receiver. **Decoding** is the receiver translating the message. This process can be very tricky. The meanings of various words and symbols may differ depending on the attitudes and experiences of the two groups. People need a common frame of reference to communicate effectively. Maidenform encountered this problem with its promotion aimed at working women. The company ran a series of ads depicting women stockbrokers and doctors wearing Maidenform lingerie. The men in the ads were fully dressed. Maidenform was trying to show women in positions of authority, but some women felt the ad presented them as sex objects. In this case, the promotion people who encoded the message didn't understand the attitudes of the target market and how they would decode the message.[5]

Message channel is important too

The communication process is complicated even more because the message is coming through some **message channel**—the carrier of the message. A source can use many message channels to deliver a message. The salesperson does it in person with voice and action. Advertising must do it with media such as magazines, TV, e-mail, or Internet websites. A particular message channel may enhance or detract from a message. A TV ad, for example, can *show* that Dawn dishwashing detergent "takes the grease away"; the same claim might not be very convincing if it arrived in a consumer's e-mail. On the other hand, a receiver may attach value to a product if the message comes in a well-respected medium. Some consumers buy products advertised in *Good Housekeeping* magazine, for example, because they have faith in its seal.[6]

The same message may be interpreted differently

Different audiences may interpret a message differently. Such differences are common in international marketing when cultural differences or translation are problems. In Taiwan, the translation of the Pepsi slogan "Come alive with the Pepsi Generation" came out as "Pepsi will bring your ancestors back from the dead." Worse, a campaign for Schweppes Tonic Water in Italy translated the name into Schweppes Toilet Water.[7]

Ethical issues in marketing communications

Promotion is one of the most often criticized areas of marketing. Many criticisms focus on whether communications are honest and fair. Marketers must sometimes make ethical judgments in considering these charges and in planning their promotion.

For example, when a TV news program broadcasts a video publicity release, consumers don't know it was prepared to achieve marketing objectives. They think the news staff is the source. That may make the message more credible, but is it fair? Many say yes—as long as the publicity information is truthful. But gray areas still remain.

Critics raise similar concerns about the use of celebrities in advertisements. A person who plays the role of an honest and trustworthy person on a popular TV series may be a credible message source in an ad, but is using such a person misleading to consumers? Some critics believe it is. Others argue that consumers recognize advertising when they see it and know celebrities are paid for their endorsements.

The most common criticisms of promotion relate to exaggerated claims. Some promotions do misrepresent product benefits. However, most marketing managers want to develop ongoing relationships with, and repeat purchases from, their customers. They realize that customers won't come back if the marketing mix doesn't deliver what the promotion promises. Further, consumers are becoming more skeptical about all the claims they hear and see. As a result, most marketing managers work to make promotion claims specific and believable.[8]

Integrated Direct-Response Promotion Is Very Targeted

The challenge of developing promotions that reach *specific* target customers has prompted many firms to turn to direct marketing—direct communication between a seller and an individual customer using a promotion method other than face-to-face personal selling. Most direct marketing communications are designed to prompt immediate feedback—a direct response—by customers. That's why this type of communication is often called *direct-response promotion*.

Early efforts in the direct-response area focused on direct-mail advertising. A carefully selected mailing list—perhaps from the firm's customer relationship management (CRM) database—allowed advertisers to reach customers with specific interests. And direct-mail advertising proved to be very effective when the objective was to get a direct response from the customer.

Now it's more than direct-mail advertising

Achieving a measurable, direct response from specific target customers is still the heart of direct promotion. But direct-response media now include telephone, print, e-mail, a website, broadcast, and even interactive video. The customer's response may be a purchase (or donation), a question, or a request for more information. At a website, the response may be a simple mouse-click to link to more information, a click to put an item in a virtual shopping cart, or a click to purchase.

Often the customer responds by calling a toll-free telephone number or, in the case of business markets, by sending a fax or an e-mail. Then a salesperson calls the customer and follows up. That might involve filling an order or scheduling a personal visit with a prospect. There are, however, many variations on this approach. For example, some firms route incoming information-request calls to a computerized answering system. The caller indicates what information is required by pushing a few buttons on the telephone keypad. Then the computer instantly sends requested information to the caller's fax machine.

Direct-response promotion is often an important component of integrated marketing communications programs and is closely tied to other elements of the marketing mix.[9] A promotion campaign developed for BMW illustrates this idea.

BMW and other car companies found that videotapes are a good way to provide consumers with a lot of information about a new model. However, it's too expensive to send tapes to everyone. To target the mailing, BMW first sends likely car buyers (high-income consumers who own a BMW or competing brand) personalized

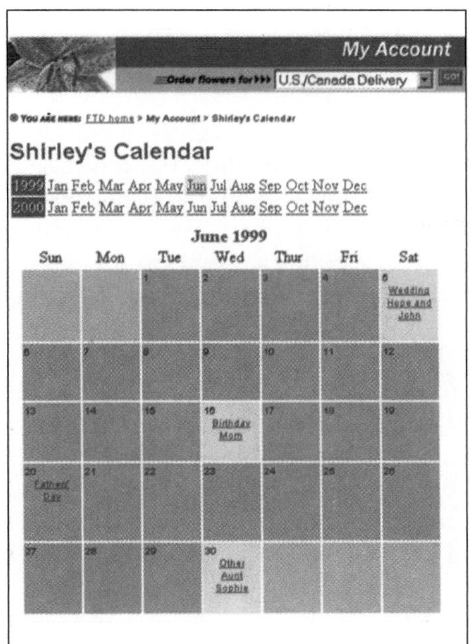

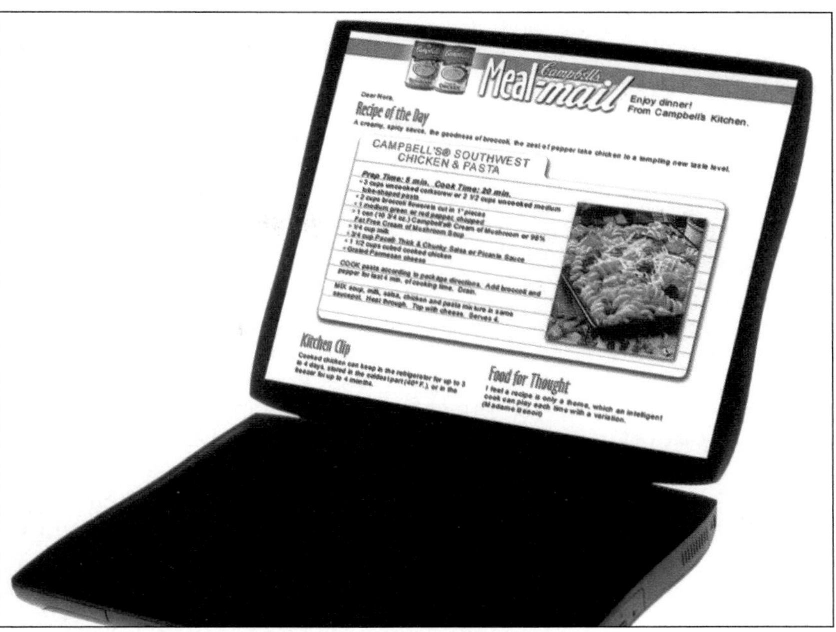

FTD's website encourages a direct response from consumers, starting with a personalized calendar where the customer can enter dates for important flower-giving occasions. Similarly, Campbell's Soup encourages consumers to sign up to receive free recipes that are e-mailed each week.

direct-mail ads that offer a free videotape. Interested consumers send back a return card. Then BMW sends the advertising tape and updates its database so a dealer will know to call the consumer.

Target customer directly with a CRM database

Direct-response promotion usually relies on a customer relationship management database to target specific prospects or customers. The CRM database includes customers' names and addresses (or telephone numbers) as well as past purchases and other segmenting characteristics. Greenpeace and the Cousteau Society send mail advertisements to people interested in environmental issues. They ask for donations or other types of support. Individuals (or segments) who respond to direct promotion are the target for additional promotion. For example, a customer who buys lingerie from a catalog or a website once is a good candidate for a follow-up. The follow-up might extend to other types of clothing.

Direct-response methods raise ethical concerns

Direct-response promotion and customer relationship management database targeting have become an important part of many marketing mixes. But some critics argue that thousands of acres of trees are consumed each week—just to make the paper for direct response "junk mail" that consumers don't want. Most e-mail users get uninvited messages—"spam." Worse, some firms have been criticized for creating websites that secretly install programs on customers' computers. Then, unknown to the user, the program gathers information about other websites the user visits and sends it back to the firm over the Internet. Other critics worry about privacy issues and how a CRM database might be used, especially if it includes details about a consumer's purchases. Similarly, many consumers don't like getting telephone solicitations so most states prohibit automatic calling systems that use prerecorded messages rather than a live salesperson. Firms that use direct-response promotion are sensitive to these concerns and most take steps to address them.[10]

The Customer May Initiate the Communication Process

In the past, marketers usually viewed the buyer as a passive message receiver—at least until the marketer has done something to stimulate attention, interest, and desire. That's one reason that targeting is so important—so that the promotion expense isn't wasted on someone who isn't interested. Moreover, most mass-selling messages are based on the idea that you can get a customer's attention for only a minute or two. Even with direct-response promotion, the marketer typically has taken the first step.

New electronic media enable interactive communication

However, this is changing. Buyers can now access a great deal of information (pictures, words, graphs, videos, sound) and place an order without the seller having been directly involved at all. The new interactive technologies enabling this change take many different forms. Some of the most important are websites, e-mail list-servers, caller-controlled fax-on-demand, computerized telephone voice-messaging systems, video kiosks in malls, CD-ROM and DVD disks on personal computers, and WebTV.

New variations on these interactive technologies are being developed all of the time. For example, in England, where interactive cable TV systems have been operating for a decade, consumers have access to a system called Teletext. With Teletext, they can use their standard TV remote control unit to search through thousands of on-screen pages of information—ranging from the schedule for flights from London's airports and the current weather to advertising for automobiles and specials at the local supermarket. The benefits of Teletext are very similar to the benefits of the World Wide Web on the Internet, but it uses a standard TV. Similar systems will become more available in other countries as government regulations change and as cable companies upgrade their equipment.

Internet

Internet Exercise Visit the Campbell's Soup website (www.campbellsoup.com). Does the website make it easy for you to get information? Does it make you want to spend more time and get more information? Explain your answer.

Work is underway to develop broadcast systems in which icons will appear on-screen as consumers watch a program or movie. For example, an icon might appear on a jacket worn by a talk show guest. A consumer who is interested in the product will be able to press a button on a remote control to get more information about the product or where to buy it—or even to place an order. The same concept is already implemented on DVDs for some movies. When this type of system is available via cable (or with streaming video over the Internet), it will provide a powerful new tool for marketers and, over time, reshape the way many marketing communications are handled.

Consider the simple model of customer ("receiver") initiated interactive communication shown in Exhibit 13-5. At first it doesn't seem very different from the traditional communication model we considered earlier (Exhibit 13-4). However, the differences are significant.

Consumer initiates communication with a search process

In the model in Exhibit 13-5, a customer initiates the communication process with a decision to search for information in a particular message channel. The most far-reaching message channel to search is the Internet. The message channel is still the carrier of the message, as was the case before, but "searchable" message

Exhibit 13-5
A Model of Customer-Initiated Interactive Communication

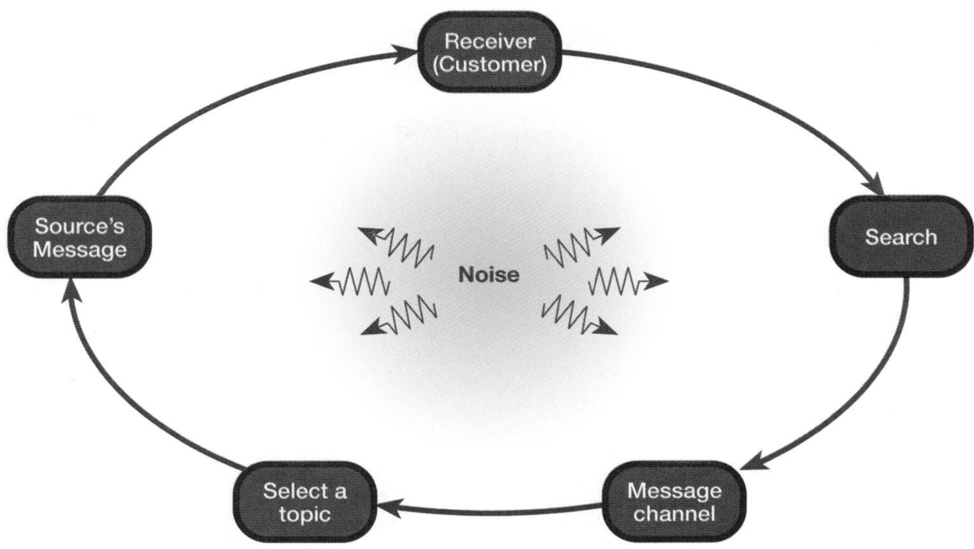

channels usually feature an archive of existing messages on a number of topics. There may be many available topics—even millions.

In the next step, the consumer selects one specific topic on which to receive a message. Selecting a topic might be done in one of a variety of ways, depending on the message channel. The most typical approaches involve using a mouse, remote control device, or keypad to highlight a selection from an initial list (like a table of contents or index). Of course, other approaches are common. Many dial-up telephone systems use voice recognition. Or, in the case of the Internet, you might type a phrase and have the computer search for a list of topics that include it.

Consumer decides how much information to get

Once a specific topic is selected, the message for that topic is displayed. Typically, the message is brief. But it may include a simple way to get more detailed information, select another related topic, return to the original selection process, or quit the search. Thus, after each message the consumer can decide whether to search further (say, to get more detail). This interactive approach makes it easy for the consumer to get as much information as desired. However, noise may still be a problem. For example, a consumer may waste time and still not find what is needed—because it is not available or is too hard to find. So some firms offer consumers a website choice that establishes communication with a real person at a 24-hour-a-day service center. Some of these systems use instant messaging so that the consumer and a customer service person can chat online. With other systems, like AT&T's "Interactive Answers" approach, a service person immediately phones the customer to provide the information or help needed. Other firms are using variations of this approach, including live teleconferencing over the Internet.

Action—including purchase—may be immediate

The action required to make a purchase by interactive media is usually fast and easy. At many Internet sites, for example, a consumer can click on an item to place it in a virtual shopping cart, charge it to a credit card, and arrange for shipping.

Custom communications will be more personalized

The traditional principles of communication discussed earlier in the chapter are still important in customer-initiated interactive communication. At the same time, the interactive approach allows the marketer to customize communication to the

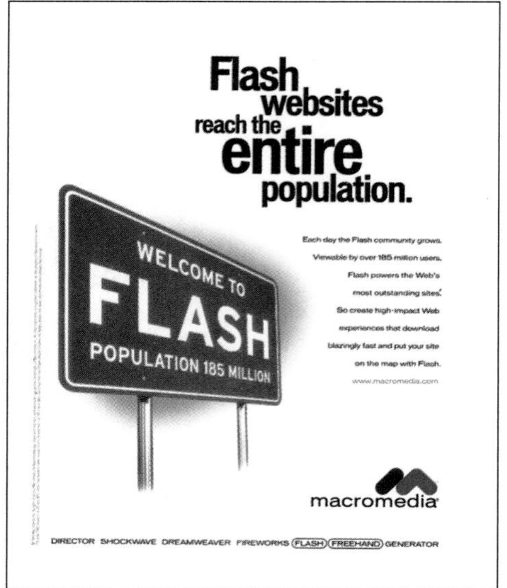

Lipstream and Macromedia offer products that help marketing managers take advantage of the interactive and multimedia potential of website communications.

needs and responses of the consumer. As new approaches develop in this arena, we are seeing more promotion targeted at single-person "segments."[11]

How Typical Promotion Plans Are Blended and Integrated

Get a push in the channel with promotion to middlemen

When a channel of distribution involves middlemen, their cooperation can be crucial to the success of the overall marketing strategy. **Pushing** (a product through a channel) means using normal promotion effort—personal selling, advertising, and sales promotion—to help sell the whole marketing mix to possible channel members. This approach emphasizes the importance of securing the wholehearted cooperation of channel members to promote the product in the channel and to the final user.

Producers usually take on much of the responsibility for the pushing effort in the channel. However, most wholesalers also handle at least some of the promotion to retailers. Similarly, retailers often handle promotion in their local markets. The overall effort is most likely to be effective when all of the individual messages are carefully integrated.

Promotion to middlemen emphasizes personal selling

Salespeople handle most of the important communication with middlemen. Middlemen don't want empty promises. They want to know what they can expect in return for their cooperation and help. A salesperson can answer questions about what promotion will be directed toward the final consumer, each channel member's part in marketing the product, and important details on pricing, markups, promotion assistance, and allowances.

When suppliers offer similar products and compete for attention and shelf space, middlemen usually pay attention to the one with the best profit potential. Sales promotions targeted at middlemen usually focus on short-term arrangements that will improve the middleman's profits. For example, a soft-drink bottler might offer a convenience store a free case of drinks with each two cases it buys. The free case improves the store's profit margin on the whole purchase.

Firms run ads in trade magazines to recruit new middlemen or to inform channel members about a new offering. Trade ads usually encourage middlemen to contact the supplier for more information, and then a salesperson takes over.

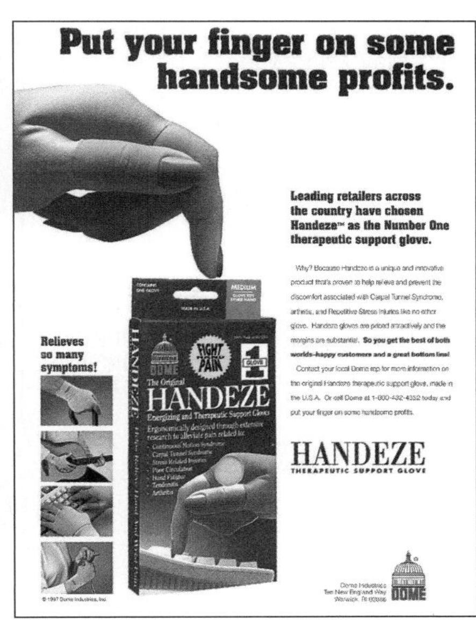

Nesquik's ad is targeted at parents and kids and designed to stimulate demand and help pull Nesquik's popular chocolate additive for milk through the channel of distribution. Dome's trade ad message is targeted at retailers and designed to persuade them to give the Handeze therapeutic support glove an extra promotional push.

Push within a firm—with promotion to employees

Some firms emphasize promotion to their own employees—especially salespeople or others in contact with customers. This type of *internal marketing* effort is basically a variation on the pushing approach. One objective of an annual sales meeting is to inform reps about important elements of the marketing strategy—so they'll work together as a team to implement it. Some firms use promotion to motivate employees to provide customer service or achieve higher sales. This is typical in services where the quality of the employees' efforts is a big part of the product. Some ads, for example, use the theme "we like to see you smile." The ads communicate to customers, but also remind employees that the service they provide is crucial to customer satisfaction.

Pulling policy—customer demand pulls the product through the channel

Most producers focus a significant amount of promotion on customers at the end of the channel. This helps to stimulate demand and pull the product through the channel of distribution. **Pulling** means getting customers to ask middlemen for the product.

Pulling and pushing are usually used in combination. See Exhibit 13-6. However, if middlemen won't work with a producer—perhaps because they're already carrying a competing brand—a producer may try to use a pulling approach by itself. This involves highly aggressive promotion to final consumers or users—perhaps using coupons or samples—temporarily bypassing middlemen. If the promotion works, the middlemen are forced to carry the product to satisfy customer requests. However, this approach is risky. Customers may lose interest before reluctant middlemen make the product available. At minimum, middlemen should be told about the planned pulling effort—so they can be ready if the promotion succeeds.[12]

Promotion to final consumers

The large number of consumers almost forces producers of consumer products and retailers to emphasize advertising and sales promotion. Sales promotion—such as coupons, contests, or free samples—builds consumer interest and short-term sales of a product. Effective mass selling may build enough brand familiarity so that little personal selling is needed—as in self-service and discount operations.[13]

Personal selling can be effective too. But aggressive personal selling to final consumers usually is found in expensive channel systems, such as those for fashionable clothing, furniture, consumer electronics, and automobiles.

Promotion to business customers

Producers and wholesalers who target business customers often emphasize personal selling. This is practical because these customers are much less numerous than final consumers and their purchases are typically larger.

Exhibit 13-6
Promotion May Encourage Pushing in the Channel, Pulling by Customers, or Both

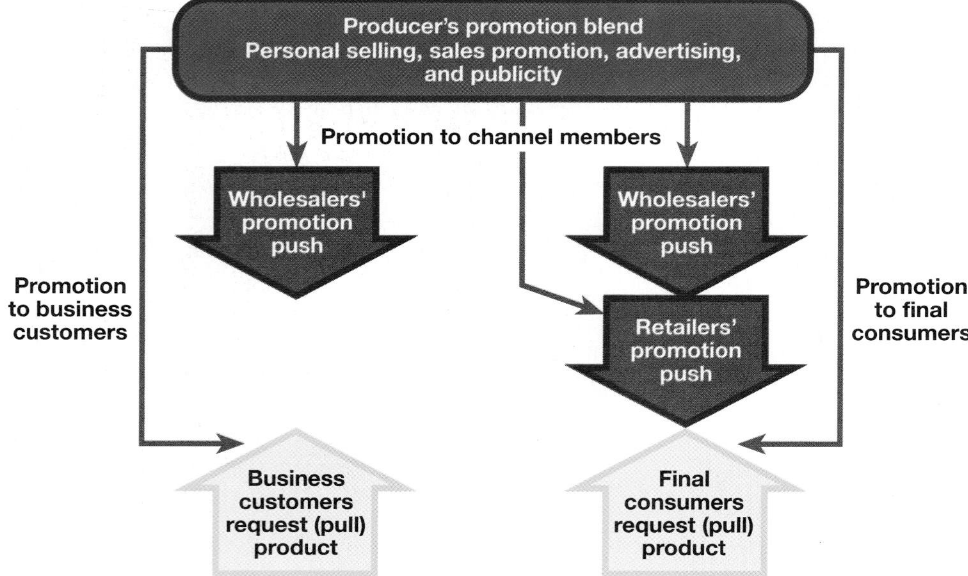

Sales reps can be more flexible in adjusting their companies' appeals to suit each customer—and personal contact is usually required to close a sale. A salesperson is also able to call back later to follow up, resolve any problems, and nurture the relationship with the customer.

While personal selling dominates in business markets, mass selling is necessary too. A typical sales call on a business customer costs about $200.[14] That's because salespeople spend less than half their time actually selling. The rest is consumed by such tasks as traveling, paperwork, sales meetings, and strictly service calls. So it's seldom practical for salespeople to carry the whole promotion load.

Ads in trade magazines or at a B2B e-commerce website, for instance, can inform potential customers that a product is available. Most trade ads give a toll-free telephone number, fax number, or website address to stimulate direct inquiries. Domestic and international trade shows also help identify prospects. Even so, most sellers who target business customers spend only a small percentage of their promotion budget on mass selling and sales promotion.

Each market segment may need a unique blend

Knowing what type of promotion is typically emphasized with different targets is useful in planning the promotion blend. But each unique market segment may need a separate marketing mix and a different promotion blend. Some mass-selling specialists miss this point. They think mainly in terms of mass marketing rather than target marketing. Aiming at large markets is desirable in some situations, but promotion aimed at everyone can end up hitting no one. In developing the promotion blend, you should be careful not to slip into a shotgun approach when what you really need is a rifle approach—with a more careful aim.

Adoption Processes Can Guide Promotion Planning

The AIDA and adoption processes look at individuals. This emphasis on individuals helps us understand how promotion affects the way that people behave. But it's also useful to look at markets as a whole. Different segments of customers within a market may behave differently—with some taking the lead in trying new products and, in turn, influencing others.

Exhibit 13-7
The Adoption Curve

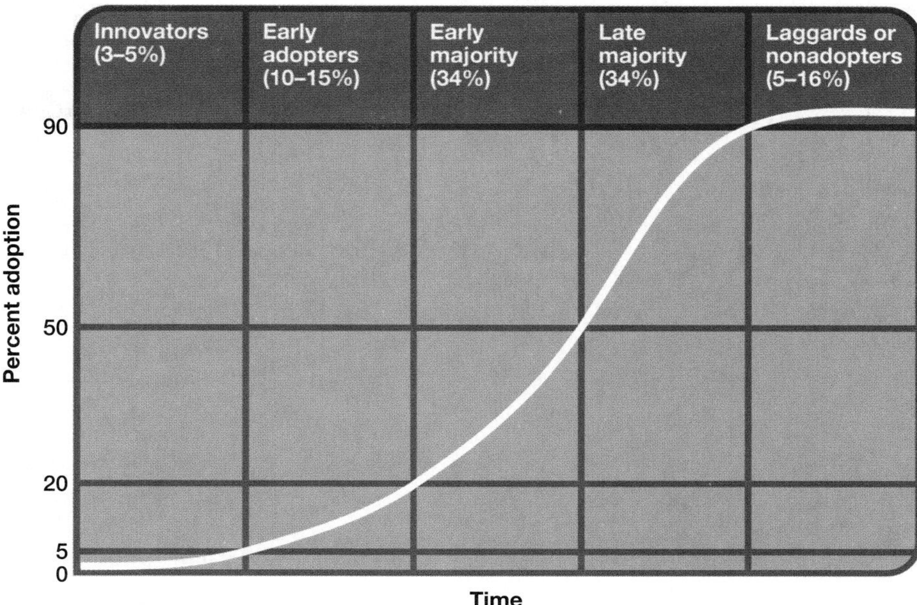

Promotion must vary for different adopter groups

Research on how markets accept new ideas has led to the adoption curve model. The **adoption curve** shows when different groups accept ideas. It emphasizes the relations among groups—and shows that individuals in some groups act as leaders in accepting a new idea. It also shows the need to change the promotion effort as time passes.

Exhibit 13-7 shows the adoption curve for a typical successful product. Some of the important characteristics of each of these customer groups are discussed below. Which one are you?

Innovators don't mind taking some risks

The **innovators** are the first to adopt. They are eager to try a new idea and willing to take risks. Innovators tend to be young and well educated. They are likely to be mobile and have many contacts outside their local social group and community. Business firms in the innovator group are often rather specialized.

Innovators tend to rely on impersonal and scientific information sources, or other innovators, rather than salespeople. They often search for information on the Internet, read articles in technical publications, or look for informative ads in special-interest magazines.

Early adopters are often opinion leaders

Early adopters are well respected by their peers and often are opinion leaders. They tend to be younger, more mobile, and more creative than later adopters. But unlike innovators, they have fewer contacts outside their own social group or community. Business firms in this category also tend to be specialized.

Of all the groups, this one tends to have the greatest contact with salespeople. Mass media are important information sources too. Marketers should be very concerned with attracting and selling the early adopter group. Their acceptance is crucial. The next group, the early majority, look to them for guidance. The early adopters can help the promotion effort by spreading *word-of-mouth* information and advice among other consumers.

The Internet is also providing companies with a low-cost way to encourage word of mouth. An interesting web page can attract attention—and customers can easily e-mail a copy to a friend. For example, a retail shop called Hot Hot Hot, which carries a very wide variety of hot sauces for food, established a website. Very quickly, largely because of word of mouth, 1,500 people were visiting the website each day.[15]

Do You Hear That Buzz, and Where Is It Coming From?

Computer viruses can spread like wildfire. Some marketers are trying to get attention for their products by promoting the same kind of "viral" spread of word-of-mouth promotion from a small set of opinion leaders to other consumers. For example, BMW commissioned famous movie directors to create a series of short (about five minutes each) action films that show BMWs in high-performance chase action. The films are available for online viewing at www.bmwfilms.com. It would be impossible to show all of the dangerous stunts in TV ads. But car enthusiasts who hear about the site love the action and tell their friends to go check it out. It's all a well-planned effort to create more buzz about BMW as the ultimate driving machine.

Lee Dungarees used a complicated viral marketing campaign to try to build a cooler image among youthful males. Lee's agency e-mailed 200,000 computer game fans a trio of grainy video clips. The videos were supposedly intended to draw people to websites about three quirky characters. But the clips were so bad that they were funny. That was intentional. Many guys who received them forwarded them to friends. Little did they know that the odd characters in the videos would later be featured in an online computer game created by Lee. Gamers who figured out the connection with the videos passed the word and the popularity of the game spread across the Web. But to win at the game guys had to enter a secret code, which could only be found on Lee's jeans labels and required a visit to a store.

It's clear why a marketer might want target consumers to hear the buzz about a product from their coolest friend—and not just dismiss it as some commercial pitch. But often the intent is to mislead consumers about where the buzz starts. Some say that makes it unethical; others say that the marketer is only planting a few seeds and that it really is consumers who spread the word. Of course, this can backfire. Sony, for instance, got bad publicity for fabricating favorable movie reviews and portraying them as coming from movie critics.[16]

Early majority group is deliberate

The **early majority** avoid risk and wait to consider a new idea after many early adopters have tried it—and liked it. Average-sized business firms that are less specialized often fit in this category. If successful companies in their industry adopt the new idea, they will too.

The early majority have a great deal of contact with mass media, salespeople, and early adopter opinion leaders. Members usually aren't opinion leaders themselves.

Late majority is cautious

The **late majority** are cautious about new ideas. Often they are older and more set in their ways, so they are less likely to follow early adopters. In fact, strong social pressure from their own peer group may be needed before they adopt a new product. Business firms in this group tend to be conservative, smaller-sized firms with little specialization.

Compaq is not targeting people who are Internet innovators but rather members of the late majority group who just want a hassle-free way to use e-mail as part of their everyday life. On the other hand, Toyota's Prius ad targets innovators and early adopters.

The late majority make little use of marketing sources of information—mass media and salespeople. They tend to be oriented more toward other late adopters rather than outside sources they don't trust.

Laggards or nonadopters hang on to tradition

Laggards or **nonadopters** prefer to do things the way they've been done in the past and are very suspicious of new ideas. They tend to be older and less well educated. The smallest businesses with the least specialization often fit this category. They cling to the status quo and think it's the safe way.

The main source of information for laggards is other laggards. This certainly is bad news for marketers.[17]

Promotion Blends Vary over the Life Cycle

Stage of product in its life cycle

The adoption curve helps explain why a new product goes through the product life-cycle stages described in Chapter 9. During these stages, promotion blends may have to change to achieve different promotion objectives.

Market introduction stage—"this new idea is good"

During market introduction, the basic promotion objective is informing. If the product is a really new idea, the promotion must build **primary demand**—demand for the general product idea—not just for the company's own brand. Video phone service and electric cars are good examples of product concepts where primary demand is just beginning to grow. There may be few potential innovators during the introduction stage, and personal selling can help find them. Firms also need salespeople to find good channel members and persuade them to carry the new product. Sales promotion may be targeted at salespeople or channel members to get them interested in selling the new product. And sales promotion may also encourage customers to try it.

Market growth stage—"our brand is best"

In the market growth stage, more competitors enter the market, and promotion emphasis shifts from building primary demand to stimulating **selective demand**—demand for a company's own brand. The main job is to persuade customers to buy, and keep buying, the company's product.

Now that there are more potential customers, mass selling may become more economical. But salespeople and personal selling must still work in the channels—expanding the number of outlets and cementing relationships with current channel members.

Market maturity stage—"our brand is better, really"

In the market maturity stage, mass selling and sales promotion may dominate the promotion blends of consumer products firms. Business products may require more aggressive personal selling—perhaps supplemented by more advertising. The total dollars allocated to promotion may rise as competition increases.

If a firm already has high sales—relative to competitors—it may have a real advantage in promotion at this stage. If, for example, Nabisco has twice the sales for a certain type of cookie as Keebler, its smaller competitor, and they both spend the same *percentage* of total sales on promotion, Nabisco will be spending twice as much and will probably communicate to more people.

Firms may use reminder-type advertising at this stage or target frequent-buyer promotions at current customers to strengthen the relationship and keep customers loyal.

In markets that are drifting toward pure competition, some companies resort to price-cutting. This *may* temporarily increase the number of units sold, but it may also reduce total revenue and the amount available for promotion *per unit*. And competitive retaliation, perhaps in the form of short-term sales promotions, may

This ad uses humor to highlight what's distinctive about 2-Alarm Chili—to stimulate selective demand in a very competitive market.

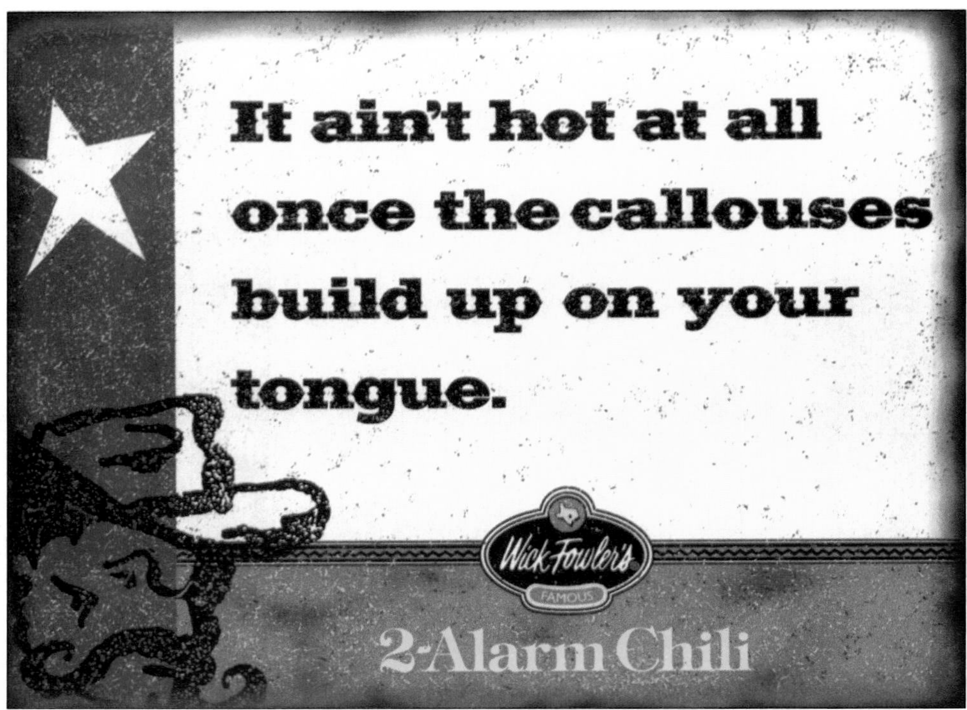

reduce the temporary sales gains and drag price levels down faster. As cash flowing into the business declines, spending may have to be cut back.

Sales decline stage—"let's tell those who still want our product"

During the sales decline stage, the total amount spent on promotion usually decreases as firms try to cut costs to remain profitable. Since some people may still want the product, firms need more targeted promotion to reach these customers.

On the other hand, some firms may increase promotion to try to slow the cycle—at least temporarily. Crayola had almost all of the market for children's crayons, but sales were slowly declining as new kinds of markers came along. Crayola increased ad spending to urge parents to buy their kids a "fresh box."[18]

Setting the Promotion Budget

Size of budget affects promotion efficiency and blend

There are some economies of scale in promotion. An ad on national TV might cost less *per person* reached than an ad on local TV. Similarly, citywide radio, TV, and newspapers may be cheaper than neighborhood newspapers or direct personal contact. But the *total cost* for some mass media may force small firms, or those with small promotion budgets, to use promotion alternatives that are more expensive per contact. For example, a small retailer might want to use local television but find that there is only enough money for a web page, an ad in the Yellow Pages, and an occasional newspaper ad.

Budgeting for promotion—50 percent, 30 percent, or 10 percent is better than nothing

The most common method of budgeting for promotion expenditures is to compute a percentage of either past sales or sales expected in the future. The virtue of this method is its simplicity.

However, just because this mechanical approach is common doesn't mean that it's smart. It leads to expanding marketing expenditures when business is good and

Many marketing managers now view promotion on the Internet as a "must buy" in a promotion budget.

cutting back when business is poor. When business is poor, this approach may just make the problem worse—if weak promotion is the reason for declining sales.

Find the task, budget for it

In the light of our continuing focus on planning marketing strategies to reach objectives, the most sensible approach to budgeting promotion expenditures is the **task method**—basing the budget on the job to be done. For example, the spending level might be based on the number of new customers desired and the percentage of current customers that the firm must retain to leverage investments in established relationships.

A practical approach is to determine which promotion objectives are most important and which promotion methods are most economical and effective for the communication tasks relevant to each objective. This approach helps you to set priorities so that the money you spend produces specific results. The costs of these tasks are then totaled—to determine how much should be budgeted for promotion (just as money is allocated for other marketing activities required by the strategy). In other words, the firm can assemble its total promotion budget directly from detailed plans rather than by simply relying on historical patterns or ratios.

This method also helps to eliminate budget fights between managers responsible for different promotion methods who see themselves as pitted against each other for limited budget dollars. The specialists may still make their own suggestions about how to perform tasks. But then the budget allocations are based on the most effective ways of getting things done, not on what the firm did last year, what some competitor does, or even on internal politics. With this approach, different promotion specialists are also more likely to recognize that they must all work together to achieve truly integrated marketing communications.[19]

Conclusion

Promotion is an important part of any marketing mix. Most consumers and intermediate customers can choose from among many products. To be successful, a producer must not only offer a good product at a reasonable price but also inform potential customers about the product and where they can buy it. Further, producers must tell wholesalers and retailers in the channel about their product and their marketing mix. These middlemen, in turn, must use promotion to reach their customers.

The promotion blend should fit logically into the strategy being developed to satisfy a particular target market. Strategy planning needs to state *what* should be communicated to them and *how*. The overall promotion objective is to affect buying behavior, but the basic promotion objectives are informing, persuading, and reminding.

Three basic promotion methods can be used to reach these objectives. Behavioral science findings can help firms combine various promotion methods for effective communication. In particular, what we know about the communication process and how individuals and groups adopt new products is important in planning promotion blends.

An action-oriented framework called AIDA can help marketing managers plan promotion blends. But the marketing manager has the final responsibility for combining the promotion methods into one integrated promotion blend for each marketing mix.

In this chapter, we considered some basic concepts that apply to all areas of promotion. In the next two chapters, we'll discuss personal selling, advertising, and sales promotion in more detail.

Questions and Problems

1. Briefly explain the nature of the three basic promotion methods available to a marketing manager. What are the main strengths and limitations of each?
2. In your own words, discuss the integrated marketing communications concept. Explain what its emphasis on "consistent" and "complete" messages implies with respect to promotion blends.
3. Relate the three basic promotion objectives to the four jobs (AIDA) of promotion using a specific example.
4. Discuss the communication process in relation to a producer's promotion of an accessory product—say, a new electronic security system businesses use to limit access to areas where they store confidential records.
5. If a company wants its promotion to appeal to a new group of target customers in a foreign country, how can it protect against its communications being misinterpreted?
6. Promotion has been the target of considerable criticism. What specific types of promotion are probably the object of this criticism? Give a specific example that illustrates your thinking.
7. With direct-response promotion, customers provide feedback to marketing communications. How can a marketing manager use this feedback to improve the effectiveness of the overall promotion blend?
8. How can a promotion manager target a message to a certain target market with electronic media (like the Internet) when the customer initiates the communication? Give an example.
9. What promotion blend would be most appropriate for producers of the following established products? Assume average- to large-sized firms in each case and support your answer.
   a. Chocolate candy bar.
   b. Car batteries.
   c. Panty hose.
   d. Castings for truck engines.
   e. A special computer used by manufacturers for control of production equipment.
   f. Inexpensive plastic rainhats.
   g. A digital tape recorder that has achieved specialty-product status.
10. A small company has developed an innovative new spray-on glass cleaner that prevents the buildup of electrostatic dust on computer screens and TVs. Give examples of some low-cost ways the firm might effectively promote its product. Be certain to consider both push and pull approaches.
11. Would promotion be successful in expanding the general demand for: *(a)* almonds, *(b)* air travel, *(c)* golf clubs, *(d)* walking shoes, *(e)* high-octane unleaded gasoline, *(f)* single-serving, frozen gourmet dinners, and *(g)* bricks? Explain why or why not in each case.
12. Explain how an understanding of the adoption process would help you develop a promotion blend for digital tape recorders, a new consumer electronics product that produces high-quality recordings. Explain why you might change the promotion blend during the course of the adoption process.
13. Discuss how the adoption curve should be used to plan the promotion blend(s) for a new automobile accessory—an electronic radar system that alerts a driver if he or she is about to change lanes into the path of a car that is passing through a blind spot in the driver's mirrors.

14. If a marketing manager uses the task method to budget for marketing promotions, are competitors' promotion spending levels ignored? Explain your thinking and give an example that supports your point of view.

15. Discuss the potential conflict among the various promotion managers. How could this be reduced?

Suggested Cases

13. Mixed Media Technologies, Inc.
17. myWedding.com
18. Outdoor World, Inc.

Computer-Aided Problem

13. **Selecting a Communications Channel**

Helen Troy, owner of three Sound Haus stereo equipment stores, is deciding what message channel (advertising medium) to use to promote her newest store. Her current promotion blend includes direct-mail ads that are effective for reaching her current customers. She also has knowledgeable salespeople who work well with consumers once they're in the store. However, a key objective in opening a new store is to attract new customers. Her best prospects are professionals in the 25–44 age range with incomes over $38,000 a year. But only some of the people in this group are audiophiles who want the top-of-the-line brands she carries. Troy has decided to use local advertising to reach new customers.

Troy narrowed her choice to two advertising media: an FM radio station and a biweekly magazine that focuses on entertainment in her city. Many of the magazine's readers are out-of-town visitors interested in concerts, plays, and restaurants. They usually buy stereo equipment at home. But the magazine's audience research shows that many local professionals do subscribe to the magazine. Troy doesn't think that the objective can be achieved with a single ad. However, she believes that ads in six issues will generate good local awareness with her target market. In addition, the magazine's color format will let her present the prestige image she wants to convey in an ad. She thinks that will help convert aware prospects to buyers. Specialists at a local advertising agency will prepare a high-impact ad for $2,000, and then Troy will pay for the magazine space.

The FM radio station targets an audience similar to Troy's own target market. She knows repeated ads will be needed to be sure that most of her target audience is exposed to her ads. Troy thinks it will take daily ads for several months to create adequate awareness among her target market. The FM station will provide an announcer and prepare a tape of Troy's ad for a one-time fee of $200. All she has to do is tell the station what the message content for the ad should say.

Both the radio station and the magazine gave Troy reports summarizing recent audience research. She decides that comparing the two media in a spreadsheet will help her make a better decision.

a. *Based on the data displayed on the initial spreadsheet, which message channel (advertising medium) would you recommend to Troy? Why?*
b. *The agency that offered to prepare Troy's magazine ad will prepare a fully produced radio ad—including a musical jingle—for $2,500. The agency claims that its musical ad will have much more impact than the ad the radio station will create. The agency says its ad should produce the same results as the station ad with 20 percent fewer insertions. If the agency claim is correct, would it be wise for Troy to pay the agency to produce the ad?*
c. *The agency will not guarantee that its custom-produced radio ad will reach Troy's objective—making 80 percent of the prospects aware of the new store. Troy wants to see how lower levels of awareness—between 50 percent and 70 percent—would affect the advertising cost per buyer and the cost per aware prospect. Use the results feature to vary the percent of prospects who become aware. Prepare a table showing the effect on the two kinds of costs. What are the implications of your analysis?*

For additional questions related to this problem, see Exercise 13-3 in the *Learning Aid for Use with Essentials of Marketing*, 9th edition.

.When You Finish This Chapter, You Should

1. Understand the importance and nature of personal selling.

2. Know the three basic sales tasks and what the various kinds of salespeople can be expected to do.

3. Know how sales technology affects the way sales are performed.

4. Know what the sales manager must do—including selecting, training, and organizing salespeople—to carry out the personal selling job.

5. Understand how the right compensation plan can help motivate and control salespeople.

6. Understand when and where to use the three types of sales presentations.

7. Understand the important new terms (shown in red).

Chapter Fourteen
Personal Selling

Cisco Systems, Inc., has enjoyed enormous growth by "empowering the Internet generation." Cisco sells the backroom gear and systems that businesses, government agencies, schools, and other organizations need to support their computer networks, websites, and e-commerce applications. Eighty percent of the traffic over the Internet runs on Cisco equipment.

Cisco takes care of customers with cutting-edge e-commerce technology at its website (www.cisco.com) whenever it can. Distributors also handle some needs. But Cisco's own salespeople handle the job of getting and keeping major accounts. Cisco's sales force is as central to its success as its technology. Decisions to invest millions of dollars in information technology involve top management. Cisco's sales professionals, like Sue Bostrom, work with these executives to learn about their needs and then sell business solutions rather than "gear." Of course, a firm's IT specialists may also get in the act—and they want to know about technical details ("Will Cisco's router work with our systems security software?"). Technical specialists from Cisco's local sales office might handle some of these concerns as part of the sales team effort. And when the sales rep

place price promotion produ

identifies a prospect that has the potential to become one of Cisco's "premier partners," Cisco's top brass may help cement a close relationship. Cisco faces tough competition, so even with all this help Cisco salespeople need real skill to get the order and close a deal. And to keep the relationship going, top-notch sales support is needed whenever a customer has a problem that can't be quickly handled online.

To be certain that these challenging jobs are done well, Cisco's sales managers recruit talented people using a wide variety of methods. For example, the Hot Jobs@Cisco section of its website collects job applicant profiles on an ongoing basis. When a position opens up, qualified candidates are notified. After the best people are selected, Cisco provides the sales training to make them even better. New people may need training to build professional problem-solving and sales presentation skills as well as technical knowledge. Even experienced sales reps need ongoing training. For example, Cisco gives its salespeople training in everything from the firm's policies on expenses to the latest developments in technology—with approaches ranging from traditional instructor-led workshops to cutting-edge e-learning opportunities.

Cisco's salespeople have an array of different skills and experience. And Cisco has customers and sales offices all over the world. So Cisco must carefully match each salesperson to particular territories, industries, customers, and product lines. And to be sure that each salesperson is highly motivated, Cisco's sales managers must make certain that sales compensation arrangements and benefits reward salespeople for producing needed results.[1]

The Importance and Role of Personal Selling

Salespeople are communicators who build relationships

Promotion is communicating with potential customers. As the Cisco case suggests, personal selling is often the best way to do it. While face-to-face with prospects, salespeople can get more attention than an advertisement or a display. They can adjust what they say to the prospect's feedback and questions. If, and when, the prospect is ready to buy, the salesperson is there to ask for the order. And afterward, the salesperson works to be certain that the customer is satisfied with the relationship and will buy again in the future.

Personal selling requires strategy decisions

In this chapter, we'll discuss the importance and nature of personal selling so you'll understand the strategy decisions sales and marketing managers face. These strategy decisions are shown in Exhibit 14-1.

We'll also discuss a number of frameworks and how-to approaches that guide these strategy decisions. Because these approaches apply equally to domestic and international markets, we won't emphasize that distinction in this chapter. This does not mean, however, that personal selling techniques don't vary from one country to another. To the contrary, in dealing with *any* customer, the salesperson must be very sensitive to cultural influences and other factors that might affect communication. For example, a Japanese customer and an Arab customer might respond differently to subtle aspects of a salesperson's behavior. The Arab customer might expect to be very close to a salesperson, perhaps only 2 feet away, while they talk. The Japanese customer might consider that distance rude. Similarly, what topics of discussion are considered sensitive, how messages are

Exhibit 14-1 Strategy Planning for Personal Selling

interpreted, and which negotiating styles are used vary from one country to another. A salesperson must know how to communicate effectively with each customer—wherever and whoever that customer is.[2]

Personal selling is important

Personal selling is absolutely essential in the promotion blends of some firms. Consider how you would feel if you regularly had to meet payrolls and somehow, almost miraculously, your salespeople kept coming in with orders just in time to keep the business profitable.

Personal selling is often a company's largest single operating expense. This is another reason why it is important to understand sales management decisions. Bad ones are costly both in lost sales and in actual out-of-pocket expenses.

Every economy needs and uses many salespeople. In the United States, one person out of every ten in the total labor force is involved in sales work. By comparison, that's about 20 times more people than are employed in advertising. Any activity that employs so many people and is so important to the economy deserves study. Looking at what salespeople do is a good way to start.

Helping to buy is good selling

Good salespeople don't just try to *sell* the customer. Rather, they try to *help the customer buy*—by understanding the customer's needs and presenting the advantages and disadvantages of their products. Such helpfulness results in satisfied customers and long-term relationships. And strong relationships often form the basis for a competitive advantage, especially for firms that target business markets.

You may think of personal selling in terms of an old-time stereotype of a salesperson: a bag of wind with no more to offer than a funny story, a big expense account, and an engaging grin. But that isn't true any more. Old-time salespeople are being replaced by real professionals—problem solvers—who have something definite to contribute to their employers *and* their customers.

Salespeople represent the whole company—and customers too

The salesperson is often seen as a representative of the whole company—responsible for explaining its total effort to customers rather than just pushing products. The salesperson may provide information about products, explain and interpret company policies, and even negotiate prices or diagnose technical problems.

The sales rep is often the only link between the firm and its customers—especially if customers are far away. When a number of people from the firm are involved in communications with the customer organization, it is usually the sales rep who coordinates the relationship. See Exhibit 6-5.

The salesperson also represents the *customer* back inside the selling firm. Recall that feedback is an essential part of both the communication process *and* the basic management process of planning, implementing, and control. For example, the sales rep is the likely one to explain to the production manager why a customer is unhappy with product quality—or to the e-commerce specialist how better order status information available on the website could help the customer save money.

As evidence of these changing responsibilities, some companies give their salespeople such titles as field manager, sales consultant, market specialist, account representative, or sales engineer.

Sales force aids in market information function as well

The sales force can aid in the marketing information function too. The sales rep may be the first to hear about a new competitor or a competitor's new strategy.

Sales reps who are well attuned to customers' needs can be a key source of ideas for new products. Ballard Medical Products competes with international giants in the hospital supply business. Its salespeople have a lot of say in what products the company produces and how they are designed. At each hospital, they work closely with the doctor and nurse specialists who use Ballard products. And when one of them says "we need a product that would solve this problem," the Ballard sales rep probes the customer's needs and then follows up with Ballard's new product group.[3]

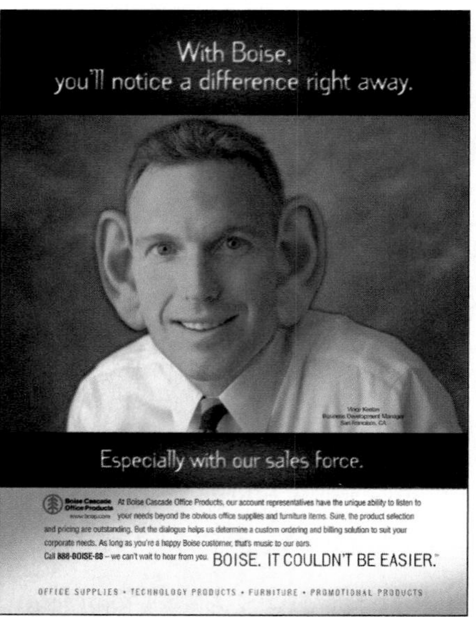

Good salespeople try to help the customer solve problems and meet needs—and often that requires both careful listening to really understand the customer and then effective service after the sale.

Salespeople can be strategy planners too

Some salespeople are expected to be marketing managers in their own territories. And some become marketing managers by default because top management hasn't provided detailed strategy guidelines. Either way, salespeople may have choices about (1) what target customers to aim at, (2) which particular products to emphasize, (3) which middlemen to call on or to work with the hardest, (4) how to use promotion money, and (5) how to adjust prices.

A salesperson who can put together profitable strategies and implement them well can rise very rapidly. The opportunity is there for those prepared and willing to work.[4]

What Kinds of Personal Selling Are Needed?

If a firm has too few salespeople, or the wrong kind, some important personal selling tasks may not be completed. And having too many salespeople wastes money. A sales manager needs to find a good balance—the right number and the right kind of salespeople. This balance may change over time with changes in the market environment; that's why many firms have to restructure their sales forces.

One of the difficulties of determining the right balance is that every sales job is different. While an engineer or accountant can look forward to fairly specific duties, the salesperson's job changes constantly. However, there are three basic types of sales tasks. This gives us a starting point for understanding what selling tasks need to be done and how many people are needed to do them.

Personal selling is divided into three tasks

The three **basic sales tasks** are order-getting, order-taking, and supporting. For convenience, we'll describe salespeople by these terms—referring to their primary task—*although one person may do all three tasks in some situations*.

Order Getters Develop New Business Relationships

Order getters are concerned with establishing relationships with new customers and developing new business. **Order-getting** means seeking possible buyers with a well-organized sales presentation designed to sell a good, service, or idea.

Order getters must know what they're talking about, not just be personal contacts. Order-getting salespeople normally are well paid—many earn more than $80,000 a year.

Producer's order getters—find new opportunities

Producers of all kinds of products, especially business products, have a great need for order getters. They use order getters to locate new prospects, open new accounts, see new opportunities, and help establish and build channel relationships.

Top-level customers are more interested in ways to save or make more money than in technical details. Good order getters cater to this interest. They help the customer identify ways to solve problems; then they sell concepts and ideas, not just physical products. The goods and services they supply are merely the means of achieving the customer's end.

For example, Circadian, Inc., sells high-tech medical equipment. Changes in Medicare rules mean that doctors can no longer routinely order expensive tests in hospitals because the costs can't be recovered easily. But the doctors *can* be paid for tests done in their offices—if they have the right equipment. When Circadian order getters call on doctors, they show how the firm's testing equipment can improve patient care and office profits. Reps can often get a $20,000 order on the spot because they can show that the equipment will pay for itself in the first year.[5]

Order getters for professional services—and other products where service is a crucial element of the marketing mix—face a special challenge. The customer usually can't inspect a service before deciding to buy. The order getter's communication and relationship with the customer may be the only basis on which to evaluate the quality of the supplier.

An order getter in business markets often needs to understand a customer's whole business as well as technical details about the product and its applications. For example, a salesperson for automated manufacturing equipment must understand a prospect's production process as well as the technical details of converting to computer-controlled equipment.

Wholesalers' order getters—almost hand it to the customer

Agent middlemen often are order getters—particularly the more aggressive manufacturers' agents and brokers. They face the same tasks as producers' order getters. But, unfortunately for them, once the order-getting is done and the customers become established and loyal, producers may try to eliminate the agents and save money with their own order takers.

Progressive merchant wholesaler sales reps should be consultants and store advisors rather than just order takers. Such order getters become retailers' partners in the job of moving goods from the wholesale warehouse through the retail store to consumers. These order getters almost become a part of the retailer's staff—helping to solve consumers' problems, train employees, conduct demonstrations, and plan advertising, special promotions, and other retailing activities.

Retail order getters—influence consumer behavior

Convincing consumers about the value of products they haven't seriously considered takes a high level of personal selling ability. Order getters for unsought products must help customers see how a new product can satisfy needs now being filled by something else. Without order getters, many common products—ranging from mutual funds to air conditioners—might have died in the market introduction stage. The order getter helps bring products out of the introduction stage into the market growth stage.

Order getters are also helpful for selling *heterogeneous* shopping products. Consumers shop for many of these items on the basis of suitability and value. They welcome useful information.

Producers sometimes aid in the personal selling effort by providing innovative displays that communicate not only the features but also the benefits of their products. To help salespeople explain the benefits of its new Profile washer and dryer, GE places this interactive display in dealers' stores.

Order Takers Nurture Relationships to Keep the Business Coming

Order takers sell to the regular or established customers, complete most sales transactions, and maintain relationships with their customers. After a customer becomes interested in a firm's products through an order getter or supporting salesperson or through advertising or sales promotion, an order taker usually answers any final questions and completes the sale. **Order-taking** is the routine completion of sales made regularly to the target customers. The routine completion of sales usually requires ongoing follow-up to make certain that the customer is satisfied and that the relationship will continue.

Producers' order takers—train, explain, and collaborate

Once industrial, wholesale, or retail accounts are established, regular follow-up is necessary. Order takers work on improving the whole relationship with the customer, not just on completing a single sale. Even in e-commerce, where customers place routine orders with computerized order systems and EDI, order takers do a variety of important jobs that are essential to the business relationship. Someone has to explain details, make adjustments, handle complaints, explain or negotiate new prices and terms, place sales promotion materials, and keep customers informed of new developments. All these activities are part of the order taker's job. A failure to meet a customer's expectations on any of them might jeopardize the relationship and future sales.

Producers' order takers often have a regular route with many calls. To handle these calls well, they must have energy, persistence, enthusiasm, and a friendly personality that wears well over time. They sometimes have to take the heat when something goes wrong with some other element of the marketing mix.

Firms sometimes use order-taking jobs to train potential order getters and managers. Such jobs give them an opportunity to meet key customers and to better understand their needs. And frequently, they run into some order-getting opportunities.[6]

Good retail order takers can play an important role in building good relations with customers.

Wholesalers' order takers—not getting orders but keeping them

While producers' order takers usually handle relatively few items, wholesalers' order takers may sell 125,000 items or more. They have so many items that they can't possibly give aggressive sales effort to many—except perhaps newer or more profitable items. There are just too many items to single any out for special attention.

The wholesale order taker's main job is to write up orders and maintain close contact with customers. The order taker normally checks to be sure the company fills the order promptly, handles any adjustments or complaints, and generally acts as a liaison between the company and its customers.

Such salespeople are usually the low-pressure type—friendly and easygoing. Usually these jobs aren't as high paying as the order-getting variety—but they attract many because they aren't as taxing. There can be a social aspect too. The salesperson sometimes becomes good friends with customers.

Retail order takers—often they are poor salesclerks

Order-taking may be almost mechanical at the retail level—for example, at the supermarket checkout counter. Some retail clerks are poor order takers because they aren't paid much—often only the minimum wage. But they may be paid little because they do little. Even so, retail order takers play a vital role in a retailer's marketing mix. Customers expect prompt and friendly service. They will find a new place to shop, or to do their banking or have their car serviced, rather than deal with a salesclerk who is rude or acts annoyed by having to complete a sale.

Supporting Sales Force Informs and Promotes in the Channel

Supporting salespeople help the order-oriented salespeople—but they don't try to get orders themselves. Their activities are aimed at enhancing the relationship with the customer and getting sales in the long run. For the short run, however, they are ambassadors of goodwill who may provide specialized services and information. Almost all supporting salespeople work for producers or middlemen who do this supporting work for producers. There are two types of supporting salespeople: missionary salespeople and technical specialists.

Missionary salespeople can increase sales

Missionary salespeople are supporting salespeople who work for producers—calling on their middlemen and their customers. They try to develop goodwill and stimulate demand, help the middlemen train their salespeople, and often take orders for delivery by the middlemen. Missionary salespeople are sometimes called *merchandisers* or *detailers*.

Producers who rely on merchant wholesalers or e-commerce to obtain widespread distribution often use missionary salespeople. The sales rep can give a promotion boost to a product that otherwise wouldn't get much attention because it's just one of many. A missionary salesperson for Vicks' cold remedy products, for example, might visit druggists during the cold season and encourage them to use a special end-of-aisle display for Vicks' cough syrup—and then help set it up. The wholesaler that supplies the drugstore would benefit from any increased sales, but might not take the time to urge use of the special display.

An imaginative missionary salesperson can double or triple sales. Naturally, this doesn't go unnoticed. Missionary sales jobs are often a route to order-oriented jobs.

Technical specialists are experts who know product applications

Technical specialists are supporting salespeople who provide technical assistance to order-oriented salespeople. Technical specialists usually are science or engineering graduates with the know-how to understand the customer's applications and explain the advantages of the company's product. They are usually more skilled in showing the technical details of their product than in trying to persuade customers to buy it. Before the specialist's visit, an order getter probably has stimulated interest. The technical specialist provides the details.

Three tasks may have to be blended

We have described three sales tasks—order-getting, order-taking, and supporting. However, a particular salesperson might be given two, or all three, of these tasks. Ten percent of a particular job may be order-getting, 80 percent order-taking, and the additional 10 percent supporting. Another company might have many different people handling the different sales tasks. This can lead to **team selling**—when different sales reps work together on a specific account. Sometimes one or more of the people on a team are not from the sales department at all. If improving the relationship with the customer calls for technical support from the quality control manager, then that person becomes a part of the team, at least temporarily.

Producers of high-ticket items often use team selling. AT&T uses team selling to sell office communications systems for a whole business. Different specialists handle different parts of the job—but the whole team coordinates its efforts to achieve the desired result.[7]

The Right Structure Helps Assign Responsibility

A sales manager must organize the sales force so that all the necessary tasks are done well. A large organization might have different salespeople specializing by different selling tasks *and* by the target markets they serve.

The Clorox sales team responsible for the launch of liquid bleach in the Brazilian market drew on people from R&D, marketing, and sales.

Different target markets need different selling tasks

Sales managers often divide sales force responsibilities based on the type of customer involved. For example, Bigelow—a company that makes quality carpet for homes and office buildings—divided its sales force into two groups of specialists. Some Bigelow salespeople call only on architects to help them choose the best type of carpet for new office buildings. These reps know all the technical details, such as how well a certain carpet fiber will wear or its effectiveness in reducing noise from office equipment. Often no selling is involved because the architect only suggests specifications and doesn't actually buy the carpet.

Other Bigelow salespeople call on retail carpet stores. These reps encourage the store manager to keep a variety of Bigelow carpets in stock. They also introduce new products, help train the store's salespeople, and try to solve any problems that occur.

Big accounts get special treatment

Very large customers often require special selling effort—and relationships with them are treated differently. Moen, a maker of plumbing fixtures, has a regular sales force to call on building material wholesalers and an elite **major accounts sales force** that sells directly to large accounts—like Lowe's or other major retail chains that carry plumbing fixtures.

You can see why this sort of special attention is justified when you consider Procter & Gamble's relationship with Wal-Mart. Although P&G is an international powerhouse, its total sales in every country except the U.S. and Germany add up to less than its sales to Wal-Mart. That's why the P&G sales team that calls on Wal-Mart lives in Bentonville, Arkansas, where Wal-Mart is based.[8]

Some salespeople specialize in telephone selling

Some firms have a group of salespeople who specialize in **telemarketing**—using the telephone to "call" on customers or prospects. A phone call has many of the benefits of a personal visit—including the ability to modify the message as feedback is received. The big advantage of telemarketing is that it saves time and money. A telemarketing sales force can often build profitable relationships with small or hard-to-reach customers the firm might otherwise have to ignore. Telemarketing is also important when many prospects have to be contacted to reach one actually interested in buying. On the other hand, many people object to the growing number of uninvited solicitations.[9]

Sales tasks are done in sales territories

Often companies organize selling tasks on the basis of a **sales territory**—a geographic area that is the responsibility of one salesperson or several working together. A territory might be a region of a country, a state, or part of a city—depending on the market potential. An airplane manufacturer like Boeing might consider a whole country as *part* of a sales territory for one salesperson.

Carefully set territories can reduce travel time and the cost of sales calls, as well as confusion about who has responsibility for a set of selling tasks. Consider the Hyatt Hotel chain. Until recently, each hotel had its own salespeople to get bookings for big conferences. That meant that people who had responsibility for selecting meeting locations might be called on by sales reps from 20 different Hyatt hotels. Now, the Hyatt central office divides up responsibility for working with specific accounts; one rep calls on an account and then tries to sell space in the Hyatt facility that best meets the customer's needs.

Size of sales force depends on workload

Once the important selling tasks are specified and the responsibilities divided, the sales manager must decide how many salespeople are needed. The first step is estimating how much work can be done by one person in some time period. Then the sales manager can make an educated guess about how many people are required in total, as the following example shows.

For many years, the Parker Jewelry Company was very successful selling its silver jewelry to department and jewelry stores in the southwestern region of the United States. But top managers wanted to expand into the big urban markets in the northeastern states. They realized that most of the work for the first few years would require order getters. They felt that a salesperson would need to call on each account at least once a month to get a share of this competitive business. They estimated that a salesperson could make only five calls a day on prospective buyers and still allow time for travel, waiting, and follow-up on orders that came in. This meant that a sales rep who made calls 20 days a month could handle about 100 stores (5 a day × 20 days).

The managers used a personal computer and a CD-ROM database that included all of the telephone Yellow Pages listings for the country. Then they simply divided the total number of stores by 100 to estimate the number of salespeople needed. This also helped them set up territories—by defining areas that included about 100 stores for each salesperson. Obviously, managers might want to fine-tune this estimate for differences in territories—such as travel time. But the basic approach can be adapted to many different situations.[10]

Some managers forget that over time the right number of salespeople may change—as selling tasks change. Then when a problem becomes obvious, they try to change everything in a hurry—a big mistake.

E-commerce sometimes substitutes for personal selling

Some tasks that have traditionally been handled by a salesperson can now be handled effectively and at lower cost by e-commerce systems. The selling situation that the firm faces may influence which approach makes the most sense and how many salespeople are really needed. See Exhibit 14-2.

A salesperson is likely to be required in important selling situations where there is a need to create and build relationships. Here the salesperson focuses on tasks like creative problem solving, persuading, coordinating, and supporting the customer. On the other hand, information technology is cost effective for handling the recurring exchange of standardized information (such as inventory, orders, and delivery status). Similarly, details of product specifications and prices can be organized at a website. Of course, there should be some way to provide good customer service when needs arise. In a complex relationship, using technology for standard information frees the sales rep to spend time on value-added communication.

When relationship building is not required and there is not a recurring need for routine information, a firm may be able to meet customer needs best by providing digital self-service. This is basically the role of ATMs for banks—to service customers who don't want to wait until a teller is available. Similarly, Amazon's virtual

Exhibit 14-2
Examples of Possible Personal Selling Emphasis in Some Different Business-Market Selling Situations

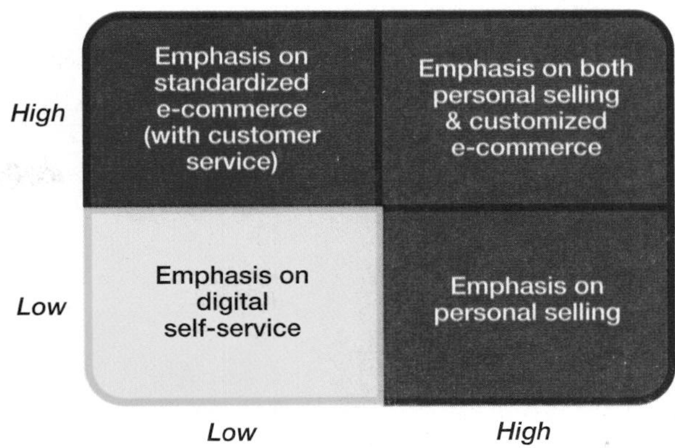

shopping carts play this role. But digital self-service can be more sophisticated. Some firms provide "intelligent agents" at their websites. An intelligent agent is a computer program that helps customers solve their own problems. At the CompUSA website, a customer who wants to buy a laptop can respond to a series of structured questions about how the laptop will be used, and the intelligent agent recommends which features are most important and what brands have those features. Similarly, a wholesaler's website might provide an agent to help retailers forecast demand for a new product based on information about their local market areas.

The total amount of personal selling effort justified in any of these situations may depend on other factors, including how important the customer is. Further, we've focused on technology that substitutes for personal contact by a salesperson. But marketing managers also need to make decisions about providing sales technology support to help salespeople communicate more effectively.

Sales Technology Provides Tools to Do the Job

Changes in how sales tasks are handled

How sales tasks and responsibilities are planned and handled is changing in many companies because of the new sales technology tools that are available. It is usually the sales manager's job—perhaps with help from specialists in technology—to decide what types of tools are needed and how they will be used.

To get a sense of what is involved, consider a day in the life of a sales representative for a large consumer packaged goods firm. Over a hasty breakfast, she plans the day's sales calls on her laptop's organizer, logs onto the company network, and sorts through the dozen e-mail messages. One is from a buyer for a supermarket chain. Sales in the chain's paper towel category are off 10 percent, and he wants to know if the rep can help. The rep downloads sales trend data for the chain and its competitors from her firm's intranet. A spreadsheet analysis of the data reveals that the sales decline is due to increased competition from warehouse clubs. After a conference call with a brand manager and a company sales promotion specialist to seek advice, she prepares a PowerPoint presentation, complete with a proposed shelf-space plan, that recommends that the buyer promote larger-size packages of both her company's and competitors' brands. Before leaving home, the rep e-mails an advance copy of the report to her manager. In her car, she calls the buyer to schedule an appointment.

New information technologies are making the modern sales force more efficient and giving salespeople communication tools that are creating totally new ways to meet the needs of their customers while achieving the objectives of their jobs.

New software and hardware provide a competitive advantage

As in this example, sales reps today rely on support from an array of software and hardware that was hardly imaginable even a decade ago. Software for spreadsheet analysis, electronic presentations, time management, sales forecasting, customer contact, and shelf-space management is at the salesperson's fingertips. Still new but already commonplace hardware includes everything from wireless phones, fax machines, laptop computers, and pagers to personalized videoconferencing systems. In many situations these technologies give sales reps new ways to meet customer needs while achieving the objectives of their jobs.

The basic sales tasks are not different, but the tools change how well the job is done. Yet this is not simply a matter that is best left to individual sales reps. Use of these tools may be necessary just to compete effectively. For example, if a customer expects a sales rep to access data on past sales and provide an updated sales forecast, a sales organization that does not have this capability will be at a real disadvantage in keeping that customer's business.

On the other hand, these tools have costs. There is an obvious expense of buying the technology. But there is also the training cost of keeping everyone up-to-date. Often that is not a simple matter. Some salespeople who have done the sales job well for a long time "the old-fashioned way" resent being told that they have to change what they are doing—even if it's what customers expect. So if a firm expects salespeople to be able to use these technologies that requirement needs to be included in selecting and training people for the job.[11]

Sound Selection and Training to Build a Sales Force

Selecting good salespeople takes judgment, plus

It is important to hire *good, well-qualified* salespeople. But the selection in many companies is done without serious thought about exactly what kind of person the firm needs. Managers may hire friends and relations, or whoever is available, because they feel that the only qualifications for sales jobs are a friendly personality. This approach leads to poor sales and costly sales force turnover.

Progressive companies are more careful. They constantly update a list of possible job candidates. They invite applications at the company's website. They schedule candidates for multiple interviews with various executives, and do thorough background

Salespeople Work Smarter—With Their Fingertips

Laptop computers help more salespeople work smarter, not just harder. Salespeople use computers in many different ways.

Without a laptop, it was impossible for a wholesaler's salespeople to master Cincinnati Milacron's product line. Now a computer asks a series of questions and then helps the salesperson figure out which of 65,000 grinding wheels and hundreds of cutting fluids to sell to each metal shop. After adding this system, Milacron doubled its market share—without adding any new salespeople.

Laptops help keep salespeople for London Fog clothing up-to-date when they're on the road calling on accounts. Early each morning before leaving the hotel, the sales reps call into the company's central computer. It downloads to their laptops all the latest information about product availability, prices, customers' accounts, and the like. Later in the day, when a customer has a question about product delivery, the sales rep can answer it instantly—without scheduling another appointment or even calling the home office.

Salespeople for Metropolitan Life Insurance company use laptops to help customers analyze the financial implications of different investments. For example, when the manager of a pension fund wanted to see what would happen if she switched money from one investment to another, the salesperson used spreadsheet software on the laptop to do the analysis—on the spot. The customer was convinced, and the sales rep closed a $633,000 sale.

Herman Miller, the office equipment company, provides dealers who sell its furniture with software that allows their sales reps to do a better job in a variety of tasks ranging from competitor analysis to preparation of realistic three-dimensional graphics that show an arrangement of furniture in a customer's office space. The competitor database provides very useful information about the limitations of office furniture available from many other firms. For instance, a sales rep learned that a prospect was leaning toward buying a competitor's office cubicles. She got back on track when the database revealed that the cubicles had no electrical outlets.

Results like these explain why the number of companies equipping salespeople with laptops is growing so rapidly. New laptops that feature built-in DVD drives (to handle massive amounts of information, including full-motion video for demonstrations and presentations), wireless Internet access, and the power to handle e-commerce applications are attracting even more attention.[12]

www.mhhe.com/fourps

checks. Unfortunately, such techniques can't guarantee success. But a systematic approach based on several different inputs results in a better sales force.

One problem in selecting salespeople is that two different sales jobs with identical titles may involve very different selling tasks and require different skills. A carefully prepared job description helps avoid this problem.

Job descriptions should be in writing and specific

A **job description** is a written statement of what a salesperson is expected to do. It might list 10 to 20 specific tasks—as well as routine prospecting and sales report writing. Each company must write its own job specifications. And it should provide clear guidelines about what selling tasks the job involves. This is critical to determine the kind of salespeople who should be selected—and later it provides a basis for seeing how they should be trained, how well they are performing, and how they should be paid.

Good salespeople are trained, not born

The idea that good salespeople are born may have some truth—but it isn't the whole story. A salesperson needs to be taught about the company and its products, about giving effective sales presentations, and about building strong relationships with customers. But this isn't always done. Many salespeople do a poor job because they haven't had good training. Firms often hire new salespeople and immediately send them out on the road, or the retail selling floor, with no grounding in the basic selling steps and no information about the product or the customer. They just get a price list and a pat on the back. This isn't enough![13]

Sales training should be modified based on the experience and skills of the group involved. But the company's sales training program should cover at least the following areas: (1) company policies, (2) product information, (3) building relationships with customer firms, and (4) professional selling skills.

La-Z-Boy operates a sales training institute to help furniture retailers train their salespeople. VCampus provides efficient online learning and training in a variety of fields, including sales.

Selling skills can be learned

Many companies spend the bulk of their training time on product information and company policy. They neglect training in selling techniques because they think selling is something anyone can do. But training in selling skills can pay off. Estée Lauder, for example, has selling skills for the "beauty advisors" who sell its cosmetics down to a fine art—and its training manual and seminars cover every detail. Its advisors who take the training seriously immediately double their sales.[14] Training can also help salespeople learn how to be more effective in cold calls on new prospects, in listening carefully to identify a customer's real objections, and in closing the sale.

Internet

Internet Exercise The Motivating Tape Company sells various sales training videos. Go to the firm's website (www.achievement.com) and then scroll down and select *Sales Training Videos.* Review the list of sales training videos offered. If a sales manager were going to rely on some of these tapes for training people just moving into a sales career, what key areas of sales training would he have to cover by some other approach?

Training on selling techniques often starts in the classroom with lectures, case studies, and videotaped trial presentations and demonstrations. But a complete training program adds on-the-job observation of effective salespeople and coaching from sales supervisors. Many companies also use weekly sales meetings or work sessions, annual conventions, and regular e-mail messages and newsletters, as well as ongoing training sessions, to keep salespeople up-to-date.[15]

Compensating and Motivating Salespeople

To recruit and keep good salespeople, a firm has to develop an attractive compensation plan designed to motivate. Ideally, sales reps should be paid in such a way that what they want to do—for personal interest and gain—is in the company's interest too. Most companies focus on financial motivation—but public recognition, sales contests, and simple personal recognition for a job well done can be highly effective in encouraging greater sales effort.[16] Our main emphasis here, however, will be on financial motivation.[17]

Two basic decisions must be made in developing a compensation plan: (1) the level of compensation and (2) the method of payment.

Compensation varies with job and needed skills

To attract good salespeople, a company must pay at least the going market wage for different kinds of salespeople. To be sure it can afford a specific type of salesperson, the company should estimate—when the job description is written—how valuable such a salesperson will be. A good order getter may be worth $50,000 to $100,000 to one company but only $15,000 to $25,000 to another—just because the second firm doesn't have enough to sell! In such a case, the second company should rethink its job specifications, or completely change its promotion plans, because the going rate for order getters is much higher than $15,000 a year.

If a job requires extensive travel, aggressive pioneering, or contacts with difficult customers, the pay may have to be higher. But the salesperson's compensation level should compare, at least roughly, with the pay scale of the rest of the firm. Normally, salespeople earn more than the office or production force but less than top management.

Payment methods vary

Given some general level of compensation, there are three basic methods of payment: (1) *straight salary*, (2) *straight commission*, or (3) a *combination plan*. Straight salary normally supplies the most security for the salesperson—and straight commission the most incentive. Most companies want to offer their salespeople some balance between incentive and security, so the most popular method is a combination plan that includes some salary and some commission. Bonuses, profit sharing, pensions, stock plans, insurance, and other fringe benefits may be included too.

Salary gives control—if there is close supervision

A salesperson on straight salary earns the same amount regardless of how he or she spends time. So the salaried salesperson is expected to do what the sales manager asks—whether it is order-taking, supporting sales activities, solving customer problems, or completing sales call reports. However, the sales manager maintains control *only* by close supervision. As a result, straight salary or a large salary element in the compensation plan increases the amount of sales supervision needed.

If such personal supervision would be difficult, a firm may get better control with a compensation plan that includes some commission, or even a straight commission plan with built-in direction. For example, if a company wants its salespeople to devote more time to developing new accounts, it can pay higher commissions for first orders from a new customer. However, a salesperson on a straight commission tends to be his or her own boss. The sales manager is less likely to get help on sales activities that won't increase the salesperson's earnings.

Incentives can be direct or indirect

The incentive effect of compensation works best when there is a direct relationship between the salesperson's effort and results. Otherwise, a salesperson in a growing territory might have rapidly increasing earnings—while the sales rep in a poor area will have little to show for the same amount of work. Such a situation isn't fair—and it can lead to high turnover and much dissatisfaction. A sales manager can take such differences into consideration when setting a salesperson's **sales quota**—the specific sales or profit objective a salesperson is expected to achieve.

The relationship between individual effort and results is less direct if a number of people are involved in the sale—engineers, top management, or supporting salespeople. In this case, each one's contribution is less obvious—and greater emphasis on salary may make more sense.

Exhibit 14-3
Relation between Personal Selling Expenses and Sales Volume—for Three Basic Personal Selling Compensation Alternatives

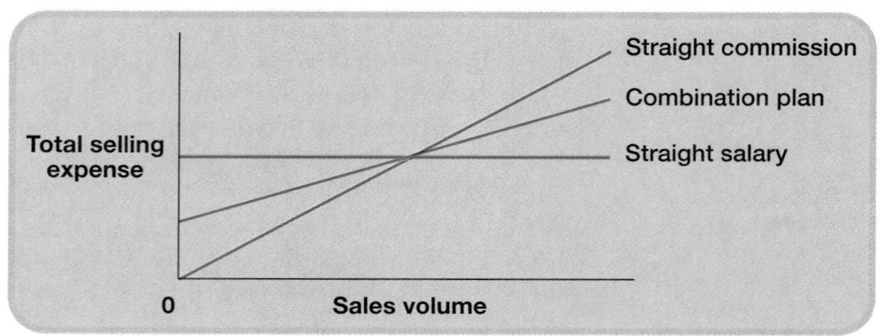

An incentive compensation plan can help motivate salespeople, but you have to be certain that the incentives are really aligned with the firm's objectives. For example, IBM's old sales commission plan resulted in IBM salespeople pushing customers to buy computers they didn't need. Sales reps got the sale and income, but then customers who were dissatisfied with what they'd purchased broke off their relationship with IBM and turned to other suppliers. Now IBM is trying to align its incentive plan with a customer orientation. For example, most IBM sales reps receive incentive pay based on customer satisfaction ratings and the profitability of the sales they get. Finding the right balance between these two criteria isn't easy. But many other firms use variations of this approach—because incentives that just focus on one-time sales may not be what is best to motivate sales reps to develop long-term, need-satisfying relationships with their customers.

Commissions are paid only if sales are made

Companies with limited working capital and uncertain markets often prefer straight commission, or combination plans with a large commission element. When sales drop off, costs do too. Such flexibility is similar to using manufacturers' agents who get paid only if they deliver sales. This advantage often dominates in selecting a sales compensation method. Exhibit 14-3 shows the general relation between personal selling expense and sales volume for each of the basic compensation alternatives.

Simplicity shows the link between effort and income

A final consideration is the need for *simplicity*. Complicated plans are hard for salespeople to understand. Salespeople become dissatisfied if they can't see a direct relationship between their effort and their income.

Simplicity is best achieved with straight salary. But in practice, it's usually better to sacrifice some simplicity to gain some incentive, flexibility, and control.

One way to increase flexibility and still make it easy for a sales rep to see the relationship between effort and compensation is to provide that information online. For example, Oracle, a company that sells database systems, has developed sales compensation software so its own sales reps can check a website at any point and see how they are doing. As new sales results come in, the report at the website is updated. Sales managers can also make changes quickly—for example, by putting a higher commission on a product or more weight on customer satisfaction scores.[18]

Personal Selling Techniques—Prospecting and Presenting

We've stressed the importance of training in selling techniques. Now let's discuss these ideas in more detail so you understand the basic steps each salesperson should follow—including prospecting and selecting target customers, planning

Exhibit 14-4
Key Steps in the Personal Selling Process

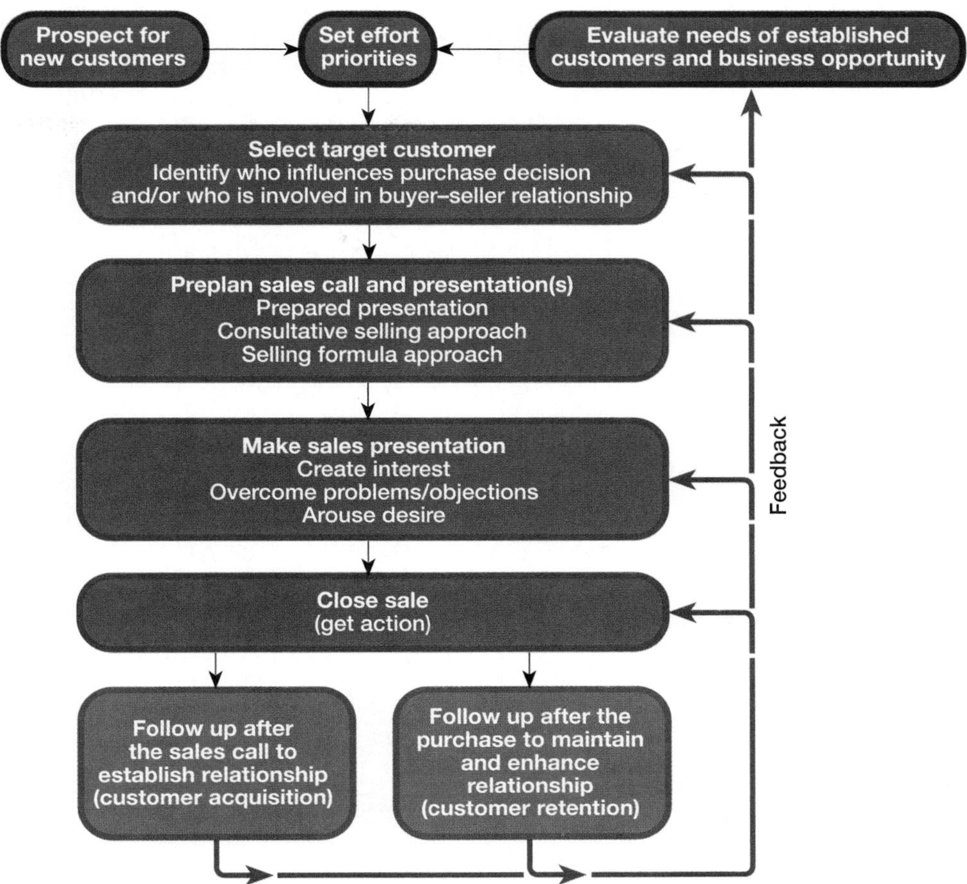

sales presentations, making sales presentations, and following up after the sale. Exhibit 14-4 shows the steps we'll consider. You can see that the salesperson is just carrying out a planned communication process—as we discussed in Chapter 13.[19]

Prospecting—narrowing down to the right target

Narrowing the personal selling effort down to the right target requires constant, detailed analysis of markets and much prospecting. Basically, **prospecting** involves following all the leads in the target market to identify potential customers.

Finding live prospects who will help make the buying decision isn't as easy as it sounds. In business markets, for example, the salesperson may need to do some hard detective work to find the real purchase decision makers.

Some companies provide prospect lists to make this part of the selling job easier. Inquiries that come in at the firm's website, for example, can be passed along to a sales rep for follow-up. A more indirect approach may be required. For example, one insurance company checks the local newspaper for marriage announcements—then a salesperson calls to see if the new couple is interested in finding out more about life insurance.

All customers are not equal

While prospecting focuses on identifying new customers, established customers require attention too. It's often time-consuming and expensive to establish a relationship with a customer, so once established it makes sense to keep the relationship healthy. That requires the rep to routinely review active accounts, rethink customers' needs, and reevaluate each customer's long-term business potential.

Sales managers are always looking for ways to make their salespeople more efficient and more effective.

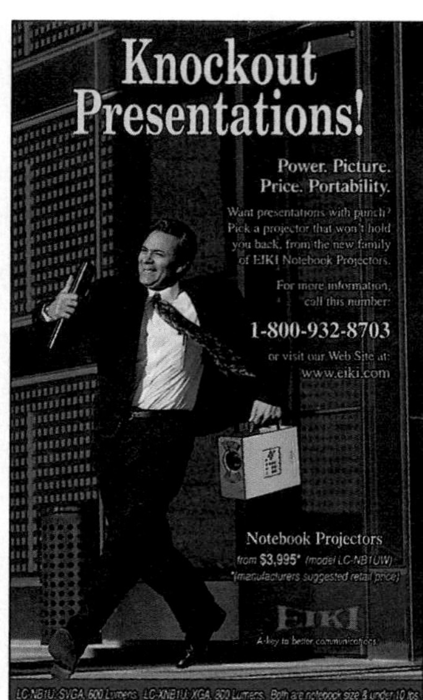

Some small accounts may have the potential to become big accounts, and some accounts that previously required a lot of costly attention may no longer warrant it. So a sales rep may need to set priorities both for new prospects and existing customers.

Internet

Internet Exercise Interact Commerce Corporation sells various software products, including ACT! personal management software that is used by many salespeople to organize information about their customers, sales calls, and tasks they need to do. Visit the ACT! website (www.act.com) for information about this product. Give a few specific examples of ways that a salesperson could use ACT! to build better relationships with customers.

How long to spend with whom?

Once a set of possible prospects, and customers who need attention, has been identified, the salesperson must decide how much time to spend with each one. A sales rep must qualify customers—to see if they deserve more effort. The salesperson usually makes these decisions by weighing the potential sales volume as well as the likelihood of a sale. This requires judgment. But well-organized salespeople usually develop some system because they have too many demands on their time.[20]

Many firms provide their reps with specially developed computer programs to help with this process. Most of them use some grading scheme. A sales rep might estimate how much each prospect is likely to purchase and the probability of getting and keeping the business given the competition. The computer then combines this information and grades each prospect. Attractive accounts may be labeled A—and the salesperson may plan to call on them weekly until the sale is made, the relationship is in good shape, or the customer is moved into a lower category. B customers might offer somewhat lower potential and be called on monthly. C accounts might be called on only once a year—unless they happen to contact the salesperson. And D accounts might be transferred to a telemarketing group.[21]

Exhibit 14-5
Prepared Approach to Sales Presentation

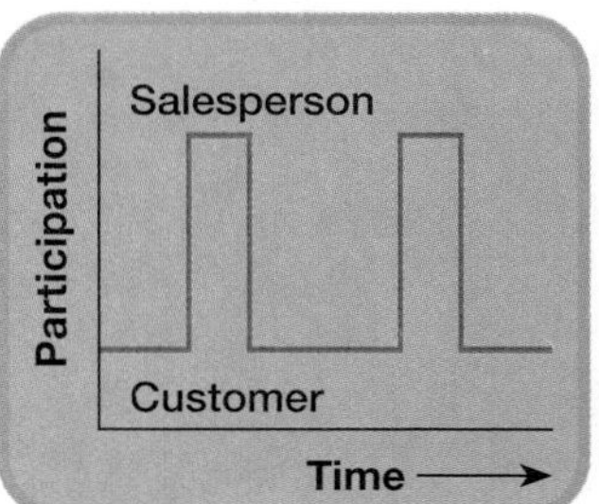

Exhibit 14-6
Consultative Selling Approach to Sales Presentation

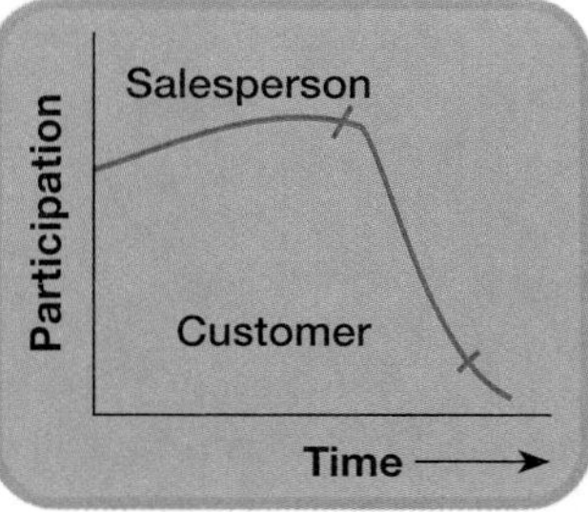

Exhibit 14-7
Selling Formula Approach to Sales Presentation

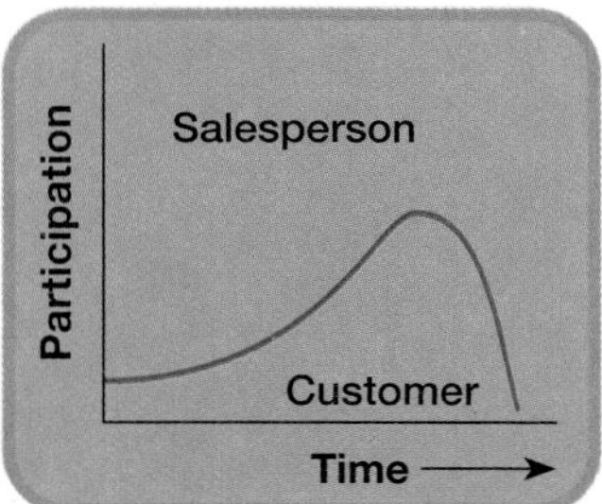

Three kinds of sales presentations may be useful

Once the salesperson selects a target customer, it's necessary to make a **sales presentation**—a salesperson's effort to make a sale or address a customer's problem. But someone has to plan what kind of sales presentation to make. This is a strategy decision. The kind of presentation should be set before the sales rep goes calling. And in situations where the customer comes to the salesperson—in a retail store, for instance—planners have to make sure that prospects are brought together with salespeople.

A marketing manager can choose two basically different approaches to making sales presentations: the prepared approach or the consultative selling approach. Another approach—the selling formula approach—is a combination of the two. Each of these has its place.

The prepared sales presentation

The **prepared sales presentation** approach uses a memorized presentation that is not adapted to each individual customer. This approach says that a customer faced with a particular stimulus will give the desired response—in this case, a yes answer to the salesperson's prepared statement, which includes a **close,** the salesperson's request for an order.

If one trial close doesn't work, the sales rep tries another prepared presentation and attempts another closing. This can go on for some time—until the salesperson runs out of material or the customer either buys or decides to leave. Exhibit 14-5 shows the relative participation of the salesperson and customer in the prepared approach. Note that the salesperson does most of the talking.

Firms may rely on the canned approach when only a short presentation is practical. It's also sensible when salespeople aren't very skilled. The company can control what they say and in what order. For example, Novartis uses missionary salespeople to tell doctors about new drugs when they're introduced. Doctors are busy, so they only give the rep a minute or two. That's just enough time to give a short, prepared pitch and leave some samples. To get the most out of the presentation, Novartis refines it based on feedback from doctors whom it pays to participate in focus groups.[22]

But a canned approach has a weakness. It treats all potential customers alike. It may work for some and not for others—and the salespeople probably won't know why or learn from experience. A prepared approach may be suitable for simple order-taking—but it is no longer considered good selling for complicated situations.

Consultative selling—builds on the marketing concept

The **consultative selling approach** involves developing a good understanding of the individual customer's needs before trying to close the sale. This name is used because the salesperson is almost acting as a consultant to help identify and solve the customer's problem. With this approach, the sales rep makes some general benefit statements to get the customer's attention and interest. Then the salesperson asks questions and *listens carefully* to understand the customer's needs. Once they agree on needs, the seller tries to show the customer how the product fills those needs and to close the sale. This is a problem-solving approach—in which the customer and salesperson work together to satisfy the customer's needs. That's why it's sometimes called the need-satisfaction approach. Exhibit 14-6 shows the participation of the customer and the salesperson during such a sales presentation.

The consultative selling approach takes skill and time. The salesperson must be able to analyze what motivates a particular customer and show how the company's offering would help the customer satisfy those needs. The sales rep may even conclude that the customer's problem is really better solved with someone else's product. That might result in one lost sale, but it also is likely to build real trust and more sales opportunities over the life of the relationship with the customer. That's why this kind of selling is typical in business markets when a salesperson already has established a close relationship with a customer.

Selling formula approach—some of both

The **selling formula approach** starts with a prepared presentation outline—much like the prepared approach—and leads the customer through some logical steps to a final close. The prepared steps are logical because we assume that we know something about the target customer's needs and attitudes.

Exhibit 14-7 shows the selling formula approach. The salesperson does most of the talking at the beginning of the presentation—to communicate key points early. This part of the presentation may even have been prepared as part of the marketing strategy. As the sales presentation moves along, however, the salesperson brings the customer into the discussion to help clarify just what needs this customer has. The salesperson's job is to discover the needs of a particular customer to know how to proceed. Once it is clear what kind of customer this is, the salesperson comes back to show how the product satisfies this specific customer's needs and to close the sale.

AIDA helps plan sales presentations

AIDA—Attention, Interest, Desire, Action: Most sales presentations follow this AIDA sequence. The time a sales rep spends on each of the steps might vary depending on the situation and the selling approach being used. But it is still necessary to begin a presentation by getting the prospect's *attention* and, hopefully, to move the customer to *action*.[23]

Each sales manager and salesperson needs to think about this sequence in deciding what sales approach to use and in evaluating a possible presentation. Does the presentation get the prospect's attention quickly? Will it be interesting? Will the benefits be clear? Does the presentation consider likely objections so the sales rep can act to close the sale when the time is right? These may seem like simple things. But too frequently they aren't done at all—and a sale is lost.

Ethical issues may arise

As in every other area of marketing communications, ethical issues arise in the personal selling area. The most basic issue, plain and simple, is whether a salesperson's presentation is honest and truthful. But addressing that issue is a no-brainer. No company is served well by a salesperson who lies or manipulates customers to get their business.

On the other hand, most sales reps sooner or later face a sales situation in which they must make more difficult ethical decisions about how to balance company interests, customer interests, and personal interests. Conflicts are less likely to arise if the firm's marketing mix really meets the needs of its target market. Similarly, they are less likely to arise when the firm sees the value of developing a longer-term relationship with the customer. Then the salesperson is arranging a happy marriage. By contrast, ethical conflicts are more likely when the sales rep's personal outcomes

Keebler salespeople use an interactive tool called Instant Data Evaluation Access ("IDEA") Wizard on their laptop computers. It provides research data related to the marketing of cookies and crackers on topics such as shelf space management and consumer purchase patterns. The sales rep can use the Wizard to support a consultative selling approach in working to develop closer relationships with retailers.

(such as commission income) or the selling firm's profits hinge on making sales to customers whose needs are only partially met by the firm's offering.

Ideally, companies can avoid the whole problem by supporting their salespeople with a marketing mix that really offers target customers unique benefits. Moreover, top executives, marketing managers, and sales managers set the tone for the ethical climate in which a salesperson operates. If they set impossible goals or project a "do-what-you-need-to-do" attitude, a desperate salesperson may yield to the pressure of the moment. When a firm clearly advocates ethical selling behavior and makes it clear that manipulative selling techniques are not acceptable, the salesperson is not left trying to swim "against the flow."[24]

Conclusion

In this chapter, we discussed the importance and nature of personal selling. Selling is much more than just getting rid of the product. In fact, a salesperson who is not given strategy guidelines may have to become the strategy planner for the market he or she serves. Ideally, however, the sales manager and marketing manager work together to set some strategy guidelines: the kind and number of salespersons needed, what sales technology support will be provided, the kind of sales presentation desired, and selection, training, and motivation approaches.

We discussed the three basic sales tasks: (1) order-getting, (2) order-taking, and (3) supporting. Most sales jobs combine at least two of these three tasks. Once a firm specifies the important tasks, it can decide on the structure of its sales organization and the number of salespeople it needs. The nature of the job and the level and method of compensation also depend on the blend of these tasks. Firms should develop a job description for each sales job. This, in turn, provides guidelines for selecting, training, and compensating salespeople.

Once the marketing manager agrees to the basic plan and sets the budget, the sales manager must implement the plan—including directing and controlling the sales force. This includes assigning sales territories and controlling performance. You can see that the sales manager has more to do than jet around the country sipping martinis and entertaining customers. A sales manager is deeply involved with the basic management tasks of planning and control—as well as ongoing implementation of the personal selling effort.

We also reviewed some basic selling techniques and identified three kinds of sales presentations. Each has its place—but the consultative selling approach seems best for higher-level sales jobs. In these kinds of jobs, personal selling is achieving a new, professional status because of the competence and level of personal responsibility required of the salesperson. The day of the old-time glad-hander is passing in favor of the specialist who is creative, industrious, persuasive, knowledgeable, highly trained, and therefore able to help the buyer. This type of salesperson always has been, and probably always will be, in short supply. And the demand for high-level salespeople is growing.

Questions and Problems

1. What strategy decisions are needed in the personal selling area? Why should the marketing manager make these strategy decisions?
2. What kind of salesperson (or what blend of the basic sales tasks) is required to sell the following products? If there are several selling jobs in the channel for each product, indicate the kinds of salespeople required. Specify any assumptions necessary to give definite answers.
   a. Laundry detergent.
   b. Costume jewelry.
   c. Office furniture.
   d. Men's underwear.
   e. Mattresses.
   f. Corn.
   g. Life insurance.
3. Distinguish among the jobs of producers', wholesalers', and retailers' order-getting salespeople. If one order getter is needed, must all the salespeople in a channel be order getters? Illustrate.
4. Discuss the role of the manufacturers' agent in a marketing manager's promotion plans. What kind of salesperson is a manufacturers' agent? What type of compensation plan is used for a manufacturers' agent?
5. Discuss the future of the specialty shop if producers place greater emphasis on mass selling because of the inadequacy of retail order-taking.
6. Compare and contrast missionary salespeople and technical specialists.
7. Explain how a compensation plan could be developed to provide incentives for experienced salespeople and yet make some provision for trainees who have not yet learned the job.
8. Cite an actual local example of each of the three kinds of sales presentations discussed in the chapter. Explain for each situation whether a different type of presentation would have been better.
9. Are the benefits and limitations of a canned presentation any different if it is supported with a slide show or videotape than if it is just a person talking? Why or why not?
10. Describe a consultative selling sales presentation that you experienced recently. How could it have been improved by fuller use of the AIDA framework?
11. How would our economy operate if personal salespeople were outlawed? Could the economy work? If so, how? If not, what is the minimum personal selling effort necessary? Could this minimum personal selling effort be controlled by law?

Suggested Cases

16. Enviro Pure Water, Inc.
19. Chemical International, Inc.
20. Cable Designs, Inc.
22. PlastiForm Mfg., Inc.
24. PCT, Inc.

Computer-Aided Problem

14. Sales Compensation

Franco Welles, sales manager for Nanek, Inc., is trying to decide whether to pay a sales rep for a new territory with straight commission or a combination plan. He wants to evaluate possible plans—to compare the compensation costs and profitability of each. Welles knows that sales reps in similar jobs at other firms make about $36,000 a year.

The sales rep will sell two products. Welles is planning a higher commission for Product B—because he wants it to get extra effort. From experience with similar products, he has some rough estimates of expected sales volume under the different plans and various ideas about commission rates. The details are found in the spreadsheet. The program computes compensation and how much the sales rep will contribute to profit. "Profit contribution" is equal to the total revenue generated by the sales rep minus sales compensation costs and the costs of producing the units.

a. *For the initial values shown in the spreadsheet, which plan—commission or combination—would give the rep the highest compensation, and which plan would give the greatest profit contribution to Nanek, Inc.?*

b. *Welles thinks a sales rep might be motivated to work harder and sell 1,100 units of Product B if the commission rate (under the commission plan) were increased to 10 percent. If Welles is right (and everything else stays the same), would the higher commission rate be a good deal for Nanek? Explain your thinking.*

c. *A sales rep interested in the job is worried about making payments on her new car. She asks if Welles would consider paying her with a combination plan but with more guaranteed income (an $18,000 base salary) in return for taking a 3 percent commission on Products B and A. If this arrangement results in the same unit sales as Welles originally estimated for the combination plan, would Nanek, Inc., be better off or worse off under this arrangement?*

d. *Do you think the rep's proposal will meet Welles' goals for Product B? Explain your thinking.*

For additional questions related to this problem, see Exercise 14-3 in the *Learning Aid for Use with Essentials of Marketing*, 9th edition.

Chapter Fifteen

Advertising and Sales Promotion

When You Finish This Chapter, You Should

1. Understand why a marketing manager sets specific objectives to guide the advertising effort.

2. Understand when the various kinds of advertising are needed.

3. Understand how to choose the "best" medium.

4. Understand the main ways that advertising on the Internet differs from advertising in other media.

5. Understand how to plan the "best" message—that is, the copy thrust.

6. Understand what advertising agencies do and how they are paid.

7. Understand how to advertise legally.

8. Understand the importance and nature of sales promotion.

9. Know the advantages and limitations of different types of sales promotion.

10. Understand the important new terms (shown in red).

Over the years, Frito-Lay brands—like Doritos, Fritos, and Lay's—had captured half of all snack sales. However, low-priced dealer brands were stealing market share. Worse, the bulging growth from snacks was tapering off. Aging consumers were cutting back on fat, and snacks, in their diet. So Rebecca Johnson, product manager for Lay's Potato Chips, had to figure out how to fend off the price cutters and attract new snackers.

The main weapon in her battle was a line of low-fat products that were in product development. Baked Lay's, a low-fat potato crisp, had great potential. They had only about 15 percent of the fat in regular Lay's Potato Chips and fewer calories. They had also fared well in consumer taste tests. Consumers simply wouldn't compromise on good taste.

There were still some challenges. The retail price of Baked Lay's would be about one-third more than regular chips. That was the difference in the cost to produce them. Further, because of FTC rules, Baked Lay's could not be called potato "chips." Chips are slices from

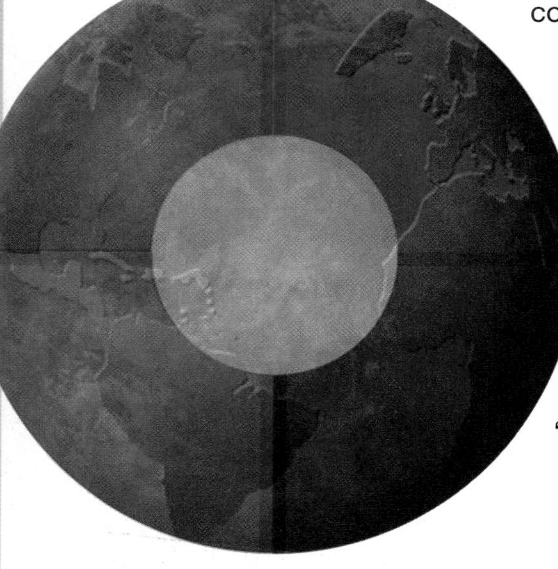

place price promotion produ

potatoes, but Baked Lay's were cut from a thin sheet of dough made from potato flakes. No one knew if people would pay a higher price for a crisp; it was a new unsought product.

Baked Lay's went into national distribution in the late fall, but initial sales were only one-third of the forecast. Trade promotion and personal selling helped get Baked Lay's on store shelves, but without TV ads to give a reason to buy, the packages were collecting dust. By contrast, regular Lay's were selling well even though there had been little advertising since the "bet you can't eat just one" campaign over a year earlier. Yet it usually does take more ad weight to introduce a new product—even one with a famous name—than to support an existing one. And Johnson knew that it would take effective advertising to win back the support of Frito-Lay salespeople and to interest consumers in baked crisps.

Johnson worked with BBDO—Lay's long-time ad agency—to set specific objectives for the campaign and to create an attention-getting ad that would interest women with a low-fat pitch, but not turn off men—who are the biggest snackers. The launch of the campaign was on New Year's Day with an ad that showed a trio of supermodels doing unlikely things like chowing down on the crisps. The tagline "Now you can eat like one of the guys and still look like one of the girls" gave consumers permission to indulge their cravings without the guilt. That copy thrust hit the right chord with women, and it didn't turn off men. It was also consistent with the "better for you" positioning of Frito-Lay's whole low-fat line. A heavy flight of ads ran on targeted media throughout the spring.

Research on the effectiveness of the ads showed strong results, but the ads didn't carry the whole load in generating interest and trial. For example, the trio of supermodels also appeared on a crisp-covered float that Frito-Lay sponsored for the nationally televised New Year's Rose Parade. And to encourage trial, a million samples were sent to households for Super Bowl Sunday. Those were followed during the next two weekends with ads and coupons in newspaper free-standing inserts.

Two weeks into the campaign, sales started to surge and supply ran short. Consumers were even asking friends to keep an eye out for them. Some cynical critics said that the shortages were just another advertising gimmick contrived for the publicity. But the firm simply couldn't keep up with demand—even with all four factories working full tilt 24 hours a day.

There's no doubt that clever ads and timely sales promotion spurred consumer interest in Baked Lay's. But in the end, what kept customers coming back, even at a premium price, was the superior value of a product that really met their needs.[1]

Advertising, Sales Promotion, and Marketing Strategy Decisions

The Baked Lay's case shows that carefully planned advertising and sales promotion can be critical to the success of a strategy.

Unfortunately, the results that marketers *actually achieve* are very uneven. It's often said that half of the money spent on advertising and sales promotion is wasted—but that too few managers know which half. Mass selling can be exciting and involving or it can be downright obnoxious. Sometimes it's based on careful research, yet much of it is just based on someone's pet idea. A creative idea may produce great results or be a colossal waste of money. Ads can stir deep emotions or go unnoticed.

Many managers do a poor job with advertising and sales promotion. So, just copying how lots of other firms handle these important strategy decisions is not "good enough." There's no sense in imitating bad practices. Instead, it makes sense to understand the important strategy decisions involved in each of these areas.

As the Lay's case illustrates, marketing managers and the advertising agencies that work with them have important advertising decisions to make, including (1) who their target audience is, (2) what kind of advertising to use, (3) how to reach customers (via which types of media), (4) what to say to them (the copy thrust), and (5) who will do the work—the firm's own advertising department or outside agencies. See Exhibit 15-1.

International dimensions are important

The basic strategy planning decisions for advertising and sales promotion are the same regardless of where in the world the target market is located. However, the choices available to a marketing manager within each of the decision areas may vary dramatically from one country to another.

Commercial television may not be available. If it is, government rules may limit the type of advertising permitted or when ads can be shown. Radio broadcasts in a market area may not be in the target market's language. The target audience may not be able to read. Access to interactive media like the Internet may be nonexistent. Cultural influences may limit ad messages. Ad agencies that already know a nation's unique advertising environment may not be available.

Exhibit 15-1 Strategy Planning for Advertising

International dimensions also impact sales promotion. A typical Japanese grocery retailer with only 250 square feet of space, for example, doesn't have room for *any* special end-of-aisle displays. Consumer promotions may be affected too. Polish consumers, for example, are skeptical about product samples. They figure that if it's free something's amiss. In some developing nations samples can't be distributed through the mail—because they're stolen before they get to customers. And some countries ban consumer sweepstakes—because they see them as a form of gambling.

In this chapter we'll consider a number of these international issues, but we'll focus on the array of choices available in the U.S. and other advanced economies.[2]

Traditional media choices are more limited in some international markets, so marketers must be creative to communicate their messages. In North Africa and the Middle East, Coke uses hot-air balloons. The 12-stories-tall Ariel shirt was mounted on a building in China.

Exhibit 15-2 Advertising Spending as Percent of Sales for Illustrative Product Categories

Category	Advertising as percent of sales
PRODUCERS:	
Petroleum refining	0.8
Bakery products	1.4
Computers and office equipment	1.5
Plastic products	1.8
Dairy products	2.5
Motor vehicles and car bodies	2.7
Greeting cards	3.0
Cable and other pay TV services	4.2
Sporting and athletic goods	4.4
Business services	4.8
Footwear (except rubber)	5.0
Soft drinks, water	5.3
Investment advice	5.7
Transportation services	6.2
Malt beverages	8.6
Games and toys	10.3
Soap and detergent	12.5
Perfumes and cosmetics	12.8
RETAILERS:	
Grocery stores	1.2
Hotels and motels	1.2
Eating places	3.8
Videotape rental	4.5
Women's clothing stores	5.6
Amusement parks	7.5
Catalog, mail-order houses	9.1
Furniture stores	9.4

Total spending is big—and growing internationally

As an economy grows, advertising becomes more important—because more consumers have income and advertising can get results. But good advertising results cost money. And spending on advertising is significant. In 1946, U.S. advertising spending was slightly more than $3 billion. By 2001 it was about $250 billion.

During the last decade, the rate of advertising spending has increased even more rapidly in other countries. However, advertising in the U.S. accounts for roughly half of worldwide ad spending. Europe accounts for 23 percent, and Asia about 22 percent. For most countries in other regions, advertising spending has traditionally been quite low.[3]

Most advertisers aren't really spending that much

While total spending on advertising seems high, it represents a small portion of what people pay for the goods and services they buy. U.S. corporations spend an average of only about 2.5 percent of their sales dollar on advertising. Worldwide, the percentage is even smaller.

Exhibit 15-2 shows, however, that advertising spending as a percent of sales dollars varies significantly across product categories. Producers of consumer products generally spend a larger percent than firms that produce business products. For example, U.S. companies that make perfume and cosmetics spend a whopping 12.8 percent. At the other extreme, companies that sell plastics to manufacturers spend only about 1.8 percent.

In general, the percent is smaller for retailers and wholesalers than for producers. Large chains like Kmart and JCPenney spend about 3 percent, but many retailers and wholesalers spend 1 percent or less.

Of course, percentages don't tell the whole story. Nissan, which spends less than 1 percent of sales on advertising, is among the top 50 advertisers worldwide. The really big spenders are very important to the advertising industry because they account for a large share of total advertising spending. Worldwide, the top 50 global advertisers spend about $50 billion a year. The three top spenders are Unilever, Procter & Gamble, and Nestlé.[4]

Advertising doesn't employ that many people

While total advertising expenditures are large, the advertising industry itself employs relatively few people. The major expense is for media time and space. In the United States, the largest share of this—24 percent—goes for television (including cable). Newspapers take about 20 percent of the total and direct mail about 18 percent. The shares for radio (8 percent), the Yellow Pages (5 percent), magazines (5 percent), and the Internet (2 percent) are much smaller. However, spending for advertising on the Internet is growing very fast.[5]

Many students hope for a glamorous job in advertising, but there are fewer jobs in advertising than you might think. In the United States, only about 500,000 people work directly in the advertising industry. Advertising agencies employ only about half of all these people.[6]

Advertising Objectives Are a Strategy Decision

Advertising objectives must be specific

Every ad and every advertising campaign should have clearly defined objectives. These should grow out of the firm's overall marketing strategy and the promotion jobs assigned to advertising. It isn't enough for the marketing manager to say "Promote the product." The marketing manager must decide exactly what advertising should do.

Advertising objectives should be more specific than personal selling objectives. One of the advantages of personal selling is that a salesperson can shift the presentation for a specific customer. Each ad, however, must be effective not just for one customer but for thousands, or millions, of them.

The marketing manager sets the overall direction

The marketing manager might give the advertising manager one or more of the following specific objectives, along with the budget to accomplish them:

1. Help position the firm's brand or marketing mix by informing and persuading target customers or middlemen about its benefits.
2. Help introduce new products to specific target markets.
3. Help obtain desirable outlets and tell customers where they can buy a product.
4. Provide ongoing contact with target customers—even when a salesperson isn't available.
5. Prepare the way for salespeople by presenting the company's name and the merits of its products.
6. Get immediate buying action.
7. Help to maintain relationships with satisfied customers and encourage more purchases.

If you want half the market, say so!

The objectives listed above highlight that a balancing act may be required. The first objective is quite broad and relates to the basic decisions about how the marketing manager wants to differentiate and position the whole marketing mix. That should guide decisions about what other specific objectives are most important. In fact, some of the objectives listed are not as specific as they could be. If a marketing manager really wants specific results, they should be clearly stated. A general objective is "To help expand market share." This could be rephrased more specifically: "To increase shelf space in our cooperating retail outlets by 25 percent during the next three months."

Exhibit 15-3 Examples of Different Types of Advertising over Adoption Process Stages

Awareness	Interest	Evaluation and trial	Decision	Confirmation
Teaser campaigns Pioneering ads Jingles/slogans Internet banners Announcements	Informative or descriptive ads Image/celebrity ads Flash ads Demonstration of benefits	Competitive ads Persuasive copy Comparative ads Testimonials	Direct-action retail ads Point-of-purchase ads Price deal offers	Reminder ads Informative "why" ads

Objectives guide type of advertising

The specific objectives obviously affect what type of advertising is best. Exhibit 15-3 shows that the type of advertising that achieves objectives for one stage of the adoption process may be off target for another. For example, most advertising for cameras in the United States, Germany, and Japan focuses on fool-proof pictures or state-of-the-art design because most consumers in these countries already own *some* camera. In Africa, where only about 20 percent of the population owns a camera, ads must sell the whole concept of picture-taking.

Objectives Determine the Kinds of Advertising Needed

The advertising objectives largely determine which of two basic types of advertising to use—product or institutional.

Product advertising tries to sell a product. It may be aimed at final users or channel members.

Institutional advertising tries to promote an organization's image, reputation, or ideas rather than a specific product. Its basic objective is to develop goodwill or improve an organization's relations with various groups—not only customers but also current and prospective channel members, suppliers, shareholders, employees, and the general public. The British government, for instance, uses institutional advertising to promote England as a place to do business.

Product advertising—know us, like us, remember us

Product advertising falls into three categories: pioneering, competitive, and reminder advertising.

Pioneering advertising—builds primary demand

Pioneering advertising tries to develop primary demand for a product category rather than demand for a specific brand. Pioneering advertising is usually done in the early stages of the product life cycle; it informs potential customers about the new product and helps turn them into adopters. When Merrell Dow Pharmaceutical introduced a prescription drug to help smokers break the habit, its pioneering ad didn't even mention the name of the drug. Instead it informed smokers who wanted to quit that doctors had a new way to help them.

Competitive advertising—emphasizes selective demand

Competitive advertising tries to develop selective demand for a specific brand. A firm is forced into competitive advertising as the product life cycle moves along—to hold its own against competitors.

Competitive advertising may be either direct or indirect. The **direct type** aims for immediate buying action. The **indirect type** points out product advantages to affect future buying decisions.

Comparative ads make direct comparisons with other brands using actual product names. For example, the Baby Orajel ad touts its fast relief compared to Children's Tylenol. Buster Brown uses a different approach. It is a well-known brand with a hundred-year history, but at back-to-school, shoe-buying time it ran print and outdoor ads to remind parents of their positive feelings about Buster Brown shoes. Ads featured a toll-free number to call or website address so consumers could learn the location of the closest retailer.

Most of Delta Airlines' advertising is of the competitive variety. Much of it tries for immediate sales—so the ads are the direct type with prices, timetables, and phone numbers to call for reservations. Some of its ads are the indirect type. They focus on the quality of service—and suggest you mention Delta's name when you talk to your travel agent.

Comparative advertising is even rougher. **Comparative advertising** means making specific brand comparisons—using actual product names. A recent comparative ad for a Kia Optima implied that a Toyota Camry with the same features was a great car but not as good a value as the Optima, which costs $5,000 less.

Many countries forbid comparative advertising, but that situation is changing. For example, Japan banned comparative advertising until about 15 years ago, when the restrictions were relaxed. Japan's move followed an earlier change in the United States. The Federal Trade Commission decided to encourage comparative ads, after banning them for years—because it thought they would increase competition and provide consumers with more useful information.

In the United States, superiority claims are supposed to be supported by research evidence—but the guidelines aren't clear. When P&G's Dryel did not fare well in independent test comparisons with stain removal by professional dry cleaners, P&G changed its ad claims. However, some firms just keep running tests until they get the results they want. Others talk about minor differences that don't reflect a product's overall benefits.[7]

Reminder advertising—reinforces a favorable relationship

Reminder advertising tries to keep the product's name before the public. It may be useful when the product has achieved brand preference or insistence—perhaps in the market maturity or sales decline stages. It is used primarily to reinforce previous promotion. Here the advertiser may use soft-sell ads that just mention or show the name—as a reminder. Sunkist, for example, often relies on reminder ads because most consumers already know the brand name and, after years of promotion, associate it with high product quality.

Institutional advertising—remember our name

Institutional advertising usually focuses on the name and prestige of an organization or industry. It may seek to inform, persuade, or remind.

Japanese firms, like Hitachi, emphasize institutional advertising, in part because they often use the company name as a brand name.

Companies sometimes rely on institutional advertising to present the company in a favorable light—perhaps to overcome image problems. Oil giant BP, for example, ran ads in a bid to be seen as more pro-environmental. However, in this case, they just drew more criticism.[8]

Some organizations use institutional advertising to advocate a specific cause or idea. Insurance companies and organizations like Mothers Against Drunk Driving, for example, use these advocacy ads to encourage people not to drink and drive.[9]

Coordinating Advertising Efforts with Cooperative Relationships

Vertical cooperation—advertising allowances, cooperative advertising

Sometimes a producer knows that an advertising job can be done more effectively or more economically by someone further along in the channel. Alternatively, a retail chain like Best Buy may approach a manufacturer like Panasonic with an ad program and tell them how much it will cost to participate. In either case, the producer may offer **advertising allowances**—price reductions to firms further along in the channel to encourage them to advertise or otherwise promote the firm's products locally.

Cooperative advertising involves middlemen and producers sharing in the cost of ads. This helps wholesalers and retailers compete in their local markets. It also helps the producer get more promotion for the advertising dollar because media usually give local advertisers lower rates than national or international firms. In addition, a retailer or wholesaler who is paying a share of the cost is more likely to follow through.

Integrated communications from cooperative relationships

Coordination and integration of ad messages in the channel is another reason for cooperative advertising. One big, well-planned, integrated advertising effort is often better than many different, perhaps inconsistent, local efforts. Many franchise operations like the idea of communicating with one voice. KFC, for example, encourages its franchises to use a common advertising program. Before, many developed their own local ads—with themes like "Eight clucks for four bucks"—that didn't fit with the company's overall marketing strategy.

To get this coordination, producers often provide a master of an ad on a videotape, cassette tape, website, or printed sheets. The middlemen add their identification before turning the ad over to local media.[10]

Ethical concerns may arise

Ethical issues sometimes arise concerning advertising allowance programs. For example, a retailer may run one producer's ad to draw customers to the store but then sell them another brand. Is this unethical? Some producers think it is. A different view is that retailers are obligated to the producer to run the ad but obligated to consumers to sell them what they want, no matter whose brand it may be. A producer can often avoid the problem by setting the allowance amount as a percent of the retailer's *actual sales*. That way, a retailer who doesn't produce sales doesn't get the allowance. Smart producers also insist on proof that the advertising was really done.[11]

Choosing the "Best" Medium—How to Deliver the Message

What is the best advertising medium? There is no simple answer to this question. Effectiveness depends on how well the medium fits with the rest of a marketing strategy—that is, it depends on (1) your promotion objectives, (2) what target

Does Advertising That's Everywhere Get Us Anywhere?

It's everywhere. You get to the beach, look down, and huge versions of the Skippy peanut butter logo are embossed in the sand. You roll your eyes in dismay and catch a view of a plane pulling MCI's 100-foot-long banner with Mr. T demanding "Call home, fool." You go in the bathroom to change into your swimsuit, but the walls are adorned with posters for Good Humor ice-cream bars. Forget that. Maybe you should just eat your picnic lunch. Oops, the whole back of the bench you're going to sit on is an ad for a check-cashing service—and just for good measure the banana you pull out of your lunch bag has a sticker advertising Florida oranges. So you jump in your car to escape the onslaught. But when you stop to pump gas a miniature video screen by the credit card slot urges you to get a Visa debit card from a local bank (first in English and then in Spanish). The billboards you ignore along the way seem pretty civilized compared to the towering trucks whose trailers are rolling billboards. Back at the ranch, at last, you know you can watch the Grammy Awards show in peace because you taped it on your VCR—so you can zap past the ads. But no, you can't see the celebrities arrive without staring at virtual logos digitally superimposed on the entry canopy and sidewalk by the front door. So there's no alternative but to pull the plug on the VCR and check for e-mail from your sweetie. Wrong move. A pop-up ad for a video cam covers half of the screen—and why can't you make it go away? You can drag it to the side, but then there's so much spam in your mailbox that you've run out of disk space.

There are certainly many cases where promotion benefits both the consumer and the firm, and after all it is revenues from advertising that cover the cost of lots of great stuff consumers get for free. Yet sometimes you can't help but wish that you were not the target that somebody else is aiming at![12]

www.mhhe.com/fourps

markets you want to reach, (3) the funds available for advertising, and (4) the nature of the media—including who they *reach*, with what *frequency*, with what *impact*, and at what *cost*.

Exhibit 15-4 shows some pros and cons of major kinds of media and some examples of costs. However, some of the advantages noted in this table may not apply in all markets. For example, direct mail may not be a flexible choice in a country with a weak postal system. Internet ads might be worthless if few target customers have access to the Internet. Similarly, TV audiences are often less selective and targeted, but a special-interest cable TV show may reach a very specific audience.[13]

Specific promotion objectives

The medium should support the promotion objectives. If the objective requires demonstrating product benefits, TV may be the best alternative. If the objective is to inform—telling a detailed story and using precise pictures—then Internet advertising might be right. Alternatively, with a broad target market, print media may be better. For example, Jockey switched its advertising to magazines from television when it decided to show the variety of styles of its men's briefs. Jockey worried that there were problems with modeling men's underwear on television. However, Jockey might have stayed with TV if it had been targeting consumers in France or Brazil—where nudity in TV ads is common.[14]

Match your market with the media

To guarantee good media selection, the advertiser first must *clearly* specify its target market. Then the advertiser can choose media that reach target customers.

The media available in a country may limit the choices. In less-developed nations, for example, radio is often the only way to reach a broad-based market of poor consumers who can't read or afford television.

In most cases, however, the major problem is to select media that effectively reach the target audience. Most of the major media use marketing research to develop profiles of the people who buy their publications or live in their broadcasting area.

Another problem is that the audience for media that *do* reach your target market may also include people who are *not* in the target group. But *you pay for the whole audience the media delivers*—including those who aren't potential customers. For example, Delta Faucet, a faucet manufacturer that wanted its ads to reach plumbers, placed ads on ESPN's Saturday college football telecasts. Research showed

Exhibit 15-4 Relative Size and Costs, and Advantages and Disadvantages, of Major Kinds of Media

Kinds of Media	Sales Volume, 2000 ($ billions)	Typical Costs, 2000	Advantages	Disadvantages
Television and Cable	$59.2	$4,500 for a 30-second spot, prime time, Phoenix	Demonstrations, good attention, wide reach	Expensive in total, "clutter," less-selective audience
Newspaper	49.0	$42,570 for one-page (black/white) weekday, *Arizona Republic*	Flexible, timely, local market	May be expensive, short life, no "pass-along"
Direct mail	44.6	$215 per 1,000 for listing of 114,000 human resource executives by industry or employee size	Selected audience, flexible, can personalize	Relatively expensive per contact, "junk mail"—hard to retain attention
Radio	19.3	$350–$400 for one-minute drive time, Phoenix	Wide reach, segmented audience, inexpensive	Weak attention, many different rates, short exposure
Yellow Pages	13.2	$2,760 a year for a ⅛-page display ad in a directory for a city with .5 million population	Reaches local customers seeking purchase information	Many other competitors listed in same place, hard to differentiate
Magazine	12.4	$192,000 for one-page, four-color in *Time* (national)	Very targeted, good detail, good "pass-along"	Inflexible, long lead times
Outdoor	5.2	$5,000 (painted) for prime billboard, 30- to 60-day showings, Phoenix	Flexible, repeat exposure, inexpensive	"Mass market," very short exposure
Internet	4.3	Banner ads average $34 for every 1,000 ad impressions on the site	Ads link to more detailed website, some "pay for results"	Hard to compare costs with other media

that many plumbers watched the ESPN games. Yet plumbers are only a very small portion of the total college football audience—and the size of the total audience determined the cost of the advertising time.[15]

The cost of reaching the real target market goes up fastest when the irrelevant audience is very large. For example, the last episode of the wildly popular "Seinfeld" sitcom drew about 75 million viewers and NBC charged $1.5 million for a 30-second ad slot. It may have been worth that for Visa to reach such a large, mainly adult, audience.[16] On the other hand, tiny Gardenburger, Inc., bought an ad slot in a shoot-for-the-moon effort to turn the audience on to its veggie patties. Yet only about 8 percent of consumers have ever tasted a veggie burger. A 30-second ad, even a memorable one, isn't likely to change a basic mind-set for most people. So in betting the farm on its "Seinfeld" ad, Gardenburger had to pay to reach a very large audience, most of whom were not interested in what the company had to offer.[17]

Because it's hard to pick the best media, media analysts often focus on the cost per thousand of audience size or circulation. But advertisers preoccupied with keeping these costs down may ignore the relevant segmenting dimensions and slip into mass marketing.

Some media help zero in on specific target markets

Today the major media direct more attention to reaching smaller, more defined target markets. The most obvious evidence of this is in the growth of spending on direct-mail advertising to consumers in databases. However, other media—even traditional ones—are becoming more targeted as well.

TV is a good example. Cable TV channels—like MTV, Cable News Network (CNN), Nickelodeon, and ESPN—are taking advertisers away from the networks because they target specific audiences. For example, British Sky Broadcasting does a good job of reaching homemakers with young children.

Infomercials—long commercials that are broadcast with a TV show format—give a glimpse of how targeted cable TV will become now that more consumers have access to hundreds of TV channels. With many channels competing for attention, most will succeed only if they offer programs and commercials to the specific interests of smaller, more homogeneous target markets.

Radio has also become a more specialized medium. Some stations cater to particular ethnic and racial groups—such as Hispanics, African Americans, or French Canadians. Others aim at specific target markets with rock, country, or classical music. Now that radio stations can get their programming to a larger number of consumers over the Internet and via satellite broadcast systems, expect even more targeting.

Many magazines serve only special-interest groups—such as fishermen, new parents, and personal computer users. In fact, the most profitable magazines seem to be the ones aimed at clearly defined markets.

There are also trade magazines in many fields—such as chemical engineering, furniture retailing, electrical wholesaling, farming, and the aerospace market. *Standard Rate and Data* provides a guide to the thousands of magazines now available in the United States. Similar guides exist in most other countries.

Many of the national print media offer specialized editions. *Time* magazine, for example, offers not only several regional and metropolitan editions but also special

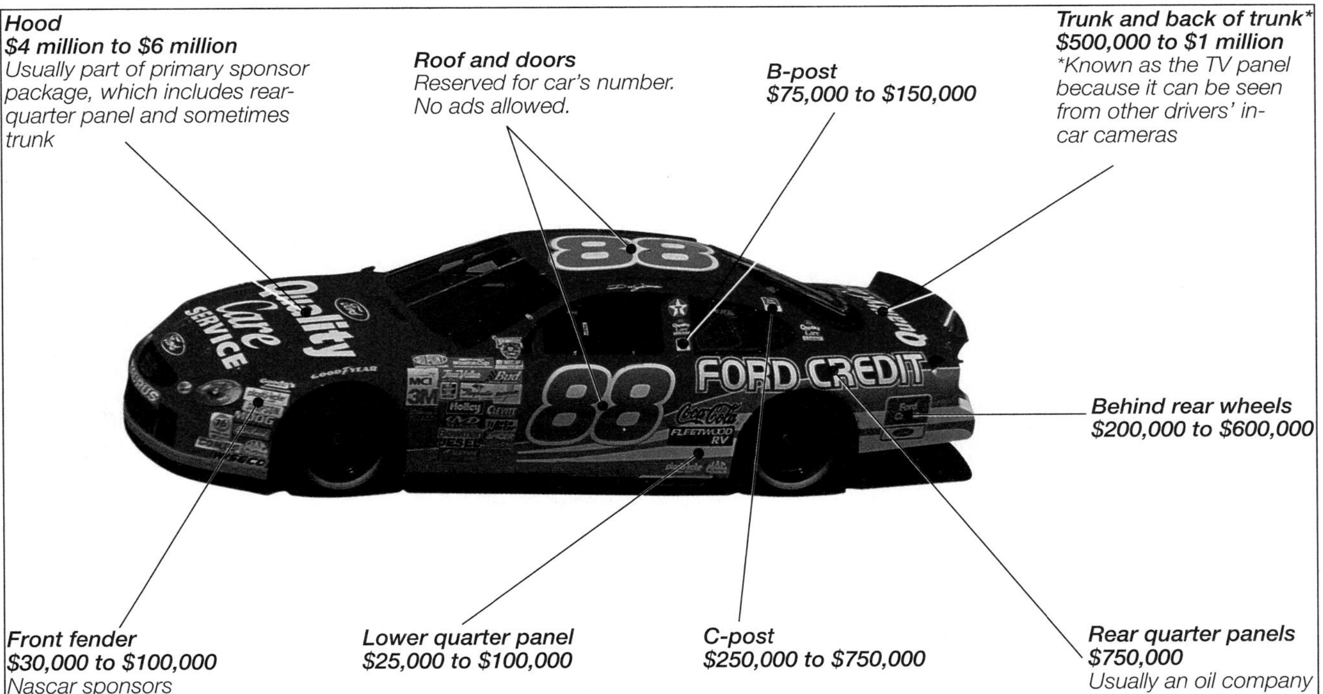

Advertising space on a race car reaches racing fans and often benefits from extended TV coverage. But the cost for primary sponsors can be millions of dollars.

editions for college students, educators, doctors, and business managers. Magazines like *Newsweek*, France's *Paris Match International*, and Germany's *Wirtschaftwoche* provide international editions.

Specialized media are small—but gaining

The advertising media listed in Exhibit 15-4 are attracting the vast majority of advertising media budgets. But advertising specialists always look for cost-effective new media that will help advertisers reach their target markets. For example, one company successfully sells space for signs on bike racks that it places in front of 7-Eleven stores. In Eastern Europe, where major media are still limited, companies like Campbell's pay to put ads on bus shelters. A new generation of ATMs being placed in shopping centers show video ads while customers wait to get their money. Some gas station pumps have similar displays.[18]

And, of course, the Internet is a fast-growing medium that has the potential to be highly targeted.

"Must buys" may use up available funds

Selecting which media to use is still pretty much an art. The media buyer starts with a budgeted amount and tries to buy the best blend to reach the target audience.

Some media are obvious "must buys"—like *the* local newspaper for a retailer in a small town. Most firms serving local markets view a Yellow Pages listing as a must buy. Website advertising is increasingly seen as a must buy. It may be the only medium for firms trying to reach business buyers in overseas markets. Must buy ads may even use up the available funds.

For many firms, even national advertisers, the high cost of television may eliminate it from the media blend. The average cost just to produce a national TV ad is now about $250,000. In the United States, a 30-second commercial on a popular prime-time show like "Friends" is well over $500,000.[19]

Advertising on the Internet: New Opportunities and New Challenges

Internet ads take many forms

Advertising on the Internet is growing rapidly as more mainstream advertisers join the quest for a more efficient medium. Internet ads take many forms, ranging from display ads that look like traditional print ads to button and banner ads. An Internet *banner ad* is a headline that appears on a web page. Its purpose is to attract the interest of people in the advertiser's target market and encourage them to visit the advertiser's website for more information. A button is usually much smaller—perhaps just showing the advertiser's name or symbol.

Internet ads seek a direct response—a click

Whatever specific form an ad takes, it is usually "linked" to the advertiser's website. When a viewer responds to an ad by clicking on it with a mouse, more detailed information appears. The information may include pictures, videos, sound, text, a product database, order entry procedures, and much more.

Content on a website can be very different from traditional advertising. The advertiser can put up more information and allow viewers to self-direct to those pages that interest them the most. The website can also provide links to other outside sources of information. Or it can invite the viewer to e-mail or start a chat session for more detailed information on a particular topic. It can even offer a sign-up for e-mail updates when there is some sort of news. We talked about this sort of interactive communication in Chapter 13.

Some websites generate more exposure

Some advertisers are primarily interested in placing ads on websites that will give their ads a lot of exposure—almost without regard to the content of the website or who visits it. Although there are millions of websites on the Internet, a small subset accounts for a large percent of the potential audience. For example, many people

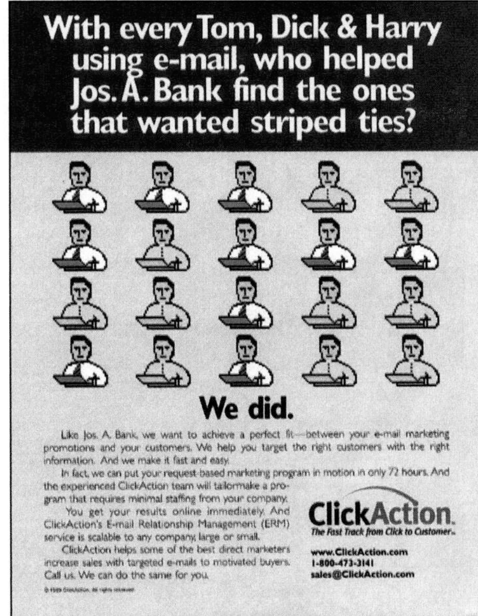

Advertising managers are always looking for cost-effective new media that will help them reach their specific target markets.

see the AOL or Yahoo website every time they use the Internet. The software ("browser") they use to view Internet information starts at these websites. Some people refer to such websites as *portals* because they act like doorways to the Internet.

A few portal websites are becoming for the Internet what the networks once were for television: *the* place where an advertiser is willing to pay high rates because they are uniquely able to reach a very large, broad market. For example, Dell might want its computer ads on the AOL or Yahoo home page so they will be viewed by the large number of computer user visitors. But what makes sense for Dell in that situation might not make sense for a firm with a different strategy. As with traditional media, getting lots of exposure for an Internet ad doesn't help if viewers are not in the firm's target market. At most websites, rates are set based on number of exposures, and you pay for an exposure regardless of who it is.

Some websites are better for reaching target customers

Bristol-Myers Squibb's experiment with web advertising is typical of what many other firms are trying to do—place ads on websites that attract the desired target market. In the middle of income tax season, Bristol-Myers Squibb ran ads on financial websites extolling Excedrin as "the tax headache medicine." The ads offered a free sample of Excedrin. Within a month, more than 30,000 people clicked on the ad and typed their names into the firm's customer database. The cost of obtaining those names was half that of traditional methods. Now the firm can follow up the Excedrin samples with other database-directed promotions, either by e-mail or other methods.

Context advertising links ad to content being viewed

Targeting on the Internet can be even more precise. For example, ads for Fragrance Counter (a cosmetics retailer) pop up when an Internet user does a search on a term such as *perfume* or *Estée Lauder.* This approach is called *context advertising*—monitoring the content a net surfer is viewing and then serving up related ads. For example, if a consumer visits a website with information about cars, an ad for Amazon.com might appear and note that it carries books on buying a car. If the consumer clicks on the Amazon ad, a list of links to relevant books appears on screen.

Pointcasting determines which customers see an ad

Another approach that offers more precise targeting is pointcasting. Pointcasting means displaying an ad *only* to an individual who meets certain qualifications—perhaps a person who has previously expressed interest in the topic of the advertising. A pointcasting ad is usually included with other information that the customer wants and that a pointcasting service provides for free. An example shows how this works. A woman who is interested in financial planning might sign up with Time-Warner's Road Runner service and request that it routinely send her newly published articles on independent retirement accounts. When the service sends her that information over the Internet, it might include an ad from a mutual fund company. The pointcasting service matches ads to customer interests. Many advertisers like this concept but worry that pointcasting may overwhelm the recipient with too much clutter.

Sending ads directly to the target customer via e-mail is a simpler approach. A limitation of e-mail is that a person's e-mail software may reformat messages in different ways. That is changing with increased use of e-mail in HTML format. However, a different problem will continue: Most people resent being "spammed" with a lot of unsolicited e-mail.

Internet

Internet Exercise ValueClick is a firm that provides services for firms that want to advertise on the Internet and also for website publishers that host Internet advertising. Go to its website (www.valueclick.com) and read about its service. Briefly describe the main benefits it provides for advertisers and the main benefits it provides for publishers.

Some viewers get benefits if they agree to look at ads

Some websites offer people a benefit—like free e-mail or a chance to enter a contest—if they provide information about themselves and agree to view ads selected to match their interests. Juno, a firm that offers a free e-mail service, uses this approach. When people sign up for e-mail accounts, they also provide detailed information for a database. The information might include demographics as well as interests, what products they use, where they shop, and where they live. Then a specific ad is displayed based on characteristics in the database. For example, a cosmetics firm might specify that its ads be shown only to females who are 16 or older and who routinely wear nail polish.

At some websites, ads are free if they don't get results

While the number of firms interested in putting ads on websites has grown, the number of websites that are chasing their ad dollars has grown at an even faster pace. Many websites charge advertisers a fee based on how frequently or how long an ad is shown. Competition for advertisers has prompted some websites to display an ad for free and charge a fee only if the ad gets results. The fee the advertiser pays is sometimes based on "clickthrough"—the number of people who actually click on the ad and link to the advertiser's website. Some websites set fees based on actual sales that result from the clickthrough. This is a big shift from traditional media where firms have to pay for their ads whether they work or not. More firms will put ads on websites if there is a direct relationship between costs and results. Moreover, the arrangement gives websites more incentive to attract an audience that some specific advertiser wants to reach.[20]

Planning the "Best" Message—What to Communicate

Specifying the copy thrust

Once you decide *how* the messages will reach the target audience, you have to decide on the **copy thrust**—what the words and illustrations should communicate.

The right copy thrust helps an ad clearly communicate to its target market.

Carrying out the copy thrust is the job of advertising specialists. But the advertising manager and the marketing manager need to understand the process to be sure that the job is done well.

Let AIDA help guide message planning

Basically, the overall marketing strategy should determine *what* the message should say. Then management judgment—perhaps aided by marketing research—can help decide how to encode this content so it will be decoded as intended.

As a guide to message planning, we can use the AIDA concept: getting Attention, holding Interest, arousing Desire, and obtaining Action.

Getting attention

Getting attention is an ad's first job. Many readers leaf through magazines without paying attention to any of the ads, and viewers often get snacks during TV commercials. On the Internet, they may click on the next website before the ad message finishes loading onto the screen.

Many attention-getting devices are available. A large headline, computer animations, shocking statements, attractive models, animals, special effects—anything different or eye-catching—may do the trick. However, the attention-getting device can't detract from, and hopefully should lead to, the next step, holding interest.

Holding interest

Holding interest is more difficult. A humorous ad, an unusual video effect, or a clever photo may get your attention—but once you've seen it, then what? If there is no relation between what got your attention and the marketing mix, you'll move on. To hold interest, the tone and language of the ad must fit with the experiences and attitudes of the target customers. As a result, many advertisers develop ads that relate to specific emotions. They hope that the good feeling about the ad will stick—even if its details are forgotten.

To hold interest, informative ads need to speak the target customer's language. Persuasive ads must provide evidence that convinces the customer. For example, TV ads often demonstrate a product's benefits.

Layouts for print ads should be arranged to encourage the eye to move smoothly through the ad—perhaps from a headline to the illustration or body copy in the

Billboards are good for getting attention with a simple copy thrust.

middle and finally to the lower right corner where the ad's "signature" usually gives the company or brand name, toll-free number, and website address.[21]

Arousing desire

Arousing desire to buy a particular product is one of an ad's most difficult jobs. The ad must convince customers that the product can meet their needs. Testimonials may persuade a consumer that other people with similar needs like the product. Product comparisons may highlight the advantages of a particular brand.

Although products may satisfy certain emotional needs, many consumers find it necessary to justify their purchases on some logical basis. Snickers candy bar ads helped ease the guilt of calorie-conscious snackers by assuring them that "Snickers satisfies you when you need an afternoon energy break."

An ad should usually focus on a *unique selling proposition* that aims at an important unsatisfied need. This can help differentiate the firm's marketing mix and position its brand as offering superior value to the target market. For example, Altoids' ads use humor to highlight the "curiously strong" flavor of its mints.

Obtaining action

Getting action is the final requirement—and not an easy one. From communication research, we now know that prospective customers must be led beyond considering how the product *might* fit into their lives—to actually trying it.

Direct-response ads can sometimes help promote action by encouraging consumers to do *something* even if they're not ready to make a purchase. For example, an ad that includes a toll-free telephone number or website address might prompt some consumers to at least call or visit the website for more information. It seeks to get action one step at a time, where the first step provides a "foot in the door" for subsequent communication efforts.

Careful research on attitudes in the target market may help uncover strongly felt *unsatisfied* needs. Appealing to important needs can get more action and also provide the kind of information buyers need to confirm the correctness of their decisions. Some customers seem to read more advertising *after* a purchase than before.

Can global messages work?

Many international consumer products firms try to use one global advertising message all around the world. Of course, they translate the message or make other

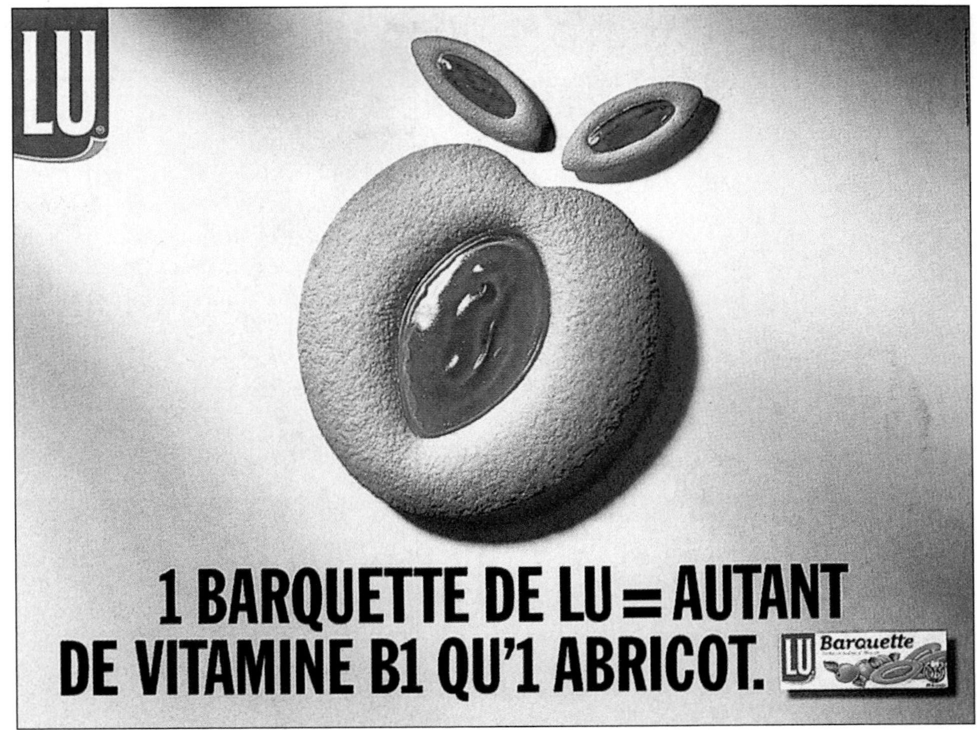

Ads that feature a unique selling proposition help consumers focus on what is different and better about a firm's marketing mix. LU wants health-conscious European consumers to know that its cookie has as much vitamin B1 as an apricot.

minor adjustments—but the focus is one global copy thrust. Some do it to cut the cost of developing different ads for each country. Others feel their customers' basic needs are the same, even in different countries. Some just do it because it's fashionable to "go global."

This approach works for some firms. Coca-Cola and IBM, for example, feel that the needs their products serve are very similar for customers around the world. They focus on the similarities among customers who make up their target market rather than the differences. However, most firms who use this approach experience terrible results. They may save money by developing fewer ads, but they lose sales because they don't develop advertising messages, and whole marketing mixes, aimed at specific target markets. They just try to appeal to a global "mass market."

Combining smaller market segments into a single, large target market makes sense if the different segments can be served with a single marketing mix. But when that is not the case, the marketing manager should treat them as different target markets and develop different marketing mixes for each target.[22]

Advertising Agencies Often Do the Work

An advertising manager manages a company's advertising effort. Many advertising managers—especially those working for large retailers—have their own advertising departments that plan specific advertising campaigns and carry out the details. Others turn over much of the advertising work to specialists—the advertising agencies.

Ad agencies are specialists

Advertising agencies are specialists in planning and handling mass-selling details for advertisers. Agencies play a useful role. They are independent of the advertiser and have an outside viewpoint. They bring experience to an individual client's problems because they work for many other clients. They can often do the job more economically than a company's own department. And if an agency isn't doing a good job, the client can select another. However, ending a relationship with an agency is a serious decision. Too many marketing managers just use their advertising agency as a scapegoat. Whenever anything goes wrong, they blame the agency.

Some full-service agencies handle any activities related to advertising, publicity, or sales promotion. They may even handle overall marketing strategy planning as well as marketing research, product and package development, and sales promotion. Other agencies are more specialized. For example, in recent years there has been rapid growth of firms that specialize in developing websites and Internet banner ads.

The biggest agencies handle much of the advertising

The vast majority of advertising agencies are small—with 10 or fewer employees. But the largest agencies account for most of the billings. Over the past decade many of the big agencies merged—creating mega-agencies with worldwide networks.

The mega-agency can offer varied services—wherever in the world a marketing manager needs them. This may be especially important for managers in large corporations—like Toyota, Renault, Unilever, NEC, and PepsiCo—that advertise worldwide.[23]

The really big agencies are less interested in smaller accounts. Smaller agencies will continue to appeal to customers who want more personal attention and a close relationship that is more attuned to their marketing needs.

Are they paid too much?

Traditionally, U.S. advertising agencies have been paid a commission of about 15 percent on media and production costs. This arrangement evolved because media usually have two prices: one for national advertisers and a lower rate for local advertisers, such as local retailers. The advertising agency gets a 15 percent commission on national rates but not on local rates. This makes it worthwhile for producers and national middlemen to use agencies. National advertisers have to pay the full media rate anyway, so it makes sense to let the agency experts do the work and earn their commission. Local retailers—allowed the lower media rate—seldom use agencies.

Many firms—especially big producers of consumer packaged goods—resist the idea of paying agencies the same way regardless of the work performed or *the results achieved*. The commission approach also makes it hard for agencies to be completely objective about inexpensive media. Agencies don't always like a commission arrangement, either. Some try to charge additional fees when advertisers spend relatively little on media or need extra services—like preparation of materials to support a website or the personal selling effort. About half of all advertisers now pay agencies some sort of labor-based fee.

Some firms pay the agency based on results

A number of advertisers now grade the work done by their agencies—and the agencies' pay depends on the grade. General Foods was the first to do this. It lowered its basic commission to about 13 percent. However, it paid the agency a bonus of about 3 percent on campaigns that earned an A rating. If the agency only earned a B, it lost the bonus. If it earned a C, it had to improve fast or GF removed the account. Variations on this approach are becoming common. For example, Carnation directly links its agency's compensation with how well its ads score in market research tests.[24]

Ethical conflicts may arise

Ad agencies usually work closely with their clients, and they often have access to confidential information. This can create ethical conflicts if an agency is working with two or more competing clients. Most agencies are sensitive to the potential problems and keep people and information from competing accounts separated. But many advertisers refuse to work with an agency that handles any competing accounts, even when they're handled in different offices. For example, a top executive for the Budweiser brand ended a 79-year relationship with an agency when one of the agency's subsidiaries accepted an assignment to buy media space for a competing brand of beer.[25]

Measuring Advertising Effectiveness Is Not Easy

Success depends on the total marketing mix

It would be convenient if we could measure the results of advertising by looking at sales. Some breakthrough ads do have a very direct effect on a company's sales—and the advertising literature is filled with success stories that "prove" advertising increases sales. Similarly, market research firms like Information Resources can sometimes compare sales levels before and after the period of an ad campaign. Yet we usually can't measure advertising success just by looking at sales. The total marketing mix—not just advertising—is responsible for the sales result. Only with direct-response advertising can a company make a direct link between advertising and sales results.

Research and testing can improve the odds

Ideally, advertisers should pretest advertising before it runs rather than relying solely on their own guesses about how good an ad will be. The judgment of creative people or advertising experts may not help much. They often judge only on the basis of originality or cleverness of the copy and illustrations.

Many progressive advertisers now demand research to evaluate an ad's effectiveness.[26] For example, split runs on cable TV systems in test markets are an important approach for testing ads in a normal viewing environment. Scanner sales data from retailers in those test markets can provide an estimate of how an ad is likely to affect sales. This approach will become even more powerful in the future as more cable systems allow viewers to provide immediate feedback to an ad as it appears on the TV.

Hindsight may lead to foresight

After ads run, researchers may try to measure how much consumers recall about specific products or ads. The response to radio or television commercials or magazine readership can be estimated using various survey methods to check the size and composition of audiences (the Nielsen and Starch reports are examples). Similarly, most Internet advertisers keep track of how many "hits" on the firm's website come from ads placed at other websites.[27]

Mercedes used the ad (above) to help introduce its new model and attract younger customers in Latin America. A bad economy dampened sales, but the ad did pull the target market into showrooms. This increased names in the dealers' customer database, used to target other promotions, by 50 percent. Firms like QuickTake.com do research to help advertisers determine if a creative ad is also effective. More and more research is being done online.

How to Avoid Unfair Advertising

Government agencies may say what is fair

In most countries, the government takes an active role in deciding what kinds of advertising are allowable, fair, and appropriate. For example, France and Japan limit the use of cartoon characters in advertising to children, and Canada bans *any* advertising targeted directly at children. Greece and Sweden have had similar policies and want the rest of the European Union to adopt them. In Switzerland, an advertiser cannot use an actor to represent a consumer. New Zealand and Switzerland limit political ads on TV. In the United States, print ads must be identified so they aren't confused with editorial matter; in other countries ads and editorial copy can be intermixed.

What is seen as positioning in one country may be viewed as unfair or deceptive in another. For example, when Pepsi was advertising its cola as "the choice of the new generation" in most countries, Japan's Fair Trade Committee didn't allow it—because in Japan Pepsi was not "the choice."[28]

Differences in rules mean that a marketing manager may face very specific limits in different countries, and local experts may be required to ensure that a firm doesn't waste money developing ads that will never be shown or which consumers will think are deceptive.

FTC controls unfair practices in the United States

In the United States, the Federal Trade Commission (FTC) has the power to control unfair or deceptive business practices—including deceptive advertising. The FTC has been policing deceptive advertising for many years. And it may be getting results now that advertising agencies as well as advertisers must share equal responsibility for false, misleading, or unfair ads.

This is a serious matter. If the FTC decides that a particular practice is unfair or deceptive, it has the power to require affirmative disclosures—such as the health warnings on cigarettes—or **corrective advertising**—ads to correct deceptive advertising. Years ago the FTC forced Listerine to spend millions of dollars on advertising to "correct" earlier ads that claimed the mouthwash helped prevent colds. That may explain why Microsoft quickly settled when the FTC charged the firm with deceptive advertising concerning WebTV.[29]

What is unfair or deceptive is changing

What constitutes unfair and deceptive advertising is a difficult question. Laws provide some guidelines, but the marketing manager must make personal judgments as well. The social and political environment is changing worldwide. Practices considered acceptable some years ago are now questioned or considered deceptive. Saying or even implying that your product is best may be viewed as deceptive. And a 1988 revision of the Lanham Act protects firms whose brand names are unfairly tarnished in comparative ads. A little puffing is acceptable—and probably always will be. But marketing managers need to put a stop to the typical production-oriented approach of trying to use advertising to differentiate me-too products that are not different and don't offer customers better value.[30]

Sales Promotion: Do Something Different to Stimulate Change

The nature of sales promotion

Sales promotion refers to those promotion activities—other than advertising, publicity, and personal selling—that stimulate interest, trial, or purchase by final customers or others in the channel. Exhibit 13-2 shows examples of typical sales promotions targeted at final customers, channel members, or a firm's own employees.

Sony's interactive kiosk provides special in-store sales promotion support for memory sticks used by portable electronic devices like the new MS Walkman.

While advertising campaigns and sales force strategy decisions tend to have longer-term effects, a particular sales promotion activity usually lasts for only a limited time period. But sales promotion can often be implemented quickly and get sales results sooner than advertising. Further, sales promotion objectives usually focus on prompting some short-term action. For a middleman, such an action might be a decision to stock a product, provide a special display space, or give extra sales emphasis. For a consumer, the desired action might be to try a new product, switch from another brand, or buy more of a product. The desired action by an employee might be a special effort to satisfy customers.

Sales promotion objectives and situation should influence decision

There are many different types of sales promotion, but what type is appropriate depends on the situation and objectives. For example, Exhibit 15-5 shows some possible ways that a short-term promotion might affect sales. The sales pattern in the graph on the left might occur if Hellmann's issues coupons to help clear its excess mayonnaise inventory. Some consumers might buy earlier to take advantage of the coupon, but unless they use extra mayonnaise their next purchase will be delayed. In the center graph, kids might convince parents to eat more Big Macs while McDonald's has a Star Wars promotion, but when it ends things go back to normal. The graph on the right shows a Burger King marketer's dream come true: free samples of a new style of french fries quickly pull in new customers who like what they try and keep coming back after the promotion ends. This is also the kind of long-term result that is the aim of effective advertising. From these examples, you can see that the situation and the objective of the promotion should determine what specific type is best.

Sales promotion spending has grown in mature markets

Sales promotion involves so many different types of activities that it is difficult to estimate accurately how much is spent in total. There is general consensus, however, that the total spending on sales promotion exceeds spending on advertising. Companies that sell frequently purchased consumer products shifted their promotion blends to put more emphasis on sales promotion during the 1990s.[31]

One reason for increased use of sales promotion by many consumer products firms is that they are generally competing in mature markets. There's only so much

Exhibit 15-5 Some Possible Effects of a Sales Promotion on Sales

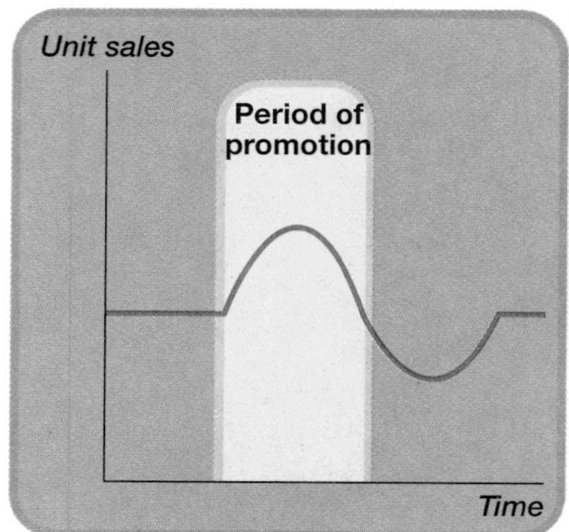

Sales temporarily increase, then decrease, then return to regular level

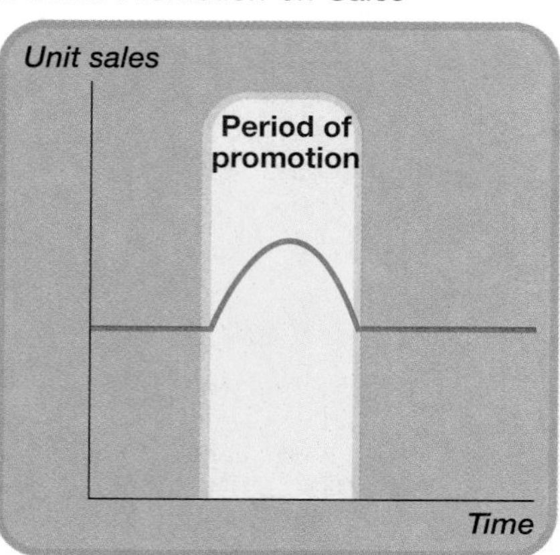

Sales temporarily increase and then return to regular level

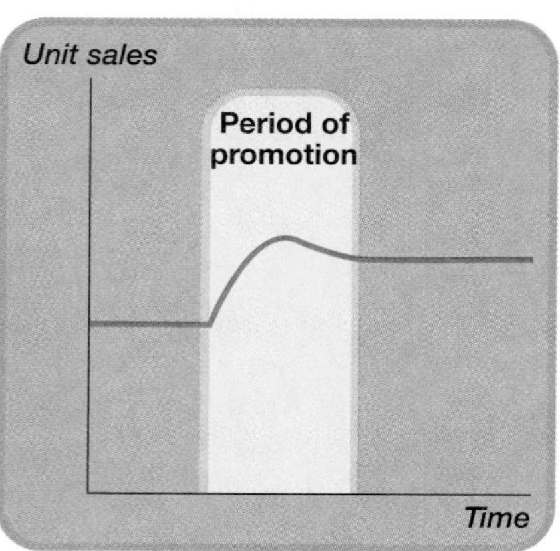

Sales increase and then remain at higher level

soap consumers want to buy—regardless of how many brands are vying for their dollars. There's also only so much shelf space that retailers will allocate to a particular product category.

The competitive situation is intensified by the growth of large, powerful retail chains. They have put more emphasis on their own dealer brands and also demanded more sales promotion support for the manufacturer brands they do carry.

Perhaps in part because of this competition, many consumers have become more price sensitive. Many sales promotions, like coupons, have the effect of lowering the prices consumers pay. So sales promotion has been used as a tool to overcome consumer price resistance.

Changes in technology have also made sales promotion more efficient. For example, with scanners at retail checkout counters, it's possible to instantly pinpoint a customer who is the target for a particular coupon. If a customer buys a bottle of Kraft salad dressing, Kraft can have the retailer's computerized cash register print out a coupon, on the spot, to encourage the customer to buy Kraft again the next time.

The growth of sales promotion has also been fostered by the availability of more agencies and specialists who plan and implement sales promotion programs. Of course, the most basic reason for the growth of spending on sales promotion is that it can be very effective if it is done properly. But there are problems in the sales promotion area.

Problems in Managing Sales Promotion

Does sales promotion erode brand loyalty?

Some experts think that marketing managers—especially those who deal with consumer packaged goods—put too much emphasis on sales promotions. They argue that the effect of most sales promotions is temporary and that money spent on advertising and personal selling helps the firm more over the long term. Their view is that most sales promotions don't help develop close relationships with consumers and instead erode brand loyalty.

There is heavy use of sales promotion in mature markets where competition is fierce. When the market is not growing, sales promotions may just encourage "deal-prone" customers (and middlemen) to switch back and forth among brands. Here, all the expense of the sales promotions simply contributes to lower profits. It also increases the prices that consumers pay because it increases selling costs.

However, once a marketing manager is in this situation there may be little choice other than to continue. In a mature market, frequent sales promotions may be needed just to offset the effects of competitors' promotions. One escape from this competitive rat race is for the marketing manager to seek new opportunities—with a strategy that doesn't rely solely on short-term sales promotions for competitive advantage.

There are alternatives

Procter & Gamble is a company that changed its strategy, and promotion blend, to decrease its reliance on sales promotion targeted at middlemen. It is offering middlemen lower prices on many of its products and supporting those products with more advertising and promotion to final consumers. P&G believes that this approach builds its brand equity, serves consumers better, and leads to smoother-running relationships in its channels. Not all retailers are happy with P&G's changes. However, many other producers are following P&G's lead.[32]

Sales promotion is hard to manage

Another problem in the sales promotion area is that it is easy to make big, costly mistakes. Because sales promotion includes a wide variety of activities—each of which may be custom-designed and used only once—it's difficult for the typical company to develop skill in this area. Mistakes caused by lack of experience can be very costly too. One promotion sponsored jointly by Polaroid and Trans World Airlines (TWA) proved to be a disaster. The promotion offered a coupon worth 25 percent off the price of any TWA ticket with the purchase of a $20 Polaroid camera. The companies intended to appeal to vacationers who take pictures when they travel. Instead, travel agents bought up many of the cameras. For the price of the $20 camera, they made an extra 25 percent on every TWA ticket they sold. And big companies bought thousands of the cameras to save on travel expenses. This is not an isolated example. Such problems are common.[33]

Not a sideline for amateurs

Sales promotion mistakes are likely to be worse when a company has no sales promotion manager. If the personal selling or advertising managers are responsible for sales promotion, they often treat it as a "stepchild." They allocate money to sales promotion if there is any "left over" or if a crisis develops.

Making sales promotion work is a learned skill, not a sideline for amateurs. That's why specialists in sales promotion have developed—both inside larger firms and as outside consultants. Some of these people are real experts. But it's the marketing manager's responsibility to set sales promotion objectives and policies that will fit in with the rest of each marketing strategy.[34]

Different Types of Sales Promotion for Different Targets

Sales promotion for final consumers or users

Much of the sales promotion aimed at final consumers or users tries to increase demand, perhaps temporarily, or speed up the time of purchase. Such promotion might involve developing materials to be displayed in retailers' stores—including banners, sample packages, calendars, and various point-of-purchase materials. It might include sweepstakes contests as well as coupons designed to get customers to buy a product by a certain date. Each year, about 300 billion coupons are distributed—and consumers redeem enough of them to save, in total, nearly $4 billion. Coupon distribution has dropped off some in recent years but still averages over 3,000 coupons per household in America![35]

Sales promotions such as the price-off coupon from Soft Scrub in the U.S. and the free product samples and coupons from Ajax in Greece prompt consumers to try a product—and a consumer who is satisfied with the trial is likely to become a regular customer.

Internet

Internet Exercise Catalina Marketing Corporation is a supplier of in-store, at-home, and online consumer promotions. Go to the Catalina website (www.catalinamktg.com) and select the shopping cart icon for in-store. Then review information about its Retail programs. Briefly describe, in your own words, how the Direct Mail program works, and describe a situation in which a manufacturer might find it useful.

All of these sales promotion efforts are aimed at specific objectives. For example, if customers already have a favorite brand, it may be hard to get them to try anything new. A free trial-sized bottle of mouthwash might be just what it takes to get cautious consumers to try the new product.

Once a product is established, consumer sales promotion usually focuses on short-term sales increases. For example, after a price-off coupon for a soft drink is distributed, sales might temporarily pick up as customers take advantage of buying at a lower price. When the objective of the promotion is focused primarily on producing a short-term increase in sales, it's sensible for the marketing manager to evaluate the cost of the promotion relative to the extra sales expected. If the increase in sales won't at least cover the cost of the promotion, it probably doesn't make sense to do it. Otherwise, the firm is "buying sales" at the cost of reduced profit.

Sales promotion directed at industrial customers might use the same kinds of ideas. In addition, the sales promotion people might set up and staff trade show exhibits. Here, attractive models are often used to encourage buyers to look at a firm's product—especially when it is displayed near other similar products in a circuslike atmosphere. Trade shows are a cost-effective way to reach target customers and generate a list of "live" prospects for sales rep follow-up. However, many firms handle these leads badly. A recent study says that 85 percent of the leads never get followed up by anybody.[36]

Sales promotion for middlemen

Sales promotion aimed at middlemen—sometimes called *trade promotion*—emphasizes price-related matters. The objective may be to encourage middlemen to stock new items, buy in larger quantity, buy early, or stress a product in their own promotion efforts.

The tools used here include merchandise allowances, promotion allowances, and perhaps sales contests to encourage retailers or wholesalers to sell specific items or the company's whole line. Offering to send contest winners to Hawaii, for example, may increase sales.

About half of the sales promotion spending targeted at middlemen has the effect of reducing the price that they pay for merchandise. So we'll go into more detail on different types of trade discounts and allowances in the next chapter.[37]

Sales promotion for own employees

Sales promotion aimed at the company's own sales force might try to encourage better service, getting new customers, selling a new product, or selling the company's whole line. Depending on the objectives, the tools might be contests, bonuses on sales or number of new accounts, and holding sales meetings at fancy resorts to raise everyone's spirits.

Ongoing sales promotion work might also be aimed at the sales force—to help sales management. Sales promotion might be responsible for preparing sales portfolios, videotapes on new products, displays, and other sales aids, as well as sales training material.

Service-oriented firms, such as hotels or restaurants, now use sales promotions targeted at their employees. Some, for example, give a monthly cash prize for the employee who provides the "best service." And the employee's picture is displayed to give recognition.[38]

Conclusion

It may seem simple to develop an advertising campaign. Just pick the medium and develop a message. But it's not that easy. Effectiveness depends on using the "best" available medium and the "best" message considering (1) promotion objectives, (2) the target markets, and (3) the funds available for advertising.

Specific advertising objectives determine what kind of advertising to use—product or institutional. If product advertising is needed, then the particular type must be decided—pioneering, competitive (direct or indirect), or reminder. And advertising allowances and cooperative advertising may be helpful.

Many technical details are involved in mass selling, and specialists—advertising agencies—handle some of these jobs. But specific objectives must be set for them, or their advertising may have little direction and be almost impossible to evaluate.

Effective advertising should affect sales. But the whole marketing mix affects sales—and the results of advertising usually can't be measured by sales changes alone. By contrast, sales promotion tends to be more action-oriented.

Sales promotion spending is big and growing. This approach is especially important in prompting action—by customers, middlemen, or salespeople. There are many different types of sales promotion, and it is a problem area in many firms because it is difficult for a firm to develop expertise with all of the possibilities.

Advertising and sales promotion are often important parts of a promotion blend—but in most blends personal selling also plays an important role. Further, promotion is only a part of the total marketing mix a marketing manager must develop to satisfy target customers. So to broaden your understanding of the four Ps and how they fit together, in the next two chapters we'll go into more detail on the role of Price in strategy decisions.

Questions and Problems

1. Identify the strategy decisions a marketing manager must make in the advertising area.
2. Discuss the relation of advertising objectives to marketing strategy planning and the kinds of advertising actually needed. Illustrate.
3. List several media that might be effective for reaching consumers in a developing nation with low per capita income and a high level of illiteracy. Briefly discuss the limitations and advantages of each medium you suggest.

4. Give three examples where advertising to middlemen might be necessary. What are the objective(s) of such advertising?
5. What does it mean to say that "money is invested in advertising"? Is all advertising an investment? Illustrate.
6. Find advertisements to final consumers that illustrate the following types of advertising: *(a)* institutional, *(b)* pioneering, *(c)* competitive, and *(d)* reminder. What objective(s) does each of these ads have? List the needs each ad appeals to.
7. Describe the type of media that might be most suitable for promoting: *(a)* tomato soup, *(b)* greeting cards, *(c)* a business component material, and *(d)* playground equipment. Specify any assumptions necessary to obtain a definite answer.
8. Briefly discuss some of the pros and cons an advertising manager for a producer of sports equipment might want to think about in deciding whether to advertise on the Internet.
9. Discuss the use of testimonials in advertising. Which of the four AIDA steps might testimonials accomplish? Are they suitable for all types of products? If not, for which types are they most suitable?
10. Find a magazine ad that you think does a particularly good job of communicating to the target audience. Would the ad communicate well to an audience in another country? Explain your thinking.
11. Johnson & Johnson sells its baby shampoo in many different countries. Do you think baby shampoo would be a good product for Johnson & Johnson to advertise with a single global message? Explain your thinking.
12. Discuss the future of smaller advertising agencies now that many of the largest are merging to form mega-agencies.
13. Does advertising cost too much? How can this be measured?
14. How would your local newspaper be affected if local supermarkets switched their weekly advertising and instead used a service that delivered weekly, free-standing ads directly to each home?
15. Is it unfair to criticize a competitor's product in an ad?
16. Explain why P&G and other consumer packaged goods firms are trying to cut back on some types of sales promotion like coupons for consumers and short-term trade promotions such as "buy a case and get a case free."
17. Discuss some ways that a firm can link its sales promotion activities to its advertising and personal selling efforts—so that all of its promotion efforts result in an integrated effort.
18. Indicate the type of sales promotion that a producer might use in each of the following situations and briefly explain your reasons:
    a. A firm has developed an improved razor blade and obtained distribution, but customers are not motivated to buy it.
    b. A competitor is about to do a test market for a new brand and wants to track sales in test market areas to fine tune its marketing mix.
    c. A big grocery chain won't stock a firm's new popcorn-based snack product because it doesn't think there will be much consumer demand.
19. Why wouldn't a producer of toothpaste just lower the price of its product rather than offer consumers a price-off coupon?
20. If sales promotion spending continues to grow—often at the expense of media advertising—how do you think this might affect the rates charged by mass media for advertising time or space? How do you think it might affect advertising agencies?

Suggested Cases

17. myWedding.com
18. Outdoor World, Inc.
28. Lever, Ltd.

Computer-Aided Problem

15. **Sales Promotion**

As a community service, disc jockeys from radio station WMKT formed a basketball team to help raise money for local nonprofit organizations. The host organization finds or fields a competing team and charges $5 admission to the game. Money from ticket sales goes to the nonprofit organization.

Ticket sales were disappointing at recent games—averaging only about 300 people per game. When WMKT's marketing manager, Bruce Miller, heard about the problem, he suggested using sales promotion to improve ticket sales. The PTA for the local high school—the sponsor for the next game—is interested in the idea but is concerned that its budget doesn't include any promotion money. Miller tries to help them by reviewing his idea in more detail.

Specifically, he proposes that the PTA give a free T-shirt (printed with the school name and date of the game) to the first 500 ticket buyers. He thinks the T-shirt giveaway will create a lot of interest. In fact, he says he is almost certain the promotion would help the PTA sell 600 tickets—double the usual number. He speculates that the PTA might even have a sellout of all 900 seats in the school gym. Further, he notes that the T-shirts will more than pay for themselves if the PTA sells 600 tickets.

A local firm that specializes in sales promotion items agrees to supply the shirts and do the printing for $2.40 a shirt if the PTA places an order for at least 400 shirts. The PTA thinks the idea is interesting but wants to look at it more closely to see what will happen if the promotion doesn't increase ticket sales. To help the PTA evaluate the alternatives, Miller sets up a spreadsheet with the relevant information.

a. *Based on the data from the initial spreadsheet, does the T-shirt promotion look like a good idea? Explain your thinking.*
b. *The PTA treasurer worries about the up-front cost of printing the T-shirts and wants to know where they would stand if they ordered the T-shirts and still sold only 300 tickets. He suggests it might be safer to order the minimum number of T-shirts (400). Evaluate his suggestion.*
c. *The president of the PTA thinks the T-shirt promotion will increase sales but wonders if it wouldn't be better just to lower the price. She suggests $2.60 a ticket, which she arrives at by subtracting the $2.40 T-shirt cost from the usual $5.00 ticket price. How many tickets would the PTA have to sell at the lower price to match the money it would make if it used the T-shirt promotion and actually sold 600 tickets? (Hint: Change the selling price in the spreadsheet and then vary the quantity using the results feature.)*

For additional questions related to this problem, see Exercise 15-3 in the *Learning Aid for Use with Essentials of Marketing*, 9th edition.

Chapter Sixteen
Pricing Objectives and Policies

When You Finish This Chapter, You Should

1. Understand how pricing objectives should guide strategy planning for pricing decisions.

2. Understand choices the marketing manager must make about price flexibility.

3. Know what a marketing manager should consider when setting the price level for a product in the early stages of the product life cycle.

4. Understand the many possible variations of a price structure, including discounts, allowances, and who pays transportation costs.

5. Understand the value pricing concept and its role in obtaining a competitive advantage and offering target customers superior value.

6. Understand the legality of price-level and price flexibility policies.

7. Understand the important new terms (shown in red).

For years, the Chevy Suburban utility vehicle was a low-price, no-frills, work truck targeted at commercial users. Then changes in the marketing environment presented a new opportunity. To turn the opportunity into profits, marketing managers planned a new strategy for the Suburban—and new price policies were a crucial aspect of the strategy.

In the early 1990s, luxury car sales to the high-income, baby-boomer crowd were growing fast. BMW, Lexus, and Mercedes sedans seemed to be the ultimate yuppie status symbol and the leaders in customer satisfaction. Yet sales of luxury sedans slowed as affluent consumers looked for other ways to meet their needs. One clear sign of this shift was the growth in demand for fancy utility vehicles like the Jeep Grand Cherokee.

As consumer preferences changed, marketing managers for the Chevy Suburban changed their strategy. They turned the Suburban into an upscale utility vehicle targeted at families for hauling special cargo—like kids, toys, and pets. And this target market wanted to do its hauling in style.

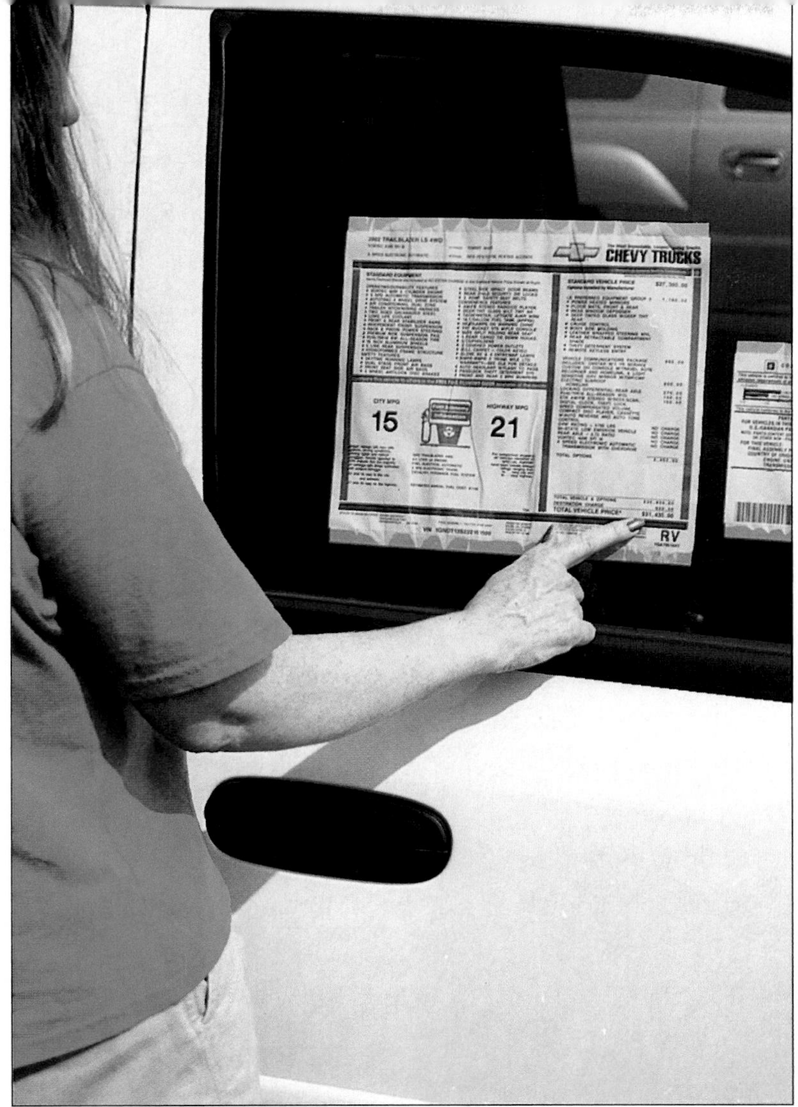

So marketing managers for the Suburban added many luxury features and options—like leather interiors and power everything. They also significantly raised the suggested list price; a fully equipped Suburban cost about $40,000. In 1996, Suburbans could command that price because no other model was as big, plush, and powerful. If a consumer really wanted jumbo-sized luxury, Suburban was the only choice.

Even at its steep price, demand for the Suburban was so hot that supply couldn't keep up. Yet GM managers didn't want to build a new factory. They realized that other firms were scrambling to develop competing models that would cut into Suburban's sales and lofty prices. If a new factory turned into excess capacity and high overhead costs, it would be hard to cut Suburban prices and still make a profit. That risk didn't seem worth it when the profit on each Suburban was about $8,000—much higher than for most cars.

Dealers couldn't get all the Suburbans they could sell, so many sold the ones they could get at a premium of $1,000 or more above the suggested list price. This jacking up of prices irritated buyers—and many switched to Ford Explorers or other vehicles. Yet GM's marketing managers couldn't *make* dealers charge the suggested list price—and it's not legal to charge uncooperative dealers a higher price for the Suburbans that they buy.

In 1997, two new jumbo luxury haulers—the Lincoln Navigator and the Ford Expedition—hit the market. They were instant successes. They attracted a lot of the people who had walked away when Suburban dealers tried to extract an unreasonable price. Other customers just liked the smoother ride. It also didn't hurt that gasoline prices

place price promotion product

www.mhhe.com/fourps

were at a 25-year low. That pulled new consumers into the market who earlier had thought that the high operating cost of a gas guzzler made it a bad value, no matter how useful it might be.

By 2002, more competitors had come on the scene. Toyota redesigned its Land Cruiser for more interior space and luxury in 1998 and then hit even harder with a new Sequoia model. The exchange rate of the Japanese yen against the dollar gave Toyota a price advantage as the economy was shifting into lower gear. And Mercedes introduced its ML320 luxury sport-ute. It is smaller than the Suburban, but many consumers think that its styling, safety features, and low price make it a better value. Suburban sales were even cannibalized by other brands in the GM product line—including Cadillac's Escalade, which gave GM an offering at the next price line up from Suburban.

The economy, high gas prices, and competition cooled the demand for Suburbans. A special website (www.chevrolet.com/suburban) promotion offered Suburban buyers in the West (where the economic and competitive situation was the worst) financing at a 1.9 percent annual interest rate. However, some buyers from other regions saw the website and complained to dealers that the low financing rate wasn't available to them. In the end, to move inventory, many of these dealers just took a price cut or threw in free options.[1]

Price Has Many Strategy Dimensions

Guided by the company's objectives, marketing managers must develop a set of pricing objectives and policies. They must spell out what price situations the firm will face and how it will handle them. These policies should explain (1) how flexible prices will be, (2) at what level they will be set over the product life cycle, (3) to whom and when discounts and allowances will be given, and (4) how transportation costs will be handled. See Exhibit 16-1. These Price-related

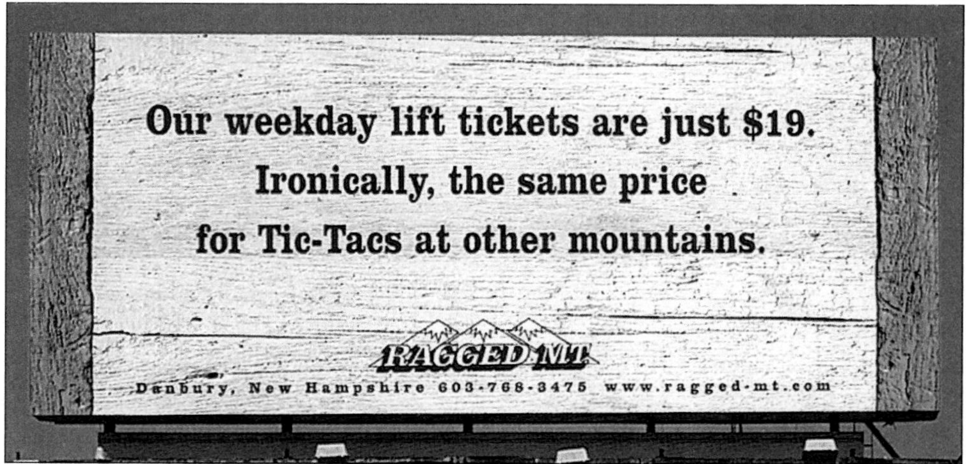

Ragged Mountain wants its customers to know that its price is a good value compared to what they get at other ski resorts.

Exhibit 16-1
Strategy Planning for Price

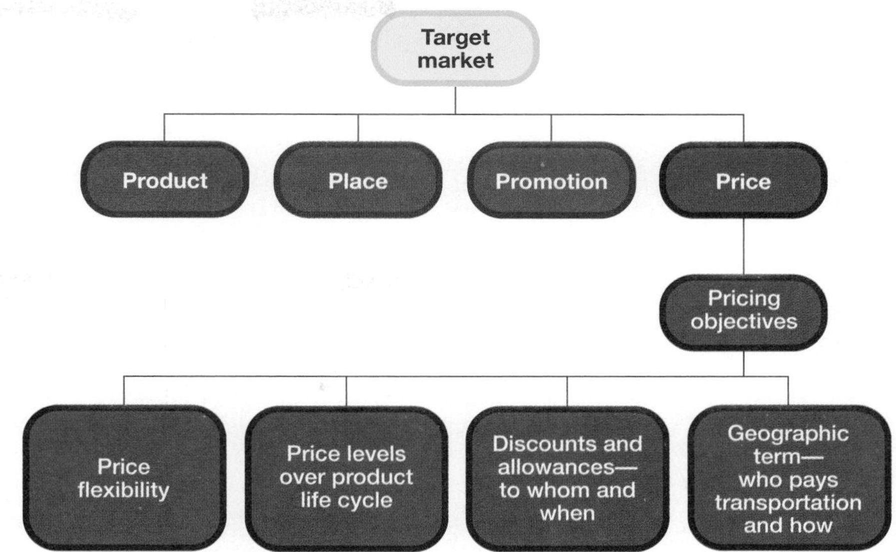

strategy decision areas are the focus of this chapter. After we've looked at specific decision areas, we will discuss how they combine to impact customer value as well as laws that are relevant. In the next chapter, we will discuss how specific prices are set.

It's not easy to define price in real-life situations because prices reflect many dimensions. People who don't realize this can make big mistakes.

Suppose you've been saving to buy a new car and you see in an ad that the base price for the new-year model has dropped to $16,494—5 percent lower than the previous year. At first this might seem like a real bargain. However, your view of this deal might change if you found out you also had to pay a $400 transportation charge and an extra $480 for an extended service warranty. The price might look even less attractive if you discovered the options you wanted—a CD player, side airbags, and a moonroof—cost $1,200 more than the previous year. The sales tax on all of this might come as an unpleasant surprise too. Further, how would you feel if you bought the car anyway and then learned that a friend who just bought the exact same model got a much lower price from the dealer by using a broker he found on the Internet?[2]

The price equation: price equals something of value

This example emphasizes that when a seller quotes a price, it is related to *some* assortment of goods and services. So **Price** is the amount of money that is charged for "something" of value. Of course, price may be called different things in different settings. Colleges charge tuition. Landlords collect rent. Motels post a room rate. Country clubs get dues. Banks ask for interest when they loan money. Airlines have fares. Internet providers set fees. People may call it different things, but *almost every business transaction in our modern economy involves an exchange of money—the Price—for something.*

The nature and extent of this something determines the amount of money exchanged. Some customers pay list price. Others obtain large discounts or allowances because something is *not* provided. Exhibit 16-2 summarizes some possible variations for consumers or users, and Exhibit 16-3 does the same for channel members. These variations are discussed more fully below, and then we'll consider the customer value concept more fully—in terms of competitive advantage. But here it should be clear that Price has many dimensions. How each of these dimensions

Exhibit 16-2
Price as Seen by Consumers or Users

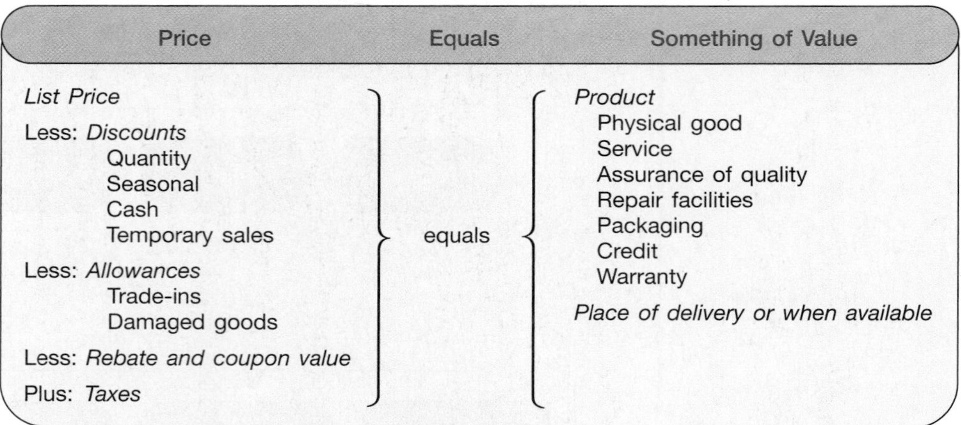

is handled affects customer value. If a customer sees greater value in spending money in some other way, no exchange will occur.

Objectives Should Guide Strategy Planning for Price

Pricing objectives should flow from, and fit in with, company-level and marketing objectives. Pricing objectives should be *explicitly stated* because they have a direct effect on pricing policies as well as the methods used to set prices. Exhibit 16-4 shows the various types of pricing objectives we'll discuss.

Profit-Oriented Objectives

Target returns provide specific guidelines

A **target return objective** sets a specific level of profit as an objective. Often this amount is stated as a percentage of sales or of capital investment. A large manufacturer like Motorola might aim for a 15 percent return on investment. The target for Safeway and other grocery chains might be a 1 percent return on sales.

Exhibit 16-3
Price as Seen by Channel Members

Price	Equals	Something of Value
List Price Less: *Discounts* Quantity Seasonal Cash Trade or functional Temporary "deals" Less: *Allowances* Damaged goods Advertising Push money Stocking Plus: *Taxes and tariffs*	equals	*Product* Branded—well known Guaranteed Warranted Service—repair facilities Convenient packaging for handling *Place* Availability—when and where *Price* Price-level guarantee Sufficient margin to allow chance for profit *Promotion* Promotion aimed at customers

Exhibit 16-4
Possible Pricing Objectives

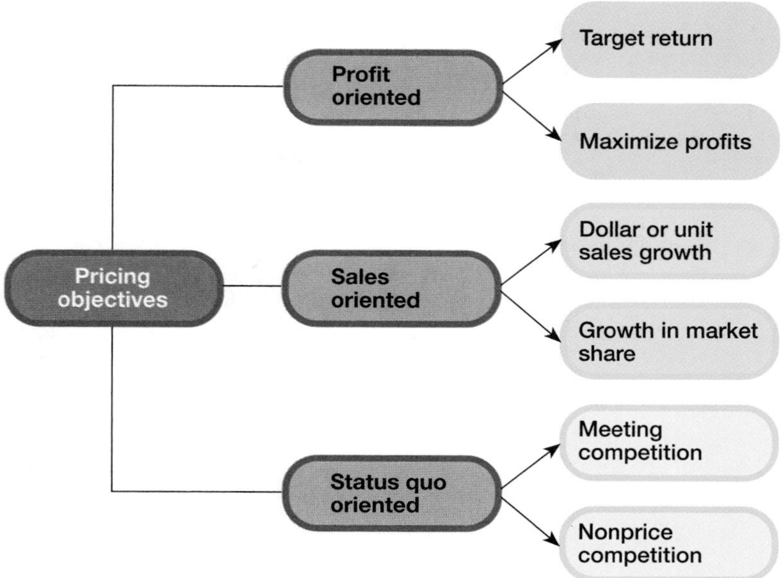

A target return objective has administrative advantages in a large company. Performance can be compared against the target. Some companies eliminate divisions, or drop products, that aren't yielding the target rate of return. For example, General Electric sold its small appliance division to Black & Decker because it felt it could earn higher returns in other product-markets.

Some just want satisfactory profits

Some managers aim for only satisfactory returns. They just want returns that ensure the firm's survival and convince stockholders they're doing a good job. Similarly, some small family-run businesses aim for a profit that will provide a comfortable lifestyle.[3]

Many private and public nonprofit organizations set a price level that will just recover costs. In other words, their target return figure is zero. For example, a government agency may charge motorists a toll for using a bridge but then drop the toll when the cost of the bridge is paid.

Similarly, firms that provide critical public services—including many utility and insurance companies, transportation firms, and defense contractors—sometimes pursue only satisfactory long-run targets. They are well aware that the public expects them to set prices that are in the public interest. They may also have to face public or government agencies that review and approve prices.[4]

This kind of situation can lead to decisions that are not in the public interest. For example, some critics argue that some power companies that serve California were not motivated to keep costs low or expand capacity. After deregulation, there were big shortages, and even price gouging by some firms, because it takes a long time to add new power systems.

Profit maximization can be socially responsible

A **profit maximization objective** seeks to get as much profit as possible. It might be stated as a desire to earn a rapid return on investment—or, more bluntly, to charge all the traffic will bear.

Pricing to achieve profit maximization doesn't always lead to high prices. Low prices may expand the size of the market and result in greater sales and profits. For example, when prices of VCRs were very high, only innovators and wealthy people bought them. When producers lowered prices, nearly everyone bought one.

Some politicians want to control the prices of drugs, but that may not be in the public interest if it reduces the incentive for firms to make the big investment required to develop innovative new medicines that people need. That, in turn, would reduce consumer choices.

If a firm is earning a very large profit, other firms will enter the market. Frequently, this leads to lower prices. IBM sold its original personal computer for about $4,500 in 1981. As Compaq, Dell, and other competitors started to copy IBM, it added more power and features and cut prices. By 2002, customers could buy a personal computer with more than 50 times the power, speed, and data storage for about $500, and prices continue to drop.[5]

Sales-Oriented Objectives

A **sales-oriented objective** seeks some level of unit sales, dollar sales, or share of market—*without referring to profit.*

Sales growth doesn't necessarily mean big profits

Some managers are more concerned about sales growth than profits. They think sales growth always leads to more profits. This kind of thinking causes problems when a firm's costs are growing faster than sales. Some major corporations have had declining profits in spite of growth in sales. At the extreme, many dot-coms kept lowering prices to increase market share but never earned any profits. Pets.com had growing sales until it burned through investors' money and went bankrupt. Generally, however, business managers now pay more attention to profits, not just sales.[6]

Some nonprofit organizations set prices to increase market share—precisely because they are *not* trying to earn a profit. For example, many cities set low fares to fill up their buses. Buses cost the same to run empty or full, and there's more benefit when they're full even if the total revenue is no greater.

Market share objectives are popular

Many firms seek to gain a specified share (percent) of a market. If a company has a large market share, it may have better economies of scale than its competitors. In addition, it's usually easier to measure a firm's market share than to determine if profits are being maximized.

A company with a longer-run view may aim for increased market share when the market is growing. The hope is that future volume will justify sacrificing some profit in the short run. In the early days of the Internet, Netscape took this approach with its browser software. And companies as diverse as 3M and Coca-Cola look at opportunities in Eastern Europe this way.

Of course, market share objectives have the same limitations as straight sales growth objectives. A larger market share, if gained at too low a price, may lead to profitless "success."

Status Quo Pricing Objectives

Don't-rock-the-boat objectives

Managers satisfied with their current market share and profits sometimes adopt **status quo objectives**—don't-rock-the-*pricing*-boat objectives. Managers may say that they want to stabilize prices, or meet competition, or even avoid competition. This don't-rock-the-boat thinking is most common when the total market is not growing.

Or stress nonprice competition instead

A status quo pricing objective may be part of an aggressive overall marketing strategy focusing on **nonprice competition**—aggressive action on one or more of the Ps other than Price. Fast-food chains like McDonald's, Wendy's, and Burger King experienced very profitable growth by sticking to nonprice competition for many years. However, when Taco Bell and others started to take away customers with price-cutting, the other chains also turned to price competition.[7]

Most Firms Set Specific Pricing Policies—To Reach Objectives

Administered prices help achieve objectives

Price policies usually lead to **administered prices**—consciously set prices. In other words, instead of letting daily market forces decide their prices, most firms set their own prices. They may hold prices steady for long periods or change them frequently if that's what's required to meet objectives.

If a firm doesn't sell directly to final customers, it usually wants to administer both the price it receives from middlemen and the price final customers pay. After all, the price final customers pay will ultimately affect its sales. Yet it is often difficult to administer prices throughout the channel. Other channel members may also wish to administer prices to achieve their own objectives. This is what happened to Alcoa, one of the largest aluminum producers. To reduce its excess inventory, Alcoa offered its wholesalers a 30 percent discount off its normal price. Alcoa expected the wholesalers to pass most of the discount along to their customers to stimulate sales throughout the channel. Instead, wholesalers bought *their* aluminum at the lower price but passed on only a small discount to customers. As a result, the quantity Alcoa sold didn't increase much, and it still had excess inventories, while the wholesalers made much more profit on the aluminum they did sell.[8]

Some firms don't even try to administer prices. They just meet competition—or worse, mark up their costs with little thought to demand. They act as if they have no choice in selecting a price policy.

Remember that Price has many dimensions. Managers usually *do* have many choices. They *should* administer their prices. And they should do it carefully because, ultimately, customers must be willing to pay these prices before a whole marketing mix succeeds. In the rest of this chapter, we'll talk about policies a marketing manager must set to do an effective job of administering Price.[9]

Price Flexibility Policies

One-price policy—the same price for everyone

One of the first decisions a marketing manager has to make is about price flexibility. A **one-price policy** means offering the same price to all customers who purchase products under essentially the same conditions and in the same quantities. The majority of U.S. firms use a one-price policy—mainly for administrative convenience and to maintain goodwill among customers.

A one-price policy makes pricing easier. But a marketing manager must be careful to avoid a rigid one-price policy. This can amount to broadcasting a price that competitors can undercut—especially if the price is somewhat high. One reason for the growth of mass-merchandisers is that conventional retailers rigidly applied traditional margins and stuck to them.

Flexible-price policy—different prices for different customers

A **flexible-price policy** means offering the same product and quantities to different customers at different prices. When computers are used to implement flexible pricing, the decisions focus more on what type of customer will get a price break.

Pricing databases make flexible pricing easier

Various forms of flexible pricing are more common now that most prices are maintained in a computer database. Frequent changes are easier. You see this when grocery chains give frequent-shopper club members reduced prices on weekly specials. The checkout scanner reads the code on the package and looks up the club price or the regular price depending on whether a club card has been scanned.

Some marketing managers have set up relationships with Internet companies whose ads invite customers to "set your own price." For example, Priceline operates a website at www.priceline.com. Visitors to the website specify the desired schedule for an airline flight and what price they're willing to pay. Priceline electronically forwards the information to airlines and if one accepts the offer the consumer is notified.

It may appear that these marketing managers have given up on administering prices. Just the opposite is true. They are carefully administering a flexible price. Most airlines, for example, set a very high list price. Not many people pay it. Travelers who plan ahead or who accept nonpeak flights get a discount. Business travelers who want high-demand flights on short notice pay the higher prices. However, it doesn't make sense to stick to a high price and fly the plane half empty. So the airline continuously adjusts the price on the basis of how many seats are left to fill. If seats are still empty at the last minute, the website offers a rock-bottom fare. Other firms, especially service businesses, use this approach when they have excess capacity.[10]

Salespeople can adjust prices to the situation

Flexible pricing is most common in the channels, in direct sales of business products, and at retail for expensive shopping products. Retail shopkeepers in less-developed economies typically use flexible pricing. These situations usually involve personal selling, not mass selling. The advantage of flexible pricing is that the salesperson can adjust price—considering competitors' prices, the relationship with the customer, and the customer's bargaining ability.[11]

Flexible pricing does have disadvantages. A customer who finds that others paid lower prices for the same marketing mix will be unhappy. This can cause real conflict in channels. For example, the Winn-Dixie supermarket chain stopped carrying products of some suppliers who refused to give Winn-Dixie the same prices available to chains in other regions of the country. Similarly, companies that post different prices for different segments on a website that all can see often get complaints.[12]

To reach its objectives, Carnival uses flexible pricing—including discounts for retired people. By contrast, *Professional Carwashing & Detailing,* a trade magazine, wants advertisers to know that it charges everyone the same price for ad space.

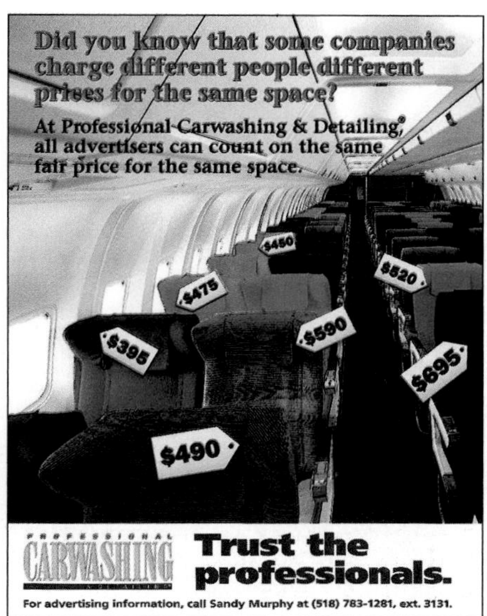

If buyers learn that negotiating can be in their interest, the time needed for bargaining will increase. This can increase selling costs and reduce profits.

Too much price-cutting erodes profits

Some sales reps let price-cutting become a habit. This can lead to a lower price level and lower profit. A small price cut may not seem like much; but keep in mind that all of the revenue that is lost would go to profit. If salespeople for a producer that usually earns profits equal to 15 percent of its sales cut prices by an average of about 5 percent, profits would drop by a third!

Price-Level Policies—Over the Product Life Cycle

Marketing managers who administer prices must consciously set a price-level policy. As they enter the market, they have to set introductory prices that may have long-run effects. They must consider where the product life cycle is and how fast it's moving. And they must decide if their prices should be above, below, or somewhere in between relative to the market.

Skimming pricing—feeling out demand at a high price

A **skimming price policy** tries to sell the top (skim the cream) of a market—the top of the demand curve—at a high price before aiming at more price-sensitive customers. Skimming may maximize profits in the market introduction stage for an innovation, especially if there are few substitutes or if some customers are not price sensitive.

Skimming is also useful when you don't know very much about the shape of the demand curve. It's sometimes safer to start with a high price that customers can refuse and then reduce it if necessary.

Skimming has critics

Some critics argue that firms should not try to maximize profits by using a skimming policy on new products that have important social consequences—a patent-protected, life-saving drug or a genetic technique that increases crop yields, for example. Many of those who need the product may not have the money to buy it. This is a serious concern. However, it's also a serious problem if firms don't have any incentive to take risks and develop new products.[13]

Exhibit 16-5 Alternative Introductory Pricing Policies

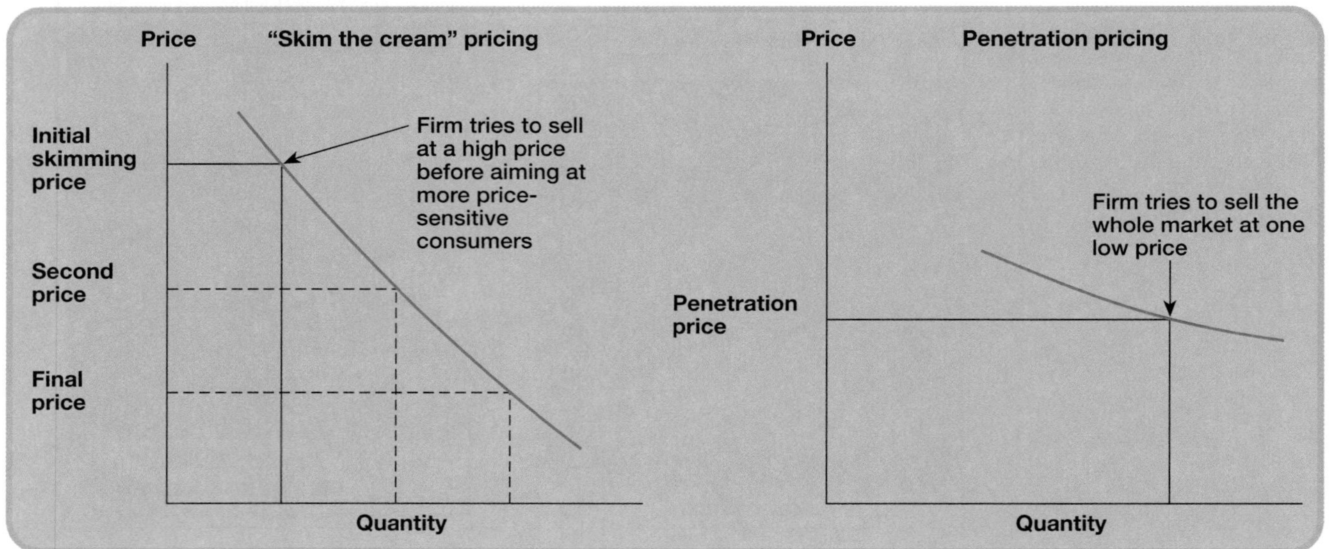

Price moves down the demand curve

A skimming policy usually involves a slow reduction in price over time. See Exhibit 16-5. Note that as price is reduced, new target markets are probably being sought. So as the price level steps down the demand curve, new Place, Product, and Promotion policies may be needed too.

When McCaw Cellular Communications pioneered cellular phone service, it set a high price. A wireless minute cost about $1 and customers had to pay about $675 for a phone. McCaw used dealers to sell the premium-priced packages mainly to firms for their on-the-go executives. When competitors entered the market, McCaw bought large quantities of phones from Motorola at low cost and packaged them with a service contract at a high discount. As the market grew, economies of scale kicked in. McCaw did more advertising and started to sell cellular services through retail outlets. Prices on phones had come down so much that retailers appealed to families by giving them free phones with one-year service contracts. Now cellular providers continue to cut prices and offer new services like Internet messaging. And some providers are bypassing retailers with TV ads that encourage consumers to subscribe at a website.[14]

Penetration pricing—get volume at a low price

A **penetration pricing policy** tries to sell the whole market at one low price. See Exhibit 16-5. Such an approach might be wise when the elite market—those willing to pay a high price—is small. A penetration policy is even more attractive if selling larger quantities results in lower costs because of economies of scale. Penetration pricing may be wise if the firm expects strong competition very soon after introduction.

When the first version of the PalmPilot was introduced, competitors were close behind. In addition, Apple had failed when it tried to introduce the Newton at a skimming price of $1,000. So the focus for Palm was on a combination of features and price that would be a good value and help penetrate the market quickly. The initial price of about $250 resulted in sales of a million units in 24 months.[15]

Introductory price dealing—temporary price cuts

Low prices do attract customers. Therefore, marketers often use **introductory price dealing**—temporary price cuts—to speed new products into a market and get customers to try them. However, don't confuse these *temporary* price cuts with low penetration prices. The plan here is to raise prices as soon as the introductory offer is over. Established competitors often choose not to meet introductory price dealing—as long as the introductory period is not too long or too successful.

Marketers often use introductory price dealing—in the form of temporary price cuts or introductory coupons—to speed new products into a market.

Different price-level policies through the channel

A manufacturer may set different price-level policies for different levels in the channel. For example, a producer of a slightly better product might set a price level that is low relative to competitors when selling to retailers, while suggesting an above-the-market retail price. This encourages retailers to emphasize the product because it yields higher profits.

The price of money may affect the price level

We've been talking about the price level of a firm's product. But a nation's money also has a price level—what it is worth in some other currency. For example, on April 16, 2001, one U.S. dollar was worth 0.70 British pounds. In other words, the exchange rate for the British pound against the U.S. dollar was 0.70. Exhibit 16-6 lists exchange rates for money from several countries over a number of years. From this exhibit you can see that exchange rates change over time—and sometimes the changes are significant. For example, during 1995, a U.S. dollar was worth, on average, 24.92 Thai bhat; in April 2001 it was worth 45.65 Thai bhat. That exchange rate moved up rapidly starting in 1997 because of economic problems that hit Thailand and the rest of Asia.

Exchange rate changes can have a significant effect on international trade. From a manager's viewpoint, they also affect whether or not a price level has the expected result. As the following example shows, this can be an important factor even for a small firm that sells only in its own local market.

Exhibit 16-6 Exchange Rates for Various Currencies against the U.S. Dollar over Time

	Number of Units of Base Currency per U.S. Dollar*							
Base Currency	1987	1989	1991	1993	1995	1997	1999	2001
British pound	0.61	0.62	0.57	0.67	0.67	0.61	0.62	0.70
Thai bhat	25.76	25.72	25.53	25.33	24.92	31.07	37.40	45.65
Japanese yen	144.60	138.07	134.59	111.08	94.11	121.09	117.86	124.58
Australian dollar	1.43	1.26	1.32	1.47	1.35	1.34	1.55	1.96
Canadian dollar	1.33	1.18	1.15	1.29	1.37	1.38	1.49	1.56
German mark	1.80	1.88	1.66	1.65	1.43	1.73		
Euro							1.07	1.13

*Units shown are the average for each year 1987–1997. For 1999 and 2001, units shown are for April 16, 1999, and April 16, 2001.

In 1995 the marketing manager for EControl, Inc.—a small firm that produces electronic controllers for producers of satellite TV receiving dishes—set a meeting-competition wholesale price of about $100 for a carton of the controllers. The profit margin on the controllers at that price was about $10 per carton. The wholesalers who distribute the controllers also carried a product by a British firm. Its wholesale price was also $100, which means that the British firm got about 67 British pounds ($100 × 0.67 pounds per dollar) per carton. Prices were stable for some time. However, when the exchange rate for the pound against the dollar fell from 0.67 to 0.61, the British producer got 6 fewer pounds for each $100 carton of controllers (67 pounds − 61 pounds = 6 pounds).

Because EControl's marketing manager was only selling controllers in the domestic market, she didn't pay any attention to the drop in the exchange rate at first. However, she did pay attention when the British producer decided to raise its wholesale price to $110 a carton. At the $110 price, the British firm got about 67.1 pounds per carton ($110 × 0.61 pounds per dollar)—about the same as it was getting before the exchange rate change. EControl's market share and sales increased substantially—at the British competitor's expense—because EControl's price was $10 lower than its British competitor. EControl's marketing manager concluded that it would probably take a while for the British firm to lower its price, even if the exchange rate went up again. So she decided that she could safely raise her price level by 5 percent—up to $105—and still have a solid price advantage over the British supplier. At a price of $105 per carton, EControl's profit per carton jumped from $10 to $15, a 50 percent increase in profit.

Things turned out well for EControl even though the manager initially ignored exchange rates. Note, however, that during the 1999–2001 period the exchange rate for the British pound against the U.S. dollar *increased*. So in the 1999–2001 period EControl's situation might have been reversed![16]

Internet

Internet Exercise Xenon Laboratories has set up a website with a system that uses current exchange rates to convert one country's currency to another. Go to the website (www.ausmall.com.au), scroll down and click on *International Currency Converter.* How much is $100 U.S. worth now in Thai bhats, British pounds, and German marks? How do those numbers compare with April 2001 (see Exhibit 16-6)?

Most Price Structures Are Built around List Prices

Prices start with a list price

Most price structures are built around a base price schedule or price list. **Basic list prices** are the prices final customers or users are normally asked to pay for products. In this book, unless noted otherwise, list price refers to basic list price.

In the next chapter, we discuss how firms set these list prices. For now, however, we'll consider variations from list price and why they are made.

Discount Policies—Reductions from List Prices

Discounts are reductions from list price given by a seller to buyers who either give up some marketing function or provide the function themselves. Discounts can be useful in marketing strategy planning. In the following discussion, think about what function the buyers are giving up, or providing, when they get each of these discounts.

Vietnamese Smugglers Set Prices to Brush Off Competition

P&G and Unilever were among the first multinational firms to spend millions to set up factories in Vietnam. Now the factories are mostly idle. It's not because the Vietnamese aren't buying their brands. Rather, they're buying the same products at lower prices from low-cost smugglers. For example, smugglers get crates of Tide detergent and Close-Up toothpaste produced in a P&G factory in Thailand. Then they pile them high on bicycles and plod across the jungle and Cambodia's border to where Vietnamese consumers wait.

There is an explanation for this unusual and unauthorized channel of distribution. The Thai bhat was weakened by the Asian economic crisis. By contrast, the crisis didn't have much effect on the Vietnamese dong because the Communist government doesn't allow it to be converted into foreign currency. As a result, the same goods produced in Vietnam now cost about 35 percent more. The smugglers exploit this difference. After their "mark up" to cover transportation and profit, a tube of Close-Up smuggled from the P&G factory in Thailand sells for about 11,000 Vietnamese dong (67 cents), while a tube from the Vietnamese factory sells for about 14,000 dong. In Vietnam, where annual per capita income is only about $370, the cheaper tube has an edge. Moreover, some Vietnamese consumers are so weary of second-rate, Communist-made goods that they assume that anything made in Thailand is better. So at the market in Ho Chi Minh City, Thai soap is priced higher and still sells faster.

Smuggling is affecting everything from lipstick to toilets. It's still 30 percent of sales for some products, even though the Vietnamese border patrols have shut down all the dirt paths through the jungle to Cambodia. Many firms have been discounting prices to match the smugglers' prices. Those discounts probably weren't in the marketing plan![17]

Quantity discounts encourage volume buying

Quantity discounts are discounts offered to encourage customers to buy in larger amounts. This lets a seller get more of a buyer's business, or shifts some of the storing function to the buyer, or reduces shipping and selling costs—or all of these.

Cumulative quantity discounts apply to purchases over a given period—such as a year—and the discount usually increases as the amount purchased increases. Cumulative discounts encourage *repeat* buying by reducing the customer's cost for additional purchases. For example, a Lowe's lumberyard might give a cumulative quantity discount to a building contractor who is not able to buy all of the needed materials at once. Lowe's wants to reward the contractor's patronage and discourage shopping around.

Noncumulative quantity discounts apply only to individual orders. Such discounts encourage larger orders but do not tie a buyer to the seller after that one purchase. Lowe's lumberyard may resell insulation products made by several competing producers. Owens-Corning might try to encourage Lowe's to stock larger quantities of its pink insulation by offering a noncumulative quantity discount.

While quantity discounts are usually given as price cuts, sometimes they are given as free or bonus products. Airline frequent flier programs use this approach.

Cargill uses a seasonal discount to encourage its customers to stock products earlier than present demand requires. China's Coolbid.com used a quantity discount to launch its shopping site; the greater the number of people who applied to buy a product, the more the price was discounted.

Seasonal discounts—buy sooner

Seasonal discounts are discounts offered to encourage buyers to buy earlier than present demand requires. If used by a manufacturer, this discount tends to shift the storing function further along in the channel. It also tends to even out sales over the year. For example, Kyota offers wholesalers a lower price on its garden tillers if they buy in the fall—when sales are slow.

Service firms that have excess capacity often use seasonal discounts. For example, ski resorts offer lower weekday rates when attendance would otherwise be down.

Payment terms and cash discounts set payment dates

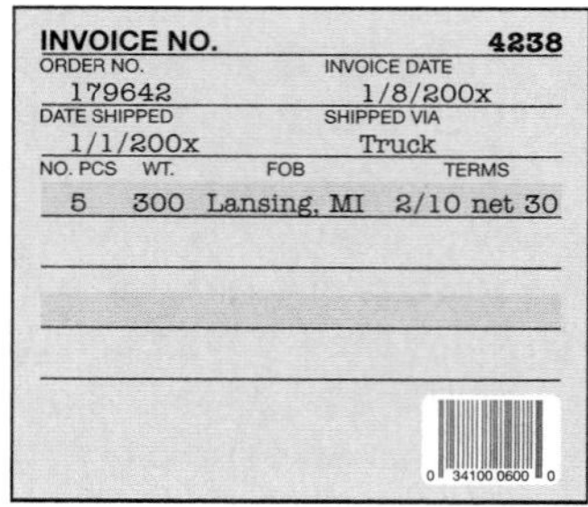

INVOICE NO. 4238
ORDER NO. 179642 INVOICE DATE 1/8/200x
DATE SHIPPED 1/1/200x SHIPPED VIA Truck
NO. PCS 5 WT. 300 FOB Lansing, MI TERMS 2/10 net 30

Most sales to businesses are made on credit. The seller sends a bill (invoice) by mail or electronically, and the buyer's accounting department processes it for payment. Some firms depend on their suppliers for temporary working capital (credit). Therefore, it is very important for both sides to clearly state the terms of payment—including the availability of cash discounts—and to understand the commonly used payment terms.

Net means that payment for the face value of the invoice is due immediately. These terms are sometimes changed to net 10 or net 30—which means payment is due within 10 or 30 days of the date on the invoice.

Cash discounts are reductions in price to encourage buyers to pay their bills quickly. The terms for a cash discount usually modify the net terms.

2/10, net 30 means the buyer can take a 2 percent discount off the face value of the invoice if the invoice is paid within 10 days. Otherwise, the full face value is due within 30 days. And it usually is stated or understood that an interest charge will be added after the 30-day free-credit period.

Why cash discounts are given and should be evaluated

Smart buyers carefully evaluate cash discounts. A discount of 2/10, net 30 may not look like much at first. But the buyer earns a 2 percent discount for paying the invoice just 20 days sooner than it should be paid anyway. By not taking the discount, the company in effect is borrowing at an annual rate of 36 percent. That is, assuming a 360-day year and dividing by 20 days, there are 18 periods during which the company could earn 2 percent—and 18 times 2 equals 36 percent a year.

Consumers say "charge it"

Credit sales are also important to retailers. Most retailers use credit card services, such as Visa or MasterCard, and pay a percent of the revenue from each credit sale for this service. For this reason, some retailers offer discounts to consumers who pay cash.

Many consumers like the convenience of credit card buying. But some critics argue that the cards make it too easy for consumers to buy things they really can't afford. Credit card interest charges can increase the total costs to consumers.

Trade discounts often are set by tradition

A **trade (functional) discount** is a list price reduction given to channel members for the job they are going to do.

A manufacturer, for example, might allow retailers a 30 percent trade discount from the suggested retail list price to cover the cost of the retailing function and their profit. Similarly, the manufacturer might allow wholesalers a *chain* discount of 30 percent and 10 percent off the suggested retail price. In this case, the wholesalers would be expected to pass the 30 percent discount on to retailers.[18]

Special sales reduce list prices—temporarily

A **sale price** is a temporary discount from the list price. Sale price discounts encourage immediate buying. In other words, to get the sale price, customers give up the convenience of buying when they want to buy and instead buy when the seller wants to sell.

Many stores guarantee that they have the lowest price and promise a refund if a customer finds an item lower somewhere else. Sun Television and Appliances woos customers to its stores with automatic refunds. Sun hires an outside firm to do daily price checks. When a customer is due a refund, it is sent automatically.

Special sales provide a marketing manager with a quick way to respond to changing market conditions—without changing the basic marketing strategy. For example, a retailer might use a sale to help clear extra inventory.

In recent years, sale prices and deals have become much more common. At first it may seem that consumers benefit from all this. But prices that change constantly may confuse customers and erode brand loyalty.

To avoid these problems, some firms that sell consumer convenience products offer **everyday low pricing**—setting a low list price rather than relying on frequent discounts or allowances. Many grocery stores use this approach.

Sale prices should be used carefully, consistent with well-thought-out pricing objectives and policies. A marketing manager who constantly uses temporary sales to adjust the price level probably has not done a good job setting the normal price.[19]

Allowance Policies—Off List Prices

Allowances, like discounts, are given to final consumers, customers, or channel members for doing something or accepting less of something.

Advertising allowances—something for something

Advertising allowances are price reductions given to firms in the channel to encourage them to advertise or otherwise promote the supplier's products locally. For example, General Electric gave an allowance (1.5 percent of sales) to its wholesalers of housewares and radios. They, in turn, were expected to spend the allowance on local advertising.

Stocking allowances—get attention and shelf space

Stocking allowances—sometimes called slotting allowances—are given to a middleman to get shelf space for a product. For example, a producer might offer a retailer cash or free merchandise to stock a new item. Stocking allowances are used mainly to get supermarket chains to handle new products. They're more willing to give space to a new product if the supplier will offset their handling costs and risks.

With a big stocking allowance, the middleman makes a profit—even if a new product fails and the producer loses money.

Are stocking allowances ethical?

Critics say that retailer demands for big stocking allowances slow new product introductions and make it hard for small producers to compete. Some producers feel that retailers' demands are just a different form of extortion. Retailers, on the other hand, point out that the fees protect them from producers that simply want to push more me-too products onto their shelves. Perhaps the best way for a producer to cope with the problem is to develop new products that really do offer consumers superior value. Then it benefits everyone in the channel, including retailers, to get the products to the target market.[20]

PMs—push for cash

Push money (or prize money) allowances—sometimes called PMs or spiffs—are given to retailers by manufacturers or wholesalers to pass on to the retailers' salesclerks for aggressively selling certain items. PM allowances are used for new items, slower-moving items, or higher-margin items. They are often used for pushing furniture, clothing, consumer electronics, and cosmetics. A salesclerk, for example, might earn an additional $5 for each new model Pansonic DVD player sold.

Bring in the old, ring up the new—with trade-ins

A **trade-in allowance** is a price reduction given for used products when similar new products are bought. Trade-ins give the marketing manager an easy way to lower the effective price without reducing list price. Proper handling of trade-ins is important when selling durable products.

Some Customers Get Something Extra

Clipping coupons—more for less

Many producers and retailers offer discounts (or free items) through coupons distributed in packages, mailings, print ads, or at the store. By presenting a coupon to a retailer, the consumer is given a discount off list price. This is especially common

Rebates give the producer a way to be certain that final consumers—not others in the channel—actually get the price reduction. Coupons are typically used for consumer products, but marketers for ThunkDesign offered a coupon for a $30,000 discount to prompt business customers to action.

in the consumer packaged goods business—but the use of price-off coupons is growing in other lines of business too.

Retailers are willing to redeem producers' coupons because it increases their sales—and they usually are paid for the trouble of handling the coupon. For example, a retailer who redeems a 50 cents off coupon might be repaid 75 cents.

Internet

Internet Exercise Catalina, a firm that specializes in targeted sales promotions, set up an online system called "ValuPage." Consumers can print out a sheet with a list of discounts that sponsoring supermarkets redeem with "web bucks"—which the consumer can then use for any future purchase at the store. Go to the website (www.supermarkets.com), type in your *Zip Code* only, and press *Enter* to review the system. Do you think this system will be more or less susceptible to fraud than regular coupons? Explain your thinking.

Cash rebates when you buy

Some producers offer **rebates**—refunds paid to consumers after a purchase. Rebates give the producer a way to be certain that final consumers actually get the price reduction. If the rebate amount were just taken off the price charged middlemen, they might not pass the savings along to consumers. In addition, many consumers buy because of the rebate—but then never ask for the refund.[21]

List Price May Depend on Geographic Pricing Policies

Retail list prices sometimes include free delivery. Or free delivery may be offered to some customers as an aid to closing the sale. But deciding who pays the freight charge is more important on sales to business customers than to final consumers because more money is involved. Purchase orders usually specify place, time, method of delivery, freight costs, insurance, handling, and other charges. There are many possible variations for an imaginative marketing manager, and some specialized terms have developed.

F.O.B. pricing is easy

A commonly used transportation term is **F.O.B.**—which means free on board some vehicle at some place. Typically, F.O.B. pricing names the place—often the location of the seller's factory or warehouse—as in F.O.B. Taiwan or F.O.B. mill. This means that the seller pays the cost of loading the products onto some vehicle, then title to the products passes to the buyer. The buyer pays the freight and takes responsibility for damage in transit.

If a firm wants to pay the freight for the convenience of customers, it can use F.O.B. delivered or F.O.B. buyer's factory. In this case, title does not pass until the products are delivered. If the seller wants title to pass immediately but is willing to prepay freight (and then include it in the invoice), F.O.B. seller's factory-freight prepaid can be used.

F.O.B. shipping point pricing simplifies the seller's pricing—but it may narrow the market. Since the delivered cost varies depending on the buyer's location, a customer located farther from the seller must pay more and might buy from closer suppliers.

Zone pricing smooths delivered prices

Zone pricing means making an average freight charge to all buyers within specific geographic areas. The seller pays the actual freight charges and bills each customer for an average charge. For example, a company in Canada might divide the United States into seven zones, then bill all customers in the same zone the same amount for freight even though actual shipping costs might vary.

Zone pricing reduces the wide variation in delivered prices that results from an F.O.B. shipping point pricing policy. It also simplifies transportation charges.

Uniform delivered pricing—one price to all

Uniform delivered pricing means making an average freight charge to all buyers. It is a kind of zone pricing—an entire country may be considered as one zone—that includes the average cost of delivery in the price. Uniform delivered pricing is most often used when (1) transportation costs are relatively low and (2) the seller wishes to sell in all geographic areas at one price—perhaps a nationally advertised price.

Freight-absorption pricing—competing on equal grounds in another territory

When all firms in an industry use F.O.B. shipping point pricing, a firm usually competes well near its shipping point but not farther away. As sales reps look for business farther away, delivered prices rise and the firm finds itself priced out of the market.

This problem can be reduced with **freight-absorption pricing**—which means absorbing freight cost so that a firm's delivered price meets the nearest competitor's. This amounts to cutting list price to appeal to new market segments. Some firms look at international markets this way; they just figure that any profit from export sales is a bonus.

Pricing Policies Combine to Impact Customer Value

Look at Price from the customer's viewpoint

We've discussed pricing policies separately so far, but from the customer's view they all combine to impact customer value. So, when we talk about Price we are really talking about the whole set of price policies that define the real price level. On the other hand, superior value isn't just based on having a lower price than some competitor but rather on the whole marketing mix.

Value pricing leads to superior customer value

Smart marketers look for the combination of Price decisions that result in value pricing. **Value pricing** means setting a fair price level for a marketing mix that really gives the target market superior customer value.

Value pricing doesn't necessarily mean cheap if cheap means bare-bones or low-grade. It doesn't mean high prestige either if the prestige is not accompanied by the right quality goods and services. Rather, the focus is on the customer's requirements and how the whole marketing mix meets those needs.

Toyota is a firm that has been effective with value pricing. It has different marketing mixes for different target markets. But from the low-price Echo to the $30,000 Avalon, the Japanese automaker consistently offers better quality and lower prices than its competitors.

Companies that use value pricing deliver on their promises. They try to give the consumer pleasant surprises—like an unexpected service—because it increases value and builds customer loyalty. They return the price if the customer isn't completely satisfied. They avoid unrealistic price levels—prices that are high only because consumers already know the brand name. They build relationships so customers will come back time and again.

There are Price choices in most markets

Some marketing managers miss the advantages of value pricing. They've heard economists say that in perfect competition it's foolish to offer products above or below the market price. But most firms *don't* operate in perfect competition where what firms offer is exactly the same.

Most operate in monopolistic competition, where products and whole marketing mixes are not exactly the same. This means that there are pricing options. At one

Marketers for Luvs diapers want consumers to know that Luvs' value price, compared to the pricey brands, is equivalent to getting 275 diapers a year for free.

extreme, some firms are clearly above the market—they may even brag about it. Tiffany's is well known as one of the most expensive jewelry stores in the world. Other firms emphasize below-the-market prices in their marketing mixes. Prices offered by mass-merchandisers, such as Wal-Mart and Tesco, illustrate this approach. They may even promote their pricing policy with catchy slogans like "guaranteed lowest prices."

Value pricers define the target market and the competition

In making price decisions and using value pricing, it is important to clearly define the *relevant target market* and *competitors* when making price comparisons.

Consider Wal-Mart prices again from this view. Wal-Mart may have lower camera prices than conventional camera retailers, but it offers less help in the store, less selection, and it won't take old cameras in trade. Wal-Mart may be appealing to budget-oriented shoppers who compare prices *and* value among different mass-merchandisers. But a specialty camera store may be trying to appeal to different customers and not even be a direct competitor!

A camera producer with this point of view might offer the specialty store models that are not available to Wal-Mart—to ensure that customers don't view price as the only difference between the two stores.

Further, the specialty store needs to communicate clearly to its target market *how* it offers superior value. Wal-Mart is certainly going to communicate that it offers low prices. If that's all customers hear, it's no wonder that they just focus on price. The specialty retailer has to be certain that consumers understand that price is not the only thing of value that is different. This same logic applies to comparisons between Internet sellers and brick-and-mortar competitors. Each may have advantages or disadvantages that relate to value.

Meeting competitors' prices may be necessary

In a mature market there is downward pressure on both prices and profit margins. Moreover, differentiating the value a firm offers may not be easy when competitors can quickly copy new ideas. Extending our camera example, if our speciality store is in a city with a number of similar stores with the same product, there may not be a way to convince consumers that one beats all of the others. In such circumstances there may be no real pricing choice other than to "meet the competition." With profit margins already thin, they would quickly disappear or turn

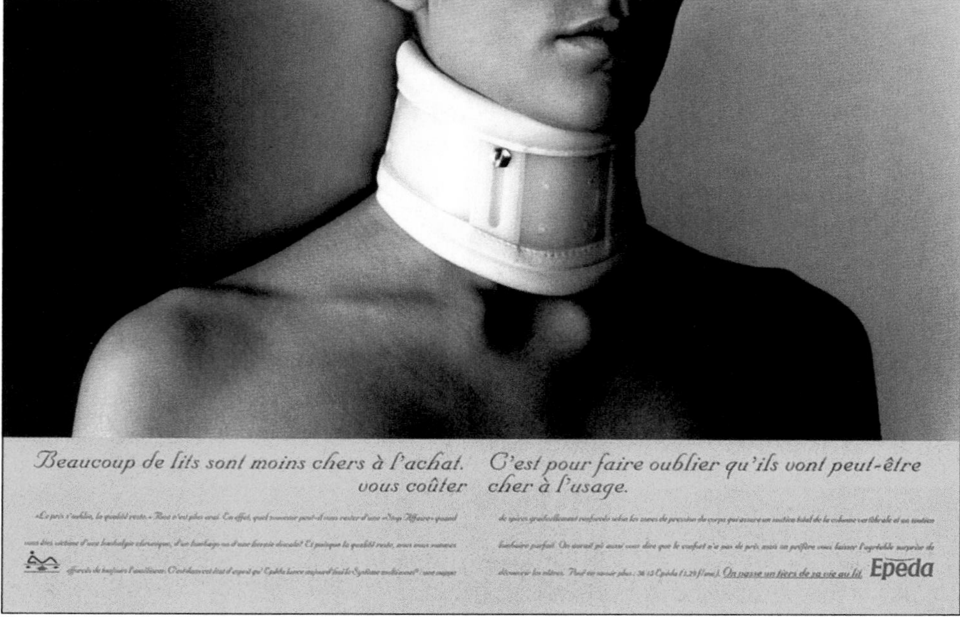

Epeda sells high-quality mattresses. It wants customers to know that its higher price is worth it. This ad says, "Lots of mattresses are cheap to buy. The reason is to make you forget how much sleeping on them is going to cost you."

into losses at a lower price. And a higher price would simply prompt competitors to promote their price advantage.[22]

Similarly, a B2B supplier may have a better marketing mix than competitors; but if buyers have decided to use a procurement hub and reverse auction as the only way to buy, the supplier may not have any choice but to decide what the lowest price is that it will bid to get the business. Winning the bid at a profit-losing price doesn't help.

Even though competition can be intense, too many marketers give up too easily. They often can find a way to differentiate, even if it's something that competitors dismiss as less important. Research showed that many McDonald's customers actually prefer the burgers at Burger King. But they judge the bathrooms at McDonald's to be cleaner and assume that the kitchen is cleaner too.[23]

There may be little choice about Price in oligopoly situations. Pricing at the market—that is, meeting competition—may be the only sensible policy. To raise prices might lead to a large loss in sales—unless competitors adopt the higher price too. And cutting prices would probably lead to similar reductions by competitors—downward along an inelastic industry demand curve. This can only lead to a decrease in total revenue for the industry and probably for each firm. The major airlines faced these problems recently.

To avoid these problems, each oligopolist may choose a status quo pricing objective and set its price at the competitive level. Some critics call this pricing behavior conscious parallel action, implying it is unethical and the same as intentional conspiracy among firms. As a practical matter, however, that criticism seems overly harsh. It obviously isn't sensible for firms to ignore their competitors.

Value pricing fits with market-oriented strategy planning

There are times when the marketing manager's hands are tied and there is little that can be done to differentiate the marketing mix. However, most marketing managers do have choices—many choices. They can vary strategy decisions with respect to all of the marketing mix variables, not just Price, to offer target customers superior value. And when a marketer's hands are really tied, it's time to look for new opportunities that offer more promise.

Legality of Pricing Policies

This chapter discusses the many pricing decisions that must be made. However, some pricing decisions are limited by government legislation. The first step to understanding pricing legislation is to know the thinking of legislators and the courts. To get a better idea of the "why" of legislation, we'll focus on U.S. legislation here, but many other countries have similar pricing laws.[24]

Minimum prices are sometimes controlled

Unfair trade practice acts put a lower limit on prices, especially at the wholesale and retail levels. They have been passed in more than half the states in the United States. Selling below cost in these states is illegal. Wholesalers and retailers are usually required to take a certain minimum percentage markup over their merchandise-plus-transportation costs. The practical effect of these laws is to protect certain limited-line food retailers—such as dairy stores—from the kind of "ruinous" competition supermarkets might offer if they sold milk as a leader, offering it below cost for a long time.

The United States and most other countries control the minimum price of imported products with antidumping laws. **Dumping** is pricing a product sold in a foreign market below the cost of producing it or at a price lower than in its domestic market. These laws are usually designed to protect the country's domestic producers and jobs. But there is debate about how well they work.[25]

Even very high prices may be OK

Generally speaking, firms can charge high prices—even outrageously high prices—as long as they don't conspire with their competitors to fix prices, discriminate against some of their customers, or lie.

Of course, there are exceptions. Firms in regulated businesses may need to seek approval for their prices. For example, in the United States, most states regulate automobile insurance rates. Some countries impose more general price controls—to reduce inflation or try to control markets. However, most countries have followed the move toward a market-directed economy. That doesn't mean, however, that there aren't important regulations in the pricing area.

Local media in China claim that both Fuji from Japan and Kodak from the U.S. are dumping their products in China, even though China's Lucky brand of film and paper has a price that is 50 percent lower.

You can't lie about prices

Phony list prices are prices customers are shown to suggest that the price has been discounted from list. Some customers seem more interested in the supposed discount than in the actual price. Most businesses, trade associations, and government agencies consider the use of phony list prices unethical. In the United States, the FTC tries to stop such pricing—using the **Wheeler Lea Amendment,** which bans "unfair or deceptive acts in commerce."[26]

In recent years some electronics retailers, like Best Buy, have been criticized on these grounds. They'd advertise a $300 discount on a computer when the customer signed up for an Internet service provider, but it might not be clear to the consumer that a three-year commitment—costing over $700—was required.

Price fixing is illegal—you can go to jail

Difficulties with pricing—and violations of pricing legislation—usually occur when competing marketing mixes are quite similar. When the success of an entire marketing strategy depends on price, there is pressure (and temptation) to make agreements with competitors (conspire). And **price fixing**—competitors getting together to raise, lower, or stabilize prices—is common and relatively easy. *But it is also completely illegal in the United States.* It is considered "conspiracy" under the Sherman Act and the Federal Trade Commission Act. To discourage price fixing, both companies and individual managers are held responsible. Some executives have already gone to jail![27]

Different countries have different rules concerning price fixing, and this has created problems in international trade. Japan, for example, allows price fixing—especially if it helps Japanese firms.

U.S. antimonopoly laws ban price discrimination unless . . .

Price-level and price flexibility policies can lead to price discrimination. The **Robinson-Patman Act** (of 1936) makes illegal any **price discrimination**—selling the same products to different buyers at different prices—*if it injures competition.* The law does permit some price differences—but they must be based on (1) cost differences or (2) the need to meet competition. Both buyers and sellers are considered guilty if they know they're entering into discriminatory agreements. This is a serious matter—price discrimination suits are common.

What does "like grade and quality" mean?

The Robinson-Patman Act allows a marketing manager to charge different prices for similar products if they are *not* of "like grade and quality." The FTC says that if the physical characteristics of a product are similar, then they are of like grade and quality. A landmark U.S. Supreme Court ruling against the Borden Company upheld the FTC's view that a well-known label *alone* does not make a product different from one with an unknown label. The company agreed that the canned milk it sold at different prices under different labels was basically the same.

But the FTC's victory in the Borden case was not complete. The U.S. Court of Appeals found no evidence of injury to competition and further noted that there could be no injury unless Borden's price differential exceeded the "recognized consumer appeal of the Borden label." How to measure "consumer appeal" was not spelled out and may lead to additional suits. For now, however, producers who want to sell several brands—or dealer brands at lower prices than their main brand—probably should offer physical differences, and differences that are really useful.[28]

Can cost analysis justify price differences?

The Robinson-Patman Act allows price differences if there are cost differences—say, for larger quantity shipments or because middlemen take over some of the physical distribution functions. But justifying cost differences is a difficult job. And the justification must be developed *before* different prices are set. The seller can't wait until a competitor, disgruntled customer, or the FTC brings a charge. At that point, it's too late.[29]

Can you legally meet price cuts?

Under the Robinson-Patman Act, meeting a competitor's price is permitted as a defense in price discrimination cases. A major objective of antimonopoly laws is to protect competition, not competitors. And "meeting competition in good faith" still seems to be legal.

Special promotion allowances might not be allowed

Some firms violate the Robinson-Patman Act by providing push money, advertising allowances, and other promotion aids to some customers and not others. The act prohibits such special allowances—*unless they are made available to all customers on "proportionately equal" terms.*[30]

How to avoid discriminating

Because price discrimination laws are complicated and penalties for violations heavy, many business managers follow the safest course by offering few or no quantity discounts and the same cost-based prices to *all* customers. This is *too* conservative a reaction. But when firms consider price differences, they may need a lawyer involved in the discussion!

Conclusion

The Price variable offers an alert marketing manager many possibilities for varying marketing mixes. What pricing policies should be used depends on the pricing objectives. We looked at profit-oriented, sales-oriented, and status quo-oriented objectives.

A marketing manager must set policies about price flexibility, price levels over the product life cycle, who will pay the freight, and who will get discounts and allowances. While doing this, the manager should be aware of legislation that affects pricing policies.

In most cases, a marketing manager must set prices—that is, administer prices. Starting with a list price, a variety of discounts and allowances may be offered to adjust for the something of value being offered in the marketing mix.

Throughout this chapter, we talk about what may be included or excluded in the something of value and what objectives a firm might set to guide its pricing policies. We discuss how pricing policies combine to impact customer value. Price setting itself is not discussed. It will be covered in the next chapter—where we show ways to carry out the various pricing objectives and policies.

Questions and Problems

1. Identify the strategy decisions a marketing manager must make in the Price area. Illustrate your answer for a local retailer.
2. How should the acceptance of a profit-oriented, a sales-oriented, or a status quo-oriented pricing objective affect the development of a company's marketing strategy? Illustrate for each.
3. Distinguish between one-price and flexible-price policies. Which is most appropriate for a hardware store? Why?
4. What pricing objective(s) is a skimming pricing policy most likely implementing? Is the same true for a penetration pricing policy? Which policy is probably most appropriate for each of the following products: *(a)* a new type of home lawn-sprinkling system, *(b)* a skin patch drug to help smokers quit, *(c)* a DVD of a best-selling movie, and *(d)* a new children's toy?
5. How would differences in exchange rates between different countries affect a firm's decisions concerning the use of flexible-price policies in different foreign markets?
6. Are seasonal discounts appropriate in agricultural businesses (which are certainly seasonal)?
7. What are the effective annual interest rates for the following cash discount terms: *(a)* 1/10, net 20; *(b)* 1/5, net 10; and *(c)* net 25?

8. Do stocking allowances increase or reduce conflict in a channel of distribution? Explain your thinking.
9. Why would a manufacturer offer a rebate instead of lowering the suggested list price?
10. How can a marketing manager change a firm's F.O.B. terms to make an otherwise competitive marketing mix more attractive?
11. What type of geographic pricing policy is most appropriate for the following products (specify any assumptions necessary to obtain a definite answer): *(a)* a chemical by-product, *(b)* nationally advertised candy bars, *(c)* rebuilt auto parts, and *(d)* tricycles?
12. How would a ban on freight absorption (that is, requiring F.O.B. factory pricing) affect a producer with substantial economies of scale in production?
13. Give an example of a marketing mix that has a high price level but that you see as a good value. Briefly explain what makes it a good value.
14. Think about a business from which you regularly make purchases even though there are competing firms with similar prices. Explain what the firm offers that improves value and keeps you coming back.
15. Cite two examples of continuously selling above the market price. Describe the situations.
16. Explain the types of competitive situations that might lead to a meeting-competition pricing policy.
17. Would consumers be better off if all nations dropped their antidumping laws? Explain your thinking.
18. How would our marketing system change if manufacturers were required to set fixed prices on *all* products sold at retail and *all* retailers were required to use these prices? Would a manufacturer's marketing mix be easier to develop? What kind of an operation would retailing be in this situation? Would consumers receive more or less service?
19. Is price discrimination involved if a large oil company sells gasoline to taxicab associations for resale to individual taxicab operators for 2½ cents a gallon less than the price charged to retail service stations? What happens if the cab associations resell gasoline not only to taxicab operators but to the general public as well?

Suggested Cases

12. Paper Supplies Corporation
22. PlastiForm Mfg., Inc.

Computer-Aided Problem

16. Cash Discounts

Joe Tulkin owns Tulkin Wholesale Co. He sells paper, tape, file folders, and other office supplies to about 120 retailers in nearby cities. His average retailer customer spends about $900 a month. When Tulkin started business in 1991, competing wholesalers were giving retailers invoice terms of 3/10, net 30. Tulkin never gave the issue much thought—he just used the same invoice terms when he billed customers. At that time, about half of his customers took the discount. Recently, he noticed a change in the way his customers were paying their bills. Checking his records, he found that 90 percent of the retailers were taking the cash discount. With so many retailers taking the cash discount, it seems to have become a price reduction. In addition, Tulkin learned that other wholesalers were changing their invoice terms.

Tulkin decides he should rethink his invoice terms. He knows he could change the percent rate on the cash discount, the number of days the discount is offered, or the number of days before the face amount is due. Changing any of these, or any combination, will change the interest rate at which a buyer is, in effect, borrowing money if he does not take the discount. Tulkin decides that it will be easier to evaluate the effect of different invoice terms if he sets up a spreadsheet to let him change the terms and quickly see the effective interest rate for each change.

a. *With 90 percent of Tulkin's customers now taking the discount, what is the total monthly cash discount amount?*
b. *If Tulkin changes his invoice terms to 1/5, net 20, what interest rate is each buyer paying by not taking the cash discount? With these terms, would fewer buyers be likely to take the discount? Why?*

c. *Tulkin thinks 10 customers will switch to other wholesalers if he changes his invoice terms to 2/10, net 30, while 60 percent of the remaining customers will take the discount. What interest rate does a buyer pay by not taking this cash discount? For this situation, what will the total gross sales (total invoice) amount be? The total cash discount? The total net sales receipts after the total cash discount? Compare Tulkin's current situation with what will happen if he changes his invoice terms to 2/10, net 30.*

For additional questions related to this problem, see Exercise 16-3 in the *Learning Aid for Use with Essentials of Marketing*, 9th edition.

When You Finish This Chapter, You Should

1. Understand how most wholesalers and retailers set their prices—using markups.

2. Understand why turnover is so important in pricing.

3. Understand the advantages and disadvantages of average-cost pricing.

4. Know how to use break-even analysis to evaluate possible prices.

5. Understand the advantages of marginal analysis and how to use it for price setting.

6. Understand the various factors that influence customer price sensitivity.

7. Know the many ways that price setters use demand estimates in their pricing.

8. Understand the important new terms (shown in red).

Chapter Seventeen

Price Setting in the Business World

In the spring of 2001, Kmart's prices on products like toothpaste, light bulbs, laundry soap, and beauty products were 10 to 15 percent higher than at Wal-Mart. Shoppers buy these items frequently and know what they pay. To provide equal value, marketing managers for Kmart decided that they needed to cut prices on 4,000 products. And to highlight their price-cutting they revived Kmart's hourly Blue Light Specials, a surprise sale on an item that usually lasts about 15 minutes. It didn't take long for Wal-Mart to announce that it would be putting even more emphasis on price rollbacks. By taking a longer-term look at how Wal-Mart has grown so fast in the past, you'll get a pretty good idea how this wrestling match is going to turn out.

To put the big picture in perspective, Wal-Mart's current sales are about five times Kmart's. By the year 2005, Wal-Mart sales should exceed $330 billion—double what they were in 1999 and 13 times what they were in 1990. Back then,

place price promotion produ

Wal-Mart earned about twice as much profit as Kmart even though they had about the same sales revenue.

What explains the big difference in growth and profits when the two chains are in many ways similar? Part of the answer is that Wal-Mart has more sales volume in each store. Wal-Mart's sales revenue per square foot is more than twice that at Kmart. Wal-Mart's lower prices on similar products increases demand in its stores. But it also reduces its fixed operating costs as a percentage of sales. That means it can add a smaller markup, still cover its operating expenses, and make a larger profit. And as lower prices pull in more and more customers, its percent of overhead costs to sales continues to drop—from about 20.2 percent in 1980 to about 16 percent now.

In the past few years, Wal-Mart has also improved profits by cutting unnecessary inventory by over $2 billion, thereby saving $150 million in carrying cost and reducing markdowns. Wal-Mart also has lower costs for the goods it sells. Its buyers are tough in negotiating the best prices from suppliers—to be able to offer Wal-Mart customers the brands they want at low prices. But Wal-Mart also works closely with producers to reduce costs in the channel. For example, Wal-Mart was one of the first major retailers to insist that all orders be placed by computer; that helps to reduce stock-outs on store shelves and lost sales at the checkout counter. Wal-Mart also works with vendors to create private-label brands, such as Sam's Choice Cola. Its low price—about 15 percent below what consumers expect to pay for well-known colas—doesn't leave a big profit margin. Yet when customers come in to buy it they also pick up other, more profitable, products.

Even with its lower costs, Wal-Mart isn't content to take the convenient route to price setting by just adding a standard percentage markup on different items. The company was one of the first retailers to give managers in every department in every store frequent, detailed information about what is selling and what isn't. They drop items that are collecting dust and roll back prices on the ones with the fastest turnover and highest margins. That not only increases stockturn but also puts the effort behind products with the most potential. For example, every department manager in every Wal-Mart store has a list of special VPIs (volume producing items). They give VPIs special attention and display space—to get a bigger sales and profit boost. For instance, Wal-Mart's analysis of checkout-scanner sales data revealed that parents often pick up more than one kid's video at a time. So now they are certain that special displays feature several videos and that the rest of the selection is close by.

Wal-Mart was the first major retailer to move to online selling (www.walmart.com). Its online sales still account for only a small percent of its total sales, so there's lots of room to grow there too. Further, Wal-Mart is aggressively taking its low-price approach to other countries—ranging from Mexico to China.

To return to where we started, Kmart is now copying many of Wal-Mart's innovations. However, Wal-Mart has such advantages on sales volume, unit costs, and margins that it will be difficult for Kmart to win in any price war—unless Wal-Mart somehow stumbles because of its enormous size.[1]

Price Setting Is a Key Strategy Decision

In the last chapter, we discussed the idea that pricing objectives and policies should guide pricing decisions. We accepted the idea of a list price and went on to discuss variations from list and how they combine to impact customer value. Now we'll see how the basic list price is set in the first place—based on information about costs, demand, and profit margins. See Exhibit 17-1.

There are many ways to set list prices. But for simplicity they can be reduced to two basic approaches: *cost-oriented* and *demand-oriented* price setting. We will discuss cost-oriented approaches first because they are most common. Also, understanding the problems of relying only on a cost-oriented approach shows why a marketing manager must also consider demand to make good Price decisions. Let's begin by looking at how most retailers and wholesalers set cost-oriented prices.

Some Firms Just Use Markups

Markups guide pricing by middlemen

Some firms, including most retailers and wholesalers, set prices by using a **markup**—a dollar amount added to the cost of products to get the selling price. For example, suppose that a CVS drugstore buys a bottle of Pert Plus shampoo for $2.

Exhibit 17-1
Key Factors That Influence Price Setting

To make a profit, the drugstore obviously must sell the shampoo for more than $2. If it adds $1 to cover operating expenses and provide a profit, we say that the store is marking up the item $1.

Markups, however, usually are stated as percentages rather than dollar amounts. And this is where confusion sometimes arises. Is a markup of $1 on a cost of $2 a markup of 50 percent? Or should the markup be figured as a percentage of the selling price—$3.00—and therefore be 33⅓ percent? A clear definition is necessary.

Markup percent is based on selling price—a convenient rule

Unless otherwise stated, **markup (percent)** means percentage of selling price that is added to the cost to get the selling price. So the $1 markup on the $3.00 selling price is a markup of 33⅓ percent. Markups are related to selling price for convenience.

There's nothing wrong with the idea of markup on cost. However, to avoid confusion, it's important to state clearly which markup percent you're using.

A manager may want to change a markup on selling price to one based on cost, or vice versa. The calculations used to do this are simple. (See the section on markup conversion in Appendix B on marketing arithmetic.)[2]

Many use a standard markup percent

Many middlemen select a standard markup percent and then apply it to all their products. This makes pricing easier. When you think of the large number of items the average retailer and wholesaler carry—and the small sales volume of any one item—this approach may make sense. Spending the time to find the best price to charge on every item in stock (day to day or week to week) might not pay.

Moreover, different companies in the same line of business often use the same markup percent. There is a reason for this: Their operating expenses are usually similar. So a standard markup is acceptable as long as it's large enough to cover the firm's operating expenses and provide a reasonable profit.

Specialized products that rely on selective distribution and sell in smaller volume usually offer retailers higher markups, in part to offset the retailer's higher carrying costs and marketing expenses.

Markups are related to gross margins

How does a manager decide on a standard markup in the first place? A standard markup is often set close to the firm's *gross margin*. Managers regularly see gross margins on their operating (profit and loss) statements. The gross margin is the amount left—after subtracting the cost of sales (cost of goods sold) from net sales—to cover the expenses of selling products and operating the business. (See Appendix B on marketing arithmetic if you are unfamiliar with these ideas.) Our CVS manager knows that there won't be any profit if the gross margin is not large enough. For this reason, CVS might accept a markup percent on Pert Plus shampoo that is close to the store's usual gross margin percent.

Smart producers pay attention to the gross margins and standard markups of middlemen in their channel. They usually allow trade (functional) discounts similar to the standard markups these middlemen expect.

Markup chain may be used in channel pricing

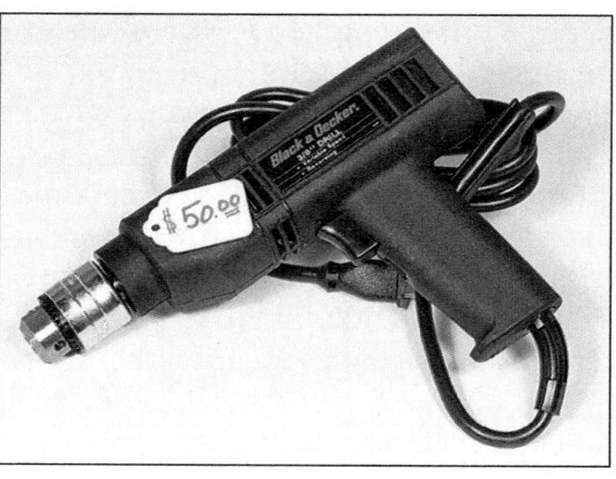

Different firms in a channel often use different markups. A **markup chain**—the sequence of markups firms use at different levels in a channel—determines the price structure in the whole channel. The markup is figured on the *selling price* at each level of the channel.

For example, Black & Decker's selling price for an electric drill becomes the cost the Ace Hardware wholesaler pays. The wholesaler's selling price becomes the hardware retailer's cost. And this cost plus a retail markup becomes the retail selling price. Each markup should cover the costs of running the business and leave a profit.

Exhibit 17-2 illustrates the markup chain for an electric drill at each level of the channel system. The production (factory) cost of the drill is $21.60. In this case, the producer takes a 10 percent markup and sells the product for $24. The markup is 10 percent of $24 or $2.40. The producer's selling price now becomes the wholesaler's cost—$24. If the wholesaler is used to taking a 20 percent markup on selling price, the markup is $6—and the wholesaler's selling price becomes $30. The $30

Exhibit 17-2 Example of a Markup Chain and Channel Pricing

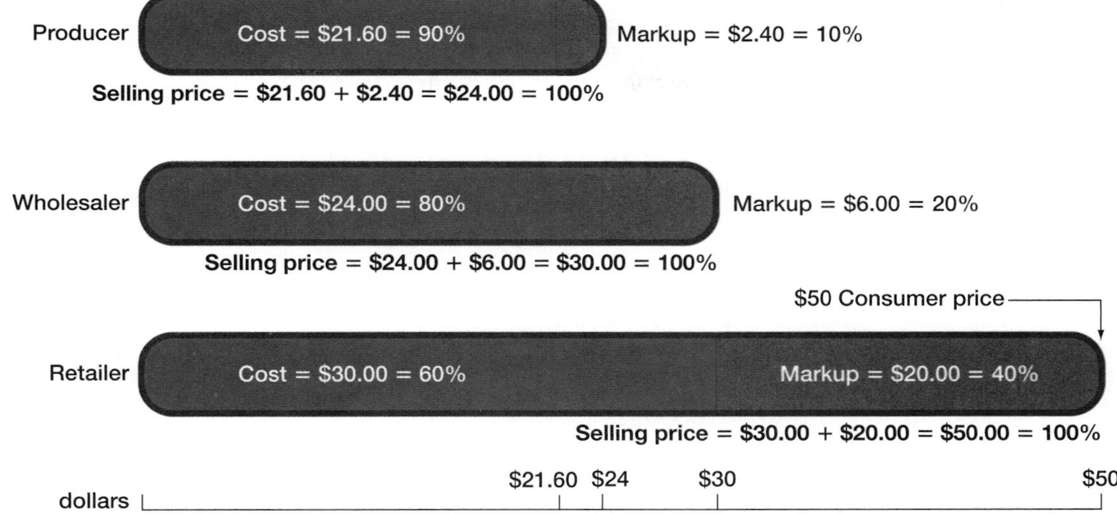

now becomes the cost for the hardware retailer. And a retailer who is used to a 40 percent markup adds $20, and the retail selling price becomes $50.

High markups don't always mean big profits

Some people, including many conventional retailers, think high markups mean big profits. Often this isn't true. A high markup may result in a price that's too high—a price at which few customers will buy. You can't earn much if you don't sell much, no matter how high your markup on a single item. So, high markups may lead to low profits.

Lower markups can speed turnover and the stockturn rate

Some retailers and wholesalers, however, try to speed turnover to increase profit—even if this means reducing their markups. They realize that a business runs up costs over time. If they can sell a much greater amount in the same time period, they may be able to take a lower markup and still earn higher profits at the end of the period.

An important idea here is the **stockturn rate**—the number of times the average inventory is sold in a year. Various methods of figuring stockturn rates can be used (see the section "Computing the Stockturn Rate" in Appendix B). A low stockturn rate may be bad for profits.

At the very least, a low stockturn increases inventory carrying cost and ties up working capital. If a firm with a stockturn of 1 (once per year) sells products that cost it $100,000, it has that much tied up in inventory all the time. But a stockturn of 5 requires only $20,000 worth of inventory ($100,000 cost ÷ 5 turnovers a year). If annual inventory carrying cost is about 20 percent of the inventory value, that reduces costs by $16,000 a year. That's a big difference on $100,000 in sales!

Whether a stockturn rate is high or low depends on the industry and the product involved. A NAPA auto parts wholesaler may expect an annual rate of 1—while a Safeway supermarket might expect 20 to 30 stockturns for soaps and detergents and 70 to 80 stockturns for fresh fruits and vegetables.

Mass-merchandisers run in fast company

Although some middlemen use the same standard markup percent on all their products, this policy ignores the importance of fast turnover. Mass-merchandisers know this. They put low markups on fast-selling items and higher markups on items that sell less frequently. For example, Wal-Mart may put a small markup on fast-selling health and beauty aids (like toothpaste or shampoo) but higher markups on appliances and clothing.

Where does the markup chain start?

Some markups eventually become standard in a trade. Most channel members tend to follow a similar process—adding a certain percentage to the previous price. But who sets price in the first place? The firm that brands a product is usually the one that sets its basic list price. It may be a large retailer, a large wholesaler, or most often, the producer.

Some producers just start with a cost per unit figure and add a markup—perhaps a standard markup—to obtain their selling price. Or they may use some rule-of-thumb formula such as:

$$\text{Selling price} = \text{Average production cost per unit} \times 3$$

A producer who uses this approach might develop rules and markups related to its own costs and objectives. Yet even the first step—selecting the appropriate cost per unit to build on—isn't easy. Let's discuss several approaches to see how cost-oriented price setting really works.

Average-Cost Pricing Is Common and Can Be Dangerous

Average-cost pricing means adding a reasonable markup to the average cost of a product. A manager usually finds the average cost per unit by studying past records. Dividing the total cost for the last year by all the units produced and sold in that period gives an estimate of the average cost per unit for the next year. If the cost was $32,000 for all labor and materials and $30,000 for fixed overhead expenses—such as selling expenses, rent, and manager salaries—then the total cost is $62,000. If the company produced 40,000 items in that time period, the average cost is $62,000 divided by 40,000 units, or $1.55 per unit. To get the price, the producer decides how much profit per unit to add to the average cost per unit. If the company considers 45 cents a reasonable profit for each unit, it sets the new price at $2.00. Exhibit 17-3A shows that this approach produces the desired profit—if the company sells 40,000 units.

Exhibit 17-3 Results of Average-Cost Pricing

A. Calculation of Planned Profit if 40,000 Items Are Sold		B. Calculation of Actual Profit if Only 20,000 Items Are Sold	
Calculation of Costs:		**Calculation of Costs:**	
Fixed overhead expenses	$30,000	Fixed overhead expenses	$30,000
Labor and materials ($.80 a unit)	32,000	Labor and materials ($.80 a unit)	16,000
Total costs	$62,000	Total costs	$46,000
"Planned" profit	18,000		
Total costs and planned profit	$80,000		
Calculation of Profit (or Loss):		**Calculation of Profit (or Loss):**	
Actual unit sales × price ($2.00*)	$80,000	Actual unit sales × price ($2.00*)	$40,000
Minus: total costs	62,000	Minus: total costs	46,000
Profit (loss)	$18,000	Profit (loss)	($6,000)
Result:		**Result:**	
Planned profit of $18,000 is earned if 40,000 items are sold at $2.00 each.		Planned profit of $18,000 is not earned. Instead, $6,000 loss results if 20,000 items are sold at $2.00 each.	

*Calculation of "reasonable" price: $\frac{\text{Expected total costs and planned profit}}{\text{Planned number of items to be sold}} = \frac{\$80,000}{40,000} = \$2.00$

Are Women Consumers Being Taken to the Cleaners?

Women have complained for years that they pay more than men for dry cleaning, haircuts, shoes, and a host of other products. For example, a laundry might charge $2.25 to launder a woman's white cotton shirt and charge only $1.25 for an identical shirt delivered by a man.

A survey in California found that of 25 randomly chosen dry cleaners, 64 percent charged more to launder women's cotton shirts than men's; 28 percent charged more to dry clean women's suits. And 40 percent of 25 hair salons surveyed charged more for basic women's haircuts. Soon after the survey, California passed a law banning such gender-based differences in prices—and New York and Massachusetts followed suit. On the other hand, there's nothing in any law to say that Mennen antiperspirant for men, priced at $2.89 for 2.25 ounces, can't be a better deal than Mennen's Lady Speed Stick, which is $2.69 for one-third fewer ounces. Such differences are common with health and beauty aids.

Critics argue that firms are discriminating against women by arbitrarily charging them higher prices. Not everyone shares this view. A spokesperson for an association of launderers says that "the automated equipment we use fits a certain range of standardized shirts. A lot of women's blouses have different kinds of trim . . . and it all has to be hand-finished. If it involves hand-finishing, we charge more." Some cleaners charge more for doing women's blouses because the average cost is higher than the average cost for men's shirts. Some just charge more because women buy anyway.

There are no federal laws to regulate the prices that dry cleaners, hair salons, or tailors charge. Still, most experts argue that any such laws are unnecessary. After all, customers who don't like a particular cleaner's rates are free to go to a competitor who may charge less.

Other firms face the issue of how to set prices when the average costs are different to serve different customers. For example, poor, inner-city consumers often pay higher prices for food. But inner-city retailers also face higher average costs for facilities, shoplifting, and insurance. Some firms don't like to charge different consumers different prices, but they also don't want to charge everyone a higher average price—to cover the expense of serving high-cost customers.[3]

www.mhhe.com/fourps

It does not make allowances for cost variations as output changes

It's always a useful input to pricing decisions to understand how costs operate at different levels of output. Further, average-cost pricing is simple. But it can also be dangerous. It's easy to lose money with average-cost pricing. To see why, let's follow this example further.

First, remember that the average cost of $2.00 per unit was based on output of 40,000 units. But if the firm is only able to produce and sell 20,000 units in the next year, it may be in trouble. Twenty thousand units sold at $2.00 each ($1.55 cost plus 45 cents for expected profit) yield a total revenue of only $40,000. The overhead is still fixed at $30,000, and the variable material and labor cost drops by half to $16,000—for a total cost of $46,000. This means a loss of $6,000, or 30 cents a unit. The method that was supposed to allow a profit of 45 cents a unit actually causes a loss of 30 cents a unit. See Exhibit 17-3B.

The basic problem with the average-cost approach is that it doesn't consider cost variations at different levels of output. In a typical situation, costs are high with low output, and then economies of scale set in—the average cost per unit drops as the quantity produced increases. This is why mass production and mass distribution often make sense. It's also why it's important to develop a better understanding of the different types of costs a marketing manager should consider when setting a price.

Marketing Manager Must Consider Various Kinds of Costs

Average-cost pricing may lead to losses because there are a variety of costs—and each changes in a *different* way as output changes. Any pricing method that uses cost must consider these changes. To understand why, we need to define six types of costs.

Average fixed costs are lower when a larger quantity is produced.

There are three kinds of total cost

1. **Total fixed cost** is the sum of those costs that are fixed in total—no matter how much is produced. Among these fixed costs are rent, depreciation, managers' salaries, property taxes, and insurance. Such costs stay the same even if production stops temporarily.
2. **Total variable cost,** on the other hand, is the sum of those changing expenses that are closely related to output—expenses for parts, wages, packaging materials, outgoing freight, and sales commissions.

   At zero output, total variable cost is zero. As output increases, so do variable costs. If Levi's doubles its output of jeans in a year, its total cost for denim cloth also (roughly) doubles.

3. **Total cost** is the sum of total fixed and total variable costs. Changes in total cost depend on variations in total variable cost—since total fixed cost stays the same.

There are three kinds of average cost

The pricing manager usually is more interested in cost per unit than total cost because prices are usually quoted per unit.

1. **Average cost** (per unit) is obtained by dividing total cost by the related quantity (that is, the total quantity that causes the total cost).
2. **Average fixed cost** (per unit) is obtained by dividing total fixed cost by the related quantity.
3. **Average variable cost** (per unit) is obtained by dividing total variable cost by the related quantity.

An example shows cost relations

A good way to get a feel for these different types of costs is to extend our average-cost pricing example (Exhibit 17-3A). Exhibit 17-4 shows the six types of cost and how they vary at different levels of output. The line for 40,000 units is highlighted because that was the expected level of sales in our average-cost pricing example. For simplicity, we assume that average variable cost is the same for each unit. Notice, however, that total variable cost increases when quantity increases.

Exhibit 17-5 shows the three average cost curves from Exhibit 17-4. Notice that average fixed cost goes down steadily as the quantity increases. Although the average variable cost remains the same, average cost decreases continually too. This is because average fixed cost is decreasing. With these relations in mind, let's reconsider the problem with average-cost pricing.

Exhibit 17-4 Cost Structure of a Firm

Quantity (Q)	Total Fixed Costs (TFC)	Average Fixed Costs (AFC)	Average Variable Costs (AVC)	Total Variable Costs (TVC)	Total Cost (TC)	Average Cost (AC)
0	$30,000	—	—	—	$ 30,000	—
10,000	30,000	$3.00	$0.80	$ 8,000	38,000	$3.80
20,000	30,000	1.50	0.80	16,000	46,000	2.30
30,000	30,000	1.00	0.80	24,000	54,000	1.80
40,000	30,000	0.75	0.80	32,000	62,000	1.55
50,000	30,000	0.60	0.80	40,000	70,000	1.40
60,000	30,000	0.50	0.80	48,000	78,000	1.30
70,000	30,000	0.43	0.80	56,000	86,000	1.23
80,000	30,000	0.38	0.80	64,000	94,000	1.18
90,000	30,000	0.33	0.80	72,000	102,000	1.13
100,000	30,000	0.30	0.80	80,000	110,000	1.10

110,000 (TC)
−80,000 (TVC)
30,000 (TFC)

0.30 (AFC)
(Q) 100,000 ⟌ 30,000 (TFC)
0.80 (AVC)

100,000 (Q)
×0.80 (AVC)
80,000 (TVC)

30,000 (TFC)
+80,000 (TVC)
110,000 (TC)

1.10 (AC)
(Q) 100,000 ⟌ 110,000 (TC)

Ignoring demand is the major weakness of average-cost pricing

Average-cost pricing works well if the firm actually sells the quantity it used to set the average-cost price. Losses may result, however, if actual sales are much lower than expected. On the other hand, if sales are much higher than expected, then profits may be very good. But this will only happen by luck—because the firm's demand is much larger than expected.

To use average-cost pricing, a marketing manager must make *some* estimate of the quantity to be sold in the coming period. Without a quantity estimate, it isn't possible to compute average cost. But unless this quantity is related to price—that is, unless the firm's demand curve is considered—the marketing manager may set a price that doesn't even cover a firm's total cost! You saw this happen in Exhibit 17-3B, when the firm's price of $2.00 resulted in demand for only 20,000 units and a loss of $6,000.

The demand curve is still important even if management doesn't take time to think about it. For example, Exhibit 17-6 shows the demand curve for the firm we're discussing. This demand curve shows *why* the firm lost money when it tried to use

Exhibit 17-5
Typical Shape of Cost (per unit) Curves When Average Variable Cost per Unit Is Constant

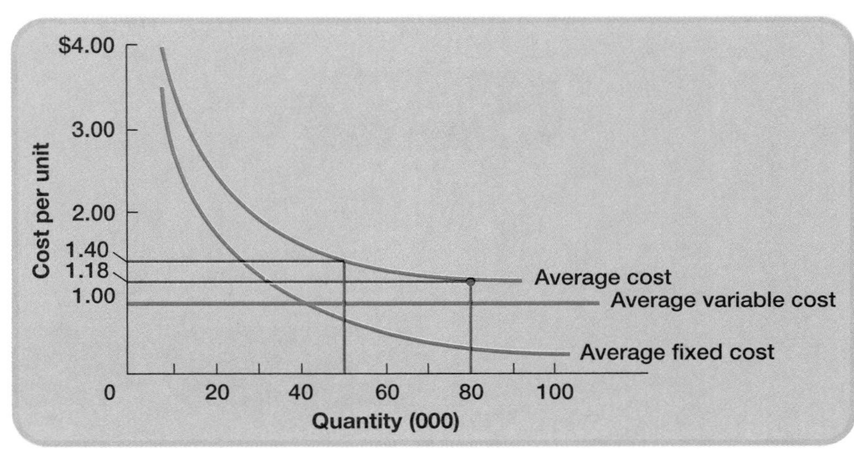

Exhibit 17-6
Evaluation of Various Prices along a Firm's Demand Curve

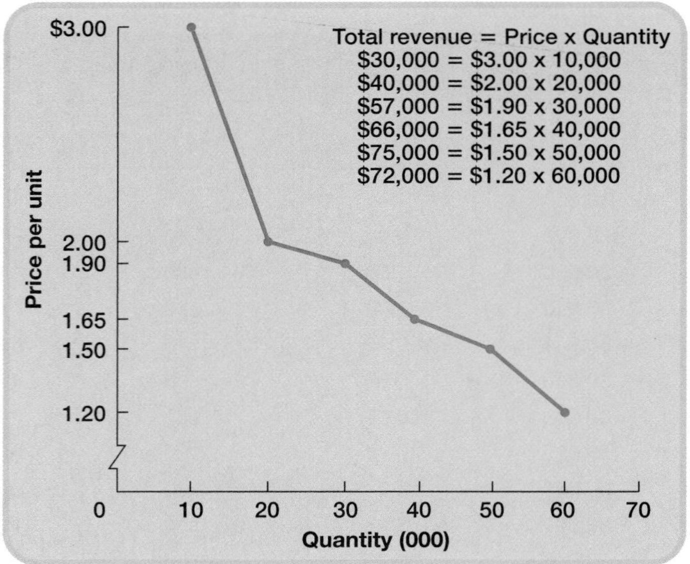

average-cost pricing. At the $2.00 price, quantity demanded is only 20,000. With this demand curve and the costs in Exhibit 17-4, the firm will incur a loss whether management sets the price at a high $3 or a low $1.20. At $3, the firm will sell only 10,000 units for a total revenue of $30,000. But total cost will be $38,000—for a loss of $8,000. At the $1.20 price, it will sell 60,000 units—at a loss of $6,000. However, the curve suggests that at a price of $1.65 consumers will demand about 40,000 units, producing a profit of about $4,000.

In short, average-cost pricing is simple in theory but often fails in practice. In stable situations, prices set by this method may yield profits but not necessarily *maximum* profits. And note that such cost-based prices may be higher than a price that would be more profitable for the firm, as shown in Exhibit 17-6. When demand conditions are changing, average-cost pricing is even more risky.

Exhibit 17-7 summarizes the relationships discussed above. Cost-oriented pricing requires an estimate of the total number of units to be sold. That estimate determines

Exhibit 17-7
Summary of Relationships among Quantity, Cost, and Price Using Cost-Oriented Pricing

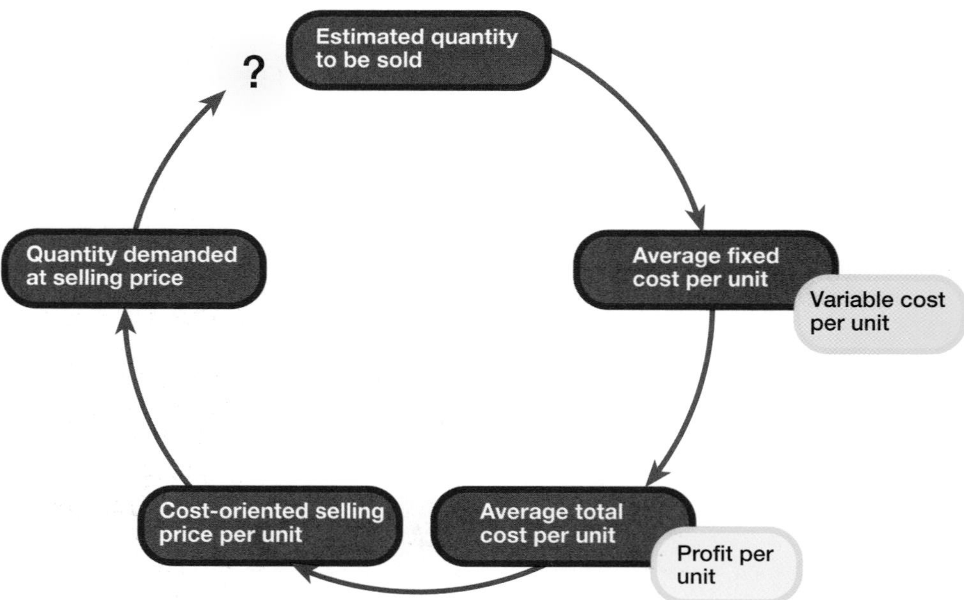

the *average* fixed cost per unit and thus the average total cost. Then the firm adds the desired profit per unit to the average total cost to get the cost-oriented selling price. How customers react to that price determines the actual quantity the firm will be able to sell. But that quantity may not be the quantity used to compute the average cost![4]

Break-Even Analysis Can Evaluate Possible Prices

Some price setters use break-even analysis in their pricing. **Break-even analysis** evaluates whether the firm will be able to break even—that is, cover all its costs—with a particular price. This is important because a firm must cover all costs in the long run or there is not much point being in business. This method focuses on the **break-even point (BEP)**—the quantity where the firm's total cost will just equal its total revenue.

Break-even charts help find the BEP

To help understand how break-even analysis works, look at Exhibit 17-8, an example of the typical break-even chart. *The chart is based on a particular selling price*—in this case $1.20 a unit. The chart has lines that show total costs (total variable plus total fixed costs) and total revenues at different levels of production. The break-even point on the chart is at 75,000 units—where the total cost and total revenue lines intersect. At that production level, total cost and total revenue are the same—$90,000.

The difference between the total revenue and total cost at a given quantity is the profit—or loss! The chart shows that below the break-even point, total cost is higher than total revenue and the firm incurs a loss. The firm would make a profit above the break-even point. However, the firm would only reach the break-even point, or get beyond it into the profit area, *if* it could sell at least 75,000 units at the $1.20 price.

Break-even analysis can be very helpful if used properly, so let's look at this approach more closely.

How to compute a break-even point

A break-even chart is an easy-to-understand visual aid, but it's also useful to be able to compute the break-even point.

Exhibit 17-8
Break-Even Chart for a Particular Situation

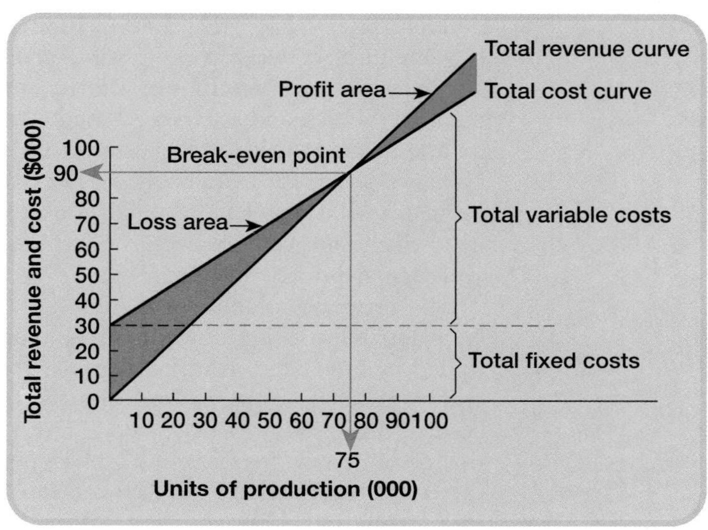

The BEP, in units, can be found by dividing total fixed costs (TFC) by the **fixed-cost (FC) contribution per unit**—the assumed selling price per unit minus the variable cost per unit. This can be stated as a simple formula:

$$\text{BEP (in units)} = \frac{\text{Total fixed cost}}{\text{Fixed cost contribution per unit}}$$

This formula makes sense when we think about it. To break even, we must cover total fixed costs. Therefore, we must figure the contribution each unit will make to covering the total fixed costs (after paying for the variable costs to produce the item). When we divide this per-unit contribution into the total fixed costs that must be covered, we have the BEP (in units).

To illustrate the formula, let's use the cost and price information in Exhibit 17-8. The price per unit is $1.20. The average variable cost per unit is 80 cents. So the FC contribution per unit is 40 cents ($1.20 − 80 cents). The total fixed cost is $30,000 (see Exhibit 17-8). Substituting in the formula:

$$\text{BEP} = \frac{\$30{,}000}{.40} = 75{,}000 \text{ units}$$

From this you can see that if this firm sells 75,000 units, it will exactly cover all its fixed and variable costs. If it sells even one more unit, it will begin to show a profit—in this case, 40 cents per unit. Note that once the fixed costs are covered, the part of revenue formerly going to cover fixed costs is now *all profit*.

Break-even analysis is a useful tool for analyzing costs and evaluating what might happen to profits in different market environments. But it is a cost-oriented approach. Like other cost-oriented approaches, it does not consider the effect of price on the quantity that consumers will want—that is, the demand curve.

So to really zero in on the most profitable price, marketers are better off estimating the demand curve itself and then using marginal analysis, which we'll discuss next.[5]

Marginal Analysis Considers Both Costs and Demand

Marginal analysis helps find the right price

The best pricing tool marketers have for looking at costs and revenue (demand) at the same time is marginal analysis. **Marginal analysis** focuses on the changes in total revenue and total cost from selling one more unit to find the most profitable price and quantity. Marginal analysis shows how costs, revenue, and profit change at different prices. The price that maximizes profit is the one that results in the greatest difference between total revenue and total cost.

Since the price determines what quantity will be sold, a manager needs an estimate of the demand curve to compute total revenue. A practical approach here is for the manager to think about a price that appears to be too high and one that is too low. Then, for a number of prices between these two extremes, the manager estimates what quantity it might be possible to sell. You can think of this as a summary of the answers to a series of what-if questions—*what* quantity will be sold *if* a particular price is selected?

The first two columns of Exhibit 17-9 give quantity and price combinations for an example firm. Total revenue in Column 3 of Exhibit 17-9 is equal to a price multiplied by its related quantity. Costs at the different quantities are also shown. The profit at each quantity and price is the difference between total revenue and total cost. In this example, the best price is at $79 (and a quantity of 6 units sold) because that combination results in the highest profit ($106). In Exhibit 17-10, which graphs the data from Exhibit 17-9, you can see that the best price is the one that has the greatest distance between the total revenue and total cost curves.

Exhibit 17-9
Revenue, Cost, and Profit at Different Prices for a Firm

(1) Quantity (Q)	(2) Price (P)	(3) Total Revenue (TR)	(4) Total Variable Cost (TVC)	(5) Total Cost (TC)	(6) Profit (TR − TC)
0	$150	$ 0	$ 0	$200	$ − 200
1	140	140	96	296	− 156
2	130	260	116	316	− 56
3	117	351	131	331	+ 20
4	105	420	144	344	+ 76
5	92	460	155	355	+ 105
6	79	474	168	368	+ 106
7	66	462	183	383	+ 79
8	53	424	223	423	+ 1
9	42	378	307	507	− 129
10	31	310	510	710	− 400

A profit range is reassuring

Marginal analysis focuses on the best price—the one that earns the highest profit. But a slight miss doesn't mean failure because demand estimates don't have to be exact. There is usually a range of profitable prices. You can see this in Exhibit 17-9 and in the section of Exhibit 17-10 that is shown in blue. Although the price that would result in the highest profit is $79, this firm's strategy would be profitable all the way from a price of $53 to $117. So, the effort of trying to estimate demand will probably lead to being someplace in the profitable range. In contrast, mechanical use of average-cost pricing could lead to a price that is much too high—or much too low. This is why estimating demand isn't just desirable—it's essential.[6]

Exhibit 17-10
Graphic Determination of the Price Giving the Greatest Total Profit for a Firm

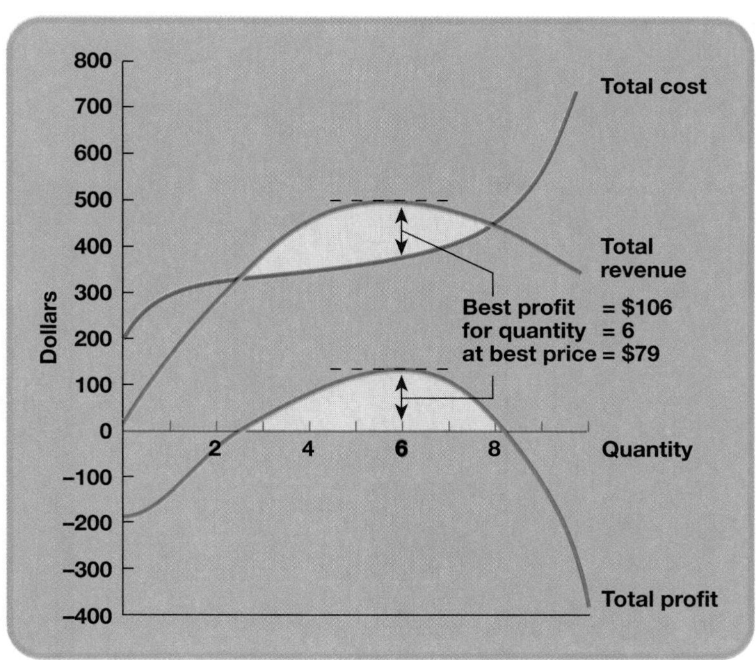

Demand-Oriented Approaches for Setting Prices

Evaluating the customer's price sensitivity

A manager who knows what influences target customers' price sensitivity can do a better job estimating the demand curve that the firm faces. Marketing researchers have identified a number of factors that influence price sensitivity across many different market situations.

The first is the most basic. When customers have *substitute ways* of meeting a need, they are likely to be more price sensitive. A cook who wants a cappuccino maker to be able to serve something distinctive to guests at a dinner party may be willing to pay a high price. However, if different machines are available and our cook sees them as pretty similar, price sensitivity will be greater. It's important not to ignore dissimilar alternatives if the customer sees them as substitutes. If a machine for espresso were much less expensive than one for cappuccino, our cook might decide that an espresso machine would meet her needs just as well.

The impact of substitutes on price sensitivity is greatest when it is easy for customers to *compare prices*. For example, unit prices make it easier for our cook to compare the prices of espresso and cappuccino grinds on the grocery store shelf. Many people believe that the ease of comparing prices on the Internet will increase price sensitivity and ultimately bring down prices. If nothing else, it may make sellers more aware of competing prices.

People tend to be less price sensitive when someone else pays the bill or *shares the cost*. Perhaps this is just human nature. Insurance companies think that consumers would reject high medical fees if they were paying all of their own bills. And executives might plan longer in advance to get better discounts on airline flights if their companies weren't footing the bills.

Customers tend to be more price sensitive the greater the *total expenditure*. Sometimes a big expenditure can be broken into smaller pieces. Mercedes knows this. When its ads focused on the cost of a monthly lease rather than the total price of the car, more consumers got interested in biting the bullet.

Customers are less price sensitive the greater the *significance of the end benefit* of the purchase. Computer makers will pay more to get Intel processors if they believe that having an "Intel inside" sells more machines. Positioning efforts often focus on

Value in use pricing considers what a customer will save by buying a product. Axilok's ad reminds its business customers that its wheel bearing nut system can cut labor costs by 50 percent. Similarly, Emerson Electric invites prospective customers to use computer models available on the PlantWeb Internet site to calculate project savings for their plants.

emotional benefits of a purchase to increase the significance of a benefit. Ads for L'Oreal hair color, for example, show closeups of beautiful hair while popular celebrities tell women to buy it "because you're worth it." A consumer who cares about the price of a bottle of hair color might still have no question that she's worth the difference in price.

Customers are sometimes less price sensitive if they already have a *sunk investment* that is related to the purchase. This is especially relevant with business customers. For example, once managers of a firm have invested to train employees to use Microsoft Excel, they are less likely to resist the high price of a new version of that software.

These factors apply in many different purchase situations, so it makes sense for a marketing manager to consider each of them in refining estimates of how customers might respond at different prices.[7]

Value in use pricing—how much will the customer save?

Organizational buyers think about how a purchase will affect their total costs. Many marketers who aim at business markets keep this in mind when estimating demand and setting prices. They use **value in use pricing**—which means setting prices that will capture some of what customers will save by substituting the firm's product for the one currently being used.

For example, a producer of computer-controlled machines used to assemble cars knows that the machine doesn't just replace a standard machine. It also reduces labor costs, quality control costs, and—after the car is sold—costs of warranty repairs. The marketer can estimate what each auto producer will save by using the machine—and then set a price that makes it less expensive for the auto producer to buy the computerized machine than to stick with the old methods. The number of customers who have different levels of potential savings also provides some idea about the shape of the demand curve.

Creating a product that could save customers money doesn't guarantee that customers will be willing to pay a higher price. To capture the value created, the seller must convince buyers of the savings—and buyers are likely to be skeptical. A salesperson needs to be able to show proof of the claims.[8]

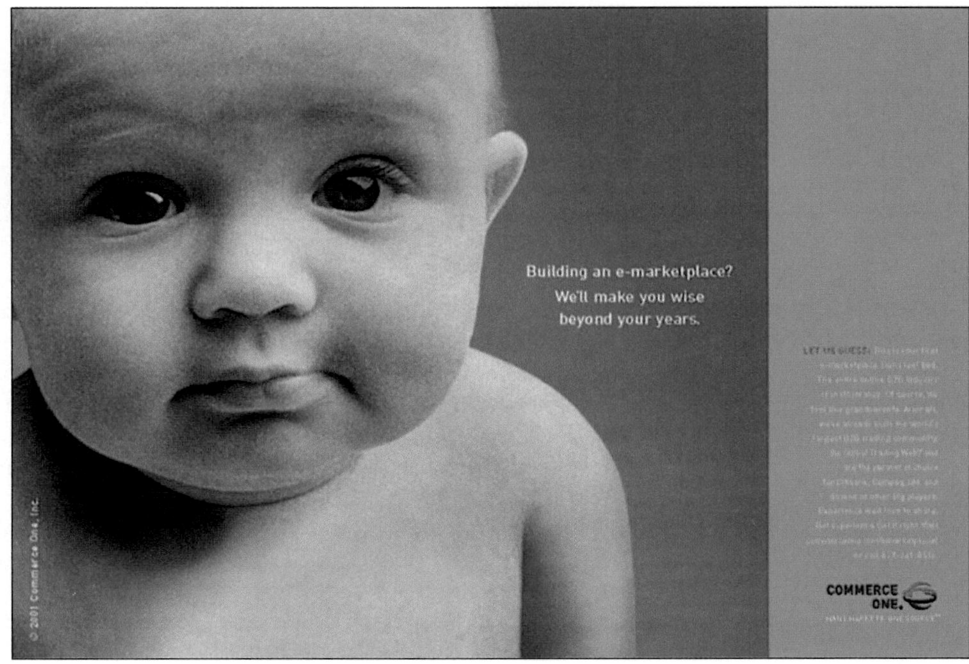

Internet-based auctions have quickly become a very important force in business-to-business markets.

Hallmark's ad prompts consumers to think of the reference price for a greeting card in terms of the value it creates for the person who receives the card. eCampus.com wants consumers to view its prices more economically. By pricing its products lower than the target market's reference price, eCampus.com hopes consumers will view its products as offering better customer value.

Auctions are coming online fast

Auctions have always been a way to determine exactly what some group of potential customers would pay, or not pay, for a product. However, as we discussed in Chapter 12, auctions were traditionally used for specific types of products and drew only local buyers. That has changed with the development of online auctions on the Internet. New firms are setting up auctions that specialize in categories of products ranging from vacation trips to electric energy. Some firms are setting up their own auctions, especially for products in short supply. Recently government agencies in the U.S. and Europe have used auctions to sell rights to use transmission frequencies (air waves) for a new type of wireless phone service. The bidding among communications companies was more intense than anyone had imagined. Count on more growth in online auctions, not only for business products but also for consumer products.[9]

Internet

Internet Exercise SportStop launched an Internet auction site for many different categories of sporting goods. Go to the auction website (www.sportstop.com) and review the activities in two auction categories, one for a sport that is in season and another sport that is not. For example, you might compare snowboarding and golfing. Do you think that season makes a difference in the bidding activity? Explain your thinking.

Customers may have reference prices

Some people don't devote much thought to what they pay for the products they buy—including some frequently purchased goods and services. But most consumers have a **reference price**—the price they expect to pay—for many of the products they purchase. And different customers may have different reference prices for the same basic type of purchase. For example, a person who really enjoys reading might have a higher reference price for a popular paperback book than another person who is only an occasional reader.[10]

If a firm's price is lower than a customer's reference price, customers may view the product as a better value and demand may increase. See Exhibit 17-11. Sometimes a firm will try to position the benefits of its product in such a way that consumers compare it with a product that has a higher reference price. Public Broadcasting System TV stations do this when they ask viewers to make donations that

Exhibit 17-11 How Customer's Reference Price Influences Perceived Value (for a marketing mix with a given set of benefits and costs)

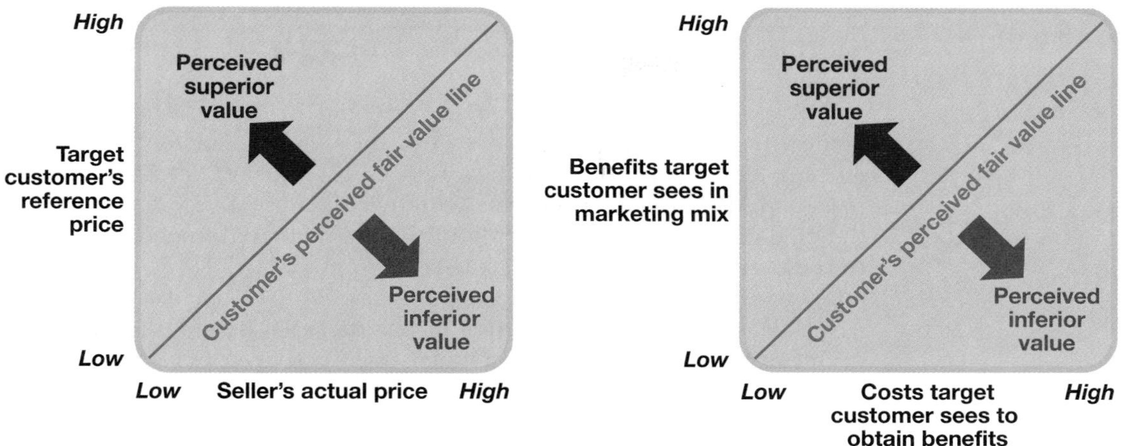

match what they pay for "just one month of cable service." Insurance companies frame the price of premiums for homeowners' coverage in terms of the price to repair flood damage—and advertising makes the damage very vivid.

Leader pricing—make it low to attract customers

Leader pricing means setting some very low prices—real bargains—to get customers into retail stores. The idea is not only to sell large quantities of the leader items but also to get customers into the store to buy other products. Certain products are picked for their promotion value and priced low—but above cost. In food stores, the leader prices are the "specials" that are advertised regularly to give an image of low prices. Leader pricing is normally used with products for which consumers do have a specific reference price.

Leader pricing can backfire if customers buy only the low-priced leaders. To avoid hurting profits, managers often select leader items that aren't directly competitive with major lines—as when bargain-priced videotapes are a leader for an electronics store.[11]

Bait pricing—offer a steal, but sell under protest

Bait pricing is setting some very low prices to attract customers but trying to sell more expensive models or brands once the customer is in the store. For example, a furniture store may advertise a color TV for $199. But once bargain hunters come to the store, salespeople point out the disadvantages of the low-priced TV and try to convince them to trade up to a better, and more expensive, set. Bait pricing is something like leader pricing. But here the seller *doesn't* plan to sell many at the low price.

If bait pricing is successful, the demand for higher-quality products expands. This approach may be a sensible part of a strategy to trade up customers. And customers may be well served if—once in the store—they find a higher-priced product offers features better suited to their needs. But bait pricing is also criticized as unethical.

Is bait pricing ethical?

Extremely aggressive and sometimes dishonest bait-pricing advertising has given this method a bad reputation. Some stores make it very difficult to buy the bait item. The Federal Trade Commission considers this type of bait pricing a deceptive act and has banned its use in interstate commerce. Even well-known chains like Sears have been criticized for bait-and-switch pricing.

Psychological pricing—some prices just seem right

Psychological pricing means setting prices that have special appeal to target customers. Some people think there are whole ranges of prices that potential customers see as the same. So price cuts in these ranges do not increase the quantity sold. But

Exhibit 17-12
Demand Curve When Psychological Pricing Is Appropriate

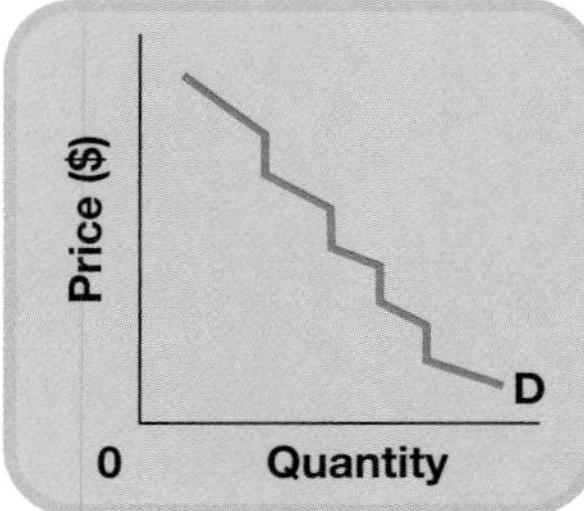

just below this range, customers may buy more. Then, at even lower prices, the quantity demanded stays the same again—and so on. Exhibit 17-12 shows the kind of demand curve that leads to psychological pricing. Vertical drops mark the price ranges that customers see as the same. Pricing research shows that there *are* such demand curves.[12]

Odd-even pricing is setting prices that end in certain numbers. For example, products selling below $50 often end in the number 5 or the number 9—such as 49 cents or $24.95. Prices for higher-priced products are often $1 or $2 below the next even dollar figure—such as $99 rather than $100.

Some marketers use odd-even pricing because they think consumers react better to these prices—perhaps seeing them as "substantially" lower than the next highest even price. Marketers using these prices seem to assume that they have a rather jagged demand curve—that slightly higher prices will substantially reduce the quantity demanded. Long ago, some retailers used odd-even prices to force their clerks to make change. Then the clerks had to record the sale and could not pocket the money.[13]

Price lining—a few prices cover the field

Price lining is setting a few price levels for a product line and then marking all items at these prices. This approach assumes that customers have a certain reference price in mind that they expect to pay for a product. For example, many neckties are priced between $20 and $50. In price lining, there are only a few prices within this range. Ties will not be priced at $20, $21, $22, $23, and so on. They might be priced at four levels—$20, $30, $40, and $50.

Price lining has advantages other than just matching prices to what consumers expect to pay. The main advantage is simplicity—for both salespeople and customers. It is less confusing than having many prices. Some customers may consider items in only one price class. Their big decision, then, is which item(s) to choose at that price.

For retailers, price lining has several advantages. Sales may increase because (1) they can offer a bigger variety in each price class and (2) it's easier to get customers to make decisions within one price class. Stock planning is simpler because demand is larger at the relatively few prices. Price lining can also reduce costs because inventory needs are lower.

Prestige pricing is often used with luxury products like jewelry and high-end consumer electronics to suggest high quality. But Paradigm wants consumers to view its low price as a sign of good quality and good value, not as a signal of low quality.

Demand-backward pricing and prestige pricing

Demand-backward pricing is setting an acceptable final consumer price and working backward to what a producer can charge. It is commonly used by producers of consumer products—especially shopping products such as women's clothing and appliances. It is also used with gift items for which customers will spend a specific amount—because they are seeking a $10 or a $15 gift. Here a reverse cost-plus pricing process is used. This method has been called market-minus pricing.

The producer starts with the retail (reference) price for a particular item and then works backward—subtracting the typical margins that channel members expect. This gives the approximate price the producer can charge. Then the average or planned marketing expenses can be subtracted from this price to find how much can be spent producing the item. Candy companies do this. They alter the size of the candy bar to keep the bar at the expected price.

Exhibit 17-13
Demand Curve Showing a Prestige Pricing Situation

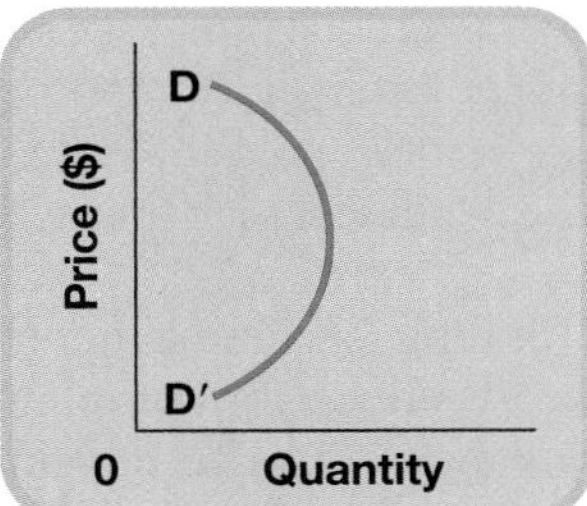

Prestige pricing is setting a rather high price to suggest high quality or high status. Some target customers want the best, so they will buy at a high price. But if the price seems cheap, they worry about quality and don't buy. Prestige pricing is most common for luxury products such as furs, jewelry, and perfume.

It is also common in service industries—where the customer can't see the product in advance and relies on price to judge its quality. Target customers who respond to prestige pricing give the marketing manager an unusual demand curve. Instead of a normal down-sloping curve, the curve goes down for a while and then bends back to the left again.[14] See Exhibit 17-13.

Internet

Internet Exercise Tiffany & Co. is widely recognized as one of the world's premiere jewelers. It commands high prices for what it offers. Go to the Tiffany website (www.tiffany.com) and review the different sections. Do you think that the website communicates superior customer value to the Tiffany target market? Explain your opinion and which specific aspects of the website support your view.

Pricing a Full Line

Our emphasis has been, and will continue to be, on the problem of pricing an individual product mainly because this makes our discussion clearer. But most marketing managers are responsible for more than one product. In fact, their "product" may be the whole company line! So we'll discuss this matter briefly.

Full-line pricing—market- or firm-oriented?

Full-line pricing is setting prices for a whole line of products. How to do this depends on which of two basic situations a firm is facing.

In one case, all products in the company's line are aimed at the same general target market, which makes it important for all prices and value to be logically related. This is a common approach with shopping products. A producer of TV sets might offer several models with different features at different prices to give its target customers some choice. The difference among the prices and benefits should appear reasonable when the target customers are evaluating them. Customer perceptions can be important here. A low-priced item, even one that is a good value at that price, may drag down the image of the higher end of the line. Alternatively, one item that consumers do not see as a good value may spill over to how they judge other products in the line.

In other cases, the different products in the line are aimed at entirely different target markets so there doesn't have to be any relation between the various prices.

A chemical producer of a wide variety of products with several target markets, for example, probably should price each product separately.

Costs are complicated in full-line pricing

The marketing manager must try to recover all costs on the whole line—perhaps by pricing quite low on more competitive items and much higher on ones with unique benefits. However, estimating costs for each product is a challenge because there is no single right way to assign a company's fixed costs to each of the products. Regardless of how costs are allocated, any cost-oriented pricing method that doesn't consider demand can lead to very unrealistic prices. To avoid mistakes, the marketing manager should judge demand for the whole line as well as demand for each individual product in each target market.

Complementary product pricing

Complementary product pricing is setting prices on several products as a group. This may lead to one product being priced very low so that the profits from another product will increase, thus increasing the product group's total profits. A new Gillette shaver, for example, may be priced low to sell the blades, which must be replaced regularly.

Complementary product pricing differs from full-line pricing because different production facilities may be involved—so there's no cost allocation problem. Instead, the problem is really understanding the target market and the demand curves for each of the complementary products. Then various combinations of prices can be tried to see what set will be best for reaching the company's pricing objectives.

Product-bundle pricing—one price for several products

A firm that offers its target market several different products may use **product-bundle pricing**—setting one price for a set of products. Firms that use product-bundle pricing usually set the overall price so that it's cheaper for the customer to buy the products at the same time than separately. Drugstores sometimes bundle the cost of a roll of film and the cost of the processing. A bank may offer a product-bundle price for a safe-deposit box, traveler's checks, and a savings account. Sprint bundles wireless minutes and long distance. Bundling encourages customers to spend more and buy products that they might not otherwise buy—because the added cost of the extras is not as high as it would normally be, so the value is better.

Most firms that use product-bundle pricing also set individual prices for the unbundled products. This may increase demand by attracting customers who want one item in a product assortment but don't want the extras. Many firms treat services this way. A software company may have a product-bundle price for its software and access to a toll-free telephone assistance service. However, customers who don't need help can pay a lower price and get just the software.[15]

Bid Pricing and Negotiated Pricing Depend Heavily on Costs

A new price for every job

We introduced the issue of competitive bidding and reverse auctions in Chapter 6. But now let's take a closer look at bid pricing. **Bid pricing** means offering a specific price for each possible job rather than setting a price that applies for all customers. In an e-commerce reverse auction for a standardized product, this may just require that the manager decide the firm's lowest acceptable selling price. But in many situations bid pricing is more complicated. For example, building contractors usually must bid on possible projects. And many companies selling services (like cleaning or data processing) must submit bids for jobs they would like to have.

A big problem in bid pricing on a complicated job is estimating all the costs that will apply. This may sound easy, but a complicated bid may involve thousands of

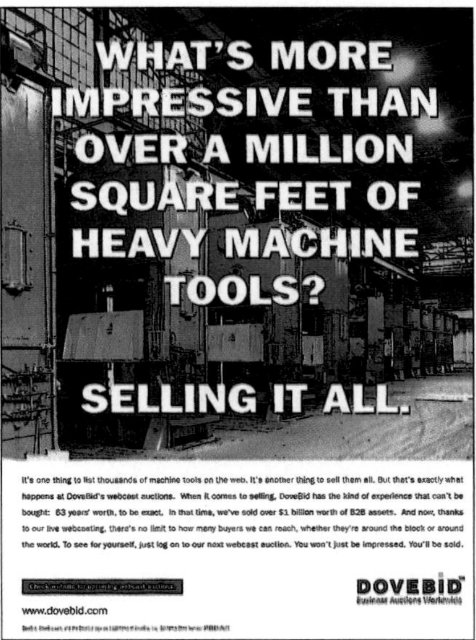

The Internet is making it fast and easy for customers to communicate their needs to a larger number of suppliers and to use competitively based bid pricing.

cost components. Further, management must include an overhead charge and a charge for profit.

Because many firms use an e-mail distribution list or website to solicit bids, the process is fast and easy for the buyer. But a seller has to be geared up to set a price and respond quickly. However, this system does allow the seller to set a price based on the precise situation and what marginal costs and marginal revenue are involved.

Bids are usually based on purchase specifications provided by the customer. The specs may be sent as an attachment to an e-mail message, or increasingly, they are posted on a website. Sometimes the seller can win the business, even with a higher bid price, by suggesting changes in the specs that save the customer money.

Sometimes it isn't possible to figure out specs or costs in advance. This may lead to a negotiated contract where the customer agrees to pay the supplier's total cost plus an agreed-on profit figure (say, 10 percent of costs or a dollar amount)—after the job is finished.

Ethical issues in cost-plus bid pricing

Some unethical sellers give bid prices based on cost-plus contracts a bad reputation by faking their records to make costs seem higher than they really are. In other cases, there may be honest debate about what costs should be allowed. We've already considered, for instance, the difficulties in allocating fixed costs.

Demand must be considered too

Competition must be considered when adding in overhead and profit for a bid price. Usually, the customer will get several bids and accept the lowest one. So unthinking addition of typical overhead and profit rates should be avoided. Some bidders use the same overhead and profit rates on all jobs, regardless of competition, and then are surprised when they don't get some jobs.[16]

Negotiated prices—what will a specific customer pay?

Sometimes the customer asks for bids and then singles out the company that submits the *most attractive* bid, not necessarily the lowest, for further bargaining. What a customer will buy—if the customer buys at all—depends on the **negotiated price,** a price set based on bargaining between the buyer and seller. As with simple bid pricing, negotiated pricing is most common in situations where the marketing mix is adjusted for each customer—so bargaining may involve the whole marketing mix, not just the price level.

Sellers must know their costs to negotiate prices effectively. However, negotiated pricing is a demand-oriented approach. Here the seller analyzes very carefully a particular customer's position on a demand curve, or on different possible demand curves based on different offerings, rather than the overall demand curve for a group of customers.

Conclusion

In this chapter, we discussed various approaches to price setting. Generally, retailers and wholesalers use markups. Some just use the same markups for all their items. Others find that varying the markups increases turnover and profit. In other words, they consider demand and competition!

Many firms use average-cost pricing to help set their prices. But this approach sometimes ignores demand completely. A more realistic approach to average-cost pricing requires a sales forecast—maybe just assuming that sales in the next period will be roughly the same as in the last period. This approach *does* enable the marketing manager to set a price—but the price may or may not cover all costs and earn the desired profit.

Break-even analysis is useful for evaluating possible prices. But management must estimate demand to evaluate the chance of reaching these possible break-even points.

The major difficulty with demand-oriented pricing is estimating the demand curve. But experienced managers, aided perhaps by marketing research, can estimate the nature of demand for their products. Such estimates are useful even if they aren't exact. They get you thinking in the right ballpark. Sometimes, when all you need is a decision about raising or lowering price, even rough demand estimates can be very revealing. Further, a firm's demand curve does not cease to exist simply because it's ignored. Some information is better than none at all. And marketers should consider demand in their pricing. We see this with value in use pricing, online auctions, leader pricing, bait pricing, odd-even pricing, psychological pricing, full-line pricing, and even bid pricing. Understanding the factors that influence price sensitivity can make these approaches more effective.

Throughout the book, we stress that firms must consider the customer before they do anything. This certainly applies to pricing. It means that when managers are setting a price, they have to consider what customers will be willing to pay. This isn't always easy. But it's nice to know that there is a profit range around the best price. Therefore, even rough estimates about what potential customers will buy at various prices will probably lead to a better price than mechanical use of traditional markups or cost-oriented formulas.

While our focus in this chapter is on price setting, it's clear that pricing decisions must consider the cost of offering the whole marketing mix. Smart marketers don't just accept costs as a given. Target marketers always look for ways to be more efficient—to reduce costs while improving the value that they offer customers.

Questions and Problems

1. Why do many department stores seek a markup of about 40 percent when some discount houses operate on a 20 percent markup?
2. A producer distributed its riding lawn mowers through wholesalers and retailers. The retail selling price was $800, and the manufacturing cost to the company was $312. The retail markup was 35 percent and the wholesale markup 20 percent. *(a)* What was the cost to the wholesaler? To the retailer? *(b)* What percentage markup did the producer take?
3. Relate the concept of stock turnover to the growth of mass-merchandising. Use a simple example in your answer.
4. If total fixed costs are $200,000 and total variable costs are $100,000 at the output of 20,000 units, what are the probable total fixed costs and total variable costs at an output of 10,000 units? What are the average fixed costs, average variable costs, and average costs at these two output levels? Explain what additional information you would want to determine what price should be charged.
5. Construct an example showing that mechanical use of a very large or a very small markup might still lead to unprofitable operation while some intermediate price would be profitable. Draw a graph and show the break-even point(s).

6. The Davis Company's fixed costs for the year are estimated at $200,000. Its product sells for $250. The variable cost per unit is $200. Sales for the coming year are expected to reach $1,250,000. What is the break-even point? Expected profit? If sales are forecast at only $875,000, should the Davis Company shut down operations? Why?
7. Distinguish between leader pricing and bait pricing. What do they have in common? How can their use affect a marketing mix?
8. Cite a local example of psychological pricing and evaluate whether it makes sense.
9. Cite a local example of odd-even pricing and evaluate whether it makes sense.
10. How does a prestige pricing policy fit into a marketing mix? Would exclusive distribution be necessary?
11. Is a full-line pricing policy available only to producers? Cite local examples of full-line pricing. Why is full-line pricing important?

Suggested Cases

11. ChemTech
16. Enviro Pure Water, Inc.
21. Wire Solutions, Inc.

Computer-Aided Problem

17. **Price Setting and Profit Analysis**

This problem lets you see the dynamics of break-even analysis. The starting values (costs, revenues, etc.) for this problem are from the break-even analysis example in this chapter (see Exhibit 17-8).

The first column computes a break-even point. You can change costs and prices to figure new break-even points (in units and dollars). The second column goes further. There you can specify target profit level, and the unit and dollar sales needed to achieve your target profit level will be computed. You can also estimate possible sales quantities, and the program will compute costs, sales, and profits. Use this spreadsheet to address the following issues.

a. *Vary the selling price between $1.00 and $1.40. Prepare a table showing how the break-even point (in units and dollars) changes at the different price levels.*
b. *If you hope to earn a target profit of $15,000, how many units would you have to sell? What would total cost be? Total sales dollars? (Note: Use the right-hand ["profit analysis"] column in the spreadsheet.)*
c. *Using the "profit analysis" column (column 2) and the results feature, allow your estimate of the sale quantity to vary between 64,000 and 96,000. Prepare a table that shows, for each quantity level, what happens to average cost per unit and profit. Explain why average cost changes as it does over the different quantity values.*

For additional questions related to this problem, see Exercise 17-4 in the *Learning Aid for Use with Essentials of Marketing*, 9th edition.

When You Finish This Chapter, You Should

1. Understand, in detail, all of the elements of the marketing strategy planning process and the strategy decisions for the four Ps.

2. Know how to prepare a marketing plan and how it relates to the marketing strategy planning process.

3. Understand why marketing must be evaluated differently at the micro and macro levels.

4. Understand why the text argues that micro-marketing costs too much.

5. Understand why the text argues that macro-marketing does not cost too much.

6. Know some of the key challenges marketers face as they work to develop ethical marketing strategies that serve consumers' needs.

Chapter Eighteen

Developing Innovative Marketing Plans: Appraisal and Challenges

Marketing managers recently went through the marketing strategy planning process to develop an innovative plan that created profitable growth for Maytag by offering target customers superior value. Let's look at what they did. This case is longer than others we've covered—to help you review what is in a marketing plan and the process of creating one. As you read the case, relate it to the ideas you've studied throughout the text.

Changes in the external environment called for a new strategy. The U.S. Department of Energy (DOE) was considering new regulations to require that clothes washers use less water and energy. The U.S. uses three times as much water a day—1,300 gallons per person—as the average European country. One reason is that front-loading clothes washers have long been standard in Europe. This is in part an economic issue. Front-loaders heat

place price promotion produ

less water so less energy is used, and Europeans face steeper energy costs. There is also a cultural difference. North Americans are more convenience-oriented, but front-loaders make you stoop, they spill water on the floor, and you can't throw in a stray sock during the wash cycle.

Maytag's R&D people thought that they could use technology to improve the design of a front-loading washer to make it more convenient and to conserve water and energy as well. With inputs from marketers about broader needs in the clothes care product-market they looked at needs beyond just cleaning. It appeared that a consumer-oriented design could improve basic benefits like easier loading and gentler care of fabrics.

Competitors were also on the move. Frigidaire came out with a front-load unit just in time to be the only one tested for a *Consumer Reports* article. It tested well on cleaning, but Maytag thought it fell short in improving other customer benefits. GE was further behind in working on a front-loader. But these were strong competitors, so if Maytag didn't move quickly they could get a lead.

Maytag formed a cross-functional new-product development team to quickly focus the effort. It screened various product ideas and strategies on criteria such as potential for superior customer value, initial costs, long-term growth, social responsibility, and profitability. Using nearly 40 pieces of consumer research, the team refined what the strategy might be and what it would cost.

S.W.O.T. analysis showed that Maytag's advantages included a strong dealer network, the technical skills to develop the product, and the financial resources to do it. Major threats were mainly related to competitors' efforts and consumers' prior attitudes about front-loading machines. Addressing those threats would take informing and real persuading.

Market segmentation helped to narrow down to a target market. Various segments could be identified. For example, there was a homogeneous business market. It consisted of owners of coin-operated laundries who were mainly interested in operating costs and attracting customers. Consumer segments were more varied. Relevant needs focused on cleaning, removing stains, caring for fabric, and saving water or energy. Some people just wanted less hassle on wash days and a care-free washer. Maytag decided not to target just the segment that conserved energy; that was not a qualifying dimension. Instead they combined several segments into a larger target market. The main qualifying dimension was the ability to pay for a dependable washer that provided superior cleaning. Determining dimensions were interests in saving time, hassle, and expense while getting better results.

The design of the washing machine evolved from target consumers' needs, so it is different from most washers. The stainless steel tub tilts at a 15-degree angle, which improves visibility and reach. Cutting out the normal agitator increases load capacity by about a third while decreasing damage to clothes. It also increases access space for bulky items and makes loading and unloading easier. Fins inside lift the clothes and then plop them back in the shallow basin of water. This eliminates spills because the water level is below the door. In fact, it uses half the water and energy of regular machines but removes tough stains better. As Maytag's design progressed, consumer tests showed that consumers liked the unique benefits and were willing to pay for them. Financial analysis of the marketing plan for this new product indicated that it could meet Maytag's objectives, so Maytag invested the money to put the plan into action.

The new product needed a memorable brand name—Neptune. The existing marketing program positioned Maytag as "the dependability people," so the plan called for a strategy that would build on that base but also position the new product as really new and superior—as "the washer for the new millennium."

The plan called for a warranty that would signal real dependability to consumers. It specified a 10-year warranty on the drive motor or rust damage and lifetime coverage on the stainless steel wash basket.

The plan also differentiated Neptune with an unprecedented level of after-sale support. Neptune buyers would get Priority One Service that offers dedicated toll-free assistance and priority scheduling should any in-home calls be required. The plan also got down to details: The easy-to-remember toll-free number is 888-4-MAYTAG.

In stores, the washer is displayed out of the carton, so the plan focused on a package designed to protect the product during handling and, by using bar codes and clear model labels, make logistics in the channel more efficient. But the thrust of the packaging was to protect, not promote.

While our focus here is on the washer, the plan also considered product-line issues. It called for a matching dryer designed so that the length of wash and dry cycles would be virtually the same. This means that a user can move load after load from washer to dryer without the waiting that's typical with conventional laundry pairs. What's more, the dryer handles Neptune's extra large loads with ease and uses the same angled styling—so transferring a load to the dryer is easier than ever.

To reduce start-up costs and keep the effort focused, the initial plan called for only one model of the Neptune washer. However, a full-sized stacked version of a combination washer/dryer was planned for later.

The plan called for a national rollout using Maytag's established dealers. Making a product available in so many places at once added difficulties, but it was consistent with the plan of using national promotion to give the product a big introduction.

To help coordinate efforts in the channel, Maytag released stories in *Merchandiser*, a magazine it publishes for dealers. As channel captain, Maytag kept dealers informed about the specific timing of the program, including when stock would be available. Maytag salespeople got dealers' orders and helped them to plan their own strategies.

The plan anticipated that product availability could be a constraint if the introduction went extremely well. So dealers could participate in a program that allowed consumers to reserve one of the early units off the production line. This preselling activity improved inventory management, reduced stock-outs, and got sales early in the program.

Even with these efforts at coordination, the promotion portion of the plan was developed recognizing that some independent dealers were skeptical about carrying and promoting a premium-price front-loader. So the plan called for a mix of push and pull promotion.

Details of promotion planning was handled as a team effort by Maytag and Leo Burnett, its Chicago agency. The plan called for integrated marketing communications. To make it easy for the sales force, dealers, customers, and potential customers to remember all of Neptune's benefits, the promotion effort consistently focused on Neptune's four Cs—Cleaning, Convenience, Clothes Care, and Conservation. (You can probably figure out where a group of marketing folks got the idea of using a catchy acronym like that.)

The plan relied on different promotion methods to emphasize different benefits and objectives. For example, much of the prerelease publicity focused on conservation of water, energy, and related costs. Then initial advertising focused on availability and cleaning benefits. The marketing plan also specified tests by independent laboratories so that there would be evidence to support claims of superiority.

The distinctive advantages of the Neptune offered a particularly good opportunity to use publicity to create broad awareness and generate interest. Thus, the plan set out an extensive set of public relations events, including a glitzy media launch at New York's Lincoln Center. It featured famous TV moms talking about the Maytag washer they used—followed by the introduction of the Neptune, "the washer for the next millennium." This garnered widespread media attention just a few weeks before the product launch.

The plan also laid out an attention-getting venture with the Department of Energy that involved benchmarking the water and energy usage of all of the washers in a small, water-starved town in Kansas and then replacing half of them with Neptune washers. The test showed that the Neptune produced savings of 39 percent in water usage and 58 percent in energy usage. Media coverage ranged from "NBC Nightly News" to the front page of *USA Today*.

An unknown new product calls for attention-getting advertising, and that is exactly what the plan specified. A big-budget TV commercial debuted at precisely the same moment on both CBS and NBC and then was scheduled for frequent repetitions over the next three months. The ad features Maytag's Lonely Repairman out for a late-night walk with his dog. Ol' Lonely spills a cupful of coffee down his front when the pooch starts racing in circles. You see why when a spaceship appears overhead, beaming down a Neptune washer and three happy little aliens. In a flash, they strip the coffee-stained uniform off Ol' Lonely and throw it in the washer. Following a demo of the washer's tumbling action, the now-spotless uniform reappears on the famous repairman. As the Neptunians depart in their spaceship, Ol' Lonely says, "They're never gonna believe this. A washer that removes stains."

The plan also called for promotion support for dealers. For example, to attract attention Maytag dealers received 20-foot-high balloons that looked like Ol' Lonely to put on top of their stores, as well as in-store banners, posters, and brochures.

Maytag didn't miss the opportunity to plan interactive marketing communications. At the website (www.maytag.com) consumers could see pictures and read about the benefits of the Neptune. A website visitor who was ready to buy could even reserve a Neptune that would be delivered by the local dealer or use an interactive dealer locator to find a store.

The plan didn't ignore the coin-laundry segment. The website featured a special section on how the Neptune could help improve profits for those firms. It went into detail about savings on energy, water, and sewer costs, as well as technical matters related to maintenance.

Of course, the plan called for dealers to pitch in with some promotion efforts of their own, such as setting up displays to demo the Neptune in action. Dealers were required to correctly and attractively display point-of-purchase materials. And salespeople were brought up-to-speed about Neptune's four Cs so they could explain its benefit and help customers determine if it met their needs.

The plan called for an initial suggested list price of $1,099, which was high relative to most washers. The washer-dryer combination was about $1,700. Some dealers, however, cut that price because the plan allowed dealers a higher than normal dollar profit.

The plan anticipated that Frigidaire and GE might cut prices when faced with competition (and in fact that later happened). However, Maytag stuck with its planned higher price because many consumers viewed its design as offering a better value. Further, the plan provided information to help salespeople reduce price sensitivity by reminding consumers that water and energy savings from the Neptune are about $100 a year, so it pays for itself in 10 years.

Bounty can probably get a reasonably good forecast of sales for its improved paper towels based on experience with similar products that it already sells. By contrast, satellite navigation is a newer concept and it will probably be more difficult for Garmin to accurately forecast how quickly sales for its new eTrex product will grow.

The plan did not include use of rebates, but some utility companies offered rebates to customers who purchased a Neptune. For example, one water company handed out 1,500 rebates of $50 each. It figures that those Neptunes save 18,000 gallons of water a day.

With the plan finally in operation, Neptunes flew off the dealers' floors and truckload orders began rolling in. This caused some implementation problems, but Maytag production workers went into overdrive and moved Neptunes off the loading docks around the clock. Swiftly, new tooling was installed to raise plant production rates.

As this product-market moves along in the growth stage, competition could get tough. So far, however, Maytag marketers have developed creative strategies and thorough plans that have stimulated growth in sales and profit. And along the way, they've helped raise the social responsibility bar on conservation.[1]

Marketing Strategy Planning Process Requires Logic and Creativity

As the Maytag case shows, developing a good marketing strategy and turning the strategy into a marketing plan requires creative blending of the ideas we've discussed throughout this text. We'll start this chapter with a brief review of these ideas, then we'll show how you bring them together to prepare a marketing plan. We'll conclude by considering how effective marketing is—at both the micro and macro levels—and the opportunities and challenges that marketing managers face. Exhibit 18-1 provides a broad overview of the major areas we've been talking about. You've seen this before in Chapter 3—before you learned what's really involved in each idea. Now we must integrate ideas about these different areas to narrow down to logical marketing strategies and marketing plans.

Marketing strategy planning process brings focus to efforts

As suggested in Exhibit 18-1, developing an effective marketing strategy involves a process of narrowing down to a specific target market and marketing mix that represents a real opportunity. This narrowing-down process requires a thorough

Exhibit 18-1
Overview of Marketing Strategy Planning Process

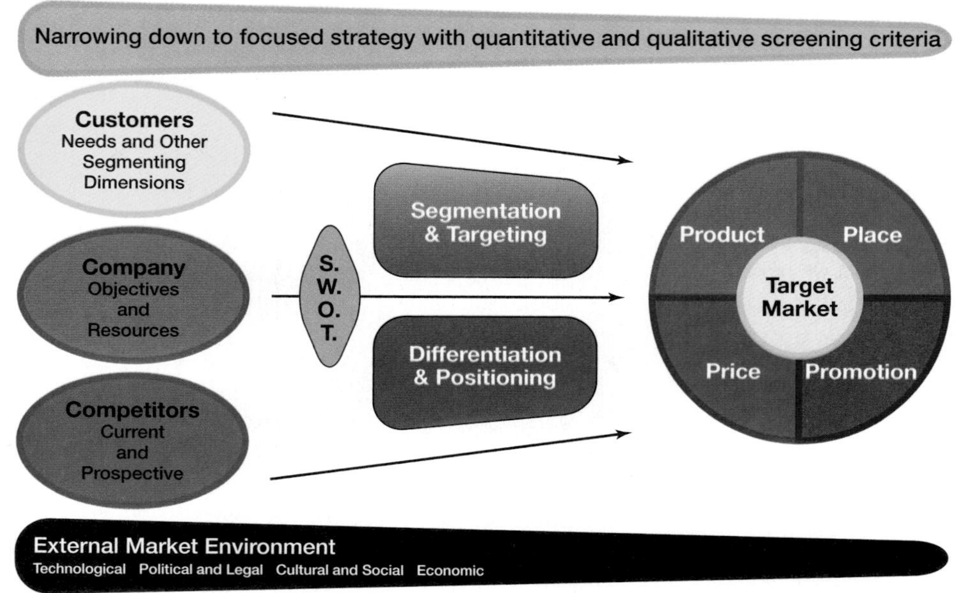

understanding of the market. That understanding is enhanced by careful analysis of customers' needs, current or prospective competitors, and the firm's own objectives and resources. Similarly, trends in the external market environment may make a potential opportunity more or less attractive.

There are usually more different strategy possibilities than a firm can pursue. Each possible strategy usually has a number of different potential advantages and disadvantages. This can make it difficult to zero in on the best target market and marketing mix. However, developing a set of specific qualitative and quantitative screening criteria—to define what business and markets the firm wants to compete in—can help eliminate potential strategies that are not well suited for the firm.

Careful analysis helps the manager focus on a strategy that takes advantage of the firm's opportunities and strengths while avoiding its weaknesses and threats to its success. These can be compared with the pros and cons of strategies that are considered. For example, if a firm is considering a target market that is already satisfied by a competitor's offering, finding a competitive advantage might require an innovative new product, improved distribution, more effective promotion, or a better price. Just offering a marketing mix that is like what is available from competitors usually doesn't provide any real basis for the firm to position or differentiate its marketing mix as offering superior customer value.

Marketing manager must blend the four Ps

Exhibit 18-2 reviews the major marketing strategy decision areas organized by the four Ps. Each of these requires careful decision making. Yet marketing planning involves much more than just independent decisions and assembling the parts into a marketing mix. The four Ps must be creatively *blended*—so the firm develops the best mix for its target market. In other words, each decision must work well with all of the others to make a logical whole.

In our discussion, we've given the job of integrating the four Ps strategy decisions to the marketing manager. Now you should see the need for this integrating role. It is easy for specialists to focus on their own areas and expect the rest of the company to work for or around them. This is especially true in larger firms where the size of the whole marketing job is too big for one person. Yet the ideas of the product manager, the advertising manager, the sales manager, the logistics

Exhibit 18-2
Strategy Decision Areas Organized by the Four Ps

Product
- Physical good
- Service
- Features
- Benefits
- Quality level
- Accessories
- Installation
- Instructions
- Warranty
- Product lines
- Packaging
- Branding

Place
- Objectives
- Channel type
- Market exposure
- Kinds of middlemen
- Kinds and locations of stores
- How to handle transporting and storing
- Service levels
- Recruiting middlemen
- Managing channels

Promotion
- Objectives
- Promotion blend
- Salespeople
  - Kind
  - Number
  - Selection
  - Training
  - Motivation
- Advertising
  - Targets
  - Kinds of ads
  - Media type
  - Copy thrust
  - Prepared by whom
- Sales promotion
- Publicity

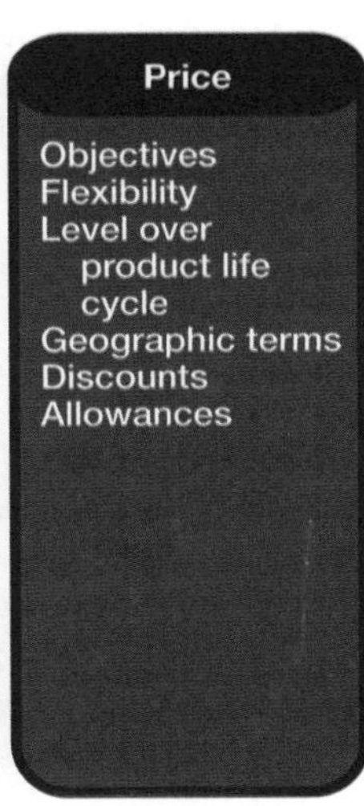

manager, and whoever makes pricing decisions may have to be adjusted to improve the whole mix. It's critical that each marketing mix decision work well with all of the others. A breakdown in any one decision area may doom the whole strategy to failure.

The Marketing Plan Brings All the Details Together

Marketing plan provides a blueprint for implementation

Once the manager has selected the target market, decided on the (integrated) marketing mix to meet that target market's needs, and developed estimates of the costs and revenue for that strategy, it's time to put it all together in the marketing plan. As we explained in Chapter 2, a marketing plan includes the time-related details—including costs and revenues—for a marketing strategy. Thus, the plan basically serves as a blueprint for what the firm will do.

Exhibit 18-3 provides a summary outline of the different sections of a complete marketing plan. You can see that this outline is basically an abridged overview of the topics we've covered throughout the text. Thus, you can flesh out your thinking for any portion of a marketing plan by reviewing the section of the book where that topic is discussed in more detail. Further, the Maytag case at the beginning of this chapter also gives you a real example of the types of thinking and detail that are included.

Marketing plan spells out the timing of the strategy

Some time schedule is implicit in any strategy. A marketing plan simply spells out this time period and the time-related details. Usually, we think in terms of some reasonable length of time—such as six months, a year, or a few years. But it might be only a month or two in some cases—especially when rapid changes in fashion or technology are important. Or a strategy might be implemented over several years—perhaps the length of a product life cycle or at least the early stages of the product's life.

Although the outline in Exhibit 18-3 does not explicitly show a place for the time frame for the plan or the specific costs for each decision area, these should be included in the plan—along with expected estimates of sales and profit—so that the plan can be compared with *actual performance* in the future. In other words, the plan not only makes it clear to everyone what is to be accomplished

Exhibit 18-3 Summary Outline of Different Sections of Marketing Plan

Name of Product-Market

Major screening criteria relevant to product-market opportunity selected
- Quantitative (ROI, profitability, risk level, etc.)
- Qualitative (nature of business preferred, social responsibility, etc.)
- Major constraints

Analysis of Other Aspects of External Market Environment (favorable and unfavorable factors and trends)

Economic environment
Technological environment
Political and legal environment
Cultural and social environment

Customer Analysis (organizational and/or final consumer)

Possible segmenting dimensions (customer needs, other characteristics)
- Identification of qualifying dimensions and determining dimensions

Identification of target market(s) (one or more specific segments)
- Operational characteristics (demographics, geographic locations, etc.)
- Potential size (number of people, dollar purchase potential, etc.) and likely growth

Key psychological and social influences on buying
Type of buying situation
Nature of relationship with customers

Competitor Analysis

Nature of current/likely competition
Current and prospective competitors (and/or rivals)
- Current strategies and likely responses to plan

Competitive barriers to overcome and sources of potential competitive advantage

Company Analysis

Company objectives and overall marketing objectives
Company resources
S.W.O.T.: Identification of major *s*trengths, *w*eaknesses, *o*pportunities, and *t*hreats (based on above analyses of company resources, customers, competitors, and other aspects of external market environment)

Marketing Information Requirements

Marketing research needs (with respect to customers, marketing mix effectiveness, external environment, etc.)
Secondary data and primary data needs
Marketing information system needs, models to be used, etc.

Product

Product class (type of consumer or business product)
Current product life cycle stage
New-product development requirements (people, dollars, time, etc.)
- Product liability, safety and social responsibility considerations

Specification of core physical good and/or service
- Features, quality, etc.

Supporting customer service(s) needed
Warranty (what is covered, timing, who will support, etc.)
Branding (manufacturer versus dealer, family brand versus individual brand, etc.)
Packaging
- Promotion and labeling needs
- Protection needs

Cultural sensitivity of product
Fit with product line

Place

Objectives
- Degree of market exposure required
- Distribution customer service level required

Type of channel (direct, indirect)
- Other channel members and/or facilitators required
  - Type/number of wholesalers (agent, merchant, etc.)
  - Type/number of retailers
- How discrepancies and separations will be handled
- How marketing functions will be shared

Coordination needed in company, channel, and supply chain
- Information requirements (EDI, the Internet, e-mail, etc.)

Transportation requirements
Inventory product-handling requirements
Facilities required (warehousing, distribution centers, etc.)
Reverse channels (for returns, recalls, etc.)

Promotion

Objectives
Major message theme(s) for integrated marketing communications (desired "positioning")
Promotion blend
- Advertising (type, media, copy thrust, etc.)
- Personal selling (type and number of salespeople, how compensated, how effort will be allocated, etc.)
- Sales promotion (for channel members, customers, employees)
- Publicity
- Interactive media

Mix of push and pull required
Who will do the work

Price

Nature of demand (price sensitivity, price of substitutes)
Demand and cost analyses (marginal analysis)
Markup chain in channel
Price flexibility
Price level(s) (under what conditions) and impact on customer value
Adjustments to list price (geographic terms, discounts, allowances, etc.)

Special Implementation Problems to Be Overcome

People required
Manufacturing, financial, and other resources needed

Control

Marketing information system needs
Criterion measures comparison with objectives (customer satisfaction, sales, cost, performance analysis, etc.)

Forecasts and Estimates

Costs (all elements in plan, over time)
Sales (by market, over time, etc.)
Estimated operating statement *(pro forma)*

Timing

Specific sequence of activities and events, etc.
Likely changes over the product life cycle

and how—but it also provides a basis for the control process after the plan is implemented.

A complete plan spells out the reasons for decisions

The plan outline shown in Exhibit 18-3 is quite complete. It doesn't just provide information about marketing mix decisions—it also includes information about customers (including segmenting dimensions), competitors' strategies, other aspects of the marketing environment, and the company's objectives and resources. This material provides important background relevant to the "why" of the marketing mix and target market decisions.

Some managers do not include this information; their plans just lay out the details of the target market and the marketing mix strategy decisions. This shortcut approach is more common when the plan is really just an update of a strategy that has been in place for some time. However, that approach can be risky.

Managers too often make the mistake of casually updating plans in minor ways—perhaps just changing some costs or sales forecasts—but otherwise sticking with what was done in the past. A big problem with this approach is that it's easy to lose sight of why those strategy decisions were made in the first place. When the market situation changes, the original reasons may no longer apply. Yet if the logic for those strategy decisions is not retained, it's easy to miss changes taking place that should result in a plan being reconsidered. For example, a plan that was established in the growth stage of the product life cycle may have been very successful for a number of years. But a marketing manager can't be complacent and assume that success will continue forever. When market maturity hits, the firm may be in for big trouble—unless the basic strategy and plan are modified. If a plan spells out the details of the market analysis and logic for the marketing mix and target market selected, then it is a simple matter to routinely check and update it. Remember: The idea is for all of the analysis and strategy decisions to fit together as an integrated whole. Thus, as some of the elements of the plan or marketing environment change, the whole plan may need a fresh approach.

Internet

Internet Exercise Go to the Maytag website (www.maytag.com) and review the information about the Neptune line. Do you see any indication that the strategy for Neptune is changing from what is described in the case that introduces this chapter? Explain your point of view.

How Should Marketing Be Evaluated?

We've been emphasizing the role of marketing in organizations. But now that you have a better understanding of what marketing is all about—and how the marketing manager contributes to the macro-marketing process—you should be able to decide whether marketing is effective—or if it costs too much.

Your answer is very important. It will affect your own business career and the economy in which you live.

We must evaluate at two levels

As we saw in Chapter 1, it's useful to distinguish between two levels of marketing: the *micro* level (how individual firms run) and the *macro* level (how the whole system works). Some complaints against marketing are aimed at only one of these levels at a time. In other cases, the criticism *seems* to be directed to one level but actually is aimed at the other. Some critics of specific ads, for example, probably wouldn't be satisfied with *any* advertising. When evaluating marketing, we must treat each of these levels separately.

Nation's objectives affect evaluation

Different nations have different social and economic objectives. Dictatorships, for example, may be mainly concerned with satisfying the needs of society as seen by the political elite. In a socialist state, the objective might be to satisfy society's needs as defined by government planners. In a society that has recently broken the chains of communism, the objective may be to make the transition to a market-directed economy as quickly as possible—before there are more revolts.

Consumer satisfaction is the objective in the United States

In the United States, *the basic objective of our market-directed economic system has been to satisfy consumer needs as they, the consumers, see them.* This objective implies that political freedom and economic freedom go hand in hand and that citizens in a free society have the right to live as they choose. The majority of American consumers would be unwilling to give up the freedom of choice they now enjoy. The same can be said for Canada, Great Britain, and most other countries in the European Union. However, for focus we will concentrate on marketing as it exists in American society.

Planetfeedback.com is a website that makes it easy for consumers to give feedback to companies. Of course, some feedback is clear from customers' choices in the marketplace. For example, Camry marketing managers gain very positive feedback from the fact that Camry is the number one selling car and that it has more repeat buyers than any other car.

1. ***Video:*** An office. People at work.

2. ***Audio*** (MVO): "If you are now waiting for something amusing to happen, ..."

3. "... you'll be disappointed. A bank is not a theater."

4. ***Video*** (cut): Under one of the desks a cat is napping.
Audio (MVO): "Rikk Bank. The most boring bank in the world."

5. ***Video:*** Cut to view of the whole office.
Audio (MVO): "The people are working. The money is working."

6. ***Video:*** Cut to the logo of Rikk Bank.
Audio (MVO): "And that's all."

In the U.S., banks provide all kinds of special services to meet customer expectations. In Russia, consumer expectations about banks are different, so Rikk uses TV ads to emphasize that it's not going to do anything unusual, it's just going to be a solid bank.

Therefore, let's try to evaluate the operation of marketing in the American economy—where the present objective is to satisfy consumer needs *as consumers see them.* This is the essence of our system. The business firm that ignores this fact is asking for trouble.

Can Consumer Satisfaction Be Measured?

Since consumer satisfaction is our objective, marketing's effectiveness must be measured by *how well* it satisfies consumers. There have been various efforts to measure overall consumer satisfaction not only in the United States but also in other countries. For example, a team of researchers at the University of Michigan has created the American Customer Satisfaction Index based on regular interviews with thousands of customers of about 200 companies and 34 industries. The 2001 index was lower than it was when the effort started seven years earlier. Similar studies are available for member countries of the European Union.

Satisfaction depends on individual aspirations

This sort of index makes it possible to track changes in consumer satisfaction measures over time and even allows comparison among countries. That's potentially useful. Yet there are limits to interpreting any measure of consumer satisfaction when we try to evaluate macro-marketing effectiveness in any absolute sense. One basic issue is that satisfaction depends on and is *relative to* your level of aspiration or expectation. Less prosperous consumers begin to expect more out of an economy as they see the higher living standards of others. Also, aspiration levels tend to rise with repeated successes and fall with failures. Products considered satisfactory one day may not be satisfactory the next day, or vice versa. A few years ago, most of us were more than satisfied with a 19-inch color TV that pulled in three or four channels. But once you've watched one of the newer large-screen models and enjoyed all the options possible with a digital satellite receiver or a DVD, that old TV is never the same again. And when high-definition digital TVs and interactive broadcast systems become more widespread, today's most satisfying units won't seem quite so acceptable.

In addition, consumer satisfaction is a highly personal concept—and looking at the "average" satisfaction of a whole society does not provide a complete picture for evaluating macro-marketing effectiveness. At a minimum, some consumers are more satisfied than others. So although efforts to measure satisfaction are useful, any evaluation of macro-marketing effectiveness has to be largely subjective.

Probably the supreme test is whether the macro-marketing system satisfies enough individual consumer-citizens so that they vote—at the ballot box—to keep it running. So far, we've done so in the United States.[2]

There are many measures of micro-marketing effectiveness

Measuring micro-marketing effectiveness is also difficult, but it can be done. Expectations may change just as other aspects of the market environment change—so firms have to do a good job of coping with the change. Individual business firms can and should try to measure how well their marketing mixes satisfy their customers (or why they fail). In fact, most large firms now have some type of ongoing effort to determine whether they're satisfying their target markets. For example, the J. D. Power marketing research firm is well known for its studies of consumer satisfaction with different makes of automobiles and computers. And the American Customer Satisfaction Index is also used to rate individual companies. For example, in the 2001 results, McDonald's ranked among the poorest performing retailers. While managers at McDonald's take issue with that result, the firm's own internal satisfaction studies say that on the average day 11 percent of McDonald's customers complain to the restaurant about some dissatisfaction (for example, because of slow service, wrong orders, dirty stores, or employees who have forgotten the company's "we love to see you smile" slogan). It's reported that 70 percent of those dissatisfied customers are further dissatisfied with the way McDonald's handled the complaint.[3]

Many large and small firms measure customer satisfaction with attitude research studies. Other widely used methods include comment cards, e-mail response features on websites, unsolicited consumer responses (usually complaints), opinions of middlemen and salespeople, market test results, and profits. Of course, customers may be very satisfied about some aspects of what a firm is doing but dissatisfied about other dimensions of performance.[4]

In our market-directed system, it's up to each customer to decide how effectively individual firms satisfy his or her needs. Usually, customers will buy more of the products that satisfy them—and they'll do it repeatedly. That's why firms that develop really satisfying marketing mixes are able to develop profitable long-term relationships with the customers that they serve. Because efficient marketing plans can increase profits, profits can be used as a rough measure of a firm's efficiency in satisfying customers. Nonprofit organizations have a different bottom line, but they too will fail if they don't satisfy supporters and get the resources they need to continue to operate.

Evaluating marketing effectiveness is difficult—but not impossible

It's easy to see why opinions differ concerning the effectiveness of micro- and macro-marketing. If the objective of the economy is clearly defined, however—and the argument is stripped of emotion—the big questions about marketing effectiveness probably *can* be answered.

In this chapter, we argue that micro-marketing (how individual firms and channels operate) frequently *does* cost too much but that macro-marketing (how the whole marketing system operates) *does not* cost too much, *given the present objective of the American economy—consumer satisfaction*. Don't accept this position as *the* answer but rather as a point of view. In the end, you'll have to make your own judgment.[5]

Micro-Marketing Often Does Cost Too Much

Throughout the text, we've explored what marketing managers could or should do to help their firms do a better job of satisfying customers—while achieving company objectives. Many firms implement highly successful marketing programs, but others are still too production-oriented and inefficient. For customers of these latter firms, micro-marketing often does cost too much.

Research shows that many consumers are not satisfied. But you know that already. All of us have had experiences when we weren't satisfied—when some firm didn't deliver on its promises. And the problem is much bigger than some marketers want to believe. Research suggests that the majority of consumer complaints are never reported. Worse, many complaints that are reported never get fully resolved.

The failure rate is high

Further evidence that too many firms are too production-oriented—and not nearly as efficient as they could be—is the fact that so many new products fail. New and old businesses—even ones that in the past were leaders in their markets—fail regularly too.

Maxwell House ready-to-drink coffee came in a package that looked like a milk carton, but it had an inner foil liner that caused problems when consumers heated the carton in a microwave. There was no mention on the package that it might make good iced coffee. Fixing these problems might not have made the product a success, but they certainly contributed to its failure.

Generally speaking, marketing inefficiencies are due to one or more of three reasons:

1. Lack of interest in or understanding of the sometimes fickle customer.
2. Improper blending of the four Ps—caused in part by overemphasis on internal problems as contrasted with a customer orientation.
3. Lack of understanding of or adjustment to the marketing environment, especially what competitors do.

Any of these problems can easily be a fatal flaw—the sort of thing that leads to death-wish marketing and business failures. A firm can't create value if it doesn't have a clue what customers think or say. Even if a firm listens to the "voice of the customer," there's no incentive for the customer to buy if the benefits of the marketing mix don't exceed the costs. And if the firm succeeds in coming up with a marketing mix with benefits greater than costs, it still won't be a superior value unless it's better than what competitors offer.

The high cost of missed opportunities

Another sign of failure is the inability of firms to identify new target markets and new opportunities. A new marketing mix that isn't offered doesn't fail—but the lost opportunity can be significant for both a firm and society. Too many managers seize on whatever strategy seems easiest rather than seeking really new ways to satisfy customers. Too many companies stifle really innovative thinking. Layers of bureaucracy and a "that's not the way we do things" mentality just snuff it out.

On the other hand, not every new idea is a good idea for every company. For example, there is little doubt that e-commerce and online systems are having a dramatic effect in improving how many firms serve their customers. But in the last few years, hundreds of firms have lost millions of dollars with failed efforts to capitalize on the Internet or some "hot" website idea. Just jumping on the "what's new" bandwagon—without stopping to figure out how it is going to really satisfy the customer and result in profit for the firm—is as much a ticket for failure as being too slow or bureaucratic.

Micro-marketing does cost too much—but things are changing

For reasons like these, marketing does cost too much in many firms. Despite much publicity, the marketing concept is not really applied in many places.

But not all firms and marketers deserve criticism. More of them *are* becoming customer-oriented. And many are paying more attention to market-oriented planning to carry out the marketing concept more effectively. Throughout the text, we've highlighted firms and strategies that are making a difference. The successes of innovative firms—like Wal-Mart, 3M, Cisco, AOL, Dell, Tesco, UPS, and Frito-Lay—do not go unnoticed. Yes, they make some mistakes. That's human—and marketing is a human enterprise. But they have also showed the results that market-oriented strategy planning can produce.

Another encouraging sign is that more companies are recognizing that it often takes a diverse set of backgrounds and talents to meet the increasingly varied needs of their increasingly global customers. They're shedding "not-invented-here" biases and embracing technologies like the Internet and information systems, comparing what they do with the best practices of firms in totally different industries, and teaming up with outside specialists who can bring a fresh perspective.

Managers who adopt the marketing concept as a way of business life do a better job. They look for target market opportunities and carefully blend the elements of the marketing mix to meet their customers' needs. As more of these managers rise in business, we can look forward to much lower micro-marketing costs and strategies that do a better job of satisfying customer needs.

Internet

Internet Exercise Ikea is an innovative furniture company that is using its website to refine its strategy. It has always relied on information technology to keep costs low by tracking sales at individual stores and using the information to control inventory and reduce shipping costs between the factory, distribution centers, and its massive retail stores. Go to the Ikea website (www.ikea.com). What else does the website tell you about Ikea's strategy? Does the website help Ikea offer superior value? Explain your answer.

Macro-Marketing Does Not Cost Too Much

Some critics of marketing take aim at the macro-marketing system. They typically argue that the macro-marketing system causes poor use of resources and leads to an unfair distribution of income. Most of these complaints imply that some micro-marketing activities should not be permitted—and because they are, our macro-marketing system does a poor job. Let's look at some of these positions to help you form your own opinion.

Micro-efforts help the economy grow

Some critics feel that marketing helps create a monopoly or at least monopolistic competition. Further, they think this leads to higher prices, restricted output, and reduction in national income and employment.

It's true that firms in a market-directed economy try to carve out separate monopolistic markets for themselves with new products. But consumers do have a choice. They don't *have* to buy the new product unless they think it's a better value. The old products are still available. In fact, to meet the new competition, prices of the old products usually drop. And that makes them even more available.

Over several years, the innovator's profits may rise—but rising profits also encourage further innovation by competitors. This leads to new investments—which contribute to economic growth and higher levels of national income and employment. Around the world, many countries failed to achieve their potential for economic

Marketing stimulates innovation and the development of new ways to meet customers' needs.

growth under centrally planned systems because this type of profit incentive didn't exist. Even now, many of the regulations that are imposed by the developed countries are left over from old ways of thinking and get in the way of progress.

Is advertising a waste of resources?

Advertising is the most criticized of all micro-marketing activities. Indeed, many ads *are* annoying, insulting, misleading, and downright ineffective. This is one reason why micro-marketing often does cost too much. However, advertising can also make both the micro- and macro-marketing processes work better.

Advertising is an economical way to inform large numbers of potential customers about a firm's products. Provided that a product satisfies customer needs, advertising can increase demand for the product—resulting in economies of scale in manufacturing, distribution, and sales. Because these economies may more than offset advertising costs, advertising can actually *lower* prices to the consumer.[6]

Does marketing make people buy things they don't need?

Some critics feel that advertising manipulates consumers into buying products that they don't need. This, of course, raises a question. How should a society determine which products are unnecessary and shouldn't be produced or sold? One critic suggested that Americans could and should do without such items as pets, newspaper comic strips, second family cars, motorcycles, snowmobiles, campers, recreational boats, beer cans, and hats.[7] You may agree with some of these. But who should determine minimum material requirements of life—individual consumers or critics?

Needs and wants change

Consumer needs and wants change constantly. Few of us would care to live the way our grandparents lived when they were our age. Marketing's job is not just to satisfy consumer wants as they exist at any particular point in time. Rather, marketing must keep looking for new and better ways to create value and serve consumers.[8]

Does marketing make people materialistic?

There is no doubt that marketing caters to materialistic values. However, people disagree as to whether marketing creates these values or simply appeals to values already there.

Even in the most primitive societies, people want to accumulate possessions. The tendency for ancient pharaohs and kings to surround themselves with wealth and treasures can hardly be attributed to the persuasive powers of advertising agencies![9]

Clearly, the quality of life can't be measured just in terms of quantities of material goods. But when we view products as the means to an end rather than the end itself, they *do* make it possible to satisfy higher-level needs. Microwave ovens, for example, greatly reduced the amount of time and effort people must spend preparing meals—leaving them free to pursue other interests. The Internet empowers people with information in ways that few could have even imagined a few years ago.

Not all needs are met

Some critics argue that our macro-marketing system is flawed because it does not provide solutions to important problems, such as questions about how to help the homeless, the uneducated, dependent children, minorities who have suffered discrimination, the elderly poor, and the sick. Many of these people do live in dire circumstances. But is that the result of a market-directed system?

There is no doubt that many firms focus their effort on people who can pay for what they have to offer. But as the forces of competition drive down prices, more people are able to afford more of what they need. And the matching of supply and demand stimulates economic growth, creates jobs, and spreads income among more people. In other words, a market-directed economy makes efficient use of resources. However, it can't guarantee that government aid programs are effective. It doesn't ensure that all voters and politicians agree on which problems should be solved first—or how taxes should be set and allocated. It can't eliminate the possibility of a child being ignored.

These are important societal issues. But citizen-consumers in a democratic society assign some responsibilities to business and some to government. Ultimately

Some critics argue that people are bombarded with too much advertising—ranging from posters that cover a whole building to messages pressed into the sand on public beaches—and that it tends to cater to materialistic values. However, in a free market consumers have choices, and so advertising tends to reflect society's values rather than create them.

consumer-citizens vote in the ballot box for how they want governments to deal with these concerns—just as they vote with their dollars for which firms to support. As more managers in the public sector understand and apply marketing concepts, we should be able to do a better job meeting the needs of all people.

Challenges Facing Marketers

We've said that our macro-marketing system does *not* cost too much—given the present objective of our economy. But we admit that the performance of many business firms leaves a lot to be desired. This presents a challenge to serious-minded students and marketers. What needs to be done—if anything?

Change is the only thing that's constant

Many firms are still production-oriented. Some hardly plan at all, and others simply extend one year's plans into the next. Progressive firms are beginning to realize that this doesn't work in our fast-changing markets. Market-oriented strategy planning is becoming more important in many companies. Firms are paying more attention to changes in the market—including trends in the marketing environment—and how marketing strategies need to be adapted to consider these changes. Exhibit 18-4 lists some of the important trends and changes we've discussed throughout this text.

Most of the changes and trends summarized in Exhibit 18-4 are having a positive effect on how marketers serve society. And this ongoing improvement is self-directing. As consumers shift their support to firms that do meet their needs, laggard businesses are forced to either improve or get out of the way.

If it ain't broke, improve it

Marketing managers must constantly evaluate their strategies to be sure they're not being left in the dust by competitors who see new and better ways of doing things. It's crazy for a marketing manager to constantly change a strategy that's working well. But too many managers fail to see or plan for needed changes. They're afraid to do anything different and adhere to the idea that "if it ain't broke, don't fix it." But a firm can't always wait until a problem becomes completely obvious to do something about it. When customers move on and profits disappear, it may be too late to fix the problem. Marketing managers who take the lead in finding innovative new markets and approaches get a competitive advantage.

Exhibit 18-4 Some Important Changes and Trends Affecting Marketing Strategy Planning

Communication Technologies
The Internet and intranets
Satellite communications
HTML e-mail and instant messaging
Videoconferencing and Internet telephone
Cellular telephones

Role of Computerization
E-commerce, websites
Computers and PDAs
Spreadsheet analysis
Wireless networks
Scanners and bar codes for tracking
Multimedia integration

Marketing Research
Search engines
Growth of marketing information systems
Decision support systems
Single source data (and scanner panels)
Data warehouses and data mining
Multimedia data and questionnaires
Customer relationship management (CRM) systems

Demographic Patterns
"Wired" households
Explosion in teen and ethnic submarkets
Aging of the baby boomers
Population growth slowdown in U.S.
Geographic shifts in population
Slower real income growth in U.S.

Business and Organizational Customers
Closer relationships and single sourcing
Just-in-time inventory systems/EDI
Web portals and Internet sourcing
Interactive bidding and proposal requests
Shift to NAICS
ISO 9000
E-commerce and supply chain management

Product Area
More attention to "really new" products
Faster new-product development
Computer-aided design (CAD)
R&D teams with market-driven focus
More attention to quality
More attention to service technologies
More attention to design, including packages
Category management

Channels and Logistics
Internet selling (wholesale and retail)
More vertical marketing systems
Clicks and bricks
Larger, more powerful retail chains
More attention to distribution service
Real-time inventory replenishment
Rapid response, JIT, and ECR
Automated warehousing and handling
Cross-docking at distribution centers
Logistics outsourcing
Cross-channel logistics coordination
Growth of mass-merchandising

Sales Promotion
Database-directed promotion
Point-of-purchase promotion
Trade promotion becoming more sensible
Event sponsorships
Better support from agencies
Customer loyalty programs
Customer acquisition cost analysis

Personal Selling
Sales technology
Automated order-taking
Use of laptop computers
Major accounts specialization
More telemarketing and team selling
Use of e-mail, fax, and voice mail

Mass Selling
Interactive media (websites, etc.)
Integrated marketing communication
More targeted media
  Pointcasting
  Specialty publications
  Specialty radio and TV (cable, satellite)
  Point-of-purchase
Growth of interactive agencies
Consolidation of global agencies
Consolidation of media companies
Changing agency compensation
Direct-response advertising
Shrinking media budgets

Pricing
Electronic bid pricing and auctions
Value pricing
Overuse of sales and deals
Bigger differences in functional discounts
More attention to exchange rate effects
Lower markups on higher stockturn items
Spreadsheets for marginal analysis

International Marketing
Struggles of post-communist economies
More international market development
Global competitors—at home and abroad
Global communication over Internet
New trade rules (NAFTA, WTO, EU, etc.)
More attention to exporting by small firms
International expansion by retailers
Impact of "pop" culture on traditional cultures
Tensions between "have" and "have-not" cultures
Growing role of airfreight

General
Explicit mission statements
SWOT analysis
Collapse of many dot-com startups
Benchmarking and total quality management
More attention to positioning and differentiation
Less regulation of business
Increased use of alliances
Shift away from diversification
More attention to profitability, not just sales
Greater attention to superior value
Addressing environmental concerns

We need to welcome international competition

Increasingly, marketing managers face global competition. Some managers hate that thought. Worldwide competition creates even more pressure on marketing managers to figure out what it takes to gain a competitive advantage—both at home and in foreign markets. But with the challenge comes opportunities. The forces of competition in and among market-directed economies will help speed the diffusion of marketing advances to consumers everywhere. As macro-marketing systems improve worldwide, more consumers will have income to buy products—from wherever in the world those products come.

We need to use technology wisely

We live in a time of dramatic new technologies. For example, in just a few short years the Internet has opened the door to radical new approaches for e-commerce. Too many feel that it's the job of the technical specialist to figure out how a new technology can help the firm serve its customers. But identifying and understanding new ways of satisfying customers and meeting their needs *is* a basic marketing responsibility. Marketers can't just pawn that responsibility off on "somebody else." If that means learning about new technologies, then that is just part of the marketing job. It's better for the marketer to have to struggle to understand the implications of a new technology than it is to just assume that the technology specialists will struggle to understand customers' needs. More often than not, that's a really bad assumption. And when no one is worrying about the customers' point of view, everybody suffers the consequences.

At a broader level, firms face the challenge of determining what technologies are acceptable and which are not. For example, gene research has opened the door to lifesaving medicines, genetically altered crops that resist drought or disease, and even cloning of human beings. Yet in all of these arenas there is intense conflict among different groups about what is appropriate. The fact that science allows us to do something doesn't necessarily mean that it should be done. On the other hand, how should these decisions be made? There is no simple answer to this question, but it's clear that old production-oriented views are *not* the answer. Perhaps we will move toward developing answers if some of the marketing ideas that have been applied to understanding individual needs can be extended to better understand the needs of society as a whole.

May need more social responsibility

Good business managers put themselves in the consumer's position. A useful rule to follow might be: Do unto others as you would have others do unto you.

Marketers need to understand and be sensitive to consumer concerns. Issues like protecting the environment are important and firms that look for better ways to address this issue may find that they can do well by doing good.

Promotion Managers Go Back to School

Schools are a targeted place for youth-oriented marketers to promote their products to the U.S.'s 45 million elementary and secondary students. Coke and Pepsi are eager to contribute scoreboards (or is that billboards?) for high school sports fields. In school cafeterias, which serve 30 million meals a day, Kellogg's cereal and Dannon's yogurt sponsor programs to motivate learning (and increase consumption). A school district in Colorado got national attention for selling advertising space on the sides of its school buses. This is not a new idea. The National Dairy Council has promoted dairy products in the schools since 1915.

Even so, the launch of the Channel One television network with ads and programming for schools brought new attention to the issue. Many critics saw it as a crass attempt to exploit captive students. Some schools even hand out coupons tied in with the ads. Channel One notes that schools get benefits. Besides the excellent news programs, they get video equipment and chances to win support for Internet access. Even Internet access is a mixed blessing. It's a great research tool, but there are virtually no limits on Internet advertising banners or websites. A teacher who does an in-class search on an innocent topic like "Asian teens" may click on one of the websites listed and instantly face a screen full of explicit pictures from a Japanese website that sells porno videos. To prevent that sort of thing, many schools use a web-filtering program from N2H2, Inc. But critics are troubled that N2H2 sells information about student surfing habits collected by the program.

To find more targeted ways of reaching students, some consumer products firms turn to promotion specialists, like Sampling Corporation of America (SCA). About 70 percent of all schools participate in SCA programs. For example, every Halloween SCA provides schools with safety literature wrapped around product samples or coupons provided by sponsor companies. Other firms create teaching materials. Dole Foods' nutrition curriculum, for example, centers on a multimedia CD-ROM featuring 30 animated fruits and vegetables. Dole also urges supermarket produce managers to contact their local schools to arrange special tours. More than 750,000 elementary school students have taken in-store produce tours.

There is no question that in-school promotion efforts do provide budget-strapped educators with added resources, including useful teaching materials. Yet promotions targeted at students also raise sensitive issues of educational standards, ethics, and taste. Marketers who are not sensitive to these issues can provoke a hostile public backlash, including a host of new regulations.[10]

www.mhhe.com/fourps

In practice, this means developing satisfying marketing mixes for specific target markets. It may mean building in more quality or more safety. The consumer's long-run satisfaction should be considered too. How will the product hold up in use? What about service guarantees? While trying to serve the needs of some target market, does the marketing strategy disregard the rights and needs of other consumers or create problems that will be left for future generations?[11]

The environment is everyone's need

Marketers need to work harder and smarter at finding ways to satisfy consumer needs without sacrificing the current or future environment. All consumers need the environment—whether they realize it yet or not. We are only beginning to understand the consequences of the environmental damage that's already been done. Acid rain, depletion of the ozone layer, global warming, and toxic waste in water supplies—to mention but a few current environmental problems—have catastrophic effects. Many top executives now say that preserving and protecting the environment will be one of the major challenges, if not *the* major challenge, of business firms in the new millennium.

In the past, most firms didn't pass the cost of environmental damage on to consumers in the prices that they paid. Pollution was a hidden and unmeasured cost for most companies. That is changing. Some firms are already paying billions of dollars to correct problems—including problems created years ago. The government isn't accepting the excuse that "nobody knew it was a big problem." Consider yourself warned: Businesspeople who fail to anticipate the coming public backlash on this issue put their careers and businesses at risk!

Creative marketers should be able to figure out how to preserve the environment, meet customer needs, and make profits all at the same time. Aveda, a cosmetics company, uses seeds from a shrub in the Amazon rain forest for the reddish pigment in its lipstick. By giving natives of the Amazon a way to make a living without further clearing of the rain forest, Aveda is helping to preserve the forest and also meeting the needs of consumers who want to buy environmentally friendly products.[12]

May need attention to consumer privacy

Marketers also must be sensitive to consumers' rights and privacy. Today, sophisticated marketing research methods, the Internet, and other new technologies make it easier to abuse these rights. For example, credit card records—which reveal much about consumers' purchases and private lives—are routinely computerized and sold to anybody who pays for the list.

Marketing managers should use technology responsibly to improve the quality of life, not disrupt it. If you don't think privacy is a serious matter, enter your social security number in an Internet search engine and see what pops up. You may be surprised.[13]

May need to change laws and how they are enforced

One of the advantages of a market-directed economic system is that it operates automatically. But in our version of this system, consumer-citizens provide certain constraints (laws), which can be modified at any time. Managers who ignore consumer attitudes must realize that their actions may cause new restraints.

Before piling on too many new rules, however, some of the ones we have may need to be revised and others may need to be enforced more carefully. Antitrust laws, for example, are often applied to protect competitors from each other—when they were really intended to encourage competition.

On the other hand, U.S. antitrust laws were originally developed so that all firms in a market would compete on a level playing field. That is no longer always true. In many markets individual U.S. firms compete with foreign firms whose governments urge them to cooperate with each other.

Internet

Internet Exercise Obvious Implementations Corp. is a small consulting and manufacturing firm. Go to its website (www.obviously.com) and then select *How to stop junk mail, e-mail, and phone calls.* Read through the information and, if you wish, follow some of the links to other sites listed. Should it be easier to avoid mail, spam, and calls you don't want? Explain your thinking.

Laws merely define minimal ethical standards

Whether a marketer is operating in his or her own country or in a foreign nation, the legal environment sets the *minimal* standards of ethical behavior as defined by a society. But marketing managers constantly face ethical issues where there are no clearly defined answers. Every marketing manager should make a personal commitment to carefully evaluate the ethical consequences of marketing strategy decisions.

On the other hand, innovative new marketing strategies *do* sometimes cause problems for those who have a vested interest in the old ways. Some people try to portray anything that disrupts their own personal interest as unethical. But that is not an appropriate ethical standard. The basic ethical charge to marketers is to find new and better ways to serve society's needs.

Need socially responsible consumers

We've stressed that marketers should act responsibly—but consumers have responsibilities too. Some consumers abuse policies about returning goods, change price tags in self-service stores, and are downright abusive to salespeople. Others think nothing of ripping off businesses because "they're rich." Shoplifting is a major problem for most traditional retailers and honest consumers pay for the cost of this theft in higher prices.[14]

Americans tend to perform their dual role of consumer-citizens with a split personality. We often behave one way as consumers, then take the opposite position at the ballot box. For example, we cover our beaches and parks with garbage and litter, while urging our legislators to take stiff action to curb pollution.

Unethical or illegal behavior is widespread. In a major survey of workers, managers, and executives from a wide range of industries, 48 percent admitted to taking unethical or illegal actions in the past year. Offenses included things like cheating

Increasingly, marketing managers face global competition. Lotus software allows managers in different locations, including different countries, to quickly share information, which helps to make implementation and control faster and more effective.

on expense accounts, paying or accepting kickbacks, trading sex for sales, lying to customers, leaking company secrets, and looking the other way when environmental laws are violated. Think about it—we're talking about half of the workforce.[15]

As consumer-citizens, each of us shares the responsibility for preserving an effective macro-marketing system. And we should take this responsibility seriously. That even includes the responsibility to be smarter customers. Let's face it, a majority of consumers ignore most of the available information that could help them spend money (and guide the marketing process) more wisely.

How Far Should the Marketing Concept Go?

Should marketing managers limit consumers' freedom of choice?

Achieving a better macro-marketing system is certainly a desirable objective. But what part should a marketer play in deciding what products to offer?

This is extremely important, because some marketing managers, especially those in large corporations, can have an impact far larger than they do in their roles as consumer-citizens. For example, should they refuse to produce hazardous products, like skis or motorcycles, even though such products are in strong demand? Should they install safety devices that increase costs but that customers don't want?

These are difficult questions to answer. Some things marketing managers do clearly benefit both the firm and consumers because they lower costs and/or improve consumers' options. But other choices may actually reduce consumer choice and conflict with a desire to improve the effectiveness of our macro-marketing system.

Consumer-citizens should vote on the changes

It seems fair to suggest, therefore, that marketing managers should be expected to improve and expand the range of goods and services they make available—always trying to add value and better satisfy consumers' needs and preferences. This is the job we've assigned to business.

If pursuing this objective makes excessive demands on scarce resources or has an unacceptable ecological effect, then consumer-citizens have the responsibility to vote for laws restricting individual firms that are trying to satisfy consumers' needs. This is the role that we, as consumers, have assigned to the government—to ensure that the macro-marketing system works effectively.

The Domino's logo shown here behind home plate does not actually exist on the playing field of this major league baseball game—but rather is created electronically. The advertiser pays the TV broadcaster to get the exposure. As new imaging technologies emerge, companies will have to decide what is fair and appropriate.

It is important to recognize that some *seemingly minor* modifications in our present system *might* result in very big, unintended problems. Allowing some government agency to prohibit the sale of products for seemingly good reasons could lead to major changes we never expected and could seriously reduce consumers' present rights to freedom of choice—including "bad" choices.

Conclusion

We started this chapter with a brief review of the strategy planning process. We stressed the importance of developing whole marketing mixes—not just developing policies for the individual four Ps and hoping they will fit together. The marketing manager is responsible for developing a workable blend—integrating all of a firm's efforts into a coordinated whole that makes effective use of the firm's resources and guides it toward its objectives. We went on to show that the marketing manager must develop a marketing plan for carrying out each strategy.

Now that you know more about marketing and what it involves, it's time to step back and evaluate how effective it is.

We argue that macro-marketing does *not* cost too much. Consumers have assigned business the role of satisfying their needs. Customers find it satisfactory and even desirable to permit businesses to cater to them and even to stimulate wants. As long as consumers are satisfied, macro-marketing will not cost too much—and business firms will be permitted to continue as profit-making entities.

But business exists at the consumer's discretion. It's mainly by satisfying the consumer that a particular firm—and *our* economic system—can justify its existence and hope to keep operating.

In carrying out this role—granted by consumers—business firms are not always as effective as they could be. Many business managers don't understand the marketing concept or the role that marketing plays in our way of life. They seem to feel that business has a God-given right to operate as it chooses. And they proceed in their typical production-oriented ways. Further, many managers have had little or no training in business management and are not as competent as they should be. Others fail to adjust to the changes taking place around them. And a few dishonest or unethical managers can do a great deal of damage before consumer-citizens take steps to stop them. As a result, micro-marketing often *does* cost too much. But the situation is improving. More business training is now available, and more competent people are being attracted to marketing and business generally. Clearly, *you* have a role to play in improving marketing activities in the future.

To keep our system working effectively, individual firms should implement the marketing concept in a more efficient, ethical, and socially responsible way. At the same time, we—as consumers—should consume goods and services in an intelligent and socially responsible way. Further, we have the responsibility to vote and ensure that we get the kind of macro-marketing system we want. What kind do you want? What should you do to ensure that fellow consumer-citizens will vote for your system? Is your system likely to satisfy you as well as another macro-marketing system? You don't have to answer these questions right now—but your answers will affect the future you'll live in and how satisfied you'll be.

Questions and Problems

1. Distinguish clearly between a marketing strategy and a marketing plan. If a firm has a really good strategy, does it need to worry about developing a written plan?
2. Review the Maytag case and then give examples of Maytag's strategy decisions that relate to the strategy planning process shown in Exhibit 18-1.
3. Explain why marketing must be evaluated at two levels. What criteria should be used to evaluate each level of marketing? Defend your answer. Explain why your criteria are better than alternative criteria.
4. Discuss the merits of various economic system objectives. Is the objective of the American economic system sensible? Could it achieve more consumer satisfaction if sociologists or public officials determined how to satisfy the needs of lower-income or less-educated consumers? If so, what education or income level should be required before an individual is granted free choice?
5. Should the objective of our economy be maximum efficiency? If your answer is yes, efficiency in what? If not, what should the objective be?
6. Discuss the conflict of interests among production, finance, accounting, and marketing executives. How does this conflict affect the operation of an individual firm? The economic system? Why does this conflict exist?
7. Why does adoption of the marketing concept encourage a firm to operate more efficiently? Be specific about the impact of the marketing concept on the various departments of a firm.
8. In the short run, competition sometimes leads to inefficiency in the operation of our economic system. Many people argue for monopoly in order to eliminate this inefficiency. Discuss this solution.
9. How would officially granted monopolies affect the operation of our economic system? Consider the effect on allocation of resources, the level of income and employment, and the distribution of income. Is the effect any different if a firm obtains a monopoly by winning out in a competitive market?
10. Comment on the following statement: "Ultimately, the high cost of marketing is due only to consumers."
11. How far should the marketing concept go? How should we decide this issue?
12. Should marketing managers, or business managers in general, refrain from producing profitable products that some target customers want but that may not be in their long-run interest? Should firms be expected to produce "good" but less profitable products? What if such products break even? What if they are unprofitable but the company makes other profitable products—so on balance it still makes some profit? What criteria are you using for each of your answers?
13. Should a marketing manager or a business refuse to produce an "energy-gobbling" appliance that some consumers are demanding? Should a firm install an expensive safety device that will increase costs but that customers don't want? Are the same principles involved in both these questions? Explain.
14. Discuss how one or more of the trends or changes shown in Exhibit 18-4 is affecting marketing strategy planning for a specific firm that serves the market where you live.
15. Discuss how slower economic growth or no economic growth would affect your college community—in particular, its marketing institutions.

Suggested Cases

16. Enviro Pure Water, Inc.
24. PCT, Inc.
25. Metal Works, Inc.
26. DeLuxe Foods, Ltd.
27. Expert Nursing Services, Inc. (ENS)
28. Lever, Ltd.
29. Huntoon & Balbiera P.C.

Economics Fundamentals

When You Finish This Appendix, You Should

1. Understand the "law of diminishing demand."

2. Understand demand and supply curves and how they set the size of a market and its price level.

3. Know about elasticity of demand and supply.

4. Know why demand elasticity can be affected by availability of substitutes.

5. Know the different kinds of competitive situations and understand why they are important to marketing managers.

6. Recognize the important new terms (shown in red).

A good marketing manager should be an expert on markets and the nature of competition in markets. The economist's traditional analysis of demand and supply is a useful tool for analyzing markets. In particular, you should master the concepts of a demand curve and demand elasticity. A firm's demand curve shows how the target customers view the firm's Product—really its whole marketing mix. And the interaction of demand and supply curves helps set the size of a market and the market price. The interaction of supply and demand also determines the nature of the competitive environment, which has an important effect on strategy planning. These ideas are discussed more fully in the following sections.

Products and Markets as Seen by Customers and Potential Customers

Economists provide useful insights

How potential customers (not the firm) see a firm's product (marketing mix) affects how much they are willing to pay for it, where it should be made available, and how eager they are for it—if they want it at all. In other words, their view has a very direct bearing on marketing strategy planning.

Economists have been concerned with market behavior for years. Their analytical tools can be quite helpful in summarizing how customers view products and how markets behave.

Economists see individual customers choosing among alternatives

Economics is sometimes called the dismal science—because it says that most customers have a limited income and simply cannot buy everything they want. They must balance their needs and the prices of various products.

Economists usually assume that customers have a fairly definite set of preferences and that they evaluate alternatives in terms of whether the alternatives will make them feel better (or worse) or in some way improve (or change) their situation.

But what exactly is the nature of a customer's desire for a particular product?

Usually economists answer this question in terms of the extra utility the customer can obtain by buying more of a particular product—or how much utility would be lost if the customer had less of the product. It is easier to understand the idea of utility if we look at what happens when the price of one of the customer's usual purchases changes.

The law of diminishing demand

Suppose that consumers buy potatoes in 10-pound bags at the same time they buy other foods such as bread and rice. If the consumers are mainly interested in buying a certain amount of food and the price of the potatoes drops, it seems reasonable to expect that they will switch some of their food money to potatoes and away from some other foods. But if the price of potatoes rises, you expect our consumers to buy fewer potatoes and more of other foods.

The general relationship between price and quantity demanded illustrated by this food example is called the **law of diminishing demand**—which says that if the price of a product is raised, a smaller quantity will be demanded and if the price of a product is lowered, a greater quantity will be demanded. Experience supports this relationship between prices and total demand in a market, especially for broad product categories or commodities such as potatoes.

The relationship between price and quantity demanded in a market is what economists call a "demand schedule." An example is shown in Exhibit A-1. For each row in the table, Column 2 shows the quantity consumers will want (demand) if they have to pay the price given in Column 1. The third column shows that the total revenue (sales) in the potato market is equal to the quantity demanded at a given price times that price. Note that as prices drop, the total *unit* quantity increases, yet the total *revenue* decreases. Fill in the blank lines in the third column

Exhibit A-1
Demand Schedule for Potatoes (10-pound bags)

Point	(1) Price of Potatoes per Bag (P)	(2) Quantity Demanded (bags per month) (Q)	(3) Total Revenue per Month (P × Q = TR)
A	$1.60	8,000,000	$12,800,000
B	1.30	9,000,000	________
C	1.00	11,000,000	11,000,000
D	0.70	14,000,000	________
E	0.40	19,000,000	________

and observe the behavior of total revenue—an important number for the marketing manager. We will explain what you should have noticed, and why, a little later.

The demand curve—usually down-sloping

If your only interest is seeing at which price the company will earn the greatest total revenue, the demand schedule may be adequate. But a demand curve shows more. A **demand curve** is a graph of the relationship between price and quantity demanded in a market—assuming that all other things stay the same. Exhibit A-2 shows the demand curve for potatoes—really just a plotting of the demand schedule in Exhibit A-1. It shows how many potatoes potential customers will demand at various possible prices. This is a "down-sloping demand curve."

Most demand curves are down-sloping. This just means that if prices are decreased, the quantity customers demand will increase.

Demand curves always show the price on the vertical axis and the quantity demanded on the horizontal axis. In Exhibit A-2, we have shown the price in dollars. For consistency, we will use dollars in other examples. However, keep in mind that these same ideas hold regardless of what money unit (dollars, yen, francs, pounds, etc.) is used to represent price. Even at this early point, you should keep in mind that markets are not necessarily limited by national boundaries—or by one type of money.

Note that the demand curve only shows how customers will react to various possible prices. In a market, we see only one price at a time, not all of these prices. The curve, however, shows what quantities will be demanded—depending on what price is set.

You probably think that most businesspeople would like to set a price that would result in a large sales revenue. Before discussing this, however, we should consider the demand schedule and curve for another product to get a more complete picture of demand-curve analysis.

Exhibit A-2
Demand Curve for Potatoes (10-pound bags)

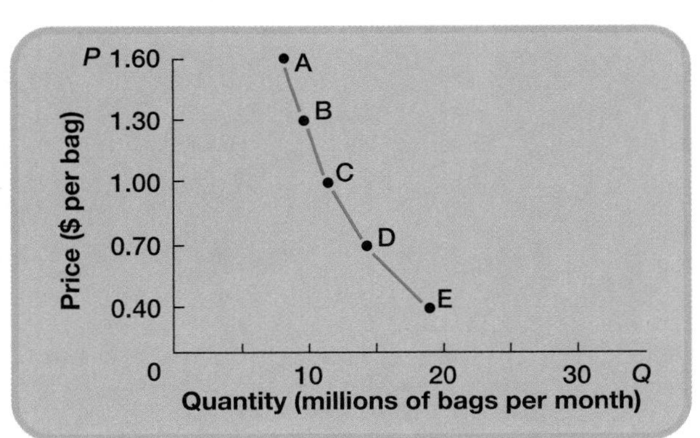

Exhibit A-3
Demand Schedule for 1-Cubic-Foot Microwave Ovens

Point	(1) Price per Microwave Oven (P)	(2) Quantity Demanded per Year (Q)	(3) Total Revenue (TR) per Year (P × Q = TR)
A	$300	20,000	$ 6,000,000
B	250	70,000	15,500,000
C	200	130,000	26,000,000
D	150	210,000	31,500,000
E	100	310,000	31,000,000

Microwave oven demand curve looks different

A different demand schedule is the one for standard 1-cubic-foot microwave ovens shown in Exhibit A-3. Column 3 shows the total revenue that will be obtained at various possible prices and quantities. Again, as the price goes down, the quantity demanded goes up. But here, unlike the potato example, total revenue increases as prices go down—at least until the price drops to $150.

Every market has a demand curve—for some time period

These general demand relationships are typical for all products. But each product has its own demand schedule and curve in each potential market—no matter how small the market. In other words, a particular demand curve has meaning only for a particular market. We can think of demand curves for individuals, groups of individuals who form a target market, regions, and even countries. And the time period covered really should be specified—although this is often neglected because we usually think of monthly or yearly periods.

The difference between elastic and inelastic

The demand curve for microwave ovens (see Exhibit A-4) is down-sloping—but note that it is flatter than the curve for potatoes. It is important to understand what this flatness means.

We will consider the flatness in terms of total revenue—since this is what interests business managers.*

When you filled in the total revenue column for potatoes, you should have noticed that total revenue drops continually if the price is reduced. This looks undesirable

Exhibit A-4
Demand Curve for 1-Cubic-Foot Microwave Ovens

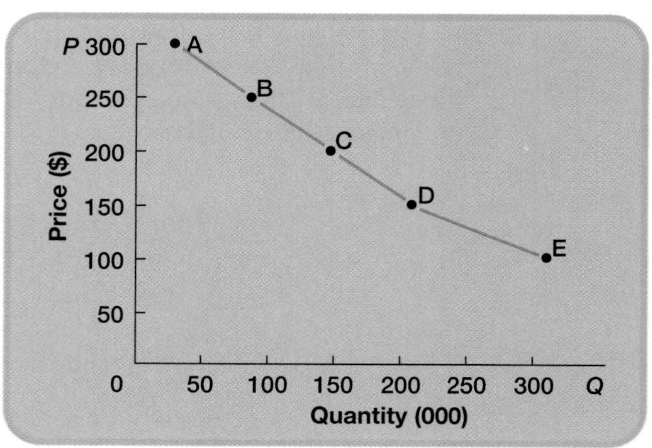

*Strictly speaking, two curves should not be compared for flatness if the graph scales are different, but for our purposes now we will do so to illustrate the idea of "elasticity of demand." Actually, it would be more accurate to compare two curves for one product—on the same graph. Then both the shape of the demand curve and its position on the graph would be important.

for sellers and illustrates inelastic demand. **Inelastic demand** means that although the quantity demanded increases if the price is decreased, the quantity demanded will not "stretch" enough—that is, it is not elastic enough—to avoid a decrease in total revenue.

In contrast, **elastic demand** means that if prices are dropped, the quantity demanded will stretch (increase) enough to increase total revenue. The upper part of the microwave oven demand curve is an example of elastic demand.

But note that if the microwave oven price is dropped from $150 to $100, total revenue will decrease. We can say, therefore, that between $150 and $100, demand is inelastic—that is, total revenue will decrease if price is lowered from $150 to $100.

Thus, elasticity can be defined in terms of changes in total revenue. *If total revenue will increase if price is lowered, then demand is elastic. If total revenue will decrease if price is lowered, then demand is inelastic.* (Note: A special case known as "unitary elasticity of demand" occurs if total revenue stays the same when prices change.)

Total revenue may increase if price is raised

A point often missed in discussions of demand is what happens when prices are raised instead of lowered. With elastic demand, total revenue will *decrease* if the price is *raised*. With inelastic demand, however, total revenue will *increase* if the price is *raised*.

The possibility of raising price and increasing dollar sales (total revenue) at the same time is attractive to managers. This only occurs if the demand curve is inelastic. Here total revenue will increase if price is raised, but total costs probably will not increase—and may actually go down—with smaller quantities. Keep in mind that profit is equal to total revenue minus total costs. So when demand is inelastic, profit will increase as price is increased!

The ways total revenue changes as prices are raised are shown in Exhibit A-5. Here total revenue is the rectangular area formed by a price and its related quantity. The larger the rectangular area, the greater the total revenue.

P_1 is the original price here, and the total potential revenue with this original price is shown by the area with blue shading. The area with red shading shows the total revenue with the new price, P_2. There is some overlap in the total revenue areas, so the important areas are those with only one color. Note that in

Exhibit A-5
Changes in Total Revenue as Prices Increase

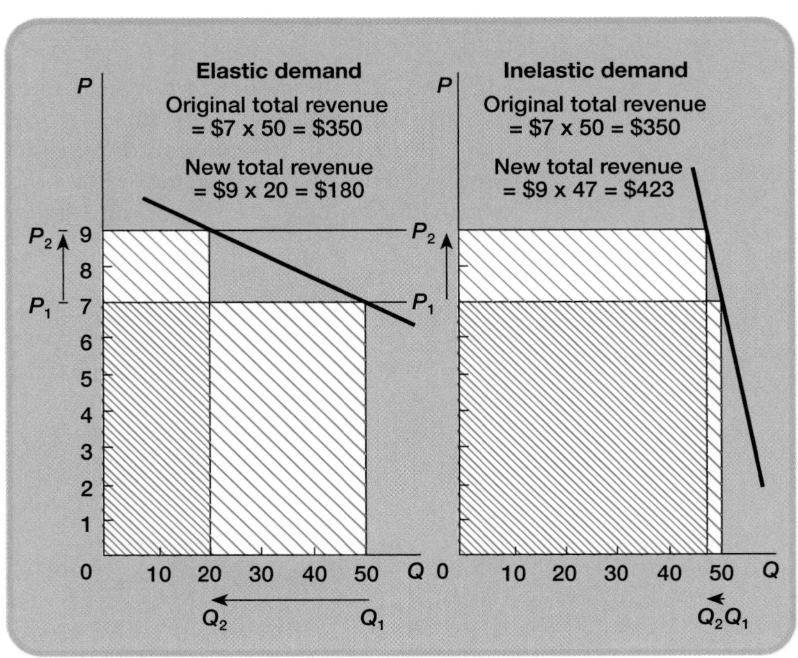

the left-hand figure—where demand is elastic—the revenue added (the red-only area) when the price is increased is less than the revenue lost (the blue-only area). Now let's contrast this to the right-hand figure, when demand is inelastic. Only a small blue revenue area is given up for a much larger (red) one when price is raised.

An entire curve is not elastic or inelastic

It is important to see that it is *wrong to refer to a whole demand curve as elastic or inelastic*. Rather, elasticity for a particular demand curve refers to the change in total revenue between two points on the curve, not along the whole curve. You saw the change from elastic to inelastic in the microwave oven example. Generally, however, nearby points are either elastic or inelastic—so it is common to refer to a whole curve by the degree of elasticity in the price range that normally is of interest—the *relevant range*.

Demand elasticities affected by availability of substitutes and urgency of need

At first, it may be difficult to see why one product has an elastic demand and another an inelastic demand. Many factors affect elasticity—such as the availability of substitutes, the importance of the item in the customer's budget, and the urgency of the customer's need and its relation to other needs. By looking more closely at one of these factors—the availability of substitutes—you will better understand why demand elasticities vary.

Substitutes are products that offer the buyer a choice. For example, many consumers see grapefruit as a substitute for oranges and hot dogs as a substitute for hamburgers. The greater the number of "good" substitutes available, the greater will be the elasticity of demand. From the consumer's perspective, products are "good" substitutes if they are very similar (homogeneous). If consumers see products as extremely different, or heterogeneous, then a particular need cannot easily be satisfied by substitutes. And the demand for the most satisfactory product may be quite inelastic.

As an example, if the price of hamburger is lowered (and other prices stay the same), the quantity demanded will increase a lot—as will total revenue. The reason is that not only will regular hamburger users buy more hamburger, but some consumers who formerly bought hot dogs or steaks probably will buy hamburger too. But if the price of hamburger is raised, the quantity demanded will decrease—perhaps sharply. Still consumers will buy some hamburger—depending on how much the price has risen, their individual tastes, and what their guests expect (see Exhibit A-6).

In contrast to a product with many "substitutes"—such as hamburger—consider a product with few or no substitutes. Its demand curve will tend to be inelastic. Motor oil is a good example. Motor oil is needed to keep cars running. Yet no one person or family uses great quantities of motor oil. So it is not likely that the quantity of motor oil purchased will change much as long as price changes are *within a*

Exhibit A-6
Demand Curve for Hamburger (a product with many substitutes)

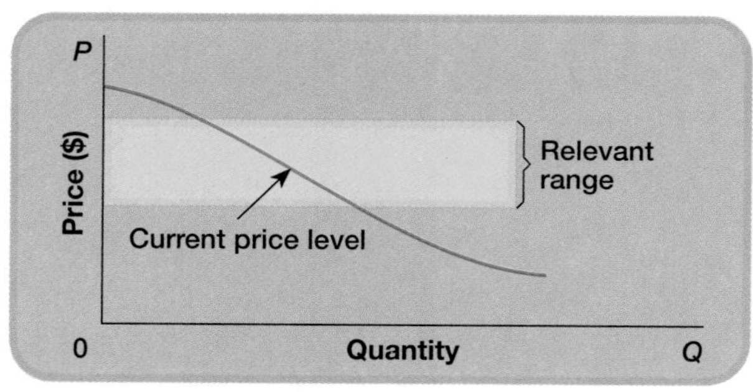

Exhibit A-7
Demand Curve for Motor Oil (a product with few substitutes)

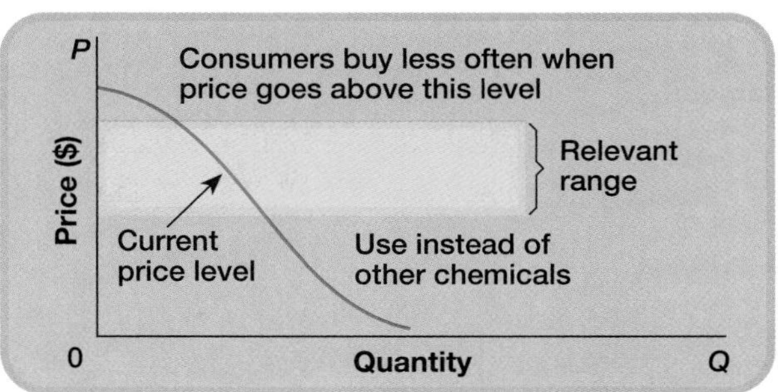

reasonable range. Of course, if the price is raised to a staggering figure, many people will buy less oil (change their oil less frequently). If the price is dropped to an extremely low level, manufacturers may buy more—say, as a lower-cost substitute for other chemicals typically used in making plastic (Exhibit A-7). But these extremes are outside the relevant range.

Demand curves are introduced here because the degree of elasticity of demand shows how potential customers feel about a product—and especially whether they see substitutes for the product. But to get a better understanding of markets, we must extend this economic analysis.

Markets as Seen by Suppliers

Customers may want some product—but if suppliers are not willing to supply it, then there is no market. So we'll study the economist's analysis of supply. And then we'll bring supply and demand together for a more complete understanding of markets.

Economists often use the kind of analysis we are discussing here to explain pricing in the marketplace. But that is not our intention. Here we are interested in how and why markets work and the interaction of customers and potential suppliers. Later in this appendix we will review how competition affects prices, but how individual firms set prices, or should set prices, is discussed fully in Chapters 16 and 17.

Supply curves reflect supplier thinking

Generally speaking, suppliers' costs affect the quantity of products they are willing to offer in a market during any period. In other words, their costs affect their supply schedules and supply curves. While a demand curve shows the quantity of products customers will be willing to buy at various prices, a **supply curve** shows the quantity of products that will be supplied at various possible prices. Eventually, only one quantity will be offered and purchased. So a supply curve is really a hypothetical (what-if) description of what will be offered at various prices. It is, however, a very important curve. Together with a demand curve, it summarizes the attitudes and probable behavior of buyers and sellers about a particular product in a particular market—that is, in a product-market.

Some supply curves are vertical

We usually assume that supply curves tend to slope upward—that is, suppliers will be willing to offer greater quantities at higher prices. If a product's market price is very high, it seems only reasonable that producers will be anxious to produce more of the product and even put workers on overtime or perhaps hire more workers to

Exhibit A-8
Supply Schedule for Potatoes (10-pound bags)

Point	Possible Market Price per 10-lb. Bag	Number of Bags Sellers Will Supply per Month at Each Possible Market Price
A	$1.60	17,000,000
B	1.30	14,000,000
C	1.00	11,000,000
D	0.70	8,000,000
E	0.40	3,000,000

Note: This supply curve is for a month to emphasize that farmers might have some control over when they deliver their potatoes. There would be a different curve for each month.

increase the quantity they can offer. Going further, it seems likely that producers of other products will switch their resources (farms, factories, labor, or retail facilities) to the product that is in great demand.

On the other hand, if consumers are only willing to pay a very low price for a particular product, it's reasonable to expect that producers will switch to other products—thus reducing supply. A supply schedule (Exhibit A-8) and a supply curve (Exhibit A-9) for potatoes illustrate these ideas. This supply curve shows how many potatoes would be produced and offered for sale at each possible market price in a given month.

In the very short run (say, over a few hours, a day, or a week), a supplier may not be able to change the supply at all. In this situation, we would see a vertical supply curve. This situation is often relevant in the market for fresh produce. Fresh strawberries, for example, continue to ripen, and a supplier wants to sell them quickly—preferably at a higher price—but in any case, they must be sold.

If the product is a service, it may not be easy to expand the supply in the short run. Additional barbers or medical doctors are not quickly trained and licensed, and they only have so much time to give each day. Further, the prospect of much higher prices in the near future cannot easily expand the supply of many services. For example, a hit play or an "in" restaurant or nightclub is limited in the amount of "product" it can offer at a particular time.

Elasticity of supply

The term *elasticity* also is used to describe supply curves. An extremely steep or almost vertical supply curve, often found in the short run, is called **inelastic supply** because the quantity supplied does not stretch much (if at all) if the price is raised. A flatter curve is called **elastic supply** because the quantity supplied does stretch

Exhibit A-9
Supply Curve for Potatoes (10-pound bags)

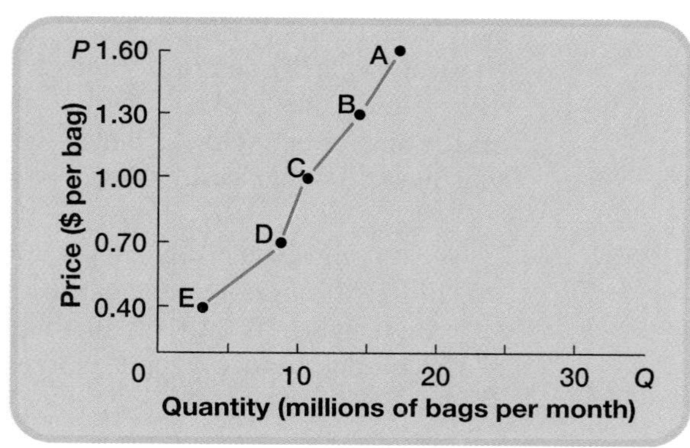

more if the price is raised. A slightly up-sloping supply curve is typical in longer-run market situations. Given more time, suppliers have a chance to adjust their offerings, and competitors may enter or leave the market.

Demand and Supply Interact to Determine the Size of the Market and Price Level

We have treated market demand and supply forces separately. Now we must bring them together to show their interaction. The *intersection* of these two forces determines the size of the market and the market price—at which point (price and quantity) the market is said to be in *equilibrium*.

The intersection of demand and supply is shown for the potato data discussed above. In Exhibit A-10, the demand curve for potatoes is now graphed against the supply curve in Exhibit A-9.

In this potato market, demand is inelastic—the total revenue of all the potato producers would be greater at higher prices. But the market price is at the **equilibrium point**—where the quantity and the price sellers are willing to offer are equal to the quantity and price that buyers are willing to accept. The $1.00 equilibrium price for potatoes yields a smaller *total revenue* to potato producers than a higher price would. This lower equilibrium price comes about because the many producers are willing to supply enough potatoes at the lower price. *Demand is not the only determiner of price level. Cost also must be considered—via the supply curve.*

Some consumers get a surplus

Presumably, a sale takes place only if both buyer and seller feel they will be better off after the sale. But sometimes the price a consumer pays in a sales transaction is less than what he or she would be willing to pay.

The reason for this is that demand curves are typically down-sloping, and some of the demand curve is above the equilibrium price. This is simply another way of showing that some customers would have been willing to pay more than the equilibrium price—if they had to. In effect, some of them are getting a bargain by being able to buy at the equilibrium price. Economists have traditionally called these bargains the **consumer surplus**—that is, the difference to consumers between the value of a purchase and the price they pay.

Some business critics assume that consumers do badly in any business transaction. In fact, sales take place only if consumers feel they are at least getting their money's worth. As we can see here, some are willing to pay much more than the market price.

Exhibit A-10
Equilibrium of Supply and Demand for Potatoes (10-pound bags)

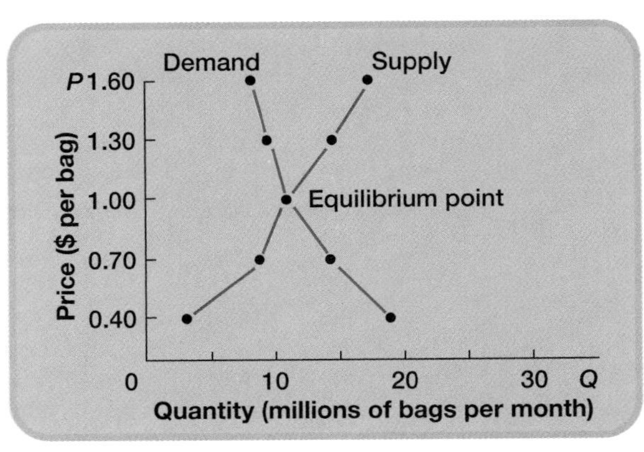

Demand and Supply Help Us Understand the Nature of Competition

The elasticity of demand and supply curves and their interaction help predict the nature of competition a marketing manager is likely to face. For example, an extremely inelastic demand curve means that the manager will have much choice in strategy planning, especially price setting. Apparently customers like the product and see few substitutes. They are willing to pay higher prices before cutting back much on their purchases.

Clearly, the elasticity of a firm's demand curves makes a big difference in strategy planning, but other factors also affect the nature of competition. Among these are the number and size of competitors and the uniqueness of each firm's marketing mix. Understanding these market situations is important because the freedom of a marketing manager, especially control over price, is greatly reduced in some situations.

A marketing manager operates in one of four kinds of market situations. We'll discuss three kinds: pure competition, oligopoly, and monopolistic competition. The fourth kind, monopoly, isn't found very often and is like monopolistic competition. The important dimensions of these situations are shown in Exhibit A-11.

When competition is pure

Many competitors offer about the same thing

Pure competition is a market situation that develops when a market has

1. Homogeneous (similar) products.
2. Many buyers and sellers who have full knowledge of the market.
3. Ease of entry for buyers and sellers; that is, new firms have little difficulty starting in business—and new customers can easily come into the market.

More or less pure competition is found in many agricultural markets. In the potato market, for example, there are thousands of small producers—and they are in pure competition. Let's look more closely at these producers.

Although the potato market as a whole has a down-sloping demand curve, each of the many small producers in the industry is in pure competition, and each of them faces a flat demand curve at the equilibrium price. This is shown in Exhibit A-12.

Exhibit A-11
Some Important Dimensions Regarding Market Situations

	Types of Situations			
Important Dimensions	Pure Competition	Oligopoly	Monopolistic Competition	Monopoly
Uniqueness of each firm's product	None	None	Some	Unique
Number of competitors	Many	Few	Few to many	None
Size of competitors (compared to size of market)	Small	Large	Large to small	None
Elasticity of demand facing firm	Completely elastic	Kinked demand curve (elastic and inelastic)	Either	Either
Elasticity of industry demand	Either	Inelastic	Either	Either
Control of price by firm	None	Some (with care)	Some	Complete

Exhibit A-12 Interaction of Demand and Supply in the Potato Industry and the Resulting Demand Curve Facing Individual Potato Producers

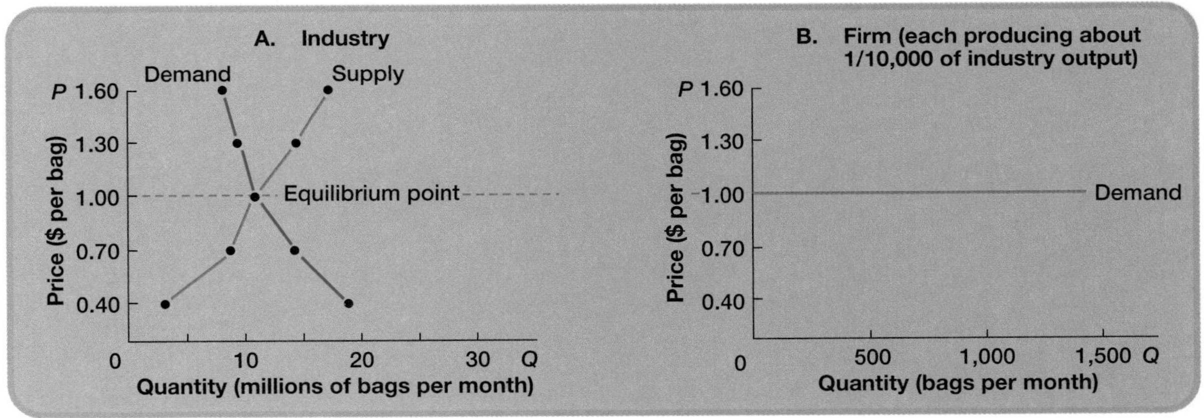

As shown at the right of Exhibit A-12, an individual producer can sell as many bags of potatoes as he chooses at $1—the market equilibrium price. The equilibrium price is determined by the quantity that all producers choose to sell given the demand curve they face.

But a small producer has little effect on overall supply (or on the equilibrium price). If this individual farmer raises 1/10,000th of the quantity offered in the market, for example, you can see that there will be little effect if the farmer goes out of business—or doubles production.

The reason an individual producer's demand curve is flat is that the farmer probably couldn't sell any potatoes above the market price. And there is no point in selling below the market price! So in effect, the individual producer has no control over price.

Markets tend to become more competitive

Not many markets are *purely* competitive. But many are close enough so we can talk about "almost" pure competition situations—those in which the marketing manager has to accept the going price.

Such highly competitive situations aren't limited to agriculture. Wherever *many* competitors sell *homogeneous* products—such as textiles, lumber, coal, printing, and laundry services—the demand curve seen by *each producer* tends to be flat.

Markets tend to become more competitive, moving toward pure competition (except in oligopolies—see below). On the way to pure competition, prices and profits are pushed down until some competitors are forced out of business. Eventually, in long-run equilibrium, the price level is only high enough to keep the survivors in business. No one makes any profit—they just cover costs. It's tough to be a marketing manager in this situation!

When competition is oligopolistic

A few competitors offer similar things

Not all markets move toward pure competition. Some become oligopolies. **Oligopoly** situations are special market situations that develop when a market has

1. Essentially homogeneous products—such as basic industrial chemicals or gasoline.
2. Relatively few sellers—or a few large firms and many smaller ones who follow the lead of the larger ones.
3. Fairly inelastic industry demand curves.

The demand curve facing each firm is unusual in an oligopoly situation. Although the industry demand curve is inelastic throughout the relevant range, the demand

Exhibit A-13
Oligopoly—Kinked Demand Curve—Situation

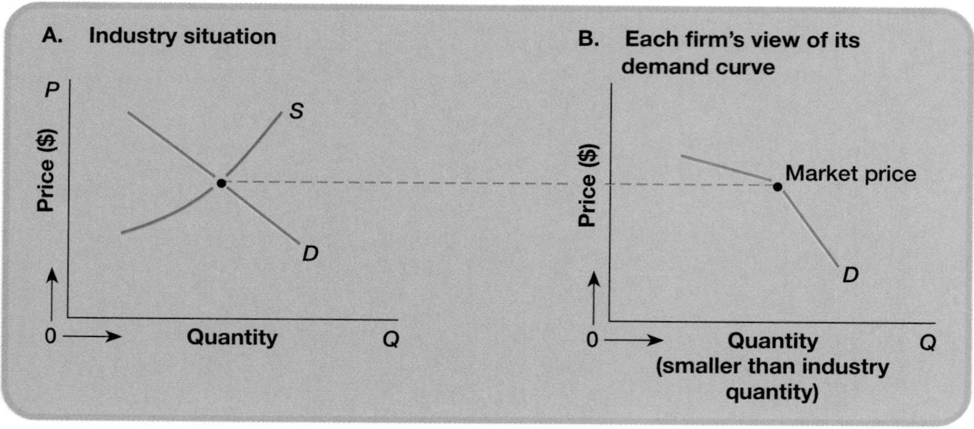

curve facing each competitor looks "kinked." See Exhibit A-13. The current market price is at the kink.

There is a market price because the competing firms watch each other carefully—and they know it's wise to be at the kink. Each firm must expect that raising its own price above the market price will cause a big loss in sales. Few, if any, competitors will follow the price increase. So the firm's demand curve is relatively flat above the market price. If the firm lowers its price, it must expect competitors to follow. Given inelastic industry demand, the firm's own demand curve is inelastic at lower prices—assuming it keeps its share of this market at lower prices. Since lowering prices along such a curve will drop total revenue, the firm should leave its price at the kink—the market price.

Actually, however, there are price fluctuations in oligopolistic markets. Sometimes this is caused by firms that don't understand the market situation and cut their prices to get business. In other cases, big increases in demand or supply change the basic nature of the situation and lead to price cutting. Price cuts can be drastic—such as Du Pont's price cut of 25 percent for Dacron. This happened when Du Pont decided that industry production capacity already exceeded demand, and more plants were due to start production.

It's important to keep in mind that oligopoly situations don't just apply to whole industries and national markets. Competitors who are focusing on the same local target market often face oligopoly situations. A suburban community might have several gas stations—all of which provide essentially the same product. In this case, the "industry" consists of the gas stations competing with each other in the local product-market.

As in pure competition, oligopolists face a long-run trend toward an equilibrium level—with profits driven toward zero. This may not happen immediately—and a marketing manager may try to delay price competition by relying more on other elements in the marketing mix.

When competition is monopolistic

A price must be set

You can see why marketing managers want to avoid pure competition or oligopoly situations. They prefer a market in which they have more control. **Monopolistic competition** is a market situation that develops when a market has

1. Different (heterogeneous) products—in the eyes of some customers.
2. Sellers who feel they do have some competition in this market.

The word *monopolistic* means that each firm is trying to get control in its own little market. But the word *competition* means that there are still substitutes. The vigorous competition of a purely competitive market is reduced. Each firm has its own down-sloping demand curve. But the shape of the curve depends on the similarity of competitors' products and marketing mixes. Each monopolistic competitor has freedom—but not complete freedom—in its own market.

Judging elasticity will help set the price

Since a firm in monopolistic competition has its own down-sloping demand curve, it must make a decision about price level as part of its marketing strategy planning. Here, estimating the elasticity of the firm's own demand curve is helpful. If it is highly inelastic, the firm may decide to raise prices to increase total revenue. But if demand is highly elastic, this may mean many competitors with acceptable substitutes. Then the price may have to be set near that of the competition. And the marketing manager probably should try to develop a better marketing mix.

Conclusion

The economist's traditional demand and supply analysis provides a useful tool for analyzing the nature of demand and competition. It is especially important that you master the concepts of a demand curve and demand elasticity. How demand and supply interact helps determine the size of a market and its price level. The interaction of supply and demand also helps explain the nature of competition in different market situations. We discuss three competitive situations: pure competition, oligopoly, and monopolistic competition. The fourth kind, monopoly, isn't found very often and is like monopolistic competition.

The nature of supply and demand—and competition—is very important in marketing strategy planning. We discuss these topics more fully in Chapters 3 and 4 and then build on them throughout the text. This appendix provides a good foundation on these topics.

Questions and Problems

1. Explain in your own words how economists look at markets and arrive at the "law of diminishing demand."
2. Explain what a demand curve is and why it is usually down-sloping. Then give an example of a product for which the demand curve might not be down-sloping over some possible price ranges. Explain the reason for your choice.
3. What is the length of life of the typical demand curve? Illustrate your answer.
4. If the general market demand for men's shoes is fairly elastic, how does the demand for men's dress shoes compare to it? How does the demand curve for women's shoes compare to the demand curve for men's shoes?
5. If the demand for perfume is inelastic above and below the present price, should the price be raised? Why or why not?
6. If the demand for shrimp is highly elastic below the present price, should the price be lowered?
7. Discuss what factors lead to inelastic demand and supply curves. Are they likely to be found together in the same situation?
8. Why would a marketing manager prefer to sell a product that has no close substitutes? Are high profits almost guaranteed?
9. If a manufacturer's well-known product is sold at the same price by many retailers in the same community, is this an example of pure competition? When a community has many small grocery stores, are they in pure competition? What characteristics are needed to have a purely competitive market?
10. List three products that are sold in purely competitive markets and three that are sold in monopolistically competitive markets. Do any of these products have anything in common? Can any generalizations be made about competitive situations and marketing mix planning?
11. Cite a local example of an oligopoly—explaining why it is an oligopoly.

Appendix B

Marketing Arithmetic

When You Finish This Appendix, You Should

1. Understand the components of an operating statement (profit and loss statement).

2. Know how to compute the stockturn rate.

3. Understand how operating ratios can help analyze a business.

4. Understand how to calculate markups and markdowns.

5. Understand how to calculate return on investment (ROI) and return on assets (ROA).

6. Understand the basic forecasting approaches and why they are used.

7. Understand the important new terms (shown in red).

Marketing students must become familiar with the essentials of the language of business. Businesspeople commonly use accounting terms when talking about costs, prices, and profit. And using accounting data is a practical tool in analyzing marketing problems.

The Operating Statement

An **operating statement** is a simple summary of the financial results of a company's operations over a specified period of time. Some beginning students may feel that the operating statement is complex, but as we'll soon see, this really isn't true. *The main purpose of the operating statement is determining the net profit figure and presenting data to support that figure.* This is why the operating statement is often referred to as the *profit and loss statement.*

Exhibit B-1 shows an operating statement for a wholesale or retail business. The statement is complete and detailed so you will see the framework throughout the

Exhibit B-1 An Operating Statement (profit and loss statement)

Smith Company
Operating Statement
For the Year Ended December 31, 200X

Gross sales			$540,000
Less: Returns and allowances			40,000
Net sales			$500,000
Cost of sales:			
Beginning inventory at cost		$ 80,000	
Purchases at billed cost	$310,000		
Less: Purchase discounts	40,000		
Purchases at net cost	270,000		
Plus: freight-in	20,000		
Net cost of delivered purchases		290,000	
Cost of goods available for sale		370,000	
Less: Ending inventory at cost		70,000	
Cost of sales			300,000
Gross margin (gross profit)			200,000
Expenses:			
Selling expenses:			
Sales salaries	60,000		
Advertising expense	20,000		
Website updates	10,000		
Delivery expense	10,000		
Total selling expense		100,000	
Administrative expense:			
Office salaries	30,000		
Office supplies	10,000		
Miscellaneous administrative expense	5,000		
Total administrative expense		45,000	
General expense:			
Rent expense	10,000		
Miscellaneous general expenses	5,000		
Total general expense		15,000	
Total expenses			160,000
Net profit from operation			$ 40,000

Detailed Analysis of Sections of the Operating Statement

Cost of sales for a wholesale or retail company

The cost of sales section includes details that are used to find the cost of sales ($300,000 in our example).

In Exhibit B-1, you can see that beginning and ending inventory, purchases, purchase discounts, and freight-in are all necessary to calculate costs of sales. If we pull the cost of sales section from the operating statement, it looks like this:

Cost of sales:			
Beginning inventory at cost		$ 80,000	
Purchases at billed cost	$310,000		
Less: Purchase discounts	40,000		
Purchases at net cost	270,000		
Plus: Freight-in	20,000		
Net cost of delivered purchases		290,000	
Cost of goods available for sale		370,000	
Less: Ending inventory at cost		70,000	
Cost of sales			$300,000

Cost of sales is the cost value of what is *sold*, not the cost of goods on hand at any given time.

Inventory figures merely show the cost of goods on hand at the beginning and end of the period the statement covers. These figures may be obtained by physically counting goods on hand on these dates or estimated from perpetual inventory records that show the inventory balance at any given time. The methods used to determine the inventory should be as accurate as possible because these figures affect the cost of sales during the period and net profit.

The net cost of delivered purchases must include freight charges and purchase discounts received since these items affect the money actually spent to buy goods and bring them to the place of business. A **purchase discount** is a reduction of the original invoice amount for some business reason. For example, a cash discount may be given for prompt payment of the amount due. We subtract the total of such discounts from the original invoice cost of purchases to get the *net* cost of purchases. To this figure we add the freight charges for bringing the goods to the place of business. This gives the net cost of *delivered* purchases. When we add the net cost of delivered purchases to the beginning inventory at cost, we have the total cost of goods available for sale during the period. If we now subtract the ending inventory at cost from the cost of the goods available for sale, we get the cost of sales.

One important point should be noted about cost of sales. The way the value of inventory is calculated varies from one company to another—and it can cause big differences in the cost of sales and the operating statement. (See any basic accounting textbook for how the various inventory valuation methods work.)

Cost of sales for a manufacturing company

Exhibit B-1 shows the way the manager of a wholesale or retail business arrives at his cost of sales. Such a business *purchases* finished products and resells them. In a manufacturing company, the purchases section of this operating statement is replaced by a section called cost of production. This section includes purchases of raw materials and parts, direct and indirect labor costs, and factory overhead charges

Exhibit B-2
Cost of Sales Section of an Operating Statement for a Manufacturing Firm

Cost of sales:			
Finished products inventory (beginning)		$ 20,000	
Cost of production (Schedule 1)		100,000	
Total cost of finished products available for sale		120,000	
Less: Finished products inventory (ending) . .		30,000	
Cost of sales			$ 90,000
Schedule 1, Schedule of cost of production			
Beginning work in process inventory			15,000
Raw materials:			
Beginning raw materials inventory		10,000	
Net cost of delivered purchases		80,000	
Total cost of materials available for use		90,000	
Less: Ending raw materials inventory		15,000	
Cost of materials placed in production		75,000	
Direct labor		20,000	
Manufacturing expenses:			
Indirect labor	$4,000		
Maintenance and repairs	3,000		
Factory supplies	1,000		
Heat, light, and power	2,000		
Total manufacturing expenses		10,000	
Total manufacturing costs			105,000
Total work in process during period			120,000
Less: Ending work in process inventory			20,000
Cost of production			$100,000

(such as heat, light, and power) that are necessary to produce finished products. The cost of production is added to the beginning finished products inventory to arrive at the cost of products available for sale. Often, a separate cost of production statement is prepared, and only the total cost of production is shown in the operating statement. See Exhibit B-2 for an illustration of the cost of sales section of an operating statement for a manufacturing company.

Expenses

Expenses go below the gross margin. They usually include the costs of selling and the costs of administering the business. They do not include the cost of sales—either purchased or produced.

There is no right method for classifying the expense accounts or arranging them on the operating statement. They can just as easily be arranged alphabetically or according to amount, with the largest placed at the top and so on down the line. In a business of any size, though, it is clearer to group the expenses in some way and use subtotals by groups for analysis and control purposes. This was done in Exhibit B-1.

Summary on operating statements

The statement presented in Exhibit B-1 contains all the major categories in an operating statement—together with a normal amount of supporting detail. Further detail can be added to the statement under any of the major categories without changing the nature of the statement. The amount of detail normally is determined by how the statement will be used. A stockholder may be given a sketchy operating statement—while the one prepared for internal company use may have a lot of detail.

Computing the Stockturn Rate

A detailed operating statement can provide the data needed to compute the **stockturn rate**—a measure of the number of times the average inventory is sold during a year. Note that the stockturn rate is related to the *turnover during a year,* not the length of time covered by a particular operating statement.

The stockturn rate is a very important measure because it shows how rapidly the firm's inventory is moving. Some businesses typically have slower turnover than others. But a drop in turnover in a particular business can be very alarming. It may mean that the firm's assortment of products is no longer as attractive as it was. Also, it may mean that the firm will need more working capital to handle the same volume of sales. Most businesses pay a lot of attention to the stockturn rate—trying to get faster turnover (and lower inventory costs).

Three methods—all basically similar—can be used to compute the stockturn rate. Which method is used depends on the data available. These three methods, which usually give approximately the same results, are shown below.*

$$(1) \qquad \frac{\text{Cost of sales}}{\text{Average inventory at cost}}$$

$$(2) \qquad \frac{\text{Net sales}}{\text{Average inventory at selling price}}$$

$$(3) \qquad \frac{\text{Sales in units}}{\text{Average inventory in units}}$$

Computing the stockturn rate will be illustrated only for Formula 1, since all are similar. The only difference is that the cost figures used in Formula 1 are changed to a selling price or numerical count basis in Formulas 2 and 3. Note: Regardless of the method used, you must have both the numerator and denominator of the formula in the same terms.

If the inventory level varies a lot during the year, you may need detailed information about the inventory level at different times to compute the average inventory. If it stays at about the same level during the year, however, it's easy to get an estimate. For example, using Formula 1, the average inventory at cost is computed by adding the beginning and ending inventories at cost and dividing by 2. This average inventory figure is then divided into the cost of sales (in cost terms) to get the stockturn rate.

For example, suppose that the cost of sales for one year was $1,000,000. Beginning inventory was $250,000 and ending inventory $150,000. Adding the two inventory figures and dividing by 2, we get an average inventory of $200,000. We next divide the cost of sales by the average inventory ($1,000,000 ÷ $200,000) and get a stockturn rate of 5. The stockturn rate is covered further in Chapter 17.

Operating Ratios Help Analyze the Business

Many businesspeople use the operating statement to calculate **operating ratios**—the ratio of items on the operating statement to net sales—and to compare these ratios from one time period to another. They can also compare their own operating

*Differences occur because of varied markups and nonhomogeneous product assortments. In an assortment of tires, for example, those with low markups might have sold much better than those with high markups. But with Formula 3, all tires would be treated equally.

ratios with those of competitors. Such competitive data is often available through trade associations. Each firm may report its results to a trade association, which then distributes summary results to its members. These ratios help managers control their operations. If some expense ratios are rising, for example, those particular costs are singled out for special attention.

Operating ratios are computed by dividing net sales into the various operating statement items that appear below the net sales level in the operating statement. The net sales is used as the denominator in the operating ratio because it shows the sales the firm actually won.

We can see the relation of operating ratios to the operating statement if we think of there being another column to the right of the dollar figures in an operating statement. This column contains percentage figures—using net sales as 100 percent. This approach can be seen below.

Gross sales	$540,000	
Less: Returns and allowances	40,000	
Net sales	500,000	100%
Less: Cost of sales	300,000	60
Gross margin	200,000	40
Less: Total Expenses	160,000	32
Net profit	$ 40,000	8%

The 40 percent ratio of gross margin to net sales in the above example shows that 40 percent of the net sales dollar is available to cover sales expenses and administering the business and provide a profit. Note that the ratio of expenses to sales added to the ratio of profit to sales equals the 40 percent gross margin ratio. The net profit ratio of 8 percent shows that 8 percent of the net sales dollar is left for profit.

The value of percentage ratios should be obvious. The percentages are easily figured and much easier to compare than large dollar figures.

Note that because these operating statement categories are interrelated, only a few pieces of information are needed to figure the others. In this case, for example, knowing the gross margin percent and net profit percent makes it possible to figure the expenses and cost of sales percentages. Further, knowing just one dollar amount and the percentages lets you figure all the other dollar amounts.

Markups

A **markup** is the dollar amount added to the cost of sales to get the selling price. The markup usually is similar to the firm's gross margin because the markup amount added onto the unit cost of a product by a retailer or wholesaler is expected to cover the selling and administrative expenses and to provide a profit.

The markup approach to pricing is discussed in Chapter 17, so it will not be discussed at length here. But a simple example illustrates the idea. If a retailer buys an article that costs $1 when delivered to his store, he must sell it for more than this cost if he hopes to make a profit. So he might add 50 cents onto the cost of the article to cover his selling and other costs and, hopefully, to provide a profit. The 50 cents is the markup.

The 50 cents is also the gross margin or gross profit from that item *if* it is sold. But note that it is *not* the net profit. Selling expenses may amount to 35 cents,

45 cents, or even 55 cents. In other words, there is no guarantee the markup will cover costs. Further, there is no guarantee customers will buy at the marked-up price. This may require markdowns, which are discussed later in this appendix.

Markup conversions

Often it is convenient to use markups as percentages rather than focusing on the actual dollar amounts. But markups can be figured as a percent of cost or selling price. To have some agreement, *markup (percent)* will mean percentage of selling price unless stated otherwise. So the 50-cent markup on the \$1.50 selling price is a markup of 33⅓ percent. On the other hand, the 50-cent markup is a 50 percent markup on cost.

Some retailers and wholesalers use markup conversion tables or spreadsheets to easily convert from cost to selling price—depending on the markup on selling price they want. To see the interrelation, look at the two formulas below. They can be used to convert either type of markup to the other.

$$(4) \qquad \text{Percent markup on selling price} = \frac{\text{Percent markup on cost}}{100\% + \text{Percent markup on cost}}$$

$$(5) \qquad \text{Percent markup on cost} = \frac{\text{Percent markup on selling price}}{100\% - \text{Percent markup on selling price}}$$

In the previous example, we had a cost of \$1, a markup of 50 cents, and a selling price of \$1.50. We saw that the markup on selling price was 33⅓ percent—and on cost, it was 50 percent. Let's substitute these percentage figures—in Formulas 4 and 5—to see how to convert from one basis to the other. Assume first of all that we only know the markup on selling price and want to convert to markup on cost. Using Formula 5, we get

$$\text{Percent markup on cost} = \frac{33\tfrac{1}{3}\%}{100\% - 33\tfrac{1}{3}\%} = \frac{33\tfrac{1}{3}\%}{66\tfrac{2}{3}\%} = 50\%$$

On the other hand, if we know only the percent markup on cost, we can convert to markup on selling price as follows:

$$\text{Percent markup on selling price} = \frac{50\%}{100\% + 50\%} = \frac{50\%}{150\%} = 33\tfrac{1}{3}\%$$

These results can be proved and summarized as follows:

Markup \$0.50	=	50% of cost, or 33⅓% of selling price
+ Cost \$1.00	=	100% of cost, or 66⅔% of selling price
Selling price \$1.50	=	150% of cost, or 100% of selling price

Note that when the selling price (\$1.50) is the base for a markup calculation, the markup percent (33⅓ percent = \$.50/\$1.50) must be less than 100 percent. As you can see, that's because the markup percent and the cost percent (66⅔ percent = \$1.00/\$1.50) sums to exactly 100 percent. So if you see a reference to a markup percent that is greater than 100 percent, it could not be based on the selling price and instead must be based on cost.

Markdown Ratios Help Control Retail Operations

The ratios we discussed above were concerned with figures on the operating statement. Another important ratio, the **markdown ratio,** is a tool many retailers use to measure the efficiency of various departments and their whole business. But note that it is *not directly related to the operating statement*. It requires special calculations.

A **markdown** is a retail price reduction required because customers won't buy some item at the originally marked-up price. This refusal to buy may be due to a variety of reasons—soiling, style changes, fading, damage caused by handling, or an original price that was too high. To get rid of these products, the retailer offers them at a lower price.

Markdowns are generally considered to be due to business errors—perhaps because of poor buying, original markups that are too high, and other reasons. (Note, however, that some retailers use markdowns as a way of doing business rather than a way to correct errors. For example, a store that buys out overstocked fashions from other retailers may start by marking each item with a high price and then reduce the price each week until it sells.) Regardless of the reason, however, markdowns are reductions in the original price—and they are important to managers who want to measure the effectiveness of their operations.

Markdowns are similar to allowances because price reductions are made. Thus, in computing a markdown ratio, markdowns and allowances are usually added together and then divided by net sales. The markdown ratio is computed as follows:

$$\text{Markdown \%} = \frac{\$\text{ Markdowns} + \$\text{ Allowances}}{\$\text{ Net sales}} \times 100$$

The 100 is multiplied by the fraction to get rid of decimal points.

Returns are *not* included when figuring the markdown ratio. Returns are treated as consumer errors, not business errors, and therefore are not included in this measure of business efficiency.

Retailers who use markdown ratios usually keep a record of the amount of markdowns and allowances in each department and then divide the total by the net sales in each department. Over a period of time, these ratios give management one measure of the efficiency of buyers and salespeople in various departments.

It should be stressed again that the markdown ratio is not calculated directly from data on the operating statement since the markdowns take place before the products are sold. In fact, some products may be marked down and still not sold. Even if the marked-down items are not sold, the markdowns—that is, the reevaluations of their value—are included in the calculations in the time period when they are taken.

The markdown ratio is calculated for a whole department (or profit center), *not* individual items. What we are seeking is a measure of the effectiveness of a whole department, not how well the department did on individual items.

Return on Investment (ROI) Reflects Asset Use

Another off-the-operating-statement ratio is **return on investment (ROI)**—the ratio of net profit (after taxes) to the investment used to make the net profit, multiplied by 100 to get rid of decimals. Investment is not shown on the operating statement. But it is on the **balance sheet** (statement of financial condition), another accounting statement, which shows a company's assets, liabilities, and net worth. It may take some digging or special analysis, however, to find the right investment number.

Investment means the dollar resources the firm has invested in a project or business. For example, a new product may require $4 million in new money—for inventory, accounts receivable, promotion, and so on—and its attractiveness may be judged by its likely ROI. If the net profit (after taxes) for this new product is expected to be $1 million in the first year, then the ROI is 25 percent—that is, ($1 million ÷ $4 million) × 100.

There are two ways to figure ROI. The *direct* way is

$$\text{ROI (in \%)} = \frac{\text{Net profit (after taxes)}}{\text{Investment}} \times 100$$

The *indirect* way is

$$\text{ROI (in \%)} = \frac{\text{Net profit (after taxes)}}{\text{Sales}} = \frac{\text{Sales}}{\text{Investment}} \times 100$$

This way is concerned with net profit margin and turnover—that is

$$\text{ROI (in \%)} = \text{Net profit margin} \times \text{Turnover} \times 100$$

This indirect way makes it clearer how to *increase* ROI. There are three ways:

1. Increase profit margin (with lower costs or a higher price).
2. Increase sales.
3. Decrease investment.

Effective marketing strategy planning and implementation can increase profit margins and/or sales. And careful asset management can decrease investment.

ROI is a revealing measure of how well managers are doing. Most companies have alternative uses for their funds. If the returns in a business aren't at least as high as outside uses, then the money probably should be shifted to the more profitable uses.

Some firms borrow more than others to make investments. In other words, they invest less of their own money to acquire assets—what we called *investments*. If ROI calculations use only the firm's own investment, this gives higher ROI figures to those who borrow a lot—which is called *leveraging*. To adjust for different borrowing proportions—to make comparisons among projects, departments, divisions, and companies easier—another ratio has come into use. **Return on assets (ROA)** is the ratio of net profit (after taxes) to the assets used to make the net profit—times 100. Both ROI and ROA measures are trying to get at the same thing—how effectively the company is using resources. These measures became increasingly popular as profit rates dropped and it became more obvious that increasing sales volume doesn't necessarily lead to higher profits—or ROI or ROA. Inflation and higher costs for borrowed funds also force more concern for ROI and ROA. Marketers must include these measures in their thinking or top managers are likely to ignore their plans and requests for financial resources.

Forecasting Target Market Potential and Sales

Effective strategy planning and developing a marketing plan require estimates of future sales, costs, and profits. Without such information, it's hard to know if a strategy is potentially profitable.

The marketing manager's estimates of sales, costs, and profits are usually based on a forecast (estimate) of target **market potential**—what a whole market segment might buy—and a **sales forecast**—an estimate of how much an industry or firm hopes to sell to a market segment. Usually we must first try to judge market potential before we can estimate what share a particular firm may be able to win with its particular marketing mix.

Three levels of forecasts are useful

We're interested in forecasting the potential in specific market segments. To do this, it helps to make three levels of forecasts.

Some economic conditions affect the entire global economy. Others may influence only one country or a particular industry. And some may affect only one company or one product's sales potential. For this reason, a common top-down approach to forecasting is to

1. Develop a *national income forecast* (for each country in which the firm operates) and use this to
2. Develop an *industry sales forecast*, which then is used to
3. Develop forecasts for a *specific company*, its *specific products*, and the *segments* it targets.

Generally, a marketing manager doesn't have to make forecasts for a national economy or the broad industry. This kind of forecasting—basically trend projecting—is a specialty in itself. Such forecasts are available in business and government publications, and large companies often have their own technical specialists. Managers can use just one source's forecast or combine several. Unfortunately, however, the more targeted the marketing manager's earlier segmenting efforts have been, the less likely that industry forecasts will match the firm's product-markets. So managers have to move directly to estimating potential for their own companies and for their specific products.

Two approaches to forecasting

Many methods are used to forecast market potential and sales, but they can all be grouped into two basic approaches: (1) extending past behavior and (2) predicting future behavior. The large number of methods may seem confusing at first, but this variety has an advantage. Forecasts are so important that managers often develop forecasts in two or three different ways and then compare the differences before preparing a final forecast.

Extending past behavior can miss important turning points

When we forecast for existing products, we usually have some past data to go on. The basic approach—called **trend extension**—extends past experience into the future. With existing products, for example, the past trend of actual sales may be extended into the future. See Exhibit B-3.

Ideally, when extending past sales behavior, we should decide why sales vary. This is the difficult and time-consuming part of sales forecasting. Usually we can gather a lot of data about the product or market or about changes in the marketing environment. But unless we know the *reason* for past sales variations, it's hard to predict in what direction, and by how much, sales will move. Graphing the data and statistical techniques—including correlation and regression analysis—can be useful here. (These techniques, which are beyond our scope, are discussed in beginning statistics courses.)

Once we know why sales vary, we can usually develop a specific forecast. Sales may be moving directly up as population grows in a specific market segment, for example. So we can just estimate how population is expected to grow and project the impact on sales.

The weakness of the trend extension method is that it assumes past conditions will continue unchanged into the future. In fact, the future isn't always like the

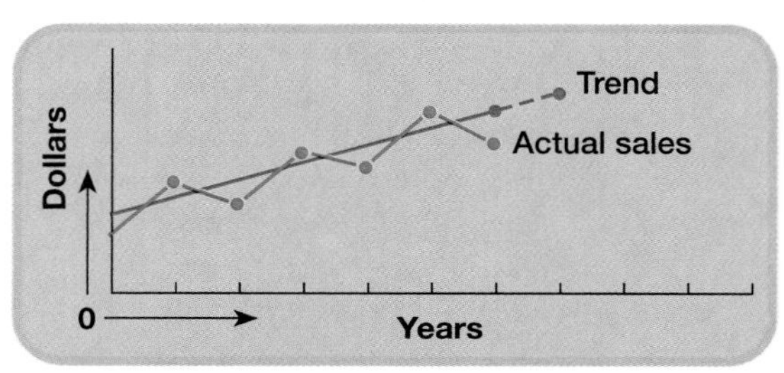

Exhibit B-3
Straight-Line Trend Projection—Extends Past Sales into the Future

past. An agent wholesaler's business may have been on a steady path, but the development of the Internet adds a totally new factor. The past trend for the agent's sales changed because the agent could quickly reach a broader market.

As another example, for years the trend in sales of disposable diapers moved closely with the number of new births. However, as the number of women in the workforce increased and as more women returned to jobs after babies were born, use of disposable diapers increased, and the trend changed. As in these examples, trend extension estimates will be wrong whenever big changes occur. For this reason—although they may extend past behavior for one estimate—most managers look for another way to help them forecast sharp market changes.

Predicting future behavior takes judgment

When we try to predict what will happen in the future, instead of just extending the past, we have to use other methods and add more judgment. Some of these methods (to be discussed later) include juries of executive opinion, salespeople's estimates, surveys, panels, and market tests.

Forecasting Company and Product Sales by Extending Past Behavior

Past sales can be extended

At the very least, a marketing manager ought to know what the firm's present markets look like and what it has sold to them in the past. A detailed sales analysis for products and geographic areas helps to project future results.

Just extending past sales into the future may not seem like much of a forecasting method. But it's better than just assuming that next year's total sales will be the same as this year's.

Factor method includes more than time

A simple extension of past sales gives one forecast. But it's usually desirable to tie future sales to something more than the passage of time.

The factor method tries to do this. The **factor method** tries to forecast sales by finding a relation between the company's sales and some other factor (or factors). The basic formula is: something (past sales, industry sales, etc.) *times* some factor *equals* sales forecast. A **factor** is a variable that shows the relation of some other variable to the item being forecast. For instance, in our example above, both the birthrate and the number of working mothers are factors related to sales of disposable diapers.

A bread producer example

The following example—about a bread producer—shows how firms can make forecasts for many geographic market segments using the factor method and available data. This general approach can be useful for any firm—producer, wholesaler, or retailer.

Analysis of past sales relationships showed that the bread manufacturer regularly sold one-tenth of 1 percent (0.001) of the total retail food sales in its various target markets. This is a single factor. By using this single factor, a manager could estimate the producer's sales in a new market for the coming period by multiplying a forecast of expected retail food sales by 0.001.

Sales & Marketing Management magazine makes retail food sales estimates each year. Exhibit B-4 shows the kind of geographically detailed data available.

Let's carry this bread example further—using the data in Exhibit B-4 for the Denver, Colorado, metro area. Denver's food sales were $3,591,232,000 for the previous year. By simply accepting last year's food sales as an estimate of next year's sales and multiplying the food sales estimate for Denver by the 0.001 factor (the firm's usual share of food purchases in such markets), the manager would have an estimate of next year's bread sales in Denver. That is, last year's food sales estimate ($3,591,232,000) times 0.001 equals this year's bread sales estimate of $3,591,232.

Exhibit B-4 Sample of Pages from *Sales & Marketing Management's* Survey of Buying Power: Metro and County Totals

COLORADO CONT'D

METRO AREA County City	Population						Retail Sales by Store Group ($000)						Effective Buying Income					
	Total Population (000s)	% of Population by Age Group 18–24	25–34	35–49	50 +	House-holds (000s)	Total Retail Sales	Food	Eating & Drinking Places	General Mdse.	Furniture/ Furnish. Appliance	Auto-motive	Total EBI ($000)	Median Hsld. EBI	% of Hslds: by EBI Group A $20,000–$34,999	B $35,000–$49,999	C $50,000– & Over	Buying Power Index
COLORADO																		
BOULDER-LONGMONT	**260.2**	**12.2**	**17.3**	**27.9**	**19.2**	**103.6**	**2,999,501**	**525,192**	**432,303**	**304,860**	**182,133**	**660,874**	**5,024,497**	**39,919**	**21.3**	**18.0**	**38.1**	**.1163**
BOULDER	260.2	12.2	17.3	27.9	19.2	103.6	2,999,501	525,192	432,303	304,860	182,133	660,874	5,024,497	39,919	21.3	18.0	38.1	.1163
• Boulder	84.2	23.7	18.4	24.6	17.8	35.5	1,602,708	268,101	246,771	142,011	129,516	304,425	1,618,013	33,409	21.8	14.7	33.3	.0452
• Longmont	57.4	7.6	16.4	25.4	22.4	22.2	771,282	132,991	85,375	61,538	31,383	227,700	916,833	36,965	24.5	21.0	31.9	.0247
COLORADO SPRINGS	**476.8**	**10.1**	**17.2**	**24.4**	**20.1**	**178.3**	**4,883,063**	**703,957**	**557,021**	**685,402**	**279,106**	**1,170,529**	**6,624,809**	**30,020**	**28.4**	**19.4**	**22.4**	**.1747**
EL PASO	476.8	10.1	17.2	24.4	20.1	178.3	4,883,063	703,957	557,021	685,402	279,106	1,170,529	6,624,809	30,020	28.4	19.4	22.4	.1747
• Colorado Springs	331.6	9.2	17.9	24.7	20.8	132.3	4,560,947	661,538	475,447	624,435	272,996	1,141,550	4,793,827	29,398	27.8	18.7	22.2	.1379
DENVER	**1,880.2**	**7.5**	**17.0**	**27.0**	**22.1**	**756.1**	**19,355,163**	**3,591,232**	**2,546,761**	**2,243,175**	**1,399,533**	**4,898,564**	**33,489,662**	**36,606**	**23.3**	**19.4**	**32.9**	**.7783**
ADAMS	313.6	8.4	17.3	24.0	20.8	114.3	2,518,700	574,523	252,072	357,779	155,806	609,381	4,180,008	32,518	27.3	22.3	23.4	.1042
Thornton	70.7	8.0	19.0	26.4	13.3	24.6	642,216	203,950	63,444	104,042	14,744	170,337	954,782	36,563	26.6	25.2	27.5	.0246
Westminster	97.2	8.4	20.1	27.5	14.1	36.3	842,545	144,824	80,403	233,108	81,905	143,178	1,563,416	39,286	24.6	24.1	33.4	.0363
ARAPAHOE	458.7	7.3	16.9	28.7	19.8	183.8	6,560,505	1,049,222	575,350	668,476	465,750	2,418,123	9,187,206	40,923	22.6	19.8	38.7	.2245
Aurora	255.8	8.2	19.3	27.4	17.0	104.5	2,959,057	613,693	308,304	373,495	264,448	769,394	4,284,060	36,665	25.9	22.3	30.4	.1066
DENVER	499.5	8.3	18.0	24.3	27.0	228.4	4,075,124	740,723	918,989	222,440	322,954	616,803	8,397,781	27,458	25.3	16.3	22.2	.1878
• Denver	499.5	8.3	18.0	24.4	26.9	228.4	4,075,124	740,723	918,989	222,440	322,954	616,803	8,397,781	27,458	25.3	16.3	22.2	.1878
DOUGLAS	112.3	4.7	17.2	32.3	14.9	39.3	752,159	163,177	93,281	140,967	63,492	83,206	2,447,689	54,826	14.3	19.3	57.6	.0469
JEFFERSON	496.1	7.1	16.0	28.8	21.6	190.3	5,448,675	1,063,587	707,069	853,513	391,531	1,171,051	9,276,978	43,093	21.1	21.3	40.5	.2149
Arvada	97.0	7.4	14.8	28.1	22.3	36.2	796,133	238,354	102,088	170,176	49,836	27,179	1,655,557	42,897	21.1	22.0	39.5	.0368
Lakewood	123.7	8.7	16.7	26.1	26.2	51.2	1,723,111	229,333	232,966	211,165	130,278	527,661	2,259,951	37,695	25.0	21.1	33.0	.0574
DENVER-BOULDER-GREELEY **CONSOLIDATED AREA** . .	**2,292.9**	**8.3**	**17.0**	**26.8**	**21.8**	**914.6**	**23,486,046**	**4,301,572**	**3,097,926**	**2,738,836**	**1,638,229**	**5,864,367**	**40,369,337**	**36,332**	**23.3**	**19.2**	**32.7**	**.9421**

Factor method can use several factors

The factor method is not limited to just one factor; several factors can be used together. For example, *Sales & Marketing Management* regularly gives a "buying power index" (BPI) as a measure of the potential in different geographic areas. See Exhibit B-4. This index considers (1) the population in a market, (2) the retail sales in that market, and (3) income in that market. The BPI for the Denver, Colorado, metro area, for example, is 0.7783—that is, Denver accounts for 0.7783 percent of the total U.S. buying power. This means that consumers who live in Denver have higher than average buying power. We know this because Denver accounts for about 0.6681 percent of the U.S. population. We can calculate this figure by using Denver's total population of 1,880,200 (in Exhibit B-4) and dividing it by the total population of the U.S.—281,422,000 (in Exhibit 4-4). So the people in Denver have buying power that is about 16 percent higher than average.

Using several factors rather than only one uses more information. And in the case of the BPI, it gives a single measure of a market's potential. Rather than falling back on using population only, or income only, or trying to develop a special index, the BPI can be used in the same way that we used the 0.001 factor in the bread example.

Predicting Future Behavior Calls for More Judgment and Some Opinions

These past-extending methods use quantitative data—projecting past experience into the future and assuming that the future will be like the past. But this is risky in competitive markets. Usually, it's desirable to add some judgment to other forecasts before making the final forecast yourself.

Jury of executive opinion adds judgment

One of the oldest and simplest methods of forecasting—the **jury of executive opinion**—combines the opinions of experienced executives, perhaps from marketing, production, finance, purchasing, and top management. Each executive estimates market potential and sales for the *coming years*. Then they try to work out a consensus.

The main advantage of the jury approach is that it can be done quickly and easily. On the other hand, the results may not be very good. There may be too much extending of the past. Some of the executives may have little contact with outside market influences. But their estimates could point to major shifts in customer demand or competition.

Estimates from salespeople can help too

Using salespeople's estimates to forecast is like the jury approach. But salespeople are more likely than home office managers to be familiar with customer reactions and what competitors are doing. Their estimates are especially useful in some business markets where the few customers may be well known to the salespeople. But this approach may be useful in any type of market.

However, managers who use estimates from salespeople should be aware of the limitations. For example, new salespeople may not know much about their markets. Even experienced salespeople may not be aware of possible changes in the economic climate or the firm's other environments. And if salespeople think the manager is going to use the estimates to set sales quotas, the estimates may be low!

Surveys, panels, and market tests

Special surveys of final buyers, retailers, and/or wholesalers can show what's happening in different market segments. Some firms use panels of stores—or final consumers—to keep track of buying behavior and to decide when just extending past behavior isn't enough.

Surveys are sometimes combined with market tests when the company wants to estimate customers' reactions to possible changes in its marketing mix. A market test might show that a product increased its share of the market by 10 percent when its price was dropped 1 cent below competition. But this extra business might be quickly lost if the price were increased 1 cent above competition. Such market experiments help the marketing manager make good estimates of future sales when one or more of the four Ps is changed.

Accuracy depends on the marketing mix

Forecasting can help a marketing manager estimate the size of possible market opportunities. But the accuracy of any sales forecast depends on whether the firm selects and implements a marketing mix that turns these opportunities into sales and profits.

Questions and Problems

1. Distinguish between the following pairs of items that appear on operating statements: *(a)* gross sales and net sales, and *(b)* purchases at billed cost and purchases at net cost.
2. How does gross margin differ from gross profit? From net profit?
3. Explain the similarity between markups and gross margin. What connection do markdowns have with the operating statement?
4. Compute the net profit for a company with the following data:

Beginning inventory (cost)	$ 150,000
Purchases at billed cost	330,000
Sales returns and allowances	250,000
Rent	60,000
Salaries	400,000
Heat and light	180,000
Ending inventory (cost)	250,000
Freight cost (inbound)	80,000
Gross sales	1,300,000

5. Construct an operating statement from the following data:

Returns and allowances	$150,000
Expenses	20%
Closing inventory at cost	600,000
Markdowns	2%
Inward transportation	30,000
Purchases	1,000,000
Net profit (5%)	300,000

6. Compute net sales and percent of markdowns for the following data:

Markdowns	$ 40,000
Gross sales	400,000
Returns	32,000
Allowances	48,000

7. *(a)* What percentage markups on cost are equivalent to the following percentage markups on selling price: 20, 37½, 50, and 66⅔? *(b)* What percentage markups on selling price are equivalent to the following percentage markups on cost: 33⅓, 20, 40, and 50?
8. What net sales volume is required to obtain a stockturn rate of 20 times a year on an average inventory at cost of $100,000 with a gross margin of 25 percent?
9. Explain how the general manager of a department store might use the markdown ratios computed for her various departments. Is this a fair measure? Of what?
10. Compare and contrast return on investment (ROI) and return on assets (ROA) measures. Which would be best for a retailer with no bank borrowing or other outside sources of funds; that is, the retailer has put up all the money that the business needs?
11. Explain the difference between a forecast of market potential and a sales forecast.
12. Suggest a plausible explanation for sales fluctuations for *(a)* computers, *(b)* ice cream, *(c)* washing machines, *(d)* tennis rackets, *(e)* oats, *(f)* disposable diapers, and *(g)* latex for rubber-based paint.
13. Explain the factor method of forecasting. Illustrate your answer.
14. Based on data in Exhibit B-4, discuss the relative market potential of the city of Boulder, Colorado, and the city of Lakewood, Colorado, for *(a)* prepared cereals, *(b)* automobiles, and *(c)* furniture.

Appendix C

Career Planning in Marketing

When You Finish This Appendix, You Should

1. Know that there is a job or a career for you in marketing.

2. Know that marketing jobs can be rewarding, pay well, and offer opportunities for growth.

3. Understand the difference between "people-oriented" and "thing-oriented" jobs.

4. Know about the many marketing jobs you can choose from.

5. Know some ways to use the Internet to help with career planning.

One of the hardest jobs facing most college students is the choice of a career. Of course, no one can make this decision for you. You must be the judge of your own objectives, interests, and abilities. Only you can decide what career *you* should pursue. However, you owe it to yourself to at least consider the possibility of a career in marketing.

There's a Place in Marketing for You

We're happy to tell you that many opportunities are available in marketing. There's a place in marketing for everyone—from a service provider in a fast-food restaurant to a vice president of marketing in a large company such as Microsoft or Procter & Gamble. The opportunities range widely—so it will help to be more specific. In the following pages, we'll discuss (1) the typical pay for different marketing jobs, (2) setting your own objectives and evaluating your interests and abilities, and (3) the kinds of jobs available in marketing. We'll also provide some ideas about how to use the Internet to get more information and perhaps even to apply for a job or post your own information; this material is in the special box with the title "Getting Wired for a Career in Marketing."

There Are Many Marketing Jobs, and They Can Pay Well

There are many interesting and challenging jobs for those with marketing training. You may not know it, but 60 percent of graduating college students take their initial job in a sales, marketing, or customer service position regardless of their stated major. So you'll have a head start because you've been studying marketing, and companies are always looking for people who already have skills in place. In terms of upward mobility, more CEOs have come from the sales and marketing side than all other fields combined. The sky is the limit for those who enter the sales and marketing profession prepared for the future!

Further, marketing jobs open to college-level students do pay well. At the time this went to press, marketing undergraduates were being offered starting salaries around $30,000—with a range from about $18,000 to $40,000 a year. Students with a master's in marketing averaged about $45,000; those with an MBA averaged about $55,000. Starting salaries can vary considerably—depending on your background, experience, and location.

Starting salaries in marketing compare favorably with many other fields. They are lower than those in such fields as computer science and electrical engineering where college graduates are currently in demand. But there is even better opportunity for personal growth, variety, and income in many marketing positions. The *American Almanac of Jobs and Salaries* ranks the median income of marketers number 10 in a list of 125 professions. Marketing also supplies about 50 percent of the people who achieve senior management ranks.

How far and fast your career and income rise above the starting level, however, depends on many factors—including your willingness to work, how well you get along with people, and your individual abilities. But most of all, it depends on *getting results*—individually and through other people. And this is where many marketing jobs offer the newcomer great opportunities. It is possible to show initiative, ability, creativity, and judgment in marketing jobs. And some young people move up very rapidly in marketing. Some even end up at the top in large companies or as owners of their own businesses.

Marketing is often the route to the top

Marketing is where the action is! In the final analysis, a firm's success or failure depends on the effectiveness of its marketing program. This doesn't mean the other functional areas aren't important. It merely reflects the fact that a firm won't have much need for accountants, finance people, production managers, and so on if it can't successfully meet customers' needs and sell its products.

Because marketing is so vital to a firm's survival, many companies look for people with training and experience in marketing when filling key executive positions. In general, chief executive officers for the nation's largest corporations are more likely to have backgrounds in marketing and distribution than in other fields such as production, finance, and engineering.

Develop Your Own Personal Marketing Strategy

Now that you know there are many opportunities in marketing, your problem is matching the opportunities to your own personal objectives and strengths. Basically the problem is a marketing problem: developing a marketing strategy to sell a product—yourself—to potential employers. Just as in planning strategies for products, developing your own strategy takes careful thought. Exhibit C-1 shows how you can organize your own strategy planning. This exhibit shows that you should evaluate yourself first—a personal analysis—and then analyze the environment for opportunities. This will help you sharpen your own long- and short-run objectives—which will lead to developing a strategy. Finally, you should start implementing your own personal marketing strategy. These ideas are explained more fully below.

Exhibit C-1
Organizing Your Own Personal Marketing Strategy Planning

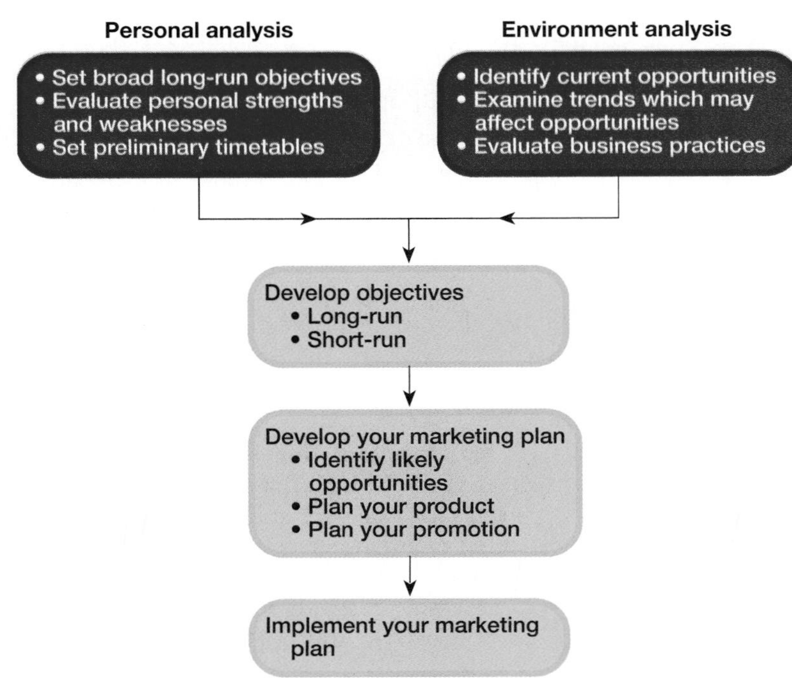

Conduct Your Own Personal Analysis

You are the Product you are going to include in your own marketing plan. So first you have to decide what your long-run objectives are—what you want to do, how hard you want to work, and how quickly you want to reach your objectives. Be honest with yourself—or you will eventually face frustration. Evaluate your own personal strengths and weaknesses—and decide what factors may become the key to your success. Finally, as part of your personal analysis, set some preliminary timetables to guide your strategy planning and implementation efforts. Let's spell this out in detail.

Set broad long-run objectives

Strategy planning requires much trial-and-error decision making. But at the very beginning, you should make some tentative decisions about your own objectives—what you want out of a job and out of life. At the very least, you should decide whether you are just looking for a job or whether you want to build a career. Beyond this, do you want the position to be personally satisfying—or is the financial return enough? And just how much financial return do you need? Some people work only to support themselves and their leisure-time activities. Others work to support themselves and their families. These people seek only financial rewards from a job. They try to find job opportunities that provide adequate financial returns but aren't too demanding of their time or effort.

Other people look first for satisfaction in their job—and they seek opportunities for career advancement. Financial rewards may be important too, but these are used only as measures of success. In the extreme, the career-oriented individual may be willing to sacrifice a lot, including leisure and social activities, to achieve success in a career.

Once you've tentatively decided these matters, then you can get more serious about whether you should seek a job or a career in marketing. If you decide to pursue a career, you should set your broad long-run objectives to achieve it. For example, one long-run objective might be to pursue a career in marketing management (or marketing research). This might require more academic training than you planned, as well as a different kind of training. If your objective is to get a job that pays well, on the other hand, then this calls for a different kind of training and different kinds of job experiences before completing your academic work.

Evaluate personal strengths and weaknesses

What kind of a job is right for you?

Because of the great variety of marketing jobs, it's hard to generalize about what aptitudes you should have to pursue a career in marketing. Different jobs attract people with various interests and abilities. We'll give you some guidelines about what kinds of interests and abilities marketers should have. However, if you're completely lost about your own interests and abilities, see your campus career counselor and take some vocational aptitude and interest tests. These tests will help you to compare yourself with people who are now working in various career positions. They will *not* tell you what you should do, but they can help—especially in eliminating possibilities you are less interested in or less able to do well in.

Are you people-oriented or thing-oriented?

One of the first things you need to decide is whether you are basically "people-oriented" or "thing-oriented." This is a very important decision. A people-oriented person might be very unhappy in an inventory management job, for example, while a thing-oriented person might be miserable in a personal selling or retail management job that involves a lot of customer contact.

Marketing has both people-oriented and thing-oriented jobs. People-oriented jobs are primarily in the promotion area—where company representatives must make contact with potential customers. This may be direct personal selling or customer

Getting Wired for a Career in Marketing

The Internet is a great resource at every stage of career planning and job hunting. It can help you learn: how to do a self-assessment, the outlook for different industries and jobs, what firms have jobs open, how to improve a résumé and post it online for free, and just about anything else you can imagine. Here we'll highlight just a few ideas and websites that can help you get started. However, if you start with some of these suggestions, each website you visit will provide links to other relevant sites that will give you new ideas to think about.

One good place to start is at Yahoo (www.yahoo.com). Select *jobs* under the business and economy heading, and then click on *careers and jobs.* Take a look at all of the information and services that are available when you select the *Yahoo! Careers* link (which takes you to careers.yahoo.com). For example, you can browse résumé tools and salary information, look at job listings, and much more. Yahoo also has a link to a listing of career fields, including a section on advertising and marketing. You may also want to study the information on *career planning,* with a special section for students and recent grads.

Another website to check is at www.marketingjobs.com. It has listings of marketing jobs, links to a number of companies with openings, a résumé center with ideas for preparing a résumé and posting it on the Internet, and lists of helpful periodicals. You might also go to www.careerjournal.com. There are job listings, job-hunting advice, career articles from *The Wall Street Journal,* and more. You can create and post a résumé here as well. Professional associations are another great resource. For example, the American Marketing Association website is at www.ama.org, and the Sales and Marketing Executives International website is at www.smei.com. The Council of Logistics Management website is at www.clm1.org.

Another good website address is www.collegegrad.com. It has links to the best sites on the Web for posting a résumé, information on writing cover letters and getting references, and ideas about how to find a company with job openings. To get a sample of what's possible in tracking down jobs, visit the website at www.thejobresource.com and experiment with its search engine, which lets you look at what's available by state. For example, you might want to search through job listings that mention terms such as *entry level, marketing, advertising,* and *sales.*

This should get you started. Remember, however, that in Chapter 7 we gave addresses for a number of websites with search engines. You can use one of them to help find more detail on any topic that interests you. For example, you might go to www.altavista.digital.com and do a search on terms such as *marketing jobs, salary surveys, post a résumé,* or *entry level position.*

service activities—for example, in technical service or installation and repair. Thing-oriented jobs focus more on creative activities and analyzing data—as in advertising and marketing research—or on organizing and scheduling work—as in operating warehouses, transportation agencies, or the back-end of retailers.

People-oriented jobs tend to pay more, in part because such jobs are more likely to affect sales—the lifeblood of any business. Thing-oriented jobs, on the other hand, are often seen as cost generators rather than sales generators. Taking a big view of the whole company's operations, the thing-oriented jobs are certainly necessary—but without sales no one is needed to do them.

Thing-oriented jobs are usually done at a company's facilities. Further, especially in lower-level jobs, the amount of work to be done and even the nature of the work may be spelled out quite clearly. The time it takes to design questionnaires and tabulate results, for example, can be estimated with reasonable accuracy. Similarly, running a warehouse, analyzing inventory reports, scheduling outgoing shipments, and so on are more like production operations. It's fairly easy to measure an employee's effectiveness and productivity in a thing-oriented job. At the least, time spent can be used to measure an employee's contribution.

A sales rep, on the other hand, might spend all weekend thinking and planning how to make a half-hour sales presentation on Monday. For what should the sales rep be compensated—the half-hour presentation, all of the planning and thinking that went into it, or the results? Typically, sales reps are rewarded for results—and this helps account for the sometimes extremely high salaries paid to effective order getters. At the same time, some people-oriented jobs can be routinized and are lower paid. For example, salespeople in some retail stores are paid at or near the minimum wage.

Managers needed for both kinds of jobs

Here we have oversimplified deliberately to emphasize the differences among types of jobs. Actually, of course, there are many variations between the two extremes. Some sales reps must do a great deal of analytical work before they make a presentation. Similarly, some marketing researchers must be extremely people-sensitive to get potential customers to reveal their true feelings. But the division is still useful because it focuses on the primary emphasis in different kinds of jobs.

Managers are needed for the people in both kinds of jobs. Managing others requires a blend of both people and analytical skills—but people skills may be the more important of the two. Therefore, people-oriented individuals are often promoted into managerial positions more quickly.

What will differentiate your Product?

After deciding whether you're generally people-oriented or thing-oriented, you're ready for the next step—trying to identify your specific strengths (to be built on) and weaknesses (to be avoided or remedied). It is important to be as specific as possible so you can develop a better marketing plan. For example, if you decide you are more people-oriented, are you more skilled in verbal or written communication? Or if you are more thing-oriented, what specific analytical or technical skills do you have? Are you good at working with numbers, using a computer, solving complex problems, or coming to the root of a problem? Other possible strengths include past experience (career-related or otherwise), academic performance, an outgoing personality, enthusiasm, drive, motivation, and so on.

It is important to see that your plan should build on your strengths. An employer will be hiring you to do something—so promote yourself as someone who is able to do something *well.* In other words, find your competitive advantage in your unique strengths—and then communicate these unique things about *you* and what you can do. Give an employer a reason to pick you over other candidates by showing that you'll add superior value to the company.

While trying to identify strengths, you also must realize that you may have some important weaknesses—depending on your objectives. If you are seeking a career that requires technical skills, for example, then you need to get those skills. Or if you are seeking a career that requires independence and self-confidence, then you should try to develop those characteristics in yourself—or change your objectives.

Set some timetables

At this point in your strategy planning process, set some timetables to organize your thinking and the rest of your planning. You need to make some decisions at this point to be sure you see where you're going. You might simply focus on getting your first job, or you might decide to work on two marketing plans: (1) a short-run plan to get your first job and (2) a longer-run plan—perhaps a five-year plan—to show how you're going to accomplish your long-run objectives. People who are basically job-oriented may get away with only a short-run plan—just drifting from one opportunity to another as their own objectives and opportunities change. But those interested in careers need a longer-run plan. Otherwise, they may find themselves pursuing attractive first job opportunities that satisfy short-run objectives—but quickly leave them frustrated when they realize that they can't achieve their long-run objectives without additional training or other experiences that require starting over again on a new career path.

Environment Analysis

Strategy planning is a matching process. For your own strategy planning, this means matching yourself to career opportunities. So let's look at opportunities available in the marketing environment. (The same approach applies, of course, in the whole business area.) Exhibit C-2 shows some of the possibilities and salary ranges.

Exhibit C-2 Some Career Paths and Salary Ranges

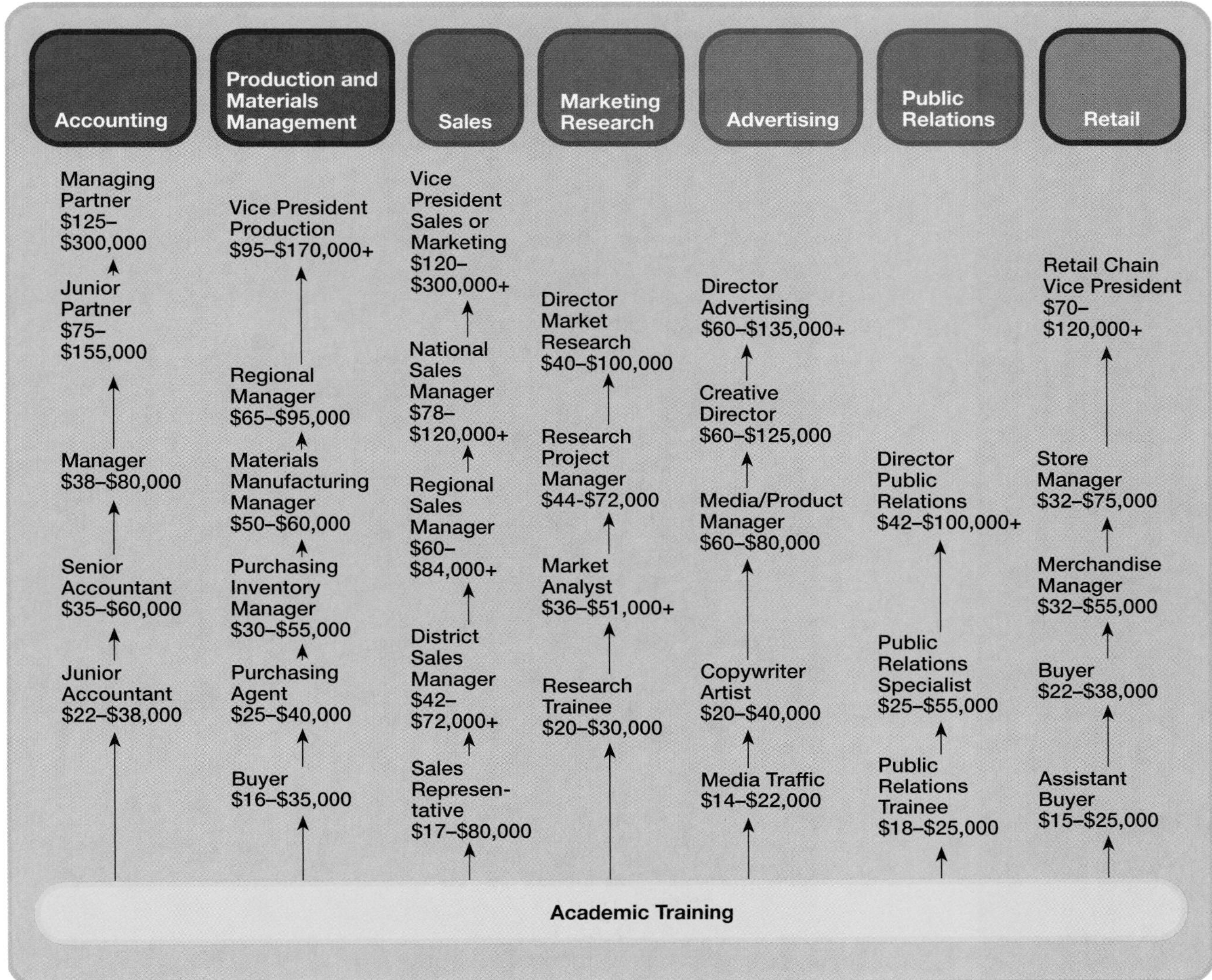

Keep in mind that the salary ranges in Exhibit C-2 are rough estimates. Salaries for a particular job often vary depending on a variety of factors, including company size, industry, and geographic area. People in some firms also get big bonuses that are not counted in salary. In recent years *Advertising Age* has been publishing an annual survey of salary levels for different marketing and advertising jobs—with breakdowns by company size and other factors. Many trade associations—across a variety of different industries—also publish surveys. If you use the Internet search engine at www.yahoo.com and do a search on *salary survey*, you will find that there are hundreds of such surveys available on the Internet for a number of different industries.

Identifying current opportunities in marketing

Because of the wide range of opportunities in marketing, it's helpful to narrow your possibilities. After deciding on your own objectives, strengths, and weaknesses, think about where in the marketing system you might like to work. Would you like to work for manufacturers, or wholesalers, or retailers? Or does it really matter? Do you want to be involved with consumer products or business products? By analyzing your feelings about these possibilities, you can begin to zero in on the kind of job and the functional area that might interest you most.

One simple way to get a better idea of the kinds of jobs available in marketing is to review the chapters of this text—this time with an eye for job opportunities rather than new concepts. The following paragraphs contain brief descriptions of job areas that marketing graduates are often interested in with references to specific chapters in the text. Some, as noted below, offer good starting opportunities, while others do not. While reading these paragraphs, keep your own objectives, interests, and strengths in mind.

Marketing manager (Chapter 2)

This is usually not an entry-level job, although aggressive students may move quickly into this role in smaller companies.

Customer or market analyst (Chapters 3, 4, and 5)

Opportunities as consumer analysts and market analysts are commonly found in large companies, marketing research organizations, advertising agencies, and some consulting firms. Investment banking firms also hire entry-level analysts; they want to know what the market for a new business is like before investing. Beginning market analysts start in thing-oriented jobs until their judgment and people-oriented skills are tested. The job may involve collecting or analyzing secondary data or preparation of reports and plans. Because knowledge of statistics, computer software, Internet search techniques, and/or behavioral sciences is very important, marketing graduates often find themselves competing with majors from statistics, sociology, computer science, and economics. Graduates who have courses in marketing *and* one or more of these areas may have the best opportunities.

Purchasing agent/buyer (Chapter 6)

Entry-level opportunities are commonly found in large companies, and there are often good opportunities in the purchasing area. Many companies are looking for bright newcomers who can help them find new and better ways to work with suppliers. To get off on the right track, beginners usually start as trainees or assistant buyers under the supervision of experienced buyers. That's good preparation for a promotion to more responsibility.

Marketing research opportunities (Chapter 7)

There are entry-level opportunities at all levels in the channel (but especially in large firms where more formal marketing research is done in-house), in advertising agencies, and in marketing research firms. Some general management consulting firms also have marketing research groups. Quantitative and behavioral science skills are extremely important in marketing research, so some firms are more interested in business graduates who have studied statistics or psychology as electives. But there still are many opportunities in marketing research for marketing graduates, especially if they have some experience in working with computers and statistical software. A recent graduate might begin in a training program—conducting interviews or summarizing open-ended answers from questionnaires and helping to prepare electronic slide presentations for clients—before being promoted to a position as an analyst, assistant project manager, account representative, and subsequent management positions.

Packaging specialists (Chapter 8)

Packaging manufacturers tend to hire and train interested people from various backgrounds—there is little formal academic training in packaging. There are many sales opportunities in this field—and with training, interested people can become specialists fairly quickly in this growing area.

Product/brand manager (Chapters 8 and 9)

Many multiproduct firms have brand or product managers handling individual products—in effect, managing each product as a separate business. Some firms hire marketing graduates as assistant brand or product managers, although larger firms typically recruit MBAs for these jobs. Many firms prefer that recent college graduates spend some time in the field doing sales work or working with an ad agency or sales promotion agency before moving into brand or product management positions.

Product planner (Chapter 9)

This is usually not an entry-level position. Instead, people with experience on the technical side of the business or in sales might be moved onto a new-product development team as they demonstrate judgment and analytical skills. However, new employees with winning ideas for new products don't go unnoticed—and they sometimes have the opportunity to grow fast with ideas they spearhead. Having a job that puts you in contact with customers is often a good way to spot new needs.

Distribution channel management (Chapter 10)

This work is typically handled or directed by sales managers and therefore is not an entry-level position. However, many firms form teams of specialists who work closely with their counterparts in other firms in the channel to strengthen coordination and relationships. Such a team often includes new people in sales or purchasing because it gives them exposure to a different part of the firm's activities. It's also not unusual for people to start working in a particular industry and then take a different job at a different level in the channel. For example, a graduate who has trained to be a store manager for a chain of sporting goods stores might go to work for a manufacturers' representative that handles a variety of sports equipment.

Logistics opportunities (Chapter 11)

There are many sales opportunities with physical distribution specialists—but there are also many thing-oriented jobs involving traffic management, warehousing, and materials handling. Here training in accounting, finance, and computer methods could be very useful. These kinds of jobs are available at all levels in channels of distribution.

Retailing opportunities (Chapter 12)

Not long ago, most entry-level marketing positions in retailing involved some kind of sales work. That has changed rapidly in recent years because the number of large retail chains is expanding and they often recruit graduates for their management training programs. Retailing positions tend to offer lower-than-average starting salaries—but they often provide opportunities for very rapid advancement. In a fast-growing chain, results-oriented people can move up very quickly. Most retailers require new employees to have some selling experience before managing others—or buying. A typical marketing graduate can expect to work as an assistant manager or do some sales work and manage one or several departments before advancing to a store management position—or to a staff position that might involve buying, advertising, location analysis, and so on.

Wholesaling opportunities (Chapter 12)

Entry-level jobs with merchant wholesalers typically fall into one of two categories. The first is in the logistics area—working with transportation management, inventory control, distribution customer service, and related activities. The other category usually involves personal selling and customer support. Agent wholesalers typically focus on selling, and entry-level jobs often start out with order-taking responsibilities that grow into order-getting responsibilities. Many wholesalers are moving much of their information to the Internet, so marketing students with skills and knowledge in this arena may find especially interesting opportunities.

Personal selling opportunities (Chapter 14)

Because there are so many different types of sales jobs and so many people are employed in sales, there are many good entry-level opportunities in personal selling. This might be order-getting, order-taking, or missionary selling. Many sales jobs now rely on sales technology, so some of the most challenging opportunities will go to students who know how to prepare spreadsheets and presentation materials using software programs like Microsoft Office. Many students are reluctant to get into personal selling—but this field offers benefits that are hard to match in any other field. These include the opportunity to earn extremely high salaries and commissions quickly, a chance to develop your self-confidence and resourcefulness, an opportunity to work with minimal supervision—almost to the point of being your own boss—and a chance to acquire product and customer knowledge that many firms consider necessary for a successful career in product/brand management, sales management, and marketing management. On the other hand, many salespeople prefer to spend their entire careers in selling. They like the freedom and earning potential that go with a sales job over the headaches and sometimes lower salaries of sales management positions.

Advertising opportunities (Chapters 13 and 15)

Job opportunities in this area are varied and highly competitive. And because the ability to communicate and a knowledge of the behavioral sciences are important, marketing graduates often find themselves competing with majors from fields such as English, communication, psychology, and sociology. There are thing-oriented jobs such as copywriting, media buying, art, and so on. Competition for these jobs is very competitive—and they go to people with a track record. So the entry-level positions are as assistant to a copywriter, media buyer, or art director. There are also people-oriented positions involving work with clients—which are probably of more interest to marketing graduates. This is a glamorous but small and extremely competitive industry where young people can rise very rapidly—but they can also be as easily displaced by new bright young people. Entry-level salaries in advertising are typically low. There are sometimes good opportunities to get started in advertising with a retail chain that prepares its advertising internally. Another way to get more experience with advertising is to take a job with one of the media—perhaps in sales or as a customer consultant. Selling advertising space on a website or cable TV station or newspaper may not seem as glamorous as developing TV ads, but media salespeople help their customers solve promotion problems and get experience dealing with both the business and creative side of advertising.

Sales promotion opportunities (Chapters 13 and 15)

The number of entry-level positions in the sales promotion area is growing because the number of specialists in this area is growing. For example, specialists might help a company plan a special event for employees, figure out procedures to distribute free samples, or perhaps set up a database to send customers a newsletter. Because clients' needs are often different, creativity and judgment are required. It is usually difficult for an inexperienced person to show evidence of these skills right out of school, so entry-level people often work with a project manager until they learn the ropes. In companies that handle their own sales promotion work, a beginner usually starts by getting some experience in sales or advertising.

Pricing opportunities (Chapters 16 and 17)

Pricing decisions are usually handled by experienced executives. However, in some large companies and consulting firms there are opportunities as pricing analysts for marketing graduates who have quantitative skills. These people work as assistants to higher-level executives and collect and analyze information about competitors' prices and costs, as well as the firm's own costs. Thus, being able to work with accounting numbers and computer spreadsheets is often important in these jobs. However, sometimes the route to these jobs is through experience in marketing research or product management.

Credit management opportunities

Specialists in credit have a continuing need for employees who are interested in evaluating customers' credit ratings and ensuring that money gets collected. Both people skills and thing skills can be useful here. Entry-level positions normally involve a training program and then working under the supervision of others until your judgment and abilities are tested.

International marketing opportunities

Many marketing students are intrigued with the adventure and foreign travel promised by careers in international marketing. Some firms hire recent college graduates for positions in international marketing, but more often these positions go to MBA graduates. However, that is changing as more and more firms are pursuing international markets. It's an advantage in seeking an international marketing job to know a second language and to know about the culture of countries where you would like to work. Your college may have courses or international exchange programs that would help in these areas. Graduates aiming for a career in international marketing usually must spend time mastering the firm's domestic marketing operations before being sent abroad. So a good way to start is to focus on firms that are already involved in international marketing, or that are planning to move in that direction soon. On the other hand, there are many websites with listings of international jobs. For example, you might want to visit www.overseasjobs.com.

Customer relations/consumer affairs opportunities (Chapters 13 and 18)

Most firms are becoming more concerned about their relations with customers and the general public. Employees in this kind of work, however, usually have held various positions with the firm before doing customer relations.

Study trends that may affect your opportunities

A strategy planner should always be evaluating the future because it's easier to go along with trends than to buck them. This means you should watch for political, technical, or economic changes that might open, or close, career opportunities.

If you can spot a trend early, you may be able to prepare yourself to take advantage of it as part of your long-run strategy planning. Other trends might mean you should avoid certain career options. For example, rapid technological changes in computers and communications, including the Internet, are leading to major changes in retailing and advertising, as well as in personal selling. Cable television, telephone selling, and direct-mail selling may reduce the need for routine order takers—while increasing the need for higher-level order getters. More targeted and imaginative sales presentations for delivery by mail, e-mail, phone, or even by Internet websites may be needed. The retailers who survive may need a better understanding of their target markets. And they may need to be supported by wholesalers and manufacturers who can plan targeted promotions that make economic sense. This will require a better understanding of the production and physical distribution side of business, as well as the financial side. And this means better training in accounting, finance, inventory control, and so on. So plan your personal strategy with such trends in mind.

One good way to get more detailed analysis is to go to the U.S. Bureau of Labor Statistics website at http://stats.bls.gov and use the search procedure to look for the term *occupational outlook*. The Bureau provides detailed comments about the outlook for employment and growth in different types of jobs, industries, and regions.

Evaluate business practices

Finally, you need to know how businesses really operate and the kind of training required for various jobs. We've already seen that there are many opportunities in marketing—but not all jobs are open to everyone, and not all jobs are entry-level jobs. Positions such as marketing manager, brand manager, and sales manager are higher rungs on the marketing career ladder. They become available only when you have a few years of experience and have shown leadership and judgment. Some positions require more education than others. So take a hard look at your long-run objectives—and then see what degree you may need for the kinds of opportunities you might like.

Develop Objectives

Once you've done a personal analysis and environment analysis—identifying your personal interests, your strengths and weaknesses, and the opportunities in the environment—define your short-run and long-run objectives more specifically.

Develop long-run objectives

Your long-run objectives should clearly state what you want to do and what you will do for potential employers. You might be as specific as indicating the exact career area you want to pursue over the next 5 to 10 years. For example, your long-run objective might be to apply a set of marketing research and marketing management tools to the food manufacturing industry—with the objective of becoming director of marketing research in a small food manufacturing company.

Your long-run objectives should be realistic and attainable. They should be objectives you have thought about and for which you think you have the necessary skills (or the capabilities to develop those skills) as well as the motivation to reach the objectives.

Your long-run objectives should clearly state what you want to do and what you will do for potential employers.

Develop short-run objectives

To achieve your long-run objective(s), you should develop one or more short-run objectives. These should spell out what is needed to reach your long-run objective(s). For example, you might need to develop a variety of marketing research skills *and* marketing management skills—because both are needed to reach the longer-run objective. Or you might need an entry-level position in marketing research for a large food manufacturer to gain experience and background. An even shorter-run objective might be to take the academic courses that are necessary to get that desired entry-level job. In this example, you would probably need a minimum of an undergraduate degree in marketing, with an emphasis on marketing research. (Note that, given the longer-run objective of managerial responsibility, a business degree would probably be better than a degree in statistics or psychology.)

Developing Your Marketing Plan

Now that you've developed your objectives, move on to developing your own personal marketing plan. This means zeroing in on likely opportunities and developing a specific marketing strategy for these opportunities. Let's talk about that now.

Identify likely opportunities

An important step in strategy planning is identifying potentially attractive opportunities. Depending on where you are in your academic training, this can vary all the way from preliminary exploration to making detailed lists of companies that offer the kinds of jobs that interest you. If you're just getting started, talk to your school's career counselors and placement officers about the kinds of jobs being offered to your school's graduates. Your marketing instructors can help you be realistic about ways you can match your training, abilities, and interests to job opportunities. Also, it helps to read business publications such as *Business Week*, *Fortune*, *The Wall Street Journal*, and *Advertising Age*. *Applications in Basic Marketing*, which comes shrinkwrapped with this text, provides reprints of recent articles from these publications. If you are interested in opportunities in a particular industry, check at your library or on the Internet to see if there are trade publications or websites that can bring you up to speed on the marketing issues in that area. Your library or college may also have an online service to make it easier to search for articles about specific companies or industries. And many companies have their own websites that can be a very useful source of information.

Don't overlook the business sections of your local newspapers to keep in touch with marketing developments in your area. And take advantage of any opportunity to talk with marketers directly. Ask them what they're doing and what satisfactions they find in their jobs. Also, if your college has a marketing club, join it and participate actively in the club's programs. It will help you meet marketers and students with serious interest in the field. Some may have had interesting job experiences and can provide you with leads on part-time jobs or exciting career opportunities.

If you're far along in your present academic training, list companies that you know something about or are willing to investigate—trying to match your skills and interests with possible opportunities. Narrow your list to a few companies you might like to work for.

If you have trouble narrowing down to specific companies, make a list of your personal interest areas—sports, travel, reading, music, or whatever. Think about the companies that compete in markets related to these interests. Often your own knowledge about these areas and interest in them can give you a competitive advantage in getting a job. This helps you focus on companies that serve needs you think are important or interesting. A related approach is to do a search on the Internet for websites related to your areas of interest. Websites often display ads or links to firms that are involved in that specific interest area. Further, many companies post job openings on their own websites or at websites that specialize in promoting job searches by many companies.

Then do some research on these companies. Find out how they are organized, their product lines, and their overall strategies. Try to get clear job descriptions for the kinds of positions you're seeking. Match these job descriptions against your understanding of these jobs and your objectives. Jobs with similar titles may offer very different opportunities. By researching job positions and companies in depth, you should begin to have a feel for where you would be comfortable as an employee. This will help you narrow your target market of possible employers to perhaps five firms. For example, you may decide that your target market for an entry-level position consists of large corporations with (1) in-depth training programs, (2) a wide product line, and (3) a wide variety of marketing jobs that will enable you to get a range of experiences and responsibilities within the same company.

Planning your Product

Just like any strategy planner, you must decide what Product features are necessary to appeal to your target market. Identify which credentials are mandatory and which are optional. For example, is your present academic program enough, or will you need more training? Also, identify what technical skills are needed—such as computer programming or accounting. Further, are there any business experiences or extracurricular activities that might help make your Product more attractive to employers? This might involve active participation in college organizations or work experience, either on the job or in internships.

Planning your Promotion

Once you identify target companies and develop a Product you hope will be attractive to them, you have to tell these potential customers about your Product. You can write directly to prospective employers—sending a carefully developed résumé that reflects your strategy planning. Or you can visit them in person (with your résumé). Many colleges run well-organized interviewing services. Seek their advice early in your strategy planning effort.

Implementing Your Marketing Plan

When you complete your personal marketing plan, you have to implement it—starting with working to accomplish your short-run objectives. If, as part of your plan, you decide that you need specific outside experience, then arrange to get it. This may mean taking a low-paying job or even volunteering to work in political organizations or volunteer organizations where you can get that kind of experience. If you decide that you need skills you can learn in academic courses, plan to take these courses. Similarly, if you don't have a good understanding of your opportunities, then learn as much as you can about possible jobs by talking to professors, taking advanced courses, and talking to businesspeople. Of course, trends and opportunities can change—so continue to read business publications, talk with professionals in your areas of interest, and be sure that the planning you've done still makes sense.

Strategy planning must adapt to the environment. If the environment changes or your personal objectives change, you have to develop a new plan. This is an ongoing process—and you may never be completely satisfied with your strategy planning. But even trying will make you look much more impressive when you begin your job interviews. Remember, while all employers would like to hire a Superman or a Wonder Woman, they are also impressed with candidates who know what they want to do and are looking for a place where they can fit in and make a contribution. So planning a personal strategy and implementing it almost guarantee you'll do a better job of career planning, and this will help ensure that you reach your own objectives, whatever they are.

Whether or not you decide to pursue a marketing career, the authors wish you the best of luck in your search for a challenging and rewarding career, wherever your interests and abilities may take you.

Video Cases

Guide to the Use of These Cases

Essentials of Marketing includes two different types of marketing cases: the 7 special video cases in this section and the 30 traditional cases in the next section. All of the cases offer you the opportunity to evaluate marketing concepts at work in a variety of real-world situations. However, the video cases add a multimedia dimension because we have produced a special video to accompany each of the written cases. An abbreviated version of the video for each case is available on the *Student CD-ROM to Accompany Essentials of Marketing*. The full-length videos are available to professors who adopt *Essentials of Marketing* for use in their course. (These case-based videos are in addition to 19 other video segments we have custom produced and made available to instructors for possible use with other parts of the text.)

The videos bring to life many of the issues considered in each case. However, you can read and analyze the written case descriptions even if there is no time or opportunity to view the video. Either way, you'll find the case interesting and closely tied to the important concepts you've studied in the text.

The set of questions at the end of each case will get you started in thinking about the marketing issues in the case. Further, we provide instructors with a number of suggestions on using the video cases—both for group discussion in class or individual assignments. Thus, as is also true with the traditional cases in the next section, the video cases can be used in many different ways and sequences. You can analyze all of the cases, or only a subset. In fact, the same case can be analyzed several times for different purposes. As your understanding of marketing deepens throughout the course, you'll "see" many more of the marketing issues considered in each case.

 Marketing in the Hardwood Industry*

Logs cut from hardwood forests are an important raw material used by many domestic and foreign producers. Unlike pine and other softwoods, which are used mostly for general construction, the demand for oak, black walnut, black cherry, white ash, maple, and other hardwoods derives from consumer demand for high-value products such as hardwood furniture, cabinets, flooring, millwork, and moldings. When properly finished, hardwoods offer a finish that is both durable and beautiful. The wood is also very strong, so even pieces that do not have a perfect appearance are well suited for making frames of chairs, sofas, and other furniture that are covered with various upholstery materials.

Hardwood forests cover many of the rural areas of the eastern United States—areas where there is often little other industry. Thus, the forest products industry is important to economic development and to the employment and quality of life of people who live and work in these areas.

Unfortunately, that potential for economic development is not always achieved. A key reason for this is that many of the firms that harvest logs do not focus on any particular target market or specific customers. Rather, they just see the market opportunity in terms of the products they have always produced: hardwood logs or perhaps "green" roughsawn lumber cut from the logs. As a result, they sell a commodity product to distant customers who view logs from one supplier as like all of the others on the market and simply purchase logs at the lowest price.

Under this production-oriented, commodity approach, the hardwood produced in rural regions of the U.S. has usually been shipped to other regions—including foreign countries—before the wood is processed into intermediate and finished products. But when the wood is sold and shipped out of the region as an unfinished commodity, the profit opportunities—and associated employment—relevant to the secondary processing are exported as well.

Historically, in this commodity-market environment, successful producers were those who could operate with the lowest total cost. The major cost areas are raw material (lumber), labor, any processing that is done, transportation, and, of course, any marketing-related expenses. Small- and medium-sized producers are at an inherent disadvantage in this competitive, cost-oriented environment. They cannot achieve economies of scale because they can't spread their overhead expenses over a large number of units produced. As a result, there is little way for them to obtain a competitive advantage in production or distribution.

Some hardwood producers, including some smaller ones, were able to improve sales and profits—in both the U.S. and international markets—by differentiating their offerings with higher-quality products and service. For example, firms that worked to keep lumber dry and clean were better able to meet the needs of some customers. Further, some customers appreciated supplier firms that did a good job of sorting and grading different types of woods. And some suppliers focused on supplying species of wood that were desirable but less-readily available.

In spite of such efforts, in the past most hardwood from U.S. producers was just sold as a commodity in a very competitive market. However, some people in the hardwood industry are applying marketing concepts to help change this situation. They are focusing attention on ways to expand the market for existing hardwood products and also trying to identify markets with specific needs so that they can increase the value added to the hardwood lumber—by producing finished or semi-processed products—before it is shipped out of the region where the trees are cut.

These efforts are having an effect. For example, some companies have found markets for hardwood-based composite materials for use as beams, columns, or rafters in building construction. Traditional materials for structural framing include softwood lumber and nonrenewable resources such as steel and aluminum. These structural hardwood composites are manufactured by breaking lower quality hardwood logs into small pieces such as strands, flakes, or thin sheets of wood (veneer) and reforming the pieces into large members with names like "parallel-strand lumber" or "laminated veneer lumber" for the construction market. By finding market opportunities for structural hardwood composites, companies add value by using small or poorly formed logs, less desirable hardwood species, and sometimes even the hardwood waste from other industrial processes. Development of value-added markets for structural hardwood composites also has resulted in job creation and economic development in rural, forested areas.

However, producing structural hardwood composites is just one way to meet customer needs that were not previously being satisfied. An increasing number of customers want to buy kiln-dried boards rather than green lumber that isn't immediately ready to use for their own production purposes. So, many firms that cut and sell hardwood are taking the step of adding value to their product by doing the kiln-drying process. But numerous other opportunities to add value also exist. To uncover them, U.S. hardwood suppliers are asking basic questions like: What are the needs of different customers in the broad product-market for hardwood? Who are these customers and where are they located? What kind of hardwood products—beyond the commodity lumber we've sold in the past—do they want? What are the opportunities to differentiate what we sell and add more value to our product through additional processing that meets the needs of specific target segments? How do we go about finding the answers to these questions?

One opportunity for expanding both the market and value-added product opportunities lies in the area of international exports. Prior to 1980, many firms that supplied hardwood ignored the export market. Domestic demand was sufficiently large to sustain growth and profitability. However, as domestic demand softened and competition grew more intense, U.S. suppliers began to rethink entry into the international marketplace. In the last decade, efforts to market hardwood products to foreign markets have expanded significantly, and the value of exported hardwood products has increased substantially.

*This case and the script for the accompanying video were prepared by Thomas G. Ponzurick and James P. Armstrong.

Despite some recent success, there is still a vital need for more U.S. suppliers to adopt the marketing concept, especially in targeting the export marketplace. Currently, international buyers are focusing most of their attention on the higher-grade hardwood products. But growth of sales and profits from exporting will depend on the U.S. industry's ability to find markets for more of their available product inventory—including lower grades and species of hardwood. In fact, finding markets for value-added products may be the best way to improve sales of the lower grades and species. This would not only result in more efficient and profitable use of hardwood resources, but it could also reduce costs by improving economies of scale in production.

However, the question that should be uppermost in marketers' minds is: What do these customers want in the way of hardwood products? To answer this question, one must first determine the needs of these international buyers. In the case of U.S. hardwood suppliers, Canadian buyers are currently the largest market for these products.

Most of the Canadian firms that import U.S. hardwood to Canada are concentrated in a few geographic areas: over 75 percent are located in either Ontario or Quebec. Much of the imported lumber is purchased by Canadian manufacturers who use it to produce their own products—including furniture, cabinets, hardwood flooring, and molding and millwork for the construction industry. However, these customers account for only about 31 percent of U.S. imports. Canadian wholesalers—especially brokers and agents—account for more than half of the Canadian hardwood lumber purchased from U.S. sources. Many of these middlemen specialize in international sales. In fact, nearly 20 percent of all U.S. hardwood lumber imported by Canada is subsequently resold and exported to Europe—usually after some value-adding activities such as grading, sorting, repackaging, or additional product processing.

Red oak, hard maple, and white oak are the principal hardwood species that Canadian customers import from the United States. However, there are also markets for some species of lesser value—including soft maple and yellow poplar.

All types of lumber are graded according to quality, and this grading is important to Canadian buyers who have different hardwood needs. About 70 percent of the total volume of hardwood lumber purchased by Canadian firms is the higher-quality Number 1 Common grade or better. The other 30 percent of lumber imported is graded as Number 2 Common or lower. Firms that purchase the lower grades of lumber are mostly flooring manufacturers, furniture manufacturers, and brokers.

Marketing research studies indicate that Canadian hardwood lumber buyers are relatively satisfied with the quality of products and services now being provided by U.S. suppliers. However, the research reveals that suppliers could enhance customer satisfaction and their competitive advantage by improving their product quality through more accurate grading and reporting of moisture content as well as by providing cleaner and straighter lumber. Buyers would also like to see better distribution customer service from U.S. suppliers. This includes improving the reliability of lumber supplies and reducing order cycle time—that is, the time from when a customer orders lumber until it is delivered. And of course, organizational buyers are always interested in competitive pricing.

Importantly, the research also shows that over one-third of the firms that import hardwood lumber from the United States are potentially interested in purchasing finished hardwood parts from U.S. suppliers. Examples in the area of finished hardwood parts include parts for making furniture, doors, stairways, and railings. Organizations showing an interest in these finished products include importers, export brokers, and manufacturers of various hardwood products. These results indicate that there may be a good opportunity for U.S. suppliers of hardwood products to custom produce such parts for specific customers. Yet it is still unknown how substantial this opportunity might be, how eager Canadian buyers might be to purchase value-added finished hardwood products, and at what prices. To begin to answer these questions, U.S. suppliers need to determine the types and specifications of the finished hardwood products desired by individual buyers. That will require that supplier firms do more marketing research or have more direct personal selling contact with buyers for specific firms than has been typical in the past. Alternatively, working with these customers may require closer relationships—partnerships—with middlemen who can help producers with some of the required marketing functions.

It appears that U.S. hardwood firms face a variety of possible opportunities to expand sales and improve profits. Export markets, including Canada, appear to offer greater potential than has been captured. Further, some of the opportunities are ones that focus on the value-added products that have the potential to foster economic development in rural areas of the U.S. where such activities have in the past been limited. However, just having access to hardwood forests alone isn't enough to turn these opportunities into profitable business. Developing international markets for value-added hardwood products requires that individual supplier firms adapt their marketing strategies to marketplace needs. Producers need to identify specific target markets and understand the unique needs and buying behavior of these markets. They also need to get beyond production-oriented thinking and develop whole marketing mixes to serve their target customers. That means figuring out what type of products and services to offer. It also means making decisions about how to price specific offerings—because firms that are doing something unique for their customers won't just face perfect competition and a price that is set by the market. A firm that does a good job with this marketing strategy planning has the potential to satisfy some target customers very well and in the process gain a sustainable competitive advantage. And, of course, as more firms do that they will not only make better profits, but also contribute to the economic development of the areas in which they operate.

1. Why is it important for firms that produce and supply hardwood to adopt the marketing concept?
2. What are some of the ways hardwood products can be adapted to meet value-added market needs?
3. In what ways is the marketing strategy different for hardwood suppliers who focus on a specific target market than for firms that just sell roughsawn logs or green lumber in the commodity market?

4. What are some of the potential target markets for U.S. hardwood suppliers selling to the Canadian market? Which marketing mix variables are likely to be most important to the target markets you have identified?

2 Celestial Seasonings*

In the late 1960s, the era of Woodstock and Summer of Love music festivals, Mo and Peggy Siegel and two friends began picking herbs in the mountains around Aspen, Colorado. They decided to start a company that they named after one of their friends—Lucinda Ziesing, whose nickname was Celestial. The next year, 10,000 muslin bags of Mo's 36 Herb Tea were sewn, filled, and sold to a health-food store in Boulder, Colorado. A year later, Sleepytime Herb Tea was created, and the business was moved to a barn in Boulder. But that didn't last long. Mo and his friends were onto something hot! Soon they were purchasing herbs around the world and learning how to mass produce their product in a factory. Loose-pack tea was eventually replaced with single-serve tea bags, and additional flavors were created—all of which fueled sales. Today, Celestial Seasonings is recognized as a leader in herbal products, accounting for half the herbal tea market in the United States and expanding worldwide.

Celestial Seasonings' core business is herbal teas. Along with Mo's 36 Herb, Red Zinger, and their best-selling product, Sleepytime, the company has created over 60 different herbal teas.

The tea market is comprised of black teas, herbal and medicinal teas, diet teas, iced teas, and Chai, a sweet Indian spiced blend. The U.S. tea market has an annual growth rate of about 10 percent in recent years. Herbal and medicinal teas represent two-thirds of the total tea market and are growing at about 12 percent a year. Celestial Seasonings is the leading competitor in the herbal tea category, holding 50 percent market share. Other herbal tea competitors include Republic of Tea, Tazo (Starbucks), Yogi Tea, and Oregon Chai.

Herbal teas compete with traditional black teas, dominated by Lipton Tea Company. In the 70s, Celestial revolutionized the tea industry when it introduced the idea of herbal teas as flavorful, healthy beverages for everyday consumption. At that time, herbal teas were perceived as foul-tasting medicinal brews. Few retail stores carried a complete line of herbal teas, so creating awareness, favorable image, and distribution posed a daunting challenge to the company. Initially, Celestial Seasonings promoted and distributed its products through health-food stores.

In 1984, food industry giant Kraft Foods bought Celestial Seasonings. With its marketing muscle and channel power, Kraft expanded distribution of Celestial Seasonings and added a line of gourmet black teas under the Celestial brand name. Shortly after the Kraft buyout, Mo Siegel retired from the company, and Barney Feinblum was named successor. However, the Kraft way of doing business sometimes conflicted with Celestial's culture, which from the beginning was influenced by "hippie-style" entrepreneurship, employee involvement, and earth-friendly community initiatives.

*This case and the script for the accompanying video were prepared by Professor Davis Folsom of USC Beaufort.

The values of the company are epitomized in its belief statement:

> We believe in marketing and selling healthful and naturally oriented products that nurture people's bodies and uplift their souls. Our products must be superior in quality, of good value, beautifully artistic, and philosophically inspiring.

In 1988, Celestial Seasonings management along with a venture capital firm bought the company back from Kraft. A new board of directors was created, and new headquarters were constructed outside of Boulder, Colorado. In 1991, Mo Siegel returned as CEO and chairman of the board and agreed to stay until 1997.

During Mo's second period of leadership, Celestial Seasonings went public and attempted a variety of product diversifications. A partnership with Perrier was formed to license and produce a line of ready-to-drink bottled teas under the Celestial Seasonings brand. A line of After Dinner Teas was launched, targeting more upscale consumers than Celestial's original back-to-the-earth customers and promoting tea as an after-dinner beverage. Iced Delight teas were created and marketed as "Brews in Your Fridge." A licensing agreement with Warner-Lambert produced Celestial Seasonings Soothers, herbal throat drops. In 1995, with HP Hood Company, Celestial created iced tea flavored frozen popsicles, but they were not a market success. That same year, Celestial developed its first medicinal herb tea—Herbal Comfort. In 1997, based on the success of Herbal Comfort, Celestial Seasonings expanded the line of medicinal teas to include Echinacea, Green Tea, GinkoSharp, Diet Partner, GingerEase, Detox A.M., LaxaTea, and Melatonin P.M. Celestial Seasonings now has 46 percent (up from 24 percent in June 1998) of the fast-growing medicinal tea category.

In 1998, Celestial acquired Mountain Chai, a Boulder-based manufacturer of concentrated Indian-style tea. Six varieties of Mountain Chai were reformulated and introduced under the Celestial logo. That same year, a line of six green teas was launched. Green teas have been used in Asian cultures for hundreds of years and are known for their curative qualities. Green teas were introduced to the American market in the 60s but were not widely successful due to their bland taste.

In 1997, Mo Siegel's commitment to manage the company ended, and Steve Hughes, known in the industry for growing the Healthy Choice line of food products, became Celestial's CEO. With Hughes at the helm, Celestial Seasonings entered a new phase. Saying that Celestial was "a $500 million brand trapped in a $100 million business," Hughes initiated a series of efforts to leverage the Celestial brand name, including the creation of herbal supplements. According to Hughes,

> For 25 years we've cared about one thing—creating healthy, natural products that make our customers feel good. Our herbal supplement line is a natural extension of that mission. We know the power of herbs and the simple solutions they provide for good health. We want to share that.

Launched in April 1998 in capsule form, the herbal supplements line included nine single-herb extracts and eight advanced-formula blend products. The timing seemed perfect. Herbal supplements were rapidly gaining consumer acceptance as alternatives and additions to traditional health and wellness products. A 1998 Market Facts survey showed the percentage of Americans who reported using herbal supplements had grown from just 3 percent in 1990 to 37 percent in 1998, and almost 80 percent of respondents felt herbal supplements were safe to take. Herbal supplements also have a number of logical synergies with Celestial's existing products. Many of the same ingredients are used, and herbal supplements can be sold through the same distribution channels.

Herbal supplements are promoted on the company's Natural Wellness website (www.celestialseasonings.com):

> We do our best to eat right, get enough rest, and exercise, and the benefits are undeniable. But our health can be affected by things we can't control. Environmental toxins, emotional and physical stress and simply getting older create concerns that show up in many ways—as wrinkles, low energy, a flagging mood, and more. We're not defenseless, though. Nature, as usual, provides what we need.

Clearly, Celestial Seasonings is appealing to specific target market segments, like aging baby boomers and health-conscious consumers of all ages. In fact, whenever a new Celestial product or service is proposed, the first question asked is "What will Tracy think?" Tracy Jones is the company's nickname for their primary target market: a 35- to 54-year-old, college-educated, socially involved woman with a focus on healthy lifestyle and household income greater than $50,000. Tracy also is not a major viewer of television. Herbal supplements are primarily targeted to Tracy and secondarily targeted to other health-conscious consumers. With labels that talk about "Tummy Mint" and "Tension Tamer," these new herbal supplements are designed to strike an emotional chord in Tracy.

Launched with a $4 million dollar campaign and priced at a premium, the herbal supplements line brought in 21 percent of Celestial's revenues in 1998. But just as things looked as bright as a summer day in the Rockies, Celestial learned a classic marketing lesson. The market for herbal supplements peaked at the same time two major competitors, One a Day and Centrum, entered the market. Also, 1999 SPINS and AC-Nielsen market research data indicated a variety of changes in the herbal market. Green teas, medicinal blend teas, and Chai were gaining sales, but previously popular single-herb supplements, including St. John's Wort and Ginseng, showed sharp declines.

In response, Celestial restaged the herbal supplements line in 1999 by dropping six products, reducing the advertising budget, and doubling the number of capsules per bottle. Celestial's herbal supplements line still represents a major part of company sales, but initial enthusiasm has mellowed, and the marketing team has begun to look for new opportunities. Also, companies specializing in herbal supplements face several ethical and legal issues.

Almost 80 percent of American consumers believe that herbal supplements are *safe*. However, as one FDA director has stated, "Realize that the label term 'natural' doesn't guarantee that a product is safe. Think of poisonous mushrooms. They're natural." Herbal supplements companies must abide by FDA rules regarding claims of effectiveness of their products; they cannot represent their products as medicines. Mike Gross, Celestial's regulatory expert, explains, "What it all boils down to is that you cannot make any claim to cure, treat, prevent, mitigate, or diagnose any disease state—or even mention a disease! For example, you cannot say 'for the treatment of prostate enlargement' but you can say 'to keep your prostate healthy.'"

One new direction under consideration at most consumer goods companies is the Internet. Surprisingly, the Internet initiative at Celestial started in the Information Technology division of the organization. Celestial started a modest web storefront designed to educate consumers and sell seasonal items and gifts from its mail-order catalog. Then the catalog manager got onboard and the marketing group joined in to build this alternative channel.

Part of the success of Celestial's catalog and Internet sales is attributable to the company kitchen! Started in 1973 as a free lunch program for employees, outsiders began to drift in, wanting to buy products. As more and more customers visited the factory, the idea of a factory tour gained favor. Between 1994 and 1999, over 350,000 people took Celestial's factory tour, creating a huge database for catalog and Internet marketing strategies.

1. What kinds of synergies do herbal supplements have with herbal teas?
2. What environmental trends seem to be fueling sales growth for herbal supplements? What environmental trends pose threats to the sales and profits of herbal supplements?
3. What kinds of new products should Celestial Seasonings develop? What criteria would you use to evaluate new product ideas for Celestial Seasonings? Why?

3 Briggs & Stratton Corporation*

Briggs & Stratton is the world's largest producer of air-cooled gasoline engines for outdoor power equipment, mainly for lawn mowers. The company designs, manufactures, markets, and services these products—which are sold as components to original equipment manufacturers (OEMs) in 85 countries.

Steve Briggs and Harry Stratton started the company in 1909 to produce a six-cylinder, two-cycle engine similar to one Briggs had developed a few years earlier as an engineering student in college. The engine turned out to be too expensive to mass produce, so the partners turned their attention to designing and producing electrical parts for automobiles—including switches, starters, and regulators.

Later B&S acquired the patent for the Motor Wheel—a gasoline engine designed to fit on a bicycle. It was a market success and ultimately proved to be a good way to power several other types of vehicles. In some parts of Asia it was even used on rickshas.

To build on the success of the Motor Wheel, B&S looked for new markets for engines. Its search led to the development of a stationary utility engine for use on such products as garden

*This case and the script for the accompanying video were prepared by Roger C. Shoenfeldt.

cultivators and reel-type mowers. Before utility companies brought electricity to rural parts of the U.S., these B&S engines even powered refrigerators, milking machines, and elevators.

After World War II, the booming U.S. economy, the shift of population to the suburbs, and the growth of leisure time prompted new consumer interest in lawn and garden equipment. B&S saw this growth opportunity and shifted its focus to producing motors for the lawn mower manufacturers who served that market. But B&S didn't just try to push engines it was already producing.

At that time, most power mowers used two-cycle engines; their light weight made mowers easy to push. However, two-cycles weren't reliable and needed a mix of gas and oil—which was inconvenient for consumers. Four-cycle engines like the ones B&S produced were very reliable, but they were made from cast iron and very heavy. Marketing people at B&S realized that consumers wanted *both* reliability and light weight, so the firm designed a new lawn mower engine from aluminum alloy.

Over time, the Briggs & Stratton name has become almost synonymous with the lawn mower. Top producers such as Toro, Snapper, and John Deere proudly proclaim in their ads that their mowers are powered by a Briggs & Stratton engine. In fact, Briggs & Stratton is often the most prominent brand name on the mower, even though the engine is just a component. The Briggs & Stratton name helps sell the mowers because it means quality, reliability, and performance to consumers. Because of this reputation—and consumer demand—many retailers won't sell a mower unless it uses a Briggs & Stratton motor.

Early in the 1980s B&S faced a serious competitive threat. A shift in international exchange rates made Japanese products less expensive in the U.S. and other parts of the world. This gave Japanese motorcycle producers a pricing edge to expand into the market for small engines. Because B&S was the leading producer of small engines, any competitive inroads would be at its expense.

Marketers at B&S realized that to keep competitors from carving up its market they would need to fine tune the firm's offerings for specific market segments. A starting point for that effort was to develop new product lines—actually, whole marketing strategies—for each type of need rather than just trying to get economies of scale by serving bigger, but heterogeneous, product-markets. B&S invested $250 million to develop carefully targeted new products, build new plants, and develop new processes to improve quality and reduce costs.

B&S' new-product development effort for specific segments cut short the Japanese invasion and increased customer satisfaction and brand loyalty. That put B&S in a better position to deal with another change—a big shift in the channel of distribution for lawn mowers. In the past, most consumers bought lawn mowers from independent lawn and garden equipment dealers. However, over time mass-merchandisers have taken away almost all of that business. In fact, five of the largest retail chains now account for half of all the lawn mowers sold in the U.S.—and about 80 percent of B&S' lawn and garden equipment sales are through mass-merchandisers.

This concentration of purchasing power has given the big retail chains new clout in the channel of distribution. Retail buyers pressure lawn mower producers to keep costs and prices low; and the producers in turn expect B&S to keep its prices in check. While this has probably reduced the price premium that the B&S brand commands, it hasn't eliminated it. Retailers know that consumers want lawn mowers with B&S engines. So brand loyalty by final consumers gives B&S an advantage in negotiations with its producer-customers. Even so, the squeeze on profit margins throughout the channel—and intense competition—means that B&S must continue to find better ways to meet customers' needs if it is to maximize market share and earn attractive profits. And for B&S, developing innovative new products has long been the key to meeting needs better. Its skill in this arena is illustrated by its success in developing a 4-horsepower motor to fill a gap in its product line.

In 1993 B&S had four main lines of lawn mower engines. B&S' Classic 3.5-horsepower (HP) engine was at the low end of the price range and it was found on mowers priced at about $99. As the name implies, this reliable model has been popular for many years. If a customer wanted a bit more power and a mower that took less pulling effort to start, B&S' 3.75-HP Sprint engine was available on mowers that sell for about $119. For consumers who wanted an easy-starting engine that quietly conquered even the thickest grass, the Quantum 5.0-HP Plus line was the choice—on a mower that cost from $160 up to $500. Finally, B&S offered a top-of-the-line Diamond Plus model with about 6.0 HP, unique European styling, and all the bells and whistles. A customer who had to ask how much it cost probably couldn't afford it.

In spite of multiple models in each of these lines, B&S did not have a good 4-HP mower engine. Yet there was a clear market for one. B&S' main competitor, Tecumseh, proved that. Its 4-HP engine was a market leader. And B&S needed to develop a new engine if it wanted to compete for the segment of customers who wanted a 4-HP engine. To take customers away from Tecumseh, B&S marketers knew they needed to develop a cost-effective engine that was better than the Tecumseh model on all operating and performance criteria. Research also showed that styling was becoming an important purchase criterion for many customers—perhaps because that was the one difference in engines that consumers could see while shopping.

Although they had a clear idea of what the market wanted, marketing managers at B&S faced a real challenge. Creating a superior new engine wouldn't do much good if lawn mower producers and retailers didn't know about it, and *the* time and place to introduce an important new lawn and garden product was at a big, national trade show that was less than a year away. If they missed that date, they'd effectively lose a year. So getting the new product to market fast—without making costly mistakes—was critical.

To speed up development and also reduce costs, B&S designers created a contemporary, aerodynamic look with a computer-aided design (CAD) system; the tooling of the parts—direct from the computer drawings—was very fast. Further, B&S engineers used standard parts from other B&S engines when they could. This helped to control costs, reduce development time, cut inventory requirements, and later would make after-the-sale service easier and faster. As a result of efforts like these, the new product went from the concept stage to production in about nine months—in time for the trade show deadline.

While the new product team was developing the engine, B&S marketing people had other work to do. To emphasize the new engine's distinct identity, they used an individual brand name, Quattro, which means four in Spanish. They also developed promotional materials to use at the trade show, and started work on ads and other cooperative promotional materials so they would be ready for producers and retailers to use when the Quattro started to appear on lawn mowers in retail stores.

The B&S salespeople also started to call on their top OEM customers. Besides explaining the advantages of the new Quattro motor and answering questions, they provided hundreds of sample motors. That made it possible for the producers to get a head start in creating prototypes of new mowers to show their retailer-customers. And since the retailers have a big influence on the producer's purchase decisions, B&S salespeople also promoted the features of the new motor—and the pull appeal of the Briggs & Stratton name—to retail buyers.

The salespeople also explained the benefits of the B&S cooperative advertising arrangements and how they work. B&S provides cooperative advertising allowances and materials to all of its OEM customers and to the retailers who sell their products.

As a result of all this front-end planning, the Quattro got off to a very successful start. In fact, customer reaction to the new engine's sleek appearance, power, and reliability was so strong that demand was double what B&S had forecast. By mid-1995, the company was hard-pressed to keep up with demand.

That's one reason that during the first year B&S decided to focus the marketing effort for the Quattro primarily on the U.S. market. It didn't make sense to spend money promoting the product in foreign markets if supply would be limited. However, exports account for 21 percent of all B&S engine and parts sales, and the Quattro isn't likely to be an exception to that pattern. When the time comes for the Quattro's international rollout some changes in the domestic marketing strategies may be required. For example, while lawn and garden equipment is important in nations with developed economies, in less-developed countries the Quattro is likely to be used for other types of applications—in agricultural, marine, and other commercial markets.

1. Are there any disadvantages to Briggs & Stratton's decision to hold off introducing its new Quattro engine in international markets? Explain your thinking.
2. What are the marketing implications for Briggs & Stratton of the fact that the U.S. market for lawn mowers is in the market maturity stage?
3. Given that engines are such an important component in manufacturing lawn mowers, would it make sense for Briggs & Stratton to develop and market its own line of mowers? Explain your thinking.
4. Given B&S' ability to compete well with Japanese motorcycle producers when they tried to take market share away from Briggs & Stratton's small engines, would it make sense for Briggs & Stratton to produce a small motorcycle—or perhaps a motorscooter—to market in India and other countries where incomes are low but demand for personal transportation is increasing? Explain your thinking.

4 Frog's Leap Winery*

In order to save a $2.00 camping fee, John Williams rode his motorcycle into a field in the Napa Valley, pitched his tent, and was enjoying a good night's sleep until he was rudely awakened early the next morning by the owner of the property, Larry Turley, a local doctor. In order to make amends, John offered to share a bottle of wine with the doctor, and by the time the bottle was empty, the two had discovered they both shared a strong desire to make wine.

Having grown up on a dairy farm in western New York, John originally went to Cornell University to extend his studies as a dairyman. However, a fortuitous work-study program at Taylor Wine Company—and a few bottles of wine later—made John realize he was more interested in making wine than in returning to the family dairy farm. His newfound interest led him to enroll in the Enology and Viticulture Masters Program at the University of California, Davis. After concluding his studies at Davis, John returned to the Finger Lakes area of New York as the start-up winemaker at Glenora Wine Cellars. But having been exposed to the superior climate and soils of the Napa Valley, John eventually headed back to the Napa Valley to assume winemaking duties at Spring Mountain Vineyards.

Back in the Napa Valley, John reacquainted himself with the good doctor whose land he had poached on several years before, Larry Turley. Larry was now living on a small parcel of land called The Frog Farm, so named because an old ledger revealed that around the turn of the century frogs were raised there and sold for $.33 per dozen, destined no doubt for the tables of Victorian San Francisco restaurants. As a lark, they gathered some grapes and made a small quantity of wine. They called the Wine "Frog's Leap," a combination of a good-natured dig at Stag's Leap, the classy Napa Valley winery, and a tribute to The Frog Farm where Larry lived.

Because of their love of winemaking, they continued to make small quantities of the wine for several years and managed to sell a few cases each year to help defray expenses. John and Larry continued to produce the wine as a hobby—they both were still working full-time in their real jobs—and probably wouldn't have changed except for the fact that a wine writer from *The New York Times* picked up a bottle and wrote a column entitled "Frog's Leap: A Prince of a Wine." The free publicity resulted in hundreds of telephone calls and the sale of their entire year's production.

The opportunity to attempt to grow the winery was too hard to resist, and, according to John, the hobby became a real business when "We made the ultimate male sacrifice and decided to sell our motorcycles in order to raise the capital necessary to start the winery as a commercial venture."

Production grew from 700 cases of wine at its inception in 1982, to 2,900 cases in 1983, to 4,400 cases in 1984. By 1985, the winery was doing well enough for John to quit his paid employment at Spring Mountain Winery and make Frog's

---

*Peter Rainsford prepared this case and the script for the accompanying video. He would like to thank John Williams, founder and owner of Frog's Leap Winery, for providing information in the case and for his constructive suggestions during its preparation.

Leap his full-time job. Frog's Leap has continued to grow and produced more than 50,000 cases in 2000. There are a variety of reasons for its success, but the overriding theme is best summed up by the following paragraph from the company's mission statement:

> We will strive to produce wines of excellent value that are fresh, delicious, and natural using the best of Napa Valley's organically grown grapes. Our professional presentation will be juxtaposed with our image of irreverent humor, fun, genuine hospitality, openness, and honest caring.

The winery has always been committed to quality and has refused to compromise with respect to quality. As John says, "Our goal is to have fun making elegant wines with superb balance."

While the contents of the bottle may be award-winning quality, the exterior of the bottle reflects the fun and humor of the company. The company's motto is "Time's Fun When You're Having Flies." Each bottle's label—which won a prestigious wine label award at the time it was designed—features an elongated frog in mid leap; it also contains the instructions, "Open Other End," at the base of the label. The humor continues when the bottle is opened as the word "ribbit" is clearly marked on every cork. But make no mistake, their first objective is to produce world-class wines, and if awards are any indication, they are clearly meeting this objective.

Dan Berger described the quality of the wines in the holiday 1995 issue of *Wine Enthusiast*. In an article about the 10 most underrated wineries on the West Coast, Berger states,

> I don't know why people don't see the utter greatness in the wines John Williams makes. His Cabernets are packed with fruit and elegance, his Zinfandel is among the best made anywhere, and his Sauvignon Blanc is a world-beater. This is simply one of the best producers in California and it never seems to get the acclaim it deserves. Maybe John's label note "Open Other End" is too subtle for the number of reviewers. (For that matter, his cork says it all!)

Speaking of the label, John looked for an unknown artist who would be willing to design a label for $100 and several cases of wine. Charles House agreed to do the job and was specifically told not to put a frog on the label. But that's exactly what House created—a captivating, eye-catching rendition of a frog in full leap—a frog "going for it" all out! The label went on to win one of the nation's top graphic design awards, House became famous, and Frog's Leap wine labels became part of the Smithsonian's permanent collection.

By 1994, the winery was not only successful but was bursting at the seams. The company was still located at The Frog Farm, but the business had "succeeded far beyond our expectations." According to John, "Frog's Leap was faced with a lack of production space, a lack of office space, and the need to make the winery accessible to the public." There was also a sense that John and Larry had different goals for both the winery and their personal lives. Larry wanted to spend less time being a doctor and more time involved in the day-to-day aspects of making wine—but on a much smaller scale. They decided, in a very amicable agreement, to split the winery in half. Larry, who owned the property where Frog's Leap had been located, kept the winery, all the winemaking equipment, and the one acre of sauvignon blanc vines located at the site. John retained the Frog's Leap brand, the wine inventory, and the marketing program.

The only problem with the split was the fact that John needed a place to put his winery—it was a winery in name only. He quickly found the ideal spot, a 38-acre parcel on the Rutherford Crossroad with a 8,000-square-foot barn, The Red Barn, which had been built in 1884 as a winery. Although the barn needed a great deal of renovation, it was restorable for use as a winery. The site also provided John with the land he needed to grow some of his own grapes and to practice sustainable agriculture and organic farming.

In the six years since John moved the winery to The Red Barn location, Frog's Leap has continued to improve both its reputation and the quality of its wines. And it has been able to succeed even though more and more wineries have been built in the Napa Valley and as more and more big corporate wineries (e.g., Sutter Home, Robert Mondavi, and Kendall-Jackson, just to name a few) have dominated the Napa and Sonoma Valleys.

1. How would you describe the position strategy for Frog's Leap? How do you think it differs from a large, corporate winery such as Sutter Home?
2. How has Frog's Leap grown over the years? What are the growth strategies that John Williams plans to follow in the future?
3. Do you think the first half of the twenty-first century will be a hospitable environment for winemakers in the U.S.? Why or why not?

5 Girl Scouts*

Girl Scouting is dedicated to and available to all girls age 5 to 17. Today there are approximately 3.6 million Girl Scouts in the U.S., including over 2.7 million girls and nearly 900,000 adult members, most of whom are volunteers. Membership categories for the girls are

Category	*Age*	*Grade*
Daisy	5–6	K, 1
Brownie	6, 7, 8	1, 2, 3
Junior Girl Scout	8, 9, 10, 11	3, 4, 5, 6
Cadette Girl Scout	11, 12, 13, 14	6, 7, 8, 9
Senior Girl Scout	14–17	9–12

Membership is at an all-time high. In 1999, as a result of specific target market initiatives, growth was especially strong among Hispanic (a 6.3 percent increase) and African-American (5.9 percent increase) girls. And membership is not just limited to the United States. Through its membership in the World Association of Girl Guides and Girl Scouts, Girl Scouts of the U.S.A. (GSUSA) is part of a larger entity of over 10 million girls in 140 countries. Although some programs for

---

*This case and accompanying video script were prepared by Dr. George Prough, the University of Akron, with assistance from Lori Arguelles, Communications Director, GSUSA, and Mary Kintz, Director of Member Services, Western Reserve Girl Scouts Council.

overseas travel and adventure exist, the international link is still being developed and is not nearly as strong as the link between GSUSA and the local councils.

As is true for many nonprofit organizations, the Girl Scouts organization operates on two levels. At the corporate or headquarters level is Girl Scouts of the U.S.A., located in New York. A board of directors, a national president, and a national executive director run GSUSA. From these offices, plans are made for the national parent and for the local councils. These local councils may be thought of as strategic business units (SBUs) for the Girl Scouts. Over 300 local councils serve to direct the activities of the more than 226,000 troops in the United States and overseas. A local board of directors and an executive director manages each of these local councils. To become a part of GSUSA, each of these local councils must go through a type of accreditation review by the national organization. Every four years each council is reviewed, and if it continues to meet the established criteria, it will be rechartered. This chartering process provides GSUSA with a strong weapon to maintain some level of consistency for the strategies and actions of the member Girl Scout councils.

Strategic marketing planning clearly is necessary to run such a large organization. GSUSA does extensive corporate-level planning and also provides the local councils with assistance for their own formulation and execution of plans. Strategic marketing planning at the corporate level is the responsibility of the president and the board, with input from board committees, board task groups, community leaders, and community groups. Four steps are involved. The first step is a S.W.O.T. analysis, a review of internal strengths and external trends. This includes using the database maintained by GSUSA that details membership, program attendance, financial and development data, and similar benchmarks. The study of external trends results in the *Environmental Scanning Report,* which uses social, economic, political, and technological data from a variety of sources. This document is then made available to corporate- and council-level planners. One result of this S.W.O.T. analysis is the identification of a set of critical issues facing GSUSA. These issues are then used in the second step: to develop corporate goals covering a six-year period. These goals are reviewed at the midpoint of the planning period. In the third step, the group develops strategic guidelines, strategies, and long-range projects. Finally, the group develops long-range resource strategies that are needed to support the projects identified in the third step.

Staff and volunteers involved in implementing the strategic plans are responsible for the development of one-year plans (tactical planning). At this fourth step, priorities are established; specific operational goals are set; action plans are developed, including decisions about who, how, what, and when; and the operational budget is determined.

The completed corporate plan shapes all efforts and programs at the national level. However, local planners can exercise some discretion in planning for their markets. To accomplish local planning, some councils hold planning retreats with local board and community experts; some hold planning sessions for just staff; and some limit the efforts to a committee of the board. Whatever the process, the council board develops a set of five-year goals that it reviews annually. While these usually mirror national goals, each local council has the opportunity to change priorities or to add other goals peculiar to their local efforts. Using these goals, the staff develops proposals for specific objectives and action steps for board approval. These approved objectives and action steps form the basis for the local council's annual operating plan.

During the year, results are measured, compared to objectives, and subjected to corrective actions. Also during the year, the staff has the opportunity to reevaluate the goals that have been set by the board for the coming year and may provide suggestions to the board. The board then meets again early in the following year to plan for that year and to add goals for the fifth year in the current plan. Thus, the local council board always has a plan that looks five years ahead.

Marketing plans and efforts must be directed at three distinct groups. First, plans must be developed for recruiting and marketing efforts directed to the target market for Scouting: girls and their families. In addition, marketing plans also must target volunteers. Scouting could not function nearly as effectively without its giant network of volunteers, both at the local and national levels. There are over 880,000 adult members of Girl Scouting and most all of them are volunteers. Many of these volunteers were involved in scouting when they were young. Others are parents of current scouts.

Finally, the community at large represents an important stakeholder group. This group includes donors, both corporate and individual, who provide financial and other resources; schools and school counselors; church organizations and the like. During the S.W.O.T. analysis, all three groups are studied, and this provides input for recruitment plans and for the ongoing marketing efforts.

Quite clearly, young girls in the target demographic are the most important marketing target. Marketing efforts aimed at this group include recruitment efforts as well as retention efforts (keeping existing Scouts delighted with their experiences).

Plans of both types must consider the competition faced by Girl Scouting. All organizations face competition of various sorts, but Girl Scouts planners face an unusual situation. Essentially, the competition for Scouting is other activities that compete for a girl's time. This includes school clubs and other school-related activities; sports; private lessons such as piano, ballet, and music; church; and other social activities, including dating boys. However, the thinking about competition at Girl Scouts is different. Girl Scouting does not attempt to defeat the competition. Instead, Scouting embraces many of these competing activities and offers them as part of their product mix. If it finds that a certain activity is becoming more important to young girls, then Scouting looks at the possibility of incorporating that activity into its product mix of activities.

As girls mature, this kind of competition grows more intense. Older girls have more choices, making retention in these categories more difficult. As a result, there has been a growing concern that the programs and offerings of Girl Scouting, especially in the older age categories, is not sufficiently contemporary. Retention of these older girls is a problem. For instance, analysis of the U.S. membership shows the following data regarding the number of girls served by the Girl Scouts in each membership category:

Category	*Girls Served in the Category*
Daisy	1 of every 8
Brownie	1 of every 4
Junior Girl Scout	1 of every 7
Cadette Girl Scout	1 of every 25
Senior Girl Scout	1 of every 73

To better understand customers and the competing demands on their lives, Girl Scouts USA is beginning to do extensive market and customer research among young girls. During the fall of 2000, GSUSA launched the Girl Scout Research Institute, a research and public policy information center focusing on the healthy development of girls. Through this Institute, the GSUSA hopes to develop a large database of information on girls, with the additional goal of positioning itself as an information resource and expert on girls.

Within this competitive market, the GSUSA uses a variety of plans and strategies in order to attract new girls. The national website offers an overview for interested girls; however, it is not very interactive and has limited recruiting value. Nationally prepared brochures and literature are also available. Often these can be useful as stuffers in store, mall, and other point-of-sale display units. But many councils choose to localize and personalize these efforts. For these councils, most of the recruitment and marketing efforts are planned and developed at the local level. Local websites, school visits, locally prepared fliers, recruiting efforts at malls, churches, and other similar local activities lend a more personal touch to their recruiting.

Specific to certain types of competition, GSUSA has responded with a changing product mix. Each year, Girl Scouts adds to its diversity of activities and merit badges, all awarded for participation and mastery of particular tasks. With the increase in girls participating in sporting activities, Girl Scouts developed *GirlSports*, a program offering senior Girl Scouts from around the country a chance to spend a week during the summer developing certain sporting skills. During the 2000 version, 26 girls met in Oakland, California, with local athletes and trainers, learned 13 extreme sports, and met with and studied with ESPN fitness experts and Olympic athletes. An expanded version of *GirlSports* is being developed to include over 100,000 girls competing in nearly 2,300 different sporting events in over 300 councils.

Another trend identified was the increasing interest of girls in the sciences. As a result, the *Girl at the Center* program was developed. This is a science and technology program in which local councils can take advantage of partnerships between the Girl Scouts and over 31 science museums, encouraging families and girls to explore and to learn more about the sciences. The *Girl at the Center* and the *GirlSports* programs are examples of how the Girl Scouts organization is forming partnerships with others to make their programs relevant and successful.

Girl Scouting uses several methods to appeal to volunteers, both to attract them and to keep them motivated and involved. To attract volunteers at the national level, the website offers valuable insight as do the nationally prepared brochures highlighting the benefits of volunteering and the many ways of doing so. But again, the local councils often develop their own marketing efforts. Parents are targeted by maintaining a parents' network and involving parents in meetings and events. When the local council has events at malls or churches, the council staff involved makes every attempt to sell volunteering to adults as much as they do scouting to young girls. Additionally, many local councils work with area organizations in an attempt to generate volunteers. Universities, schools, the local housing authority, and other volunteer-based organizations have proven to be excellent sources of interns or other types of volunteers.

To keep volunteers motivated and involved, GSUSA national offers a variety of adult development and training opportunities. These include programs at the corporate training center, a number of online training offerings, and certification programs that support and enable the volunteers to improve their abilities to perform their functions.

The third stakeholder group consists of the community at large. Efforts to interact with this stakeholder group can be planned, and suggestions are made at the national level; however, many of these efforts involve personal contacts and one-on-one relationships with donors or other partnership targets. As a result, many of these efforts are developed and conducted by people at the local council level.

1. Compare strategic marketing planning by the Girl Scouts with planning by for-profit organizations. What are the similarities? What are the differences?
2. What changes would you suggest to improve the planning process in the Girl Scouts?

6 Volkswagen's New Beetle*

Volkswagen management was very surprised at the reaction to their latest design study, the Concept 1. Unveiled in Detroit at the North American International Auto Show in January 1994, the car was an instant hit with the public. Throngs of people crowded around the viewing stand to get a close look at what VW designers had created, a 90s version of the much-loved Beetle. The original Beetle had been sold in the U.S. from 1948 to 1981, and is still sold in some countries such as Mexico and Brazil.

Automotive design studies are used to gauge public reaction to styling and design ideas. The overwhelming response to the Concept 1, which closely resembled the looks of the original Beetle, prompted VW to study what was behind the strong consumer response. They wanted to know if the favorable response was because of the uniquely identifiable profile of the Beetle, the fond memories of the millions of U.S. Beetle owners, or simple nostalgia—a desire to be carried back to a "different" time.

It was clear that the Concept 1 touched the buying public at the auto show. The number of phone calls and letters to U.S. Volkswagen headquarters was so overwhelming that VW management promptly put a product-development team into

*This case and the script for the accompanying video were prepared by Professor Jim Burley.

action. The charge was to create a thoroughly modern version of the beloved Beetle, a car that would utilize the latest cutting-edge technologies housed in the uniquely identifiable shape of the most widely produced car in history.

Twenty-one million original Beetles have been built since the original idea for the car was shown to the German government in 1934 by Dr. Ferdinand Porsche. Porsche's dream was to build a simple, high-quality car for the masses, a car that even the average owner could learn to care for and maintain with minimal expense. That was the formula that had worked so well in the United States when Henry Ford introduced the Model T and put America on wheels.

Porsche's dream for the "people's car" (or Volkswagen) would not become a commercial reality until after World War II, though some prototypes and early production units had reached the public prior to the war's outbreak. By 1948, the war-damaged factory was rebuilt and the Beetle was being produced in full scale in Europe. It was also in that year that the Beetle was shown to the U.S. public at the N.Y. Auto Show. By the late 1950s the Beetle was the leading imported car in America, and hundreds of thousands of Americans were driving the small cars with air-cooled engines. Many people loved the simplicity and economy of the car, and the quality was very high. The car represented a very good value for the consumer's money.

Japanese auto manufacturers took notice of Volkswagen's success in the United States and designed their own competing models of small, economical cars. But they were different in character than the Beetle. The Japanese-produced small cars were more like shrunken versions of full-sized cars. They had big car styling and incorporated many features that U.S. car buyers of the 60s wanted, including power-assisted steering, power windows, and automatic transmissions. The small cars introduced by Toyota, Nissan, and Honda quickly cut into Volkswagen's sales volume. Although sales in the small-car category grew rapidly, increased competition left smaller sales volume for the previously dominant Beetle.

VW management held steadfastly to the "simple is beautiful" positioning that was carefully reinforced in the Beetle's advertising campaign. Advertisements with headlines such as "Ugly is only skin deep" reminded customers that the real beauty of the VW was its simplicity, reliability, and the economical ownership experience it produced. Despite this message, many people in the market were attracted to the larger choice of options and features found on the Japanese entries. After the Beetle's U.S. sales peaked at 423,000 units in 1968, sales began to decline.

Volkswagen responded to the market changes that were taking place by introducing the Rabbit, a small European hatchback that was refined to incorporate many of the features Americans wanted. The Rabbit was an immediate hit. Even though it did not have the instant recognizability of the Beetle, it benefited from the Beetle's reputation.

The decline of the Beetle in the U.S. was complete in 1981 when VW management removed it from sale in the U.S. market. However, VW continued to produce and sell the car in Mexico and South America. These were strong markets for the car because the Beetle was ideally suited to developing economies where simple and reliable transportation was more important than a long list of fancy accessories.

Although the original Beetle was a simple car, the New Beetle is not. As VW marketers began to develop the concept for the "New Beetle" they realized that the affluent American consumer expected features such as air-conditioning, stereo systems, and security features—as well as government-mandated safety items such as airbags and 5-MPH bumpers. The New Beetle would clearly require a degree of complexity and sophistication that Dr. Porsche could never have imagined.

The product development process incorporated customers' reactions from auto shows around the world. The reaction to the Concept 1 was nearly uniform worldwide, so VW management knew they would have a winner if they could build a street vehicle that incorporated the looks of the Concept 1 with an affordable platform. They found that platform in the one they were developing for the Golf, Europe's most popular car. With a few modifications, a New Beetle body could be built over a Golf chassis. This eliminated much of the time and expense of developing a completely new automobile. The use of the Golf platform also made it possible for VW to bring the New Beetle to market more quickly.

Just four years after first showing the Concept 1, VW management unveiled the New Beetle at the 1998 North American International Auto Show. The response to the "real" car was overwhelming. During much of the show it wasn't even possible to get near the car because of the crowds.

Executives from competing auto producers were astonished at consumers' reaction to the car, and were even more concerned when they learned more about VW's marketing strategy. Preintroduction guesses by the automotive media had suggested a price of $18,000 for the base car, but VW management priced the New Beetle at a low $15,200. This price included airbags, air-conditioning, power door locks, a multispeaker stereo system, tilt and telescoping steering, and many other attractive features. The automotive press in attendance at the unveiling applauded loudly when the price was announced.

Volkswagen marketers had crafted a very desirable new product that their dealers and customers were anxious to have. A promotional strategy was created to build enthusiasm for the car's official arrival in showrooms in spring 1998. Dealers were shown the car at a special party at Disney World in Orlando, Florida. There they not only got to drive the car but also to participate in Disney-style clinics on the attitudes and expectations of the New Beetle target market. Nostalgia was an important component of the target customers' feelings toward the car, but testing also revealed a broad demographic and psychographic appeal that included many young buyers who had never owned an older-style Beetle.

The dealers thought that the 50,000 units scheduled for production the first year would not be enough to satisfy the demand, but they were hopeful that some of the visitors to their showrooms could be switched to other VW products. VW's product line included cars that were either more economical or more spacious depending on the customers' needs. Jeff Williams, a VW dealer, explained the problems and the excitement associated with the new car:

> I'm sure we'll have trouble meeting the demand that seems to be in the market. The car is really exciting customers. I have one customer who's ordered one for his 19-year-old daughter. He hopes she can have as much fun with her car as he did with his Beetle 30 years ago.

1. Why didn't VW managers more accurately forecast the sales potential for the New Beetle?
2. Is styling really what sells cars or is it other factors?

7 Royal Appliance Manufacturing Company: Dirt Devil*

> You've just arrived on campus for the fall semester at college. Whether you're in a dorm room, apartment, or a rented home, in no time at all the place is sure to be a mess. And, looking at your current roommate situation, you probably won't get much help with the cleaning. You can either live with the disorder or get a new roommate—the Dirt Devil RoomMate. This new, lightweight upright vacuum may very well be the best companion a college student could ever have.

So begins an August 1997 press release from Dirt Devil, a subsidiary of Royal Appliance Manufacturing Company. The once staid and boring vacuum cleaner industry now sees college students as an interesting, vital target market.

The Dirt Devil brand has been responsible, in large part, for this new-found excitement. New product introductions and a groundbreaking advertising campaign are the latest chapters in the story of arguably the oldest vacuum cleaner manufacturing company in the world.

The first Royal vacuum cleaners were made by the P. A. Geier Company of Cleveland, Ohio, in 1905. As was the case with home computer companies in the 1970s and 1980s, Royal has its roots in a backyard garage. The company grew quickly and moved from the garage to a large, four-story structure where it produced vacuum cleaners, mixers, hair dryers, and washing machine units.

The core business of the P. A. Geier Company, however, continued to be vacuum cleaners. The industry's first hand-held vacuum, the Royal Prince, was introduced in 1937. The Geier company maintained its position in the vacuum cleaner industry until the firm was acquired in 1953 and renamed the Royal Appliance Manufacturing Company. The newly named organization was purchased by a group of employees in 1954 and moved to Highland Heights, Ohio, in 1969.

In 1984 Royal Appliance introduced another innovative product, the Dirt Devil Hand Vac, which was touted as a cleaner for couch cushions, stairs, and other hard-to-reach places. Between 1984 and 1997, its light weight, low price, and attractive red plastic body combined to create total sales of over 17 million units, making it the largest selling hand vac in the world. Royal now claims over 95 percent brand name awareness of the Dirt Devil name (up from 4 percent in 1990 and 21 percent in 1992), and it now commands 42 percent of the U.S. market for hand-held vacuums.

Of course, there have been some stumbles along the way. In 1990, Royal began to market Dirt Devil products throughout Europe and Great Britain. However, the European market did not take to the new products as well as Royal had hoped. And, on the domestic front, expensive promotion did not deliver a focused, unified message to American consumers. For example, dispersed promotion efforts in the U.S. in 1991 included advertising on Paul Harvey's radio program and sponsorship of race cars on the Indy Car and Nascar circuits. Because of problems such as these, performance began to dip. By 1995 mounting financial losses necessitated a change in company management and the sale of Royal's European operations. Royal's stock price at the end of 1995 was $2.50 per share, but it rebounded to $9 per share by the end of 1996—a year that saw $286 million in sales and $9.4 million in profit.

A revitalized Royal states its mission on its website.

> The company's mission is to bring innovative household products to the marketplace and thrill customers. It strives to recognize the needs of its customers and supply them with quality products that solve their cleaning problems. . . . The success of the company depends upon the continued introduction and promotion of new, innovative, high-quality products (www.dirtdevil.com).

This mission is associated with the Dirt Devil name—now used on virtually all of the company's consumer goods. The Royal brand name is reserved for high-end, heavy-duty, mostly industrial products. Most manufacturing is contracted out, leaving only some assembly to be done at corporate-owned facilities. This structure allows for the versatility and flexibility needed for the introduction and management of innovative products.

One of these new, innovative products is the Broom Vac. Launched in 1996, the Broom Vac was seen to be as creative as the original Royal Prince was at its debut. It also represented the type of newsworthy breakthrough that the Dirt Devil group needed. The Dirt Devil Broom Vac is a cordless, rechargeable broom that has a vacuum in the center of the unit's bristles to suck up dirt and dust in seconds. It does a better job of sweeping, and the user needs only to empty the filter and dirt compartment when full instead of bending over a dustpan.

Traditionally, the vacuum industry's products are classified as canister, upright, stick, or extractor cleaners. Hoover is recognized as the industry leader, emphasizing middle- and upper-end canisters, uprights, and sticks for an overall U.S. market share of 27 percent, followed by Eureka at 22 percent. Royal's strategy of innovative designs and distribution through mass-merchandisers has earned the company third place in the market and an 18 percent share.

But the industry doesn't know how to classify the Broom Vac. It is usually categorized as a stick vacuum by retailers and in industry sales figures, but it does not really fit in that market sector.

The development team at Dirt Devil was also concerned about how consumers would view the product. Would they perceive sufficient advantage over the usual broom and dustpan to pay a premium price? How much of a premium would they be willing to pay? Where would they want to purchase the product? How should the product be promoted? What should be the message?

In the past, Royal has distributed its products through independent vacuum cleaner dealers, regional retail chains, mass-merchants, and electronic and discount stores. However, none of these was considered to be completely adequate for introducing a high-volume product that would require demonstration of its advantages.

*This case and the script for the accompanying video were prepared by Professor Douglas Hausknecht. He expresses appreciation to Thomas F. Sherer, who assisted in developing the case.

The decision was made to introduce the Broom Vac using direct-response television advertising. This enabled Dirt Devil to control the demonstrations that were seen by prospective purchasers and to experiment with marketing variables. In test markets, variables such as price, shipping cost, and payment options were manipulated. A $50 price point was selected for the direct-response introduction. As the product moved into regular retail channels, this price was expected to be retained throughout the first year of sales.

In order to demonstrate the product fully, a two-minute infomercial was developed. The longer format allowed for a more complete explanation of the features and advantages. Dirt Devil and its advertising agency took pains to produce a high-quality infomercial to counter consumers' possible negative stereotypes of this advertising form. The infomercials concluded with toll-free telephone numbers and shipping information.

Most of the infomercials aired during lower-cost daytime and late-night hours. This provided added cost efficiency in the media purchase. Later, 15-second lifts (excerpts) from the infomercial were aired during prime time for the retail launch of the product.

At first, retailers were concerned that direct-response TV ads would just compete for their customers, but that did not happen. Dirt Devil's retailers found that customers came in looking for the product that they had seen on television. This exposed consumers to the Dirt Devil displays, which featured bright, colorful packaging and plenty of product information. Retailers found that sales volumes were enhanced and that customers required less "selling effort."

Retailers were also encouraged to use special shelf or floor displays of the product. Additionally, some retailers used newspaper inserts or other retail advertising in which Dirt Devil participated on a cooperative advertising basis. Eventually, as the original Broom Vac diffused throughout the market, retailers discounted the product from its original $50 price point.

As 1996 drew to a close, Dirt Devil was poised to once again agitate the industry. This time the shock would come not from a product innovation but rather from attention-getting communication. The grungy, boring, mature vacuum cleaner industry was to be represented in the showcase of American advertising—the Super Bowl.

On January 26, 1997, Dirt Devil aired three 15-second spots during the Super Bowl. Each spot highlighted a different product: the Broom Vac, the Ultra Hand Vac, and the Ultra MVP upright vacuum. This was the first Super Bowl exposure not only for Royal but for any vacuum cleaner.

The commercials featured these products acting as "dance partners" with the late Fred Astaire. The ad campaign, designed by Cleveland advertising agency Meldrum and Fewsmith, achieved several technical breakthroughs in its execution.

Although requested many times in the past, Fred Astaire's image had never been licensed to market any product. An agreement was reached with Astaire's widow based, in part, on the fact that actual dance footage would be used and that Mr. Astaire would not be seen as verbally endorsing any product. In fact, he does not speak in any of the commercials.

Why use Fred Astaire? In his films, Astaire often danced with props. Atomic Films SME of Los Angeles created the movie magic that substituted Dirt Devil products for the props originally used in the films, *Royal Wedding* (1951) and *Easter Parade* (1948). The message to be communicated was that using Dirt Devil products could make cleaning appear to be effortless, even fun!

Royal Appliance and its ad agency felt that the campaign needed to be both attention getting and entertaining in order to be successful. Happily, it was both! Independent tests immediately following the Super Bowl credited the Dirt Devil commercials with achieving good brand name recall (fifth overall among Super Bowl advertisers) and excellent recall of celebrity/brand name pairing (second among the advertisers using this technique). Separate research found the Astaire commercials finishing number one for correct sponsor identification and celebrity association with the brand. The performance was particularly notable since the Dirt Devil brand had relatively little exposure time (45 total seconds) compared to the other advertisers (ranging from one- to four-minute on-air times). Yet Dirt Devil had higher-ranked recall scores. The Bruzzone Research Company, which has extensively studied Super Bowl advertising since 1992, concluded that the Dirt Devil spots were "noticed by more people per dollar investment in airtime than anything we've seen in the past six years."

The commercials were also well received by the broadcasting and advertising industries. *Advertising Age* and other trade outlets gave favorable exposure and reviews. In addition to the 130 million plus Super Bowl viewers, the commercials were shown and/or described on *Entertainment Tonight*, *CBS Evening News*, *NBC Today Show*, *Good Morning America* (ABC), and *Dateline NBC*, and in over 200 additional television stories and 1,100 newspaper and magazine articles.

Concurrently, retail insert advertising was increased. Mr. Astaire was featured in the print advertising as well as in retail display material and on product packaging. Retailers were given advance notice of the campaign so that they could be prepared with adequate stock and have the option to participate in cooperative advertising. In most states, a Dirt Devil free standing insert (FSI) also promoted a sweepstakes with a $1 million grand prize. Finally, positive publicity was generated when Mrs. Astaire announced that the campaign was the first outcome of a joint effort by the Astaire estate and Dirt Devil to sponsor the Arthritis Foundation. The "ease of use" benefit delivered by Dirt Devil's products was a natural linkage to the arthritis cause. Royal executives, for their part, promised a redoubled effort to be responsive to the needs of consumers with arthritis in the design of new and modified products.

During 1997, some of these new products were tested and launched. The Mop Vac was introduced in April as a natural extension of the Broom Vac. With the Mop Vac, consumers could clean up by releasing a cleaning solution where needed from a container on the mop handle, scrubbing, then vacuuming the fluid through a squeegee to leave a clean, dry, streak-free floor. This new household tool was also introduced using direct-response advertising, at a $100 price point. The retail rollout was to follow in time for Christmas shopping in the fall.

Other products flesh out the Dirt Devil line, ranging from two old-fashioned carpet sweepers (using only rollers and brushes, no electricity required) to a new Broom Vac Extra (more suction and more dirt capacity than the original). Two wet/dry vacuums also are available, both featuring a detachable leaf blower (when the suction motor detaches from the storage "tank"). This foray into the outdoors was followed late in 1997 with the Dirt Devil Pick-up. This is a plastic wheelbarrow that was test-marketed via direct-response television. Its unique feature is the lift-and-load wheel mechanism, which allows the container to be flush to the ground for loading and unloading, then lift up to 400 pounds. The pick-up also includes a front trap door that makes the wheelbarrow easy to empty. Another nonvacuum product that was tested, this time without advertising, was a rug cleaner spray. Dirt Devil Carpet Stain Remover was marketed in Wal-Mart stores without manufacturer advertising beyond point of sale.

With all of these products and more on the way, it is no wonder that the Royal Appliance Manufacturing Company's well-known tagline boasts, "Nothing escapes the power of a Dirt Devil!"

1. Describe Dirt Devil's pricing strategy for its recent product introductions.
2. Explain how Dirt Devil integrated its marketing mix in the introduction of the Broom Vac.
3. Was the use of Fred Astaire in television commercials a good idea?
4. What kinds of products might Dirt Devil introduce next?
5. What problems might arise with retailers if Dirt Devil continues to expand its product line beyond basic floor care?

Cases

Guide to the Use of These Cases

Cases can be used in many ways. And the same case can be analyzed several times for different purposes.

"Suggested cases" are listed at the end of most chapters, but these cases can also be used later in the text. The main criterion for the order of these cases is the amount of technical vocabulary—or text principles—that are needed to read the case meaningfully. The first cases are "easiest" in this regard. This is why an early case can easily be used two or three times—with different emphasis. Some early cases might require some consideration of Product and Price, for example, and might be used twice, perhaps regarding product planning and later pricing. In contrast, later cases, which focus more on Price, might be treated more effectively *after* the Price chapters are covered.

In some of the cases, we have disguised certain information—such as names or proprietary financial data—at the request of the people or firms involved in the case. However, such changes do not alter the basic substantive problems you will be analyzing in a case.

1 McDonald's "Seniors" Restaurant

Suzanne Drolet is manager of a McDonald's restaurant in a city with many "seniors." She has noticed that some senior citizens have become not just regular patrons—but patrons who come for breakfast and stay on until about 3 pm. Many of these older customers were attracted initially by a monthly breakfast special for people aged 55 and older. The meal costs $1.99, and refills of coffee are free. Every fourth Monday, between 100 and 150 seniors jam Suzanne's McDonald's for the special offer. But now almost as many of them are coming every day—turning the fast-food restaurant into a meeting place. They sit for hours with a cup of coffee, chatting with friends. On most days, as many as 100 will stay from one to four hours.

Suzanne's employees have been very friendly to the seniors, calling them by their first names and visiting with them each day. In fact, Suzanne's McDonald's is a happy place—with her employees developing close relationships with the seniors. Some employees have even visited customers who have been hospitalized. "You know," Suzanne says, "I really get attached to the customers. They're like my family. I really care about these people." They are all "friends" and it is part of McDonald's corporate philosophy (as reflected in its website, www.mcdonalds.com) to be friendly with its customers and to give back to the communities it serves.

These older customers are an orderly group and very friendly to anyone who comes in. Further, they are neater than most customers and carefully clean up their tables before they leave. Nevertheless, Suzanne is beginning to wonder if anything should be done about her growing "non-fast-food" clientele. There's no crowding problem yet, during the time when the seniors like to come. But if the size of the senior citizen group continues to grow, crowding could become a problem. Further, Suzanne is concerned that her restaurant might come to be known as an "old people's" restaurant—which might discourage some younger customers. And if customers felt the restaurant was crowded, some might feel that they wouldn't get fast service. On the other hand, a place that seems busy might be seen as "a good place to go" and a "friendly place."

Suzanne also worries about the image she is projecting. McDonald's is a fast-food restaurant (there are over 29,000 of them in 120 countries), and normally customers are expected to eat and run. Will allowing people to stay and visit change the whole concept? In the extreme, Suzanne's McDonald's might become more like a European-style restaurant where the customers are never rushed and feel very comfortable about lingering over coffee for an hour or two! Suzanne knows that the amount her senior customers spend is similar to the average customer's purchase—but the seniors do use the facilities for a much longer time. However, most of the older customers leave McDonald's by 11:30—before the noon crowd comes in.

Suzanne is also concerned about another possibility. If catering to seniors is OK, then should she do even more with this age group? In particular, she is considering offering bingo games during the slow morning hours—9 AM to 11 AM. Bingo is popular with some seniors, and this could be a new revenue source—beyond the extra food and drink purchases that probably would result. She figures she could charge $5 per person for the two-hour period and run it with two underutilized employees. The prizes would be coupons for purchases at her store (to keep it legal) and would amount to about two-thirds of the bingo receipts (at retail prices). The party room area of her McDonald's would be perfect for this use and could hold up to 150 persons.

Evaluate Suzanne Drolet's current strategy regarding senior citizens. Does this strategy improve this McDonald's image? What should she do about the senior citizen market—that is, should she encourage, ignore, or discourage her seniors? What should she do about the bingo idea? Explain.

2 Healthy Foods, Inc.

It is 2002, and Don Warren, newly elected president of Healthy Foods, Inc., faces a severe decline in profits. Healthy Foods, Inc., is a 127-year-old California-based food processor. Its multiproduct lines are widely accepted under the Healthy Foods brand. The company and its subsidiaries prepare, package, and sell canned and frozen foods—including fruits, vegetables, pickles, and condiments. Healthy Foods, which operates more than 30 processing plants in the United States, is one of the larger U.S. food processors—with annual sales (in 2001) of about $650 million.

Until 2000, Healthy Foods was a subsidiary of a major midwestern food processor, and many of the present managers came from the parent company. Healthy Foods' last president recently said:

> The influence of our old parent company is still with us. As long as new products look like they will increase the company's sales volume, they are introduced. Traditionally, there has been little, if any, attention paid to margins. We are well aware that profits will come through good products produced in large volume.

Frederico Montegro, a 25-year employee and now production manager, agrees with the multiproduct-line policy. As he puts it: "Volume comes from satisfying needs. We will can or freeze any vegetable or fruit we think consumers might want." Frederico Montegro also admits that much of the expansion in product lines was encouraged by economics. The typical plants in the industry are not fully used. By adding new products to use this excess capacity, costs are spread over greater volume. So the production department is always looking for new ways to make more effective use of its present facilities.

Healthy Foods has a line-forcing policy, which requires that any store wanting to carry its brand name must be willing to carry all 65 items in the Healthy Foods line. This policy, coupled with its wide expansion of product lines, has resulted in 88 percent of the firm's sales coming from supermarket chain stores—such as Safeway, Kroger, and A&P. Smaller stores are generally not willing to accept the Healthy Foods policy. Frederico Montegro explains, "We know that only large stores can afford to stock all our products. But the large stores are the volume! We give consumers the choice of any Healthy Foods product they want, and the result is maximum sales." Many small retailers have complained about Healthy Foods' policy, but they have been ignored because they are considered too small in potential sales volume per store to be of any significance.

In late 2001, a stockholders' revolt over low profits (in 2001, they were only $500,000) resulted in Healthy Foods' president and two of its five directors being removed. Don Warren, an accountant from the company's outside auditing firm, was brought in as president. One of the first things he focused on was the variable and low levels of profits in the past several years. A comparison of Healthy Foods' results with comparable operations of some large competitors supported his concern. In the past 13 years, Healthy Foods' closest competitors had an average profit return on shareholders' investment of 6 to 12 percent, while Healthy Foods averaged only 2.5 percent. Further, Healthy Foods' sales volume, $650 million in 2001, has not increased much from the 1983 level (after adjusting for inflation)—while operating costs have soared upward. Profits for the firm were about $8 million in 1983. The closest Healthy Foods has come since then is about $6 million—in 1991. The outgoing president blamed his failure on an inefficient sales department. He said, "Our sales department has deteriorated. I can't exactly put my finger on it, but the overall quality of salespeople has dropped, and morale is bad. The team just didn't perform." When Don Warren e-mailed Lars Svensson, the vice president of sales, with this charge, his reply was,

> It's not our fault. I think the company made a key mistake in the late 70s. It expanded horizontally—by increasing its number of product offerings—while major competitors were expanding vertically, growing their own raw materials and making all of their packing materials. They can control quality and make profits in manufacturing that can be used in promotion. I lost some of my best people from frustration. We just aren't competitive enough to reach the market the way we should with a comparable product and price.

In a lengthy e-mail from Lars Svensson, Don Warren learned more about the nature of Healthy Foods' market. Although all the firms in the food-processing industry advertise heavily, the size of the market for most processed foods hasn't grown much for many years. Further, most consumers are pressed for time and aren't very selective. If they can't find the brand of food they are looking for, they'll pick up another brand rather than go to some other store. No company in the industry has much effect on the price at which its products are sold. Chain store buyers are very knowledgeable about prices and special promotions available from all the competing suppliers, and they are quick to play one supplier against another to keep the price low. Basically, they have a price they are willing to pay—and they won't exceed it. However, the chains will charge any price they wish on a given brand sold at retail. (That is, a 48-can case of beans might be purchased from any supplier for $18.10, no matter whose product it is. Generally, the shelf price for each is no more than a few pennies different, but chain stores occasionally attract customers by placing a well-known brand on sale.)

Besides insisting that processors meet price points, like for the canned beans, some chains require price allowances if special locations or displays are desired. They also carry nonadvertised brands and/or their own brands at lower price—to offer better value to their customers. And most will willingly accept producers' cents-off coupons—which are offered by Healthy Foods as well as most of the other major producers of full lines.

At this point, Don Warren is trying to decide why Healthy Foods, Inc., isn't as profitable as it once was. And he is puzzled about why some competitors are putting products on the market with low potential sales volume. (For example, one major competitor recently introduced a line of exotic foreign vegetables with gourmet sauces.) And others have been offering frozen dinners or entrees with vegetables for several years. Apparently, Healthy Foods' managers considered trying such products several years ago but decided against it because of the small potential sales volumes and the likely high costs of new-product development and promotion.

Evaluate Healthy Foods' present situation. What would you advise Don Warren to do to improve Healthy Foods' profits? Explain why.

3 Pillsbury's Häagen-Dazs

Jan Phillips is the newly hired ice cream product-market manager for the United States for Häagen-Dazs—the world's leading brand of super premium ice cream (now available in 55 countries) and the market leader in the U.S. Pillsbury says Häagen-Dazs (www.pillsbury.com/main/brands/haagen) is profitable globally, with total sales of more than $900 million. The company saw its sales grow rapidly during the 1990s, but now its markets are facing significant change and very aggressive competition. Phillips is responsible for Häagen-Dazs' ice cream strategy planning for the United States.

Other product-market managers are responsible for Europe, Japan, and other global markets. Therefore, Phillips will be expected to focus only on the United States while knowing that "everyone" will be watching her (and the United States) for clues about what may happen elsewhere.

Overall, ice cream sales in the U.S. have been off 1 to 2 percent in recent years. Still, some new entries have made a big splash. Starbucks, the coffee king, is one such brand. In its first year in grocery-store freezer sections, its Frappuccino bars—in several flavors—were a big hit. In addition, the Starbucks brand quickly became the nation's top-selling premium coffee ice cream. Häagen-Dazs, along with a few other super premium producers, are continuing to grow at rates of 2 to 3 percent. But most other U.S. super premium producers are reporting flat sales—and some are going out of business. The easy availability of super premium ice cream in supermarkets has hurt some of these producers who sell through ice cream stores, which specialize in take-out cones, sundaes, and small containers of ice cream. It is also thought that, at least in part, the decline in sales growth of super premium ice cream in the U.S. since the early 1990s is due to competition from other products such as lower-calorie yogurts and low-fat ice cream.

Despite a real concern about healthy diets, Americans seem to swing back and forth in their yearnings for low fat and rich taste. There is some evidence that "dessert junkies" who want to indulge without too much guilt are turning to low-fat frozen yogurt and low-fat ice cream. This has encouraged a number of super premium ice cream competitors to offer these products too. Pillsbury's Häagen-Dazs, International Dairy Queen, and Baskin Robbins are selling frozen yogurt. And Kraft—which makes Frusen Glädjè, Edy's, and Dreyer's Grand

Ice Cream—is among many other ice cream makers who are promoting gourmet versions of low-fat ice cream.

Because of the competition from low-fat products, Häagen-Dazs recently introduced a line of low-fat super premium ice cream. The new low-fat line contains no more than three grams of fat per serving. That compares with six times that or more grams of fat in a half-cup serving of its full-fat versions. Häagen-Dazs believes that its low-fat super premium ice cream is better tasting than other alternatives. Its belief is that "people like to make every calorie count." Having worked on the low-fat item for more than two years, it developed a process whereby a concentration of dairy proteins from lactose-reduced skim milk gives a mouth-feel that approximates that of a higher-fat product. Häagen-Dazs sells its low-fat products in a variety of flavors.

Most ice cream products are considered economy and regular brands—priced at $2 to $5 a half gallon. Super premium ice cream retails for $2.50 to $3.50 a *pint,* or $8 to $10 a half gallon. The retail price for a pint of Häagen-Dazs is usually over $3.00. The low-fat version is comparably priced to the full-fat product.

Many other U.S. ice cream producers have turned to frozen yogurt for growth. Frozen yogurt sales were in a slump for a long time because many people didn't like the tart taste. But after the product was reformulated it started to win customers. The difference is that today's frozen yogurt tastes more like ice cream.

The yogurt market leader, TCBY Enterprises, Inc. (www.tcby.com), which had sales of only about $2 million in 1983, has risen to over $100 million in sales. It numbers over 2,800 stores worldwide and is franchised in over 60 countries. In the U.S., yogurt makers are using aggressive promotion against ice cream. TCBY ads preach: "Say goodbye to high calories—say goodbye to ice cream" and "All the pleasure, none of the guilt." And the ads for its nonfat frozen yogurt emphasize: "Say goodbye to fat and high calories with the great taste of TCBY Nonfat Frozen Yogurt."

Baskin Robbins has introduced yogurt in many of its U.S. stores and has even changed its name to Baskin Robbins Ice Cream and Yogurt. Häagen-Dazs also offers yogurt in most of its stores.

Although the flurry of consumer interest in low-fat yogurt and low-fat ice cream certainly created some new market opportunities, it is not clear how consumers will react to these products over the longer term. One reason is that many consumers who were initially excited about being able to buy a good tasting, low-fat frozen dessert have realized that low fat does not necessarily mean low calorie. In fact, Jan Phillips has been trying to identify a product that Häagen-Dazs could produce that would offer consumers great taste, low fat, and low calories all at the same time. One possibility she is seriously considering is to introduce a line of sorbets based on exotic fruits like kiwi and mango and that use low-calorie sweeteners.

A sorbet is basically the same as sherbet, but European sorbets usually have an icy texture and include less milk. This is the sort of product that Jan Phillips has in mind. She thinks that it might have an upscale appeal and also be different from what is already in the premium ice cream case.

On the other hand, calling a product by a different name doesn't make it really new and different, and basic sherbet has been around for a long time and never been a big seller. Further, consumers don't think of sorbet in the same way that they think about a rich-tasting bowl of ice cream. You don't have to convince people that they might like premium ice cream. Sorbet, on the other hand, isn't something that consumers crave and make a special trip to buy.

Further, Phillips is very conscious that the Häagen-Dazs brand should stand for high quality and the best ingredients. Yet, it's not clear that consumers will think of sorbet as a premium product. Rather, they might just see it as ground-up ice with some flavoring thrown in. But if sorbet isn't the right way to go with new-product development, how should Häagen-Dazs counter the competition from other low-fat ice cream brands like Ben & Jerry's and other new entries to the super premium category like Starbucks?

Evaluate what is happening in the ice cream market, especially regarding the apparent leveling off of super premium ice cream sales and the possibilities for growth of the sorbet market. Is Jan Phillips' idea about rolling out a low-cal fruit sorbet a good idea? Would it be better to use the Häagen-Dazs brand name or a different brand name? What else, if anything, would need to be different about the strategy? Why?

4 Bidwell Carpet Cleaning, Inc.

Sharon Bidwell is getting desperate about her new business. She's not sure she can make a go of it—and she really wants to stay in her hometown of Petoskey, Michigan, a beautiful summer resort area along the eastern shore of Lake Michigan. The area's permanent population of 10,000 more than triples in the summer months and doubles at times during the winter skiing and snowmobiling season.

Sharon spent four years in the Navy after college graduation, returning home in June 2000. She decided to go into business for herself because she couldn't find a good job in the Petoskey area. She set up Bidwell Carpet Cleaning, Inc. She thought that her savings would allow her to start the business without borrowing any money. Her estimates of required expenditures were $9,000 for a used panel truck, $625 for a steam-cleaning machine adaptable to carpets and furniture, $400 for a heavy-duty commercial vacuum cleaner, $50 for special brushes and attachments, $100 for the initial supply of cleaning fluids and compounds, and $500 for insurance and other incidental expenses. This total of $10,675 still left Sharon with about $4,000 in savings to cover living expenses while getting started.

One of the reasons Sharon chose the cleaning business was her previous work experience. From the time she was 16 until she finished college, Sharon had worked part-time for Peter Kittany. Kittany operates the only successful complete (carpet, furniture, walls, etc.) cleaning company in Petoskey. (There is one other carpet-cleaning company in Petoskey, but it is rumored to be near bankruptcy.)

Kittany prides himself on quality work and has a loyal clientele. Specializing in residential carpet cleaning and furniture care, Kittany has built a strong customer franchise. For 35 years, Kittany's major source of new business—besides retailer recommendations—has been satisfied customers who tell friends about his quality service. He is so highly thought of that the leading carpet and furniture stores in Petoskey always recommend Kittany for preventive maintenance in quality carpet and furniture care. Often Kittany is given the keys to the area's finest homes for months at a time—when owners are out of town and want his services. Kittany's customers are so loyal, in fact, that Vita-Clean—a national household carpet-cleaning franchise—found it impossible to compete with him. Even price-cutting was not an effective weapon against Kittany.

Sharon Bidwell thought that she knew the business as well as Kittany—having worked for him many years. Sharon was anxious to reach her $60,000-per-year sales objective because she thought this would provide her with a comfortable living in Petoskey. While aware of cleaning opportunities in businesses such as office buildings and motels, Sharon felt that the sales volume available there was small because most businesses had their own cleaning staffs. As Sharon saw it, her only opportunity was direct competition with Kittany.

To get started, Sharon spent $1,400 to advertise her business in the local newspaper and on an Internet website. With this money she bought two large announcement ads and 52 weeks of daily ads in the classified section—listed under Miscellaneous Residential Services. The website simply listed businesses in the Petoskey area and gave a telephone number, e-mail address, and brief description. She put magnetic sign boards on her truck and waited for business to take off.

Sharon had a few customers and was able to gross about $150 a week. Of course, she had expected much more. These customers were usually Kittany regulars who, for one reason or another (usually stains, spills, or house guests), weren't able to wait the two weeks until Kittany could work them in. While these people agreed that Sharon's work was of the same quality as Kittany's, they preferred Kittany's "quality-care" image and they had an ongoing relationship with him. Sometimes Sharon did get more work than she could handle. This happened during April and May—when seasonal businesses were preparing for summer openings and owners of summer homes and condos were ready to "open the cottage." The same rush occurred in September and October—as many of these places were being closed for the winter. During these months, Sharon was able to gross about $130 to $150 a day—working 10 hours.

Toward the end of her discouraging first year in business, Sharon Bidwell is thinking about quitting. While she hates to think about leaving Petoskey, she can't see any way of making a living there in the carpet- and furniture-cleaning business. Kittany seems to have dominated the market—except in the rush seasons and for people who need emergency cleaning. And the resort housing market is not growing very fast, so there is little hope of a big increase in potential customers.

Evaluate Sharon Bidwell's strategy planning for her new business. Why wasn't she able to reach her objective of $60,000? What should Sharon do now? Explain.

5 Republic Polymer Company

Gary Walden, a chemist in Republic Polymer's polymer resins laboratory, is trying to decide how hard to fight for the new product he has developed. Walden's job is to find new, more profitable applications for the company's present resin products—and his current efforts are running into unexpected problems.

During the last four years, Walden has been under heavy pressure from his managers to come up with an idea that will open up new markets for the company's foamed polystyrene.

Two years ago, Walden developed the "foamed-dome concept"—a method of using foamed polystyrene to make dome-shaped roofs and other structures. He described the procedure for making domes as follows: The construction of a foamed dome involves the use of a specially designed machine that bends, places, and bonds pieces of plastic foam together into a predetermined dome shape. In forming a dome, the machine head is mounted on a boom, which swings around a pivot like the hands of a clock, laying and bonding layer upon layer of foam board in a rising spherical form.

According to Walden, polystyrene foamed boards have several advantages:

1. Foam board is stiff—but can be formed or bonded to itself by heat alone.
2. Foam board is extremely lightweight and easy to handle. It has good structural rigidity.
3. Foam board has excellent and permanent insulating characteristics. (In fact, the major use for foam board is as an insulator.)
4. Foam board provides an excellent base on which to apply a variety of surface finishes, such as a readily available concrete-based stucco that is durable and inexpensive.

Using his good selling abilities, Walden easily convinced his managers that his idea had potential.

According to a preliminary study by the marketing research department, the following were areas of construction that could be served by the domes:

1. Bulk storage.
2. Cold storage.
3. Educational construction.
4. Covers for industrial tanks.
5. Light commercial construction.
6. Planetariums.
7. Recreational construction (such as a golf-course starter house).

The marketing research study focused on uses for existing dome structures. Most of the existing domes are made of cement-based materials. The study showed that large savings would result from using foam boards—due to the reduction of construction time.

Because of the new technology involved, the company decided to do its own contracting (at least for the first four to five years). Walden thought this was necessary to make sure that no mistakes were made by inexperienced contractor crews. (For example, if not applied properly, the plastic may burn.)

After building a few domes in the United States to demonstrate the concept, Walden contacted some leading U.S. architects. Reactions were as follows:

> "It's very interesting, but we're not sure the fire marshal of Chicago would ever give his OK."

"Your tests show that foamed domes can be protected against fires, but there are no *good* tests for unconventional building materials as far as I am concerned."

"I like the idea, but foam board does not have the impact resistance of cement."

"We design a lot of recreational facilities, and kids will find a way to poke holes in the foam."

"Building codes in our area are written for wood and cement structures. Maybe we'd be interested if the codes change."

After this unexpected reaction, management didn't know what to do. Walden still thinks they should go ahead with the project. He wants to build several more demonstration projects in the United States and at least three each in Europe and Japan to expose the concept in the global market. He thinks architects outside the United States may be more receptive to really new ideas. Further, he says, it takes time for potential users to "see" and accept new ideas. He is sure that more exposure to more people will speed acceptance. And he is convinced that a few reports of well-constructed domes in leading trade papers and magazines will go a long way toward selling the idea. He is working on getting such reports right now. But his managers aren't sure they want to OK spending more money on "his" project. His immediate boss is supportive, but the rest of the review board is less sure about more demonstration projects or going ahead at all—just in the United States or in global markets.

Evaluate how Republic Polymer got into the present situation. What should Gary Walden do? What should Walden's managers do? Explain.

6 Three Rivers Steel Company

Three Rivers Steel Company is one of two major producers of wide-flange beams in the United States. The other producer is United Steel Corporation (now USX). A few small firms also compete, but they tend to compete mainly on price in nearby markets where they can keep transport costs low. Typically, all interested competitors charge the same delivered price, which varies some depending on how far the customer is from either of the two major producers. In other words, local prices are higher in more remote geographic markets.

Wide-flange beams are one of the principal steel products used in construction. They are the modern version of what are commonly known as I-beams. USX rolls a full range of wide flanges from 6 to 36 inches. Three Rivers entered the field about 20 years ago—when it converted an existing mill to produce this product. Three Rivers' mill is limited to flanges up to 24 inches, however. At the time of the conversion, Three Rivers felt that customer usage of sizes over 24 inches was likely to be small. In recent years, however, there has been a definite trend toward the larger and heavier sections.

The beams produced by the various competitors are almost identical—since customers buy according to standard dimensional and physical-property specifications. In the smaller size range, there are a number of competitors. But above 14 inches, only USX and Three Rivers compete. Above 24 inches, USX has no competition.

All the steel companies sell these beams through their own sales forces. The customer for these beams is called a structural fabricator. This fabricator typically buys unshaped beams and other steel products from the mills and shapes them according to the specifications of each customer. The fabricator sells to the contractor or owner of the structure being built.

The structural fabricator usually must sell on a competitive-bid basis. The bidding is done on the plans and specifications prepared by an architectural or structural engineering firm—and forwarded to the fabricator by the contractor who wants the bid. Although thousands of structural fabricators compete in the U.S., relatively few account for the majority of wide-flange tonnage in the various geographical regions. Since the price is the same from all producers, they typically buy beams on the basis of availability (i.e., availability to meet production schedules) and performance (i.e., reliability in meeting the promised delivery schedule).

Several years ago, Three Rivers' production schedulers saw that they were going to have an excess of hot-rolled plate capacity in the near future. At the same time, development of a new production technology allowed Three Rivers to weld three plates together into a section with the same dimensional and physical properties and almost the same cross-section as a rolled wide-flange beam. This development appeared to offer two key advantages to Three Rivers: (1) It would enable Three Rivers to use some of the excess plate capacity, and (2) larger sizes of wide-flange beams could be offered. Cost analysts showed that by using a fully depreciated plate mill and the new welding process it would be possible to produce and sell larger wide-flange beams at competitive prices—that is, at the same price charged by USX.

Three Rivers' managers were excited about the possibilities—because customers usually appreciate having a second source of supply. Also, the new approach would allow the production of up to a 60-inch flange. With a little imagination, these larger sizes might offer a significant breakthrough for the construction industry.

Three Rivers decided to go ahead with the new project. As the production capacity was converted, the salespeople were kept well informed of the progress. They, in turn, promoted this new capability to their customers—emphasizing that soon they would be able to offer a full range of beam products. Three Rivers sent several general information letters to a broad mailing list but did not advertise. The market development section of the sales department was very busy explaining the new possibilities of the process to fabricators—at engineering trade associations and shows.

When the new production line was finally ready to go, the market reaction was disappointing. No orders came in and none were expected. In general, customers were wary of the new product. The structural fabricators felt they couldn't use it without the approval of their customers—because it would involve deviating from the specified rolled sections. And as long as they could still get the rolled section, why make the extra effort for something unfamiliar—especially with no price advantage. The salespeople were also bothered with a very common question: How can you take plate that you sell for about $460 per ton and make a product that you can sell for $470? This question came up frequently and tended to divert the whole discussion to the cost of production rather than to the way the new product might be used or its value in the construction process.

Evaluate Three Rivers' situation. What should Three Rivers do?

 Lilybank Lodge

Nestled in the high country of New Zealand's South Island is a getaway adventure playground aimed unashamedly at the world's very wealthy. Presidents, playboys, and other such globe-trotters are the prime targets of this fledgling tourism business developed by Lilybank Lodge. The lodge offers this exclusive niche the opportunity of a secluded holiday in a little-known paradise. Guests, commonly under public scrutiny in their everyday lives, can escape such pressures at a hunting retreat designed specifically with their needs in mind.

A chance meeting between a New Zealand Department of Conservation investigator and the son of the former Indonesian president marked the beginning of this specialty tourist operation. Recognizing that "filthy rich" public figures are constantly surrounded by security and seldom have the luxury of going anywhere incognito, the New Zealander, Gerard Olde-Olthof, suggested that he and his new friend purchase a high-country station and hunting-guide company that was for sale. Olde-Olthof believed that the facilities, and their secluded and peaceful environment, would make an ideal holiday haven for this elite group. His Indonesian partner concurred.

Olde-Olthof, who was by now the company's managing director, developed a carefully tailored package of goods and services for the property. Architecturally designed accommodations, including a game trophy room and eight guest rooms, were constructed using high-quality South Island furniture and fittings, to create the ambience necessary to attract and satisfy the demands of their special clientele.

Although New Zealand had an international reputation for being sparsely populated and green, Olde-Olthof knew that rich travelers frequently complained that local accommodations were below overseas standards. Since the price (NZ$700 a night) was not a significant variable for this target market, sumptuous guest facilities were built. These were designed to be twice the normal size of most hotel rooms, with double-glazed windows that revealed breathtaking views. Ten full-time staff and two seasonal guides were recruited to ensure that visitors received superior customized service, in fitting with the restrained opulence of the lodge.

The 28,000 hectares of original farmland that made up the retreat and backed onto the South Island's Mount Cook National Park were converted into a big-game reserve. All merino sheep on the land were sold, and deer, elk, chamois, and wapiti were brought in and released. This was a carefully considered plan. Olde-Olthof, the former conservationist, believed that financially and environmentally this was the correct decision. Not only do tourists, each staying for one week and taking part in safari shooting, inject as much cash into the business as the station's annual wool clip used to fetch, but the game does less harm to the environment than sheep. Cattle, however, once part of the original station, were left to graze on lower riverflat areas.

For those high-flying customers seeking less bloodthirsty leisure activities, Lilybank developed other product-line extensions. Horse-trekking, golfing on a nearby rural course (with no need for hordes of security forces), world-class photographic opportunities, helicopter trips around nearby Lake Tekapo, nature walks, and other such activities formed part of the exclusive package.

While still in the early stages of operation, this retreat has already attracted a steady stream of visitors. To date the manager has relied solely on positive word of mouth, publicity, and public relations to draw in new customers. Given the social and business circles in which his potential target market moves, Olde-Olthof considers these to be the most appropriate forms of marketing communication. The only real concern for Lilybank Lodge has been the criticism of at least one New Zealand lobby group that the company is yet another example of local land passing into "foreign" hands, and that New Zealanders are prevented from using the retreat and excluded from its financial returns. However, this unwelcome attention has been fairly short-lived.

Identify the likely characteristics of the market segment being targeted by the company. Why are most target customers likely to be foreigners rather than New Zealanders? Suggest what expectations target customers are likely to have regarding the quality, reliability, and range of services. What are the implications for Lilybank Lodge? How difficult is it for Lilybank Lodge to undertake market research? Elaborate.

 Sophia's Ristorante

Sophia Manderino, the owner and manager of Sophia's Ristorante, is reviewing the slow growth of her restaurant. She's also thinking about the future and wondering if she should change her strategy. In particular, she is wondering if she should join a fast-food or family restaurant franchise chain. Several are located near her, but there are many franchisors without local restaurants. After doing some research on the Internet, she has learned that with help from the franchisors, some of these places gross $500,000 to $1 million a year. Of course, she would have to follow someone else's strategy and thereby lose her independence, which she doesn't like to think about. But those sales figures do sound good, and she has also heard that the return to the owner-manager (including salary) can be over $100,000 per year. She has also considered putting a web page for Sophia's Ristorante on the Internet but is not sure how that will help.

Sophia's Ristorante is a fairly large restaurant—about 2,000 square feet—located in the center of a small shopping center completed early in 2000. Sophia's sells mainly full-course "home-cooked" Italian-style dinners (no bar) at moderate prices. In addition to Sophia's restaurant, other businesses in the shopping center include a supermarket, a hair salon, a liquor store, a video rental store, and a vacant space that used to be a hardware store. The hardware store failed when a Home Depot located nearby. Sophia has learned that a pizzeria is considering locating there soon. She wonders how that competition will affect her. Ample parking space is available at the shopping center, which is located in a residential section of a growing suburb in the East, along a heavily traveled major traffic route.

Sophia graduated from a local high school and a nearby university and has lived in this town with her husband and two children for many years. She has been self-employed in the restaurant business since her graduation from college in 1979. Her most recent venture before opening Sophia's was a large restaurant that she operated successfully with her brother from 1990 to 1996. In 1996, Sophia sold out her share because of illness. Following her recovery, she was anxious for something to do and opened the present restaurant in April 2000. Sophia feels her plans for the business and her opening were well thought out. When she was ready to start her new restaurant, she looked at several possible locations before finally deciding on the present one. Sophia explained: "I looked everywhere, but here I particularly noticed the heavy traffic when I first looked at it. This is the crossroads for practically every main road statewide. So obviously the potential is here."

Having decided on the location, Sophia signed a 10-year lease with option to renew for 10 more years, and then eagerly attacked the problem of outfitting the almost empty store space in the newly constructed building. She tiled the floor, put in walls of surfwood, installed plumbing and electrical fixtures and an extra washroom, and purchased the necessary restaurant equipment. All this cost $100,000—which came from her own cash savings. She then spent an additional $1,500 for glassware, $2,000 for an initial food stock, and $2,125 to advertise Sophia's Ristorante's opening in the local newspaper. The paper serves the whole metro area, so the $2,125 bought only three quarter-page ads. These expenditures also came from her own personal savings. Next she hired five waitresses at $175 a week and one chef at $350 a week. Then, with $24,000 cash reserve for the business, she was ready to open. Reflecting her sound business sense, Sophia knew she would need a substantial cash reserve to fall back on until the business got on its feet. She expected this to take about one year. She had no expectations of getting rich overnight. (Her husband, a high school teacher, was willing to support the family until the restaurant caught on.)

The restaurant opened in April and by August had a weekly gross revenue of only $1,800. Sophia was a little discouraged with this, but she was still able to meet all her operating expenses without investing any new money in the business. By September business was still slow, and Sophia had to invest an additional $2,000 in the business just to survive.

Business had not improved in November, and Sophia stepped up her advertising—hoping this would help. In December, she spent $800 of her cash reserve for radio advertising—10 late-evening spots on a news program at a station that aims at middle-income America. Sophia also spent $1,100 more during the next several weeks for some metro newspaper ads.

By April 2001, the situation had begun to improve, and by June her weekly gross was up to between $2,100 and $2,300. By March 2002, the weekly gross had risen to about $2,800. Sophia increased the working hours of her staff six to seven hours a week and added another cook to handle the increasing number of customers. Sophia was more optimistic for the future because she was finally doing a little better than breaking even. Her full-time involvement seemed to be paying off. She had not put any new money into the business since summer 2001 and expected business to continue to rise. She had not yet taken any salary for herself, even though she had built up a small surplus of about $6,000. Instead, she planned to put in a bigger air-conditioning system at a cost of $4,000 and was also planning to use what salary she might have taken for herself to hire two new waitresses to handle the growing volume of business. And she saw that if business increased much more she would have to add another cook.

Evaluate Sophia's past and present marketing strategy. What should she do now? Should she seriously consider joining some franchise chain?

9 SleepyTime Motel

Eng Huang is trying to decide whether he should make some minor changes in the way he operates his SleepyTime Motel or if he should join either the Days Inn or Holiday Inn motel chains. Some decision must be made soon because his present operation is losing money. But joining either of the chains will require fairly substantial changes, including new capital investment if he goes with Holiday Inn.

Huang bought the recently completed 60-room motel two years ago after leaving a successful career as a production manager for a large producer of industrial machinery. He was looking for an interesting opportunity that would be less demanding than the production manager job. The SleepyTime is located at the edge of a very small town near a rapidly expanding resort area and about one-half mile off an interstate highway. It is 10 miles from the tourist area, with several nationally franchised full-service resort motels suitable for "destination" vacations. There is a Best Western, a Ramada Inn, and a Hilton Inn, as well as many mom and pop and limited-service, lower-priced motels—and some quaint bed and breakfast facilities—in the tourist area. The interstate highway near the SleepyTime carries a great deal of traffic, since the resort area is between several major metropolitan areas. No development has taken place around the turnoff from the interstate highway. The only promotion for the tourist area along the interstate highway is two large signs near the turnoffs. They show the popular name for the area and that the area is only 10 miles to the west. These signs are maintained by the tourist area's Tourist Bureau. In addition, the state transportation department maintains several small signs showing (by symbols) that near this turnoff one can find gas, food, and lodging. Huang does not have any signs advertising SleepyTime except the two on his property. He has been relying on people finding his motel as they go toward the resort area.

Initially, Huang was very pleased with his purchase. He had traveled a lot himself and stayed in many different hotels and motels—so he had some definite ideas about what travelers wanted. He felt that a relatively plain but modern room with a comfortable bed, standard bath facilities, and free cable TV would appeal to most customers. Further, Huang thought a swimming pool or any other nonrevenue-producing additions were not necessary. And he felt a restaurant would be a greater management problem than the benefits it would offer. However, after many customers commented about the lack of convenient breakfast facilities, Huang served a free continental breakfast of coffee, juice, and rolls in a room next to the registration desk.

Day-to-day operations went fairly smoothly in the first two years, in part because Huang and his wife handled registration and office duties as well as general management. During the first year of operation, occupancy began to stabilize around 55 percent of capacity. But according to industry figures, this was far below the average of 68 percent for his classification—motels without restaurants.

After two years of operation, Huang was concerned because his occupancy rates continued to be below average. He decided to look for ways to increase both occupancy rate and profitability and still maintain his independence.

Huang wanted to avoid direct competition with the full-service resort motels. He stressed a price appeal in his signs and brochures and was quite proud of the fact that he had been able to avoid all the "unnecessary expenses" of the full-service resort motels. As a result, Huang was able to offer lodging at a very modest price—about 40 percent below the full-service hotels and comparable to the lowest-priced resort area motels. The customers who stayed at SleepyTime said they found it quite acceptable. But he was troubled by what seemed to be a large number of people driving into his parking lot, looking around, and not coming in to register.

Huang was particularly interested in the results of a recent study by the regional tourist bureau. This study revealed the following information about area vacationers:

1. 68 percent of the visitors to the area are young couples and older couples without children.
2. 40 percent of the visitors plan their vacations and reserve rooms more than 60 days in advance.
3. 66 percent of the visitors stay more than three days in the area and at the same location.
4. 78 percent of the visitors indicated that recreational facilities were important in their choice of accommodations.
5. 13 percent of the visitors had family incomes of less than $24,000 per year.
6. 38 percent of the visitors indicated that it was their first visit to the area.

After much thought, Huang began to seriously consider affiliating with a national motel chain in hopes of attracting more customers and maybe protecting his motel from the increasing competition. There were constant rumors that more motels were being planned for the area. After some investigating, he focused on two national chain possibilities: Days Inn and Holiday Inn. Neither had affiliates in the area even though they have numerous units nationwide: Days Inn has about 1,900 units and Holiday Inn about 1,600.

Days Inn of America, Inc., is an Atlanta-based chain of economy lodgings. It has been growing rapidly and is willing to take on new franchisees. A major advantage of Days Inn is that it would not require a major capital investment by Huang. The firm is targeting people interested in lower-priced motels—in particular, senior citizens, the military, school sports teams, educators, and business travelers. In contrast, Holiday Inn would probably require Huang to upgrade some of his facilities, including adding a swimming pool. The total new capital investment would be between $300,000 and $500,000, depending on how fancy he got. But then Huang would be able to charge higher prices—perhaps $75 per day on the average rather than the $45 per day per room he's charging now.

The major advantages of going with either of these national chains would be their central reservation system and their national names. Both companies offer nationwide, toll-free reservation lines, which produce about 40 percent of all bookings in affiliated motels. Both companies also offer websites (www.daysinn.com and www.holiday-inn.com) that help find a specific hotel by destination, rate, amenities, quality rating, and availability.

A major difference between the two national chains is their method of promotion. Days Inn uses little TV advertising and less print advertising than Holiday Inn. Instead, Days Inn emphasizes sales promotions. In a recent campaign, for example, Blue Bonnet margarine users could exchange proof-of-purchase seals for a free night at a Days Inn. This tie-in led to the Days Inn system *selling* an additional 10,000 rooms. Further, Days Inn operates a September Days Club for travelers 50 and over who receive such benefits as discount rates and a quarterly travel magazine.

Days Inn also has other membership programs, including its InnCentives loyalty club for frequent business and leisure travelers. Other programs targeted to business travelers include two Corporate Rate programs and its new Days Business Place hotels. Not to be outdone, Holiday Inn has a membership program called Priority Club Worldwide.

Both firms charge 8 percent of gross room revenues for belonging to their chain—to cover the costs of the reservation service and national promotion. This amount is payable monthly. In addition, franchise members must agree to maintain their facilities and make repairs and improvements as required. Failure to maintain facilities can result in losing the franchise. Periodic inspections are conducted as part of supervising the whole chain and helping the members operate more effectively.

Evaluate Eng Huang's present strategy. What should he do? Explain.

 10 Runners World

Sue Koenig, owner of Runners World, is trying to decide what she should do with her retail business and how committed she should be to her current target market.

Sue is 39 years old, and she started her Runners World retail store in 1987 when she was only 24 years old. She was a nationally ranked runner herself and felt that the growing interest in jogging offered real potential for a store that provided serious runners with the shoes and advice they needed. The jogging boom quickly turned Runners World into a profitable business selling high-end running shoes—and Sue made a very good return on her investment for the first 10 years. From 1987 until 1997, Sue emphasized Nike shoes, which were well accepted and seen as top quality. Nike's aggressive promotion and quality shoes resulted in a positive image that made it possible to get a $5 to $7 per pair premium for Nike shoes. Good volume and good margins resulted in attractive profits for Sue Koenig.

Committing so heavily to Nike seemed like a good idea when its marketing and engineering was the best available. In addition to running shoes, Nike had other athletic shoes Sue could sell. So even though they were not her primary focus, Sue did stock other Nike shoes including walking shoes, shoes for aerobic exercise, basketball shoes, tennis shoes, and cross-trainers. She also added more sportswear to her store and put more emphasis on fashion rather than just function.

Even with this broadened product line, Sue's sales flattened out—and she wasn't sure what to do to get her business back in growth mode. She realized that she was growing older and so were many of her longer-term customers. Many of them were finding that jogging isn't just hard work—it's hard on the body, especially the knees. So many of her previously loyal runner-customers were switching to other, less demanding exercise programs. However, when she tried to orient her store and product line more toward these people she wasn't as effective in serving the needs of serious runners—still an important source of sales for the store.

She was also facing more competition on all fronts. Many consumers who don't really do any serious exercise buy running shoes as their day-to-day casual shoes. As a result, many department stores, discount stores, and regular shoe stores have put more and more emphasis on athletic shoes in their product assortment. When Sue added other brands and put more emphasis on fashion she found that she was in direct competition with a number of other stores—which put more pressure on her to lower prices and cut her profit margins. For example, in Sue's area there are a number of local and online retail chains offering lower-cost and lower-quality versions of similar shoes as well as related fashion apparel. Even Wal-Mart has expanded its assortment of athletic shoes—and it offers rock-bottom prices. Other chains, like Foot Locker, have focused their promotion and product lines on specific target markets. Still, all of them (including Sue's Runners World, the local chains, Wal-Mart, and Foot Locker) are scrambling to catch up with rival category killers whose selections are immense.

In the spring of 2000 Sue tried an experiment. She took on a line of high-performance athletic shoes that were made to order. The distinctive feature of these shoes was that the sole was molded to precisely fit the customer's foot. A pair of these custom-made shoes cost about $170, so the market was not large. Further, Sue didn't put much promotional emphasis on this line. However, when a customer came in the store with a serious interest in high-performance shoes, Sue's sales clerks would tell them about the custom shoe alternative and show a sample. When a customer was interested, a mold of the customer's bare foot was made at the store—using an innovative material that hardened in just a few minutes without leaving a sticky mess. Sue sent the mold off to the manufacturer by UPS, and about two weeks later the finished shoes arrived. Customers who tried these shoes were delighted with the result. However, the company that offered them ran into financial trouble and went out of business.

Sue recently learned about another company that is offering a very similar custom shoe program. However, that company requires more promotion investment by retailers and in return provides exclusive sales territories. Another requirement is that the store establish a website promoting the shoes and providing more detail on how the order process works. All of a retailer's salesclerks are also required to go through a special two-day training program so that they know how to present the benefits of the shoe and do the best job creating the molds. The training program is free, but Sue would have to pay travel, hotel, and food expenses for her salespeople. So before even getting started, the new program would cost her several thousand dollars.

Sue is uncertain about what to do. Although sales have dropped, she is still making a reasonable profit and has a relatively good base of repeat customers—with the serious runners still more than half of her sales and profits. She thinks that the custom shoe alternative is a way to differentiate her store from the mass-merchandisers and to sharpen her focus on the target market of serious runners. On the other hand, that doesn't really solve the problem that the "runners" market seems to be shrinking. It also doesn't address the question of how best to keep a lot of the aging customers she already serves who seem to be shifting away from an emphasis on running. She also worries that she'll lose the loyalty of her repeat customers if she shifts the store further away from her running niche and more toward fashionable athletic shoes or fashionable casual wear. Yet athletic wear—women's, in particular—has come a long way in recent years. Designers like Donna Karan, Calvin Klein, Georgio Armani, and Ralph Lauren are part of the fast-growing women's wear business.

So Sue is trying to decide if there is anything else she can do to better promote her current store and product line, or if she should think about changing her strategy in a more dramatic way. Any change from her current focus would involve retraining her current salespeople and perhaps hiring new salespeople. Adding and maintaining a website isn't an insurmountable challenge, but it is not an area where she has either previous experience or skill.

Clearly, a real shift in emphasis would require that Sue make some hard decisions about her target market and her whole marketing mix. She's got some flexibility—it's not like she's a manufacturer of shoes with a big investment in a factory that can't be changed. On the other hand, she's not certain she's ready for a big change—especially a change that would mean starting over again from scratch. She started Runners World because she was interested in running and felt she had something special to offer. Now she worries that she's just clutching at straws without a real focus or any obvious competitive advantage. She also knows that she is already much more successful than she ever dreamed when she started her business—and in her heart she wonders if she wasn't just spoiled by growth that came fast and easy at the start.

Evaluate Sue Koenig's present strategy. Evaluate the alternative strategies she is considering. Is her primary problem her emphasis on running shoes, her emphasis on trying to hang on to her current customers, or is it something else? What should she do? Why?

11 ChemTech

Jeannie Trenton, a new product manager for ChemTech, must decide what to do with a new engine cooling system product that is not doing well compared to the company's other cooling system products. ChemTech is one of the large chemical companies in the United States—making a wide line of organic and inorganic chemicals and plastics. Technical research has played a vital role in the company's growth.

Recently, one of ChemTech's researchers developed a new engine cooling system product—EC-301. Much time and money was spent on the technical phase, involving various experiments concerned with the quality of the new product. Then Jeannie Trenton took over and has been trying to develop a strategy for the product.

The engine coolant commonly used now is ethylene glycol. If it leaks into the crankcase oil, it forms a thick, pasty sludge that can cause bearing damage, cylinder scoring, or a dozen other costly and time-consuming troubles for both the operator and the owner of heavy-duty engines.

ChemTech researchers believed that the new product—EC-301—would be very valuable to the owners of heavy-duty diesel and gasoline trucks, as well as other heavy-equipment owners. Chemically, EC-301 uses a propanol base instead of the conventional glycol and alcohol bases. It cannot prevent leakage, but if it does get into the crankcase, it won't cause serious problems.

The suggested list price of EC-301 is $22 per gallon—more than twice the price of regular coolants. The higher price was set because of higher production costs and to obtain a "premium" for making a better engine coolant.

At first, Trenton thought she had two attractive markets for EC-301: (1) the manufacturers of heavy-duty trucks and (2) the users of heavy-duty trucks. ChemTech sales reps have made numerous calls. So far neither type of customer has shown much interest, and the sales manager is discouraging any more calls for EC-301. He feels there are more profitable uses for the sales reps' time. The truck manufacturer prospects are reluctant to show interest in the product until it has been proven in actual use. The maintenance managers for truck fleets, construction companies, and other users of heavy-duty trucks have also been hesitant. Some say the suggested price is far too high for the advantages offered. Others don't understand what is wrong with the present coolants and refuse to talk any more about paying extra for just another me-too product.

Explain what has happened so far. What should Jeannie Trenton do? Why?

12 Paper Supplies Corporation*

Diane Chin, marketing manager for Paper Supplies Corporation, must decide whether she should permit her largest customer to buy some of Paper Supplies' commonly used file folders under the customer's brand rather than Paper Supplies' own FILEX brand. She is afraid that if she refuses, this customer—Office Center, Inc.—will go to another file folder producer and Paper Supplies will lose this business.

Office Center, Inc., is a major distributor of office supplies and has already managed to put its own brand on more than 45 high-sales-volume office supply products. It distributes these products—as well as the branded products of many manufacturers—through its nationwide distribution network, which includes 150 retail stores. Now Ken Sawyer, vice president of marketing for Office Center, is seeking a line of file folders similar in quality to Paper Supplies' FILEX brand, which now has over 60 percent of the market.

This is not the first time that Office Center has asked Paper Supplies to produce a file folder line for Office Center. On both previous occasions, Diane Chin turned down the requests and Office Center continued to buy. In fact, Office Center not only continued to buy the file folders but also the rest of Paper Supplies' lines. And total sales continued to grow as Office Center built new stores. Office Center accounts for about 30 percent of Diane Chin's business. And FILEX brand file folders account for about 35 percent of this volume.

In the past Paper Supplies consistently refused such dealer-branding requests—as a matter of corporate policy. This policy was set some years ago because of a desire (1) to avoid excessive dependence on any one customer and (2) to sell its own brands so that its success is dependent on the quality of its products rather than just a low price. The policy developed from a concern that if it started making products under other customers' brands, those customers could shop around for a low price and the business would be very fickle. At the time the policy was set, Diane Chin realized that it might cost Paper Supplies some business. But it was felt wise nevertheless—to be better able to control the firm's future.

Paper Supplies Corporation has been in business 28 years and now has a sales volume of $40 million. Its primary products are file folders, file markers and labels, and a variety of indexing systems. Paper Supplies offers such a wide range of size, color, and type that no competition can match it in its part of the market. About 40 percent of Paper Supplies' file folder business is in specialized lines such as files for oversized blueprint and engineer drawings; see-through files for medical markets; and greaseproof and waterproof files for marine, oil field, and other hazardous environmental markets. Paper Supplies' competitors are mostly small paper converters. But excess capacity in the industry is substantial, and these converters are always hungry for orders and willing to cut price. Further, the raw materials for the FILEX line of file folders are readily available.

Paper Supplies' distribution system consists of 10 regional stationery suppliers (40 percent of total sales), Office Center, Inc. (30 percent), and more than 40 local stationers who have wholesale and retail operations (30 percent). The 10 regional stationers each have about six branches, while the local stationers each have one wholesale and three or four retail locations. The regional suppliers sell directly to large corporations and to some retailers. In contrast, Office Center's main volume comes from sales to local businesses and walk-in customers at its 150 retail stores.

Diane Chin has a real concern about the future of the local stationers' business. Some are seriously discussing the formation of buying groups to obtain volume discounts from vendors and thus compete more effectively with Office Center's 150 retail stores, the large regionals, and the superstore chains, which are spreading rapidly. These chains—for example, Staples, Office World, Office Max, and Office Depot—operate stores of 16,000 to 20,000 square feet (i.e., large stores compared to the usual office supply stores) and let customers wheel through high-stacked shelves to supermarket-like checkout

*Adapted from a case written by Professor Hardy, University of Western Ontario, Canada.

counters. These chains stress convenience, wide selection, and much lower prices than the typical office supply retailers. They buy directly from manufacturers, such as Paper Supplies, bypassing wholesalers like Office Center. It is likely that the growing pressure from these chains is causing Office Center to renew its proposal to buy a file line with its own name.

None of Diane's other accounts is nearly as effective in retailing as Office Center—which has developed a good reputation in every major city in the country. Office Center's profits have been the highest in the industry. Further, its brands are almost as well known as those of some key producers—and its expansion plans are aggressive. And now, these plans are being pressured by the fast-growing superstores—which are already knocking out many local stationers.

Diane is sure that Paper Supplies' brands are well entrenched in the market, despite the fact that most available money has been devoted to new-product development rather than promotion of existing brands. But Diane is concerned that if Office Center brands its own file folders it will sell them at a discount and may even bring the whole market price level down. Across all the lines of file folders, Diane is averaging a 35 percent gross margin, but the commonly used file folders sought by Office Center are averaging only a 20 percent gross margin. And cutting this margin further does not look very attractive to Diane.

Diane is not sure whether Office Center will continue to sell Paper Supplies' FILEX brand of folders along with Office Center's own file folders if Office Center is able to find a source of supply. Office Center's history has been to sell its own brand and a major brand side by side, especially if the major brand offers high quality and has strong brand recognition.

Diane is having a really hard time deciding what to do about the existing branding policy. Paper Supplies has excess capacity and could easily handle the Office Center business. And she fears that if she turns down this business, Office Center will just go elsewhere and its own brand will cut into Paper Supplies' existing sales at Office Center stores. Further, what makes Office Center's offer especially attractive is that Paper Supplies' variable manufacturing costs would be quite low in relation to any price charged to Office Center—that is, there are substantial economies of scale, so the extra business could be very profitable—if Diane doesn't consider the possible impact on the FILEX line. This Office Center business will be easy to get, but it will require a major change in policy, which Diane will have to sell to Paul Jennings, Paper Supplies' president. This may not be easy. Paul is primarily interested in developing new and better products so the company can avoid the "commodity end of the business."

Evaluate Paper Supplies' current strategy. What should Diane Chin do about Office Center's offer? Explain.

13 Mixed Media Technologies, Inc.

Josh Sullivan, manager of Mixed Media Technologies, Inc., is looking for ways to increase profits. But he's turning cautious after the poor results of his last effort—during the previous Christmas season. Mixed Media Technologies, Inc. (MMT), is located along a busy crosstown street about two miles from the downtown of a metropolitan area of 1 million and near a large university. It sells a wide variety of products used for its different types of multimedia presentations. Its lines include high-quality still, video, and digital cameras, color scanners for use with computers, and projection equipment—including 35-mm slide projectors, overhead projectors, and electronic projectors that produce large-screen versions of computer output. Most of the sales of this specialized equipment are made to area school boards for classroom use, to industry for use in research and sales, and to the university for use in research and instruction.

Mixed Media Technologies also offers a good selection of production-quality video media (including hard-to-get betacam tapes and recordable CDs), specialized supplies (such as the acetates used with full-color computer printers), video and audio editing equipment, and a specialized video editing service. Instead of just duplicating videos on a mass production basis, MMT gives each video editing job individual attention—to add an audio track or incorporate computer graphics as requested by a customer. This service is really appreciated by local firms that need help producing high-quality videos—for example, for training or sales applications.

To encourage the school and industrial trade, MMT offers a graphics consultation service. If a customer wants to create a video or computerized presentation, professional advice is readily available. In support of this free service, MMT carries a full line of computer software for multimedia presentations and graphics work.

MMT has four full-time store clerks and two outside sales reps. The sales reps call on business firms, attend trade shows, make presentations for schools, and help both present and potential customers in their use and choice of multimedia materials. Most purchases are delivered by the sales reps or the store's delivery truck. Many orders come in by phone or mail.

The people who make most of the over-the-counter purchases are (1) serious amateurs and (2) some professionals who prepare videos or computerized presentation materials on a fee basis. MMT gives price discounts of up to 25 percent of the suggested retail price to customers who buy more than $2,000 worth of goods per year. Most regular customers qualify for the discount.

In recent years, many amateur photo buffs have started to buy relatively inexpensive new digital cameras to capture family pictures. Frequently, the buyer is a computer user who wants to use the computer as a digital darkroom—and the cameras now available make this easy. MMT has not previously offered the lower-priced and lower-quality digital models such buyers commonly want. But Josh Sullivan knew that lots of such digital cameras were bought and felt that there ought to be a good opportunity to expand sales during the Christmas gift-giving season. Therefore, he planned a special pre-Christmas sale of two of the most popular brands of digital cameras and discounted the prices to competitive discount store levels—about $169 for one and $229 for the other. To promote the sale, he posted large signs in the store windows and ran ads in a Christmas gift-suggestion edition of the local newspaper. This edition appeared each Wednesday during the four weeks before Christmas. At these prices and with this promotion, Josh hoped to sell at least 100 cameras. However, when the Christmas returns were in, total sales were five cameras. Josh was extremely disappointed with these results—especially because trade experts suggested that sales of digital cameras in these price and quality ranges were up 200 percent over last year—during the Christmas selling season.

Evaluate what Mixed Media Technologies is doing and what happened with the special promotion. What should Josh Sullivan do to increase sales and profits?

14 Modern Horizons, Inc.

Melita Sanchez, owner of Modern Horizons, Inc., is deciding whether to take on a new line. She is very concerned, however, because although she wants more lines she feels that something is wrong with her latest possibility.

Melita Sanchez graduated from a large midwestern university in 1998 with a B.S. in business. She worked selling cellular telephones for a year. Then Melita decided to go into business for herself and formed Modern Horizons, Inc. Looking for opportunities, Melita placed several ads in her local newspaper in Columbus, Ohio, announcing that she was interested in becoming a sales representative in the area. She was quite pleased to receive a number of responses. Eventually, she became the sales representative in the Columbus area for three local computer software producers: Accto Company, which produces accounting-related software; Saleco, Inc., a producer of sales management software; and Invo, Inc., a producer of inventory control software. All of these companies were relatively small and were represented in other areas by other sales representatives like Melita Sanchez.

Melita's main job was to call on possible customers. Once she made a sale, she would fax the signed license agreement to the respective producer, who would then UPS the programs directly to the customer. The producer would bill the customer, and Sanchez would receive a commission varying from 5 to 10 percent of the dollar value of the sale. Sanchez was expected to pay her own expenses. And the producers would handle any user questions—either by using 800 numbers for out-of-town calls or by e-mail queries to a technical support group.

Sanchez called on anyone in the Columbus area who might use the products she sold. At first, her job was relatively easy, and sales came quickly because she had little competition. Many national companies offer similar products, but at that time they were not well represented in the Columbus area. Most small businesses needed someone to demonstrate what the software could do.

In 2000, Sanchez sold $250,000 worth of Accto software, earning a 10 percent commission; $100,000 worth of Saleco software, also earning a 10 percent commission; and $200,000 worth of Invo software, earning a 5 percent commission. She was encouraged with her progress and looked forward to expanding sales in the future. She was especially optimistic because she had achieved these sales volumes without overtaxing herself. In fact, she felt she was operating at about 60 percent of her capacity and could easily take on new lines. So she began looking for other products she could sell in the Columbus area. Recently, a manufacturer of small lift trucks approached her, but Melita wasn't too enthusiastic about this offer because the commission was only 2 percent on potential annual sales of $150,000.

Now Melita Sanchez is faced with another decision. The owner of the Metclean Company, also in Columbus, has made what looks like an attractive offer. She called on Metclean to see if the firm might be interested in buying her accounting software. The owner didn't want the software, but he was very impressed with Melita. After two long discussions, he asked if she would like to help Metclean solve its current problem. Metclean is having trouble with marketing and the owner would like Melita Sanchez to take over the whole marketing effort.

Metclean produces solvents used to make coatings for metal products. It sells mainly to industrial customers in the mid-Ohio area and faces many competitors selling essentially the same products and charging the same low prices. Metclean is a small manufacturer. Last year's sales were $400,000. It could handle at least four times this sales volume with ease, and is willing to expand to increase sales—its main objective in the short run. Metclean's owner is offering Melita a 12 percent commission on all sales if she will take charge of their pricing, advertising, and sales efforts. Melita is flattered by the offer, but she is a little worried because the job might require a great deal more traveling than she is doing now. For one thing, she would have to call on new potential customers in mid-Ohio, and she might have to travel up to 200 miles around Columbus to expand the solvent business. Further, she realizes that she is being asked to do more than just sell. But she did have marketing courses in college, and thinks the new opportunity might be challenging.

Evaluate Melita Sanchez's current strategy and how the proposed solvent line fits in with what she is doing now. What should she do? Why?

15 Morgan Company

Timothy Morgan, owner of Morgan Company, feels his business is threatened by a tough new competitor. And now Timothy must decide quickly about an offer that may save his business.

Timothy Morgan has been a sales rep for lumber mills for about 20 years. He started selling in a clothing store but gave it up after two years to work in a lumberyard because the future looked much better in the building materials industry. After drifting from one job to another, Timothy finally settled down and worked his way up to manager of a large wholesale building materials distribution warehouse in Buffalo, New York. In 1982, he formed Morgan Company and went into business for himself, selling carload lots of lumber to lumberyards in western New York and Pennsylvania.

Timothy works with five large lumber mills on the West Coast. They notify him when a carload of lumber is available to be shipped, specifying the grade, condition, and number of each size board in the shipment. Timothy isn't the only person selling for these mills—but he is the only one in his area. He isn't required to take any particular number of carloads per month—but once he tells a mill he wants a particular shipment, title passes to him and he has to sell it to someone. Timothy's main function is to find a buyer, buy the lumber from the mill as it's being shipped, and have the railroad divert the car to the buyer.

Having been in this business for 20 years, Timothy knows all of the lumberyard buyers in his area very well and is on good working terms with them. He does most of his business over the telephone or by e-mail from his small office, but he tries to see each of the buyers about once a month. He has been marking up the lumber between 4 and 6 percent—the standard markup, depending on the grades and mix in each car—and has been able to make a good living for himself and his family. The going prices are widely publicized in trade publications and are listed on the Internet, so the buyers can easily check to be sure Timothy's prices are competitive.

In the last few years, a number of Timothy's lumberyard customers have gone out of business—and others have lost sales. The main problem is competition from several national home-improvement chains that have moved into Timothy's market area. These chains buy lumber in large quantities direct from a mill, and their low prices, available inventory, and one-stop shopping are taking some customers away from the traditional lumberyards. Some customers think the quality of the lumber is not quite as good at the big chains, and some contractors stick with the lumberyards out of loyalty or because they get better service, including rush deliveries when they're needed. However, if it weren't for a boom in the construction market—helping to make up for lost market share—Timothy's profits would have taken an even bigger hit.

Six months ago, things got worse. An aggressive young salesman set up in the same business, covering about the same area but representing different lumber mills. This new salesman charges about the same prices as Timothy but undersells him once or twice a week in order to get the sale. On several occasions he even set up what was basically an e-mail-based auction to quickly sell excess wood that was not moving fast enough. Many lumber buyers—feeling the price competition from the big chains and realizing that they are dealing with a homogeneous product—seem to be willing to buy from the lowest-cost source. This has hurt Timothy financially and personally—because even some of his old friends are willing to buy from the new competitor if the price is lower. The near-term outlook seems dark, since Timothy doubts that there is enough business to support two firms like his, especially if the markup gets shaved any closer. Now they seem to be splitting the shrinking business about equally—as the newcomer keeps shaving his markup.

A week ago, Timothy was called on by Mr. DeBeer of Good Timber Mfg. Co., a large manufacturer of windows, raised-panel doors, and accessories. Good Timber doesn't sell to the big chains and instead distributes its quality line only through independent lumberyards. DeBeer knows that Timothy is well acquainted with the local lumberyards and wants him to become Good Timber's exclusive distributor (sales rep) of residential windows and accessories in his area. DeBeer gave Timothy several brochures on the Good Timber product lines. He also explained Good Timber's new support program, which will help train and support Timothy and interested lumberyards on how to sell the higher markup accessories. Later, in a lengthy e-mail, DeBeer explained how this program will help Timothy and interested lumberyards differentiate themselves in this very competitive market.

Most residential windows of specified grades are basically "commodities" that are sold on the basis of price and availability, although some premium and very low end windows are sold also. The national home-improvement chains usually stock and sell only the standard sizes. Most independent lumberyards do not stock windows because there are so many possible sizes. Instead, the lumberyards custom order from the stock sizes each factory offers. Stock sizes are not set by industry standards; they vary from factory to factory, and some offer more sizes. Most factories can deliver these custom orders in two to six weeks—which is usually adequate to satisfy contractors who buy and install them according to architectural plans. This part of the residential window business is well established, and most lumberyards buy from several different window manufacturers—to ensure sources of supply in case of strikes, plant fires, and so on. How the business is split depends on price and the personality and persuasiveness of the sales reps. And given that prices are usually similar, the sales rep–customer relationship can be quite important.

Good Timber Mfg. Co. gives more choice than just about any other supplier. It offers many variations in ⅛-inch increments—to cater to remodelers who must adjust to many situations. Good Timber has even set up a special system on an Internet website. The lumberyard can connect to the website, enter the specs for a window online, and within seconds get a price quote and estimated delivery time.

One reason DeBeer has approached Timothy Morgan is because of Timothy's many years in the business. But the other reason is that Good Timber is aggressively trying to expand—relying on its made-to-order windows, a full line of accessories, and a newly developed factory support system to help differentiate it from the many other window manufacturers.

To give Timothy a quick big picture of the opportunity he is offering, DeBeer explained the window market as follows:

1. For commercial construction, the usual building code ventilation requirements are satisfied with mechanical ventilation. So the windows do not have to operate to permit natural ventilation. They are usually made with heavy-grade aluminum framing. Typically, a distributor furnishes and installs the windows. As part of its service, the distributor provides considerable technical support, including engineered drawings and diagrams to the owners, architects, and/or contractors.
2. For residential construction, on the other hand, windows must be operable to provide ventilation. Residential windows are usually made of wood, frequently with light-gauge aluminum or vinyl on the exterior. The national chains get some volume with standard size windows, but lumberyards are the most common source of supply for contractors in Timothy's area. These lumberyards do not provide any technical support or engineered drawings. A few residential window manufacturers do have their own sales centers in selected geographic areas, which provide a full range of support and engineering services, but none are anywhere near Timothy's area.

Good Timber Mfg. Co. feels a big opportunity exists in the commercial building repair and rehabilitation market (sometimes called the retrofit market) for a crossover of residential windows to commercial applications—and it has designed some accessories and a factory support program to help lumberyards get this "commercial" business. For applications such as nursing homes and dormitories (which must meet commercial codes), the wood interior of a residential window is desired, but the owners and architects are accustomed to commercial grades and building systems. And in some older facilities, the windows may have to provide supplemental ventilation for a deficient mechanical system. So what is needed is a combination of the residential *operable* window with a heavy-gauge commercial exterior frame that is easy to specify and install. And this is what Good Timber Mfg. Co. is offering with a combination of its basic windows and easily adjustable accessory frames. Two other residential window manufacturers offer a similar solution, but neither has pushed its products aggressively and neither offers technical support to lumberyards or trains sales reps like Timothy to do the necessary job. DeBeer feels this could be a unique opportunity for Timothy.

The sales commission on residential windows would be about 5 percent of sales. Good Timber Mfg. Co. would do the billing and collecting. By getting just 20 to 30 percent of his lumberyards' residential window business, Timothy could earn about half of his current income. But the real upside would come from increasing his residential window share. To do this, Timothy would have to help the lumberyards get a lot more (and more profitable) business by invading the commercial market with residential windows and the bigger markup accessories needed for this market. Timothy would also earn a 20 percent commission on the accessories—adding to his profit potential.

Timothy is somewhat excited about the opportunity because the retrofit market is growing. And owners and architects are seeking ways of reducing costs (which Good Timber's approach does—over usual commercial approaches). But he is also concerned that a lot of sales effort will be needed to introduce this new idea. He is not afraid of work, but he is concerned about his financial survival.

Timothy thinks he has three choices:

1. Take DeBeer's offer and sell both window and lumber products.
2. Take the offer and drop lumber sales.
3. Stay strictly with lumber and forget the offer.

DeBeer is expecting an answer within one week, so Timothy has to decide soon.

Evaluate Timothy Morgan's current strategy and how the present offer fits in. What should he do now? Why?

16 Enviro Pure Water, Inc.*

Manish (Manny) Krishna established his company, Enviro Pure Water, Inc. (Enviro), to market a product designed to purify drinking water. The product, branded as the PURITY II Naturalizer Water Unit, is produced by Environmental Control, Inc., a corporation that focuses primarily on water purification and filtering products for industrial markets.

Enviro Pure Water is a small but growing business. Manny started the business with initial capital of only $20,000—which came from his savings and loans from several relatives. Manny manages the company himself. He has a secretary and six full-time salespeople. In addition, he employs two college students part-time; they make telephone calls to prospect for customers and set up appointments for a salesperson to demonstrate the unit in the consumer's home. By holding spending to a minimum, Manny has kept the firm's monthly operating budget at only $4,500—and most of that goes for rent, his secretary's salary, and other necessities like computer supplies and telephone bills.

The PURITY II system uses a reverse osmosis purification process. Reverse osmosis is the most effective technology known for improving drinking water. The device is certified by the Environmental Protection Agency to reduce levels of most foreign substances, including mercury, rust, sediment, arsenic, lead, phosphate, bacteria, and most insecticides.

Each PURITY II unit consists of a high-quality 1-micron sediment removal cartridge, a carbon filter, a sediment filter, a housing, a faucet, and mounting hardware. The compact system fits under a kitchen sink or a wet bar sink. An Enviro salesperson can typically install the PURITY II in about a half hour. Installation involves attaching the unit to the cold-water supply line, drilling a hole in the sink, and fastening the special faucet. It works equally well with water from a municipal system or well water and it can purify up to 15 gallons daily. Enviro sells the PURITY II to consumers for $395, which includes installation.

The system has no movable parts or electrical connections and it has no internal metal parts that will corrode or rust. However, the system does use a set of filters that must be replaced after about two years. Enviro sells the replacement filters for $80. Taking into consideration the cost of the filters, the system provides water at a cost of approximately $.05 per gallon for the average family.

There are two major benefits from using the PURITY II system. First, water treated by this system tastes better. Blind taste tests confirm that most consumers can tell the difference between water treated with the PURITY II and ordinary tap-water. Consequently, the unit improves the taste of coffee, tea, frozen juices, ice cubes, mixed drinks, soup, and vegetables cooked in water. Perhaps more important, the PURITY II's ability to remove potentially harmful foreign matter makes the product of special interest to people who are concerned about health and the safety of the water they consume.

The number of people with those concerns is growing. In spite of increased efforts to protect the environment and water supplies, there are many problems. Hundreds of new chemical compounds—ranging from insecticides to industrial chemicals to commercial cleaning agents—are put into use each year. Some of the residue from chemicals and toxic waste eventually enters water supply sources. Further, floods and hurricanes have damaged or completely shut down water treatment facilities in some cities. Problems like these have led to rumors of possible epidemics of such dread diseases as cholera and typhoid—and more than one city has recently experienced near-panic buying of bottled water.

Given these problems and the need for pure water, Manny believes that the market potential for the PURITY II system is

*The original version of this case was developed by Professor Ben Enis of the University of Southern California, and it is adapted for use here with his permission.

very large. Residences, both single-family and apartment, are one obvious target. The unit is also suitable for use in boats and recreational vehicles; in fact, the PURITY II is standard equipment on several upscale RVs. And it can be used in taverns and restaurants, in institutions such as schools and hospitals, and in commercial and industrial buildings.

There are several competing ways for customers to solve the problem of getting pure water. Some purchase bottled water. Companies such as Ozarka deliver water monthly for an average price of $.60 per gallon. The best type of bottled water is distilled water; it is absolutely pure because it is produced by the process of evaporation. However, it may be *too pure*. The distilling process removes needed elements such as calcium and phosphate—and there is some evidence that removing these trace elements contributes to heart disease. In fact, some health-action groups recommend that consumers not drink distilled water.

A second way to obtain pure water is to use some system to treat tapwater. PURITY II is one such system. Another system uses an ion exchange process that replaces ions of harmful substances like iron and mercury with ions that are not harmful. Ion exchange is somewhat less expensive than the PURITY II process, but it is not well suited for residential use because bacteria can build up before the water is used. In addition, there are a number of other filtering and softening systems. In general, these are less expensive and less reliable than the PURITY II. For example, water softeners remove minerals but do not remove bacteria or germs.

Manny's first year with his young company has gone quite well. Customers who have purchased the system like it, and there appear to be several ways to expand the business and increase profits. For example, so far he has had little time to make sales calls on potential commercial and institutional users or residential builders. He also sees other possibilities such as expanding his promotion effort or targeting consumers in a broader geographic area.

At present, Enviro distributes the PURITY II in the 13-county gulf coast region of Texas. Because of the Robinson-Patman Act, the manufacturer cannot grant an exclusive distributorship. However, Enviro is currently the only PURITY II distributor in this region. In addition, Enviro has the right of first refusal to set up distributorships in other areas of Texas. The manufacturer has indicated that it might even give Enviro distribution rights in a large section of northern Mexico.

The agreement with the manufacturer allows Enviro to distribute the product to retailers, including hardware stores, plumbing supply dealers, and the like. Manny has not yet pursued this channel, but a PURITY II distributor in Florida reported some limited success selling the system to retailers at a wholesale price of $275. Retailers for this type of product typically expect a markup of about 33 percent of their selling price.

Environmental Control, Inc., ships the PURITY II units directly from its warehouse to the Enviro office via UPS. The manufacturer's $200 per unit selling price includes the cost of shipping. Enviro only needs to keep a few units on hand because the manufacturer accepts faxed orders and then ships immediately—so delivery never takes more than a few days. Further, the units are small enough to inventory in the back room of the Enviro sales office. Several of the easy-to-handle units will fit in the trunk of a salesperson's car.

Manny is thinking about recruiting additional salespeople. Finding capable people has not been a problem so far. However, there has already been some turnover, and one of the current salespeople is complaining that the compensation is not high enough. Manny pays salespeople on a straight commission basis. A salesperson who develops his or her own prospects gets $100 per sale; the commission is $80 per unit on sales leads generated by the company's telemarketing people. For most salespeople, the mix of sales is about half and half. Enviro pays the students who make the telephone contacts $4 per appointment set up and $10 per unit sold from an appointment.

An average Enviro salesperson can easily sell 20 units per month. However, Manny believes that a really effective and well-prepared salesperson can sell much more, perhaps 40 units per month.

Enviro and its salespeople get good promotion support from Environmental Control, Inc. For example, Environmental Control supplies sales training manuals and sales presentation flip charts. The materials are also well done, in part because Environment Control's promotion manager previously worked for Electrolux vacuum cleaners, which are sold in a similar way. The company also supplies print copy for magazine and newspaper advertising and tapes of commercials for radio and television. Thus, all Enviro has to do is buy media space or time. In addition, Environmental Control furnishes each salesperson with a portable demonstration unit, and the company recently gave Enviro three units to be placed in models of condominium apartments.

Manny has worked long hours to get his company going, but he realizes that he has to find time to think about how his strategy is working and to plan for the future.

Evaluate Manish Krishna's current marketing strategy for Enviro Pure Water. How do you think he's doing so far, and what should he do next? Why?

myWedding.com

Gray Hunter is happy with her life but disappointed that the idea she had for starting her own business hasn't taken off as expected. Within a few weeks she either has to renew the contract for her Internet website or decide not to put any more time and money into her idea. She knows that it doesn't make sense to renew the contract if she doesn't come up with a plan to make her website-based business profitable—and she doesn't like to plan. She's a "doer," not a planner.

Gray's business, myWedding.com, started as an idea 18 months ago as she was planning her own wedding. She attended a bridal fair at the convention center in Raleigh, North Carolina, to get ideas for a wedding dress, check out catering companies and florists, and in general learn more about the various services available to newlyweds. While there she and her fiancé went from one retailer's booth to another to sign up for their wedding gift registries. Almost every major retailer in the city—ranging from the Home Depot warehouse to the Belk's department store to the specialty shops that handle imported crystal glassware—offered a gift registry. Some had computers set up to provide access to their online registries. Being listed in all of the registries improved the odds that her wedding gifts would be items she wanted and could use—and it saved time and hassle for gift-givers. On the way back from the fair, Gray and her fiancé discussed the idea that it would be a lot easier to register gift preferences once on a central Internet site than to provide lots of different stores with bits and pieces of information. A list at a website would also make it easier for gift-givers—at least those who were computer users.

When Gray got back home, she did an Internet search and found several sites that focused on weddings. The biggest seemed to be www.weddingchannel.com. It had features for couples who were getting married, including a national gift registry. The site featured products from a number of companies, especially large national retail chains; however, there was a search feature to locate people who provide wedding-related services in a local ZIP code area. Gray thought that the sites she found looked quite good, but that they were not as helpful as a site could be with a more local focus.

The more Gray and her fiancé discussed the idea of a website offering local wedding-related services, the more it looked like an interesting opportunity. Except for the annual bridal fair, there was no other obvious local place for consumers to get information about planning a wedding and buying wedding-related services. And for local retailers, florists, catering companies, insurance agents, home builders, and many other types of firms, there was no other central place to target promotion at newlyweds. Further, the amount of money spent on weddings and wedding gifts is very substantial, and right before and after getting married many young couples make many important purchase decisions for everything from life insurance to pots and pans. Spending on the wedding itself can easily exceed the cost of a year of college.

Gray was no stranger to the Internet. She worked as a website designer for a small firm whose one and only client was IBM. That IBM was the only client was intentional rather than accidental. A year earlier IBM had decided that it wanted to outsource certain aspects of its website development work and have it handled by an outside contractor. After negotiating a three-year contract to do IBM's work, several IBM employees quit their jobs and started the business. IBM was a good client, and all indications were that IBM could give the firm as much work as it could handle as it hired new people and prospected for additional accounts over the next few years. Gray especially liked the creative aspects of designing the "look" of a website, and technical specialists handled a lot of the subtle details.

Before joining this new company, Gray had several marketing-related jobs—but none had been the glamorous ad agency job she dreamed of in college as an advertising major. Her first job as a college graduate was with an ad agency, but she was in a backroom operation handling a lot of the arrangements for printing and mailing large-scale direct-mail promotions. In spite of promises that it was a path to other jobs at the agency, the pay was bad, the work was always pressured, and every aspect of what she had to do was boring. After six punishing months, she quit and went looking for something else.

When a number of job applications didn't turn up something quickly, she took a part-time job doing telemarketing calls for a life insurance company. Gray's boss told her that she was doing a great job reeling in prospects—but she hated disturbing people at night and just didn't like making sales pitches. Fortunately for her, that pain didn't last long. A neighbor in Gray's apartment complex got Gray an interview for a receptionist position at an ad agency. That, at least, got her foot in the door. Her job description wasn't very interesting, but in a small agency she had the opportunity to learn a lot about all aspects of the business—ranging from working on client proposals and media plans to creative sessions for new campaigns. In fact, it was from a technician at that agency that she learned to work with the graphics software used to create ad layouts and website pages. When the website design job came open at the new firm, her boss gave her a glowing recommendation, and in two days she was off on her new career.

Although Gray's jobs had not been high-profile positions, they did give her some experience in sales promotion, personal selling, and advertising. Those skills were complemented by the technical computer skills of her fiancé (now husband), who made a living as a database programmer for a large software consulting firm. Taking everything as a whole, they thought that they could get a wedding-related website up and running and make it profitable.

There were a number of different facets to the original plan for myWedding.com. One part focused on recruiting local advertisers and "sponsors" who would pay to be listed at the website and be allocated a web page (which Gray would design) describing their services, giving contact information, and links to their own websites. Another facet focused on services for people who were planning to be married. In addition to an online wedding gift registry, sections of the website provided information about typical wedding costs, planning checklists, details about how to get a required marriage license, and other helpful information (including a discussion forum with comments about the strengths and weaknesses of various local suppliers). A man and woman could sign up for the service online and could pay the modest $20 "membership" fee for a year by credit card. Friends, family, and invited guests could visit the website at no charge and get information about wedding preferences, local hotels, discounts on local car rentals, and even printable maps to all of the churches and synagogues in the area.

When Gray told friends about her plan they all thought it sounded like a great idea. In fact, each time she discussed it someone came up with another idea for a locally oriented feature to add to the website. Several friends said that they had tried national websites but that the information was often too general. But generating more new ideas was not the problem. The problem was generating revenue. Gray had already contracted for space from an Internet service provider and created some of the initial content for the website, but she only had four paying sponsors—two of whom happened to be family friends.

Gray started by creating a colorful flyer describing the website and sent it to most of the firms that had participated in the bridal fair. When no one sent back the reply coupon for more information, Gray started to make calls (mainly during her lunch hour at her full-time job). Some stores seemed intrigued by the concept, but no one seemed ready to sign up. One reason was that they all seemed surprised at the cost to participate and get ad space at the website—$2,400 a year (about the same as a 1/16-page display ad in the Raleigh Yellow Pages). Another problem was that no one wanted to be the first to sign up. As one florist shop owner put it, "If you pull this off and other florists sign up, then come back and I will too."

Getting couples to sign up went slowly too. Gray paid for four display ads in local Sunday newspapers in the society section, sent information sheets about the website to clergy in the area, listed the website with about 25 Internet search engines, and sent carefully crafted press releases announcing the service to almost every publication in the area. One article that resulted from a press release got some attention, and for a few weeks there was a flurry of e-mail inquiries about her web page. But after that it slowed to a trickle again.

Gray's diagnosis of the problem was simple. Most people thought it was a great idea, but few couples knew to look on the Internet for such a service. Similarly, potential advertisers—many of them small local businesses—were not accustomed to the idea of paying for Internet advertising. They didn't know if the cost was reasonable or if her site would be effective in generating business.

Gray's life as a married person was going great and her job as a web page designer kept her very busy. Her free time outside of work was always in short supply because the young crowd at her office always had some scheme for how to keep entertained. So she wasn't about to quit her job to devote full time to her business idea. Further, she thought that once it got rolling she would only have to devote 10 hours a week to it to earn an extra $30,000 a year. She didn't have delusions of becoming a "dot-com millionaire." She just wanted a good locally oriented business.

However, it still wasn't clear how to get it rolling. After a year of trying on and off, she only had four paying ad sponsors, and one of them had already notified her that he didn't plan to sign up again because it wasn't clear that the website had generated any direct leads or sales. Further, it looked like anything she could do to attract more "members" would end up being expensive and inefficient.

Gray thinks the idea has real potential, and she's willing to do the work. But she's not certain if she can make it pay off. She has to decide soon, however, because the bill for the Internet service provider is sitting on her desk.

What is Gray's strategy? What should she do? If she were to move forward, what strategy would you recommend? Does her financial goal seem realistic? Why?

18 Outdoor World, Inc.

Jamie McCullough, owner of Outdoor World, Inc., is worried about his business' future. He has tried various strategies for two years now, and he's still barely breaking even.

Two years ago, Jamie McCullough bought the inventory, supplies, equipment, and business of Outdoor World—located on the edge of Minneapolis, Minnesota. The business is in an older building along a major highway leading out of town—several miles from any body of water. The previous owner had sales of about $400,000 a year but was just breaking even. For this reason—plus the desire to retire to Arizona—the owner sold to Jamie for roughly the value of the inventory.

Outdoor World had been selling two well-known brands of small pleasure boats, a leading outboard motor, two brands of snowmobiles and jet-skis, and a line of trailer and pickup-truck campers. The total inventory was valued at $150,000—and Jamie used all of his own savings and borrowed some from two friends to buy the inventory and the business. At the same time, he took over the lease on the building—so he was able to begin operations immediately.

Jamie had never operated a business of his own before, but he was sure that he would be able to do well. He had worked in a variety of jobs—as a used-car salesman, an auto repairman, and a jack-of-all-trades in the maintenance departments of several local businesses.

Soon after starting his business, Jamie hired his friend, Omar, who had a similar background. Together, they handle all selling and setup work on new sales and do maintenance work as needed. Sometimes the two are extremely busy—at the peaks of each sport season. Then both sales and maintenance keep them going up to 16 hours a day. At these times it's difficult to have both new and repaired equipment available as soon as customers want it. At other times, however, Jamie and Omar have almost nothing to do.

Jamie usually charges the prices suggested by the various manufacturers—except at the end of a weather season when he is willing to make deals to clear the inventory. He is annoyed that some of his competitors sell mainly on a price basis—offering 10 to 30 percent off a manufacturer's suggested list prices—even at the beginning of a season! Jamie doesn't want to get into that kind of business, however. He hopes to build a loyal following based on friendship and personal service. Further, he doesn't think he really has to cut price because all of his lines are exclusive for his store. No stores within a five-mile radius carry any of his brands, although nearby retailers offer many brands of similar products.

To try to build a favorable image for his company, Jamie occasionally places ads in local papers and buys some radio spots. The basic theme of this advertising is that Outdoor World is a friendly, service-oriented place to buy the equipment needed for the current season. Sometimes he mentions the brand names he carries, but generally Jamie tries to build an image for concerned, friendly service—both in new sales and repairs—stressing "We do it right the first time." He chose this approach because, although he has exclusives on the brands he carries, there generally are 10 to 15 different manufacturers' products being sold in the area in each product category—and most of the products are quite similar. Jamie feels that this similarity among competing products almost forces him to try to differentiate himself on the basis of his own store's services.

The first year's operation wasn't profitable. In fact, after paying minimal salaries to Omar and himself, the business just about broke even. Jamie made no return on his $150,000 investment.

In hopes of improving profitability, Jamie jumped at a chance to add a line of lawn mowers, tractors, and trimmers as he was starting into his second year of business. This line was offered by a well-known equipment manufacturer who wanted to expand into the Minneapolis area. The equipment is similar to that offered by other lawn equipment manufacturers. The manufacturer's willingness to do some local advertising and to provide some point-of-purchase displays appealed to Jamie. And he also liked the idea that customers probably would want this equipment sometime earlier than boats and other summer items. So he thought he could handle this business without interfering with his other peak selling seasons.

It's two years since Jamie bought Outdoor World—and he's still only breaking even. Sales have increased a little, but costs have gone up too because he had to hire some part-time help. The lawn equipment helped to expand sales—as he had expected—but unfortunately, it did not increase profits as he had hoped. Jamie needed part-time helpers to handle this business—in part because the manufacturer's advertising had generated a lot of sales inquiries. Relatively few inquiries resulted in sales, however, because many people seemed to be shopping for deals. So Jamie may have even lost money handling the new line. But he hesitates to give it up because he doesn't want to lose that sales volume, and the manufacturer's sales rep has been most encouraging—assuring Jamie that things will get better and that his company will be glad to continue its promotion support during the coming year.

Jamie is now considering the offer of a mountain bike producer that has not been represented in the area. The bikes have become very popular with students and serious bikers in the last several years. The manufacturer's sales rep says industry sales are still growing (but not as fast as in the past) and probably will grow for many more years. The sales rep has praised Jamie's service orientation and says this could help him sell lots of bikes because many mountain bikers are serious about buying a quality bike and then keeping it serviced. He says Jamie's business approach would be a natural fit with bike customers' needs and attitudes. As a special inducement to get Jamie to take on the line, the sales rep says Jamie will not have to pay for the initial inventory of bikes, accessories, and repair parts for 90 days. And, of course, the company will supply the usual promotion aids and a special advertising allowance of $10,000 to help introduce the line to Minneapolis. Jamie kind of likes the idea of carrying mountain bikes because he has one himself and knows that they do require some service year-round. But he also knows that the proposed bikes are very similar in price and quality to the ones now being offered by the bike shops in town. These bike shops are service- rather than price-oriented, and Jamie feels that they are doing a good job on service—so he is concerned with how he could be "different."

Evaluate Jamie McCullough's overall strategy(ies) and the mountain bike proposal. What should he do now?

19 Chemical International, Inc.

Chemical International, Inc., is a multinational producer of various chemicals and plastics with plants in the United States, England, France, and Germany. It is run from its headquarters in New Jersey.

Kevin Duryea is marketing manager of Chemical International's plastics business. Kevin is reconsidering his promotion approach. He is evaluating what kind of promotion—and how much—should be directed to car producers and to other major plastics customers worldwide. Currently, Kevin has one salesperson who devotes most of his time to the U.S. car industry. This man is based in the Detroit area and focuses on GM, Ford, and Chrysler—as well as the various firms that mold plastics to produce parts to supply the car industry. This approach worked well when relatively little plastic was used in each car *and* the auto producers did all of the designing themselves and then sent out specifications for very price-oriented competitive bidding. But now the whole product planning and buying system is changing—and of course foreign producers with facilities in the U.S. are much more important.

How the present system works can be illustrated in terms of the approach Chrysler used on its project to design the Sebring.

Instead of the old five-year process of creating a new automobile in sequential steps, the new system is a team approach. Under the old system, product planners would come up with a general concept and then expect the design team to give it artistic form. Next engineering would develop the specifications and pass them on to manufacturing and suppliers. There was little communication between the groups and no overall project responsibility.

Under the new approach, representatives from all the various functions—planning, design, engineering, purchasing, marketing, and manufacturing—work together. In fact, representatives from key suppliers are usually involved from the outset. The whole team takes final responsibility for a car. Because all of the departments are involved from the start, problems are resolved as the project moves on—before they cause a crisis. Manufacturing, for example, can suggest changes in design that will result in higher productivity or better quality.

In the Sebring project, Chrysler engineers followed the Japanese lead and did some reverse engineering of their own. They dismantled several competitors' cars, piece by piece, looking for ideas they could copy or improve. This helped them learn how the parts were assembled and how they were designed. Eventually, Chrysler incorporated almost all of the best features into its design of the Sebring.

In addition to reverse engineering, Chrysler researchers conducted a series of market studies. This led to the inclusion of additional features, such as easier-to-read gauges, oil dipsticks painted a bright yellow for faster identification, and a net in the trunk to hold grocery bags upright.

Chrysler also asked assembly-line workers for suggestions before the car was redesigned and then incorporated their ideas into the new car. All bolts had the same-size head, for example, so workers didn't have to switch from one wrench to another.

Finally, Chrysler included its best suppliers as part of the planning effort. Instead of turning to a supplier after the car's design was completed, the Chrysler team signed long-term contracts with suppliers and invited them to participate in product planning.

Most other vehicles are now developed with an approach similar to this, and Chrysler is not alone in the effort. Ford, for example, used a very similar team approach to redesign its Taurus. And major firms in most other industries are using similar approaches. A major outgrowth of this effort has been a trend by these producers to develop closer working relationships with a smaller number of suppliers.

For example, the suppliers selected for the Sebring project were major suppliers who had already demonstrated a serious commitment to the car industry. They had not only the facilities, but also the technical and professional managerial staff who could understand—and become part of—the program management approach. Chrysler expected these major suppliers to join in its total quality management push and to be able to provide just-in-time delivery systems. Chrysler dropped suppliers whose primary sales technique was to entertain buyers and then submit bids on standard specifications.

Because many firms have moved to these team-oriented approaches and developed closer working relationships with a subset of their previous suppliers, Kevin Duryea is trying to determine if Chemical International's present effort is still appropriate. Kevin's strategy has focused primarily on responding to inquiries and bringing in Chemical International technical people as the situation seems to require. Potential customers with technical questions are sometimes referred to other noncompeting customers already using the materials or to a Chemical International plant—to be sure that all questions are answered. But basically, all producer-customers are treated more or less alike. The sales reps make calls and try to find good business wherever they can.

Each Chemical International sales rep usually has a geographic area. If an area like Detroit needs more than one rep, each may specialize in one or several similar industries. But Chemical International uses the same basic approach—call on present users of plastic products and try to find opportunities for getting a share (or bigger share) of existing purchases or new applications. The sales reps are supposed to be primarily order getters rather than technical specialists. Technical help can be brought in when the customer wants it or sometimes the sales rep simply sets up a conference call between Chemical International's technical experts, the buyer, and the users at the buyer's facility.

Kevin sees that some of his major competitors—including General Electric and Dow Chemical—are becoming more aggressive. They are seeking to affect specifications and product design from the start rather than after a product design is completed. This takes a lot more effort and resources, but Kevin thinks it may get better results. A major problem he sees, however, is that he may have to drastically change the nature of Chemical International's promotion. Instead of focusing primarily on buyers and responding to questions, it may be necessary to try to contact *all* the multiple buying influences and not only answer their questions but help them understand what questions to raise—and help answer them. Such a process may even require more technically trained sales reps. In fact, it may require that people from Chemical International's other departments—engineering, manufacturing, R&D, and distribution—get actively involved in discussions with their counterparts in customer firms. Further, use of e-mail and an Internet website might make ongoing contacts faster and easier.

While Kevin doesn't want to miss the boat if changes are needed, he also doesn't want to go off the deep end. After all, many of the firm's customers don't seem to want Chemical International to do anything very different from what it's been doing. In fact, some say that they're very satisfied with their current supply arrangements and really have no interest in investing in a close relationship with a single supplier.

Contrast Chrysler's previous approach to designing and producing cars to its program management approach, especially as it might affect suppliers' promotion efforts. Given that many other major producers have moved in the program management direction, what promotion effort should Kevin Duryea develop for Chemical International? Should every producer in every geographic area be treated alike—regardless of size? Explain.

20 Cable Designs, Inc.

Steve Russell, vice president of marketing for Cable Designs, Inc., is deciding how to organize and train his sales force—and what to do about Ron Pittman.

At its plant in Pittsburgh, Pennsylvania, Cable Designs, Inc., produces wire cable—ranging from ½ inch to 4 inches in diameter. Cable Designs sells across the United States and Canada. Customers include firms that use cranes and various other overhead lifts in their own operations—ski resorts and amusement parks, for example. The company's main customers, however, are cement plants, railroad and boat yards, heavy-equipment manufacturers, mining operations, construction companies, and steel manufacturers.

Cable Designs employs its own sales specialists to call on and try to sell the buyers of potential users. All of Cable Designs' sales reps are engineers who go through an extensive training program covering the different applications, product strengths, and other technical details concerning wire rope and cable. Then they are assigned their own district—the size depending on the number of potential customers. They are paid a good salary plus generous travel expenses—with small bonuses and prizes to reward special efforts.

Ron Pittman went to work for Cable Designs in 1982, immediately after receiving an engineering degree from the University of Wisconsin. After going through the training program, he took over as the only company rep in the Illinois district. His job was to call on and give technical help to present customers of wire cable. He was also expected to call on new customers, especially when inquiries came in. But his main activities were to (1) service present customers and supply the technical assistance needed to use cable in the most efficient and safe manner, (2) handle complaints, and (3) provide evaluation reports to customers' management regarding their use of cabling.

Ron Pittman soon became Cable Designs' outstanding representative. His exceptional ability to handle customer complaints and provide technical assistance was noted by many of the firm's customers. This helped Ron bring in more sales dollars per customer and more in total from present customers than any other rep. He also brought in many new customers—mostly heavy equipment manufacturers in northern Illinois. Over the years, his sales have been about twice the sales rep average, and always at least 20 percent higher than the next best rep—even though each district is supposed to have about the same sales potential.

Ron's success established Illinois as Cable Designs' largest-volume district. Although the company's sales in Illinois have not continued to grow as fast in the last few years because Ron seems to have found most of the possible applications and won a good share for Cable Designs, the replacement market has been steady and profitable. This fact is mainly due to Ron Pittman. As one of the purchasing managers for a large machinery manufacturer mentioned,

> When Ron makes a recommendation regarding use of our equipment and cabling, even if it is a competitor's cable we are using, we are sure it's for the best of our company. Last week, for example, a cable of one of his competitors broke, and we were going to

> give him a contract. He told us it was not a defective cable that caused the break, but rather the way we were using it. He told us how it should be used and what we needed to do to correct our operation. We took his advice and gave him the contract as well!

Four years ago, Cable Designs introduced a unique and newly patented wire sling device for holding cable groupings together. The sling makes operations around the cable much safer—and its use could reduce both injuries and lost-time costs due to accidents. The slings are expensive—and the profit margin is high. Cable Designs urged all its representatives to push the sling, but the only sales rep to sell the sling with any success was Ron Pittman. Eighty percent of his customers are currently using the wire sling. In other areas, sling sales are disappointing.

As a result of Ron's success, Steve Russell is now considering forming a separate department for sling sales and putting Ron Pittman in charge. His duties would include traveling to the various sales districts and training other representatives to sell the sling. The Illinois district would be handled by a new rep.

Evaluate Steve Russell's strategy(ies). What should he do about Ron Pittman and his sales force? Explain.

 21 Wire Solutions, Inc.

Myra Martinez, marketing manager of consumer products for Wire Solutions, Inc., is trying to set a price for her most promising new product—a space-saving shoe rack suitable for small homes or apartments.

Wire Solutions, Inc.—located in Ft. Worth, Texas—is a custom producer of industrial wire products. The company has a lot of experience bending wire into many shapes and also can chrome- or gold-plate finished products. The company was started 13 years ago and has slowly built its sales volume to $3.2 million a year. Just one year ago, Myra Martinez was appointed marketing manager of the consumer products division. It is her responsibility to develop this division as a producer and marketer of the company's own branded products—as distinguished from custom orders, which the industrial division produces for others.

Martinez has been working on a number of different product ideas for almost a year now and has developed several designs for CD holders, cassette holders, plate holders, doll stands, collapsible book ends, and other such products. Her most promising product is a shoe rack for crowded homes and apartments. The wire rack attaches to the inside of a closet door and holds eight pairs of shoes.

The rack is very similar to one the industrial division produced for a number of years for another company. That company sold the shoe rack and hundreds of other related items out of its "products for organizing and storing" mail-order catalog. Managers at Wire Solutions were surprised by the high sales volume the catalog company achieved with the rack. In fact, that is what interested Wire Solutions in the consumer market and led to the development of the separate consumer products division.

Martinez has sold hundreds of the shoe racks to various local hardware, grocery, and general merchandise stores, and wholesalers on a trial basis, but each time she has negotiated a price—and no firm policy has been set. Now she must determine what price to set on the shoe rack—which she plans to push aggressively wherever she can. Actually, she hasn't decided on exactly which channels of distribution to use. But trials in the local area have been encouraging, and as noted above, the experience in the industrial division suggests that there is a large market for this type of product. Further, she noticed that a Wal-Mart store in her local area was selling a similar rack made of plastic. When she talked casually about her product with the store manager, he suggested that she contact the chain's houseware buyers in the home office in Arkansas. The manufacturing cost on this product—when made in reasonable quantities—is approximately $2.80 if it is painted black and $3.60 if it is chromed. Similar products have been selling at retail in the $9.95 to $19.95 range. The sales and administrative overhead to be charged to the division will amount to $90,000 a year. This will include Martinez's salary and some office expenses. She expects that a number of other products will be developed in the near future. But for the coming year, she hopes the shoe rack will account for about half the consumer products division's sales volume.

Evaluate Myra Martinez's strategy planning so far. What should she do now? What price should she set for the shoe rack? Explain.

 22 PlastiForm Mfg., Inc.

David Houston, the marketing manager of PlastiForm Mfg., Inc., wants to increase sales by adding sales reps rather than "playing with price." That's how David describes what Will Houston, his father and PlastiForm's president, is suggesting. Will is not sure what to do either. But he does want to increase sales, so something new is needed.

PlastiForm Mfg., Inc.—of Long Beach, California—is a leading producer in the plastic forming machinery industry. It has patents covering over 200 variations, but PlastiForm's customers seldom buy more than 30 different types in a year. The machines are sold to plastic forming manufacturers to increase production capacity or replace old equipment.

Established in 1970, the company has enjoyed a steady growth to its present position with annual sales of $50 million.

Twelve U.S. firms compete in the U.S. plastic forming machinery market. Several Japanese, German, and Swedish firms compete in the global market, but the Houstons have not seen much of them on the West Coast. Apparently the foreign firms rely on manufacturers' agents who have not provided an ongoing presence. They are not good about following up on inquiries, and their record for service on the few sales they have made on the East Coast is not satisfactory. So the Houstons are not worried about them right now.

Each of the 12 U.S. competitors is about the same size and manufactures basically similar machinery. Each has tended to specialize in its own geographic region. None has exported much because of high labor costs in the United States. Six of the competitors are located in the East, four in the Midwest, and two—including PlastiForm—on the West Coast. The other West Coast firm is in Tacoma, Washington. All of the competitors offer similar prices and sell F.O.B. their factories.

Demand has been fairly strong in recent years. As a result, all of the competitors have been satisfied to sell in their geographic areas and avoid price-cutting. In fact, price-cutting is not a popular idea in this industry. About 15 years ago, one firm tried to win more business and found that others immediately met the price cut—but industry sales (in units) did not increase at all. Within a few years, prices returned to their earlier level, and since then competition has tended to focus on promotion and avoid price.

PlastiForm's promotion depends mainly on six company sales reps, who cover the West Coast. In total, these reps cost about $660,000 per year including salary, bonuses, supervision, travel, and entertaining. When the sales reps are close to making a sale, they are supported by two sales engineers—at a cost of about $120,000 per year per engineer. PlastiForm does some advertising in trade journals—less than $50,000—and occasionally uses direct mailings and trade show exhibits. It also has a simple home page on the Internet. But the main promotion emphasis is on personal selling. Any personal contact outside the West Coast market is handled by manufacturers' agents who are paid 4 percent on sales—but sales are very infrequent.

Will Houston is not satisfied with the present situation. Industry sales have leveled off and so have PlastiForm's sales—although the firm continues to hold its share of the market. Will would like to find a way to compete more effectively in the other regions because he sees great potential outside the West Coast.

Competitors and buyers agree that PlastiForm is the top-quality producer in the industry. Its machines have generally been somewhat superior to others in terms of reliability, durability, and productive capacity. The difference, however, usually has not been great enough to justify a higher price—because the others are able to do the necessary job—unless a PlastiForm sales rep convinces the customer that the extra quality will improve the customer's product and lead to fewer production line breakdowns. The sales rep also tries to sell the advantages of PlastiForm's better sales engineers and technical service people—and sometimes is successful. But if a buyer is mainly interested in comparing delivered prices for basic machines—the usual case—PlastiForm's price must be competitive to get the business. In short, if such a buyer has a choice between PlastiForm's and another machine *at the same price*, PlastiForm will usually win the business in its part of the West Coast market. But it's clear that PlastiForm's price has to be at least competitive in such cases.

The average plastic forming machine sells for about $220,000, F.O.B. shipping point. Shipping costs within any of the three major regions average about $4,000—but another $3,000 must be added on shipments between the West Coast and the Midwest (either way) and another $3,000 between the Midwest and the East.

Will Houston is thinking about expanding sales by absorbing the extra $3,000 to $6,000 in freight cost that occurs if a midwestern or eastern customer buys from his West Coast location. By doing this, he would not actually be cutting price in those markets but rather reducing his net return. He thinks that his competitors would not see this as price competition and therefore would not resort to cutting prices themselves.

David Houston, the marketing manager, disagrees. David thinks that the proposed freight absorption plan would stimulate price competition in the Midwest and East and perhaps on the West Coast. He proposes instead that PlastiForm hire some sales reps to work the Midwest and Eastern regions—selling quality—rather than relying on the manufacturers' agents. He argues that two additional sales reps in each of these regions would not increase costs too much and might greatly increase the sales from these markets over that brought in by the agents. With this plan, there would be no need to absorb the freight and risk disrupting the status quo. Adding more of PlastiForm's own sales reps is especially important, he argues, because competition in the Midwest and East is somewhat hotter than on the West Coast—due to the number of competitors (including foreign competitors) in those regions. A lot of expensive entertaining, for example, seems to be required just to be considered as a potential supplier. In contrast, the situation has been rather quiet in the West—because only two firms are sharing this market and each is working harder near its home base. The eastern and midwestern competitors don't send any sales reps to the West Coast—and if they have any manufacturers' agents, they haven't gotten any business in recent years.

Will Houston agrees that his son has a point, but industry sales are leveling off and Will wants to increase sales. Further, he thinks the competitive situation may change drastically in the near future anyway, as global competitors get more aggressive and some possible new production methods and machines become more competitive with existing ones. He would rather be a leader in anything that is likely to happen rather than a follower. But he is impressed with David's comments about the greater competitiveness in the other markets and therefore is unsure about what to do.

Evaluate PlastiForm's current strategies. Given Will Houston's sales objective, what should PlastiForm Mfg. do? Explain.

Rainbow Packers, Inc.

Hans Fleming, president of Rainbow Packers, Inc., is not sure what he should propose to the board of directors. His recent strategy change isn't working. And Niels Sondergaard, Rainbow's only sales rep (and a board member), is so frustrated that he refuses to continue his discouraging sales efforts. Sondergaard wants Hans Fleming to hire a sales force or do *something*.

Rainbow Packers, Inc., is a long-time processor in the highly seasonal vegetable canning industry. Rainbow packs and sells canned beans, peas, carrots, corn, peas and carrots mixed, and kidney beans. It sells mainly through food brokers to merchant wholesalers, supermarket chains (such as Kroger, Safeway, A&P, and Jewel), cooperatives, and other outlets—mostly in the Midwest. Of less importance, by volume, are sales to local institutions, grocery stores, and supermarkets—and sales of dented canned goods at low prices to walk-in customers.

Rainbow is located in Wisconsin's Devil's River Valley. The company has more than $28 million in sales annually (exact sales data are not published by the closely held corporation). Plants are located in strategic places along the valley—with main offices in Riverside. The Rainbow brand is used only on canned goods sold in the local market. Most of the goods are sold and shipped under a retailer's label or a broker's/wholesaler's label.

Rainbow is well known for the consistent quality of its product offerings. And it's always willing to offer competitive prices. Strong channel relations were built by Rainbow's former chairman of the board and chief executive officer Dane Christian. Christian—who owns controlling interest in the firm—worked the Chicago area as the company's sales rep in its earlier years, before he took over from his father as president in 1972. Christian was an ambitious and hard-working top manager—the firm prospered under his direction. He became well known within the canned food processing industry for technical/product innovations.

During the off-canning season, Christian traveled widely. In the course of his travels, he arranged several important business deals. His 1986 and 1997 trips resulted in the following two events: (1) inexpensive pineapple was imported from Formosa and sold by Rainbow, primarily to expand the product line, and (2) a technically advanced continuous process cooker (65 feet high) was imported from England and installed at one of the Rainbow plants. It was the first of its kind in the United States and cut processing time sharply while improving quality.

Christian retired in 2001 and named his son-in-law, 35-year-old Hans Fleming, as his successor. Fleming is intelligent and hard-working. He was concerned primarily with the company's financial matters and only recently with marketing problems. During his seven years as financial director, the firm received its highest credit rating and was able to borrow working capital ($5 million to meet seasonal can and wage requirements) at the lowest rate ever.

The fact that the firm isn't unionized allows some competitive advantage. However, changes in minimum wage laws have increased costs. And these and other rising costs have squeezed profit margins. This led to the recent closing of two plants as they became less efficient to operate. Rainbow expanded capacity of the remaining two plants (especially warehouse facilities) so they could operate more profitably with maximum use of existing processing equipment.

Shortly after Christian's retirement, Hans Fleming reviewed the company's situation with his managers. He pointed to narrowing profit margins, debts contracted for new plants and equipment, and an increasingly competitive environment. Even considering the temporary labor-saving competitive advantage of the new cooker system, there seemed to be no way to improve the status quo unless the firm could sell direct—as they do in the local market—thereby eliminating the food brokers' 5 percent commission on sales. This was the plan decided on, and Niels Sondergaard was given the new sales job. An inside salesperson was retained to handle incoming orders and do some telemarketing to smaller accounts.

Niels Sondergaard, the only full-time outside sales rep for the firm, lives in Riverside. Other top managers do some selling but not much. Being a nephew of Christian, Niels Sondergaard is also a member of the board of directors. He is well qualified in technical matters and has a college degree in food chemistry. Although Niels Sondergaard formerly did call on some important customers with the brokers' sales reps, he is not well known in the industry or even by Rainbow's usual customers.

It is now five months later. Niels Sondergaard is not doing very well. He has made several selling trips, placed hundreds of telephone calls, and maintained constant e-mail contacts with prospective customers—all with discouraging results. He is unwilling to continue sales efforts on his own. There seem to be too many potential customers for one person to reach. And much negotiating, wining, and dining seems to be needed—certainly more than he can or wants to do.

Sondergaard insists that Rainbow hire a sales force to continue the present way of operating. Sales are down in comparison both to expectations and to the previous year's results. Some regular supermarket chain customers have stopped buying—though basic consumer demand has not changed. Further, buyers for some supermarket chains that might be potential new customers have demanded quantity guarantees much larger than Rainbow Packers can supply. Expanding supply would be difficult in the short run—because the firm typically must contract with growers to ensure supplies of the type and quality they normally offer.

Christian, still the controlling stockholder, has asked for a special meeting of the board in two weeks to discuss the present situation.

Evaluate Rainbow's past and current strategy planning. What should Hans Fleming tell Mr. Christian? What should Rainbow do now?

 24 PCT, Inc.

Ben Colavito, president and marketing manager of Prime Cutting Tools, Inc., is deciding what strategy, or strategies, to pursue.

Prime Cutting Tools (PCT) is a manufacturer of industrial cutting tools. These tools include such items as lathe blades, drill press bits, and various other cutting edges used in the operation of large metal cutting, boring, or stamping machines. Ben Colavito takes great pride in the fact that his company—whose $5,200,000 sales in 2001 is small by industry standards—is recognized as a producer of a top-quality line of cutting tools.

Competition in the cutting-tool industry is intense. PCT competes not only with the original machine manufacturers, but also with many other larger domestic and foreign manufacturers offering cutting tools as one of their many different product lines. This has had the effect, over the years, of standardizing the price, specifications, and, in turn, the quality of the competing products of all manufacturers. It has also led to fairly low prices on standard items.

About a year ago, Ben was tiring of the financial pressure of competing with larger companies enjoying economies of scale. At the same time, he noted that more and more potential cutting-tool customers were turning to small tool-and-die shops that used computer-controlled equipment to meet specialized needs that could not be met by the mass production firms. Ben thought perhaps he should consider some basic strategy changes. Although he was unwilling to become strictly a custom producer, he thought that the recent trend toward buying customized cutting edges suggested new markets might be developing—markets too small for the large, multiproduct-line companies to serve profitably but large enough to earn a good profit for a flexible company of PCT's size.

Ben hired a marketing research company, Fennell Associates, to study the feasibility of serving these markets. The initial results were encouraging. It was estimated that PCT might increase sales by 65 percent and profits by 90 percent by serving the emerging markets. This research showed that there are many large users of standard cutting tools who buy directly from large cutting-tool manufacturers (domestic or foreign) or wholesalers who represent these manufacturers. This is the bulk of the cutting-tool business (in terms of units sold and sales dollars). But there are also many smaller users all over the United States who buy in small but regular quantities. And some of these needs are becoming more specialized. That is, a special cutting tool may make a machine and/or worker much more productive, perhaps eliminating several steps with time-consuming setups. This is the area that the research company sees as potentially attractive.

Next, Ben had the sales manager hire two technically oriented market researchers (at a total cost of $60,000 each per year, including travel expenses) to maintain continuous contact with potential cutting-tool customers. The researchers were supposed to identify any present or future needs that might exist in enough cases to make it possible to profitably produce a specialized product. The researchers were not to take orders or sell PCT's products to the potential customers. Ben felt that only through this policy could these researchers talk to the right people.

The initial feedback from the market researchers was most encouraging. Many firms (large and small) had special needs—although it often was necessary to talk to the shop foreman or individual machine operators to find these needs. Most operators were making do with the tools available. Either they didn't know customizing was possible or doubted that their supervisors would do anything about it if they suggested that a more specialized tool would increase productivity. But these operators were encouraging because they said that it would be easier to persuade supervisors to order specialized tools if the tools were already produced and in stock than if they had to be custom made. So Ben decided to continually add high-quality products to meet the ever-changing, specialized needs of users of cutting tools and edges.

PCT's potential customers for specialized tools are located all over the United States. The average sale per customer is likely to be less than $500, but the sale will be repeated several times within a year. Because of the widespread market and the small order size, Ben doesn't think that selling direct—as is done by small custom shops—is practical. At the present time, PCT sells 90 percent of its regular output through a large industrial wholesaler—National Mill Supplies, Inc.—which serves the area east of the Mississippi River and carries a very complete line of industrial supplies (to "meet every industrial need"). National Mill Supplies carries over 10,000 items. Some sales come from customers who know exactly what they want and just place orders directly by fax or at the firm's Internet website. But most of the selling is by National's sales reps, who work from an electronic catalog on a laptop computer. National Mill Supplies, although very large and well known, is having trouble moving cutting tools. National is losing sales of cutting tools in some cities to newer wholesalers specializing in the cutting-tool industry. The new wholesalers are able to give more technical help to potential customers and therefore better service. National's president is convinced that the newer, less-experienced concerns will either realize that a substantial profit margin can't be maintained along with their aggressive strategies, or they will eventually go broke trying to overspecialize.

From Ben's standpoint, the present wholesaler has a good reputation and has served PCT well in the past. National Mill Supplies has been of great help in holding down Ben's inventory costs—by increasing the inventory in National's 35 branch locations. Although Ben has received several complaints about the lack of technical assistance given by National's sales reps—as well as their lack of knowledge about PCT's new special products—he feels that the present wholesaler is providing the best service it can. All its sales reps have been told about the new products at a special training session, and a new page has been added to the catalog they carry with them. So regarding the complaints, Ben says: "The usual things you hear when you're in business."

Ben thinks there are more urgent problems than a few complaints. Profits are declining, and sales of the new cutting tools are not nearly as high as forecast—even though all research reports indicate that the company's new products meet the intended markets' needs perfectly. The high costs involved in producing small quantities of special products and in adding the market research team—together with lower-than-expected sales—have significantly reduced PCT's profits. Ben is wondering whether it is wise to continue to try to cater to the needs of many specific target markets when the results are this discouraging. He also is considering increasing advertising expenditures in the hope that customers will pull the new products through the channel.

Evaluate PCT's situation and Ben Colavito's present strategy. What should he do now?

 Metal Works, Inc.

Victor Carrington, marketing manager for Metal Works, Inc., is trying to figure out how to explain to his boss why a proposed new product line doesn't make sense for them. Victor is sure it's wrong for Metal Works, Inc., but isn't able to explain why.

Metal Works, Inc., is a producer of malleable iron castings for automobile and aircraft manufacturers and a variety of other users of castings. Last year's sales of castings amounted to over $70 million.

Metal Works also produces about 30 percent of all the original equipment bumper jacks installed in new U.S.-made automobiles each year. This is a very price-competitive business, but Metal Works has been able to obtain its large market share with frequent personal contact between the company's executives and its customers—supported by very close cooperation between the company's engineering department and its customers' buyers. This has been extremely important because the wide variety of models and model changes frequently requires alterations in the specifications of the bumper jacks. All of Metal Works' bumper jacks are sold directly to the automobile manufacturers. No attempt has been made to sell bumper jacks to final consumers through hardware and automotive channels—although they are available through the manufacturers' automobile dealers.

Tom Gaines, Metal Works' production manager, now wants to begin producing hydraulic garage jacks for sale through automobile-parts wholesalers to retail auto parts stores. Gaines saw a variety of hydraulic garage jacks at a recent automotive show and knew immediately that his plant could produce these products. This especially interested him because of the possibility of using excess capacity. Further, he says "jacks are jacks," and the company would merely be broadening its product line by introducing hydraulic garage jacks. (Note: Hydraulic garage jacks are larger than bumper jacks and are intended for use in or around a garage. They are too big to carry in a car's trunk.)

As Tom Gaines became more enthusiastic about the idea, he found that Metal Works' engineering department already had a design that appeared to be at least comparable to the products now offered on the market. None of these products have any patent protection. Further, Gaines says that the company would be able to produce a product that is better made than the competitive products (i.e., smoother castings)—although he agrees that most customers probably wouldn't notice the difference. The production department estimates that the cost of producing a hydraulic garage jack comparable to those currently offered by competitors would be about $48 per unit.

Victor Carrington, the marketing manager, has just received an e-mail from George Daggett, the company president, explaining the production department's enthusiasm for broadening Metal Works' present jack line into hydraulic jacks. George Daggett seems enthusiastic about the idea too, noting that it would be a way to make fuller use of the company's resources and increase its sales. Daggett's e-mail asks for Victor's reaction, but George Daggett already seems sold on the idea.

Given Daggett's enthusiasm, Victor Carrington isn't sure how to respond. He's trying to develop a good explanation of why he isn't excited about the proposal. The firm's six sales reps are already overworked with their current accounts. And Victor couldn't possibly promote this new line himself—he's already helping other reps make calls and serving as sales manager. So it would be necessary to hire someone to promote the line. And this sales manager would probably have to recruit manufacturers' agents (who probably will want 10 to 15 percent commission on sales) to sell to automotive wholesalers who would stock the jack and sell to the auto parts retailers. The wholesalers will probably expect trade discounts of about 20 percent, trade show exhibits, some national advertising, and sales promotion help (catalog sheets, mailers, and point-of-purchase displays). Further, Victor Carrington sees that Metal Works' billing and collection system will have to be expanded because many more customers will be involved. It will also be necessary to keep track of agent commissions and accounts receivable.

Auto parts retailers are currently selling similar hydraulic garage jacks for about $99. Victor Carrington has learned that such retailers typically expect a trade discount of about 35 percent off of the suggested list price for their auto parts.

All things considered, Victor Carrington feels that the proposed hydraulic jack line is not very closely related to the company's present emphasis. He has already indicated his lack of enthusiasm to Tom Gaines, but this made little difference in Tom's thinking. Now it's clear that Victor will have to convince the president or he will soon be responsible for selling hydraulic jacks.

Contrast Metal Works, Inc.'s current strategy and the proposed strategy. What should Victor Carrington say to George Daggett to persuade him to change his mind? Or should he just plan to sell hydraulic jacks? Explain.

26 Deluxe Foods, Ltd.*

Jessica Walters, marketing manager of Deluxe Foods, Ltd.—a Canadian company—is being urged to approve the creation of a separate marketing plan for Quebec. This would be a major policy change because Deluxe Foods' international parent is trying to move toward a global strategy for the whole firm and Jessica has been supporting Canada-wide planning.

Jessica Walters has been the marketing manager of Deluxe Foods, Ltd., for the last four years—since she arrived from international headquarters in Minneapolis. Deluxe Foods, Ltd., headquartered in Toronto, is a subsidiary of a large U.S.-based consumer packaged-food company with worldwide sales of more than $2 billion in 1997. Its Canadian sales are just over $350 million—with the Quebec and Ontario markets accounting for 69 percent of the company's Canadian sales.

The company's product line includes such items as cake mixes, puddings, pie fillings, pancakes, prepared foods, and frozen dinners. The company has successfully introduced at least six new products every year for the last five years. Products from Deluxe Foods are known for their high quality and enjoy much brand preference throughout Canada—including the Province of Quebec.

The company's sales have risen every year since Jessica Walters took over as marketing manager. In fact, the company's market share has increased steadily in each of the product categories in which it competes. The Quebec market has closely followed the national trend except that, in the past two years, total sales growth in that market began to lag.

According to Walters, a big advantage of Deluxe Foods over its competitors is the ability to coordinate all phases of the food business from Toronto. For this reason, Walters meets at least once a month with her product managers—to discuss developments in local markets that might affect marketing plans. While each manager is free to make suggestions and even to suggest major changes, Jessica Walters has the responsibility of giving final approval for all plans.

One of the product managers, Marie LeMans, expressed great concern at the last monthly meeting about the poor performance of some of the company's products in the Quebec market. While a broad range of possible reasons—ranging from inflation and the threat of job losses to politics—were reviewed to try to explain the situation, LeMans insisted that it was due to a basic lack of understanding of that market. She felt not enough managerial time and money had been spent on the Quebec market—in part because of the current emphasis on developing all-Canada plans on the way to having one global strategy.

Marie LeMans felt the current marketing approach to the Quebec market should be reevaluated because an inappropriate marketing plan may be responsible for the sales slowdown. After all, she said, "80 percent of the market is French-speaking. It's in

*This case was adapted from one written by Professor Roberta Tamilia, University of Windsor, Canada.

Table 1 Per Capita Consumption Index, Province of Quebec (Canada = 100)

Cake mixes	107	Soft drinks	126
Pancakes	87	Pie fillings	118
Puddings	114	Frozen dinners	79
Salad dressings	85	Prepared packaged foods	83
Molasses	132	Cookies	123

the best interest of the company to treat that market as being separate and distinct from the rest of Canada."

Marie LeMans supported her position by showing that Quebec's per capita consumption of many product categories (in which the firm competes) is above the national average (see Table 1). Research projects conducted by Deluxe Foods also support the "separate and distinct" argument. Over the years, the firm has found many French–English differences in brand attitudes, lifestyles, usage rates, and so on.

LeMans argued that the company should develop a unique Quebec marketing plan for some or all of its brands. She specifically suggested that the French-language advertising plan for a particular brand be developed independently of the plan for English Canada. Currently, the Toronto agency assigned to the brand just translates its English-language ads for the French market. Jessica Walters pointed out that the present advertising approach assured Deluxe Foods of a uniform brand image across Canada. Marie LeMans said she knew what the agency is doing, and that straight translation into Canadian-French may not communicate the same brand image. The discussion that followed suggested that a different brand image might be needed in the French market if the company wanted to stop the brand's decline in sales.

The managers also discussed the food distribution system in Quebec. The major supermarket chains have their lowest market share in that province. Independents are strongest there—the "mom-and-pop" food stores fast disappearing outside Quebec remain alive and well in the province. Traditionally, these stores have stocked a higher proportion (than supermarkets) of their shelf space with national brands—an advantage for Deluxe Foods.

Finally, various issues related to discount policies, pricing structure, sales promotion, and cooperative advertising were discussed. All of this suggested that things were different in Quebec and that future marketing plans should reflect these differences to a greater extent than they do now.

After the meeting, Jessica Walters stayed in her office to think about the situation. Although she agreed with the basic idea that the Quebec market was in many ways different, she wasn't sure how far the company should go in recognizing this fact. She knew that regional differences in food tastes and brand purchases existed not only in Quebec but in other parts of Canada as well. But people are people, after all, with far more similarities than differences, so a Canadian and eventually a global strategy makes some sense too.

Jessica Walters was afraid that giving special status to one region might conflict with top management's objective of achieving standardization whenever possible—one global strategy for Canada, on the way to one worldwide global strategy. She was also worried about the long-term effect of such a policy change on costs, organizational structure, and brand image. Still, enough product managers had expressed their concern over the years about the Quebec market to make her wonder if she shouldn't modify the current approach. Perhaps they could experiment with a few brands—and just in Quebec. She could cite the language difference as the reason for trying Quebec rather than any of the other provinces. But Walters realizes that any change of policy could be seen as the beginning of more change, and what would Minneapolis think? Could she explain it successfully there?

Evaluate Deluxe Foods, Ltd.'s present strategy. What should Jessica Walters do now? Explain.

 27 Expert Nursing Services, Inc.

Carol Crane, executive director of Expert Nursing Services, Inc., is trying to clarify her strategies. She's sure some changes are needed, but she's less sure about how *much* change is needed and/or whether it can be handled by her people.

Expert Nursing Services, Inc. (ENS), is a nonprofit organization that has been operating—with varying degrees of success—for 25 years, offering nursing services in clients' homes. Some of its funding comes from the local United Way—to provide emergency nursing services for those who can't afford to pay. The balance of the revenues—about 90 percent of the $2.2 million annual budget—comes from charges made directly to the client or to third-party payers, including insurance companies, health maintenance organizations (HMOs), and the federal government, for Medicare or Medicaid services.

Carol Crane has been executive director of ENS for two years. She has developed a well-functioning organization able to meet most requests for service that come from some local doctors and from the discharge officers at local hospitals. Some business also comes by self-referral—the client finds the ENS name in the Yellow Pages of the local phone directory.

The last two years have been a rebuilding time—because the previous director had personnel problems. This led to a weakening of the agency's image with the local referring agencies. Now the image is more positive. But Carol is not completely satisfied with the situation. By definition, Expert Nursing Services is a nonprofit organization. But it still must cover all its costs: payroll, rent payments, phone expenses, and so on, including Carol's own salary. She can see that while ENS is growing slightly and is now breaking even, it doesn't have much of a cash cushion to fall back on if (1) the demand for ENS nursing services declines, (2) the government changes its rules about paying for ENS' kind of nursing services, either cutting back what it will pay for or reducing the amount it will pay for specific services, or (3) new competitors enter the market. In fact, the last possibility concerns Carol greatly. Some hospitals, squeezed for revenue, are expanding into home health care—especially nursing services as patients are being released earlier from hospitals because of payment limits set by government guidelines. For-profit organizations (e.g., Kelly Home Care Services) are expanding around the country to provide a complete line of home health care services—including nursing services of the kind offered by

ENS. These for-profit organizations appear to be efficiently run—offering good service at competitive and sometimes even lower prices than some nonprofit organizations. And they seem to be doing this at a profit—which suggests that it would be possible for these for-profit companies to lower their prices if nonprofit organizations try to compete on price.

Carol is considering whether she should ask her board of directors to let her offer a complete line of home health care services—that is, move beyond just nursing services into what she calls "care and comfort" services.

Currently, ENS is primarily concerned with providing professional nursing care in the home. But ENS nurses are much too expensive for routine home health care activities—helping fix meals, bathing and dressing patients, and other care and comfort activities. The full cost of a nurse to ENS, including benefits and overhead, is about $65 per hour. But a registered nurse is not needed for care and comfort services. All that is required is someone who is honest, can get along with all kinds of people, and is willing to do this kind of work. Generally, any mature person can be trained fairly quickly to do the job—following the instructions and under the general supervision of a physician, a nurse, or family members. The full cost of aides is $8 to $15 per hour for short visits and as low as $65 per 24 hours for a live-in aide who has room and board supplied by the client.

The demand for all kinds of home health care services seems to be growing. With more dual-career families and more single-parent households, there isn't anyone in the family to take over home health care when the need arises—due to emergencies or long-term disabilities. Further, hospitals send patients home earlier than in the past. And with people living longer, there are more single-survivor family situations where there is no one nearby to take care of the needs of these older people. But often some family members—or third-party payers such as the government or insurers—are willing to pay for some home health care services. Carol now occasionally recommends other agencies or suggests one or another of three women who have been doing care and comfort work on their own, part-time. But with growing demand, Carol wonders if ENS should get into this business, hiring aides as needed.

Carol is concerned that a new, full-service home health care organization may come into her market and be a single source for both nursing services *and* less-skilled home care and comfort services. This has happened already in two nearby but somewhat larger cities. Carol fears that this might be more appealing than ENS to the local hospitals and other referrers. In other words, she can see the possibility of losing nursing service business if ENS does not begin to offer a complete home health care service. This would cause real problems for ENS—because overhead costs are more or less fixed. A loss in revenue of as little as 10 percent would require some cutbacks—perhaps laying off some nurses or secretaries, giving up part of the office, and so on.

Another reason for expanding beyond nursing services—using paraprofessionals and relatively unskilled personnel—is to offer a better service to present customers *and* make more effective use of the computer systems and organization structure that she has developed over the last two years. Carol estimates that the administrative and office capabilities could handle twice as many clients without straining the system. It would be necessary to add some clerical help—if the expansion were quite large—as well as expanding the hours when the switchboard is open. But these increases in overhead would be minor compared to the present proportion of total revenue that goes to covering overhead. In other words, additional clients or more work for some clients could increase revenue and ensure the survival of ENS, provide a cushion to cover the normal fluctuations in demand, and ensure more job security for the administrative personnel.

Further, Carol thinks that if ENS were successful in expanding its services—and therefore could generate some surplus—it could extend services to those who aren't now able to pay. Carol says one of the worst parts of her job is refusing service to clients whose third-party benefits have run out or for whatever reason can no longer afford to pay. She is uncomfortable about having to cut off service, but she must schedule her nurses to provide revenue-producing services if she's going to meet the payroll every two weeks. By expanding to provide more services, she might be able to keep serving more of these nonpaying clients. This possibility excites Carol because her nurse's training has instilled a deep desire to serve people in need—whether they can pay or not. This continual pressure to cut off service because people can't pay has been at the root of many disagreements and even arguments between the nurses serving the clients and Carol, as executive director and representative of the board of directors.

Carol knows that expanding into care and comfort services won't be easy. Some decisions would be needed about relative pay levels for nurses, paraprofessionals, and aides. ENS would also have to set prices for these different services and tell the present customers and referral agencies about the expanded services.

These problems aren't bothering Carol too much, however—she thinks she can handle them. She is sure that care and comfort services are in demand and could be supplied at competitive prices.

Her primary concern is whether this is the right thing for Expert Nursing Services—basically a nursing organization—to do. ENS' whole history has been oriented to supplying *nurses' services*. Nurses are dedicated professionals who bring high standards to any job they undertake. The question is whether ENS should offer less-professional services. Inevitably, some of the aides will not be as dedicated as the nurses might like them to be. And this could reflect unfavorably on the nurse image. At a minimum, she would need to set up some sort of training program for the aides. As Carol worries about the future of ENS, and her own future, it seems that there are no easy answers.

Evaluate ENS' present strategy. What should Carol Crane do? Explain.

28 Lever, Ltd.*

Alan Cooke is product manager for Guard Deodorant Soap. He was just transferred to Lever, Ltd., a Canadian subsidiary of Lever Group, Inc., from world headquarters in New York. Alan is anxious to make a good impression because he is hoping to transfer to Lever's London office. He is working on developing and securing management approval of next

*Adapted from a case prepared by Daniel Aronchick, who at the time of its preparation was marketing manager at Thomas J. Lipton, Limited.

Table 1 Past 12-Month Share of Bar Soap Market (percent)

	Maritimes	Quebec	Ontario	Manitoba/Saskatchewan	Alberta	British Columbia
Deodorant segment						
Zest	21.3%	14.2%	24.5%	31.2%	30.4%	25.5%
Dial	10.4	5.1	12.8	16.1	17.2	14.3
Lifebuoy	4.2	3.1	1.2	6.4	5.8	4.2
Guard	2.1	5.6	1.0	4.2	4.2	2.1
Beauty bar segment						
Camay	6.2	12.3	7.0	4.1	4.0	5.1
Lux	6.1	11.2	7.7	5.0	6.9	5.0
Dove	5.5	8.0	6.6	6.3	6.2	4.2
Lower-priced bars						
Ivory	11.2	6.5	12.4	5.3	5.2	9.0
Sunlight	6.1	3.2	8.2	4.2	4.1	8.0
All others (including stores' own brands)	26.9	30.8	18.6	17.2	16.0	22.6
Total bar soap market	100.0%	100.0%	100.0%	100.0%	100.0%	100.0%

year's marketing plan for Guard. His first job is submitting a draft marketing plan to Wendy Lee, his recently appointed group product manager, who is responsible for several such plans from product managers like Alan.

Alan's marketing plan is the single most important document he will produce on this assignment. This annual marketing plan does three main things:

1. It reviews the brand's performance in the past year, assesses the competitive situation, and highlights problems and opportunities for the brand.
2. It spells out marketing strategies and the plan for the coming year.
3. Finally, and most importantly, the marketing plan sets out the brand's sales objectives and advertising/promotion budget requirements.

In preparing this marketing plan, Alan gathered the information in Table 1.

Alan was somewhat surprised at the significant regional differences in the bar soap market:

1. The underdevelopment of the deodorant bar segment in Quebec, with a corresponding overdevelopment of the beauty bar segment. But some past research suggested that this is due to cultural factors—English-speaking people have been more interested than others in cleaning, deodorizing, and disinfecting. A similar pattern is seen in most European countries, where the adoption of deodorant soaps has been slower than in North America. For similar reasons, the perfumed soap share is highest in French-speaking Quebec.
2. The overdevelopment of synthetic bars in the Prairies. These bars, primarily in the deodorant segment, lather better in the hard water of the Prairies. Nonsynthetic bars lather very poorly in hard-water areas and leave a soap film.
3. The overdevelopment of the "all-other" segment in Quebec. This segment, consisting of smaller brands, fares better in Quebec, where 43 percent of the grocery trade is done by independent stores. Conversely, large chain grocery stores dominate in Ontario and the Prairies.

Alan's brand, Guard, is a highly perfumed deodorant bar. His business is relatively weak in the key Ontario market. To confirm this share data, Alan calculated consumption of Guard per thousand people in each region (see Table 2).

These differences are especially interesting since per capita sales of all bar soap products are roughly equal in all provinces.

A consumer attitude and usage research study was conducted approximately a year ago. This study revealed that consumer "top-of-mind" awareness of the Guard brand differed greatly across Canada. This was true despite the even—by population—expenditure of advertising funds in past years. Also, trial of Guard was low in the Maritimes, Ontario, and British Columbia (see Table 3).

Table 2 Standard Cases of 3-Ounce Bars Consumed per 1,000 People in 12 Months

	Maritimes	Quebec	Ontario	Manitoba/ Saskatchewan	Alberta	British Columbia
Guard	4.1	10.9	1.9	8.1	4.1	6.2
Sales index	66	175	31	131	131	100

Table 3 Usage Results (in percent)

	Maritimes	Quebec	Ontario	Manitoba/ Saskatchewan	Alberta	British Columbia
Respondents aware of Guard	20%	58%	28%	30%	32%	16%
Respondents ever trying Guard	3	18	2	8	6	4

The attitude portion of the research revealed that consumers who had heard of Guard were aware that its deodorant protection came mainly from a high fragrance level. This was the main selling point in the copy, and it was well communicated by Guard's advertising. The other important finding was that consumers who had tried Guard were satisfied with the product. About 70 percent of those trying Guard had repurchased the product at least twice.

Alan has also discovered that bar soap competition is especially intense in Ontario. It is Canada's largest market, and many competitors want a share of it. The chain stores are also quite aggressive in promotion and pricing—offering specials, in-store coupons, and so on. They want to move goods. And because of this, two key Ontario chains have put Guard on their pending delisting sheets. These chains, which control about half the grocery volume in Ontario, are dissatisfied with how slowly Guard is moving off the shelves.

Now Alan feels he is ready to set a key part of the brand's marketing plan for next year: how to allocate the advertising/sales promotion budget by region.

Guard's present advertising/sales promotion budget is 20 percent of sales. With forecast sales of $4 million, this would amount to an $800,000 expenditure. Traditionally such funds have been allocated in proportion to population (see Table 4).

Alan feels he should spend more heavily in Ontario where the grocery chain delisting problem exists. Last year, 36 percent of Guard's budget was allocated to Ontario, which accounted for only 12 percent of Guard's sales. Alan wants to increase Ontario spending to 48 percent of the total budget by taking funds evenly from all other areas. Alan expects this will increase business in the key Ontario market, which has over a third of Canada's population, because it is a big increase and will help Guard "outshout" the many other competitors who are promoting heavily.

Alan presented this idea to Wendy, his newly appointed group product manager. Wendy strongly disagrees. She has also been reviewing Guard's business and feels that promotion funds have historically been misallocated. It is her strong belief that, to use her words, "A brand should spend where its business is." Wendy believes that the first priority in allocating funds regionally is to support the areas of strength. She suggested to Alan that there may be more business to be had in the brand's strong areas, Quebec and the Prairies, than in chasing sales in Ontario. The needs and attitudes toward Guard, as well as competitive pressures, may vary a lot among the provinces. Therefore, Wendy suggested that spending for Guard in the coming year be proportional to the brand's sales by region rather than to regional population.

Alan is convinced this is wrong, particularly in light of the Ontario situation. He asked Wendy how the Ontario market should be handled. Wendy said that the conservative way to build business in Ontario is to invest incremental promotion funds. However, before these incremental funds are invested, a test of this Ontario investment proposition should be conducted. Wendy recommended that some of the Ontario money should be used to conduct an investment-spending market test in a small area or town in Ontario for 12 months. This will enable Alan to see if the incremental spending results in higher sales and profits—profits large enough to justify higher spending. In other words, an investment payout should be ensured before spending any extra money in Ontario. Similarly, Wendy would do the same kind of test in Quebec—to see if more money should go there.

After several e-mails back and forth, Alan feels this approach would be a waste of time and unduly cautious, given the importance of the Ontario market and the likely delistings in two key chains.

Evaluate the present strategy for Guard and Alan's and Wendy's proposed strategies. How should the promotion money be allocated? Should investment-spending market tests be run first? Why? Explain.

Table 4 Allocation of Advertising/Sales Promotion Budget, by Population

	Maritimes	Quebec	Ontario	Manitoba/ Saskatchewan	Alberta	British Columbia	Canada
Percent of population	10%	27%	36%	8%	8%	11%	100%
Possible allocation of budget based on population (in 000s)	$80	$216	$288	$64	$64	$88	$800
Percent of Guard business at present	7%	51%	12%	11%	11%	8%	100%

29 Huntoon & Balbiera, P.C.

The partners of Huntoon & Balbiera are having a serious discussion about what the firm should do in the near future.

Huntoon & Balbiera, P.C. (H&B) is a large regional certified public accounting firm based in Grand Rapids, Michigan—with branch offices in Lansing and Detroit. Huntoon & Balbiera has nine partners and a professional staff of approximately 105 accountants. Gross service billings for the fiscal year ending June 30, 2001, were $6.9 million. Financial data for 1999, 2000, and 2001 are presented in Table 1.

H&B's professional services include auditing, tax preparation, bookkeeping, and some general management consulting. Its client base includes municipal governments (cities, villages, and townships), manufacturing companies, professional organizations (attorneys, doctors, and dentists), and various other small businesses. A good share of revenue comes from the firm's municipal practice. Table 1 gives H&B's gross revenue by service area and client industry for 1999, 2000, and 2001.

At the monthly partners' meeting held in July 2001, Pat Hogan, the firm's managing partner (CEO), expressed concern about the future of the firm's municipal practice. Hogan's presentation to his partners appears below:

> Although our firm is considered to be a leader in municipal auditing in our geographic area, I am concerned that as municipals attempt to cut their operating costs, they will solicit competitive bids from other public accounting firms to perform their annual audits. Four of the six largest accounting firms in the world have local offices in our area. Because they concentrate their practice in the manufacturing industry—which typically has December 31 fiscal year-ends—they have "available" staff during the summer months.
>
> Therefore, they can afford to low-ball competitive bids to keep their staffs busy and benefit from on-the-job training provided by municipal clientele. I am concerned that we may begin to lose clients in our most established and profitable practice area.*

Ann Yost, a senior partner in the firm and the partner in charge of the firm's municipal practice, was the first to respond to Pat Hogan's concern.

> Pat, we all recognize the potential threat of being underbid for our municipal work by our four large accounting competitors. However, H&B is a recognized leader in municipal auditing in Michigan, and we have much more local experience than our competitors. Furthermore, it is a fact that we offer a superior level of service to our clients—which goes beyond the services normally expected during an audit to include consulting on financial and other operating issues. Many of our less sophisticated clients depend on our nonaudit consulting assistance. Therefore, I believe, we have been successful in differentiating our services from our competitors. In many recent situations, H&B was selected over a field of as many as 10 competitors even though our proposed prices were much higher than those of our competitors.

*Organizations with December fiscal year-ends require audit work to be performed during the fall and in January and February. Those with June 30 fiscal year-ends require auditing during the summer months.

Table 1 Fiscal Year Ending June 30

	2001	2000	1999
Gross billings	$6,900,000	$6,400,000	$5,800,000
Gross billings by service area:			
Auditing	3,100,000	3,200,000	2,750,000
Tax preparation	1,990,000	1,830,000	1,780,000
Bookkeeping	1,090,000	745,000	660,000
Other	720,000	625,000	610,000
Gross billings by client industry:			
Municipal	3,214,000	3,300,000	2,908,000
Manufacturing	2,089,000	1,880,000	1,706,000
Professional	1,355,000	1,140,000	1,108,000
Other	242,000	80,000	78,000

The partners at the meeting agreed with Ann Yost's comments. However, even though H&B had many success stories regarding their ability to retain their municipal clients—despite being underbid—they had lost three large municipal clients during the past year. Ann Yost was asked to comment on the loss of those clients. She explained that the lost clients are larger municipalities with a lot of in-house financial expertise and therefore less dependent on H&B's consulting assistance. As a result, H&B's service differentiation went largely unnoticed. Ann explained that the larger, more sophisticated municipals regard audits as a necessary evil and usually select the low-cost reputable bidder.

Pat Hogan then requested ideas and discussion from the other partners at the meeting. One partner, Joe Reid, suggested that H&B should protect itself by diversifying. Specifically, he felt a substantial practice development effort should be directed toward manufacturing. He reasoned that since manufacturing work would occur during H&B's off-season, H&B could afford to price very low to gain new manufacturing clients. This strategy would also help to counter (and possibly discourage) low-ball pricing for municipals by the four large accounting firms mentioned earlier.

Another partner, Bob LaMott, suggested that "if we have consulting skills, we ought to promote them more, instead of hoping that the clients will notice and come to appreciate us. Further, maybe we ought to be more aggressive in calling on smaller potential clients."

Another partner, John Smith, agreed with LaMott, but wanted to go further. He suggested that they recognize that there are at least two types of municipal customers and that two (at least) different strategies be implemented, including lower prices for auditing only for larger municipal customers and/or higher prices for smaller customers who are buying consulting too. This caused a big uproar from some who said this would lead to price-cutting of professional services and H&B didn't want to be price cutters: "One price for all is the professional way."

However, another partner, Megan Cullen, agreed with John Smith and suggested they go even further—pricing consulting services separately. In fact, she suggested that the partners consider setting up a separate department for consulting—like the four large accounting firms have done. This can be very profitable business. But it is a different kind of business and eventually may require different kinds of people and a different organization. For now, however, it may be desirable to appoint a manager for consulting services—with a budget—to be sure it gets proper attention. This suggestion too caused serious disagreement. Some of the partners knew that having a separate consulting arm had led to major conflicts in some firms. The main problem seemed to be that the consultants brought in more profit than the auditors, but the auditors controlled the partnership and did not properly reward the successful consultants—at least as they saw it!

Pat Hogan thanked everyone for their comments and encouraged them to debate these issues in smaller groups and to share ideas by e-mail before coming to a one-day retreat (in two weeks) to continue this discussion and come to some conclusions.

Evaluate Huntoon & Balbiera's situation. What strategy(ies) should the partners select? Why?

30 Aluminum Basics Co.*

Mark Parcells, newly hired VP of marketing for Aluminum Basics Co., is reviewing the firm's international distribution arrangements because they don't seem to be very well thought out. He is not sure if anything is wrong, but he feels that the company should follow a global strategy rather than continuing its current policies.

Aluminum Basics, based in Atlanta, Georgia, produces finished aluminum products, such as aluminum ladders, umbrella-type clothes racks, scaffolding, and patio tables and chairs that fold flat. Sales in 2001 reached $25 million—primarily to U.S. customers.

In 1997, Aluminum Basics decided to try foreign markets. The sales manager, Bonnie Pope, believed the growing affluence of European workers would help the company's products gain market acceptance quickly.

Bonnie's first step in investigating foreign markets was to join a trade mission to Europe—a tour organized by the U.S. Department of Commerce. This trade mission visited Italy, Germany, Denmark, Holland, France, and England. During this trip, Bonnie was officially introduced to leading buyers for department store chains, import houses, wholesalers, and buying groups. The two-week trip convinced Bonnie that there was ample buying power to make exporting a profitable opportunity.

On her return to Atlanta, Bonnie's next step was to obtain credit references for the firms she considered potential distributors. To those who were judged creditworthy, she sent letters expressing interest and samples, brochures, prices, and other relevant information.

The first orders were from a French wholesaler. Sales in this market totaled $70,000 in 1998. Similar success was achieved in Germany and England. Italy, on the other hand, did not produce any sales. Bonnie felt the semiluxury nature of the company's products and the lower incomes in Italy encouraged a "making do" attitude rather than purchase of goods and services that would make life easier.

In the United States, Aluminum Basics distributes through fairly aggressive and well-organized merchant hardware distributors and buying groups, such as cooperative and voluntary hardware chains, which have taken over much of the strategy planning for cooperating producers and retailers. In its foreign markets, however, there is no recognizable pattern. Channel systems vary from country to country. To avoid mixing channels of distribution, Aluminum Basics has only one account in each country. The chosen distributor is the exclusive distributor.

In France, Aluminum Basics distributes through a wholesaler based in Paris. This wholesaler has five salespeople covering the country. The firm specializes in small housewares and has contacts with leading buying groups, wholesalers, and department stores. Bonnie is impressed with the firm's aggressiveness and knowledge of merchandising techniques.

In Germany, Aluminum Basics sells to a Hamburg-based buying group for hardware wholesalers throughout the country. Bonnie felt this group would provide excellent coverage of the market because of its extensive distribution network.

In Denmark, Aluminum Basics' line is sold to a buying group representing a chain of hardware retailers. This group recently expanded to include retailers in Sweden, Finland, and Norway. Together this group purchases goods for about 500 hardware retailers. The buying power of Scandinavians is quite high, and it is expected that Aluminum Basics' products will prove very successful there.

In the United Kingdom, Aluminum Basics uses an importer-distributor, who both buys on his own account and acts as a sales agent. This firm sells to department stores and hardware wholesalers. This firm has not done very well overall, but it has done very well with Aluminum Basics' line of patio tables and chairs.

Australia is handled by an importer who operates a chain of discount houses. It heard about Aluminum Basics from a United Kingdom contact. After extensive e-mailing, this firm discovered it could land aluminum patio furniture in Melbourne at prices competitive with Japanese imports. So it started ordering because it wanted to cut prices in a high-priced garden furniture market.

The Argentina market is handled by an American who came to the United States from Buenos Aires in search of new lines. Aluminum Basics attributes success in Argentina to the efforts of this aggressive and capable agent. He has built a sizable trade in aluminum ladders.

In Trinidad and Jamaica, Aluminum Basics' products are handled by traders who carry such diversified lines as insurance, apples, plums, and fish. They have been successful in selling aluminum ladders. This business grew out of inquiries sent to the U.S. Department of Commerce and in researching its website (www.doc.gov), which Bonnie Pope followed up by mail.

Bonnie Pope's export policies for Aluminum Basics are as follows:

1. Product: No product modifications will be made in selling to foreign customers. This may be considered later after a substantial sales volume develops.

*Adapted from a case written by Professor Peter Banting, McMaster University, Canada.

2. Price: The company does not publish suggested list prices. Distributors add their own markup to their landed costs. Supply prices will be kept as low as possible. This is accomplished by *(a)* removing advertising expenses and other strictly domestic overhead charges from price calculations, *(b)* finding the most economical packages for shipping (smallest volume per unit), and *(c)* bargaining with carriers to obtain the lowest shipping rates possible.
3. Promotion: The firm does no advertising in foreign markets. Brochures and sales literature already being used in the United States are supplied to foreign distributors, who are encouraged to adapt them or create new materials as required. Aluminum Basics will continue to promote its products by participating in overseas trade shows. These are handled by the sales manager. All inquiries are forwarded to the firm's distributor in that country.
4. Distribution: New distributors will be contacted through foreign trade shows. Bonnie Pope considers large distributors desirable. She feels, however, that they are not as receptive as smaller distributors to a new, unestablished product line. Therefore, she prefers to appoint small distributors. Larger distributors may be appointed after the company has gained a strong consumer franchise in a country.
5. Financing: Aluminum Basics sees no need to provide financial help to distributors. The company views its major contribution as providing good products at the lowest possible prices.
6. Marketing and planning assistance: Bonnie Pope feels that foreign distributors know their own markets best. Therefore, they are best equipped to plan for themselves.
7. Selection of foreign markets: The evaluation of foreign market opportunities for the company's products is based primarily on discretionary income and lifestyle patterns. For example, Bonnie fails to see any market in North Africa for Aluminum Basics' products, which she thinks are of a semi-luxury nature. She thinks that cheaper products such as wood ladders (often homemade) are preferred to prefabricated aluminum ladders in regions such as North Africa and Southern Europe. Argentina, on the other hand, she thinks is a more highly industrialized market with luxury tastes. Thus, Bonnie sees Aluminum Basics' products as better suited for more highly industrialized and affluent societies.

Evaluate Aluminum Basics' present foreign markets strategies. Should it develop a global strategy? What strategy or strategies should Mark Parcells (the new VP of marketing) develop? Explain.

Computer-Aided Problems

Guide to the Use of the Computer-Aided Problems

Computer-Aided Problem Solving

Marketing managers are problem solvers who must make many decisions. Solving problems and making good decisions usually involves analysis of marketing information. Such information is often expressed in numbers—like costs, revenues, prices, and number of customers or salespeople. Most marketing managers use a computer to help keep track of the numbers and speed through tedious calculations. The computer can also make it easier to look at a problem from many different angles—for example, to see how a change in the sales forecast might impact expected sales revenue, costs, and profit.

The computer can only take a manager so far. The manager is the one who puts it all together—and it still takes skill to decide what the information means. The computer-aided problems at the end of the chapters in this text were specially developed by the authors to help you develop this skill. To work on the problems, you use the computer-aided problem (CAP) software that is included on the *Student CD-ROM to Accompany Essentials of Marketing* shrinkwrapped with this text.

The problems are short descriptions of decisions faced by marketing managers. Each description includes information to help make the decision. With each problem there are several questions for you to answer. Further, the *Learning Aid for Use with Essentials of Marketing* includes additional questions related to each problem.

Although you will use the computer program to do an analysis, most problems ask you to indicate what decision you would make and why. Thus, in these problems—as in the marketing manager's job—the computer is just a tool to help you make better decisions.

Each problem focuses on one or more of the marketing decision areas discussed in the corresponding chapter. The earlier problems require less marketing knowledge and are simpler in terms of the analysis involved. The later problems build on the principles already covered in the text. The problems can be used in many ways. And the same problem can be analyzed several times for different purposes. Although it is not necessary to do all of the problems or to do them in a particular order, you will probably want to start with the first problem. This practice problem is simpler than the others. In fact, you could do the calculations quite easily without a computer. But this problem will help you see how the program works and how it can help you solve the more complicated problems that come later.

Spreadsheet Analysis of Marketing Problems

Marketing managers often use spreadsheet analysis to evaluate their alternatives—and the program for the computer-aided problems does computerized spreadsheet analysis. In spreadsheet analysis, costs, revenue, and other data related to a marketing problem are organized into a data table—a spreadsheet. The spreadsheet analysis allows you to change the value of one or more of the variables in the data table—to see how each change affects the value of other variables. This is possible because the relationships among the variables are already programmed into the computer. You do not need to do any programming. Let's look at an overly simple example.

You are a marketing manager interested in the total revenue that will result from a particular marketing strategy. You are considering selling your product at $10.00 per unit. You expect to sell 100 units. In our CAP analysis, this problem might be shown in a (very simple) spreadsheet that looks like this:

Variable	Value
Selling price	$10.00
Units sold	100
Total revenue	$1,000.00

There is only one basic relationship in this spreadsheet: Total revenue is equal to the selling price multiplied by the number of units sold. If that relationship has been programmed into the computer (as it is in these problems), you can change the selling price or the number of units you expect to sell, and the program will automatically compute the new value for total revenue.

But now you can ask questions like: What if I raise the price to $10.40 and still sell 100 units? What will happen to total revenue? To get the answer, all you have to do is enter the new price in the spreadsheet, and the program will compute the total revenue for you.

You may also want to do many "what-if" analyses—for example, to see how total revenue changes over a range of prices. Spreadsheet analysis allows you to do this quickly and easily. For instance, if you want to see what happens to total revenue as you vary the price between some minimum value (say, $8.00) and a maximum value (say, $12.00), the program will provide the results table for a what-if analysis showing total revenue for 11 different prices in the range from $8.00 to $12.00.

In a problem like this—with easy numbers and a simple relationship between the variables—the spreadsheet does not do that much work for you. You could do it in your head. But with more complicated problems, the spreadsheet makes it very convenient to more carefully analyze different alternatives or situations.

Using the Program

You don't have to know about computers or using a spreadsheet to use the computer-aided problems program. It was designed to be easy to learn and use. The Help button will give you more detailed information if you need it. But it's best to just try things out to see how it works. A mistake won't hurt anything.

You're likely to find that it's quicker and easier to just use the program than it is to read the instructions—especially if you've used a Windows program before. So you may want to go ahead and install the CD-ROM on your own computer and try the practice problem now. Check the label on the CD-ROM for instructions about how to install the software. It takes just a few minutes and there's nothing to it.

The Spreadsheet Is Easy to Use

The spreadsheet software is very easy to use and specifically designed for the computer-aided problems. Like the other software on the Student CD-ROM, it follows conventions that are standard to browser programs (like Microsoft Internet Explorer or Netscape Navigator). If you have used a browser to surf the Internet, using this will be the same. Even if you have not used a browser or other Windows software before, using this program will make it easy for you to learn. However, if you want more general information about using Microsoft Windows software, you can review the Help file or tutorial that comes with the Windows operating system.

As with other browser-based programs, you typically use a mouse to move around in the program and select options. When you move the mouse, the cursor (which appears on your screen as an arrow) also moves. If you move the mouse so that the cursor is over one of the options on the screen and quickly press and release the left button on the mouse, the program will perform the action associated with that option. This process of using the mouse to position the cursor and then quickly pressing and releasing the left button is called "clicking" or "selecting." In these instructions, we'll refer to this often. For example, we'll say things like "click the Results button" or "select a problem from the list."

Let's use the first problem to illustrate how the program works.

Start by selecting a problem

When you start the *Essentials of Marketing* CD-ROM software, the first screen displayed is a home page with the title of the book and various options. Click on the label that says CAPs (short for computer-aided problems).

The computer-aided problem page will appear, and you will see a small window in the upper-left corner with the phrase "Choose a problem by clicking on the arrow." When you click the small arrow to the right of that label, a drop-down list of problems will appear. Select the problem you want to work (in this case, select the first one, "Revenue, Cost, and Profit Relationships").

Note: When you first select a problem, be patient while the program loads. It may take a minute or so. Once the program has loaded, calculations are immediate.

Once you select a problem, the problem description window appears. This is simply a convenient reminder of the problem description found in this text. (The assignment questions for each problem are in this book, so it's useful to have your book with you at the computer when you're working on a problem.)

Across the top of the box in which the problem description appears you will see buttons labeled Description, Spreadsheet, Results, Graph, and Calculator. After you've reviewed the problem description, click the Spreadsheet button.

Each spreadsheet consists of one or two columns of numbers. Each column and row is labeled. Look at the row and column labels carefully to see what variable is represented by the value (number) in the spreadsheet. Study the layout of the spreadsheet, and get a feel for how it organizes the information from the problem description. The spreadsheet displays the starting values for the problem. Keep in mind that sometimes the problem description does not provide as much detail about the starting values as is provided in the spreadsheet.

You will see that some of the values in the spreadsheet appear in a highlighted edit box. These are usually values related to the decision variables in the problem you are solving. You can change any value (number) that appears in one of these boxes. When you make a change, the rest of the values (numbers) in that column are recalculated to show how a change in the value of that one variable affects the others. Think about how the numbers relate to each other.

Making changes in values is easy. When the spreadsheet first appears your cursor appears as a free-floating arrow; however, when you pass the cursor over the box for the value that you want to change the cursor changes to the shape of an I-beam. When you click on the value in that box you can change it. Or to move the cursor to a value in a different box, just click on that box.

When you have selected the box with the value (number) you want to change, there are different ways to type in your new number. A good approach is to position the I-beam cursor before the first digit, and while depressing the mouse button drag the cursor across all of the digits in the number. This will highlight the entire number. Then simply type in the new number and the old one will be replaced. Alternatively, you can use other keys to edit the number. For example, you can use the backspace key to erase digits to the left of the I-beam cursor; similarly, you can use the Del key to erase digits to the right of the cursor. Or you can use the arrow keys to move the cursor to the point where you want to change part of a number. Then you just type in your change. You may want to experiment to see which of these editing approaches you like the best.

When you are finished typing the new number, press the Enter key and the other values in the spreadsheet will be recalculated to show the effect of your new value. Similarly, the other numbers will recalculate if you click on a different box after you have entered a number.

When you are typing numbers into the edit boxes, you'll probably find it most convenient to type the numbers and the decimal point with the keys on the main part of the keyboard (rather than those on the cursor control pad). For example, a price of one thousand dollars and 50 cents would be typed as 1000.50 or just 1000.5—using the number keys on the top row of the keyboard and the period key for the decimal point. *Do not type in the dollar sign or the commas to indicate thousands*. Be careful not to type the letters o or l (lowercase L) instead of the numbers 0 or 1.

Typing percent values is a possible point of confusion—since there are different ways to think about a percent. For example, "ten and a half" percent might be represented by 10.5 or .105. To avoid confusion, the program always expects you to enter percents using the first approach—which is the way percents are discussed in the problems. Thus, if you want to enter the value for ten and a half percent you would type 10.5.

To help prevent errors, each problem is programmed with a set of permitted values for each boxed field. After you click on a specific edit box, the range of permitted values is shown in the line at the bottom left corner of the spreadsheet window. It may be useful to explain what we mean by "permitted values." For example, if you accidentally type a letter when the computer program expects a number, the entry will turn red and what you typed will not be accepted. Further, the program won't allow you to enter a new value for a variable that is outside of a permitted range of values.

For example, if you try to type −10.00 as the price of a product, the entry will turn red. (It doesn't make sense to set the price as a negative number!) If you make an error, check what range of values is permitted—and then retype a new number that is in the permitted range, and press the Enter key to recompute the spreadsheet. When you have entered a permitted value, the value will no longer appear in red.

Remember that a value on the spreadsheet stays changed until you change it again. Some of the questions that accompany the problems ask you to evaluate results associated with different sets of values. It's good practice to check that you have entered all the correct values on a spreadsheet before interpreting the results.

In addition to changing values (numbers) on the spreadsheet itself, there are other options on the spreadsheet menu bar. If you click the Print button, the current spreadsheet will be printed—assuming of course that a graphics printer is properly hooked up to your computer and that it is configured for Windows. *Before you select the Print option, make sure that the printer is turned on and loaded with paper.*

Click the Description button to go back and review the problem description—or you can use the drop-down list again to select another problem. If you click the Results button, a new window will appear that shows the results table for a what-if analysis.

Results of a what-if analysis

The Results button makes it easy for you to study in more detail the effect of changing the value of a particular variable. It systematically changes the value of one variable (which you select) and displays the effect that variable has on two other variables. You could do the same thing manually at the spreadsheet—by entering a value for a variable, checking the effect on other variables, and then repeating the process over and over again. But the manual approach is time-consuming and requires you to keep track of the results after each change. A what-if analysis does all this very quickly and presents the results table summary; you can also print or graph the results table if you wish.

Now let's take a step-by-step look at how you can get the exact what-if analysis that you want. The first step is to decide what variable (value) you want to vary and what result values you want to see in the results table.

You select the variables for your analysis by simply clicking the circle ("radio button") beside the number of interest. Click the radio button beside the value of the variable in an edit box that you want to vary. The radio button for the selected value is filled in. You can only select one variable to vary at a time. So if you want to vary some other variable, simply click on your new selection.

When you select a value to vary, the program computes a default "suggested" minimum value and maximum value for the range over which that variable may vary. The minimum value is usually 20 percent smaller than the value shown on the spreadsheet, and the maximum value is 20 percent larger. These default values are used as the minimum and maximum values to compute the results table for a what-if analysis (when you click the Results button).

You can also select the two variables that you want to display in the results table of the what-if analysis. Typically, you will want to display the results (computed values) for variables that will be affected by the variable you select to vary. Remember the example we used earlier. If you had specified that price was going to vary, you might want to display total revenue—to see how it changes at different price levels.

You select a variable to display in the same way that you select the variable you are going to vary. Simply click on the radio button beside a number on the spreadsheet that is not in an edit box. Then use this approach to select a second variable to be displayed in the results table. If you change your mind, you can click on the radio button for another variable. When you have completed this step, you will see a solid radio button next to the variable you chose to vary and solid radio buttons next to the two variables that you want to display.

Now you can let the computer take over. On the button bar at the top of the spreadsheet window, click the Results button and the results table for the what-if analysis will appear. Each row in the first column of the results table will show a different value for the variable you wanted to vary. The minimum value will be in the first row. The maximum value will be in the bottom row. Evenly spaced values between the minimum and maximum will be in the middle rows. The other columns show the calculated results for the values you selected to display. Each column of values is labeled at the top to identify the column and row from the spreadsheet. The row portion of the label is a short version of the label from the spreadsheet. The results are based on the values that were in the spreadsheet when you selected the Results button—except for the value you selected to vary.

After the results table is displayed, you have the option to type in your own minimum value and maximum value in the edit boxes below the results table. To do that, just use the same approach you use to enter new values in the spreadsheet. When you enter a new minimum or maximum, the results table will be updated based on the new range of values between the minimum and maximum you entered.

At this point you will want to study the results of your analysis. You can also print a copy of the results table by clicking the Print button. The button bar also shows other possibilities. For example, if you select the Spreadsheet button, the spreadsheet will reappear. The radio buttons will still show the values you selected in the previous analysis. From there you can make additional changes in the values in the spreadsheet, check the results table for a new what-if analysis, or select another problem to work. Or you can look at (and print) a graph of values in the results table for the what-if analysis.

Viewing a graph of your results

You can create a graph of values in the results table by clicking the Graph button. The horizontal axis for the graph will be the variable in the first column of the display. The vertical axis on the left side is based on the first variable you selected to display in the results table. The vertical axis on the right side of the graph is for the second variable. There will be a line on the graph that corresponds to each axis. When the graph is displayed, you can select the Print button to print a copy or you can go back to the spreadsheet and select other values to vary or select another column to graph.

What to do next

The next section gives additional tips on the program. You will probably want to look through it after you have done some work with the practice problem. For now, however, you're probably tired of reading instructions. So work a problem or two. It's easier and faster to use the program than to read about it. Give it a try, and don't be afraid to experiment. If you have problems, remember that the Help button is available when you need it.

Some Tips on Using the CAP Program

Resetting the spreadsheet to the initial values

The initial spreadsheet for each problem gives the "starting values" for the problem. While working a problem, you will often change one or more of the starting values to a new number. A changed value stays in effect—unless you change it again. This is a handy feature. But after you make several changes, you may not be able to remember the starting values. There is a simple solution—you can click the button to return to the home page, then click the CAPs label again, and reselect the problem you want. The spreadsheet will appear with the original set of starting values.

Checking the computer's calculations

Some values appear in the spreadsheet as whole numbers, and others appear with one or more digits to the right of a decimal point. For example, dollar values usually have two digits to the right of the decimal point—indicating how many cents

Notes

Chapter 1

1. Eric H. Shaw, "A Review of Empirical Studies of Aggregate Marketing Costs and Productivity in the United States," *Journal of the Academy of Marketing Science*, Fall 1990, pp. 285–92; Christopher H. Lovelock and Charles B. Weinberg, *Marketing for Public and Nonprofit Managers* (New York: John Wiley & Sons, 1984).

2. Gregory D. Upah and Richard E. Wokutch, "Assessing Social Impacts of New Products: An Attempt to Operationalize the Macromarketing Concept," *Journal of Public Policy and Marketing* 4 (1985), pp. 166–78.

3. An American Marketing Association committee developed a similar—but more complicated—definition of marketing: "Marketing is the process of planning and executing conception, pricing, promotion, and distribution of ideas, goods, and services to create exchanges that satisfy individual and organizational objectives." See *Marketing News*, March 1, 1985, p. 1. See also Ernest F. Cooke, C. L. Abercrombie, and J. Michael Rayburn, "Problems With the AMA's New Definition of Marketing Offer Opportunity to Develop an Even Better Definition," *Marketing Educator*, Spring 1986, p. 1ff.

4. George Fisk, "Editor's Working Definition of Macromarketing," *Journal of Macromarketing* 2, no. 1 (1982), pp. 3–4; Shelby D. Hunt and John J. Burnett, "The Macromarketing/Micromarketing Dichotomy: A Taxonomical Model," *Journal of Marketing*, Summer 1982, pp. 11–26.

5. For an historical review of this topic see Robert W. Nason and Phillip D. White, "The Visions of Charles C. Slater: Social Consequences of Marketing," *Journal of Macromarketing* 1, no. 2 (1981), pp. 4–18.

6. "Russia's Middle Class," *Business Week*, October 16, 2000, pp. 78–85; "Capitalism in a Cold Climate," *Fortune*, June 12, 2000, pp. 195–216; "Special Report: Europe Ten Years Later . . . ," *Business Week*, November 8, 1999, pp. 56–88; "Glow Is Wearing Off in the East," *USA Today*, October 11, 1999, p. 1Aff.; "World Business: Ten Years Later," *The Wall Street Journal Reports*, September 27, 1999; "From Worry to Worse: Revisiting a Family in Russia 7 Years Later," *The Wall Street Journal*, September 28, 1998, p. A1ff.; "World Business: Playing the New Europe," *The Wall Street Journal Reports*, September 28, 1998. See also Stanislaw Gajewski, "Consumer Behavior in Economics of Shortage," *Journal of Business Research*, January 1992, pp. 5–10; Krystyna Iwinska-Knop, "Distribution as a Barrier to Application of Marketing in the Centrally Planned Economy (Case Study of Poland)," *Journal of Business Research*, January 1992, pp. 19–26; "Russia's New Capitalism," *Business Week*, October 10, 1994, pp. 68–80.

7. Victor V. Cordell, "Effects of Public Policy on Marketing," *Journal of Macromarketing*, Spring 1993, pp. 20–32; James M. Carman and Robert G. Harris, "Public Regulation of Marketing Activity, Part III: A Typology of Regulatory Failures and Implications for Marketing and Public Policy," *Journal of Macromarketing*, Spring 1986, pp. 51–64.

8. "Is The Digital Divide a Problem or an Opportunity?" *Business Week* (Special Section), December 18, 2000; "Global Capitalism: Can It Be Made to Work Better?" *Business Week*, November 6, 2000, pp. 72–100; "It Takes a Cell Phone," *The Wall Street Journal*, June 25, 1999, p. B1ff.

9. "Who Will Profit from the Internet Agora?" *Business Week E.Biz*, June 5, 2000, pp. EB56–74; "First E-Shopping, Now E-Swapping," *The Wall Street Journal*, January 17, 2000, p. B1ff.

10. Clifford J. Shultz and Anthony Pecotich, "Marketing and Development in the Transition Economies of Southeast Asia: Policy Explication, Assessment, and Implications," *Journal of Public Policy & Marketing*, Spring 1997, pp. 55–68; Charles R. Taylor and Glenn S. Omura, "An Evaluation of Alternative Paradigms of Marketing and Economic Development, Part 1," *Journal of Macromarketing*, Fall 1994, pp. 6–20; Van R. Wood and Scott J. Vitell, "Marketing and Economic Development: Review, Synthesis and Evaluation," *Journal of Macromarketing* 6, no. 1 (1986), pp. 28–48.

11. "Making Sense of India," *Newsweek*, August 4, 1997, pp. 41–46; "In Rural India, Video Vans Sell Toothpaste and Shampoo," *The Wall Street Journal*, January 10, 1996, p. B1ff.

12. Available from World Wide Web: <http://www.odci.gov/cia/publications/factbook/geos>; "A Shrinking Trade Gap Looks Good Stateside," *Business Week*, May 7, 2001, pp. 35–36; "U.S. Slowdown Would Ripple around Globe," *USA Today*, January 22, 2001, p. 1Bff.; "American Economy Offers a Model Others Both Envy and Fear," *The Wall Street Journal*, January 18, 2001, p. A1ff.; "Exporting Management Savvy," *The Wall Street Journal*, October 24, 2000, p. B1ff.; "The Big Myth about U.S. Manufacturing," *Fortune*, October 2, 2000, pp. 244BB–PP; "This Trade Deficit Was Made in the U.S.A.," *The Wall Street Journal*, August 7, 2000, p. A1; "The Atlantic Century?" *Business Week*, February 8, 1999, pp. 64–72; "Global Capitalism, R.I.P.?" *Newsweek*, September 14, 1998, pp. 40–42; "A Whole New Wave of Japanese Exports Is Headed Westward," *The Wall Street Journal*, November 14, 1997, p. A1ff.; "Trade Wars Aside, U.S. and Europe Buy More of Each Other's Foods," *The Wall Street Journal*, November 4, 1997, p. A1ff.; "These Are the Good Old Days," *Fortune*, June 9, 1997, pp. 74–87.

13. "Betting on Free Trade," *Business Week*, April 23, 2001, pp. 60–62; Saeed Samiee, "Globalization, Privatization, and Free Market Economy," *Journal of the Academy of Marketing Science*, Summer 2001, pp. 319–23.

14. "Ready to Burn Rubber in Russia," *Business Week*, March 31, 1997, pp. 52–53; "BMW, Mercedes, Rolls-Royce—Could This Be Russia?" *Business Week*, August 2, 1993, p. 40.

15. "Tariffs Shield Some U.S. Products," *USA Today*, May 6, 1999, p. 1Bff.

16. Available from World Wide Web: <http://www. barternews.com>; and <http://www.cob.ohio-state.edu /citm/ expa/countertrade.html>; and <http://www.fita.org/ioma/ countertrade.html>; Bureau of the Census, *Statistical Abstract of the United States 2000* (Washington, DC: U.S. Government Printing Office, 2001), pp. 821–56; Laura B. Forker, "Internationalizing Procurement: Determinants of Countertrade Involvement," *International Journal of Purchasing & Materials Management,* Spring 1997, pp. 27–34; Aspy P. Palia and Peter W. Liesch, "Survey of Countertrade Practices in Australia," *Industrial Marketing Management,* July 1997, pp. 301–13; Dorothy A. Paun, Larry D. Compeau, and Dhruv Grewal, "A Model of the Influence of Marketing Objectives on Pricing Strategies in International Countertrade," *Journal of Public Policy & Marketing,* Spring 1997, pp. 69–82; Sam C. Okoroafo, "Implementing International Countertrade: A Dyadic Approach," *Industrial Marketing Management,* July 1994, pp. 229–34; Abla M. Abdel-Latif and Jeffrey B. Nugent, "Countertrade as Trade Creation and Trade Diversion," *Contemporary Economic Policy,* January 1994, pp. 1–11.

17. Available from World Wide Web: <http://www. wto.org/ wto/about/cover.htm>; "China Takes a Great Leap toward the WTO," *The Wall Street Journal,* June 22, 2001, p. A13; "Troubled Trade Group Sees Slight Chance for Progress," *USA Today,* November 29, 2000, p. 1Bff.; "Will China Follow WTO Rules?" *Business Week,* June 5, 2000, pp. 42–43; "There's Something Happening Here," *Fortune,* May 15, 2000, pp. 232–44; "Backlash: Behind the Anxiety over Globalization," *Business Week,* April 24, 2000, pp. 38–48; "The Siege of Seattle," *Newsweek,* December 13, 1999, pp. 30–40; "WTO's Failure in Bid to Launch Trade Talks Emboldens Protesters," *The Wall Street Journal,* December 6, 1999, p. A1ff.; "Welcome to the Club," *Business Week,* November 29, 1999, pp. 34–37; "WTO or Bust," *Business Week,* November 22, 1999, pp. 60–61; "In Historic Pact, U.S. Opens Way for China to Finally Join WTO," *The Wall Street Journal,* November 16, 1999, p. A1ff.; "Who Stands to Win, Lose under Trade Treaty," *USA Today,* December 1, 1994, p. 4B; "Trade Pact Is Set by 117 Nations, Slashing Tariffs, Subsidies Globally," *The Wall Street Journal,* December 16, 1993, p. A3ff.

18. William McInnes, "A Conceptual Approach to Marketing," in *Theory in Marketing,* second series, ed. Reavis Cox, Wroe Alderson, and Stanley J. Shapiro (Homewood, IL: Richard D. Irwin, 1964), pp. 51–67.

19. *1990 Annual Report,* Tandem; "The New Germany's Glowing Future," *Fortune,* December 3, 1990, pp. 146–54; "Berlin Tries to Raze Its Great Divide," *Insight,* October 15, 1990, pp. 8–17; "West Brands Rain on East's Parade," *Advertising Age,* October 1, 1990, p. 15ff.

20. "Technology: Overload," *The Wall Street Journal Reports,* June 21, 1999; "Technology Is 'Demolishing' Time, Distance," *USA Today,* April 24, 1997, p. 1Bff.; see also Roger A. Layton, "Measures of Structural Change in Macromarketing Systems," *Journal of Macromarketing,* Spring 1989, pp. 5–15.

21. "Too Much Corporate Power?" *Business Week,* September 11, 2000, pp. 144–58; "Ad Nauseam," *Advertising Age,* July 10, 2000, p. 1ff.

22. Stanley J. Shapiro, "Ethical Decision Making in Marketing," *Journal of Public Policy & Marketing,* Fall 1996, pp. 321–23; Oswald A. Mascarenhas, "Exonerating Unethical Marketing Executive Behaviors: A Diagnostic Framework," *Journal of Marketing,* April 1995, pp. 43–57; Gina Vega, "Caveat Emptor: Ethical Chauvinism in the Global Economy," *Journal of Business Ethics,* September 1997, pp. 1353–62; George G. Brenkert, "Competing With Integrity in International Business," *Journal of Business Ethics,* January 1997, pp. 6, 22ff. For a discussion of some criticisms of advertising, see Banwari Mittal, "Public Assessment of TV Advertising: Faint Praise and Harsh Criticism," *Journal of Advertising Research,* January/February 1994, pp. 35–53. For a discussion of ethical issues in marketing, see Anusorn Singhapakdi et al., "The Perceived Importance of Ethics and Social Responsibility on Organizational Effectiveness: A Survey of Marketers," *Journal of the Academy of Marketing Science,* Spring 1995, pp. 49–56; Ishmael P. Akaah and Daulatram Lund, "The Influence of Personal and Organizational Values on Marketing Professionals' Ethical Behavior," *Journal of Business Ethics,* June 1994, pp. 417–30.

Chapter 2

1. Available from World Wide Web: <http://www.dell.com>; "The Mother of All Price Wars," *Business Week,* July 20, 2001, pp. 32–35; "Why Dell Isn't Dumb," *Fortune,* July 9, 2001, pp. 134–36; "Automate or Die," *Ecompany,* July 2001, pp. 60–67; "How Dell Fine-Tunes Its PC Pricing to Gain Edge in a Slow Market," *The Wall Street Journal,* June 8, 2001, p. A1ff.; "How Dell Keeps from Stumbling," *Business Week,* May 14, 2001, pp. 38B–D; "How Dell, Starwood and Teva Fight, Win in Commodity-Priced Business," *Investor's Business Daily,* May 4, 2001, p. A1; "Dell Dethrones Compaq as Global PC Sales Leader," *Investor's Business Daily,* April 23, 2001, p. A6; "Dell, Gateway Seen Turning Up the Heat in PC Price Wars," *Investor's Business Daily,* March 28, 2001, p. A7; "Price War Squeezes PC Makers," *The Wall Street Journal,* March 26, 2001, p. B1ff.; "Thinking Outside the Beige PC Box," *Investor's Business Daily,* March 6, 2001, p. A1; "Be like Mike," *Ecompany,* December 2000, pp. 85–86; "How a Low-Cost Provider like Dell also Delivers Best Customer Service," *Investor's Business Daily,* November 13, 2000, p. A1; "Going Digital? Think First," *Fortune,* November 13, 2000, pp. 190–98; "Can Michael Dell Escape the Box?" *Fortune,* October 16, 2000, pp. 92–120; "Dell's Second Web Revolution," *Business Week E.Biz,* September 18, 2000, pp. EB62–EB63; "Dell Looks for Ways to Rekindle the Fire It Had as an Upstart," *The Wall Street Journal,* August 31, 2000, p. A1ff.; "Direct PC Seller Dell Computer Aims to Sell Its Web Expertise," *Investor's Business Daily,* April 13, 2000, p. A6; "Dell to Offer Hosting of Small-Business Web Sites," *The Wall Street Journal,* February 22, 2000, p. B23; "Dell's Big New Act," *Fortune,* December 6, 1999, pp. 152–56; "Dell Cracks China," *Fortune,* June 21, 1999, pp. 120–24; "Nine Ways to Win on the Web," *Fortune,* May 24, 1999, pp. 112–25; "Dell Builds an Electronics Superstore on the Web," *The Wall Street Journal,* March 3, 1999, p. B1ff.; "The Internet: Leading the PC Pack," *The Wall Street Journal Reports,* December 7, 1998, p. R27; "Michael Dell Rocks," *Fortune,* May 11, 1998, pp. 58–70; "No Big Deal: Why Michael Dell Isn't Afraid of The New Compaq," *Fortune,* March 2, 1998, pp. 189–92;

"Dell's Profit Leaps 52% as Asian Sales Soar," *The Wall Street Journal,* February 19, 1998, p. B20; "Asia: Why Business Is Still Bullish," *Fortune,* October 27, 1997, pp. 139–42; "And Give Me an Extra-Fast Modem with That, Please," *Business Week,* September 29, 1997, p. 38; "Now Everyone in PCs Wants to Be like Mike," *Fortune,* September 8, 1997, pp. 91–92; "Michael Dell Turns the PC World Inside Out," *Fortune,* September 8, 1997, pp. 76–86; "Dell Fights PC Wars by Emphasizing Customer Service," *The Wall Street Journal,* August 15, 1997, p. B4; Joan Magretta, "The Power of Virtual Integration: An Interview With Dell Computer's Michael Dell," *Harvard Business Review,* March–April 1998, pp. 72–84.

2. Charles R. Weiser, "Championing the Customer," *Harvard Business Review,* November 1995–December 1995, pp. 113–16; Stanley F. Slater and John C. Narver, "Market Orientation and the Learning Organization," *Journal of Marketing,* July 1995, pp. 63–74; Regina F. Maruca, "Getting Marketing's Voice Heard," *Harvard Business Review,* January–February 1998, pp. 10–11; Vikas Mittal, "Driving Customer Equity: How Customer Lifetime Value Is Reshaping Corporate Strategy," *Journal of Marketing,* April 2001, pp. 107–110; Christine Steinman, "Beyond Market Orientation: When Customers and Suppliers Disagree," *Journal of the Academy of Marketing Science,* Winter 2000, pp. 109–120; Francis J. Gouillart and Frederick D. Sturdivant, "Spend a Day in the Life of Your Customers," *Harvard Business Review,* January 1994–February 1994, pp. 116–20ff; George S. Day, "The Capabilities of Market-Driven Organizations," *Journal of Marketing,* October 1994, pp. 37–52; R. W. Ruekert, "Developing a Market Orientation: An Organizational Strategy Perspective," *International Journal of Research in Marketing,* August 1992, pp. 225–46; J. David Lichtenthal and David T. Wilson, "Becoming Market Oriented," *Journal of Business Research,* May 1992, pp. 191–208; George J. Avlonitis and Spiros P. Gounaris, "Marketing Orientation and Company Performance: Industrial Vs. Consumer Goods Companies," *Industrial Marketing Management,* September 1997, pp. 385–402; Bernard J. Jaworski and Ajay K. Kohli, "Market Orientation: Antecedents and Consequences," *Journal of Marketing,* July 1993, pp. 53–70. See also "The Marketing Revolution at Procter & Gamble," *Business Week,* July 25, 1988, pp. 72–73ff.; Frederick E. Webster, Jr., "The Changing Role of Marketing in the Corporation," *Journal of Marketing,* October 1992, pp. 1–17; Franklin S. Houston, "The Marketing Concept: What It Is and What It Is Not," *Journal of Marketing,* April 1986, pp. 81–87; George S. Day, "The Capabilities of Market-Driven Organizations," *Journal of Marketing,* October 1994, pp. 37–52.

3. For more on the marketing concept in the banking industry, see "What's Next—The Bank of Burger King," *Business Week,* June 18, 2001, p. 150; "Could Citi Make Money by Sending Money?" *Business Week,* July 16, 2001, p. 83; "What a Bank Should Be," *Business Week Small Biz,* July 16, 2001, pp. 23–28; "Altering Course, Banks Welcome Check Cashers," *The Wall Street Journal,* July 6, 2001, p. B1ff.; "Banks Cozy Up to Customers," *The Wall Street Journal,* April 26, 2001, p. B1ff.; "Online or Off-Line Banking: Where to Stash Your Cash?" *Ecompany,* January/February 2001, pp. 174–76; "A Small Chain Grows by Borrowing Ideas from Burger Joints," *The Wall Street Journal,* May 17, 2000, p. A1ff.; "On the Road with a Rolling Bank Branch," *The Wall Street Journal,* November 6, 1997, p. B1ff.; "Have You Noticed All of Those ATMs Suddenly Appearing?" *The Wall Street Journal,* October 7, 1997, p. A1ff. For more on the marketing concept and churches, see "The Glorious Rise of Christian Pop," *Newsweek,* July 16, 2001, pp. 38–43; "God, Mammon and 'Bibleman,'" *Newsweek,* July 16, 2001, pp. 44–48: "Rappin' and Rockin' for the Lord," *The Wall Street Journal,* February 28, 2001, p. B1ff.; "Registers Ring in Sanctuary Stores," *The Wall Street Journal,* December 17, 1999, p. B1ff.; "Religious Advertising Converts, Moving Toward a Tougher Sell," *The Wall Street Journal,* February 24, 1998, p. B2; "Bringing the Good Book to the Outlet Mall," *The Wall Street Journal,* December 2, 1997, p. B1ff.; "Churches Launch 'In Your Face' Pitches," *The Wall Street Journal,* November 7, 1997, p. B8. For more on the marketing concept and the academic community, see "The New U: A Tough Market Is Reshaping Colleges," *Business Week,* December 22, 1997, pp. 96–102; "Some Small Colleges Hire Recruiters to Get Bigger Freshman Class," *The Wall Street Journal,* September 5, 1995, p. A1ff. For more on the marketing concept and the medical profession, see "Grocery List: Milk, Bread, QuickMedx," *USA Today,* January 23, 2001, p. 3B; "See the Doctor, Get a Toaster," *Business Week,* December 8, 1997, pp. 86–87; "Hospitals Use TV Spots to Boost Business," *The Wall Street Journal,* September 26, 1996, p. B10; "Rx: Thirty Minutes on the StairMaster Twice Weekly," *Newsweek,* March 17, 1997, p. 46; "Designing a New Hospital? Let Malls Be Your Muse," *The Wall Street Journal,* August 1, 1994, p. B1ff.; "Offering Aerobics, Karate, Aquatics, Hospitals Stress Business of 'Wellness,'" *The Wall Street Journal,* August 9, 1993, P. B1ff.; "Pediatric Centers Spring Up to Provide Off-Hour Care," *The Wall Street Journal,* February 13, 1989, p. B1. See also Gary D. Hailey, "The Federal Trade Commission, the Supreme Court and Restrictions on Professional Advertising," *International Journal of Advertising* 8, no. 1 (1989), pp. 1–16; Betsy D. Gelb, Samuel V. Smith, and Gabriel M. Gelb, "Service Marketing Lessons from the Professionals," *Business Horizons,* September–October 1988, pp. 29–34; Valarie A. Zeithaml, A. Pasasuraman, and Leonard L. Berry, "Problems and Strategies in Services Marketing," *Journal of Marketing,* Spring 1985, pp. 33–46.

4. "Remedies for an Economic Hangover," *Fortune,* June 25, 2001, pp. 130–39; "The Best Little Grocery Store in America," *Inc.,* June 2001, pp. 54–61; "Fanatics!" *Inc.,* April 2001, pp. 36–48; "Internet Nirvana," *Ecompany,* December 2000, pp. 99–108; "The *Inc.* Web Awards," *Inc.* Tech, No. 4, 2000, pp. 45–86; "The Bride Wore Swag," *Ecompany,* October 2000, pp. 201–202; "Why Women Find Lauder Mesmerizing," *Fortune,* May 25, 1998, pp. 96–106; "Smart Managing: The Power of Reflection," *Fortune,* November 24, 1997, pp. 291–96; "Why Some Customers Are More Equal than Others," *Fortune,* September 19, 1994, pp. 215–24; Stanley F. Slater and John C. Narver, "Market Orientation, Customer Value, and Superior Performance," *Business Horizons,* March–April 1994, pp. 22–28; "Relationships: Six Steps to Success," *Sales & Marketing Management,* April 1992, pp. 50–58; Stanley F. Slater, "Developing a Customer Value-Based Theory of the Firm," *Journal of the Academy of Marketing Science,* Spring 1997, pp. 162–67; Sharon E. Beatty, "Keeping Customers," *Journal of Marketing,* April 1994, pp. 124–25; Thomas W. Gruen, "Relationship Marketing: The Route to Marketing Efficiency and Effectiveness," *Business Horizons,* November–December 1997, pp. 32–38; A. Parasuraman,

"Reflections on Gaining Competitive Advantage Through Customer Value," *Journal of the Academy of Marketing Science*, Spring 1997, pp. 154–61; Alan W. H. Grant and Leonard A. Schlesinger, "Realize Your Customers' Full Profit Potential," *Harvard Business Review*, September–October 1995, pp. 59–72; Diana L. Deadrick, R. B. McAfee, and Myron Glassman, "'Customers for Life': Does It Fit Your Culture?" *Business Horizons*, July–August 1997, pp. 11–16; Robert B. Woodruff, "Customer Value: The Next Source for Competitive Advantage," *Journal of the Academy of Marketing Science*, Spring 1997, pp. 139–53; Robert M. Morgan, "Aftermarketing: How to Keep Customers for Life Through Relationship Marketing," *Journal of the Academy of Marketing Science*, Winter 1997, pp. 92–93.

5. Available from World Wide Web: <http://www.llbean.com>; "Here's the Maine Store for the Great Outdoors," *The Blade*, (Toledo, Ohio), August 26, 1990; "L.L. Bean Scales Back Expansion Goals to Ensure Pride in Its Service Is Valid," *The Wall Street Journal*, July 31, 1989, p. B3; "Training at L.L. Bean," *TRAINING, The Magazine of Human Resources Development*, October 1988; "Using the Old (L.L.) Bean," *The Reader's Digest*, June 1986.

6. "Dot-Com Decline Turns into Lift for the Dot-Orgs," *The Wall Street Journal*, March 12, 2001, p. B1ff.; "With Recruiting Slow, the Air Force Seeks a New Ad Campaign," *The Wall Street Journal*, February 14, 2001, p. A1ff.; "Big Retailers Cutting into Nonprofits' Tree Sales," *The Wall Street Journal*, December 19, 2000, p. B1ff.; "Dot-Coop, Dot-Museum, Dot-Pro? Enter Domain of New Web Names," *Investor's Business Daily*, November 21, 2000, p. A10; "Uncle Sam Wants You—and So Does Pepsi," *Business Week*, September 4, 2000, p. 52; "When Nonprofits Go After Profits," *Business Week*, June 26, 2000, pp. 173–78; "Army Enlists Net to Be All It Can Be," *USA Today*, April 19, 2000, p. 10B; "Uncle Sam Wants You . . . to Have Fun!" *Business Week*, February 21, 2000, pp. 98–101; "Modern Marketing Helps Sell Life as a Nun," *The Wall Street Journal*, May 11, 1999, p. B1ff.; "This Exhibit Is Brought to You by . . . ," *Business Week*, November 10, 1997, pp. 91–94; "In Funding Squeeze, PBS Cozies Up to Madison Avenue 'Sponsors,'" *The Wall Street Journal*, July 3, 1996, p. B1ff.; "Non-Profits Get Market-Savvy," *Advertising Age*, May 29, 1995, p. 1ff.; William G. Bowen, "When a Business Leader Joins a Nonprofit Board," *Harvard Business Review*, September–October 1994, pp. 38–44; "Charities Draw Younger Donors with Hip Events and Door Prizes," *The Wall Street Journal*, April 25, 1994, p. B1; "Nonprofits Dig into Databases for Big Donors," *The Wall Street Journal*, September 8, 1992, p. B1ff.; William A. Sutton, "Sports Marketing: Competitive Business Strategies for Sports," *Journal of the Academy of Marketing Science*, Spring 1996, pp. 176–77; Russell W. Jones, Carolyn Marshall, and Thomas P. Bergman, "Can a Marketing Campaign Be Used to Achieve Public Policy Goals?" *Journal of Public Policy & Marketing*, Spring 1996, pp. 98–107; J. G. Dees, "Enterprising Nonprofits," *Harvard Business Review*, January–February 1998, pp. 55–67; W. C. Kim and Renee Mauborgne, "Value Innovation: The Strategic Logic of High Growth," *Harvard Business Review*, January–February 1997, pp. 102–12; Gerald E. Smith and Paul D. Berger, "The Impact of Direct Marketing Appeals on Charitable Marketing Effectiveness," *Journal of the Academy of Marketing Science*, Summer 1996, pp. 219–31; Shohreh A. Kaynama, "Fundraising for Non-Profits," *Journal of the Academy of Marketing Science*, Spring 1997, p.173; C. Scott Greene and Paul Miesing, "Public Policy, Technology, and Ethics: Marketing Decisions for NASA's Space Shuttle," *Journal of Marketing*, Summer 1984, pp. 56–67; Alan R. Andreasen, "Nonprofits: Check Your Attention to Customers," *Harvard Business Review*, May–June 1982, pp. 105–10.

7. "The Black Market Vs. the Ozone," *Business Week*, July 7, 1997, pp. 128–30; "CFC-Span: Refrigerant's Reign Nears an End," *USA Today*, August 22, 1994, p. 5B; "Who Scores Best on the Environment," *Fortune*, July 26, 1993, pp. 114–22; "Quick, Save the Ozone," *Business Week*, May 17, 1993, pp. 78–79; "Air-Conditioner Firms Put Chill on Plans to Phase Out Use of Chlorofluorocarbons," *The Wall Street Journal*, May 10, 1993, p. B1ff. See also Alan R. Andreasen, "Social Marketing: Its Definition and Domain," *Journal of Public Policy & Marketing*, Spring 1994, pp. 108–14.

8. For more on Wal-Mart's efforts, see "Wrestling with Your Conscience," *Time*, November 15, 1999, pp. 72–73; "Wal-Mart Provides Many an Introduction to Sport Shooting," *The Wall Street Journal*, April 15, 1999, p. A1ff. For more on Kmart's efforts, see "Kmart Sells Out: Ammo Sales End, under Pressure from PC Prankster," *Investor's Business Daily*, July 10, 2001, p. A18. For more on Green Mountain, see "GreenMountain.com Makes Pitch for Clean Energy," *The Wall Street Journal*, May 1, 2000, p. A36; "Energy: Green Fees," *The Wall Street Journal Reports*, September 13, 1999, p. R12. For more on overseas sweatshops, see "Global Capitalism: A World of Sweatshops," *Business Week* (Special Report), November 6, 2000, pp. 84–86; "A Life of Fines and Beating," *Business Week*, October 2, 2000, pp. 122–28; "The Root of All Good," *Time*, October 18, 1999, pp. 88–91; "Nike's Image Problem," *USA Today*, October 4, 1999, p. 1Bff.

9. Edward J. O'Boyle and Lyndon E. Dawson, Jr., "The American Marketing Association Code of Ethics: Instructions for Marketers," *Journal of Business Ethics*, December 1992, pp. 921–30; Ellen J. Kennedy and Leigh Lawton, "Ethics and Services Marketing," *Journal of Business Ethics*, October 1993, pp. 785–96; Michael R. Hyman, Robert Skipper, and Richard Tansey, "Ethical Codes Are Not Enough," *Business Horizons*, March/April, 1990, pp. 15–22; John Tsalikis and David J. Fritzsche, "Business Ethics: A Literature Review with a Focus on Marketing Ethics," *Journal of Business Ethics*, September, 1989, pp. 695–702; G. R. Laczniak, R. F. Lusch, and P. E. Murphy, "Social Marketing: Its Ethical Dimensions," *Journal of Marketing*, Spring 1979, pp. 29–36.

10. Mary Anne Raymond and Hiram C. Barksdale, "Corporate Strategic Planning and Corporate Marketing: Toward an Interface," *Business Horizons*, September/October, 1989, pp. 41–48; George S. Day, "Marketing's Contribution to the Strategy Dialogue," *Journal of the Academy of Marketing Science*, Fall 1992, pp. 323–30; P. Rajan Varadarajan and Terry Clark, "Delineating the Scope of Corporate, Business, and Marketing Strategy," *Journal of Business Research*, October–November 1994, pp. 93–106.

11. Available from World Wide Web: <http://www.learningco.com>; "Broderbund: Identify an Need, Turn a Profit," *Fortune*, November 30, 1992, pp. 78–79.

12. "With the Telecom Industry on Hold, Nextel Sends Out a Different Signal," *Investor's Business Daily*, March 2, 2001, p. A1; "Keep 'Em Coming Back," *Business Week E. Biz*, May 15, 2000,

p. EB20; "Marketers Put a Price on Your Life," *USA Today,* July 7, 1999, p. 3B.

13. Orville C. Walker, Jr., and Robert W. Ruekert, "Marketing's Role in the Implementation of Business Strategies: A Critical Review and Conceptual Framework," *Journal of Marketing,* July 1987, pp. 15–33; Thomas V. Bonoma, "A Model of Marketing Implementation," *1984 AMA Educators' Proceedings* (Chicago: American Marketing Association, 1984), pp. 185–89; Kevin Romer and Doris C. Van Doren, "Implementing Marketing in a High-Tech Business," *Industrial Marketing Management,* August 1993, pp. 177–86.

14. *2000 Annual Report,* Gillette Company.

15. "For the Wrist that Has Everything," *Newsweek,* June 25, 2001, p. 80; "Now That's Good Timing," *Business Week Small Biz,* April 23, 2001, p. 14; "You Can Be a New-Product Dynamo: Medtronic, Pizza Hut, ADT Tell How," *Investor's Business Daily,* April 9, 2001, p. A1; "Movado Winds Up Lifestyle Effort, Expanded Line, with $15M in Print," *Brandweek,* April 2, 2001, p. 4; "Catching Up to Dick Tracy," *Business Week,* February 12, 2001, p. 100E4; "Timex Pursues Hip, Younger Set in Ads for Its New iControl Watch," *The Wall Street Journal,* May 19, 2000, p. B2; "Swatch: Ready for Net Time," *Business Week,* February 14, 2000, p. 61; "Timex Puts 'Iron' into TV with $5M," *Brandweek,* September 22, 1997, p. 6; "Timex Lines Goes for Museum-Goers," *Brandweek,* July 21, 1997, p. 8; "Timex Back to Basics to Retro-fit Gen X," *Brandweek,* August 5, 1996, p. 3; "Swatch Adds Metal Watch," *Advertising Age,* November 7, 1994, p. 60; Benetton Readies Watch Campaign," *Brandweek,* August 8, 1994, p. 5; "Indiglo Watch Lights Up Better Times for Timex," *Brandweek,* April 25, 1994, pp. 30–32.

Chapter 3

1. Available from World Wide Web: <http://www.i-zone.com>; "Photo Op: Nike, Polaroid Pair Up for Footwear Line," *Advertising Age,* April 2, 2001, p. 8; "Polaroid Teen Focus Advances I-Zone Effort," *Brandweek,* February 26, 2001, p. 8B; "From Kids to Adults, the USA Is Stuck on Stickers," *USA Today,* February 14, 2001, p. 1Dff.; "Hazy Picture at Polaroid," *Business Week,* December 4, 2000, pp. 95–96; "Polaroid Preps I-Zone's Next Step, as Scanner, Combo Cam Get Jiggy," *Brandweek,* October 2, 2000, p. 18; "Polaroid Combo Cam Targets Teens," *Advertising Age,* July 17, 2000, p. 65; "The Techies Grumbled, but Polaroid's Pocket Turned into a Huge Hit," *The Wall Street Journal,* May 2, 2000, p. A1ff.; "Camera Makers Aim to Snap Up Teens' Attention," *Advertising Age,* May 1, 2000, p. 14; "Re-Imaged Image Maker," *Brandweek,* March 13, 2000, pp.22–23; "Targeting Teens Pays Off for Polaroid," *Advertising Age,* March 6, 2000, p. 16; *2000 Annual Report,* Polaroid.

2. Mark B. Houston, "Competing for the Future: Breakthrough Strategies for Seizing Control of Your Industry and Creating the Markets of Tomorrow," *Journal of the Academy of Marketing Science,* Winter 1996, pp. 77–79; George S. Day and Robin Wensley, "Assessing Advantage: A Framework for Diagnosing Competitive Superiority," *Journal of Marketing,* April 1988, pp. 1–20; Kevin P. Coyne, "Sustainable Competitive Advantage—What It Is, What It Isn't," *Business Horizons,* January/February 1986, pp. 54–61; Michael E. Porter, *Competitive Advantage—Creating and Sustaining Superior Performance* (New York: Free Press, MacMillan, 1986).

3. For an unsuccessful differentiation example, see "GM Warms Up Its Branding Iron," *Business Week,* April 16, 2001, pp. 56–58; "GM Still Pushing Lame-Duck Oldsmobiles," *USA Today,* February 19, 2001, p. 4B; "One Last Look at Oldsmobile," *Brandweek,* Janary 8, 2001, pp. 28–32; "GM: 'Out with the Olds' Is Just the Start," *Business Week,* December 25, 2000, p. 57; "In Order to Grow, GM Finds that the Order of the Day Is Cutbacks," *The Wall Street Journal,* December 18, 2000, p. A1ff.; "How to Sell a Dying Brand," *Advertising Age,* December 18, 2000, p. 4ff.; "After Decades of Brand Bodywork, GM Parks Oldsmobile—for Good," *The Wall Street Journal,* December 13, 2000, p. B1ff.; "GM Decides to Shutter Oldsmobile," *USA Today,* December 13, 2000, p. 3B; "Oldsmobile to Go as GM Outlines Cost-Cutting Steps," *Investor's Business Daily,* December 13, 2000, p. A13.

4. "Taking On Procter & Gamble," *Inc.,* October 2000, pp. 66–71.

5. Brian Wansink and Michael L. Ray, "Advertising Strategies to Increase Usage Frequency," *Journal of Marketing,* January 1996, pp. 31–46; Ian C. MacMillan and Rita G. McGrath, "Discover Your Products' Hidden Potential," *Harvard Business Review,* May–June 1996, pp. 58–73; Ian C. MacMillan and Rita G. McGrath, "Discovering New Points of Differentiation," *Harvard Business Review,* July–August 1997, pp. 133–38ff.; Des Thwaites, Keith Walley, and Steve Foots, "Systematic Management of Differential Advantage," *Industrial Marketing Management,* May 1996, pp. 209–22.

6. For more on Coleman, see "Events Light Coleman's Fire," *Advertising Age,* June 18, 2001, p. 61; "Growing to Match Its Brand Name," *Fortune,* June 13, 1994, p. 114; "Coleman's Familiar Name Is Both Help and Hindrance," *The Wall Street Journal,* May 17, 1990, p. B2.

7. For more on E-Z-Go, see "Off-Roading, Golf-Cart Style," *The Wall Street Journal,* June 14, 2001, p. B1ff. For more on McDonald's, see "Disney Orders McDonald's Burger Joint for New Park," *USA Today,* January 15, 2001, p. 1B; "For East German Pair, McDonald's Serves Up an Economic Parable," *The Wall Street Journal,* November 8, 1999, p. A1ff.; "Fast-food Icon Wants Shine Restored to Golden Arches," *USA Today,* May 1, 1998, p. 1Bff.; "McD's Eyes Rollout of Loyalty Card," *Advertising Age,* April 27, 1998, p. 3; "A Really Big Mac," *Newsweek,* November 17, 1997, pp. 56–58; "Why You Won't Find Any Egg McMuffins for Breakfast in Brazil," *The Wall Street Journal,* October 23, 1997, p. A1ff.; "Burger Wars Sizzle as McDonald's Clones the Whopper," *The Wall Street Journal,* "September 17, 1997, p. B1ff.; "Toilet Paper and a Big Mac," *American Demographics,* July 1996, p. 15–16; "McDonald's Conquers the World," *Fortune,* October 17, 1994, pp. 103–16.

8. For more on Heinz EZ Squirt, see "Heinz Picks Purple as New EZ Squirt Color," *Brandweek,* June 25, 2001, p. 7; "Kids Salivate for New, Yucky, Weirdly Colored Food," *USA Today,* April 23, 2001, p. 7B; "Do E-Ads Have a Future?" *Business Week E.Biz,* January 22, 2001, pp. EB46–EB50; "Squeezing New from Old," *USA Today,* January 4, 2001, p. 1Bff.; "Bottled Up," *Fortune,* September 18, 2000, pp. 194–206; "EZ Being Green:

Kids Line Is Latest Heinz Innovation," *Advertising Age*, July 10, 2000, p. 3ff.; *2000 Annual Report*, Heinz. For more on ski resorts, see "It's All Downhill: Sugar Mountain Opens Slopes to Mountain Bikers," *Raleigh News & Observer*, July 25, 1999, p. 1Hff.; "Bikers Give Ski Resorts Summer Time Lift," *The Wall Street Journal*, July 7, 1994, p. B1ff. For more on Nike, see "Nike Puts Its Swoosh on MP3 Players, Walkie-Talkies, Heart Monitors," *The Wall Street Journal*, May 10, 2000, p. B1ff.; *2000 Annual Report*, Nike; "It's Not Just about Shoes," *Newsweek*, May 18, 1998, pp. 50–51.

9. For more on McDonald's and its hotel diversification effort, see "Would You Like a Bed with Your Burger?" *Ad Age Global*, February 2001, p. 12; "The Golden Arches: Burgers, Fries and 4-Star Rooms," *The Wall Street Journal*, November 17, 2000, p. B1ff.; *2000 Annual Report*, McDonald's.

10. For more on Purafil, see "Small Businesses Find International Success," *USA Today*, June 30, 2000, p. 1Bff.

11. For more on JLG, see "The Secret of U.S. Exports: Great Products," *Fortune*, January 10, 2000, pp. 154C-J.

12. Susan P. Douglas, "Exploring New Worlds: the Challenge of Global Marketing," *Journal of Marketing*, January 2001, pp. 103–108; Catharine M. Curran, "Selling to Newly Emerging Markets," *Journal of the Academy of Marketing Science*, Summer 2001, pp. 324–27; "Key Ingredient in Going Global Is Acquiring Local Tastes," *USA Today*, December 2, 1997, p. 15A; Judith Clair, "International Marketing: Your Company's Next Stage of Growth," *Journal of the Academy of Marketing Science*, Summer 1997, pp. 257–58; C. P. Rao, "Marketing to China: One Billion New Customers," *Journal of the Academy of Marketing Science*, Spring 1997, pp. 171–72; Dana-Nicoleta Lascu, "Total Global Strategy: Managing for Worldwide Competitive Advantage," *Journal of Marketing*, July 1994, pp. 121–23.

13. Available from World Wide Web: <http://www.hallmark.com>; *2000 Annual Report*, Hallmark; "American Greetings Thinks Time for 'Anytime' Is Now," *The Wall Street Journal*, March 24, 1998, p. B9; "American Greeting, Hallmark's Cards Will Send an Earful," *The Wall Street Journal*, November 5, 1993, p. B10B; "Old-Fashioned Sentiments Go High-Tech," *The Wall Street Journal*, November 9, 1992, p. B1ff.

14. Shelby D. Hunt and Robert M. Morgan, "Resource-Advantage Theory: A Snake Swallowing Its Tail or a General Theory of Competition?" *Journal of Marketing*, October 1997, pp. 74–82; Stavros P. Kalafatis and Vicki Cheston, "Normative Models and Practical Applications of Segmentation in Business Markets," *Industrial Marketing Management*, November 1997, pp. 519–30; Lisa R. Adam, "Nichecraft: Using Your Specialness to Focus Your Business, Corner Your Market, and Make Customers Seek You Out," *Journal of the Academy of Marketing Science*, Summer 1997, pp. 259–60; S. Ratneshwar, Cornelia Pechmann, and Allan D. Shocker, "Goal-Derived Categories and the Antecedents of Across-Category Consideration," *Journal of Consumer Research*, December 1996, pp. 240–50; George S. Day, A. D. Shocker, and R. K. Srivastava, "Customer-Oriented Approaches to Identifying Product-Markets," *Journal of Marketing*, Fall 1979, pp. 8–19; Rajendra K. Srivastava, Mark I. Alpert, and Allan D. Shocker, "A Customer-Oriented Approach for Determining Market Structures," *Journal of Marketing*, Spring 1984, pp. 32–45.

15. For more on both Nividia and Check Point, see "Little Niches that Grew," *Business Week*, June 18, 2001, pp. 100–01. See also "The Riches in Market Niches," *Fortune*, April 27, 1987, pp. 227–30; Robert E. Linneman and John L. Stanton, Jr., "Mining for Niches," *Business Horizons*, May–June 1992, pp. 43–51; Michael E. Raynor, "The Pitfalls of Niche Marketing," *The Journal of Business Strategy*, March/April, 1992, pp. 29–32.

16. Terry Elrod and Russell S. Winer, "An Empirical Evaluation of Aggregation Approaches for Developing Market Segments," *Journal of Marketing*, Fall 1982, pp. 32–34; Frederick W. Winter, "A Cost-Benefit Approach to Market Segmentation," *Journal of Marketing*, Fall 1979, pp. 103–11; Andrew Hilton, "Mythology, Markets, and the Emerging Europe," *Harvard Business Review*, November–December 1992, pp. 50–127. For a successful segmenting example, see, available from World Wide Web: <http://www.kaepa.com>; "Tapping into Cheerleading," *Adweek's Marketing Week*, March 2, 1992, p. 17.

17. Philip A. Dover, "Segmentation and Positioning for Strategic Marketing Decisions," *Journal of the Academy of Marketing Science*, Summer 2000, pp. 438–41; John Hogan, "Defining Your Market: Winning Strategies for High-Tech, Industrial, and Service Firms," *Journal of the Academy of Marketing Science*, Summer 2000, pp. 442–4; Hershey H. Friedman and Linda W. Friedman, "Reducing the 'Wait' in Waiting-Line Systems: Waiting Line Segmentation," *Business Horizons*, July–August 1997, pp. 54–58; Alex Chernev, "The Effect of Common Features on Brand Choice: Moderating Role of Attribute Importance," *Journal of Consumer Research*, March 1997, pp. 304–11; Dianne S. P. Cermak, Karen Maru File, and Russ Alan Prince, "A Benefit Segmentation of the Major Donor Market," *Journal of Business Research*, February 1994, pp. 121–30; Robert L. Armacost and Jamshid C. Hosseini, "Identification of Determinant Attributes Using the Analytic Hierarchy Process," *Journal of the Academy of Marketing Science*, Fall 1994, pp. 383–92; Joel S. Dubow, "Occasion-based vs. User-based Benefit Segmentation, A Case Study," *Journal of Advertising Research*, March/April 1992, pp. 11–19; Peter R. Dickson and James L. Ginter, "Market Segmentation, Product Differentiation, and Marketing Strategy," *Journal of Marketing*, April 1987, pp. 1–10; Russell I. Haley, "Benefit Segmentation—20 Years Later," *Journal of Consumer Marketing* 1, no. 2 (1984), pp. 5–14.

18. For more on General Mills, see "General Mills Intends to Reshape Doughboy in Its Own Image," *The Wall Street Journal*, July 18, 2000, p. A1ff. See also "Food Marketing," *Brandweek*, April 30, 2001, pp. 20–26. For another determining dimension example, see "New at the Inn: Remote-Control Curtains," *The Wall Street Journal*, April 27, 2001, p. W9; "Find Wired Hotels at Bargain Prices," *Investor's Business Daily*, September 15, 2000, p. A1; "Hotels Add Fast Internet to Room Services," *Investor's Business Daily*, July 5, 2000, p. A8; "Hotels Target Generation X," *USA Today*, February 10, 2000, p. 1Bff.; "Hotels Fired Up to Get Wired Up," *USA Today*, September 2, 1999, p. 1Bff.; "For Hotel Guests with Glitches, High-Tech Room Service," *The Wall Street Journal*, August 30, 1999, p. B1ff.

19. "Marketers Find 'Tweens' Too Hot to Ignore," *USA Today*, July 10, 2001, p. 13A; "Yamada Card Gives Credit to Struggling Brazilians," *The Wall Street Journal*, March 27, 2001, p. B1ff.; "Grown-Up Drinks for Tender Taste Buds," *Business Week*, March 5, 2001, p. 96; "Boosting Diageo's Spirits," *The Wall Street*

Journal, February 12, 2001, p. B1ff.; "Soda Pop That Packs a Punch," *Newsweek*, February 19, 2001, p. 45; "New Web Sites Let Kids Shop, Like, Without Credit Cards," *The Wall Street Journal*, June 14, 1999, p. B1ff.; "How Big Liquor Takes Aim at Teens," *Business Week*, May 19, 1997, p. 92; "How 'Medicaid Moms' Became a Hot Market for Health Industry," *The Wall Street Journal*, May 1, 1997, p. A1ff.; Suzeanne Benet, Robert E. Pitts, and Michael LaTour, "The Appropriateness of Fear Appeal Use for Health Care Marketing to the Elderly: Is It OK to Scare Granny?" *Journal of Business Ethics*, January 1993, pp. 45–56; "New Converse Shoe Named Run 'N Gun Is Angering Critics," *The Wall Street Journal*, February 8, 1993, p. B5; "'Black Death' Becomes 'Black Hat' so that Vodka Can Stay on Shelves," *The Wall Street Journal*, May 12, 1992, p. B6; "Malt Liquor Makers Find Lucrative Market in the Urban Young," *The Wall Street Journal*, March 9, 1992, p. A1ff.; Richard W. Pollay, S. Siddarth, Michael Siegel, Anne Haddix et al., "The Last Straw? Cigarette Advertising and Realized Market Shares Among Youths and Adults, 1979–1993," *Journal of Marketing*, April 1996, pp. 1–16; N. C. Smith and Elizabeth Cooper-Martin, "Ethics and Target Marketing: The Role of Product Harm and Consumer Vulnerability," *Journal of Marketing*, July 1997, pp. 1–20.

20. Girish Punj and David W. Stewart, "Cluster Analysis in Marketing Research: Review and Suggestions for Application," *Journal of Marketing Research*, May 1983, pp. 134–48; Fernando Robles and Ravi Sarathy, "Segmenting the Computer Aircraft Market with Cluster Analysis," *Industrial Marketing Management*, February 1986, pp. 1–12.

21. Available from World Wide Web: <http://www.hermanmillerred.com>; "Herman Miller Inc. Has Small Businesses Seeing Red," *The Wall Street Journal*, June 18, 2001, p. B4; "New Technology Reconditions Herman Miller, *Investor's Business Daily*, March 8, 2001, p. A8; "The Ultimate Sitting Machine," *Ecompany*, October 2000, pp. 65–66; "Reinventing Herman Miller," *Business Week E.Biz*, April 3, 2000, pp. EB89–EB96; *2000 Annual Report*, Herman Miller; "Where 'Build to Order' Works Best," *Fortune*, April 26, 1999, pp. 160A-V.

22. For more on CRM, see Chapter 7, footnote #5. For more on Amazon, see "This Race Isn't Even Close," *Business Week*, December 18, 2000, pp. 208–10; "Amazon: King of the On-Line Jungle, Master of All Domains," *DSNRetailing Today*, November 20, 2000, pp. 18–22; "The Amazon Way Is Still the Best Model for Web Shopping," *The Wall Street Journal*, September 21, 2000, p. B1; "Amazon: Creative Coddling, Great Word of Mouth," *Business Week E. Biz*, September 16, 2000; "E-Commerce: At Your Service," *Wall Street Journal Reports*, April 17, 2000, p. R12ff.; "Secrets of the New Brand Builders," *Fortune*, June 22, 1998, pp. 167–70. For more on privacy, see Chapter 13, footnote #10 and Chapter 18, footnote #13.

23. David A. Aaker and J. Gary Shansby, "Positioning Your Product," *Business Horizons*, May/June, 1982, pp. 56–62; Al Ries and Jack Trout, *Positioning: The Battle for Your Mind* (New York: McGraw-Hill, 1981), p. 53. For some current examples of positioning, see "Getting Corian Out of the Kitchen," *The Wall Street Journal*, December 12, 2000, p. B1ff.; "Corian Refashions," *Advertising Age*, September 18, 2000, pp. 74–76; "Pie in the Sky," *Brandweek*, December 16, 1996, pp. 23–24; "From the Horse's Mouth: Try a Little Hoof Fix on Your Nails," *The Wall Street Journal*, July 29, 1994, p. B1ff.; Hans Muhlbacher, Angelika Dreher, and Angelika Gabriel-Ritter, "MIPS-Managing Industrial Positioning Strategies," *Industrial Marketing Management*, October 1994, pp. 287–98.

Chapter 4

1. Available from World Wide Web: <http://www.ups.com>; "Got Mail?" *The Wall Street Journal*, June 22, 2001, p. B1ff.; "The Total Package," *Ecompany*, June 2001, pp. 90–97; "FedEx Pushes the Right Buttons to Remain No. 1 in Fast Shipping," *Investor's Business Daily*, May 25, 2001, p. A7; "Ground Wars," *Business Week*, May 21, 2001, pp. 64–68; "Federal Expressive," *Ecompany*, May 2001, pp. 45–48; "UPS Targets Logistics Business in Asia," *The Wall Street Journal*, April 26, 2001, p. A17; "Outside the Box," *The Wall Street Journal* (Special Report: E-Commerce), February 12, 2001, p. R20; "FedEx, UPS Join Forces to Stave Off Foreign Push into U.S. Markets," *The Wall Street Journal*, February 1, 2001, p. B1ff.; "A Deal No More, Priority Mail Is Prey for Rivals, *The Wall Street Journal*, January 24, 2001, p. B1ff.; "FedEx, Postal Service Reach Delivery Partnership," *The Wall Street Journal*, January 11, 2001, p. A6; "FedEx, UPS Teach Dot-Coms Ways to Get Gifts under Tree on Time," *The Wall Street Journal*, December 18, 2000, p. B1ff.; "Shippers Brace for E-Commerce," *Investor's Business Daily*, November 24, 2000, p. A5; "When Germans Open the Mail, They Get Message on Capitalism," *The Wall Street Journal*, November 20, 2000, p. A1ff.; "UPS Logistics: Delivering Solutions, Not Packages," *Fortune*, October 30, 2000, pp. T208L-R; "Who's Got Mail?" *Time*, October 16, 2000, pp. 86–88; "UPS Appears Set to Win Battle for China Routes," *The Wall Street Journal*, September 22, 2000, p. A14; "UPS Launches Package-Return Service for Web Purchases that Tracks Progress," *The Wall Street Journal*, September 21, 2000, p. B4; "Big Brown's Big Coup," *Business Week E.Biz*, September 18, 2000, pp. EB76–EB77; "Postal Service, FedEx in Talks to Share Tasks," *The Wall Street Journal*, September 7, 2000, p. B1ff.; "UPS Is in Talks to Buy 2 Logistics Firms," *The Wall Street Journal*, June 12, 2000, p. A3ff.; "They've Got Mail!" *Fortune*, February 7, 2000, pp. 100–112; "Ford Is Hiring UPS to Track Vehicles as They Move from Factories to Dealers," *The Wall Street Journal*, February 2, 2000, p. A6; "Going Nowhere Fast in Cyberspace," *Business Week*, January 31, 2000, pp. 58–59; "Men in Brown," *Forbes*, January 10, 2000; *2000 Annual Report*, UPS; "Overnight, Everything Changed for FedEx: Can It Reinvent Itself?" *The Wall Street Journal*, November 4, 1999, p. A1ff.; "National Mail Services Foil UPS's Big Strategy for Dominating Europe," *The Wall Street Journal*, January 18, 1999, p. A1ff.; *1999 Annual Report*, UPS.

2. See Peter F. Drucker, *Management: Tasks, Responsibilities, Practices, and Plans* (New York: Harper and Row, 1973); Sev K. Keil, "The Impact of Business Objectives and the Time Horizon of Performance Evaluation on Pricing Behavior," *International Journal of Research in Marketing*, June 2001, p. 67; Kenneth E. Clow, "Marketing Strategy: The Challenge of the External Environment," *Journal of the Academy of Marketing Science*, Summer 2000, pp. 437–9. See also T. Levitt, "Marketing Myopia," *Harvard Business Review*, September–October 1975, p. 1ff.; David J. Morris, Jr., "The Railroad and Movie Industries: Were They Myopic?" *Journal of the Academy of Marketing Science*, Fall, 1990, pp. 279–84.

3. Lance Leuthesser and Chiranjeev Kohli, "Corporate Identity: The Role of Mission Statements," *Business Horizons*, May–June 1997, pp. 59–66; Christopher K. Bart, "Sex, Lies, and Mission Statements," *Business Horizons*, November–December 1997, pp. 9–18; Christopher K. Bart, "Industrial Firms and the Power of Mission," *Industrial Marketing Management*, July 1997, pp. 371–83.

4. "Why Inflation Is Not Inevitable," *Fortune*, September 12, 1988, pp. 117–24. See also "Behind Cisco's Woes Are Some Wounds of Its Own Making," *The Wall Street Journal*, April 18, 2001, p. A1ff.; Robert Jacobson and David A. Aaker, "Is Market Share All That It's Cracked Up to Be?" *Journal of Marketing*, Fall 1985, pp. 11–22; Carolyn Y. Woo, "Market-Share Leadership—Not Always So Good," *Harvard Business Review*, January–February 1984, pp. 50–55; "Reichhold Chemicals: Now the Emphasis Is on Profits Rather than Volume," *Business Week*, June 20, 1983, pp. 178–79.

5. Available from World Wide Web: <http://www.harley-davidson.com>; "Harley Davidson's Jeffrey Bleustein: Communication Focus Keeps His Company Roaring," *Investor's Business Daily*, February 28, 2001, p. A4; *2000 Annual Report*, Harley-Davidson; "Motorcycle Madness Revvs Up Ad Budgets," *Advertising Age*, November 8, 1999, p. 38; "Gearing Up for the Cruiser Wars," *Fortune*, August 3, 1998, pp. 128B–L; "Motorcycle Maker Caters to the Continent," *USA Today*, April 22, 1998, p. 8B; "That Vroom! You Hear May Not Be a Harley," *Business Week*, October 20, 1997, pp. 159–60; "Have Brands, Will Travel," *Brandweek*, October 6, 1997, pp. 22–26; "Japan's Bikers: The Tame Ones," *Business Week*, October 6, 1997, pp. 30D-F; "Killer Strategies that Make Shareholders Rich," *Fortune*, June 23, 1997, pp. 70–84; "Aided by Research, Harley Goes Whole Hog," *Marketing News*, December 2, 1996, pp. 16–17; "Tune-Up Time for Harley," *Business Week*, April 8, 1996, pp. 90–94; "The Rumble Heard Round the World," *Business Week*, May 24, 1993, p. 58–60; "Put to the Test," *Adweek*, December 7, 1992, pp. 28–32; "Yuppies Help Fuel Demand," *USA Today*, July 22, 1991, p. 1Bff.; "Harley-Davidson's U-Turn," *USA Today*, March 2, 1990, p. 1Bff.; "How Harley Beat Back the Japanese," *Fortune*, September 25, 1989, pp. 155–64.

6. For more on Starbucks, see "Remedies for an Economic Hangover," *Fortune*, June 25, 2001, pp. 130–39; "Starbucks Joins Microsoft to Serve Web with Its Coffee," *The Wall Street Journal*, January 4, 2001, p. B8; "Starbucks Takes North America, Seeks Broader Sphere of Influence," *Investor's Business Daily*, July 11, 2000, p. A12; "Starbucks Fills Asia's Cup," *USA Today*, June 7, 2000, p. 10B; "Now, Starbucks Uses Its Bean," *Business Week*, February 14, 2000, pp. 92–93; "Starbucks in Pact with Kozmo.com on Using Stores," *The Wall Street Journal*, February 14, 2000, p. A34; "Trouble Brewing," *Newsweek*, July 19, 1999, pp. 40–41; "Schultz' Caffeinated Crusade," *Brandweek*, July 5, 1999, pp. 20–25; "Battle Grounds," *Inc.*, July 1999, pp. 52–58; "Still Perking after All These Years," *Fortune*, May 24, 1999, pp. 203–10; "Starbucks Brews Broader Base," *Raleigh News & Observer*, March 23, 1999, p. 1Dff.; "Some Meatloaf with That Decaf Latte?" *The Wall Street Journal*, March 16, 1999, p. B1ff.; "Starbucks Cultivates Caffeine Rush," *USA Today*, April 30, 1998, p. 1Bff.; "Starbucks.com Will Let Coffee Drinkers Get Wired," *Brandweek*, April 27, 1998, p. 33; "Starbucks Ships Its Coffee Craze to Pacific Rim," *Advertising Age*, April 27, 1998, p. 28; "Starbucks: Making Values Pay," *Fortune*, September 29, 1997, pp. 261–72; "Starbucks Gives Vitamin Jolt to Frappuccino Drink," *Advertising Age*, September 15, 1997, p. 82; "Restaurant Brands Fill Supermarkets," *USA Today*, August 26, 1997, p. 1Bff.; "Starbucks Does Not Live by Coffee Alone," *Business Week*, August 5, 1996, p. 76; "Japan's Staid Coffee Bars Wake Up and Smell Starbucks," *The Wall Street Journal*, July 25, 1996, p. B1ff.

7. For more on patents, see "Would You Buy a Patent License from This Man?" *Ecompany*, April 2001, pp. 104–10; "Prilosec-Time Is Just About Up," *Business Week*, January 8, 2001, p. 47; "Eli Lilly Loses Prozac Patent-Protection Battle," *The Wall Street Journal*, August 10, 2000, p. A3ff.; "Businesses Battle over Intellectual Property," *USA Today*, August 2, 2000, p. 1Bff.; "Qualcomm Hits the Big Time," *Fortune*, May 15, 2000, pp. 213–29; "New Teeth for Old Patents," *Business Week*, November 30, 1998, pp. 92–95; "What's Next—A Patent for the 401(K)?" *Business Week*, October 26, 1998, pp. 104–107; "Drug Pirates," *Fortune*, October 12, 1998, pp. 146–48.

8. For more on Microsoft's Xbox, see "This Game's Not Over Yet," *Fortune*, July 9, 2001, p. 164; ". . . Games," *The Wall Street Journal Reports*, June 25, 2001, p. R6; "Game Wars 5.0," *Newsweek*, May 28, 2001, pp. 65–66; "Let the Game-System War Begin," *USA Today*, May 21, 2001, p. 3D; "The Battle of Seattle," *Time*, May 21, 2001, pp. 58–59; "Sony, AOL Join Up to Link PlayStation 2 to Internet in Move to Outflank Microsoft," *The Wall Street Journal*, May 15, 2001, p. A3; "Xbox Marks the Spot for Launch of Microsoft's Game," *USA Today*, April 23, 2001, p. 1B; "As Microsoft's Xbox Debut Nears, Fan Sites Get Cocky, Rivals—Wary," *The Wall Street Journal*, April 12, 2001, p. B1ff.; "How Microsoft Hopes to Win with Xbox," *The Wall Street Journal*, January 31, 2001, p. B1ff.; "Game Wars," *Time*, March 20, 2000, pp. 44–45; "How Four Renegades Persuaded Microsoft to Make a Game Machine," *The Wall Street Journal*, March 10, 2000, p. B1ff.

9. Peter J. Williamson, "Asia's New Competitive Game," *Harvard Business Review*, September–October 1997, pp. 55–67; David J. Collis and Cynthia A. Montgomery, "Competing on Resources: Strategy in the 1990s," *Harvard Business Review*, July–August 1995, pp. 118–28; "How Goodyear Forecast a Great Decade," *American Demographics*, March 1995, p. 39; "Firms Analyze Rivals to Help Fix Themselves," *The Wall Street Journal*, May 3, 1994, p. B1ff.; Thomas S. Gruca and D Sudharshan, "A Framework for Entry Deterrence Strategy: The Competitive Environment, Choices, and Consequences," *Journal of Marketing*, July 1995, pp. 44–55; Venkatram Ramaswamy, Hubert Gatignon, and David J. Reibstein, "Competitive Marketing Behavior in Industrial Markets," *Journal of Marketing*, April 1994, pp. 45–55; Z. S. Deligonul and S. T. Cavusgil, "Does the Comparative Advantage Theory of Competition Really Replace the Neoclassical Theory of Perfect Competition?" *Journal of Marketing*, October 1997, pp. 65–73; J. S. Armstrong, "Co-Opetition," *Journal of Marketing*, April 1997, pp. 92–95; John L. Haverty and Myroslaw J. Kyj, "What Happens when New Competitors Enter an Industry," *Industrial Marketing Management* 20, no. 1 (1991), pp. 73–80; Arch G. Woodside and Elizabeth J. Wilson, "Diagnosing Customer Comparisons of Competitors' Marketing Mix Strategies," *Journal of Business Research*, October–November

1994, pp. 133–44; David W. Cravens and Shannon H. Shipp, "Market-Driven Strategies for Competitive Advantage," *Business Horizons*, January/February, 1991, pp. 53–61; William W. Keep, Glenn S. Omura, and Roger J. Calantone, "What Managers Should Know about Their Competitors' Patented Technologies," *Industrial Marketing Management*, July 1994, pp. 257–64.

10. *Kao* (Cambridge, MA: Harvard Business School Press, 1984); Bruce R. Klemz, "Managerial Assessment of Potential Entrants: Processes and Pitfalls," *International Journal of Research in Marketing*, June 2001, p. 37.

11. For more on P&G, see "P&G Wins Lawsuit, Loses Market," *Advertising Age*, September 18, 1989, p. 72. For more on corporate spying, see "More Firms Hire Sleuths to Avoid Nasty Surprises," *USA Today*, June 26, 2001, p. 1Bff.; "Your Employees Love IM. Should You Worry?" *Ecompany*, June 2001, pp. 102–106; "Spooked: Is That Salesman Really a Spy?" *Fortune*, January 8, 2001, p. 192; Adam L. Penenberg and Marc Barry, *Spooked: Espionage in Corporate America* (New York: HarperCollins, 2000); "Hey, It's Not Prying; It's Competitive Intelligence," *Raleigh News & Observer*, August 6, 2000, p. 14E; "Call It Mission Impossible Inc.—Corporate-Spying Firms Thrive," *The Wall Street Journal*, July 3, 2000, p. B1ff.; "Protecting Corporate Secrets: Does Your Company Own What You Know?" *USA Today*, January 19, 2000, p. 1Aff.; "Eyeing the Competition," *Time*, March 22, 1999, pp. 58–60; "How Safe Are Your Secrets?" *Fortune*, September 8, 1997, pp. 114–20; "High-Tech Tools Usher in Stolen-Information Age," *USA Today*, April 10, 1997, p. 1Bff. For more on the Oracle/Microsoft case, see "Oracle Case Shines Light on Corporate Spying," *Investor's Business Daily*, June 30, 2000, p. A7; "Oracle-Style Investigations Common, Experts Say," *USA Today*, June 29, 2000, p. 3B; "How Piles of Trash Became Latest Focus in Bitter Software Feud," *The Wall Street Journal*, June 29, 2000, p. A1ff.; "Oracle Hired Firm to Probe Microsoft Allies, *The Wall Street Journal*, June 28, 2000, p. A3ff. For more on other specific cases, see "System Breach Is Stirring Up Airline Rivalry," *The Wall Street Journal*, June 27, 2000, p. B1ff.; "China's Spies Target Corporate America," *Fortune*, March 30, 1998, pp. 118–22; "In the Debris of a Failed Merger: Trade Secrets," *The Wall Street Journal*, March 10, 1998, p. B1ff.; "Ex-Kodak Manager Is Sentenced to Jail; Company Sues Scherer," *The Wall Street Journal*, November 17, 1997, p. B17. See also Shaker A. Zahra, "Unethical Practices in Competitive Analysis: Patterns, Causes and Effects," *Journal of Business Ethics*, January 1994, pp. 53–62.

12. "A Whole New Wave of Japanese Exports Is Headed Westward," *The Wall Street Journal*, November 14, 1997, p. A1ff.

13. Rajdeep Grewal, "Building Organizational Capabilities for Managing Economic Crisis: The Role of Market Orientation and Strategic Flexibility," *Journal of Marketing*, April 2001, pp. 67–81; "Gas Prices May Level Off—Until Next Summer," *USA Today*, May 22, 2001, p. 1Aff.; "Daimler Thinks Small: With Gas Prices Soaring, Will Americans Get 'Smart'?" *Newsweek*, May 21, 2001, p. 48; "Europeans Unmoved by USA's Energy Plight," *USA Today*, May 17, 2001, p. 8A; "Diesel-Sippers Win Fans as Gas Prices Soar," *USA Today*, Mary 15, 2001, p. 1B; "Shock at the Wheel: Wonder Why Gas Prices Suddenly Got So High?" *The Wall Street Journal*, May 14, 2001, p. A1ff.; "Wary Consumers Watch as Inflation Nudges Prices Up," *USA Today*, April 30, 2001, p. 1Bff.; "Time for a Reality Check," *Business Week*, December 2, 1996, pp. 58–67; "Industry Covets Potential of Pacific Rim," *USA Today*, June 17, 1996, p. 1Bff.; "Biggest Show of Force in a Decade Halts Slide of the Dollar—for Now," *The Wall Street Journal*, May 5, 1994, p. A1ff.; "Demand for Wood Leads to Building Panic," *USA Today*, March 17, 1993, p. 1Bff.

14. "New Frontiers: A New Brand of Tech Cities," *Newsweek*, April 30, 2001, pp. 44–70; "Technology: The Era of Living Wirelessly," *USA Today Bonus*, June 26, 2001; "Technology: What's Ahead," *The Wall Street Journal Reports*, June 25, 2001; "tough Times in Techland," *The Wall Street Journal*, December 28, 2000, p. B1ff.; "Tech Extra: Consumer Electronics," *Investor's Business Daily*, December 8, 2000; "Technology: How Technology Has Changed the Way We . . . ," *The Wall Street Journal Reports*, November 13, 2000; "Telecommunications: Untangling the Cord," *The Wall Street Journal Reports*, September 18, 2000; "Tech Extra: The Web Goes Wireless," *Investor's Business Daily*, September 15, 2000; "Gadget Envy," *The Wall Street Journal*, August 3, 2000, p. B1ff.; "Special Report: Wireless in Cyberspace," *Business Week*, May 29, 2000, pp. 136–64; "Special Report: Digital Wheels," *Business Week*, April 10, 2000, pp. 114–24; "Entertainment + Technology: Together at Last," *The Wall Street Journal Reports*, March 20, 2000; "Technology: Cleaning Out Your Desk," *The Wall Street Journal Reports*, November 15, 1999; "The Internet Age," *Business Week*, October 4, 1999, pp. 69–98; "Beyond the PC," *Business Week*, March 8, 1999, pp. 79–88; "Technology: Thinking about Tomorrow," *The Wall Street Journal Reports*, November 16, 1998; "Digital D-Day," *Business Week*, October 26, 1998, pp. 144–58; "Technology: In the Chips," *The Wall Street Journal Reports*, June 15, 1998; Robert A. Peterson, Sridhar Balasubramanian, and Bart J. Bronnenberg, "Exploring the Implications of the Internet for Consumer Marketing," *Journal of the Academy of Marketing Science*, Fall 1997, pp. 329–46; John Deighton, "Commentary on 'Exploring the Implications of the Internet for Consumer Marketing'," *Journal of the Academy of Marketing Science*, Fall 1997, pp. 347–51; D L. Andrus, "Inside the Tornado: Marketing Strategies From Silicon Valley's Cutting Edge," *Journal of Marketing*, April 1997, pp. 97–99; Kim Schatzel, "The Dynamics of Technological Innovation: The Evolution and Development of Information Technology," *Journal of Product Innovation Management*, January 1998, pp. 103–04; Karen A. Graziano, "The Innovator's Dilemma: When New Technologies Cause Great Firms to Fail," *Journal of Product Innovation Management*, January 1998, pp. 95–97; Thomas Kiely, "Obeying the Laws of Cyberspace," *Harvard Business Review*, September–October 1997, pp. 12–13; Edward McDonough, "Strategic Management of Technology and Innovation," *Journal of Product Innovation Management*, November 1997, pp. 533–34.

15. "Chips: Breaking the Light Barrier," *Business Week*, April 16, 2001, pp. 74–75; "Handhelds That Do It All," *Business Week*, February 12, 2001, pp. 98–99; "Will Light Bulbs Go the Way of the Victrola?" *Business Week*, January 22, 2001, p. 94H; "Dick Tracy, Meet '3G,'" *The Wall Street Journal*, January 18, 2001, p. B1ff.; "Raft of New Wireless Technologies Could Lead to Airwave Gridlock," *The Wall Street Journal*, January 8, 2001, p. B1ff.; "Drive-by-Wire Technology Promises Simpler and Safer Car Control," *The Wall Street Journal*, January 12, 2001, p. B1ff.; "Wireless Telephones Shed Keypads to Make Way for Bigger

Screens," *The Wall Street Journal*, January 11, 2001, p. B1ff.; "GSM, CDMA, TDMA Make for a Wireless Tower of Babel," *Investor's Business Daily*, December 28, 2000, p. A5; "High-Tech Applications Transform Old Economy," *USA Today*, September 7, 2000, p, 3B; "In Dot-Com World, the Hot New Thing Is the Old Telephone," *The Wall Street Journal*, June 30, 2000, p. A1ff.; "In Japan, the World Goes Flat," *The Wall Street Journal*, June 29, 2000, p. B1ff.; "The World Is Your Office," *Fortune*, June 12, 2000, pp. 227–34; "Wireless Summer," *Time*, May 29, 2000, pp. 58–66; "Wireless Gets Easier and Faster," *Business Week*, May 29, 2000, p. 34; "An Efficiency Drive: Fast-Food Lanes Are Getting Even Faster," *The Wall Street Journal*, May 18, 2000, p. A1ff.; "E-Novel Approach Promises New Chapter for Book Lovers," *USA Today*, May 9, 2000, p. 1Bff.; "Chips for the Post-PC Era," *Business Week*, March 27, 2000, pp. 96–104; "Welcome to 2010," *Business Week*, March 6, 2000, pp. 102–12; "Wireless Option Opens Door to a New E-World," *USA Today*, February 18, 2000, p. 1Aff.; "Wireless Takes to the High Wire," *Business Week*, February 14, 2000, pp. 68–70; "This Frame Fetches Photos from the Net, Staging a Slide Show," *The Wall Street Journal*, February 3, 2000, p. B1; "The Soul of a New Refrigerator," *Business Week*, January 17, 2000, p. 42; "Driving a Stick," *Brandweek*, January 10, 2000, pp. 28–33; "Will the Future Be Written in E-Ink?" *The Wall Street Journal*, January 4, 2000, p. B1ff.; "Made in Japan," *Fortune*, December 6, 1999, pp. 190–202; "GM Will Connect Drivers to the World Wide Web," *The Wall Street Journal*, November 3, 1999, p. B1ff.; "Here Come Smart Phones," *Business Week*, October 25, 1999, pp. 167–94; "Here Come PVRs: Is Network TV Doomed?" *Time*, September 27, 1999, pp. 62–63; "So Many Megabytes, So Little Space," *The Wall Street Journal*, September 3, 1999, p. B1ff.; "Battle of the Batteries," *Business Week*, August 9, 1999, pp. 87–88; "Forget Microwaves: 'Speed Cookers' Also Crisp and Brown," *The Wall Street Journal*, June 30, 1999, p. B1ff.; "Evolutionary Wars," *Brandweek*, January 11, 1999, pp. 20–25; "A PC in Your Car? Why?" *Fortune*, September 7, 1998, pp. 113–15; "In HDTV Age, Successor to VCR Is a Long Way Off," *The Wall Street Journal*, April 8, 1998, p. B1ff.; "The Automakers' Big-Time Bet on Fuel Cells," *Fortune*, March 30, 1998, pp. 122C-P; "Take the Internet with You in a Phone, Watch or Shoe," *USA Today*, March 19, 1998, p. 1Bff.; "Detroit's Impossible Dream," *Business Week*, March 2, 1998, pp. 66–68; "Computer Industry Races to Conquer the Automobile," *The Wall Street Journal*, February 23, 1998, p. B1ff.; "Let's Talk: Speech Technology," *Business Week*, February 23, 1998, pp. 61–80; "Technology, Not Fashion, Now Seen as Crucial to Selling Athletic Shoes," *Brandweek*, February 16, 1998, p. 16; "How Smart Sensors Keep Factories Humming," *Fortune*, March 17, 1997, pp. 144A-H; "In Digital Dorm, Click on Return for Soda," *The Wall Street Journal*, January 23, 1997, p. B1ff.; Noel Capon and Rashi Glazer, "Marketing and Technology: A Strategic Coalignment," *Journal of Marketing*, July 1987, pp. 1–14. For more on privacy, see Chapter 13, footnote #10 and Chapter 18, footnote #13.

16. "Lessons of a Crisis," *Business Week*, April 23, 2001, pp. 56–57; "Made in Japan? Not for Home Team," *The Wall Street Journal*, February 18, 1998, p. A6; "U.S. Backpedals on Law that Hung 'Made in China' Tag on European Goods," *The Wall Street Journal*, August 8, 1997, p. A2; Gopalkrishnan R. Iyer, "Anticompetitive Practices in Japan: Their Impact on the Performance of Foreign Firms," *Journal of Marketing*, October 1997, pp. 97–99; Michael G. Harvey, "Buy American": Economic Concept or Political Slogan?" *Business Horizons*, May– June 1993, pp. 40–46; "Made in America Becomes a Boast in Europe," *The Wall Street Journal*, January 19, 1994, p. B1ff.; Terry Clark, "National Boundaries, Border Zones, and Marketing Strategy: A Conceptual Framework and Theoretical Model of Secondary Boundary Effects," *Journal of Marketing*, July 1994, pp. 67–80.

17. For more on Lands' End example, see "Border Crossings," *The Wall Street Journal* (Special Report: E-Commerce), November 22, 1999, p. R41. For more on EU, see "Ready, Set, Euros!" *Business Week*, July 2, 2001, pp. 48–50; "Blair's Euro Dilemma," *Business Week*, June 25, 2001, pp, 48–49; "Euro Leaves U.S. Investors Under the Weather," *The Wall Street Journal*, June 14, 2001, p. C1ff.; "There's Really No Reason to Worry about the Euro," *Business Week*, June 11, 2001, pp. 60–62; "Future of Euro Sparks a Marketing Contest," *Ad Age Global*, March 2001, p. 21; "Back from the Depths," *Business Week*, January 8, 2001, pp. 52–53; "The Euro: A Dismal Failure, a Ringing Success," *The Wall Street Journal*, November 6, 2000, p. A29ff.; "The Euro Mess," *Business Week*, October 2, 2000, pp. 140–46; "What's Really Wrong with the Euro? It's Not the Currency, But the Gov'ts," *Investor's Business Daily*, September 29, 2000, p. A9; "Is Currency Intervention Enough to Hold Up Euro?" *USA Today*, September 25, 2000, p. 1Bff.; "In Drug-Cost Debate, Europe Offers U.S. a Telling Side Effect," *The Wall Street Journal*, July 21, 2000, p. A1ff.; "The End of a Free Ride for Carmakers?" *Business Week*, June 26, 2000, p. 70; "Why the Euro Keeps Shriveling," *Business Week*, March 27, 2000, pp. 218–19; "Bon Voyage! Weak Euro Is Bonanza for U.S. Tourists," *The Wall Street Journal*, July 16, 1999, p. B1ff.; "Emergence of Euro Embodies Challenge and Hope for Europe," *The Wall Street Journal*, January 4, 1999, p. A1ff.; "Countdown to New Currency," *USA Today*, December 28, 1998, p. 1Bff.; "The Euro: Are You Ready?" *Business Week*, December 14, 1998, pp. 62–72; "As the Euro's Arrival Nears, Europe Braces for Lots of Headaches," *The Wall Street Journal*, November 30, 1998, p. A1ff.; "Au Revoir, Malaise: Europe's Economies Are Back in Business," *The Wall Street Journal*, April 9, 1998, p. A1ff.; "A Tale of Two Nations Shows Europe's Union Has Differing Sides," *The Wall Street Journal*, July 28, 1997, p. A1ff.; "Europe's Borders Fade and People and Goods Can Move More Freely," *The Wall Street Journal*, May 18, 1993, p. A1ff.; Valerie L. Vaccaro, "European Retailing's Vanishing Borders," *Journal of the Academy of Marketing Science*, Fall 1996, pp. 386–88.

18. Available from World Wide Web: <http://www.nafta.org>. For more on NAFTA, see "Border Crossing? No Problema," *Business Week Small Biz*, July 16, 2001, p. 10; "NAFTA Scorecard: So Far, So Good," *Business Week*, July 9, 2001, pp. 54–56; "Mexican Trucks Won't Fill the U.S. Soon," *The Wall Street Journal*, February 16, 2001, p. C4; "Mexican Truckers Face U.S. Obstacle Course," *USA Today*, February 5, 2001, p. 1Bff.; "Car Power," *Business Week*, October 23, 2000, pp. 72–82; "Mexico Thrives under NAFTA, Seeks More," *USA Today*, August 28, 2000, p. 1B; "Mexico Pulls Off Another Trade Coup," *Business Week*, February 7, 2000, p. 56; "Job Shift to Mexico Lets U.S. Firms Upgrade," *The Wall Street Journal*, November 15, 1999, p. A28; "Mexico Builds a Home-Appliance Bonanza," *The Wall Street Journal*, August 23, 1999, p. A12; "In the Wake of NAFTA, a Family Firm Sees Business Go South," *The Wall Street*

Journal, February 23, 1999, p. A1; "Mexican Makeover," *Business Week*, December 21, 1998, pp. 50–52; "NAFTA Jam," *USA Today*, April 3, 1998, p. 1Bff.; Kent Jones, "NAFTA Chapter 19: Is There Hope for Bilateral Dispute Resolution of Unfair Trade Law Decisions?" *Journal of Public Policy & Marketing*, Fall 1994, pp. 300–6.

19. Thomas L. Osterhus, "Pro-Social Consumer Influence Strategies: When and How Do They Work?" *Journal of Marketing*, October 1997, pp. 16–29; Roger Swagler, "Evolution and Applications of the Term Consumerism: Theme and Variations," *Journal of Consumer Affairs*, Winter 1994, pp. 347–60; Alan Morrison, "The Role of Litigation in Consumer Protection," *The Journal of Consumer Affairs*, Winter, 1991, pp. 209–20; William K. Darley and Denise M. Johnson, "Cross-National Comparison of Consumer Attitudes Toward Consumerism in Four Developing Countries," *Journal of Consumer Affairs*, Summer 1993, pp. 37–54.

20. For more on Beech-Nut, see "What Led Beech-Nut Down the Road to Disgrace," *Business Week*, February 22, 1988, pp. 124–28. See also David A. Balto, "Emerging Antitrust Issues in Electronic Commerce," *Journal of Public Policy & Marketing*, Fall 2000, pp. 277–87; Shelby D. Hunt, "Competition as an Evolutionary Process and Antitrust Policy," *Journal of Public Policy & Marketing*, Spring 2001, Vol. 20, 1, pp.15–27; "Europe: A Different Take on Antitrust," *Business Week*, June 25, 2001, p. 40; "Trustbusting's Top Cop," *Business Week*, April 30, 2001, pp. 88–89; "A Different Kind of Trustbuster," *Business Week*, April 16, 2001, pp. 66–68; "Antitrust: Laying the Tracks a Bit to the Right," *Business Week*, February 12, 2001, p. 36; "Is the FTC Defending Goliath?" *Business Week*, December 18, 2000, pp. 160–62; "How a Whistle-Blower Spurred Pricing Case Involving Drug Makers," *The Wall Street Journal*, May 12, 2000, p. A1ff.; "Invasion of the Cartel Cops," *Business Week*, May 8, 2000, pp. 130–32; "By Any Other Name, a Monopoly.Com," *Business Week*, April 19, 1999, p. 154; "A Little Internet Firm Got a Big Monopoly; Is That Such a Bad Thing?" *The Wall Street Journal*, October 8, 1998, p. A1ff.; "In Archer-Daniels Saga, Now the Executives Face Trial," *The Wall Street Journal*, July 9, 1998, p. B10; "The FTC's Eager Sheriff," *Business Week*, July 6, 1998, pp. 65–66; Gregory T. Gundlach, "Exchange Relationships and the Efficiency Interests of the Law," *Journal of Public Policy & Marketing*, Fall 1996, pp. 185–202; Tara J. Schleicher, "The U.S. Supreme Court's Use of Post-Chicago Antitrust Theory in Eastman Kodak V. Image Technical Services: Implications for Marketing Practice," *Journal of Public Policy & Marketing*, Fall 1997, pp. 310–18; Ann C. Morales, "Corporate Officer Liability: FTC Expands Its Remedial Reach Over Deceptive Marketing Practices," *Journal of the Academy of Marketing Science*, Spring 1998, pp. 163–64; Jef I. Richards, "Legal Potholes on the Information Superhighway," *Journal of Public Policy & Marketing*, Fall 1997, pp. 319–26; Dan A. Fuller and Debra L. Scammon, "Newly Evolving Organizational Structures in the Health Care Industry: Principles of Antitrust Enforcement and Implications for Marketing," *Journal of Public Policy & Marketing*, Spring 1996, pp. 128–35; G. S. Erickson, "Export Controls: Marketing Implications of Public Policy Choices," *Journal of Public Policy & Marketing*, Spring 1997, pp. 83–92; Thomas A. Hemphill, "The New Era of Business Regulation," *Business Horizons*, July–August 1996, pp. 26–30; Rita M. Cain, "Recent Developments in Telemarketing Regulation," *Journal of Public Policy & Marketing*, Spring 1996, pp. 135–41; Charles S. Gulas, "Marketing Strategies for Services: Globalization, Client-Orientation, Deregulation," *Journal of the Academy of Marketing Science*, Spring 1996, pp. 178–79; Joan T. A. Gabel, "Lanham Act Not Limited to Advertisements Aimed at the Ultimate Consumer," *Journal of the Academy of Marketing Science*, Spring 1997, p.178. See also Louis W. Stern and Thomas L. Eovaldi, *Legal Aspects of Marketing Strategy: Antitrust and Consumer Protection Issues* (Englewood Cliffs, N.J.: Prentice-Hall, 1984).

21. For more on Firestone, see Chapter 8, footnote #15. For more on auto safety, see "Smash, Bang, Crunch, Screech—Wow, What a Car!" *The Wall Street Journal*, April 13, 2001, p. B1ff.; "Safety First," *Newsweek*, October 30, 2000, pp. 56–59; "Formula Predicts Rollover Risk," *USA Today*, July 17, 2000, p. 1Bff.; "New Clan of Crash Dummies Ready for Lab Mayhem," *USA Today*, July 5, 2000, p. 6B; "The Safest Cars? It's in the Bag," *The Wall Street Journal*, May 12, 2000, p. W1; "The Side Air Bag Controversy: No Safety Regulations Mean Risk Levels Differ by Design," *USA Today*, February 11, 1999, p. 1Bff.; For more on food and drug safety, see "Pills on a Pedestal," *USA Today*, February 6, 2001, p. 1Dff.; "Move to Import Medicines: Boon or Boondoggle?" *The Wall Street Journal*, October 13, 2000, p. B1ff.; "Complex Drug Labels Bury Safety Messages," *USA Today*, May 3, 2000, p. 1Aff.; "Many Medicines Prove Potent for Years Past Their Expiration Dates," *The Wall Street Journal*, March 28, 2000, p. A1ff.; "Splitting Hairs on Supplement Claims," *The Wall Street Journal*, February 22, 2000, p. B1ff.; Foul-Ups by Asthma-Drug Maker Draw FDA Fire," *The Wall Street Journal*, January 28, 2000, p. B1ff.; "In Boom for Home Drug Tests, One Runs Afoul of FDA," *The Wall Street Journal*, August 24, 1999, p. B1ff.; "Supplement or Additive? Issue Is on FDA's Plate," *USA Today*, November 4, 1998, p. 1Bff.; "Rush to Judgment? Policy Speeds Approvals, but Some Say It's Risky," *USA Today*, July 10, 1998, p. 1Aff.; "Meat Safety: Critics Say New Regulations Won't Work," *USA Today*, October 8, 1997, p. 1Aff.; "Fine Print in Drug Ads Sparks a Debate," *The Wall Street Journal*, April 1, 1997, p. B1ff.

22. "Marketing Law: A Marketer's Guide to Alphabet Soup," *Business Marketing*, January 1990, pp. 56–58; Ray O. Werner, "Marketing and the Supreme Court in Transition, 1982–1984," *Journal of Marketing*, Summer 1985, pp. 97–105; Ray O. Werner, "Marketing and the United States Supreme Court, 1975–1981," *Journal of Marketing*, Spring 1982, pp. 73–81; Dorothy Cohen, "Trademark Strategy," *Journal of Marketing*, January 1986, pp. 61–74.

23. Based on U.S. Census data and United Nations statistical data including *Global Population Profile: 2000* and *World Population Profile: 1998* (Washington, DC: Government Printing Office) and *World Population at a Glance: 1998 and Beyond, IB/98-4*; and other Census data available from World Wide Web: <http://www.census.gov/ipc>; *World Population Prospects: The 1999 Revision of the UN Population Division* (New York: United Nations, 2000); World Bank data including, *World Development Indicators: 2000* (Washington, DC: International Bank for Reconstruction and Development/The World Bank, 2000) and available from World Wide Web: <http://www.worldbank.org/data/wdi2000> and <http://devdata.worldbank.org/data-query>; Central Intelligence Agency data and available from World Wide Web: <http://www.odci.gov/cia/ publications/ factbook>; Population Reference Bureau data, including *2000 World Population Data Sheet* (Washington, DC: Population Reference Bureau, 2000) and available from World Wide Web: <http://www. prb.org/pubs/wpds2000>; and CountryWatch, available from World Wide Web: <http://www. countrywatch. com>; "How Rich Nations Can Defuse the Population Bomb," *Business Week*, May 28, 2001, p. 28; "China Tries Easing Once-Brutal Approach to Family Planning," *The Wall Street Journal*, February 2, 2001, p. A1ff.; "These Oldies Look Golden to Japan Inc.," *Business Week*, August 7, 2000, p. 59; "Rough Translation: 'No English, No Job'—A Reality Many of Asia's Workers Face," *USA Today*, July 21, 2000, p. 1Bff.; "The Big Crunch," *Time* (Special Issue), April–May 2000, pp. 44–47; "On the Move," *The Wall Street Journal*, January 1, 2000, p. R42ff.; Michel J. Weiss, *The Cluttered World* (Little, Brown and Company, 2000); "Parallel Universe," *American Demographics*, October 1999, pp. 58–63; "Six Billion Served," *American Demographics*, June 1999, pp. 14–16; Tamer S. Cavusgil, "Measuring the Potential of Emerging Markets: An Indexing Approach," *Business Horizons*, January–February 1997, pp. 87–91; E. B. Keehn, "A Yen to Spend," *Harvard Business Review*, March–April 1996, pp. 154–59; Tarun Khanna and Krishna Palepu, "Why Focused Strategies May Be Wrong for Emerging Markets," *Harvard Business Review*, July–August 1997, pp. 41–51.

24. Based on U.S. Census data and "Population of Rural America Is Swelling," *The Wall Street Journal*, July 21, 1996, p. B1ff.; "The Rural Rebound," *American Demographics*, May 1994, pp. 24–29.

25. "China Coping with Its New Power," *Business Week*, April 16, 2001, pp. 28–36; "China's Coming Telecom Battle," *Fortune*, November 27, 2000, pp. 209–14; "Gates & Co. Attack Asia," *Fortune*, April 17, 2000, pp. 197–208; "China's 'Little Emperors': The Offspring of Policy," *USA Today*, February 23, 2000, p. 10D; "PC Legend in the Making," *USA Today*, December 6, 1999, p. 1Bff.; "Dell Cracks China," *Fortune*, June 21, 1999, pp. 120–24; "How Legend Lives Up to Its Name," *Business Week*, February 15, 1999, pp. 75–78.

26. Based on World Bank GNP and GDP data and available from World Wide Web: <http://www.worldbank.org/data/wdi>; and Central Intelligence Agency GDP data available from World Wide Web: <http://www.odci.gov/cia/publications/ factbook>. Discussion of difference in GNP/GDP available from World Wide Web: <http://www.cyberus.ca/choose.sustain/ Question/GDP-GNP.html>.

27. Based on United Nations statistical data including statistical data from UNESCO available from World Wide Web: <http://unescostat.unesco.org/statsen/statistics/yearbook/tables>; statistical data from World Bank available from World Wide Web: <http://www.worldbank.org/data/wdi2000/illiteracy>; "The Lowdown on Literacy," *American Demographics*, June 1994, p. 6; Lee D. Dahringer and Hans Muhlbacher, *International Marketing: A Global Perspective* (Reading, MA: Addison-Wesley, 1991), p. 182.

28. Based on U. S. Census data including, "Table 2. Resident Population of the 50 States, the District of Columbia, and Puerto Rico: Census 2000," and "Table 5. Resident Population of the 50 States, the District of Columbia, and Puerto Rico: April 1, 2000 (Census 2000) and April 1, 1990 (1990 Census)," and "Figure 1. Percent Change in Resident Population for the 50 States, the District of Columbia, and Puerto Rico:1990 to 2000," and available from World Wide Web: <http://www.census.gov/population/ www/cen2000/respop>; and "Census Bureau Projects Doubling of Nation's Population by 2100" (Press Release); "Exploring a Nation of Extremes," *The Wall Street Journal*, May 25, 2001, p. B1ff.; "Census Tracks Geographical Generation Gap," *USA Today*, May 25, 2001, p. 3A; "Lust for Statistics," *American Demographics*, March 2001, pp. 68–70; "Census Shows Record Growth," *USA Today*, December 29, 2000, P. 1Aff.; "Sun Belt Is Still Hot, but Census Finds a Big Shift," *The Wall Street Journal*, December 29, 2000, p. 6A; "Census Shows Gains in South and West," *The Wall Street Journal*, December 29, 2000, p. A2ff. Also based on data from Population Reference Bureau and Ameristat, available from World Wide Web: <http://www.prb.org> and <http://www.ameristat.org>.

29. Based on U.S. Census data, including "Geographical Mobility: March 1998 to March 1999 (Update), P20–531" and available from World Wide Web: <http://www.census.gov/ population/www/socdemo/migrate>; Roberto Suro, "Movement at Warp Speed," *American Demographics*, August 2000, pp. 61–64.

30. Based on U.S. Census data and "Minorities Reshape Suburbs," *USA Today*, July 9, 2001, p. 1Aff.; "Counting Change," *Advertising Age*, May 14, 2001, pp. 16–20; "U.S. Cities Buck Trend with Boom Downtown," *USA Today*, May 7, 2001, p. 1Aff.; "Downtowns Make Cities Winners," *USA Today*, May 7, 2001, p. 3A; "Census Gainers and Losers: What Now?" *The Wall Street Journal*, April 11, 2001, p. B13; "Immigration Helped Restore Cities," *USA Today*, March 19, 2001, p. 3A

31. Based on U.S. Census data and Rebecca Gardyn, "Retirement Redefined," *American Demographics*, November 2000, pp. 52–57; "Northern Exposure," *Fortune*, August 14, 2000, pp. 164–78; "After 54 Years, Baby Boom on the Wane," *The Wall Street Journal*, July 25, 2000, p. 3A; "A Design with Twists and Turns," *The Wall Street Journal*, February 3, 2000, p. B1ff.; Michelle Krebs, "Shifting Gears," *American Demographics*, January 2000, pp. 52–55; "Hell No, We Won't Go!" *Fortune*, July 19, 1999, pp. 102–108; "Home of the Gray," *Newsweek*, March 1, 1999, pp. 50–53; Jeff Brazil, "You Talkin' to Me?" *American Demographics*, December 1998, pp. 55–59; "The Latest Home Accessory: Garden Tools," *The Wall Street Journal*, April 10, 1998, p. W8; "Off Target?" *USA Today*, December 8, 1997, p. 1Bff.; "More than Meets the Eye," *Brandweek*, October 20, 1997, pp. 24–30; "Boomer Women Fuel Surge in Fashionable Plus-Sizes," *Advertising Age*, July 7, 1997, p. 24; "Entrepreneurs Cater to a Growing Nation," *The Wall Street Journal*, April 10, 1997, p. B1ff.; William R. Swinyard and Heikki J. Rinne, "The Six Shopping Worlds of Baby Boomers," *Business Horizons*, September–October 1994, pp. 64–69.

32. Based on U.S. Census data and Pamela Paul, "Echoboomerang," *American Demographics*, June 2001, pp. 44–49; "Marketers Tweak Strategies as Age Groups Realign," *The Wall Street Journal*, May 15, 2001, p. B1ff.; *Teen Fact Book* (Channel One Network, 2000) and available from World Wide Web: <http://www.TeenFactBook.com>; Susan Mitchell, "The Next Baby Boom," *American Demographics*, October 1995, pp. 22–31; "Teens, the Most Global Market of All," *Fortune*, May 16, 1994, pp. 90–97.

33. For more on the changing nature of families, see "In 24-Hour Workplace, Day Care Is Moving to the Night Shift," *The Wall Street Journal*, July 6, 2001, p. A1ff.; Rebecca Gardyn, "Granddaughters of Feminism," *American Demographics*, April 2001, pp. 42–47; "The Changing Face of Super Sunday," *USA Today*, January 25, 2001, p. 1Bff.; "Eyes on the Prize," *American Demographics*, November 2000, pp. 48–49; "High-Tech List for India's Women," *The Wall Street Journal*, November 1, 2000, p. B1ff.; "Net Lets Japanese Women Join Work Force at Home," *The Wall Street Journal*, February 29, 2000, p. B1ff.; "The New Debate Over Working Moms," *Business Week*, September 18, 2000, pp. 102–16; "Mommy, Do You Love Your Company More Than Me?" *Business Week*, December 20, 1999, p. 175; "Aiming to Please Women," *USA Today*, June 10, 1999, p. 1Bff.; "Women's Site iVillage Woos Busy Female Fitness Buffs," *Advertising Age*, May 3, 1999, p. S26; "Soap and Diaper Makers Pitch to Masses of Web Women," *The Wall Street Journal*, July 20, 1998, p. B1ff.; "Gillette's New Strategy Is to Sharpen Pitch to Women," *The Wall Street Journal*, May 11, 1998, p. B1ff.; "Advertisers Target Women, but Market Remains Elusive," *Advertising Age*, November 10, 1997, p. 1ff.; "More Dads Raise Families without Mom," *The Wall Street Journal*, October 3, 1997, p. B1ff.; "Ads that Portray Women," *USA Today*, September 9, 1996, p. 4B; Gerry Myers, "Selling a Man's World to Women," *American Demographics*, April 1996, pp. 36–41; "In Fitful Pursuit of American Women," *Advertising Age*, January 8, 1996, P. S4ff.; "High-Tech Marketers Try to Attract Women without Causing Offense," *The Wall Street Journal*, March 17, 1994, p. B1ff; "Narrowcast in Past, Women Earn Revised Role in Advertising," *Advertising Age*, October 4, 1993, p. S1ff.; "Stay-at-Home Moms Are Fashionable Again in Many Communities," *The Wall Street Journal*, July 23, 1993, p. A1ff. For more on changing food habits, see "Skip the Tofu—More Americans Tear into Steaks," *The Wall Street Journal*, March 8, 2001, p. B1ff.; "Food Industry Battles for Moms Who Want to Cook—Just a Little," *The Wall Street Journal*, March 7, 2001, p. A1ff.; "Personal Chefs Are No Longer Just for the Rich," *USA Today*, February 9, 2001, p. 1Aff.; "Can Tyson Fight 'Chicken Fatigue' with Pork, Beef?" *The Wall Street Journal*, January 10, 2001, p. B1ff.; "Takeout Turkey on More Tables as Cooks Relax," *The Wall Street Journal*, November 24, 2000, p. A11ff.; "Bring on the Junk Food," *Newsweek*, July 10, 2000, p. 44; "Breakfast Eats Time, So Workers Gobble at the Office," *USA Today*, June 22, 2000, p. 6B; "Stewing in a Tough Market: Beef Industry Hopes New Ideas . . . ," *USA Today*, July 8, 1999, p. 1Bff.; "On the Run," *Advertising Age*, August 24, 1998, p. 1ff. For more on poverty of time, see "Can Workplace Stress Get Worse?" *The Wall Street Journal*, January 16, 2001, pp. B1ff.; "Telecommuters' Lament," *The Wall Street Journal*, October 31, 2000, p. B1ff.; "The Price of Speed," *USA Today*, August 3, 2000, p. 10D; "Why Everyone Is So Short-Tempered," *USA Today*, July 18, 2000, p. 1Aff.; "The End of Leisure," *American Demographics*, July 2000, pp. 50–56; "Home Is Where the Office Is," *American Demographics*, June 2000, pp. 54–60; "Surviving Commuting," *American Demographics*, July 1998, pp. 51–55. See also Eric Panitz, "Marketing in a Multicultural World: Ethnicity, Nationalism and Cultural Identity," *Journal of the Academy of Marketing Science*, Spring 1997, pp. 169–71; Victoria D. Bush and Thomas Ingram, "Adapting to Diverse Customers: A Training Matrix for International Marketers," *Industrial Marketing Management*, September 1996, pp. 373–83.

34. Frank R. Bacon, Jr., and Thomas W. Butler, Jr., *Planned Innovation*, rev. ed. (Ann Arbor: Institute of Science and Technology, University of Michigan, 1980).

35. Paul F. Anderson, "Marketing, Strategic Planning and the Theory of the Firm," *Journal of Marketing*, Spring 1982, pp. 15–26; George S. Day, "Analytical Approaches to Strategic Market Planning," in *Review of Marketing 1981*, ed. Ben M. Enis and Kenneth J. Roering (Chicago: American Marketing Association, 1981), pp. 89–105; Ronnie Silverblatt and Pradeep Korgaonkar, "Strategic Market Planning in a Turbulent Business Environment," *Journal of Business Research*, August 1987, pp. 339–58.

36. Keith B. Murray and Edward T. Popper, "Competing under Regulatory Uncertainty: A U.S. Perspective on Advertising in the Emerging European Market," *Journal of Macromarketing*, Fall 1992, pp. 38–54; "Inside Russia—Business Most Unusual," *UPS International Update*, Spring 1994, p. 1ff.; "Freighted with Difficulties," *The Wall Street Journal*, December 10, 1993, p. R4; "Russia Snickers after Mars Invades," *The Wall Street Journal*, July 13, 1993, p. B1ff.; Michael G. Harvey and James T. Rothe, "The Foreign Corrupt Practices Act: The Good, the Bad and the Future," in *1983 American Marketing Association Educators' Proceedings*, ed. P. E. Murphy et al. (Chicago: American Marketing Association, 1983), pp. 374–79.

37. "Sensitive Export: Seeking New Markets for Tampons, P&G Faces Cultural Barriers," *The Wall Street Journal*, December 8, 2000, p. A1ff.; "Pizza Queen of Japan Turns Web Auctioneer," *The Wall Street Journal*, March 6, 2000, p. B1ff.; "What Makes Italy Easier?" *Going Global—Italy* (supplement to *Inc.*), 1994; "Jean Cloning," *Brandweek*, May 30, 1994, pp. 15–22; "Double Entendre: The Life and the Life of Pepsi Max," *Brandweek*, April 18, 1994, p. 40; "Global Ad Campaigns, After Many Missteps, Finally Pay Dividends," *The Wall Street Journal*, August 27, 1992, p. A1ff.; Kamran Kashani, "Beware the Pitfalls of Global Marketing," *Harvard Business Review*, September–October 1989, pp. 91–98.

Chapter 5

1. Available from World Wide Web: <http://www.yoplait.com>; "You've Got Surveys," *American Demographics*, November 2000, pp. 42–45; "Marketers of the Year: Groove Tube," *Brandweek* (SuperBrands Issue), October 16, 2000, pp. M111–M116; "Yoplait's Revenge Is Portable Yogurt that Kids Slurp Up," *Advertising Age*, September 11, 2000, pp. 28–30; "Dannon Struggles against Go-Gurt's Market Incursions," *Advertising Age*, September 11, 2000, pp. 28–30; "General Mills Intends to Reshape Doughboy in Its Own Image," *The Wall Street Journal*, July 18, 2000, p. A1ff.; "Squeezable Yogurt? Eggs on a Stick? You Got It!" *USA Today*, March 31, 2000, p. 1D; *Annual Report 2000*, General Mills; "Yogurt Goes Tubular," *Newsweek*, October 11, 1999, p. 63.

2. "Marketing to the New Millionaire," *The Wall Street Journal*, October 11, 2000, p. B1ff.; "New Face of Luxury: Who's Wealthy Now?" *Advertising Age*, May 15, 2000, pp. 44–46; "The Lure of the Entrepreneur," *American Demographics*, February 1998, p. 41;

"Spending at Our Discretion," *American Demographics*, August 1997, p. 2; Peter K. Francese, "Big Spenders," *American Demographics*, August 1997, pp. 51–57; "Disposable Dollars Determine Spending," *American Demographics*, June 1997, pp. 18–19; "Indulging in Inconspicuous Consumption," *The Wall Street Journal*, April 14, 1997, p. B1ff.

3. Based on U.S. Census data, including "Press Briefing on 1999 Income and Poverty Estimates, September 26, 2000" and "Poverty Rate Lowest in 20 Years, Household Income at Record High," (Press Release) and available from World Wide Web: <http://www.census.gov/hhes/income/income99> and <http://www.census.gov/hhes/poverty/poverty99>. For more on income, see Alison Stein Wellner, "The Money in the Middle," *American Demographics*, April 2000, pp. 56–64; "Finally, U.S. Median Income Approaches Old Heights," *The Wall Street Journal*, September 25, 1998, p., B1. For more on poverty, see "Down and Out in the Midst of a Boom," *Business Week*, May 28, 2001, p. 24; "Poverty at a 21-Year Low; Income Up, But Gap Wider," *Investor's Business Daily*, September 27, 2000, p. A1; "Poverty Rate Falls to 11.8%, the Lowest Level since 1979," *The Wall Street Journal*, September 27, 2000, p. A2; "Poverty in America," *Business Week*, October 18, 1999, pp. 156–66; "Charting the Pain Behind the Gain," *The Wall Street Journal*, October 1, 1999, p. B1ff.; "How Hard Are Hard Times?" *American Demographics*, February 1998, pp. 30–32; "Income Gap between Rich and Poor Grows Nationwide," *The Wall Street Journal*, December 17, 1997, p. B2.

4. Kristina D. Frankenberger, "Consumer Psychology for Marketing," *Journal of the Academy of Marketing Science*, Summer 1996, pp. 279–81; K. H. Chung, *Motivational Theories and Practices* (Columbus, Ohio: Grid, 1977), pp. 40–43; A. H. Maslow, *Motivation and Personality* (New York: Harper & Row, 1970).

5. "What Works for One Works for All," *Business Week*, April 20, 1992, pp. 112–13.

6. For more on Ben & Jerry's, see "Ben & Jerry's Keeps Its Folksy Focus," *Advertising Age*, February 12, 2001, p. 4ff. See also Jennifer Gregan-Paxton and Deborah R. John, "Consumer Learning by Analogy: A Model of Internal Knowledge Transfer," *Journal of Consumer Research*, December 1997, pp. 266–84; M. C. Macklin, "Preschoolers' Learning of Brand Names From Visual Cues," *Journal of Consumer Research*, December 1996, pp. 251–61; Jaideep Sengupta, Ronald C. Goodstein, and David S. Boninger, "All Cues Are Not Created Equal: Obtaining Attitude Persistence Under Low-Involvement Conditions," *Journal of Consumer Research*, March 1997, pp. 351–61; John Kim, Jeen-Su Lim, and Mukesh Bhargava, "The Role of Affect in Attitude Formation: A Classical Conditioning Approach," *Journal of the Academy of Marketing Science*, Spring 1998, pp. 143–52; Paul S. Speck and Michael T. Elliott, "Predictors of Advertising Avoidance in Print and Broadcast Media," *Journal of Advertising*, Fall 1997, pp. 61–76; Frances K. McSweeney and Calvin Bierley, "Recent Developments in Classical Conditioning," *Journal of Consumer Research*, September 1984, pp. 619–31; Scott A. Hawkins and Stephen J. Hoch, "Low-Involvement Learning: Memory without Evaluation," *Journal of Consumer Research*, September 1992, pp. 212–25.

7. "Purina Dog Chow: Grand Effie Winner, Pet Care/Gold Winner," *Brandweek*, (Special Effies Winner Supplement), 1997. See also Edward Rosbergen, Rik Pieters, and Michel Wedel, "Visual Attention to Advertising: A Segment-Level Analysis," *Journal of Consumer Research*, December 1997, pp. 305–14; Gavan J. Fitzsimons and Vicki G. Morwitz, "The Effect of Measuring Intent on Brand-Level Purchase Behavior," *Journal of Consumer Research*, June 1996, pp. 1–11; Ellen C. Garbarino and Julie A. Edell, "Cognitive Effort, Affect, and Choice," *Journal of Consumer Research*, September 1997, pp. 147–58.

8. Vikas Mittal, William T. Ross, and Patrick M. Baldasare, "The Asymmetric Impact of Negative and Positive Attribute-Level Performance on Overall Satisfaction and Repurchase Intentions," *Journal of Marketing*, January 1998, pp. 33–47; Mary F. Luce, "Choosing to Avoid: Coping With Negatively Emotion-Laden Consumer Decisions," *Journal of Consumer Research*, March 1998, pp. 409–33; Calvin P. Duncan and Richard W. Olshavsky, "External Search: The Role of Consumer Beliefs," *Journal of Marketing Research*, February 1982, pp. 32–43; M. Joseph Sirgy, "Self-Concept in Consumer Behavior: A Critical Review," *Journal of Consumer Research*, December 1982, pp. 287–300.

9. "Living Larger," *USA Today*, March 16, 1998, p. 4D; "It's Not Easy Being Lean in Cairo Today, but Women Do Try," *The Wall Street Journal*, March 4, 1998, p. A1ff.; "If Fat-Free Pork Is Your Idea of Savory, It's a Bright Future," *The Wall Street Journal*, January 29, 1998, p. A1ff.; "Pork Is Tasty, Say National Ads that Shift Focus from Nutrition," *The Wall Street Journal*, August 13, 1997, p. B5; "Americans Develop More Discriminating Taste," *USA Today*, June 6, 1997, p. 1Bff.; "Hershey Craves Gumdrops, Hard Candy amid Fat Fear," *The Wall Street Journal*, October 23, 1996, p. B1ff.; "Three Diet Firms Settle False-Ad Case; Two Others Vow to Fight FTC Charges," *The Wall Street Journal*, October 1, 1993, p. B5.

10. "The Dirt on At-Home Dry Cleaning," *The Wall Street Journal*, September 15, 2000, p. W14; "Does P&G Still Matter?" *Advertising Age*, September 25, 2000, pp. 48–54; "P&G Shifts Strategy for Dryel," *Advertising Age*, January 24, 2000, p. 4; "Novel P&G Product Brings Dry Cleaning Home," *The Wall Street Journal*, November 19, 1997, p. B1ff.

11. For more on Van Heusen, see "Men Are Taking a Cotton to Wrinkle-Free Pants," *USA Today*, June 16, 1994, p. 5D; "'Wrinkle-Free' Shirts Don't Live Up to the Name," *The Wall Street Journal*, May 11, 1994, p. B1ff. See also "Rogaine Urges the Nonbald to Use Ounces of Prevention," *The Wall Street Journal*, September 20, 1999, p. B1ff. For more on service quality, see Chapter 8, footnote #4. For more on service expectations, see "Customer Service with a :-)," *USA Today*, December 6, 2000, p. 1Eff.; "Spotty Service Irks Cellphone Users," *USA Today*, November 6, 2000, p. 1Aff.; "Why Service Stinks," *Business Week*, October 23, 2000, pp. 118–28; "Cliff-Hanger Christmas," *Business Week E.Biz*, October 23, 2000, pp. 30–38; "It's the People, Stupid," *Business Week E.Biz*, October 23, 2000, p. EB138; "Service, Please," *Business Week E.Biz*, October 23, 2000, pp. EB48–EB50; "Seller of Suits Loosens Collar, Breathes Easier," *Investor's Business Daily*, October 19, 2000, p. A12; "On a Power Trip, They Arrive with Grating Expectations," *USA Today*, September 22, 2000, p. 1Dff.; "Customer Service: Rewriting the Rules of the Road," *Business Week E.Biz*, September 18,

2000, p. EB86; "How to Lose a Customer in a Matter of Seconds," *Fortune*, June 12, 2000, p. 326; "Special Report: E-Tailing," *Business Week E.Biz*, May 15, 2000, pp. EB103–EB118; "It's the Service, Stupid," *Business Week E.Biz*, April 3, 2000, p. EB118; "Just Another Medium," *Business Week E.Biz*, September 27, 1999, p. EB78; "Internet Businesses Customize to Survive," *Investor's Business Daily*, April 27, 2000, p. A8; "You'll Wanna Hold Their Hands," *Business Week E.Biz*, March 22, 1999, pp. EB30–EB31; "Online with the Operator," *American Demographics*, February 1999, pp. 36–39. See also A. Parasuraman, Valarie A. Zeithaml, and Leonard L. Berry, "Reassessment of Expectations As a Comparison Standard in Measuring Service Quality: Implications for Further Research," *Journal of Marketing*, January 1994, pp. 111–24; Alain Genestre and Paul Herbig, "Service Expectations and Perceptions Revisited: Adding Product Quality to SERVQUAL," *Journal of Marketing Theory & Practice*, Fall 1996, pp. 72–82; Valarie A. Zeithaml, Leonard L. Berry, and A. Parasuraman, "The Nature and Determinants of Customer Expectations of Service," *Journal of the Academy of Marketing Science*, Winter 1993, pp. 1–12.

12. Harold H. Kassarjian and Mary Jane Sheffet, "Personality and Consumer Behavior: An Update," in H. Kassarjian and T. Robertson, *Perspectives in Consumer Behavior* (Glenview, IL: Scott, Foresman, 1981), p. 160; Todd A. Mooradian and James M. Olver, "'I Can't Get No Satisfaction:' The Impact of Personality and Emotion on Postpurchase Processes," *Psychology & Marketing*, July 1997, pp. 379–93.

13. "Chock Full of Peanuts," *American Demographics*, April 1997, p. 60.

14. "Generation Next," *Advertising Age*, January 15, 2001, pp. 14–16; "Head Trips," *American Demographics*, October 2000, pp. 38–40; "Label-Crazy Marketers Have Got You Pegged," *USA Today*, August 1, 2000, p. 1Bff.; "Simple Sells," *USA Today*, June 1, 2000, p. 1Aff.; "Make Room for Daddy," *American Demographics*, June 2000, pp. 34–36; "Join the Club," *Brandweek*, February 15, 1999, pp. 26–32; Annetta Miller, "The Millennial Mind-Set," *American Demographics*, January 1999, pp. 60–65; Rebecca Piirto Heath, "The Frontier of Psychographics," *American Demographics*, July 1996, pp. 38–43; "Making Generational Marketing Come of Age," *Fortune*, June 26, 1995, pp. 110–13; Robert A. Mittelstaedt, "Economics, Psychology, and the Literature of the Subdiscipline of Consumer Behavior," *Journal of the Academy of Marketing Science*, Fall, 1990, pp. 303–12; W. D. Wells, "Psychographics: A Critical Review," *Journal of Marketing Research*, May 1975, pp. 196–213.

15. Available from World Wide Web: <http://future.sri.com/vals>; Judith Waldrop, "Markets with Attitude," *American Demographics*, July 1994, pp. 22–33; "New VALS 2 Takes Psychological Route," *Advertising Age*, February 13, 1989, p. 24; Lynn R. Kahle, Sharon E. Beatty, and Pamela Homer, "Alternative Measurement Approaches to Consumer Values: The List of Values (LOV) and Values and Life Styles (VALS)," *Journal of Consumer Research*, December 1986, pp. 405–10.

16. Jan Larson, "The New Face of Homemakers," *American Demographics*, September 1997, pp. 45–50; "Work & Family" (Special Section), *The Wall Street Journal*, March 31, 1997, pp. 1–20; "Family Values: Some Surprises," *USA Today*, March 11, 1997, P. 6D; Margaret K. Ambry, "Receipts from a Marriage," *American Demographics*, February 1993, pp. 30–37; "A Snapshot of Younger Lifestage Group Purchases," *American Demographics*, November 9, 1992, p. 28; Patrick E. Murphy and William A. Staples, "A Modernized Family Life Cycle," *Journal of Consumer Research*, June 1979, pp. 12–22.

17. Based on U.S. Census data and "Unmarried with Children," *Newsweek*, May 28, 2001, pp. 46–55; "Single-Father Households in USA Increase 62% in '90s," *USA Today*, May 18, 2001, p. 1A; "Census 2000: The New Demographics," *The Wall Street Journal*, May 15, 2001, p. B1ff.; "Advertisers Are Cautious as Household Makeup Shifts," *The Wall Street Journal*, May 15, 2001, p. B1ff.; "For Whom the Bell Tolls," *Brandweek*, May 7, 2001, p. 22; Joan Raymond, "The Ex-Files," *American Demographics*, February 2001, pp. 60–64; "Houses Aren't Just for Couples," *Business Week*, January 8, 2001, p. 142; Rebecca Gardyn, "Unmarried Bliss," *American Demographics*, December 2000, pp. 56–61; "Demographics on Wall Street," *American Demographics*, December 2000, p. 6; "In Unwedded Bill: More Couples Decide To Avoid the Altar," *The Wall Street Journal*, August 2, 2000, P. S3; "The Heralded Return of Traditional Families Is Not What It Seems," *The Wall Street Journal*, May 31, 2000, p. B1; "Changing the Shape of the American Family," *USA Today*, April 18, 2000, p. 1Bff; Alison Stein Wellner, "Who Is in the House?" *American Demographics*, January 2000, pp. 48–51; "A Home of Their Own," *American Demographics*, September 1999, pp. 35–38; "The Ties that Bind," *Time*, August 18, 1997, pp. 48–50; "Mobility Mangles Marriage," *USA Today*, September 11, 1996, p. 15A; Frank F. Fustenberg, Jr., "The Future of Marriage," *American Demographics*, June 1996, pp. 34–40.

18. Based on U.S. Census data and "Just How Deep Are Those Teen Pockets?" *Business Week*, July 30, 2001, p. 39; "Special Report: Teen Marketing," *Advertising Age*, June 25, 2001, pp. S1–12; "Marketers Have a Crush on Teens," *USA Today*, November 27, 2000, p. 10B; "To Reach the Unreachable Teen," *Business Week*, September 18, 2000, pp. 78–80; "Rushing to Cash In on the New Baby Boom," *The Wall Street Journal*, August 9, 2000, p. B1ff.; "Stores Roll Out Welcome Mat for Mall Rats," *The Wall Street Journal*, August 9, 2000. p. B1ff.; "My, You've Grown: The Teen Economy Is Like Totally Awesome," *The Wall Street Journal*, June 28, 2000, p. S3; "The Six Value Segments of Global Youth," *Brandweek*, May 22, 2000, pp. 38–50; "Can Levi's Be Cool Again?" *Business Week*, March 13, 2000, pp. 144–48; Elissa Moses, *The $100 Billion Allowance: Accessing the Global Teen Market* (John Wiley & Sons, 2000); Jeff Brazil, "Play Dough," *American Demographics*, December 1999, pp. 56–61; "Generation Y," *Business Week*, February 15, 1999, pp. 80–88; "Teen Retailing: The Underground Tastemakers," *The Wall Street Journal*, December 9, 1998, p. B1ff.; "Teen-Magazine Boom: Beauty, Fashion, Stars and Sex," *The Wall Street Journal*, December 7, 1998, p. B1ff.; "Apartments Replace the Dorm," *The Wall Street Journal*, October 28, 1998, p. B18; "Generation Y: Boomers' Kids a Booming Market," *USA Today*, October 6, 1998, p. 1Aff.; "The Boom Tube," *Adweek*, May 18, 1998, pp. 44–52; "Girl Power," *Fortune*, December 8, 1997, pp. 132–40; "In Developing Nations, Many Youths Splurge, Mainly on U.S. Goods," *The Wall Street Journal*, June 26, 1997, p. A1ff.; Soyeon Shim, "Adolescent Consumer Decision-Making Styles: The

Consumer Socialization Perspective," *Psychology & Marketing*, September 1996, pp. 547–69.

19. Based on U.S. Census data and Joan Raymond, "The Joy of Empty Nesting," *American Demographics*, May 2000, pp. 48–54; "Take My Stuff, Please!" *The Wall Street Journal*, March 31, 2000, P. W1ff.; "The Big House Backlash," *The Wall Street Journal*, March 17, 2000, p. W1ff.; "Big Footprints: Hey, Baby Boomers Need Their Space, OK? Look at All Their Stuff," *The Wall Street Journal*, January 7, 2000, p. A1ff.; "Extreme Nesting," *The Wall Street Journal*, January 7, 2000, p. W1ff.; Don Fost, "Growing Older, But Not Up," *American Demographics*, September 1998, pp. 59–65.

20. For more on kids' influence in purchase decisions, see "Marketers Find 'Tweens' Too Hot to Ignore," *USA Today*, July 10, 2001, p. 13A; "Marketers Call on Kids to Help Design Web Sites," *USA Today*, June 5, 2001, p. 1Bff.; "Special Report: Marketing to Kids and Tweens," *Advertising Age*, 2001, S2–S14; "Kid-Fluence," *USA Today*, December 29, 2000, p. 1Eff.; "Baby's Booty," *Newsweek*, December 4, 2000, pp. 55–56; "Young Girls Targeted by Makeup Companies," *Advertising Age*, November 27, 2000, p. 15; "Retailers Reaching Out to Capture Kids' Clout," *Advertising Age*, October 9, 2000, p. 16; Alison Stein Wellner, "Generation Z," *American Demographics* September 2000, pp. 60–64; "Fashion's Littlest Victims," *Brandweek*, July 17, 2000, p. 24; "In Quest for Prettiest Baby, Parents Snap Up Pricey Kids' Cosmetics," *The Wall Street Journal*, June 9, 2000, p. B1ff.; "One Size Doesn't Fit All," *American Demographics*, May 2000, pp. 44–45; "Special Report: Youth Marketing," *Advertising Age*, February 14, 2000, pp. 38–45; Jeff Brazil, "Play Dough," *American Demographics*, December 1999, pp. 56–61; "Nickelodeon Makes Deals with Grown-Up Products," *The Wall Street Journal*, November 19, 1999, p. B1ff.; "Kids Shopping On Line," *USA Today*, August 25, 1999, p. 1B; "Foods Targeting Children Aren't Just Child Play," *Advertising Age*, March 1, 1999, p. 16; "Makeup for Moppets: Lots of Glitter, Hot Sales," *The Wall Street Journal*, December 4, 1998, p. B1ff.; "Little Big Spenders: As Children Become More Sophisticated, Marketers Think Older," *The Wall Street Journal*, October 13, 1998, p. A1ff.; James U. McNeal, "Tapping the Three Kids' Markets," *American Demographics*, April 1998, pp. 37–41; "Software Firms Coddle a Growing Market: The Preschool Crowd," *The Wall Street Journal*, April 2, 1998, p. A1ff.; "Not All Approve of Barbie's MasterCard," *USA Today*, March 30, 1998, p. 6B; "Hey Kid, Buy This!" *Business Week*, June 30, 1997, pp. 62–69; "Kodak Focuses on Putting Kids behind a Camera," *The Wall Street Journal*, May 6, 1997, p. B8; "Special Report: Reaching Kids," *Advertising Age*, February 10, 1997, pp. 25–28; "The Rise of the Net-Generation," *Advertising Age*, October 14, 1996, p. 31ff.; Sharon E. Beatty and Salil Talpade, "Adolescent Influence in Family Decision Making: A Replication with Extension," *Journal of Consumer Research*, September 1994, pp. 332–41. See also Ugur Yavas, Emin Babakus, and Nejdet Delener, "Family Purchasing Roles in Saudi Arabia: Perspectives from Saudi Wives," *Journal of Business Research*, September 1994, pp. 75–86; Rosemary Polegato and Judith L. Zaichkowsky, "Family Food Shopping: Strategies Used by Husbands and Wives," *Journal of Consumer Affairs*, Winter 1994, pp. 278–99; Eric H. Shaw and Stephen F. I. Pirog, "A Systems Model of Household Behavior," *Journal of Marketing Theory & Practice*, Summer 1997, pp. 17–30; Kay M. Palan and Robert E. Wilkes, "Adolescent-Parent Interaction in Family Decision Making," *Journal of Consumer Research*, September 1997, pp. 159–69; Mary C. Gilly, John L. Graham, Mary F. Wolfinbarger, and Laura J. Yale, "A Dyadic Study of Interpersonal Information Search," *Journal of the Academy of Marketing Science*, Spring 1998, pp. 83–100; Conway L. Lackman, David P. Hanson, and John M. Lanasa, "Social Relations in Culture and Marketing," *Journal of Marketing Theory & Practice*, Winter 1997, pp. 144–52; Ellen R. Foxman, Patriya S. Tansuhaj, and Karin M. Ekstrom, "Adolescents' Influence in Family Purchase Decisions: A Socialization Perspective," *Journal of Business Research*, March 1989, pp. 159–72; C. Lackman and J. M. Lanasa, "Family Decision-Making Theory: An Overview and Assessment," *Psychology & Marketing*, March/April 1993, pp. 81–94. For more on women's influence in purchase decisions, see U.S. Census data, including "Women in the United States: A Profile, March 2000," and available from World Wide Web: <http://www.census.gov/population/www/socdemo/women>; "Women Hold Power of Purse Strings," *USA Today*, June 26, 2000, p. 11B; "A Guide to Who Holds the Purse Strings," *The Wall Street Journal*, June 22, 2000, p. A14; "How to Market to Women," *Advertising Age*, June 12, 2000, pp. 24–26; Faith Popcorn and Lyn Marigold, *EVEolution: The Eight Truths of Marketing to Women* (Hyperion, 2000); "Plugging into Women," *Brandweek*, March 15, 1999, pp. 25–26.

21. "Luxury for the Masses," *Brandweek*, June 25, 2001, pp. 16–34; "Special Report: Luxury Marketing," *Advertising Age*, June 11, 2001, pp. S1–14; "Which Is Luxury?" *USA Today*, May 4, 2001, p. 1Bff.; Hassan Fattah, "The Rising Tide," *American Demographics*, April 2001, pp. 48–53; "Despite Downturn, Japanese Are Still Having Fits for Luxury Goods," *The Wall Street Journal*, April 24, 2001, p. B1ff.; "The Rise of the Comfortable," *Advertising Age*, October 16, 2000, pp. 60–62; "90s Luxury Beyond Top of the Line," *USA Today*, July 6, 1999, p. 1Aff.; Debra Goldman, "Paradox of Pleasure," *American Demographics*, May 1999, pp. 50–53; "Culture Class: How America's Youth Defines Luxury," *Brandweek*, April 19, 1999, pp. 67–76; Rebecca Piirto Heath, "The New Working Class," *American Demographics*, January 1998, pp. 51–55; "Education Marks a Widening Income Divide," *The Wall Street Journal*, June 28, 1996, p. R2; "Class in America," *Fortune*, February 7, 1994, pp. 114–26; Basil G. Englis and Michael R. Solomon, "To Be and Not to Be: Lifestyle Imagery, Reference Groups, and the Clustering of America," *Journal of Advertising*, Spring 1995, pp. 13–28; Greg J. Duncan, Timothy M. Smeeding, and Willard Rodgers, "The Incredible Shrinking Middle Class," *American Demographics*, May 1992, pp. 34–38; Dennis L. Rosen and Richard W. Olshavsky, "The Dual Role of Informational Social Influence: Implications for Marketing Management," *Journal of Business Research*, April 1987, pp. 123–44; Terry L. Childers and Akshay R. Rao, "The Influence of Familial and Peer-based Reference Groups on Consumer Decisions," *Journal of Consumer Research*, September 1992, pp. 198–211; Basil G. Englis and Michael R. Solomon, "To Be and Not to Be: Lifestyle Imagery, Reference Groups, and The Clustering of America," *Journal of Advertising*, Spring 1995, pp. 13–28.

22. "Auto Makers Find They Don't Want to Avoid Collisions in Movies," *The Wall Street Journal*, July 5, 2001, p. B1ff.; "Small Wonder," *The Wall Street Journal*, June 25, 2001, p. R; Rebecca Gardyn, "Granddaughters of Feminism," *American Demographics*,

April 2001, pp. 43–47; "A Wide Web of Advice," *Business Week E.Biz*, January 22, 2001, pp. EB18–EB20; "How to Generate Buzz to Sell Your Product," *Investor's Business Daily*, October 3, 2000, p. A1; "Word of Mouth in the Digital Age: Marketers Win when Friends Hit 'Send'," *Brandweek*, October 2, 2000, pp. 24–26; "Ebola. Smallpox. Christina Aguilera." *Ecompany*, October 2000, pp. 48–52; "Steering to the Right Sites for the Best Buy," *Time Digital*, May 2000, p. 92; "Marketing Superstars: Aki Maita, Tamagotchi," *Advertising Age International*, December 1997, p. 10; James H. Myers and Thomas S. Robertson, "Dimensions of Opinion Leadership," *Journal of Marketing Research*, February 1972, pp. 41–46.

23. "Art of Noise," *Brandweek*, November 1, 1999, p. 78.

24. For an overview of ethnic populations in the U.S., see *Racial and Ethnic Diversity* (Ithaca, NY: New Strategist, 2000); Geng Cui, "Marketing to Ethnic Minority Consumers: An Historical Journey (1932–1997)," *Journal of Macromarketing*," June 2001, Vol. 21, 1, pp. 23–21; Marilyn Halter, *Shopping for Identity: The Marketing of Ethnicity* (Schocken Books, 2000); "An Almost-Invisible $1 Trillion Market," *Business Week*, June 11, 2001, p. 151; William H. Frey, "Micro Melting Pots," *American Demographics*, June 2001, pp. 20–23; "Spanish Study Booms in USA," *USA Today*, May 9, 2001, p. 1Aff.; "Color Them Beautiful— and Visible," *USA Today*, May 2, 2001, p. 1Bff.; "The New Age of Ethnic Marketing," *Brandweek*, March 19, 2001, pp. 24–28; "Impact of Census' Race Data Debated," *USA Today*, March 13, 2001, p. 1Aff.; "Even 126 Sizes Don't Fit All," *The Wall Street Journal*, March 2, 2001, p. B1ff.; "Census to Define Multiracial in Myriad Ways," *USA Today*, February 28, 2001, p. 8D; "The New America: The New Face of Race," *Newsweek*, September 18, 2000, pp. 38–65; "Won't You Be My Neighbor?" *American Demographics*, June 2000, pp. 60–62; "A Consumer in Every Pot," *Brandweek*, April 24, 2000, pp. 32–36; "In the Land of Bratwurst, a New Hispanic Boom," *The Wall Street Journal*, March 16, 2000, p. B1ff.; "Diversity in Advertising," *Advertising Age* (Special Report), February 21, 2000, pp. S1–20; "Our New Look: The Colors of Race," *Newsweek*, January 1, 2000, pp. 28–30; "The Web Goes Multicultural," *Advertising Age* (Special Report), November 29, 1999, pp. S1–14; Roberto Suro, "Mixed Doubles," *American Demographics*, November 1999, pp. 56–62; "The New Face of America," *USA Today*, September 7, 1999, p. 1Aff.; "Time and the Melting Pot," *American Demographics*, June 1998, pp. 18–23; William O'Hare, "Managing Multiple-Race Data," *American Demographics*, April 1998, pp. 42–52; "Multicultural," (Special Report) *Advertising Age*, November 17, 1997, pp. S1–S34. For more on the African-American market, see "U.S. Census data including "The Black Population in the United States: March 1999, P20–530" and available from World Wide Web: <http://www.census.gov/population/www/socdemo/race>; "Black Boom in the 'Burbs," *American Demographics*, July 2001, pp. 20–21; Alison Stein Wellner, "The Forgotten Baby Boom," *American Demographics*, February 2001, pp. 46–51; "The New Demographics of Black Americans," *Business Week*, December 4, 2000, p. 14; Carol M. Motley, "Aunt Jemima, Uncle Ben, and Rastus: Blacks in Advertising, Yesterday, Today, and Tomorrow," *Journal of Marketing*, April 1995, pp. 111–13; "Close Vs. Safe: Rivals Prepare to Market New Razors," *The Wall Street Journal*, September 29, 1997, p. B1ff.; "The New Black Power," *Fortune*, August 4, 1997, pp. 46–83; "Spike Lee: Madison Ave.'s Gotta Have Him," *Fortune*, April 14, 1997, pp. 84–86; "Black America in 2001," *American Demographics*, November 1996, pp. 14–15; "Marketing to African-Americans" (Special Report), *Advertising Age*, July 17, 1995, pp. S1–S4. For more on the Hispanic market, see U.S. Census data, including "The Hispanic Population in the United States: March 2000" and available from World Wide Web: <http://www.census.gov/population/www/socdemo/race>; "The New Frontier," *Time*, June 11, 2001, pp. 36–79; "Hispanics Stump for Success," *USA Today*, May 21, 2001, p. 1Bff.; "U.S. Marketers Adopt Cinco de Mayo as National Fiesta," *The Wall Street Journal*, May 1, 2001, p. B1ff.; "Welcome Mat Rolls Out for Hispanic Workers," *USA Today*, April 12, 2001, p. 1Bff.; "For Hispanic Marketers, Census Says It All," *The Wall Street Journal*, April 24, 2001, p. B8; Rebecca Gardyn, "Habla English?" *American Demographics*, April 2001, pp. 54–57; "Hispanic Growth Reveals Isolation," *USA Today*, March 26, 2001, p. 1Aff.; M. Isabel Valdes, *Marketing to American Latinos* (Ithaca, NY: Paramount, 2000); "P&G Reaches Out to Hispanics," *The Wall Street Journal*, October 13, 2000, p. B1ff.; "Why the Latino Market Is So Hard to Count," *The Wall Street Journal*, October 13, 2000, p. B1ff.; "Hispanic Sector Is Booming—In Unlikely Places," *The Wall Street Journal*, October 11, 2000, p. S3; "Hispanic TV Takes Off in the U.S.," *The Wall Street Journal*, September 7, 2000, p. B1ff.; Cristina Merrill, "Where the Cars Are Caliente!" *American Demographics*, January 2000, pp. 56–59; "Marketing to Hispanics," *Advertising Age* (Special Report), August 30, 1999, pp. S1–20; "Latino America," *Newsweek*, July 12, 1999, pp. 48–58; Helene Stapinski, "Generacion Latino," *American Demographics*, July 1999, pp. 62–68; "Attention, Shoppers: Target Makes a Play for Minority Group Sears Has Cultivated," *The Wall Street Journal*, April 12, 1999, p. A1ff.; "Special Report: Marketing to Hispanics," *Advertising Age*, August 24, 1998, pp. S1–27; "Housing Industry Courts Hispanics like Alas Family," *The Wall Street Journal*, October 2, 1997, p. B1ff.; "Targeting the Hispanic Market," *Advertising Age*, March 31, 1997, pp. A1–A16; "Hispanic Americans in 2001," *American Demographics*, January 1997, pp. 16–17. For more on the Asian-American market, see U.S. Census data, including "The Asian and Pacific Islander Population in the United States: March 1999, P20–529" and available from World Wide Web: <http:// www.census.gov/population/www/socdemo/race>; "The Asian American Blind Spot," *American Demographics*, July 2001, pp. 16–17; "U.S. Asian Population Grew and Diversified, Census Shows," *The Wall Street Journal*, May 15, 2001, p. B4; "Cars: Dealing with Asians," *Brandweek*, January 5, 1998, pp. 15–17; "Asian Americans in 2001," *American Demographics*, February 1997, pp. 16–17; Marcia Mogelonsky, "Asian-Indian Americans," *American Demographics*, August 1995, pp. 32–39; "Two English-Speaking Magazines Target Affluent Asian-Americans," *The Wall Street Journal*, October 1, 1993, p. A5A; Charles R. Taylor and Barbara B. Stern, "Asian-Americans: Television Advertising and the 'Model Minority' Stereotype," *Journal of Advertising*, Summer 1997, pp. 47–61; Charles R. Taylor and Ju Yung Lee, "Not in *Vogue*: Portrayals of Asian Americans in Magazine Advertising," *Journal of Public Policy & Marketing*, Fall 1994, pp. 239–45. See also Scott D. Roberts and H. S. Hart, "A Comparison of Cultural Value Orientations As Reflected by

Advertisements Directed at the General U.S. Market, the U.S. Hispanic Market, and the Mexican Market," *Journal of Marketing Theory & Practice*, Winter 1997, pp. 91–99; Geng Cui, "Marketing Strategies in a Multi-Ethnic Environment," *Journal of Marketing Theory & Practice*, Winter 1997, pp. 122–34; Michael Laroche, Chung K. Kim, and Madeleine Clarke, "The Effects of Ethnicity Factors on Consumer Deal Interests: An Empirical Study of French- and English-Canadians," *Journal of Marketing Theory & Practice*, Winter 1997, pp. 100–12.

25. "Overcoming the Stigma of Dishwashers in Japan," *The Wall Street Journal*, May 19, 2000, p. B1ff.; Sydney Roslow, "International Consumer Behavior: Its Impact on Marketing Strategy Development," *Journal of the Academy of Marketing Science*, Summer 1996, pp. 278–79; R. Mead, "Where is the Culture of Thailand?" *International Journal of Research in Marketing*, September 1994, pp. 401–04.

26. John L. Graham, "How Culture Works," *Journal of Marketing*, April 1996, pp. 134–35; Gary D. Gregory and James M. Munch, "Cultural Values in International Advertising: An Examination of Familial Norms and Roles in Mexico," *Psychology & Marketing*, March 1997, pp. 99–119; Shiretta F. Ownbey and Patricia E. Horridge, "Acculturation Levels and Shopping Orientations of Asian-American Consumers," *Psychology & Marketing*, January 1997, pp. 1–18; Jennifer L. Aaker and Durairaj Maheswaran, "The Effect of Cultural Orientation on Persuasion," *Journal of Consumer Research*, December 1997, pp. 315–28; Grant McCracken, "Culture and Consumption: A Theoretical Account of the Structure and Movement of the Cultural Meaning of Consumer Goods," *Journal of Consumer Research*, June 1986, pp. 71–84. For some examples, see "Starbucks Hits a Humorous Note in Pitching Iced Coffee to Brits," *The Wall Street Journal*, September 1, 1999, p. B7; "Will the British Warm Up to Iced Tea? Some Big Marketers Are Counting on It," *The Wall Street Journal*, August 22, 1994, p. B1ff.

27. "No More Shoppus Interruptus," *American Demographics*, May 2001, pp. 39–40; "No Buy? Then Bye-Bye," *Business Week E.Biz*, April 16, 2001, p. EB6; "Ok, Forget the Whole Damn Thing," *Ecompany*, December 2000, pp. 185–88; "Clinching the Holiday E-Sale," *The Wall Street Journal*, October 9, 2000, p. B1ff.; "A New Cure for Shoppus Interruptus," *American Demographics*, August 2000, pp. 44–47; "Special Report: E-Tailing," *Business Week E.Biz*, May 15, 2000, pp. EB103–EB118; "Many Web Shoppers Abandon Virtual Carts," *Investor's Business Daily*, May 11, 2000, p. A8; Charles S. Areni, Pamela Kiecker, and Kay M. Palan, "Is It Better to Give Than to Receive? Exploring Gender Differences in the Meaning of Memorable Gifts," *Psychology & Marketing*, January 1998, pp. 81–109; Russell W. Belk, "Situational Variables and Consumer Behavior," *Journal of Consumer Research* 2, 1975, pp. 157–64; John F. Sherry, Jr., "Gift Giving in Anthropological Perspective," *Journal of Consumer Research*, September 1983, pp. 157–68.

28. Adapted and updated from James H. Myers and William H. Reynolds, *Consumer Behavior and Marketing Management* (Boston: Houghton Mifflin, 1967), p. 49. See also Ronald E. Goldsmith, "A Theory of Shopping," *Journal of the Academy of Marketing Science*, Fall 2000, pp. 541–4; Judith Lynne Zaichkowsky, "Consumer Behavior: Yesterday, Today, and Tomorrow," *Business Horizons*, May/June 1991, pp. 51–58.

29. Ravi Dhar and Steven J. Sherman, "The Effect of Common and Unique Features in Consumer Choice," *Journal of Consumer Research*, December 1996, pp. 193–203; Victor V. Cordell, "Consumer Knowledge Measures As Predictors in Product Evaluation," *Psychology & Marketing*, May 1997, pp. 241–60; John V. Petrof and Naoufel Daghfous, "Evoked Set: Myth or Reality?" *Business Horizons*, May–June 1996, pp. 72–77; Wayne D. Hoyer, "An Examination of Consumer Decision Making for a Common Repeat Purchase Product," *Journal of Consumer Research*, December 1984, pp. 822–29; James R. Bettman, *An Information Processing Theory of Consumer Choice* (Reading, Mass.: Addison-Wesley Publishing, 1979); Richard W. Olshavsky and Donald H. Granbois, "Consumer Decision Making—Fact or Fiction?" *Journal of Consumer Research*, September 1979, pp. 93–100.

30. Cele Otnes, Tina M. Lowrey, and L. J. Shrum, "Toward an Understanding of Consumer Ambivalence," *Journal of Consumer Research*, June 1997, pp. 80–93; Ronald E. Goldsmith, "Consumer Involvement: Concepts and Research," *Journal of the Academy of Marketing Science*, Summer 1996, pp. 281–83; Jeffrey B. Schmidt and Richard A. Spreng, "A Proposed Model of External Consumer Information Search," *Journal of the Academy of Marketing Science*, Summer 1996, pp. 246–56; Judith L. Zaichkowsky, "The Personal Involvement Inventory: Reduction, Revision, and Application to Advertising," *Journal of Advertising*, December 1994, pp. 59–70; Raj Arora, "Consumer Involvement—What It Offers to Advertising Strategy," *International Journal of Advertising* 4, no. 2 (1985), pp. 119–30; J. Brock Smith and Julia M. Bristor, "Uncertainty Orientation: Explaining Differences in Purchase Involvement and External Search," *Psychology & Marketing*, November/December 1994, pp. 587–608; Don R. Rahtz and David L. Moore, "Product Class Involvement and Purchase Intent," *Psychology and Marketing*, Summer 1989, pp. 113–28.

31. Adapted from E. M. Rogers with F. Shoemaker, *Communication of Innovation: A Cross Cultural Approach* (New York: Free Press, 1968). For some sampling (trial) examples, see "Small Wonder," *The Wall Street Journal*, June 25, 2001, p. R; "Freebies Take on Brash New Form," *USA Today*, May 15, 2001, p. 1Bff.; "A Bull's Market," *Brandweek*, May 28, 2001, pp. 21–24; "Red Bull's Good Buzz," *Newsweek*, May 14, 2001, p. 39; "Time to Make the Donuts," *American Demographics*, May 2001, p. 8; "Marketers of the Next Generation: Krispy Kreme," *Brandweek*, March 26, 2001, p. 21; "Use of Samples in Drug Industry Raises Concern," *The Wall Street Journal*, July 19, 2000, p. B1ff.; "Auto Site Rolls Out a Vintage Campaign," *The Wall Street Journal*, July 11, 2000, p. B12; "PepsiCo Tries to Clarify Pepsi One's Image," *The Wall Street Journal*, February 25, 2000, p. B7; "Canine Cuisine Fetches Success," *USA Today*, February 17, 2000, p. 12B; "Try It. You'll Like It," *The Wall Street Journal*, September 27, 1999, p. 15; "How a Confection Became a Trendy Fashion Accessory," *The Wall Street Journal*, September 29, 1998, p. B1ff.; "Secrets of the New Brand Builders," *Fortune*, June 22, 1998, pp. 167–70; "The Internet Is Mr. Case's Neighborhood," *Fortune*, March 30, 1998, pp. 69–80; "The Cookie Queen," *The Wall Street Journal*, March 30, 1998, p. 6; "Brand Builders: Progresso Warriors," *Brandweek*,

June 23, 1997, pp. 20–22; "Read This. It's Free," *Brandweek*, June 16, 1997, p. 42.

32. William Cunnings and Mark Venkatesan, "Cognitive Dissonance and Consumer Behavior: A Review of the Evidence," *Journal of Marketing Research*, August 1976, pp. 303–8; Sarah Fisher Gardial et al., "Comparing Consumers' Recall of Prepurchase and Postpurchase Product Evaluation Experience," *Journal of Consumer Research*, March 1994, pp. 548–60.

33. Robert M. March, *The Honourable Customer: Marketing and Selling to the Japanese in the 1990s* (Melbourne, Vic.: Longman Professional, 1990); Robert Gottliebsen, "Japan's Stark Choices," *Business Review Weekly*, October 16, 1992.

Chapter 6

1. "Outsourcing Is More than Cost Cutting," *Fortune*, October 26, 1998, pp. 238C–V; *2000 Annual Report*, Deere & Company; *1999 Annual Report*, Deere & Company.

2. "Detroit to Suppliers: Quality or Else," *Fortune*, September 30, 1996, p. 134Cff.; G. M. Naidu, V. K. Prasad, and Arno Kleimenhagen, "Purchasing's Preparedness for ISO 9000 International Quality Standards," *International Journal of Purchasing & Materials Management*, Fall 1996, pp. 46–53; Wade Ferguson, "Impact of the ISO 9000 Series Standards on Industrial Marketing," *Industrial Marketing Management*, July 1996, pp. 305–10.

3. "The Push to Streamline Supply Chains," *Fortune*, March 3, 1997, pp. 108C–R; P. F. Johnson, Michiel R. Leenders, and Harold E. Fearon, "Evolving Roles and Responsibilities of Purchasing Organizations," *International Journal of Purchasing & Materials Management*, Winter 1998, pp. 2–11; "Purchasing's New Muscle," *Fortune*, February 20, 1995, pp. 75–83; Harry R. Page, "Revolution in Purchasing: Building Competitive Power Through Proactive Purchasing," *International Journal of Purchasing & Materials Management*, Fall 1996, p. 56; Joseph R. Carter and Ram Narasimhan, "Purchasing and Supply Management: Future Directions and Trends," *International Journal of Purchasing & Materials Management*, Fall 1996, pp. 2–12; Joseph R. Carter and Ram Narasimhan, "A Comparison of North American and European Future Purchasing Trends," *International Journal of Purchasing & Materials Management*, Spring 1996, pp. 12–22.

4. Jeffrey E. Lewin, "The Effects of Downsizing on Organizational Buying Behavior: An Empirical Investigation," *Journal of the Academy of Marketing Science*, Spring 2001, pp. 151–165; Larry C. Giunipero and Judith F. Vogt, "Empowering the Purchasing Function: Moving to Team Decisions," *International Journal of Purchasing & Materials Management*, Winter 1997, pp. 8–15; Jerome M. Katrichis, "Exploring Departmental Level Interaction Patterns in Organizational Purchasing Decisions," *Industrial Marketing Management*, March 1998, pp. 135–46; Robert D. McWilliams, Earl Naumann, and Stan Scott, "Determining Buying Center Size," *Industrial Marketing Management*, February 1992, pp. 43–50; Ajay Kohli, "Determinants of Influence in Organizational Buying: A Contingency Approach," *Journal of Marketing*, July 1989, pp. 50–65; Melvin R. Mattson, "How to Determine the Composition and Influence of a Buying Center," *Industrial Marketing Management*, August 1988, pp. 205–14.

5. W. E. I. Patton, "Use of Human Judgment Models in Industrial Buyers' Vendor Selection Decisions," *Industrial Marketing Management*, March 1996, pp. 135–49; Minette E. Drumwright, "Socially Responsible Organizational Buying: Environmental Concern As a Noneconomic Buying Criterion," *Journal of Marketing*, July 1994, pp. 1–19; Lisa M. Ellram, "A Structured Method for Applying Purchasing Cost Management Tools," *International Journal of Purchasing & Materials Management*, Winter 1996, pp. 11–19; Morgan P. Miles, Linda S. Munilla, and Gregory R. Russell, "Marketing and Environmental Registration/Certification: What Industrial Marketers Should Understand About ISO 14000," *Industrial Marketing Management*, July 1997, pp. 363–70; Morry Ghingold and Bruce Johnson, "Technical Knowledge As Value Added in Business Markets," *Industrial Marketing Management*, May 1997, pp. 271–80; Sime Curkovic and Robert Handfield, "Use of ISO 9000 and Baldrige Award Criteria in Supplier Quality Evaluation," *International Journal of Purchasing & Materials Management*, Spring 1996, pp. 2–11; M. Bixby Cooper, Cornelia Droge, and Patricia J. Daugherty, "How Buyers and Operations Personnel Evaluate Service," *Industrial Marketing Management* 20, no. 1 (1991), pp. 81–90.

6. Jeanette J. Arbuthnot, "Identifying Ethical Problems Confronting Small Retail Buyers During the Merchandise Buying Process," *Journal of Business Ethics*, May 1997, pp. 745–55; Gail K. McCracken and Thomas J. Callahan, "Is There Such a Thing As a Free Lunch?" *International Journal of Purchasing & Materials Management*, Winter 1996, pp. 44–50; Robert W. Cooper, Garry L. Frank, and Robert A. Kemp, "The Ethical Environment Facing the Profession of Purchasing and Materials Management," *International Journal of Purchasing & Materials Management*, Spring 1997, pp. 2–11; I. Fredrick Trawick, John E. Swan, Gail W. McGee, and David R. Rink, "Influence of Buyer Ethics and Salesperson Behavior on Intention to Choose a Supplier," *Journal of the Academy of Marketing Science*, Winter 1991, pp. 17–24; Michael J. Dorsch and Scott W. Kelley, "An Investigation into the Intentions of Purchasing Executives to Reciprocate Vendor Gifts," *Journal of the Academy of Marketing Science*, Fall 1994, pp. 315–327; J. A. Badenhorst, "Unethical Behaviour in Procurement: A Perspective on Causes and Solutions," *Journal of Business Ethics*, September 1994, pp. 739–46.

7. H. L. Brossard, "Information Sources Used by an Organization During a Complex Decision Process: An Exploratory Study," *Industrial Marketing Management*, January 1998, pp. 41–50; Michele D. Bunn, "Taxonomy of Buying Decision Approaches," *Journal of Marketing*, January 1993, pp. 38–56; Patricia M. Doney and Gary M. Armstrong, "Effects of Accountability on Symbolic Information Search and Information Analysis by Organizational Buyers," *Journal of the Academy of Marketing Science*, Winter 1996, pp. 57–65; Thomas G. Ponzurick, "International Buyers Perspective Toward Trade Shows and Other Promotional Methods," *Journal of Marketing Theory & Practice*, Winter 1996, pp. 9–19; Mark A. Farrell and Bill Schroder, "Influence Strategies in Organizational Buying Decisions," *Industrial Marketing Management*, July 1996, pp. 293–303; R. Venkatesh, Ajay K. Kohli, and Gerald Zaltman, "Influence Strategies in Buying Centers," *Journal of Marketing*, October 1995, pp. 71–82; Richard G. Newman, "Monitoring

Price Increases With Economic Data: A Practical Approach," *International Journal of Purchasing & Materials Management,* Fall 1997, pp. 35–40; Barbara Kline and Janet Wagner, "Information Sources and Retailer Buyer Decision-Making: The Effect of Product-Specific Buying Experience," *Journal of Retailing,* Spring 1994, p. 75; Ellen Day and Hiram C. Barksdale, Jr., "How Firms Select Professional Services," *Industrial Marketing Management,* May 1992, pp. 85–92; H. Michael Hayes and Steven W. Hartley, "How Buyers View Industrial Salespeople," *Industrial Marketing Management* 18, no. 2 (1989), pp. 73–80; Peter Banting et al., "Similarities in Industrial Procurement Across Four Countries," *Industrial Marketing Management,* May 1985, pp. 133–44; Edward F. Fern and James R. Brown, "The Industrial/Consumer Marketing Dichotomy: A Case of Insufficient Justification," *Journal of Marketing,* Spring 1984, pp. 68–77; Rowland T. Moriarty, Jr. and Robert E. Spekman, "An Empirical Investigation of the Information Sources Used During the Industrial Buying Process," *Journal of Marketing Research,* May 1984, pp. 137–47.

8. "Strong Brands Lure Web Buyers," *Investor's Business Daily,* May 30, 2001, p. A5; "With Promise of Big Savings, Net Bill Paying Could Soon Win Fans among U.S. Businesses," *Investor's Business Daily,* February 26, 2001, p. A7; "How Baxter, PNC, Pratt & Whitney Make the Internet Work for Them," *Investor's Business Daily,* February 12, 2001, p. A1; "Look, Ma, No Humans," *Business Week E.Biz,* November 20, 2000, p. EB132; "Hewlett-Packard's Slick Procurement System," *Ecompany,* November 2000, pp. 236–38; "Schools Are Buying Online; The Savings Could Add Up," *Investor's Business Daily,* July 7, 2000, p. A4; "E-Purchasing Saves Businesses Billions," *USA Today,* February 7, 2000, p. 1Bff.; "Supply Side," *The Wall Street Journal,* November 15, 1999, p. R22; "Purchasing in Packs," *Business Week E.Biz,* November 1, 1999, pp. EB32–EB38; "From Regineering to E-Engineering," *Business Week E.Biz,* March 22, 1999, pp. EB14–EB18; "Setting Standards for Corporate Purchasing on the Internet," *Fortune,* September 8, 1997, pp. 156–58; "Invoice? What's an Invoice?" *Business Week,* June 10, 1996, pp. 110–12; "On-Line Service Offers Fast Lane to Small Businesses," *The Wall Street Journal,* October 11, 1994, p. B2; Earl D. Honeycutt, Theresa B. Flaherty, and Ken Benassi, "Marketing Industrial Products on the Internet," *Industrial Marketing Management,* January 1998, pp. 63–72; A. C. Samli, James R. Wills, and Paul Herbig, "The Information Superhighway Goes International: Implications for Industrial Sales Transactions," *Industrial Marketing Management,* January 1997, pp. 51–58; Barbara C. Perdue, "The Size and Composition of the Buying Firm's Negotiation Team in Rebuys of Component Parts," *Journal of the Academy of Marketing Science,* Spring 1989, pp. 121–28.

9. "The New Golden Rule of Business," *Fortune,* February 21, 1994, pp. 60–64; Janet L. Hartley and Thomas Y. Choi, "Supplier Development: Customers As a Catalyst of Process Change," *Business Horizons,* July–August 1996, pp. 37–44; Theodore P. Stank, Margaret A. Emmelhainz, and Patricia J. Daugherty, "The Impact of Information on Supplier Performance," *Journal of Marketing Theory & Practice,* Fall 1996, pp. 94–105.

10. "The Push to Streamline Supply Chains," *Fortune,* March 3, 1997, pp. 108C-R; "Push from Above," *The Wall Street Journal,* May 23, 1996, p. R24; "The New Golden Rule of Business," *Fortune,* February 21, 1994, pp. 60–64.

11. Much of the discussion in this section is based on research reported in Joseph P. Cannon and William D. Perreault, Jr., "Buyer-Seller Relationships in Business Markets," *Journal of Marketing Research,* November 1999; Joseph P. Cannon, "Buyer-Supplier Relationships and Customer Firm Costs," *Journal of Marketing,* January 2001, pp. 29–44; Alexandra J. Campbell, "What Affects Expectations of Mutuality in Business Relationships?" *Journal of Marketing Theory & Practice,* Fall 1997, pp. 1–11; James C. Anderson, Hakan Hakansson, and Jan Johanson, "Dyadic Business Relationships Within a Business Network Context," *Journal of Marketing,* October 1994, pp. 1–15; Patricia M. Doney and Joseph P. Cannon, "An Examination of the Nature of Trust in Buyer-Seller Relationships," *Journal of Marketing,* April 1997, pp. 35–51; James M. Comer and B. J. Zirger, "Building a Supplier-Customer Relationship Using Joint New Product Development," *Industrial Marketing Management,* March 1997, pp. 203–11; Arun Sharma and Jagdish N. Sheth, "Supplier Relationships: Emerging Issues and Challenges," *Industrial Marketing Management,* March 1997, pp. 91–100; William W. Keep, Stanley C. Hollander, and Roger Dickinson, "Forces Impinging on Long-Term Business-to-Business Relationships in the United States: An Historical Perspective," *Journal of Marketing,* April 1998, pp. 31–45.

12. "Purchasing's New Muscle," *Fortune,* February 20, 1995, pp. 75–83; Rosemary P. Ramsey and Ravipreet S. Sohi, "Listening to Your Customers: The Impact of Perceived Salesperson Listening Behavior on Relationship Outcomes," *Journal of the Academy of Marketing Science,* Spring 1997, pp. 127–37.

13. For more on outsourcing, see "Why Some Sony Gear Is Made in Japan—by Another Company," *The Wall Street Journal,* June 14, 2001, p. A1ff.; "Inside Out-Sourcing," *Fortune*/CNET Technology Review, Summer 2001, pp. 85–92; "Taiwan Goes after the World's Chip Business," *Fortune,* May 14, 2001, pp. 216T–HH; "Outsourcing as a Strategic Option: It's about More than Saving Money," *Investor's Business Daily,* May 7, 2001, p. A1; "The Tech Slump's Next Victim?" *Business Week,* March 5, 2001, pp. 104–105; "Solectron, All Along the Chain Except the Ends," *Fortune,* October 30, 2000, pp. T208T–Z; "You Order It, They'll Make It," *Business Week,* May 29, 2000, pp. 218D–J; "The Low-Tech King of High Tech," *Fortune,* October 25, 1999, pp. 339–43; "New Saturn Is Heavy on Outsourcing," *USA Today,* July 5, 1996, p. 1Bff. For more on supplier speeds and costs, see "When Cool Heads Prevail," *Business Week,* June 11, 2001, p. 114; "Should Suppliers Be Partners?" *Business Week,* June 4, 2001, pp. 30B–D; "Machete Time," *Business Week,* April 9, 2001, pp. 42–43; "Can Chrysler Get Blood from a Supplier?" *Business Week,* December 25, 2000, p. 56; "Chrysler's Checks to Suppliers, Shoppers to Shrink," *The Wall Street Journal,* December 8, 2000, p. B4; "Firms Boost Suppliers' Speeds, Win Investors' Hearts," *The Wall Street Journal,* April 6, 1998, p. A20; "Stores' Demands Squeeze Apparel Companies," *The Wall Street Journal,* July 15, 1997, p. B1ff.; "Hardball Is Still GM's Game," *Business Week,* August 8, 1994, p. 26; "Big Customers' Late Bills Choke Small Suppliers," *The Wall Street Journal,* June 22, 1994, p. B1. For more on JIT, see "As Christmas Approaches, Parts Shortages Plague Electronic Makers," *The Wall Street Journal,* October 10, 2000, p. B1ff.; "Parts Shortages Hamper Electronics Makers," *The Wall*

Street Journal, July 7, 2000, p. B5. For some excellent examples, see "The Web at Work: Clorox Co." *The Wall Street Journal,* October 9, 2000, p. B21; "Kimberly-Clark Keeps Costco in Diapers, Absorbing Costs Itself," *The Wall Street Journal,* September 7, 2000, p. A1ff.; "At Ford, E-Commerce Is Job 1," *Business Week,* February 28, 2000, pp. 74–78; "Where 'Build to Order' Works Best," *Fortune,* April 26, 1999, pp. 160C-V. For more on relationship-specific adaptations, see "Why Toyota Wins Such High Marks on Quality Surveys," *The Wall Street Journal,* March 15, 2001, p. A1ff. See also "Japanese Auto Makers Help U.S. Suppliers Become More Efficient," *The Wall Street Journal,* September 9, 1991, p. A1ff.; David L. Blenkhorn and A. Hamid Noori, "What It Takes to Supply Japanese OEMs," *Industrial Marketing Management,* February, 1990, pp. 21–30. See also John Ramsay, "The Case Against Purchasing Partnerships," *International Journal of Purchasing & Materials Management,* Fall 1996, pp. 13–19; George S. Day, "Managing Market Relationships," *Journal of the Academy of Marketing Science,* Winter 2000, pp. 24–31; John V. Petrof, "Relationship Marketing—the Emperor in Used Clothes," *Business Horizons,* March–April 1998, pp. 79–82; Shankar Ganesan, "Determinants of Long-Term Orientation in Buyer-Seller Relationships," *Journal of Marketing,* April 1994, pp. 1–19; Brian K. H. Low, "Long-Term Relationship in Industrial Marketing: Reality or Rhetoric?" *Industrial Marketing Management,* January 1996, pp. 23–35; Allan J. Magrath and Kenneth G. Hardy, "Building Customer Partnerships," *Business Horizons,* January–February 1994, pp. 24–28; Paul Dion, Debbie Easterling, and Shirley Jo Miller, "What is Really Necessary in Successful Buyer/Seller Relationships?" *Industrial Marketing Management,* January 1995, pp. 1–10.

14. For other examples of big/small partnerships, see "A Fruitful Relationship," *Business Week E.Biz,* November 20, 2000, pp. EB94–EB96; "Automating an Automaker," *Inc. Tech 2000,* No. 4, p. 86. See also "Polaroid Corp. Is Selling Its Technique for Limiting Supplier Price Increases," *The Wall Street Journal,* February 13, 1985, p. 36; "Making Honda Parts, Ohio Company Finds, Can Be Road to Ruin," *The Wall Street Journal,* October 5, 1990, p. A1ff.; "Toshiba Official Finds Giving Work to Firms in U.S. Can Be Tricky," *The Wall Street Journal,* March 20, 1987, p. 1ff.

15. "A Blaze in Albuquerque Sets Off Major Crisis for Cell-Phone Giants," *The Wall Street Journal,* January 29, 2001, p. A1ff.; "Toyota's Fast Rebound after Fire at Supplier Shows Why It Is Tough," *The Wall Street Journal,* May 8, 1997, p. A1ff.; Larry R. Smeltzer and Sue P. Siferd, "Proactive Supply Management: The Management of Risk," *International Journal of Purchasing & Materials Management,* Winter 1998, pp. 38–45; Paul D. Larson and Jack D. Kulchitsky, "Single Sourcing and Supplier Certification: Performance and Relationship Implications," *Industrial Marketing Management,* January 1998, pp. 73–81; Rasmus F. Olsen and Lisa M. Ellram, "A Portfolio Approach to Supplier Relationships," *Industrial Marketing Management,* March 1997, pp. 101–13; Cathy Owens Swift, "Preferences for Single Sourcing and Supplier Selection," *Journal of Business Research,* February 1995, pp. 105–12.

16. "You Buy My Widgets, I'll Buy Your Debt," *Business Week,* August 1, 1988, p. 85; Robert E. Weigand, "The Problems of Managing Reciprocity," *California Management Review,* Fall 1973, pp. 40–48.

17. "Who Will Profit from the Internet Agora?" *Business Week E.Biz,* June 5, 2000, pp. EB56–EB74; Rajdeep Grewal, "An Investigation into the Antecedents of Organizational Participation in Business-to-Business Electronic Markets," *Journal of Marketing,* July 2001, pp. 17–34; for discussion of steel industry online, see "Is the Internet Stronger than Steel?" *Fortune,* May 15, 2000, pp. 148–76; "Let's Build an Online Supply Network," *The Wall Street Journal,* April 17, 2000, p. B1ff.; "Industries, from Steel to Chemicals, Say One Internet Site May Not Meet Needs," *The Wall Street Journal,* February 28, 2000, p. A16ff.; "Web Sites Made of Steel," *The Wall Street Journal,* September 16, 1999, p. B1ff. See also "The Missing Link," *Ecompany,* May 2001, pp. 82–88; "Manufacturers Turning to B2B," *Investor's Business Daily,* March 20, 2001, p. A6; "Can Carmakers Corral the Web?" *Investor's Business Daily,* February 21, 2001, p. A6; "Finally, the Net Gets Real," *Newsweek,* December 25, 2000, pp. 66–67; "Amid Downturn, B2B Eyes B2G," *Investor's Business Daily,* December 19, 2000, p. A6; "Let's Keep This Exchange to Ourselves," *Business Week,* December 4, 2000, p. 48; "B2B Is Long on Promise, but Still Short on Results," *Investor's Business Daily,* October 12, 2000, p. A6; "How Ariba Got Airborne," *Business Week E.Biz,* September 18, 2000, pp. EB127–EB130; "IBM-Led Trio Begins Campaign Touting Its E-Commerce Services," *The Wall Street Journal,* August 17, 2000, p. B18; "Old MacDonald Has a Web Site," *Business Week E.Biz,* May 15, 2000, pp. EB82–EB88; "Despite the Hype, B2B Marketplaces Struggle," *USA Today,* May 10, 2000, p. 1Bff.; "E-I-E-I-E-Farming," *Business Week,* May 1, 2000, p. 202; "Farm B2Bs Find Fertile Soil on Net," *USA Today,* April 20, 2000, p. 1Bff.; "Where the Money Is," *The Wall Street Journal,* April 17, 2000, p. R30ff.; "Detroit Goes Digital," *Fortune,* April 17, 2000, pp. 170–74; "In the New Economy, Who Are the Hunters and Who the Hunted?" *The Wall Street Journal,* April 12, 2000, p. A1ff.; "Online Exchanges Also Suffer from a Glut of Players," *The Wall Street Journal,* April 7, 2000, p. B1ff.; "The B2B Tool That Really Is Changing the World," *Fortune,* March 20, 2000, pp. 132–45; "E-Malls for Business," *Business Week,* March 13, 2000, pp. 32–34; "Big Three Car Makers Plan Net Exchange," *The Wall Street Journal,* February 28, 2000, p. A3ff.; "Old-Line Companies Grab a Piece of the 'B2B' Pie," *The Wall Street Journal,* February 28, 2000, p. B1ff.; "A Web Auctioneer Roils the Rust Belt," *The Wall Street Journal,* January 5, 2000, p. B1ff.; "How GM, Ford Think Web Can Make Splash on the Factory Floor," *The Wall Street Journal,* December 3, 1999, p. A1ff.; "Internet Changes the Face of Supply and Demand," *The Wall Street Journal,* October 18, 1999, p. A43Q; "Bidding for E-Nuts and E-Bolts on the Net," *The Wall Street Journal,* March 12, 1999, p. B1ff. See also Li-Pheng Khoo, Shu B. Tor, and Stephen S. G. Lee, "The Potential of Intelligent Software Agents in the World Wide Web in Automating Part Procurement," *International Journal of Purchasing & Materials Management,* Winter 1998, pp. 46–52; Rodney L. Stump and Ven Sriram, "Employing Information Technology in Purchasing: Buyer-Supplier Relationships and Size of the Supplier Base," *Industrial Marketing Management,* March 1997, pp. 127–36; Richard E. Plank, et al., "The Impact of Computer Usage by Purchasing," *Industrial Marketing Management,* August 1992, pp. 243–48; Joel Herche, " Innovations in Procurement Management," *Journal of the Academy of Marketing Science,* Summer 2000, pp. 450–2.

18. Available from World Wide Web: <http://www.national.com>. See also "Web Masters," *Sales & Marketing Management*, 2000 and 2001.

19. Available from World Wide Web: <http://www.getradeweb.com> and <http://www.gegxs.com>. "Sales Are Clicking on Manufacturing's Internet Mart," *Fortune*, July 7, 1997, pp. 136C–T.

20. "Heroes of U.S. Manufacturing," *Fortune*, March 19, 2001, pp. 178C–HH; "Better Machine Tools Give Manufacturers Newfound Resilience," *The Wall Street Journal*, February 15, 2001, p. A1ff.; "The Big Myth about U.S. Manufacturing," *Fortune*, October 2, 2000, pp. 244BB–PP. See also U.S. Bureau of the Census, *Statistical Abstract of the United States 2000* (Washington, DC: U.S. Government Printing Office, 2000); U.S. Bureau of the Census, *County Business Patterns 1998, United States* (Washington, DC: U.S. Government Printing Office, 2000); U.S. Bureau of the Census, *1997 Census of Manufacturers, Subject Series, General Summary* (Washington, DC: U.S. Government Printing Office, 2001).

21. Available from World Wide Web: <http://www.naics.com>. See also "Classified Information," *American Demographics*, July 1999, p. 16; "SIC: The System Explained," *Sales and Marketing Management*, April 22, 1985, pp. 52–113; "Enhancement of SIC System Being Developed," *Marketing News Collegiate Edition*, May 1988, p. 4.

22. U.S. Bureau of the Census, *Statistical Abstract of the United States 2000* (Washington, DC: U.S. Government Printing Office, 2000); U.S. Bureau of the Census, *County Business Patterns 1998, United States* (Washington, DC: U.S. Government Printing Office, 2000). For more on Canon, see "Perfecting the Pitch," *The Wall Street Journal*, May 23, 1996, p. R26ff.; *1996 Annual Report*, Canon; "Can Anyone Duplicate Canon's Personal Copiers' Success?" *Marketing and Media Decisions*, Special Issue, Spring 1985, pp. 97–101.

23. *2000 Annual Report*, Safeway; *2000 Annual Report*, Food Lion; *2000 Annual Report*, Winn-Dixie; *2000 Annual Report*, A&P; Daulatram B. Lund, "Retail Scanner Checkout System: How Buying Committees Functioned," *Industrial Marketing Management* 18, no. 3 (1989), pp. 179–86; Janet Wagner, Richard Ettenson, and Jean Parrish, "Vendor Selection Among Retail Buyers: An Analysis by Merchandise Division," *Journal of Retailing*, Spring 1989, pp. 58–79.

24. "Create Open-to-Buy Plans the Easy Way," *Retail Control*, December 1984, pp. 21–31.

25. Based on U.S. Census data and "How Not to Buy 300,000 Personal Computers," *Business Week*, March 8, 1993, p. 36; Kevin W. Westbrook, "Risk Coordinative Maneuvers During Buyer-Seller Negotiations," *Industrial Marketing Management*, July 1996, pp. 283–92; Sheryl B. Ball and Catherine C. Eckel, "Buying Status: Experimental Evidence on Status in Negotiation," *Psychology & Marketing*, July 1996, pp. 381–405; Robert Gulbro and Paul Herbig, "Negotiating Successfully in Cross-Cultural Situations," *Industrial Marketing Management*, May 1996, pp. 235–41; William C. Perkins, James C. Hershauer, Abbas Foroughi, and Michael M. Delaney, "Can a Negotiation Support System Help a Purchasing Manager?" *International Journal of Purchasing & Materials Management*, Spring 1996, pp. 37–45; Warren H. Suss, "How to Sell to Uncle Sam," *Harvard Business Review*, November–December, 1984, pp. 136–44.

26. For a detailed discussion of business ethics in a number of countries, see *Journal of Business Ethics*, (Special Issue) October 1997. See also "How Can a U.S. Company Go International, Avoid the Economic Disaster of a Thai Baht . . . and Pay No Bribes?" *USA Today*, November 17, 1997, p. 5B; Larry R. Smeltzer and Marianne M. Jennings, "Why an International Code of Business Ethics Would Be Good for Business," *Journal of Business Ethics*, January 1998, pp. 57–66; James J. Kellaris, Robert F. Dahlstrom, and Brett A. Boyle, "Contextual Bias in Ethical Judgment of Marketing Practices," *Psychology & Marketing*, October 1996, pp. 677–94; Massoud M. Saghafi, Fanis Varvoglis, and Tomas Vega, "Why U.S. Firms Don't Buy from Latin American Companies," *Industrial Marketing Management* 20, no. 3 (1991), pp. 207–14; Peter Banting, Jozsef Beracs, and Andrew Gross, "The Industrial Buying Process in Capitalist and Socialist Countries," *Industrial Marketing Management* 20, no. 2 (1991), pp. 105–14.

Chapter 7

1. Available from World Wide Web: <http://www.lenscrafters.com>; "LensCrafters Hits One Billion in Sales," *Business Wire*, February 3, 1998; "LensCrafters Polishes Image with Style," *Chain Store Age Executive*, October 1996, p. 144ff.; "'SuperOpticals' Edge out the Corner Optician," *Adweek's Marketing Week*, October 1, 1990, p. 36; "LensCrafters Takes the High Road," *Adweek's Marketing Week*, April 30, 1990, pp. 26–27.

2. "How an Intranet Opened Up the Door to Profits," *Business Week E. Biz*, July 26, 1999, pp. EB32–EB38; "Here Comes the Intranet," *Business Week*, February 26, 1996, pp. 76–84.

3. "Virtual Management," *Business Week*, September 21, 1998, pp. 80–82; John T. Mentzer and Nimish Gandhi, "Expert Systems in Marketing: Guidelines for Development," *Journal of the Academy of Marketing Science*, Winter, 1992, pp. 73–80; William D. Perreault, Jr., "The Shifting Paradigm in Marketing Research," *Journal of the Academy of Marketing Science*, Fall 1992, pp. 367–76; J. M. McCann, W. G. Lahti, and J. Hill, "The Brand Manager's Assistant: A Knowledge-Based System Approach to Brand Management," *International Journal of Research in Marketing*, April 1991, pp. 51–74.

4. Stanley F. Slater, "Intelligence Generation and Superior Customer Value," *Journal of the Academy of Marketing Science*, Winter 2000, pp. 120–128; Philip B. Evans and Thomas S. Wurster, "Strategy and the New Economics of Information," *Harvard Business Review*, September–October 1997, pp. 70–82; Deborah Utter, "Information-Driven Marketing Decisions: Development of Strategic Information Systems," *Journal of the Academy of Marketing Science*, Spring 1998, pp. 157–58; James M. Sinkula, "Market Information Processing and Organizational Learning," *Journal of Marketing*, January 1994, pp. 35–45; Lawrence B. Chonko, John F. Tanner, Jr., and Ellen Reid Smith, "The Sales Force's Role in International Marketing Research and Marketing Information Systems," *Journal of Personal Selling and Sales Management*, Winter, 1991, pp. 69–80; James C. Bondra and Tim R. V. Davis, "Marketing's Role in Cross-Functional Information Management," *Industrial Marketing Management*, May 1996, pp. 187–95; Alfred C. Holden, "How to Locate and Communicate with Overseas Customers," *Industrial Marketing Management* 20, no. 3 (1991), pp. 161–68.

5. For more on CRM, see Chapter 3, footnote #22. "Marketers Hone Targeting," *Advertising Age*, June 18, 2001, p. T16; "Data Miners Reel after Wal-Mart Snub," *Brandweek*, May 21, 2001, p. 9; "Closer Than Ever," *Business Week Small Biz*, May 21, 2001, pp. 14–15; "CRM: Shooting Holes in the Hype," *Advertising Age*, April 16, 2001, p. 1ff.; "Firms See Value of CRM Software, but Adoption Can Be Costly," *Investor's Business Daily*, April 4, 2001, p. A7; "A Singular Sensation," *Brandweek*, February 28, 2001, pp. 32–38; "Product by Design," *American Demographics*, February 2001, pp. 38–41; "CRM Firms Adjust to Downturn," *Investor's Business Daily*, December 28, 2000, p. A4; "The New Software Whizzes," *Business Week E.Biz*, December 11, 2000, pp. EB30–EB42; "Mystery Shoppers," *American Demographics*, December 2000, pp. 41–43; "Mountains to Mine," *American Demographics*, August 2000, pp. 40–44; "With All Companies Lured to Web, Enterprise Software Is a Must-Have," *Investor's Business Daily*, April 17, 2000, p. A10; "Mining Everyone's Business," *Brandweek*, February 28, 2000, pp. 32–56; "An Eagle Eye on Customers," *Business Week*, February 21, 2000, pp. 66–76; "The Information Gold Mine," *Business Week E.Biz*, July 26, 1999, pp. EB16–EB30; "Data Mining Digs In," *American Demographics*, July 1999, pp. 38–45; "Looking for Patterns," *The Wall Street Journal*, June 21, 1999, p. R16ff.; "Know Your Customer," *The Wall Street Journal*, June 21, 1999, p. R18. See also Siva K. Balasubramanian, "The New Marketing Research Systems—How to Use Strategic Database Information for Better Marketing Decisions," *Journal of the Academy of Marketing Science*, Spring 1996, pp. 179–81; John I. Hagel and Jeffrey F. Rayport, "The Coming Battle for Customer Information," *Harvard Business Review*, January–February 1997, pp. 53–65; "What's the Best Source of Market Research?" *Inc.*, June 1992, p. 108; James M. Sinkula, "Perceived Characteristics, Organizational Factors, and the Utilization of External Market Research Suppliers," *Journal of Business Research*, August, 1990, pp. 1–18. For more on privacy, see Chapter 13, footnote #10 and Chapter 18, footnote #13.

6. For a discussion of ethical issues in marketing research, see "How 'Tactical Research' Muddied Diaper Debate: a Case," *The Wall Street Journal*, May 17, 1994, p. B1ff.; John R. Sparks and Shelby D. Hunt, "Marketing Researcher Ethical Sensitivity: Conceptualization, Measurement, and Exploratory Investigation," *Journal of Marketing*, April 1998, pp. 92–109; Naresh K. Malhotra and Gina L. Miller, "An Integrated Model for Ethical Decisions in Marketing Research," *Journal of Business Ethics*, February 1998, pp. 263–80; Stephen B. Castleberry, Warren French and Barbara A. Carlin, "The Ethical Framework of Advertising and Marketing Research Practitioners: A Moral Development Perspective," *Journal of Advertising*, June 1993, pp. 39–46; Ishmael P. Akaah, "Attitudes of Marketing Professionals toward Ethics in Marketing Research: A Cross-National Comparison," *Journal of Business Ethics*, January, 1990, pp. 45–54.

7. Linda I. Nowak, Paul D. Boughton, and Arun J. A. Pereira, "Relationships Between Businesses and Marketing Research Firms," *Industrial Marketing Management*, November 1997, pp. 487–95; Peter M. Chisnall, "The Effective Use of Market Research: A Guide for Management to Grow the Business," *International Journal of Market Research*, Summer 2000, Vol. 42, 3, p. 359; Seymour Sudman and Edward Blair, *Marketing Research: A Problem Solving Approach* (Burr Ridge, IL: Irwin/McGraw-Hill, 1998). See also Christine Moorman, Rohit Deshpande, and Gerald Zaltman, "Factors Affecting Trust in Market Research Relationships," *Journal of Marketing*, January 1993, pp. 81–101.

8. "Special Report: 2001 David Ogilvy Research Awards," *American Demographics*, March 2001, pp. S1–21; "Special Report: 2000 David Ogilvy Research Awards," *American Demographics*, March 2000, pp. S1–22; "What Consumer Research Won't Tell You," *Brandweek*, November 1, 1999, pp. 40–48; "Intelligence Agents," *American Demographics*, March 1999, pp. 52–60; "Grandma Got Run Over by Bad Research," *Inc.*, January 1998, p. 27.

9. Available from World Wide Web: <http://www.windweaver.com/searchtools> and <http://www.windweaver.com/searchengines>; "What's Ahead for Search Engines," *The Wall Street Journal*, June 25, 2001, p. R17; "Avoid Quagmires with Simple Web Search Tactics," *Investor's Business Daily*, April 4, 2001, p. A9; "Google Is Smart, Fast, Honest and May Be Best Sleuth on the Web," *The Wall Street Journal*, March 1, 2001, p. B1; "Browser Beware," *Inc. Tech 2001*, No. 2, pp. 77–81; "The Internet: The Best Way to Search," *The Wall Street Journal Reports*, November 27, 2000, p. R26ff.; "Vroom Vroom," *Adweek*, November 27, 2000, p. IQ10; "Shop Bots Can Save You Money," *Ecompany*, October 2000, pp. 221–22; "In Search of Google," *Time*, August 21, 2000, pp. 66–67; "Successful Net Search Starts with Need," *USA Today*, January 24, 2000, p. 3D; "The Internet: The Best Way to Search Online," *The Wall Street Journal Reports*, December 6, 1999, p. R25; Shikhar Ghosh, "Making Business Sense of the Internet," *Harvard Business Review*, March–April 1998, pp. 126–35.

10. An excellent review of commercially available secondary data may be found in William R. Dillon, Thomas J. Madden, and Neil H. Firtle, *Marketing Research in a Marketing Environment*, 3rd ed. (Burr Ridge, IL: Irwin/McGraw-Hill, 1993). For more on Census data, see "The National Headcount," *American Demographics*, March 2001, p. S12; "Counting on the Census," *The Wall Street Journal*, February 14, 2001, p. B1ff.; "Census 2000: Math, Not Politics, Please," *Business Week*, September 22, 1997, p. 42; "Two Words and a Number," *American Demographics*, February 1997, pp. 10–15; "Preparing for 2000, Census Bureau Tests Carrots vs. Sticks," *The Wall Street Journal*, May 2, 1996, p. B1ff.; Jackson Morton, "Census on the Internet," *American Demographics*, March 1995, p. 52. See also "Library Sites Can Be Useful when Doing Online Research," *Investor's Business Daily*, April 5, 2001, p. A13; "Hey, It's Not Prying; It's Competitive Intelligence," *Raleigh News & Observer*, August 6, 2000, p. 14E.

11. Available from World Wide Web: <http://www.burke.com/ice/online>; "Heinz Picks Purple as New EZ Squirt Color," *Brandweek*, June 25, 2001, p. 7; "Web Enhances Market Research," *Advertising Age*, June 18, 2001, p. T18; "Marketers Call on Kids to Help Design Web Sites," *USA Today*, June 5, 2001, p. 1Bff.; "Speaking Up: One Focus Group Revealed," *The Wall Street Journal*, November 27, 2000, p. B21; "Double Play," *Business Week E.Biz*, October 23, 2000, pp. EB42–EB46; "More Marketers

Bypass Focus Groups," *USA Today*, August 23, 1999, p. 6B. See also William J. McDonald, "Focus Group Research Dynamics and Reporting: An Examination of Research Objectives and Moderator Influences," *Journal of the Academy of Marketing Science*, Spring 1993, pp. 161; Thomas Kiely, "Wired Focus Groups," *Harvard Business Review*, January–February 1998, pp. 12–16.

12. "Japan's High-School Girls Excel in Art of Setting Trends," *The Wall Street Journal*, April 24, 1998, p. B1ff.

13. "Selling Sibelius Isn't Easy," *American Demographics*, The 1994 Directory, pp. 24–25; "Symphony Strikes a Note for Research as It Prepares to Launch a New Season," *Marketing News*, August 29, 1988, p. 12.

14. Available from World Wide Web: <http://www.sawtooth.com/pages/glossary>; "Friendly Spies on the Net," *Business Week E.Biz*, July 9, 2001, pp. EB26–EB28; "You've Got Surveys," *American Demographics*, November 2000, pp. 42–45; "A Matter of Opinion," *The Wall Street Journal Reports*, October 23, 2000, p. R46; "Pollster Aims at One-Stop Marketing Shop," *The Wall Street Journal*, September 7, 2000, p. B6ff; "Online Testing Rated," *Advertising Age*, May 8, 2000, p. 64; "Western Pair's Madeforchina.com Clicks into Consumer Mind There," *The Wall Street Journal*, May 5, 2000, p. B6; "The Surfer in the Family," *American Demographics*, April 2000, pp. 34–36; "Market Research for the Internet Has Its Drawbacks," *The Wall Street Journal*, March 2, 2000, p. B4; "Safe at Any Speed?" *Advertising Age*, January 24, 2000, p. 1ff.; "High Level of Comfort Leads to Truthful Research Worth a Mint," *USA Today*, May 17, 1999, p. 1Aff.; "Surprise! A Home Builder (Finally) Surveys Buyers," *The Wall Street Journal*, February 11, 1998, p. B1ff.; Christine M. Fox, K. L. Robinson, and Debra Boardley, "Cost-Effectiveness of Follow-Up Strategies in Improving the Response Rate of Mail Surveys," *Industrial Marketing Management*, March 1998, pp. 127–33; Kathy E. Green, "Sociodemographic Factors and Mail Survey Response," *Psychology & Marketing*, March 1996, pp. 171–84; Terry L. Childers and Steven J. Skinner, "Toward a Conceptualization of Mail Survey Response Behavior," *Psychology & Marketing*, March 1996, pp. 185–209; Frederick Wiseman and Maryann Billington, "Comment on a Standard Definition of Response Rates," *Journal of Marketing Research*, August 1984, pp. 336–38.

15. Available from World Wide Web: <http://www.whirlpool.com> and <http://acsi.asqc.org>; "Firms Hope to Clean Up Taking Housework High-Tech," *The Wall Street Journal*, March 16, 2001, p. B4; "As I Was Saying to My Refrigerator . . . ," *Business Week E.Biz*, September 18, 2000, pp. EB40–EB41; "Now Are You Satisfied?" *Fortune*, February 16, 1998, pp.161–64; "Your Customers Are Telling the Truth," *Fortune*, February 16, 1998, pp. 164–66; "Product Pampering," *Brandweek*, June 16, 1997, pp. 29–40; Deborah Duarte and Nancy Snyder, "From Experience: Facilitating Global Organizational Learning in Product Development at Whirlpool Corporation," *Journal of Product Innovation Management*, January 1997, pp. 48–55.

16. "P&G Checks Out Real Life," *The Wall Street Journal*, May 17, 2001, p. B1ff.; "Research on a Shoestring," *American Demographics*, April 2001, pp. 38–39; "Consumers in the Mist," *Business Week*, February 26, 2001, pp. 92–94; "Under the Lens," *American Demographics*, September 2000, pp. 42–45; "O&M Turns Reality TV into Research Tool," *Advertising Age*, July 10, 2000, p. 6; "How Do You Like Your Beef?" *American Demographics*, January 2000, pp. 35–37; "Attention Shoppers: This Man Is Watching You," *Fortune*, July 19, 1999, pp. 131–34; "What Shoppers Want," *Inc.*, July 1999, pp. 72–82; "New Ways to Get into Our Heads," *USA Today*, March 2, 1999, p. 1Bff.; "The New Market Research," *Inc.*, July 1998, pp. 87–94. See also Stephen J. Grove and Raymond P. Fisk, "Observational Data Collection Methods for Services Marketing: An Overview," *Journal of the Academy of Marketing Science*, Summer 1992, pp. 217–24; "Coupon Clippers, Save Your Scissors," *Business Week*, June 20, 1994, pp. 164–66; Magid M. Abraham and Leonard M. Lodish, "An Implemented System for Improving Promotion Productivity Using Store Scanner Data," *Marketing Science*, Summer 1993, pp. 248–69; "The Nitty-Gritty of ECR Systems: How One Company Makes It Pay," *Advertising Age*, May 2, 1994, pp. S1ff.; Peter J. Danaher and Terence W. Beed, "A Coincidental Survey of People Meter Panelists: Comparing What People Say with What They Do," *Journal of Advertising Research*, January/February 1993, p. 86.

17. "Will Your Web Business Work? Take It for a Test Drive," *Ecompany*, May 2001, pp. 101–104; "Ads Awaken to Fathers' New Role in Family Life," *Advertising Age*, January 10, 1994, p. S8; "AT&T's Secret MultiMedia Trials Offer Clues to Capturing Interactive Audiences," *The Wall Street Journal*, July 28, 1993, p. B1ff.; "Experimenting in the U.K.: Phone, Cable Deals Let U.S. Test Future," *USA Today*, June 28, 1993, p. 1Bff. See also Raymond R. Burke, "Virtual Shopping: Breakthrough in Marketing Research," *Harvard Business Review*, March–April 1996, pp. 120–31; Glen L. Urban, Bruce D. Weinberg, and John R. Hauser, "Premarket Forecasting of Really-New Products," *Journal of Marketing*, January 1996, pp. 47–60; "Bar Wars: Hershey Bites Mars," *Fortune*, July 8, 1985, pp. 52–57.

18. "Nielsen Plans New Pricing as Part of Bid to Double People Meters," *The Wall Street Journal*, June 29, 2001, p. B6; "Confessions of a Nielsen Household," *American Demographics*, May 2001; "Trying to Clean Up Sweeps," *American Demographics*, May 2001, pp. 42–49; "The Metrics System," *Brandweek*, November 13, 2000, pp. 106–10; "Special Report: Top 25 Global Research Organizations," *Advertising Age*, August 24, 2000; "We're Being Watched," *American Demographics*, October 1998, pp. 52–58; "Special Report: 100 Leading Research Companies," *Advertising Age*, May 19, 1997; "Rivals Duel Bitterly for Job of Supplying Market Information," *The Wall Street Journal*, November 15, 1993, p. A1ff.

19. For more detail on data analysis techniques, see William R. Dillon, Thomas J. Madden, and Neil H. Firtle, *Marketing Research in a Marketing Environment*, 3rd ed. (Burr Ridge, IL: Irwin/McGraw-Hill, 1993) or other current marketing research texts. See also "Merry Maids Clean Up Territories with MapInfo System," *Investor's Business Daily*, February 20, 2001, p. A8; Michael D. Johnson and Elania J. Hudson, "On the Perceived Usefulness of Scaling Techniques in Market Analysis," *Psychology & Marketing*, October 1996, pp. 653–75; Milton D. Rosenau, "Graphing Statistics and Data: Creating Better Charts," *Journal of Product Innovation Management*, March 1997, p. 144.

20. "Careful What You Ask For," *American Demographics*, July 1998, pp. 8–15; See also John G. Keane, "Questionable

Statistics," *American Demographics*, June 1985, pp. 18–21. Detailed treatment of confidence intervals is beyond the scope of this text, but it is covered in most marketing research texts, such as Donald R. Lehmann, *Analysis for Marketing Planning* 4th ed. (Burr Ridge, IL: Irwin/McGraw-Hill, 1997).

21. E. Jerome McCarthy et al., *Basic Marketing: A Managerial Approach*, 1st Australasian ed. (Burr Ridge, IL: Richard D. Irwin, 1994), pp. 128–29.

22. Alan R. Andreasen, "Cost-Conscious Marketing Research," *Harvard Business Review*, July–August, 1983, pp. 74–81; A. Parasuraman, "Research's Place in the Marketing Budget," *Business Horizons*, March/April 1983, pp. 25–29; Jack J. Honomichl, "Point of View: Why Marketing Information Should Have Top Executive Status," *Journal of Advertising Research*, November/ December 1994, pp. 61–66; Jim Bessen, "Riding the Marketing Information Wave," *Harvard Business Review*, September–October 1993, pp. 150–61.

Chapter 8

1. Available from World Wide Web: <http://www.kodak.com>; "Price Wars, Shift to Digital Photos Leaving Kodak Out of the Picture," *Investor's Business Daily*, March 19, 2001, p. A1; "Will Kodak's Carp Miss His Photo Op?" *Business Week*, October 9, 2000, p. 52; "Kodak Hires Web Guru to Develop Its Digital Plans," *The Wall Street Journal*, October 9, 2000, p. B1ff.; "With Polaroid Film, You're Seconds from Digital Fun," *USA Today*, September 20, 2000, p. 3D; "Affordable Digital Cameras Arrive, Bringing Decent Quality under $150," *Investor's Business Daily*, September 8, 2000, p. A4; "Digital Video Cameras Give Amateurs Entree to Real Movie-Making," *The Wall Street Journal*, August 31, 2000, p. B1; "Shutterbugs Ditch 35mm Gear for Digital Cameras, Computer Printers," *The Wall Street Journal*, May 8, 2000, p. B1ff.; "Businesses Prove the Focus of Big Digital Camera Sales," *Investor's Business Daily*, April 25, 2000, p. A6; "Wall Street Left to Wonder Whether Kodak's Getting the Digital Picture," *Investor's Business Daily*, April 11, 2000, p. A1; "Eastman Kodak Splits Focus Between Old, New Film Worlds," *USA Today*, February 14, 2000, p. 5B; "Fuji: Beyond Film," *Business Week*, November 22, 1999, pp. 132–38; "Film vs. Digital: Can Kodak Build a Bridge?" *Business Week*, August 2, 1999, pp. 66–69; "Shutter Snaps on Fisher's Leadership at Kodak," *The Wall Street Journal*, June 10, 1999, p. B1ff.; "Momentous Shifts," *Brandweek*, June 1, 1998, pp. 26–30; "For New Film, a Brighter Picture," *The Wall Street Journal*, May 5, 1998, p. B1ff.; "For Kodak's Advantix, Double Exposure as Company Relaunches Camera System," *The Wall Street Journal*, April 23, 1997, p. B1ff.; "APS Camera Brands Make Picture-Imperfect Debut," *Ad Age International*, January 1997, p. 12ff.; "Camera System Is Developed but Not Delivered," *The Wall Street Journal*, August 7, 1996, p. B1ff.

2. Available from World Wide Web: <http://www.hertz.com>; *2000 Annual Report*, Hertz; "How Market Leaders Keep Their Edge," *Fortune*, February 6, 1995, pp. 88–98.

3. Joseph M. Juran, "Made In U.S.A.: A Renaissance in Quality," *Harvard Business Review*, July–August 1993, pp. 42–53; "Measuring Quality Perception of America's Top Brands," *Brandweek*, April 4, 1994, pp. 24–26; Ajay Menon, Bernard J. Jaworski, and Ajay K. Kohli, "Product Quality: Impact of Interdepartmental Interactions," *Journal of the Academy of Marketing Science*, Summer 1997, pp. 187–200; Neil A. Morgan and Nigel F. Piercy, "Market-Led Quality," *Industrial Marketing Management*, May 1992, pp. 111–18; H. Michael Hayes, "ISO9000: The New Strategic Consideration," *Business Horizons*, May–June 1994, pp. 52–60.

4. For more on service expectations, see Chapter 5, footnote #11. For more on service quality, see Leonard L. Berry, "Cultivating Service Brand Equity," *Journal of the Academy of Marketing Science*, Winter 2000, pp. 128–138; Dwayne D. Gremler, "Discovering the Soul of Service: The Nine Drivers of Sustainable Business Success," *Journal of the Academy of Marketing Science*, Spring 2000, pp. 311–13; *2000 Annual Report*, MCI; *2000 Annual Report*, Merrill Lynch; "Air Service Faces Heat from Fliers," *USA Today*, June 1, 2000, p. 3B; "Airlines and Airwaves: Services Take Off," *Advertising Age*, May 1, 2000, pp. 18–20; "The Death of the Bellman," *The Wall Street Journal*, March 10, 2000, p. W11; "Avis to Try Even Harder with Ads Touting High Quality of Service," *The Wall Street Journal*, February 18, 2000, p. B9; "Better Service or Lip Service?" *USA Today*, December 16, 1999, p. 1Bff.; "How Does Low Unemployment Affect Service?" *Raleigh News & Observer*, December 5, 1999, pp. 27A–28A; "Price Isn't Everything," *The Wall Street Journal*, July 12, 1999, p. R20; "Only Extra Nice Will Suffice," *The Wall Street Journal*, June 14, 1999, p. 16ff.; "Buckling Up the Business Traveler," *American Demographics*, December 1998, pp. 48–52; "Service Is Everybody's Business," *Fortune*, June 27, 1994, pp. 48–60; James Golleher, "Value-Added Customer Service," *Journal of Personal Selling & Sales Management*, Spring 1997, p.71; James Reardon, Chip Miller, Ronald Hasty, and Blaise J. Waguespack, "A Comparison of Alternative Theories of Services Marketing," *Journal of Marketing Theory & Practice*, Fall 1996, pp. 61–71; Kirk Smith, "Service Aspects of Industrial Products Lead to Future Product Purchase Intentions," *Industrial Marketing Management*, January 1998, pp. 83–93; James C. Anderson and James A. Narus, "Capturing the Value of Supplementary Services," *Harvard Business Review*, January 1995–February 1995, pp. 75–83; Banwari Mittal and Walfried M. Lassar, "The Role of Personalization in Service Encounters," *Journal of Retailing*, Spring 1996, pp. 95–109; Barry J. Babin and James S. Boles, "Employee Behavior in a Service Environment: A Model and Test of Potential Differences Between Men and Women," *Journal of Marketing*, April 1998, pp. 77–91; Mary Jo Bitner, Bernard H. Booms, and Lois A. Mohr, "Critical Service Encounters: The Employee's Viewpoint," *Journal of Marketing*, October 1994, pp. 95–106; Leonard L. Berry, A. Parasuraman, and Valarie A. Zeithaml, "The Service-Quality Puzzle," *Business Horizons*, September/October 1988, pp. 35–43; Leonard L. Berry, "Services Marketing Is Different," in Christopher H. Lovelock, *Services Marketing* (Englewood Cliffs, NJ: Prentice-Hall, 1984), pp. 29–37.

5. *2000 Annual Report*, Sara Lee; *2000 Annual Report*, Enterprise.

6. For example, see "Russian Maneuvers Are Making Palladium Ever More Precious," *The Wall Street Journal*, March 6, 2000, p. A1ff. See also William S. Bishop, John L. Graham, and Michael H. Jones, "Volatility of Derived Demand in Industrial Markets and Its Management Implications," *Journal of Marketing*, Fall 1984, pp. 95–103.

7. Edward M. Tauber, "Why Do People Shop?" *Journal of Marketing*, October 1972, pp. 46–49; Christopher H. Lovelock, "Classifying Services to Gain Strategic Marketing Insights," *Journal of Marketing*, Summer 1983, pp. 9–20. Tom Boyt and Michael Harvey, "Classification of Industrial Services," *Industrial Marketing Management*, July 1997, pp. 291–300.

8. Dennis W. Rook, "The Buying Impulse," *Journal of Consumer Research*, September 1987, pp. 189–99; Cathy J. Cobb and Wayne D. Hoyer, "Planned Versus Impulse Purchase Behavior," *Journal of Retailing*, Winter 1986, pp. 384–409.

9. William B. Wagner and Patricia K. Hall, "Equipment Lease Accounting in Industrial Marketing Strategy," *Industrial Marketing Management* 20, no. 4 (1991), pp. 305–10; Robert S. Eckley, "Caterpillar's Ordeal: Foreign Competition in Capital Goods," *Business Horizons*, March/April 1989, pp. 80–86; M. Manley, "To Buy or Not to Buy," *Inc.*, November 1987, pp. 189–90.

10. P. Matthyssens and W. Faes, "OEM Buying Process for New Components: Purchasing and Marketing Implications," *Industrial Marketing Management*, August 1985, pp. 145–57; Paul A. Herbig and Frederick Palumbo, "Serving the Aftermarket in Japan and the United States," *Industrial Marketing Management*, November 1993, pp. 339–46; Ralph W. Jackson and Philip D. Cooper, "Unique Aspects of Marketing Industrial Services," *Industrial Marketing Management*, May 1988, pp. 111–18; Timothy L. Wilson and Frank E. Smith, "Business Services 1982–1992: Growth, Industry Characteristics, Financial Performance," *Industrial Marketing Management*, March 1996, pp. 162–71.

11. Ruth H. Krieger and Jack R. Meredith, "Emergency and Routine MRO Part Buying," *Industrial Marketing Management*, November 1985, pp. 277–82; Warren A. French et al., "MRO Parts Service in the Machine Tool Industry," *Industrial Marketing Management*, November 1985, pp. 283–88. See also "The Web's New Plumbers," *Ecompany*, March 2001, pp. 126–28.

12. For more on brand extensions, see "Cookie Makers Bake Up New Twists," *USA Today*, March 27, 2001, p. 3B; "Much about History," *Brandweek*, March 12, 2001, pp. 19–20; "Watershed Crystal," *Brandweek*, October 30, 2000, pp. 22–25; "Reposition: Simplifying the Customer's Brandscape," *Brandweek*, October 2, 2000, pp. 36–48; "The Joy of Laundry," *Business Week*, July 17, 2000, p. 8; "Crackers Say Cheese," *Advertising Age*, April 24, 2000, p. 32; "M&M/Mars Ice Cream Sees Red for Its Debut," *Advertising Age*, March 13, 2000, p. 33; "Clorox Tries Formula 409 for Carpets," *Advertising Age*, March 10, 1997, p. 6; "Can Betty Crocker Heat Up General Mills' Cereal Sales?" *The Wall Street Journal*, July 19, 1996, p. B1ff.; "Nabisco to Bring Top Cookie Brands to Breakfast Line," *The Wall Street Journal*, February 23, 1994, p. B5; "Multiple Varieties of Established Brands Muddle Consumers, Make Retailers Mad," *The Wall Street Journal*, January 24, 1992, p. B1ff. For more on brand equity and brand value, see "When Designers Attack!" *Ecompany*, June 2001, pp. 45–46; "Designated Shopper," *Brandweek*, May 28, 2001, p. 40; "Brand Building: Chairman of the Board," *Business Week*, May 28, 2001, p. 96; "In the Movie 'Foodfight,' Mr. Clean Plays Bit Part That Worries His Agent," *The Wall Street Journal*, April 30, 2001, p. A1ff.; "Mission, Message and Monitoring: How the Best Build, Nurture Brands," *Investor's Business Daily*, March 12, 2001, p. A1; David F. D'Alessandro, *Brand Warfare: 10 Rules for Building the Killer Brand* (2001); "Making the Emotional Connection," *Brandweek*, January 29, 2001, pp. 23–27; "What to Do with a Brand Gone Bland?" *The Wall Street Journal*, December 14, 2000, p. B14; "Pledge of Allegiance," *American Demographics*, November 2000, pp. 40–42; Marc Gob, *Emotional Branding: The New Paradigm for Connecting Brands to People* (New York: Watson-Gruptill, 2000); Marc Braunstein and Edward H. Levine, *Deep Branding on the Internet* (2000); "Making Your Mark Online," *Advertising Age*, October 9, 2000, pp. 46–48; "A Word of Advice to Body Shop: Don't Undermine Your Fine Branding with an Inconsistent Internet Effort," *Brandweek*, September 25, 2000, pp. 34–36; "Brands in a Bind," *Business Week*, August 28, 2000, pp. 234–38; "Branded Blooms Find Fertile Market," *Advertising Age*, January 24, 2000, p. 16; "Two Ways to Destroy a Valuable Brand," *Brandweek*, November 15, 1999, p. 26; "Creating the New Gold Standard," *Brandweek*, July 27, 1998, pp. 27–30. See also Elise K. Prosser, "Brand Marketing: Building Winning Brand Strategies That Deliver Value and Customer Satisfaction," *Journal of the Academy of Marketing Science*, Winter 1996, pp. 86–87; David A. Aaker, "Should You Take Your Brand to Where the Action Is?" *Harvard Business Review*, September–October 1997, pp. 135–43; Richard C. Leventhal, "Branding Strategy," *Business Horizons*, September–October 1996, pp. 17–23; Deborah R. John, Barbara Loken, and Christopher Joiner, "The Negative Impact of Extensions: Can Flagship Products Be Diluted?" *Journal of Marketing*, January 1998, pp. 19–32; Cathy J. Cobb-Walgren, Cynthia A. Ruble, and Naveen Donthu, "Brand Equity, Brand Preference, and Purchase Intent," *Journal of Advertising*, Fall 1995, pp. 25–40; Vijay Vishwanath and Jonathan Mark, "Your Brand's Best Strategy," *Harvard Business Review*, May–June 1997, pp. 123–29; Michael A. Kamins and Nancy A. Frost, "A 'Brand' New Language," *Journal of Marketing*, April 1994, pp. 129–30; John A. Quelch and David Kenny, "Extend Profits, Not Product Lines," *Harvard Business Review*, September 1994–October 1994, pp. 153–60; Linda B. Samuels and Jeffery M. Samuels, "Famous Marks Now Federally Protected Against Dilution," *Journal of Public Policy & Marketing*, Fall 1996, pp. 307–10; Pamela W. Henderson and Joseph A. Cote, "Guidelines for Selecting or Modifying Logos," *Journal of Marketing*, April 1998, pp. 14–30; Erich Joachimsthaler and David A. Aaker, "Building Brands Without Mass Media," *Harvard Business Review*, January–February 1997, pp. 39–50; Kevin Lane Keller, "Conceptualizing, Measuring, and Managing Customer-Based Brand Equity," *Journal of Marketing*, January 1993, pp. 1–22.

13. "Global Products Require Name-Finders," *The Wall Street Journal*, April 11, 1996, p. B8; Martin S. Roth, "Effects of Global Market Conditions on Brand Image Customization and Brand Performance," *Journal of Advertising*, Winter 1995, pp. 55–75.

14. Available from World Wide Web: <http://www.yahoo.com>; "Coterie of Early Hires Made Yahoo! A Hit but an Insular Place," *The Wall Street Journal*, March 9, 2001, p. A1ff.; "Yahoo Drops Bomb with Koogle's Exit," *USA Today*, March 8, 2001, p. 1Bff.; "Voulez-vous Yahoo Avec Moi?" *Fortune*, October 16, 2000, pp. 245–54; "Yahoo's Grand Vision for Web Advertising Takes Some Hard Hits," *The Wall Street Journal*, September 1, 2000, p. A1ff.; "Yahoo Stands Alone in Web Wars," *USA Today*, August 24, 2000, p. 1Bff.; "Surprise! Yahoo Goes Broadband,"

Fortune, May 29, 2000, pp. 182–92; "The Two Grown-Ups behind Yahoo!'s Surge," *The Wall Street Journal,* April 10, 1998, p. B1ff.; "Yahoo! Challenges AOL as a Portal to World Wide Web," *The Wall Street Journal,* March 19, 1998, p. B1; "How Yahoo! Won the Search Wars," *Fortune,* March 2, 1998, pp. 148–54; "*Brandweek's* Marketers of the Year: Yahoo!, Karen Edwards," *Superbrands '98,* October 20, 1997, pp. 70–74; "What Hath Yahoo Wrought?" *Business Week,* February 12, 1996, pp. 88–89.

15. "Highway Safety: Time for Tougher Cops," *Business Week,* July 2, 2001, p. 42; "Firestone Plans to Close Troubled Decatur Factory," *The Wall Street Journal,* June 28, 2001, p. A3ff.; "First, Crunch Time for Jac," *Fortune,* June 25, 2001, pp. 34–35; "Ford: Why It's Worse than You Think," *Business Week,* June 25, 2001, pp. 80–89; "Ford: Other Firestone Tires Fail, Too," *USA Today,* June 14, 2001, p. 1B; "Firestone: Is This Brand beyond Repair?" *Business Week,* June 11, 2001, p. 48; "Ford Vs. Firestone: A Corporate Whodunit," *Business Week,* June 11, 2001, pp. 46–47; "Ford's Gamble: Will It Backfire?" *Business Week,* June 4, 2001, pp. 40–41; "Tired of Each Other," *Time,* June 4, 2001, pp. 50–56; "Ford Has Big Problem Beyond the Tire Mess: Making Quality Cars," *The Wall Street Journal,* May 25, 2001, p. A1ff.; "Confused Drivers May Have Trouble Trusting Either Firm," *USA Today,* May 23, 2001, p. 1Bff.; "Ford to Replace Up to 13 Million Firestone Tires," *Investor's Business Daily,* May 23, 2001, p. A9; "Firestone Quits as Tire Supplier to Ford," *The Wall Street Journal,* May 22, 2001, p. A3ff.; "Meet the New Face of Firestone," *Business Week,* April 30, 2001, pp. 64–66; "Facing or Fearing a Publicity Crisis? Right Steps to Get Past the Trouble," *Investor's Business Daily,* April 23, 2001, p. A1; "After Tireless Efforts, Ford Launches All-New Explorer," *USA Today,* March 29, 2001, p. 1Bff.; "Under Glare of Recall, Tire Makers Are Giving New Technology a Spin," *The Wall Street Journal,* March 23, 2001, p. A1ff.; "Industry Report: Tires," *Investor's Business Daily,* February 12, 2001, p. B22; "More Firestone Tires Peel," *USA Today,* February 8, 2001, p. 1Bff.; "What Japan's CEOs Can Learn from Bridgestone," *Business Week,* January 29, 2001, p. 50; "Firestone Leaves an Indelible Mark," *USA Today,* December 26, 2000, p. 1Bff.; "Cost Hinders Wider Use of Nylon to Make Steel-Belted Tires Safer," *The Wall Street Journal,* December 20, 2000, p. A8; "Firestone Admits Manufacturing Problems But Also Scrutinizes Tire-Inflation Levels," *The Wall Street Journal,* December 20, 2000, p. A3ff; "Firestone Recall Fuels Interest in 'Smart' Tires," *The Wall Street Journal,* November 22, 2000, p. B1ff.; "Drivers Complained of Tread Problems Years before Recall," *USA Today,* November 15, 2000, p. 1Bff.; "Firestone Dealers Step Up to Defend Tiremaker," *USA Today,* November 10, 2000, p. 10B; "Can Courts' Cloak of Secrecy Be Deadly?" *USA Today,* October 16, 2000, p. 1Bff.; "The Tire Flap: Behind the Feeding Frenzy," *Business Week,* October 16, 2000, pp. 126–28; "Firestone Team Faces Challenge of Steering Company Past Crisis," *The Wall Street Journal,* October11, 2000, p. A1ff.; "Squabbles between Ford and Firestone May Hurt Their Legal Defense," *The Wall Street Journal,* October 9, 2000, p. B1ff.; "Documents Imply Firestone Knew of Tire Trouble in '94," *USA Today,* October 4, 2000, p. 1Bff.; "Would You Buy One?" *Business Week,* September 25, 2000, pp. 46–47; "Jac Nasser's Biggest Test," *Fortune,* September 18, 2000, pp. 123–28; "Ford: A Crisis of Confidence," *Business Week,* September 18, 2000, pp. 40–42; "Answers Still Elusive in Tire Crisis," *The Wall Street Journal,* September 15, 2000, p. B1ff.; "Anatomy of a Recall," *Time,* September 11, 2000, pp. 28–32; "How Ford, Firestone Let the Warnings Slide By as Debacle Developed," *The Wall Street Journal,* September 6, 2000, p. A1ff.; "Tension between Ford and Firestone Mounts amid Recall Efforts," *The Wall Street Journal,* August 28, 2000, p. A1ff.; "More People Die Despite Recall," *USA Today,* August 22, 2000, p. 1Bff.; "Ford CEO Takes Recall Reins as More Questions Arise," *USA Today,* August 17, 2000, p. 1Bff.; "What You Don't Know about Your Tires," *USA Today,* August 11, 2000, p. 1Bff.; "Bridgestone/Firestone Handling of Recall Results in Consumer Confusion, Chaos," *The Wall Street Journal,* August 11, 2000, p. A3ff.; "How the Tire Problem Turned into a Crisis for Firestone and Ford," *The Wall Street Journal,* August 10, 2000, p. A1ff.; "Could $1 Worth of Nylon Have Saved People's Lives?" *USA Today,* August 9, 2000, p. 1Bff.; "A Blowout Blindsides Bridgestone," *The Wall Street Journal,* August 7, 2000, p. A8ff.

16. "Road to Foreign Franchises Is Paved with New Problems," *The Wall Street Journal,* May 14, 2001, p. B10; "Tiger Fight Sees Kellogg, ExxonMobil Clash in Court," *Ad Age Global,* November 2000; "Wrestling, Wildlife Fund Battle over WWF Site," *USA Today,* October 25, 2000, p. 1A; "More Firms Flash New Badge," *USA Today,* October 4, 2000, p. 3B; "Name Lawsuit Prompts AppleSoup to Become Flycode," *USA Today,* September 11, 2000, p. 6B; Charles H. Schwepker, "Trademark Problems and How to Avoid Them," *Journal of the Academy of Marketing Science,* Winter 1997, pp. 89–90; Lee B. Burgunder, "Trademark Protection of Product Characteristics: A Predictive Model," *Journal of Public Policy & Marketing,* Fall 1997, pp. 277–88; Itamar Simonson, "Trademark Infringement from the Buyer Perspective: Conceptual Analysis and Measurement Implications," *Journal of Public Policy & Marketing,* Fall 1994, pp. 181–99; "Asian Trademark Litigation Continues," *The Wall Street Journal,* February 16, 1994, p. B8.

17. "Product Piracy Poses Biggest Threat to China's Economic Status," *USA Today,* June 28, 2001, p. 6B; "Beijing's Phony War on Fakes," *Fortune,* October 30, 2000, pp. 188–208; "Knocking Out the Knockoffs," *Fortune,* October 2, 2000, pp. 213–18; "Can Microsoft Stamp Out Piracy?" *Business Week,* October 2, 2000, p. 28; "China's Piracy Plague," *Business Week,* June 5, 2000, pp. 44–48; "Hackers, Pirates Thrive in Russia's Tech Underworld," *USA Today,* June 1, 2000, p. 17A; "Why Tommy Hilfiger Just Can't Seem to Stay Out of Local Wal-Mart," *The Wall Street Journal,* January 28, 1999, p. A1ff.; "In China's Software Market, a Hundred Microsoft-Bashers Bloom," *The Wall Street Journal,* December 31, 1999, p. B1ff.; "In Pursuit of Pokemon Pirates," *The Wall Street Journal,* November 8, 1999, p. B1ff.; "Software Piracy Ahoy!" *USA Today,* September 22, 1999, p. 1Bff.; "Europe Piracy!" *Business Week,* July 26, 1999, pp. 90–94; "Private Eye Stalks Mexico's Mall Pirates," *The Wall Street Journal,* December 2, 1998, p. B1ff.; "A Crackdown on Smugglers—and Foreign Companies," *Business Week,* November 9, 1998, p. 70; "Originals Increasingly Taking Knockoffs to Court," *USA Today,* October 26, 1998, p. 6B; "China's Antismuggling Drive to Hurt U.S. Exporters that Support Crackdown," *The Wall Street Journal,* August 5, 1998, p. A12; "China's CD Pirates Find a New Hangout," *Business Week,* December 15, 1997, p. 138F; "Busting Bogus Merchandise Peddlers with the Logo Cops," *The Wall Street Journal,* October 24, 1997, p. B1ff.; "Reebok Tussles with Venezuelan Company over Name, Designs," *Ad Age International,* September 1997, p. I38;

"CD Piracy Flourishes in China, and West Supplies Equipment," *The Wall Street Journal*, April 24, 1997, p. A1ff.; Janeen E. Olsen and Kent L. Granzin, "Using Channels Constructs to Explain Dealers' Willingness to Help Manufacturers Combat Counterfeiting," *Journal of Business Research*, June 1993, pp. 147–70; Ronald F. Bush, Peter H. Bloch, and Scott Dawson, "Remedies for Product Counterfeiting," *Business Horizons*, January–February 1989, pp. 59–65; Alexander Nill and Clifford J. Clifford J II, "The Scourge of Global Counterfeiting," *Business Horizons*, November–December 1996, pp. 37–42.

18. For more on licensing, see "Washed Up at Warnaco?" *Time*, June 25, 2001, pp. 36–37; "Jordan Leaps into Palm of Your Hand," *USA Today*, June 18, 2001, p. 4B; "Ford Buys Beanstalk for Licensing Magic," *The Wall Street Journal*, June 11, 2001, p. B6; "New Jeep Is Sure to Turn Heads, on the Playground," *The Wall Street Journal*, January 9, 2001, p. B1ff.; "Brand New Goods," *Time*, November 1, 1999; "Deals that Go Bump in the Night," *Business Week*, February 16, 1998, p. 84; "Brand Builders: Licensing, the Color of Money," *Brandweek*, September 15, 1997, pp. 22–23; "Toy Makers Offer the Moon for New 'Star Wars' Licenses," *The Wall Street Journal*, August 19, 1997, p. B1ff.; "Arm & Hammer's Owner Looks at Licensing to Freshen Results," *The Wall Street Journal*, August 6, 1997, p. B2.

19. Amitabh Mungale, "Managing Product Families," *Journal of Product Innovation Management*, January 1998, pp. 102–03; Gloria Barczak, "Product Management," *Journal of Product Innovation Management*, September 1997, pp. 425–26; "Brand Managing's New Accent," *Adweek's Marketing Week*, April 15, 1991, pp. 18–22; "Brand Managers: 90s Dinosaurs?" *Advertising Age*, December 19, 1988, p. 19.

20. "Ten Years May Be Generic Lifetime," *Advertising Age*, March 23, 1987, p. 76; Brian F. Harris and Roger A. Strang, "Marketing Strategies in the Age of Generics," *Journal of Marketing*, Fall 1985, pp. 70–81.

21. Kusum L. Ailawadi, "Pursuing the Value-Conscious Consumer: Store Brands Versus National Brand Promotions," *Journal of Marketing*, January 2001, pp. 71–90; "White Clouds Could Bring Rain on P&G," *Advertising Age*, July 2, 2001, p. 4; "Black Eye in Store for Big Brands," *Advertising Age*, April 30, 2001, p. 1ff.; "National Tool Brands Vie for Maximum Exposure," *DSN Retailing Today*, March 5, 2001, p. 26ff.; "New Private-Label Alternatives Bring Changes to Supercenters, Clubs," *DSN Retailing Today*, February 5, 2001, p. 66; "Target Signs Exclusive Deal with *Parents* Magazine for Educational Toy Line," *DSN Retailing Today*, December 11, 2000, p. 7ff.; "Popularity of PL Toys Stems from Benefits in Cost, Exclusivity," *DSN Retailing Today*, November 20, 2000, p. 4ff.; "Wal-Mart Stores Go Private (Label)," *Advertising Age*, November 29, 1999, p. 1ff.; "For Wal-Mart, a Soap War Looms Against Mighty P&G," *The Wall Street Journal*, August 6, 1999, p. B1ff.; "Dr. Pop and Frisk Help a Grocery Chain Grow," *The Wall Street Journal*, April 13, 1998, p. B1ff.; Marcia Mogelonsky, "When Stores Become Brands," *American Demographics*, February 1995, pp. 32–38; "Big Firms Come Out Fighting, Slow Sales of Private-Label Rivals," *The Wall Street Journal*, July 7, 1994, p. B8; "Exposing the Five Myths of Private Label Brands," *Brandweek*, June 20, 1994, p. 17; R. Sethuraman and J. Mittelstaedt, "Coupons and Private Labels: A Cross-Category Analysis of Grocery Products," *Psychology & Marketing*, November/December 1992, pp. 487–500; "Store-Brand Sales Have Their Ups and Downs as Buying Habits Shift," *The Wall Street Journal*, May 12, 1994, p. B6; John A. Quelch and David Harding, "Brands Versus Private Labels: Fighting to Win," *Harvard Business Review*, January–February 1996, pp. 99–109.

22. "Many-Flavored Milk Competes with Sodas," *USA Today*, January 26, 2001, p. 1D; "Chug-a-Mania," *Brandweek*, June 22, 1998, pp. 22–23; "Dean Foods Attempts to Reintroduce Milk to Consumers," *The Wall Street Journal*, March 26, 1998, p. B4; "The Hip New Drink: Milk," *Business Week*, February 16, 1998, p. 44; "Milk Marches into New Era with Branded Product Push," *Advertising Age*, January 26, 1998, p. 14.

23. "Getting a Grip on Consumer Tastes," *Business Week*, July 16, 2001, p. 12; "Color Me Popular: Marketers Shape Up Packaging," *USA Today*, February 8, 2001, p. 7B; "See-Through Stuff Sells Big," *USA Today*, December 26, 2000, p. 6B; "This Potion's Power Is in Its Packaging," *The Wall Street Journal*, December 21, 2000, p. B12; "APPEX Show Features Top Auto Products," *DSN Retailing Today*, November 20, 2000, p. 4ff.; "Heinz Puts Squeeze on Places Refilling Its Ketchup Bottles," *The Wall Street Journal*, June 22, 2000, p. A1ff.; "Online Sales Pack a Crunch," *USA Today*, December 6, 1999, p. 1Dff.; "Hefty's Plastic Zipper Bag Is Rapping Rivals," *The Wall Street Journal*, April 16, 1999, p. B1ff.; "Excedrin Is Upfront about New Package," *The Wall Street Journal*, April 8, 1998, p. B8; "Quaker, Coca-Cola Introduce Colorful Drink Contenders," *Advertising Age*, January 26, 1998, p. 52; "What's Foiling the Aluminum Can," *Business Week*, October 6, 1997, pp. 106–8; "Breakthrough Bottles," *Brandweek*, May 20, 1996, pp. 32–52; "If Your Brand's Number Two, Get with the Package Program," *Brandweek*, June 27, 1994, pp. 26–27; Brian Wansink, "Can Package Size Accelerate Usage Volume?" *Journal of Marketing*, July 1996, pp. 1–14.

24. "UPC Registers Retailing Impact," *Advertising Age*, April 7, 1986, p. 3ff.; "Bar Codes: Beyond the Checkout Counter," *Business Week*, April 8, 1985, p. 90; Ronald C. Goodstein, "UPC Scanner Pricing Systems: Are They Accurate?" *Journal of Marketing*, April 1994, pp. 20–30; "Firms Line Up to Check Out Bar Codes," *USA Today*, December 4, 1985, pp. B1–2.

25. Bruce A. Silverglade, "The Nutrition Labeling and Education Act—Progress to Date and Challenges for the Future," *Journal of Public Policy & Marketing*, Spring 1996, pp. 148–50; Sandra J. Burke, Sandra J. Milberg, and Wendy W. Moe, "Displaying Common but Previously Neglected Health Claims on Product Labels: Understanding Competitive Advantages, Deception, and Education," *Journal of Public Policy & Marketing*, Fall 1997, pp. 242–55; Scott B. Keller, Mike Landry, Jeanne Olson, Anne M. Velliquette et al., "The Effects of Nutrition Package Claims, Nutrition Facts Panels, and Motivation to Process Nutrition Information on Consumer Product Evaluations," *Journal of Public Policy & Marketing*, Fall 1997, pp. 256–69; Paul J. Petruccelli, "Consumer and Marketing Implications of Information Provision: The Case of the Nutrition Labeling and Education Act of 1990," *Journal of Public Policy & Marketing*, Spring 1996, pp. 150–53; Christine Moorman, "A Quasi Experiment to Assess the Consumer and Informational Determinants of Nutrition Information Processing Activities: The Case of the Nutrition Labeling and Education Act," *Journal of Public Policy & Marketing*, Spring 1996, pp. 28–44.

26. "Open at Your Own Risk," *USA Today*, July 13, 2001, p. 1Aff.; "Pushing Paper in a Plastic World," *The Wall Street Journal*, February 24, 1998, p. B1ff.; "Record Makers Giving Retailers the Blues," *The Wall Street Journal*, March 16, 1992, p. B1ff.; "Shed the Egg, Spare the Image," *Adweek's Marketing Week*, July 15, 1991, p. 9; "New Packaging That's Thriftier! Niftier! and Cooks Your Food!" *Fortune*, September 5, 1994, p. 109.

27. Paula Fitzgerald, Bone Corey, and Robert J. Corey, "Ethical Dilemmas in Packaging: Beliefs of Packaging Professionals," *Journal of Macromarketing*, Spring 1992, pp. 45–54. For more on downsizing, see "Big Trend: Smaller Packaging," *USA Today*, April 1, 1993, p. 1Bff.; "State AGs Attack Downsized Brands," *Advertising Age*, February 18, 1991, p. 1ff.; "Critics Call Cuts in Package Size Deceptive Move," *The Wall Street Journal*, February 5, 1991, p. B1ff. For more discussion on disposable products, see "Disposing of the Green Myth," *Adweek's Marketing Week*, April 13, 1992, pp. 20–21; "The Waste Land," *Adweek*, November 11, 1991, p. 26; "Ridding the Nation of Polystyrene Peanuts," *Adweek's Marketing Week*, October 22, 1990, p. 17.

28. J. E. Russo, "The Value of Unit Price Information," *Journal of Marketing Research*, May 1977, pp. 193–201; David A. Aaker and Gary T. Ford, "Unit Pricing Ten Years Later: A Replication," *Journal of Marketing*, Winter 1983, pp. 118–22.

29. For more on service guarantees, see "Got a Gripe? Amtrak Patrons Get Free Ride," *USA Today*, July 7, 2000, p. 2B; "Amtrak Rolls Out Service Guarantee, New Logo," *Investor's Business Daily*, July 7, 2000, p. A7; "Biztravel.com Promises Money Back for Flight Delays," *USA Today*, May 23, 2000, p. 1Bff.; "It's Service in a Box from Hewlett-Packard," *Advertising Age*, May 10, 1993, p. 5; "More Firms Pledge Guaranteed Service," *The Wall Street Journal*, July 17, 1991, p. B1ff. For more on warranties, see M. E. Blair and Daniel E. Innis, "The Effects of Product Knowledge on the Evaluation of Warranted Brands," *Psychology & Marketing*, August 1996, pp. 445–56; Ellen M. Moore and F. Kelly Shuptrine, "Warranties: Continued Readability Problems After the 1975 Magnuson-Moss Warranty Act," *Journal of Consumer Affairs*, Summer 1993, pp. 23–36; M. A. J. Menezes and I. S. Currim, "An Approach for Determination of Warranty Length," *International Journal of Research in Marketing*, May 1992, pp. 177–96; "Service Dealers Complain about Warranty Business," *The Wall Street Journal*, February 20, 1992, p. B2.

Chapter 9

1. Available from World Wide Web: <http://www.palm.com>; "Palm Slips to No. 2 in Revenue as iPaq Grabs the Top Spot," *Investor's Business Daily*, June 19, 2001, p. A6; "Jordan Leaps into Palm of Your Hand," *USA Today*, June 18, 2001, p. 4B; "Palm's Fortune Take a Tumble, Pressuring CEO," *The Wall Street Journal*, June 4, 2001, p. B1ff.; "The 411 on PDAs," *Ecompany*, June 2001, pp. 133–35; "Has Palm Lost Its Grip?" *Fortune*, May 28, 2001, pp. 104–108; "Palm Shares Sink as One-Time Star Says Sales Fading," *Investor's Business Daily*, May 21, 2001, p. A6; "HandEra's Hand-Held Puts Some New Twists on the Usual Formula," *The Wall Street Journal*, May 10, 2001, p. B1; "Hand-Helds that Are Less of a Handful," *Business Week*, April 9, 2001, p. 18; "PDA Wars: Round 2," *Time*, April 2, 2001, pp. 40–41; "No Cartwheels for Handspring," *Business Week*, April 2, 2001, pp. 56–58; "Palm and Handspring Offer Welcome Updates to Hand-Held Models," *The Wall Street Journal*, March 29, 2001, p. B1; "New Devices Shrink Difference in Price for Palm, Pocket PC," *Investor's Business Daily*, March 21, 2001, p. A6; "Palm and Handspring Lead a Sector that Hardly Had to Sweat," *Investor's Business Daily*, January 2, 2001, p. A6; "Palm, Microsoft Extend Rivalry to Wireless Arena," *Investor's Business Daily*, November 20, 2000, p. A6; "Seeding Demand for Handspring," *Advertising Age*, November 6, 2000, p. S36; "Palm Hopes to Blaze a New Image in Major Campaign," *The Wall Street Journal*, November 1, 2000, p. B10; "Hard Cell," *Fortune*, October 30, 2000, pp. 305–308; "Hand-Held Makers Spring Free from Parent," *Investor's Business Daily*, October 4, 2000, p. A12; "Palm and Handspring Go Hand to Hand," *Fortune*, September 18, 2000, pp. 319–20; "Palm Puts Up Its Fists as Microsoft Attacks Hand-Held PC Market," *The Wall Street Journal*, August 8, 2000, p. A1ff.; "Army of Programmers Helps Palm Keep Its Edge," *The Wall Street Journal*, June 1, 2000, p. B1ff.; "Improved Hand-Helds Still Don't Capture the Magic of Palms," *The Wall Street Journal*, May 4, 2000, p. B1; "If at First You Don't Succeed . . . ," *Business Week*, April 24, 2000, pp. 120–30; "Palm Gets Ready for New Hands," *The Wall Street Journal*, February 28, 2000, p. B1ff.; "3Com Tries to Solve Its Palm Problem," *Fortune*, October 11, 1999, pp. 167–68; "Palm Has the Whole World in Its Hand," *USA Today*, September 14, 1999, p. 1Bff.; "Putting Fluff over Function," *Fortune*, March 15, 1999, pp. 163–65; "The Palm Pilot Sequel Is a Hit," *Fortune*, April 13, 1998, pp. 154–56; "3Com Again Changes Name of Hot-Selling PalmPilot," *Advertising Age*, March 9, 1998, p. 4; "Apple Drops Newton, an Idea Ahead of Its Time," *The Wall Street Journal*, March 2, 1998, p. B1ff.; "What's in a Name? Ask 3Com," *Business Week*, January 26, 1998, p. 6; "Little Computers, Big New Marketing Battle," *The Wall Street Journal*, November 17, 1997, p. B1ff.; "A Rocket in Its Pocket," *Business Week*, September 9, 1996, pp. 111–14; "How Palm Computing Became an Architect," *Harvard Business Review*, September–October 1997, p. 89.

2. Lee G. Cooper, "Strategic Marketing Planning for Radically New Products," *Journal of Marketing*, January 2000, pp. 1–16; Robert W. Veryzer, "Key Factors Affecting Customer Evaluation of Discontinuous New Products," *Journal of Product Innovation Management*, March 1998, pp. 136–50; Laura Birou, Stanley E. Fawcett, and Gregory M. Magnan, "Integrating Product Life Cycle and Purchasing Strategies," *International Journal of Purchasing & Materials Management*, Winter 1997, pp. 23–31; Frank H. Alpert and Michael A. Kamins, "An Empirical Investigation of Consumer Memory, Attitude and Perceptions Toward Pioneer and Follower Brands," *Journal of Marketing*, October 1995, pp. 34–45; Neil A. Morgan, "Managing Imitation Strategies: How Later Entrants Seize Market Share From Pioneers," *Journal of Marketing*, October 1995, pp. 104–06; David M. Szymanski, Lisa C. Troy, and Sundar G. Bharadwaj, "Order of Entry and Business Performance: An Empirical Synthesis and Reexamination," *Journal of Marketing*, October 1995, pp. 17–33; George Day, "The Product Life Cycle: Analysis and Applications Issues," *Journal of Marketing*, Fall 1981, pp. 60–67; John E. Swan and David R. Rink, "Fitting Marketing Strategy to Varying Product Life Cycles," *Business Horizons*, January/February 1982, pp. 72–76; Igal Ayal, "International Product Life Cycle: A Reassessment and Product Policy Implications," *Journal of Marketing*, Fall 1981, pp. 91–96; Edward T. Popper and Bruce D. Buskirk, "Technology Life Cycles in Industrial Markets," *Industrial Marketing Management*, February 1992, pp. 23–32; Vijay Mahajan, Subhash Sharma, and Robert D. Buzzell, "Assessing the Impact of Competitive Entry on Market Expansion and Incumbent Sales," *Journal of Marketing*, July 1993, pp. 39–52; Mary Lambkin and George S. Day, "Evolutionary Processes in Competitive Markets: Beyond the Product Life Cycle," *Journal of Marketing*, July 1989, pp. 4–20.

3. Jorge Alberto Sousa De Vasconcellos, "Key Success Factors in Marketing Mature Products," *Industrial Marketing Management* 20, no. 4 (1991), pp. 263–78; Paul C.N. Michell, Peter Quinn, and Edward Percival, "Marketing Strategies for Mature Industrial Products," *Industrial Marketing Management* 20, no. 3 (1991), pp. 201–6; "Computers Become a Kind of Commodity, to Dismay of Makers," *The Wall Street Journal*, September 5, 1991, p. A1ff.; Peter N. Golder and Gerard J. Tellis, "Pioneer Advantage: Marketing Logic or Marketing Legend?" *Journal of Marketing Research*, May 1993, pp. 158–70; "As Once Bright Market for CAT Scanners Dims, Smaller Makers of the X-Ray Devices Fade Out," *The Wall Street Journal*, May 6, 1980, p. 40.

4. U.S. Bureau of the Census, *Statistical Abstract of the United States 2000* (Washington, DC: U.S. Government Printing Office, 2000), p. 726.

5. "Netscape's Plan: Survive, Thrive—New Focus Is on Digital Economy," *USA Today*, April 21, 1998, p. 1Bff.; "Netscape to Share Browser Program Code," *The Wall Street Journal*, January 23, 1998, p. B6; "Special Report: The Internet," *The Wall Street Journal*, December 8, 1997, pp. R1–32; "Netspeed at Netscape," *Business Week*, February 10, 1997, pp. 78–86; "A Sea Change for Netscape: Internet Upstart Shows Muscle on the Web," *USA Today*, February 6, 1996, p. 1Bff.

6. "Would You Buy a Patent License from This Man?" *Ecompany*, April 2001, pp. 104–10; "Businesses Battle Over Intellectual Property," *USA Today*, August 2, 2000, p. 1Bff.; "Rivals Square Off Toe to Toe," *USA Today*, August 24, 1993, p. 1Bff.; "The Patent Pirates Are Finally Walking the Plank," *Business Week*, February 17, 1992, pp. 125–27; "Is It Time to Reinvent the Patent System?" *Business Week*, December 2, 1991, pp. 110–15; C. C. Baughn, Michael Bixby, and L. S. Woods, "Patent Laws and the Public Good: IPR Protection in Japan and the United States," *Business Horizons*, July–August 1997, pp. 59–65; Karen Bronikowski, "Speeding New Products to Market," *The Journal of Business Strategy*, September/October 1990, pp. 34–37.

7. For an example, see "Betamax Wars All Over Again," *Business Week*, September 29, 1997, pp. 35–36; "The Next Great Gadget," *Time*, January 20, 1997, p. 66; "Sony Isn't Mourning the 'Death' of Betamax," *Business Week*, January 25, 1988, p. 37. See also Sigvald J. Harryson, "How Canon and Sony Drive Product Innovation Through Networking and Application-Focused R&D," *Journal of Product Innovation Management*, July 1997, pp. 288–95; M. Lambkin, "Pioneering New Markets: A Comparison of Market Share Winners and Losers," *International Journal of Research in Marketing*, March 1992, pp. 5–22.

8. "Retailers Seek Higher Profits in Low-Rise Jeans," *The Wall Street Journal*, June 28, 2001, p. B1ff.; "Recipe for a Fashion Brand?" *The Wall Street Journal*, June 25, 2001, p. B1ff.; "Dusting Off Fashion's Old Bags," *Time* (Special Issue: Your Business), June 2001, pp. Y2–Y4; "Retailers' Holiday Leather Fetish," *The Wall Street Journal*, November 29, 2000, p. B1ff.; "Designers Howl for Fur," *The Wall Street Journal*, September 22, 2000, p. B1ff.; "Goose Bumps Define the Height of Fashion as Fall Tinges the Air," *The Wall Street Journal*, September 12, 2000, p. A1ff.; "More Teens Get Hung Up on Cellphones," *USA Today*, July 18, 2000, p. 3B; "Like, Be Hip or Be Gone in Teen Clothes Market," *USA Today*, July 5, 2000, p. 8B; "To Track Fickle Fashion, Apparel Firms Go Online," *The Wall Street Journal*, May 11, 2000, p. B1ff.; "Blue Collar No More," *Time*, May 8, 2000, p. 80; "Frilly and Full," *USA Today*, April 10, 2000, p. 8D; "Claiborne Patches Together an Empire," *The Wall Street Journal*, February 2, 2000, p. B1ff.; "Pokemon Makes a Monster Splash," *USA Today*, December 7, 1999, p. 1Dff.; "Forget the Clothes—Fashion Fortunes Turn on Heels and Purses," *The Wall Street Journal*, November 23, 1999, p. A1ff.; "Pokemon Poised to Stomp Elmo, Furby," *USA Today*, November 10, 1999, p. 1Bff.; "True Grit, or How Sights Denim Makes Money in Dirty Jeans," *The Wall Street Journal*, October 12, 1999, p. A1ff.; "Beanie Brouhaha," *Advertising Age*, September 6, 1999, p. 1ff.; "The Latest Trend in Newfangled Bangles," *The Wall Street Journal*, September 2, 1999, p. B1ff.; "It's Lustrous, It's Chic, It's Plastic," *The Wall Street Journal*, September 1, 1999, p. B1ff.; "Nokia Shoots for the Stars with New Phone," *The Wall Street Journal*, August 24, 1999, p. B7; "Fashion Coup at Dawson's Creek," *The Wall Street Journal*, June 22, 1999, p. B1ff.; "Sheer Marketing: Bare Pantyhose," *The Wall Street Journal*, May 24, 1999, p. B1ff.; "Banana Republic's Answer to Khaki Overdose: Chino!" *The Wall Street Journal*, March 26, 1999, p. B1ff.; "Fashion Understatement: That's So 5 Minutes Ago," *USA Today*, March 23, 1999, p. 1Dff.; "A Fad Flames Out, and Retailers Get Burned," *The Wall Street Journal*, January 21, 1999, p. B1ff.; "Urban Wear Goes Suburban," *Fortune*, December 21, 1998, pp. 169–72; "Despite Hype, There Are No Endangered Furbies," *USA Today*, December 15, 1998, p. 1D; "Army Pants with Pouchy Pockets Storm Fashion World," *The Wall Street Journal*, July 9, 1998, p. B1ff.; "At McDonald's, a Case of Mass Beaniemania," *The Wall Street Journal*, June 5, 1998, p. B1ff.; "Fidel Meets Naomi," *The Wall Street Journal*, March 2, 1998, p. B1ff.; "Updating a Classic: The Man in the Gray Spandex Suit," *The Wall Street Journal*, January 27, 1998, p. B1ff.; "Teletubbies Are Coming: Brit Hit Sets U.S. Invasion," *Advertising Age*, January 19, 1998, p. 12; "Rural Kids Like Hip Clothes, Too, Hot Chain Discovers," *The Wall Street Journal*, January 15, 1998, p. B1ff.; "A Grumpy Old Lady Becomes a Big Hit for Hallmark," *The Wall Street Journal*, December 24, 1997, p. B1ff.; "How Belgian Engineer Created a Global Backpack Trend," *The Wall Street Journal*, December 10, 1997, p. B1ff.; "Will Working Women Wear This Stuff?" *The Wall Street Journal*, October 8, 1997, p. B1ff.; "Virtual Pets Are Some Campers' Best Friends," *USA Today*, July 29, 1997, p. 1D; "The Beanie Factor," *Brandweek*, June 16, 1997, pp. 22–27. See also Martin G. Letscher, "How to Tell Fads from Trends," *American Demographics*, December 1994, pp. 38–45; R. E. Goldsmith, J. B. Freiden, and J. C. Kilsheimer, "Social Values and Female Fashion Leadership: A Cross-Cultural Study," *Psychology & Marketing*, September/October 1993, pp. 399–412; "Special Report: Fashion Marketing," *Advertising Age*, August 22,

1994, pp. 23–28; Craig J. Thompson and Diana L. Haytko, "Speaking of Fashion: Consumers' Uses of Fashion Discourses and the Appropriation of Countervailing Cultural Meanings," *Journal of Consumer Research*, June 1997, pp. 15–42.

9. For more on Zara, see "Just-in-Time Fashion," *The Wall Street Journal*, May 18, 2001, p. B1ff.; "The Fashion Cycle Hits High Gear," *Business Week E.Biz*, September 18, 2000, p. EB66; "Zara Has a Made-to-Order Plan for Success," *Fortune*, September 4, 2000, p. 80; "The Mark of Zara," *Business Week*, May 29, 2000, pp. 98–100.

10. "Pioneer, Panasonic Drive toward Recordable DVD," *Investor's Business Daily*, June 26, 2001, p. A7; "Blockbuster Tests Postvideo Future," *The Wall Street Journal*, June 18, 2001, p. B1ff.; "DVDs Aren't Ready for Home Movies Yet," *Business Week*, May 7, 2001, p. 28; "DVDs' Popularity Gives Studio Earnings Much-Needed Spin," *USA Today*, April 30, 2001, p. 4B; "Vivastar's DVD System Is Affordable, Recordable," *Investor's Business Daily*, April 20, 2001, p. A4; "Apple and Compaq Give a Sneak Preview of DVD Recording," *The Wall Street Journal*, April 5, 2001, p. B1; "Is It Time to Hop on the DVD Bandwagon?" *Ecompany*, March 2001, pp. 162–64; "Sales of DVD Players Boom, but Makers Record Little Profit," *Investor's Business Daily*, January 22, 2001, p. A6; "DVD Makers Battle over Recording Standard," *The Wall Street Journal*, November 9, 2000, p. B6ff.; "To DVD—or Not to DVD?" *The Wall Street Journal*, November 3, 2000, p. W1ff.; "Those Great DVD Sets Are Hitting the Market, but Don't Buy One Yet," *The Wall Street Journal*, August 24, 2000, p. B1ff.; "DVD Sales Energize Home Video Market," *USA Today*, April 30, 2000, p. 3B; "Don't Throw Away Those CDs Yet, Recordable DVDs a Long Way Off," *Investor's Business Daily*, April 13, 2000, p. A6; "DVD Players: Don't Toss That VCR Yet," *Business Week*, March 6, 2000, p. 160H; "As Prices Tumble, Sales of DVD Players Explode for the Holidays," *The Wall Street Journal*, December 9, 1999, p. B1ff.; "Thou Shalt Buy DVD," *Fortune*, November 8, 1999, pp. 201–208; "DVD Acceptance Picks Up Pace," *Discount Store News*, August 9, 1999, pp. 29–34; "With a Clear Path Ahead, DVD Readies for Mass Rule," *Discount Store News*, July 12, 1999, pp. 29–44; "DVD and Conquer: Why One Technology Prevailed," *Business Week*, July 5, 1999, p. 34; "Divx: The Video Technology That Geeks Love to Hate," *Fortune*, June 21, 1999, p. 177; "Circuit City Pulls the Plug on Its Divx Videodisk Venture," *The Wall Street Journal*, June 17, 1999, p. B10; "8–Tracks, Betamax—and Divx?" *Business Week*, November 9, 1998, pp. 108–10; "DVDs Catch On (but Don't Junk the VCR Yet)," *The Wall Street Journal*, September 8, 1998, p. B1ff.; "A New Spin," *Time*, August 24, 1998, pp. 60–61.

11. For an example, see "Video Games Win Respect as Researchers Adapt Features for Computer Programs," *The Wall Street Journal*, August 29, 1991, p. B1ff.; "Multimedia Goes Mainstream," *Business Marketing*, June 1991, pp. 20–22; "A New Spin on Videodiscs," *Newsweek*, June 5, 1989, pp. 68–69.

12. *2000 Annual Report*, RJR Nabisco; "Oreo, Ritz Join Nabisco's Low-Fat Feast," *Advertising Age*, April 4, 1994, p. 3ff.; "They're Not Crying in Their Crackers at Nabisco," *Business Week*, August 30, 1993, p. 61; "Nabisco Unleashes a New Batch of Teddies," *Adweek's Marketing Week*, September 24, 1990, p. 18.

13. For more on Tide, see *2000 Annual Report*, Procter & Gamble; "Detergent Tablets of the '70s Make a Comeback," *USA Today*, July 27, 2000, p. 9B; "Boom in Liquid Detergents Has P&G Scrambling," *The Wall Street Journal*, September 25, 1997, p. B1ff.; "Ultra-Clean—Retail Cheers Still More P&G Concentrates," *Advertising Age*, August 22, 1994, p. 1ff.; "Detergent Industry Spins into New Cycle," *The Wall Street Journal*, January 5, 1993, p. B1ff.; "P&G Unleashes Flood of New Tide Products," *Advertising Age*, June 16, 1986, p. 3ff. For more on Dryel, see "The Dirt on At-Home Dry Cleaning," *The Wall Street Journal*, September 15, 2000, p. W14; "Does P&G Still Matter?" *Advertising Age*, September 25, 2000, pp. 48–54; "P&G Shifts Strategy for Dryel," *Advertising Age*, January 24, 2000, p. 4; "Novel P&G Product Brings Dry Cleaning Home," *The Wall Street Journal*, November 19, 1997, p. B1ff. For more on rescuing products online, see "How the Web Rescued Quisp from a Cereal Killing," *The Wall Street Journal*, April 24, 2000, p. B1ff.; "Oh, Heavenly Tastes: We Miss You Back on Earth," *USA Today*, March 24, 2000, p. 5D. See also "The Hard Life of Orphan Brands," *The Wall Street Journal*, April 13, 2001, p. B1ff.; "Orphan Relief," *Advertising Age*, March 19, 2001, p. 3ff.

14. For more on rejuvenating mature products, see "Dawn Gets Grease Out of Traffic's Way after Tanker Truck Spill," *Raleigh News & Observer*, May 6, 1998, p. 1Aff.; Brian Wansink, "Making Old Brands New," *American Demographics*, December 1997, pp. 53–58; "Classic Roller Skates Return as Safety Fears Dull Blades," *The Wall Street Journal*, October 24, 1997, p. B1ff.; "Dusting Off the *Britannica*," *Business Week*, October 20, 1997, pp. 143–46; "Never Say 'Old and Lousy,'" *Fortune*, October 13, 1997, p. 40; "At Du Pont, Time to Both Sow and Reap," *Business Week*, September 29, 1997, pp. 107–8; "A Boring Brand Can Be Beautiful," *Fortune*, November 18, 1991, pp. 169–77; "Teflon Is 50 Years Old, but Du Pont Is Still Finding New Uses for Invention," *The Wall Street Journal*, April 7, 1988, p. 34; Stephen W. Miller, "Managing Imitation Strategies: How Later Entrants Seize Markets From Pioneers," *Journal of the Academy of Marketing Science*, Summer 1996, pp. 277–78; Richard E. Anderson, "Phased Product Development Friend or Foe?" *Business Horizons*, November–December 1996, pp. 30–36; Regina Fazio Maruca and Amy L. Halliday, "When New Products and Customer Loyalty Collide," *Harvard Business Review*, November–December 1993, pp. 22–36.

15. "Too Many Choices," *The Wall Street Journal*, April 20, 2001, p. B1ff.; "Reposition: Simplifying the Customer's Brandscape," *Brandweek*, October 2, 2000, pp. 36–48; "Consumers to GM: You Talking to Me?" *Business Week*, June 19, 2000, pp. 213–16; "How Growth Destroys Differentiation," *Brandweek*, April 24, 2000, pp. 42–50; "P&G, Seeing Shoppers Were Being Confused, Overhauls Marketing," *The Wall Street Journal*, January 15, 1997, p. A1ff.; "Make It Simple," *Business Week*, September 9, 1996, pp. 96–104; "Diaper Firms Fight to Stay on the Bottom," *The Wall Street Journal*, March 23, 1993, p. B1ff.; "Multiple Varieties of Established Brands Muddle Consumers, Make Retailers Mad," *The Wall Street Journal*, January 24, 1992, p. B1ff.

16. "Too Many Choices," *The Wall Street Journal*, April 20, 2001, p. B1ff.; "Special Report: New Products," *Ad Age International*, April 13, 1998, pp. 17–20; "The Ghastliest Product

Launches," *Fortune*, March 16, 1998, p. 44; "New and Improved," *American Demographics*, March 1998, p. 32; "Seems the Only Problem with New Products Is That They're New," *Brandweek*, August 22, 1994, pp. 36–40; "Flops: Too Many New Products Fail. Here's Why—and How to Do Better," *Business Week*, August 16, 1993, pp. 76–82; Brian D. Ottum and William L. Moore, "The Role of Market Information in New Product Success/Failure," *Journal of Product Innovation Management*, July 1997, pp. 258–73.

17. "Makers of Chicken Tonight Find Many Cooks Say, 'Not Tonight,'" *The Wall Street Journal*, May 17, 1994, p. B1ff.; "Failure of Its Oven Lovin' Cookie Dough Shows Pillsbury Pitfalls of New Products," *The Wall Street Journal*, June 17, 1993, p. B1ff.; Sharad Sarin and Gour M. Kapur, "Lessons From New Product Failures: Five Case Studies," *Industrial Marketing Management*, November 1990, pp. 301–14.

18. "How Top Software Firms Dominate," *Investor's Business Daily*, June 12, 2001, p. A1; "Opening the Spigot," *Business Week E.Biz*, June 4, 2001, pp. EB16–Eb20; "Digital Workflow Speeds Time to Shelf," *Brand Packaging*, March/April 2001, pp. 24–26; "Shelf Life Is Short for Innovations: How to Speed Products to Market," *Investor's Business Daily*, February 26, 2001, p. A1; "How the Web Is Retooling Detroit," *Business Week*, November 27, 2000, pp. 194B–D; "How Fast Can This Baby Go?" *Business Week*, April 10, 2000, pp. 38–40; Kathleen M. Eisenhardt and Shona L. Brown, "Time Pacing: Competing in Markets That Won't Stand Still," *Harvard Business Review*, March–April 1998, pp. 59–69; Marco Iansiti and Alan MacCormack, "Developing Product on Internet Time," *Harvard Business Review*, September–October 1997, pp. 108–17; Bryan Lilly and Rockney Walters, "Toward a Model of New Product Preannouncement Timing," *Journal of Product Innovation Management*, January 1997, pp. 4–20; Richard Bauhaus, "Developing Products in Half the Time," *Journal of Product Innovation Management*, January 1997, pp. 68–69; "Fast-Selling Software that Hurries Products to Market," *Fortune*, April 29, 1996, p. 150Cff.; Joseph T. Vesey, "Time-to-Market: Put Speed in Product Development," *Industrial Marketing Management*, May 1992, pp. 151–58. For more on P&G's efforts to bring products to market faster, see "Brands in a Bind," *Business Week*, August 28, 2000, pp. 234–238; "Warm and Fuzzy Won't Save Procter & Gamble," *Business Week*, June 26, 2000, pp. 48–50; "Is P&G's Makeover Only Skin-Deep?" *Business Week*, November 15, 1999, p. 52; "P&G and Unilever's Giant Headaches," *Advertising Age*, May 24, 1999, pp. 22–28.

19. "How Burger King Got Burned in Quest to Make the Perfect Fry," *The Wall Street Journal*, January 16, 2001, p. A1ff.; "Tailoring World's Cars to U.S. Tastes," *The Wall Street Journal*, January 15, 2001, p. B1ff.; "From Research Dollars to Riches," *Investor's Business Daily*, December 5, 2000, p. A1ff; "Look Who's Doing R&D," *Fortune*, November 27, 2000, pp. 232C-Z; "Why Dow Chemical Finds Slime Sublime," *The Wall Street Journal*, November 15, 1999, p. B1ff.; "Product Development Is Always Difficult; Consider the Frito Pie," *The Wall Street Journal*, October 25, 1999, p. A1ff.; Robert Polk, Richard E. Plank, and David A. Reid, "Technical Risk and New Product Success: An Empirical Test in High Technology Business Markets," *Industrial Marketing Management*, November 1996, pp. 531–43; X. M. Song and Mark E. Parry, "A Cross-National Comparative Study of New Product Development Processes: Japan and the United States," *Journal of Marketing*, April 1997, pp. 1–18; Robert G. Cooper, "Overhauling the New Product Process," *Industrial Marketing Management*, November 1996, pp. 465–82; Jeffrey B. Schmidt and Roger J. Calantone, "Are Really New Product Development Projects Harder to Shut Down?" *Journal of Product Innovation Management*, March 1998, pp. 111–23; S. N. Wasti and Jeffrey K. Liker, "Risky Business or Competitive Power? Supplier Involvement in Japanese Product Design," *Journal of Product Innovation Management*, September 1997, pp. 337–55; Cheryl Nakata and K Sivakumar, "National Culture and New Product Development: An Integrative Review," *Journal of Marketing*, January 1996, pp. 61–72; William H. Murphy and Linda Gorchels, "How to Improve Product Management Effectiveness," *Industrial Marketing Management*, January 1996, pp. 47–58; Gary S. Lynn, Joseph G. Morone, and Albert S. Paulson, "Marketing and Discontinuous Innovation: The Probe and Learn Process," *California Management Review*, Spring 1996, pp. 8–37; Dorothy Leonard and Jeffrey F. Rayport, "Spark Innovation Through Empathic Design," *Harvard Business Review*, November–December 1997, pp. 102–8ff.; Gary L. Ragatz, Robert B. Handfield, and Thomas V. Scannell, "Success Factors for Integrating Suppliers into New Product Development," *Journal of Product Innovation Management*, May 1997, pp. 190–202; X. M. Song and Mitzi M. Montoya-Weiss, "Critical Development Activities for Really New Versus Incremental Products," *Journal of Product Innovation Management*, March 1998, pp. 124–35.

20. "Hallmark Hits the Mark," *USA Today*, June 14, 2001, p. 1Dff.; "Pickups Get Women's Touch," *USA Today*, June 13, 2001 p. 1Bff.; "Windstar's Designing Women," *USA Today*, July 19, 1999, p. 3B; "Where Great Ideas Come From," *Inc.*, April 1998, pp. 76–94; Ari-Pekka Hameri and Jukka Nihtila, "Distributed New Product Development Project Based on Internet and World-Wide Web: A Case Study," *Journal of Product Innovation Management*, March 1997, pp. 77–87; "Seeing the Future First," *Fortune*, September 5, 1994, pp. 64–70; "Detroit's New Strategy to Beat Back Japanese Is to Copy Their Ideas," *The Wall Street Journal*, October 1, 1992, p. A1ff.

21. "It Was a Hit in Buenos Aires—So Why Not Boise?" *Business Week*, September 7, 1998, pp. 56–58; Don R. Graber, "How to Manage a Global Product Development Process," *Industrial Marketing Management*, November 1996, pp. 483–89; "U.S. Companies Shop Abroad for Product Ideas," *The Wall Street Journal*, March 14, 1990, p. B1ff.

22. Eric von Hippel, *The Sources of Innovation* (New York: Oxford University Press, 1988).

23. "Gun Makers to Push Use of Gun Locks," *The Wall Street Journal*, May 9, 2001, p. B12; "U.S. Recalls Millions of Evenflo 'Joyride' Infant Seats, Carriers," *The Wall Street Journal*, May 2, 2001, p. B6; "Cosco's History Reads Like Recipe for Recalls," *USA Today*, April 4, 2001, p. 1Bff.; "Stand Up and Fight," *Business Week*, September 11, 2000, pp. 54–55; "Why One Jury Dealt a Big Blow to Chrysler in Minivan-Latch Case," *The Wall Street Journal*, November 19, 1997, p. A1ff.; "Chinese Discover Product-Liability Suits," *The Wall Street Journal*, November 13, 1997, p. B1ff.; Paula Mergenhagen, "Product Liability: Who Sues?" *American Demographics*, June 1995, pp. 48–55; "How a Jury Decided that a Coffee Spill Is Worth $2.9 Million," *The*

Wall Street Journal, September 1, 1994, p. A1ff.; Paul A. Herbig and James E. Golden, "Innovation and Product Liability," *Industrial Marketing Management*, July 1994, pp. 245–56; Robert N. Mayer and Debra L. Scammon, "Caution: Weak Product Warnings May Be Hazardous to Corporate Health," *Journal of Business Research*, June 1992, pp. 347–60; Thomas V. Greer, "Product Liability in the European Community: The Legislative History," *Journal of Consumer Affairs*, Summer 1992, pp. 159–76.

24. "Want Shelf Space at the Supermarket? Ante Up," *Business Week*, August 7, 1989, pp. 60–61; "Grocer 'Fee' Hampers New-Product Launches," *Advertising Age*, August 3, 1987, p. 1ff; Frank H. Alpert, Michael A. Kamins, and John L. Graham, "An Examination of Reseller Buyer Attitudes Toward Order of Brand Entry," *Journal of Marketing*, July 1992, pp. 25–37.

25. Fred Langerak, Ed Peelen, and Harry Commandeur, "Organizing for Effective New Product Development," *Industrial Marketing Management*, May 1997, pp. 281–89; Keith Goffin, "Evaluating Customer Support During New Product Development—An Exploratory Study," *Journal of Product Innovation Management*, January 1998, pp. 42–56; Paul S. Adler, Avi Mandelbaum, Vien Nguyen, and Elizabeth Schwerer, "Getting the Most Out of Your Product Development Process," *Harvard Business Review*, March–April 1996, pp. 134–52; Frank R. Bacon, Jr., and Thomas W. Butler, Jr., *Planned Innovation*, rev. ed. (Ann Arbor: Institute of Science and Technology, University of Michigan, 1980); Christer Karlsson and Par Ahlstrom, "Perspective: Changing Product Development Strategy—A Managerial Challenge," *Journal of Product Innovation Management*, November 1997, pp. 473–84.

26. "Torture Testing," *Fortune*, October 2, 2000, pp. 244B–X; "Industry's Amazing New Instant Prototypes," *Fortune*, January 12, 1998, pp. 120E–L; "Secrets of Product Testing," *Fortune*, November 28, 1994, pp. 166–72; "A Smarter Way to Manufacture," *Business Week*, April 30, 1990, pp. 110–17; "Oops! Marketers Blunder Their Way through the 'Herb Decade'," *Advertising Age*, February 13, 1989, p. 3ff.

27. For more on Gillette's razor costs, see "Gillette's Edge," *Brandweek*, May 28, 2001, p. 5; "No New CEO, but Gillette Does Have a New Product," *Advertising Age*, November 6, 2000, p. 25; "Brands in a Bind," *Business Week*, August 28, 2000, pp. 234–38; "Gillette Loses Face," *Fortune*, November 8, 1999, pp. 147–52; "Everything's at a Premium," *Advertising Age*, August 2, 1999, pp. 12–15; "Would You Spend $1.50 for a Razor Blade?" *Business Week*, April 27, 1998, p. 46; "The Men Who Broke Mach3," *Time*, April 27, 1998, p. 4; "Gillette Puts $300 Mil behind Its Mach3 Shaver," *Advertising Age*, April 20, 1998, p. 6; "How Gillette Brought Its MACH3 to Market," *The Wall Street Journal*, April 15, 1998, p. B1ff.; "Gillette Finally Reveals Its Vision of the Future, and It Has 3 Blades," *The Wall Street Journal*, April 14, 1998, p. A1ff. For more on Gillette's toothbrush costs, see "All About Gadgets and Gizmosity," *Fortune*, February 19, 2001, p. 264; "Gillette Lines Up Oral-B Ad Push," *Advertising Age*, December 4, 2000, p. 22; "Fashionable Mouths Bristle at the Ordinary," *USA Today*, May 10, 2000, p. 5D; "Oral-B Hopes New Toothbrush Scrubs the Competition," *USA Today*, January 4, 1999, p. 10B; "New Toothbrush Is Big-Ticket Item," *The Wall Street Journal*, October 27, 1998, p. B1ff.

28. "Oops! Marketers Blunder Their Way Through the 'Herb Decade,'" *Advertising Age*, February 13, 1989, p. 3ff.

29. "An Rx for Drug Trials," *Business Week E.Biz*, December 11, 2000, pp. EB66–EB68; "Web Sites Give Retailers Better Way to Test-Market Products," *USA Today*, August 29, 2000, p. 3B; "Can Procter & Gamble Change Its Culture, Protect Its Market Share, and Find the Next Tide?" *Fortune*, April 26, 1999, pp. 146–52; "To Test or Not to Test . . . ," *American Demographics*, June 1998, p. 64; John R. Dickinson and Carolyn P. Wilby, "Concept Testing With and Without Product Trial," *Journal of Product Innovation Management*, March 1997, pp. 117–25; "Born to Be a Little Too Wild," *Business Week*, December 18, 2000, pp. 69–70.

30. William E. Souder, David Buisson, and Tony Garrett, "Success Through Customer-Driven New Product Development: A Comparison of U.S. and New Zealand Small Entrepreneurial High Technology Firms," *Journal of Product Innovation Management*, November 1997, pp. 459–72; Artemis March, "Usability: The New Dimension of Product Design," *Harvard Business Review*, September 1994–October 1994, pp. 144–49; Peter H. Bloch, "Seeking the Ideal Form: Product Design and Consumer Response," *Journal of Marketing*, July 1995, pp. 16–29; Roger J. Calantone, "Engines of Innovation: U.S. Industrial Research at the End of an Era," *Journal of Product Innovation Management*, July 1997, pp. 315–17; George M. Chryssochoidis and Veronica Wong, "Rolling Out New Products Across Country Markets: An Empirical Study of Causes of Delays," *Journal of Product Innovation Management*, January 1998, pp. 16–41; Erik J. Hultink, Abbie Griffin, Susan Hart, and Henry S. Robben, "Industrial New Product Launch Strategies and Product Development Performance," *Journal of Product Innovation Management*, July 1997, pp. 243–57; Alan Flaschner, "Technology Fountainheads: The Management Challenge of R&D Consortia," *Journal of Product Innovation Management*, July 1997, pp. 309–12; William Q. Judge, Gerald E. Fryxell, and Robert S. Dooley, "The New Task of R&D Management: Creating Goal-Directed Communities for Innovation," *California Management Review*, Spring 1997, pp. 72–85; John P. Workman, Jr., "Marketing's Limited Role in New Product Development in One Computer Systems Firm," *Journal of Marketing Research*, November 1993, pp. 405–21.

31. Available from World Wide Web: <http://www.3m.com>; *2000 Annual Report*, 3M; "How to Get the Most Out of R&D: Balance Funds Against Risk, Timing" *Investor's Business Daily*, May 11, 2001, p. A1; "3M: Glued to the Web," *Business Week E.Biz*, November 20, 2000, pp. EB65–EB70; "3M's Big Cleanup," *Business Week*, June 5, 2000, pp. 96–98; "3M: The Heat Is on the Boss," *Business Week*, March 15, 1999, pp. 82–84; "Steel Wool Dino Roars a Powerful Message," *Advertising Age*, September 16, 1996, p. 55; "3M Eyes Retail Software with E-Post-it Notes," *Brandweek*, March 11, 1996, p. 12; "How 3M, by Tiptoeing into Foreign Markets, Became a Big Exporter," *The Wall Street Journal*, March 29, 1991, p. A1ff.

32. "Brands at Work," *Brandweek*, April 13, 1998, pp. 27–35; "Special Report: Auto Marketing & Brand Management," *Advertising Age*, April 6, 1998, pp. S1–28; "P&G Redefines the Brand Manager," *Advertising Age*, October 13, 1997, p1ff.; Don Frey, "Learning the Ropes: My Life as a Product Champion,"

Harvard Business Review, September/October 1991, pp. 46–57; Stephen K. Markham, "New Products Management," *Journal of Product Innovation Management*, July 1997, pp. 312–14; Manfred F. Maute and William B. Locander, "Innovation as a Socio-Political Process: An Empirical Analysis of Influence Behavior among New Product Managers," *Journal of Business Research*, June 1994, pp. 161–74.

33. The restaurant case is adapted from Marie Gaudard, Roland Coates and Liz Freeman, "Accelerating Improvement," *Quality Progress*, October 1991, pp. 81–88. For more on quality management and control, see "Miller Brewing: Beer with a Good Head on Its Shoulders," *Business Week E.Biz*, September 18, 2000, p. EB64; "How to Bring Out Better Products Faster," *Fortune*, November 23, 1998, pp. 238B–T. See also Roland T. Rust, Anthony J. Zahorik, and Timothy L. Keiningham, "Return on Quality (ROQ): Making Service Quality Financially Accountable," *Journal of Marketing*, April 1995, pp. 58–70; "TQM: More than a Dying Fad?" *Fortune*, October 18, 1993, pp. 66–72; "Quality Control from Mars," *The Wall Street Journal*, January 27, 1992, p. A12; William B. Locander and Daniel J. Goebel, "The Quality Train Is Leaving and Marketers Are Nodding Off in the Club Car," *Journal of Marketing Theory & Practice*, Summer 1996, pp. 1–10; William C. LaFief, "Total Quality Marketing: The Key to Regaining Market Shares," *Journal of the Academy of Marketing Science*, Fall 1996, pp. 377–78; David W. Finn, Julie Baker, Greg W. Marshall, and Roy Anderson, "Total Quality Management and Internal Customers: Measuring Internal Service Quality," *Journal of Marketing Theory & Practice*, Summer 1996, pp. 36–51; Robert F. Hurley, Melissa T. Gropper, and Gianpaolo Roma, "The Role of TQM in Advertising: A Conceptualization and a Framework for Application," *Journal of Marketing Theory & Practice*, Summer 1996, pp. 11–23; Teresa A. Swartz, "Why TQM Fails and What to Do About It," *Journal of the Academy of Marketing Science*, Fall 1996, pp. 380–81; Iris Mohr-Jackson, "Managing a Total Quality Orientation: Factors Affecting Customer Satisfaction," *Industrial Marketing Management*, March 1998, pp. 109–25; Cengiz Haksever, "Total Quality Management in the Small Business Environment," *Business Horizons*, March–April 1996, pp. 33–40; Michael P. Bigwood, "Total Quality Management at Work: Development of an Effective Competitive Analysis Process," *Industrial Marketing Management*, September 1997, pp. 459–66.

34. For examples of empowerment, see "Whole Foods Vs. Wild Oats Markets: A Study in Culture, Vision, Execution," *Investor's Business Daily*, June 29, 2001, p. A1; "Glass Act: How a Window Maker Rebuilt Itself," *Fortune*, November 13, 2000, pp. 384B–V. See also Roland T. Rust, Anthony J. Zahorik, and Timothy L. Keiningham, *Return on Quality* (Chicago: Probus, 1994); Valarie A. Zeithaml, "Service Quality, Profitability, and the Economic Worth of Customers: What We Know and What We Need to Learn," *Journal of the Academy of Marketing Science*, Winter 2000, pp. 67–86; Warren S. Martin and Wendy K. Martin, "The Application of Benchmarking to Marketing," *Journal of Marketing Theory & Practice*, Summer 1996, pp. 52–59; J. J. Cronin and Steven A. Taylor, "SERVPERF Versus SERVQUAL: Reconciling Performance-Based and Perceptions-Minus-Expectations Measurement of Service Quality," *Journal of Marketing*, January 1994, pp. 125–31; Timothy C. Johnston and Molly A. Hewa, "Fixing Service Failures," *Industrial Marketing Management*, September 1997, pp. 467–73; Shirley Taylor, "Waiting for Service: The Relationship Between Delays and Evaluations of Service," *Journal of Marketing*, April 1994, pp. 56–69; Mary J. Bitner, Bernard H. Booms, and Lois A. Mohr, "Critical Service Encounters: The Employee's Viewpoint," *Journal of Marketing*, October 1994, pp. 95–106; G T. M. Hult, "Service Quality: New Directions in Theory and Practice," *Journal of the Academy of Marketing Science*, Summer 1997, pp. 264–65; Scott W. Kelley, Timothy Longfellow, and Jack Malehorn, "Organizational Determinants of Service Employees' Exercise of Routine, Creative, and Deviant Discretion," *Journal of Retailing*, Summer 1996, pp. 135–57; Pierre Filiatrault, Jean Harvey, and Jean-Charles Chebat, "Service Quality and Service Productivity Management Practices," *Industrial Marketing Management*, May 1996, pp. 243–55; Joseph H. Foegen, "Are Managers Losing Control?" *Business Horizons*, March–April 1998, pp. 2–5; Robert Simons, "Control in an Age of Empowerment," *Harvard Business Review*, March 1995–April 1995, pp. 80–88; "Finding, Training & Keeping the Best Service Workers," *Fortune*, October 3, 1994, pp. 110–22; Timothy L. Keiningham, Roland T. Rust, and M. Marshall Weems, "The Bottom Line on Quality," *Financial Executive*, September/October 1994, pp. 50–52.

Chapter 10

1. Available from World Wide Web: <http://www.bn.com> and <http://www.amazon.com>; "Ingram Book Group and Valley Media Partner," *Nashville Business Journal*, May 29, 2001; "Ingram Book Group Shifts Distribution from Chino, Calif. To Roseburg, Ore.," *The Business Journal Portland*, May 2, 2001; "Booking Space on the Net," *USA Today*, January 28, 1998, p. 4D; "Virtual Bookstores Start to Get Real," *Business Week*, October 27, 1997, pp. 146–48; "Why the Bookstore Wars Are Good," *Fortune*, October 27, 1997, pp. 50–54; "Stop Your Whining," *Fortune*, October 13, 1997, pp. SB3–6; "Why Barnes & Noble May Crush Amazon," *Fortune*, September 29, 1997, pp. 248–50; "A Haven for the Intellect," *USA Today*, July 10, 1997, p. 1Dff.; "Bookstore Survival Stunts Have Scant Literary Merit," *The Wall Street Journal*, June 3, 1997, p. B1ff.; "Book Superstores Bring Hollywood-Like Risks to Publishing Business," *The Wall Street Journal*, May 29, 1997, p. A1ff.; "Superstores, Megabooks—and Humongous Headaches," *Business Week*, April 14, 1997, pp. 92–94; "Volume Business," *Inc. Tech*, No. 2, 1997, pp. 54–61.

2. *2000 Annual Report*, Colgate-Palmolive; *2000 Annual Report*, Procter & Gamble; "After Gobbling Up Iams, P&G Finds People Who Have Bones to Pick," *The Wall Street Journal*, June 14, 2000, p. B1ff.; "For Online Pet Stores, It's Dog-Eat-Dog," *Business Week*, March 6, 2000, pp. 78–80; "P&G Is Out to Fetch Distribution Gains for Iams Pet Food," *The Wall Street Journal*, January 6, 2000, p. A6; "Pet Supplies: Pure-Plays Teach Old Dogs New Tricks," *Discount Store News*, December 13, 1999, p. 49; "Big Pet-Supply Retailers Try to Tame the Competition," *The Wall Street Journal*, August 20, 1999, p. B4; "P&G to Buy Iams: Will Pet-Food Fight Follow?" *The Wall Street Journal*, August 12, 1999, p. B1ff.; "A Web Surfer's Best Friend," *The Wall Street Journal*, July 12, 1999, p. R45; "It's Becoming a Dogfight for the $15 Billion Pet Supply Market," *Raleigh News &*

Observer, September 25, 1994, p. 5F; "Pet Superstores Collar Customers from Supermarkets, Small Shops," *The Wall Street Journal*, November 18, 1993, p. B12.

3. "Apple Gambles with Retail Plan," *Advertising Age*, June 4, 2001, p. 45; "Sorry, Steve: Here's Why It Won't Work," *Business Week*, May 21, 2001, pp. 44–45; "Apple to Open 25 Retail Stores This Year in a Bid to Reach Out to New Customers," *The Wall Street Journal*, May 16, 2001, p. B8; "Mac Sales Coming to Mall Near You," *USA Today*, May 16, 2001, p. 3D.

4. For a discussion of the advantages and disadvantages of direct channel systems, see Donald Bowersox and M. Bixby Cooper, *Strategic Marketing Channel Management*, 2nd ed. (Burr Ridge, IL: Irwin/McGraw-Hill, 1992). See also David Shipley, Colin Egan, and Scott Edgett, "Meeting Source Selection Criteria: Direct versus Distributor Channels," *Industrial Marketing Management* 20, no. 4 (1991), pp. 297–304; Thomas L. Powers, "Industrial Distribution Options: Trade-Offs to Consider," *Industrial Marketing Management* 18, no. 3 (1989), pp. 155–62.

5. For more on Avon as example, see "Sears Says Stores Won't Sell Makeup, a Setback for Avon's New Line," *The Wall Street Journal*, July 11, 2001, p. B1ff.; "Avon Thinks Younger, Wealthier," *Advertising Age*, October 2, 2000, p. 69; "Avon Expects Boutiques in Sears, Penneys to Break Even by 2002," *The Wall Street Journal*, September 28, 2000, p. B14; "Avon: The New Calling," *Business Week*, September 18, 2000, pp. 136–48; "Avon Goes Store to Store," *The Wall Street Journal*, September 18, 2000, p. B1ff.; "Avon's Calling Beyond In-House," *Advertising Age*, June 19, 2000, p. 1ff.; "Tour de Face," *Brandweek*, May 29, 2000, pp. 34–36; *2000 Annual Report*, Avon; "Ding-Dong, Avon Calling (on the Web, Not Your Door)," *The Wall Street Journal*, December 28, 1999, p. B4; "Deck the Mall with Kiosks," *Business Week*, December 13, 1999, pp. 86–88; "Is the Bell Tolling for Door-to-Door Selling?" *Business Week E.Biz*, November 1, 1999, pp. EB58–EB60; "Not Your Mother's Avon," *Fortune*, May 24, 1999, pp. 44–46; *1999 Annual Report*, Avon; "Avon Malling," *American Demographics*, April 1999, pp. 38–40; "Avon Is Calling with a New Way to Make a Sale," *The Wall Street Journal*, October 27, 1997, p. B1ff.; "Avon's New Calling: Sell Barbie in China," *The Wall Street Journal*, May 1, 1997, p. B1ff.

6. Edward L. Nash, *Direct Marketing* (New York: McGraw-Hill, 1986).

7. For a discussion of indirect channel systems, see Frederick E. Webster, Jr., "Understanding the Relationships among Brands, Consumers, and Resellers," *Journal of the Academy of Marketing Science*, Winter 2000, pp. 17–24; Richard Parker and G. R. Funkhouser, "The Consumer As an Active Member of the Channel: Implications for Relationship Marketing," *Journal of Marketing Theory & Practice*, Spring 1997, pp. 72–79; Gordon C. Bruner, "Cyberspace: The Marketing Frontier," *Journal of Marketing*, January 1997, pp. 112–13; Lou E. Pelton, David Strutton, and James R. Lumpkin, *Marketing Channels: A Relationship Management Approach* (Burr Ridge, IL: Irwin/McGraw-Hill, 1997). See also Bert Rosenbloom and Trina L. Larsen, "How Foreign Firms View Their U.S. Distributors," *Industrial Marketing Management*, May 1992, pp. 93–102; Frank Lynn, "The Changing Economics of Industrial Distribution," *Industrial Marketing Management*, November 1992, pp. 355–60. For more on middlemen intermediaries and their functions, see Richard Greene, "Wholesaling," *Forbes*, January 2, 1984, pp. 226–28; James D. Hlavacek and Tommy J. McCuistion, "Industrial Distributors—When, Who, and How?" *Harvard Business Review*, January–February 1983, pp. 96–101; Elizabeth J. Wilson and Arch G. Woodside, "Marketing New Products with Distributors," *Industrial Marketing Management*, February 1992, pp. 15–22; W. Benoy et al., "How Industrial Distributors View Distributor-Supplier Partnership Arrangements," *Industrial Marketing Management*, January 1995, pp. 27–36.

8. For a classic discussion of the discrepancy concepts, see Wroe Alderson, "Factors Governing the Development of Marketing Channels," in *Marketing Channels for Manufactured Goods*, ed. Richard M. Clewett (Homewood, IL: Richard D. Irwin, 1954), pp. 7–9.

9. "Cellular Carriers Bypass Dealers, Creating Static," *The Wall Street Journal*, March 9, 1998, p. B1ff.

10. For some examples on how channels change to adjust discrepancies, see "How Magazines Arrive on Shelves, and Why Some Soon May Not," *The Wall Street Journal*, February 26, 1998, p. A1ff.; "Blockbuster Seeks a New Deal with Hollywood," *The Wall Street Journal*, March 25, 1998, p. B1ff.; Robert A. Mittelstaedt and Robert E. Stassen, "Structural Changes in the Phonograph Record Industry and Its Channels of Distribution, 1946–1966," *Journal of Macromarketing*, Spring 1994, pp. 31–44; Arun Sharma and Luis V. Dominguez, "Channel Evolution: A Framework for Analysis," *Journal of the Academy of Marketing Science*, Winter 1992, pp. 1–16.

11. "What's Wrong with Selling Used CDs?" *Business Week*, July 26, 1993, p. 38.

12. Jakki J. Mohr, Robert J. Fisher, and John R. Nevin, "Collaborative Communication in Interfirm Relationships: Moderating Effects of Integration and Control," *Journal of Marketing*, July 1996, pp. 103–15; Joseph P. Cannon, "Contracts, Norms, and Plural Form Governance," *Journal of the Academy of Marketing Science*, Spring 2000, pp. 180–195; Amy E. Cox and Orville C. Walker, "Reactions to Disappointing Performance in Manufacturer-Distributor Relationships: The Role of Escalation and Resource Commitments," *Psychology & Marketing*, December 1997, pp. 791–821; Rajiv P. Dant and Patrick L. Schul, "Conflict Resolution Processes in Contractual Channels of Distribution," *Journal of Marketing*, January 1992, pp. 38–54.

13. "Get Great Results from Salespeople by Finding What Really Moves Them," *Investor's Business Daily*, July 2, 2001, p. A1.

14. "For Two Tire Makers, a Flat-Out Pitch for Safer Wheels," *The Wall Street Journal*, July 3, 1997, p. B4; "Bridgestone Takes on Goodyear in Aggressive Campaign," *The Wall Street Journal*, April 16, 1997, p. B2; "Goodyear Revs Image," *Brandweek*, February 10, 1997, p. 12; "Goodyear Wins Court Dispute with Dealers," *The Wall Street Journal*, July 2, 1996, p. B6; "Stan Gault's Designated Driver," *Business Week*, April 8, 1996, pp. 128–30; "Goodyear Drives Home Lifetime Promise," *The Wall Street Journal*, March 7, 1996, p. B8; "Goodyear Expands Just Tires by Converting Full Service Centers," *Discount Store News*, May 16, 1994, p. 6; "Goodyear Plans to Sell Its Tires at

Sears Stores," *The Wall Street Journal,* March 3, 1992, p. B1ff.; Thomas L. Baker, "Leaders in Selling and Sales Management: An Analysis of the Impact of Sales and Marketing Principles on the Career of Stanley C. Gault," *Journal of Personal Selling & Sales Management,* Spring 1993, pp. 91–94; Wujin Chu and Paul R. Messinger, "Information and Channel Profits," *Journal of Retailing,* Winter 1997, pp. 487–99; Donald V. Fites, "Make Your Dealers Your Partners," *Harvard Business Review,* March–April 1996, pp. 84–95; John F. Tanner, Rick E. Ridnour, and Stephen B. Castleberry, "Types of Vertical Exchange Relationships: An Empirical Re-Examination of the Cadre/Hired-Hand Distinction," *Journal of Marketing Theory & Practice,* Summer 1997, pp. 109–25; Zhan G. Li and Rajiv P. Dant, "An Exploratory Study of Exclusive Dealing in Channel Relationships," *Journal of the Academy of Marketing Science,* Summer 1997, pp. 201–13.

15. For more on what's happening in the beer industry, see "How Big Brewers Are Sidling into Retail," *The Wall Street Journal,* May 18, 1998, p. B1ff.; "Amid Probe, Anheuser Conquers Turf," *The Wall Street Journal,* March 9, 1998, p. B1ff.; "Some Liquor Makers Are Happy if You Switch to Beer—as Long as It's Theirs," *The Wall Street Journal,* May 23, 1996, p. B1ff. See also "Making the Middleman an Endangered Species," *Business Week,* June 6, 1994, pp. 114–15; Jule B. Gassenheimer et al., "Models of Channel Maintenance: What Is the Weaker Party to Do?" *Journal of Business Research,* July 1994, pp. 225–36; Gregory T. Gundlach, Ravi S. Achrol, and John T. Mentzer, "The Structure of Commitment in Exchange," *Journal of Marketing,* January 1995, pp. 78–92; Jan B. Heide, "Interorganizational Governance in Marketing Channels," *Journal of Marketing,* January 1994, pp. 71–85; Jean L. Johnson et al., "The Exercise of Interfirm Power and Its Repercussions in U.S.-Japanese Channel Relationships," *Journal of Marketing,* April 1993, pp. 1–10.

16. "Kimberly-Clark Keeps Costco in Diapers, Absorbing Costs Itself," *The Wall Street Journal,* September 7, 2000, p. A1ff.

17. "Mothers Work: Giving the Lady What She Wants," *Fortune,* October 30, 2000, pp. T208BB–HH.

18. Ravi S. Achrol, "Changes in the Theory of Interorganizational Relations in Marketing: Toward a Network Paradigm," *Journal of the Academy of Marketing Science,* Winter 1997, pp. 56–71; Aric Rindfleisch and Jan B. Heide, "Transaction Cost Analysis: Past, Present, and Future Applications," *Journal of Marketing,* October 1997, pp. 30–54; Robert F. Lusch and James R. Brown, "Interdependency, Contracting, and Relational Behavior in Marketing Channels," *Journal of Marketing,* October 1996, pp. 19–38; Robert D. Buzzell, "Is Vertical Integration Profitable?" *Harvard Business Review,* January–February 1983, pp. 92–102; Michael Etgar and Aharon Valency, "Determinants of the Use of Contracts in Conventional Marketing Channels," *Journal of Retailing,* Winter 1983, pp. 81–92; Louis W. Stern and Torger Reve, "Distribution Channels as Political Economies: A Framework for Comparative Analysis," *Journal of Marketing,* Summer 1980, pp. 52–64.

19. "Special Report: Partners," *Business Week,* October 25, 1999, pp, 106–30.

20. "A Talk with the Man Who Got Rayovac All Charged Up," *Business Week,* February 21, 2000, pp. 32F–32H.

21. "Esprit's Spirited Style Is Hot Seller," *USA Today,* March 25, 1986, p. B5; "Apparel Firm Makes Profits, Takes Risks by Flouting Tradition," *The Wall Street Journal,* June 11, 1985, p. 1ff; David Rylander, David Strutton, and Lou E. Pelton, "Toward a Synthesized Framework of Relational Commitment: Implications for Marketing Channel Theory and Practice," *Journal of Marketing Theory & Practice,* Spring 1997, pp. 58–71; Gary L. Frazier and Walfried M. Lassar, "Determinants of Distribution Intensity," *Journal of Marketing,* October 1996, pp. 39–51; Adam J. Fein and Erin Anderson, "Patterns of Credible Commitments: Territory and Brand Selectivity in Industrial Distribution Channels," *Journal of Marketing,* April 1997, pp. 19–34.

22. "Antitrust Issues and Marketing Channel Strategy" and "Case 1—Continental T.V., Inc., et al. v. GTE Sylvania, Inc.," in Louis W. Stern and Thomas L. Eovaldi, *Legal Aspects of Marketing Strategy* (Englewood Cliffs, NJ: Prentice-Hall, 1984), pp. 300–361.

23. For more on Reebok, see *2000 Annual Report,* Reebok; "Reebok's Direct Sales Spark a Retail Revolt," *Adweek's Marketing Week,* December 2, 1991, p. 7. See also Saul Sands and Robert J. Posch, Jr., "A Checklist of Questions for Firms Considering a Vertical Territorial Distribution Plan," *Journal of Marketing,* Summer 1982, pp. 38–43; Debra L. Scammon and Mary Jane Sheffet, "Legal Issues in Channels Modification Decisions: The Question of Refusals to Deal," *Journal of Public Policy and Marketing* 5 (1986), pp. 82–96. For more on VW Beetle sales online, see "Volkswagen Drives Some Beetle Sales Online," *Investor's Business Daily,* June 21, 2000, p. A8; "VW Rides a Hot Streak," *Newsweek,* May 22, 2000, pp. 48–50; "VW Targets Web-Savvy with Online Beetle Offer," *Advertising Age,* May 8, 2000, p. 18. For more on Volvo sales online, see "Driving through the Clutter," *Brandweek,* November 27, 2000, pp. IQ34–IQ36; "Volvo Plans Online Ad Campaign for Latest Launch," *The Wall Street Journal,* September 25, 2000, p. B1ff.; "Volvo, Seeking Younger Buyers, Tries to Create a Sexier Image," *The Wall Street Journal,* August 26, 1999, p. B1ff.

24. Gregory T. Gundlach and Patrick E. Murphy, "Ethical and Legal Foundations of Relational Marketing Exchanges," *Journal of Marketing,* October 1993, pp. 35–46; Craig B. Barkacs, "Multilevel Marketing and Antifraud Statutes: Legal Enterprises or Pyramid Schemes?" *Journal of the Academy of Marketing Science,* Spring 1997, pp. 176–77; Robert A. Robicheaux and James E. Coleman, "The Structure of Marketing Channel Relationships," *Journal of the Academy of Marketing Science,* Winter 1994, pp. 38–51; Brett A. Boyle and F. Robert Dwyer, "Power, Bureaucracy, Influence and Performance: Their Relationships in Industrial Distribution Channels," *Journal of Business Research,* March 1995, pp. 189–200.

25. "It's Getting Easier to Return Items Bought on the Web," *Investor's Business Daily,* May 1, 2001, p. A8; "Returning Gifts Bought Online Presents Fewer Problems," *Investor's Business Daily,* January 22, 2001, p. A8.

26. See, for example, "P&G to Stores: Keep the Dented Crisco Cans," *The Wall Street Journal,* March 21, 1997, p. B1ff.; "Turning Trash into Cash," *Traffic Management,* October 1993, pp. 46–48; Harvey Alter, "Cost of Recycling Municipal Solid Waste With and Without a Concurrent Beverage Container Deposit Law," *Journal of Consumer Affairs,* Summer 1993, pp. 166–86.

Chapter 11

1. "Coca-Cola Gets Hip to the 'Net," *Advertising Age*, July 2, 2001, p. 21; "Coke and Pepsi Escalate Their Water Fight," *The Wall Street Journal*, May 18, 2001, p. B8; "Sports Drinks Refresh Rivalry for Coke, Pepsi," *The Wall Street Journal*, May 8, 2001, p. B1ff.; "Will Coke.net Be the Real Thing to Put Fizz into Fountain Sales?" *Investor's Business Daily*, May 4, 2001, p. A5; "Coke Hopes to Add Fizz to Future with New Structure, Management," *Investor's Business Daily*, April 18, 2001, p. A1; "Why Coke Indulges (the Few) Fans of Tab," *The Wall Street Journal*, April 13, 2001, p. B1ff.; "Guess Who's Winning the Cola Wars," *Fortune*, April 2, 2001, pp. 164–65; "Coca-Cola Readies Global Assault," *Advertising Age*, April 2, 2001, p. 1ff.; "Repairing the Coke Machine," *Business Week*, March 19, 2001, pp. 86–88; "Coke and P&G's Shotgun Wedding," *Ad Age Global*, March 2001, p. 6; "Coke's 'Think Local' Strategy Has Yet to Prove Itself," *The Wall Street Journal*, March 1, 2001, p. B6; "Is Coke Getting as Good as It Gives in P&G Partnership?" *The Wall Street Journal*, February 22, 2001, p. B4; "Coke and P&G Plan to Create $4.2 Billion Juice and Snack Company," *The Wall Street Journal*, February 21, 2001, p. B1ff.; "Coke Retains Top Spot in U.S. Soda Sales," *The Wall Street Journal*, February 16, 2001, p. B8; "Coke Shifts Strategy as Surge Fizzles," *Advertising Age*, February 12, 2001, p. 1ff.; "Coke to Acquire Maker of Coffee, Bottled Drinks," *The Wall Street Journal*, January 12, 2001, p. B4; "Tea Is a Hit for Coke," *Ad Age Global*, January 2001, p. 5; "Pepsi, Coke Still at War, but on Different Fronts," *Advertising Age*, December 11, 2000, p. 4; "Coke and Pepsi Do Battle on the Web," *Ad Age Global*, November 2000, p. 48; "Pepsi, Coke Duke It Out in India, China," *Ad Age Global*, October 2000, p. 6; "Consumers Lose Some Appetite for Fizzy Drinks," *The Wall Street Journal*, September 19, 2000, p. B1ff.; "Brands in a Bind," *Business Week*, August 28, 2000, pp. 234–38; "Coca-Cola Light Employs Local Edge," *Advertising Age*, August 21, 2000, p. 18ff.; "For Coke, Local Is It," *Business Week*, July 3, 2000, p. 122; "To Fix Coca-Cola, Daft Sets Out to Get Relationships Right," *The Wall Street Journal*, June 23, 2000, p. A1ff.; "Coke Looses Ad Reins," *Ad Age International*, April 2000, p. 1ff.; "Now, Coke Is No Longer It," *Business Week*, February 28, 2000, pp. 148–51; "Guess Who Wants to Make a Splash in Water," *Business Week*, March 1, 1999, p. 36; "The China Card," *Fortune*, May 25, 1998, p. 82; "For Pepsi, a Battle to Capture Coke's Fountain Sales," *The Wall Street Journal*, May 11, 1998, p. B1ff.; "Pepsi Hits Coca-Cola with an Antitrust Lawsuit," *The Wall Street Journal*, May 8, 1998, p. A3ff.; "For Coke in India, Thums Up Is the Real Thing," *The Wall Street Journal*, April 29, 1998, p. B1ff.; "I'd Like the World to Buy a Coke," *Business Week*, April 13, 1998, pp. 70–76; "If You Can't Beat 'Em, Copy 'Em," *Business Week*, November 17, 1997, p. 50; "Where Coke Goes from Here," *Fortune*, October 13, 1997, pp. 88–91; "Advertising Breezes along the Nile River with Signs for Sails," *The Wall Street Journal*, July 18, 1997, p. A1ff.; "Coke Recruits Paraplegics to Help Fight PepsiCo in Soda War in India," *The Wall Street Journal*, June 10, 1997, p. B9; "A Coke and a Perm? Soda Giant Is Pushing into Unusual Locales," *The Wall Street Journal*, May 8, 1997, p. A1ff.; "For Coca-Cola in Japan, Things Go Better with Milk," *The Wall Street Journal*, January 20, 1997, p. B1ff.; "Coke Pours into Asia," *Business Week*, October 28, 1996, p. 72ff.; "Coke's Soda Fountain for Offices Fizzles, Dashing High Hopes," *The Wall Street Journal*, June 14, 1993, p. A1ff.; "The World's Best Brand," *Fortune*, May 31, 1993, pp. 44–54. For more on Pepsi's distribution, see "Playing for Time," *Brandweek*, June 11, 2001, p. 4; "Beverage Marketers See Refreshing Distribution Possibilities," *The Wall Street Journal*, May 29, 2001, p. B2; "FTC Could Try to Block Pepsi-Quaker Merger," *USA Today*, May 10, 2001, p. 1B.; "Necessity and Invention," *Brandweek*, February 19, 2001, pp. 22–25; "Done Duo," *Brandweek*, January 15, 2001, p. 1ff.; "Quaker Accepts Pepsi's $13.4B Bid," *USA Today*, December 5, 2000, p. 3B; "Race to Buy Gatorade Stirs Up Drink Market," *Investor's Business Daily*, December 4, 2000, p. A10; "Regulators to Keep Close Eye on PepsiCo after Deal," *USA Today*, December 4, 2000, p. 14A; "PepsiCo Hopes to Feast on Profits from Quaker Snacks," *The Wall Street Journal*, December 4, 2000, p. B4; "Behind the Coke Board's Refusal to Let CEO Daft Buy Quaker Oats," *The Wall Street Journal*, November 30, 2000, p. B1ff.; "Gotta Get That Gator," *Business Week*, November 27, 2000, pp. 91–94; "Cadbury's Snapple Testing Out Bottled Beer," *Advertising Age*, November 27, 2000, p. 26; "New Age Dawns as Soda Giants Go Alternative," *Advertising Age*, November 6, 2000, p. 96; "Pepsi Edges Past Coke, and It Has Nothing to Do with Cola," *The Wall Street Journal*, November 6, 2000, p. A1ff.; "Pepsi Edges Coke in Deal to Buy New Age SoBe," *The Wall Street Journal*, October 30, 2000, p. B1ff.; "Pucker Up! Pepsi's Latest Weapon Is Lemon-Lime," *The Wall Street Journal*, October 13, 2000, p. B1ff.; "Snapple vs. SoBe," *Brandweek*, July 10, 2000, p. 1ff.; "PepsiCo's New Formula: How Roger Enrico Is Remaking the Company . . . and Himself," *Business Week*, April 10, 2000, pp. 172–84; "Lizard Wizards," *Brandweek*, November 22, 1999, pp. 30–32; "A Fruity Kind of Cola War," *USA Today*, August 3, 1999, p. 1Bff.; "Between Coke and a Hard Place," *Brandweek*, June 22, 1998, pp. 34–38; "Pepsi Gets Back in the Game," *Time*, April 26, 1999, pp. 44–46; "Herbal-Tonic Bottler Has Healthy Start," *Inc.*, June 1999, pp. 21–22.

2. Available from World Wide Web: <http://www.transora.com> and <http://www.fmi.org/media/bg/ecr1>; "How to Make a Frozen Lasagna (with Just $250 Million)," *Fortune*, April 30, 2001, pp. 149–54; "Delivering the Goods," *Fortune*, November 28, 1994, pp. 64–78; "Making the Middleman an Endangered Species," *Business Week*, June 6, 1994, pp. 114–15; "The Nitty-Gritty of ECR Systems: How One Company Makes It Pay," *Advertising Age*, May 2, 1994, pp. S1ff.; "Behind the Tumult at P&G," *Fortune*, March 7, 1994, pp. 74–82.

3. "Compaq Stumbles as PCs Weather New Blow," *The Wall Street Journal*, March 9, 1998, p. B1ff.; "At What Profit Price?" *Brandweek*, June 23, 1997, pp. 24–28; "Delivering the Goods," *Fortune*, November 28, 1994, pp. 64–78; Brian F. O'Neil and Jon L. Iveson, "Strategically Managing the Logistics Function," *The Logistics and Transportation Review*, December 1991, pp. 359–78; Lloyd M. Rinehart, M. Bixby Cooper, and George D. Wagenheim, "Furthering the Integration of Marketing and Logistics Through Customer Service in the Channel," *Journal of the Academy of Marketing Science*, Winter 1989, pp. 63–72; Philip B. Schary, "A Concept of Customer Service," *The Logistics and Transportation Review*, December 1992, pp. 341–52; Edward A. Morash and John Ozment, "Toward Management of Transportation Service Quality," *The Logistics and Transportation Review*, June 1994, pp. 115–40; Michael H. Morris and Duane L. Davis, "Measuring and Managing Customer Service in Industrial

Firms," *Industrial Marketing Management*, November 1992, pp. 343–54; Gary L. Frazier, Robert E. Spekman, and Charles R. O'Neal, "Just-In-Time Exchange Relationships in Industrial Markets," *Journal of Marketing*, October 1988, pp. 52–67; William D. Perreault, Jr., and Frederick A. Russ, "Physical Distribution Service in Industrial Purchase Decisions," *Journal of Marketing*, April 1976, pp. 3–10.

4. Daniel J. Flint, "Logiticians as Marketers: Their Role When Customers' Desired Value Changes," *Journal of Business Logistics*, 2000, Vol. 21, 2, pp. 19–46; "Logistics Gets a Little Respect," *Business Week E.Biz*, November 20, 2000, pp. EB112–EB116; "One Smart Cookie," *Business Week E.Biz*, November 20, 2000, p. EB120; "A Cereal Maker Hitches Its Wagons to the Web," *Business Week E.Biz*, September 18, 2000, p. EB80; "Costs Too High? Bring in the Logistics Experts," *Fortune*, November 10, 1997, pp. 200C–T; "Ryder Sees the Logic of Logistics," *Business Week*, August 5, 1996, p. 56; Carol J. Emerson and Curtis M. Grimm, "The Relative Importance of Logistics and Marketing Customer Service: A Strategic Perspective," *Journal of Business Logistics*, 1998, pp. 17–32; Edward A. Morash, Cornelia L. M. Droge, and Shawnee K. Vickery, "Strategic Logistics Capabilities for Competitive Advantage and Firm Success," *Journal of Business Logistics*, 1996, pp. 1–22; John L. Kent and Daniel J. Flint, "Perspectives on the Evolution of Logistics Thought," *Journal of Business Logistics*, 1997, pp. 15–29; Jonathan W. Kohn and Michael A. McGinnis, "Logistics Strategy: A Longitudinal Study," *Journal of Business Logistics*, 1997, pp. 1–14; Steven R. Clinton and David J. Closs, "Logistics Strategy: Does It Exist?" *Journal of Business Logistics*, 1997, pp. 19–44; Prabir K. Bagchi and Helge Virum, "Logistical Alliances: Trends and Prospects in Integrated Europe," *Journal of Business Logistics*, 1998, pp. 191–213.

5. For more on Clorox, see *2000 Annual Report*, Clorox; "The Web @ Work/Clorox Co.," *The Wall Street Journal*, October 9, 2000, p. B21; also available from World Wide Web: <http://www.clorox.com>. See also Forrest E. Harding, "Logistics Service Provider Quality: Private Measurement, Evaluation, and Improvement," *Journal of Business Logistics*, 1998, pp. 103–20; Carol C. Bienstock, John T. Mentzer, and Monroe M. Bird, "Measuring Physical Distribution Service Quality," *Journal of the Academy of Marketing Science*, Winter 1997, pp. 31–44; G. T. M. Hult, "Measuring Cycle Time of the Global Procurement Process," *Industrial Marketing Management*, September 1997, pp. 403–12; R. Mohan Pisharodi, "Preference for Supplier When Supplier and Customer Perceptions of Customer Service Levels Differ," *The Logistics and Transportation Review*, March 1994, pp. 31–54; Benson P. Shapiro, V. K. Rangan, and J. J. Sviokla, "Staple Yourself to an Order," *Harvard Business Review*, July–August, 1992, pp. 113–22; J. B. Fuller, J. O'Conor, and R. Rawlinson, "Tailored Logistics: The Next Advantage," *Harvard Business Review*, May–June 1993, pp. 87–98.

6. Lisa M. Ellram and Sue P. Siferd, "Total Cost of Ownership: A Key Concept in Strategic Cost Management Decisions," *Journal of Business Logistics*, 1998, pp. 55–84; Scott R. Swenseth and Michael R. Godfrey, "Estimating Freight Rates for Logistics Decisions," *Journal of Business Logistics*, 1996, pp. 213–31; Philip T. Evers, "The Impact of Transshipments on Safety Stock Requirements," *Journal of Business Logistics*, 1996, pp. 109–33.

7. For more on JIT, see "As Christmas Approaches, Parts Shortages Plague Electronic Makers," *The Wall Street Journal*, October 10, 2000, p. B1ff.; "Parts Shortages Hamper Electronics Makers," *The Wall Street Journal*, July 7, 2000, p. B5; Richard Germain, Cornelia Droge, and Nancy Spears, "The Implications of Just-in-Time for Logistics Organization Management and Performance," *Journal of Business Logistics*, 1996, pp. 19–34; Claudia H. Pragman, "JIT II: A Purchasing Concept for Reducing Lead Times in Time-Based Competition," *Business Horizons*, July–August 1996, pp. 54–58; Faye W. Gilbert, Joyce A. Young, and Charles R. O'Neal, "Buyer-Seller Relationships in Just-in-Time Purchasing Environments," *Journal of Business Research*, February 1994, pp. 111–20; Steve McDaniel, Joseph G. Ormsby, and Alicia B. Gresham, "The Effect of JIT on Distributors," *Industrial Marketing Management*, May 1992, pp. 145–50; "Allen-Edmonds Shoe Tries 'Just-in-Time' Production," *The Wall Street Journal*, March 4, 1993, p. B2.

8. Available from World Wide Web: <http://silmaril.smeal.psu.edu/misc/supply_chain>; Rakesh Niraj, "Customer Profitability in a Supply Chain," *Journal of Marketing*, July 2001, pp. 1–17; William F. Crittenden, "Business Success: A Way of Thinking about Strategy, Critical Supply Chain Assets and Operational Best Practices," *Journal of the Academy of Marketing Science*, Summer 2000, pp. 446–8; Donald J. Bowersox, "Ten Mega-Trends That Will Revolutionize Supply Chain Logistics," *Journal of Business Logistics*, 2000, Vol. 21, 2, pp. 1–17; "New Victories in the Supply-Chain Revolution," *Fortune*, October 30, 2000, pp. T208C–HH; "How a Tighter Supply Chain Extends the Enterprise," *Fortune*, November 8, 1999, pp. 272A–DD; "Wrestling New Wealth from the Supply Chain," *Fortune*, November 9, 1998, pp. 204C–204Z; "The Push to Streamline Supply Chains," *Fortune*, March 3, 1997, pp. 108C–R; Chickery J. Kasouf and Kevin G. Celuch, "Interfirm Relationships in the Supply Chain: The Small Supplier's View," *Industrial Marketing Management*, November 1997, pp. 475–86; William H. Borghesani, Peter L. de la Cruz, and David B. Berry, "Controlling the Chain: Buyer Power, Distributive Control, and New Dynamics in Retailing," *Business Horizons*, July–August 1997, pp. 17–24; Jeffrey H. Dyer, Dong S. Cho, and Wujin Chu, "Strategic Supplier Segmentation: The Next 'Best Practice' in Supply Chain Management," *California Management Review*, Winter 1998, pp. 57–77; Noel P. Greis and John D. Kasarda, "Enterprise Logistics in the Information Era," *California Management Review*, Summer 1997, pp. 55–78; Craig R. Carter and Lisa M. Ellram, "Reverse Logistics: A Review of the Literature and Framework for Future Investigation," *Journal of Business Logistics*, 1998, pp. 85–102; Harry L. Sink and C. J. Langley, "A Managerial Framework for the Acquisition of Third-Party Logistics Services," *Journal of Business Logistics*, 1997, pp. 163–89; Robert C. Lieb and Hugh L. Randall, "A Comparison of the Use of Third-Party Logistics Services by Large American Manufacturers, 1991, 1994, and 1995," *Journal of Business Logistics*, 1996, pp. 305–20; B. C. Arntzen, G. C. Brown, T. P. Harrison et al., "Global Supply Chain Management at Digital Equipment Corporation," *Interfaces*, January–February, 1995.

9. Cornelia Droge, "The Relationship of Electronic Data Interchange with Inventory and Financial Performance," *Journal of Business Logistics*, 2000, Vol. 21, 2, pp. 209–31; Lisa R.

Williams, Avril Nibbs, Dimples Irby, and Terence Finley, "Logistics Integration: The Effect of Information Technology, Team Composition, and Corporate Competitve Positioning," *Journal of Business Logistics*, 1997, pp. 31–41; Paul R. Murphy and James M. Daley, "International Freight Forwarder Perspectives on Electronic Data Interchange and Information Management Issues," *Journal of Business Logistics*, 1996, pp. 63–84; Kenneth B. Kahn and John T. Mentzer, "EDI and EDI Alliances: Implications for the Sales Forecasting Function," *Journal of Marketing Theory & Practice*, Spring 1996, pp. 72–78; Ira Lewis and Alexander Talalayevsky, "Logistics and Information Technology: A Coordination Perspective," *Journal of Business Logistics*, 1997, pp. 141–57.

10. "A Smart Cookie at Pepperidge," *Fortune*, December 22, 1986, pp. 67–74.

11. "As Stores Scrimp More and Order Less, Suppliers Take on Greater Risks, Costs," *The Wall Street Journal*, December 10, 1991, p. B1ff.

12. Douglas Lambert, James R. Stock, and Lisa M. Ellram, *Fundamentals of Logistics* (Burr Ridge, IL: Irwin/McGraw-Hill, 1998).

13. For more detail on deregulation of transportation, see Paul D. Larson, "Transportation Deregulation, JIT, and Inventory Levels," *The Logistics and Transportation Review*, June 1991, pp. 99–112; James C. Nelson, "Politics and Economics in Transport Regulation and Deregulation—A Century Perspective of the ICC's Role," *The Logistics and Transportation Review*, March, 1987, pp. 5–32; Karl M. Ruppentha, "U.S. Airline Deregulation-Winners and Losers," *The Logistics and Transportation Review*, March 1987, pp. 65–82.

14. For a more detailed comparison of mode characteristics, see Robert Dahlstrom, Kevin M. McNeilly, and Thomas W. Speh, "Buyer-Seller Relationships in the Procurement of Logistical Services," *Journal of the Academy of Marketing Science*, Spring 1996, pp. 110–24; Roger Dale Abshire and Shane R. Premeaux, "Motor Carriers' and Shippers' Perceptions of the Carrier Choice Decision," *The Logistics and Transportation Review*, December 1991, pp. 351–58; Brian J. Gibson, Harry L. Sink, and Ray A. Mundy, "Shipper-Carrier Relationships and Carrier Selection Criteria," *The Logistics and Transportation Review*, December 1993, pp. 371–82.

15. "Trains: Industry Report," *Investor's Business Daily*, May 7, 2001, p. B6; "Railroads: Asleep at the Switch," *Business Week*, April 2, 2001, pp. 78B-78D; "Tired of Costs, Delays of Railroads, Firms Lay Their Own Tracks," *The Wall Street Journal*, February 6, 1998, p. A1ff.; "America's Railroads Struggle to Recapture Their Former Glory," *The Wall Street Journal*, December 5, 1997, p. A1ff.; "The Rails: Trouble Behind, Trouble Ahead," *Business Week*, November 24, 1997, pp. 40–42; "An Unsolved Mystery: Where Are Shippers' Rail Cars?" *The Wall Street Journal*, October 13, 1997, p. B1ff.; "Union Pacific Tie-Ups Reach across Economy," *The Wall Street Journal*, October 8, 1997, p. B1ff.; "The Great Train Game," *Fortune*, November 11, 1996, pp. 151–54; "High Tech Puts Them Back on Track," *USA Today*, November 2, 1994, p. 1Bff.

16. "Inside the Race to Get Hot Video Games on Shelves," *The Wall Street Journal*, December 20, 2000, p. B1ff.

17. "Trucking: Rig and Roll," *The Wall Street Journal*, October 23, 2000, p. R51; "Diesel Is Fueling a New Kind of Road Rage," *Business Week*, September 18, 2000, pp. 154–56; "Trucking Gets Sophisticated," *Fortune*, July 24, 2000, pp. T270B–R; "Forward Air Corp.: Hauler Gets Freight from Jets to Businesses," *Investor's Business Daily*, June 6, 2000, p. A14; "Making Sure Big Rigs Have Something to Carry," *Business Week*, June 12, 2000, p. 168F; "Trucking Finds the Internet," *Heavy Duty Trucking*, October 1999, pp. 116–20; "Hauling Super Freight Takes Ingenuity and a Huge Rig," *The Wall Street Journal*, April 13, 1998, p. B1ff.; "Extra-Big Rigs Could Barrel Down More Roads," *The Wall Street Journal*, June 16, 1997, p. B1ff.; "More Trucks Shake Residential America," *The Wall Street Journal*, April 29, 1997, p. B1ff.; "Riding the Data Highway," *Newsweek*, March 21, 1994, p. 54–55; "Hauling It for Less," *Nation's Business*, January 1994, pp. 46–48. For trucking's role in e-commerce, see "Bekins Worldwide," *Ecompany*, April 2001, p. 126; "Gunning for the Heavy Weights in National Delivery," *Fortune*, June 12, 2000, p. 322; "How E-Tailers Deliver within Hours," *Fortune*, May 29, 2000, pp. T210B-N; "E-Commerce's Newest Portals: Truck Drivers," *The Wall Street Journal*, January 3, 2000, p. A11ff.; "Getting the Goods," *The Wall Street Journal*, November 22, 1999, p. R39.

18. "Shipping Firms' Web Sites Help You Track Items," *Investor's Business Daily*, July 6, 2001, p. A6; "Why FedEx Is Flying High," *Fortune*, November 10, 1997, pp. 155–60; "UPS Puts Its Back into It," *Business Week*, October 27, 1997, p. 50; "FedEx Hears International Opportunity Knocking," *USA Today*, October 7, 1997, p. 3B; "Federal Express, UPS Battle for a Foothold in Asia," *The Wall Street Journal*, January 22, 1997, p. B1ff.; "UPS, Feeling Boxed In, Stages Its Own Coming Out," *The Wall Street Journal*, September 17, 1996, p. B4.

19. K. Raguraman and Claire Chan, "The Development of Sea-Air Intermodal Transportation: An Assessment of Global Trends," *The Logistics and Transportation Review*, December 1994, p. 379; "Cargo that Phones Home," *Fortune*, November 15, 1993, p. 143; "Grain Processor Improvises to Stay Afloat," *The Wall Street Journal*, July 21, 1993, p. B1ff.

20. "Hospital Cost Cutters Push Use of Scanners to Track Inventories," *The Wall Street Journal*, June 10, 1997, p. A1ff.; "Retired General Speeds Deliveries, Cuts Costs, Help Sears Rebound," *The Wall Street Journal*, July 16, 1996, p. A1ff.; Paul Zinszer, "Supply Chain Strategies for Managing Excess Inventories," *Journal of Marketing Theory & Practice*, Spring 1996, pp. 55–60; Paul A. Dion, Loretta M. Hasey, Patrick C. Dorin, and Jean Lundin, "Consequences of Inventory Stockouts," *Industrial Marketing Management* 20, no. 1 (1991), pp. 23–28.

21. Anita Lahey, "Brand Revolution," from World Wide Web: <http://www.fmi.org>.

22. "Compaq Borrows Wal-Mart's Idea to Boost Production," *The Wall Street Journal*, June 17, 1994, p. B4; Wade Ferguson, "Buying an Industrial Service Warehouse Space," *Industrial Marketing Management*, February 1983, pp. 63–66; Arnold B. Maltz, "Outsourcing the Warehousing Function: Economics and Strategic Considerations," *The Logistics and Transportation Review*, September 1994, pp. 245–66; Patricia J. Daugherty, Dale S. Rogers, and Theodore P. Stank, "Benchmarking: Strategic

Implications for Warehousing Firms," *The Logistics and Transportation Review*, March 1994, pp. 55–72.

23. "Hot New Technologies for American Factories," *Fortune*, June 26, 2000, pp. 288A–K; "Smart Labels Do What Bar Codes Do, Only Better," *Raleigh News & Observer*, November 22, 1999, p. 6D; "Cotter DC Rides the Wave of Technology into the Future," *Hardware Age*, October 1995, p. 50ff.; "Scanning the Distribution Horizon," *Foodservice Equipment & Supplies Specialist*, June 1994, pp. 44–52.

24. "Distribution Center Doubles Output with Paperless System," *Modern Materials Handling/Scan Tech News*, September 1994, pp. S17–19; Maureen E. Lynch, Sharon J. Imada, and James H. Bookbinder, "The Future of Logistics in Canada: A Delphi-Based Forecast" *The Logistics and Transportation Review*, March 1994, p. 95.

Chapter 12

1. Available from World Wide Web: <http://www.friedas.com>; "How Lower-Tech Gear Beat Web 'Exchanges' at Their Own Game," *The Wall Street Journal*, March 16, 2001, p. A1ff.; "Family Firms Confront Calamities of Transfer," *USA Today*, August 29, 2000, p. 1Bff.; "Business, Too Close to Home," *Time*, July 17, 2000, pp. B24–B27; "The Kiwi to My Success," *Hemispheres*, July 1999; "Searching for the Next Kiwi: Frieda's Branded Produce," *Brandweek*, May 2, 1994, pp. 46–48; "Strange Fruits," *Inc.*, November 1989, pp. 80–90; "The Produce Marketer," *Savvy*, June 1988, pp. 26–28.

2. Available from World Wide Web: <http://www.census.gov>; U.S. Bureau of the Census, *Statistical Abstract of the United States 2000* (Washington, DC: U.S. Government Printing Office, 2000); U.S. Bureau of the Census, *County Business Patterns 1998, United States* (Washington, DC: U.S. Government Printing Office, 2000); "Remedies for an Economic Hangover," *Fortune*, June 25, 2001, pp. 130–39; "Outlet Centers Go Upmarket with Amenities," *The Wall Street Journal*, June 6, 2001, p. B12; "Designer Stores, in Extra Large," *The Wall Street Journal*, June 6, 2001, p. B1ff.; "Special Report: The New Leaders," *DSN Retailing Today*, May 8, 2000, pp. 37–130; "Feisty Mom-and-Pops of Gotham Strike Back at Drugstore Chains," *The Wall Street Journal*, March 20, 2000, p. A1ff.; "Making Malls (Gasp!) Convenient," *The Wall Street Journal*, February 8, 2000, p. B1ff.; "Look Who's Thinking Small," *Business Week*, May 17, 1999, pp. 66–70; "Revolution in the Showroom," *Business Week*, February 19, 1996, pp. 70–76; "The Future of Retailing," *American Demographics*, September 1995, p. 26ff.

3. "99 Cents Only Stores: So You Think It's Funny? Well, Come On In," *Investor's Business Daily*, July 13, 2001, p. A6; "Family Dollar Uses 'Hardline' Stance to Get a Leg Up in Discount Battles," *Investor's Business Daily*, May 23, 2001, p. A1; "Family Dollar's Howard Levine: Information Helps Him Keep His Company on Top," *Investor's Business Daily*, May 18, 2001, p. A3; "Cheap Thrills for Shoppers," *Newsweek*, April 16, 2001, p. 45; "Dollar General Hits Milestone," *DSN Retailing Today*, February 19, 2001, p. 1ff.; "In Modest Times, 'Dollar' Stores Remain Upbeat," *The Wall Street Journal*, December 22, 2000, p. B1ff.; "The Buck Stops Here," *Advertising Age*, November 6, 2000, p. 1ff.; "Penny Pinchers Propel a Retail Star," *The Wall Street Journal*, March 20, 1998, p. B1ff.; "The Best Retailer You've Never Heard Of," *Fortune*, March 16, 1998, pp. 110–12; "For You, Toto, 10% Off on the Lamp," *Fortune*, February 2, 1998, pp. 148D–F; "Ikea's New Game Plan," *Business Week*, October 6, 1997, pp. 99–102; "Beyond the Database: Sales and Service on a First-Name Basis," *Colloquy*, No. 1, 1997, pp. 8–9; "Neiman Marcus, Saks Wage Expensive Battle for Upscale Shoppers," *The Wall Street Journal*, November 21, 1996, p. A1ff.; Eric R. Spangenberg, Ayn E. Crowley, and Pamela W. Henderson, "Improving the Store Environment: Do Olfactory Cues Affect Evaluations and Behaviors?" *Journal of Marketing*, April 1996, pp. 67–80; Richard L. Oliver, Roland T. Rust, and Sajeev Varki, "Customer Delight: Foundations, Findings, and Managerial Insight," *Journal of Retailing*, Fall 1997, pp. 311–36; William R. Darden and Barry J. Babin, "Exploring the Concept of Affective Quality: Expanding the Concept of Retail Personality," *Journal of Business Research*, February 1994, pp. 101–10; Jeffrey S. Conant, Denise T. Smart, and Roberto Solano-Mendez, "Generic Retailing Types, Distinctive Marketing Competencies, and Competitive Advantage," *Journal of Retailing*, Fall, 1993, pp. 254–79; Robert J. Donovan et al., "Store Atmosphere and Purchasing Behavior," *Journal of Retailing*, Fall 1994, p. 283; John P. Dickson and Douglas L. MacLachlan, "Social Distance and Shopping Behavior," *Journal of the Academy of Marketing Science*, Spring 1990, pp. 153–62.

4. "Small Retailers Outfox Big Rivals," *Investor's Business Daily*, November 28, 2000, p. A1; "Urban Rarity: Stores Offering Spiffy Service," *The Wall Street Journal*, July 25, 1996, p. B1ff.; "Airports: New Destination for Specialty Retailers," *USA Today*, January 11, 1996, p. 5B; "Buoyant Shoppers Boost Specialty Sales," *The Wall Street Journal*, December 15, 1992, p. B1ff.; Sharon E. Beatty, Morris Mayer, James E. Coleman, Kristy E. Reynolds, and Jungki Lee, "Customer-Sales Associate Retail Relationships," *Journal of Retailing*, Fall 1996, pp. 223–47.

5. Available from World Wide Web: <http://www.census.gov>; U.S. Bureau of the Census, *County Business Patterns 1998, United States*,; U.S. Bureau of the Census, *1997 Census of Retail Trade, Subject Series, Establishment and Firm Size* (Washington, DC: U.S. Government Printing Office, 2000); "Department Stores and Designer Tenants Jockey Over Real Estate," *The Wall Street Journal*, October 31, 2000, p. A1ff.; "They Tried to Save It, but This Penney Store Is Set to Close Forever," *The Wall Street Journal*, March 31, 1998, p. A1ff.; "Bright Lights, Big Store," *Business Week*, March 17, 1997, p. 43; "Reinventing Sears," *Time*, December 23, 1996, pp. 53–55; "Department Stores, Seemingly Outmoded, Are Perking Up Again," *The Wall Street Journal*, January 4, 1994, p. A1ff.; Richard A. Rauch, "Retailing's Dinosaurs: Department Stores and Supermarkets," *Business Horizons*, September/October 1991, pp. 21–25.

6. David Appel, "The Supermarket: Early Development of an Institutional Innovation," *Journal of Retailing*, Spring 1972, pp. 39–53.

7. Available from World Wide Web: <http://www.census.gov> and <http://www.fmi.org/food/superfact>; "Grocery Shoppers Can Be Own Cashiers," *USA Today*, March 9, 1998, p. 6B; "The Taste of the Nation," *USA Today*, March 9, 1998, p. 1Dff.; "Finally, Supermarkets Find Ways to Increase Their Profit Margins," *The Wall Street Journal*, May 29, 1997, p. A1ff.; "Special

Report: Grocery Marketing," *Advertising Age*, May 8, 1995, pp. S1–10; U.S. Bureau of the Census, *1997 Census of Retail Trade, Subject Series, Establishment and Firm Size* (Washington, DC: U.S. Government Printing Office, 2000). See also "How Growth Destroys Differentiation," *Brandweek*, April 24, 2000, pp. 42–50.

8. "Ahold's Supermarkets 'Go Native' to Succeed in U.S.," *The Wall Street Journal*, October 4, 1994, p. B4; "Supermarkets Mimic Warehouse Clubs," *Advertising Age*, July 12, 1993, p. 20; "Supermarkets Want to Join the Club," *Adweek*, July 5, 1993, p. 10; "Supermarkets Can Beat Warehouse Clubs, but Not on Price Alone," *Brandweek*, January 4, 1993, p. 25.

9. For more on Wal-Mart, see Chapter 17, footnote #1. For more on Target, see "Why Is Target So Cool," *DSN Retailing Today*, April 2, 2001, p. A4; "Special Report: Target," *DSN Retailing Today*, April 2, 2001, pp. 43–64; "Marketer of the Year: On Target," *Advertising Age*, December 11, 2000, p. 1ff.; "Special Report: Target," *DSN Retailing Today*, July 24, 2000, pp. 45–72; "How Target Got Hot," *Fortune*, May 24, 1999, pp. 169–74; "Power Retailer: Target," *Discount Store News*, April 19, 1999, pp. 53–86; "Power Retailer: Target," *Discount Store News*, April 6, 1998, pp. 59–96. See also James Reardon, Ron Hasty, and Barbara Coe, "The Effect of Information Technology on Productivity in Retailing," *Journal of Retailing*, Winter 1996, pp. 445–61; Christopher D. Norek, "Mass Merchant Discounters: Drivers of Logistics Change," *Journal of Business Logistics*, 1997, pp. 1–17.

10. "Super Stores: Land for Plenty," *Raleigh News & Observer*, March 3, 2001, p. 1Dff.; "SuperTarget Grows Grocery," *Discount Store News*, March 20, 2000, p. 1ff.; "Target's Aim: Bring Fashion to Food on a National Scale," *The Wall Street Journal*, March 1, 2000, p. B4; "How Grocers Are Fighting Giant Rivals," *The Wall Street Journal*, March 27, 1997, p. B1ff.; "Wal-Mart's Super Day: 23 Supercenters in 14 States," *Discount Store News*, February 6, 1995, p. 1ff.

11. "Warehouse Clubs: When the Going Gets Tough . . . ," *Business Week*, July 16, 2001, p. 60; "BJ's Wholesale Club: Exclusive Club Has Retailer Raising the Stakes," *Investor's Business Daily*, February 28, 2001, p. A12; "Costco's In-Store Foodservice Operations Add Relish to the Company's Overall Sales," *DSN Retailing Today*, January 22, 2001, p. 24; "Gasoline Fuels Heavier Traffic at Clubs," *DSN Retailing Today*, January 1, 2001, p. 7; "Costco Cooks Up Factory Concept," *DSN Retailing Today*, November 6, 2000, p. 3ff.; "Costco to Bridge Coastal Presence with Aggressive 3-Year Plan," *DSN Retailing Today*, October 23, 2000, p. 1ff.; "Sharpening Its Razor-Thin Margins Is Costco's Way of Doing Business," *Investor's Business Daily*, April 13, 2000, p. A1; "Inside the Cult of Costco," *Fortune*, September 6, 1999, pp. 184–90; "Why Sam's Wants Businesses to Join the Club," *Business Week*, June 27, 1994, p. 48; "Warehouse-Club War Leaves Few Standing, and They Are Bruised," *The Wall Street Journal*, November 18, 1993, p. A1ff.

12. "Category Killers Go from Lethal to Lame in the Space of a Decade," *The Wall Street Journal*, March 9, 2000, p. A1ff.; "U.S. Superstores Find Japanese Are a Hard Sell," *The Wall Street Journal*, February 14, 2000, p. B1ff.; "Look Who's Thinking Small," *Business Week*, May 17, 1999, pp. 66–70; "Office-Supply Superstores Find Bounty in the Boonies," *The Wall Street Journal*, September 1, 1998, p. B1ff.; "Health-Care Superstores Experience Growing Pains," *The Wall Street Journal*, May 12, 1997, p. B1ff.; "New Sneaker Superstores Aim to Step on Their Competition," *The Wall Street Journal*, March 19, 1997, p. B1ff.; "Bridal Superstores Woo Couples with Miles of Gowns and Tuxes," *The Wall Street Journal*, February 14, 1996, p. B1ff.; "Superstore Sells Every Necessity for Reading, 'Riting, 'Rithmetic," *The Wall Street Journal*, May 16, 1994, p. B1ff.; "This Do-It-Yourself Store Is Really Doing It," *Business Week*, May 2, 1994, p. 108; "Pet Superstores Collar Customers from Supermarkets, Small Shops," *The Wall Street Journal*, November 18, 1993, p. B12.

13. For more on 7-Eleven in Japan, see "From Convenience Store to Online Behemoth?" *Business Week*, April 10, 2000, p. 64; "Japan Goes Web Crazy," *Fortune*, February 7, 2000, pp. 115–18; "Seven-Eleven Japan, Sony Set E-Commerce Plan," *The Wall Street Journal*, January 7, 2000, p. A13; "In Japan, the Hub of E-Commerce Is a 7-Eleven," *The Wall Street Journal*, November 1, 1999, p. B1ff. For more on 7-Eleven in the U.S., see "New Banking Hours: From 7 a.m. to 11 p.m.," *Newsweek*, May 7, 2001, p. 79; "7-Eleven Kiosk Program Banks on Shifts in Strategy," *DSN Retailing Today*, March 19, 2001, p. 2; "Mobile Phone with That Slurpee? Holiday Shoppers Buy on the Run," *USA Today*, December 15, 2000, p. 1B; "Now at 7-Eleven: Gas, Food and Christmas Shopping," *The Wall Street Journal*, November 28, 2000, p. B1ff.; "New 7-Eleven Kiosks Bring On-Line Transactions Home," *Discount Store News*, February 21, 2000, p. 2ff.; "7-Eleven Stores Face Fresh Food Showdown," *Brandweek*, February 28, 1994, p. 1ff.

14. "Kodak Rages in Favor of the Machines," *Brandweek*, February 26, 2001, p. 6; "Push-Button Lover," *The Economist*, November 16, 1991, p. 88; "Machines Start New Fast-Food Era," *USA Today*, July 19, 1991, pp. 1B–2B; "High-Tech Vending Machines Cook Up a New Menu of Hot Fast-Food Entrees," *The Wall Street Journal*, May 13, 1991, p. B1ff.

15. "New Page in E-Retailing: Catalogs," *The Wall Street Journal*, November 30, 2000, p. B1ff.; "Beyond Mail Order: Catalogs Now Sell Image, Advice," *The Wall Street Journal*, July 29, 1997, p. B1ff.; "Catalogers Expand in Asia," *USA Today*, October 18, 1996, p. 4B; "Spiegel's Book Is a Real Page-Turner," *Business Week*, September 12, 1994, pp. 74–76; "U.S. Catalogers Test International Waters," *The Wall Street Journal*, April 19, 1994, p. B1; C. R. Jasper and P. N. R. Lan, "Apparel Catalog Patronage: Demographic, Lifestyle, and Motivational Factors," *Psychology & Marketing*, July/August 1992, pp. 275–96; "Shoppers Seem to Prefer Mail over Mall," *USA Today*, August 12, 1993, p. 4B.

16. "Is There a Future for the TV Mall?" *Brandweek*, March 25, 1996, pp. 24–26; "QVC Draws Wares from Everywhere," *USA Today*, November 1, 1994, p. 1Dff.; "Battling for Buck$," *Profiles*, November 1994, pp. 49–52; "MTV Home Shopping Picks Model Host," *The Wall Street Journal*, July 18, 1994, p. B5; "TV or Not TV," *Inc.*, June 1994, pp. 63–68; "Purchasing Power," *U.S. News & World Report*, January 31, 1994, pp. 56–59; "Home Shoppers to Be Given Yet Another Service," *The Wall Street Journal*, January 14, 1994, p. B1ff.

17. "Etoys to Close Up Shop This Spring," *DSN Retailing Today*, February 19, 2001, p. 6ff.; "The eToys Saga: Costs Kept Rising But Sales Slowed," *The Wall Street Journal*, January 22,

2001, p. B1ff.; "Bridging the Loyalty Gap," *Business Week E.Biz*, January 22, 2001, p. EB10; "Etoys' Disappointing Holiday Spells Disaster for Pure-Players," *DSN Retailing Today*, January 1, 2001, p. 11ff.; "Toy Stores Make Their Own Hits," *The Wall Street Journal*, December 20, 2000, p. B1ff.; "Etoys' Disappointing Forecast Prompts Hard Look at Rest of E-Commerce Sector," *The Wall Street Journal*, December 18, 2000, p. A3ff.; "E-Tailers Alter Marketing Plans, Invest New Dollars in Old Medium," *DSN Retailing Today*, December 11, 2000, p. 6ff.; "Santa's Middleman Takes Stock," *The Wall Street Journal*, December 8, 2000, p. B1ff.; "Etoys Isn't Playing Around in Strategy," *USA Today*, November 24, 2000, p. 5B; "Toby Lenk," *Brandweek*, October 30, 2000, pp. IQ36–46; "The Last e-Store on the Block," *Fortune*, September 18, 2000, pp. 214–20; "He's Not Playing," *Business Week E.Biz*, July 24, 2000, pp. EB92–EB96; "Etoys' Strategy to Stay in the Game," *The Wall Street Journal*, April 25, 2000, p. B1ff.; "Stocking a Giant Toybox," *USA Today*, November 24, 1999, p. 1Bff.; "Amazon, Etoys Make Big, Opposing Bets; Which One Is Right?" *The Wall Street Journal*, November 2, 1999, p. A1ff.; "On the Internet, Toys R Us Plays Catch-Up," *The Wall Street Journal*, August 19, 1999, p. B1ff.; "This Toy War Is No Game," *Business Week*, August 9, 1999, p. 86ff.; "Etoys Story," *The Wall Street Journal*, July 12, 1999, p. R38.

18. "Has Growth of the Net Flattened?" *The Wall Street Journal*, July 16, 2001, p. B1ff.; "Remedies for an Economic Hangover," *Fortune*, June 25, 2001, pp. 130–39; "An Internet Model That Works," *Inc.*, May 2001, pp. 25–26; "Battle-Tested Rules of Online Retail," *Ecompany*, April 2001, pp. 72–80; Matthew L. Meuter, "Self-Service Technologies: Understanding Customer Satisfaction with Technology-Based Service Encounters," *Journal of Marketing*, July 2000, pp. 50–65; "Special Report: Rethinking the Internet," *Business Week*, March 26, 2001, pp. 117–41; "Online America," *American Demographics* March 2001, pp. 53–60; "The Broad Backlash Against E-Tailers," *Business Week*, February 5, 2001, p. 102; "Bricks vs. Clicks," *The Wall Street Journal*, December 11, 2000, p. R10; "Clinching the Holiday E-Sale," *The Wall Street Journal*, October 9, 2000, p. B1ff.; "Are You Web Smart?" *Business Week E.Biz*, September 18, 2000, pp. EB36– EB38; "Toil and Trouble: Online Shopping Is Still a Muddle," *Fortune*, September 4, 2000, pp. 374–76; "Special Report: E-Tailing," *Business Week E.Biz*, May 15, 2000, pp. 102–25; "Wooing the Newbies," *Business Week E.Biz*, May 15, 2000, pp. 116–19; "Revamping the Model: Clicks and Bricks," *The Wall Street Journal*, April 17, 2000, p. R8ff.; "The Lessons Learned," *The Wall Street Journal*, April 17, 2000, p. R6ff.; "Xtreme Retailing," *Business Week*, December 20, 1999, pp. 120–28; "Nothing Like the Real Thing," *The Wall Street Journal*, November 22, 1999, p. R25; "A New Model: Buying Frenzy," *The Wall Street Journal*, July 12, 1999, p. R6ff.; "The Impact of Electronic Commerce on Marketing," *Harvard Business Review*, May–June 1996, p.137; Raymond R. Burke, "Do You See What I See? The Future of Virtual Shopping," *Journal of the Academy of Marketing Science*, Fall 1997, pp. 352–60; Joseph Alba, John Lynch, Barton Weitz, Chris Janiszewski et al., "Interactive Home Shopping: Consumer, Retailer, and Manufacturer Incentives to Participate in Electronic Marketplaces," *Journal of Marketing*, July 1997, pp. 38–53; Birud Sindhav, "Net Gain: Expanding Markets Through Virtual Communities," *Journal of Marketing*, January 1998, pp. 120–21; "Doing Business in the Internet Age," *Business Week*, June 22, 1998, pp. 121–72; "Entrepreneurs Reap Riches from Net Niches," *USA Today*, April 20, 1998, p. 3B; "Shopping On-Line? Here's Why You Should—and Shouldn't," *The Wall Street Journal*, November 20, 1997, p. B4.

19. Chip E. Miller, "The Effects of Competition on Retail Structure: an Examination of Intratype, Intertype, and Intercategory Competition," *Journal of Marketing*, October 1999, pp. 107–21; "Latest Supermarket Special—Gasoline," *The Wall Street Journal*, April 30, 2001, p. B1ff.; "Barnes & Noble Plots Way to Sell Magazines Via Web," *Investor's Business Daily*, April 30, 2001, p. A6; "Levi's Doesn't Fancy Selling with Cukes," *The Wall Street Journal*, April 10, 2001, p. B10; "Price Wars, Shift to Digital Photos Leaving Kodak Out of the Picture," *Investor's Business Daily*, March 19, 2001, p. A1; "Barnes & Noble Finds Grinch Effect in Games Strategy," *The Wall Street Journal*, December 20, 2000, p. B4; "Now at 7-Eleven: Gas, Food and Christmas Shopping," *The Wall Street Journal*, November 28, 2000, p. B1ff.; "Fill 'Er Up with Regular in Aisle 9," *Business Week*, October 23, 2000, p. 14; "Savoring Chocolate," *Advertising Age*, September 4, 2000, pp. 24–26; "In Aisle 10, Soup, Tea—and Bikinis?" *The Wall Street Journal*, June 28, 2000, p. B1ff.; "Grocery List: Peas, Veal, Throat Culture," *The Wall Street Journal*, May 20, 1998, p. B1ff.; "7-Eleven Follows Trend, Brews High-End Coffee," *USA Today*, April 22, 1998, p. 5B; "Fill It Up and a Cheeseburger, Please," *The Wall Street Journal*, October 15, 1997, p. B18; "Cued by Mini-Marts, Supermarkets Try Pumping Gas," *The Wall Street Journal*, October 14, 1997, p. B4; "Shoppers Park Their Grocery Carts and Eat a Little Dinner," *Marketing News*, May 20, 1996, p. 10; "Stung by Mass Merchandisers, Drugstores Try New Remedies," *The Wall Street Journal*, February 11, 1993, p. B1ff.; Jack M. Cadeaux, "Industry Product Volatility and Retailer Assortments," *Journal of Macromarketing*, Fall 1992, pp. 28–37; Ronald Savitt, "The 'Wheel of Retailing' and Retail Product Management," *European Journal of Marketing* 18, no. 6/7 (1984), pp. 43–54.

20. "How Did Sears Blow This Gasket?" *Business Week*, June 29, 1992, p. 38; "An Open Letter to Sears Customers," *USA Today*, June 25, 1992, p. 8A; see also John Paul Fraedrich, "The Ethical Behavior of Retail Managers," *Journal of Business Ethics*, March 1993, pp. 207–18.

21. Available from World Wide Web: <http://www.census.gov>; *County Business Patterns 1998, United States;* U.S. Bureau of the Census, *1997 Census of Retail Trade, Subject Series, Establishment and Firm Size;* "Retailers Grab Power, Control Marketplace," *Marketing News*, January 16, 1989, pp. 1–2; Dale D. Achabal, John M. Heineke, and Shelby H. McIntyre, "Issues and Perspectives on Retail Productivity," *Journal of Retailing*, Fall 1984, p. 107ff.; Charles A. Ingene, "Scale Economies in American Retailing: A Cross-Industry Comparison," *Journal of Macromarketing* 4, no. 2 (1984), pp. 49–63; "Mom-and-Pop Videotape Shops Are Fading Out," *Business Week*, September 2, 1985, pp. 34–35.

22. "European Inns Take the Hilton Route," *The Wall Street Journal*, April 23, 2001, p. B1ff.; "Forging Ahead with Custom Contracts," *Foodservice Equipment & Supplies Specialist*, June 1994, p. 52; "Manufacturers Start to Spurn Big Discounters," *The Wall Street Journal*, November 30, 1993, p. B1ff.; "CLOUT! More and More, Retail Giants Rule the Marketplace," *Business Week*, December 21, 1992, pp. 66–73.

23. "Why Subway Is 'The Biggest Problem in Franchising,'" *Fortune*, March 16, 1998, pp. 126–34; "Fast-Food Fight," *Business Week*, June 2, 1997, pp. 34–36; "Rattling the Chains," *Brandweek*, April 21, 1997, pp. 28–40; "Lawsuit Spoils the Party at Tupperware," *The Wall Street Journal*, November 29, 1996, p. B1ff.; "Court Decides Franchisees Get Elbow Room," *The Wall Street Journal*, August 14, 1996, p. B1ff.; "Chicken and Burgers Create Hot New Class: Powerful Franchisees," *The Wall Street Journal*, May 21, 1996, p. A1ff.; "Some Franchisees Say Moves by McDonald's Hurt Their Operations," *The Wall Street Journal*, April 17, 1996, p. A1ff.; Robert Dahlstom, "Franchising: Contemporary Issues and Research," *Journal of Public Policy & Marketing*, Spring 1996, pp. 159–61; Surinder Tikoo, "Assessing the Franchise Option," *Business Horizons*, May–June 1996, pp. 78–82; Rajiv P. Dant, Audhesh K. Paswan, and Patrick J. Kaufman, "What We Know About Ownership Redirection in Franchising: A Meta-Analysis," *Journal of Retailing*, Winter 1996, pp. 429–44; Alessandro Baroncelli and Angelo Manaresi, "Franchising As a Form of Divestment: An Italian Study," *Industrial Marketing Management*, May 1997, pp. 223–35; Roger D. Blair and Jill B. Herndon, "Franchise Supply Agreements: Quality Control or Illegal Tying?" *Journal of the Academy of Marketing Science*, Spring 1997, pp. 177–78; Richard C. Hoffman and John F. Preble, "Franchising into the Twenty-First Century," *Business Horizons*, November–December 1993, pp. 35–43; "Trouble in Franchise Nation," *Fortune*, March 6, 1995, pp. 115–29; Francine Lafontaine and Patrick J. Kaufmann, "The Evolution of Ownership Patterns in Franchise Systems," *Journal of Retailing*, Summer 1994, pp. 97–114; "The Franchise Hall of Fame," *Inc.*, April 1994, pp. 86–95.

24. Arieh Goldman, "The Transfer of Retail Formats into Developing Economies: The Example of China," *Journal of Retailing*, Summer 2001, Vol. 77, 2, p. 221; Valerie Severin, "The Stability of Retail Shopping Choices Over Time and Across Countries," *Journal of Retailing*, Summer 2001, Vol. 77, 2, p. 185; "European Inns Take the Hilton Route," *The Wall Street Journal*, April 23, 2001, p. B1ff.; "U.S. Superstores Find Japanese Are a Hard Sell," *The Wall Street Journal*, February 14, 2000, p. B1ff.; Philip R. Cateora, *International Marketing*, 10th ed. (Burr Ridge, IL: Irwin/McGraw-Hill, 1999); Foo N. Ho, Beng S. Ong, and Seonsu Lee, "A Multicultural Comparison of Shopping Patterns Among Asian Consumers," *Journal of Marketing Theory & Practice*, Winter 1997, pp. 42–51; Saeed Samiee, "Retailing and Channel Considerations in Developing Countries: A Review and Research Propositions," *Journal of Business Research*, June 1993, pp. 103–30; "In Guam, Shopping Sprees Are Replacing Tanning," *The Wall Street Journal*, August 23, 1996, p. B4; "How's This for a Cultural Revolution? Chinese Are Getting Home Shopping," *The Wall Street Journal*, January 4, 1996, p. A6; "Retailers Go Global," *Fortune*, February 20, 1995, pp. 102–8; "Russians Say 'Ja' to Swedish Shops," *Advertising Age*, November 7, 1994, p. 47; "A Different World," *The Wall Street Journal*, October 28, 1994, p. R6; "Wal-Mart Is Slowed by Problems of Price and Culture in Mexico," *The Wall Street Journal*, July 29, 1994, p. A1ff.; "A Bargain Basement Called Japan," *Business Week*, June 27, 1994, pp. 42–43; "From Men's Suits to Sake, Discounting Booms in Japan," *Advertising Age International*, March 21, 1994, p. I1ff.; "Europe's Smaller Food Shops Face Finis," *The Wall Street Journal*, May 12, 1993, p. B1ff.

25. "Why the Web Can't Kill the Middleman," *Ecompany*, April 2001, p. 75; "Not Dead Yet," *Inc. Tech*, No. 1, 2001, pp. 58–59; "Electronics Distributors Are Reporting Record Profits," *The Wall Street Journal*, July 13, 2000, p. B4; "Chow (On)Line," *Business Week E.Biz*, June 5, 2000, pp. EB84–EB90; "Why Online Distributors—Once Written Off—May Thrive," *Fortune*, September 6, 1999, pp. 270–72; "Middlemen Find Ways to Survive Cyberspace Shopping," *The Wall Street Journal*, December 12, 1996, p. B6; "Invoice? What's an Invoice?" *Business Week*, June 10, 1996, pp. 110–12; "Computer Wholesalers Face Shakeout and Consolidation," *The Wall Street Journal*, August 26, 1994, p. B4; "Electric Power Brokers Create New Breed of Business," *The Wall Street Journal*, August 2, 1994, p. B4; Allan J. Magrath, "The Hidden Clout of Marketing Middlemen," *Journal of Business Strategy*, March/April 1990, pp. 38–41; Paul Herbig and Bradley S. O'Hara, "Industrial Distributors in the Twenty-First Century," *Industrial Marketing Management*, July 1994, pp. 199–204.

26. "Cold War: Amana Refrigeration Fights Tiny Distributor," *The Wall Street Journal*, February 26, 1992, p. B2. For another example, see "Quickie-Divorce Curbs Sought By Manufacturers' Distributors," *The Wall Street Journal*, July 13, 1987, p. 27; "Merger of Two Bakers Teaches Distributors a Costly Lesson (3–parts)," *The Wall Street Journal*, September 14, 1987, p. 29; October 19, 1987, p. 35; November 11, 1987, p. 33.

27. Available from World Wide Web: <http://www.census.gov>; U.S. Bureau of the Census, *County Business Patterns 1998, United States;* U.S. Bureau of the Census, *1997 Census of Wholesale Trade, Geographic Area Series, United States* (Washington, DC: U.S. Government Printing Office, 2000); "Why Manufacturers Are Doubling as Distributors," *Business Week*, January 17, 1983, p. 41. See also "Who Is Bob Kierlin—and Why Is He So Successful?" *Fortune*, December 8, 1997, pp. 245–48; Robert F. Lusch, Deborah S. Coykendall, and James M. Kenderdine, *Wholesaling in Transition: An Executive Chart Book* (Norman, OK: Distribution Research Program, University of Oklahoma, 1990).

28. "Revolution in Japanese Retailing," *Fortune*, February 7, 1994, pp. 143–46; Arieh Goldman, "Evaluating the Performance of the Japanese Distribution System," *Journal of Retailing*, Spring 1992, pp. 11–39; "Japan Begins to Open the Door to Foreigners, a Little," *Brandweek*, August 2, 1993, pp. 14–16.

29. Available from World Wide Web: <http://www.rell.com>; "Richardson Electronics Ltd.: Maker of Ancient Tech Finds a Way to Prosper," *Investor's Business Daily*, June 27, 2000, p. A12; *2000 Annual Report*, Richardson Electronics.

30. Available from World Wide Web: <http://www.inmac.com> and <http://www.grainger.com>; "B2B: Yesterday's Darling," *The Wall Street Journal*, October 23, 2000, p. R8; "W. W. Grainger's Web Investments: Money Well Spent? Don't Ask Street," *Investor's Business Daily*, September 19, 2000, p. A1; "Junk That Catalog and Get On the Web," *Business Week*, June 26, 2000, pp. 28B–D.

31. For more on manufacturers' agents being squeezed, see "Wal-Mart Draws Fire: Reps, Brokers Protest Being Shut Out by New Policy," *Advertising Age*, January 13, 1992, p. 3ff.; Patrick R. Mehr, "Identifying Independent Reps," *Industrial Marketing*

Management, November 1992, pp. 319–22; "Independent Sales Reps Are Squeezed by the Recession," *The Wall Street Journal*, December 27, 1991, p. B1. For more discussion on wholesaling abroad, see "Japan Rises to P&G's No. 3 Market," *Advertising Age*, December 10, 1990, p. 42; "'Papa-Mama' Stores in Japan Wield Power to Hold Back Imports," *The Wall Street Journal*, November 14, 1988, p. 1ff.; Yoo S. Yang, Robert P. Leone, and Dana L. Alden, "A Market Expansion Ability Approach to Identify Potential Exporters," *Journal of Marketing*, January 1992, pp. 84–96; Daniel C. Bello and Ritu Lohtia, "The Export Channel Design: The Use of Foreign Distributors and Agents," *Journal of the Academy of Marketing Science*, Spring 1995, pp. 83–93; Jim Gibbons, "Selling Abroad with Manufacturers' Agents," *Sales & Marketing Management*, September 9, 1985, pp. 67–69; Evelyn A. Thomchick and Lisa Rosenbaum, "The Role of U.S. Export Trading Companies in International Logistics," *Journal of Business Logistics*, September 1984, pp. 85–105; D. Steven White, "Behind the Success and Failure of U.S. Export Intermediaries: Transactions, Agents and Resources," *Journal of the Academy of Marketing Science*, Summer 2001, pp. 18–20.

32. "Keep the Excess Moving," *Business Week E.Biz*, November 20, 2000, pp. EB78–EB82; "Good-Bye to Fixed Pricing?" *Business Week*, May 4, 1998, pp. 71–84; "Sales Are Clicking on Manufacturing's Internet Mart," *Fortune*, July 7, 1997, pp. 136C–T.

33. "Sick of Checkout Lines? These Guys Can Help," *Investor's Business Daily*, July 9, 2001, p. A7; "What's Ahead for Retailing," *The Wall Street Journal*, June 25, 2001, p. R16; "Digital ID Cards," *The Wall Street Journal*, June 25, 2001, p. R16; "Get Smart: Target Will Be First Among Big Stores to Issue Cards," *The Wall Street Journal*, June 20, 2001, p. B6; "Now, Harried Shoppers Can Take Control at Supermarkets," *USA Today*, June 7, 2001, p. 1Aff.; "Leave It in the Box," *Business Week E.Biz*, December 11, 2000, pp. EB82–EB83; "Master Plan," *Brandweek*, October 18, 1999, pp. 52–54.

Chapter 13

1. Available from World Wide Web: <http://www.chrysler.com/pt-cruiser>; "Special Report: Buzz Marketing," *Business Week*, July 30, 2001, pp. 50–56; "Fuel Standards: How to Plug the Leaks," *Business Week*, May 28, 2001, p. 36; "A Risky Mass-Market Move for the PT," *Business Week*, May 7, 2001, p. 14; "Ford Seeks 'PT-Style' Buzz for T-Bird Via Relationship Efforts, Not TV," *Brandweek*, January 15, 2001, p. 4; "Focusing on the Front End," *Brandweek* (Marketers of the Year Special Issue), October 16, 2000, pp. M66–M74; "PT Cruiser Crash Tests Produce Mixed Results," *USA Today*, July 26, 2000, p. 3B; "Too Cool for Chrysler?" *The Wall Street Journal*, July 20, 2000, p. B1ff.; "An Economy Car in Hot Rod's Clothing," *The Wall Street Journal*, June 30, 2000, p. W11C; "Pricey PT Cruisers Land NHTSA in Hot Water," *USA Today*, June 29, 2000, p. 8B; "Safety Testers Pay $20,000 Above Sticker for Cruisers," *USA Today*, May 25, 2000, p. 1B; "Chrysler PT Cruises by Fair Pricing," *USA Today*, May 22, 2000, p. 24A; "PT Cruiser Drives Some Buyers Wild," *USA Today*, May 16, 2000, p. 1Aff.; "Chrysler Hits Right Buttons to Unveil Novel PT Cruiser," *Advertising Age*, April 17, 2000, p. 73; "Hearst Designs Promotion for Chrysler's PT Cruiser," *Advertising Age*, March 27, 2000, p. 20; "New Cruiser Stirs Beetle-Like Buzz," *USA Today*, March 17, 2000, p. 1Bff.; "EPA Labels PT Cruiser a Car, Creating Potential Trouble for Some Auto Makers," *The Wall Street Journal*, March 3, 2000, p. A3; "Sampling: PT Barnstorm," *Brandweek*, October 25, 1999, pp. 26–28.

2. "Wary Over Harry," *Brandweek*, June 11, 2001, p. 1ff.; "Inside the Halls of Hogwarts," *On Magazine*, June 2001, pp. 74–75; "Harry Potter and the Marketing Whiz-Kids," *Ad Age Global*, March 2001, p. 5; "Potter Fans Put Hex of a Boycott on Warner Bros.," *USA Today*, February 22, 2001, p. 1D; "Warner Bros. Chooses Coke to Bestow Marketing Magic on Harry Potter Film," *The Wall Street Journal*, February 20, 2001, p. A3ff.; "Transportation," *Business Week*, January 8, 2001, P. 130; "Next Up for Wizard Fans: Harry Potter and the Contested Domains," *The Wall Street Journal*, December 21, 2000, p. B1ff.; "Potter Cognoscenti All Know a Muggle When They See One," *The Wall Street Journal*, October 18, 2000, p. A1ff.; "Buzzmeisters of the Year," *Brandweek* (Marketers of the Year Special Issue), October 16, 2000, pp. M8–M18; "Harry Potter, Meet 'Ha-li Bo-te,'" *The Wall Street Journal*, September 21, 2000, p. B1ff.; "Creative Coddling, Great Word of Mouth," *Business Week E.Biz*, September 18, 2000; "Wizard of Marketing," *Business Week*, July 24, 2000, pp. 84–87; "Wizard for a Day: Now Young Muggles Act Out 'Potter' Online," *The Wall Street Journal*, July 31, 2000, p. B1; "Marketers Count on Potter Film for Golden Touch," *USA Today*, July 18, 2000, p. 1Bff.; "Web Booksellers Give Potter Fans Rush Delivery," *The Wall Street Journal*, June 22, 2000, p. B1ff.; "Harry Potter and the Booksellers," *The Wall Street Journal*, June 16, 2000, p. B1ff.; "Mattel and Hasbro Get Licenses for Harry Potter," *The Wall Street Journal*, February 11, 2000, p. B6.

3. "Old-Fashioned PR Gives General Mills Advertising Bargains," *The Wall Street Journal*, March 20, 1997, p. A1ff.; "Name That Chintz! How Shelter Magazines Boost Brands," *The Wall Street Journal*, March 14, 1997, p. B1ff.; "Rosie and 'Friends' Make Drake's Cakes a Star," *The Wall Street Journal*, February 10, 1997, p. B1ff.; "Toy Story: How Shrewd Marketing Made Elmo a Hit," *The Wall Street Journal*, December 16, 1996, p. B1ff.; "PR Shouldn't Mean 'Poor Relations'," *Industry Week*, February 3, 1992, p. 51; Siva K. Balasubramanian, "Beyond Advertising and Publicity: Hybrid Messages and Public Policy Issues," *Journal of Advertising*, December 1994, pp. 29–46; Thomas H. Bivins, "Ethical Implications of the Relationship of Purpose to Role and Function in Public Relations," *Journal of Business Ethics*, January, 1989, pp. 65–74.

4. "Small Wonder," *The Wall Street Journal*, June 25, 2001, p. R; "Minute Maid Opens Juicy Site to Promote New Drink," *Brandweek*, April 30, 2001, p. B; "PMA Reggie Awards 2001," *Brandweek* (Supplement), March 12, 2001, pp. R1–R22; "Mystery Shoppers," *American Demographics*, December 2000, pp. 41–43; "Sweet Deals," *Inc. Tech*, No. 4, 2000, pp. 98–109; "Hot Wheels," *American Demographics*, August 2000, pp. 48–49; "Calling All Car Worms," *Brandweek*, March 6, 2000, pp. 22–23; "Sharp Curves Ahead for Car Marketers," *Brandweek*, January 3, 2000, pp. 18–19; "Talbots Mounting Its Biggest Integrated Marketing Push," *Advertising Age*, August 11, 1997, p. 29; "Olds' Intrigue Stars in Web Game Based on NBC TV Show," *Advertising Age*, July 28, 1997, p. 16ff.; "Product Program Flea Control," *Advertising Age*, Special Issue, 1997, p. E8; "Promotion Marketing," *Brandweek*, March 4, 1996, pp. 22–26; J. R. Shannon, "The

New Promotions Mix: A Proposed Paradigm, Process, and Application," *Journal of Marketing Theory & Practice*, Winter 1996, pp. 56–68; Kathleen J. Kelly, "Integrated Marketing Communication: Putting It Together & Making It Work," *Journal of the Academy of Marketing Science*, Winter 1997, pp. 83–85.

5. "High-Tech Branding: Pushing Digital PCS," *Brandweek*, August 4, *1997, pp. 30–34;* "Brand Builders: Delivery Guy Chic," *Brandweek*, June 30, 1997, pp. 18–19; "Eye-Catching Logos All Too Often Leave Fuzzy Images in Minds of Consumers," *The Wall Street Journal*, December 5, 1991, p. B1ff.; David I. Gilliland and Wesley J. Johnston, "Toward a Model of Business-to-Business Marketing Communications Effects," *Industrial Marketing Management*, January 1997, pp. 15–29; Michel T. Pham and Gita V. Johar, "Contingent Processes of Source Identification," *Journal of Consumer Research*, December 1997, pp. 249–65; Louisa Ha and Barry R. Litman, "Does Advertising Clutter Have Diminishing and Negative Returns?" *Journal of Advertising*, Spring 1997, pp. 31–42; Barbara B. Stern, "A Revised Communication Model for Advertising: Multiple Dimensions of the Source, the Message, and the Recipient," *Journal of Advertising*, June 1994, pp. 5–15; Ronald E. Dulek, John S. Fielden, and John S. Hill, "International Communication: An Executive Primer," *Business Horizons*, January/February 1991, pp. 20–25; Kaylene C. Williams, Rosann L. Spiro, and Leslie M. Fine, "The Customer-Salesperson Dyad: An Interaction/Communication Model and Review," *Journal of Personal Selling and Sales Management*, Summer 1990, pp. 29–44; Susan Mitchell, "How to Talk to Young Adults," *American Demographics*, April 1993, p. 50; Richard F. Beltramini and Edwin R. Stafford, "Comprehension and Perceived Believability of Seals of Approval Information in Advertising," *Journal of Advertising*, September 1993, pp. 3–14; Jacob Jacoby and Wayne D. Hoyer, "The Comprehension/Miscomprehension of Print Communication: Selected Findings," *Journal of Consumer Research*, March 1989, pp. 434–43.

6. "Good Housekeeping Unveils Web Site Review Program," *Brandweek*, May 29, 2000, p. 52; "Good Housekeeping to Offer 'Seal' to Autos," *Advertising Age*, June 29, 1998, p. 18; "Marketing in Which We Bash a Baby Seal," *Fortune*, September 8, 1997, p. 36ff; Jagdish Agrawal and Wagner A. Kamakura, "The Economic Worth of Celebrity Endorsers: An Event Study Analysis," *Journal of Marketing*, July 1995, pp. 56–62; David J. Moore, John C. Mowen, and Richard Reardon, "Multiple Sources in Advertising Appeals: When Product Endorsers Are Paid by the Advertising Sponsor," *Journal of the Academy of Marketing Science*, Summer 1994, pp. 234–43.

7. "Global Branding: Same, But Different," *Brandweek*, April 9, 2001, p. 25; "When You Translate 'Got Milk' for Latinos, What Do You Get?" *The Wall Street Journal*, June 3, 1999, p. A1ff.; "Cash, Cache, Cachet: All 3 Seem to Matter When You Buy a PC," *The Wall Street Journal*, December 18, 1998, p. A1ff.; "Hey, #!@*% Amigo, Can You Translate the Word 'Gaffe'?" *The Wall Street Journal*, July 8, 1996, p. B2; "Lost in Translation: How to 'Empower Women' in Chinese," *The Wall Street Journal*, September 13, 1994, p. A1ff.; "In World Cup Games, Words Get Lost and Gained in Translation," *The Wall Street Journal*, July 14, 1994, p. B1ff.; "Too Many Computer Names Confuse Too Many Buyers," *The Wall Street Journal*, June 29, 1994, p. B1ff.; "Go Ask Alice," *Adweek*, January 17, 1994, p. 32.

8. "The Corruption of TV Health News," *Business Week*, February 28, 2000, pp. 66–68; "Collagen Corp.'s Video Uses News Format," *The Wall Street Journal*," March 29, 1994, p. B8; "Totally Hidden Video," *Inside PR*, August 1990, pp. 11–13; "'News' Videos That Pitch Drugs Provoke Outcry for Regulations," *The Wall Street Journal*, February 8, 1990, p. B6; Thomas H. Bivins, "Public Relations, Professionalism, and the Public Interest," *Journal of Business Ethics*, February 1993, pp. 117–26; Siva K. Balasubramanian, "Beyond Advertising and Publicity: Hybrid Messages and Public Policy Issues," *Journal of Advertising*, December 1994, pp. 47–58.

9. "Escalade Got Game," *Advertising Age*, June 11, 2001, p. 42; "All Juiced Up," *American Demographics*, January 2001, pp. 42–44; Albert Schofield, "Alternative Reply Vehicles in Direct-Response Advertising," *Journal of Advertising Research*, September/October 1994, pp. 28–34. For an electronic direct mail example, see "Web Slice," *Brandweek*, May 26, 1997, pp. 22–23; Judy F. Davis, "Maintaining Customer Relationships Through Effective Database Marketing: A Perspective for Small Retailers," *Journal of Marketing Theory & Practice*, Spring 1997, pp. 31–42; Craig A. Conrad, "Response! The Complete Guide to Direct Marketing," *Journal of the Academy of Marketing Science*, Winter 1998, pp. 70–71; Kapil Bawa, "Influences on Consumer Response to Direct Mail Coupons: An Integrative Review," *Psychology & Marketing*, March 1996, pp. 129–56; William J. Carner, "Direct Marketing Through Broadcast Media: TV, Radio, Cable, Infomercials, Home Shopping, and More," *Journal of the Academy of Marketing Science*, Winter 1997, pp. 86–87.

10. For more on privacy, see Chapter 18, footnote #13. "Why Those Companies Are So Eager to Get Your E-Mail Address," *The Wall Street Journal*, February 12, 2001, p. B1; "Direct Mail That Really Sells Hinges on Data Smarts and Clever Content," *The Wall Street Journal*, January 22, 2001, p. A1; "When E-Mail Ads Aren't Spam," *Business Week*, October 16, 2000, pp. 112–14; "Special Report: Direct and Database Marketing," *Advertising Age*, October 16, 2000, pp. S1–22; "Jupiter Projects E-Mail Marketing Will Jump to $7.3 Billion by 2005," *Advertising Age*, May 8, 2000, p. 80ff.; "E-Mail Direct," *Brandweek*, April 10, 2000, pp. 108–12; "You've Got Snail Mail!" *American Demographics*, March 2000, pp. 54–56; "Special Report: Direct and Database Marketing," *Advertising Age*, October 18, 1999, pp. S1–8; "Special Report: Direct Marketing," *Advertising Age*, October 12, 1998, pp. S1–8; "Customers Are Eager, Infrastructure Lags," *Advertising Age*, October 5, 1998, p. 12; George R. Milne and Mary Ellen Gordon, "Direct Mail Privacy-Efficiency Trade-Offs Within an Implied Social Contract Framework," *Journal of Public Policy & Marketing*, Fall 1993, pp. 206–15.

11. Donna L. Hoffman and Thomas P. Novak, "Marketing in Hypermedia Computer-Mediated Environments: Conceptual Foundations," *Journal of Marketing*, July 1996, pp. 50–68; Gregory C. Mosier and James M. Jackman, "Personal Jurisdiction: Is Internet Presence Enough?" *Journal of the Academy of Marketing Science*, Spring 1998, p.164; Pierre Berthon, Leyland Pitt, and Richard T. Watson, "Marketing Communication and the World Wide Web," *Business Horizons*, September–October 1996, pp. 24–32.

12. For more on DTC advertising, see "While Critics May Fret, Public Likes DTC Ads," *Advertising Age*, March 26, 2001, p. 24;

"Drug Firms, Stymied in the Lab, Become Marketing Machines," *The Wall Street Journal*, July 6, 2000, p. A1ff.; "New Venture Aims to Measure Effectiveness of DTC Drug Work," *Advertising Age*, May 29, 2000, pp. 16–18; "An Overdose of Drug Advertising?" *Business Week*, May 22, 2000, p. 52; "DTC Execs Quick to Learn Upfront Value," *Advertising Age*, May 15, 2000, p. S58; "Drug Makers Prescribed Direct-Mail Pitch," *The Wall Street Journal*, December 16, 1999, p. B16; "Flu Season Will Arrive with Two New Drugs and Ad Blitz by Makers," *The Wall Street Journal*, September 22, 1999, p. A1ff.; "Prescription for Profit," *Advertising Age*, March 15, 1999, pp. S1–20; "Ads Reveal New Side to Drug Industry," *Raleigh News & Observer*, January 24, 1999, p. 13E; "A Little Knowledge," *The Wall Street Journal*, October 19, 1998, p. R8; "The Fine Print," *The Wall Street Journal*, October 19, 1998, p. R6ff.; "But First, Call Your Drug Company," *American Demographics*, October 1998, pp. 27–30; "Are Drug Ads a Cure-All?" *Business Week*, March 30, 1998, pp. 59–60; "Prescription for Profit," *Advertising Age*, March 16, 1998, pp. S1–30; "Campaign for Prozac Targets Consumers," *The Wall Street Journal*, July 1, 1997, p. B1ff. See also Steven W. Kopp and Mary J. Sheffet, "The Effect of Direct-to-Consumer Advertising of Prescription Drugs on Retail Gross Margins: Empirical Evidence and Public Policy Implications," *Journal of Public Policy & Marketing*, Fall 1997, pp. 270–76; Mary C. Gilly and Mary Wolfinbarger, "Advertising's Internal Audience," *Journal of Marketing*, January 1998, pp. 69–88; S. A. Erdem and L. J. Harrison-Walker, "Managing Channel Relationships: Toward an Identification of Effective Promotional Strategies in Vertical Marketing Systems," *Journal of Marketing Theory & Practice*, Spring 1997, pp. 80–87; Michael Levy, John Webster, and Roger Kerin, "Formulating Push Marketing Strategies: A Method and Application," *Journal of Marketing*, Winter 1983, pp. 25–34.

13. "Decker Scores with Sweepstakes to Promote Days Inn," *USA Today*, November 6, 1997, p. B10; "Biore: The Nose Knew at Lilith Fair," *Brandweek*, September 15, 1997, p. 28; "Brand Builders: Progresso Warriors," *Brandweek*, June 23, 1997, pp. 20–22; "Advertisers Often Cheer the Loudest," *USA Today*, March 27, 1997, p. 1Aff.; "Crossing the Border," *Brandweek*, December 16, 1996, pp. 17–22; "Brand Builders: Pie in the Sky," *Brandweek*, December 16, 1996, pp. 23–24; "Tractor Dealers Get Down in the Dirt Promoting Machines," *The Wall Street Journal*, July 16, 1996, p. A1ff.; "Pepsi Cancels an Ad Campaign as Customers Clamor for Stuff," *The Wall Street Journal*, June 27, 1996, p. B1ff.

14. "Compensation and Expenses," *Sales & Marketing Management*, June 28, 1993, p. 65; "The Cost of Selling Is Going Up," *Boardroom Reports*, December 15, 1991, p. 15; "An In-House Sales School," *Inc.*, May 1991, pp. 85–86.

15. For an example of Toyota's Prius targeting innovators and early adopters, see "Changing Lanes," *The Wall Street Journal*, April 23, 2001, p. R32; "Green Cars," *American Demographics*, January 2001, pp. 56–61; "Hybrid Power," *Time*, December 11, 2000, pp. 94–95; "Prius Pumps Up Luxury of Efficiency," *USA Today*, November 17, 2000, p. 13D; "Another Way to Beat High Gas Prices," *Fortune*, October 30, 2000, p. 58; "U.S. Auto Makers to Rev Up Output of 'Hybrid' Vehicles," *The Wall Street Journal*, October 24, 2000, p. B4; "The World's Most Admired Companies," *Fortune*, October 2, 2000, pp. 183–89; "The Eco-Car," *Business Week*, August 14, 2000, pp. 63–70; "Toyota Makes a Bet on New Hybrid Prius," *The Wall Street Journal*, July 20, 2000, pp. B18; "Forget Electric—Hydrogen Is Cars' Future," *Investor's Business Daily*, July 7, 2000, p. A6; "California May Soften Electric Car Mandate," *The Wall Street Journal*, June 2, 2000, p. 3B; "Attention Techies and Assorted Geniuses: Toyota Prius Wants You," *Brandweek*, May 8, 2000, p. 113; "Toyota To Sell Prius Hybrid Only on Net," *USA Today*, April 19, 2000, p. 3B; "Toyota, Honda Start to Push Hybrid Vehicles," *Advertising Age*, June 28, 1999, p. 20; "Toyota's Green Machine," *Business Week*, December 15, 1997, pp. 108–110; "How Toyota Defies Gravity," *Fortune*, December 8, 1997, pp. 100–108. For more on word of mouth, see "Auto Makers Find They Don't Want to Avoid Collisions in Movies," *The Wall Street Journal*, July 5, 2001, p. B1, "Small Wonder," *The Wall Street Journal*, June 25, 2001, p. R; "Word of Mouth Makes Nike Slip-On Sneakers Take Off," *The Wall Street Journal*, June 7, 2001, p. B1ff.; "Bristol-Myers Builds Buzz for True Intense Color Line," *Advertising Age*, April 23, 2001, p. 18; "Improbable Eastern Hit Proves It Can Fly in U.S.," *Advertising Age*, March 26, 2001, p. S2; "How Sony Marketers Gave 'Crouching Tiger' an Early Leg Up," *The Wall Street Journal*, January 11, 2001, p. A1ff.; "How an Idea Spreads Like Flu," *Advertising Age*, May 8, 2000, pp. 42–46; "Street Marketing Hits the Internet," *Advertising Age*, May 1, 2000, p. 32; "Ad Budget: Zero. Buzz: Deafening," *The Wall Street Journal*, December 29, 1999, p. B1ff.; "Word of Mouth Makes Kansas Store a Star," *The Wall Street Journal*, November 7, 1997, p. B1ff.; "Why the Veterinarian Really Recommends that 'Designer' Chow," *The Wall Street Journal*, November 3, 1997, p. A1ff.; "Foot Soldiers Help Sell Street Chic," *USA Today*, June 16, 1997, p. 1Bff. See also Jagdip Singh, "Voice, Exit, and Negative Word-of-Mouth Behaviors: An Investigation Across Three Service Categories," *Journal of the Academy of Marketing Science*, Winter 1990, pp. 1–16; Jeffrey G. Blodgett, Donald H. Granbois, and Rockney G. Walters, "The Effects of Perceived Justice on Complainants' Negative Word-of Mouth Behavior and Repatronage Intentions," *Journal of Retailing*, Winter 1993, pp. 399–428; Paula Fitzgerald Bone, "Word-of-Mouth Effects on Short-term and Long-term Product Judgments," *Journal of Business Research*, March 1995, pp. 213–24; Bruce MacEvoy, "Change Leaders and the New Media," *American Demographics*, January 1994, pp. 42–49; Dale F. Duhan, Scott D. Johnson, James B. Wilcox, and Gilbert D. Harrell, "Influences on Consumer Use of Word-of-Mouth Recommendation Sources," *Journal of the Academy of Marketing Science*, Fall 1997, pp. 283–95; Russell N. Laczniak, Thomas E. DeCarlo, and Carol M. Motley, "Retail Equity Perceptions and Consumers' Processing of Negative Word-of-Mouth Communication," *Journal of Marketing Theory & Practice*, Fall 1996, pp. 37–48.

16. "Special Report: Buzz Marketing," *Business Week*, July 30, 2001, pp. 50–56; "Viral Marketing Breaks Through," *Advertising Age*, June 25, 2001, p. S10; Barbara Bickart, "Internet Forums as Influential Sources of Consumer Information," *Journal of Interactive Marketing*, Summer 2001, p. 31; "Marketers Find 'Tweens' Too Hot to Ignore," *USA Today*, July 10, 2001, p. 13A; "Hollywood, the Internet, and Kids," *American Demographics*, May 2001, pp. 51–55; "Viral Marketing Alert!" *Business Week E.Biz*, March 19, 2001, p. EB8; "How a Viral Marketing E-Mail Campaign Delivered for Lee Apparel," *Advertising Age*, 2000, pp. A10–A11; "This Is One Virus You Want to Spread," *Fortune*,

November 27, 2000, pp. 297–300; "Accelerating Natural Contagion," *Brandweek*, October 20, 2000, pp. 31–38; "Sneaker Shock," *Brandweek*, October 2, 2000, p. 1ff.; "Motorola's 'Silent Bill' Arrives Via E-Mail," *The Wall Street Journal*, August 3, 2000, p. B13; "Tell Me a (Digital) Story," *Business Week E.Biz*, May 15, 2000, pp. EB91–94; "Guerrilla Marketers of the Year," *Brandweek*, March 27, 2000, pp. 28–76; "Desperately Seeking Buzz," *Business Week E.Biz*, February 7, 2000, pp. EB98–EB100.

17. Meera P. Venkatraman, "Opinion Leaders, Adopters, and Communicative Adopters: A Role Analysis," *Psychology and Marketing*, Spring 1989, pp. 51–68; S. Ram and Hyung-Shik Jung, "Innovativeness in Product Usage: A Comparison of Early Adopters and Early Majority," *Psychology & Marketing*, January/February 1994, pp. 57–68; Robert J. Fisher and Linda L. Price, "An Investigation into the Social Context of Early Adoption Behavior," *Journal of Consumer Research*, December 1992, p. 477; Leisa R. Flynn, Ronald E. Goldsmith, and Jacqueline K. Eastman, "Opinion Leaders and Opinion Seekers: Two New Measurement Scales," *Journal of the Academy of Marketing Science*, Spring 1996, pp. 137–47; Everett M. Rogers and F. Floyd Shoemaker, *Communication of Innovations: A Cross-Cultural Approach* (New York: Free Press, 1971), pp. 203–9.

18. Kusum L. Ailawadi, Paul W. Farris and Mark E. Parry, "Share and Growth Are Not Good Predictors of the Advertising and Promotion/Sales Ratio," *Journal of Marketing*, January 1994, pp. 86–97.

19. Deborah Utter, "Marketing on a Budget," *Journal of the Academy of Marketing Science*, Summer 2000, pp. 441–3; Kim P. Corfman and Donald R. Lehmann, "The Prisoner's Dilemma and the Role of Information in Setting Advertising Budgets," *Journal of Advertising*, June 1994, pp. 35–48; C. L. Hung and Douglas West, "Advertising Budgeting Methods in Canada, the UK and the USA," *International Journal of Advertising* 10, no. 3 (1991), pp. 239–50; Pierre Filiatrault and Jean-Charles Chebat, "How Service Firms Set Their Marketing Budgets," *Industrial Marketing Management*, February 1990, pp. 63–68; James E. Lynch and Graham J. Hooley, "Industrial Advertising Budget Approaches in the U.K.," *Industrial Marketing Management* 18, no. 4 (1989), pp. 265–70; "Beat the Budgeting Blues," *Business Marketing*, July 1989, pp. 48–57; Douglas J. Dalrymple and Hans B. Thorelli, "Sales Force Budgeting," *Business Horizons*, July/August 1984, pp. 31–36; Peter J. Danaher and Roland T. Rust, "Determining the Optimal Level of Media Spending," *Journal of Advertising Research*, January/February 1994, pp. 28–34.

Chapter 14

1. Available from World Wide Web: <http://www.cisco.com>; "Cisco Fractures Its Own Fairy Tale," *Fortune*, May 14, 2001, pp. 105–12; "Tech Consultants: You'll Need One Sooner or Later—So Get It Right," *Investor's Business Daily*, March 5, 2001, p. A1; "How Cisco Makes Takeovers Work with Rules, Focus on Client Needs," *Investor's Business Daily*, November 20, 2000, p. A1; "Going Digital? Think First," *Fortune*, November 13, 2000, pp. 190–98; "Cisco Not the Top Choice of Every Network Builder," *Investor's Business Daily*, November 13, 2000, p. A6; "Cisco Keeps Growing, But Exactly How Fast Is Becoming an Issue," *The Wall Street Journal*, November 3, 2000, p. A1ff.; "Accelerating Natural Contagion," *Brandweek*, October 30, 2000, pp. 31–38; "Factory Marks New Optical Era for Cisco," *Investor's Business Daily*, October 4, 2000, p. A8; "At Cisco, Executives Accumulate Stakes in Clients, Suppliers," *The Wall Street Journal*, October 3, 2000, p. A1ff.; "The World's Most Admired Companies," *Fortune*, October 2, 2000, pp. 183–89; "Cisco: A Web-Profit Prophet Spreads the Word," *Business Week E.Biz*, September 18, 2000, p. EB68; "Spread the Web: Cisco Reaches Beyond Techies," *The Wall Street Journal*, June 13, 2000, p. B1ff.; "Cisco High," *Business Week E.Biz*, June 5, 2000, pp. EB102–EB104; "How to Drive an Express Train," *The Wall Street Journal*, June 1, 2000, p. B1ff.; "How Cisco and Alcoa Make Real Time Work," *Fortune*, May 29, 2000, pp. 284–86; "There's Something About Cisco," *Fortune*, May 15, 2000, pp. 114–38; "Eating Their Own Dog Food," *The Wall Street Journal*, April 19, 2000, p. B1ff.; "Ford, Cisco Team Up to Speed Wiring of 40,000 Suppliers and Dealers for Web," *The Wall Street Journal*, February 10, 2000, p. A5; "Do You Know Cisco?" *Time*, January 17, 2000, pp. 72–74; "Customers Move Into the Driver's Seat," *Business Week*, October 4, 1999, pp. 103–106; "Mr. Internet," *Business Week*, September 13, 1999, pp. 128–40; "The Corporation of the Future," *Business Week*, August 31, 1998, pp. 102–106; "The New Economy Is Still Being Driven by the Old Hard Sell," *The Wall Street Journal*, August 13, 1999, p. B1.

2. "The Seoul Answer to Selling," *Going Global* (supplement to *Inc.*), March 1994; "AIG Sells Insurance in Shanghai, Testing Service Firms' Role," *The Wall Street Journal*, July 21, 1993, p. A1ff.; "Hungarians Seeking to Find a New Way Find Instead Amway," *The Wall Street Journal*, January 15, 1993, p. A1ff.; "The Secret to Northern's Japanese Success: When in Tokyo . . . ," *Business Week*, July 27, 1992, p. 57; "U.S. Companies in China Find Patience, Persistence and Salesmanship Pay Off," *The Wall Street Journal*, April 3, 1992, p. B1ff.; Paul A. Herbig and Hugh E. Kramer, "Do's and Don'ts of Cross-Cultural Negotiations," *Industrial Marketing Management*, November 1992, pp. 287–98; Alan J. Dubinsky et al., "Differences in Motivational Perceptions among U.S., Japanese, and Korean Sales Personnel," *Journal of Business Research*, June 1994, pp. 175–86; Carl R. Ruthstrom and Ken Matejka, "The Meanings of 'YES' in the Far East," *Industrial Marketing Management*, August 1990, pp. 191–92.

3. Tom Richman, "Seducing the Customer: Dale Ballard's Perfect Selling Machine," *Inc.*, April, 1988, pp. 96–104; *1987 Annual Report*, Ballard Medical Products.

4. Thomas R. Wotruba, "The Transformation of Industrial Selling: Causes and Consequences," *Industrial Marketing Management*, September 1996, pp. 327–38; William M. Strahle, Rosann L. Spiro, and Frank Acito, "Marketing and Sales: Strategic Alignment and Functional Implementation," *Journal of Personal Selling & Sales Management*, Winter 1996, pp. 1–20; Paul Boughton, "Winning Customers, Building Accounts: Some Do It Better Than Others," *Journal of the Academy of Marketing Science*, Spring 1996, pp. 175–76; Jerome A. Colletti and Lawrence B. Chonko, "Change Management Initiatives: Moving Sales Organizations From Obsolescence to High Performance," *Journal of Personal Selling & Sales Management*, Spring 1997, pp. 1–30; Marvin A. Jolson, "Broadening the Scope of Relationship Selling," *Journal of Personal Selling & Sales Management*, Fall 1997, pp. 75–88; Douglas M. Lambert, Howard Marmorstein, and Arun Sharma, "Industrial Salespeople as a Source of Market Information," *Industrial Marketing Management*, May 1990, pp. 141–48.

5. "Pushing Doctors to Buy High Tech for the Office," *Business Week*, September 2, 1985, pp. 84–85.

6. For an example, see "NationsBank Asks Tellers to Branch Out," *Raleigh News & Observer*, September 12, 1993, p. 1Fff.

7. Mark A. Moon and Susan F. Gupta, "Examining the Formation of Selling Centers: A Conceptual Framework," *Journal of Personal Selling & Sales Management*, Spring 1997, pp. 31–41; S. Joe Puri and Pradeep Korgaonkar, "Couple the Buying and Selling Teams," *Industrial Marketing Management* 20, no. 4 (1991), pp. 311–18; "P&G Rolls Out Retailer Sales Teams," *Advertising Age*, May 21, 1990, p. 18.

8. Dan C. Weilbaker and William A. Weeks, "The Evolution of National Account Management: A Literature Perspective," *Journal of Personal Selling & Sales Management*, Fall 1997, pp. 49–59; C. J. Lambe and Robert E. Spekman, "National Account Management: Large Account Selling or Buyer-Supplier Alliance?" *Journal of Personal Selling & Sales Management*, Fall 1997, pp. 61–74; Catherine Pardo, "Key Account Management in the Business to Business Field: The Key Account's Point of View," *Journal of Personal Selling & Sales Management*, Fall 1997, pp. 17–26; Sanjit Sengupta, Robert E. Krapfel, and Michael A. Pusateri, "Switching Costs in Key Account Relationships," *Journal of Personal Selling & Sales Management*, Fall 1997, pp. 9–16; Paul Dishman and Philip S. Nitse, "National Accounts Revisited: New Lessons From Recent Investigations," *Industrial Marketing Management*, January 1998, pp. 1–9.

9. "Telephone Sales Reps Do Unrewarding Jobs that Few Can Abide," *The Wall Street Journal*, September 9, 1993, p. A1ff.; Brett A. Boyle, "The Importance of the Industrial Inside Sales Force: A Case Study," *Industrial Marketing Management*, September 1996, pp. 339–48; "How to Unite Field and Phone Sales," *Inc.*, July 1992, p. 115; "Telemarketers Take Root in the Country," *The Wall Street Journal*, February 2, 1989, p. B1; "FCC Adopts Rules to Curb Telemarketing," *The Wall Street Journal*, September 18, 1992, p. B1; "Congress' 'Cure' for Junk Calls Faces a Skeptical FCC," *The Wall Street Journal*, May 19, 1992, p. B6.

10. "How to Remake Your Sales Force," *Fortune*, May 4, 1992, pp. 98–103; "What Flexible Workers Can Do," *Fortune*, February 13, 1989, pp. 62–64; "Apparel Makers Play Bigger Part on Sales Floor," *The Wall Street Journal*, March 2, 1988, p. 31; Ravipreet S. Sohi, Daniel C. Smith, and Neil M. Ford, "How Does Sharing a Sales Force Between Multiple Divisions Affect Salespeople?" *Journal of the Academy of Marketing Science*, Summer 1996, pp. 195–207; David W. Cravens and Raymond W. LaForge, "Salesforce Deployment Analysis," *Industrial Marketing Management*, July 1983, pp. 179–92; Michael S. Herschel, "Effective Sales Territory Development," *Journal of Marketing*, April 1977, pp. 39–43.

11. "Supercharged Sell," *Inc. Tech*, No. 2, 1997, pp. 42–51; Mary Jo Bitner, "Technology Infusion in Service Encounters," *Journal of the Academy of Marketing Science*, Winter 2000, pp. 138–150; Allan J. Magrath, "From the Practitioner's Desk: A Comment on 'Personal Selling and Sales Management in the New Millennium'," *Journal of Personal Selling & Sales Management*, Winter 1997, pp. 45–47; Michael J. Swenson and Adilson Parrella, "Sales Technology Applications: Cellular Telephones and the National Sales Force," *Journal of Personal Selling & Sales Management*, Fall 1992, pp. 67–74; Paul Dishman and Kregg Aytes, "Exploring Group Support Systems in Sales Management Applications," *Journal of Personal Selling & Sales Management*, Winter 1996, pp. 65–77.

12. "Salespeople Say Automation Software Still Lacking," *Investor's Business Daily*, January 18, 2001, p. A4; "MarketSoft Tailors Products to Solve Problems," *The Wall Street Journal*, November 30, 2000, p. B8; "New Software's Payoff? Happier Salespeople," *Investor's Business Daily*, May 23, 2000, p. A8; "Making the Sale," *The Wall Street Journal*, November 15, 1999, p. R16; "Free Software from Anywhere?" *Business Week*, September 13, 1999, pp. 37–38; "Offices Goin' Mobile," *USA Today*, May 17, 1999, p. 3B; "Bob Schmonsees Has a Tool for Better Sales and It Ignores Excuses," *The Wall Street Journal*, March 26, 1999, p. B1; "Companies Sold on the Latest Technology for the Sales Force," *Chicago Tribune*, November 8, 1992, Sect. 19, p. 5; "New Software Is Helping Reps Fill Custom Orders without Glitches," *The Wall Street Journal*, August 11, 1992, p. B6; "Salespeople on Road Use Laptops to Keep in Touch," *The Wall Street Journal*, April 25, 1991, p. B1.

13. For an example of HP's efforts, see "Fiorina Whips H-P into Fighting Shape," *USA Today*, June 5, 2001, p. 3B; "H-P Profit Drops 66% But Tops Forecast," *The Wall Street Journal*, May 17, 2000, p. A3ff.; "H-P Woes Are Deeper Than the Downturn," *Business Week*, May 7, 2001, p. 48; "The Radical: Carly Fiorina's Bold Management Experiment at HP," *Business Week*, February 19, 2001, pp. 68–80; "The Boss," *Business Week*, August 2, 1999, pp. 76–84.

14. "The Art of the Sale," *The Wall Street Journal*, January 11, 2001, p. B1ff.

15. Available from World Wide Web: <http://www.achievement.com/sales>; Ellen B. Pullins, Leslie M. Fine, and Wendy L. Warren, "Identifying Peer Mentors in the Sales Force: An Exploratory Investigation of Willingness and Ability," *Journal of the Academy of Marketing Science*, Spring 1996, pp. 125–36; Alan J. Dubinsky, "Some Assumptions About the Effectiveness of Sales Training," *Journal of Personal Selling & Sales Management*, Summer 1996, pp. 67–76; Earl D. Honeycutt, Ashraf M. Attia, and Angela R. D. Auria, "Sales Certification Programs," *Journal of Personal Selling & Sales Management*, Summer 1996, pp. 59–65; "Systematizing Salesperson Selection," *Sales and Marketing Management*, February 1992, pp. 65–68; "The Faxable International Sales-Rep Application," *Inc.*, November 1993, pp. 95–97; Patrick L. Schul and Brent M. Wren, "The Emerging Role of Women in Industrial Selling: A Decade of Change," *Journal of Marketing*, July 1992, pp. 38–54; William A. Weeks and Carl G. Stevens, "National Account Management Sales Training and Directions for Improvement: A Focus on Skills/Abilities," *Industrial Marketing Management*, September 1997, pp. 423–31; Earl D. Honeycutt, Jr., John B. Ford, and John F. Tanner, Jr., "Who Trains Salespeople? The Role of Sales Trainers and Sales Managers," *Industrial Marketing Management*, February 1994, pp. 65–70; Jeffrey K. Sager, "Recruiting and Retaining Committed Salespeople," *Industrial Marketing Management* 20, no. 2 (1991), pp. 99–104; S. Joe Puri,

"Where Industrial Sales Training Is Weak," *Industrial Marketing Management,* May 1993, pp. 101–8.

16. Douglas M. Lambert, Arun Sharma, and Michael Levy, "What Information Can Relationship Marketers Obtain From Customer Evaluations of Salespeople?" *Industrial Marketing Management,* March 1997, pp. 177–87; Erin Anderson and Thomas S. Robertson, "Inducing Multiline Salespeople to Adopt House Brands," *Journal of Marketing,* April 1995, pp. 16–31; Stephen B. Knouse and David Strutton, "Molding a Total Quality Salesforce Through Managing Empowerment, Evaluation, and Reward and Recognition Processes," *Journal of Marketing Theory & Practice,* Summer 1996, pp. 24–35; Ajay K. Kolhi and Bernard J. Jaworksi, "The Influence of Coworker Feedback on Salespeople," *Journal of Marketing,* October 1994, pp. 82–94; "Fire Up Your Sales Force," *Business Marketing,* July 1990, pp. 52–55; William L. Cron, Alan J. Dubinsky, and Ronald E. Michaels, "The Influence of Career Stages on Components of Salesperson Motivation," *Journal of Marketing,* January 1988, pp. 78–92.

17. Goutam Ghallagalla, "Supervisory Orientations and Salesperson Work Outcomes: the Moderating Effect of Salesperson Location," *The Journal of Personal Selling & Sales Management,* Summer 2000, pp. 161–172; "Creating Incentives Down in Ranks: Marriott Ties Pay to Guest Replies," *Investor's Business Daily,* July 6, 2001, p. A1; "Get Great Results from Salespeople by Finding What Really Moves Them," *Investor's Business Daily,* July 2, 2001, p. A1; "Medical Gear Sales Force Works on Commission," *Investor's Business Daily,* July 25, 2000, p. A14; Rene Y. Darmon, "Selecting Appropriate Sales Quota Plan Structures and Quota-Setting Procedures," *Journal of Personal Selling & Sales Management,* Winter 1997, pp. 1–16; Thomas E. Tice, "Managing Compensation Caps in Key Accounts," *Journal of Personal Selling & Sales Management,* Fall 1997, pp. 41–47; Joseph Kissan and Manohar U. Kalwani, "The Role of Bonus Pay in Salesforce Compensation Plans," *Industrial Marketing Management,* March 1998, pp. 147–59; Russell Abratt and Michael R. Smythe, "A Survey of Sales Incentive Programs," *Industrial Marketing Management,* August 1989, pp. 209–14; "Incentive Pay Isn't Good for Your Company," *Inc.,* September 1994, pp. 23–24; "The Few, the True, the Blue," *Business Week,* May 30, 1994, pp. 124–26; Arun Sharma, "Customer Satisfaction-Based Incentive Systems: Some Managerial and Salesperson Considerations," *Journal of Personal Selling & Sales Management,* Spring 1997, pp. 61–70; William Strahle and Rosann L. Spiro, "Linking Market Share Strategies to Salesforce Objectives, Activities, and Compensation Policies," *Journal of Personal Selling and Sales Management,* August 1986, pp. 11–18.

18. "New Software's Payoff? Happier Salespeople," *Investor's Business Daily,* May 23, 2000, p. A8. See also Richard L. Oliver and Erin Anderson, "An Empirical Test of the Consequences of Behavior- and Outcome-Based Sales Control Systems," *Journal of Marketing,* October 1994, pp. 53–67; Susan K. DelVecchio, "The Salesperson's Operating Freedom: A Matter of Perception," *Industrial Marketing Management,* January 1998, pp. 31–40; Vlasis Stathakopoulos, "Sales Force Control: A Synthesis of Three Theories," *Journal of Personal Selling & Sales Management,* Spring 1996, pp. 1–12; Gregory A. Rich, "The Constructs of Sales Coaching: Supervisory Feedback, Role Modeling and Trust," *Journal of Personal Selling & Sales Management,* Winter 1998, pp. 53–63; Goutam N. Challagalla and Tasadduq A. Shervani, "Dimensions and Types of Supervisory Control: Effects on Salesperson Performance and Satisfaction," *Journal of Marketing,* January 1996, pp. 89–105; Steven P. Brown and Robert A. Peterson, "The Effect of Effort on Sales Performance and Job Satisfaction," *Journal of Marketing,* April 1994, pp. 70–80; Paul A. Dion, Debbie Easterling, and Raj Javalgi, "Women in the Business-to-Business Salesforce: Some Differences in Performance Factors," *Industrial Marketing Management,* September 1997, pp. 447–57; Frederick A. Russ, Kevin M. McNeilly, and James M. Comer, "Leadership, Decision Making and Performance of Sales Managers: A Multi-Level Approach," *Journal of Personal Selling & Sales Management,* Summer 1996, pp. 1–15; Jhinuk Chowdhury, "The Motivational Impact of Sales Quotas on Effort," *Journal of Marketing Research,* February 1993, pp. 28–41; Alan J. Dubinsky, Francis J. Yammarino, and Marvin A. Jolson, "Closeness of Supervision and Salesperson Work Outcomes: An Alternate Perspective," *Journal of Business Research,* March 1994, pp. 225–38; David W. Cravens et al., "Behavior-Based and Outcome-Based Salesforce Control Systems," *Journal of Marketing,* October 1993, pp. 47–59; Daniel A. Sauers, James B. Hunt, and Ken Bass, "Behavioral Self-Management as a Supplement to External Sales Force Controls," *Journal of Personal Selling and Sales Management,* Summer 1990, pp. 17–28; Douglas N. Behrman and William D. Perreault, Jr., "A Role Stress Model of the Performance and Satisfaction of Industrial Salespersons," *Journal of Marketing,* Fall 1984, pp. 9–21; Richard T. Hise and Edward L. Reid, "Improving the Performance of the Industrial Sales Force in the 1990s," *Industrial Marketing Management,* October 1994, pp. 273–80.

19. "Chief Executives Are Increasingly Chief Salesmen," *The Wall Street Journal,* August 6, 1991, p. B1ff.; Joe F. Alexander, Patrick L. Schul, and Emin Babakus, "Analyzing Interpersonal Communications in Industrial Marketing Negotiations," *Journal of the Academy of Marketing Science,* Spring 1991, pp. 129–40.

20. Andris A. Zoltners, "Sales Territory Alignment: An Overlooked Productivity Tool," *The Journal of Personal Selling & Sales Management,* Summer 2000, pp. 139–151; Sanjit Sengupta, "An Empirical Investigation of Key Account Salesperson Effectiveness," *The Journal of Personal Selling & Sales Management,* Fall 2000, pp. 253–62; Ken Grant, "The Role of Satisfaction with Territory Design on the Motivation, Attitudes, and Work Outcomes of Salespeople," *Journal of the Academy of Marketing Science,* Spring 2001, pp. 165–179; William C. Moncrief, et al., "Examining the Roles of Telemarketing in Selling Strategy," *Journal of Personal Selling and Sales Management,* Fall 1989, pp. 1–12; J. David Lichtenthal, Saameer Sikri, and Karl Folk, "Teleprospecting: An Approach for Qualifying Accounts," *Industrial Marketing Management,* February 1989, pp. 11–18.

21. "When Should I Give Up on a Sales Prospect?" *Inc.,* May 1998, p. 129; "Downloading Their Dream Cars," *Business Week,* March 9, 1998, pp. 93–94; "The New Wave of Sales Automation," *Business Marketing,* June 1991, pp. 12–16; L. Brent Manssen, "Using PCs to Automate and Innovate Marketing Activities," *Industrial Marketing Management,* August 1990, pp. 209–14; Doris C. Van Doren and Thomas A. Stickney, "How to Develop a Database for Sales Leads," *Industrial Marketing Management,* August 1990, pp. 201–8.

22. "Novartis' Marketing Doctor," *Business Week,* March 5, 2001, p. 56.

23. For more on sales presentation approaches, see "Advise and Conquer," *Brandweek,* May 14, 2001, p. 1ff.; "Rick Francolini, TV Guide," *Brandweek,* October 25, 1999, p. 22; "The 60-Second Sales Pitch," *Inc.*, October 1994, pp. 87–89; David M. Szymanski, "Modality and Offering Effects in Sales Presentations for a Good Versus a Service," *Journal of the Academy of Marketing Science,* Spring 2001, pp. 179–190; Cathy Waters, "Customer Centered Selling: Eight Steps to Success from the World's Best Sales Force," *Journal of the Academy of Marketing Science,* Fall 2000, pp. 546–8; Jon M. Hawes, James T. Strong, and Bernard S. Winick, "Do Closing Techniques Diminish Prospect Trust?" *Industrial Marketing Management,* September 1996, pp. 349–60; Stephen B. Castleberry and C. David Shepherd, "Effective Interpersonal Listening and Personal Selling," *Journal of Personal Selling & Sales Management,* Winter 1993, pp. 35–50; Morgan P. Miles, Danny R. Arnold, and Henry W. Nash, "Adaptive Communication: The Adaption of the Seller's Interpersonal Style to the Stage of the Dyad's Relationship and the Buyer's Communication Style," *Journal of Personal Selling and Sales Management,* Winter 1990, pp. 21–28; Harish Sujan, Barton A. Weitz, and Nirmalya Kumar, "Learning Orientation, Working Smart, and Effective Selling," *Journal of Marketing,* July 1994, pp. 39–52.

24. For more on pharmaceutical company selling tactics, see "Doctors Step Out; Drug Salesmen Step In," *USA Today,* July 5, 2001, p. 11A; "Why Some Dialysis Patients Take $12-a-Day Drug Instead of Tums," *The Wall Street Journal,* June 26, 2001, p. B1ff.; "Sales Pitch: Drug Firms Use Perks to Push Pills," *USA Today,* May 16, 2001, p. 1Bff.; "Drug Database for Doctors Sells Ads to Sponsors," *The Wall Street Journal,* June 19, 2000, p. B1ff.; "Who's Teaching the Doctors?" *USA Today,* March 9, 2000, p. 1Dff.; "Web Links Give Drug Reps Foot in Doctors' Door," *The Wall Street Journal,* May 18, 1999, p. B1ff.; "In Marketing of Drugs, Genentech Tests Limits of What Is Acceptable," *The Wall Street Journal,* January 10, 1995, p. A1ff.; "Pharmacy Chain's Successful Sales Pitch Dismays Some Doctors and Drug Firms," *The Wall Street Journal,* February 26, 1993, p. B1ff. For more on Sears' selling tactics, see "Did Sears Take Other Customers for a Ride?" *Business Week,* August 3, 1992, pp. 24–25. See also Barry J. Babin, " Representing the Perceived Ethical Work Climate among Marketing Employees," *Journal of the Academy of Marketing Science,* Summer 2000, pp. 345–359; Bulent Menguc, "Organizational Consequences, Marketing Ethics and Salesforce Supervision: Further Empirical Evidence," *Journal of Business Ethics,* March 1998, pp. 333–52; David Strutton, J. B. I. Hamilton, and James R. Lumpkin, "An Essay on When to Fully Disclose in Sales Relationships: Applying Two Practical Guidelines for Addressing Truth-Telling Problems," *Journal of Business Ethics,* April 1997, pp. 545–60; Lawrence B. Chonko, John F. Tanner, and William A. Weeks, "Ethics in Salesperson Decision Making: A Synthesis of Research Approaches and an Extension of the Scenario Method," *Journal of Personal Selling & Sales Management,* Winter 1996, pp. 35–52; Alan J. Dubinsky, Marvin A. Jolson, Masaaki Kotabe, and Chae Un Lim, "A Cross-National Investigation of Industrial Salespeople's Ethical Perceptions," *Journal of International Business Studies,* Winter 1991, pp. 651–70.

Chapter 15

1. "Lays Chips Lands at DDB Needham," *Advertising Age,* May 12, 1997, p. 1ff.; "Rebecca Johnson: Frito-Lay," *Brandweek,* November 4, 1996, pp. 74–76; "Frito-Lay Named New Product Marketer of 1995," *Marketing News,* May 6, 1996, p. E2ff.; "Baked Chips Are Such a Hit, There's a Crunch," *USA Today,* March 20, 1996, p. 1Bff.

2. "Special Report: U.S. Multinationals," *Ad Age International,* January 1998, pp. 17–26; "Colgate-Palmolive Is Really Cleaning Up in Poland," *Business Week,* March 15, 1993, pp. 54–56; Charles R. Taylor, Gordon E. Miracle, and R. D. Wilson, "The Impact of Information Level on the Effectiveness of U.S. and Korean Television Commercials," *Journal of Advertising,* Spring 1997, pp. 1–18; Ann M. Barry, "Advertising and Culture: Theoretical Perspectives," *Journal of the Academy of Marketing Science,* Winter 1998, pp. 67–68; Siew M. Leong, Sween H. Ang, and Leng L. Tham, "Increasing Brand Name Recall in Print Advertising Among Asian Consumers," *Journal of Advertising,* Summer 1996, pp. 65–81; Ronald E. Taylor, Mariea G. Hoy, and Eric Haley, "How French Advertising Professionals Develop Creative Strategy," *Journal of Advertising,* Spring 1996, pp. 1–14; Nan Zhou and Mervin Y. T. Chen, "A Content Analysis of Men and Women in Canadian Consumer Magazine Advertising: Today's Portrayal, Yesterday's Image?" *Journal of Business Ethics,* April 1997, pp. 485–95; Johny K. Johansson, "The Sense of 'Nonsense': Japanese TV Advertising," *Journal of Advertising,* March 1994, pp. 17–26; Yong Zhang and Betsy D. Gelb, "Matching Advertising Appeals to Culture: The Influence of Products' Use Conditions," *Journal of Advertising,* Fall 1996, pp. 29–46; John L. Graham, Michael A. Kamins and Djoko S. Oetomo, "Content Analysis of German and Japanese Advertising in Print Media from Indonesia, Spain, and the United States," *Journal of Advertising,* June 1993, pp. 5–16; Bob D. Cutler and Rajshekhar G. Javalgi, "A Cross-Cultural Analysis of the Visual Components of Print Advertising: The United States and the European Community," *Journal of Advertising Research,* January/February 1992, p.71; Terence Nevett, "Differences Between American and British Television Advertising: Explanations and Implications," *Journal of Advertising,* December 1992, pp. 61–72; Bob D. Cutler and Rajshekhar G. Javalgi, "Comparison of Business-to-Business Advertising: The United States and the United Kingdom," *Industrial Marketing Management,* April 1994, pp. 117–24.

3. "Write It Off," *Advertising Age,* July 2, 2001, p. 1ff.; "Turn Signals," *Advertising Age,* June 25, 2001, p. 44; "Forecast: Hazy," *Advertising Age,* June 18, 2001, p. 4ff.; "Europe's Ad-Spending Picture Gets Darker," *The Wall Street Journal,* June 14, 2001, p. B5; "Top Forecaster Sees Lower Ad Growth," *Advertising Age,* June 11, 2001, p. 1ff.; "A Lot of Subtraction in Ad Game," *Raleigh News & Observer,* April 6, 2001, p. 1Dff.; "The Party's Over," *Advertising Age,* January 1, 2001, p. 1ff.; "Asian Industry Has High Hopes for 2001," *The Wall Street Journal,* December 29, 2000, p. A10.

4. "Unilever Leapfrogs P&G, Takes Ad Lead Outside U.S.," *Advertising Age,* November 13, 2000, p. 21; "Special Report: Global Marketers, the World's Biggest Spenders," *Ad Age Global,* November 2000, pp. 35–44. "2000 Advertising-to-Sales Ratios for the 200 Largest Ad Spending Industries," *Advertising Age,*

June 2000; Kip D. Cassino, "An Advertising Atlas," *American Demographics*, August 1994, pp. 44–55; Kusum L. Ailawadi, Paul W. Farris, and Mark E. Parry, "Share and Growth Are Not Good Predictors of the Advertising and Promotion/Sales Ratio," *Journal of Marketing*, January 1994, pp. 86–97.

5. "Forecast: Hazy," *Advertising Age*, June 18, 2001, p. 4ff.; "Top Forecaster Sees Lower Ad Growth," *Advertising Age*, June 11, 2001, p. 1ff.; "Economic Mood Channels Tough Talk on TV Ad Sales," *USA Today*, May 9, 2001, p. 1Bff.; "The Party's Over," *Advertising Age*, January 1, 2001, p. 1ff.

6. Exact data on this industry are elusive, but see U.S. Bureau of the Census, *Statistical Abstract of the United States 1997* (Washington, DC: U.S. Government Printing Office, 1997), pp. 410–15

7. For more on Dryel, see "The Dirt on At-Home Dry Cleaning," *The Wall Street Journal*, September 15, 2000, p. W14. See also "Sour Dough: Pizza Hut v. Papa John's," *Brandweek*, May 21, 2001, pp. 26–30; Kenneth C. Manning, "Understanding the Mental Representations Created by Comparative Advertising," *Journal of Advertising*, Summer 2001, pp. 27–40; "Irate Firms Take Comparisons to Court," *The Wall Street Journal*, December 22, 1999, p. B8; "Survey: Comparative Ads Can Dent Car's Credibility," *Advertising Age*, May 4, 1998, p. 26; "Rivals Take the Gloves Off as Taste-Test Wars Heat Up," *The Wall Street Journal*, March 30, 1998, p. B10; "Industry Panel Refers FedEx Case to FTC," *The Wall Street Journal*, April 11, 1997, p. B6; Diana L. Haytko, "Great Advertising Campaigns: Goals and Accomplishments," *Journal of Marketing*, April 1995, pp. 113–15; Carolyn Tripp, "Services Advertising: An Overview and Summary of Research, 1980–1995," *Journal of Advertising*, Winter 1997, pp. 21–38; Dhruv Grewal, Sukumar Kavanoor, Edward F. Fern, Carolyn Costley, and James Barnes, "Comparative Versus Noncomparative Advertising: A Meta-Analysis," *Journal of Marketing*, October 1997, pp. 1–15; Marla R. Stafford and Ellen Day, "Retail Services Advertising: The Effects of Appeal, Medium, and Service," *Journal of Advertising*, Spring 1995, pp. 57–71; For more on AT&T, MCI, and Sprint's comparative ads, see "Best Phone Discounts Go to Hardest Bargainers," *The Wall Street Journal*, February 13, 1997, p. B1ff.; "Fighting for Customers Gets Louder," *USA Today*, January 9, 1995, p. 1Bff.; "Discount War Can Be Confusing," *USA Today*, September 23, 1994, p. 1Bff.; "AT&T Tweaks MCI's 'Friends'," *Advertising Age*, March 2, 1992, p. 4. For other examples of comparative advertising, see "Allergy Drugs Wage a Bitter War of the Noses," *The Wall Street Journal*, May 23, 1996, p. B1ff.; "New Drug Ads Give Doctors Heartburn," *The Wall Street Journal*, April 25, 1996, p. B9; "Bitter Ads to Swallow," *Time*, April 1, 1996, pp. 48–49; "More Heartburn Relief Unsettles Market," *The Wall Street Journal*, February 7, 1996, p. B6; "New Ammo for Comparative Ads," *Advertising Age*, February 14, 1994, p. 26; Thomas E. Barry, "Comparative Advertising: What Have We Learned in Two Decades?" *Journal of Advertising Research*, March/April 1993, pp. 19–29; Naveen Donthu, "Comparative Advertising Intensity," *Journal of Advertising Research*, November/December 1992, pp. 53–58.

8. "As BP Goes Green, the Fur Is Flying," *The Wall Street Journal*, April 16, 2001, p. B1ff.

9. "Brawl Erupts Over Do-Good Advertising," *The Wall Street Journal*, September 29, 1997, p. B1ff.; "Cause and Effects Marketing," *Brandweek*, April 22, 1996, pp. 38–40; "Are Good Causes Good Marketing?" *Business Week*, March 21, 1994, pp. 64–66; "Chemical Firms Press Campaigns to Dispel Their 'Bad Guy' Image," *The Wall Street Journal*, September 20, 1988, p. 1ff.; "Spiffing up the Corporate Image," *Fortune*, July 21, 1986, pp. 68–72; Minette E. Drumwright, "Company Advertising With a Social Dimension: The Role of Noneconomic Criteria," *Journal of Marketing*, October 1996, pp. 71–87; Eric Haley, "Exploring the Construct of Organization As Source: Consumer's Understandings of Organizational Sponsorship of Advocacy Advertising," *Journal of Advertising*, Summer 1996, pp. 19–35; John K. Ross III, Larry T. Patterson, and Mary Ann Stutts, "Consumer Perceptions of Organizations That Use Cause-Related Marketing," *Journal of the Academy of Marketing Science*, Winter 1992, pp. 93–98.

10. For more on Benetton's co-op ads, see "Store Owners Rip into Benetton," *Advertising Age*, February 6, 1995, p. 1; "Benetton, German Retailers Squabble," *Advertising Age*, February 6, 1995, p. 46; "Benetton Brouhaha," *Advertising Age*, February 17, 1992, p. 62. For more on Intel's co-op ads, see "Intel Inside at 10," *Advertising Age*, April 30. 2001, p. 4ff.; "Co-op Crossroads," *Advertising Age*, November 15, 1999, p. 1ff.; "Intel Will Help Pay Costs of PC Makers' Web Ads," *USA Today*, August 5, 1997, p. 1B; "Changes to Intel's Co-op Program Could Boost Web Advertising 40%," *The Wall Street Journal*, August 5, 1997, p. B7; "Intel Co-op Could Bring $150 Million to the Web," *Advertising Age*, July 28, 1997, p. 16; "How Strong Is the Case Against Intel?" *Business Week*, June 22, 1998, p. 42; "Intel Proposal Is Angering Web Publishers," *The Wall Street Journal*, January 16, 1998, p. B1ff.; "Trade Bait," *Brandweek*, December 1, 1997, pp. 36–44; "Intel's Amazing Profit Machine," *Fortune*, February 17, 1997, pp. 60–72. For more on GM's co-op ads, see "Still Pulling the Strings, But Locally, Too," *Brandweek*, April 17, 2000, pp. 34–42; "GM Dealers Rebel Against Local Ad Structure," *Advertising Age*, January 24, 2000, p. 3ff.; "GM Dealers Aren't Buying It," *Business Week*, February 8, 1999, pp. 46–50.

11. For more on co-op ads, see "Big Blue Offers Solutions with $60 Mil Co-op Effort," *Advertising Age*, April 30, 2001, p. 8; "Revlon Plans Another Makeover," *The Wall Street Journal*, November 21, 2000, p. B1ff.; "Retailers Open Doors Wide for Co-op," *Advertising Age*, August 1, 1994, p. 30; John P. Murry and Jan B. Heide, "Managing Promotion Program Participation Within Manufacturer-Retailer Relationships," *Journal of Marketing*, January 1998, pp. 58–68. For more on joint promotions, see "Joint Marketing with Retailers Spreads," *The Wall Street Journal*, October 24, 1996, p. B6; "Joint Promotions Spawn Data Swap," *Advertising Age*, October 7, 1991, p. 44; "H&R Block, Excedrin Discover Joint Promotions Can Be Painless," *The Wall Street Journal*, February 28, 1991, p. B3.

12. "Firms Pitch New Place to Park Ads," *The Wall Street Journal*, July 11, 2001, p. B10; "Look Up, Down, All Around—Ads Fill Airports, Planes," *USA Today*, July 10, 2001, p. 12B; "It's an Ad, Ad, Ad, Ad World," *Time*, July 9, 2001, p. 17; "Ads Are Here, There, Everywhere," *USA Today*, June 19, 2001, p. 1Bff.; "Ahh, the Sun, the Surf . . . and Tons of Ads," *USA Today*, May 24, 2001, p. 3B; "Video Venue Joins the Line for Gas-Pump Advertising," *Advertising Age*, April 23, 2001, p. 8; "Think Graffiti Is All That's Hanging in Subway Tunnels? Look Again," *The*

Wall Street Journal, April 4, 2001, p. B1ff.; "Ads Show Up in Unexpected Places," *USA Today,* March 23, 2001, p. 1Bff.; "Ad-Packed TVs May Soon Be Boarding City Buses," *The Wall Street Journal,* February 21, 2001, p. B1ff.; "Signage-itis: More Buildings Sport Billboards," *The Wall Street Journal,* January 10, 2001, p. B10; "Happy Meal?" *Brandweek,* November 13, 2000, p. 98; "From Elevators to Gas Stations, Ads Multiplying," *Advertising Age,* November 13, 2000, pp. 40–42; "Moving Targets," *American Demographics,* October 2000, pp. 32–36; "Motorists Finding Logos a Gas," *USA Today,* September 15, 2000, p. 3A; "From Cell Phones to Sell Phones," *Business Week,* September 11, 2000, pp. 88–90; "New Gas Pumps Deliver Ads Via the Net," *Investor's Business Daily,* June 23, 2000, p. A6; "Advertisers Find One of the Last Clutter-Free Places," *The Wall Street Journal,* June 15, 2000, p. B1ff.; "Believe Your Eyes? Ads Bend Reality," *USA Today,* April 24, 2000, p. 1Bff.; "Virtual Ads Grab More Attention from Marketers," *Advertising Age,* May 29, 2000; "It's an Ad, Ad, Ad, Ad World," *Inc.,* March 2000, pp. 23–26; "The Omnipresent Persuaders," *The Wall Street Journal,* January 1, 2000, p. R26; "P&G's Tide Rolls Into Pizza Shops," *Brandweek,* July 26, 1999, p. 9; "Bright Idea Has Business Looking Up for Ad Blimps," *The Wall Street Journal,* October 14, 1997, p. B1ff.

13. *Standard Rate and Data,* 2000; "Special Report: Media Outlook 2001," *Adweek,* September 25, 2000. For more on the Yellow Pages medium, see "Print Yellow Pages Are Still Profitable," *The Wall Street Journal,* May 22, 2000, p. B16; "The Truth About Yellow Pages: Making Them Work for You," *Journal of the Academy of Marketing Science,* Winter 1998, pp. 71–72; "'Sleeping Giant,' the Yellow Pages, Tries to Waken Madison Avenue," *The Wall Street Journal,* August 19, 1993, p. B6. For more on videotape medium, see "Are Spots on Home Video Badvertising?" *Brandweek,* January 29, 1996, p. 40; "Special Report: Direct Marketing," *Advertising Age,* October 28, 1996, pp. S1–6; "Direct Marketers Press Fast-Forward on Videotape Use," *The Wall Street Journal,* October 31, 1994, p. B8B. For more on the outdoor medium, see "A Market on the Move," *Ad Age Global,* April 2001, p. 38; "Billboards Help Media Firms Weather Slowdown," *USA Today,* December 12, 2000, p. 6B; "New Technology, Improved Image Draw Companies to Billboard Ads," *The Wall Street Journal,* July 31, 2000, p. B10; "Look Up! Seeing Is Believing," *Advertising Age,* August 2, 1999, p. S2; "The Great Outdoors," *Fortune,* March 1, 1999, pp. 150–57; "Billboards Aren't Boring Anymore," *Business Week,* September 21, 1998, pp. 86–90. See also Charles R. Taylor and John C. Taylor, "Regulatory Issues in Ourdoor Advertising: A Content Analysis of Billboards," *Journal of Public Policy & Marketing,* Spring 1994, pp. 97–107. For more on the radio medium, see "Old Media Get a Web Windfall," *The Wall Street Journal,* September 17, 1999, p. B1ff.; "TV Commercials Turn Obscure Songs into Radio Hits," *The Wall Street Journal,* October 9, 1998, p. B1ff.; "Radio's New Spin on an Oldie: Pay-for-Play," *The Wall Street Journal,* March 16, 1998, p. B1ff. See also Darryl W. Miller and Lawrence J. Marks, "Mental Imagery and Sound Effects in Radio Commercials," *Journal of Advertising,* December 1992, pp. 83–94. For more on the newspaper medium, see "Special Report: Newspaper Industry," *Advertising Age,* April 30, 2001, pp. S1–7; "Special Report: Newspapers," *Adweek,* April 30, 2001, pp. SR1–14; "Special Report: Newspapers," *Advertising Age,* May 8, 2000, pp. S1–20; "Publish or Perish?" *Fortune,* January 10, 2000, pp. 140–54; "Special Report: Newspapers," *Adweek,* April 26, 1999, pp. 1–28; "Newspapers," *Advertising Age,* April 26, 1999, pp. S1–22. See also Lawrence C. Soley and Robert L. Craig, "Advertising Pressures on Newspapers: A Survey," *Journal of Advertising,* December 1992, pp. 1–10; Srini S. Srinivasan, Robert P. Leone, and Francis J. Mulhern, "The Advertising Exposure Effect of Free Standing Inserts," *Journal of Advertising,* Spring 1995, pp. 29–40; Karen W. King, Leonard N. Reid, and Margaret Morrison, "Large-Agency Media Specialists' Opinions on Newspaper Advertising for National Accounts," *Journal of Advertising,* Summer 1997, pp. 1–17. For more on the magazine medium, see "To Sell Ad Pages, Magazines Offer Extra Services," *The Wall Street Journal,* July 9, 2001, p. B1ff.; "O Sister, Where Art Thou? Buying O," *USA Today,* January 18, 2001, p. 10D; "Special Report: Magazine Forecast," *Advertising Age,* October 23, 2000, pp. S1–36; "Magazines Think Outside the Rack," *USA Today,* November 15, 1999, p. 1Bf.; "Special Report: Magazines," *Advertising Age,* October 25, 1999, pp. S1–28. For more on the television and cable medium, see "MTV Networks Chief Juggles Expectations," *USA Today,* June 11, 2001, p. 1Bff.; "Special Report: TV's Upfront," *Advertising Age,* May 14, 2001, pp. S1–54; "Special Report: Cable TV," *Ad Age Global,* May 1, 2001, pp. 25–38; "Special Report: Cable TV," *Advertising Age,* April 16, 2001, pp. S1–28; "Special Report: TV's Upfront," *Advertising Age,* May 15, 2000, pp. S1–60; "Special Report: Cable TV Convergence," *Advertising Age,* April 10, 2000, pp. S1–38; "Special Report: Cable TV," *Advertising Age,* December 6, 1999, pp. S1–28. See also Jean L. Rogers, "Mail Advertising and Consumer Behavior," *Psychology & Marketing,* March 1996, pp. 211–33; Elizabeth C. Hirschman and Craig J. Thompson, "Why Media Matter: Toward a Richer Understanding of Consumers' Relationships With Advertising and Mass Media," *Journal of Advertising,* Spring 1997, pp. 43–60; Richard J. Fox and Gary L. Geissler, "Crisis in Advertising?" *Journal of Advertising,* December 1994, pp. 79–84; Roland T. Rust and Richard W. Oliver, "The Death of Advertising," *Journal of Advertising,* December 1994, pp. 71–77.

14. "Sex-Themed Ads Often Don't Travel Well," *The Wall Street Journal,* March 31, 2000, p. B7; "U.S. Admakers Cover It Up; Others Don't Give a Fig Leaf," *USA Today,* June 27, 1997, p. 1Bff.; "Mars *Inc.* Dips into Sex to Lure Consumers into Arms of M&M's," *The Wall Street Journal,* January 21, 1997, p. B9; "Underwear Ads Caught in Bind over Sex Appeal," *Advertising Age,* July 8, 1996, p. 27; "No Sexy Sales Ads, Please—We're Brits and Swedes," *Fortune,* October 21, 1991, p. 13.

15. "Looking for Mr. Plumber," *MediaWeek,* June 27, 1994, p. 7ff.; "Those Really Big Shows Are Often Disappointing to Those Who Advertise," *The Wall Street Journal,* June 14, 1994, p. B1ff.

16. "Yech and Yada in 'Seinfeld' Ads," *Advertising Age,* May 18, 1998, p. 63; "'Seinfeld' Finale Advertisers Put on Game Faces," *USA Today,* April 29, 1998, p. 1B; "NBC May Get Only $1.5 Million for Ad Spots on 'Seinfeld' Finale," *The Wall Street Journal,* March 4, 1998, p. B6.

17. "Gardenburger's Ad May Help Its Rival," *The Wall Street Journal,* May 20, 1998, p. B8; "Gardenburger Bets the (Soybean) Farm on the Last 'Seinfeld,'" *The Wall Street Journal,* April 13, 1998, p. A1ff..

18. For more on ATM ads, see "Ads on Automated Teller Machines Multiply as Technology Improves," *Investor's Business Daily,* October 5, 2000, p. A6; "ATMs Are Latest Place-Based Medium," *Advertising Age,* November 24, 1997, p. 1ff. For more on Nascar ads, see "Revved-Up Prices Stall Fox Nascar Spots," *The Wall Street Journal,* March 26, 2001, p. B8; "On-Track Tragedy May Create Hazard for Future Nascar Sponsorships," *Brandweek,* February 26, 2001, p. 8; "Nascar's New Deal: Will Street Ride Along?" *Investor's Business Daily,* February 16, 2001, p. A8; "Forget Football," *American Demographics,* February 2001, pp. 34–36; "Start the Engines!" *Brandweek,* October 9, 2000, p. 1ff.; "Speed Sells," *Fortune,* April 12, 1999, pp. 56–70; "Babes, Bordeaux, and Billy Bobs," *Time,* May 31, 1999, pp. 70–76; "Sports Marketing: Stock Rising," *Brandweek,* March 22, 1999, pp. 24–26; "The Green Flag Is Up," *American Demographics,* April 1999, pp. 33–36; "Smile, You're a Winner!" *Time,* June 15, 1998, pp. 42–43; "Speed Sells," *Business Week,* August 11, 1997, pp. 86–90; "New Breed of Sponsors Race to NASCAR," *USA Today,* April 5, 1996, p. 1Bff. See also Alan J. Greco and Linda E. Swayne, "Sales Response of Elderly Consumers to Point-of-Purchase Advertising," *Journal of Advertising Research,* September/October 1992, pp. 43–53.

19. "Ads Held Viewers the Super Bowl Bored," *The Wall Street Journal,* February 2, 2001, p. B6; "Super Bowl Ad Meter," *USA Today,* January 29, 2001, p. 8Bff.; "Super Bowl Accepts No Half-Hearted Effort," *USA Today,* January 26, 2001, p. 1Bff.; "Super Bowl's 30-Second Ad Rush," *The Wall Street Journal,* January 26, 2001, p. B1ff.; "No Gain," *Advertising Age,* January 25, 2001, p. 1ff.; "Diageo Designs Sneak Ad Play for Super Bowl," *The Wall Street Journal,* January 15, 2001, p. B1ff.; "CBS Eyes Windfall from Record Rates for 'Survivor' Ads," *The Wall Street Journal,* January 12, 2001, p. B4; "Edgy Spots Stir Controversy, and Results," *The Wall Street Journal,* January 11, 2001, p. B13; "Super Bowl Ads Are Latest Victim of Downturn," *The Wall Street Journal,* January 9, 2001, p. B1ff.; "Firms Pick Super Bowl as Prime Time for Kickoff Ads," *USA Today,* January 2, 2001, p. 1B; "VW + XXXV = $uper Bowl $trategy," *USA Today,* December 20, 2000, p. 2B; "ER Tops Price Charts, Regis Wears the Crown," *Advertising Age,* October 2, 2000, p. 1ff.; "ABC Tally for Oscar: $62.4 Mil," *Advertising Age,* March 20, 2000, pp. 40–42.

20. Kim Bartel Sheehan, "Re-Weaving the Web: Integrating Print and Online Communications," *Journal of Interactive Marketing,* Spring 2001, p. 47; Lee Sherman, "Banner Advertising: Measuring Effectiveness and Optimizing Placement," *Journal of Interactive Marketing,* Spring 2001, p. 60; "Behind the Wheel Driving the Web," *Advertising Age,* July 23, 2001, pp. 10–12; "Web Ads Getting in Your Way? Try Blocking Software," *Investor's Business Daily,* July 12, 2001, p. A6; "Aggressive Web Ads Push Ahead," *Investor's Business Daily,* July 3, 2001, p. A5; "The Bright Future of Web Advertising," *Ecompany,* June 2001, pp. 51–60; "Can You Say 'Cheese'? Intrusive Web Ads Could Drive Us Nuts," *The Wall Street Journal,* May 21, 2001, p. B1; "Choices, Choices . . . Web Advertising," *The Wall Street Journal,* April 23, 2001, p. R12; "Ad Nauseam," *The Wall Street Journal,* April 23, 2001, p. R8ff.; "Advertisers Have a Banner Year," *Investor's Business Daily,* March 9, 2001, p. A4; "Web's Next Phase Will Weave Through Your Life," *USA Today,* March 2, 2001, p. 1Bff.; "Looking Beyond Banners to Revive Web Advertising," *The Wall Street Journal,* February 26, 2001, p. B1ff.; "Dot-Com Rarity: NextCard Finds Online Ads Work," *The Wall Street Journal,* January 29, 2001, p. B1f.; "Do e-Ads Have a Future?" *Business Week E.Biz,* January 22, 2001, pp. EB46–EB50; "Beyond the Banner Ad," *Business Week E.Biz.,* December 11, 2000, p. EB16; "As Ads Fail to Heat Up, Sites Turning to Paid Subscribers," *Investor's Business Daily,* December 11, 2000, p. A8; "Content on Web Is Under Fire for Losing Cash," *The Wall Street Journal,* October 9, 2000, p. B1ff.; "Web Sites Toot Their Horns Amid Ad Chill," *The Wall Street Journal,* June 27, 2000, p. B1ff.; "Online Ads Turn to Hand-Held Devices," *The Wall Street Journal,* February 4, 2000, p. B6; "The Silicon Alley Heart of Internet Advertising," *Fortune,* December 6, 1999, pp. 166–68; "Banner Ads Are Driving Web Purchases," *The Wall Street Journal,* November 24, 1999, p. B9ff.; "Now It's Time for a Commercial," *The Wall Street Journal,* November 22, 1999, p. R28ff.; "Internet Waves Hit Asia Shores," *Ad Age International,* November 1999, p. 43ff.; "The Net Chases the Networks," *Fortune,* October 11, 1999, p. 296; "Humor Is Used to Slow Down Web Surfers," *The Wall Street Journal,* August 17, 1999, p. B9; "P&G Lathers On-Line Ad Revolution," *USA Today,* July 15, 1999, p. 3B; "Getting Noticed," *The Wall Street Journal,* July 12, 1999, p. R16ff.; "Online Persuaders," *The Wall Street Journal,* July 12, 1999, p. R12ff.; "Wacky Internet Ads Ride Creative Wave," *USA Today,* June 9, 1999, p. 1Bff.; "The Trouble with Web Advertising," *Fortune,* April 12, 1999, pp. 147–48; "Clicks for Free," *American Demographics,* February 1999, pp. 54–55; "Ads Click for Net Retailers," *USA Today,* January 28, 1999, p. 3B; "Your Message Here," *Inc. Tech,* No. 1, 1999, pp. 76–80; "Web Sites Say: Your Ad Sells or It's on Us," *The Wall Street Journal,* June 27, 1997, p. B9; "How Net Is Becoming More Like Television to Draw Advertisers," *The Wall Street Journal,* December 13, 1996, p. A1ff.; Richard T. Watson, Sigmund Akselsen, and Leyland F. Pitt, "Attractors: Building Mountains in the Flat Landscape of the World Wide Web," *California Management Review,* Winter 1998, pp. 36–56; W. W. Kassaye, "Global Advertising and the World Wide Web," *Business Horizons,* May–June 1997, pp. 33–42.

21. For more on Jordan's celebrity ads, see "Jordan Leaps into Palm of Your Hand," *USA Today,* June 18, 2001, p. 4B; "Marketers Drool over a Jordan Return," *USA Today,* April 11, 2001, p. 1B; "Jordan Trades Pitches for Piece of the Action," *Advertising Age,* March 27, 2000, p. 1ff.; "Jordan Tires of Ad Gigs," *USA Today,* March 23, 2000, p. 3B; "MJ's Court," *Newsweek,* January 25, 1999, pp. 46–55; "Birth of an Icon," *Advertising Age,* January 25, 1999, pp. 22–24; "Michael Jordan Isn't Retiring from Hot Deals," *The Wall Street Journal,* January 15, 1999, p. B1ff.; "The Jordan Effect," *Fortune,* June 22, 1998, pp. 124–38; "NBA Bravely Plans for Post-Jordan Era," *The Wall Street Journal,* February 6, 1998, p. B1ff. For more on Woods' celebrity ads, see "The Dominator," *Newsweek,* June 18, 2001, pp. 44–49; "Nike: Great Balls Afire. Will Golf Clubs Be Next?" *Business Week,* February 26, 2001, p. 109; "Tiger Vs. the PGA: How Serious Is It?" *Business Week,* November 27, 2000, pp. 102–106; "The Yin and Yang of the Tiger Effect," *Business Week,* October 16, 2000, p. 110; "Woods' Latest Trophy: $100 Million Nike Deal," *USA Today,* September 15, 2000, p. 1A; "Can Tiger Make Buick Roar?" *USA Today,* December 15, 1999, p. 1Bff.; "Woods Brand Gets New Look," *USA Today,* September 18, 1998,p. 1Bff. For more on the Williams Sisters' celebrity ads, see "Ad-Vantage: the

Williams Sisters," *Business Week*, February 5, 2001, p. 71; "Venus and Serena Become Avon's New Leading Ladies," *Advertising Age*, January 22, 2001, p. 8; "Deal Sealed, Venus Endorses Fee Idea," *USA Today*, December 22, 2000, p. 1Cff.; "Girl Power: Advertisers Shift Focus to Female Athletes," *USA Today*, December 12, 2000, p. 1B; "Show Them the Money," *Time*, December 4, 2000, p. 63. See also "Subaru's Forester Takes Female Athletes on a New $18M Ad Ride," *Brandweek*, April 30, 2001, p. 16; "Why Sports Should Fear the Hand that Feeds It," *Ad Age Global*, October 2000, p. 29; "Holly Wired," *Time Digital*, May 2000, pp. 78–81; "Meet Lycra's New Face," *Brandweek*, April 24, 2000, p. 1ff.; "Kwan Spins Silver into Gold," *USA Today*, February 9, 2000, p. 1Bff.; "Battle of the Golf Shirts," *The Wall Street Journal*, January 6, 2000, p. B1ff.; "Golfing with Troy, and Other Perks," *The Wall Street Journal*, October 4, 1999, p. B1ff.; "Sports Bra's Flash Could Cash In," *USA Today*, July 13, 1999, p. 1Aff.; "Show Me the Money," *The Wall Street Journal*, May 17, 1999, p. B1ff.; "Home-Run Heroes Bring In Few Endorsements," *The Wall Street Journal*, October 21, 1998, p. B1ff.; "In the NBA, Shoe Money Is No Longer a Slam-Dunk," *The Wall Street Journal*, May 14, 1998, p. B1ff. See also "Dip Ad Stirs Church Ire," *Advertising Age*, July 2, 2001, p., 8ff.; "Ghosts of Cannes," *Advertising Age*, June 11, 2001, p. 1ff.; "Duck Ads Have New Customers," *USA Today*, September 18, 2000, p. 13B; "Cough Syrup Touts 'Awful' Taste in U.S.," *The Wall Street Journal*, December 15, 1999, p. B10; "Honda Hopes Mr. Clean Helps to Make Its Image Sparkle," *The Wall Street Journal*, September 26, 1997, p. B20; "Madison Avenue Picks an Average Joe as '90s Pitchman," *The Wall Street Journal*, September 11, 1996, p. B1ff. See also Erik L. Olson, "How Magazine Articles Portrayed Advertising From 1900 to 1940," *Journal of Advertising*, Fall 1995, pp. 41–54; Audhesh K. Paswan, "Marketing to the Mind: Right Brain Strategies for Advertising and Marketing," *Journal of the Academy of Marketing Science*, Winter 1998, pp. 68–69; Avery M. Abernethy and George R. Franke, "The Information Content of Advertising: A Meta-Analysis," *Journal of Advertising*, Summer 1996, pp. 1–17; James H. Leigh, "The Use of Figures of Speech in Print Ad Headlines," *Journal of Advertising*, June 1994, pp. 17–33; Bruce A. Huhmann and Timothy P. Brotherton, "A Content Analysis of Guilt Appeals in Popular Magazine Advertisements," *Journal of Advertising*, Summer 1997, pp. 35–45; Margaret F. Callcott and Wei-Na Lee, "A Content Analysis of Animation and Animated Spokes-Characters in Television Commercials," *Journal of Advertising*, December 1994, pp. 1–12; Alan J. Bush and Victoria D. Bush, "The Narrative Paradigm As a Perspective for Improving Ethical Evaluations of Advertisements," *Journal of Advertising*, September 1994, pp. 31–41; L. W. Turley and Scott W. Kelley, "A Comparison of Advertising Content: Business to Business Versus Consumer Services," *Journal of Advertising*, Winter 1997, pp. 39–48; Eleonora Curlo and Robert Chamblee, "Ad Processing and Persuasion: The Role of Brand Identification," *Psychology & Marketing*, May 1998, pp. 279–99; V. C. Broach, Thomas J. Page, and R. D. Wilson, "Television Programming and Its Influence on Viewers' Perceptions of Commercials: The Role of Program Arousal and Pleasantness," *Journal of Advertising*, Winter 1995, pp. 45–54; Laurie A. Babin and Alvin C. Burns, "Effects of Print Ad Pictures and Copy Containing Instructions to Imagine on Mental Imagery That Mediates Attitudes," *Journal of Advertising*, Fall 1997, pp. 33–44; Noel M. Murray and Sandra B. Murray, "Music and Lyrics in Commercials: A Cross-Cultural Comparison Between Commercials Run in the Dominican Republic and in the United States," *Journal of Advertising*, Summer 1996, pp. 51–63; Barbara B. Stern, "Advertising Intimacy: Relationship Marketing and the Services Consumer," *Journal of Advertising*, Winter 1997, pp. 7–19; Baba Shiv, Julie A. Edell, and John W. Payne, "Factors Affecting the Impact of Negatively and Positively Framed Ad Messages," *Journal of Consumer Research*, December 1997, pp. 285–94; Harlan E. Spotts, Marc G. Weinberger, and Amy L. Parsons, "Assessing the Use and Impact of Humor on Advertising Effectiveness: A Contingency Approach," *Journal of Advertising*, Fall 1997, pp. 17–32; Martha Rogers and Kirk H. Smith, "Public Perceptions of Subliminal Advertising: Why Practitioners Shouldn't Ignore This Issue," *Journal of Advertising Research*, March/April 1993, pp. 10–18; Kathryn T. Theus, "Subliminal Advertising and the Psychology of Processing Unconscious Stimuli: A Review of Research," *Psychology & Marketing*, May/June 1994, pp. 271–90; Carolyn A. Lin, "Cultural Differences in Message Strategies: A Comparison between American and Japanese TV Commercials," *Journal of Advertising Research*, July/August 1993, pp. 40–49; Robert Chamblee and Dennis M. Sandler, "Business-to-Business Advertising: Which Layout Style Works Best?" *Journal of Advertising Research*, November/December 1992, pp. 39–46.

22. Fahad S. Al-Olayan, "A Content Analysis of Magazine Advertisements from the United States and the Arab World," *Journal of Advertising*, Fall 2000, pp. 69–83; "Exxon Centralizes New Global Campaign," *The Wall Street Journal*, July 11, 2001, p. B6; "McCann Finds Global a Tough Sell in Japan," *The Wall Street Journal*, June 19, 1997, p. B2; "Microsoft Global Image Campaign Is Dizzying without a Hard Sell," *The Wall Street Journal*, November 11, 1994, p. B7; Fred Zandpour et al., "Global Reach and Local Touch: Achieving Cultural Fitness in TV Advertising," *Journal of Advertising Research*, September/October 1994, pp. 35–63; Michael G. Harvey, "A Model to Determine Standardization of the Advertising Process in International Markets," *Journal of Advertising Research*, July/August 1993, pp. 57–64; Barbara Mueller, "Standardization vs. Specialization: An Examination of Westernization in Japanese Advertising," *Journal of Advertising Research*, January/February 1992, pp. 15–24; Dana L. Alden, Wayne D. Hoyer, and Chol Lee, "Identifying Global and Culture-Specific Dimensions of Humor in Advertising: A Multinational Analysis," *Journal of Marketing*, April 1993, pp. 64–75; "International Special Report: Global Media," *Advertising Age International*, July 18, 1994, p. I11–16; Ali Kanso, "International Advertising Strategies: Global Commitment to Local Vision," *Journal of Advertising Research*, January/February 1992, pp. 10–14; "Professor Stands by His Theory on Global Advertising," *The Wall Street Journal*, October 13, 1992, p. B10; Theodore Levitt, "The Globalization of Markets," *Harvard Business Review*, May–June 1983, pp. 92–102; Kamran Kashani, "Beware the Pitfalls of Global Marketing," *Harvard Business Review*, September/October 1989, pp. 91–98; Ludmilla G. Wells, "Western Concepts, Russian Perspectives: Meanings of Advertising in the Former Soviet Union," *Journal of Advertising*, March 1994, pp. 83–95; William L. Shanklin and David A. Griffith, "Crafting Strategies for Global Marketing in the New Millennium," *Business Horizons*, September–October 1996, pp 11–16.

23. "Will Ad Agencies Survive Slowdown?" *Investor's Business Daily*, May 8, 2001, p. A1; "IBD Corporate Leaders: Advertising Agencies," *Investor's Business Daily*, May 8, 2001, p. B20; "Agency Report," *Advertising Age*, April 23, 2001, pp. S1–36; "Interpublic Still Faces Hurdles in True North Deal," *Advertising Age*, March 26, 2001, p. 3fff.; "Slim Selection Is Seen for Takeover Targets," *The Wall Street Journal*, March 21, 2001, p. B14; "Slow Ad Period Likely to Spur More Deals," *The Wall Street Journal*, March 20, 2001, p. B2; "A Chill Hits Madison Avenue," *The Wall Street Journal*, March 19, 2001, p. B1ff.; "Culture Shock," *Advertising Age*, January 8, 2001, p. 1ff.; "How the Internet Gave Big Edge to Tiny Ad Firm," *The Wall Street Journal*, June 22, 2000, p. B1ff.; "Road Less Traveled Leads Cappelli to Success," *USA Today*, May 11, 2000, p. 3B; "Agencies Teach Skill Building," *Advertising Age*, May 1, 2000, p. 12; "Agencies Form Group to Help Set Guidelines for Ads on the Web," *The Wall Street Journal*, April 19, 2000, p. B7; "Special Report: Interactive," *Advertising Age*, March 6, 2000, pp. S1–48; "It's Splitsville When Dot-Coms Irk Ad Agencies," *The Wall Street Journal*, December 8, 1999, p. B1ff.; "Agencies Left in Cold as Marketers Expand Online," *Advertising Age*, July 26, 1999, pp. S26–30; "The Old Order Blurreth," *Brandweek*, April 19, 1999, pp. 54–64; "Agencies Centralize Web Ad Serving," *Advertising Age*, March 1, 1999, pp. S1–12; "IQ's Leading Agencies," *Brandweek*, January 18, 1999, pp. IQ20–41; "The Race to Inter-Activity," *Advertising Age*, January 4, 1999, p. 1ff. See also Louise Ripley, "Why Industrial Advertising is Often Done in House," *Industrial Marketing Management*, November 1992, pp. 331–34; Murray Young and Charles Steilen, "Strategy-Based Advertising Agency Selection: An Alternative to 'Spec' Presentations," *Business Horizons*, November–December 1996, pp. 77–80; Douglas C. West, "Purchasing Professional Services: The Case of Advertising Agencies," *International Journal of Purchasing & Materials Management*, Summer 1997, pp. 2–9; Douglas W. LaBahn and Chiranjeev Kohli, "Maintaining Client Commitment in Advertising Agency-Client Relationships," *Industrial Marketing Management*, November 1997, pp. 497–508; Alan T. Shao and John S. Hill, "Executing Transnational Advertising Campaigns: Do U.S. Agencies Have the Overseas Talent?" *Journal of Advertising Research*, January/February 1992, pp. 49–58.

24. "Feeling the Squeeze," *Advertising Age*, June 4, 2001, p.1ff.; "Unilever Reviews the Way It Pays for Ads," *The Wall Street Journal*, April 27, 2001, p. B6; "Kraft Folds $800 Million into Starcom," *Advertising Age*, December 18, 2000, p. 1ff.; "Agencies, Beware a Downturn," *Advertising Age*, July 10, 2000, p. 30; "Performance Pays," *Advertising Age*, February 28, 2000, pp. S14–S16; "Agencies Get Dot-Com Stock for Hot Spots," *The Wall Street Journal*, February 8, 2000, p. B1ff.; "Dot-Compensation: Ad Agencies Feel Net Effect," *Advertising Age*, February 7, 2000, p. 1ff.; "P&G Expands Its Program to Tie Agency Pay to Brand Performance," *The Wall Street Journal*, September 16, 1999, p. B12; "Nissan Ties TBWA's Pay to Car Sales," *Advertising Age*, June 7, 1999, p. 1ff.; "Incentive Compensation: A Trend or a Tsunami?" *Advertising Age*, March 1, 1999, p. 26; "P&G to Test Ad-Agency Pay Tied to Sales," *The Wall Street Journal*, November 9, 1998, p. B10; "Price Becomes Prime Issue," *Advertising Age*, September 14, 1998, p. 24; "ANA Survey: Under 50% Pay Agency Commissions," *Advertising Age*, June 15, 1998, p. 18; "Becoming Strategic Partners in the 1990s," *Advertising Age*, June 8, 1998, p. 28; "P&G Poised to Rewrite Ad Agency Pay Policies," *Advertising Age*, February 16, 1998, p. 1ff. See also R. Susan Ellis and Lester W. Johnson, "Agency Theory as a Framework for Advertising Agency Compensation Decisions," *Journal of Advertising Research*, September/October 1993, p. 76; Thorolf Helgesen, "Advertising Awards and Advertising Agency Performance Criteria," *Journal of Advertising Research*, July/August 1994, pp. 43–53.

25. "Can An Agency Be Guilty of Malpractice?" *Advertising Age*, January 31, 2000, pp. 24–25; "Bowl Postmortem: Tadpoles, Ad Polls," *Advertising Age*, February 6, 1995, p. 44; "Why A-B Bounced Bud," *Advertising Age*, November 21, 1994, p. 1ff.; "Ties that Bind Agency, Client Unravel," *The Wall Street Journal*, November 16, 1994, p. B9; Paul C. N. Mitchell, Harold Cataquet, and Stephen Hague, "Establishing the Causes of Disaffection in Agency-Client Relations," *Journal of Advertising Research*, March/April 1992, pp. 41–48.

26. For an example of pretesting ads, see "Behind the Scenes at an American Express Commercial," *Business Week*, May 20, 1985, pp. 84–88.

27. Ann Marie Barry, "How Advertising Works: The Role of Research," *Journal of the Academy of Marketing Science*, Winter 2001, p.1036. For one specific example, see "Dog-Gone Days: FCB Creates Ads for Taco Bell Acc't," *Advertising Age*, July 24, 2000, p. 4; "Taco Bell Drops the Chihuahua in Management Shuffle," *USA Today*, July 19, 2000, p. 1B; "Taco Bell Fences in Chihuahua for Ads," *Advertising Age*, July 3, 2000, p. 32; "Chihuahua Gets Muzzled as Taco Bell Pushes Value," *Advertising Age*, November 29, 1999, p. 26; "Taco Bell Ads to Focus on Food, Not Dog," *The Wall Street Journal*, October 11, 1999, p. B10; "Say Bark in Hindi!" *Advertising Age*, January 11, 1999, p. 1ff.; "Taco Bell Finds a Dog's Life Quite Fetching," *USA Today*, October 22, 1998, p. 1Bff.; "Chiat's New Day," *Newsweek*, August 3, 1998. See also "How Terrific Ads Propelled Colgate, Dethroned Longtime Leader P&G," *Investor's Business Daily*, April 20, 2001, p. A1ff.; "MasterCard Learns Ads Can Be Tricky," *The Wall Street Journal*, February 23, 2001, p. B8; "Measuring Up," *Advertising Age*, February 5, 2001, p. 1ff.; "Does Creativity Count?" *Brandweek*, December 11, 2000, pp. 32–44; "The Metrics System," *Brandweek*, November 13, 2000, pp. 106–10; "Protests Let Air Out of Nike Ads," *USA Today*, November 13, 2000, p. 6B; "Nike Rescinds Ad, Apologizes to Disabled People," *The Wall Street Journal*, October 26, 2000, p. B20; "Hard Selling on the Net," *Advertising Age*, October 23, 2000, pp. 48–52; "Jazzy Sprint Ads Fail to Connect," *USA Today*, August 28, 2000, p. 5B; "Uncle Sam Wants Who? New Report Calls Military's Ads Off Target," *The Wall Street Journal*, July 6, 2000, p. B1ff.; "Where Have All the Gerbils Gone?" *The Wall Street Journal*, March 30, 2000, p. B1ff.; "Shock Treatment," *Newsweek*, November 1, 1999, pp. 58–59; "Omnicom Group to Measure How Ads Do," *The Wall Street Journal*, October 21, 1999, p. B16; "Glamour Sets Out to Prove Its Ads Work," *The Wall Street Journal*, August 26, 1999, p. B8; "Where's the Commercial?" *USA Today*, June 25, 1999, p. 1Bff.; "I'd Like to Teach the World to Sell," *Business Week*, June 7, 1999, p. 59; "Traditional Marketing Is Dead," *Advertising Age*, May 31, 1999, pp. 24–26; "ADKnowledge Goes Beyond Clicks to Measurable Results," *Advertising Age*, March 1, 1999, p. S14 "Nissan's Crisis Was Made in the U.S.A.," *The Wall Street Journal*, November 25,

1998, p. B1ff.; "Great Ad! What's It For?" *Business Week*, July 20, 1998, pp. 118–20; "When Ads Get Creative, Some Click, Some Bomb," *USA Today*, December 15, 1997, p. 1Bff. See also Gerald J. Tellis and Doyle L. Weiss, "Does TV Advertising Really Affect Sales? The Role of Measures, Models, and Data Aggregation," *Journal of Advertising*, Fall 1995, pp. 1–12; John H. Holmes, "When Ads Work," *Journal of the Academy of Marketing Science*, Winter 1997, pp. 88–89; Karen Whitehill King, John D. Pehrson, and Leonard N. Reid, "Pretesting TV Commercials: Methods, Measures, and Changing Agency Roles," *Journal of Advertising*, September 1993, p. 85; "Researchers Probe Ad Effectiveness Globally," *Marketing News*, August 29, 1994, pp. 6–7. See also Erik du Plessis, "Recognition versus Recall," *Journal of Advertising Research*, May/June 1994, pp. 75–91.

28. "In Asia, It's Not a Wide-Open Web," *The Wall Street Journal*, July 9, 2001, p. B1ff.; "Chinese Officials Force Magazines to Go Without Famous Names," *The Wall Street Journal*, February 2, 2000, p. B1ff.; "Sweden Presses EU for Further Ad Restrictions," *Advertising Age*, April 12, 1999, p. 2; "Vietnamese Police Raid Bates' Ho Chi Minh Office," *Advertising Age*, May 4, 1998, p. 6; "Pakistan Cracks Whip," *Ad Age International*, February 9, 1998, p. 26; "Indian Court Tells Lever to Clean Up Ad Claims," *Ad Age International*, January 1998, p. 32; "PepsiCo's Pitch in Japan Has New Twist," *The Wall Street Journal*, May 23, 1997, p. B10. See also Alexander Simonson, "The Impact of Advertising Law on Business and Public Policy," *Journal of Marketing*, October 1994, pp. 123–25; Ross D. Petty, "Advertising Law in the United States and European Union," *Journal of Public Policy & Marketing*, Spring 1997, pp. 2–13; Steve Lysonski and Michael F. Duffy, "The New Zealand Fair Trading Act of 1986: Deceptive Advertising," *Journal of Consumer Affairs*, Summer 1992, pp. 177–99; "Drop That Remote! In Britain, Watching TV Can Be a Crime," *The Wall Street Journal*, September 27, 1993, p. A1ff.; "East Europeans Adjust to Western Ads; Information after Years of Propaganda," *The Wall Street Journal*, July 17, 1993, p. A5B; Albert Schofield, "International Differences in Advertising Practices: Britain Compared with Other Countries," *International Journal of Advertising* 10, no. 4 (1991), pp. 299–308.

29. For more on deceptive ads, see "FDA Faults 'Misleading' Drug-Ad Images," *The Wall Street Journal*, May 4, 2001, p. B8; "Xenical Ads Avoid Listing Unpleasant Side Effects," *The Wall Street Journal*, April 3, 2001, p. B1ff.; "FDA's Not-So-Secret Weapon," *Advertising Age*, March 19, 2001, pp. S1–10; "FDA Scrambles to Police Drug Ads' Truthfulness," *The Wall Street Journal*, January 2, 2001, p. A24; "Microsoft WebTV Settles False-Advertising Complaint," *The Wall Street Journal*, October 26, 2000, p. B16; "Amex, Ogilvy Face the Music over Tune," *The Wall Street Journal*, May 1, 1998, p. B4; "Claim by Gerber for Baby Food Was Simply Mush, FTC Alleges," *The Wall Street Journal*, March 13, 1997, p. B15; "Ford Threatens Lawsuit over GM Test-Drive Video," *USA Today*, January 30, 1998, p. 1Bff.; "Competition in Sippy-Cup Market Spills into Court," *The Wall Street Journal*, August 19, 1997, p. B1ff.; "FDA Ruling Gives Colgate Cause to Smile," *The Wall Street Journal*, July 15, 1997, p. B3; "Ad Watchdogs Track Untruths, Sometimes Bite," *The Wall Street Journal*, July 7, 1997, p. B1ff.; "Vacuums Make Sweeping Health Claims," *The Wall Street Journal*, September 25, 1996, p. B1ff.; "FTC Hammers Pain Relievers to Keep Their Claims in Check," *The Wall Street Journal*, June 28, 1996, p. B12. See also Boris W. Becker, "The Tangled Web They Weave: Truth, Falsity, & Advertisers," *Journal of Advertising*, Summer 1996, pp. 83–85; Elizabeth K. LaFleur, R. E. Reidenbach, Donald P. Robin, and PJ Forrest, "An Exploration of Rule Configuration Effects on the Ethical Decision Processes of Advertising Professionals," *Journal of the Academy of Marketing Science*, Winter 1996, pp. 66–76; Barbara B. Stern, "'Crafty Advertisers': Literary Versus Literal Deceptiveness," *Journal of Public Policy & Marketing*, Spring 1992, pp. 72–81; Joel J. Davis, "Ethics in Advertising Decision-making: Implications for Reducing the Incidence of Deceptive Advertising," *Journal of Consumer Affairs*, Winter 1994, pp. 380–402. For more on unfair ads, see "Kids Ads: To Regulate or Not?" *Advertising Age*, October 9, 2000, pp. 58–60; "Can Hollywood Shelter Kids from Its Ads?" *The Wall Street Journal*, September 29, 2000, p. B1ff.; "Studios Admit to Targeting Children," *USA Today*, September 28, 2000, p. 1Aff.; "FTC Report on Violence Stokes Regulatory Fires," *Advertising Age*, September 18, 2000, p. 3ff.; "Selling to Kids Blurs Ethical Picture," *USA Today*, March 20, 2000, p. 7D; "A Virtual Playground," *USA Today*, September 28, 1999, p. 1Bff.; "California Sues Reynolds Over Magazine Ads," *The Wall Street Journal*, March 20, 2001, p. A3ff.; "Top Ad Agency Defends Tossing Joe Camel Files," *The Wall Street Journal*, April 30, 1998, p. B1ff.; "Anheuser-Busch Amphibian Ads Called Cold-Blooded by Doctors," *The Wall Street Journal*, April 10, 1998, p. B8; "How the Beer Industry Uses TV Ads to Mollify Critics, Buff Its Image," *The Wall Street Journal*, August 14, 1997, p. A1ff.; "With Joe Camel Out, Goverment Wants the Marlboro Man 'Down,'" *Advertising Age*, July 14, 1997, p. 3ff.; "Liquor Industry Votes to Rescind Ban on TV Ads," *The Wall Street Journal*, November 8, 1996, p. B1ff.; "25 Years of Self-Regulation," *Advertising Age*, December 2, 1996, pp. C1–7; "TV Advertising Aimed at Kids Is Filled with Fat," *The Wall Street Journal*, November 9, 1993, p. B1; Mary C. Martin, "Children's Understanding of the Intent of Advertising: A Meta-Analysis," *Journal of Public Policy & Marketing*, Fall 1997, pp. 205–16; Avery M. Abernethy, "Advertising Clearance Practices of Radio Stations: A Model of Advertising Self-Regulation," *Journal of Advertising*, September 1993, pp. 15–26.

30. Ivan L. Preston, "Regulatory Positions Toward Advertising Puffery of the Uniform Commercial Code and the Federal Trade Commission," *Journal of Public Policy & Marketing*, Fall 1997, pp. 336–44; Claude R. Martin, Jr., "Ethical Advertising Research Standards: Three Case Studies," *Journal of Advertising*, September 1994, pp. 17–30; William K. Darley and Robert E. Smith, "Advertising Claim Objectivity: Antecedents and Effects," *Journal of Marketing*, October 1993, pp. 100–13; George M. Zinkhan, "Advertising Ethics: Emerging Methods and Trends," *Journal of Advertising*, September 1994, pp. 1–4; Alexander Simonson and Morris B. Holbrook, "Permissible Puffery Versus Actionable Warranty in Advertising and Salestalk: An Empirical Investigation," *Journal of Public Policy & Marketing*, Fall 1993, pp. 216–33.

31. Nancy Spears, "Time Pressure and Information in Sales Promotion Strategy: Conceptual Framework and Content Analysis," *Journal of Advertising*, Spring 2001, pp. 67–77; "Not Just Cereal Material: Prizes Pop Up in More CDs," *The Wall Street Journal*, May 31, 2001, p. B1ff.; "Events & Promotions," *Advertising Age*, March 17, 1997, pp. S1–6; "Special Report: Promotional Marketing," *Advertising Age*, March 21, 1994, pp. S1–14. See also K. Sivakumar, "Tradeoff Between Frequency and Depth of Price Promotions: Implications for High- and Low-Priced Brands," *Journal of Marketing Theory & Practice*, Winter 1996, pp. 1–8.

32. "Too Many Choices," *The Wall Street Journal*, April 20, 2001, p. B1ff.; "Reposition: Simplifying the Customer's Brandscape," *Brandweek*, October 2, 2000, pp. 36–48; "Make It Simple," *Business Week*, September 9, 1996, pp. 96–104; "Pay for Performance Picking Up Speed," *Advertising Age*, August 9, 1993, p. 19; Donald R. Lichtenstein, Scot Burton, and Richard G. Netemeyer, "An Examination of Deal Proneness Across Sales Promotion Types: A Consumer Segmentation Perspective," *Journal of Retailing*, Summer 1997, pp. 283–97; Donald R. Glover, "Distributor Attitudes Toward Manufacturer-Sponsored Promotions," *Industrial Marketing Management* 20, no. 3 (1991), pp. 241–50; A. S. C. Ehrenberg, Kathy Hammond, and G. J. Goodhardt, "The After-Effects of Price-related Consumer Promotions," *Journal of Advertising Research*, July/August 1994, pp. 11–21; Jean J. Boddewyn and Monica Leardi, "Sales Promotions: Practice, Regulation and Self-Regulation Around the World," *International Journal of Advertising* 8, no. 4 (1989), pp. 363–74.

33. For another example, see "Shopper Turns Lots of Pudding into Free Miles," *The Wall Street Journal*, January 24, 2000, p. B1ff.; "The Pudding Guy Flies Again (and Again) Over Latin America," *The Wall Street Journal*, March 16, 2000, p. B1. See also P. Rajan Varadarajan, "Horizontal Cooperative Sales Promotion: A Framework for Classification and Additional Perspectives," *Journal of Marketing*, April, 1986 pp. 61–73.

34. J. F. Engel, M. R. Warshaw, and T. C. Kinnear, *Promotional Strategy* (Homewood, IL: Richard D. Irwin, 1988).

35. "Cybercoupons," *Discount Store News*, March 9, 1998, p. 18; "The Scoop on Coupons," *Brandweek*, March 17, 1997, pp. 34–48; "Many Companies Are Starting to Wean Shoppers Off Coupons," *The Wall Street Journal*, January 22, 1997, p. B1ff.; "Internet Coupons offer H.O.T! Deals," *USA Today*, December 13, 1996, p. 17D; "First, Green Stamps. Now, Coupons?" *Business Week*, April 22, 1996, p. 68; "P&G Ad Chief Plots Demise of the Coupon," *The Wall Street Journal*, April 17, 1996, p. B1ff; Judy F. Graham, "Increasing Repurchase Rates: A Reappraisal of Coupon Effects," *Psychology & Marketing*, November/December 1994, pp. 533–48; A. Krishna and R. W. Shoemaker, "Estimating the Effects of Higher Coupon Face Values on the Timing of Redemptions, the Mix of Coupon Redeemers, and Purchase Quality," *Psychology & Marketing*, November/December 1992, pp. 453–68; Venkatram Ramaswamy and Srini S. Srinivasan, "Coupon Characteristics and Redemption Intentions: A Segment-Level Analysis," *Psychology & Marketing*, January 1998, pp. 59–80.

36. "The Cyber-Show Must Go On," *Trade Media*, May 7, 2001, pp. SR3–4; "Getting the Most from a Trade-Show Booth," *Investor's Business Daily*, April 25, 2000, p. 1; Marnik G. Dekimpe, Pierre Francois, Srinath Gopalakrishna, Gary L. Lilien, and Christophe Van den Bulte, "Generalizing About Trade Show Effectiveness: A Cross-National Comparison," *Journal of Marketing*, October 1997, pp. 55–64; Scott Barlass, "How to Get the Most Out of Trade Shows," *Journal of Product Innovation Management*, September 1997, pp. 423–24; Srinath Gopalakrishna, Gary L. Lilien, Jerome D. Williams, and Ian K. Sequeira, "Do Trade Shows Pay Off?" *Journal of Marketing*, July 1995, pp. 75–83; Ronald C. Curhan and Robert J. Kopp, "Obtaining Retailer Support for Trade Deals: Key Success Factors," *Journal of Advertising Research*, December 1987–January 1988, pp. 51–60; Donald W. Jackson, Janet E. Keith, and Richard K. Burdick, "The Relative Importance of Various Promotional Elements in Different Industrial Purchase Situations," *Journal of Advertising* 16, no. 4 (1987), pp. 25–33.

37. "Trade Promotion Rises," *Advertising Age*, April 3, 2000, p. 24; "Getting Tough on Trade," *Adweek*, April 13, 1992, pp. 20–30; "A Shift in Direction?" *Adweek's Marketing Week*, April 13, 1992, pp. 26–27; Mary A. Raymond and Jong W. Lim, "Promotion and Trade Mix Considerations for Entering and Competing in the Korean Market," *Journal of Marketing Theory & Practice*, Winter 1996, pp. 44–55; Sunil Gupta, "Impact of Sales Promotions on When, What, and How Much to Buy," *Journal of Marketing Research*, November 1988, pp. 342–55.

38. "Creating Incentives Down in Ranks: Marriott Ties Pay to Guest Replies," *Investor's Business Daily*, July 6, 2001, p. A1; "Get Great Results from Salespeople by Finding What Really Moves Them," *Investor's Business Daily*, July 2, 2001, p. A1.

Chapter 16

1. Available from World Wide Web: <http://www.chevrolet.com/suburban>; "A Super-Size Station Wagon," *The Wall Street Journal*, February 11, 2000, p. W15C; "Toyota: Overdue for a Tune-Up?" *Business Week*, May 4, 1998, pp. 158F–J; "You'll Charge What I Tell You to Charge," *Business Week*, October 6, 1997, pp. 118–20; "Automakers Draft New Designs in Global Mission," *USA Today*, September 11, 1997, p. 1Bff.; "Cadillac and Lincoln Try to Regain Their Cachet," *The Wall Street Journal*, July 3, 1997, p. B1ff.; "Navigator Overcomes Looks with Inner Beauty," *USA Today*, June 4, 1997, p. 6B; "Which Bigger Is Better?" *Fortune*, November 25, 1996, pp. 226–27; "Honk If You're Building a Sport-Utility Vehicle," *Business Week*, September 30, 1996, p. 35; "Ford's New Expedition Heads into Suburban's Terrain," *The Wall Street Journal*, June 24, 1996, p. B1ff.; "Even Luxury Models Join Rugged Race," *USA Today*, January 5, 1996, p. 1Bff.; "Demand in Overdrive for Top Models," *USA Today*, November 18, 1994, p. 1Aff.; "World War II Workhorse Started Trend," *USA Today*, June 6, 1994, p. 1Bff.

2. "Adding Options Helps Car Firms Increase Prices," *The Wall Street Journal*, December 27, 1993, p. 9ff.; "Car Makers Seek to Mask Price Increases," *The Wall Street Journal*, August 16, 1989, p. B1.

3. Alfred Rappaport, "Executive Incentives versus Corporate Growth," *Harvard Business Review*, July–August 1978, pp. 81–88; David M. Szymanski, Sundar G. Bharadwaj, and P. Rajan Varadarajan, "An Analysis of the Market Share-Profitability Relationship," *Journal of Marketing*, July 1993, pp. 1–18.

4. Pricing "in the public interest" is often an issue in pricing government services; for an interesting example, see "Price Policy on Space Shuttle's Commercial Use Could Launch—or Ground—NASA's Rockets," *The Wall Street Journal*, March 21, 1985, p. 64.

5. "The Mother of All Price Wars," *Business Week*, July 30, 2001, pp. 32–35; "Cheap PCs," *Business Week*, March 23, 1998, pp. 28–32; "Good-Quality Laptops Are Starting to Get a Little Less Expensive," *The Wall Street Journal*, March 26, 1998, p. B1; "Crashing Prices," "Five Easy PCs," *Fortune*, November 10, 1997, pp. 311–12; "I'm Not Going to Pay a Lot for This Aptiva," *Business Week*, October 13, 1997, p. 59; "Now PC Buyers Are Getting More for Even Less," *The Wall Street Journal*, June 18, 1996, p. B1ff.

6. "Applying Old Pricing Lessons to a New Investing World," *The Wall Street Journal*, May 21, 2001, p. C1ff.; Stephen E. Frank, *Net Worth* (2001); "E-Assets for Sale," *Business Week E.Biz*, May 14, 2001, pp. EB20–EB22; "Last Guys Finish First," *Ecompany*, May 2001, pp. 93–97; "After the Wild Ride," *Business Week E.Biz*, April 16, 2001, pp. EB29–EB30; "Study: Net Start-Ups Ignored Economics 101," *Investor's Business Daily*, March 2, 2001, p. A8; "12 Months When the Dot Turned into a Dark Period," *Investor's Business Daily*, January 2, 2001, p. A6; "We're Heading into Something Big—but What?" *USA Today*, December 29, 2000, p. 1Bff.; "What Detonated Dot-Bombs?" *USA Today*, December 4, 2000, p. 1Bff.; "Dot-Bombs," *Brandweek*, November 27, 2000, pp. IQ16–IQ20; "Pets.com's Demise: Too Much Litter, Too Few Funds," *The Wall Street Journal*, November 8, 2000, p. B1ff.; "Dot-Coms, What Have We Learned?" *Fortune*, October 30, 2000, pp. 82–137; "Sock Dogma," *Brandweek*, June 5, 2000, pp. IQ28–IQ34; "Shakeout E-Tailers," *Business Week E.Biz*, May 15, 2000, pp. EB102–EB118; "E-Tail Gets Derailed: How Web Upstarts Misjudged the Game," *The Wall Street Journal*, April 5, 2000, p. A1ff.

7. "What Are Price Wars Good For? Absolutely Nothing," *Fortune*, May 12, 1997, p. 156; "Price Wars," *Adweek's Marketing Week*, June 8, 1992, pp. 18–22; "A Remarkable Gamble in an Industry Slump Pays Off Fast for Agco," *The Wall Street Journal*, August 19, 1997, p. A1ff.; "Why the Price Wars Never End," *Fortune*, March 23, 1992, pp. 68–78; "Avis, Sidestepping Price Wars, Focuses on the Drive Itself," *Adweek's Marketing Week*, February 12, 1990, p. 24.

8. "Aluminum Firms Offer Wider Discounts but Price Cuts Stop at Some Distributors," *The Wall Street Journal*, November 16, 1984, p. 50.

9. Michael V. Marn and Robert L. Rosiello, "Managing Price, Gaining Profit," *Harvard Business Review*, September–October 1992, pp. 84–94; Subhash C. Jain and Michael B. Laric, "A Framework for Strategic Industrial Pricing," *Industrial Marketing Management* 8 (1979), pp. 75–80; Peter R. Dickson and Joel E. Urbany, "Retailer Reactions to Competitive Price Changes," *Journal of Retailing*, Spring 1994, pp. 1–22; Mary Karr, "The Case of the Pricing Predicament," *Harvard Business Review*, March–April, 1988, pp. 10–23; Saeed Samiee, "Pricing in Marketing Strategies of U.S. and Foreign-Based Companies," *Journal of Business Research*, February 1987, pp. 17–30; Gerard J. Tellis, "Beyond the Many Faces of Price: An Integration of Pricing Strategies," *Journal of Marketing*, October 1986, pp. 146–60.

10. For more on Priceline, see "Fasten Your Seat Belt!" *Time Digital*, 2001; "Inside Jay Walker's House of Cards," *Fortune*, November 13, 2000, pp. 127–38; "Live Long and Prosper?" *The Wall Street Journal*, October 23, 2000, p. R22ff.; "How Jay Walker Built WebHouse on a Theory that He Couldn't Prove," *The Wall Street Journal*, October 16, 2000, p. 1Aff.; "Letting the Masses Name Their Price," *Business Week E.Biz*, September 18, 2000, p. EB44; "Be Yor Own Barcode," *Time*, July 10, 2000, pp. 96–97; "Name Your Price—for Everything?" *Business Week*, April 17, 2000, pp. 72–78; "The Hype Is Big, Really Big, at Priceline," *Fortune*, September 6, 1999, pp. 193–202. For more on other online travel sites, see "Orbitz Doesn't Soar," *Business Week E.Biz*, July 9, 2001, p. EB8; "Southwest Limits Most Travel Data to Own Web Site," *USA Today*, July 6, 2001, p. 3B; "Your Family May Be Too Big for Orbitz," *USA Today*, June 29, 2001, p. 5D; "Airlines Jettison Incentives for Making Reservations Over the Internet," *The Wall Street Journal*, June 25, 2001, p. B1; "Hotel Reservation Network: Travel Site Enjoys Solid Profits," *Investor's Business Daily*, June 20, 2001, p. A5; "Good Fares Await Travelers Buying Tickets Online," *Investor's Business Daily*, June 12, 2001, p. A8; "Where the Net Delivers: Travel," *Business Week*, June 11, 2001, pp. 142–44; "Southwest Pushes Its Online Booking, Says Internet Rivals Come Up Short," *Brandweek*, June 11, 2001, p. 16; "Orbitz Puts New Spin on Airfares," *USA Today*, June 8, 2001, p. 8D; "Big Airlines Officially Open Online Outlet," *USA Today*, June 4, 2001, p. 1Bff.; "Airlines to Offer Cheap Tickets on the Internet," *The Wall Street Journal*, June 29, 2000, p. B1ff.

11. Stephen P. Bradley, "Ebay, Inc.," *Journal of Interactive Marketing*, Autumn 2000, p. 73; "Ebay Allows Sellers to Set Up 'Storefronts' Online in Bid to Expand Beyond Auctions," *The Wall Street Journal*, June 12, 2001, p. B8; "Corporate Sellers Put the Online Auctioneer on Even Faster Track," *The Wall Street Journal*, June 1, 2001, p. A1ff.; "One Man's Economic Gotterdammerung Is Another's Clearance Sale," *Ecompany*, May 2001, pp. 106–108; "Ebay's Bid to Conquer All," *Time*, February 5, 2001, pp. 48–51; "A Revolution in Pricing? Not Quite," *Business Week*, November 20, 2000, pp. 48–49; "Will Auction Frenzy Cool?" *Business Week E. Biz*, September 18, 2000, p. EB140; "Going, Going, Gone," *Business Week*, April 12, 1999, pp. 30–32; "Good-Bye to Fixed Pricing," *Business Week*, May 4, 1998, pp. 71–84; "One-Price Deals Save Time, Hassles, but Not Money," *USA Today*, March 11, 1998, p. 1Bff; "Airlines Raise Their Class Consciousness," *Business Week*, February 23, 1998, p. 40; "Haggling in Cyberspace Transforms Car Sales," *The Wall Street Journal*, December 30, 1997, p. B1ff.; "Car Hagglers May Still Drive Best Car Deals," *The Wall Street Journal*, October 12, 1994, p. B1ff. See also Eric Matson, "Customizing Prices," *Harvard Business Review*, November–December 1995, pp. 13–14; Sanjay K. Dhar and Stephen J. Hoch, "Price Discrimination Using In-Store Merchandising," *Journal of Marketing*, January 1996, pp. 17–30; Michael H. Morris, "Separate Prices as a Marketing Tool," *Industrial Marketing Management*, May 1987, pp. 79–86; P. Ronald Stephenson, William L. Cron, and Gary L. Frazier, "Delegating Pricing Authority to the Sales Force: The Effects on Sales and Profit Performance," *Journal of Marketing*, Spring 1979, pp. 21–24.

12. For more on Amazon offering different prices to different customers, see "Price? For You, $2; For the Rich Guy, $5," *Investor's Business Daily*, September 29, 2000, p. A8. For more on the Winn-Dixie example, see "Squeezin' the Charmin," *Fortune*, January 16, 1989, pp. 11–12; "Grocers Join Winn-Dixie," *Advertising Age*, November 7, 1988, p. 3; "Grocery Chains Pressure Suppliers for Uniform Prices," *The Wall Street Journal*, October 21, 1988, p. B1.

13. "What's a Fair Price for Drugs?" *Business Week*, April 30, 2001, pp. 105–106; "AIDS Gaffes in Africa Come Back to Haunt Drug Industry at Home," *The Wall Street Journal*, April 23, 2001, p. A1ff.; "Vaccine's Price Drives a Debate about Its Use," *The Wall Street Journal*, February 16, 2000, p. B1ff.; "Price Tag for Schering-Plough Drug Angers Activists," *The Wall Street Journal*, August 24, 1999, p. B6; "AZT Price Cut for Third World Mothers-to-Be," *The Wall Street Journal*, March 5, 1998, p. B1ff.; "Breakthrough in Birth Control May Elude Poor," *The Wall Street Journal*, March 4, 1991, p. B1ff; "Burroughs Wellcome Reaps Profits, Outrage from Its AIDS Drug," *The Wall Street Journal*, September 15, 1989, p. A1ff; Richard A. Spinello, "Ethics, Pricing and the Pharmaceutical Industry," *Journal of Business Ethics*, August 1992, pp. 617–26; Dhruv Grewal and Larry D. Compeau, "Comparative Price Advertising: Informative or Deceptive?" *Journal of Public Policy & Marketing*, Spring 1992, pp. 52–62.

14. "Mobile Warfare," *Time*, May 26, 1997, pp. 52–54; "Motorola Goes for the Hard Cell," *Business Week*, September 23, 1996, p. 39; "Why Motorola Has Nonworking Numbers," *Business Week*, July 22, 1996, p. 39; "Cell-Phone Service May Be Getting Cheaper," *The Wall Street Journal*, January 11, 1996, p. B1ff.; Alan Reynolds, "A Kind Word for 'Cream Skimming,'" *Harvard Business Review*, November–December 1974, pp. 113–20.

15. For more on Palm, see Chapter 9, footnote #1. See also "A Best Seller Gets Better," *Newsweek*, March 16, 1998, p. 79; "Apple Drops Newton, an Idea Ahead of Its Time," *The Wall Street Journal*, March 2, 1998, p. B1ff.; "A Rocket in Its Pocket," *Business Week*, September 9, 1996, pp. 111–14.

16. Check out foreign exchange rates on the World Wide Web: <http://www.imf.org> and <http://www.federal reserve.gov>; "One Dollar Is Worth One Dollar, but That Wasn't Always So," *The Wall Street Journal*, January 13, 1998, p. A1ff.; "The Buck Bites Back," *Newsweek*, May 5, 1997, p. 47; "Luxury Prices for U.S. Goods No Longer Pass Muster in Japan," *The Wall Street Journal*, February 28, 1996, p. B1ff.; Timothy A. Luehrman, "Exchange Rate Changes and the Distribution of Industry Value," *Journal of International Business Studies*, Winter, 1991, pp. 619–50; James K. Weekly, "Pricing in Foreign Markets: Pitfalls and Opportunities," *Industrial Marketing Management*, May 1992, p. 173.

17. "Soap Smugglers Clean Up in Vietnam," *The Wall Street Journal*, April 1, 1998, p. B1ff.

18. "Discounts Follow Dip in Business Travel," *USA Today*, June 21, 2001, p. 1Bff.; "Sailing on Sale: Travelers Ride a Wave of Discounts on Cruise Ships," *The Wall Street Journal*, July 17, 2000, p. B1ff.; "Competing Online, Drugstore Chains Virtually Undersell Themselves," *The Wall Street Journal*, January 10, 2000, p. B1ff.; "Prescription: Cash Only, Some Doctors Offer Discounts," *USA Today*, December 22, 1999, p. 1Bff.; "Printer Wars: Toner Discount Incites Rivals," *The Wall Street Journal*, April 10, 1998, p. B1ff.; "Snaring Cheap Fares on the Internet," *The Wall Street Journal*, October 10, 1997, p. B10; "Ask and It Shall Be Discounted," *Business Week*, October 6, 1997, pp. 116–18; "The Latest Weapon in the Price Wars," *Fortune*, July 7, 1997, p. 200; "Owens Corning: Back from the Dead," *Fortune*, May 26, 1997, pp. 118–26; "Travelers Take Internet Route for Discounts," *USA Today*, January 13, 1997, p. 3B; Douglas D. Davis and Charles A. Holt, "List Prices and Discounts: The Interrelationship Between Consumer Shopping Patterns and Profitable Marketing Strategies," *Psychology & Marketing*, July 1996, pp. 341–63; David W. Arnesen, C. P. Fleenor, and Rex S. Toh, "The Ethical Dimensions of Airline Frequent Flier Programs," *Business Horizons*, January–February 1997, pp. 47–56; K. J. Blois, "Discounts in Business Marketing Management," *Industrial Marketing Management*, April 1994, pp. 93–100; James B. Wilcox et al., "Price Quantity Discounts: Some Implications for Buyers and Sellers," *Journal of Marketing*, July 1987, pp. 60–70; Mark T. Spriggs and John R. Nevin, "The Legal Status of Trade and Functional Price Discounts," *Journal of Public Policy & Marketing*, Spring 1994, pp. 61–75; Judith Waldrop, "The Seasons of Business," *American Demographics*, May 1992, pp. 40–45; "Cash Discounts," *Electrical Wholesaling*, May 1989, pp. 90–96.

19. For more on P&G's everyday low pricing, see "P&G, Others Try New Uses for Coupon-Heavy Media," *Advertising Age*, September 22, 1997, p. 20; "Move to Drop Coupons Puts Procter & Gamble in Sticky PR Situation," *The Wall Street Journal*, April 17, 1997, p. A1ff.; "Zeroing In on Zero Coupons," *Brandweek*, June 3, 1996, pp. 30–36; "Company Makes Big Cuts to Stay Fit," *USA Today*, July 16, 1993, p. 1Bff.; "P&G Plays Pied Piper on Pricing," *Advertising Age*, March 9, 1992, p. 6; Stephen J. Hoch, Xavier Dreze, and Mary E. Purk, "EDLP, Hi-Lo, and Margin Arithmetic," *Journal of Marketing*, October 1994, pp. 16–27; George S. Bobinski, Dena Cox, and Anthony Cox, "Retail 'Sale' Advertising, Perceived Retailer Credibility, and Price Rationale," *Journal of Retailing*, Fall 1996, pp. 291–306; Francis J. Mulhern and Daniel T. Padgett, "The Relationship Between Retail Price Promotions and Regular Price Purchases," *Journal of Marketing*, October 1995, pp. 83–90.

20. Paul N. Bloom, "Slotting Allowances and Fees: Schools of Thought and the Views of Practicing Managers," *Journal of Marketing*, April 2000, pp. 92–109. For an example of company that refuses to pay slotting fees, see "Green Mountain Coffee: Bad Break Room Coffee Stirs Opportunity Here," *Investor's Business Daily*, May 11, 2001, p. A8; "Green Mountain Coffee: Starbucks Proliferation Sweetens Wholesaler," *Investor's Business Daily*, November 1, 2000, p. A12. See also "Clorox Gives In on Glad, Hikes Trade Promotion," *Advertising Age*, November 27, 2000, p. 22; "Beer Makers Frothing over Plan to Charge for Retail Shelf Space," *The Wall Street Journal*, April 22, 1994, p. B1ff.

21. For more on coupons on the Web, see "Penny-Pinchers' Paradise," *Business Week E.Biz*, January 22, 2001, p. EB12; "E-Tailers Missing the Mark with Flood of Web Coupons," *Advertising Age*, September 25, 2000, p. 104. For more on rebates on the Web, see "Free-with-Rebate Costs Web Buyers Some Big Bucks," *The Wall Street Journal*, May 18, 2001, p. B1ff.; "One Web Retailer's Watchword: 'Free after Rebate,'" *The Wall Street Journal*, March 5, 2001, p. B1ff. For more on rebates on green cars, see "How to Get Green Cars on the Road," *Business Week*, November 20, 2000, p. 89; "If You Paid Half Price for That New SUV, You Must Be in Arizona," *The Wall Street Journal*, October 26, 2000, p. A1ff. See also William D. Diamond, "Just What Is a 'Dollar's Worth'? Consumer Reactions to Price Discounts vs. Extra Product Promotions," *Journal of Retailing*, Fall 1992, pp. 254–70; Kenneth A. Hunt and Susan M. Keaveney, "A Process Model of the Effects of Price Promotions on Brand Image," *Psychology & Marketing*, November/December 1994, pp. 511–32; "Coupon

Scams Are Clipping Companies," *Business Week*, June 15, 1992, pp. 110–11; "Rebates' Secret Appeal to Manufacturers: Few Consumers Actually Redeem Them," *The Wall Street Journal*, February 10, 1998, p. B1ff.; Peter K. Tat, "Rebate Usage: A Motivational Perspective," *Psychology & Marketing*, January/February 1994, pp. 15–26; Abdul Ali, Marvin A. Jolson, and Rene Y. Darmon, "A Model for Optimizing the Refund Value in Rebate Promotions," *Journal of Business Research*, March 1994, pp. 239–46.

22. "Two-Tier Marketing," *Business Week*, March 17, 1997, pp. 82–90; "Makeup Ads Downplay Glamour for Value," *The Wall Street Journal*, June 20, 1994, p. B5; "Value Pricing Kicks off Model Year," *USA Today*, October 1, 1993, p. 1Bff.; "Value Pricing Comes to Funerals," *USA Today*, July 14, 1993, p. 5B; "Tide, Cheer Join P&G 'Value Pricing' Plan," *Advertising Age*, February 15, 1993, p. 3ff.; "More Stores Switch from Sales to 'Everyday Low Prices,'" *The Wall Street Journal*, November 12, 1992, p. B1ff.; "Value Marketing," *Business Week*, November 11, 1991, pp. 132–40; Louis J. De Rose, "Meet Today's Buying Influences with Value Selling," *Industrial Marketing Management* 20, no. 2 (1991), pp. 87–90.

23. "At What Profit Price?" *Brandweek*, June 23, 1997, pp. 24–28.

24. For an excellent discussion of laws related to pricing, see Louis W. Stern and Thomas L. Eovaldi, *Legal Aspects of Marketing Strategy: Antitrust and Consumer Protection Issues* (Englewood Cliffs, NJ: Prentice-Hall, 1984); Joseph P. Guiltinan and Gregory T. Gundlach, "Aggressive and Predatory Pricing: A Framework for Analysis," *Journal of Marketing*, July 1996, pp. 87–102.

25. For more on dumping, see "Will Kodak Get Lucky in China?" *Business Week*, July 28, 1997, p. 48; "Antidumping Laws Keep Out Goods that Pacts Would Ordinarily Let In," *The Wall Street Journal*, February 26, 1993, p. A11.

26. For more on phony list prices, see Larry D. Compeau, Dhruv Grewal, and Diana S. Grewal, "Adjudicating Claims of Deceptive Advertised Reference Prices: The Use of Empirical Evidence," *Journal of Public Policy & Marketing*, Fall 1994, pp. 312–18; Patrick J. Kaufmann, N. Craig Smith, and Gwendolyn K. Ortmeyer, "Deception in Retailer High-Low Pricing: A 'Rule of Reason' Approach," *Journal of Retailing*, Summer 1994, pp. 115–38.

27. For more on airline pricing, see "Is American-United Rivalry Too Friendly?" *USA Today*, June 27, 2001, p. 1Bff.; "Predatory Pricing: Cleared for Takeoff," *Business Week*, May 14, 2001, p. 50; "American Airlines Secures Antitrust Win," *The Wall Street Journal*, April 30, 2001, p. A3ff.; "Caveat Predator?" *Business Week*, May 22, 2000, pp. 116–18. For more on credit card pricing, see "House of Cards?" *Time*, October 23, 2000, pp. B10–B11; "Breaking Up the Old Card Game," *Business Week*, June 12, 2000, pp. 98–102; "Antitrust Suit Targeting MasterCard and Visa Puts the Pair at Odds," *The Wall Street Journal*, June 12, 2000, p. B1ff.; "Facing Its Own Antitrust Trial, Visa Lashes Out at American Express," *The Wall Street Journal*, May 10, 2000, p. B1ff. For more on CD pricing, see "Prices of CDs Likely to Drop, Thanks to FTC," *The Wall Street Journal*, May 11, 2000, p. B1ff. See also "Online Booksellers Abound in Japan, But Legal Price Fixing Poses Challenge," *The Wall Street Journal*, July 31, 2000, p. B8; "Up Against the Wall, Monopolist," *Business Week*, March 23, 1998, p. 35; "P&G Calls the Cops as It Strives to Expand Sales in Latin America," *The Wall Street Journal*, March 20, 1998, p. A1ff.; "Independent Bookstores Are Suing Borders Group and Barnes & Noble," *The Wall Street Journal*, March 19, 1998, p. B10; "Antitrust Crackdown Frustrates Businesses," *USA Today*, March 12, 1998, p. 1Bff.; "Are Corporate Predators on the Loose," *Business Week*, February 23, 1998, pp. 124–25; "Antitrust Enforcers Drop the Ideology, Focus on Economics," *The Wall Street Journal*, February 27, 1997, p. A1ff.; "The ADM Scandal: Betrayal," *Fortune*, February 3, 1997, pp. 82–91; "Frito-Lay under Snack Attack," *Time*, June 10, 1996, pp. 62–63; "FTC Says Toys "R" Us Competes Unfairly," *The Wall Street Journal*, May 23, 1996, p. A3; "Archer-Daniels Cuts Surprisingly Good Deal in Price-Fixing Suit," *The Wall Street Journal*, April 12, 1996, p. A1ff.; Larry L. Miller, Steven P. Schnaars, and Valerie L. Vaccaro, "The Provocative Practice of Price Signaling: Collusion Versus Cooperation," *Business Horizons*, July–August 1993, pp. 59–65; Mary Jane Sheffet, "The Supreme Court and Predatory Pricing," *Journal of Public Policy & Marketing*, Spring 1994, pp. 163–67; Michael L. Ursic and James G. Helgeson, "Using Price as a Weapon: An Economic and Legal Analysis of Predatory Pricing," *Industrial Marketing Management*, April 1994, pp. 125–32; Robert L. Cutts, "Capitalism In Japan: Cartels and Keiretsu," *Harvard Business Review*, July–August 1992, pp. 48–129; Daniel T. Ostas, "Ethics of Contract Pricing," *Journal of Business Ethics*, February 1992, pp. 137–46; Mary Jane Sheffet and Debra L. Scammon, "Resale Price Maintenance: Is It Safe to Suggest Retail Prices?" *Journal of Marketing*, Fall 1985, pp. 82–91.

28. Richard L. Pinkerton and Deborah J. Kemp, "The Industrial Buyer and the Robinson-Patman Act," *International Journal of Purchasing & Materials Management*, Winter 1996, pp. 29–36.

29. "Is the Cost Defense Workable?" *Journal of Marketing*, January 1965, pp. 37–42; B. J. Linder and Allan H. Savage, "Price Discrimination and Cost Defense—Change Ahead?" *MSU Business Topics*, Summer 1971, pp. 21–26; "Firms Must Prove Injury from Price Bias to Qualify for Damages, High Court Says," *The Wall Street Journal*, May 19, 1981, p. 8.

30. "Booksellers Say Five Publishers Play Favorites," *The Wall Street Journal*, May 27, 1994, p. B1ff.; Joseph P. Vaccaro and Derek W. F. Coward, "Managerial and Legal Implications of Price Haggling: A Sales Manager's Dilemma," *Journal of Personal Selling & Sales Management*, Summer 1993, pp. 79–86; John R. Davidson, "FTC, Robinson-Patman and Cooperative Promotion Activities," *Journal of Marketing*, January 1968, pp. 14–18; L. X. Tarpey, Sr., "Buyer Liability under the Robinson-Patman Act: A Current Appraisal," *Journal of Marketing*, January 1972, pp. 38–42.

Chapter 17

1. For more on Wal-Mart International, see "Wal*Mart International, the Division that Defines the Future," *DSN Retailing Today* (Special Issue), June 2001; "Wal-Mart Gets Aggressive about Brazil," *The Wall Street Journal*, May 25, 2001, p. A8ff.; "Wal-Mart to Add Japan to Global Lineup," *DSN Retailing Today*, January 22, 2001, p. 1ff.; "Wal-Mart de Mexico to Grow Stores by 10%," *DSN Retailing Today*, March 19, 2001, p. 3ff.; "Wal-Mart Fumes at Argentine Legislation," *The Wall Street Journal*, November 28, 2000, p. A23; "Stores Told to Lift Prices in Germany," *The Wall Street Journal*, September 11, 2000,

p. A27ff.; "Wal-Mart Girds for Major German Expansion," *The Wall Street Journal*, July 20, 2000, p. A21ff.; "Who's Afraid of Wal-Mart," *Fortune*, June 26, 2000, pp. 186–96; "With ASDA in Tow, Wal-Mart Shakes Up Supermarket World," *Ad Age International*, February 2000, p. 4; "Wal-Mart's Not-So-Secret British Weapon," *Business Week*, January 24, 2000, p. 132; "As Wal-Mart Invades Europe, Rivals Rush to Match Its Formula," *The Wall Street Journal*, October 6, 1999, p. A1ff.; "For French Retailers, a Weapon against Wal-Mart," *The Wall Street Journal*, September 27, 1999, p. B1ff.; "En Garde, Wal-Mart," *Business Week*, September 13, 1999, pp. 54–55; "French Retailers Create New Wal-Mart Rival," *The Wall Street Journal*, August 31, 1999, p. A14; "Wal-Mart Rocks European Retailing as It Rolls into United Kingdom," *Discount Store News*, July 12, 1999, p. 1ff.; "Watch Out: Here Comes Wal-Mart," *Business Week*, June 28, 1999, pp. 48–49; "Wal-Mart Goes Shopping in Europe," *Fortune*, June 7, 1999, pp. 105–12; "Wal-Mart Ends Speculation with Euro Entry, Acquires German Chain," *Discount Store News*, January 5, 1998, p. 1ff.; "The Wal-Mart Way Sometimes Gets Lost in Translation Overseas," *The Wall Street Journal*, October 8, 1997, p. A1ff.; "Wal-Mart Spoken Here," *Business Week*, June 23, 1997, pp. 138–44; "Wal-Mart International Reshapes the World Retailing Order," *Discount Store News*, January 20, 1997, pp. 21–28. For more on Wal-Mart's Neighborhood Markets, see "Neighborhood Market Redefines Convenience," *DSN Retailing Today*, February 5, 2001, p. 5ff.; "Store Distinctions Blur at Wal-Mart," *Discount Store News*, February 7, 2000, p. 6ff; "Wal-Mart Upgrades Neighborhood Market," *Discount Store News*, November 22, 1999, p. 1ff.; "Wal-Mart's 'Small-Marts' May Make It Biggest Grocer," *The Wall Street Journal*, June 21, 1999, p. B4; "Wal-Mart Goes Express with 'Market' Concept," *Discount Store News*, February 22, 1999, p. 1ff.; "Look Out, Supermarkets—Wal-Mart Is Hungry," *Business Week*, September 14, 1998, pp. 98–100. For more on Wal-Mart on the Web, see "Amazon + Wal-Mart = Win/Win," *Business Week*, March 19, 2001, p. 42; "Walmart.com Purchases Garden.com Content Assets," *DSN Retailing Today*, February 5, 2001, p. 8; "Will Walmart.com Get It Right This Time?" *Business Week*, November 6, 2000, pp. 104–12; "Wal-Mart Launches Web Site a Third Time, This Time Emphasizing Speed and Ease," *The Wall Street Journal*, October 31, 2000, p. B12; "Preparing for Net-Speed, Walmart. com Names CEO," *Discount Store News*, March 20, 2000, p. 1ff.; "A Matchmaker for 'Bricks' and 'Clicks,'" *The Wall Street Journal*, March 13, 2000, p. B1ff.; "Overhauling Its Web Site, Wal-Mart Will Push Toys and Electronics," *The Wall Street Journal*, October 1, 1999, p. B1ff.; "Wal-Mart's Goal: To Reign over Web," *Advertising Age*, July 5, 1999, p. 1ff.; "When Wal-Mart Flexes Its Cybermuscles . . . ," *Business Week*, July 26, 1999, pp. 82–85; "As Web Retailing Surges, Where's Wal-Mart?" *The Wall Street Journal*, May 17, 1999, p. B1ff. For more on Wal-Mart in the U.S., see "Kmart, Wal-Mart Face Off in Price-Cutting Fight," *USA Today*, June 8, 2001, p. 1B; "How Wal-Mart Transfers Power," *The Wall Street Journal*, March 27, 2001, p. B1ff.; "After Legendary Sprint to the Top, Wal-Mart Finally Hits Speed Bump," *Investor's Business Daily*, March 14, 2001, p. A1; "Super Stores: Land for Plenty," *Raleigh News & Observer*, March 3, 2001, p. 1Dff.; "Wal-Mart Wows with Growth Plan," *DSN Retailing Today*, October 23, 2000, p. 3ff.; "Big Three Redirect Efforts, Let Spoils Go to Regionals, Smaller-Format Chains," *DSN Retailing Today*, August 7, 2000, pp. 31–32; "Wal-Mart 'Imagines' Even Greater Growth," *DSN Retailing Today*, June 19, 2000, p. 1ff.; "Sam Would Be Proud," *Fortune*, April 17, 2000, pp. 130–44; "Wal-Mart Wins Reversal in Trademark Lawsuit," *The Wall Street Journal*, March 23, 2000, p. A3ff.; "Bankers Assail Mint for Deal with Wal-Mart," *The Wall Street Journal*, February 9, 2000, p. B1ff.; "Someday, Lee, This May All Be Yours," *Business Week*, November 15, 1999, pp. 84–92; *2000 Annual Report*, Wal-Mart; "Wal*Mart, Retailer of the Century," *Discount Store News* (Special Issue), October 1999; "Wal-Mart Sets Computer Doctor Centers," *The Wall Street Journal*, September 20, 1999, p. A3; "Power Retailer: Wal-Mart," *Discount Store News*, June 7, 1999, pp. 81–147; "Logistics Whiz Rises at Wal-Mart," *The Wall Street Journal*, March 11, 1999, p. B1ff.; "An Unstoppable Marketing Force," *USA Today*, November 6, 1998, p. 1Bff.; "Wal-Mart's Garth-Quake May Spur Sales," *The Wall Street Journal*, November 2, 1998, p. B1ff. See also Norman W. Hawker, "Wal-Mart and the Divergence of State and Federal Predatory Pricing Law," *Journal of Public Policy & Marketing*, Spring 1996, pp. 141–47. For more on Kmart Bluelight, see "Battle-Tested Rules of Online Retail," *Ecompany*, April 2001; "No Bluelight Special as Kmart Is Forced into Free ISP Field," *Investor's Business Daily*, December 5, 2000, p. A6; "Going for Gold at BlueLight," *Business Week E.Biz*, November 20, 2000, pp. EB43–EB46; "Attention Kmart Bashers," *Fortune*, November 13, 2000, pp. 213–22; "BlueLight, Green Light," *Brandweek*, October 2, 2000, pp. 21–22; "Kmart Gives Green Light to Bluelight Business Model," *DSN Retailing Today*, July 24, 2000, p. 18ff.; "BlueLight.com Aims to Coax Kmart Shoppers Online," *The Wall Street Journal*, June 19, 2000, p. B4; "It's All Net," *Brandweek*, May 1, 2000, pp. IQ18–IQ22. For more on Kmart, see "CEO Rings Up Plan to Restore Kmart," *USA Today*, June 27, 2001, p. 3B; "Turning Up the Intensity on a Storied Turnaround," *DSN Retailing Today*, May 21, 2001, pp. 17–18; "Super K Showcases the Future," *DSN Retailing Today*, May 21, 2001, p. 1ff.; "Kmart's Bright Idea," *Business Week*, April 19, 2001, pp. 50–52; "Kmart Turns to Blue Light to Boost Image," *DSN Retailing Today*, April 16, 2001, p. 1ff.; "Code Blue," *Advertising Age*, April 9, 2001, p. 1ff.; "Kmart: On the Threshold of a New Era," *DSN Retailing Today*, March 5, 2001, pp. 33–68; "Kmart Targets Target as It Taps TBWA for Ads," *Advertising Age*, October 2, 2000, p. 20; "A Kmart Special: Better Service," *Business Week*, September 4, 2000, pp. 80–84; "Kmart's New CEO Outlines Plans for Fast Changes," *The Wall Street Journal*, July 27, 2000, p. B4; "Attention, Kmart Investors: Retailer Is Likely to Be Second Fiddle Awhile," *Investor's Business Daily*, May 2, 2000, p. 1; "Ms. Stewart's Advice for How to Improve Kmart: Ask Martha," *The Wall Street Journal*, May 1, 2000, p. A1ff.; "Power Retailer: Kmart," *Discount Store News*, March 6, 2000, pp. 49–81; "Kmart Food Supply Deal Whets Retailer's Appetite," *Discount Store News*, August 9, 1999, p. 1ff.; "Power Retailer: Kmart," *Discount Store News*, March 22, 1999, pp. 21–71.

2. Marvin A. Jolson, "A Diagrammatic Model for Merchandising Calculations," *Journal of Retailing*, Summer 1975, pp. 3–9; C. Davis Fogg and Kent H. Kohnken, "Price-Cost Planning," *Journal of Marketing*, April 1978, pp. 97–106.

3. "Women Pay More for Haircuts, Dry Cleaning, and Clothing Alterations, a New York City Council Study Shows," *New York Daily News*, September 28, 1996, p. 7; Emerald Yeh and Christine McMurry, "The Cost of the Gender Gap" and "Gender

Pricing-Part 1" and "Gender Pricing-Part 2" available from World Wide Web: <http://www.kron.com/nc4/contact4/stories/gender>; "Why Women Pay More," *American Demographics*, April 1996, pp. 40–41; "Women Demand Fair Shear," *U. Magazine*, May 1995, p. 8; "State May Ban Bias in Pricing Hairdos, Wash," *The Wall Street Journal*, May 11, 1994, p. B1ff.

4. "The Little Extras That Count (Up)," *The Wall Street Journal*, July 12, 2001, p. B1ff.; "CEO Rings Up Plan to Restore Kmart," *USA Today*, June 27, 2001, p. 3B; "Battle-Tested Rules of Online Retail," *Ecompany*, April 2001; "The Return of Pricing Power," *Business Week*, May 8, 2000, pp. 50–51; "The Power of Smart Pricing," *Business Week*, April 10, 2000, pp. 160–64. See also Mary L. Hatten, "Don't Get Caught with Your Prices Down: Pricing in Inflationary Times," *Business Horizons*, March 1982, pp. 23–28; Douglas G. Brooks, "Cost Oriented Pricing: A Realistic Solution to a Complicated Problem," *Journal of Marketing*, April 1975, pp. 72–74; Steven M. Shugan, "Retail Product-Line Pricing Strategy When Costs and Products Change," *Journal of Retailing*, Spring 2001, Vol. 77, 1, p. 17.

5. G. Dean Kortge, "Inverted Breakeven Analysis for Profitable Marketing Decisions," *Industrial Marketing Management*, October 1984, pp. 219–24; Thomas L. Powers, "Breakeven Analysis with Semifixed Costs," *Industrial Marketing Management*, February 1987, pp. 35–42.

6. Approaches for estimating price–quantity relationships are reviewed in Kent B. Monroe, *Pricing: Making Profitable Decisions* (New York: McGraw-Hill, 1979). For a specific example see Frank D. Jones, "A Survey Technique to Measure Demand under Various Pricing Strategies," *Journal of Marketing*, July 1975, pp. 75–77; or Gordon A. Wyner, Lois H. Benedetti, and Bart M. Trapp, "Measuring the Quantity and Mix of Product Demand," *Journal of Marketing*, Winter 1984, pp. 101–9. See also Michael H. Morris and Mary L. Joyce, "How Marketers Evaluate Price Sensitivity," *Industrial Marketing Management*, May, 1988, pp. 169–76. David E. Griffith and Roland T. Rust, "The Price of Competitiveness in Competitive Pricing," *Journal of the Academy of Marketing Science*, Spring 1997, pp. 109–16; Robert J. Dolan, "How Do You Know When the Price Is Right?" *Harvard Business Review*, September 1995–October 1995, pp. 174–83; S. C. Choi, "Price Competition in a Duopoly Common Retailer Channel," *Journal of Retailing*, Summer 1996, pp. 117–35.

7. "Latest Supermarket Special—Gasoline," *The Wall Street Journal*, April 30, 2001, p. B1ff.; "Who Really Needs a Pentium 4?" *Fortune*, January 8, 2001, pp. 217–18; "Extra $75 a Month Helps the Medicine Go Down," *USA Today*, October 30, 2000, p. 1Bff.; "Marriott International: A Hotel That Clicks with Guests," *Business Week E.Biz*, September 18, 2000, p. EB58; "The Paradox of Value," *Brandweek*, June 5, 2000, pp. 40–56; Watts Wacker and Jim Taylor, *The Visionary's Handbook: Nine Paradoxes That Will Shape the Future of Your Business* (HarperCollins, 2000); "Selling Pears at $5 a Pound," *USA Today*, December 3, 1999, p. 1Bff.; "How Low Should They Go?" *The Wall Street Journal*, November 22, 1999, p. R20ff.; "Your Room Costs $250 . . . No! $200 . . . No . . . ," *The Wall Street Journal*, May 5, 1999, p. B1ff. See also Dhruv Grewal, Kent B. Monroe, and R. Krishnan, "The Effects of Price-Comparison Advertising on Buyers' Perceptions of Acquisition Value, Transaction Value, and Behavioral Intentions," *Journal of Marketing*, April 1998, pp. 46–59; John T. Gourville, "Pennies-a-Day: The Effect of Temporal Reframing on Transaction Evaluation," *Journal of Consumer Research*, March 1998, pp. 395–408; Joel E. Urbany, Rosemary Kalapurakal, and Peter R. Dickson, "Price Search in the Retail Grocery Market," *Journal of Marketing*, April 1996, pp. 91–104; Venkatesh Shankar and Lakshman Krishnamurthi, "Relating Price Sensitivity to Retailer Promotional Variables and Pricing Policy: An Empirical Analysis," *Journal of Retailing*, Fall 1996, pp. 249–72; Chakravarthi Narasimhan, Scott A. Neslin, and Subrata K. Sen, "Promotional Elasticities and Category Characteristics," *Journal of Marketing*, April 1996, pp. 17–30; K. Sivakumar and S. P. Raj, "Quality Tier Competition: How Price Change Influences Brand Choice and Category Choice," *Journal of Marketing*, July 1997, pp. 71–84.

8. "Fram Pays Up Now," *Brandweek*, July 20, 1998, pp. 16–17; "New Long-Life Bulbs May Lose Brilliance in a Crowded Market," *The Wall Street Journal*, June 2, 1992, p. B4; Benson P. Shapiro and Barbara P. Jackson, "Industrial Pricing to Meet Customer Needs," *Harvard Business Review*, November–December 1978, pp. 119–27; "The Race to the $10 Light Bulb," *Business Week*, May 19, 1980, p. 124; see also Michael H. Morris and Donald A. Fuller, "Pricing an Industrial Service," *Industrial Marketing Management*, May 1989, pp. 139–46.

9. "Good-Bye to Fixed Pricing?" *Business Week*, May 4, 1998, pp. 71–84.

10. Thomas T. Nagle, *The Strategy and Tactics of Pricing* (Englewood Cliffs, NJ: Prentice-Hall, 2001), pp. 249–55; Hooman Estelami, "The Impact of Research Design on Consumer Price Recall Accuracy: An Integrative Review," *Journal of the Academy of Marketing Science*, Winter 2001, pp. 36–50; Richard A. Briesch, Lakshman Krishnamurthi, Tridib Mazumdar, and S. P. Raj, "A Comparative Analysis of Reference Price Models," *Journal of Consumer Research*, September 1997, pp. 202–14; Tracy A. Suter and Scot Burton, "Believability and Consumer Perceptions of Implausible Reference Prices in Retail Advertisements," *Psychology & Marketing*, January 1996, pp. 37–54; K. N. Rajendran and Gerard J. Tellis, "Contextual and Temporal Components of Reference Price," *Journal of Marketing*, January 1994, pp. 22–34; Abhijit Biswas, Elizabeth J. Wilson, and Jane W. Licata, "Reference Pricing Studies in Marketing: A Synthesis of Research Results," *Journal of Business Research*, July 1993, pp. 239–56; Daniel S. Putler, "Incorporating Reference Price Effects into a Theory of Consumer Choice," *Marketing Science*, Summer 1992, pp. 287–309; Kristina D. Frankenberger and Ruiming Liu, "Does Consumer Knowledge Affect Consumer Responses to Advertised Reference Price Claims?" *Psychology & Marketing*, May/June 1994, pp. 235–52; Tridib Mazumdar and Kent B. Monroe, "Effects of Inter-store and In-store Price Comparison on Price Recall Accuracy and Confidence," *Journal of Retailing*, Spring 1992, pp. 66–89.

11. For an example applied to a high-price item, see "Sale of Mink Coats Strays a Fur Piece from the Expected," *The Wall Street Journal*, March 21, 1980, p. 30.

12. Noel M. Noel and Nessim Hanna, "Benchmarking Consumer Perceptions of Product Quality With Price: An Exploration," *Psychology & Marketing*, September 1996, pp. 591–604; Niraj Dawar and Philip Parker, "Marketing

Universals: Consumers' Use of Brand Name, Price, Physical Appearance, and Retailer Reputation As Signals of Product Quality," *Journal of Marketing*, April 1994, pp. 81–95; Tung-Zong Chang and Albert R. Wildt, "Impact of Product Information on the Use of Price As a Quality Cue," *Psychology & Marketing*, January 1996, pp. 55–75; B. P. Shapiro, "The Psychology of Pricing," *Harvard Business Review*, July–August 1968, pp. 14–24; Lutz Hildebrandt, "The Analysis of Price Competition Between Corporate Brands," *International Journal of Research in Marketing*, June 2001, p. 139.

13. Robert M. Schindler and Patrick N. Kirby, "Patterns of Rightmost Digits Used in Advertised Prices: Implications for Nine-Ending Effects," *Journal of Consumer Research*, September 1997, pp. 192–201; Mark Stiving and Russell S. Winer, "An Empirical Analysis of Price Endings With Scanner Data," *Journal of Consumer Research*, June 1997, pp. 57–67; Robert M. Schindler and Alan R. Wiman, "Effects of Odd Pricing on Price Recall," *Journal of Business Research*, November 1989, pp. 165–78.

14. "Keeping the Cachet," *The Wall Street Journal*, April 23, 2001, p. R28; "Luxury Sites Get Scrappy," *The Wall Street Journal*, December 4, 2000, p. B1ff.; "Online Luxury Has Limits," *Business Week E.Biz*, September 18, 2000, p. EB24; "Special Report: Luxury Marketing," *Advertising Age*, August 14, 2000, pp. S1–14; "The Galloping Gourmet Chocolate," *Brandweek*, July 31, 2000, pp. 32–37. See also Rebecca Piirto Heath, "Life on Easy Street," *American Demographics*, April 1997, pp. 33–38; K. M. Monroe and S. Petroshius, "Buyers' Subjective Perceptions of Price: An Update of the Evidence," in *Perspectives in Consumer Behavior*, ed. T. Robertson and H. Kassarjian (Glenview, IL: Scott Foresman, 1981), pp. 43–55; G. Dean Kortge and Patrick A. Okonkwo, "Perceived Value Approach to Pricing," *Industrial Marketing Management*, May 1993, pp. 133–40; Valarie A. Zeithaml, "Consumer Perceptions of Price, Quality, And Value: A Means-End Model and Synthesis of Evidence," *Journal of Marketing*, July 1988, pp. 2–22.

15. "Combatting a Fading Signal," *Brandweek*, November 27, 2000, pp. 37–42; "Why 'Bundling' Its Consumer Services Hasn't Benefited AT&T," *The Wall Street Journal*, October 24, 2000, p. B1ff.; "Soda Marketers Pour Out Fast-Feeding Frenzy of Ads," *Advertising Age*, September 11, 2000, p. 14; "PeoplePC Taps 9-Year-Old to Front $40 Mil Campaign," *Advertising Age*, May 8, 2000, p. 1ff.; Andrea Ovans, "Make a Bundle Bundling," *Harvard Business Review*, November–December 1997, pp. 18–20; Preyas S. Desai and Kannan Srinivasan, "Aggregate Versus Product-Specific Pricing: Implications for Franchise and Traditional Channels," *Journal of Retailing*, Winter 1996, pp. 357–82; Manjit S. Yadav and Kent B. Monroe, "How Buyers Perceive Savings in a Bundle Price: An Examination of a Bundle's Transaction Value," *Journal of Marketing Research*, August 1993, pp. 350–58; Dorothy Paun, "When to Bundle or Unbundle Products," *Industrial Marketing Management*, February 1993, pp. 29–34.

16. Peter E. Connor and Robert K. Hopkins, "Cost Plus What? The Importance of Accurate Profit Calculations in Cost-Plus Agreements," *International Journal of Purchasing & Materials Management*, Spring 1997, pp. 35–40; Daniel T. Ostas, "Ethics of Contract Pricing," *Journal of Business Ethics*, February 1992, pp. 137–46; J. Steve Davis, "Ethical Problems in Competitive Bidding: The Paradyne Case," *Business and Professional Ethics Journal*, 7, no. 2 (1988), pp. 3–26; David T. Levy, "Guaranteed Pricing in Industrial Purchases: Making Use of Markets in Contractual Relations," *Industrial Marketing Management*, October 1994, pp. 307–14; Akintola Akintoye and Martin Skitmore, "Pricing Approaches in the Construction Industry," *Industrial Marketing Management*, November 1992, pp. 311–18.

Chapter 18

1. Available from World Wide Web: <http://www.maytag.com>; "Sears to Defend Appliance Business with New Washer," *The Wall Street Journal*, June 25, 2001, p. B4; "Maytag Picks Ralph Hake as Chairman and CEO," *The Wall Street Journal*, June 20, 2001, p. B9; "Maytag to Buy Rival Amana Appliances from Goodman Global for $325 Million," *The Wall Street Journal*, June 6, 2001, p. B6; "Maytag Chairman Ward Resigns after Tenure Lasting 15 Months," *The Wall Street Journal*, November 10, 2000, p. B8; "Maytag Through the Wringer," *Business Week*, September 27, 1999, p. 54; "The Saga of Lloyd Ward," *Business Week*, August 9, 1999, pp. 58–70; "A New Spin on Clothes Washers," *Consumer Reports*, July 1998, pp. 50–54.; "Maytag's Top Officer, Expected to Do Little, Surprises His Board," *The Wall Street Journal*, June 23, 1998, p. A1ff.; "New Spin on an Old Chore: New Front-Loader Is Water-Stingy," *USA Today*, March 25, 1998, p. 1Aff.; "Maytag's Neptune Takes the Market by Storm," *Maytag Merchandiser*, No. 3, 1997; "Product Pampering," *Brandweek*, June 16, 1997, pp. 29–40.

2. *The American Customer Satisfaction Index, 2000*; "Now Are You Satisfied? The 1998 American Customer Satisfaction Index," *Fortune*, February 16, 1998, pp. 161–68; Claes Fornell, Michael D. Johnson, Eugene W. Anderson, Jaesung Cha, and Barbara E. Bryant, "The American Customer Satisfaction Index: Nature, Purpose, and Findings," *Journal of Marketing*, October 1996, pp. 7–18; Eugene W. Anderson, Claes Fornell, and Donald R. Lehmann, "Customer Satisfaction, Market Share, and Profitability: Findings From Sweden," *Journal of Marketing*, July 1994, pp. 53–66; John F. Gaski and Michael J. Etzel, "The Index of Consumer Sentiment Toward Marketing," *Journal of Marketing*, July 1986, pp. 71–81; "The Limits of Customer Satisfaction," *Brandweek*, March 3, 1997, p. 17; Hiram C. Barksdale et al., "A Cross-National Survey of Consumer Attitudes Toward Marketing Practices, Consumerism, and Government Regulations," *Columbia Journal of World Business*, Summer 1982, pp. 71–86; Hiram C. Barksdale and William D. Perreault, Jr., "Can Consumers Be Satisfied?" *MSU Business Topics*, Spring 1980, pp. 19–30.

3. "McDonald's Finds Angry Customers on Its Menu," *The Wall Street Journal*, July 16, 2001, p. A14.

4. Michael Brady, "Improving Your Measurement of Customer Satisfaction: A Guide to Creating, Conducting, Analyzing, and Reporting Customer Satisfaction Measurement Programs," *Journal of the Academy of Marketing Science*, Spring 2000, p. 315; David M. Szymanski, "Customer Satisfaction: A Meta-Analysis of the Empirical Evidence," *Journal of the Academy of Marketing Science*, Winter 2001, pp. 16–36; Janelle Barlow and Claus Moller, *A Complaint Is a Gift: Using Customer Feedback as a Strategic Tool* (2000); "A Satisfied Customer Isn't Enough,"

Fortune, July 21, 1997, pp. 112–13; Theodore P. Stank, Patricia J. Daugherty, and Alexander E. Ellinger, "Voice of the Customer: The Impact on Customer Satisfaction," *International Journal of Purchasing & Materials Management*, Fall 1997, pp. 2–9; Jeffrey G. Blodgett, Donna J. Hill, and Stephen S. Tax, "The Effects of Distributive, Procedural, and Interactional Justice on Postcomplaint Behavior," *Journal of Retailing*, Summer 1997, pp. 185–210; Thorsten Hennig-Thurau and Alexander Klee, "The Impact of Customer Satisfaction and Relationship Quality on Customer Retention: A Critical Reassessment and Model Development," *Psychology & Marketing*, December 1997, pp. 737–64; Scott W. Hansen, Thomas L. Powers, and John E. Swan, "Modeling Industrial Buyer Complaints: Implications for Satisfying and Saving Customers," *Journal of Marketing Theory & Practice*, Fall 1997, pp. 12–22; Paul G. Patterson, Lester W. Johnson, and Richard A. Spreng, "Modeling the Determinants of Customer Satisfaction for Business-to-Business Professional Services," *Journal of the Academy of Marketing Science*, Winter 1997, pp. 4–17; Stanley F. Slater, Eric M. Olson, and Venkateshwar K. Reddy, "Strategy-Based Performance Measurement," *Business Horizons*, July–August 1997, pp. 37–44; Stephen S. Tax, Stephen W. Brown, and Murali Chandrashekaran, "Customer Evaluations of Service Complaint Experiences: Implications for Relationship Marketing," *Journal of Marketing*, April 1998, pp. 60–76; Sunder Narayanan, "Customer Satisfaction Measurement and Management," *Journal of the Academy of Marketing Science*, Summer 1996, pp. 276–77; Mary C. Gilly, William B. Stevenson, and Laura J. Yale, "Dynamics of Complaint Management in the Service Organization," *The Journal of Consumer Affairs*, Winter 1991, pp. 295–322; F. Gouillart and F. Sturdivant, "Spend a Day in the Life of Your Customers," *Harvard Business Review*, January–February 1994, pp. 116–27; Erdener Kaynak, Orsay Kucukemiroglu, and Yavuz Odabasi, "Consumer Complaint Handling in an Advanced Developing Economy: An Empirical Investigation," *Journal of Business Ethics*, November 1992, pp. 813–30; Jagdip Singh, "Industry Characteristics and Consumer Dissatisfaction," *The Journal of Consumer Affairs*, Summer 1991, pp. 19–56; A. Parasuraman, Valarie A. Zeithaml, and Leonard L. Berry, "SERVQUAL: A Multiple-Item Scale for Measuring Consumer Perceptions of Service Quality," *Journal of Retailing*, Spring 1988, pp. 12–40.

5. Kevin J. Clancy and Robert S. Shulman, *Marketing Myths that are Killing Business: The Cure for Death Wish Marketing* (New York: McGraw-Hill, 1994); Regina E. Herzlinger, "Can Public Trust in Nonprofits and Governments Be Restored?" *Harvard Business Review*, March–April 1996, pp. 97–107; Michael S. Minor, "Relentless: The Japanese Way of Marketing," *Journal of the Academy of Marketing Science*, Spring 1998, pp. 160–61; Charles C. Snow, "Twenty-First-Century Organizations: Implications for a New Marketing Paradigm," *Journal of the Academy of Marketing Science*, Winter 1997, pp. 72–74; Frederick F. Reichheld, "Learning From Customer Defections," *Harvard Business Review*, March–April 1996, pp. 56–61ff. For a classic discussion of the problem and mechanics of measuring the efficiency of marketing, see Reavis Cox, *Distribution in a High-Level Economy* (Englewood Cliffs, NJ: Prentice-Hall, 1965).

6. For more on criticisms of advertising, see Barbara J. Phillips, "In Defense of Advertising: A Social Perspective," *Journal of Business Ethics*, February 1997, pp. 109–18; Charles Trappey, "A Meta-Analysis of Consumer Choice and Subliminal Advertising," *Psychology & Marketing*, August 1996, pp. 517–30; Karl A. Boedecker, Fred W. Morgan, and Linda B. Wright, "The Evolution of First Amendment Protection for Commercial Speech," *Journal of Marketing*, January 1995, pp. 38–47; Thomas C. O. Guinn and L. J. Shrum, "The Role of Television in the Construction of Consumer Reality," *Journal of Consumer Research*, March 1997, pp. 278–94; see also Robert B. Archibald, Clyde A. Haulman, and Carlisle E. Moody, Jr., "Quality, Price, Advertising, and Published Quality Ratings," *Journal of Consumer Research*, March 1983, pp. 347–56.

7. Donald F. Dixon, "The Economics of Conspicuous Consumption: Theory and Thought Since 1700," *Journal of Macromarketing*, June 2001, Vol. 21, 1, pp. 101–4; Guliz Ger, "Human Development and Humane Consumption: Well-Being Beyond the 'Good Life,'" *Journal of Public Policy & Marketing*, Spring 1997, pp. 110–25; Ronald P. Hill and Sandi Macan, "Consumer Survival on Welfare With an Emphasis on Medicaid and the Food Stamp Program," *Journal of Public Policy & Marketing*, Spring 1996, pp. 118–27; Dennis J. Cahill, "The Refinement of America: Persons, Houses, Cities," *Journal of Marketing*, October 1994, pp. 121–22; Arnold J. Toynbee, *America and World Revolution* (New York: Oxford University Press, 1966), pp. 144–45. See also John Kenneth Galbraith, *Economics and the Public Purpose* (Boston: Houghton Mifflin, 1973), pp. 144–45 and Russell J. Tomsen, "Take It Away," *Newsweek*, October 7, 1974, p. 21.

8. Thomas O. Jones and W E. Sasser, "Why Satisfied Customers Defect," *Harvard Business Review*, November 1995–December 1995, pp. 88–99; "The Satisfaction Trap," *Harvard Business Review*, March–April 1996, pp. 58–59.

9. Priscilla A. La Barbera and Zeynep Gurhan, "The Role of Materialism, Religiosity, and Demographics in Subjective Well-Being," *Psychology & Marketing*, January 1997, pp. 71–97; Dennis J. Cahill, "Consumption and the World of Goods," *Journal of Marketing*, April 1994, pp. 131–32; Jacqueline K. Eastman, Bill Fredenberger, David Campbell, and Stephen Calvert, "The Relationship Between Status Consumption and Materialism: A Cross-Cultural Comparison of Chinese, Mexican and American Students," *Journal of Marketing Theory & Practice*, Winter 1997, pp. 52–66; James A. Muncy and Jacqueline K. Eastman, "Materialism and Consumer Ethics: An Exploratory Study," *Journal of Business Ethics*, January 1998, pp. 137–45; See also Frederick Webster, *Social Aspects of Marketing* (Englewood Cliffs, NJ: Prentice-Hall, 1974), p. 32; Terrence H. Witkowski, "The Early American Style: A History of Marketing and Consumer Values," *Psychology & Marketing*, March 1998, pp. 125–43.

10. "Coke Finds Its Exclusive School Contracts Aren't So Easily Given Up," *The Wall Street Journal*, June 26, 2001, p. B1ff.; "Web-Filter Data from Schools Put Up for Sale," *The Wall Street Journal*, January 26, 2001, p. B1ff.; "On Many Campuses, Big Brewers Play a Role in New Alcohol Policies," *The Wall Street Journal*, November 2, 2000, p. A1ff.; "Pepsi Hits High Note with Schools," *Advertising Age*, October 9, 2000, p. 30; "If It's Marketing, Can It Also Be Education?" *Fortune*, October 2, 2000, p. 274; "AOL to Announce This Week the Launch of Free Online Service Aimed at Schools," *The Wall Street Journal*, May 16, 2000, p. B6; "Mouse-Trapping the Student Market," *American*

Demographics, May 2000, pp. 30–34; "Grad Students Match Wits in Marketing Competition," *The Wall Street Journal*, February 9, 2000, p. S1ff.; "Pitching Saturns to Your Classmates—for Credit," *The Wall Street Journal*, January 31, 2000, p. B1ff.; "Marketers on Campus: A New Bag of Tricks," *The Wall Street Journal*, January 31, 2000, p. B1ff.; "Tobacco Money Sparks a New Fight," *The Wall Street Journal*, December 10, 1999, p. B1ff.; "Schools for Sale," *Advertising Age*, October 25, 1999, pp. 22–26; "Big Cards on Campus," *Business Week*, September 20, 1999, p. 138; "Cola Contracts Lose Fizz in Schools," *USA Today*, August 18, 1999, p. 9D; "Ads in Schools: Lesson in Failure?" *Advertising Age*, June 7, 1999, p. 26; "Classrooms for Sale," *Time*, April 19, 1999, pp. 44–45; "Big Car on Campus?" *Business Week*, August 31, 1998, p. 32; "Are We Selling Our Students?" *Raleigh News & Observer*, August 2, 1998, p. 25Aff.; "This School Was Sponsored by . . . ," *Parenting*, March 1998, p. 23; "Channel One Taps Principals as Promoters," *The Wall Street Journal*, September 15, 1997, p. B1ff.; "School's Back, and So Are the Marketers," *The Wall Street Journal*, September 15, 1997, p. B1ff.; "Hey Kid, Buy This!" *Business Week*, June 30, 1997, pp. 62–69; "This Class Brought to You by . . . ," *USA Today*, January 3, 1997, p. 3A; "New Ad Vehicles: Police Car, School Bus, Garbage Truck," *The Wall Street Journal*, February 20, 1996, p. B1ff.; "A Lesson in Sample Arithmetic," *Advertising Age*, January 2, 1995, p. 22; "Companies Teach All Sorts of Lessons with Educational Tools They Give Away," *The Wall Street Journal*, April 19, 1994, p. B1ff.

11. "Can Business Still Save the World?" *Inc.*, April 2001, pp. 58–71; "Apparel Makers Back New Labor Inspection Group," *The Wall Street Journal*, April 10, 2001, p. B1ff.; "The Man Who Sold Silicon Valley on Giving," *Fortune*, November 27, 2000, pp. 182–90; "The Fight Against Latin Poverty," *Business Week*, May 1, 2000, pp. 72–84; "Corporate Charity: Why It's Slowing," *Business Week*, December 18, 2000, pp. 164–66.

12. For more on Aveda, see "From the Amazon to Your Armrest," *The Wall Street Journal*, May 1, 2001, p. B1ff. For other environmental issues, see "It May Be Time to Toss Old Ideas on Recycling," *USA Today*, July 2, 2001, p. 7D; "Battle Breaks Out over Rival Seals for 'Green' Wood," *The Wall Street Journal*, May 23, 2001, p. B1ff.; "As BP Goes Green, the Fur Is Flying," *The Wall Street Journal*, April 16, 2001, p. A10ff.; "Once Is Not Enough," *Business Week*, April 16, 2001, pp. 128B–F; "Earth-Shell Saw Big Macs and Big Bucks—Got Big Woes," *The Wall Street Journal*, April 10, 2001, p. B2; "Recycling Redefined," *The Wall Street Journal*, March 6, 2001, p. B1ff.; "More Gas-Powered Autos on 'Green' List," *USA Today*, February 9, 2001, p. 3B; "Saving the Earth, One Click at a Time," *American Demographics*, January 2001, pp. 30–33; "Life After Death," *Ecompany*, December 2000, pp. 167–78; "A Terrible Thing to Waste," *Time Digital*, December 2000, pp. 50–53; "Nonprofits—and Landfills—Deluged with Old PCs," *Investor's Business Daily*, November 27, 2000, p. A6; "Conservation: Been There, Doing That," *Business Week*, November 27, 2000, pp. 194F-H; "Where TVs Go When They Die," *The Wall Street Journal*, July 14, 2000, p. B1ff.; "Are Old PCs Poisoning Us?" *Business Week*, June 12, 2000, pp. 78–80; "A Clean Technology Powers Up," *Business Week*, May 8, 2000, pp. 102–105; "It's Not Trendy Being Green," *Advertising Age*, April 10, 2000, p. 16; "Recycler's Nightmare: Beer in Plastic," *The Wall Street Journal*, November 16, 1999, p. B1ff.; "Diesel Vehicles, in Greener Mode, May Stage Comeback," *The Wall Street Journal*, April 9, 1998, p. B4; "As Old Pallets Pile Up, Critics Hammer Them as a New Eco-Menace," *The Wall Street Journal*, April 1, 1998, p. A1ff.; "A Maine Forest Firm Prospers by Earning Eco-Friendly Label," *The Wall Street Journal*, November 26, 1997, p. A1ff.; "When Green Begets Green," *Business Week*, November 10, 1997, pp. 98–104. See also Anil Menon and Ajay Menon, "Enviropreneurial Marketing Strategy: The Emergence of Corporate Environmentalism As Market Strategy," *Journal of Marketing*, January 1997, pp. 51–67; William E. Kilbourne, "Green Advertising: Salvation or Oxymoron?" *Journal of Advertising*, Summer 1995, pp. 7–19.

13. For more on privacy, see Chapter 13, footnote #10. See also "Internet Insecurity," *Time*, July 2, 2001, pp. 44–50; "Mixed Signals," *American Demographics*, July 2001, pp. 44–49; "Swap Meet," *American Demographics*, July 2001, pp. 50–57; "Technology . . . Privacy," *The Wall Street Journal Reports*, June 25, 2001, p. R17; "What's Ahead for Cellular Phones," *The Wall Street Journal Reports*, June 25, 2001, p. R8ff.; "Why Privacy Notices Are a Sham," *Business Week*, June 18, 2001, pp. 82–83; "Marketing Gurus Clash on Internet Privacy Rules," *USA Today*, April 27, 2001, p. 1Bff.; "Silicon Valley's Open Secrets," *The Wall Street Journal*, April 27, 2001, p. B1ff.; "You've Got Mail (You Don't Want)," *The Wall Street Journal*, April 23, 2001, p. R21; "I'm Not Paranoid, But . . . ," *Business Week E.Biz*, April 16, 2001, p. EB38; "If the FBI Hopes to Get the Goods on You, It May Ask ChoicePoint," *The Wall Street Journal*, April 13, 2001, p. A1ff.; "Privacy Options Are a Blur," *USA Today*, April 10, 2001, p. 3D; "To Annoyance of Cellphone Users, Text Messages May Well Be Spam," *The Wall Street Journal*, March 28, 2001, p. B1ff.; "Microsoft's Web Effort Raises Questions," *The Wall Street Journal*, March 23, 2001, p. B5; "The Battle Over Web Privacy," *The Wall Street Journal*, March 21, 2001, p. B1ff.; "Private Matters," *The Wall Street Journal*, February 12, 2001, p. R24ff.; "Network Solutions Sells Marketers Its Web Database," *The Wall Street Journal*, February 16, 2001, p. B1ff.; "Wireless, with Strings Attached," *USA Today*, February 7, 2001, p. 1Dff.; "Continental Air Loses Some Accounts after Data-Disclosure Demand," *The Wall Street Journal*, February 6, 2001, p. B1ff.; "The Secret (Server) Service," *Brandweek*, January 1, 2001, pp. IQ31–32; "Who's Prying Now," *Business Week E.Biz*, December 11, 2000, p. EB80; "Someone to Watch over You," *The Wall Street Journal*, December 11, 2000, p. R8; "You're Being Followed (This Is Not News)," *Ecompany*, December 2000, pp. 63–64; "Chances Are, Somebody's Watching You," *USA Today*, November 30, 2000, p. 1Aff.; "It's Not Big Brother Invading Kids' Privacy, It's Mom and Dad," *The Wall Street Journal*, November 6, 2000, p. A1ff.; "TrustUs.com," *American Demographics*, November 2000, p. 47; "You Have No Secrets," *The Wall Street Journal*, October 23, 2000, p. R32; "Big Brother Calling," *Business Week*, September 25, 2000, pp. 92–98; "Freedom Software Lets You Get Some Privacy while Surfing the Web," *The Wall Street Journal*, August 10, 2000, p. B1; "Keep Away from My Cookies, More Marketers Say," *The Wall Street Journal*, March 20, 2000, p. B1ff.; "It's Time for Rules in Wonderland," *Business Week*, March 20, 2000, pp. 82–96; "Targeted Ads: Consumer Trap or a Net Necessity?" *USA Today*, February 25, 2000, p. 1Bff.; "Privacy: Outrage on the Web," *Business Week*, February 14, 2000, pp. 38–40; "We'll Be Watching You," *The Wall Street*

Journal, January 1, 2000, p. R26; "A Secret Cat-and-Mouse Game Online," *The Wall Street Journal*, October 13, 1999, p. B1ff.; "The New Gatekeepers," *American Demographics*, June 1999, pp. 41–42; "Special Report: Privacy," *Business Week*, April 5, 1999, pp. 84–90.; "Knowing You All Too Well," *Newsweek*, March 29, 1999, pp. 48–50; Ellen R. Foxman and Paula Kilcoyne, "Information Technology, Marketing Practice, and Consumer Privacy: Ethical Issues," *Journal of Public Policy & Marketing*, Spring 1993, pp. 106–19; Robert E. Thomas and Virginia G. Maurer, "Database Marketing Practice: Protecting Consumer Privacy," *Journal of Public Policy & Marketing*, Spring 1997, pp. 147–55; Marren J. Roy, "Regulation of Automatic Dialing and Announcing Devices Upheld," *Journal of the Academy of Marketing Science*, Summer 1997, pp. 269–70.

14. For more on online fraud, see "Credit-Card Scams Bedevil E-Stores," *The Wall Street Journal*, September 19, 2000, p. B1ff.; "Fraud on the Internet," *Business Week E.Biz*, April 3, 2000, pp. EB58–EB64; "Online Scambusters," *Business Week E.Biz*, April 3, 2000, p. EB66; "Card Sharps," *Business Week E.Biz*, April 3, 2000, pp. EB68–EB76. For more on in-store fraud, see "Stores Battle Employee Theft," *Raleigh News & Observer*, October 15, 2000, p. 1Eff.; "As Thievery by Insiders Overtakes Shoplifting, Retailers Crack Down," *The Wall Street Journal*, September 8, 2000, p. A1ff.; "Electronic Tags Are Beeping Everywhere," *The Wall Street Journal*, April 20, 1998, p. B1ff.; "A Time to Steal," *Brandweek*, February 16, 1998, p. 24; Scott Dawson, "Consumer Responses to Electronic Article Surveillance Alarms," *Journal of Retailing*, Fall 1993, pp. 353–62.

15. For more on socially responsible and ethical behavior, see W. P. Cunningham, "The Golden Rule As Universal Ethical Norm," *Journal of Business Ethics*, January 1998, pp. 105–09; 'Ethnic Pricing' Means Unfair Air Fares," *The Wall Street Journal*, December 5, 1997, p. B1ff.; William P. Cordeiro, "Suggested Management Responses to Ethical Issues Raised by Technological Change," *Journal of Business Ethics*, September 1997, pp. 1393–400; Eli P. I. Cox, Michael S. Wogalter, Sara L. Stokes, and Elizabeth J. T. Murff, "Do Product Warnings Increase Safe Behavior? A Meta-Analysis," *Journal of Public Policy & Marketing*, Fall 1997, pp. 195–204; "On the Net, Anything Goes," *Newsweek*, July 7, 1997, pp. 28–30; "'Levi's As Ye Sew, So Shall Ye Reap," *Fortune*, May 12, 1997, pp. 104–16; "48% of Workers Admit to Unethical or Illegal Acts," *USA Today*, April 4, 1997, p. 1Aff.; H. R. Dodge, Elizabeth A. Edwards, and Sam Fullerton, "Consumer Transgressions in the Marketplace: Consumers' Perspectives," *Psychology & Marketing*, December 1996, pp. 821–35; David W. Stewart, "Internet Marketing, Business Models, and Public Policy," *Journal of Public Policy & Marketing*, Fall 2000, pp. 287–297; Albert A. Foer, "E-commerce Meets Antitrust: A Primer," *Journal of Public Policy & Marketing*, Spring 2001, pp. 51–64; "Ethics for Hire," *Business Week*, July 15, 1996, pp. 26–28; "How a Drug Firm Paid for University Study, Then Undermined It," *The Wall Street Journal*, April 25, 1996, p. A1ff.; James A. Roberts, "Will the Real Socially Responsible Consumer Please Step Forward?" *Business Horizons*, January–February 1996, pp. 79–83; John Priddle, "Marketing Ethics, Macromarketing, and the Managerial Perspective Reconsidered," *Journal of Macromarketing*, Fall 1994, pp. 47–62; Bernard Avishai, "What is Business's Social Compact?" *Harvard Business Review*, January–February 1994, pp. 38–49; Paul N. Bloom, George R. Milne, and Robert Adler, "Avoiding Misuse of New Information Technologies: Legal and Societal Considerations," *Journal of Marketing*, January 1994, pp. 98–110; James A. Muncy and Scott J. Vitell, "Consumer Ethics: An Investigation of the Ethical Beliefs of the Final Consumer," *Journal of Business Research*, June 1992, pp. 297–312; Gene R. Laczniak and Patrick E. Murphy, "Fostering Ethical Marketing Decisions," *Journal of Business Ethics*, April 1991, pp. 259–72.

Illustration Credits

Chapter 1

Exhibits: *P.* 13, 1-2, adapted from Wroe Alderson, "Factors Governing the Development of Marketing Channels," in *Marketing Channels for Manufactured Products*, ed. Richard M. Clewett (Homewood, IL: Richard D. Irwin, 1954), p. 7. *P.* 18, 1-3, adapted from William McInnes, "A Conceptual Approach to Marketing," in *Theory in Marketing*, 2d ser., ed. Reavis Cox, Wroe Alderson, and Stanley J. Shapiro (Homewood, IL: Richard D. Irwin, 1964), pp. 51–67. *P.* 20, 1-4, model suggested by Professor A. A. Brogowicz, Western Michigan University.

Photos/ads: *P.* 3, Ben Stechschulte/Contact Press Images; *P.* 4 (left), "GLAD and STAND & ZIP are trademarks of The Glad Products Company. Advertisement ©2000 The Glad Products Company. Used with permission; (right), Courtesy Ogilvy & Mather/Paris; *P.* 6, Robert Azzi/Woodfin Camp & Associates; P.10, Courtesy Alcoa; *P.* 11 (left), Courtesy The Clorox Company; (right), ©The Procter & Gamble Company; *P.* 12 (left), Steven Begleiter; (right), Greg Girardi/Contact Press Images; *P.* 17, Agency: Hal Riney & Partners; Art Director: Chris Chaffin; Copywriter: Tony Barlow; photographer: Bob Mizono; *P.* 19 (left), Courtesy of Maryland Aviation Administration; (right), Courtesy Big Vine; *P.* 21 (left), Courtesy 3m; (right), ©2000 CarParts Technologies. Artwork supplied courtesy Schwartz Rahman Candelaria.

Chapter 2

Exhibits: *P.* 33, 2-2, adapted from R. F. Vizza, T. E. Chambers, and E. J. Cook, *Adoption of the Marketing Concept—Fact or Fiction* (New York: Sales Executive Club, Inc., 1967), pp. 13–15. *P.* 38, 2-4, adapted from discussions of an American Marketing Association Strategic Planning Committee. *P.* 47, 2-11, Copernicus: The Marketing Investment Strategy Group, Inc., 450 Lexington Street, Auburndale, MA 02166.

Photos/ads: *P.* 27, © Brian Coats, All rights reserved; *P.* 29, Courtesy of Bell Sports; Agency: Goodby Silverstein & Partners; *P.* 31 (left), Courtesy Burst.com; (right), Courtesy The Valvoline Company; *P.* 34 (left), Courtesy Payless ShoeSource, Inc.; Agency: Barkley Evergreen & Partners, Inc.; (right), Courtesy Williams-Sonoma, Inc.; Agency: Garner, Geary, Coll & Young; *P.* 35, Courtesy L.L. Bean, Inc.; *P.* 36, Courtesy CMG Communications; *P.* 43 (left and right), Courtesy Pennzoil-Quaker State Co.; *P.* 46, Courtesy Timex Corporation.

Chapter 3

Exhibits: *P.* 56, 3-2, Igor Ansoff, *Corporate Strategy* (New York; McGraw-Hill, 1965). *P.* 72, 3-12, Russell I. Haley, "Benefit Segmentation: A Decision-Oriented Research Tool," *Journal of Marketing*, July 1968, p. 33.

Photos/ads: *P.* 51, ©Kimberly Holcombe; *P.* 52 (left), S.C. Johnson & Son, Inc.; (right), Creme Savers is a trademark owned by Nabisco Brands Company and used by permission; *P.* 54, Courtesy of Audi of Norway; Agency: Bates Reklamebyra/Oslo; *P.* 56, Ilja C. Hendel/The Image Works; *P.* 57 (left), Courtesy Unilever P.L.C.; (right), ©1999 Barry Lewis/Network; *P.* 58 (top), Courtesy of Hallmark Cards, Inc.; (bottom left) Courtesy Olympus America, Inc.; (bottom center) Courtesy of Vivitar Corporation; Potter, Katz,Postal and Ferguson; MGI Software, Inc.; (bottom right) Courtesy of Sony Electronics Inc.; *P.* 63, Courtesy H.J. Heinz Company. Used with permission; *P.* 67, Photographer: Steve Bonini; *P.* 69 (left), Courtesy Nabisco Brands, Inc.; (right), Courtesy Club Med; *P.* 71 (left), Courtesy Grey Worldwide/Thailand; (right), Courtesy Target Stores.

Chapter 4

Exhibits: *P.* 93, 4-4, table based on U.S. Census data, including *Global Population Profile: 2000* and *World Population Profile: 1998* (Washington, DC: U.S. Government Printing Office) and *World Population at a Glance: 1998 and Beyond, IB/98-4*; and other Census data available from World Wide Web: <http://www.census.gov/ipc>; United Nations statistical data including *World Population Prospects: The 1999 Revision of the UN Population Division* (New York: United Nations, 2000); World Bank data, including *World Development Indicators: 2000* (Washington, DC: International Bank for Reconstruction and Development/The World Bank, 2000) and available from World Wide Web: <http://www.worldbank.org/data/wdi2000> and <http://devdata.worldbank.org/data-query>; Central Intelligence Agency data and available from World Wide Web: <http://www.odci.gov/cia/publications/factbook>; Population Reference Bureau data, including *2000 World Population Data Sheet* (Washington, DC: Population Reference Bureau, 2000) and available from World Wide Web: <http://www.prb.org/pubs/wpds2000>. *P.* 97, 4-5, map developed by the authors based on U.S. Census data available from World Wide Web: <http://www.census.gov/population/www/cen2000/respop> and "Table 2. Resident Population of the 50 States, the District of Columbia, and Puerto Rico: Census 2000" and "Table 5. Resident Population of the 50 States, the District of Columbia, and Puerto Rico: April 1, 2000 (Census 2000) and April 1, 1990 (1990 Census)" and "Figure 1. Percent Change in Resident Population for the 50 States, the District of Columbia, and Puerto Rico: 1990 to 2000." *P.* 98, 4-6, graph developed by the authors based on U.S. Census data: 2000 and 2010 figures from U.S. Census Bureau, "National Population Projections—Summary Tables" (January 13, 2000) and available from World Wide Web: <http://www.census.gov/population/www/projections/natsum-T3.html> and U.S. Bureau of the Census, *Statistical Abstract of the United States 2000*, p. 15; 1990 figures from U.S. Census Bureau, *Current Population Reports*, P25-917 and P25-1095 and unpublished data and available on World Wide

Web:<http://www.census.gov/population/www/estimates/popest> and <http://www.census.gov/statab/freq/99s0014>; 1980 figures from U.S. Bureau of the Census, *Statistical Abstract of the United States 1998*, pp. 13, 15. *P.* 101, 4-9, adapted from M. G. Allen, "Strategic Problems Facing Today's Corporate Planner," speech given at the Academy of Management, 36th Annual Meeting, Kansas City, Missouri, 1976.

Photos/ads: *P.* 77, Courtesy United Parcel Service of America, Inc.; *P.* 78, ©Angelika Grundler; *P.* 81, Courtesy Harley-Davidson Motor Company; *P.* 81, ©2001 Hertz System, Inc. Hertz is a registered service mark and trademark of Hertz System, Inc.; *P.* 83, Courtesy AOL UK; *P.* 86 (left), Courtesy Smart Money; Ad created by: DiMassimo Brand Advertising, New York; (right), Courtesy CNN; *P.* 89, Courtesy Adero, Inc.; *P.* 90, Courtesy Adidas America; photo by Bob Allen; *P.* 92 (left), Courtesy SRC; (right), TETRAD Computer Applications Inc.; *P.* 94 (left), Courtesy Monsanto; (right), Courtesy Monsanto; *P.* 102 (left), Courtesy Baldor Electric; (right), Courtesy Click 2 Asia.

Chapter 5

Exhibits: *P.* 109, 5-1, graph developed by the authors based on U.S. Census data available from World Wide Web: <http://www.census.gov/hhes/income/histinc/f01.html> , Table F-1, "Income Limits for Each Fifth and Top 5 Percent of Families (All Races): 1947 to 1999" and available from World Wide Web: <http://www.census.gov/hhes/income/histinc/f02.html> , Table F-2, "Share of Aggregate Income Received by Each Fifth and Top 5 Percent of Families (All Races): 1947 to 1999." *P.* 111, 5-3, adapted from C. Glenn Walters, *Consumer Behavior*, 3d ed. (Homewood, IL: Richard D. Irwin, 1979). *P.* 117, 5-6, Joseph T. Plummer, "The Concept and Application of Life-Style Segmentation," *Journal of Marketing*, January 1974, pp. 33–37. *P.* 119, 5-7, adapted from Patrick E. Murphy and William A. Staples, "A Modern Family Life Cycle," *Journal of Consumer Research*, June 1979, p. 17. *P.* 120, 5-8, adapted from Rebecca Piirto Heath, "The New Working Class," *American Demographics*, January 1998, pp. 51–55; "Education Marks a Widening Income Divide," *The Wall Street Journal*, June 28, 1996, p. R2; "Class in America," *Fortune*, February 7, 1994, pp. 114–26; Greg J. Duncan, Timothy M. Smeeding, and Willard Rodgers, "The Incredible Shrinking Middle Class," *American Demographics*, May 1992, pp. 34–38; Richard P. Coleman, "The Continuing Significance of Social Class to Marketing," *Journal of Consumer Research*, December 1983, pp. 265–80; "What Is Happening to the Middle Class?" *American Demographics*, January 1985, pp. 18–25; Donald W. Hendon, Emelda L. Williams, and Douglas E. Huffman, "Social Class System Revisited," *Journal of Business Research*, November 1988, pp. 259–70.

Photos/ads: *P.* 107, Copyright 2001 USA TODAY. Reprinted with permission; *P.* 108, Courtesy of CBS Television Network; *P.* 110 (left), ©The Procter & Gamble Company. Used with permission; (right), Courtesy of ConAgra Foods; *P.* 113 (left), Courtesy Reckitt Benckiser, Inc.; (right), Courtesy Iomega Corporation; *P.* 115 (left), Courtesy White Wave, Inc.; (right), Courtesy PureTek Corporation; *P.* 116 (left, center, right), ©Procter & Gamble Company. Used with permission; *P.* 118, Courtesy General Mills; *P.* 120, Michael J. Hruby; *P.* 121 (top), ©2000 Jockey International, Inc. World rights reserved; (bottom), Courtesy Salton, Inc.; *P.* 123, Courtesy Colgate-Palmolive Company; *P.* 124, Courtesy Discover Card; *P.* 128 (left), Courtesy Colgate-Palmolive Company; (right), ©John Abbott.

Chapter 6

Exhibits: *P.* 135, 6-1, U.S. Bureau of the Census, *Statistical Abstract of the United States 2000*; U.S. Bureau of the Census, *County Business Patterns 1998, United States* (Washington, DC: U.S. Government Printing Office, 2000). *P.* 140, 6-4, adapted from Rowland T. Moriarty, Jr., and Robert E. Spekman, "An Empirical Investigation of the Information Sources Used During the Industrial Buying Process, *Journal of Marketing Research*, May 1984, pp. 137–47. *P.* 150, 6-7, data adapted from U.S. Bureau of the Census, *Statistical Abstract of the United States 2000*; U.S. Bureau of the Census, *County Business Patterns 1998, United States*; U.S. Bureau of the Census, *1997 Census of Manufacturers, Subject Series, General Summary* (Washington, DC: U.S. Government Printing Office, 2001). *P.* 152, 6-8, available from World Wide Web: <http://www.naics.com>.

Photos/ads: *P.* 133, ©Sonia Katchian; *P.* 136, Courtesy The Timken Company; *P.* 137 (left and right), ©Roger Ball Photography; *P.* 139, Courtesy Federal Express Corporation; *P.* 141 (left), Courtesy Hormel Foods; (right), Courtesy Rockwell International Corporation; *P.* 145 (left), Courtesy SpaceWorks, Inc.; (right), Courtesy GoCo-op; *P.* 148, Courtesy National Semiconductor; *P.* 151, (left, center, right) All photos courtesy Alcoa; *P.* 152, Courtesy Walgreen Company; *P.* 153, Courtesy Colgate-Palmolive Company.

Chapter 7

Exhibits: *P.* 176, 7-5, adapted from Paul E. Green, Frank J. Carmone, and David P. Wachpress, "On the Analysis of Qualitative Data in Marketing Research," *Journal of Marketing Research*, February 1977, pp. 52–59.

Photos/ads: *P.* 159, ©2002 LensCrafters', Inc. The United States Shoe Corporation, LensCrafters' parent company, is owner of LensCrafters' trademark and service marks; *P.* 160 (left), Courtesy of Sun Microsystems, Inc.; Agency: Lowe & Partners; (right), Courtesy of MapInfo; *P.* 164, Courtesy Zero Knowledge Systems, Inc.; *P.* 167, Alta Vista R.; *P.* 168 (left), Reprinted with permission from Northern Light Technology, Inc. Copyright 1999; (right), Courtesy Greenfield Online, Inc.; *P.* 170, Courtesy Cetia, Inc.; *P.* 171 (left and right), Courtesy Greenfield Online, Inc.; *P.* 172, Courtesy Colgate-Palmolive Company; *P.* 174 (left), Courtesy Claritas; (right), Courtesy Business Objects; *P.* 175 (left and right), Courtesy Simmons Company; *P.* 177 (left), Courtesy Survey Sampling, Inc.; (right), Courtesy Simmons Custom Research; *P.* 178, Courtesy P. Robert & Partners; P.; (right), Courtesy Quality Controlled Services-St. Louis, MO.

Chapter 8

Photos/ads: *P.* 183, ©2001 William D. Perreault, Jr.; *P.* 185, Courtesy The Hertz Corporation; *P.* 187, Crowley Webb and Associates—Buffalo, NY, for M&T Bank; *P.* 188 (left, center, right), Courtesy American Honda Motor Co.; *P.* 190, Courtesy Crate & Barrel; *P.* 191, Courtesy GE Plastics; *P.* 195 (left and right), ©The Procter & Gamble Company. Used by permission;

P. 198 (left), Courtesy Del Monte Fresh Produce N.A., Inc.; (right), Courtesy GE Lighting; *P.* 199, Michael J. Hruby; *P.* 201 (left), Used by permission of Dean's Food Company; *P.* 202 (left), Courtesy American Isuzu Motors, Inc.; (right), Sears Home Central ad: Courtesy Sears Roebuck & Co.

Chapter 9

Exhibits: *P.* 218, 9-4, adapted from Frank R. Bacon, Jr., and Thomas W. Butler, *Planned Innovation* (Ann Arbor: University of Michigan Institute of Science and Technology, 1980). *P.* 219, 9-5, adapted from Philip Kotler, "What Consumerism Means for Marketers," *Harvard Business Review*, May–June 1972, pp. 55–56. *P.* 227, 9-7, Marie Gaudard, Roland Coates, and Liz Freeman, "Accelerating Improvement," *Quality Progress*, October 1991, pp. 81–88. *P.* 228, 9-8, Marie Gaudard, Roland Coates, and Liz Freeman, "Accelerating Improvement," *Quality Progress*, October 1991, pp. 81–88.

Photos/ads: *P.* 207, 3Com, the 3Com logo and Graffiti are registered trademarks and HotSync, Palm OS, Palm Pilot, and the Palm Pilot logo are trademarks of 3Com Corporation or its subsidiaries. All other brands and product names are trademarks and registered trademarks of their respective holders. This product is not manufactured by Pilot Corporation or Pilot Corporation of America, manufacturers and distributors of writing instruments; *P.* 210, Courtesy Braun, Inc.; *P.* 211 (left), Courtesy Leo Burnett, Singapore; (right), Courtesy of Nabisco Brands, Inc.; *P.* 212, Courtesy E.I. Dupont De Nemours & Co.; *P.* 215 (left), Courtesy Unilver P.L.C.; Photographer Barry Lewis/Network; (right), Courtesy Toys "R" Us; *P.* 216 (left and right), ©The Procter & Gamble Co. Used with permission; *P.* 218 (left), Courtesy Sauder Woodworking Company; (right), Courtesy Caliber Learning Network, Inc.; *P.* 220 (left), Courtesy E.I. Dupont De Memours & Co.; (right), Courtesy Komatsu America; *P.* 221, Courtesy GE Company; *P.* 222, Courtesy Porsche Cars North America; *P.* 222, Mark Joseph Photography-Chicago. All other rights are reserved by Mark Joseph Photography except those specifically granted by this delivery memo; *P.* 224, Courtesy of Nabisco Brands, Inc.

Chapter 10

Photos/ads: *P.* 233, ©2001 William D. Perreault, Jr.; *P.* 235 (left and right), Courtesy Colgate-Palmolive Company; *P.* 236 (left, center, and right), Courtesy Unilever P.L.C.; Photographer: Bill Prentice; *P.* 237, ©2001 USA TODAY. Reprinted with permission; *P.* 239, Courtesy Office Depot; *P.* 240 (left and right), Mark Joseph Photography-Chicago. All other rights are reserved by Mark Joseph Photography except those specifically granted by this delivery memo; *P.* 243, Courtesy The Goodyear Tire & Rubber Company; *P.* 243 (left), ©The Procter & Gamble Company. Used by permission; (right), Courtesy Leisure Concepts; *P.* 247, Tom Wagner/SABA; *P.* 249 (top), Courtesy Reebok International; (bottom), Courtesy Volkswagen of America, Inc.

Chapter 11

Exhibits: *P.* 270, 11-6, adapted from Louis W. Stern and Adel I. El-Ansary, *Marketing Channels* (Englewood Cliffs, NJ: Prentice Hall, 1977), p. 150.

Photos/ads: *P.* 255, ©Fritz Hoffman; *P.* 257 (left), Courtesy Prince Castle; (right), Courtesy W.W. Grainger, Inc.; *P.* 260 (left), Courtesy Business Objects; (right), Courtesy Sauder Woodworking Company; *P.* 262, Courtesy CNF, Inc.; *P.* 266, Courtesy Ryder Systems, Inc.; *P.* 266, Courtesy Cummins, Inc.; *P.* 268, Courtesy Great Plains Software, Inc.; *P.* 274, ©Ovak Arslanian.

Chapter 12

Exhibits: *P.* 290, 12-4, available from World Wide Web: <http://www.census.gov>. U.S. Bureau of the Census, *County Business Patterns 1998, United States*; U.S. Bureau of the Census, *1997 Census of Retail Trade, Subject Series, Establishment and Firm Size* (Washington, DC: U.S. Government Printing Office, 2000). *P.* 293, 12-5, available from World Wide Web: <http://www.census.gov>. U.S. Bureau of the Census, *County Business Patterns 1998, United States*; U.S. Bureau of the Census, *1997 Census of Wholesale Trade, Geographic Area Series, United States* (Washington, DC: U.S. Government Printing Office, 2000).

Photos/ads: *P.* 275, Photo/Karen Caplan courtesy Frieda's, Inc.; *P.* 278 (left), Courtesy Toys "R" Us, Inc.; (center), Courtesy Land's End, Inc.; (right), Courtesy The Home Depot; *P.* 279 (left), Courtesy Colgate-Palmolive Company; (right), Tom Wagner/Saba; Pp. 282-283, Courtesy of Office Depot; *P.* 284, Reproduced with permission of Exxon Mobil Corporation; *P.* 287, Courtesy Barnes & Noble.com; *P.* 288, Courtesy Jersey Gardens; *P.* 291, Courtesy of Tesco Stores Ltd.; Agency: Lowe-Howard Spink/London; Photographer: Tony Campbell; *P.* 292, Courtesy CrossLink, Inc.; *P.* 295 (left), Peter Hince; (right), ©2000 Reid Horn; *P.* 296, ©Steve Niedorf; *P.* 298, Advance Bar Code Technology, Inc.

Chapter 13

Photos/ads: *P.* 305, ©Ron Kimball; *P.* 307, Courtesy Colgate-Palmolive Company; *P.* 309, Courtesy Stanley Works; *P.* 311 (left), KELLOGG'S® NUTRI-GRAIN® and KELLOGG'S® SNACK'UMS™ are trademarks of Kellogg Company. All rights reserved. Used with permission; (right), Courtesy Beech Nutrition Corporation; *P.* 315 (left), Courtesy Florists Transworld Delivery; (right), Courtesy Campbell Soup Company; *P.* 318 (left), Courtesy Lipstream Networks, Inc.; (right), Courtesy Macromedia, Inc.; *P.* 319 (left), Courtesy Nestle U.S.A.; Agency: McCann-Erickson, L.A.; (right), Courtesy of Dome Industries; *P.* 322 (left), Advertisement courtesy of Compaq Computer Corporation; Photo courtesy of Brad Harris; (right), Courtesy Oasis The Campaign Agency; *P.* 324, Courtesy Reily Food Company; *P.* 325 (left), ©2000 Network Solutions, Inc.; (right), ©Yahoo! Inc.

Chapter 14

Exhibits: *P.* 344, 14-3, exhibit suggested by Professor A. A. Brogowicz, Western Michigan University.

Photos/ads: *P.* 329, ©Timothy Archibald; *P.* 330, Photograph courtesy of Glaxo Holdings, p.l.c.; *P.* 332 (left), Courtesy Boise Cascade Office Products; (right), Courtesy of Sauder Woodworking Company; *P.* 334, Courtesy General Electric Company;

photo by Brownie Harris; *P.* 335, ©1996 Vickers & Beechler; *P.* 336, Courtesy Alcoa; Photo by Robert Feldman; *P.* 337, Courtesy The Clorox Company; Photo by Lisa Papel; *P.* 340, Courtesy Salesforce.com; *P.* 342 (left), Courtesy Ross Roy Advertising Agency; (right), Courtesy Vcampus; *P.* 346 (left), Courtesy Experian, Inc.; (right), Courtesy Eiki International, Inc.; *P.* 348, Courtesy Keebler.

Chapter 15

Exhibits: *P.* 356, 15-2, "2000 Advertising to Sales Ratios for the 200 Largest Ad Spending Industries," *Advertising Age*, July 24, 2000, and available from World Wide Web: <http://www.adage.com>. *P.* 362, 15-4, cost data from *Standard Rate and Data*, 2000, and sales estimates from "Forecast: Hazy," *Advertising Age*, June 18, 2001, p. 4ff.; "Top Forecaster Sees Lower Ad Growth," *Advertising Age*, June 11, 2001, p. 1ff.; "Choices, Choices," *The Wall Street Journal*, April 23, 2001, p. R12.

Photos/ads: *P.* 353, ©William D. Perreault, Jr.; *P.* 355 (left), Michael Goldwater/Network; (right), ©Procter & Gamble Company. Used with permission; *P.* 359 (left), Courtesy of Del Pharmaceuticals; (right), Courtesy of Brown Shoe Co., Inc.; *P.* 365 (left), Courtesy ClickAction; (right), Courtesy Tripod; *P.* 363, David Taylor/Allsport; *P.* 367, Courtesy Birdsall Voss & Kloppenburg; *P.* 368, ©Ben Van Hook; *P.* 369, Courtesy Euro RSCG; *P.* 371 (left), Courtesy Bates USA, South Miami, FL; (right), Courtesy Greenfield Online, Inc.; *P.* 373, Courtesy Circuit City; Photographer: Jerr Zaruba; *P.* 376 (left), Courtesy Catalina Marketing; (right), Courtesy Colgate-Palmolive Company.

Chapter 16

Exhibits: *P.* 391, 16-6, exchange rate data is available from the Federal Reserve Bank; see also International Monetary Fund data available from World Wide Web: <http://www.imf.org/external/np/tre/sdr/drates> and Universal Currency Converter available from World Wide Web: <http://www.xe.net/currency>.

Photos/ads: *P.* 381, ©William D. Perreault, Jr.; *P.* 382, Courtesy Clarke Goward Agency; *P.* 386, Courtesy Merck Co., Inc.; *P.* 389 (left), Courtesy Carnival Corporation; (right), Courtesy National Trade Publications, Inc.; *P.* 391 (left), Courtesy 8 in 1 Pet Products, Inc.; (right) Courtesy H.J. Heinz Company. Used with permission; *P.* 393 (left), Courtesy Cargill, Inc.; (right) Courtesy Euro RSCG/Beijing; *P.* 395, Mike Williams/ Mercury Pictures; *P.* 396 (left), Courtesy Goodyear Tire & Rubber Company; (right) Courtesy of THUNKdesign; *P.* 399, ©The Procter & Gamble Company. Used with permission; *P.* 401, Fritz Hoffman/Network.

Chapter 17

Exhibits: *P.* 423, 17-11, this exhibit is different from, but stimulated by, a graph that appears on the Satisfaction Management Systems, Inc., website <http://www.satmansys.com>.

Photos/ads: *P.* 407, ©Brian Coats. All rights reserved; *P.* 410 (top), Courtesy Kohler Co.; (bottom), Don Smetzer/Getty Images; *P.* 414, Courtesy Colgate-Palmolive Company; *P.* 420 (left), Courtesy Metform, L.L.C.; (right) Courtesy Emerson Electric Company; *P.* 421, Courtesy Commerce One; *P.* 422 (left), Courtesy Hallmark Cards. Inc.; Agency: Leo Burnett/Chicago; (right), Courtesy eCampus.com; Agency: Devito-Verdi Advertising; *P.* 424 (left), Courtesy Dior; Photo: Albert Gordan; (right), Courtesy Audio Stream; *P.* 427 (left), Courtesy Dovebid.com; (right), Courtesy Worldbid.com.

Chapter 18

Exhibits: *P.* 449, 18-4, adapted and updated from discussions of an American Marketing Association Strategic Planning Committee.

Photos/ads: *P.* 431, ©William D. Perreault, Jr.; *P.* 432, ©William D. Perreault, Jr.; *P.* 434, ©William D. Perreault, Jr.; *P.* 435 (left), ©The Procter & Gamble Company. Used with permission; (right), Courtesy Garmin International; *P.* 441, Robin Moyer/Time Magazine; *P.* 441 (left), Courtesy Planetfeedback.com; (right), Courtesy Toyota Motor Sales, USA; Agency: Saatchi & Saatchi/Los Angeles; photographer: Tim Damon; *P.* 443, Courtesy J.D. Powers & Associates; *P.* 444, Courtesy The New Products Showcase & Learning Center; *P.* 446 (left), Courtesy The Hertz Corporation; (right), Courtesy Novatel Wireless, Inc.; Creative Director: Jimmy Long; Production Coordinator: Erika Kubli; *P.* 448 (left), Lara Jo Regan/Gettsource Liaison Agency; (right), Patrick Dori/Beach 'n Billboard; *P.* 450, Courtesy Ford Motor Company; *P.* 453, Courtesy Lotus Development Corporation, an IBM Company; *P.* 454, Courtesy Princeton Video Image.

Appendix B

Exhibits: *P.* 484, B-4, "1997 Survey of Buying Power," *Sales & Marketing Management*, Supplement, 1997.

Appendix C

Exhibits: *P.* 493, C-2, available from World Wide Web: <http://www.stats.bls.gov/oco/ocos>; <http://www.adage.com/dataplace/archives>; <http://www.marketingmag.ca/content/34.97/table1>; <http://www.scip.org/salmid>; <http://www.scip.org/salgen>; <http://www.thomas-staffing.com/survey98/salary>; <http://www.mwsu.edu/htmldocs/departments/bus_admin/salary_survey>.

Photos/ads: *P.* 498, Courtesy General Motors.

Name Index

Subject Index

Glossary

Accessories Short-lived capital items—tools and equipment used in production or office activities.

Accumulating Collecting products from many small producers.

Administered channel systems Various channel members informally agree to cooperate with each other.

Administered prices Consciously set prices aimed at reaching the firm's objectives.

Adoption curve Shows when different groups accept ideas.

Adoption process The steps individuals go through on the way to accepting or rejecting a new idea.

Advertising Any *paid* form of nonpersonal presentation of ideas, goods, or services by an identified sponsor.

Advertising agencies Specialists in planning and handling mass-selling details for advertisers.

Advertising allowances Price reductions to firms in the channel to encourage them to advertise or otherwise promote the firm's products locally.

Advertising managers Managers of their company's mass-selling effort in television, newspapers, magazines, and other media.

Agent middlemen Wholesalers who do not own (take title to) the products they sell.

AIDA model Consists of four promotion jobs: (1) to get *Attention*, (2) to hold *Interest*, (3) to arouse *Desire*, and (4) to obtain *Action*.

Allowance (accounting term) Occurs when a customer is not satisfied with a purchase for some reason and the seller gives a price reduction on the original invoice (bill), but the customer keeps the goods or services.

Allowances Reductions in price given to final consumers, customers, or channel members for doing something or accepting less of something.

Assorting Putting together a variety of products to give a target market what it wants.

Attitude A person's point of view toward something.

Auction companies Agent middlemen who provide a place where buyers and sellers can come together and complete a transaction.

Automatic vending Selling and delivering products through vending machines.

Average cost (per unit) The total cost divided by the related quantity.

Average-cost pricing Adding a reasonable markup to the average cost of a product.

Average fixed cost (per unit) The total fixed cost divided by the related quantity.

Average variable cost (per unit) The total variable cost divided by the related quantity.

Bait pricing Setting some very low prices to attract customers but trying to sell more expensive models or brands once the customer is in the store.

Balance sheet An accounting statement that shows a company's assets, liabilities, and net worth.

Basic list prices The prices that final customers or users are normally asked to pay for products.

Basic sales tasks *Order-getting, order-taking,* and *supporting*.

Battle of the brands The competition between dealer brands and manufacturer brands.

Belief A person's opinion about something.

Benchmarking Picking a basis of comparison for evaluating how well a job is being done.

Bid pricing Offering a specific price for each possible job rather than setting a price that applies for all customers.

Brand equity The value of a brand's overall strength in the market.

Brand familiarity How well customers recognize and accept a company's brand.

Brand insistence Customers insist on a firm's branded product and are willing to search for it.

Brand managers Manage specific products, often taking over the jobs formerly handled by an advertising manager—sometimes called product managers.

Brand name A word, letter, or a group of words or letters.

Brand nonrecognition Final customers don't recognize a brand at all—even though middlemen may use the brand name for identification and inventory control.

Brand preference Target customers usually choose the brand over other brands, perhaps because of habit or favorable past experience.

Brand recognition Customers remember the brand.

Brand rejection Potential customers won't buy a brand—unless its image is changed.

Branding The use of a name, term, symbol, or design—or a combination of these—to identify a product.

Break-even analysis An approach to determine whether the firm will be able to break even—that is, cover all its costs—with a particular price.

Break-even point (BEP) The sales quantity where the firm's total cost will just equal its total revenue.

Breakthrough opportunities Opportunities that help innovators develop hard-to-copy marketing strategies that will be very profitable for a long time.

Brokers Agent middlemen who specialize in bringing buyers and sellers together.

Bulk-breaking Dividing larger quantities into smaller quantities as products get closer to the final market.

Business and organizational customers Any buyers who buy for resale or to produce other goods and services.

Business products Products meant for use in producing other products.

Buying center All the people who participate in or influence a purchase.

Buying function Looking for and evaluating goods and services.

Capital item A long-lasting product that can be used and depreciated for many years.

Cash-and-carry wholesalers Like service wholesalers, except that the customer must pay cash.

Cash discounts Reductions in the price to encourage buyers to pay their bills quickly.

Catalog wholesalers Sell out of catalogs that may be distributed widely to smaller industrial customers or retailers who might not be called on by other middlemen.

Central markets Convenient places where buyers and sellers can meet one-on-one to exchange goods and services.

Chain of supply The complete set of firms and facilities and logistics activities that are involved in procuring materials, transforming them into intermediate and finished products, and distributing them to customers.

Channel captain A manager who helps direct the activities of a whole channel and tries to avoid, or solve, channel conflicts.

Channel of distribution Any series of firms or individuals who participate in the flow of products from producer to final user or consumer.

Close The salesperson's request for an order.

Clustering techniques Approaches used to try to find similar patterns within sets of data.

Combination export manager A blend of manufacturers' agent and selling agent—handling the entire export function for several producers of similar but noncompeting lines.

Combined target market approach Combining two or more submarkets into one larger target market as a basis for one strategy.

Combiners Firms that try to increase the size of their target markets by combining two or more segments.

Communication process A source trying to reach a receiver with a message.

Comparative advertising Advertising that makes specific brand comparisons using actual product names.

Competitive advantage A firm has a marketing mix that the target market sees as better than a competitor's mix.

Competitive advertising Advertising that tries to develop selective demand for a specific brand rather than a product category.

Competitive barriers The conditions that may make it difficult, or even impossible, for a firm to compete in a market.

Competitive bids Terms of sale offered by different suppliers in response to the buyer's purchase specifications.

Competitive environment The number and types of competitors the marketing manager must face, and how they may behave.

Competitive rivals A firm's closest competitors.

Competitor analysis An organized approach for evaluating the strengths and weaknesses of current or potential competitors' marketing strategies.

Complementary product pricing Setting prices on several related products as a group.

Components Processed expense items that become part of a finished product.

Concept testing Getting reactions from customers about how well a new product idea fits their needs.

Consultative selling approach A type of sales presentation in which the salesperson develops a good understanding of the individual customer's needs before trying to close the sale.

Consumer panel A group of consumers who provide information on a continuing basis.

Consumer Product Safety Act A 1972 law that set up the Consumer Product Safety Commission to encourage more awareness of safety in product design and better quality control.

Consumer products Products meant for the final consumer.

Consumer surplus The difference to consumers between the value of a purchase and the price they pay.

Consumerism A social movement that seeks to increase the rights and powers of consumers.

Containerization Grouping individual items into an economical shipping quantity and sealing them in protective containers for transit to the final destination.

Continuous improvement A commitment to constantly make things better one step at a time.

Convenience (food) stores A convenience-oriented variation of the conventional limited-line food stores.

Convenience products Products a consumer needs but isn't willing to spend much time or effort shopping for.

Cooperative advertising Middlemen and producers sharing in the cost of ads.

Cooperative chains Retailer-sponsored groups, formed by independent retailers, to run their own buying organizations and conduct joint promotion efforts.

Copy thrust What the words and illustrations of an ad should communicate.

Corporate chain A firm that owns and manages more than one store—and often it's many.

Corporate channel systems Corporate ownership all along the channel.

Corrective advertising Ads to correct deceptive advertising.

Cost of sales Total value (at cost) of the sales during the period.

Countertrade A special type of bartering in which products from one country are traded for products from another country.

Cues Products, signs, ads, and other stimuli in the environment.

Cultural and social environment Affects how and why people live and behave as they do.

Culture The whole set of beliefs, attitudes, and ways of doing things of a reasonably homogeneous set of people.

Cumulative quantity discounts Reductions in price for larger purchases over a given period, such as a year.

Customer relationship management (CRM) An approach where the seller fine-tunes the marketing effort with information from a detailed customer database.

Customer satisfaction The extent to which a firm fulfills a consumer's needs, desires, and expectations.

Customer service level How rapidly and dependably a firm can deliver what customers want.

Customer value The difference between the benefits a customer sees from a market offering and the costs of obtaining those benefits.

Data warehouse A place where databases are stored so that they are available when needed.

Dealer brands Brands created by middlemen—sometimes referred to as private brands.

Decision support system (DSS) A computer program that makes it easy for marketing managers to get and use information *as they are making decisions.*

Decoding The receiver in the communication process translating the message.

Demand-backward pricing Setting an acceptable final consumer price and working backward to what a producer can charge.

Demand curve A graph of the relationship between price and quantity demanded in a market—assuming all other things stay the same.

Department stores Larger stores that are organized into many separate departments and offer many product lines.

Derived demand Demand for business products derives from the demand for final consumer products.

Determining dimensions The dimensions that actually affect the customer's purchase of a *specific* product or brand in a *product-market.*

Differentiation The marketing mix is distinct from and better than what's available from a competitor.

Direct marketing Direct communication between a seller and an individual customer using a promotion method other than face-to-face personal selling.

Direct type advertising Competitive advertising that aims for immediate buying action.

Discount houses Stores that sell hard goods (cameras, TVs, appliances) at substantial price cuts to customers who go to discounter's low-rent store, pay cash, and take care of any service or repair problems themselves.

Discounts Reductions from list price given by a seller to buyers, who either give up some marketing function or provide the function themselves.

Discrepancy of assortment The difference between the lines a typical producer makes and the assortment final consumers or users want.

Discrepancy of quantity The difference between the quantity of products it is economical for a producer to make and the quantity final users or consumers normally want.

Discretionary income What is left of income after paying taxes and paying for necessities.

Dissonance Tension caused by uncertainty about the rightness of a decision.

Distribution center A special kind of warehouse designed to speed the flow of goods and avoid unnecessary storing costs.

Diversification Moving into totally different lines of business—perhaps entirely unfamiliar products, markets, or even levels in the production-marketing system.

Door-to-door selling Going directly to the consumer's home.

Drive A strong stimulus that encourages action to reduce a need.

Drop-shippers Wholesalers who own (take title to) the products they sell but do not actually handle, stock, or deliver them.

Dual distribution When a producer uses several competing channels to reach the same target market—perhaps using several middlemen in addition to selling directly.

Dumping Pricing a product sold in a foreign market below the cost of producing it or at a price lower than in its domestic market.

Early adopters The second group in the adoption curve to adopt a new product; these people are usually well respected by their peers and often are opinion leaders.

Early majority A group in the adoption curve that avoids risk and waits to consider a new idea until many early adopters try it and like it.

E-commerce Exchanges between individuals or organizations—and activities that facilitate those exchanges—based on applications of information technology.

Economic and technological environment Affects the way firms, and the whole economy, use resources.

Economic buyers People who know all the facts and logically compare choices in terms of cost and value received—to get the greatest satisfaction from spending their time and money.

Economic needs Needs concerned with making the best use of a consumer's time and money—as the consumer judges it.

Economic system The way an economy organizes to use scarce resources to produce goods and services and distribute them for consumption by various people and groups in the society.

Economies of scale As a company produces larger numbers of a particular product, the cost for each of these products goes down.

Elastic demand If prices are dropped, the quantity demanded will stretch enough to increase total revenue.

Elastic supply The quantity supplied does stretch more if the price is raised.

Electronic data interchange (EDI) An approach that puts information in a standardized format easily shared between different computer systems.

Emergency products Products that are purchased immediately when the need is great.

Empowerment Giving employees the authority to correct a problem without first checking with management.

Empty nesters People whose children are grown and who are now able to spend their money in other ways.

Encoding The source in the communication process deciding what it wants to say and translating it into words or symbols that will have the same meaning to the receiver.

Equilibrium point The quantity and the price sellers are willing to offer are equal to the quantity and price that buyers are willing to accept.

Everyday low pricing Setting a low list price rather than relying on frequent discounts or allowances.

Exclusive distribution Selling through only one middleman in a particular geographic area.

Expectation An outcome or event that a person anticipates or looks forward to.

Expense item A product whose total cost is treated as a business expense in the year it's purchased.

Expenses All the remaining costs that are subtracted from the gross margin to get the net profit.

Experimental method A research approach in which researchers compare the responses of two or more groups that are similar except on the characteristic being tested.

Export agents Manufacturers' agents who specialize in export trade.

Export brokers Brokers who specialize in bringing together buyers and sellers from different countries.

Extensive problem solving The type of problem solving consumers use for a completely new or important need—when they put much effort into deciding how to satisfy it.

Facilitators Firms that provide one or more of the marketing functions other than buying or selling.

Factor A variable that shows the relation of some other variable to the item being forecast.

Factor method An approach to forecast sales by finding a relation between the company's sales and some other factor (or factors).

Family brand A brand name that is used for several products.

Farm products Products grown/raised by farmers, such as oranges, oats, sugar cane, and cattle.

Fashion Currently accepted or popular style.

Federal Fair Packaging and Labeling Act A 1966 law requiring that consumer goods be clearly labeled in easy-to-understand terms.

Federal Trade Commission (FTC) Federal government agency that polices antimonopoly laws.

Financing Provides the necessary cash and credit to produce, transport, store, promote, sell, and buy products.

Fishbone diagram A visual aid that helps organize cause and effect relationships for "things gone wrong."

Fixed-cost (FC) contribution per unit The selling price per unit minus the variable cost per unit.

Flexible-price policy Offering the same product and quantities to different customers at different prices.

F.O.B. A transportation term meaning free on board some vehicle at some point.

Focus group interview An interview of 6 to 10 people in an informal group setting.

Foreign Corrupt Practices Act A law passed by the U.S. Congress in 1977 that prohibits U.S. firms from paying bribes to foreign officials.

Form utility Provided when someone produces something tangible.

Franchise operation A franchisor develops a good marketing strategy, and the retail franchise holders carry out the strategy in their own units.

Freight absorption pricing Absorbing freight cost so that a firm's delivered price meets the nearest competitor's.

General merchandise wholesalers Service wholesalers who carry a wide variety of nonperishable items such as hardware, electrical supplies, drugs, cosmetics, and automobile equipment.

General stores Early retailers who carried anything they could sell in reasonable volume.

Generic market A market with *broadly* similar needs—and sellers offering various and *often diverse* ways of satisfying those needs.

Generic products Products that have no brand at all other than identification of their contents and the manufacturer or middleman.

Gross margin (gross profit) The money left to cover the expenses of selling the products and operating the business.

Gross national product (GNP) The total market value of goods and services produced in an economy in a year.

Gross sales The total amount charged to all customers during some time period.

Heterogeneous shopping products Shopping products the customer sees as different and wants to inspect for quality and suitability.

Homogeneous shopping products Shopping products the customer sees as basically the same and wants at the lowest price.

Hypermarkets Very large stores that try to carry not only food and drug items but all goods and services that the consumer purchases *routinely* (also called supercenters).

Hypotheses Educated guesses about the relationships between things or about what will happen in the future.

Ideal market exposure When a product is available widely enough to satisfy target customers' needs but not exceed them.

Implementation Putting marketing plans into operation.

Import agents Manufacturers' agents who specialize in import trade.

Import brokers Brokers who specialize in bringing together buyers and sellers from different countries.

Impulse products Products that are bought quickly as *unplanned* purchases because of a strongly felt need.

Indirect type advertising Competitive advertising that points out product advantages—to affect future buying decisions.

Individual brands Separate brand names used for each product.

Individual product A particular product within a product line.

Inelastic demand Although the quantity demanded increases if the price is decreased, the quantity demanded will not stretch enough to avoid a decrease in total revenue.

Inelastic supply The quantity supplied does not stretch much (if at all) if the price is raised.

Innovation The development and spread of new ideas and products.

Innovators The first group to adopt new products.

Installations Important capital items such as buildings, land rights, and major equipment.

Institutional advertising Advertising that tries to promote an organization's image, reputation, or ideas rather than a specific product.

Integrated marketing communications The intentional coordination of every communication from a firm to a target customer to convey a consistent and complete message.

Intensive distribution Selling a product through all responsible and suitable wholesalers or retailers who will stock and/or sell the product.

Intermediary A middleman.

Internet A system for linking computers around the world.

Intranet A system for linking computers within a company.

Introductory price dealing Temporary price cuts to speed new products into a market.

Inventory The amount of goods being stored.

ISO 9000 A way for a supplier to document its quality procedures according to internationally recognized standards.

Job description A written statement of what a salesperson is expected to do.

Jury of executive opinion Forecasting by combining the opinions of experienced executives—perhaps from marketing, production, finance, purchasing, and top management.

Just-in-time delivery Reliably getting products there *just* before the customer needs them.

Laggards Prefer to do things the way they have been done in the past and are very suspicious of new ideas—sometimes called nonadopters—see *adoption curve*.

Lanham Act A 1946 law that spells out what kinds of marks (including brand names) can be protected and the exact method of protecting them.

Late majority A group of adopters who are cautious about new ideas—see *adoption curve*.

Law of diminishing demand If the price of a product is raised, a smaller quantity will be demanded—and if the price of a product is lowered, a greater quantity will be demanded.

Leader pricing Setting some very low prices—real bargains—to get customers into retail stores.

Learning A change in a person's thought processes caused by prior experience.

Licensed brand A well-known brand that sellers pay a fee to use.

Lifestyle analysis The analysis of a person's day-to-day pattern of living as expressed in that person's Activities, Interests, and Opinions—sometimes referred to as AIOs or psychographics.

Limited-function wholesalers Merchant wholesalers who provide only *some* wholesaling functions.

Limited-line stores Stores that specialize in certain lines of related products rather than a wide assortment—sometimes called single-line stores.

Limited problem solving When a consumer is willing to put *some* effort into deciding the best way to satisfy a need.

Logistics The transporting, storing, and handling of goods to match target customers' needs with a firm's marketing mix—both within individual firms and along a channel of distribution (i.e., another name for physical distribution).

Low-involvement purchases Purchases that have little importance or relevance for the customer.

Macro-marketing A social process that directs an economy's flow of goods and services from producers to consumers in a way that effectively matches supply and demand and accomplishes the objectives of society.

Magnuson-Moss Act A 1975 law requiring that producers provide a clearly written warranty if they choose to offer any warranty.

Major accounts sales force Salespeople who sell directly to large accounts such as major retail chain stores.

Manufacturer brands Brands created by producers.

Manufacturers' agents Agent middlemen who sell similar products for several noncompeting producers for a commission on what is actually sold.

Manufacturers' sales branches Separate warehouses that producers set up away from their factories.

Marginal analysis Evaluating the change in total revenue and total cost from selling one more unit to find the most profitable price and quantity.

Markdown A retail price reduction that is required because customers won't buy some item at the originally marked-up price.

Markdown ratio A tool used by many retailers to measure the efficiency of various departments and their whole business.

Market A group of potential customers with similar needs who are willing to exchange something of value with sellers offering various goods and/or services—that is, ways of satisfying those needs.

Market development Trying to increase sales by selling present products in new markets.

Market-directed economic system The individual decisions of the many producers and consumers make the macro-level decisions for the whole economy.

Market growth A stage of the product life cycle when industry sales grow fast—but industry profits rise and then start falling.

Market information function The collection, analysis, and distribution of all the information needed to plan, carry out, and control marketing activities.

Market introduction A stage of the product life cycle when sales are low as a new idea is first introduced to a market.

Market maturity A stage of the product life cycle when industry sales level off and competition gets tougher.

Market penetration Trying to increase sales of a firm's present products in its present markets—probably through a more aggressive marketing mix.

Market potential What a whole market segment might buy.

Market segment A relatively homogeneous group of customers who will respond to a marketing mix in a similar way.

Market segmentation A two-step process of (1) *naming* broad product-markets and (2) *segmenting* these broad product-markets in order to select target markets and develop suitable marketing mixes.

Marketing company era A time when, in addition to short-run marketing planning, marketing people develop long-range plans—sometimes 5 or more years ahead—and the whole company effort is guided by the marketing concept.

Marketing concept The idea that an organization should aim *all* its efforts at satisfying its *customers*—at a *profit*.

Marketing department era A time when all marketing activities are brought under the control of one department to improve short-run policy planning and to try to integrate the firm's activities.

Marketing ethics The moral standards that guide marketing decisions and actions.

Marketing information system (MIS) An organized way of continually gathering, accessing, and analyzing information that marketing managers need to make decisions.

Marketing management process The process of (1) *planning* marketing activities, (2) directing the *implementation* of the plans, and (3) *controlling* these plans.

Marketing mix The controllable variables that the company puts together to satisfy a target group.

Marketing model A statement of relationships among marketing variables.

Marketing orientation Trying to carry out the marketing concept.

Marketing plan A written statement of a marketing strategy *and* the time-related details for carrying out the strategy.

Marketing program Blends all of the firm's marketing plans into one big plan.

Marketing research Procedures to develop and analyze new information to help marketing managers make decisions.

Marketing research process A five-step application of the scientific method that includes (1) defining the problem, (2) analyzing the situation, (3) getting problem-specific data, (4) interpreting the data, and (5) solving the problem.

Marketing strategy Specifies a target market and a related marketing mix.

Markup A dollar amount added to the cost of products to get the selling price.

Markup chain The sequence of markups firms use at different levels in a channel—determining the price structure in the whole channel.

Markup (percent) The percentage of selling price that is added to the cost to get the selling price.

Mass marketing The typical production-oriented approach that vaguely aims at everyone with the same marketing mix.

Mass-merchandisers Large, self-service stores with many departments that emphasize soft goods (housewares, clothing, and fabrics) and staples (like health and beauty aids) and selling on lower margins to get faster turnover.

Mass-merchandising concept The idea that retailers should offer low prices to get faster turnover and greater sales volume by appealing to larger numbers.

Mass selling Communicating with large numbers of potential customers at the same time.

Merchant wholesalers Wholesalers who own (take title to) the products they sell.

Message channel The carrier of the message.

Metropolitan Statistical Area (MSA) An integrated economic and social unit with a large population nucleus.

Micro-macro dilemma What is good for some producers and consumers may not be good for society as a whole.

Micro-marketing The performance of activities that seek to accomplish an organization's objectives by anticipating customer or client needs and directing a flow of need-satisfying goods and services from producer to customer or client.

Middleman Someone who specializes in trade rather than production, sometimes called an intermediary.

Mission statement Sets out the organization's basic purpose for being.

Missionary salespeople Supporting salespeople who work for producers by calling on their middlemen and their customers.

Modified rebuy The in-between process where some review of the buying situation is done—though not as much as in new-task buying or as little as in straight rebuys.

Monopolistic competition A market situation that develops when a market has (1) different (heterogeneous) products and (2) sellers who feel they do have some competition in this market.

Multiple buying influence Several people share in making a purchase decision—perhaps even top management.

Multiple target market approach Segmenting the market and choosing two or more segments, then treating each as a separate target market needing a different marketing mix.

Nationalism An emphasis on a country's interests before everything else.

Natural products Products that occur in nature—such as timber, iron ore, oil, and coal.

Needs The basic forces that motivate a person to do something.

Negotiated contract buying Agreeing to a contract that allows for changes in the purchase arrangements.

Negotiated price A price that is set based on bargaining between the buyer and seller.

Net An invoice term meaning that payment for the face value of the invoice is due immediately—also see *cash discounts*.

Net profit What the company earns from its operations during a particular period.

Net sales The actual sales dollars the company receives.

New product A product that is new *in any way* for the company concerned.

New-task buying When an organization has a new need and the buyer wants a great deal of information.

New unsought products Products offering really new ideas that potential customers don't know about yet.

Noise Any distraction that reduces the effectiveness of the communication process.

Nonadopters Prefer to do things the way they have been done in the past and are very suspicious of new ideas—sometimes called laggards—see *adoption curve*.

Noncumulative quantity discounts Reductions in price when a customer purchases a larger quantity on an *individual order*.

Nonprice competition Aggressive action on one or more of the Ps other than Price.

North American Free Trade Agreement (NAFTA) Lays out a plan to reshape the rules of trade among the U.S., Canada, and Mexico.

North American Industry Classification System (NAICS) codes Codes used to identify groups of firms in similar lines of business.

Odd-even pricing Setting prices that end in certain numbers.

Oligopoly A special market situation that develops when a market has (1) essentially homogeneous products, (2) relatively few sellers, and (3) fairly inelastic industry demand curves.

One-price policy Offering the same price to all customers who purchase products under essentially the same conditions and in the same quantities.

Open to buy A buyer has budgeted funds that he can spend during the current time period.

Operating ratios Ratios of items on the operating statement to net sales.

Operating statement A simple summary of the financial results of a company's operations over a specified period of time.

Opinion leader A person who influences others.

Order getters Salespeople concerned with establishing relationships with new customers and developing new business.

Order-getting Seeking possible buyers with a well-organized sales presentation designed to sell a good, service, or idea.

Order takers Salespeople who sell to the regular or established customers, complete most sales transactions, and maintain relationships with their customers.

Order-taking The routine completion of sales made regularly to the target customers.

Packaging Promoting, protecting and enhancing the product.

Pareto chart A graph that shows the number of times a problem cause occurs, with problem causes ordered from most frequent to least frequent.

Penetration pricing policy Trying to sell the whole market at one low price.

Perception How we gather and interpret information from the world around us.

Personal needs An individual's need for personal satisfaction unrelated to what others think or do.

Personal selling Direct spoken communication between sellers and potential customers, usually in person but sometimes over the telephone.

Phony list prices Misleading prices that customers are shown to suggest that the price they are to pay has been discounted from list.

Physical distribution (PD) The transporting, storing, and handling of goods to match target customers' needs with a firm's marketing mix—both within individual firms and along a channel of distribution (i.e., another name for logistics).

Physical distribution (PD) concept All transporting, storing, and product-handling activities of a business and a whole channel system should be coordinated as one system that seeks to minimize the cost of distribution for a given customer service level.

Physiological needs Biological needs such as the need for food, drink, rest, and sex.

Piggyback service Loading truck trailers or flat-bed trailers carrying containers on railcars to provide both speed and flexibility.

Pioneering advertising Advertising that tries to develop primary demand for a product category rather than demand for a specific brand.

Place Making goods and services available in the right quantities and locations—when customers want them.

Place utility Having the product available *where* the customer wants it.

Planned economic system Government planners decide what and how much is to be produced and distributed by whom, when, to whom, and why.

Population In marketing research, the total group you are interested in.

Positioning An approach that refers to how customers think about proposed and/or present brands in a market.

Possession utility Obtaining a good or service and having the right to use or consume it.

Prepared sales presentation A memorized presentation that is not adapted to each individual customer.

Prestige pricing Setting a rather high price to suggest high quality or high status.

Price The amount of money that is charged for "something" of value.

Price discrimination Injuring competition by selling the same products to different buyers at different prices.

Price fixing Competitors illegally getting together to raise, lower, or stabilize prices.

Price lining Setting a few price levels for a product line and then marking all items at these prices.

Primary data Information specifically collected to solve a current problem.

Primary demand Demand for the general product idea, not just the company's own brand.

Private brands Brands created by middlemen—sometimes referred to as dealer brands.

Private warehouses Storing facilities owned or leased by companies for their own use.

Product The need-satisfying offering of a firm.

Product advertising Advertising that tries to sell a specific product.

Product assortment The set of all product lines and individual products that a firm sells.

Product-bundle pricing Setting one price for a set of products.

Product development Offering new or improved products for present markets.

Product liability The legal obligation of sellers to pay damages to individuals who are injured by defective or unsafe products.

Product life cycle The stages a new product idea goes through from beginning to end.

Product line A set of individual products that are closely related.

Product managers Manage specific products, often taking over the jobs formerly handled by an advertising manager—sometimes called brand managers.

Product-market A market with *very* similar needs—and sellers offering various *close substitute* ways of satisfying those needs.

Production Actually *making* goods or *performing* services.

Production era A time when a company focuses on production of a few specific products—perhaps because few of these products are available in the market.

Production orientation Making whatever products are easy to produce and *then* trying to sell them.

Professional services Specialized services that support a firm's operations.

Profit maximization objective An objective to get as much profit as possible.

Promotion Communicating information between seller and potential buyer or others in the channel to influence attitudes and behavior.

Prospecting Following all the leads in the target market to identify potential customers.

Psychographics The analysis of a person's day-to-day pattern of living as expressed in that person's Activities, Interests, and Opinions—sometimes referred to as AIOs or lifestyle analysis.

Psychological pricing Setting prices that have special appeal to target customers.

Public relations Communication with noncustomers—including labor, public interest groups, stockholders, and the government.

Public warehouses Independent storing facilities.

Publicity Any *unpaid* form of nonpersonal presentation of ideas, goods, or services.

Pulling Using promotion to get consumers to ask middlemen for the product.

Purchase discount A reduction of the original invoice amount for some business reason.

Purchasing managers Buying specialists for their employers.

Purchasing specifications A written (or electronic) description of what the firm wants to buy.

Pure competition A market situation that develops when a market has (1) homogeneous (similar) products, (2) many buyers and sellers who have full knowledge of the market, and (3) ease of entry for buyers and sellers.

Pure subsistence economy Each family unit produces everything it consumes.

Push money (or prize money) allowances Allowances (sometimes called PMs or spiffs) given to retailers by manufacturers or wholesalers to pass on to the retailers' salesclerks for aggressively selling certain items.

Pushing Using normal promotion effort—personal selling, advertising, and sales promotion—to help sell the whole marketing mix to possible channel members.

Qualifying dimensions The dimensions that are relevant to including a customer type in a product-market.

Qualitative research Seeks in-depth, open-ended responses, not yes or no answers.

Quality A product's ability to satisfy a customer's needs or requirements.

Quantitative research Seeks structured responses that can be summarized in numbers—like percentages, averages, or other statistics.

Quantity discounts Discounts offered to encourage customers to buy in larger amounts.

Quotas The specific quantities of products that can move in or out of a country.

Rack jobbers Merchant wholesalers who specialize in hard-to-handle assortments of products that a retailer doesn't want to manage—and they often display the products on their own wire racks.

Raw materials Unprocessed expense items—such as logs, iron ore, wheat, and cotton—that are moved to the next production process with little handling.

Rebates Refunds to consumers after a purchase.

Receiver The target of a message in the communication process, usually a potential customer.

Reciprocity Trading sales for sales—that is, "if you buy from me, I'll buy from you."

Reference group The people to whom an individual looks when forming attitudes about a particular topic.

Reference price The price a consumer expects to pay.

Regrouping activities Adjusting the quantities and/or assortments of products handled at each level in a channel of distribution.

Regularly unsought products Products that stay unsought but not unbought forever.

Reinforcement Occurs in the learning process when the consumer's response is followed by satisfaction—that is, reduction in the drive.

Reminder advertising Advertising to keep the product's name before the public.

Requisition A request to buy something.

Research proposal A plan that specifies what marketing research information will be obtained and how.

Resident buyers Independent buying agents who work in central markets for several retailer or wholesaler customers based in outlying areas or other countries.

Response An effort to satisfy a drive.

Response rate The percent of people contacted in a research sample who complete the questionnaire.

Retailing All of the activities involved in the sale of products to final consumers.

Return When a customer sends back purchased products.

Return on assets (ROA) The ratio of net profit (after taxes) to the assets used to make the net profit—multiplied by 100 to get rid of decimals.

Return on investment (ROI) Ratio of net profit (after taxes) to the investment used to make the net profit—multiplied by 100 to get rid of decimals.

Reverse channels Channels used to retrieve products that customers no longer want.

Risk taking Bearing the uncertainties that are part of the marketing process.

Robinson-Patman Act A 1936 law that makes illegal any price discrimination if it injures competition.

Routinized response behavior When consumers regularly select a particular way of satisfying a need when it occurs.

Safety needs Needs concerned with protection and physical well-being.

Sale price A temporary discount from the list price.

Sales decline A stage of the product life cycle when new products replace the old.

Sales era A time when a company emphasizes selling because of increased competition.

Sales forecast An estimate of how much an industry or firm hopes to sell to a market segment.

Sales managers Managers concerned with managing personal selling.

Sales-oriented objective An objective to get some level of unit sales, dollar sales, or share of market—without referring to profit.

Sales presentation A salesperson's effort to make a sale or address a customer's problem.

Sales promotion Those promotion activities—other than advertising, publicity, and personal selling—that stimulate interest, trial, or purchase by final customers or others in the channel.

Sales promotion managers Managers of their company's sales promotion effort.

Sales quota The specific sales or profit objective a salesperson is expected to achieve.

Sales territory A geographic area that is the responsibility of one salesperson or several working together.

Sample A part of the relevant population.

Scientific method A decision-making approach that focuses on being objective and orderly in *testing* ideas before accepting them.

Scrambled merchandising Retailers carrying any product lines that they think they can sell profitably.

Search engine A computer program that helps a marketing manager find information that is needed.

Seasonal discounts Discounts offered to encourage buyers to buy earlier than present demand requires.

Secondary data Information that has been collected or published already.

Segmenters Aim at one or more homogeneous segments and try to develop a different marketing mix for each segment.

Segmenting An aggregating process that clusters people with similar needs into a market segment.

Selective demand Demand for a company's own brand rather than a product category.

Selective distribution Selling through only those middlemen who will give the product special attention.

Selective exposure Our eyes and minds seek out and notice only information that interests us.

Selective perception People screen out or modify ideas, messages, and information that conflict with previously learned attitudes and beliefs.

Selective retention People remember only what they want to remember.

Selling agents Agent middlemen who take over the whole marketing job of producers, not just the selling function.

Selling formula approach A sales presentation that starts with a prepared presentation outline—much like the prepared approach—and leads the customer through some logical steps to a final close.

Selling function Promoting the product.

Senior citizens People over 65.

Service A deed performed by one party for another.

Service mark Those words, symbols, or marks that are legally registered for use by a single company to refer to a service offering.

Service wholesalers Merchant wholesalers who provide all the wholesaling functions.

Shopping products Products that a customer feels are worth the time and effort to compare with competing products.

Single-line (or general-line) wholesalers Service wholesalers who carry a narrower line of merchandise than general merchandise wholesalers.

Single-line stores Stores that specialize in certain lines of related products rather than a wide assortment—sometimes called limited-line stores.

Single target market approach Segmenting the market and picking one of the homogeneous segments as the firm's target market.

Situation analysis An informal study of what information is already available in the problem area.

Skimming price policy Trying to sell the top of the market—the top of the demand curve—at a high price before aiming at more price-sensitive customers.

Social class A group of people who have approximately equal social position as viewed by others in the society.

Social needs Needs concerned with love, friendship, status, and esteem—things that involve a person's interaction with others.

Social responsibility A firm's obligation to improve its positive effects on society and reduce its negative effects.

Sorting Separating products into grades and qualities desired by different target markets.

Source The sender of a message.

Specialty products Consumer products that the customer really wants and makes a special effort to find.

Specialty shop A type of conventional limited-line store—usually small and with a distinct personality.

Specialty wholesalers Service wholesalers who carry a very narrow range of products and offer more information and service than other service wholesalers.

Standardization and grading Sorting products according to size and quality.

Staples Products that are bought often, routinely, and without much thought.

Statistical packages Easy-to-use computer programs that analyze data.

Status quo objectives "Don't-rock-the-*pricing*-boat" objectives.

Stocking allowances Allowances given to middlemen to get shelf space for a product—sometimes called slotting allowances.

Stockturn rate The number of times the average inventory is sold during a year.

Storing The marketing function of holding goods.

Storing function Holding goods until customers need them.

Straight rebuy A routine repurchase that may have been made many times before.

Strategic business unit (SBU) An organizational unit (within a larger company) that focuses its efforts on some product-markets and is treated as a separate profit center.

Strategic (management) planning The managerial process of developing and maintaining a match between an organization's resources and its market opportunities.

Substitutes Products that offer the buyer a choice.

Supercenters Very large stores that try to carry not only food and drug items, but all goods and services that the consumer purchases *routinely* (also called hypermarkets).

Supermarkets Large stores specializing in groceries—with self-service and wide assortments.

Supplies Expense items that do not become part of a finished product.

Supply curve The quantity of products that will be supplied at various possible prices.

Supporting salespeople Salespeople who help the order-oriented salespeople but don't try to get orders themselves.

S.W.O.T. analysis Identifies and lists the firm's strengths and weaknesses and its opportunities and threats.

Target market A fairly homogeneous (similar) group of customers to whom a company wishes to appeal.

Target marketing A marketing mix is tailored to fit some specific target customers.

Target return objective A specific level of profit as an objective.

Tariffs Taxes on imported products.

Task method An approach to developing a budget—basing the budget on the job to be done.

Task utility Provided when someone performs a task for someone else—for instance, when a bank handles financial transactions.

Team selling Different sales reps working together on a specific account.

Technical specialists Supporting salespeople who provide technical assistance to order-oriented salespeople.

Technology The application of science to convert an economy's resources to output.

Telemarketing Using the telephone to call on customers or prospects.

Telephone and direct-mail retailing Allows consumers to shop at home—usually placing orders by mail or a toll-free long-distance telephone call and charging the purchase to a credit card.

Time utility Having the product available *when* the customer wants it.

Total cost The sum of total fixed and total variable costs.

Total cost approach Evaluating each possible PD system and identifying *all* of the costs of each alternative.

Total fixed cost The sum of those costs that are fixed in total—no matter how much is produced.

Total quality management (TQM) A philosophy in which everyone in the organization is concerned about quality, throughout all of the firm's activities, to better serve customer needs.

Total variable cost The sum of those changing expenses that are closely related to output—such as expenses for parts, wages, packaging materials, outgoing freight, and sales commissions.

Trade (functional) discount A list price reduction given to channel members for the job they are going to do.

Trade-in allowance A price reduction given for used products when similar new products are bought.

Trademark Those words, symbols, or marks that are legally registered for use by a single company.

Traditional channel systems A channel in which the various channel members make little or no effort to cooperate with each other.

Transporting The marketing function of moving goods.

Transporting function The movement of goods from one place to another.

Trend extension Extends past experience to predict the future.

Truck wholesalers Wholesalers who specialize in delivering products that they stock in their own trucks.

2/10, net 30 Allows a 2 percent discount off the face value of the invoice if the invoice is paid within 10 days.

Unfair trade practice acts Put a lower limit on prices, especially at the wholesale and retail levels.

Uniform delivered pricing Making an average freight charge to all buyers.

Unit-pricing Placing the price per ounce (or some other standard measure) on or near the product.

Universal functions of marketing Buying, selling, transporting, storing, standardizing and grading, financing, risk taking, and market information.

Universal product code (UPC) Special identifying marks for each product readable by electronic scanners.

Unsought products Products that potential customers don't yet want or know they can buy.

Utility The power to satisfy human needs.

Validity The extent to which data measures what it is intended to measure.

Value in use pricing Setting prices that will capture some of what customers will save by substituting the firm's product for the one currently being used.

Value pricing Setting a fair price level for a marketing mix that really gives the target market superior customer value.

Vendor analysis Formal rating of suppliers on all relevant areas of performance.

Vertical integration Acquiring firms at different levels of channel activity.

Vertical marketing systems Channel systems in which the whole channel focuses on the same target market at the end of the channel.

Voluntary chains Wholesaler-sponsored groups that work with independent retailers.